#1799898

Contemporary Literary Criticism

Guide to Gale Literary Criticism Series

When a patron needs to review criticism of literary works, these are the Gale series to use:

If the author's death date is:	You should turn to:
After Dec. 31, 1959 (or author is still living)	**CONTEMPORARY LITERARY CRITICISM** for example: Jorge Luis Borges, Anthony Burgess, William Faulkner, Mary Gordon, Ernest Hemingway, Iris Murdoch
1900 through 1959	**TWENTIETH-CENTURY LITERARY CRITICISM** for example: Willa Cather, F. Scott Fitzgerald, Henry James, Mark Twain, Virginia Woolf
1800 through 1899	**NINETEENTH-CENTURY LITERATURE CRITICISM** for example: Fedor Dostoevski, George Sand, Gerard Manley Hopkins, Emily Dickinson
1400 through 1799	**LITERATURE CRITICISM FROM 1400 to 1800 (excluding Shakespeare)** for example: Anne Bradstreet, Pierre Corneille, Daniel Defoe, Alexander Pope, Jonathan Swift, Phillis Wheatley
	SHAKESPEAREAN CRITICISM Shakespeare plays and poetry

Gale also publishes related criticism series:

CONTEMPORARY ISSUES CRITICISM

Presents criticism on contemporary authors writing on current issues. Topics covered include the social sciences, philosophy, economics, natural science, law, and related areas.

CHILDREN'S LITERATURE REVIEW

Covers authors of all eras. Presents criticism on authors and author/illustrators who write for the preschool to junior-high audience.

Volume 26

Contemporary Literary Criticism

Excerpts from Criticism of
the Works of Today's Novelists,
Poets, Playwrights, Short Story
Writers, Filmmakers, Scriptwriters,
and Other Creative Writers

Jean C. Stine
Editor

Bridget Broderick
Daniel G. Marowski
Associate Editors

Gale Research Company
Book Tower
Detroit, Michigan 48226

STAFF

Jean C. Stine, *Editor*

Bridget Broderick, Daniel G. Marowski, *Associate Editors*

Lee Ferency, Roger Matuz, Jane E. Neidhardt,
Jane C. Thacker, Debra A. Wells, Robyn V. Young, *Assistant Editors*

Sharon R. Gunton, Phyllis Carmel Mendelson, *Contributing Editors*

Robert J. Elster, Jr., *Production Supervisor*
Lizbeth A. Purdy, *Production Coordinator*
Denise Michlewicz, *Assistant Production Coordinator*
Eric F. Berger, Paula J. DiSante, Maureen Duffy,
Amy T. Marcaccio, Yvonne Robinson, *Editorial Assistants*

Linda M. Pugliese, *Manuscript Coordinator*
Donna Craft, *Assistant Manuscript Coordinator*
Rosetta Irene Simms Carr, Colleen M. Crane, Maureen A. Puhl, *Manuscript Assistants*

Karen Rae Forsyth, *Research Coordinator*
Jeannine Schiffman Davidson, *Assistant Research Coordinator*
Victoria Cariappa, Robert J. Hill, James A. MacEachern,
Kyle Schell, Valerie Webster, *Research Assistants*

L. Elizabeth Hardin, *Permissions Supervisor*
Filomena Sgambati, *Permissions Coordinator*
Janice M. Mach, *Assistant Permissions Coordinator*
Patricia A. Seefelt, *Assistant Permissions Coordinator, Illustrations*
Susan D. Nobles, *Senior Permissions Assistant*
Margaret Chamberlain, Mary P. McGrane, Anna Maria Pertner,
Joan B. Weber, *Permissions Assistants*
Virgie T. Leavens, *Permissions Clerk*

Library of Congress Catalog Card Number 76-38938
ISBN 0-8103-4400-9
ISSN 0091-3421

Contents

Preface

The last thirty years have brought about a type of literature which is directed specifically to a young adult audience. These works recognize the uniqueness of young adult readers while preparing them for the subjects, styles, and emotional levels of adult literature. Much of this writing has also had a definite appeal for adult readers and a discernible influence on their literature. Because of the importance of this subject matter and its audience, *Contemporary Literary Criticism* devotes periodic volumes to writers whose work is directed to or appreciated by young adults. Until now, a collection of opinion has not existed which has centered on writers for the junior high to junior college age group. These special volumes of *CLC,* therefore, are meant to acknowledge this genre and its criticism as an important and serious part of recent literature.

In these special volumes we have broadened the definition of young adult literature to include not only writers who fit into the classic young adult mode, such as Kin Platt and Maia Wojciechowska, but also authors such as Robert Frost and John Knowles, whose works are received enthusiastically by the young even though they were not originally the intended audience. In the latter category are writers whose works have such relevance for the YA sensibility that they have achieved mass appeal. A distinctive feature of these special volumes is the inclusion of criticism on writers whose work is not restricted to book form. Many songwriters, for instance Carly Simon and Billy Joel, are recognized by young people as today's poets. Their lyrics have been critically analyzed and accepted as serious literary creations. Since young people look to film, television, and the theater to expand their knowledge and reflect their world view, the young adult volumes feature criticism on filmmakers, scriptwriters, and dramatists who appeal to the young, including Ralph Bakshi, John Landis, and Arthur Miller in the present volume. Humorists such as Richard Pryor, whom young people look to for both social comment and entertainment, are also included.

Each periodic special volume on young adult literature is designed to complement other volumes of *CLC* and follows the same format with some slight variations. The list of authors treated is international in scope and, as in the other *CLC* volumes, includes creative writers who are living now or have died after December 31, 1959. Since this volume of *CLC* is intended to provide a definitive overview of the careers of the authors included, the editors have included approximately fifty writers (compared to seventy authors in the standard *CLC*) in order to devote more attention to each writer.

Criticism has been selected with the reading level and interests of the young adult in mind. Many young adult authors have also written for younger children. Criticism on these works has been included when it is felt the works may be of interest to the young adult.

Format of the Work

Altogether there are about 1,000 individual excerpts in this volume—with an average of about twenty excerpts per author—taken from hundreds of literary reviews, general magazines, scholarly journals, and monographs. Contemporary criticism is loosely defined as that which is relevant to the evaluation of the author under discussion; this includes criticism written at the beginning of an author's career as well as current commentary. Students, teachers, librarians, and researchers frequently find that the generous excerpts and supplementary material provided by the editors supply them with all the information that they need to write a term paper, analyze a poem, or lead a book discussion group. However, complete bibliographical citations facilitate the location of the original source as well as provide all of the information necessary for a term paper footnote or bibliography.

A *CLC* entry consists of the following elements:

- The **author heading** contains the author's full name, followed by birth date, and death date when applicable. Pseudonyms and other forms are also listed.

- A **portrait** of the author is included when available.

- A brief **biocritical introduction** to the author and his or her work precedes the excerpted criticism. However, *CLC* is not intended to be a definitive biographical source. Therefore, *cross-references* have been included to direct the user to other useful sources published by the Gale Research Company: the *Contemporary Authors* series now includes detailed biographical and bibliographical sketches of nearly 73,000 authors; *Children's Literature Review* presents excerpted criticism on the works of authors of children's books; *Something about the Author* contains heavily illustrated biographical sketches on writers and illustrators who create books for children and young adults; *Contemporary Issues Criticism* presents excerpted commentary on the nonfiction works of authors who influence contemporary thought; and *Dictionary of Literary Biography* provides original evaluations of authors important to literary history. Previous volumes of *CLC* in which the author has been featured are also listed.

● The **excerpted criticism** represents various kinds of critical writing—a particular essay may be normative, descriptive, interpretive, textual, appreciative, comparative, or generic. It may range in form from the brief review to the scholarly monograph. Essays are selected by the editors to reflect the spectrum of opinion about a specific work or about an author's writing in general. The excerpts are presented chronologically, adding a useful perspective to the entry. All titles by the author featured in the entry are printed in boldface, which enables the user to readily ascertain the work being discussed.

● A complete **bibliographical citation** designed to facilitate location of the original essay or book follows each excerpt. An asterisk (*) at the end of a citation indicates the essay is on more than one author.

Other Features

● An **Appendix** lists the sources from which material has been reprinted in a volume. Many other sources have also been consulted during the preparation of the volume.

● A **Cumulative Index to Authors** lists the authors who have been included in previous volumes of *CLC*—more than 1,500 of the best-known creative writers in the world today.

● A **Cumulative Index to Critics** lists the critics and the author entries in which their work appears.

● A list of **Authors Forthcoming in *CLC*** previews the authors to be researched for future volumes.

Acknowledgments

The editors wish to thank the copyright holders of the excerpted articles included in this volume for permission to use the material and the photographers and individuals who provided photographs for us. We are grateful to the staffs of the following libraries for making their resources available to us: Detroit Public Library and the libraries of Wayne State University, the University of Michigan, and the University of Detroit. We also wish to thank Henrietta Epstein for her editorial assistance and Jeri Yaryan for her assistance with copyright research.

Authors Forthcoming in *CLC*

To Be Included in Volume 27

John Barth (American novelist and short story writer)—The recent publication of his novel *Sabbatical: A Romance* has generated new discussion of the theories and techniques of this innovative and critically controversial author.

Gabriel García Márquez (Colombian novelist, short story writer, and scriptwriter)—A major figure in both Latin American and world literature, García Márquez was awarded the 1982 Nobel Prize in literature. He has recently published *Chronicle of a Death Foretold,* a novel that explores the death of a young man and the minds of his murderers.

Geoffrey Hartman (German-born American literary critic)—His work, notably *Criticism in the Wilderness,* presents and defends critical expression as a creative literary act.

Kazuo Ishiguro (Japanese novelist)—His first novel, *Pale View of the Hills,* won praise for its success in capturing the emotional turmoil of postwar Nagasaki.

Thomas Keneally (Australian novelist)—His growing reputation as an important international writer is reflected in the reception of *Schindler's Ark,* the 1982 winner of the prestigious Booker McConnell Prize.

Helen MacInnes (Scottish-born American novelist and dramatist)—She is a prolific and best-selling author of novels of international intrigue that are noted for being well researched and suspenseful.

Bernard Malamud (American novelist and short story writer)—His recent novel *God's Grace* is

dramatically different from his previous works in both setting and approach. In this novel, Malamud writes of the destruction of the world by thermonuclear warfare.

Paule Marshall (Black American novelist and short story writer)—Long neglected by critics, her novels, including *Brown Girl, Brownstones* and the recent *Praisesong for the Widow,* blend her West Indian heritage and urban American experience.

Marge Piercy (American poet and novelist)—Her recent novel *Braided Lives* continues Piercy's activist attempts to raise social consciousness through fiction that merges the political with the personal.

Muriel Rukeyser (American poet)—Her death in 1980 ended a long career of political activism and innovative poetic expression.

Boris and Arkadii Strugatskii (Soviet science fiction writers)—Combining Boris's scientific background and Arkadii's literary expertise, the Strugatskii brothers produce science fiction of high quality that has won acclaim in both the Soviet Union and the West.

Alice Walker (Black American novelist, poet, and short story writer)—Her recent and much-acclaimed novel *The Color Purple* is a moving portrait of a rural black woman's struggle for identity.

Martin Walser (German novelist and dramatist)—A recipient of the prestigious Georg Büchner Prize, Walser is one of Germany's foremost authors.

To Be Included in Volume 28

Georges Bataille (French novelist, editor, and philosopher)—His controversial writings combine mysticism, horror, and eroticism and have attracted the attention of many critics, including Jacques Derrida, Michel Foucault, and Roland Barthes.

Van Wyck Brooks (American literary critic and historian)—One of the foremost critics of the early twentieth century, Brooks won the 1937 Pulitzer Prize in history for *The Flowering of New England.*

Walter Van Tilburg Clark (American novelist, short story writer, and poet)—He is known for his

western novel about mob violence, *The Oxbow Incident.*

Philip K. Dick (American novelist and short story writer)—One of the leading authors of contemporary science fiction, Dick published more than forty novels and short story collections prior to his recent death.

Hilda Doolittle (H.D.) (American poet and novelist)—Her work and life as one of the leading Imagist poets is commanding new attention with the posthumous publication of *End to Torment* and *HERmione.*

Roy Fuller (British novelist and poet)—In a career which spans over forty years, Fuller has produced work well respected by critics. His recent books include two volumes of memoirs, *Souvenirs* and *Vamp Till Ready.*

John Gardner (American novelist, short story writer, and essayist)—An accidental death in 1982 ended the career of this prominent author. Commentary on his last books, *The Art of Living and Other Stories* and *Mickelsson's Ghosts,* will be presented.

Norman Mailer (American novelist)—In his long-awaited *Ancient Evenings,* Mailer creates a panoramic portrayal of life in Egypt 3,000 years ago.

Bobbie Ann Mason (American short story writer and critic)—Her first work of fiction, *Shiloh and Other Stories,* was highly praised by critics.

Marsha Norman (American dramatist)—Considered an important new playwright when her first play, *Getting Out,* was produced in 1977, Norman won the 1983 Pulitzer Prize in drama for *'Night, Mother.*

Katha Pollitt (American poet)—Her first book, *Antarctic Traveler,* won the 1982 National Book Critics' Circle Award.

Manuel Puig (Argentine novelist)—Puig parodies popular art forms to satirize small town life. His recent *Eternal Curse on the Reader of These Pages* is his first book to be written in English.

Paul Theroux (American novelist and short story writer)—The novels of this expatriate American reflect his passion for travel and exotic settings. His most recent novel, *The Mosquito Coast,* is a potpourri of characters, myths, and adventures unified by a man's search for his own divinity.

Christa Wolf (East German novelist, short story writer, and essayist)—Her recently translated novel, *A Model Childhood,* reflects Wolf's moral impetus to understand her country's past and how it affects the present. Criticism will also be included on another recent book, *Kein Ort, Nirgends.*

James Wright (American poet and translator)—The posthumous publication of his last poems in *This Journey* enhances Wright's reputation as one of America's finest contemporary poets.

Chinua Achebe

1930-

(Born Albert Chinualumogu) Nigerian novelist, poet, short story writer, and essayist.

Achebe is considered one of the finest of contemporary African writers. In his novels he explores traditional tribal values and the cultural changes resulting from European colonization. To present these themes, Achebe fuses ancient proverbs and idioms of his native Ibo people with the political ideologies and Christian doctrines emerging in modern Nigeria.

Achebe's first novel, *Things Fall Apart,* is praised by Charles R. Larson as "the archetypal African novel" because it traces the beginnings of European colonization in Nigeria and the developing conflict between tribal and Christian cultures. *Arrow of God* examines the breakdown and inevitable failure of traditional tribal customs in resisting colonial rule. *No Longer at Ease* and *A Man of the People* discuss the materialistic influence of Western culture on Nigeria's youth and the corrupt forces behind the country's victory as an independent state.

Achebe's writings in other genres also reveal the turmoil of Nigeria. *Christmas in Biafra and Other Poems* is highly regarded for its ironic simplicity in describing the anguish of the Nigerian civil war. *Girls at War and Other Stories* bitterly reflects a disillusionment with war and nationalism.

Commenting on his work, Achebe has stated that a writer in an emergent nation could not afford to pass up the opportunity to educate his fellow countrymen. Despite this urgency to teach, however, Achebe's work is also considered by most critics to be good reading.

(See also *CLC,* Vols. 1, 3, 5, 7, 11; *Contemporary Authors,* Vols. 1-4, rev. ed.; and *Contemporary Authors New Revision Series,* Vol. 6.)

Courtesy of Chinua Achebe

old. His picture of the collapse of tribal custom is perhaps less than compassionate.

"The Centre Cannot Hold," in The Times Literary Supplement (© *Times Newspapers Ltd. (London) 1958; reproduced from* The Times Literary Supplement *by permission), No. 2938, June 20, 1958, p. 341.*

PHOEBE-LOU ADAMS

The breakup of African tribal society is the subject of [*Things Fall Apart*]. . . . This theme has been discussed before with the same melancholy conclusions, but Mr. Achebe's book is distinctive in that most of it concerns African life before any European interference occurs.

Mr. Achebe's hero and his environment are described with care, and no attempt is made to disguise their unlovable aspects. Even by the standards of his own people, Okonkwo is not a particularly attractive man: hard working and a good provider, but overambitious, short tempered, heavy handed, humorless, and self-important. (p. 101)

To Okonkwo's credit, he is honest, conscientious in his civic duties (he has risen to the honorable office of representing one of the ancestral spirits during their masked appearances in pub-

THE TIMES LITERARY SUPPLEMENT

Mr. Achebe is a young Nigerian. In *Things Fall Apart,* his first novel, he draws a fascinating picture of tribal life among his own people at the end of the nineteenth century. His literary method is apparently simple, but a vivid imagination illuminates every page, and his style is a model of clarity. He has chosen a very cunning way of getting as much authentic background into his story as he can, by making his hero a powerful and egocentric social climber who exploits every possibility of tribal life. . . .

The great interest of this novel is that it genuinely succeeds in presenting tribal life from the inside. Patterns of feeling and attitudes of mind appear clothed in a distinctively African imagery, written neither up nor down. . . . We are made to share the African's experience of his masked gods, his oracles, and even his weather.

Only at the end of the book, when the European missionaries appear on the scene, does some confusion of attitude prevail. For Mr. Achebe himself owes much to missionary education, and his sympathies are naturally more with the new than the

11

lic), fond of his wives and children despite his bullying manner, and devoted to his gods. He also has physical courage, although he is short of nerve on moral questions and always takes the easy, conventional way out.

This is the portrait of any ordinary, proper, businesslike citizen, and Mr. Achebe has been very clever in building it up in terms of mud-walled compounds, yams, and human sacrifice. . . . These affairs permit Mr. Achebe to record the habits, jokes, stories, work, and festivities of the tribesmen in detail, until the structure of their society rises as clearly as his hero's character.

Okonkwo's world is brutal in some respects, very gentle in others, highly organized but quite incapable of contending with jails and policemen. These arrive hard on the heels of the first missionary, and everything is thrown topsy-turvy. Okonkwo, a born conservative, fights for the old gods and is beaten at once. He becomes a paragraph in a projected book on *The Pacification of the Primitive Tribes of the Lower Niger*, to be written by a man who does not understand any more about the society he is busily destroying than Okonkwo does about bookkeeping. (p. 102)

Phoebe-Lou Adams, "The Onslaught of Civilization," in The Atlantic Monthly *(copyright © 1959, by The Atlantic Monthly Company, Boston, Mass.; reprinted with permission), Vol. 203, No. 2, February, 1959, pp. 101-02.*

JOHN COLEMAN

Obi, the educated young Nigerian hero [of *No Longer at Ease*], sits in a government office in Lagos and reflects on his English boss:

> He must have come originally with an ideal—
> to bring light to the heart of darkness, to tribal
> head-hunters performing weird ceremonies and
> unspeakable rites. But when he arrived Africa
> played him false. Where was his beloved bush
> full of human sacrifices?

And yet Okonkwo, Obi's grandfather, had severed heads, as readers of Chinua Achebe's previous novel [*Things Fall Apart*] may recall, and the darkness lay all around. (p. 616)

No Longer at Ease is Obi's contemporary story, another grim one. The pacification has been long completed and Nigerian independence isn't far off. The brilliant local boy returns, after several years' study in England, to find himself at odds with both his family and the well-wishers—the Umuofia Progressive Union—who subscribed to send him away. He falls in love with Clara, an *osu* or 'untouchable,' and makes himself unpopular by refusing to take the traditional bribes in his new job. But his salary is inadequate to cover his commitments. . . . Mr. Achebe's novel moves towards its inevitable catastrophe with classic directness. Nothing is wasted and it is only after the sad, understated close that one realises, once again, how much of the Nigerian context has been touched in, from the prejudice and corruption of Lagos to the warm, homiletic simplicities of village life.

Both these novels are fine in themselves, but they're bound to have an added value at the moment—as indigenous relief-maps of hardly explored cultural territory—since Chinua Achebe is a young Nigerian, himself an Ibo, writing at first hand and in lucid, uneccentric prose of his own people. He is seen to offer all the more exciting a prospect for Afro-English when one compares his decent style with the mannered solecisms of another Nigerian writer, Amos Tutuola. . . . Tutuola's swollen reputation can only remind me of how much condescension still lurks in Western attitudes to African art. The liberal mind, enraged when the cry of 'they're-just-children' goes up from smug colonials, seems oddly content to allow itself similar liberties when it comes to discuss African sculpture or literature. The cult of primitivism (its qualities vaguely sensed as 'colour,' bold lines, confident *naïveté*, and the poetry of illogic) continues to do as much harm as good by fostering essentially juvenile virtues. . . . Nothing changes quite overnight, but— as Obi and the very real achievement of Mr. Achebe's two novels imply—it will be no help in the next few years to look across the conference table thinking hectically of beloved bushes full of human sacrifices, nostalgically of marvellous feckless primitives. (pp. 616-17)

John Coleman, "Beloved Bush," in The Spectator *(© 1960 by* The Spectator; *reprinted by permission of* The Spectator*), No. 6904, October 21, 1960, pp. 616-17.*

ROBERT C. HEALEY

["**No Longer at Ease**"] is the bourgeois tragedy, African style, of the promising young urban executive who succumbs to temptation when he is no longer able to keep up appearances and make ends meet. Obi Okonkwo, the mixed-up young hero who is no longer at ease, is the grandson of the tough tribal chief who fought to the death against the white man and his ways in Chinua Achebe's first novel, "**Things Fall Apart**." Unlike his single-minded grandfather, Obi has become thoroughly confused in his loyalties and allegiances, and the white man is only indirectly to blame.

Obi has too much status, too much to live up to even on a handsome salary. He is a "been-to," the only person in his village who has been to England for a university education. . . . As a university graduate he enjoys a select civil service status and naturally has to live in a suitable European apartment and keep up a car and a chauffeur. He has certain obligations to his family in the village, and there is also Clara, another "been-to" he is most anxious to marry. As the bills and obligations pile up, little wonder that he begins to heed the siren song of the bribes that seem so much a part of the atmosphere around him.

Outwardly this might be the plight of any ambitious junior executive continually strapped for cash. But this is Lagos, and Obi, so much at home in English literature, is a halfway child ill at ease in a culture which has sedulously adopted the outer trappings of the white man without surrendering all of its old ideas. . . .

Compared to his heroic grandfather, Obi cuts a rather sorry figure and he is intended to. But Achebe is at his best in sketching significant details and backgrounds, the metropolitan bustle and temptations of Lagos or the dignified formality of a village which could adopt the white man's formal invitation for its feasts but interpret the RSVP as "Rice and Stew Very Plenty." Wholly declarative and bare of rhetorical subtlety, "**No Longer at Ease,**" which was apparently written several years before Nigerian independence, is primitive storytelling in the best sense. Its very artlessness is its greatest asset and charm.

Robert C. Healey, "Between Two Worlds," in Lively Arts and Book Review *(© I.H.T. Corporation; reprinted by permission), April 30, 1961, p. 28.*

TIME

[In *A Man of the People* Achebe] illuminates today's confused events along the opaque waters of the Niger. Life imitates art, but seldom so promptly on cue. Achebe's book sounds the obituary drums for "the fat-dripping, gummy, eat-and-let-eat regime" that history has extinguished, and makes clear why his still unstable nation should turn to military government. In fact, his novel ends with just such a military coup, the first of many, it seems. . . .

Achebe tells his story through the mouth of Odili Samalu, a sprightly rapscallion—part idealist, part young man on the make—whom it would be tempting to call a colored Candide, except that Odili has no innocence at all, only a naiveté that makes a farce both of his convictions and his ambition. He is, in fact, perhaps the most engaging character in fiction about Africa since the hero of Joyce Cary's *Mister Johnson,* who was factotum to a white colonial official. (p. 80)

But times change. The white man has gone, and Odili must emerge with his emergent nation and attach himself to black power in the person of a cynical grafter named Chief Nanga. So begins a comedy of Freedom Now. . . .

Later he joins a reform party to put Chief Nanga and his grafters out of office. It ends in debacle. Odili is beaten nearly to death by the chief's forthright constituents, and it is back to the village for him. But all is well. A military coup deposes Nanga's gang, and, with a more or less good conscience, the convalescent Odili is able to pay the "bride price" for [Nanga's] now redundant "parlor wife." He does it from party funds.

No American Negro writer has approached the comic posture that Chinua Achebe has achieved toward his own people. His book is worth a ton of documentary journalism. Indeed, he has shown that a mind that observes clearly but feels deeply enough to afford laughter may be more wise than all the politicians and journalists. (p. 84)

A review of "A Man of the People," in Time *(copyright 1966 Time Inc.; all rights reserved; reprinted by permission from* Time*), Vol. 88, No. 8, August 19, 1966, pp. 80, 84.*

PHOEBE-LOU ADAMS

[*Arrow of God*] is not comfortable reading, nor is it easy to keep track of three dozen minor characters with names like Ofuedu and Amoge, but *Arrow of God* is worth the effort. It is enormously informative. It crackles with ironic contrasts and the sour comedy of reciprocal misunderstanding. Old Ezeulu and his unreliable sons are vividly living people whose unfamiliar principles gradually become comprehensible and worthy of respect. One even grows fond of their proverbs.

Phoebe-Lou Adams, in her review of "Arrow of God," in The Atlantic Monthly *(copyright © 1967, by The Atlantic Monthly Company, Boston, Mass.; reprinted with permission), Vol. 220, No. 6, December, 1967, p. 150.*

RONALD CHRIST

Before he opens ["**Arrow of God**"], the American reader will be well advised to ask himself two basic questions. Is he about to read it because it's a new novel—or because it's written by a prominent Nigerian about Nigeria? Will he judge it as fiction, or as ethnic reporting of ancient customs in conflict with new politics? In both cases, the second approach will prove more rewarding—though even then the rewards will be on the meager side. . . .

Not that Mr. Achebe's new book lacks plot in the conventional sense. Here, once again, we have the story of the native ruler (Chief Priest Ezeulu, "god" of six Ibo villages) in conflict with the British District Officer (Captain Winterbottom). Ezeulu finds his position strengthened when Winterbottom heads off a fight with his neighbors. Determined to learn the White Man's secrets, Ezeulu sends his son to study the ways of the Christians, only to find that he has brought a new enemy into his kingdom. His last stand against the tides of change, and its tragic aftermath, bring the book to an end.

As plots go, this is familiar and acceptable. But the slender story-line is soon lost in a plethora of local color—and local color alone, whether Nigerian or Californian, is no longer adequate stuff for novels, now that the anthropologists are doing the job so much better. In "**Things Fall Apart**," for example, Achebe wrote that "Among the Ibo, the art of conversation is regarded very highly, and proverbs are the palm-oil with which words are eaten." One must go back to Cervantes and Sancho Panza to find anyone else as meaninglessly proverbial. "When an adult is in the house, the she-goat is not left to suffer the pains of parturition on its tether." Even with palm oil on the side, "parturition" is hard to swallow.

No American or English novelist could have written such sentences; unfortunately, they are even more abundant in "**Arrow of God**." Perhaps no Nigerian, at the present stage of his culture and ours, can tell us what we need to know about that country, in a way that is available to our understanding. . . .

Here and there, in flashes, Achebe can embody the power struggle he is describing—only to lose it again in folk-patter. There is no doubt that he is writing from the inside out. In the future, let us hope that he will write of his vital subject in a way commensurate with his obvious intelligence, not his slight narrative skills.

Ronald Christ, "Among the Ibo," in The New York Times Book Review *(© 1967 by The New York Times Company; reprinted by permission), December 17, 1967, p. 22.*

CHARLES MILLER

In reading *Arrow of God,* it's not . . . necessary to know that there is such a place as the African continent to recognize at once that you are in the presence of an extraordinarily mature literary artist.

In fact, I don't think it extravagant to say that the book brings to mind Joyce Cary's African novels. It must be added, however, that if Achebe should ever happen to read this he would probably dissent vigorously and take the comparison as affront rather than honor. More than once he has said, in so many words, that Cary got away with murder, that he had no real knowledge of his subject, that his characters (notably Mister Johnson) were merely caricatures, and so forth. But whether or not this is true seems hardly the point. The fact is that the works of the two men have a great deal in common, and I am far from the first to have noted the similarity.

Which, when you get down to it, is all but inevitable. Both *Arrow of God* and Cary's African writings deal pretty much with the same people, the same land, and the same period, not to mention the same problems of racial and cultural adjustment. Possibly these resemblances are superficial, but there remains (apart from both men's copious literary talents) a vitally significant common ground. This is their intense preoccupation with the individual as he comes to grips with elemental questions of ethics and personal responsibility in his relations with his fellows, his gods, and himself.

Such a pattern of conflicts dominates *Arrow of God.* (p. 30)

[The book's structure] is certainly Olympian in its rendering, and the key to its impact will, I think, be found in Achebe's clean, unerringly direct manner of saying what he has to say. His approach to the written word is completely unencumbered with verbiage. He never strives for the exalted phrase, he never once raises his voice; even in the most emotion-charged passages the tone is absolutely unruffled, the control impeccable. It is a measure of Achebe's creative gift that he has no need whatever for prose fireworks to light the flame of his intense drama.

Worthy of particular attention are the characters. Achebe doesn't create his people with fastidiously detailed line drawings; instead, he relies on a few sure strokes that highlight whatever prominent features will bring the total personality into three-dimensional life. A facet of Ezeulu's nature is revealed through the eyes of one of his sons, who "remembered what his mother used to say when she was alive, that Ezeulu's only fault was that he expected everyone—his wives, his kinsmen, his children, his friends and even his enemies—to think and act like himself. Anyone who dared say no to him was an enemy. He forgot the saying of the elders that if a man sought for a companion who acted entirely like himself he would live in solitude."

Achebe does equally well with the white man, which is more than can usually be said about whites who try to portray Africans. . . .

Achebe spent his youth in rural Ibo society at a time when he could observe ancient customs which, though even then beginning to disintegrate, were still fairly widespread. His descriptions of festivals, council meetings, family life, even (or especially) personal quarrels—in fact, the entire fabric of the Ibo community—carry not only the ring of authenticity; they evoke a dynamic, tradition-rich society that lends a vital dimension to *Arrow of God.* (p. 31)

Charles Miller, "Mixed Allegiances," in Saturday Review *(© 1968 Saturday Review Magazine Co.; reprinted by permission), Vol. LI, No. 1, January 6, 1968, pp. 30-1.*

ROBERT McDOWELL

Chinua Achebe's powerful feeling for a lost civilization has really nothing to do with that other West African turning back to tradition—that is, the NEGRITUDE of the French-language writers. It is not reversion: it is not a desire to return. It is a contemporary writer's examination of the past, made so that he may better understand himself in the present. . . . As has been oft-noted, the title of Achebe's first and finest novel,

Things Fall Apart . . . is significantly from Yeats, and is clearly indicative of the novelist's concern with the coherence of a former life. . . .

What is perhaps most striking about Achebe in *Things Fall Apart* is that he does not neglect the ugliness, the iron brutality of habitual modes of life. Writing with admirable detachment, he creates in the central character, Okonkwo, a great literary figure of the last half of the nineteenth century—a powerful and ambitious man whose faithfulness to the importance of order is so strong that we might say his destruction comes from this strength rather [than] from any weakness.

And yet Okonkwo is a man; and to be a man is to possess private fears. Okonkwo is no more free from these than, say, Macbeth. (p. 10)

As if to impress on us what is lost in the Okonkwo story, Achebe at first focuses on the closely circumscribed arena of the village, so that until the final quarter of the novel there is no real sense that a "world" exists anywhere outside the village. Okonkwo, hard and unbending in his attachment to this tribal life, which is all he knows, goes down to his destruction with all the inevitability of an Oedipus.

When the oracle states that Okonkwo's ward, Ikemefuna, must be killed, Okonkwo, despite his love for the young boy, enters into the ritual murder. Later, at the funeral of Ezeulu, Okonkwo accidentally kills the dead man's sixteen year old son. . . . Accident or not, "The only course open to Okonkwo was to flee from the clan. It was a crime against the earth goddess to kill a clansman. . . He could return to the clan after seven years." In this instance, Okonkwo serves only the seven years because his crime is a "female" one, that is, inadvertent. Achebe is plainly dealing with a highly-unified social order, one in which everything is inexorably prescribed—every offense has its traditional, accepted punishment.

What Okonkwo cannot accept, finally, is the coming of the white man to the land. . . . Okonkwo cannot understand how his countrymen could be destroyed rather than defend themselves.

A more subtle tear in the social fabric results from the coming of the missionaries. Perhaps most interesting is the fact that they are only able to convert the worthless, the castoffs, the untouchables of the tribes—all those, in short, without status in the traditional life of the village. Thus, ironically, the missionaries attack the tribe at its weakest link—where the chain of being was already broken.

Among the missionaries is Okonkwo's weak son, Nwoye. He and other missionaries disrupt life in family and village, and set one relative against another. A member of the tribe who, like Okonkwo, is an old man, sums up the entrenchment of Christianity; his speech is good evidence that Okonkwo is not alone in his conservativism; and the speech comes close to Achebe's central concern—the dissolution of the "bond of kinship." . . . European individualism has . . . clearly caught on, and a once-vital feeling for communal life is beginning to be archaic. . . . It is immediately obvious when Okonkwo returns to Umuofia from his seven years of exile that a new order has settled over his old home. The white man is now in the area in force, with his policemen, commissioners, traders, and teachers. The hope that Okonkwo has of purging the village of outside influences is vain. But he refuses to cooperate with the British, and is ultimately arrested with six other old men (again, he is never alone in his defiance). Okonkwo feels that his brutal beating and his imprisonment by the whites will surely rouse the villagers to revengeful, concerted action, but they cannot be moved. Okonkwo, obsessed with his notions of communality and pride, . . . decapitates a policeman who comes to break up (significantly) a community meeting.

Finally, in despair, Okonkwo proceeds, just after this killing, to commit the most horrendous of all offenses against the earth goddess—suicide. Thus he ends in disgrace with the community whose preservation obsessed him. His tribesmen cannot even touch or bury him; they can only attempt to cleanse the desecrated ground where he hanged himself.

Why does the man, his life and his death, move us so? It is, I think, because Okonkwo, perhaps best among his fellows, sees the imminent danger to that old order which is their life, and more stubbornly than anyone else refuses to give up the old forms for the new formlessness. Such determination as Okonkwo's is heroic. Call it obsession; but it is nonetheless, as in Melville's Ahab, the mysteriously stirring course of a man brave enough to reach beyond his fears to bold action.

In *Things Fall Apart,* while Achebe portrays the death of an old civilization, he makes no fanfare for a new order. Neither does he in *Arrow of God* . . . , his other village novel. (pp. 10-11)

Arrow of God relates how Ezeulu, out of respect for the power of the whites (after they stop a war between two communities) sends his son Oduche to the Christian white man for training. Instead of carrying back home (as his father had hoped) all the secrets of the white man's power, Oduche upon his return tampers with the traditional religion of the community, attempting in his zeal to kill a royal python, sacred in Umuaro. Finally, in trying to battle the new Christian influence, Ezeulu is destroyed both as a leader and as a man. Because of his imprisonment by the British and his ensuing stubbornness over the consumption of the sacred yams, the traditional harvest time cannot be observed, and so Ezeulu loses his power in the community. The conflict leaves "a crack in Ezeulu's mind." . . .

[By] the time the novel ends, we learn that the "natives" have been "pacified." (p. 11)

Undeniably, Achebe intends in this novel to take into account the internal weaknesses of the old order which is destroyed. We must remember that the time is now closer to 1920 than to 1870 or 1880, and that there has been a great deal of British influence contributing to the undoing of traditional life. But flaws and all, the old order in *Arrow of God* is a kind of order after all; and even at this late stage in history, the loss of it is keenly felt.

Most important for our purposes here is that old Ezeulu's downfall is symbolic of the disintegration of an ancient way of life. Perhaps nothing in the novel as strikingly supports this symbolic role as the death of Ezeulu's son Obika who makes a ritualistic, and as it turns out, fatal run for the tribe. (pp. 11-12)

With a remarkable unity of the word with the deed, the character, the time, and the place, Chinua Achebe creates in these two novels a coherent picture of coherence being lost, of the tragic consequences of the African-European collision. There is an artistic unity of all things in these books which is rare anywhere in modern English fiction.

As for Achebe's contemporary Nigerians in the novels *No Longer at Ease* . . . and *A Man of the People* . . . , we can

only conclude that the author does not view happily or hopefully the Nigerian "been to," the young person back home to work for the government as likely as not, after an education abroad. A new trauma has been inflicted upon the characters in these novels—the city. (p. 12)

Let us examine Obi Okonkwo, the "hero" of *No Longer at Ease.* When he returns home from England, the Lagos branch of the Umuofia Progressive Union meets to greet him and to arrange with him the manner in which he will pay them back the 800 pounds sterling which they advanced for his education. The President of the organization warns Obi about the city: "'. . . If you follow its sweetness, you will perish.'" And perish Obi does. Significantly, the book is encompassed by the ugly framework of a trial: beginning with Obi's trial Achebe flashes back to the events of his return and his taking bribes and then his eventual arrest. He will be sent to jail.

In all Nigerian novels set in the city we see that no urban heroes are without their ties to the village; most urban citizens in West Africa are still new enough to Lagos or Ibadan or other larger cities to have carried with them some sediment of the mythic concerns of their rural forebears. But the folk ways are nearly dissolved since Okonkwo's time. (Nwoye, for instance, has deliberately given his son Obi an anti-African education). And neither have the fancy university educations of such as Obi seemed to build any substantial moral fibre into the younger generation. Obi's criminal acts cannot be condoned in any existing code of behavior, European or African. Clearly, Obi does not possess the force of character of Okonkwo. The personal integrity, the holding fast at the center of an understood scheme of things is not possible for Obi.

In Achebe's most recent and least substantial novel, *A Man of the People,* the plight of Odili is very close to that of Obi: how to comport himself in the complex system of governmental corruption in modern Nigeria. It is impossible to admire the morality of Odili any more than we respected the morality of Obi. Odili discovers in his opposition to Nanga that the whole political sphere of Nigeria is hopelessly corrupt. He sees too that by being involved in it he is as despicable as the rest of the political crowd, and that, worst of all, Nigerians have come to accept these corrupt political facts of life. Odili survives in the story, physically. Even that is due largely to accident— that he wasn't beaten to death. He never displays any immense intelligence or any strong moral fibre of his own. And his monologue at the end of the novel about the "fat-dripping, gummy, eat-and-let-eat regime just ended" does not cover the essential characterization of Odili the opportunist. If Odili's story indicates anything it would seem to be that the amalgamation of British and Nigerian modes of life has effected no more than the destruction of the best in both cultures. The string of continuity which has stretched deep into African history has been snapped; and what is doubly disturbing, the Africans, by partaking of the European experience (for nearly a century now), have put on all of the contemporary spiritual problems of western man as well.

Confusion? Indeed it is. Perhaps the central concern of the African intellectual today is as Judith Gleason phrases it, ". . . how to go about being an African." With Obi and Odili, at least, Achebe has indicated how not to go about it. (pp. 12-13)

It may well be that only in a modernized version of older social systems (such as the Tanzanian Ujama) will there develop a meaningful and comprehensible life structure in Nigeria. It is clear how very much the Nigerians lost when the prescribed and traditional forms of society collapsed around them. Yet it seems reasonable, too, that older forms can never be revised in any purity—nor would such resuscitation be desirable in the twentieth century, when man all around the globe is fated to live in cities.

Meanwhile, out of the swift and confusing change sweeping over contemporary Nigerian life, there is emerging a new man. Such writers as Achebe are attempting to catch an image of that man as he is being formed by his society and as he in turn is molding his social milieu. (p. 13)

Robert McDowell, "Of What Is Past, or Passing, or to Come," in Studies in Black Literature, Special Issue: Chinua Achebe *(copyright 1971 by Raman K. Singh), Vol. 2, No. 1, Spring, 1971, pp. 9-13.*

KATE TURKINGTON

Achebe's first three novels, *Things Fall Apart, No Longer at Ease* and *Arrow of God* have been published as a trilogy. His last novel to date (and surely, now, there must come a book about the recent Nigerian/Biafran conflict) is *Man of the People.* Superficially, however, the novels fall into two camps. *Things Fall Apart* and *Arrow of God* are "traditional" novels in that they are situated firmly in the past, in the traditional Ibo culture and way of life. *No Longer at Ease* and *Man of the People* are present-day situation novels, dealing as they do with educated young men versus corrupt politicians. The differences are superficial, however, because the main theme as it seems to me, the tragedy of the man who can't or won't adapt, is implicit in all the novels. And it is in the deeper meanings of the novels that I would suggest that Achebe is not dealing with parochial trivia. "This no be them country" may be geographically and ethnically true for non-West Africans, but the problems and issues that Chinua Achebe raises are relevant to most peoples and cultures.

Things Fall Apart, Achebe's first novel, has probably been paid the most critical attention of the four, not only because of its position in the brief history of the Nigerian novel, but also, because it gave for the first time in English, in a strong, confident, subtle prose, a picture of an alien society that most people outside West Africa had never heard about or been interested in. The British may have 'occupied' Nigeria for 100 years, but they knew little or nothing of the indigenous culture they imposed their own civilization upon. At first glance then, *Things Fall Apart* is an historical novel. It gives us a vivid picture of an Ibo society that was dying when Achebe wrote about it, and that recent events have done little to improve. Okonkwo, "one of the greatest men of his time" in the village of Umuofia destroys himself finally because he cannot unbend himself and his traditional ways in the face of change, represented by the white man and his new religion. He kills the white man's messenger. (pp. 205-06)

Okonkwo is Everyman facing the unknown. The situation is universal, the reaction particular. Because he is the simple, inexperienced product of an ancient and ordered way of life he becomes inarticulate in the face of things he cannot understand. This inability to comprehend becomes translated into violent action which in turn will result in his own violent death. But he dies pure, because he lives up to the ideals that his background and culture have given him. But this is more than simple narrative. Achebe is delineating a problem not only concerned with Africans tragically under pressure in a changing

world. The key sentence in [one of the passages] is, "He heard voices asking: 'Why did he do it?'"

These are the voices of universal 'survivors' for whom compromise is easy. The question Achebe poses here is a subtle one. To survive you must adapt and therefore adopt some kind of compromise. But does this entail a loss of personal honour which can only be satisfied by holding on to what you believe in? Which is better, expediency equalling survival, or a failure or refusal to adapt, thus maintaining personal integrity? Okonkwo is a fine man and the hardness of his character must be judged by the standards of his day and traditional society, not ours. But there is something elemental about him which almost symbolizes man against lesser men. Achebe understandably is less sympathetic in his treatment of the white man in this book. He presents a savage satire on the bumbling District Officer and his refusal to attempt a compromise. . . . [The official's intention to write a book entitled *The Pacification of the Primitive Tribes of the Lower Niger*] is not pretty irony; there are echoes here of Robinson Crusoe's view of the black man. "I taught him to say Master, and then let him know, that was to be my name." However, Achebe does show more compassion towards Mr Brown, the missionary, who was "respected even by the clan because he trod softly on their faith".

Achebe deals with the same problem of compromise in *No Longer at Ease.* And the very titles of these first two novels underline the issue. Here the setting is the present, but the dilemma facing Obi Okonkwo, the dead Okonkwo's grandson, although more sophisticated, is basically the same. Obi returns from four years' studying in England to try to find his position in life, literally and metaphorically. But his 'been-to' experience forces him into a situation where he must mould and adapt this 'European' experience to the African and Ibo tradition. Ironically it only limits his powers of adaptation and compromise. He had been sent to England with the high hopes of Umuofia behind him. (pp. 206-07)

Achebe carefully relates back Obi's character to that of his proud grandfather, "his self-will was not new". The conflict is yet embryonic. When Obi returns to Nigeria he is unable to compromise both his own personal integrity and his new 'European' habits and ideals to what his people expect from him. . . . The irony is that Obi knows full well what is expected of him, but cannot or will not bring himself to do it. But like his grandfather in *Things Fall Apart* this is not simply a failure in humility. It is also a failure of compromise and perhaps of imagination.

In the world of Achebe's novels it does not seem possible to exist successfully in any arbitrary scheme of ideals. To do so is to invite disaster and retribution. . . . Hopelessly in debt, Obi is forced to shelve his integrity and to accept bribes in return for government scholarships, although he still tries to pretend to himself that he has not lost all his honour by only considering candidates who have satisfied the minimal educational and other requirements. Old Okonkwo refused to attempt any kind of compromise. Obi attempts a half-hearted one and fails. And just like the "survivors" in his grandfather's time who had asked "Why did he do it?" everyone now asks the same question of Obi. (pp. 208-09)

The theme is explored again in *Arrow of God.* This novel brings into conflict again, not only the old and the new, African experience confronting European experience, but also expediency versus honour. Ezeulu, the old priest, brings personal tragedy upon himself because he refuses to compromise his pride and his traditional beliefs.

In the final novel, *Man of the People,* Odili, the idealistic and honest young schoolmaster is drawn pell-mell into the whirling, robust, boisterous world of present-day African politics which is not only extremely funny but extremely sad too. Odili's motives are pure. He wants to fight corruption and right wrongs and his innocence leads him to believe that he can triumph in a political society that makes the eighteenth-century Hustings look like one of Mrs Gaskell's tea parties. He joins the new political party, C.P.C., the Common People's Convention, that has been formed by Max, his friend from University days. Odili's scruples are easily overcome. (p. 210)

These novels are not only about Nigeria. They represent too some of the issues that face us all in a world where ideals become more and more slippery in such a rapidly changing period of moral transition. But if, as I suggest, Achebe is presenting us with the recurrent theme of compromise or die, what is he then offering as a positive solution? Okonkwo failed to adapt and died. Max tried to compromise but also died. Odili and Obi die spiritual deaths when their ideals are shattered by reality. Achebe, I think, makes no arbitrary stand. He puts a relevant world problem into a West African setting and observes, reports and then leaves us to our own judgement. And although there is so much humour in his books he means them to be sad books. (pp. 211-12)

The language of Achebe's novels presents a highly skilful hand. He has a wonderful, true ear for Nigerian and English speech rhythms and a simple-seeming but very sophisticated use of metaphor. He has understood and mastered, and made it a dominant feature of his writing, the English philosophy of understatement and its concomitant bare narrative style. And much of his narrative style has its roots in a very wide literary tradition. The writings of many nations have been concerned with the effects of dramatic change on traditional ways of life. This conflict is often sharpened by glorifying or semi-deifying the 'traditional' hero. (p. 212)

Themes in literature are rarely original. It is in their individual treatment that they take on their own particular coloration. Achebe's novels define not only situations common to the Old Icelandic Sagas but ones which recur in much of modern literature. Because he places them in his own environment, which although, specifically Nigerian, is still a microcosm of a much larger world, he gives to them a fresh colour and insight. "This no be them country" may be metaphorically true of Okonkwo and Odili in that they cannot exist successfully in a period of social and moral transition, but it is not true for us, Achebe's readers, because his "country" can be for and of all of us. It is not so much a narrow canvas as one that rather affords us a sharply angled view of a familiar human condition. (p. 214)

Kate Turkington, "'This No Be Them Country'— Chinua Achebe's Novels," in English Studies in Africa, *Vol. 14, No. 2, September, 1971, pp. 205-14.*

ADRIAN A. ROSCOE

[Achebe's declared aims as a writer] are twofold: to teach his people, and to satirise them; or, as he puts it, 'to help my society regain its belief in itself' and 'to expose and attack injustice'. The first is part of his contribution to the task of giving back to Africa the pride and self-respect it lost during the years of colonialism, to repair 'the disaster brought upon the African psyche in the period of subjection to alien races'. In this way, he takes his place alongside the band of historians, anthropologists, and political scientists who are hard at work on the massive task of African rehabilitation.

The second, the satirist's vocation, is in a sense loftier than the first, since it can transcend the bounds of temporary needs and exigencies; it also suggests an important role which the author has always been called upon to play. But Achebe's espousal of it arises directly out of West Africa's current predicament, in which the sins of the former conquerors are being cynically committed by the newly liberated. . . . A satiric note is certainly heard in the first three novels; but while bearing this in mind, it is convenient here to take these works as representative of what we might call the author's more 'pedagogic' period and to see the fourth novel, *A Man of the People,* as the beginning of a phase pre-eminently satiric in nature.

Achebe's desire to teach raises a number of interesting points. It is generally agreed that African literary artists have always fulfilled this function in society, so that Achebe, ostensibly espousing a modern cause, is simply falling in line with tradition. Furthermore, teaching, by its nature, implies an audience. Achebe told the world . . . that he does have an audience; that it is large, and, in the main, indigenous. Consisting mainly of young readers, still at school or college, this audience pays him the compliment of regarding him as its teacher.

But what really concerns us here are the implications which this holds for Achebe's style and method. Proudly African, and believing his 'pupils' should share his pride, Achebe is obviously concerned to portray with all the power at his command the beauty and rhythm of African life. What is more, since this is an indigenous audience, the most successful ways of appealing to its imagination and sensibility will be those that lie closest to indigenous modes and practice. Here the characteristics of traditional African literary art and the present need for good pedagogy meet. . . . Achebe developed his technique accordingly. His books *do* have a simple narrative line; their canvas *is* dominated by one central figure; imagery *is* clear and his style has the added virtues of lucidity and economy.

But one of the most useful devices which Achebe has employed to achieve his aim has been the African proverb. (pp. 122-23)

The reasons why Achebe uses the proverb are easily found, for the gnomic tradition, familiar in western literary history since Anglo-Saxon times, has occupied a central position in African life since time immemorial, and indeed has included precisely this didactic function with which Achebe is concerned. What is more, many scholars assert that the gnomic tradition, while either dead or moribund in the West, is still vitally alive in Africa. (p. 123)

African proverbs . . . represent an astonishingly versatile device. They are guides to conduct, aids to instruction, rallying cries to tribal unity, and, in a continent where the rhetorical arts are yet vigorously in bloom, the weapons of debate and the buttresses of oratory. . . . No situation appears too unusual for [a proverb], no aspect of social behaviour lies beyond its reach.

In the society that Achebe's novels often portray, it is the tribal elders who are the great masters of the proverb and the most fervent believers in its power. . . . Thus, in *Arrow of God,* when young men are keen to fight and risk destroying the clan, an old villager tries hard to restrain them with the powerfully blunt reminder that 'the language of young men is always *pull down and destroy;* but an old man speaks of conciliation'. The elders see their instruction of the young as a natural social function. Before Obi, in *No Longer at Ease*, sets off for England, on a scholarship provided by the Umuofia Progressive Union, one of them feels it his duty to warn him not to rush into the pleasures of the world too soon, 'like the young antelope who danced herself lame when the main dance was yet to come'; nor to marry a white woman, for thus he will be lost for ever to his people, like 'rain wasted in the forest'. Versed in his clan's myths and tales, these are allusions whose meaning and force Obi readily understands. On the hero's triumphant return from overseas, with an Honours degree in English (regarded by the clansmen as a kind of modern day Golden Fleece), an illiterate elder, no doubt feeling challenged by so much erudition among the young, explains to him why he still feels competent to offer advice. (pp. 124-25)

It is not from books but from experience and from listening to old men that the young learn wisdom; such is the perpetual theme of the elders' pronouncements. (p. 125)

More often than not, Achebe's proverbs are basically images with a didactic function, and can be used in the manner imagery is commonly used in literature, to bring into focus, and then sustain, themes the writer happens to be exploring. . . . The matter of clan solidarity is a case in point. Since Achebe is rehearsing the beauty of a traditional way of life and recording the anguish of its steady disintegration, this is an important concern in two of the first three books, especially when, as in *No Longer at Ease,* the clansmen are in Lagos, far from their homes in Iboland. In unity there is security and mutual aid in times of crisis. The clansman knows that 'He who has people is richer than he who has money', and the collective wisdom of the tribe, distilled from centuries of experience, has given him the saying 'when brothers fight to death a stranger inherits their father's estate'. (p. 126)

More richly illustrated, however, is the strong sense of tragedy pervading the novels, which all recount the downfall of their central character—Okonkwo in *Things Fall Apart,* Obi in *No Longer at Ease,* and Ezeulu in *Arrow of God.* When the High Priest of Ulu is shocked into silence by the news of his son's death, which he believes is a punishment from his god, Achebe uses a proverbial comparison quite magnificent in its simplicity:

> They say a man is like a funeral ram which
> must take whatever beating comes to it without
> opening its mouth; only the silent tremor of
> pain down its body tells of its suffering.

A diligent if obstinate priest, Ezeulu cannot understand his fate; and his predicament is the more pitiful because he cannot explain it by resorting to tribal proverbs. Indeed, lying at the very heart of his grief, and potent enough to drive him insane, is a conviction that some of the fundamental precepts enshrined in the proverbs of the old dispensation—especially those governing parents' duties to their children and a god's relations with his priest—have been shockingly and brutally violated. In his final *cri de coeur*, with its weirdly impressive conclusion, he expresses amazement that his god could treat him so harshly. (pp. 126-27)

In all three novels there are brave efforts to bear up beneath the burdens of misfortune; and sometimes the hero will proceed by adopting an attitude of stoic realism, as Obi does when he tries to ease the pain of his mother's death with the reflection, 'The most horrible sight in the world cannot put out the eye' and then with an apparently negating proverb, 'The death of a mother is not like a palm tree bearing fruit at the end of its leaf, no matter how much we want to make it so'. In spite of this, however, the novels firmly insist on the inevitability of human suffering whether man accepts it or not. (p. 127)

The protean nature of the proverb makes its precise function sometimes difficult to determine. . . . But whether imposing order on chaos, rallying the tribes to brotherhood, asserting ancestral truths or evoking the pathos of man's earthly estate, it is clear that proverbs are cherished by Achebe's people as tribal heirlooms, the treasure boxes of their cultural heritage. Through them traditions are received and handed on; and when they disappear or fall into disuse (as the novelist may well fear could happen) it is a sign that a particular tradition, or indeed a whole way of life, is passing away. (p. 128)

Achebe's first three novels showed the author as teacher. His most recent book, *A Man of the People* . . . , represents the kind of writing which [his] **'The Black Writer's Burden'** manifesto led us to anticipate. The novelist is here in his new role as the scourge of villainy, the outraged *vox populi* crying out against oppression and injustice. From instructing his society to lashing it with satire; from portraying with a touching nostalgia the beauty of a vanishing world to savagely pillorying what is succeeding it—*A Man of the People* indeed marks a new departure. Achebe's former avowal of giving back to his people their self-respect has been set aside for an angry statement of their present sins; and a concern with the ills inflicted on an unwilling race by colonialism has made way for concern with the ills which that race has inflicted upon itself.

This novel, therefore, differs in aim and theme from those preceding it. . . . Equally important, it also marks a new departure in technique, for Achebe uses here for the first time (and probably in imitation of Mongo Beti) a *persona*, a mouthpiece or other-self, who can conveniently and independently narrate and comment on the events of the plot. This *persona*, a university graduate and schoolmaster, has become alienated from the common people; he inveighs against their fickleness, and, ironically, while showing moral weakness himself, reviles them for their spinelessness in face of oppression. His creator fills him with righteous indignation towards a hopelessly corrupt political élite and a cynical people who recognise evil yet will not revolt against it. Yet he is as much an object of satire as everyone else. As we have seen, it is Achebe's view that the novelist can and must influence his society; and by using the *persona* device he can safely point a finger at the warts and sores on the face of contemporary society. Readers are immediately aware that this *is* the present-day Nigerian scene, that these *are* the ugly facts of West African life.

Unfortunately, this in itself is not a guarantee of good fiction. It is the illusion of life that fascinates us in great literature, not real life itself. We have the mass media—radio, television, and, above all, journalism—to give a plain account of real life; but the work of fiction is different, it must create, not copy. 'But who cares?' Achebe says, and the reply must be, 'Literary criticism cares'. One of the main strengths in Achebe's first three novels lay in his dispassionate detachment and in a style which recalled [Walter] Pater's remark that 'the true artist may be best recognised by his tact of omission'. He called up a world, stood away from it and left us to gaze on its details. Historically, of course, the use of a *persona* has normally guaranteed detachment, too, and writers as far apart as [Jonathan Swift, Joseph Conrad, J. D. Salinger, and Keith Waterhouse] have all used the device to devastating effect. But in Achebe's hands the technique is a failure. . . . Righteous indignation with a corrupt political élite is well enough; but as a primary aim in writing it is more in line with the tradition of the political tract than with the tradition of fiction. This is indeed the contemporary scene which Achebe is mirroring; these are real people he is drawing; but they are the 'real' people of journalism rather than those whom great authors create. (pp. 129-30)

In his anxiety to solve the present problems of his society, even if it means writing 'applied art' instead of 'pure', Achebe's artistry declines alarmingly. The teaching role suits him better; it has long roots in African tradition and makes demands on those qualities for which Achebe is distinguished. The good lesson requires minute preparation and painstaking presentation; it requires the voice of persuasive reasonableness and a care for consistency, above all, perhaps, impartiality. These are demands to which Achebe is remarkably well equipped to rise. Newcomers to satire, however, are apt to feel that its only requirements are white hot zeal and a loud voice; neophytes are apt simply to cry destruction and smash idols. . . . Satire, one suspects, has not enjoyed a long history in Africa; and for Achebe the absence of this kind of strength at his back has been disastrous. The prose is uneven. Its unsteady rhythm might well be taken as reflecting the turbulence of a committed and indignant spirit; but the effect is not artistic since there is little feeling of restraint. Success at the Swiftian *saeva indignatio* requires, above all else, control; in the heat of his moral tirade this is precisely what Achebe has lost. Much has been made of the rather prophetic close to *A Man of the People:* 'But the Army obliged us by staging a coup at that point and locking up every member of the Government'. It sounds suspiciously as though Achebe is suggesting a solution. It is not, generally speaking, the job of art to provide answers; art which does so simply moves towards propaganda.

The first three novels were enough to establish Achebe's superiority over such fellow writers as Onuora Nzekwu, T. M. Aluko, Nkem Nwankwo, and Cyprian Ekwensi. Not only did the novels display the quality of his literary skill; they illustrated the successful way in which he, unlike many of his colleagues, had faced up to, and largely solved, the literary problem modern African writers must tackle: how to write, in the metropolitan language, recognisably modern literature, which reflects contemporary mores and problems, and yet retains a large measure of cultural authenticity. As we have seen, Achebe met this problem in part by using the proverbial idiom of his people— one of the most ancient and protean teaching devices which his continent had to offer. One hopes that he will, eventually, return to a style of writing that uses still further the resources of the indigenous tradition. Then the decline represented by *A Man of the People* will be remedied and the work of journalism left to the journalists themselves. (pp. 130-31)

Adrian A. Roscoe, "West African Prose," in his Mother Is Gold: A Study in West African Literature *(© Cambridge University Press 1971), Cambridge at the University Press, 1971, pp. 71-131.**

BRUCE KING

It could be argued that the real tradition of Nigerian literature in English begins with Chinua Achebe's *Things Fall Apart* . . . . It begins a tradition not only because its influence can be detected on subsequent Nigerian novelists, such as T. M. Aluko, but also because it was the first solid achievement upon which others could build. Achebe was the first Nigerian writer

to successfully transmute the conventions of the novel, a European art form, into African literature. His craftsmanship can be seen in the way he creates a totally Nigerian texture for his fiction: Ibo idioms translated into English are used freely; European character study is subordinated to the portrayal of communal life; European economy of form is replaced by an aesthetic appropriate to the rhythms of traditional tribal life. Achebe's themes reflect the cultural traits of the Ibos, the impact of European civilization upon traditional African society, and the role of tribal values in modern urban life.

Although his writing lacks the infectious spontaneity of [Amos] Tutuola's and the intellectual sophistication which is [Wole] Soyinka's trademark, Achebe is, in my opinion, the most competent literary craftsman in Nigeria today. Each of his novels is a success and shows a control in the handling of his material of a kind which often escapes Tutuola and Soyinka. Other writers may be more promising, or show signs of genius, but in the case of Achebe there is a solid body of accomplished work which is fully achieved in its own terms and which can be evaluated, judged or criticized as literature, without reference to some of the controversies which so often erupt over the evaluation of African literature.

Achebe has a sense of irony and is especially good at social satire. It is remarkable how often his evocation of society, whether the tribal past or the present, is tinged with the sharp eye of the detached observer. His first four novels trace the progressive deterioration of a traditional culture until it has become corrupt and inefficient. Many of the problems of modern Nigerian society are seen as having their roots within tribal customs and values. The tragic forces which cause the ruin of Okonkwo in *Things Fall Apart* are implicit within the tribal culture depicted and are not merely the result of European colonization. In this sense Okonkwo is destroyed, and brings ruin on others, because he is excessive in his adherence to the values of his society; those who can compromise, change with the times and adjust are seen as more sensible. This does not make Okonkwo any less tragic or heroic. Despite Achebe's objective manner of narration, his characters are portrayed with sympathy and achieve noble stature in the course of the novels; the principles they uphold are also seen as noble and engage our sympathies. But such principles are often flawed and inherently unsound in the face of social change. Achebe is like such nineteenth-century English novelists as George Eliot and Thomas Hardy in presenting a tragic universe in which exceptional individuals are crushed by larger cultural forces. One is tempted to describe it as a deterministic universe, since the causes of the tragedy are inherent within the culture itself and its relationship to larger realities.

Although *Things Fall Apart* is one of the best known books of African literature, it is not necessarily Achebe's best novel. *Arrow of God* . . . and *A Man of the People* . . . are in my opinion better. In *A Man of the People,* he allows a thoroughly corrupt politician to have an immense warmth and vitality. His zest for life is given full credit and he comes alive on the pages of the novel. The seeming hero of the book, however, is not very likeable; it is implied that his disapproval of corruption comes as much from pride, failure and jealousy as from absolute moral standards. Only an excellent craftsman would have dared to reverse our normal expectations of the sympathetic hero and the unsympathetic villain. It could be argued of course that Achebe has always cast a wary eye on his heroes, or it could be argued that *A Man of the People* attempts to satirize all of Nigerian society, whether the corrupt politician, the intellectual, or the masses who see no wrong in corruption. In either case Achebe's ability to step back from total involvement with his main characters is an example of his artistry, a sign of his concern with literature as an art, and sets his work off from those who mistake literature for journalism, sociology and anthropology. (pp. 3-5)

Bruce King, in his introduction to Introduction to Nigerian Literature, *edited by Bruce King (copyright © 1971 by University of Lagos and Evans Brothers Limited; published by Africana Publishing Company, a division of Holmes & Meier Publishers, Inc.; reprinted by permission), Africana, 1972, pp. 1-11.*

JOHN POVEY

Chinua Achebe is very clearly the best novelist in that group of writers who at Ibadan in the fifties contrived the birth of West African literature in English. He may lack the easy grace and wit of that urbane dramatist Wole Soyinka, yet his work has a structural strength and architectural coherence unmatched by other novelists. . . . So close are many African novelists to the events they record that there is none of that artistic distance which is the basis for the writer's art. Plots mirror the autobiographical information proffered in the fly-leaf of the book's dust-jacket and this causes the balance of events to be seen only through the single self-satisfied vision of the protagonist, and the end, unless it has the shock of unexpected melodrama, can be a mere finish, for the novel has failed to develop any impetus more structural than that of the author's own life. None of these criticisms can be levelled at Achebe. The mere fact that he is one of the few novelists from Africa to write his stories with an historical setting is in itself indicative of the way he has been able to separate his own immediate experience from that of his protagonists, and thus achieve artistic rather than personal expression. . . .

Undoubtedly one of the reasons for Achebe's great success as a text in schools has been the relative orthodoxy of his handling of the genre of the novel. Teachers of literature have found that although the novels are written by an African they retain a structure that allows the established tools of European literary criticism to be applied. When one can so readily make cross-comparisons with the work of Achebe and, say, Thomas Hardy or Joseph Conrad, one has the satisfying sense that the African writer can be conveniently set within the context of the much wider field of English language writing. . . . (p. 97)

Yet Achebe cannot be dismissed in this way as a minor branch on the tree of modern British writing, for he has a very real individuality. His immense competence as a writer has allowed him to tackle and largely solve the two major problems that face the African writer who chooses to employ his second language for his creativity. . . . The first problem is the difficulty of bridging the gulf between the cultural assumptions of the writer and a part of his readership, without the intermediary assistance of a translator. The second is the establishing of a suitable English-language diction that will reflect the syntax and tone appropriate to the range of African characters the writer presents, while yet retaining that international standard of English which is required if his work is to be other than merely local in its effects.

Since the writer is aware of a foreign audience, he must too often explain things which his own local readers can take for granted. . . . Achebe manages to convey the essential elements of belief, of the importance of the yam festival in *Arrow of*

God for example, without there being a sense that one is reading a series of notes in parenthesis. He makes them an integral part of the structure of his story, so that we are informed, almost, as it were, without recognizing it and our attention is not directed away from the essential elements which give the novels their power and concentration.

In the formation of a new diction Achebe is just as successful. . . . He achieves an impressive range of styles, from the extremely formal appropriate to the most educated, to the rather dislocated English of the less educated. He also employs pidgin English where appropriate, retaining sufficient comprehensibility for the works to be readily interpreted and yet retaining all the flavour of pidgin itself. This may best be seen in the speech of the characters in *A Man of the People.* One notices the range of Nanga's idiom and how exactly it reflects his sense of the degree of formality of the occasion. (pp. 98-9)

Achebe's language matches his people, from the somewhat shallow intellectualism of Odili to the powerful command sustained by the speeches of Ezeulu. His deliberate use of Igbo proverbs, at times a mannerism, more often lends density and distinction to the style and flavours it with the African speech which he knows from the vernacular of his locality. To read Achebe is to feel a deliberate and effective selection at work moulding verbal patterns to achieve specific artistic aims. . . .

[Achebe's four novels] make the most important prose achievement yet in African literature in English. (p. 99)

John Povey, "The Novels of Chinua Achebe," in Introduction to Nigerian Literature, *edited by Bruce King (copyright © 1971 by University of Lagos and Evans Brothers Limited; published by Africana Publishing Company, a division of Holmes & Meier Publishers, Inc; reprinted by permission), Africana, 1972, pp. 97-112.*

THE NEW YORKER

[The stories in **"Girls at War and Other Stories"**] show, among other things, how British colonialism, the disintegration of tribal ways, modern education, and the Biafran war have affected Nigerian life. The excellent title story is about a proud young Ibo girl who becomes completely demoralized by the war. In another story, **"The Voter,"** old rituals and new money are used to fix a local election. Mr. Achebe's writing has a kind of serene, grandfatherly quality—especially his humor, which comes at unexpected moments. These are worldly, intelligent, absorbing stories, whose only flaw is a superfluity of untranslated Ibo words and phrases. . . .

A review of "Girls at War and Other Stories," in The New Yorker *(© 1973 by The New Yorker Magazine, Inc.), Vol. XLIX, No. 8, April 14, 1973, p. 155.*

IFEANYI A. MENKITI

The mood [of *Christmas in Biafra and Other Poems*] is as varied as the subject matter. The opening section deals with the years immediately before the Nigerian Civil War, and the second section (from which the book's title is taken), with the war period. Then there are **"Poems Not About War"**—about you and me, and about gods and the things they do to men. Achebe writes with grace and clarity. The poems, throughout, reflect the attachments of a man whose roots run deep into the Ibo soil.

Ifeanyi A. Menkiti, in his review of "Christmas in Biafra and Other Poems," in Library Journal *(reprinted from* Library Journal, *May 1, 1973; published by R. R. Bowker Co. (a Xerox company); copyright © 1973 by Xerox Corporation), Vol. 98, No. 9, May 1, 1973, p. 1493.*

THE NEW YORK TIMES BOOK REVIEW

"Girls at War" is ironic, witty and complex in its consideration of various ways in which the old Africa interacts with the new.

In "Dead Man's Path," one of the best and most representative of the stories, an ambitious and "modern" young teacher is assigned to take over the school in a provincial village. A path runs through the school grounds, connecting the village with the ancestral graveyard; the teacher considers it an eyesore, and closes it off. "Look here, my son," he is told by the village priest, "this path was here before you were born and before your father was born. The whole life of this village depends on it. . . ." The teacher scoffs ("The whole purpose of our school . . . is to eradicate just such beliefs as that"), but shortly thereafter a young woman dies in childbirth; the villagers, fearful that their ancestors have been insulted, reopen the path by destroying the school grounds.

The story is very short, but it summarizes the book: the conflicts between the old and the new; between superstition, and faith, and "education"; between the wealthy and educated of the cities and the impoverished people of the countryside; between the new nations and the old tribes within them; between the white man's culture and religion and those of the African people.

Achebe is a quiet writer, and his prose is deceptively understated. Though the stories range over two decades, and some are clearly those of an apprentice writer, they are remarkable for consistency of style and point of view. "Girls at War" has a great deal to say to Americans about the new Africa, but it is first-rate fiction in its own right. (pp. 36-7)

A review of "Girls at War and Other Stories," in The New York Times Book Review *(© 1973 by The New York Times Company; reprinted by permission), May 13, 1973, pp. 36-7.*

JOSEPH BRUCHAC

[*Christmas in Biafra*], Chinua Achebe's first book of poetry, may turn out to be, like *Things Fall Apart,* a landmark in African writing. . . . Written during the long period of his silence as a novelist, the poems are a chronicle of the difficult years of a man and his nation, as well as a truly unified book of poetry which has much to offer for both African and Western readers. Divided into 5 sections, the book takes us on a journey which begins with dark omens of disaster, progresses into the nightmare of a fratricidal war, passes through the difficult transition period when both the writer's own voice and the nation of Nigeria were being reborn, and finally rises to the point where the poet has returned, full-blown, to both his power and his duty as a writer.

The book begins with a short poem, "1966." . . . The poem is rich in inference and reflects the duality of the poet's vision of Christianity. (It is the same Christianity which would be the forerunner of empire and yet also a faith possessed of a kind of gentle grace which would stir the heart of Nwoye, the son of Okonkwo in *Things Fall Apart*.) The oil which was an

important reason for the involvement of the European nations in the Nigerian War, the disappointment of Christianity in Nigeria (a land which some of the early missionaries saw as a new Eden, an Eden *they* would create), the death of Abel at the hands of Cain and the forthcoming "war between brothers" are all conjured up by these few lines. It is the type of poem which we encounter throughout the book, simple, understated, full of irony and possessing of a depth which many may miss on first reading. (pp. 23-4)

"Mango Seedling," which may be Achebe's best-known poem, . . . speaks of a mango seedling which sprouts on the concrete of an office building and then dies from lack of water. Dedicated to Christopher Okigbo . . . , the prodigiously talented young Igbo poet who was killed in the Civil War, the poem is an image of both the dead poet and the Biafran state. Without ever mentioning the now familiar clichés of malnourished babies and bombed villages, the poem achieves a feeling of the loss, the pain and suffering which those two deaths entailed. The mango seedling lives on "seed-yams" (yams stored to be planted the following season—when they are gone there will be no harvest in the following year). . . . When its death comes at last, it is tragic, yet something other than a defeat. (pp. 24-5)

In the second section of the book, "Poems About War," the irony grows even stronger. . . . [Here], for the first time in the book, we are shown the familiar image which was for most Americans the quintessence of what Biafra meant—a mother and her starving baby. Two poems in this section, "Mother and Child" and "Christmas in Biafra," concern themselves with that well-known tableau, yet they do so in a way which is most untypical, making points which few Western newsmen cared to make. Both poems relate to Christianity with quiet anger. . . . In ["Christmas in Biafra"], its title alone a colossal irony, all of the apparatus of the sacred season has gone rotten. Even the hymns broadcast over the radio are filled with messages which are the opposite of what they purport to be. . . . A mother, too poor to offer even the worthless secessionist currency, tries to show her starving child the crèche, but he turns away. . . . The repetition of "distance" in the poem emphasizes the gap between the people and the religion which was both harbinger and tool of the colonial era which led inexorably to the Biafran conflict. The child's lack of recognition and his turning away from the meaningless spectacle of a well-fed white Christ child is obviously a response which Achebe feels to be the right one.

There is no glorification of war in Achebe's poems. There is hardly even a condemnation of the "other" side. Instead, in the midst of numb agony, a finger is pointed back toward that first contact with the West which has been at the heart of much of Achebe's writing. The finger is also pointed across oceans, to England and to Russia. In "Air Raid" Achebe associates Russian MIGS used by the Federal Government with the places of ill omen in Igbo folk belief, the "Evil Forests" where malicious spirits dwell. . . . And in one of the poems in the last section of the book, "He Loves Me; He Loves Me Not," he mentions the leader of the British government which supplies arms to both the Federal Republic of Nigeria *and* South Africa. . . . (pp. 25-7)

This kind of awareness is typical of Achebe. Yet he does not blame it all on the super-powers. In "An 'If' of History" and "Remembrance Day" the burden is shifted back to the society of which Achebe himself is a part. (p. 27)

The next section of *Christmas in Biafra*, which is called **"Poems Not About War,"** might well have been subtitled: "poems about recovering from war." It chronicles the return of the poet to involvement with his duty to instruct and criticize, proceeding from the tentative words of **"Love Song"** to the strong assertions of **"Answer."** In **"Love Song"** he refers to the time when censorship and repression of the former secessionists are at their strongest and the writers must exercise caution. . . . (It should be easily seen, however, that his poem about the danger of writing politically dangerous poetry is itself very dangerous politically.)

The voice which speaks in **"Answer"** is a new and powerful one, however. There is nothing tentative about it when Achebe describes his return to power. . . . (pp. 27-8)

After [**"Beware, Soul Brother"**], Achebe returns to the vein of irony which he mines so carefully and so well throughout the book. **"Non-Commitment,"** for example, "celebrates" those "who do nothing," who use "prudence / like a diaphragm." (p. 29)

It should be clear by now that *Christmas in Biafra* is more than just a book of poems by a novelist. It is accomplished poetry which marks the return to social criticism and literature of one of the most vital voices in English today. These clear, careful lines never deny the complexity of the subjects he writes about or the commitment to society which he feels is an integral part of being a writer. (p. 30)

Since his first novel, Chinua Achebe has been a leader in the growth of that new literature which J. P. Clark, another Nigerian poet, has called "the legacy of Caliban." Thanks to Achebe and men like him, English is no longer merely a Western language expressing Western ideas and ideals. We now have available to us fine works of literature which are also doorways into other cultures, doorways through which we must pass if we wish to truly understand ourselves, our history, and the vast potential for a renewal of the human spirit which non-Western writers can offer. (p. 31)

Joseph Bruchac, "Achebe As Poet" (© copyright 1973 The Curators of the University of Missouri; reprinted by permission of the author), in New Letters, *Vol. 40, No. 1, October, 1973, pp. 23-31.*

FRANCIS M. SIBLEY

[Chinua Achebe's four novels] are all set in Nigeria. Read as a tetralogy, they reveal a theme of tragedy together with intense moral concern. The tragedy and moral concern are not just for the fictional characters in the novels, nor are they just for the people of Nigeria, who experience extreme changes in their lives as a result of colonialism and internal strife. Rather, these novels, as they focus upon tragedy and morality, transcend their setting. By being extremely provincial, Achebe projects a picture of human experience with universal applicability. His art entertains, but it entertains in order to instruct, and it instructs about the nature of tragedy and about workable morality in fiction and in life. Of course, a great deal of fiction written in English is roughly analogous in intent and function; but Achebe's novels reflect the Ibo tradition of non-separation of art from other aspects of daily living. . . . (p. 359)

[Achebe's major theme is] that he and his characters and, *mutatis mutandis*, his readers and non-readers, are indeed no longer at ease as a result of things having fallen apart to the extent that men of the people and arrows of gods play new and confusing roles. The ability to keep one's balance in such a world is predicated upon the possession of a moral gyroscope; and Achebe's tragic vision insinuates itself as just such an instrument.

Things Fall Apart presents a picture of Ibo society at the turn of the century, before and during the irruption of missionaries and colonizers. The tragic hero, Okonkwo, is a highly respected leader among his own people until the alterations wrought by colonialism make his downfall inevitable—or so a superficial reading would suggest. But a closer examination reveals a fatal flaw in Okonkwo: granted his inability to adjust to colonialism, he is equally unable to adjust to his own society. Thus, his own violations of the mores which form the amalgam of his society contribute as much as do the violations of colonialism toward his downfall.

To understand this, it is necessary to come to grips with the Ibo concept of the *chi*, or personal god, a concept which Achebe uses frequently. The kind of response his tragic figures give to this concept determines the degree of their respective tragedies. (pp. 360-61)

Achebe's central characters proceed, book by book, towards more and more tragic figures if measured by his theory of tragedy as having practical application in fiction and in life. Okonkwo wrestles with his individual *chi*. Obi wrestles with the collective *chi*, an even more formidable adversary. Ezeulu confuses his individual *chi* with the collective *chi* and wrestles with the combination. Odili wrestles with neither his individual *chi* nor the collective *chi* (he can't find them to wrestle with, anyway), he gets the girl he wants, he retains his self-respect, and he lives most tragically ever after.

Achebe is not asserting a simple tautology to the effect that life is tragedy and tragedy is life. We respond to many of his characters in a variety of ways, but we do not regard them all as tragic figures. Those who best exemplify tragedy in Achebe's novels (prime examples: Obierika and Odili) are those who, open-eyed, accept their role as sippers of wormwood and somehow endure. What is at once tragic and promising is that they do endure, and they do so not by some hedonistic calculus but by a commitment to a moral vision which derives from the very acceptance of the concept of tragedy which it delineates. (p. 372)

Francis M. Sibley, "Tragedy in the Novels of Chinua Achebe," in The Southern Humanities Review *(copyright 1975 by Auburn University), Vol. 9, No. 4, Fall, 1975, pp. 359-73.*

G. D. KILLAM

[Achebe's short stories in *Girls At War*] reveal the same interests as the longer fiction. . . .

[The stories] fall into two classes: those which show an aspect of the conflict between traditional and modern values—for example, **'The Sacrificial Egg'**, **'Dead Man's Path'**, and **'Marriage is a Private Affair'** (originally called **'The Beginning of the End'**)—and those which display the nature of custom or religious belief without attempting to probe or explain their meanings. In fact such a separation is arbitrary; in the best stories the conflict between the traditional and the modern has its base in the general beliefs which underlie the former.

To these may be added a third classification—stories which deal with aspects of the Nigeria-Biafra war, one of which stories gives the volume its title, *Girls At War*. (p. 99)

['**The Madman**'] is about village life, presumably modern village life. But that is no matter. It is a village wherein the village values obtain. Its hero is Nwibe, a man who has achieved about the same degree of success as Okonkwo when we first met him. . . . Like Okonkwo, Nwibe has a fierce temper and his judgement deserts him when he is under its full sway. . . . The story is about pride and about ambition. But it is more: it is about the nature of sanity and the nature of tolerance. (pp. 99-100)

The story asks what madness is, what just conduct is, what is fit punishment. And plainly the generality of people do not know.

Uncle Ben, the narrator of the story, '**Uncle Ben's Choice**', is a splendid fellow. . . . He tells, retrospectively, the story of the most decisive event of his life, one which took place when he was a young clerk at Umuru working for the Niger Company, of a time when hopes ran high and Ben ran with them. . . . (p. 100)

[He] has been visited by Mami Wota, the Lady of the River Niger. And by her visit she had offered Uncle Ben wealth and riches. . . . (pp. 101-02)

Achebe and Uncle Ben tease the river god here, look at local legend and fall, happily here, victim to its influence. Mami Wota casts her spell over them both (and us). . . .

'**The Sacrificial Egg**' offers yet another view of the conflict between the generations and the beliefs held by each. This is a superb example of short story writing for in some fifteen hundred words Achebe is able to suggest a locale where traditional practices in terms of belief and daily commerce are maintained yet intensified by contact with Europe, and to suggest the moment at which a young Iboman 'whose education placed him above such superstitious stuff' as belief in the presence of members of the spirit world in the world of the living, through a moment of intense violence and pain is forced to re-examine his beliefs. (p. 102)

Nothing is explained since belief of a religious kind is antipathetic to rational scrutiny. The mystery remains a mystery. But the psychological consequences of the events are left behind and promote feelings of desolation and loss. . . .

['**Dead Man's Path**'] tells the story of Michael Obi, a young teacher, who sees in his appointment as headmaster to a mission school the chance to introduce modern ideas. Obi's ideas of 'modernity' are fairly superficial and consist in part of tidying up the school yard and arranging it after the manner of European gardens. In doing this he plants across a pathway which leads to a traditional burial ground and when the villagers continue to use the path he plants it more densely and strengthens it with barbed wire. The village priest pays him a visit and tells him that the path must be left open for the use of the villagers. For both Obi and the priest the path is a symbol. (p. 103)

Achebe is impartial here: neither side is supported. Obi, despite his somewhat frivolous attitude and the seeming paucity of his idealism, is never allowed to explain himself. Nor, on the other hand, does the priest question the validity of the religion he expounds. The force of the story lies in its suggestiveness rather than any explicit statement it makes. (p. 104)

'**Vengeful Creditor**' is the longest and in many ways the most telling of the stories, or at least of those which deal with social problems. For this story creates the atmosphere of a time when a three-month experiment in universal primary education ('free

primadu' it was called) was undertaken in Nigeria and how this experiment affected the lives of various representative peoples. The examination of the theme provides Achebe with the opportunity for an amount of wry and ironic comment on the experience and self-interest of supposedly disinterested public bodies. . . . (p. 107)

'**Vengeful Creditor**' is a powerful attack on the simplistic, complacent and hypocritical attitudes of a middle-class whose private attitudes and actions belie their public professions and practices.

In '**Civil Peace**', Jonathon Iwegbu returns to Enugu after the Civil War has ended and rebuilds his life based on the conversion of his Biafran pounds into twenty Nigerian pounds which are given 'ex gratia' by the Federal Government (called *egg rasher*, 'since few could manage its proper official name'). . . . [On] the night of the day he has got his *egg rasher* he is visited by a band of thieves. . . . (pp. 108-09)

He loses the 'ex gratia' rewards of peace just as he had lost things in the war, the things he seeks now to re-achieve. And though he says that he can accept his losses in peacetime as he has accepted those in war, that he has survived and that 'Nothing puzzles God!', there is really faint consolation for him and little to distinguish 'civil peace' from civil war.

'**Girls at War**' spans nearly the whole of the time of the Civil War in Nigeria. When Reginald Nwankwo first meets Gladys it is during the first heady stages of warlike preparation. . . . When their paths cross a third time some eighteen months later, things in the country have got very bad. . . . [There is a] background of anxiety and fear and shattered standards against which the major part of the action of the story is played out. So bad in fact have things become that Nwankwo is pilfering precious food stuffs in sizeable quantities, to sustain his own family and this boldly in front of the eyes of many starving people who throw the lies of the slogans of war in his face. (pp. 109-10)

[Gladys has also] become 'a mirror reflecting a society that has gone completely rotten and maggotty at the centre'. Achebe's despair and anger proceed from the falling away of all the fundamental decencies, as the idealism which prompts to serve in the new state is replaced by an entirely self-serving attitude as the new state is battered to bits. 'You girls are really at war, aren't you?' says Nwankwo ironically, observing that Gladys' girl friend will come back from a flight from Libreville 'on an arms plane loaded with shoes, wigs, pants, bras, cosmetics and what have you, which she will sell and make thousands of pounds.' To which Gladys rejoins, 'That is what you men want us to do.'

Nwankwo's responses are as ambiguous as is his understanding of the events in which he is caught up. He is capable of virtually stealing food for his own uses in front of starving people; he is unable to see that Gladys has become what she has become in order to survive, has to become cynical in order to survive. Yet she has a deep need for compassion and understanding; and she can give this too. Nwankwo fails to see the consistency of her behaviour in an inconsistent world whose values have been shattered.

In the end all of the moral speculation is made irrelevant by war. Nwankwo and Gladys have collected a badly maimed soldier on the road and drive him with them to Owerri. A sudden air attack takes place; Nwankwo is wounded and Gladys, seeking to release the car door to free the wounded soldier, loses her life. . . . (p. 111)

That is what war is about—blood and sweat and tears and maiming and useless death. And ideologies are lost in the wake of its destruction. This story says nothing new about war; there is nothing new to say about war. But it adds to the literature of war in an important way. It will move men to pause.

Achebe says in the Preface to these stories that it came as a shock to him to realize that the first of them was written some twenty years before, that he was not what one of his countrymen described himself as being—a 'voracious writer'—and that a dozen stories was a pretty lean harvest for twenty years of writing. Perhaps he is right in thinking that the harvest is small. But I doubt he should call it lean. For Achebe displays here his full range as a writer. . . . (p. 112)

Achebe's poems [in *Beware, Soul Brother,* the original title of *Christmas in Biafra,*] exploit the intuitive Igbo sense of duality which informs all things. Whatever the thematic content of the poems, they are manifestations in various moods and tones of this 'world-view'. . . . [Among the notes attached to the poems, we] find such explications as:

> The attitude of Igbo people to their gods is sometimes ambivalent. This arises from a world-view which sees the land of the spirits as a territorial extension of the human domain. Each sphere has its functions as well as its privileges in relation to the other. Thus a man is not entirely without authority in dealing with the spirit-world, not entirely at its mercy. The deified spirits of his ancestors look after his welfare; in return he offers them sustenance regularly in the form of sacrifice. In such a reciprocal relationship one is encouraged (within reason) to try and get the better of the bargain.
>
> (p. 115)

Given the nature of these statements on the duality implicit in Igbo cosmology, it is perhaps inevitable that Achebe would turn to and cultivate an ironic approach to writing as a natural blending of the sensitivity shaped by his own culture and sharpened by his reading in and contemplation of the Western tradition in literature. Not all of the poems in the volume reflect this joining of influences. Some of them are simply ironic reflections of a familiar kind on events which admit of such sorts of reflection, as for example the first poem in the volume, **'1966'** . . . , where in the indolent present, in 'our thoughtless days', we did not think of the hatred which man could conceive for man. . . . (p. 116)

There is the same sort of irony in **'The First Shot'** . . . where although the first bullet was sent by an anonymous hand . . . this first shot which unleashed a holocaust will echo down the corridors of history more loudly than the 'greater noises' which it releases.

Or there is the dark and bitter irony about the Biafran War, in **'An If of History'** . . . , about the legitimacy of secession, the rights and wrongs of it, the moral issues, the identification of hero and villain. The poem is worked out by identifying a series of paradoxes wherein the judgements of recent history in assigning right and wrong, guilt and innocence, in making moral judgements about the conduct of war are seen to be wholly relative to current judgements. (pp. 116-17)

[Terrifying] consequences arise out of the casual judgements or determinations which make war on a **'Refugee Mother and Child'** and make a mock of the Christian Christmas Scene in Biafra. The war poems are widely allusive—they say and show that war is horrible and that its effects are always seen and experienced most powerfully by the innocent. (p. 117)

But to the familiar statements about death and dying is added the Igbo world-view and with it a new dimension is added to war poetry. Where in the Western view the obeisance paid the dead is dependent on the vitality of the recollection of those left behind (which may be passionate or perfunctory), in Achebe's Igbo poetry the living are not to become complacent in their attitudes. The dead have their own vitality and the living had better beware. (p. 119)

[The **'Poems Not About War'**, the third section of *Beware, Soul Brother,* show that] the war is ended but its aftermath shapes the lives of those who grope towards normality. There is confusion and uncertainty and fear, a need to catch and sometimes to hold the breath. Images drawn from nature inform the poems and moral concomitants are suggested as an attempt at finding peace is subsumed by a clamorous world. . . . (p. 121)

There is wit and humour here; but there is a meditative element as well for thoughts and questions about the nature of religious belief are posed implicitly. This claim may be made for **'Those Gods Are Children'** . . . which exemplifies the view put forward in the Note cited above that the world-view of the Igbo people sees the land of the spirits as a territorial extension of the human domain. . . . (p. 123)

And finally there is the poem which gives the volume its name, **'Beware, Soul Brother,'** . . . a meditation which elaborates the musings of so many of the poems we have looked at above, especially on the duality of life and death as this is made manifest in the Igbo sensibility, made visible in the masks and the dance; as these beliefs are threatened by 'the Cross', the 'lures of ascension day', the 'day of soporific levitation'; as these are expounded by the 'leaden-footed, tone-deaf passionate only for the entrails of our soil'. The mixture of Christian and non-Christian attitudes suggested in these opposing lines points a way to the need to find one's own way, to find a joy unique to one's own soul.

The poem contains within its forty-five lines the stuff of the novels, describes the process of alienation which has been and is at work to the land. The process continues—as with the novels the poem describes the various stages which are achieved and how the bifurcation goes on as beliefs are submitted to further scrutiny. (pp. 124-25)

The volume possesses an overall unity achieved by the relationship the poem bears to an examination of the speculation on the nature of individual human and extra-human existence as this is determined, directed, described by the relationship of the individual to the consequences of political action and the pressure of religious belief. These latter are determined within an African world-view which is in fact, like the novels and stories, an Igbo-African world-view. The poems reveal the same varieties of style—ranging from the colloquial to the rhetorical; the same range of imagery, derived from both an African and a Christian experience as the novels. (p. 125)

G. D. Killam, in his The Writings of Chinua Achebe *(© G. D. Killam 1969; reprinted by permission of Heinemann Educational Books, London, England), revised edition, Heinemann, 1977, 132 p. [the excerpt of Chinua Achebe's work used here was taken from* Christmas in Biafra and Other Poems *(copyright © 1971, 1973, by Chinua Achebe; reprinted by permission of Doubleday & Company, Inc., in Canada by David Bolt Associates), Doubleday, 1973].*

JONATHAN PETERS

A Man of the People, Achebe's fourth novel, embodies a major new feature in his development as a novelist. It is a first person narrative told from the limited point of view of one of the principal participants in the story, and the accounts are given not very long after the final catastrophe. The major personal conflict in the book is between Chief the Honourable M. A. Nanga, M.P., and Odili Samalu, his former pupil. In his capacity as narrator Odili begins his story with a deliberately sarcastic statement about Nanga. This sarcasm sets the tone for the satire which sometimes involves Odili himself. . . . (p. 143)

[It] is part of the novel's irony that as narrator of the incidents which lead to the political struggle with Nanga and as portrait painter of the man, Odili succeeds in exposing perhaps more of his own character and motivations than his opponent's, for the whole narrative is told from his point of view rather than from Nanga's. The result is that in the train of events we come to know Odili, in this case not as passive narrator but as active participant, through his varying responses to Nanga's personality. It is he who emerges as something of a hero in the novel's final pages. (pp. 143-44)

It is in his relations with people—notably Nanga and the women in his life—that Odili becomes himself the butt of Achebe's satire which is quite unsparing of the people and institutions that are encountered, however briefly, in *A Man of the People.* In spite of himself Odili cannot help admiring some of the alluring qualities of Nanga which he himself lacks. (p. 145)

The truth of the matter is that Odili has an admixture of personal ambition and idealism tinged with self-pride. His change of front is dictated by whichever of these forces happens to be in the ascendant. (p. 147)

At the end of the novel the whole political structure of the unnamed African country of *A Man of the People*—the connections with Nigeria are, however, obvious—is in shambles. Since much of the novel focuses on Odili's personal and political involvement with Chief Nanga, the political reality in the novel largely comes through episodes involving one or other of the two or in Odili's commentary as narrator. At the end of the book it is Odili's moral high-mindedness which gains the upper hand. Casting aside his own meddlesome and ineffectual campaign strategy, he proceeds to castigate the people for their cynicism and hypocrisy. . . . The concluding paragraphs of the novel also take on an added resonance from the fact that Achebe endorses [Odili's] position, but without any smugness on his part. Odili is no longer "exhilarated . . . by the heady atmosphere of impending violence" . . . for he has experienced the unglamorous aspects of violence. Max has been killed. He himself has been brutally manhandled. A period of anarchy has followed the election in which practically all the old politicians, including Chief Nanga, have been voted back to power and ministerial posts in spite of the fact that the elections had been called after their corruption scandals erupted. (p. 148)

Achebe's novel does not attempt to find answers . . . but it does take up the subject of individual and group responsibility weighed against limiting factors of human nature and human reality. (p. 149)

Odili's revised stand on the obligation of the individual to the group is Achebe's own unchanged interpretation of African cultural progression over the last three generations or so. There was order and peace in the archetypal society of *Things Fall Apart* before its capitulation to European colonialism. The capitulation was achieved through anarchy, that is, through the break-up of the old value patterns. In spite, however, of the breakdown of established order, life must go on. And it goes on in the succeeding generation until a new disruption again upsets the delicate balance of forces and leads to the chaos at the end of *Arrow of God.* Anarchy becomes an archetype. Thus the constant flux of values catches Obi Okonkwo off guard as he tries ineffectually to balance claims of materialism and morality in *No Longer at Ease.* (The fact that he does not belong to any group makes his tragedy a much more personal one than the tragedy of either Okonkwo or Ezeulu.) In *A Man of the People,* except for the idealism of Odili and Max, the equipoise is completely lost; unbridled and unabashed acquisitiveness leads to social and political upheaval because of its magnitude, its universality, and the total absence of any serious commitment to group values or group interest. (pp. 152-53)

The apocalyptic vision of *A Man of the People* was fulfilled when, in January 1966, the same month it was published, the first army coup in Nigeria was staged by young army officers. But not even Achebe could have foreseen the betrayals and conflicts that led to civil war, nor the terrible massacres and brutalities that both preceded it and characterized its long duration. The Earth-Mother has again been ravaged. This time, however, the perpetrators are not the legendary men of the white skin with no toes. The fact that white men had been the plunderers under slavery and colonization and that the violence is this time turned inwards on a new and inchoate nation is a sign of the changing facets of history and human relations. In his works Achebe looks beyond the immediate modalities of time, place and particularity to the perennial realities, often painful, occasionally hopeful, in this case frustrating, of human nature and the human condition. It is this feature, above all, that gives his novels their enduring quality and universal appeal. (p. 156)

Jonathan Peters, " 'Man of the People': Anarchy As Archetype," in his A Dance of Masks: Senghor, Achebe, Soyinka *(© 1978 Three Continents Press), Three Continents Press, 1978, pp. 143-58.*

BRUCE KING

With the publication of *Things Fall Apart* (1958) Nigeria had the classic book that would serve as a point of reference and comparison for future writing. The novel was not only more competent than anything that had preceded it, but it also introduced techniques that liberated future African novelists from having to imitate the conventions of a western literary genre. The omniscient narrator of the opening paragraphs is representative of the voice of the community and introduces the story with simple, somewhat repetitive sentences in an approximation of a story-teller, thus associating the novel with Igbo traditional oral literature. In contrast to the literary device of a first-person narrator which makes us see events through the eyes of the individual speaker, Achebe's narrator makes us part of the awareness and vision of a small, apparently self-enclosed community of nine villages. We are immediately introduced to the traditions of the community, its history and myths, its arts and crafts. . . . (p. 65)

The apparent simplicity of [the opening] passage is deceptive. It is artistry of a radically different order from those . . . who later tried to write novels of village life limited to repetition and simple sentences. Achebe's purpose is to situate the reader within a community governed by a rich tribal culture which, being a living culture, is undergoing changes, and the continuity of which will be challenged by the intrusions of Christianity and the white man. If his purpose is to show the dignity of traditional African culture, his job as a writer is to make the Igbo village as richly textured with manners and mores as any local community in the novels of Jane Austen or George Eliot. Indeed Achebe's Igbo village novels resemble those of Eliot or Thomas Hardy in showing the tragedy of individuals resulting from the clash between their own strength of character and the unstoppable forces of historical change. Achebe's heroes gain their stature by their excessive virtue in attempting to oppose fate. This is in contrast to the rest of the village community, which changes its ways under pressure and which may be said to illustrate the importance of communal survival in Africa. The rigidity with which Okonkwo upholds traditional values makes him heroic, but such excesses bring self-destruction because temperance and the ability to accept change are necessary with the coming of the powerful Europeans.

Things Fall Apart is remarkable for its complexity of technique and vision. . . . We become aware of the closeness of African village life to the soil, to the movement of the seasons and to the gods who are present in the elements. The tribe has its history, its social divisions, economy, ethics, customs, myth, religion, cosmology, and, most important, its traditional wisdom handed from generation to generation through proverbs. The proverbs, which are the most noticeable feature of Achebe's style, occur mostly in the first part of the novel, before the coming of the white man; they are guides to social and moral behaviour, and represent a kind of wisdom literature. Early in the novel we are told 'Proverbs are the palm-oil with which words are eaten.' Such proverbs as 'If a child washed his hands he could eat with kings' and 'A man who pays respect to the great paves the way for his own greatness' are repositories of social advice. These two proverbs, however, are somewhat contradictory in attitude: one teaches purity in selfhood, the other obedience to those in power. Achebe does not pretend that traditional Igbo culture was totally self-consistent. At various places in the novel it is mentioned that customs important in one village are ignored in the next, and that customs change. Indeed, he wants to show that traditional society was not static. Repugnance at such traditional practices as the killing of twins or the treatment of outcasts made Christianity attractive to many of the villagers. Moreover, Okonkwo, who sees himself as the upholder of traditional values, is himself out of harmony with the village, which has changed considerably during the seven years of his exile. His act of defiance in killing the messenger of the white men is in keeping with his previous excesses and his suicide which follows, is, within tribal custom, a greater crime against his society than that of which he accuses others.

There are two techniques in *Things Fall Apart* that make the novel seminal to Nigerian literature in the way that *Huckleberry Finn* is the beginning of modern American fiction. The first characteristic is Achebe's reshaping of English into a Nigerian prose style. The inclusion of Igbo words and the translation of Igbo proverbs into English has often been commented upon. Equally worthy of notice is the modification of Nigerian spoken

English to make it into a literary style; diction and word order are often based more upon Nigerian than British usage. . . . The other characteristic is the change in narration of the novel according to the kind of community it describes. The self-enclosed world of the nine villages in the opening pages is accepted on its own valuation and terms. Although Achebe describes traditional Igbo society for the benefit of the reader, recreating a now lost world, he sees it from the inside, accepting its premises.

There are several different perspectives combined within the first half of the book. Achebe as narrator describes traditional Igbo life to the reader, objectively narrates events, acts as the voice of the community and offers comment on the characters which implies judgement. In other places he indirectly presents the psychology of the characters or allows them their individuality through dramatisation. He rapidly alternates techniques to create a consistency of appearance. . . . (pp. 66-8)

If the first half of the novel is told from within the psychology of the village, the third part of the novel stylistically reflects the social and psychological changes that have occurred with the coming of the white man. There are fewer proverbs or Igbo words, fewer expressions which appear to be based on Igbo idioms. As the unity of village opinion is lost and division occurs requiring a larger perspective on events, the style becomes more distanced. . . .

In the passage describing various reactions to Okonkwo's suicide there are radical shifts of perspective ranging from Obierika's 'That man was one of the greatest men in Umuofia' to the messenger's 'Yes, suh', the latter indicative of the new political order and social hierarchy. (p. 69)

The old values no longer hold, but no stable new set of values has become accepted. It is this problem that underlies *Things Fall Apart* and that is treated more explicitly in Achebe's second novel, *No Longer at Ease* (1960).

The story of *No Longer at Ease* concerns Obi Okonkwo, the grandson of the Okonkwo of the first novel, who returns from his studies in England to become a civil servant in Nigeria a few years before the independence. . . . The novel traces the social forces that turn Obi Okonkwo from an idealist into another corrupt member of the new society that has emerged in modern Africa. After the opening pages describing Obi's trial, the narrative moves back into the past beginning with the decision to send him to England for further education. This is followed by a straightforward narrative description of his economic and social problems after his return to Nigeria. While putting the normal conclusion of the narrative at the beginning of the book is dramatically effective, its main purpose is to make the subsequent events appear determined. It focuses attention on the narrative as a study in social cause and effect; the opening pages of the novel show us a promising young Nigerian on trial in a corrupt society, and the remainder of the story will show what has made him what he is.

The quotation from T. S. Eliot's 'The Journey of the Magi' is relevant in suggesting that Obi, like the biblical wise men, is caught between two eras: an older Nigeria with its demands of responsibility towards family and clan, and a modern Nigeria, still unborn, in which individuals live their own life, follow their own conscience, and use their money to pay taxes, electricity bills, run automobiles and choose their own wife. Obi says: 'What is a pioneer? Someone who shows the way. That is what I am doing.' He has the worst of both worlds, the responsibilities of the past and the money economy of the present.

But it is perhaps wrong to view Obi as a fallen hero. . . . Obi himself warns: 'Real tragedy is never resolved. It goes on hopelessly for ever.' The tragedy in the novel has no real resolution because it began earlier when his father became a Christian, turning against the ways of *his* father, and thus destroying the cultural unity of the family and village. If *No Longer at Ease* is a study in the cultural chaos of Nigeria on the eve of independence, it also shows Achebe's nostalgia for an ordered—if imperfect—past, when there was one accepted code of values.

His third novel, *Arrow of God* (1964), contrasts a strong individual, Ezeulu the Chief Priest of Ulu, with a confused, pliant community. . . . The main irony of the novel is that Ezeulu had previously been a voice for the acceptance of social change. Ezeulu is the first in the village to send one of his sons to study at the white man's school and to the Christian church. His favourite expression to signify the need to adjust to social change is 'A man must dance the dance prevalent in his time.'

As in *Things Fall Apart,* we are told that tradition changes and is not static. Tribal facial marks were once customary but are now considered old-fashioned and no longer used. African gods and customs are made for the survival of the clan and are not of transcendent importance in themselves. Ulu, the god for whom Ezeulu is chief priest, was made when previous gods had failed the six villages. If a god fails, he is forgotten or destroyed and another god takes his place.

Ezeulu's tragedy is that he believes his god has told him to punish the villages for being influenced by the priest of the Python god. He sees himself as an arrow of his god scourging the clan. This has made him rigid, and his rigidity necessarily must be rejected by the clan if it is to survive. His excess of will and courage makes him a victim of history. (pp. 71-3)

A theme of [*Arrow of God*] is the effect of the British policy of indirect rule. Although the intentions are innocent there is, ironically, interference in African ways in the hope of strengthening African self-rule: a corrupt, semi-westernised, English-speaking class (forerunners of the future elite) is created, and old customs are accidentally weakened and destroyed. Mission-educated Africans are appointed chiefs and they use their European-given power to organise vast systems of extortion, taking bribes, creating illegal taxes, and intimidating the villages. The clan has no means of protecting itself against such chiefs created by the Europeans. And to make matters worse, the government is inconsistent and, because of the distance of the bureaucracy from the local scene, irresponsible.

It is probable that the cultural tensions and confusions of *Arrow of God,* while based on historical fact, reflect the period during which the book was written. It observes the rise of a class of Africans who, working for the state, feel free of tribal ethics, and describes the changes that have occurred in Africa as a result of western education, the Christian religion, and the impersonal apparatus of central government. The novel sets the stage for the drama depicted in *No Longer at Ease,* showing

the long historical process which created Obi Okonkwo and modern Nigeria. The tension between the six villages, their leaders and their priests is not unlike that between tribes in post-independence Nigeria. There is, however, one supposed difference between the past and the present, shown by the statement made several times in the novel that one man cannot go against the clan. Whether the clan is right or wrong—and it is often wrong—it has its social mechanisms of reconciliation, judgement, sanctions and survival; the new national state produced by colonialism, as seen in *No Longer at Ease* and *A Man of the People,* has no organic unity, no moral sense, no mechanism of purgation; its values follow from the corrupting powers given the warrant chiefs, messengers and police by the colonial government.

One difference between *A Man of the People* (1966) and Achebe's previous novels is the use of a first-person narrator, Odili. Whereas the omniscient narrator of the village novels assumed the perspective and sometimes the voice of the community, the use of the first-person narrator is significant of the lack of traditional communal values in the new nation. The conclusion of the novel makes explicit the difference between the traditional society of the past, with its sense of moral obligation, and the new state, with its uncontrolled corruption and lack of ethical sense. . . . The use of pidgin is revealing. The old moral sayings of the Igbos have no relevance to a nation made up of various tribes and cultures; pidgin, a bastard mixture of African and foreign languages, expresses the individualism, immorality and materialism which have resulted from the colonial period and the independent nation which followed. (pp. 74-6)

The novel is set in a period of growing social tensions which reflect the political crisis in Nigeria after independence. Mention is made of various strikes, rapid inflation, favouritism towards politically loyal villages and political thuggery. British companies pay vast bribes to control the economy and American neo-colonialism arrives in the form of aid, investment, willing white women and anti-communism. A radical Marxist party, supported by an Eastern European nation, is formed and its leader killed on election day. As political thuggery gets out of hand and the government loses control, the army takes over. This, Odili tells us, is no triumph of the people over its corrupt leaders. The people themselves 'had become even more cynical than their leaders and were apathetic into the bargain'. While it would be a mistake to equate Odili with Achebe, it is clear that *A Man of the People* not only reflects a growing animosity between the Nigerian intellectuals of the mid-sixties and the government, it shows that disillusionment with independence had set in; the desire of the people for western luxuries appeared as corrupt as the government. With increased political and social changes brought about by independence, the ideal of an organic, communal way of life had even more validity, although now it was used in contrast to the new national society. (pp. 76-7)

Bruce King, "Nigeria I: The Beginnings and Achebe," in his The New English Literatures: Cultural Nationalism in a Changing World *(© Bruce King 1980; reprinted by permission of Macmillan, London and Basingstoke), Macmillan, 1980, pp. 58-77.**

Roger Angell
1920-

American nonfiction writer, short story writer, critic, and editor.

Angell has a deft ability for analyzing the intricacies and subtleties of the game of baseball and for focusing on events and people that reveal the sport's ongoing human drama. Since 1960 Angell has been contributing essays and general observations on baseball to *The New Yorker.* **Several features that characterize the magazine are evident in Angell's writings: finely crafted prose, painstaking analysis, and dry humor. His pieces have been collected in three highly acclaimed works—** *The Summer Game,* **which covers the years 1961-1971;** *Five Seasons: A Baseball Companion* **(1972-1976); and** *Late Innings: A New Baseball Companion* **(1977-1981).**

Angell is most concerned that baseball maintain the traditions which have united players and fans in a continuing seasonal ritual, providing lasting memories that tie the present to the past. Critics have praised the sensitive concern and passion with which Angell chronicles an era of significant change, when many intimate midcity ballparks have been replaced by massive suburban stadiums. Angell particularly dislikes the advent of artificial turf, free agency, designated hitters, and multimillion dollar revenues, but he finds little change in the essence of the game itself. Most critics view Angell as an extraordinarily talented writer who has found his niche in writing about baseball but whose work can be appreciated by the general reader as well.

(See also *Contemporary Authors,* **Vols. 57-60.)**

Corporation), Vol. 97, No. 8, April 15, 1972, p. 1456.

KEITH CUSHMAN

Angell is simply the most elegant, stylish, and intelligent baseball writer in the country today. His annual autumn account of the World Series [that appears in the *New Yorker*] has come to be a major event for me—and on occasion it proves to be better than the World Series. Angell knows that baseball is a game deeply wedded to ritual and tradition, and the perennial smack of horsehide against leather is becoming increasingly difficult to reconcile with inflated schedules, floating franchises, and an American League club called the Texas Rangers. Money has become the name of the national pastime, and a decided elegiac note runs through Angell's expert reporting. *The Summer Game* collects Angell's *New Yorker* baseball writings, and the teams parade by—in spring training, in heated pennant races, in the World Series—from the 1962 Amazin' Mets to the 1971 world champion Pirates. Perhaps some would feel that a few of these pieces are a little too ephemeral for republication, but everyone who understands with the author that baseball is a country of the heart will recognize *The Summer Game* as the treasure it is.

> *Keith Cushman, in his review of "The Summer Game," in* Library Journal *(reprinted from* Library Journal, *April 15, 1972; published by R. R. Bowker Co. (a Xerox company); copyright © 1972 by Xerox*

CHRISTOPHER LEHMANN-HAUPT

The bare bones of Roger Angell's **"The Summer Game"** do not seem promising. Ten years' worth of reports on baseball that have already appeared in The New Yorker, where Mr. Angell is chief resident buff? Twenty-one installments on our great national pastime written during a period when—thanks to expanding teams and schedules, carpetbagging owners and Charles O. Finley—baseball has threatened to become our great national bore? Pages devoted to such forgettable episodes as the triumph of the New York Yankees over the San Francisco Giants in the 1962 World Series, or the Orioles' sweep of the A's in the 1971 divisional playoffs? Who—as the expression goes—needs it? But what such a summary of **"The Summer Game"** fails to reckon with is Mr. Angell's love of the game. It is a love that sees a fair complexion beneath the old girl's flaking make-up. It is a love that still finds the prospect of a summer without box scores to mull over "like trying to think about infinity." It is a love that sees poetry in names like Ossee Schreckengoat, Smead Jolley, Cletus Elwood Poffenberger and Luscious Easter. It wonders how many Burleigh Grimeses can dance on the head of a pin.

It is a love that had Mr. Angell chasing around the country from 1962 to 1971 attending ''grandmothers' funerals''—his euphemism for significant confrontations on emerald diamonds all the way from San Francisco Bay to Back Bay. It had him poking around the vulgar splendors of the Houston Astrodome, trying to imagine plastic worms a-wiggling beneath the pluck-proof plastic grass, or sitting at the right hand of Judge Roy Hofheinz, ''the Kublai Khan of the Domed Stadium,'' who swigged his coffee from a golden cup, dropped cigar ashes into an outstretched golden glove and expounded for Mr. Angell's benefit on the art of entertaining baseball fans with electronic scoreboards and fine restaurants, as if watching the game itself weren't entertainment enough.

[No] matter what [the owners] did to the surface of the game, there was always the game itself for Mr. Angell. . . .

So return with him here to the days when the Mets were still patsies. . . . Return to the dear days not so long ago when . . . [Spiro] Agnew was only a name on the sunshades of Oriole fans at the 1966 World Series.

Savor the gentle comedy of elderly fans watching baseball's spring exercise in the Florida sun. See Whitey Ford in the 1962 World Series, standing ''on the mound like a Fifth Avenue bank president''; or Lou Brock in the '67 Series, ''a tiny little time pill that kept going off at intervals during the entire week''; or Dick Hall in the '70 Series, pitching ''with an awkward, sidewise motion that suggests a man feeling under his bed for a lost collar stud.'' . . .

Recall **''The Flowering and Subsequent Deflowering of New England''** in 1967, when Boston Red Sox fans, after years of misery, saw their team rise almost to the pinnacle, only to be denied by Bob Gibson and the Cardinals in the seventh game of the Series. See the Mets arrive at ''downright competence'' and then go on to the larger miracle of 1969. Rarely has it all been described so well.

Mr. Angell isn't blind with love. . . . He waxes wroth on what TV has wrought. But his criticisms are subsumed beneath his love, and both in turn are servants of his wit and style.

That is finally what makes this old news so fresh and vivid—Mr. Angell's wit and style. I have a game I sometimes play while dropping off to sleep or shaving; it involves imagining certain writers as ballplayers—Norman Mailer as a sort of Yogi Berra, lofting bad pitches out of the park; John Updike as Ted Williams, a .400 hitter who never played on a World Series winner. . . . Among baseball writers, Roger Angell is a sort of Al Kaline or Billy Goodman; no star of the brightest magnitude, he does it all well and makes it all look easy. And reading all his pieces together makes one realize how well he's been playing throughout the years.

Christopher Lehmann-Haupt, ''Angell Wings Over Baseball,'' in The New York Times *(© 1972 by The New York Times Company; reprinted by permission), June 6, 1972, p. 39.*

TED SOLOTAROFF

''The Summer Game'' provides such finely observed and finely written reportage on major-league baseball during the past decade that I hope it will triumph over certain of its disadvantages. One is that it is a collection of pieces. Collections don't sell unless they have an obvious gimmick, and I don't see any in sight for Roger Angell's witty but tactful coverage. Still, **''The Summer Game''** is a genuine book, unified by its ongoing account of the new developments and distortions of the sport and integrated by Angell's consistent ability to capture the ''feel'' of the player, the game, the series, the pennant race, and by his articulate and imaginative defense of the sport itself against its adversaries, beginning with the major league owners.

All of this creates a second liability: Angell's book is written for the sophisticated fan rather than for the adolescent one—chronological or arrested—that most sports books are aimed at. A writer concerned with the nature and nuances of baseball space and baseball time, or with the social and psychological differences between the pastoral old ball parks and the new programed stadiums, or who refers, however naturally and aptly, to the ''Caligulan whims'' of the owner of the Oakland A's, or who elegantly sums up the Mets in 1968 as a team that ''went on winning, sometimes implacably, sometimes improbably,'' is not likely to reach many of the heavy consumers.

There have been a few relatively adult baseball books such as [Jim Bouton's] ''Ball Four'' and now ''The Boys of Summer'' which make the best-seller lists, mostly because they cater to the contemporary penchant for candor or nostalgia or both, and satisfy the fan's perennial question of what So-and-So is ''really like.'' Angell has none of this; his base of observation is behind first base rather than in the clubhouse or hotel room. He will tell you that Choo Choo Coleman, a catcher for the early Mets, ''handles outside curve balls like a man fighting off bees,'' but nothing about his sex life or racial attitudes. Angell's book has the further misfortune of following in the wake and glare of the similarly titled ''The Boys of Summer,'' by another Roger (Kahn) to boot. Hopefully, some readers will pick up **''The Summer Game''** and looking for the cant of the new journalism—two parts low-down, one part corn, and a dash of obscenity—they will discover the freshness, accuracy and the unexpected depths of Angell's prose—roughly the difference, in baseball parlance, between a flashy but limited thrower and a polished and versatile pitcher: Vinegar Bend Mizell going against Warren Spahn. Page for page, **''The Summer Game''** contains not only the classiest but also the most resourceful baseball writing I have ever read. . . .

Now and then Angell lapses into certain mannerisms of The New Yorker, where he is an editor and where these pieces first appeared. His genuine enthusiasm and empathy can tail off into the habitual amiability and coyness of the ''Talk of the Town'' [section of that magazine]. Angell sometimes adopts Eustace Tilley's stiff-upper-lip or cautiously balanced response to the rapacious, stupid, vulgar or mendacious policies that have been plaguing the sport, instead of letting his own anger and dismay rip as decisively as it does elsewhere. Also he is a bit fond of New Yorker status words—''équipage'' for team, ''match'' for game, etc.—and of euphonious but slightly arch expressions like ''the fealty of the fans.'' But this is nitpicking and obscures the main point of Angell's relation to The New Yorker, which is positive and bracing (in both senses). Just as he owes his full-bodied, free-wheeling, ruminative style to his magazine's willingness to allow its writers the space, time and freedom to develop the subject in their own individual way, so, too, Angell's point of view fits into and is sustained by its dominant editorial purpose: the conservation of traditions.

The primary tradition of baseball is pastoral—not just the sunshine, swept dirt and green grass but the spacious space and slow time of the game. This affects not only the dynamics of play but also the tone of conduct. (p. 1)

[As] Angell brilliantly observes, the particular charm of modern baseball has been that the old "Parks" (Shibe, Sportsmen's, etc.), "Fields" (Ebbets, Forbes, etc.) and "Grounds" (Polo) were in intensely urban settings and were filled with the resonances between the countryside of the past and the city of the present. Thus, the Polo Grounds was both a "green barn" on a lazy summer afternoon, complete with birds in the eaves, and a dirty, noisy, crowded, intimate neighborhood of "front stoops and fire escapes." . . . (p. 14)

With appropriate rue, Angell reports on the new stadiums, which are suburban—not only in location but in character: pretty, clean, unobstructed, dull, isolating. Most of the seats are remote from any part of the field and many of the fans are remote from the game, following it by portable radios and diverted between pitches and innings by baseball's answer to TV—the massive electronic scoreboard. And beyond the supermarket functionalism of Shea and Dodger Stadiums lies the first of the "giant living rooms," Angell's apt metaphor for the Houston Astrodome, "complete with manmade weather, wall-to-wall carpeting, clean floors, and unrelenting TV show."

Such décor breeds a complementary decorum: well-dressed, polite fans who never rise above a hand-clap and never descend to a boo and who dutifully respond to the programed jokes, cheers, cartoons and ads on the scoreboard. (pp. 14, 16)

Another tradition rapidly falling by the wayside in the last decade is team identity and fan loyalty. Thanks to the relocation of many teams, which has reached the point where some franchises resemble the career of a utility infielder, and the shifting around of players through expansion of the leagues, few of the clubs are left with any of the identifiable character they once had. . . .

What then is an ex-Giant fan like Angell to do? Well, there are still the pastoral roots that flower briefly each year in spring training. There are still the clarity, tautness, precision and slowly mounting tension of the close, well-played game. There are the omens which reveal the outcome of a game, a pennant race, a World Series, or even the changing character of a team. There is the mystique of "jinxes" and "luck"—the ever-present vagaries and inner logic of chance, which makes baseball such a tense, exacting and revelatory sport: its relentless testing of the players, each isolated and on his own whether at bat or in the field, each aware that success or failure will come in inches. . . .

But most of all, there is what Angell calls "the interior stadium," fostered by baseball's unique quality of clockless time, that fills with each game's own tempo, mood, character and duration. . . . This intense watching leaves a residue of memory and desire, which enables Angell to replay the great performances and games he has seen. Moreover, baseball time cancels the alterations of historical time, joins the players of the past to those of the present in a seamless, unchanging fourth dimension. (p. 16)

Ted Solotaroff, "Green and Spacious, Played in Clockless Time," in The New York Times Book Review *(© 1972 by The New York Times Company; reprinted by permission), June 11, 1972, pp. 1, 14, 16, 18.*

PAUL GRAY

Angell is a formidable humorist. Yet he sees all the current tinkering with baseball as no laughing matter. He imagines a

time when the World Series will be totally surrendered to television, transported to some domed stadium, and made the excuse for a week of canned spectaculars. If network and baseball moguls have not already dreamed up this plan, they will now. Angell protests: "We are trying to conserve something that seems as intricate and lovely to us as any river valley. . . .

True fans need no convincing. They can read *Five Seasons* for remembrances of games, pennant races and World Series past, for another chance to think about their beloved sport under the tutelage of an expert. . . .

Angell's style neatly complements the balance, pace and mathematical exactitudes of the game he celebrates. He does not throw many high, hard ones; he favors the change of pace, the roundhouse curve. (p. 95)

Five Seasons contains leisurely off-the-diamond reporting: Angell travels through the hinterlands with a major league scout, a species of rugged individualist now threatened by cooperative head-hunting and centralized data banks. He visits three hyperfans of the Detroit Tigers and comes up with a deft report on the joys of obsession. He spends time with Steve Blass, a top pitcher for the Pittsburgh Pirates until, during the winter of 1972, he inexplicably lost the knack of getting batters out. Angell quotes one of Blass's coaches: "You know, old men don't dream much, but just the other night I had this dream that Steve Blass was all over his troubles and could pitch again."

Is not such poignancy wasted on a game? Angell thinks not, for several reasons. Baseball's vivid intensity, the demands it makes on players and knowing spectators, is the very stuff of dreams. The freebooting expansion and big-money dealing have also made it a model of reality, "no longer a release from the harsh everyday American business world but its continuation and apotheosis." Angell admits the foolishness of rooting for a professional sports team, a constantly revolving roster of athletes playing for money. Except for one thing. "What is left out of this calculation," he writes, "is the business of caring—caring deeply and passionately, really *caring*—which is a capacity or an emotion that has almost gone out of our lives." *Five Seasons* radiates this capacity—and nurtures it. (p. 96)

Paul Gray, "Splendor in the Astroturf," in Time *(copyright 1977 Time Inc.; all rights reserved; reprinted by permission from* Time*), Vol. 109, No. 20, May 16, 1977, pp. 95-6.*

JONATHAN YARDLEY

Make no mistake about it, *Five Seasons* is a "baseball book." It is, in point of fact, one of the two best baseball books we have—the other being Angell's *The Summer Game,* published in 1972—and anyone who loves our national pastime is going to love *Five Seasons.* But it is also so much more than a baseball book that a grave injustice will be done if only diehard fans read it. If its central subject is a game, it is also deeply concerned with larger, and in some cases darker, questions. . . .

As one who admired *The Summer Game* with unreserved ardor, I followed Angell's dispatches [in The New Yorker] in the five years after its publication with uneasiness and apprehension; it seemed to me that he was in danger of repeating himself, and that he was becoming a member of the Baseball Establishment, that pack of journalists and assorted hangers-on who yap at the heels of the younger, handsomer and luckier men who play the game. Brought together in one volume, however, Angell's 1972-76 baseball pieces prove me resoundingly wrong. *Five Seasons* makes abundantly clear that Angell has been altering the focus of his writing rather than trading on past glories, and that he has become a ferocious and devastating critic of the game's commercialization and debasement.

It is true that Angell now talks to the men on the field rather than watching them from the stands, but what is noteworthy is that he is not primarily interested in the people everyone else is talking to. In three different pieces he introduces us to five men who love baseball profoundly and whose lives have been shaped by it to various, but in each case important, degrees. . . .

The [Steve] Blass profile is one of the finest pieces Angell has written. Without the slightest hint of sentimentality, but with compassion and sympathy, Angell explores one of the more puzzling mysteries of baseball history: "Steve Blass . . . is out of baseball, having been recently driven into retirement by two years of pitching wildness—a sudden, near-total inability to throw strikes. No one, including Blass himself, can cure or explain it." The piece, however, is far less about inexplicable failure than it is about a man of limited talent but powerful dedication who managed to fulfill the dream of a lifetime. . . .

A Steve Blass, unfortunately, is rarer and rarer in a game that has become a child of corporate America. Angell, who is drawn to baseball in large measure because of the memories it holds for him of his own childhood, is angry and bitter. . . . (p. G1)

In the end, however, Angell cannot resist the lure of the game he loves so well, and the book ends on a hopeful note. I know what he means. During this year's spring training here in Florida, my two sons and I went through a real baseball orgy of autographs and hot dogs and home runs and double plays, and if the boys felt half as rejuvenated as I did, they were in great shape. . . .

Together with *The Summer Game, Five Seasons* is an unmatched and, is and I think, unmatchable account not merely of how baseball is played but the place it occupies in the national consciousness. No other sport has ever been so well served by any other writer. (p. G2)

Jonathan Yardley, "The Diamond's Best Friend," in Book World—The Washington Post *(© 1977, The Washington Post), June 5, 1977, pp. G1-G2.*

EDWARD HOAGLAND

I've never read a sporting novel that succeeded as do novels of the sea or of the West, . . . although I've read a number that attempted to inflate one sport or another into a subject as pelagic as the sea and as enormous as the West. The solution seems to lie with a zinging new book out about baseball by Roger Angell called *Five Seasons*. . . . [It] is so jammed with glee and eagerness and lore and exact fact that they all do manage to meld together. (p. 76)

The savage element of money has invaded even the players' side of baseball lately and has lent it what may turn out to be a new dimension. Angell takes an uncertain crack at defining this, having defined all of the old dimensions already. On more mundane matters, he says that batters have been losing out to pitchers because of the many night games, because of better pitcher-coaching, better bullpens, and the invention of the slider, which can be thrown with no discernible change in motion.

He suggests an orange baseball, and shaving the edges of home plate a little, so that the .275 "slugger" can become a .350 hitter again; but no disruptive alterations like the "designated hitter," who disjoints the essential strategy of the game, or a World Series propelled into such wintry weather by wild-card play-off games that it reaches the status of a Sugar Bowl at last.

Outside the ball park, Mr. Angell is a *New Yorker* editor and over many years has helped to shape that publication's famous shrinking-violet writing style. Very occasionally he himself falls victim to it. More often he is on vacation, though, pleasuring himself with the traditional chestnuts of baseball scribes: "the starting hurler," "the starboard garden," "the visiting nine," "the pill," "a hummer," "a round-tripper," "a four-ply blow," "heavy mitting," a "rainmaking" fly. Perhaps because *The New Yorker* tends to run overlong profiles, he avoids profiles on these days off. Indeed, except for [Steve] Blass (who has a writerly "block") and a baseball scout named Ray Scarborough, we hear rather little about most of the people behind the lively feats he makes us privy to. He's short on atmosphere also, a feel for time and place, although he's so lavish with action, names, a thousand bits of memory thrown glittering in together, so full of modesty and humor and generous spirits you know he *has* it and has assumed that you do too. The only other way he might be faulted is that, except for a few overtargeted villains like Charlie Finley and Bowie Kuhn, he never says anything about anybody that might wear out his welcome anywhere; he's awfully discreet.

But this is quibbling. The book is irresistible, the best companion to the sport since Angell's own *The Summer Game* in 1972. . . . (pp. 76, 78)

Edward Hoagland, "A Fan's Notes," in Harper's *(copyright © 1977 by Edward Hoagland; reprinted by permission of Lescher & Lescher, Ltd, as agents for the author), Vol. 255, No. 1526, July, 1977, pp. 76, 78.*

DONALD HALL

Roger Angell's *Five Seasons* bears comparison with one other baseball book—Roger Angell's *The Summer Game* (1972). The new book is even better than the first, and renders the game from various places of enlightened vantage. In *The Summer Game* Angell remained largely in the stands, describing the green mural as innings transpired before him—descriptions which blended the welcome repetitions of the game with its sudden minute varieties of action. He described a painting (a strange one, with moving figures) which carried its own light with it. Now in *Five Seasons* he describes baseball as if it were sculpture, which changes as you perceive it by walking around it, or as day's light moves over the stone from pink dawn through white noon to yellow twilight. Now he writes not only observing the game itself, as the sport's most articulate fan, but observing the work of professionals on the sidelines: owner, ex-player, roving scout. He writes of lawsuits and commissioners, players' unions and free agents, lockouts and the [designated hitter] and nighttime World Series TV spectaculars; he writes of Howard Cosell and Bowie Kuhn.

Still the *best* of Angell renders the game on the field. . . . I forgot to mention that, in the course of rendering and advocating, Angell from time to time is extremely funny.

Five Seasons is a fan's notes on baseball from 1972 through 1976, five early seasons and on-going seasons, and five specimens of the World Series, featuring the 1975 epic between [Cincinnati] Reds and [Boston] Red Sox. Angell describes extraordinary things with humor and vigor, but he excels at rendering the game's Ordinary Moments—a normal July in an undistinguished year—and stops action like a good sports photograph, freezing for the perpetual album of memory not a dramatic moment but a typical one. Baseball's *echt* moment is typical or ordinary; those who cherish the game cherish repeated scenes, and Angell is Shakespeare to the diamond's archetypes. . . .

Angell's prose is graceful and pleasant, with never a misstep, never cliché or corn or overstatement or pomposity. What a pleasure it is to read him, like the pleasure of watching effortless fielding around second base. Angell can *pick it.* And the construction of his articles—as well as the dance of syntax and the proportion of analogies—makes for our pleasure. He paces his essays—up and down, slow and fast, back and forth—leading the reader lightly, giving him just enough of each subject to leave him wanting more. I watch his essayistic subtleties and shenanigans with admiration and despair, much as a Beer League softball pitcher might observe [pitcher] Luis Tiant.

When Angell comes to the subject of baseball's owners and the imperatives of television—to Howard Cosell and Bowie Kuhn—anger replaces his usual good humor, as he defends the game against the gods of hype. . . .

Criticisms of baseball's enemies form a rightful part of this book, because Angell's prose and vision serve the game. But the *plupart* of *Five Seasons* is grandly positive. (p. 1183)

Donald Hall, "A Fan's Notes," in National Review (© National Review, Inc., 1977; 150 East 35th St., New York, N.Y. 10016), Vol. XXIX, No. 40, October 14, 1977, pp. 1183-84.

ART HILL

Rather than try to match superlatives with other reviewers of Roger Angell's new baseball book [*Late Innings*] let's just say Angell is back, and the stuff is as good as ever. That should be news enough for most fans, because Angell is special to so many of us. . . .

The degree of his caring about baseball, I think, is what makes Angell so special. Quite apart from his tremendous technical knowledge and his sharp eye for a significant, generally unnoticed detail, he obviously loves the game unstintingly. And anything that threatens it—such as the inclination of some team owners to adopt a farcical playoff system in 1981—threatens him. Some of us appreciate that.

As always, Angell is mainly concerned with major league players, but there are some rewarding side trips, notably to the playing fields of Yale in the company of Smokey Joe Wood, the 91-year-old former Yale coach who won 34 games as a Red Sox pitcher in 1912, and to the big league locker rooms (or the corridors just outside them) with several bright female reporters who were trying to breach that journalistic barrier in 1979. (p. 14)

One of the most appealing aspects of Angell's reporting is the air of seeming innocence he takes with him when he talks to baseball people, whether it be in a World Series locker room or on a lazy spring afternoon at a training camp in Arizona or Florida. You don't get informative answers from players and managers unless you ask the right questions, but Angell makes it look easy—and the reader's sense of identification is enhanced by the perception, false but compelling, that he could have done it himself with hardly any effort, given the opportunity.

The part I like best is the one that strays the farthest from the megabuck world of big-time sport. Angell traces two years in the career of a 27-year-old pitcher, once a promising pro prospect, who's giving baseball one more chance to discover him after an eight-year layoff. (pp. 14, 16)

Bob Gibson is here, too, in a brilliant essay that deftly combines Angell's vivid recollections of the great Cardinal pitcher's overpowering presence on the mound with a view of him in uneasy retirement in 1980. . . .

The piquant side dishes notwithstanding, the meat and potatoes of a Roger Angell baseball book is still his expert summation of major league seasons, and, like Reggie Jackson, he peaks in October. His accounts of the World Series resemble intricately plotted morality plays in which the good guys always win—whether by skill, determination or luck—because it would be unthinkable that the good guys might lose in this best of all possible games. (p. 16)

Art Hill, "Here's the Essence of Five Baseball Seasons by a Master of Rich Detail" (reprinted by permission of the author), in Sports Illustrated, Vol. 56, No. 20, May 17, 1982, pp. 14, 16.

JONATHAN YARDLEY

Late Innings is [Angell's] third collection of baseball pieces, and on the whole it reaffirms his position as the most astute and graceful chronicler the sport has known. I say "on the whole" because, at the risk of seeming to deface a national monument, I find Angell somewhat short of his best in many of these articles, which appeared in *The New Yorker* between 1977 and 1981. He has, perhaps, stayed too long at the fair; especially in his by-now-traditional spring-training and post-season pieces, he too often seems to be going through the motions—brilliant and inimitable motions, to be sure, but familiar ones all the same. This may cause no ennui on the reader's part, but I sense some on Angell's; he is repeating himself, as in his repeated references here to "the foolish and dispiriting winter baseball news." With the exception of a fine profile of the great pitcher Bob Gibson, and several passages in other pieces, Angell's best baseball writing is not here, but in *The Summer Game* and *Five Seasons.*

But these reservations are listed only because the writer under discussion is Roger Angell; he must be held to the standards he has set for himself, and they are very high indeed. Under any other byline, *Late Innings* would be welcomed as splendid work. It provides a perceptive, opinionated, informed account of five seasons that began with the three-homer high-water mark of "the Jacksonian Era"—Reggie Jacksonian, that is—and ended with the strike ("From first to last, the crisis was an invention of the owners . . .") and the farcical split season [of 1981]. Angell has penetrating things to say about interesting subjects: the father-son relationship between baseball generations, the age of big money, the growing distance between players and fans. Above all, he is a fan who loves the game, who understands its intricacy and its mystery and its history. (p. 3)

Jonathan Yardley, "Baseline Facts for Baseball Fans," in Book World—The Washington Post *(© 1982, The Washington Post), May 23, 1982, pp. 3, 9.**

Mark Harris, "Playing the Game," in The New York Times Book Review *(© 1982 by The New York Times Company; reprinted by permission), May 23, 1982, pp. 3, 18.*

MARK HARRIS

The 16 essays in **"Late Innings"** cover the period from 1977 to 1981 and, depending upon our geography, connect to our nostalgia for a past so recent that is has not been remembered. They also re-establish a claim about which there cannot have been much doubt. Although Mr. Angell's specialty is baseball, he marvelously avoids the clichés and weary formulations that characterize baseball writing. He never draws upon the stock of jargon that has been gathering for a century. He sees things by looking at them, not by remembering what has been so often said about them. He listens hard, especially to baseball players themselves (never to publicists), and by some masterful technique writes down the things these highly informed people say. . . .

Mr. Angell respects the game these people play, and because he cares for his own style and is rather a genius at writing well without seeming to press (which must be very hard work), he feels or understands the meaning of being excellent at the work one does. . . .

The great task as one grows older (Mr. Angell was born in 1920) is to keep the signs of weariness out, to conceal from one's enemies the fact of one's tiring. In that way one might go on indefinitely. A wise fan said to Mr. Angell, "But I'm not one of those who goes around always saying that the old players were the best." Good. Nor does Mr. Angell; therefore his writing remains young. This does not contradict the fact that during the five years covered by these pages Mr. Angell's center of interest shifts slightly. There seems to be more concern for the older player as opposed to the younger, for the retired player thinking back not only upon the glory that was but also upon what might have been had he only had the sense to make more of the short moment. . . . (p. 3)

Mr. Angell is one of those few lucky writers whose working arrangements enable them to write their specialties slowly, to be on top of the news in the way of The New Yorker rather than in the way of the daily newspaper, the television interviewer or the fanatical sports magazine. Thus he sees his subject whole—each of five complete April spring-training sessions or the entire season when it is over. He avoids speaking of the future, about which so much is said on so little basis. He has worked himself free of the worst demands of journalism, which so often produce in writers that desperation turning to hatred of their very subjects. For many sports reporters a convenient object of their fury was the woman reporter's winning her right to the clubhouse interview and to equal access generally. Mr. Angell's essay on female sports reporters is a fine example of work by a writer who is at once involved, unfettered and positive.

Journalism, even for The New Yorker, is subject to limitation, and inevitably these selections, sound and solid and satisfying as they are, lack the unity of a premeditated book. The good outcome of this is that the focus is finally upon the figure who is constant throughout—the tale-teller himself. I have met Mr. Angell at last through this slightly inadvertent self-portrait. He is the artist whose respect for the art he observes exceeds every temptation to cynicism. What makes a writer great to me is longevity. (p. 18)

WILFRID SHEED

Angell is doted on by the dabblers, the people who pick baseball up and put it down as the mood strikes, but is not, I believe, fully approved of in [sports columnist] Red Smith's kingdom, the press box, because he doesn't have to meet deadlines. In fact, most journalists wouldn't know what to do with the extra time if it was granted, as their occasional books show. But the Deadline is a stern discipline which makes for a brotherhood, and Angell isn't quite in it.

In fact, as a *New Yorker* writer, he has no natural allies in the business. He talks of dedicating **Late Innings** to the fans—by which he seems to mean something very close to E. M. Forster's "the sensitive, the decent and the plucky," a band of fellow spirits which one just has to take on faith. And speaking of Forster, imagine Angell's clip being passed around a locker room to appreciative chuckles: "As E. M. Forster said (I can still see him, with one spiked foot on the top step of the dugout and his keen, Ozark-blue eyes, under the peak of the pulled-down cap, fixed on some young batter just now stepping up to the plate), Only connect."

Neither a jock nor an English major would make much of this, but Angell soldiers on gamely. In his earlier baseball musings [Angell] seemed to accept his distance, and watch baseball under glass, like the *New Yorker's* Eustace Tilley peering through his monocle. But in his later books, especially [**Late Innings**], he has decided to go out and find those allies or quit. Among the players themselves, he notes that a surprisingly large number don't really like baseball or think about it more than they have to. But every now and then, he spots one of his phantom fans disguised in a baseball uniform, and his faith is restored.

Temporarily. These chronic reconversions lend a pinch of drama to what would otherwise be a random collection of pieces. **Late Innings** records a cycle of little deaths and rebirths as each spring he determines to give up the game, not because he thinks it unworthy of him but out of a sheer Sisyphean *Angst* rare in his dodge. (p. 46)

Thus our hero, stranded between two wastelands, too sensitive for one and too hearty for the other—but look, isn't that Bob Gibson or Pete Rose or Catfish Hunter, fellow humans all, arriving just in time? Or it might be a fellow teaching the fundamentals to kids or a PhD poet persuading her husband to take up professional pitching—always our hero is rescued (John Updike would probably call the book *Angell Is Risen*) in time to enjoy another surprisingly good season and an epiphany of a World Series.

There is nothing stagey about any of this. It is exactly what many of us go through every year, and Angell is our spokesman. How good does it make him? Previously he had been a crack utility-infielder at the *New Yorker*—short-story writer, film critic, fine editor—but hardly a household word. Then suddenly he found a whole new field to himself. Baseball had no [Eudora] Weltys or Updikes or [Pauline] Kaels to go up against; Angell's natural rivals were all chained to deadlines and space limitations and the hardened expectations of sports-page readers.

Angell could write any way he liked for a bright audience with no expectations—a heaven-sent opportunity to be terrific if you're even good. But there's usually a reason for such vacuums. Just try making spring training interesting sometime, with its unknown casts, its changeless routine, and its fly-me-to-Florida (or Arizona) settings, and you will see why other writers have left it to Roger. Angell's apparent freedom is like having the run of the Gobi Desert. Yet by a kind of hunt-and-peck method, a promising rookie here, a ruminating veteran there, he floods these bleak encampments with color. In his glowing vision, there is hardly such a thing as a dull ballplayer or a meaningless game: he will spot something in a pitcher's motion or a hitter's eyes that rivets you on the inessential until it fills the canvas. The heresy that "it's only a game" which bedeviled Red Smith becomes meaningless. Anything so sweetly concentrated on as this becomes as important as anything else—while the spell lasts.

So this is not, after all, some journeyman writer stumbling on a lucky subject. Angell was born to write about baseball; it consumes him, as artists are consumed, and there's no point asking how he'd do at something else. His feel for the game is sensual, and this seems to come through even to the heathen. He can describe a batter's swing with the thoroughness and exaltation of a man carving a statue. His years under glass taught him to *see* the game as an art student should; now that he knows the players he is ready to talk to them on a much deeper level than thin post-game chitchat. Other sportswriters know all that they need to know about a dozen or so sports, but Angell is a man of one sport, one god, so reading him is quite different in intensity from reading anybody else. He is indeed the Apostle to the Gentiles, and not in the same racket as the others. (pp. 46-7)

[Angell also reverses] Red Smith's tactic for dealing with a basically trivial subject, by removing it from the world of value altogether: baseball for baseball's sake might be his motto. Small boys can daub at it if they wish: insofar as they come into it, they are all to the good. "[Watching Tom Seaver] we had become children too, and this could not be permitted to last." As for old men, Angell tells a nice story about watching a college game with Smokey Joe Wood, a hero from the trolley-car days. Angell wants breathlessly to talk about the past, but Wood is too wrapped up in the game right there in front of him to pay much attention. Gradually, watching it through the old man's eyes, the author sees that this particular Yale-St. John's game is one of the greatest ever played, if not the very greatest, and he might have missed it if he'd had his way. Angell has just been taught a lesson of a kind one usually turns to *him* for.

My one caveat about this elegant chronicle of five seasons (1977-1981) is that the extramural stuff—the baseball strike, women reporters in the clubhouse, and whatnot—could as well have been handled by any concerned citizen, and I'm only sorry that this fine pictorial writer had to be bothered with it. (p. 47)

Wilfrid Sheed, "Reds," in The New York Review of Books *(reprinted by permission of the author), Vol. XXIX, No. 14, September 23, 1982, pp. 45-8.**

Isaac Asimov

1920-

(Also wrote under the pseudonym of Paul French) Russian-born American novelist, short story writer, nonfiction writer, essayist, editor, and autobiographer.

Asimov is a prolific writer and is regarded by many critics as the most important and influential author in the science fiction genre. His novels have done much to make science fiction a critically accepted field, and his laws of robotics and the factual information in many of his stories have earned him the respect of laypersons and scientists alike. In his fiction there is an underlying concern for humanity and its survival in the face of advancing technology. His stories often deal with such contemporary social problems as overpopulation, the threat of atomic warfare, or racial prejudice.

Asimov's stories first appeared in the science fiction magazines of the 1930s and 1940s, and most have now been published in such collections as *I, Robot*, *Asimov's Mysteries*, and *The Bicentennial Man*. He is credited as the first writer to integrate successfully the properties of science fiction with those of the detective novel. *The Caves of Steel* and its sequel, *The Naked Sun*, are successful works of this type. Asimov's long-awaited sequel to the Foundation trilogy, *Foundation's Edge*, has recently been published. Like most of his fiction, it is readable, entertaining, and intellectually stimulating. His *Foundation* trilogy won the Hugo award for best all-time series in 1966 and his novel *The Gods Themselves* won both the Hugo and Nebula awards in 1972.

Asimov also writes nonfiction science books to introduce the general public to complex scientific procedures and discoveries and to alert readers to the effects of these scientific advancements.

(See also *CLC*, Vols. 1, 3, 9, 19; *Children's Literature Review*, Vol. 5; *Contemporary Authors*, Vols. 1-4, rev. ed.; *Contemporary Authors New Revision Series*, Vol. 2; *Something about the Author*, Vols. 1, 26; and *Dictionary of Literary Biography*, Vol. 8.)

NANCIE MATTHEWS

["**I, Robot**"] is an exciting science thriller, chiefly about what occurs when delicately conditioned robots are driven off balance by mathematical violations, and about man's eternal limitations. It could be fun for those whose nerves are not already made raw by the potentialities of the atomic age.

Nancie Matthews, "When Machines Go Mad," in The New York Times Book Review (© 1951 by The New York Times Company; reprinted by permission), February 4, 1951, p. 6.

ELLEN LEWIS BUELL

[In "**David Starr: Space Ranger**," a] tale of the seventieth century, Paul French ingeniously combines mystery with science fiction. His inventiveness and his use of picturesque details remind one of Robert Heinlein's books and, though his

Photograph by Jay Kay Klein

characters are not so fully developed as are Heinlein's, they are for the most part more individualized than in the usual story of this kind. There are moments, to be sure, when David Starr suggests the comic-strip hero, but he is convincing enough for the purposes of the story.

Ellen Lewis Buell, "Martian Mystery," in The New York Times Book Review (© 1952 by The New York Times Company; reprinted by permission), February 17, 1952, p. 34.

VILLIERS GERSON

["**Lucky Starr and the Oceans of Venus**"] is Paul French's best juvenile science fiction book to date. Crackling with suspense, lit by humor, sparkling with complexities of plot, and alive with interest, it is a tasty deep-sea dish for every reader who is young at heart.

The great underwater cities which harbor Earth's settlers on Venus are threatened with destruction by a hidden enemy who can control men's minds. Lucky Starr, youngest member of Earth's Council of Science, hurries to Venus with his friend, "Bigman" Jones, to discover why the Council's agent on Venus has turned traitor. Following a trail which grows increasingly complex, Starr and Bigman find themselves in fantastic danger, developed by the author both cunningly and scientifically. The identity of the book's villains is as surprising as it is inevitable. Here is a s-f juvenile guaranteed to keep young people away from the TV set—and, incidentally, to teach them facts about their solar system.

> *Villiers Gerson, "Hidden Enemy," in The New York Times Book Review, Part II (© 1954 by The New York Times Company; reprinted by permission), November 14, 1954, p. 10.*

H. H. HOLMES

It seems to be an open secret that "Paul French" is Isaac Asimov; and the latest adventure of Lucky Starr ["**Lucky Starr and the Oceans of Venus**"] is the first in this series to deserve comparison with Asimov's often admirable adult science fiction. Here he has dropped the foolish trappings which made earlier books seem like a blend of Space Patrol, Superman and the Lone Ranger, and devoted himself to a straightforward, near-Heinlein adventure on Venus—a tight, fast story, including a well-plotted detective puzzle and some excellent xenobiology—which, for the uninitiated, means the study of possible non-Earthly life forms.

> *H. H. Holmes, in a review of "Lucky Starr and the Oceans of Venus," in New York Herald Tribune Book Review (© I.H.T. Corporation), November 28, 1954, p. 16.*

H. H. HOLMES

["**Lucky Starr and the Big Sun of Mercury**"] is much the best of the Space Patrol genre this spring. It's an interplanetary detective story of sabotage on a mysterious project on Mercury, with well constructed deduction, exciting action and accurate astronomical information.

> *H. H. Holmes, in his review of "Lucky Starr and the Big Sun of Mercury," in New York Herald Tribune Book Review (© I.H.T. Corporation; reprinted by permission), May 13, 1956, p. 36.*

ROBERT BERKVIST

The swashbuckling science-fiction hero, Buck Rogers style, can be a pretty depressing fellow. In "**Lucky Starr and the Rings of Saturn**" . . . Paul French tells us how Lucky spoils the Sirians' plans to colonize one of our sun's planets. Studded with what one supposes are spaceman epithets, such as "Great Galaxy!" and "Sands of Mars!", this is a good guy vs. bad guy situation in which neat plotting is the saving grace of an otherwise ordinary effort.

> *Robert Berkvist, "Teen-Age Space Cadets," in The New York Times Book Review (© 1958 by The New York Times Company; reprinted by permission), December 14, 1958, p. 18.*

H. H. HOLMES

[In "**Lucky Starr and the Rings of Saturn**"], French-Asimov has fun with fresh variations on the Three Laws of Robotics . . . and lets David Starr contribute to future history by establishing, against the opposition of the sinister Sirians, the principal of the indivisibility of stellar systems. The novel's a mite short on plot, and much of its banter seems more childish than

youthful; but like all Asimov it is ingenious and carefully credible.

> *H. H. Holmes, "Three, Two, One, Zero and a Space Suit," in New York Herald Tribune Book Review (© I.H.T. Corporation; reprinted by permission), May 10, 1959, p. 27.**

THEODORE M. BERNSTEIN

["**Words of Science and the History Behind Them**" is] entertaining and informative. . . . Isaac Asimov, who has written science fiction and science truth, here discusses almost 1,500 scientific terms under 250 alphabetized headings, one to a page. The result is that Enzyme and Equator glare at each other incongruously from opposite pages, as they might in a dictionary. But this is no dictionary, nor even a comprehensive reference work. Yet it is packed with information about the meanings and derivations of words and the stories behind them, and it would appeal to any youthful reader with even slight scientific curiosity.

The discovery that an aneroid barometer is a "not wet" barometer, that a centrifugal force is one that flees from the center and a centripetal force is one that moves toward the center, that centigrade is the scale of "a hundred steps" from melting to boiling and that a telescope is a "distance watcher" is bound to be provocative to a young mind. And if the young mind wants a simple introduction to relativity, that is here, too—in 400 words. . . .

[In its field, this book functions] valuably in directing the attention of a new generation to words, those beautiful and useful tools of communication. (p. 63)

> *Theodore M. Bernstein, "More Than Meets the Eye and Ear," in The New York Times Book Review, Part II (© 1959 by The New York Times Company; reprinted by permission), November 1, 1959, pp. 3, 63.**

EMILY MAXWELL

["**Words of Science and the History Behind Them**"] is an alphabetically arranged collection of one-page essays on such unfamiliar words as catalysis, isomer, occultation, tantalum, and yttrium, and such quite ordinary words as artery, continent, cortisone, lever, nucleus, and planet. . . .

In addition to being a useful reference book, this is a delightful book for children of any age to read at random, because of the charm and freshness of the author's information and speculation, and his sense of the essential reasonableness and simplicity of all science.

> *Emily Maxwell, in her review of "Words of Science and the History Behind Them," in The New Yorker (© 1959 by The New Yorker Magazine, Inc.), Vol. XXXV, No. 40, November 21, 1959, pp. 236-37.*

VIRGINIA KIRKUS' SERVICE

In the lucid and information packed style that has rendered the author outstanding in the juvenile science field, Isaac Asimov describes twenty-six men and the moments at which they reversed the course of scientific thought [in *Breakthroughs in Science*]. . . . Embracing every area of science, this is a readable text which should interest even the most reluctant student, and is therefore recommended to school libraries.

> *A review of "Breakthroughs in Science," in* Virginia Kirkus' Service, *Vol. XXVIII, No. 19, October 1, 1960, p. 869.*

THEODORE C. HINES

[*Breakthroughs in Science* is a collection] of brief (1,500 words) essays on the life and work of nearly 30 important scientists and technologists. . . . Style is odd: paragraphs and sentences seem often to have been artificially shortened and most unlike Asimov's usual excellent, smooth-flowing exposition. The essays themselves seem far too short for the amount of ground covered. The whole project bears a most un-Asimov-like air, and the result is an inferior work from an author whose true excellence can usually be taken for granted. The general juvenile encyclopedias give far better coverage of the subject treated here.

> *Theodore C. Hines, in his review of "Breakthroughs in Science," in* Junior Libraries, *an appendix to* Library Journal *(reprinted from the December, 1960 issue of* Junior Libraries, *published by R. R. Bowker Co./A Xerox Corporation; copyright © 1960), Vol. 6, No. 4, December, 1960, p. 58.*

BETTY FLOWERS

[*The Rest of the Robots*] is a true delight—reprints of eight short stories and two novels all by Asimov and all written with his characteristic verve, intelligence and humor. In his introduction he gives a capsule history of the art of science fiction and its changing philosophy. He has arranged his selections by date of writing and has prefaced each with critical comments which trace his increasingly serious approach to the world of "robotics." These stories cover a span of 15 years and clearly show a growing skill in technique as well as greater depth and complexity of subject.

> *Betty Flowers, in her review of "The Rest of the Robots," in* School Library Journal, *an appendix to* Library Journal *(reprinted from the January, 1965 issue of* School Library Journal, *published by R. R. Bowker Co./A Xerox Corporation; copyright © 1965), Vol. 11, No. 5, January, 1965, p. 72.*

HILARY CORKE

In essence *I, Robot* is a collection of indifferent short stories given a spurious novelty by mechanical transformation. But SF requires re-thinking, not mere re-clothing. In the very first story, Robbie, a nursemaid robot, is described as a primitive type, made before the secret of conferring speech on them had been discovered. Yet, inferentially, his programming must have been incredibly complex, and the inclusion of speech-mechanism would have been the merest subsidiary detail. The potentially devastating point of this particular tale, that if a child thinks of its robot guardian as human then too it thinks of its human guardian as a robot, is badly fumbled.

> *Hilary Corke, in his review of "I, Robot" (© British Broadcasting Corp. 1967; reprinted by permission of Hilary Corke), in* The Listener, *Vol. LXXVII, No. 1989, May 11, 1967, p. 629.*

RICHARD W. RYAN

In [*Asimov's Mysteries*], Isaac Asimov has brought together 14 short stories illustrative of the "science fiction mystery"—a form which, he explains, he began writing in response to comments that the two could not be combined. Obviously, they can be: the puzzle as hero can be as entertaining in its way as galactic empires, alien life-forms, or social extrapolation. This book provides further evidence if it was needed. In most of the stories Mr. Asimov draws the puzzle elements from science, and the knowledgeable reader may be able to figure out whodunit or how it was done before the climax. Four of the stories feature an eccentric professor as armchair sleuth, and a couple are vehicles for Mr. Asimov's punning propensities. . . . This is a competent volume. . . .

> *Richard W. Ryan, in his review of "Asimov's Mysteries," in* Library Journal *(reprinted from* Library Journal, *December 15, 1967; published by R. R. Bowker Co. (a Xerox company); copyright © 1967 by Xerox Corporation), Vol. 92, No. 22, December 15, 1967, p. 4521.*

SCIENCE BOOKS

As the companion volume to Asimov's earlier **Breakthroughs in science** . . . , [*Great ideas of science*] is composed of short essays on famous scientists and their accomplishments. In **Great ideas of science** the major contributions of sixteen scientists . . . are discussed. Ten years ago a reviewer suggested of **Breakthroughs** that the "general juvenile encyclopedias give far better coverage to the subjects treated." We feel that the same criticism is valid for **Great ideas of science**. Asimov's theme is that "the universe behaves in accordance with certain laws of nature that cannot be altered or changed," but that "it is possible for human reason to work out the nature of the laws governing the universe." He presents this theme in his initial chapter and subsequently discusses how each scientist's contribution has extended human reason. A formal conclusion restating the theme would have been fitting. Asimov's writing is so terse that the knowledgeable student will want more information (there is no bibliography), while other readers need more information for adequate comprehension. (p. 12)

> *A review of "Great Ideas of Science: The Men and the Thinking Behind Them," in* Science Books *(copyright ©1970 by the American Association for the Advancement of Science), Vol. 6, No. 1, May, 1970, pp. 11-12.*

GEORGE MERRILL

The continuing popularity of Asimov's earlier novels should guarantee an audience for [*The Gods Themselves*]. . . . The story of earth's demands on its dwindling energy reserves is told in three tenuously linked segments. . . . The plot, which can almost be read as three short stories, reflects the contemporary search for an energy source free from dangerous side effects and demonstrates that self-serving convenience can be an overwhelming argument against probable consequences. Although this runs counter to the "new wave" in science fiction, it will no doubt be welcomed by YA's who want accurate science, an intriguing hypothesis drawn from a modern dilemma, well-detailed imaginary worlds to explore and even a dash of romance.

> *George Merrill, in his review of "The Gods Themselves," in* School Library Journal, *an appendix to*

Library Journal *(reprinted from the May, 1972 issue of* School Library Journal, *published by R. R. Bowker Co./A Xerox Corporation; copyright © 1972), Vol. 18, No. 9, May, 1972, p. 97.*

ROBERT J. ANTHONY

In "**More Words of Science,**" Isaac Asimov exhibits, as he did in his 1959 "**Words of Science**" (to which this book is a sequel), the same deep attention to the science of words as he does to science. Dr. Asimov's knowledge of his subjects embraces their etymology, lending, in most cases, a simple clarity to even the more complex definitions. . . .

From *ablation* to *zpg*, a full page is devoted to each definition. This page-length treatment permits a scope and style most dictionaries, including children's encyclopedias, do not attempt. Asimov's mode explores both the development of the term he explains and of the idea, process, theory, hardware, organ, cell, behavior or astral body he has selected, defining these subjects' importance to us. Latin and Greek roots for words (often more informative than their modern derivatives) as well as words simply examined as they are, from modern foreign languages, form part of each definition. A full amount of knowledge is packed into each of these small essays.

The need for a sequel to the 1959 edition is made evident in the new words that have followed in the traces of myriad developments since that date, or come into more common use, or acquired new meanings. . . .

In all, there is excellent balance struck among the disciplines of biology, anthropology, astronomy, chemistry and physics. Not much, if anything, has suffered neglect. This is an excellent work of modern-day reference, surely—but, more than that, a book that can be read, enjoyably, simply for the sake of reading and learning.

> *Robert J. Anthony, in his review of "More Words of Science," in* The New York Times Book Review *(© 1972 by The New York Times Company; reprinted by permission), September 10, 1972, p. 10.*

THE TIMES LITERARY SUPPLEMENT

Every author has his favourite hero, usually based on a flattering version of his own personality. In his first work of fiction for fifteen years, *The Gods Themselves,* Isaac Asimov continues with his fictional *alter ego* in the form of the questing man of science. A man, it need hardly be added, of intellect, vision, courage, and so on. In this tripartite novel there are, basically, three distinct personalities who might be said to fit these rather exacting criteria, including an exotic though blobby alien. Despite Asimov's obvious identification with his *dramatis personae,* it is Science itself that directs the proceedings, manipulating both humans and aliens as the godlike puppetmaster; the layman is soon left floundering in a swamp of scientific complexities. . . .

Between experiments there is plenty of extra-curricular activity, such as nude PT sessions, a guided tour of a moon colony by a long-legged moongirl, and a tri-sexual mating ritual. It may seem rather trite, but then the end of the world has always been a ready-made subject for ribaldry.

> *"Any More for the Apocalypse?" in* The Times Literary Supplement *(© Times Newspapers Ltd. (London) 1972; reproduced from* The Times Literary Sup-

plement *by permission), No. 3684, October 13, 1972, p. 1235.**

SCIENCE BOOKS

The language of science continues to grow at an astounding rate. When Isaac Asimov's book, *Words of Science,* was published in 1959, terms such as "quasar," "laser," and "transfer RNA" were not included; since they were not yet a part of the common scientific vocabulary. *More Words of Science* takes up where the earlier volume left off and provides the reader with 250 more clearly and interestingly written explanations. Very often, books of this sort are useful only as references; by contrast, *More Words of Science* is so well written that many people will want to read it cover to cover. The book is not a dictionary of science terms. Each word is given a page-long narrative which goes considerably beyond the minimum. Drawn from all fields of science, the terms and their explanatory essays are thoroughly indexed. Cross-references have been avoided, however, in order to do away with the annoyance of flipping from one page to another. *More Words of Science* can be highly recommended to general readers who seek a pleasant and non-threatening introduction to a broad spectrum of words from the language of science.

> *A review of "More Words of Science," in* Science Books *(copyright © 1972 by the American Association for the Advancement of Science), Vol. VIII, No. 3, December, 1972, p. 211.*

CHOICE

[*The Early Asimov or, Eleven Years of Trying* is a candid], delightful insight into Asimov's increasing maturity as a science fiction writer. His discussion of his feelings on first breaking into print could be an inspiration to any young writer. . . . The early stories are valuable to any collection of science fiction since they show Asimov's concern with the exactness and certitude of the known in our science and his uncanny ability to predict those elements in and concerning science which have since come to pass. Stories like these also show his progression from an awkward, inspired teenager to the intellectual genius and internationally known writer he has become. (The book could be used as a text for "creative writing," provided the teacher understood science fiction.) Above all, the delicious comments about the short stories, the editors he has known, the fans and bibliographers (who grow angry when he confesses to having lost some of his earliest writings), combined with the gentle sense of humor and satire of Asimov, make this book indispensable to the SF fan or collection. There is only one Asimov in science fiction and only a handful of others who can approach his stature.

> *A review of "The Early Asimov or, Eleven Years of Trying," in* Choice *(copyright © 1973 by American Library Association), Vol. 10, No. 1, March, 1973, p. 87.*

BRIAN W. ALDISS

Asimov employed the wide-angle lens for his view of life and it is a pity that his largest milestone, the *Foundation* trilogy, was written before sf authors were able to think of their books as books, rather than as short stories or serials in ephemeral magazines (or magazines that would have been ephemeral but for the dedication of fans). Conceived as one organic whole, the *Foundation* series would have undoubtedly risen to greater majesty. . . .

Asimov has developed into one of the polymaths of our day, producing a stream of popularisations of various scientific disciplines. The popularity of his novels continues. Like many another writer, Asimov began in subversive vein, prophesying change and barbarism; but, a generation later, such ideas lose their sting and become safe for a general public. Increasingly, one sees the solid conservative faith in technology in Asimov's novels. His short stories often err on the side of facetiousness. (p. 269)

> *Brian W. Aldiss, "'After the Impossible Happened':*
> *The Fifties and Onwards, and Upwards," in his* Bil-
> lion Year Spree: The True History of Science Fiction
> *(copyright © 1973 by Brian W. Aldiss; reprinted by*
> *permission of Doubleday & Company, Inc.; in Can-*
> *ada by Wallace & Sheil Agency, Inc.), Doubleday,*
> *1973, pp. 244-84.**

MARTIN SHERWOOD

On page 4 of *The Bicentennial Man,* Isaac Asimov claims to have published 175 books. By the time you read this, the score will probably have passed 200. *The Bicentennial Man* does not seem to form any particular landmark in this apparently endless plain of prose, but is still a good read, particularly if you like conjuring-trick stories about robots and are not totally switched off by the purple cotton wool introductions in which Asimov now packs his stories. Certainly, anyone who feels that the three laws of robotics had all the pith sucked from them years ago should read this collection—although none of the stories takes the pith quite as well as John Sladek's pastiche of Asimov in *The Steam-Driven Boy.* (pp. 218-19)

> *Martin Sherwood, in his review of "The Bicentennial*
> *Man," in* New Scientist *(© IPC Magazines, 1977),*
> *Vol. 74, No. 1049, April, 1977, pp. 218-19.*

MARJORIE MITHOFF MILLER

The beginning of Isaac Asimov's career as a writer of science fiction coincided closely with the beginning of the development of "social science fiction." (p. 13)

[Asimov defines "social science fiction"] as "that branch of literature which is concerned with the impact of scientific advance upon human beings." He recognizes the existence of the other types of science fiction—adventure and gadget—which do not fit this definition, but he feels that "social science fiction is the only branch of science fiction that is sociologically significant, and that those stories, which are generally accepted as science fiction . . . but do not fall within the definition I have given above, are not significant, however amusing they may be and however excellent as pieces of fiction." (p. 14)

Science fiction has often been accused of being escape literature. There is no doubt that many science fiction stories are primarily escapist in intent; however, Asimov sees a difference between science fiction and other forms of escape literature such as westerns, true romances, and mystery stories; much of science fiction encourages its readers to think about the future—an occupation that can hardly be described as "escaping"—and the possibilities that the future seems to hold. . . . For the first time in the world's history, mankind can no longer take the future for granted. Each individual's future may always

have been uncertain, but mankind has never before been concerned about the future of the whole human race. (pp. 14-15)

One of the major functions of science fiction for Asimov is to accustom its readers to the idea of change. In contemplating the possible futures presented in science fiction, the reader is forced to recognize and accept the idea that things will change, and he is helped to surrender some of his traditional human passion for the status quo. Asimov sees this as a real benefit to our society, as we try to plan and implement the changes that will do the most good for humanity. He does not claim that science fiction writers set out deliberately to propagandize their readers and make them aware of the inevitability and value of change; they write interesting stories, usually based on scientific facts, and try to extrapolate from today's society the many different possible changes for man and his world in the future. Any benefits to the readers, or to society, are simply by-products of a job well done. (p. 15)

Asimov has written some adventure and gadget stories, and some that are just plain fun, but the greatest part of his work is clearly social science fiction. . . . [Even] his earliest stories, written when he was not yet twenty, show a real concern for people, and for social issues. As he matured as a writer, he continued to be disturbed over many of the same social problems; the main difference between his early works and his later ones may be the subtlety with which he presents his message. In some of the earlier stories, the urgency of the message weakens the effectiveness of the story. Two early stories, **"Half-Breed"** . . . and **"Half-Breeds on Venus"** . . . , were clearly motivated by Asimov's distress over the prevalence of racial prejudice. . . . He sees the diminishing of racial prejudice as a service that science fiction might help to perform for society, since science fiction writers, because they are dealing with larger areas of the universe, usually speak of all the people of Earth as simply "Earthmen," making no distinction among the races. Whether a man is black, brown, red, or white is not so important when he and his fellows are facing a green monster from Mars. (pp. 16-17)

["Trends"] dealt with a theme that had not previously been used in science fiction—the possibility that people might be opposed to the idea of space flight and try to stop it. (p. 17)

The specific threat from technological advances that man might lose the ability to control his own life is a recurrent theme in the science fiction of many writers, as are the problems of atomic energy and overpopulation. This threat is part of the problem Asimov presents in **"Trends."** . . .

The theme of man versus his own technology appears in many Asimov stories, from **"Trends"** to his science fiction novel *The Gods Themselves.* Resistance to science often takes the form, in Asimov's work, of an underground group, such as the Medievalists in *The Caves of Steel,* which works in some way to resist or subvert scientific and technological advances. This distrust of technology is a basic theme in all the robot stories. Indeed, Asimov's Three Laws of Robotics ended the Frankenstein-monster era of robot stories and brought in the more scientific story, in which mankind must make the decisions about the robots' capabilities and protect himself against any possibility that his creations might rise up and destroy him. The source of the difficulties that have to be solved in the robot stories is usually an apparent conflict between the ideal of the Three Laws, and the robots' application of the Laws. (p. 18)

Reading through Asimov's works, looking for evidence of his attitude toward man and technology, one is struck by his ambivalence. He clearly takes great delight in technological advances for their own sake—he just plain likes clever new gadgets, and new-and-better ways to do things—but he also recognizes that humanity cannot survive without allowing for individuality and uncontrollability, even "orneriness." No matter how advanced a technology may become, he feels, it will still have to be possible for people to escape the control of the machines in some way for life to have any meaning. (p. 19)

[Asimov] has great faith in man's ability to use technology for his own good, as in **The Gods Themselves,** but at the same time, he has repeatedly shown that he recognizes the danger of too much control over men's lives. Many of his stories revolve around a protagonist who insists on doing something human, whether it is simply going outdoors when it is no longer necessary or proper, or learning to do something that the computers can do for you, or working to defeat the technology that controls his life. Humanity remains triumphant, if not always victorious, in the battle against an overpowering technology.

Atomic weapons and atomic energy are a unique and overwhelming part of the technology that threatens us. Asimov has frequently used atomic devastation as one aspect of the background for his stories, instead of making it a major component of the plot. (p. 24)

One Asimov story that is *about* atomic weapons, rather than using them as one aspect of the setting, is the short-short story **"Hell-Fire"** . . . , found in **Earth Is Room Enough.** A group of scientists has gathered to view the first extremely slow-motion film of the explosion of an atomic bomb. To their shock and horror, the film clearly shows the face of Satan, complete with horns and demonic grin, formed in the mushroom cloud of the explosion. Although Asimov claims no religious affiliation himself, some of his most effective works have strong religious or theological elements because he recognizes the importance of religion in man's history, and because, as he says, he is interested in religion along with many other subjects. (p. 26)

It is obvious that Asimov's stories cannot be neatly divided into discrete categories—these stories are about atomic energy, and these are about overpopulation, and so on. There is a great deal of overlap, and most stories will contain references to many different sociological concerns. Population control might be effected by technological advances or, failing that, by atomic warfare. Population growth that is *not* controlled will, on the other hand, put great demands on technology to provide enough food and shelter for everyone. Asimov's concern about atomic energy tapered off as the world seemed to adapt to the existence of this threat, and the horror of atomic war became at least a little more remote and perhaps a little less certain. At the same time, the dangers of overpopulation began to come into prominence in his work. (p. 27)

One of Asimov's most extended and chilling looks at one possible future for Earth is provided in **The Caves of Steel.** This is one of Asimov's two novels which successfully combine the mystery story and science fiction. It is laid in the fifty-first century. The population of Earth has reached eight billion; almost the entire population is crowded into the huge cities, leaving the rest of the land free for agriculture; every aspect of life is controlled in an effort to make the overcrowded conditions as bearable as possible. (pp. 27-8)

Elijah Baley, a New York City detective, is one of the heroes of the book; the other is R. Daneel Olivaw, a robot detective from Spacetown, an Outer Worlds colony set up on Earth.

Baley lives in a New York City with a population of twenty million. He sees the "first problem of living" in such an overcrowded world as being to minimize friction with all of the other people who have to live in such close proximity. The best way to do this is for people to be scrupulous in their observance of all the customs and regulations that encompass every part of daily life, so as not to offend or inconvenience their neighbors, from whom there is never any real escape. (p. 28)

The fifty Outer Worlds were settled a thousand years before the time of this story, by men from Earth. Now each world has its own civilization and resists any immigration from Earth, in order to keep its society just the way it wants it. Earth, therefore, is hemmed in with its enormous population and cannot find any real solution to its problems. Man has long since lost the urge to colonize any new unoccupied worlds, because of his closed-in existence. Robots are widely used on the Outer Worlds but are feared and distrusted on Earth, and efforts to use them are bitterly resented.

In **The Naked Sun,** the sequel to **The Caves of Steel,** we get a closeup picture of the "ideal" life on one of the Outer Worlds that figured in the earlier work. All of the Outer Worlds are thinly populated and have economies that make use of robots. Solaria, the planet to which Baley is sent to solve a murder, presents a picture of the most extreme dependence on robots. Each citizen of Solaria lives on a large estate of his own, attended by a great number of specialized robots. . . . In striking contrast to the crowded Earth, where privacy is almost impossible, Solaria has developed a society in which human contact is at an absolute minimum. Even married couples actually "see" each other (that is, are physically present in the same room) only at scheduled intervals, although they share the same estate. All social visits and business conferences are conducted by three-dimensional televiewing, rather than "seeing." (pp. 28-9)

The Naked Sun gives a picture of a society that might be regarded as ideal from the point of view of technological advancement, and yet it is clearly not ideal in the human sense. While Earth's overcrowding has led to a timid humanity, with little spirit of adventure or initiative, Solaria's artificial isolation has led to a people with little feeling for each other and no way to work together in an emergency. The advanced technology which permits easy communication with anyone on the planet has actually made real communication—communication of human understanding, empathy, and mutual helpfulness—much more difficult. (p. 29)

Many of Asimov's stories about overpopulation simply present the problem, not the solution. He appears to feel that no solution will be possible until people are thoroughly awakened to the nature of the threat posed by our growing population. (pp. 29-30)

Throughout his writing career Asimov has shown his concern for the problems that humanity has to face. By examining a few of his stories and novels we have seen the various ways in which he has expressed this concern. Some stories seem to have been written primarily to encourage the reader to recognize and think about some particular problem. Some stories present the problem but suggest no solution; other stories offer possible solutions. Occasionally, Asimov is pessimistic about man's chance of surviving and maintaining his human individuality; more often he has seemed to feel that man's determination to run his own life will somehow win out over any obstacles that science and technology might put in the way.

From 1945 on, Asimov was quite pessimistic about the prospects for avoiding atomic war, but he usually pictured humanity as surviving and rebuilding its civilization. Only an occasional story, such as **"No Connection,"** presents the possibility of man's being completely destroyed and some other species rising to an intelligent, civilized society.

Asimov's major worry in the last twenty years, as far as the fate of humanity is concerned, has been overpopulation, and he has become increasingly pessimistic. He does not believe that humanity will be able to solve this problem soon enough—if ever. But if the problem is not solved intelligently, nature will work out a solution, or series of solutions—warfare, starvation, disease.

Asimov began to write science fiction because he was determined to be a writer, and science fiction was what he knew best and enjoyed the most. As he matured as a writer, science fiction itself was coming to maturity as a serious and responsible type of literature. Asimov and other science fiction authors wrote more and more works that sought to waken humanity to the dangers it faces. (pp. 30-1)

> *Marjorie Mithoff Miller, "The Social Science Fiction of Isaac Asimov," in* Isaac Asimov, *edited by Joseph D. Olander and Martin Harry Greenberg (copyright © 1977 by Joseph D. Olander and Martin Harry Greenberg; published by Taplinger Publishing Co., Inc., New York; reprinted by permission), Taplinger, 1977, pp. 13-31.*

HAZEL PIERCE

Asimov has balanced the demands of [two genres, mystery and science fiction] by building on their common ground.

Both types impose the need for logical, analytical method and for subtle, acute reasoning—applied in the one instance to untangling a puzzle in immediate time and place, the other in speculative time and place. Both exercise the special knowledge of the author. Detective fiction demands a knowledge of police procedures and an understanding of the deductive process; science fiction, of the scientific premises on which the speculative world is based.

A second answer lies with Asimov's own track record. He has been able to draw on his ingenuity without undue strain or awkward repetition. In at least three cases he has expanded an initial appearance of his detective characters into a series without sacrificing either his powers of deduction or his scientific reasonableness. The last four of the Lucky Starr juveniles, the Robot novels, and the Wendell Urth short stories testify to this point. (p. 37)

One might quibble at the inclusion of the Lucky Starr juveniles in a discussion of Asimov's detective science fiction, but this series is worth our notice if only to follow the shift of the title character from the conventional hero of space opera and action-adventure to the hero as cool, rational space detective. The title of the first book of the series is revelatory: *David Starr: Space Ranger*. . . . It tempts us to substitute another well-known epithet, *Lone Ranger*, especially after we read the book and meet John Bigman Jones, friend and cohort of David Starr. Bigman can well serve as a space-Tonto for he, too, comes from a different culture than the main character, albeit another culture in the galaxy instead of the continent. Together they encounter many exciting adventures and solve all problems. In the second book of the series, *Lucky Starr and the Pirates of the Asteroids* . . . , our hero continues his adventurous exploits, complete with push-tube duel in outer space. (pp. 37-8)

With the third book of the series, *Lucky Starr and the Oceans of Venus*, Lucky begins the shift from space ranger to space detective. . . . Now more prone to rely on the powers of his mind and on scientific data rather than on cleverness and physical courage alone, Lucky Starr continues to solve the puzzles of his universe: intergalactic conspiracy, conspirators who use telepathic animal extensions of their power, and computers misused to control and to gain power. One brief but telling exchange between Lucky and Bigman illustrates how far Asimov has moved his duo from a Lone Ranger-Tonto relationship to a Sherlock Holmes-Dr. Watson one. At one point Bigman excitedly questions Lucky about something he doesn't understand. Lucky's answer is not the expected explanation but a sentiment worthy of the Great Detective himself: "Actually, it's only a matter of logic." (p. 38)

In the remaining three novels of the Lucky Starr series the two characters retain this relationship, but a new element enters the picture—robots.

[*Lucky Starr and the Big Sun of Mercury, Lucky Starr and the Moons of Jupiter,* and *Lucky Starr and the Rings of Saturn*] present Lucky Starr less as a trouble-shooter and more as a problem-solver for the Council of Science of Earth in their continuing confrontation with the Sirian civilization, a robot-saturated economy. The two "space detectives" solve the stolen robot caper, block the use of Venusian V-frogs to control human emotions, and finally in the last novel they avert a serious galactic struggle when the Sirians move in to establish colonies in Earth's stellar system. While this last novel moves more closely to spy-thriller conventions, the two preceding ones rely more heavily on the personal deductive process. (pp. 38-9)

In *The Caves of Steel* Asimov uses the classic pattern of detective fiction: statement of the problem, marshalling of the clues and facts, completion of the inquiry, and explanation of the proof. Setting the pattern into action is the introduction of the detective, Elijah Baley, just before Baley is summoned to Commissioner Enderby's office to receive an assignment to investigate a murder in Spacetown. (p. 39)

This assignment holds a unique challenge for Baley. He is a true product of the conditioning which the City of some 3000 years in the future imposes upon all of its inhabitants. He fears open spaces. He feels uncomfortable in open air. Most of all, he experiences mingled fear and disgust in the presence of robots because they represent an ever-growing threat that they might replace men. To all Earthmen the robots mean loss of jobs, the misery of loss of status, and the lonely sense of displacement. His new assignment requires that Baley face all of these fears. He must go to Spacetown and endure the open spaces and the unconditioned air, especially those disturbing vagrant breezes. An obligatory consideration of the case forces him to take as an assistant a Spacer robot, R. Daneel Olivaw, whose humanoid appearance is so lifelike that he passes undetected even by the chief robotics expert of Earth.

At this point Asimov had to pay considerable attention to an important imperative of science fiction. A story which takes place some 3000 years in the future obviously demands the creation of a world different from the one in which the reader lives today. Setting is always important in science fiction; it must believably fit the future. In *Caves* Asimov begins to build his world from the first page. Particularly during the phase of the investigation which deals with the collection of data and the sifting of clues, Asimov skillfully blends in necessary details of setting.

Asimov does alleviate some possible difficulties in this blending by localizing most of his action in the world of the detective, a world which is not too unfamiliar to the reader. In *Caves* New York City now covers a large area, but more importantly it has burrowed deep underground to become a "tremendous self-contained cave of steel and concrete." . . . It is a microcosm reflecting an overpopulated Earth dependent for certain strategic material on the Outer Worlds, those outlying planets and asteroids originally populated by immigrants from Earth but now closed to such settlement.

The existence of the Outer Worlds and the conflict between them and Earth is not a new invention for this novel. In 1949, Asimov wrote **"Mother Earth"** . . . , a short story foreshadowing Baley's Earth at an earlier time when some diplomatic links still existed between Earth and the Outer Worlds. (pp. 39-40)

[The short story is] evidence of Asimov's economy or utility of invention, an economy we will see over and over again in the science fiction mystery stories of Asimov. While **"Mother Earth"** does not feature Lije Baley or R. Daneel Olivaw, it could well be considered the initial story of that series, but one lacking the presence of the detective spirit.

The length of the novel afforded Asimov some benefits which he could not gain in the short story. . . . [Since Asimov] needed to blend two effects, he took advantage of the length of the novel to fix the setting firmly before turning to the serious work of solving the crime.

Asimov gives us the City in some detail. There is some exposition and direct description of the [city]. . . .

But most exhilarating for the reader is the sense of direct experience which Asimov affords us. With Baley he moves us around the City. (p. 41)

Not only do we learn to know the City physically but we learn to know the people and the things they value. Above all, privacy is jealously guarded, as one may well imagine. Status is one of the keys to happiness, not status based on money or family connections, but on one's rating as a worker. The status ratings bring greater privileges and assure a modicum of comfort for a man and his family. The successful solution of the Spacetown murder will bring Baley a higher rating. . . .

To assure this rating, Baley has only to solve the murder. But solving the murder also means working with a robot. . . . [The] investigation must proceed; gradually Lije Baley's professional training succeeds in controlling his first instinct and he accords R. Daneel a grudging cooperation. (p. 42)

Near the end of *The Caves of Steel* Asimov does weaken the blend of mystery and science fiction by introducing a new and unanticipated element. Unexpectedly, the Spacers call off the murder investigation, informing Baley of their decision through R. Daneel. Asimov would have us believe that their main objective was not to find the murderer but to woo Baley's mind toward a tolerance of robots. With this accomplished, they then widened that tolerance to the point where he could entertain, even could express to Enderby, the idea that Earth might consider a new wave of emigration to the still-empty worlds in space. By necessity, this project would involve both

leaving the safety of the City and accepting the help of robots in colonizing the new worlds.

Asimov does salvage his detective story, however, when he allows Baley to close the case in his own way. . . . The revelation of the facts as evidence shares the readers' attention with the author's concern for the "second chance" afforded the criminal. The science fiction side of the story has the last word as Daneel says to the culprit, "Go, and sin no more!"

In the sequel *The Naked Sun*, Asimov himself recognizes his accomplishment in the brief foreword to the novel in *The Rest of the Robots*. He modestly states that he once again "achieved a perfect fusion of the murder mystery and the science-fiction novel." Whether the first novel was a *perfect* fusion is debatable. . . . The sequel, on the other hand, does achieve a unity which supercedes that of the first robot novel. . . . Like its predecessor, *The Naked Sun* features Elijah Baley and R. Daneel Olivaw collaborating on a murder case, this time on one of the Outer Worlds.

The unity achieved in *The Naked Sun* is explainable in several ways. First, Asimov uses less time to present his two main characters, who are well known, at least to his fans who have read *The Caves of Steel* (one obvious advantage of a series). Second, he does not have to be so detailed in his explanations of the people in the Outer Worlds, their way of life, or their psychology. Above all, he need not spend half his book readjusting Baley's attitude toward acceptance of robot help. Since the adjustment occurred in the first book of the series, it now requires reaffirmation only. True, Baley has other new adjustments to make: he must learn to control the panic engendered by flying; he must come to terms with the unique customs of Solaria; and, most of all, he must conquer his fear of being in the open. These are problems built into the movement of the plot and are easily absorbed into the mystery pattern.

As in *Caves,* the story in *The Naked Sun* falls into the pattern of the classic detective story. A murder occurs on Solaria, one of the Outer Worlds; Elijah Baley is sent to investigate. (pp. 44-5)

The murder on Solaria is the first in two centuries. Solarian security finds itself incapable of coping with such an extraordinary occurrence. Because his success in the Spacetown murder (*The Caves of Steel*) has earned him a reputation in the Galaxy, Solaria requests Earth to send Elijah Baley to handle the investigation of their murder. An official in the Justice Department gives Baley his charge: find the murderer. He also gives a *sub rosa* assignment: keep eyes and ears open to the general situation on Solaria so that he may report to Earth upon return. In *The Naked Sun,* unlike the late introduction of the second problem in *Caves,* Asimov introduces this thread of the plot early. Also, it fits more naturally into the detective fiction pattern—the international intrigue of the spy thriller grafted onto the localized puzzle of the mystery story.

As before, R. Daneel Olivaw from Aurora, the largest and most powerful of the Outer Worlds, joins Baley as his assistant. Once on Solaria the two detectives slowly gather data, even though they are barred from visiting the scene of the crime or from interviewing suspects except by trimensional image. In Solarian society, . . . direct access to another's personal presence is practically unknown, even between spouses who meet only on "assigned days." Asimov obviously is working a science-fiction variation of the locked-room situation in detective fiction.

The bare facts of the case come from Hannis Gruer, head of Solarian security: the identity of the murdered man; the facts that no murder weapon was found but that a positronic brain-damaged robot was on the scene; the fact that the murdered man's wife was found bending over the body. The robot, governed by First Law, cannot possibly be suspected of the murder. The chances of any one person's attempting and gaining access to the man are nil because of the elaborate network of robots around each human being on Solaria—not to mention the extreme psychological aversion the murderer would have to overcome merely to approach the victim. The only possible human suspect is the murdered man's wife Gladia. But again, no weapon which could have served the purpose of murder was found, and she had had no time in which to dispose of any such weapon.

After Gruer's report Baley recognizes the seemingly insurmountable difficulties facing him. His only move now is to fall back on the commonplaces of detection, and his response is almost a cliché: "Murder rests on three legs, each equally important. They are motive, means, and opportunity. For a good case against any suspect, each of the three must be satisfied." A faithful reader of detective fiction will easily recollect this truism from speeches of countless fictional detectives, be they amateurs or professionals. At first, the statement seems almost an unwarranted one, until we recall that Asimov must also keep up the logic of the science fiction side of his tale. His character is speaking to someone from a different culture; he is operating in a country where murder is known only in an academic sense. The study of motive, means, and opportunity is unnecessary, hence forgotten. The reminder of basic police procedure illuminates both the detective and the science fiction parts of the novel.

Find motive, means, and opportunity. The path seems simple. But complications soon arise. Baley discovers the existence of subversive elements in this ostensibly tight social organization on Solaria. These people wish to change the "old ways, the good ways," the customs and traditions of which the murdered man was an advocate. The suspicion now arises that Dr. Delmarre, being a Traditionalist, was silenced for political reasons. (pp. 45-7)

The intergalactic politics smack so obviously of twentieth-century cold war or international politics that the situation threatens to jeopardize Asimov's fusion of science fiction and mystery by suddenly assuming some conventions of a thriller. (p. 47)

Surprisingly, Asimov moves us back to the original purpose—a science-fiction detective story—with the very character whose absence at the briefing allowed the digression into galactic politics. R. Daneel Olivaw's absence gives Asimov the opportunity to subordinate the robot detective more completely to the human detective than in *Caves*. No longer the "pocket-frannistan" able to store, sort, and produce instant information for Baley, the robot serves him as the source of background information: Solaria's geography; its social and cultural mores; biographical notes on Solarian officials; and any supplementary data which Baley needs. As the novel unfolds, the need for Daneel's peculiar gift lessens while the necessity for human imagination grows.

Especially is this state of affairs evident when a second murder attempt occurs, this one on Gruer himself, in full "view" (not in "sight") of Baley and R. Daneel during another interview by trimensional image. This murder attempt accomplishes several things. It partially disables R. Daneel, whose stable existence and operation depends upon his adherence to the Laws of Robotics. Seeing harm come so dramatically to a human being briefly puts Daneel into the robotic equivalent of shock. It thus reduces his effectiveness as an equal partner. By this episode Asimov turns his full attention to the human detective and to the problem calling for human deductive powers. Lije Baley, his own professional training as his sole resource, is jolted into action. Concentrating on the immediate problem—murder and attempted murder—he lets the problem of subversion sort itself out naturally in the course of the investigation.

The internal problems of Solaria and the secondary assignment given to Baley by the Justice Department prove to be mutually supportive. With their advanced robot economy, low population, and excessively long life span, the Solarians have come to a danger-point in their social existence. What seem to be Solaria's strengths in the Galaxy are in fact its weaknesses. As Lije Baley solves the original murder and the second murder attempt, he incidentally uncovers the sociological dilemma underlying these crimes, and this discovery allows him to fulfill the second assignment.

Many writers of science fiction give in to a didactic urge. Since science fiction frequently operates as prophetic vision, an author often feels impelled to use the vision to warn his readers of the portents visible in contemporary life. Asimov yields a little to this urge in Baley's report to Albert Minnim of the Justice Department. He parallels the two societies, Solaria and Earth. Earth is a "turned-inside-out" Solaria. Both worlds are at dead ends—Solaria through personal isolation, Earth through cultural isolation. Both worlds must break their molds and introduce new ways of doing things. Each world is a distorted mirror-image of the other.

The metaphor of a mirror-image led to the title of a short story in which the detectives make their third appearance. (pp. 47-9)

The problem in **"Mirror Image"** is impending death, not of a person or of a civilization, but the death of a reputation. Two eminent mathematicians possess identical scholarly papers explaining a startling discovery in their discipline. Both propose to deliver the paper at an important convention. The paper will add considerable luster to the reputation of either man by contributing to the older man's already high place in the profession and by giving impetus to the younger man's rising prominence. Each claims the paper as his own; each accuses the other of stealing it after having been invited to read it as a consultant. Each offers to forgive and forget if the other will forego all claims on the contents.

This unpleasant contention has erupted aboard a space ship enroute to the convention. In the age-old tradition of all ships, the captain as sole authority must act the part of Solomon. To avert the future scandal, he must decide to whom the paper really belongs. He enlists the aid of a passenger on the starship, one R. Daneel Olivaw of Aurora. Olivaw in turn requests and receives permission to make an unscheduled stop at Earth so that he might consult with plainclothesman Elijah Baley.

A key factor in the case, one which Baley uses to keen advantage, is the presence of two robots, property of the two mathematicians. They reinforce the title-metaphor of mirror image by being identical robots, made in the same year at the same factory to the same specifications. Unable to interview the two scientists (they are Spacers and arrogantly reject any contact with an Earthman), Baley interviews the two servant-robots. They corroborate their masters' stories, as expected. To lie and thus cause harm to the master goes against First Law; in this instance the harm to reputation is as important as injury to person. By skillful questioning based on his knowledge of the First Law, Baley pushes one of the robots to the point of stasis, out of commission, thus finding the vital clue to the guilty man.

The clue still has to be turned into evidence. Only after Olivaw has returned to the starship, faced the two men with the fact, and received the confession of one, only then does Baley know that his deduction is accurate. In this story Asimov works a variation of the classic armchair detective. Baley collects facts while sitting in his office; he plans his course while sitting in his office; and he interviews the robots via micro-receiver set up in his office. At no time does he physically work at fact-gathering. Even the final confrontation of the detective and the guilty party is done second-hand through Olivaw. Baley himself operates purely on the intellectual level, resting his case on his powers of deduction alone.

"Mirror Image" demonstrates one reality about detective fiction not illustrated by Asimov heretofore. Stories of detection need not be based on sensational situations to be good stories of detection. While murder or political intrigue may create more excitement for a reader, the less sensational but nonetheless knotty problem allows the author to place a greater emphasis on the deductive process per se. In **"Mirror Image"** the mode of detection satisfies dyed-in-the-wool devotees of both mystery and science fiction.

Yet another Asimov character, Wendell Urth, made his appearance at the same time that Lucky Starr turned space detective and Lije Baley began his association with R. Daneel. (pp. 49-50)

[Detective] fiction devotes little space to characterization, except for the detective himself. The author usually feels the responsibility to establish his detective as a person of perspicacity with the most impeccable credentials in his own field and with a record of achievement in activities requiring deductive ability. Asimov discharges this duty admirably. He draws Wendell Urth as a man of independent mind to the point of extreme eccentricity. . . . While he works semi-isolated from the world, mentally he roams the known reaches of the solar system. His personal appearance is deceiving. Certain words attach themselves to him: *round, pudgy, snubby, stubby, stumpy*. Asimov works with images of roundness: a round body, a round face, the round nubbin of a nose on which round glasses perch. But behind this unprepossessing appearance is a mind of superior quality. (p. 51)

In Wendell Urth we have an extreme case of the armchair detective. A man who refuses to stir from his own premises except to walk to his classroom is not a man one expects to do the laborious job of clue-collecting. To accommodate his character's special eccentricity, Asimov changed the sequence of his plot from that we have been used to in the previously discussed stories. For the classic pattern he substituted R. Austin Freeman's "inverted story in two parts." In the first part of each story Asimov gives his reader the commission of the crime with the criminals fully identified. In some cases, we even experience the entire situation through dialogue and action rather than through exposition. We are given all the facts which Urth later will turn into hard evidence. In the second part of the story we follow Urth in this task.

The shift to the inverted pattern eases somewhat the work of fusing detective conventions with science fiction. Since in each

of the four stories the criminal either lives or works in space, the inverted pattern allows Asimov to tell his science fiction story before any need for deduction arises. He has only to play fair with the reader by placing all necessary facts and pertinent circumstances before him. Jacques Barzun gives his opinion that "in any combination of the detective interest with anything else, the something else must remain the junior partner." This subordination need not occur with the inverted pattern. In the first part of the story science fiction can definitely be the senior partner, with the emphasis on the nonterrestrial settings, the alien life-forms, or the scientific premise on which the action later will turn. In the second part of the story, once we have met Wendell Urth in his cluttered study and have admired his artifacts from Callistan or his Galactic Lens, then detection becomes the senior partner.

In **"The Singing Bell,"** Louis Peyton, archcriminal à la Moriarty or Flambeau, plans to recover a cache of Singing Bells from the Moon and to murder the man who has enlisted his help in the project. . . . He carefully plans the trip to the Moon by scheduling it during the month in which he habitually retreats to his mountain hideout. Under the established pattern of his life he can cover up this instance of aberrant behavior which includes murder. For the reader there is nothing kept back about the trip to the Moon, the murder, the victim, or the criminal. H. Seton Davenport in the conversation with Wendell Urth reveals that the police know everything we know, except they can't *prove* it.

This situation is, of course, the Perfect Crime perpetrated by the Master Criminal which can be broken only by the Master Mind. In this story Urth does not "solve" anything. He does the only imaginative thing possible to crack the case: he sets up a simple situation in which he forces the criminal to trap himself by another established pattern of behavior, thus betraying himself to the police who then can test him with the psychoprobe.

"The Talking Stone" departs from the most common crime of mystery fiction, murder, and turns to smuggling. When a disabled spaceship stops at a repair station, the mechanic stumbles by chance on a smuggling operation being perpetrated by asteroid miners. . . . Vernadsky, the mechanic, senses a mystery and relays his suspicions to a friend, a space-patrolman. Together they track down the ship which the mechanic had only half-repaired so that it would break down in a predetermined area in space. They do find the ship. They also find a dead crew, for a meteor has hit the ship. The silicony is alive, but it also dies after giving a cryptic message about the location of its "home": "There," it says, "Over there."

The two men report their find to H. Seton Davenport, who in turn calls on Wendell Urth. . . . Without leaving his study, Urth finds the meaning of the creature's last words. Thus he is able to direct Davenport to the location of the hidden record of the coordinates of the asteroid—in a most obvious place, of course. In **"The Talking Stone"** Asimov has worked a science-fiction twist on Poe's strategy in "The Purloined Letter."

In 1956, Asimov published the third Wendell Urth story in as many years, **"The Dying Night."** First, he gives the necessary background information for motive, means, and opportunity for murder. . . . When all clues, suspects, and paradoxes have been presented to the reader, Asimov brings in Wendell Urth, this time using Professor Mandel instead of H. Seton Davenport as the "bridge" between the two parts of the story. As in **"The**

Singing Bell," Urth solves the problem by utilizing his knowledge of each man's conditioned behavior. He forces the murderer to reveal himself by an involuntary reaction to Earth's sun.

"The Dying Night" differs significantly in other respects from the two preceding stories. Here the reader does not know who the murderer is, nor has he witnessed the preplanning or the actual commission of the murder. Also, at the end of the tale Asimov breaks, or at least "bends," one of the lesser conventions of the mystery story—no love interest. After carefully building Urth up as the Brain whose sole concerns are his profession and his deductive exercises, Asimov gives him a heart. He humanizes Urth at the end when the professor requests a trip by mass transference to a place close by. To the amazed scientists he shyly explains, "I once—quite a long time ago—knew a girl there. It's been many years—but I sometimes wonder . . . ."

"The Key" brings H. Seton Davenport back to work with Wendell Urth. (pp. 51-4)

As in **"The Dying Night,"** Asimov invites his readers to close their acquaintance with Wendell Urth on a note more personal. In the conclusion of **"The Key"** we get a glimpse of a Wendell Urth who is not always in control of situations. The nature of his fee for this case is a strange one. He requests that no notice of his help be publicized. If it is, his niece may hear of it and make his life miserable. As he describes her, "She is a terribly headstrong and shrill-voiced woman who will raise public subscriptions and organize demonstrations. She will stop at nothing," including making his life unbearable. To leave our worthy detective on such a note may seem frivolous, but it indicates something about Asimov's developing attitude toward the conventions of detective fiction. He felt freer to play with them, as is witnessed by the cryptogram based on puns; he also felt freer to dilute them with other considerations. Although the early emphasis had been on Professor Urth's formidable mental powers, in the later stories the working-out of the crime shares partnership with the tactics of humanizing Urth. (p. 55)

One must accord Asimov the credit of having faced the challenge of blending science fiction with mystery fiction in several modes. He has written short stories, short-shorts, novels; he has given us the blend in single tales, in series with a detective-duo, and in series with the amateur-professional combinations. Second, he has treated many of the classic conventions of detective fiction: the locked-room plot, the "perfect crime" plot, the mistaken-identity situation, the cryptogram gimmick, and, perhaps most importantly, he has done successful variations on the personality of the detective. He has adapted his ability to write a well-planned technological story, based on solid scientific facts, to writing a well-planned deductive episode. He has successfully used the two major patterns of the mystery formula—Poe's classic pattern and Freeman's inverted pattern; to a lesser degree, he has succeeded in utilizing some of the best features of the spy thriller.

Most of all, while using the above detective or mystery story conventions, Asimov has not, for the most part, neglected to give his readers scientifically solid science fiction stories. Notable in this effort is his description of setting, both physical and psychological. Often he may interrupt the action to insert needed scientific information in the form of exposition or dialogue between two characters. This habit is not incompatible with the mystery genre, which also relies heavily on the reader's knowing all the facts, some of which must be given in

exposition. If the facts happen to be scientific ones, Asimov is most capable of supplying these in understandable prose that does not talk down to his readers. (pp. 57-8)

Hazel Pierce, "'Elementary, My Dear . . .': Asimov's Science Fiction Mysteries," in Isaac Asimov, *edited by Joseph D. Olander and Martin Harry Greenberg (copyright © 1977 by Joseph D. Olander and Martin Harry Greenberg; published by Taplinger Publishing Co., Inc., New York; reprinted by permission), Taplinger, 1977, pp. 32-58.*

DONALD WATT

Asimov is a science fiction novelist with no pretensions toward innovative techniques, hidden allusions, or occult symbolism. He is, as he professes to be, a popular writer whose work is immediately accessible to a wide audience.

It is worth asking, then, what it is about Asimov's writing that accounts for his popularity. . . . My argument is that Asimov's characters are at the center of appeal in his major fiction because they enrich and enliven the science fiction worlds he creates. (p. 135)

In Asimov's view, the stuff of science fiction is the human response to what science and the future have wrought, and this is indeed what his own novels are about.

The *Foundation* trilogy poses two special problems for a study of Asimov's characterizations—fatalism and fragmentation. First of all, the omnipresent specter of Seldon's Plan gives rise to the objection that Asimov's is a determined universe, and that genuine characters cannot come to life within such a fixed environment. Since the inhabitants of the trilogy cannot act outside the statistical probabilities of psychohistory, so the argument goes, the individuals Asimov dramatizes in the Plan must of necessity be flat, acted upon, unidimensional. Even if this argument were accurate, the success of Asimov's characterizations need not everywhere depend upon whether or not his galactic population is fated. Sophocles' Oedipus and Chaucer's Troilus are, to varying degrees, fated characters who are nonetheless aesthetically sound and very much alive. (p. 136)

Many of the important characters in the trilogy exhibit various traits and idiosyncrasies which distinguish them as stimulating personalities whether their probable world history has been foreplotted or not, and sometimes even whether their individual responses to certain situations have been rigged or not. Manipulated though many of the trilogy's characters are, their individual initiative and resourcefulness are often necessary to guide or to repair the great Plan. In this, the *Foundation* books introduce us to a number of memorable characters in the Asimov canon.

The second problem the trilogy poses for a reading of Asimov's characters is their fragmentation. The three novels span some four hundred years in future history. As a result, it is impossible for Asimov to remain very long with any of the characters because he must maintain the extended chronological perspective. . . . As in Arthur C. Clarke's *Childhood's End*, the long temporal scope of the trilogy limits the amount of development Asimov can allow for individual characters. Despite this, Charles Elkins is perhaps too severe when he says [in his essay in *Isaac Asimov*, edited by Joseph D. Olander and Martin Harry Greenberg] the trilogy's "characters are undifferentiated and one-dimensional." One may concede that Asimov does often fall back upon stereotypes, but some of the lead characters achieve memorable life in spite of their creator's self-imposed restrictions.

In the first book of the trilogy, *Foundation,* too many of the characterizations are, admittedly, incomplete or simplistic. (pp. 136-37)

But these mediocre stereotypes are incidental to the succession of thundering Asimov heroes in *Foundation.* Hari Seldon, Salvor Hardin, Limmar Ponyets, and Hober Mallow dominate their respective sections, and though Seldon and Ponyets are sketches, Hardin and Mallow are well-executed portraits, with Mallow coming close to life-size dimensions despite some of his comic-strip gestures. These men exhibit considerable ingenuity as they master the psychology of their opponents. . . . Those scenes dramatizing Hardin's crafty psychological infighting against Haut Rodric and Wienis are surely one source of Asimov's broad appeal in the trilogy.

Mallow, though, in his rough pride and robust cunning, is the climax and the triumph of *Foundation*'s heroes. He combines the attributes of a Viking chieftain and a Mississippi riverboat gambler. (pp. 137-38)

A character such as Mallow must be seen in the perspective of Asimov's early career. As Asimov embarked on his career as a science fiction writer, he came to know John W. Campbell, editor of *Astounding Stories,* well enough to recognize the new realism Campbell encouraged among his contributors. . . . Asimov credits Campbell with seeking to people his stories with "business men, space-ship crewmen, young engineers, housewives, robots that were logical machines." Mallow is perhaps a good example in Asimov's early writings of just such a credible character. Through Mallow's meeting with Onum Barr and his tactful handling of Joranne Sutt, the reader receives further insight into his character. *Foundation* offers a series of forceful heroes, ably capped by the figure of Mallow, who improvise sensibly within Seldon's benevolent Plan for the survival of civilized man.

Though uneven in the quality of its conception, *Foundation and Empire,* the second book in the trilogy, contains some of Asimov's best characterization. The first part of the book, presenting Lathan Devers' abortive efforts to thwart the young Empire general, Bel Riose, pales next to the longer second half, with the striking figures of Bayta and the Mule. Devers is supposed to be Mallow's heroic successor but, while Asimov portrays Devers' cover as an unconcerned, self-serving trader well enough, Devers' swashbuckling mien is a little too close to the arrogant, free-wheeling Army sergeant of World War II movies.

Bel Riose is probably a better characterization. . . . But the true hero of this section, Ducem Barr, is not given sufficient breadth for the character development which potentially exists.

Notably enough, Asimov here takes pains to assure his readers that his characters are not predestined. . . . These reminders come at the right time in the trilogy, for Asimov's explanation of the inevitability of the Foundation's victory over Riose and Brodrig will strike some readers as being much too pat.

The second part of *Foundation and Empire* is another story. The Mule's rise to power under his disguise as Magnifico the clown is intriguing enough by itself, but the real interest here is Asimov's excellent variation on the legend of Beauty and the Beast. Asimov makes the tale especially convincing by the care with which he draws Beauty's—Bayta's—character. Bayta is a complex, full-blooded person, perhaps one of the more

carefully developed female characterizations in science fiction before Alexei Panshin's Mia Havero in *Rite of Passage.* We see her at the opening of **"The Mule"** twitting her new husband Toran for his lapse into sentimentality. Conversely, we find she is protective and kind toward the deformed clown Magnifico. Playful and assertive, she is an informed historian, an ex-member of a rebel group on Terminus, an efficient factory supervisor on Haven. . . . Her shooting of Ebling Mis consummates Asimov's characterization of her. It is an unexpected action which is nonetheless consistent with her development in the story.

Also perfectly consistent with her character is her enchantment of the Mule and her gradual penetration of his cover as the clown. Unwittingly, she appeals to his human emotion, for which the Mule spares her his powers of mental interference. He explains his defeat to her and Toran: "I cherished the *natural* feeling too greatly." . . . The Mule, with his beaked face, spidery body, and "all but prehensile" nose, possesses the horrid traits of his mutation, but his soft, sad attraction to Bayta makes him effectively pathetic, understandable if not forgivable. He remains uncomfortably at the edge of stereotype, although he is more fully presented than Ebling Mis or that inconceivable bureaucrat, Mayor Indbur. But Bayta leavens and enlivens *Foundation and Empire* with the many-angled features of her character.

Second Foundation is in many ways the weakest of the three books in the trilogy. Asimov has admitted that by the time he reached their later stages the Foundation stories were becoming a burden to him. There are signs of its author's flagging interest throughout *Second Foundation.* The story of the search by the Mule, the first part of the book, is clever rather than convincing. The heart of **"Search by the Foundation,"** the second part, is a lengthy diversion, the Stettinian war. Asimov's handling of the historical materials and his style in presenting the Second Foundationers are alike awkward. (pp. 138-40)

Yet *Second Foundation* has moments when its characters are sharply etched. Channis is a good creation if only because the reader is not sure whether to like him or not. His cockiness with Pritcher balances well against his agony before the Mule, surely among the most powerful and dramatic of Asimov's confrontations. . . . Too, the portrait of Arcadia in the second part of the book sustains much of the reader's interest, offsetting in part Asimov's reliance upon hackneyed stereotypes in Callia, Stettin, and "Momma" Palver. . . . Though [Arcadia] has been controlled, Asimov succeeds in evoking the reader's affection for this precocious adolescent, and his humor does enrich his early presentation of her, even to the point of making delightful fun of his own grand manner.

But she is finally right in admiring her grandmother, Bayta. Arcadia's characterization does not match Bayta's, nor does the last book of the trilogy match the first two.

The robot books are Asimov's two collections of short stories about robots, *I, Robot* and *Stories from the Rest of the Robots,* and the two science fiction detective novels, *The Caves of Steel* and *The Naked Sun.* The short story collections require a place in a study of Asimov's characters chiefly because of Susan Calvin, who appears in many of the stories and links them into a loosely united whole. The detective novels of the 1950s center upon Elijah Baley, Asimov's greatest character. . . .

As Asimov points out, "dear Susan" is the central bond knitting together the stories in *I, Robot.* . . . (p. 141)

Dr. Calvin will on surface impress readers as "a caricature of the so-called female Ph.D. as they were believed to behave in the 1940's," but something there is about her that teasingly rounds her into a real person. Asimov sprinkles his descriptions of her with a liberal number of suggestions that she is not quite the life of the party. (p. 142)

The main charge against Dr. Calvin is that she has no human feelings. Bogert, in **"Lenny,"** says he would not apply the adjective "feminine" to any part of her. He thinks robots are all she loves, and he believes her long association with them "had deprived her of any appearance of humanity. She was no more to be argued out of a decision than was a triggered micropile to be argued out of operating." It seems fitting that the robot Lenny be "the only kind of baby she could ever have or love."

On the other hand, there is much to suggest that Susan Calvin's severity is a carefully sustained protective measure, not a mask or a pose, but a means of securing herself against the greed and folly of humankind. In *I, Robot* she possesses a "schooled indifference" . . . ; in *The Rest of the Robots* her office reflects "her own frigid, carefully-ordered personality." . . . The implication is that she must keep herself under tight control, she must ward off all temptations to partake in the abundance of human weakness which surrounds her.

That she fails sufficiently often to avoid such temptation and thereby proves herself human after all is what makes her character attractive. (pp. 142-43)

A last feature of Susan Calvin's character, and one which must have been instrumental in Asimov's confessed love for her, is her scientific idealism. One might even suspect Asimov has other characters mock Dr. Calvin because of his own built-in defense mechanism: she often voices ideals Asimov must cherish, and he perhaps wishes to deflect hurtful criticism from his most sensitive areas of thought. (p. 143)

Susan Calvin, then, is a deft character creation, loosely spanning a number of related short stories, though of course neither collection of robot stories is a novel. Asimov's best sustained character portrayal is Elijah Baley in *The Caves of Steel* and *The Naked Sun*. Dr. Calvin's character is too diffuse over the broad range of the stories, but Baley is in both of the detective novels very intensively drawn. Dr. Calvin conveys Asimov's message too explicitly—the didactic content of the robot stories is too obvious and intrusive, often jarring with the action. In *The Caves of Steel* and *The Naked Sun* the message melds smoothly with the natural growth and development of Baley's complex character.

Baley's characterization is quite well done. Tight and elaborate, sustained and credible, Baley challenges Dua in *The Gods Themselves* as Asimov's top creation (and Dua, of course, is nonhuman). The opening chapter of *The Caves of Steel* establishes Baley's complex, realistic character. (p. 144)

[The] combination of weakness and strength helps make Baley a stimulating character. Baley is a psychological caveman, a man entrapped in the womb-tomb cities of Asimov's future by his hostility, bias, and narrow-mindedness. Baley's relationship with his robot partner, Daneel Olivaw, is a serio-comic study in human frustration and jealousy. Olivaw's mechanical perfection accentuates Baley's vulnerability. . . . In his human eagerness to outwit his competition, Baley twice offers wrong solutions to the case of the murdered Spacer. It is entirely

consistent with his character that Baley would strain matters to accuse first the Spacers and then Olivaw of the crime.

The problem with Baley's characterization in *The Caves of Steel* is his conversion. The turning point of the novel occurs when Fastolfe explains his great hope of joining City people with progressive Outer Worlders to inject a new and vigorous strain into the human race. Fastolfe, we learn later, uses a drug to render Baley's mind more receptive to life outside the protective caves. This device is as weak as the one [Robert] Heinlein uses in *Double Star* to remove Smythe's prejudice against Martians. Asimov seems to realize the fundamental evasion of his ploy, for he has Olivaw assure Baley the drug would not make him "believe anything that was foreign to the basic pattern of your thought." . . . But this is not enough to convince us that Baley's conversion is a direct result of his character because Asimov does not give us really sufficient evidence, early in the story, of Baley's innate potential for his enlightened change of mind.

Nonetheless, the effects of Baley's exposure to a widened view of life are convincingly presented. . . . In fact, Baley's inherent reluctance to accept any argument at face value strengthens Asimov's portrayal of his development. The blunt honesty of his prejudices does render more effective his dawning recognition of the inhuman walls they have built around him. Because he is so stubbornly pragmatic, Baley's enlightenment on the colonization of space and his grudging admiration of Olivaw make a rather compelling conclusion for the novel. (pp. 144-45)

The Naked Sun . . . , a companion piece to *The Caves of Steel*, was the last novel Asimov wrote before turning seriously to nonfiction. *The Naked Sun* encompasses most of the qualities of *The Caves of Steel* and avoids its major defect. In *The Naked Sun* Asimov creates a novel where the inner workings of his lead character's mind and motives match, if not exceed, the outer story of detection. Put another way, Baley's adventure is an exploration of his individual self as well as an investigation of interstellar crime.

Baley in this novel is a fully conceived character. Asimov gives him a diversity of human moods and impulses. He is at once proud and frightened, reflective and quick-tempered, sensitive and tough, intelligent and vulnerable. (pp. 145-46)

These many sides of Baley are necessary to balance his growth as a hero in the book. For in *The Naked Sun* Asimov achieves with his main character a substantial development, with continuity, momentum, and a certain depth. Baley's heroism consists of his gritty battle against his "cave" fixation, against his need for "the feeling of being safely and warmly enclosed in the bowels and womb of the City." . . . He also wants his independence from Olivaw, he wants to snap "this nurse-infant relationship" between himself and Daneel. . . . But his exposure to the opposite phobia of the Solarians spurs Baley to see that a return to initiative and risk is essential to the future of the whole race of man.

Baley's attraction to Gladia encourages him in his struggle. Her inclusion in *The Naked Sun* is an inspiration by Asimov, for she adds far more than the predictable love-interest. There is a gentle tenderness in the later scenes between Baley and Gladia, the tenderness of two people groping for human contact to help them out of their psychological prisons. (p. 146)

The climax of Baley's internal drama occurs when he rips down the curtain to get a full view of unobstructed night: "Walls were crutches! Darkness and crowds were crutches!'' . . . It is perhaps too melodramatic that at this instant Baley gains the insight which solves the case. But his newly found freedom in the outdoors, his liberation from the womb-like caves of the City, his rebirth under the naked sun do not lack credibility. Baley's tenacity and courage dramatize Asimov's heartfelt belief that man will not, must not become the victim of inertia, that he must meet the challenge to inquire, to explore, and to learn.

Baley's character goes deeper than Susan Calvin's and transcends the inhabitants of the *Foundation* trilogy. His development in *The Naked Sun* is free of the pharmaceutical artifice which mars *The Caves of Steel*. Attractive and richly drawn, Baley of *The Naked Sun* stands at the peak of Asimov's characterizations in his longer fiction.

For better or for worse I have grouped *Pebble in the Sky, The Stars, Like Dust, The Currents of Space*, and *The End of Eternity* under the general heading of Asimov's lesser novels. Characterization in most of these novels is halting and negligible by comparison with Asimov's major achievements. In *Pebble in the Sky* . . . , for instance, Asimov makes a fair beginning on Schwartz's character, but the subsequent development is sketchy and uneven. The Synapsifier, which brings this book into the realm of gadget science fiction, intensifies Schwartz's mental acuteness to the point where he aggressively defeats the book's villain, but his growth from a comfortable old man to a psychological wizard is too abrupt to be really credible. Of the other characters, Pola is a pretty face, Shket a harried scientist, Ennius a weak-willed ambassador, Arbin a plain farmer, and Balkis a monomaniacal despot. Only Arvardan comes close to assuming real status as a character, and he is often immature. His heroism too frequently devolves into scenes, as with the hate-filled Lt. Claudy, resembling a rather low-grade western. (p. 147)

The End of Eternity contains without question the best characterization of Asimov's lesser novels. Andrew Harlan comes close to rivaling some of Asimov's top characters. . . . Harlan's development in the novel is logical, sustained, and forceful. Asimov creates a well-executed tension between Harlan's cool pride in his position and abilities and his instinctive doubts about the justice of tampering with time. Harlan's emotional range—his anger and jealousy with Finge, his guilt and anxiety as a wayward Technician, his love and fear for Nöys—lend the novel a genuine vitality. Harlan's decision to accept Nöys' position grows persuasively out of his character. He is malleable (and perhaps indistinct by comparison with Elijah Baley), but there is charm and credibility in his confused love for Nöys. He is always ''in character,'' even when surprising in his abrupt, peevish way. If not quite as rounded as Baley, Harlan still strikes us as a real person, not a cardboard stereotype. Nöys, slightly less realistic, is a rather impassive sort of future Eve seducing Andrew-Adam to taste the apple of Infinity. Neither as icily provocative as Susan Calvin nor as gay and assertive as Bayta, Nöys borders on the stereotypical misty and mysterious female creature from the beyond. Still, *The End of Eternity* is on almost every count several notches above the other books briefly mentioned in this section, and it shows what Asimov can do when he devotes real care to a character. In this respect *The End of Eternity* anticipates *The Gods Themselves*. (pp. 148-49)

The Gods Themselves is an uneven novel, but it has such offsetting richness to compensate for its weaknesses that it may well qualify as Asimov's masterpiece. To come right to the

point, *The Gods Themselves* contains—no matter what problems may be caused by its anthropomorphism—what must be ranked among the top creations of alien character in science fiction. Of particular note in this book is Asimov's craft in the integration of science, plot, and character into a pleasing and persuasive whole. In *Opus 100* he says one of the special delights in writing science fiction is ''mastering the art of interweaving science and fiction—keeping the science accurate and comprehensible without unduly stalling the plot.'' . . . Asimov masters this art with uncommon skill in *The Gods Themselves*. Not only do action and setting coordinate well with each other, but indeed the scientific content becomes a necessary condition for an understanding of the alien characters. This bears some explanation because it is crucial to a grasp of Asimov's achievement in creating his aliens.

The Gods Themselves follows a careful A-B-A pattern in its structural organization. Its three sections divide, for their respective headings, the quote from the German dramatist Schiller: ''Against stupidity, / the gods themselves / contend in vain [?].'' The question mark, absent in Schiller, is added by Asimov to the title of the final section. (pp. 150-51)

One point about this arrangement is that the inferences made in Part One about the physical composition of the para-Universe prepare the reader with remarkable detail for the shapes in which the aliens are discovered in Part Two. Another point is that the blindness and stupidity which characterize the Earthmen of Part One are effectively modified by the imagination and stability of the human hero in Part Three. This intricate dramatization of sentient, intelligent life, both human and alien, is the heart of *The Gods Themselves*. Moreover, characterization in this novel conveys the essentials of Asimov's view of human nature. Through his handling of his characters here, as in the robot detective novels, we may deduce Asimov's scientific meliorism and his implicit philosophy of life.

Part One of *The Gods Themselves* is a good study in Asimovian realism. The overriding Asimov theme of our urgent need to combat human short-sightedness, so dominant in the *Foundation* trilogy and the Baley novels, here receives even more intensive treatment. This section analyzes various human motives in its spectrum of unrelieved spite, careerism, greed, and assorted pettiness. (pp. 151-52)

Vainglory, wounded pride, and narrow self-interest govern all the significant decisions made by the characters in the first section of the book. (p. 152)

[The] presentation of teapot conflicts and peevish concerns grounds the narrative in an unflattering but realistic account of the scientific/political Establishment. Out of this nest of human vanity emerge the telling inferences of Hallam and Lamont about the physical nature of the para-Universe. In the scientific background of the story (which may pose a sturdy challenge to the comprehension of the lay reader) are two pieces of information which contribute powerfully to one's preparation for the aliens of Part Two. First, since the nuclear interaction is ten times stronger in the para-Universe than in ours, matter is held together there with ten times less the atomic density. This renders scientifically credible the interpenetration of physical bodies during certain phases of life in the para-Universe. The second crucial bit of information is that while nuclear fission is likely in our universe, nuclear fusion is likely in the alien universe. This prepares the reader for the merging of the triad into the composite Hard One, Estwald.

In Part Two the relationship between Dua's ethereal nature and the act of sexual intercourse through "melting" is a brilliant stroke by Asimov. (pp. 152-53)

Especially fine is the wealth of consistent detail giving the reader an impression of the physiognomy of the aliens. Odeen, for example, is pleased with his bodily traits as a Rational. He is "satisfactorily solid," with a "nice, sharp outline, smooth and curved into gracefully conjoined ovoids." He lacks "the strangely attractive shimmer of Dua, and the comforting stockiness of Tritt." . . . Dua's Parental, on the other hand, stands "squat and flat-surfaced. He wasn't all smooth-curved like a Rational or shuddery uneven like an Emotional . . ." . . . With these descriptions of the Rational and the Parental frame, one can easily see why the rarefied body of an Emotional is necessary to complete a triad. And Dua is the most rarefied of Emotionals. Asimov creates a charming portrait of Dua, spreading herself out laterally to absorb the pale rays of an evening sun, slithering with adolescent promiscuity over rocks and letting her edges overlap theirs, trying to dissipate in rebellion when her Parental says he must "pass on." The reader soon feels he has come to know this alien imp who, as she grew older, "retained a girlishly rarefied structure and could flow with a smoky curl no other could duplicate." . . .

Although Dua is the center of Asimov's accomplishment in Part Two, what he does with the triad as a whole is its own sort of triumph. For the difficult task Asimov undertakes is to create each of the triad's members as an individual character and yet render plausible the blending of the trio into the composite personality Estwald at the end. That he succeeds to such a large extent is a measure of what *The Gods Themselves* has added to science fiction. (pp. 153-54)

Dua is probably Asimov's consummate piece of original characterization, if only because her impulses and her actions follow so credibly from her physical identity. (This is not to say that Asimov's characters are determined by their environment). But in spite of the depiction of traits that may strike some readers as too human for genuine aliens, Asimov does succeed in rendering the impression of a different sort of life evolved in accord with the physical principles of a different sort of universe. And Dua is the nub of Asimov's success.

She is from the start a perimeter person. Mercurial in her moods and aberrant in her behavior, Dua's very strangeness, as Odeen recognizes, is linked with her "infinite capacity to induce satisfaction with life." . . . If the child's-eye view of sexual growth is overly cute at times, the relationship between Dua's thin-energy diet, her extraordinary sexiness, and the augmentation of her sensing powers by the socially taboo action of melting into rocks is tight and convincing. She is the curious member of the triad, combining Tritt's direct approach with Odeen's native intelligence. Her conclusion that the energy exchange will have ruinous effects on the other universe is inevitable, as is her guerilla campaign against the Hard Ones. Asimov creates in Dua a character with innocence and integrity whose growth to maturity encompasses responsibility as well as rebellion. At the close of the section the reader regrets the loss of Dua's ethereal youth but accepts, as she does, the obligations of social leadership which come with adulthood.

Yet, with all the traits of individuality Asimov gives the separate members of the triad, their melding into Estwald makes good sense. . . . One is tempted to apply a Freudian reading to Asimov's triad as a test of its validity as a composite personality. Odeen is the Ego, regulating the impulses from Dua,

the Id, while Tritt is the Superego who serves as the conscience, overseeing the group with an insistence on maintaining tradition and continuity. There are clear limits to such a reading, but perhaps this approach can suggest how well the triad coheres into its own single entity.

The greatest problems with *The Gods Themselves* begin with Part Three. At the close of Part Two the reader is not sure about Estwald's attitude toward the threat posed to our universe by the energy exchange. We wonder why in Part Three, Bronowski's absence notwithstanding, there is no mention of further messages from the para-Universe—are we to assume the permanently formed Estwald will pursue the policy of letting our universe explode? Some further communication between humans and aliens would satisfy our curiosity and remove our sense of incompletion. But in the third section we are transferred to the Moon and to the tale of Denison. Part of the letdown is that we get no further word at all about the para-Universe and, especially, how Dua's position affects Estwald's progress. Another part of the letdown is that the last section seems to lack the tension, the drive, and the economy of the other two parts.

If anything in Part Three counterbalances these weaknesses, it is the character of Denison. The way Asimov juxtaposes Denison against Neville as companions of Selene is a trifle too pat, but the developing relationship between Denison and Selene is possibly Asimov's most interesting love story. Low-keyed and mature, Denison surpasses the stereotypical intelligence older man (of the mold of the 1950s Cary Grant) who by his steady charm wins the perky young woman. . . . Throughout his relationship with Selene he is considerate, gentle, and tolerant. Denison's sanity and his scientific detachment are qualities fit for the hero of *The Gods Themselves*.

There are, nevertheless, other problems with the book's third section. For example, Neville's plot is less mysterious than it is vague. Much of the time it does little more than prevent Asimov from developing the situation we most want to hear about, the effect of the energy exchange and what can be done about it. Further, the tour device which gives Denison and the reader a fuller picture of the Lunar society defers for too long the resumption of the central story. Such a device is traditional and effective in introducing a new society, but by this time the reader is anxious to pursue the established story line. Asimov dangles tantalizing hints before the reader concerning some unwritten parallels between this section and the para-Universe section. Selene's intuitionism is like Dua's, exceeding the limits of the rational. Denison's character is not unlike Odeen's, and there are some similarities also between Neville and Tritt. Is this a coincidence, or is Asimov engaging in subtleties which escape most readers (including this one)? Asimov seems to toy with the number three and combinations thereof, but one finds it difficult to know precisely what to make of it all.

One leaves *The Gods Themselves* with a sense of resolution which is scientifically pleasing but aesthetically fragmented and not quite satisfying. The Moon is, we discover, convenient for the double-pump plan because it has its natural surface vacuum far enough removed from the Earth-based Electron Pump. But the fine and intriguing science context of Part One and the imaginative creativity of Part Two seem largely absent from this long final section.

For all its weaknesses, though, *The Gods Themselves* is a remarkable book. Asimov conventionally is grouped with the older wave of science fiction writers who allegedly do not achieve the sophistication of the later generation. But the integration of scientific imagination with character development in **The Gods Themselves,** at least in Part Two, rivals the accomplishment of Ursula Le Guin in *The Left Hand of Darkness* and does not suffer in comparison with Alexei Panshin's superb creation of Mia Havero in *Rite of Passage.* If in **The Naked Sun** Asimov has written a more smoothly executed, less flawed novel, in **The Gods Themselves** he has set his sights higher. **The Gods Themselves** rises above its unevenness to occupy a place at the top of the Asimov canon.

Asimov's characterizations dramatize and give life to what he has claimed to be the significance of science fiction. . . . The real Asimovian hero is the person who looks critically at his society, its technology, and himself—and is eager to modify, to learn, to improve. Asimov's constant concern is the effect of science and future advance upon the well-being of humanity. . . . Asimov casts a cold eye upon self-serving human ambitions, upon unholy allegiances to bureaucracy, and upon the abuse of technology to the stagnation of humankind. Asimov places his faith in the adventuresome spirit of human nature. He founds his best hope on the eternally inquiring human mind.

Among the dozen or so books which thus far make up his major contribution to science fiction, one finds character creation of widely ranging quality and accomplishment. Asimov's fiction offers a galaxy full of people. Many are thin stereotypes plucked out of the popular images of the mid-twentieth century, others are real enough to bump into on a downtown subway. What is perhaps surprising is that in a type of fiction which reportedly eschews the art of character depiction, we find in Asimov so many people with real hang-ups and with genuinely interesting personalities. Asimov is a shrewd psychologist in his characterizations. Surely his tart portrayal of human conflicts and his realistic handling of human motives are essential ingredients of his appeal as a writer. A reading of Asimov's major fiction leaves one with a sense of a wider universe not yet fully explored. (pp. 154-58)

> *Donald Watt, "A Galaxy Full of People: Characterization in Asimov's Major Fiction," in* Isaac Asimov, *edited by Joseph D. Olander and Martin Harry Greenberg (copyright © 1977 by Joseph D. Olander and Martin Harry Greenberg; published by Taplinger Publishing Co., Inc., New York; reprinted by permission), Taplinger, 1977, pp. 135-73.*

MARK MANSELL

Isaac Asimov's previous collection, **Buy Jupiter!,** was largely a selection of Asimovian trivia, outrageous puns and shaggy dog stories. **The Bicentennial Man,** however, shows him to be once more the master of science fiction that has written the **Foundation** trilogy and **"Nightfall".** . . .

Four of the stories are of his famed positronic robot series. One of these, **"Feminine Intuition",** even has Asimov's favorite character, Susan Calvin. The others are: **"That Thou Art Mindful of Him",** which . . . is about the final solution to the robot problem; **"The Tercentenary Incident"** is similar to his other positronic robot story **"Evidence"** in that both deal with suspicions that an important public figure is in fact a robot; and finally, **"The Bicentennial Man".** . . . It is among the best things Asimov has ever written, being a tale of freedom and humanity as told through the eyes of a robot who wanted

to be free and to become human. It is a touching story. . . . (p. 43)

Another excellent story is **"The Winnowing",** which is about a biochemist who is forced to turn over virus-like material to government officials who plan to use it to kill off 70% of the human race so the remainder won't face famine. There are excellent reasonings on both sides of the question, and the ending is a shocker. . . .

Rounding out the collection are two small items. **"Birth of a Notion"** was written for *Amazing Stories'* 50th Anniversary, and describes how a time-traveller managed to get Hugo Gernsback not to call his magazine *Scientifiction.* The other item is **"The Prime of Life",** a poem which seeks to disprove for all time that Isaac Asimov is over a hundred, several people, or a science fiction-writing computer.

Besides the excellent stories, there are Asimov's notes to each story, telling how they came to be written, and interesting facts about them. This running dialogue has come to be a trademark in Asimov's collections, and some people enjoy them as much as the stories themselves. This collection is not to be missed by anyone who enjoys science fiction, or who just likes good storytelling. (p. 44)

> *Mark Mansell, in his review of "The Bicentennial Man and Other Stories," in* Science Fiction Review *(copyright © 1979 by Richard Geis; reprinted by permission of Richard Geis and Mark Mansell), Vol. 8, No. 1, January-February, 1979, pp. 43-4.*

PUBLISHERS WEEKLY

Asimov, who has written a virtual galaxy of excellent popular science books, . . . achieves something valuable [in **Extraterrestrial Civilizations**] by making a fresh, rigorously statistical analysis of the universe as we "know" it. In a sequence of short chapters he discusses possible habitable planetary systems that may be found in the cosmos; by well-argued processes of elimination he narrows his analysis down to a startling statement: "The number of planets in our galaxy on which a technological civilization is now in being" is roughly 530,000. For all the mathematical nature of his approach, Asimov's speculations are intriguing, although his closing guesswork on far-future cosmic exploration seems a papering over of our current state of ignorance.

> *A review of "Extraterrestrial Civilizations," in* Publishers Weekly *(reprinted from the April 16, 1979 issue of* Publishers Weekly, *published by R. R. Bowker Company; copyright © 1979 by R. R. Bowker Company), Vol. 215, No. 16, April 16, 1979, p. 65.*

MARGARET L. CHATHAM

[**Saturn and Beyond** is another] in Asimov's series of astronomy books for junior high, misleadingly titled as always. The first three quarters of the book deal only with the planets known to the ancients, one supposes in order to use a historical approach, but then Asimov talks of the 1977 discovery of Chiron (an asteroid between the orbits of Saturn and Uranus) before admitting that Uranus was discovered in 1781. He spends a great deal of time on the various moons, discussing what one could see from them as well as the usual statistics about size and orbits, which makes the lack of mention of Pluto's newly discovered moon more noticeable. Asimov's **Jupiter: the Largest Planet** . . . is better organized to tell about the outer planets, but is becoming seriously dated as new information piles up, and should be replaced with **Saturn and Beyond**.

Margaret L. Chatham, in her review of "Saturn and Beyond," in School Library Journal *(reprinted from the May, 1979 issue of* School Library Journal, *published by R. R. Bowker Co./A Xerox Corporation; copyright © 1979), Vol. 25, No. 9, May, 1979, p. 69.*

CHOICE

Isaac Asimov's **In memory yet green,** [volume] 1 of a two-volume autobiography, suffers from the faults that mar Asimov's fiction; it is long on plot (708 pages of revised diary entries) and short on characterization (few of his acquaintances emerge as anything but foils for Asimov). While Asimov is candid, as in revealing his own foibles and in exploring the effects of his immigrant background and previous early life on his attitudes and actions, he too often resorts to a parody of his legendary egomania. Finally, Asimov becomes his caricature of himself. This failing is particularly disappointing since Asimov, as the indexes of names and titles clearly indicate, is at the center of the "golden age" of science fiction. His accounts of his dealings with J. W. Campbell, editor of *Astounding Science Fiction,* are ample evidence that Asimov might have explored the way he and the science fiction community of the late 1930s produced that golden age. (pp. 652-53)

A review of "In Memory Yet Green: The Autobiography of Isaac Asimov, 1920-1954," in Choice *(copyright © 1979 by American Library Association), Vol. 16, Nos. 5 & 6, July-August, 1979, pp. 652-53.*

HARRY C. STUBBS

[*Saturn and Beyond*] consists of a historical description of what we know about the outer parts of the solar system and how we found the information. The author is very careful to indicate what sort of data are still uncertain, such as the sizes, and hence the densities, of the smaller satellites of the outer planets. He also points out fallacies in various theories of the origin of the system, which are apparent if the supposedly measured values are right; and he doesn't try to push us toward a favored choice of his own. . . . The book is sufficiently up to date to have the information on Pluto's moon, though the author either missed or didn't trust the radar evidence that the particles in Saturn's rings are about snowball size (I'm not sure how far I trust it myself). I caught only one slip; it is true that eclipses of the sun as seen from Titan occur in roughly one quarter of that satellite's revolutions, but Asimov does not indicate that they are not randomly distributed in time. When Saturn is close to its equinox, they occur in every revolution; when it isn't, they don't occur at all. There are numerous useful tables for science-fiction writers, which tell how big and bright the sun looks from various planets and how big and bright the planets look from their various moons. I'm keeping the book; I *can* figure out all these things for myself, but why should I work harder than I have to?

Harry C. Stubbs, "Astronomy," in The Horn Book Magazine *(copyright © 1979 by The Horn Book, Inc., Boston), Vol. LV, No. 4, August, 1979, p. 450.*

THOMAS LECLAIR

Like a black hole, **Extraterrestrial Civilizations** contracts, moving from a billion trillion possibilities to imaginable probabilities as Asimov shows how the origins of life and the conditions that permit it to evolve limit civilization to 540 planets in our galaxy. The information, ranging from early speculation about space to pulsars and red giants, is impressive and is lucidly presented; but the chain of logic leading to the title's assertion is as unstable as a mile-long game of crack-the-whip. While I respect Asimov's resistance to UFOs, a drunk's sighting of a purple saucer is, finally, as credible as Asimov's argument.

Asimov does wonder "where is everybody" from these civilizations. In the last chapters he discusses the presently insurmountable difficulties of interstellar travel and communication. We are not alone, but we might just as well be. Even so, Asimov ends with a *Battlestar Galactica* vision of the future. A hundred years ago people believed there were holes at the poles. Using Asimov's probabilistic methods, one can believe those holes just haven't been found yet. (pp. 58-9)

Thomas Leclair, in his review of "Extraterrestrial Civilizations," in Saturday Review *(© 1979 Saturday Review Magazine Co.; reprinted by permission), Vol. 6, No. 16, August, 1979, pp. 58-9.*

MARY JO CAMPBELL

[In **Extra-Terrestrial Civilizations**] Asimov turns his talents for clear explanations of complex scientific subjects to the question of the existence of extraterrestrial life. . . . The chemical and physical bases for life are discussed in detail but never beyond the comprehension of high school students. If alien life exists, as Asimov believes it does, why have we not found any evidence of it? Asimov theorizes that cosmic distances between even the nearest stars, not to mention galaxies, are so great that visitations are highly unlikely. . . . This clearly written discussion of a topic of interest to many young people joins other good books on this subject such as *Who Goes There?* by Edward Edelson . . . and Ian Ridpath's *Messages from the Stars.* . . .

Mary Jo Campbell, in her review of "Extra-Terrestrial Civilizations," in School Library Journal *(reprinted from the September, 1979 issue of* School Library Journal, *published by R. R. Bowker Co./A Xerox Corporation; copyright © 1979), Vol. 26, No. 1, September, 1979, p. 168.*

BOOKLIST

With more than 200 books including science fact as well as science fiction and mysteries to his credit, it is not surprising that [in **Isaac Asimov's Book of Facts**] Asimov has finally turned to assembling systematically some of the facts he has accumulated. He offers 3,000 odd bits of information here to entertain as well as inform, setting them down in categories ranging from kings and eccentricities to fashions and the Civil War. Presented with a bit of Asimov's characteristic sparkle, this is a find for browser and trivia addict. Asimov invites contributions for his second fact hodgepodge—a certainty for the future.

A review of "Isaac Asimov's Book of Facts," in Booklist *(reprinted by permission of the American Library Association; copyright © 1980 by the Amer-*

ican Library Association), Vol. 76, No. 12, February
15, 1980, p. 798.

TIME

Heavy enough to produce bursitis and double the price of standard sci-fi, the second installment of Asimov's autobiography
appears formidable. It turns out to be even more entertaining
than Volume I, **In Memory Yet Green.** Covering the years between 1954 and 1978, [**In Joy Still Felt**] is a detailed account
of the writer's literary recognition, his marital failure, his thy-
roid cancer, his heart attack and the trauma of turning 40. . . .
The book may tell more than anyone wanted to ask about the
life of America's most accomplished explainer. But it does it
so disarmingly that readers should be almost as fascinated with
its subject as he is with himself.

A review of "In Joy Still Felt," in Time *(copyright
1980 Time Inc.; all rights reserved; reprinted by
permission from* Time*), Vol. 115, No. 19, May 12,
1980, p. 81.*

ALGIS BUDRYS

[Isaac Asimov] is fluent, possessed of meticulous records and
journals going back to the days of childhood, impressively
organized in his thinking, and apparently tireless. This and
more is all apparent at the surface of his massive two-volume
autobiography [**In Memory Yet Green** and **In Joy Still Felt**],
which we hope will someday be at least three. Nor is he a
stranger to any F&SF reader. Nor, in fact, is it possible to
believe that anyone with the slightest interest in SF, in science,
or for that matter any portion of the universe of intellection,
doesn't already have some depth of friendship with him.

That, I think, is the outstanding one of all of Asimov's qualities
as a writer. He is the reader's friend. His concern for your
clear understanding of his message, his fondness for you and
his trust in your ability to make good use of his message—
that gestalt of qualities rises warmly from every paragraph he
writes, whatever the mode or the subject.

He is at times bumptious. At times, he does something in his
autobiography that he has rarely done elsewhere—he goes on
too long after a particular point has been fully made. He displays one or two other less than impeccable aspects of behavior.
But he is your friend, and he is paying you the highest compliment of all.

No fool at all, he knows—he knew from the beginning of the
project—that no man can be the perfect hero of his honest
autobiography, and he trusts you to understand that. You want
to know about him, or you wouldn't have opened the book.
All right—a wordsmith of his skills could readily have devoted
his effort to some dazzling footwork. He could have sailed off
on glittering flights of generality and statesmanly pontification,
as many do. Or he could have danced an intellectual fan dance
with you, replete with enigmatic references to dark nights of
the soul, quasi-confidences about famous names whose privacy
he could (Ho! Ho!) compromise, delicious scandals he would
retail if he weren't so discreet, might retail at some future
time. . . . You know how that goes; you've seen the technique
often enough. It's a species of orchestrated performance.

Asimov doesn't do that. He tells you about the events in his
life, his responses to them, day after day, plateau after plateau
of development, and it's all there. Make of it what you will;

there he stands, your friend, paradoxically in the limelight yet,
in all this wordage, never "on stage." . . . He could have
done us a tour de force novel about his life, and few of us
would have been the wiser. Instead, he hands us his diary.

Oh, some of the pages are glued together lightly. Again paradoxically, although he uses hundreds of thousands of words,
some of them devoted to confidences, he eschews gossip. He
has apparently made a meticulous effort never to say anything
for the sake of poking fun, to make a "harmless" joke at the
expense of an uninvolved party, to titillate us with the sort of
anecdote that's the stuff of life for the late-night party.

It's not party time in these books. We sit in the afternoon
sunlight coming through the windows of a conservatively furnished parlor; we sip tea, and our host responds to our query.
Therefore, since life itself sometimes pokes fun, sometimes
juxtaposes us with circumstances that are inherently salacious
in some sense, there are things our friend does not detail. Given
the choice between not telling us the whole of the truth or
including even the appearance of deliberate gossip-mongering,
he gives us a sufficient outline of the truth and goes on to the
next thing in detail. (pp. 68-9)

Let me tell you what I wanted to know. I wanted to know what
goes on inside a genius. What I got, of course, is what a genius
is willing to say about what he thinks is going on inside himself.
This is all anyone can ever get from such a source. But because
Asimov has chosen this diarist's approach, standing back and
letting us form our own judgments from the preferred data, he
has made his essential self fruitlessly accessible in the sense
that he rebuts hardly any synthesis one might arrive at. There
he is, make of him what you will, and the acuity of whatever
you make must depend entirely on its own internal logic. You're
dealing with a man who has deliberately drawn no conclusions
of his own. So yours have nothing to push against, and had
better be self-supporting. . . .

His technical accomplishment in the construction of these books
is awesome to me, and few things are truly awesome. (p. 70)

Despite having read [these books], . . . I still know nothing
about his creative methods or about his actual writing procedures.

He tells us about sitting down at the typewriter and working
hard; about looking things up in reference books; about editorial
conferences in which projects are shaped. . . . The man sits
down, begins to type, continues to type, and when the manuscript is complete, lo, it has effective form and purpose which
the mind, through some automatic mechanism of synthesis,
imposed on the forebrain which was selecting the particular
words and paragraphs. A mind which has produced over 200
books certainly ought to be able to do that.

But what a mind in any case, because look at the result: A
structure which is the only structure a multiplex person like
Asimov could have used without getting lost in himself, and
the only structure which can be friendly and yet preserve our
friend's essential core of privacy.

Did he do it that way consciously? Of course he did! A mind
of this caliber, doing the thing for which it is particularly
trained, does not kid itself. A mind may avoid or distort responses to conscious self-examination—slippery mind—but some
totally rectitudinous portion of it delivers an objective running
report on what is going on, and I'm sure that Isaac is in excellent
contact with all facets of his personality. (p. 71)

[Read his column in the September, 1980 issue of *The Magazine of Fantasy and Science Fiction*.] Chatty, informative, witty, useful; you are getting what you came for. The professional writer has delivered what was wanted. He has gone out and examined some external aspect of the universe, and brought back a description of it which we can all handily take away with us. Point to anything—anything at all, in or under the starry sky—express interest, and he will satisfy that interest. Or he will, alternatively, come to you and say "I noticed this aspect of reality, and I thought you might like to hear about it. Now, look where I'm pointing . . . you see that? . . . let me tell you what that is."

Not this time. Not this one time, of all the times he has written for us, our friend. There is nothing we can point to, in the infinite reaches of the human mind, that does not first have to be located for us by utterances from the person possessed of that mind. It has no objective reality; all the evidence for its existence is circumstantial. Similarly, he can tell us he is pointing to it, but there is no way we can confirm that. Again, similarly, the very nature of the mind is such that not even the person most intimately connected with it can be objectively sure that what he sees in it now is the way it was.

How much easier, how much more comfortable, how much more satisfactory it would have been for us if someone who was not Isaac Asimov, but in all other respects exactly like Isaac Asimov, had been given the assignment of writing these volumes on Isaac Asimov! But then, of course, we would have been nagged by the thought that this was, after all, only a biography; we would have wanted to hear the same events, or almost certainly more accurate descriptions of those same events, recounted by Asimov himself.

The paradoxes are inescapable, and spiralling, because Asimov could not have helped but know from the very beginning that though there was tremendous interest in having a life of Asimov, once we had it there could only be heightened interest in *really* having a life of Asimov, no matter how real he made it.

And he did it anyway.

What would you like to know? Would you like to know how it sounds?

It sounds like an earnest, meticulous, ultramethodical person bumping through life. . . . It sounds like a person directing all his intelligence and energy toward forging places for himself in a sometimes circumstantially obstinate universe. It sounds like a man attaining conditions which ought by all prior logic [to] be happy conditions, but reveal themselves not to be. Or, conversely, benefiting from unpredictable fortune.

It sounds, in other words, like a human being's story. But this is not any other human being. This is a public figure whose stature is founded on public intellection. (pp. 71-2)

[We] don't read a life of Asimov to find out how to write 200 books. The chances of any of us writing 200 books are worse than our chances of landing on the Moon. Nor is writing 300 or 400 books the objective of Asimov's life. The objective of Asimov's life is to think. And, as it happens, to communicate. But there is no one particular thing he thinks about, or even one particular area. He is not a philosopher, not primarily a scientist in the common understanding of that term, not except incidentally a titled expert, not any of the classifiable things.

He is, when you come down to it, a child in a room full of unlabelled objects and unexplained events; a room so huge that the walls, the ceiling, and even the floor are immensely far away and lose their features in shadow. He is like us. But he has more energy. Those who preceded us in the room sent out search parties, explorers and librarians who, channeling their energies as they must, proceeded along defined paths and send back messages only about what those paths intersected. The messages come back at us from all sides, linear, narrow, each claiming priority. We don't know what to make of it.

Isaac tells us. Bounding happily from one thing to another, his caracolings intersecting path after path, he puts things together for us. Others tell us what is on the paths. Isaac tells us what is in the room.

And of course that is what we all desperately want to know. So Isaac is valuable to us, rightly held in great esteem, and fully entitled to the rewards we ungrudgingly give him. (pp. 72-3)

Algis Budrys, "The Autobiography of Isaac Asimov" (reprinted by permission of the author), in The Magazine of Fantasy and Science Fiction, *Vol. 59, No. 3, September, 1980, pp. 68-73.*

PATRICIA S. WARRICK

Isaac Asimov is deservedly regarded as the father of robot stories in SF. He has produced more robot and computer stories than any other writer, and the quality of his fiction is consistently high. (p. 54)

Asimov has been both comprehensive, thoughtful, and imaginative in creating his substantial body of fiction.

Asimov is optimistic about the relationship of man and intelligent machines. Asimov has labeled the fear of mechanical intelligence the "Frankenstein complex." He does not have this fear, nor does he approve of those who do. He believes that machines take over dehumanizing labor and thus allow humans to become more human. (p. 55)

In his robot stories most of the population resents robot research and resists the use of robots, so most of the development and testing goes on in outer space. In **"Profession"** . . . he summarizes this phenomenon of resistance to change by creating a future world where the phenomenon has become part of the system. In this imaginary world most people have their brains wired to tapes and are programmed like machines to function in a routine, nondeviating fashion. Rare, creative individuals are set apart in a special house where they follow the creative thrust of their imagination. Asimov's view is clear: Most members of society are rigid, like machines, and resist change; the rare individual with a creative mind is the exception. (p. 56)

Asimov's cybernetic fiction can be divided into three phases. During the first, from 1940 to 1950, he wrote a dozen stories primarily about robots, with only two computer stories. Nine of these stories were collected and published as *I, Robot* in 1950. During his second period, from 1951 to 1961, he wrote another dozen or so stories and the novels *The Caves of Steel* and *The Naked Sun*. Many of the stories and the two novels were collected and published under the title *The Rest of the Robots*. . . . *The Bicentennial Man* . . . contains a half dozen stories marking his third period and demonstrates the evolution of his ideas about the key role computers will play in man's future.

The Asimovian view gives a kind of unity to all his fiction about computers and robots, from the first story in 1940 to the last in 1976. This view holds that man will continue to develop more sophisticated technology; he will become more skillful at solving societal and environmental problems; he will expand outward and colonize space. Many of the stories share the same characters and settings. . . .

The stories are often concerned with the same themes: the political potential of the computer, the uses of computers and robots in space exploration and development, problem solving with computers, the differences between man and machine, the evolution of artificial intelligence, the ethical use of technology. This last theme is explored through Asimov's Three Laws of Robotics, first fully stated in **"Runaround,"** Asimov's fifth robot tale. They appear in many other stories and are crucial to three stories in *The Bicentennial Man.*

Asimov handles machine intelligence both realistically and metaphorically. In stories about computers, technology functions very much like existing technology. Large stationary machines store, process, and retrieve data; do mathematical calculations at incredible speeds; play mathematical games; make logical decisions. Asimov is knowledgeable in the concepts of computer science, and his portrayals are always intelligent and accurate. He has been wise enough to omit specific descriptions of computer technology, and consequently the material does not become dated—something that can easily happen if the writer portrays details of the technology because it is changing so rapidly in the real world. Asimov's robots are much more metaphorical than his computers. In the real world no robots comparable in form to those he pictures have been built, nor is there much possibility that they will be in the near future. Only specialized industrial robots performing limited functions are being developed. The all-purpose robots that Asimov pictures might be possible, but the specialized ones are economically more feasible. It is more meaningful to regard his robots as a metaphor for all the automated electronic technology—in a variety of forms—that will replace most of man's physical and routine mental work in the future.

Asimov rarely uses dramatic conflict to develop his plots; instead he relies almost entirely on puzzle or problem solving to create suspense and to move his plot forward. Through all his fiction runs the theme of faith in the ability of human reason to solve problems. His fiction is cerebral, grounded in sound science and logic. The action is more often mental than physical. In a typical story a problem or puzzle is defined; as much data as possible is collected and evaluated; a hypothesis is formed, providing a basis for a set of predictions about the solution to the problem; finally the predictions are tested. If they are incorrect, the process is reexamined until the difficulty is discovered. This procedure, of course, is the scientific method. The universe for Asimov is more mysterious than threatening. His use of the puzzle paradigm, rather than the conflict paradigm, seems related to his optimistic view of computer and robots. His short story **"The Evitable Conflict"** reflects his attitude toward conflict. The future world is one in which society has learned to avoid war. In his fiction Asimov also avoids the conflict mode.

Asimov's earliest cybernetic fiction, **"Robbie,"** is set on earth at the end of the twentieth century, where robots are manufactured as playmates for children. . . . Asimov's robots in **"Robbie"** are programmed with the First Law of Robotics: A robot may not injure a human being or, through inaction, let a human being come to harm. Robbie, the hero of the story, is a dependable playmate for an eight-year-old girl named Gloria, even though her mother dislikes him because she distrusts robots. The robot eventually saves Gloria's life.

The next group of robot stories are set in space. Feelings against robots have grown so strong on earth that they are banned. In these stories two engineers, Powell and Donovan, solve a set of problems and puzzles using robots. The robots serve a variety of functions in space. They help maintain a space station, they perform ore-mining operations on an asteroid, they operate a spaceship sent to explore Jupiter. Because these stories are set in space, not on earth, little conflict between man and robot occurs. In the hostile environment of space, machine intelligence is vital to man, and so he welcomes it.

The situation is different on earth, where the later stories are set. In **"Evidence"** . . . , one of Asimov's most profound cybernetic stories, the general population resents robots. Stephen Byerly, who is running for mayor, is charged by his opponents with being a robot and therefore unsuitable for public office. Two questions arise: Is Byerly really a robot? If so, can a machine govern effectively?

The first question gives Asimov a good opportunity to explore the logic of proof, and here he demonstrates his education and intellectual inclination. He is ever the scientist, using the scientific method of hypothesis and proof. To the second question Asimov answers *yes.* His robots and computer are programmed with the Three Laws of Robotics, which ensure that they will always aid and serve man. **"Evidence"** contains a substantial discussion of those laws. Byerly points out that they incorporate the ethical principles of the world's great religions. Because a robot mechanism cannot violate these laws, it is a more reliable device for governing than a poltician, who may be motivated by ambition and greed. (pp. 57-9)

"The Evitable Conflict" is one of science fiction's most superbly imaginative stories in envisioning the creative use of machine intelligence. In this story, set in the twenty-first century, the world has been divided into four geographic regions, with the economy of each maintained in balance by a huge computer. As a result war has been eliminated. But small errors in production schedules begin to occur. The question is whether the resulting imbalance is caused by machine error or by human error—deliberate or otherwise. An antimachine group has arisen, and its leaders may be trying to sabotage the computer by feeding it inaccurate data. Byerly's problem is to explain and then correct the imbalance in production.

As it turns out, the computer—programmed to operate heuristically—soon corrects the problem itself. It detects the inaccurate data, and then dictates the removal of the economic supervisors opposed to machine control. They are motivated not by a concern for the good of the whole but by a drive to dominate and control, a drive that will lead to war. The computer's capacity for detecting and removing the potential creators of conflict before they can cause trouble thus prevents war. Conflict is evitable; only the machine is inevitable. Asimov in this story suggests that machine control is superior to economic and sociological forces, the whims of climate, and the fortunes of war. Mankind, he intimates, has never been free; machine control is just a different—and superior—form of control. (pp. 60-1)

Asimov's cybernetic fiction uses the electronic brain in a variety of ways, none malignant. The computer is an aid in the research and development of space travel; it performs all mathematical calculations for society, predicts election results, aids in the educational process. It solves a variety of problems, and the greatest problem it undertakes is that of decreasing entropy in the universe. In what is often considered the classic computer story, **"The Last Question"** . . . , it reverses the entropic process and recreates the cosmos. In this tale man keeps asking the computer, How can entropy be reversed? He asks it six different times, first on earth, then on various galaxies, as he continually expands through the universe. The computer keeps answering, Insufficient data to give meaningful answer. Finally, trillions of years later, as entropy becomes absolute and the last star goes out, he asks it the seventh time. The computer finally has sufficient data to give the answer: Let there be light! The story is a beautiful myth of cyclic creation. Man—himself once created—creates the machine. The machine, a greater creator, finally acquires all the information in the universe. Then, omniscient like God, the machine is able to re-create the universe. (p. 62)

In his early fiction Asimov assumes that man and machine intelligence share many characteristics—hence the continued use of the human-appearing robot as a symbol of artificial intelligence. At first glance man and robot look alike, but deeper probing reveals the difference. Machines do some things that a man can, but man possesses unique characteristics that make him more than a machine. This is why a machine is always subservient to a machine, as assured in the Second Law of Robotics.

The differences between humans and machines provide subject matter for a number of stories. One difference is that human intelligence is coupled with emotion; machine intelligence is not. . . .

Another difference is that machines cannot handle ambiguity. In mathematical logic one symbol can denote only one thing. A figure of speech, where the individual meanings of a group of words are different from their sum, creates havoc for the computer. In this respect human language is unlike computer language. Any human easily grasps the meaning of a figure of speech from its context. Not so a computer. Asimov loves to play with this difference, just as he delights in puns, which are also beyond the capacity of the computer. The delight in incongruity or contradiction is the essence of humor, and Asimov's puckish humor often shimmers just above his hard, scientific thinking. But his robots are incapable of laughter because they take everything literally and thus have no sense of humor. Asimov often uses this fact as the basis for a story. (p. 63)

Creative problem solving is another area in which machine intelligence differs from human intelligence. Asimov explores this difference in **"Risk"** . . . , in which a robot is used as a test pilot in an experimental spaceship. When difficulties develop on the ship, the robot is replaced by a man because the robot can solve only problems it has been programmed to solve, while a man is able to solve unanticipated problems.

One of the differences between human and artificial intelligence is that machines do not possess consciousness or self-awareness. They may perform operations that humans define as intelligent, but they are not aware of what they are doing. They do not observe themselves in the process of thinking as humans do.

In the fiction of his first two periods Asimov raises but does not pursue the question of consciousness in his robots. . . . When Asimov was later asked about consciousness in his robots, he replied that he does think of his robots as being conscious. But the fiction of his first two periods fails to probe the ethical and moral implications of consciousness in artificial intelligence. If a robot does have consciousness, in what significant way is he different from a human being? If he is not significantly different, is it ethical to treat him like a nonhuman? Is it moral to use him as a slave when humans value their freedom so highly? What about death? Should the robot be portrayed in SF as dying or merely wearing out? Can a human "kill" a robot? In **"Liar"** Susan Calvin deliberately programs a robot so that he collapses and goes insane. Should she be condemned for driving him insane? These are complex questions that have never been considered because man has never moved so close to the technological reality of constructing artificial intelligence. Asimov raises them in the fiction of his first two periods, but not until the fiction of his recent period does he give the thoughtful reflection that consciousness, death, and freedom—either in human or high-level artificial intelligence—deserve.

The Three Laws of Robotics have attracted more attention than any other aspect of Asimov's cybernetic SF. In SF religious tales are rare. So are stories debating the niceties of various moral codes. SF has traditionally based itself on the natural and social sciences, which aim to be analytic not normative. Certainly no writer grounds his fiction more solidly in science than Asimov, yet he has formulated an ethical code now famous in and out of SF. . . . The laws are as follows:

> 1. A robot may not injure a human being nor, through inaction, allow a human being to come to harm.

> 2. A robot must obey the orders given it by human beings except where such orders would conflict with the First Law.

> 3. A robot must protect its own existence as long as such protection does not conflict with the First or Second Law.

>   (pp. 64-5)

Several of Asimov's most recent cybernetic stories, collected in *The Bicentennial Man* . . . , explore the Three Laws on a more profound level than did the works in his first two periods. Thirty-five years after his early stories, his knowledge and perceptions have evolved considerably. So has the level of machine intelligence he describes and the implications of the Three Laws for that intelligence. The most significant aspect of the Three Laws, however, is not the ways that Asimov uses them fictionally but the influence they have had in the real world. He has suggested that man needs to consider ways to implement the ethical use of technology and has provided models for doing this. Mere fictional model? Certainly fiction, but much more than that. As Asimov's stories are always grounded in accurate scientific fact, so here his ethical possibilities rest on actual capabilities of computer programming. (pp. 66-7)

Any discussion of computer programming of ethics is still highly speculative. But there is no reason why speculations could not someday become realities. Asimov's significant accomplishment is that the drama he has created with the Three Laws has set us thinking. Perhaps in the real world ethical concepts could be operationalized in computer technology. No other science fiction writer has given the world that vision.

Asimov's imagination constantly spirals forward into new possibilities. Robbie, his first robot, was a giant toy programmed to entertain and protect a child. Later his robots labored in space. In his most recent writing robots acquire characteristics previously ascribed only to humans—characteristics like creativity and the capacity to make judgments. Finally the complexity of the robots leads Asimov in *The Bicentennial Man* to suggest that ethical considerations concerning man may need to be extended to include machine intelligence.

Several of the short stories in *The Bicentennial Man* pair with earlier fiction; comparison shows how Asimov's thinking has evolved over the last thirty-five years. "Evidence" (1946) considered whether a robot might not be as efficient a mayor as a human. In "Tercentenary Incident" (1976) a robot serves as president of the United States. In both instances the general public is unaware of the substitution of machine for man but enjoys the benefits that result from more efficient government.

Another pair of stories pictures a world governance structure operated by computer. In the early story, "The Evitable Conflict," the world economy has been stabilized, underemployment and overproduction have been eliminated, and famine and war have disappeared. The recent "Life and Times of Multivac" also pictures a world system operated by computer. . . . (p. 68)

In "The Life and Times of Multivac," as in all his other stories, Asimov has a comprehensive grasp of the issues raised by the development of artificial intelligence. Machine systems can remove the drudgery of work; they can be used in planning and decision making; they can store and process vast amounts of information, thus augmenting man's mental power. But these benefits have a cost. Man must replace his image of himself as a rugged individualist free to do as he wills with an image of himself as a systems man living in symbiosis with his machines. In *The Caves of Steel* Asimov calls this supportive relationship a C/Fe culture: carbon (C) is the basis of human life and iron (Fe) of robot life. A C/Fe culture results from a combination of the best of the two forms.

In the stories of the third period artificial intelligence has evolved substantially beyond its level in the earlier works. The goal of the computer scientists in "Feminine Intuition" . . . is to develop a creative robot. The principle of uncertainty, explains Research Director Bogert, "is important in particles the mass of positrons." If this unpredictability of minute particles can be utilized in the robot design, it might be possible to have a creative robot. . . . If the uncertainty effect can be introduced into the robot brain, it will share the creativity of the human brain. The research is successful, and U.S. Robots produces the first successful design of creativity in artificial intelligence. (pp. 69-70)

"That Thou Art Mindful of Him" . . . pictures the development of the positronic brain with the capacity for judgment. Judgment is developed in the robot because it is required to cope with conflicting orders from two humans. The Second Law says he must obey—but which order? The answer is that he must obey the human most fit by mind, character, and knowledge to give that order. However, once the capacity for judgment is designed into the robots, they begin to use it in unanticipated ways. The robot George Nine decides he will "disregard shape and form in judging human beings, and . . . rise superior to the distinction between metal and flesh." . . . He concludes, after exercising his judgment, that his fellow robots are like humans, except more fit. Therefore they ought to dominate humans. The possibility that machine intelligence may be both superior to human intelligence and likely to dominate human intelligence appears for the first time in this story.

Asimov's robots have now evolved a long way from that first clumsy Robbie in 1940.

The last design for the evolution of artificial intelligence appears in "The Bicentennial Man." . . . Here pure intelligence, irrespective of carbon or metal form, appears. This story . . . is Asimov's finest fictional work. It is the longest story (fifteen thousand words) that he has produced in seventeen years. Despite its length, it is still very terse—dense with ideas—and might well benefit from expansion to novel length. Told in twenty-three episodes, it covers two hundred years in the life of the robot Andrew Martin. Asimov's approach to the puzzle of intelligence, human or machine, gives the story its power. Inverting the obvious approach—man examining artificial intelligence—he has Andrew explore the nature and implications of human intelligence. As the story opens, Andrew is an obedient household servant for the Martin family, much the role of Asimov's early Robbie. But Andrew is a mutant robot form with an unusual talent: he is creative. He produces exquisite wood carvings. Just as he has transcended the patterns of previous robots, so he aspires to transcend the limits of the role they occupied in society. He desires to be free, not a slave to man, but this seems a clear violation of the Second Law.

Andrew's struggle to evolve beyond his programmed obedience is dramatized with great economy. The Martin family represents the small group of humans who realize the potential of artificial intelligence and take actions to foster and expand it. The U.S. Robots Corporation symbolizes the economic system supported by the mass of men who wish only to exploit robot technology for profit. They feel no ethical responsibility to this emerging form of intelligence.

After a long struggle the courts declare Andrew free. Then, bit by bit over the ensuing years, Andrew moves toward fulfilling his aspiration to become like his masters. His potential, his determination, and the support of a few dedicated individuals yield slow progress. (pp. 70-1)

"The Bicentennial Man" is a powerful, profound story for several reasons. Foremost is what Asimov leaves unsaid. The story follows the movement of mechanical intelligence toward human intelligence and death. But Andrew's progress toward manhood and death unfolds against man's development of technology and movement toward artificial intelligence and immortality. Knowledge or information eventually dies in the organic brain, but it can survive indefinitely in a mechanical brain. Thus the inorganic form may well be the most likely form for the survival of intelligence in the universe. As machine intelligence evolves to human form, human intelligence is evolving toward machine form. A second implication of "The Bicentennial Man," again unstated, is that a line between the animate and the inanimate, the organic and the inorganic, cannot be drawn. . . . If the fundamental materials of the universe are matter, energy, and information patterns (or intelligence), then man is not unique. He exists on a continuum with all intelligence; he is no more than the most highly evolved form on earth. This view implies that ethical behavior should extend to all systems because any organizational pattern—human or nonhuman, organic or inorganic—represents intelligence. A sacred view of the universe, the result not of religious mysticism but of pure logic, emerges from this reading of "The Bicentennial Man." (pp. 73-4)

Patricia S. Warrick, "Science Fiction Images of Computers and Robots" in her The Cybernetic Imagination in Science Fiction *(reprinted by permission of The MIT Press, Cambridge, Massachusetts; copy-*

right © 1980 by The Massachusetts Institute of Technology), The MIT Press, 1980, pp. 53-79.*

KATHERINE THORP

[In *Asimov on Science Fiction*] Asimov's forthright views are presented in a crisp and witty style. His lifetime of experience in the field provides mature judgments. Readers of all ages who have any degree of interest in science fiction will enjoy listening to Asimov discourse on the topics he knows so well.

Katherine Thorp, in her review of "Asimov on Science Fiction," in Library Journal *(reprinted from* Library Journal, *April 1, 1981; published by R. R. Bowker Co. (a Xerox company); copyright © 1981 by Xerox Corporation), Vol. 106, No. 7, April 1, 1981, p. 797.*

KIRKUS REVIEWS

[In *Venus: Near Neighbor of the Sun*] Asimov uses the description of a single astronomical object to relate much basic astronomy in a direct, easily understood manner. The text presents a significant amount of the content of an introductory astronomy and planetary physics course clearly, and without mathematics. The wealth of figures and tables complements and clarifies the descriptions of the relative sizes of the planets when viewed from different distances, the orbital characteristics of planets and satellites, and the appearance of objects as viewed by an observer located on another planet. Most of the astronomical history and observations that constitute the story of Venus have been described before. However, Asimov uses new data, particularly from Pioneer Venus (launched in 1978), to show that astronomy is an alive scientific field, with many theories to be tested and observations to be explained. The ploy of seeing the night sky as a Sumerian astronomer did, and following the development from astronomical observation to theory, works well in leading beginners from their own casual observations of the skies to an understanding of the elementary theories. The book's subtitle is initially confusing; however, the confusion ends when Asimov takes up the description of Mercury, asteroids, and comets—other near neighbors of the sun—in the last four chapters. As a bonus, readers lulled by the regularity of terrestrial phenomena might modify their mundane geocentric world-view; the realization that there are other, comparatively bizarre phenomena (e.g., the playful, hesitant sunrises that can occur on Mercury's surface) may surprise many readers, and start them wondering about the universe. (pp. 876-77)

A review of "Venus: Near Neighbor of the Sun," in Kirkus Reviews *(copyright © 1981 The Kirkus Service, Inc.), Vol. XLIX, No. 14, July 15, 1981, pp. 876-77.*

CHOICE

It is tempting to say that [*Asimov on science fiction*] has been assembled by a robot, but accuracy—and the state-of-the-art—blames the more prosaic computer printout. Asimov has scrutinized his prodigious output of over 200 volumes on diverse subjects, and culled from them these 55 pieces on science fiction. His incentive is a sense of the historical occasion. Rather surprisingly, Asimov has never exclusively devoted a volume to the subject. Sadly, this effort is, for the most part, mechanical and superficial. More than half of these pieces

originated from Asimov's own magazine and were editorials. They convey an artificial jocularity that makes for oppressive reading after a while. This is a pity, since Asimov remains a major force in the genre, and his contribution deserves more than this bland tinkering over familiar ground. Half a dozen pieces stand out in the collection, among them a wonderfully perceptive essay on [George] Orwell's *1984* and an epistemological piece on the myth of the machine, which has the freshness and vigor expected from the author of *I, robot*. (pp. 1538-39)

A review of "Asimov on Science Fiction," in Choice *(copyright © 1981 by American Library Association), Vol. 18, Nos. 11 & 12, July-August, 1981, pp. 1538-39.*

PUBLISHERS WEEKLY

That peerless science writer Asimov here presents [*Change!*], a collection of short essays (most about three pages), all but one of which first appeared in *American Way* magazine, the inflight publication of American Airlines. The selections offer insights into what the world of tomorrow may be like, based on the knowledge and trends of today, all presented with that remarkable lucidity which is the author's trademark. And there are many messages about contemporary issues, such as that coal is a dangerous, and solar an impractical, substitute for nuclear energy, and that attempts to inhibit population growth are pernicious in the extreme. There are all manner of glimpses into space exploration and colonization and conjectures about what we may learn from meteorites, quarks and black holes. An exciting and thought-provoking book. (pp. 48, 50)

A review of "Change!: Seventy-one Glimpses of the Future," in Publishers Weekly *(reprinted from the September 4, 1981 issue of* Publishers Weekly, *published by R. R. Bowker Company, a Xerox company; copyright ©1981 by Xerox Corporation), Vol. 220, No. 10, September 4, 1981, pp. 48, 50.*

DAVID E. NEWTON

Asimov's new book on Venus [*Venus, Near Neighbor of the Sun*] is in much the same vein as his earlier works on Mars, Jupiter, and Saturn. They are all compendia of the latest information on the planets. Unannounced in the title is the fact that almost 40% of this book deals with topics other than Venus, namely Mercury, asteroids and comets. It would have been more honest to have included this information in the title or on the cover. If nothing else, Asimov is thorough, providing us with just about every conceivable bit of information on our planetary neighbors. In fact, one wonders if children are really curious about the apparent diameter of the sun as viewed from Venus . . . , the oblateness of the planets . . . , and the separation of the planet's orbital foci. . . . These are probably of more interest to older students and those with strong interest in planetary astronomy.

But Asimov does write beautifully. Even when he is discussing the most esoteric aspects of his subject, the reader is carried along by his prose. The book is of doubtful interest to the great majority of elementary children, but probably useful at the junior high and older levels.

David E. Newton, in his review of "Venus, Near Neighbor of the Sun," in Appraisal: Science Books for Young People *(copyright © 1982 by the Chil-*

dren's Science Book Review Committee), Vol. 15, No. 1, Winter, 1982, p. 17.

JOHN CLUTE

[*The Complete Robot*] collects everything from **"Robbie"** (1940), which was the first robot story of this the most famous series of robot stories in the world, down to **"The Bicentennial Man"** (1976), which is the last of any significance, and just about the best story Asimov has ever written. (This may not be saying a great deal. It has become clearer and clearer over the years that Asimov is a much better novelist than storyteller, and that his best treatments of the robot theme are in two novels, *The Caves of Steel* and *The Naked Sun,* which are not included here.)

The trouble with most of the short stories lies in Asimov's fidgety preoccupation with the famous three laws of robotics, which he concocted round about 1940, which have been an imaginative inspiration to roboticists over the years. (p. 6)

As take-off points for speculations about how to construct an artificial intelligence with feet, the laws are fine stuff; but as any close analysis of the wording would show (and has often shown), they are full of some very deep semantic pitfalls indeed. Unfortunately, Asimov has been unable to leave these pitfalls alone, and most of his robot stories are dramatized seminars about one loophole or another. So many are the loopholes, and so devastating the consequences of any robot taking advantage of them, that many readers (myself included) would do almost anything to avoid living next door to one, three laws or no three laws. (p. 8)

John Clute, in his review of "The Complete Robot," in Book World—The Washington Post *(© 1982, The Washington Post), April 25, 1982, pp. 6, 8.*

DAVID W. MOORE

Isaac Asimov displays a portion of his impressive store of science information in *Venus, Near Neighbor of the Sun*. . . . Five of the nine chapters are devoted to Venus, two to the planet Mercury, one is on asteroids, and another on comets. The information is solid on physical attributes such as circumference, surface temperature, density, axial inclination, and orbital eccentricity of the various bodies. Fifty-four tables of facts and 39 figures help organize and clarify the information, including historical accounts of how the facts were obtained. Compressing all this into 210 pages and presenting it as clearly as Asimov does is a remarkable feat.

David W. Moore, in his review of "Venus: Near Neighbor of the Sun" (copyright 1982 by the International Reading Association, Inc.; reprinted with permission of the International Reading Association and David W. Moore), in Journal of Reading, *Vol. 25, No. 8, May, 1982, p. 812.*

KIRKUS REVIEWS

The title [of *Exploring the Earth and the Cosmos*], though accurate, does not catch the flavor of this latest Asimov—which reveals his fascination with limits and man's "restless desire" to push beyond. As preamble, Asimov reviews human physical limitations: horizons defined by human eyes, legs, and so on. Then, in true Baconian scientific spirit, he celebrates the experiments, methods, and measurements that have ex-

tended human horizons in space, time, matter, and energy. The result is a bird's-eye view of history and invention, science and industry. . . . He's said many of these things before, of course; but they are condensed and tied together here in highly satisfactory fashion, with the earthy wit (black holes as "cosmic subways") and the usual scattering of Guinness record-type tidbits. Vintage Asimov that will please fans—and also a lively introduction to science for teens or pre-teens. (pp. 563-64)

A review of "Exploring the Earth and the Cosmos," in Kirkus Reviews *(copyright © 1982 The Kirkus Service, Inc.), Vol. L, No. 9, May 1, 1982, pp. 563-64.*

EUGENE LA FAILLE

[*The Complete Robot*] brings together 31 of Asimov's robotics stories from **"Robbie"** of 1940 to several which were published in 1977, including some which have never been collected. Susan Calvin, Powell and Donovan, the Three Laws of Robotics—all of these and more old friends appear in this book.

As Asimov's theories of robotics have had a profound influence upon recent industrial development, this volume can be read as more than a mere work of fiction; however, the work is flawed in terms of its arrangement. Instead of arranging the stories chronologically, so that Asimov's development of robotics could be more easily perceived, they are ordered by arbitrary and conflicting classifications: non-human robots, immobile robots, metallic robots, humanoid robots, etc. Many of the stories reveal a lesser importance upon style, especially characterization, than social commentary.

Eugene La Faille, in his review of "Complete Robot," in Voice of Youth Advocates *(copyrighted 1982 by Voice of Youth Advocates), Vol. 5, No. 3, August, 1982, p. 39.*

ROLAND GREEN

[*Foundation's Edge*] takes place several hundred years after the close of *Second Foundation*. . . . The First Foundation on Terminus and the Second Foundation on Trantor suspect each other of manipulating the Seldon Plan for the restoration of Galactic to its own advantage. Each sends out agents, and the adventures of these agents (including their search for Earth) make up the bulk of the novel. This is Asimov's longest novel and is distinctly uneven; the opening is positively sluggish and many settings and characters fail to come to life. On the other hand, a large part of the book is essentially a cross between sf and the detective story, where Asimov's skill is as great as ever. Asimov also appears to be planning future Foundation novels as part of a grand scheme to tie together into one future history his robot novels, the Foundation saga, and the Galactic Empire novels. A book in which the author's reach appears to have exceeded his grasp, but certainly destined for extreme popularity.

Roland Green, in his review of "Foundation's Edge," in Booklist *(reprinted by permission of the American Library Association; copyright © 1982 by the American Library Association), Vol. 79, No. 2, September 15, 1982, p. 73.*

E. F. BLEILER

In some respects *Foundation's Edge* is not simply a continuation of the earlier stories, but is a redirection. A certain amount of past history has had to be rewritten, notably the career of Asimov's famous Napoleonic character, the Mule. But more important is the shift of Asimov's own position toward the ideas in the stories. The previous stories, it is now clear in retrospect, emerged from the milieu of Hitler's Germany and World War II. The Foundations were a parable on Judaism: the sacred text and its rabbinical exegetes; xenophobia; persecution; existence under cover; chiliasm and the double ghetto of the Foundations. These elements have now been minimized. The Seldon Plan is now revealed to be a fraud. The Second Foundationers, despite their paranormal abilities, are no longer pious saints but humans weighted somewhat on the down side. And the female Mayor of Terminus (chief magistrate of the Foundation Federation) is an arrogant horror. The walls, it is clear, are coming down. . . .

Foundation's Edge reveals many improvements over the earlier work. The ideas are better worked out; the plotting is better; the writing is superior; and Asimov has outgrown his tendency to trick endings that didn't always work. Instead of good guys and bad guys, we now find credible motivations like arrogance, ambition, suspicion, and feelings of insecurity—all of which take form in manipulation. I could register a minor complaint, though, about some repetitiveness, and a stronger complaint about characterizations that sometimes do not gel. But suspense is high, and there is the usual Asimov clarity of expression. It will be an unusual reader who will put the book down unfinished.

> E. F. Bleiler, in a review of "Foundation's Edge,"
> in Book World—The Washington Post (© 1982, The
> Washington Post), September 26, 1982, p. 10.

JANICE TOOMAJIAN

An overview of man's search for knowledge of his world, the prolific Asimov's new book [*Exploring the Earth and the Cosmos*] deals with exploration of space (e.g. continents, oceans, atmosphere, solar system), time (e.g. calendars, life spans, time travel), matter (e.g. electrons, vacuums, size of the earth), and energy (e.g. high temperatures, absolute zero). This is a book which sparks the imagination and gives the reader a sense of the human need to discover. It is NOT an in-depth study but rather a reprise of explorers' journeys and scientific investigation throughout history. It's loaded with bits of information (e.g. a "lustrum" is a period of five years) that will delight trivia buffs.

High school students will find this useful in many ways. Its chapters are brief and well-organized, offering concise information about subjects frequently studied in secondary school. Its detailed index includes such varied topics as grandfather clock, lunar probes and bathysphere, making it a useful ready reference source. Most important, Asimov has assembled a history of ideas and exploration which will give YAs ideas for term papers and science projects.

> Janice Toomajian, in her review of "Exploring the
> Earth and the Cosmos," in Voice of Youth Advo-
> cates (copyrighted 1982 by Voice of Youth Advo-
> cates), Vol. 5, No. 4, October, 1982, p. 52.

L. J. MURPHY

Asimov's most recent book, **"Exploring the Earth and the Cosmos,"** might well have been titled, "Everyman's Condensed Encyclopedia of Scientific Knowledge." It is the es-

sence of science technica in novel-like form. It reads like the script of a feature-length NOVA.

Although Asimov lacks Carl Sagan's eloquent gift for appealing to our imaginations and for inviting personal speculation about time and space, he has compiled an awesome collection of science facts woven together with the thread of understanding the human animal, his origins and his destiny. This book will not make one dream, but it may change one's perspective, and will certainly give one more than enough ammo for the next cocktail party. This is essentially a book geared to adults, but the inquisitive, top-level high school science student may have the tenacity to stick with it in order to perceive the larger meaning.

> L. J. Murphy, in his review of "Exploring the Earth
> and the Cosmos," in Young Adult Cooperative Book
> Review Group of Massachusetts, Vol. 19, No. 1,
> October, 1982, p. 1.

GERALD JONAS

I am relieved to report that ["**Foundation's Edge**"] is a worthy sequel in every way. As before, the First Foundation wields the power of the physical sciences and technology, and the Second Foundation has the power to cloud men's minds and predict mass behavior through the statistical insights of psychohistory. Also as before, the fate of all humanity is at stake as these mighty adversaries clash—and the focus is on the actions of a handful of people who are earnest and articulate and likable even when they do bad things (for what seem to them good reasons). Mr. Asimov gives us adversaries but no villains; this is future history portrayed as a great game. The danger of such a concept is that the reader will cease to care who wins or loses. Mr. Asimov sustains interest by keeping us guessing just which side each player represents. He writes much better than he did 33 years ago [when the first novel in the series was published]—yet he has lost none of the verve that he brought to this series when he and the galaxy were much younger. What more could one ask?

> Gerald Jonas, "Other Worlds than Earth," in The
> New York Times Book Review (© 1982 by The New
> York Times Company; reprinted by permission), De-
> cember 19, 1982, pp. 13, 18.*

JAMES GUNN

The Foundation Trilogy is a basic work upon which a vast structure of stories has been built. Its assumptions provided a solid footing for a whole city of fictional constructions. The way in which it was created, then, and the way in which it came to prominence may be useful examples of the process by which science fiction was shaped in the magazines. (pp. 27-8)

How to explain the continuing popularity of the *Trilogy*? Why has the *Foundation* become a foundation? The student of science fiction who can understand the appeal and influence of the series may understand much that differentiates science fiction from other kinds of literature, and something about the basic appeal of Campbellian science fiction. The failure to provide adequate answers to these questions is the central problem of scholarship about science fiction. The circumstances of creation, for instance, may provide some measure of understanding, but much contemporary scholarship chooses to ignore such ephemera, preferring to apply to science fiction the same criteria applied to Henry James or William Faulkner or John Updike.

Another view might argue not for lesser standards but for different standards, for more useful standards. How can traditional criticism understand the *Trilogy,* for instance, if it does not take into consideration that it was a series written for one to two cents a word by a part-time writer for the readers of a single science-fiction magazine with a strong-willed editor over a period of years in which the author aged from twenty-one to twenty-eight?

Most traditional criticism consists of textual analysis. In magazine science fiction, textual analysis finds little to work with. The important aspects of science fiction are the characteristics that transcend the text. The first of these is narrative. When the *Trilogy* was being published in *Astounding Science Fiction,* piece by piece, the story was the thing, if not the whole thing, at least the main thing. An entertaining style, a bit of wit, characters who had some resemblance to real people could be added, but those elements were not essential. (p. 29)

Story in *The Foundation Trilogy* is plentiful. Events move on a grand scale, beginning with the approaching dissolution of a galactic empire that has ruled 25 million planets inhabited by humans who spread out from Earth, although they have long forgotten their origin. The Empire has brought 12,000 years of peace, but now, according to the calculations of a psychologist named Hari Seldon, who has used a new science for predicting mass behavior called "psychohistory," the Empire will fall and be followed by 30,000 years of misery and barbarity. Seldon sets up two Foundations, one of physical scientists and a Second Foundation of psychologists (about which nothing more is heard until the last book of the *Trilogy*), at "opposite ends of the Galaxy" to shorten the oncoming dark ages to only a thousand years. *The Foundation Trilogy* covers the first four hundred years of that interregnum and tells how the Foundation meets one threat to its existence after another and alone, or with the help of the Second Foundation, preserves Seldon's Plan. (pp. 29-30)

Asimov abandoned *The Foundation Trilogy* with **"Search by the Foundation"** because it had grown too difficult to bring the reader up to date on everything and because he was tired of it. In his autobiography he reveals that while he was writing **"Search by the Foundation" (". . . And Now You Don't")** he "disliked it intensely and found working on it very difficult." Even [John W.] Campbell's persistent demand for open endings that would allow sequels could not persuade Asimov. The future history that had envisioned one thousand years of Seldon's Plan ended after less than four hundred (more than thirty years later Asimov agreed to write a fourth volume). Nevertheless, Asimov used his concept of a humanly inhabited Galaxy, of an outward movement of humanity from Earth until Earth itself was forgotten, and of the rise of an Empire and its eventual fall as the background for half a dozen later novels and several dozen shorter stories.

Other authors have used the background as well, taking it not so much directly from the *Trilogy* as from the assumptions about the future (to which the *Trilogy* contributed) that became the shared property of a generation of science-fiction writers. . . . But Asimov said it best and most completely in his series of stories published in *Astounding* between 1942 and 1949. . . . Moreover, Asimov described a totally human galaxy, partly to avoid Campbell's prejudice against relationships between humans and aliens in which the humans were inferior. In some ways readers may have preferred an all-human galaxy.

This, however, does not completely explain the *Trilogy*'s popularity. The reader must delve into what the series is about and how its narrative is handled.

One significant aspect of the series is Asimov's invention of psychohistory, with its implications for determinism and free will. Psychohistory was put together out of psychology, sociology, and history—not hard sciences, which Campbell had a reputation for preferring, but at best soft sciences: a behavioral science, a social science, and a discipline that has difficulty deciding whether to define itself as a social science or a humanity. . . . Psychohistory is the art of prediction projected as a science; later it might have been called "futurology" or "futuristics."

The ability to predict or foresee the future has been a persistent notion in science fiction almost from the genre's beginnings. Hundreds of stories have been based on various mechanisms for doing it and the various outcomes of attempts. One might cite as examples Robert Heinlein's first story, "Life-Line," Lewis Padgett's "What You Need," and James Blish's "Beep." What Asimov brought to the concept was the science of probabilities as a mechanism, the element of uncertainty for suspense, and the philosophical question "what is worth predicting?" for depth. His method—statistical probability—prohibited the prediction of any actions smaller than those of large aggregates of population. . . . [Asimov] defines psychohistory, in the epigraph quoted from the *Encyclopedia Galactica,* for Section 4 of **"The Psychohistorians,"** as "that branch of mathematics which deals with the reactions of human conglomerates to fixed social and economic stimuli. . . . Implicit in all these definitions is the assumption that the human conglomerate being dealt with is sufficiently large for valid statistical treatment. . . . A further necessary assumption is that the human conglomerate be itself unaware of psychohistoric analysis in order that its reactions be truly random." Finally, Asimov answers the question "what is worth predicting?" Not individual human lives but a great event whose consequences might be avoided, such as the fall of an empire and the dark ages of barbarism, war, hunger, despair, and death that would follow. (pp. 37-40)

Exactly what Asimov had in mind may affect the critic's judgment of the work. He had not, for instance, thought out all the different permutations in idea and story; they were built, one on another, as the years passed and the *Trilogy* developed. But he must have discussed with Campbell the implications of prediction. Some critics have tried to explain "psychohistory" on philosophical bases, as "the science that Marxism never became" [Donald Wollheim] or "the vulgar, mechanical, debased version of Marxism promulgated in the Thirties" [Charles Elkins]. (p. 40)

Psychohistory had its origins not in Marxism (Asimov has called Wollheim's speculation "reading his bent into me," for Asimov has "never read anything about it") but in John Campbell's ideas about symbolic logic. Symbolic logic, if further developed, Campbell told the young Asimov . . . , would so clear up the mysteries of the human mind that human actions would be predictable. Campbell more or less forced Asimov to include some references to symbolic logic in the first story, **"Foundation"**—"forced," because Asimov knew nothing about symbolic logic and did not believe, as Campbell insisted, that symbolic logic would "unobscure the language and leave everything clear." Asimov made a comparison to the kinetic theory of gases, "where the individual molecules in the gas remain as unpredictable as ever, but the average action is completely predictable."

The spirit of the early stories, however, is determinedly anti-deterministic. If intelligent, courageous, and forceful individuals do not attempt to retrieve the situation, most crises—all but one, perhaps—will not be resolved satisfactorily. Seldon's predictions, like God's will, are hidden from all the characters except the psychologists of the Second Foundation, as they are from the reader. Seldon's prophecies are revealed only after the fact, and even the solutions that he or others say are obvious are obvious only in retrospect, as in all good histories. At the time, they are not obvious to anyone but Salvor Hardin or Hober Mallow; the reader has no feeling that the crises would have been resolved if persons such as Hardin and Mallow had not been there. Moreover, the predictions of psychohistory are expressed as probabilities, and one of the necessary ingredients of Seldon's Plan, discussed in detail in "Search by the Foundation," is the exercise of normal initiative.

As a matter of fact, Asimov has the best of both determinism and free will. Psychohistory and Seldon's Plan provide the framework for diverse episodes about a variety of characters over a period of four hundred years, and those episodes feature a number of strong-minded individuals seeking solutions to a series of problems as they arise. If determinism alone were Asimov's subject, the *Trilogy* would reveal characters continually defeated in their attempts to change events, or manipulated like puppets by godlike prophets, or unable to fight the onrushing current of necessity.

A work in which characters were inexorably defeated by psychohistorical necessity would be so depressing that it would not have remained popular for more than a quarter of a century. Bel Riose is the only character who stares into the face of determinism; only he is frustrated by psychohistorical necessity rather than by the actions of an individual. But in "The General," Bel Riose is not the viewpoint character. The basis of the story is not Riose's predicament but how he is to be stopped, and the resolution does not celebrate the victory of determinism but the survival of the Foundation, even though the efforts of the Foundation are not involved. The reader, whose sympathies are with the Foundation, sees the events as an ally of the Foundation, not as an opponent. The Foundation's unusual power of survival, however, influences both itself and its enemies; it supplies to the Foundation confidence in ultimate victory (which can become overconfidence, and thus a problem), and it discourages the Foundation's attackers (but never enough to eliminate challenges entirely). Asimov seems to be more interested in the psychological impact of Seldon's Plan than in its philosophical implications. Indeed, it is only to those looking from the outside that Seldon's Plan seems like determinism; from within, the Foundation leaders still must find solutions without Seldon's help.

Even in the second half of the *Trilogy*, questions of free will raised by the events of the story relate not to Seldon's Plan but to the psychological manipulation of minds such as that effected by the Mule and the Second Foundation psychologists. Nothing in the story happens unless someone makes it happen; the reader is told on several occasions that "Seldon's laws help those who help themselves."

The Biblical parallel is significant. Psychohistory is no more restrictive of free will than the Judeo-Christian deity. Christians are given free will by an omniscient God; characters in the *Trilogy* receive free will from an omniscient author, as an act of authorial necessity. At the end of *Second Foundation*, Seldon's Plan has been restored, events are back on their ordered course, the rise of a new and better Empire to reunite the Galaxy and the creation of a new civilization based on mental science seem assured. The Second Foundation psychologists have won; that victory, benevolent as it seems, may have ominous undertones, but if we are to accept Asimov as being as benevolent as he is omniscient, the reader can assume that the benefits of mental science will be available to everyone.

Determinism, then, is not what the *Trilogy* is about. The structure of the episodes is anti-deterministic, for the outcome of each critical event is not inevitable. The basic appeal of the stories is problem-solving, an essential replacement for the more customary narrative drives of action and romance. Each episode presents a problem, in a way much like the formal detective story, and challenges the reader to find a solution. In the first published story, "Foundation," the solution is withheld until the next episode, a strategy of Asimov's to ensure a sequel (published in the very next issue) that almost accidentally reinforced the problem-solving quality of the stories. For the reader, the fascination lies in the presentation of clues, the twists of plot, and the final solution that makes sense of it all. In the final episode of *Foundation*, Jorane Sutt says to Hober Mallow, "There is nothing straight about you; no motive that hasn't another behind it; no statement that hasn't three meanings." He might have been speaking of Asimov.

The series of searches for the Second Foundation, the various clues pursued to inconclusive ends, the near revelation by Ebling Mis of its location (though he may have been wrong), and the succession of incorrect solutions shows Asimov imitating methods of the detective novel. (pp. 41-4)

But even the problem-solving aspect of the *Trilogy* does not account completely for the success of the series. Other aspects, more peripheral to the central structure, might be cited: the characters, for instance, though scorned by some critics, engage the reader's sympathies. They are similar to each other, it is true, mostly by being men and women of action. They do not let events happen to them (as might seem more appropriate if the theme of the *Trilogy* actually was determinism); they make things happen. The *Trilogy*, after all, is a history, and history is about people who have made things happen. The characters may not be strongly differentiated—Salvor Hardin, Limmar Ponyets, Hober Mallow, and Lathan Devers may seem interchangeable—but they may be as differentiated as the personages in most histories. They got into histories by being men and women of action. Clearly Asimov's characters are adequate for the purposes they serve in the *Trilogy*.

Asimov also provides some of his philosophy of history in his storytelling. . . . Some of what Asimov says about history comes from his model, [Edward] Gibbon's *Decline and Fall of the Roman Empire*, little seems to derive from Marxism or whatever impressions of it were in the air when the *Trilogy* was being conceived and created, and a good deal seems to be Asimov's own observations. Government, for instance, never is what it appears to be: in the *Trilogy* figureheads and powers behind the throne proliferate. Every innovation rigidifies into sterile tradition, which must, in turn, be overturned: the grip of the Encyclopedists, for instance, must be broken by Salvor Hardin, and the political power of the Mayor must be broken, in its turn, by Hober Mallow, and the economic power of the Traders must then be modified by the incorporation of the independent traders, and so on. There is, to be sure, a narrative necessity to keep the series going, but the reader cannot ignore the inevitable feeling of continual change, which seems a philosophy: one generation's solution is the next generation's problem. Asimov probably would agree that this is the case in real life.

On top of this, and perhaps the most important aspect of Asimov's writing, is his rationalism. More than any other writer of his time (the Campbell era, as Asimov calls it) or even later, Asimov speaks with the voice of reason. Avoid the emotional, the irrational, the *Trilogy* says. Avoid the obvious military reaction to threats of military attack, says Salvor Hardin. Do not throw the slender military might of the Foundation against the great battleships of the Empire, says Hober Mallow, whose continual retreat before the attacking Korellian forces is considered treason.

Rationality is the one human trait that can always be trusted, the *Trilogy* says, and the reader comes to believe that that is Asimov's conviction as well. Sometimes rational decisions are based on insufficient information and turn out to be wrong, or the person making the decision is not intelligent enough to see the ultimate solution rather than the partial one, but nothing other than reason works at all. Even the antagonists are as rational as the protagonists and therefore cannot legitimately be called villains. In the stories that Asimov likes best, rationality does not triumph over irrationality or emotion but over other rationality, as in the conflict between the Mule and Bayta (though the Mule is betrayed as well by an element of emotion unnatural to him), between the Mule and the First Speaker, and between the Second Foundation and the First Foundation.

Asimov's confidence in rationality must have been comforting to him not only in personal terms but in terms of the times when the stories were written and published. He was only twenty-one when he started writing **"Foundation"** and had passed through a difficult adolescence. He was still ill at ease with women and society in general, and he was writing largely for maladjusted teenagers who had sublimated their sexual and social frustrations into various kinds of intellectual activity, including the reading of science fiction. The belief that reason could solve problems not only was desirable, it may have been necessary. Moreover, events in the larger world, though they did not encourage a belief in the rationality of human behavior, nourished the hope that rationality would prevail. The United States had just pulled itself out of the incomprehensibility of the Depression to plunge itself into the insanity of war. Just as the theory of psychohistory was for Asimov a way to make Hitler's persistent victories bearable—no matter what initial successes the Nazis managed, the logic of history (psychohistory) would eventually bring about their defeat—so reason had to eventually prove its supremacy. Later, as the Foundation stories began to appear, the success of the Allies, aided by products of scientific laboratories, confirmed that earlier faith.

The *Trilogy* also offers more isolated insights into history, politics, and human behavior. Often these surface in the epigraphs that precede most of the chapters in the form of excerpts from the 116th edition of the *Encyclopedia Galactica* published in 1020 F.E. (Foundational Era) by the Encyclopedia Galactica Publishing Co., Terminus. But Asimov also includes some illuminating concepts within the text of the stories. . . . "Seldon assumed that human reaction to stimuli would remain constant," Mis comments in **"The Mule."**

The statement by Mis sums up Asimov's own attitude toward character. His characters have been criticized for being "one-

dimensional," and unchanged from contemporary people by the passage of time and the altered conditions in which they live. But this occurs by choice rather than from lack of skill or failure of observation. Asimov divided "social science fiction" into two widely different types of stories: "chess game" and "chess puzzle." The chess game begins with "a fixed number of pieces in a fixed position" and "the pieces change their positions according to a fixed set of rules." In a chess-puzzle story, the fixed set of rules apply but the position varies. The rules by which the pieces move (common to both types) may be equated, Asimov says, "with the motions (emotions?) and impulses of humanity: hate, love, fear, suspicion, passion, hunger, lust and so on. Presumably these will not change while mankind remains Homo sapiens." Basic human characteristics remain the same.

Asimov may not be right, but his choice is defensible against the opposing Marxist view that character will change when society becomes more rational. In addition, the *Trilogy* is concerned not with the revolution, or even the evolution, of character but with the evolution of an idea. There is also a strategic narrative value in the maintenance of contemporary characteristics. The recognizability of characters reflects that the characters accept their world as commonplace. This is the technique that Heinlein perfected as an alternative to the "gee whiz!" school of writing about the future, which introduced a character from the past in order to elicit his wonder at each new future marvel.

A story of the future is not much different than a historical novel, and its problems are similar to those of a translation from a foreign language. The decision a writer must make is not of verisimilitude alone but how much and what kind. Asimov chooses what might be called the verisimilitude of feeling over the verisimilitude of language or of character, just as a historical novelist or a translator might choose the flavor of the original over a literal representation. Science-fiction stories about changes in humanity or its language have been written, but the *Trilogy* is not one of them and does not pretend to be.

Asimov creates a sense of reality in another way: by choosing appropriate but unfamiliar names for characters, objects, and processes. Every name seems foreign yet credible. The science-fiction reader values this above subtle differentiations in character. The non-science-fiction reader often finds it puzzling at best, repulsive at worst. "Psychohistory" has proved so apt a name that it has been picked up as terminology for an academic discipline, though not, to be sure, the discipline Asimov had in mind. The names of characters are subtly altered, by changing the spelling, or dropping or rearranging letters, to suggest evolution within continuity, and the subtlety increases as the series progresses: Hari Seldon leads to Hober Mallow leads to Han Pritcher leads to Bail Channis and eventually to Arkady Darell. (pp. 44-8)

[Asimov] was the master of the epigraph. Models of imitation, clarity, and dramatization, they offer some preview of his later skill at science popularization. The epigraphs serve as a medium for exposition, which became increasingly burdensome as the series continued—a long essay Arkady writes for school in **"Search by the Foundation"** serves this function (but also convinced Asimov that the series had to end there)—but which helped Asimov provide essential background information. They also provide a framework that puts events into context and lends to the structure the verisimilitude of a future perspective.

The final virtue of the *Trilogy,* and perhaps the most important to its extended popularity, is its exhaustive treatment of an idea. That idea was not psychohistory or even determinism: it was the Foundations. Each story examined one aspect of the Foundations and their relative positions in the Galaxy and in the events happening around them. In **"The Psychohistorians,"** for instance, the problem for the Foundation is how to persuade the Empire to let the Foundation be set up on Terminus and how to persuade 100,000 Encyclopedists and their families to leave the comfort and security of Trantor for the rigors and uncertainties of the frontier. This problem, of course, is concealed until the conclusion, even until after the resolution. **"The Encyclopedists"** presents the next problem: how is the Foundation to survive the power of the barbarians that surround Terminus as the Empire slowly begins to lose its control of the periphery? The first solution is to play each group of barbarians against the others; the second, to supply the barbarians with atomic energy within a religious framework centered around Terminus.

In **"The Mayors"** the problem has become: what will happen to the Foundation when the barbarians are completely equipped with atomic weapons and are restless to use them? The answer: the priests of the scientific religion will not permit an attack on Terminus. In **"The Traders"** the question has changed to how Foundation hegemony will spread once the religious framework is recognized as a political tool of the Foundation. The answer is: by trade. Economic motivations can succeed where religion fails. Sometimes two problems converge in one story, as in **"The Merchant Princes."** The political and religious structures have rigidified into useless tradition, and the location of the Foundation has been discovered by the Empire. The solutions to those problems are that the Traders seize political power and that war against the Foundation is clearly linked with economic deprivation.

Each problem solved strengthens the Foundation and its progress toward ultimate reunification of the Galaxy, but each solution contains the seed of a new problem. In **"The General,"** the Foundation faces the problem of its own success, which has made it an attractive prize for the Empire. But it is protected by the essential nature of a decaying Empire—a weak Emperor cannot permit strong generals. In **"The Mule"** and its sequel, **"Search by the Mule,"** Asimov strikes out in a new direction. With its victory by default over the Empire, the Foundation has no clear challenges to the eventual extension of its power throughout the Galaxy and the final realization of Seldon's Plan. But what about the unexpected, developments that Seldon's psychohistorical equations could not predict because they involve elements of the unique, like the genetic accident that creates the Mule and his unpredictable and Plan-destroying power? The answer: the Second Foundation. Asimov planted mention of the Second Foundation in the first Foundation story, not because he had anticipated the function of the Second Foundation but as a safety measure, a strategic reserve in case something developed in the plot and he needed a way out. In **"The Mule,"** the Second Foundation emerges as a group of psychologists to whom Seldon's Plan was entrusted and who were charged with responsibility for protecting it. Finally, in **"Search by the Foundation,"** two new questions are raised by the revelation of the Second Foundation: what will happen to the Foundation now that it knows of the existence of the Second Foundation and suspects its custody of Seldon's Plan (which destroys one of the basic requirements for the effectiveness of psychohistorical predictions), and what can the Second Foundation do to restore the previous condition and rescue Seldon's Plan? The answer is dual-purpose: the Second Foundation de-

ceives the Foundation into believing that it has located and destroyed the Second Foundation.

In **"There's Nothing Like a Good Foundation,"** Asimov wrote that "in designing each new Foundation story, I found I had to work within an increasingly constricted area, with progressively fewer and fewer degrees of freedom. I was forced to seize whatever way out I could find without worrying about how difficult I might make the next story. Then when I came to the next story, those difficulties arose and beat me over the head." The difficulties are not apparent: each story seems designed to arise out of the earlier ones, and each develops with an air of inevitability appropriate to psychohistory itself. But it is critical folly to assume that the *Trilogy* is an organic whole, conceived before it was begun, crafted in accordance with some master plan, and produced in full consideration of the contribution of each part to the whole. External and internal evidence demonstrate that Asimov moved from story to story, solving the problems of each as they arose and discovering, on his own or with the help of Campbell, new problems on which to base the next stories. The *Trilogy* succeeds by its ingenuity, and it is a tribute to Asimov's ingenuity and cool rationality that it seems so complete, so well integrated.

Foundations should be solid. They should leave no important areas uncovered. That *The Foundation Trilogy* is so solid may be the major reason it has survived and why so many later science-fiction stories have been built upon the "central myth" that it and earlier works pioneered. (pp. 48-50)

James Gunn, in his Isaac Asimov: The Foundations of Science Fiction *(copyright © 1982 by James Gunn; reprinted by permission of the author and Oxford University Press, Inc.), Oxford University Press, New York, 1982, 236 p.*

JAMES GUNN

In 1982 Isaac Asimov returned to the science-fiction world of the 1940s to produce the long-awaited fourth volume of the Foundation series [*Foundation's Edge*]. Reasons (of many kinds) for a sequel have been clear for many years; most important of them, the Trilogy itself stopped after 400 years of the thousand-year saga envisioned in Hari Seldon's psychohistorical predictions, and concluded with some uncertainty about the situation in which it left the Foundation universe. (p. 15)

[A brief summary of *Foundation's Edge* would give] little suggestion of the flavor of the novel. In style it belongs to the 1940s—not simply to science fiction's 1940s but to Asimov's 1940s. It is no novel of character—not even a *Caves of Steel* or a *Gods Themselves*—but a discursive novel of ideas, much like the rest of the *Foundation* stories. As the first extended treatment . . .—in fact the longest novel Asimov has written— it hangs together well.

Like the stories that make up the *Foundation Trilogy, Foundation's Edge* is largely dialogue, like them it contains little action, and like them it is readable, involving, and intellectually complicated. In **"The Merchant Princes,"** the final story in the first volume of the Trilogy, Jorane Sutt tells Hober Mallow, "There is nothing straight about you; no motive that hasn't another behind it; no statement that hasn't three meanings."

So it is with *Foundation's Edge.* The suspense of the novel is sustained by repeated examples of motivations within motivations, wheels within wheels. (pp. 15-16)

[Deviousness] is common to all the characters. It comes naturally to the Speakers of the Second Foundation, who are revealed in *Foundation's Edge* as intriguing for power as relentlessly as any non-mentalist. Most important, it is characteristic of Trevise, who is the most important person in the novel, if not, indeed, its hero. Trevise is continually re-evaluating the actions of other characters, particularly in his conversations with Pelorat, whose major function in the novel is to act as confidante for Trevise. . . . Pelorat, though he is better characterized and plays a more substantial role, is Trevise's "Bigman" Jones.

The motivation-behind-motivation method is appropriate to the subject of the novel. When psychological control of people's actions and even of people's thought occurs, the hiding—and questioning—of motivation is natural. Moreover, *Foundation's Edge* operates both as a novel of intrigue and as a mystery. The various political intrigues that are at work in the First Foundation's councils on Terminus and that are found on Sayshell and, by implication, on every other planet in the Galaxy thrive on actions taken ostensibly for one reason but actually for another.

More significantly, the novel functions, in characteristic Asimovian fashion, as a mystery that begins with the apparent goal of locating the Second Foundation (the mystery that sustained the last half of the Trilogy) and then is diverted to locating the power that has kept galactic events impossibly close to Seldon's Plan, with subsidiary mysteries along the way, such as why information about Earth has disappeared from the Second Foundation's (computer) library, why Gaia is feared on Sayshell and why it is not recorded in Foundation files, etc. As a mystery the major question of the novel is who (or what) done it? Various characters are presented as suspects. . . . And, indeed, more than one turns out to be something other than what he or she seems.

Some reviews noted the increased role given to women, but the women of *Foundation's Edge* are not significantly female. The leader of the First Foundation, Mayor Harla Branno, is a woman, but she is cast in the same mold as Salvor Hardin and Hober Mallow. Though she makes a critical error in judgment, it would be a mistake to categorize this as a feminine mistake; it is motivated by ambition, and the other characters, mostly male, make similar mistakes. Novi, though more complex than she appears, has a public persona much like that of Valona March of *The Currents of Space*. Bliss, the Gaian young woman with the fast quip and the erotic outlook, is a bit different from most Asimov characters, but she may or may not be a robot. Bayta of "**The Mule**" and Arkady Darell of "**Second Foundation**," though they are not socially or politically liberated, are at least as sympathetically drawn.

In *Foundation's Edge* Asimov had to cope with the same problem he had faced in the later works of the Trilogy: how to bring the reader up to date on preceding events. . . . *Foundation's Edge* handles the situation with a prologue, as he did with "**Search by the Mule**," but he abandoned the quotations from the *Encyclopedia Galactica*. In fact, the prologue is a bit like the synopses that used to precede later episodes of serials in the old *Astounding*. Asimov is good at this; it is a process of abstracting and communicating that he has perfected for his non-fiction. But he also devotes a considerable portion of the early chapters, including a substantial amount of the dialogue, to exposition, and it still seems awkward. At one point Compor

asks Trevise, "Why are you telling me all this, Golan?" And the reader is tempted to ask the author the same question. I suspect that the question no longer bothers Asimov. . . .

Early reviews pointed out that Asimov in the new novel updated his Foundation universe scientifically. This is true. Just as, in later editions of Asimov's "**Lucky Starr**" juveniles . . . , he pointed out the scientific inaccuracies that later discoveries had revealed, so in *Foundation's Edge* he made his Foundation Galaxy more scientifically plausible without going back to revise the earlier stories.

In the world of *Foundation's Edge,* however, Asimov is tidying things up. It is not so much that the Trilogy universe is scientifically inaccurate as that scientific accuracy is not that important; the speculation about future history and the prediction of events through psychohistory is what matters, and the limited use of computers (which Asimov was contemplating in greater detail in his robot stories) seems more irrelevant than a failure of the imagination. But at the age of 62, Asimov is another man with a different sense of values. He turned to the writing of science popularizations after Sputnik with a sense of urgency and dedication to increasing the general store of scientific knowledge. Now he cannot be as casual about separating the fiction writer from the scientist who knows better. In *Foundation's Edge* the computer plays a significant part—and perhaps one, if Asimov continues the series, that will grow even more significant. Asimov also neatens up the Foundation Galaxy with recent knowledge about galactic evolution and black holes, indicating in one place that the center of the galaxy is uninhabitable because of the huge black hole there, and in several other places that most of the planets in the Galaxy are inimical to human life.

Asimov also includes in *Foundation's Edge* references not only to the earlier Foundation stories but to other Asimov works: the robot stories, the Robot Novels with their future history of space colonization and robotic civilization that differs in significant respects from the other novels that fit more neatly into the Foundation future history, *Pebble in the Sky,* and *The End of Eternity.* (p. 16)

Asimov has returned the reader not just to *The Foundation Trilogy* universe of the 1940s but to the Asimov universe of the 1940s and 1950s. Asimov himself has returned, however, with a greater conviction about the importance of accurate science and of public understanding of science, and of the importance of ecology. Gaia, for instance, is ecology carried to the ultimate degree of self-awareness; it is ecology personified.

More important, *Foundation's Edge* alters the message of the Trilogy—the message that rationality is the only human trait that can be trusted and that it will, if permitted to do so, come up with the correct solution. That message is embodied not only in Seldon's psychohistory but in the actions of the men and women who work to preserve the First and Second Foundations and Seldon's Plan, and even those who try to destroy them. In the new novel, however, Asimov has allowed to creep in (or purposefully has included) a significant element of mysticism. Mysticism is present in Gaia, the planet that acts as a gigantic mind made up of variously sentient parts (although an explanation is proposed that the robots—perhaps going back to the unfortunate Herbie of "**Liar!**"—have perfected telepathy and are continuing their guardianship of humanity, as in "**The Evitable Conflict**"), and mysticism is evident in Trevise's grasp on correctness—when he is "sure" he is always right, like Paul in D. H. Lawrence's "The Rocking-Horse Winner."

Hari Seldon and his rational psychohistory are accordingly de-emphasized. Even though Seldon's thousand-year Plan is pre-served as Trevise chooses the status quo and even though Gaia (which is the mysterious force both Trevise and Gendibal have suspected) has acted to restore Seldon's Plan after the distur-bances caused by the Mule (who is revealed as a Gaian ren-egade), the Plan seems a bit inconsequential when compared to the Gaian vision of "Galaxia! . . . A living galaxy and one that can be made favorable for all life in ways that we yet cannot foresee. . . ." It is a concept that rivals that of Olaf Stapledon's *Star Maker,* but it is transcendence reached by faith rather than by reason. (pp. 16-17)

The book has a few minor flaws. On the plot level, for instance, the First Foundation's development of the "mental shield" catches the Second Foundation by surprise. Though it is de-scribed as the most secret of projects, it is the very thing—following Toran Darell's invention of the Mental Static ma-chine in **"Search by the Foundation"**—that the Second Foun-dation psychologists would have kept closest watch on and would have sabotaged.

The Mule's origin on Gaia seems inconsistent both with what we know about the Mule and what we know about Gaia. His sterility, for instance, which was revealed so dramatically at the conclusion of **"The Mule,"** is a logical outgrowth of his origin as a natural mutation. But there is nothing about origin on Gaia that would make sterility anything more than acci-dental, unless it was the reason for his becoming a renegade. But surely in a planetary gestalt dissident feelings and thought are impossible to conceal, and why would sterility disturb a member of the gestalt, who is survived by the entire planet.

An elderly Gaian points out that "there is no more desire to live past one's time than to die before it."

Finally, on the level of ideas, *Foundation's Edge* features a significant and unhealthy emphasis on the control of others. Perhaps this was an inevitable outgrowth of the abilities of Second Foundation psychologists. Perhaps it is implicit in Hari Seldon's manipulations and even in his psychohistorical pre-dictions. But . . . Seldon's manipulations are resistable and . . . it takes rational and determined people to make Seldon's Plan work. The logical persuasion practiced by Salvor Hardin and Hober Mallow, and even the subterfuges resorted to by Harla Branno, are not fearsome and repellant in the way the reader (and Asimov) views the Mule's powers, and the similar powers exercised by Second Foundation psychologists seem little more benign. That is why I expected the First Foundation to restore the balance overthrown by the success of the Second Foundation plot in **"Search by the Foundation."** I thought Asimov dreaded the Second Foundation's "benevolent dicta-torship of the mentally best" as much as I did.

In a way he did. The analysis performed near Gaia points out that the Second Foundation, if successful, would create "a paternalistic Empire, established by calculation, maintained by calculation, and in perpetual living death by calculation." On the other hand, Asimov seems to have lost his confidence in the First Foundation's rational men and women: the First Foun-dation would create "a military Empire, established by strife, maintained by strife, and eventually destroyed by strife." So we are left with Gaia's solution of "Galaxia."

Or perhaps not. Asimov promises a sequel, and perhaps it will resolve these quibbles. (p. 17)

James Gunn, "Son of Foundation," in Fantasy Newsletter *(copyright © 1983 by Florida Atlantic University), Vol. 6, No. 4, April, 1983, pp. 15-17.*

Ralph Bakshi
1938-

Palestinian-born American film director, animator, and screenwriter.

Bakshi is said to have revolutionized the concept of the animated film with features specifically designed for adult audiences. Most of his works are graphically bold, sometimes violent and obscene, commentaries on contemporary society.

Bakshi's first, perhaps most notable, film was *Fritz the Cat* (1972). Based on an underground comic strip by Robert Crumb, *Fritz the Cat* either shocked, delighted, or bored its viewers and stirred controversy because of its strong sexual content. Bakshi combined live action and animation in his second film, *Heavy Traffic*. The film is a semiautobiographical account of a young Brooklyn cartoonist and his struggle to maintain his sense of morality amid the violence that surrounds him. Bakshi utilized basic *film noir* techniques of shadowing and coarse graphics in *Heavy Traffic* to depict the unsavory side of New York City.

Turning away from urban America, Bakshi switched to fantasy in *Wizards* and *The Lord of the Rings*. In both films, he achieved a sense of realism by first filming real actors and later sketching over the film. *American Pop*, in Bakshi's words, "is about trying to make it in America." In this film, documenting an immigrant family's pursuit of the American dream, Bakshi successfully integrated popular music into his development of plot and theme. For some critics, Bakshi came of age as a filmmaker with *American Pop*.

Although his work has often been called stereotypically offensive and violent, even racist, Bakshi is recognized by many critics as an important innovator. He is, as Andrew Sarris wrote, "a conscious antithesis to Walt Disney."

Self-portrait by Ralph Bakshi; reproduced by permission of Ralph Bakshi

VINCENT CANBY

Understatement is not the method of "Fritz The Cat," which utilizes just about every four-letter word you've ever heard in any playground, and depicts Fritz's various sexual triumphs with what might be described as indelicate frenzy. However, the film is not to be confused with those soberly obscene comic books that used to feature Toots and Casper, Dick Tracy and Tillie The Toiler. It is often exuberantly vulgar, but rather less obscene than your ordinary, run-of-the-mill, R-rated Hollywood melodrama, probably because Fritz himself is essentially an innocent of the early Jack Lemmon mold. He's the kind of cat who can be rendered instantaneously impotent with guilt when a Harlem madam laughs at him and says something like: "Honey, you ain't black enough!" (pp. 1, 3)

I suspect there is something in "Fritz The Cat" to offend just about everyone over the age of 17—blacks, whites, Jews, gentiles, Catholics, radicals, conservatives. Ironically, people under 17, who won't be allowed to see the X-rated film, are probably most familiar with cartoonist [Robert] Crumb, whose work I've somehow missed. Thus I've no idea how faithful Mr. Bakshi, who wrote and directed the film . . . , [has] been to Mr. Crumb's original creations. Compared to something

like "The Yellow Submarine," the visual style of "Fritz The Cat" is almost drab, or, to put it another way, it's spectacular Terrytoon. It doesn't exactly advance the fine art of animation, which is all to the good, and it is absolutely right for Fritz's adventures, which reflect the world as a low-life cartoon and not as a psychedelic experience. There are, however, some lovely set pieces—line drawings and washes of cityscapes, highly stylized transitions between sequences (including one featuring Billie Holiday's voice singing "Yesterdays"), and an oddly moving ending in which the drawings slowly give way to sepia still photographs of ordinary streets and sidewalks, and of the real Times Square where there is not, as there is in Fritz's world, a sign proclaiming "Natural Gas Is Best." . . .

"Fritz The Cat" has its ups and downs. But its ups are of surprisingly high and witty order, and make use not only of conventional visual devices but also of a quite unconventional soundtrack that throws away more bits of sincerely lunatic dialogue than you're likely to overhear in several years of pub-crawling through Greenwich Village, Harlem and dissident points west.

At this point I suppose I should point out that "Fritz The Cat" isn't the completely dirty movie it pretends to be (POW!ZAP!), but an intelligent social satire (GULP! WEEP!). Unlike Wyatt and Billy of "Easy Rider," who went out to look for America and found it wasn't there, Fritz finds America all right, and he survives it by exercising his Priapian talents with the kind of enthusiasm that is, unfortunately, possible only to cartoon creatures. (p. 3)

*Vincent Canby, " 'Fritz' Is a Far Cry from Disney,"
in* The New York Times, *Section 2 (© 1972 by The
New York Times Company; reprinted by permission),
April 30, 1972, pp. 1, 3.*

STANLEY KAUFFMANN

The last third of *Fritz the Cat,* the first cartoon feature to be rated X, may be superb. I'll never know. Two-thirds was twice as much as I could stand. I wish I had been kinder to myself and left after the credits.

I mean to describe the very opening exactly as we see it. Three hardhats are eating lunch atop some New York steel construction. Then one of them stands, turns his back, and pees—a thick yellow stream, which falls all through the credits. Credits over, the thick stream reaches the street level, hits a young hippie on the head, and flattens him. And we're off to liberated Cartoonland.

All the characters are "played" by animals: policemen are pigs, black people are crows, students are cats, and so on. Greenwich Village and Harlem are the locales of the part I saw. Fritz is an NYU student who wants to swing (in the '60s), goes to a pot-sex orgy, a black bar, a black club. There is one fleetingly amusing sequence in a synagogue, with bloodhounds as old Jews; the rest is unbearably self-conscious "liberated" stuff without wit or point. The construction is moronic, the drawing dull, the dialogue corny, and the voices like the radio acting of the '30s on a bad night. I was going to mention the names of the people responsible for this mess, but I hope the reader has no interest.

*Stanley Kauffmann, in his review of "Fritz the Cat"
(reprinted by permission of Brandt & Brandt Literary
Agents, Inc.; copyright © 1972 by Stanley Kauffmann), in* The New Republic, *Vol. 166, No. 21, May
20, 1972, p. 34.*

ROBERT HATCH

It troubles me that I am almost totally unresponsive to *Fritz the Cat,* an animated cartoon feature, directed by Ralph Bakshi from the strip created by Robert Crumb for Head Comics. Fritz, a cat both in comic-book terms and in the current jargon, is super hip to every breeze that blew upon the country's questing youth of a few years ago, and the picture holds up his instant causes and borrowed principles to good-natured destruction. Thus Fritz, master lecher, organizes group sex in a bathtub, which exploit is raided by the prurient fuzz, and Fritz, the free-souled undergraduate, burns his lecture notes and with them one of the larger buildings on New York University's Greenwich Village campus. . . .

[One understands] that *Fritz the Cat* is bent on depreciating youthful follies, while not overlooking the worse than foolish responses of the alarmed and puzzled establishmentarian elders. In principle, I should applaud such iconoclasm, and in principle I do. It is the execution I deplore.

My spirits began to droop when the two cops sent to spoil the fun in the bathtub turned out to be pigs (Disney's little pigs grown up and turned gross), who spoke in the "da (gulp)"

accents popularly associated with mental deficiency. They fell still further when I discovered that the blacks were to be presented as crows (though the finery of these birds did trick me into some racist snickers). It isn't the bad taste I object to (I won't also be tricked into protesting the manners of a picture whose style consists in boasting that it has none), but the lack of invention. Portraying the police as pigs and the blacks as crows—or for that matter the insouciant hero as a cat—does not add much to the picturesqueness of contemporary imagery.

It occurred to me early in the proceedings that the picture expected its very high level of outrageousness to cover up its quite low level of imagination. As the one-for-one equivalents were rolled out in bold and rude succession, I felt my face turning wooden from exposure to a human comedy that never found a perspective for comment other than the mechanical one of exaggeration. There are some funny lines—whether or not Crumb originals I do not know—most of them depending on the almost infallible device of understatement. However, the episodes and characters seem to me utterly devoid of the ironic twist that makes satire the cruelest of blood sports. It is all "zap!, powie!, dirty word," and on to the next obvious foible. Even in the interest of redressing the balance, I find that procedure wearisome.

A good thing—far and away the best thing—about [*Fritz the Cat*] was the graphic treatment of the New York City background. The scenes were drawn in a sketchy, melancholy sepia, and then at the end, when the closing credits were being run, these renderings reverted to photographs of the forlorn, scaling, garbagy neighborhoods through which all New Yorkers go their ways. The artists responsible seemed to be saying that, kidding aside, New York is no joke. That's right.

Robert Hatch, in his review of "Fritz the Cat," in
The Nation *(copyright 1972 The Nation magazine,
The Nation Associates, Inc.), Vol. 214, No. 21, May
22, 1972, p. 670.*

LEE BEAUPRE

Bakshi's idea of wit [in **"Fritz the Cat"**] is to resurrect an 8-year-old Terry Southernism like "prevert," have Fritz "kill a john" by shooting at a toilet, resolve the Israeli situation by having the Zionists "return the cities of New York and Los Angeles to the United States" and paraphrase an old Elaine May-Mike Nichols routine with a bossy lady making "a big bourgeois deal out of everything."

As for the film's animation, it is a long way from what "Yellow Submarine" had let us to anticipate in future cartooning. Some of the backgrounds have a pleasing graphic quality—perhaps because they were watercolored adaptations of photographs of New York and thus relied very little on Bakshi's "imagination"—but his constant zooming and tilting hardly augments the attractiveness of these images. And when real invention is required for a sequence depicting the post-explosion apocalypse, Bakshi feebly resorts to a sepia-toned live-action shot of a desert gale.

In juxtaposition to the stylized reality of these backgrounds, the foreground figures are as cutely sentimentalized as in any Saturday morning TV cartoon—hardly surprising in that Bakshi apprenticed in just this kind of hack work. By marrying pretension with bad habits, Bakshi has made his film look like Heckle and Jeckle on a mescalin trip.

Still, **"Fritz the Cat"** is "only" a movie, and its intellectual, moral and esthetic bankruptcy would normally warrant only passing notice. Its success with the critical community, however, escalates my outrage at the inanity of this lunk-headed rip-off of the youth culture. Only two years ago reviewers were faulting a series of films that implied kids would always be kids and that their "revolution" was just the latest peer-group enthusiasm—an attitude they now applaud in **"Fritz the Cat."**

Apparently film critics felt the media-inspired pressure to be "with it" back in 1970, and they shrewdly postponed expressing their hostility both to youthful energy and to social revolution. Now, with most youths having abandoned violent activism, with the drug scene receding and with Watts and Kent State only a memory, our reviewers would seem back in their own Nixonerous element.

One hardly wants to hear another rousing chorus of "Tradition," but a sentimental approach to the past—even the very recent past—may be preferable to the spurious revulsion that infects **"Fritz the Cat."** After all, the past remains our only route to the present and our only assurance of a future. In dismissing the political turbulence and personal quest of the sixties while simultaneously exploiting the sexual freedom sired by that decade, **"Fritz the Cat"** truly bites the hand that fed it.

> *Lee Beaupre, "Phooey on 'Fritz the Cat'," in* The New York Times, *Section 2 (© 1972 by The New York Times Company; reprinted by permission), July 2, 1972, p. 7.*

VINCENT CANBY

Ralph Bakshi's mostly animated feature, **"Heavy Traffic,"** is American graffiti of a very high and unusual order, a tale of a young New York City pilgrim named Michael, half-Italian, half-Jewish, ever innocent, and his progress through a metaphor that is nowhere near as dreary as it sounds: the pinball machine called Life. It is a liberating, arrogant sort of movie, crude, tough, vulgar, full of insult and wit and an awareness of the impermanence of all things. . . .

Bakshi's **"Heavy Traffic"** is rated X, not because it's pornographic in any way but because it employs the small gestures and words of obscenity to make its rude statement about the quality of what might be dangerously described as the New York City Experience.

The opening of the film sets its moods as the screen goes from a live-action Michael, playing his pinball machine, to the animated world that lies just beyond reality. Michael, a would-be "underground" cartoonist, asks "What makes you happy? Where do you hide? Who do you trust?" And the voice carries over as two ancient jazz musicians in terrible repair meet while foraging through a garbage can. . . .

With a poet's freedom (including the freedom from the fear he might be making an ass of himself), Bakshi conducts his misery-house tour of the quintessential modern metropolis, a New York City inhabited entirely by undesirables, junkies, whores, crooked cops, crooked union leaders, Mafia soldiers, craven dads, mad moms. The only two innocents are Michael and Carole, the pretty, no-nonsense black bartender who is also beloved by Shorty, the legless bouncer at her bar.

Bakshi's first feature, **"Fritz The Cat,"** was criticized by purists for the liberties he took with a favorite underground comic strip. Now he has created his own world in **"Heavy Traffic,"** which at its best moments is as nutty and bleak and beautiful as some scenes out of early Henry Miller, with whom Bakshi shares the inability to be entirely glum in the face of disaster. (p. 1)

"Heavy Traffic" wouldn't be much fun, however, if it were nothing more than an inventory of horrors. The fascination of **"Heavy Traffic"** is the way the horrors are turned inside out, most often for laughs but occasionally for reflections on love and loss. There is a most peculiar, most moving sequence in which Michael runs into his mom at a cheap Manhattan dance hall. She's being drunk and disorderly (her left breast just won't stay inside her dress) and then she glides off into a sodden reverie in which she's confronted by real photographs out of a not-quite-forgotten childhood.

There's also a very funny and sad rooftop encounter Michael has with a deranged old black man named Moe, who tells Michael cheerfully that he has come up to the roof to kill Michael's pigeons. Says Moe, who is suddenly sad: "I ain't there. Everybody plays like he's there. But they ain't there . . ."

Everyone in **"Heavy Traffic"** seems to think he's there or that he knows how to get there, including Snowflake, the transvestite who inevitably picks up the kind of rough trade who will beat the hell out of him when the truth is revealed. Even Michael and Carole think they know how to get there, which for them is California, a plan that is cruelly interrupted because if there's one thing Angie hates more than the idea that his son is a virgin, it's the idea that his son is sleeping with a black girl.

Bakshi's background images, which often mix animation with photographs and with well-known paintings (an Edward Hopper, for example), brilliantly evoke a New York that spans the 1930s to the 1960s. Even though the time seems always immediate, when Michael sits alone in the top balcony in some now long-removed Loew's picture palace, he is watching an actual clip from the Clark Gable-Jean Harlow film, "Red Dust" (1932).

In **"Fritz The Cat,"** Bakshi's characters were animals. Here they are cartoon humans who, in themselves, are not very interesting to look at. They are the heritage of decades of Terrytoons and Looney Tunes and Max Fleischer work that never measured up to the Disney creations. . . . Yet this very ordinariness of the characters' looks, plus Bakshi's use of the most familiar sort of cartoon prerogatives (an assassinated Mafia godfather can continue to eat his spaghetti even though he is full of see-through bullet holes), are part of what I take to be a serious attempt to use the commonplace stratagems of one era to mock the nightmares of the era that came after.

"Heavy Traffic" may well turn out to be the most original American film of the year. (pp. 1-3)

> *Vincent Canby, "'Heavy Traffic' and 'American Graffiti'—Two of the Best," in* The New York Times, *Section 2 (© 1973 by The New York Times Company; reprinted by permission), September 16, 1973, pp. 1, 3.**

ANDREW SARRIS

The moral issue with **"Heavy Traffic"** is somewhat . . . complicated in that Ralph Bakshi's animated cartoon seems less concerned with beguiling its audience . . . than of bestirring it. . . . By any standard, Bakshi's achievement is spectactularly uneven. But then he is just about the only X-rated car-toonist around, and thus there is really not too much basis for comparison. As with "Fritz the Cat," the uniqueness of the genre puts the captious critic in the uncomfortable position of hunting down an endangered species. Bakshi's artistic alibi seems to be that he is a conscious antithesis to Walt Disney. He has even accelerated Disney's unfortunate evolution from pure animation to a melange of animation and live-action, but whereas Disney's clinical orientation was anal, Bakshi's seems to be genital, and whereas Disney's fantasies did not exclude children, Bakshi's seem designed to exclude even squeamish adults. But as Stuart Byron has noted in the Real Paper, Bak-shi's urban hero flashes all kinds of Bambi expressions when confronted with the absurdism of his existence. And it is still an open question whether Bakshi is any more ruthlessly Dar-winian in his big city confrontations than Disney was in his so-called "nature studies."

The notion of the hero's being afflicted with both a Rothian Jewish Mother and a machismoid mafioso father may have been suggested by the peculiar casting of parents in an Andy Milligan very-soft-core-and-hard-yell sex-ploitation opus of some years ago. Having thus disposed of the ethnic anxiety of the Jews and the Italians, Bakshi is free to cash in on much funnier but more sensitive targets, mainly raffish blacks and drag queens. . . . [But at] what point does Bakshi exploit the very horror he says he has set out to expose? This is an especially difficult question to ask of cinema with the built-in hypocrisy of its sensuous spectacle. Hence, most anti-war films glorify war, anti-crime films glorify crime, anti-rape films glorify rape, or if they don't glorify these evils, they at least celebrate them, and thus make them more thinkable.

What is especially confusing in "Heavy Traffic" is the ex-traordinary exhilaration with which evil is committed. . . . As I watched the cartoon, I did become involved with the desperate adventures of the hero, and I followed the narrative on its own terms. And then about half-way into the plot, the hero and black girl friend decide to rip off a john. The girl lures the john to a hotel room and the hero cracks the john's skull open with a piece of lead pipe, and we see all the blood streaming out, and the john plopping down dead, and I said that's all folks because you can't put humpty-dumpty together again by treating mugging and murder as mandatory courses in a ghetto education and the picture can't go on as if nothing had hap-pened. The same thing happened to me when the pool shark died in "Fritz the Cat." I simply turned off the movie and let the images float freely to oblivion. But even on the most ab-stract level, "Heavy Traffic" collapses completely when it shifts from animation to live-action for its soft-headedly scenic finale. (p. 66)

> *Andrew Sarris, "Morals through the Shredder" (re-printed by permission of* The Village Voice *and the author; copyright © The Village Voice, Inc., 1973), in* The Village Voice, *Vol. XVIII, No. 38, Sept. 20, 1973, pp. 65-6.**

STANLEY KAUFFMANN

I walked out of Ralph Bakshi's first cartoon feature *Fritz the Cat* because it was vulgar and dull. I didn't walk out of his second, *Heavy Traffic,* which is vulgar but often interesting.

It mixes animation with some live action as it tells the story of a young New York cartoonist who, while playing a pinball machine (ah, there, Saroyan), wanders off into a (cartoon)

fantasy involving a stunning black bar hostess. Subsequently, in live film, he meets her and they "find" each other in Union Square.

There are ghetto derelicts, drag queens, hookers, mafiosi, and other delectations of the New York scene [in *Heavy Traffic*]; the ambience is grubbiness. Nothing is hinted at that can be shown, including genitals, and the story gets nowhere, not very fast; still some things are extraordinary. First, it's the best mixture of animation and live photography that I've seen—the only one I've seen that had some point. Second, which *is* the point, the texture, taking us from the real into the distorted real, makes it all a metropolitan *Walpurgisnacht*. Bakshi hasn't completely avoided tenement-poetry banalities, like the sen-sitivity of the hero and the hearts of gold in some derelicts he encounters, but in the main, and in the mainline, this is hell. Done with brio and pizazz, peopled with cartoons, but still hell. Which is just how one feels at times in New York and other big cities.

> *Stanley Kauffmann, in his review of "Heavy Traffic" (originally published in* The New Republic, *Vol. 169, No. 11, September 22, 1973), in his* Living Images: Film Comment and Criticism *(reprinted by permis-sion of Brandt & Brandt Literary Agents, Inc.; copy-right © 1970, 1971, 1972, 1973, 1974, 1975 by Stanley Kauffmann), Harper & Row, Publishers, 1975, p. 222.*

HARRIET POLT

Heavy Traffic is about New York, about violence, perhaps most of all about ugliness. Shorty, a frog-faced legless man, the Godfather slurping spaghetti through enormous lips, the skinny Jewish mamma, the fat prostitutes—all are ugly and either stupid or evil, or both. Even the two good-looking characters, Michael and his sexy black girlfriend Carol, finally turn vio-lent, perhaps corrupted by all the ugliness around them. Ralph Bakshi, the film's writer and director, depicts women with particular loathing, even more than he did in *Fritz*. Those breasts that keep popping out of blouses are not sexy but disgusting, in much the same way that Kenneth Anger's Marilyn Monroe and the other women in *Hollywood Babylon*, that classic of softcore misogyny, are disgusting.

The visual devices of *Traffic* have been rightly praised. The combination of live and animated action, the color effects pro-duced through negative printing and other laboratory tech-niques, the bird's-eye shots (also used in *Fritz*), and so on make *Traffic* frequently a pleasure to look at. Yet the live-action frame story, with a live Michael and Carol who finally get together, as well as the live pin-ball machine that Michael plays and that sets off the supposed fantasies making up the central part of the film—these devices are more confusing than constructive, muddying the already obscure point of the film. It can be said to Ralph Bakshi's credit that he has achieved the difficult task of creating people-animation rather than an-imal-animation. But when the characters created are themselves stereotypes, and the action simply an extension of the violence already exploited *ad nauseam* in live films, one is forced to ask: why bother? (pp. 60-1)

> *Harriet Polt, in her review of "Heavy Traffic," in* Film Quarterly *(© 1974 by The Regents of the Uni-versity of California; reprinted by permission of The Regents), Vol. XVII, No. 2, Winter, 1973-74, pp. 60-1.*

JOHN SIMON

With *Coonskin*, Ralph Bakshi convinces me that the sum total of his talent was exhausted in *Fritz the Cat,* and that even there the chief interest lay in novelty rather than ultimate worth. . . .

As in the equally bad *Heavy Traffic,* Bakshi is once again mixing live action and cartoon footage, alternating, juxtaposing, and superimposing them by turns. This is stylistically deleterious, rather like mixing Bach and the Rolling Stones. Each genre may have its own validity, but each sets up different responses, different degrees of involvement: the cartoon sequences try to make the fantastic real, which is fair enough; but the obtrusion of live action makes the real people look out of place, ridiculous, unreal (especially since Bakshi uses a great deal of deliberate distortion and coloristic hocus-pocus), and, finally, makes even the cartoon characters diminished and impotent, dwarfed by the human presences.

Moreoover, Bakshi proves yet again that he cannot tell a story. He can occasionally make a very brief episode, not exactly funny but, at least, biting; he has no idea, however, of how to make a plot connect, unfurl, develop. And hardly any individual episode is interesting and funny enough in itself to make us overlook the poor continuity—we miss out even on that picaresque, episodic fascination that *Fritz,* to some extent, achieved. Seldom, in fact, have I sat in a crowded screening room so empty of laughs.

Worse yet, there is no overarching satirical vision here. It's no use making out all humanity as more or less stupid and corrupt unless you can do it with enough sustaining wit and a point of view, a notion of where salvation might lie. For it is only in the name of a genuine moral vision, a true and powerful outrage, that such sweeping satire becomes viable; here all we get is a sour, intermittently grinning, peevishness. Indeed, sheer intelligibility is often missing: the images are frequently inscrutable and the sound track as clotted and muddy as [Robert] Altman at his worst. I urge black protest groups to leave Bakshi to heaven, or, rather, to the hell of his dullness and insufficiency. (p. 67)

John Simon, "Nashville without Tears," in New York Magazine (copyright © 1975 by News Group Publications, Inc.; reprinted with the permission of New York Magazine), Vol. 8, No. 32, August 11, 1975, pp. 66-7.*

ARTHUR COOPER

Mr. Walt Disney
Elysian Fields

Dear Walt,

Well, old buddy, things have come to a pretty pass. A young animator named Ralph Bakshi—you might remember, he made the first two X-rated feature-length cartoons, **"Fritz the Cat"** and **"Heavy Traffic"**—anyway, he's now made **"Coonskin."** It's got an R rating, which must stand for Ripoff because what he's done is turn your Uncle Remus stories inside out.

The movie is about these three black characters who leave the South and come to Harlem where they try to take over the rackets. Along the way they have to knock off a corrupt detective named Mannigan who looks like a women's-lib caricature of Telly Savalas. And, Walt, Bakshi represents Miss America with a cartoon character who's *nekked.* Bakshi tells his story, if you want to call it a story, as he did in his earlier

movies, by intercutting the fantasy footage with live action, including black performers like singer Barry White.

The trouble is that even with his eye for detail, Bakshi has no point of view. He creates tense situation and fritters them away without tension. Nor is there much humor. Still, the movie is making a lot of people angry. . . .

I don't know why CORE is making all this fuss because it's clear that Bakshi doesn't have much affection for man or womankind—black or white. All **"Coonskin"**'s characters are grotesque except Miss America, and as I said before, she's nekked. Last night I watched an old print of your "Song of the South," with all those cute bluebirds and sharecroppers, and I think I'll send it to Bakshi. Although there were protests about that film, in this case CORE ought to just let sleeping dogs snore. Actually, if it were a question of dogs, I wouldn't be so mad. But one of the stars of **"Coonskin"** is, can you believe it, a rabbit.

Sadly, your old cottontail buddy,
Thumper

Arthur Cooper, "Color It Black," in Newsweek (copyright 1975, by Newsweek, Inc.; all rights reserved; reprinted by permission), Vol. LXXXVI, No. 7, August 18, 1975, p. 73.

PENELOPE GILLIATT

"Coonskin," written and directed by Ralph Bakshi (of **"Fritz the Cat"** and **"Heavy Traffic"**), is at its most eloquent when it does things quietly, which is to say that a work whose whole immensely talented premise is its exuberance slows down to its best when it is temperate. . . .

"Coonskin" is a full-length feature film in which things move smoothly from animation to photography or—most interesting visually—to a mixture of the two. It is made in lewd honor of Manhattan and other melting pots, in which, Bakshi suggests, the ethnic and sexual mixing has actually long since passed the molten stage to become as cool as the sort of jazz this film so much likes. . . .

"Coonskin" is a very sympathetic, tough-spirited imagining of the lower depths. We are in a world of skinny, magenta-lipped tarts in magenta bikinis; of very poor people salvaging terrific finds of wrong-sized cotton sweaters from garbage cans; of a tight, furious, foul-mouthed, and desperate black fraternity in Harlem, where Brother Rabbit decides that black-racket money is going to stay. This brings him into collision with a fat and hairy dirty-white cop called Mannigan, whose enormous flesh is drawn with a choking disparagement that sometimes makes the line of the animation seem aesthetically out of control. Mannigan demonstrates every phobic anxiety of the middle-class white male analysand about black sexual superiority and white sexual ambiguity. His key scenes begin in a Harlem joint where he falls for a beautiful black showgirl: a photographed figure, half naked, who sidles up sumptuously through the smoky air, sways for a while on a platform, and disappears. Before he knows it, Mannigan is upstairs, in a drawn sequence, with a husky-voiced androgyne lying back on a bed. Again before he knows it, the nightmare about exchange of gender has melted into one about exchange of race, and Mannigan finds his face turned black. He slaps his hands to his cheeks, and then to his chest, leaving appalled black palm prints on a torso that has suddenly become feminine. Animation has always used the device of metamorphosis: Bakshi's metamorphic scenes are centaurlike and perturbing. When his waxy line softens and slithers and changes form, there is often an element of the truly shocking in the change. (p. 47)

[The flaws in "Coonskin"] stem from the very characteristic that also generates the work: its extravagance of energy. There is a certain flailing and, I believe, unmeant vindictiveness here, and much hatred of flesh. The hatred is unlike George Grosz's, with his icy drawings of the people of early Nazi Germany: his beaky women carrying pampered poodles as if they were expensive crocodile handbags, and his prosperous men with rolls of dangerous-looking fat packed across the backs of their necks like bundles of dynamite sticks. Bakshi's vision is more gamy than that. It is less intellectual, more reckless, more debonair. "Coonskin" has been accused by some black groups of being racist, but this is true only in the sense that it is merciless to everyone: whites, women, homosexuals, sons, mothers, Italians, and however divisions go. The very flagrancy of Bakshi's tone is a cover disguising a compassion extended to the lot of us, except upholstered racketeers. People's lives are hard, he says: nearly everyone's; and if people themselves become hard, it is because of their having spent an existence in combat.

The film is very rough going, but it is vitally human, and graphically a triumph except at the banal moments when Bakshi drops his inventive doctoring of photographs so that they look like etchings, or his mixing of photographs and animation, and collapses into a form of cartoon drawing whose chief weapon is a perverse exploitation of neon vulgarity. It should be remembered that he not only wrote the equally neon-colored yet very gifted laconic dialogue but conceived the tale as well, "Coonskin" celebrates a group of poorly placed, ill-treated people pretending to themselves with all their might that they are worth something: that Harlem is a world of brothers and sisters living on top of the heap, and the hell with soft-shoe dancing and being obliging. The way Bakshi shows the harsh, jaunty dignity implicit in the click of the abandoned Harlem woman's shoe heel is piercingly admiring. It stands for the best in the film, which is the assault that Bakshi makes on privileged glumness and any dilution of bravery. In the scheme of things he consistently creates in his films, bravery and bravado amount morally to the same thing. (p. 48)

Penelope Gilliatt, "High Bravado from the Lower Depths," in The New Yorker (© 1975 by The New Yorker Magazine, Inc.), Vol. LI, No. 27, August 25, 1975, pp. 47-9.*

STANLEY KAUFFMANN

Coonskin has met with protests from some who assert that it's racist. I'm not going to comment on the justice of the protests. . . . But if there are going to be protests, then they ought to be by everyone, because the whole human race, as exemplified in this country at this time, is what is being skewered by this scintillating, vicious, outrageous and outraged film. (p. 165)

Coonskin, on any vulgarity meter, may be the worst of [Bakshi's films]—for instance, the very first words are "Fuck you," and there are such scenes as one in which a character gets tugged along by his infinitely elastic phallus—but it's hard to think of this good film as having any other tone than the one it has. I'm glad that other people had more faith in Bakshi from the start than I had. (p. 166)

The episodic story line, which lags and pants, doesn't much matter. What does matter, greatly, is the way the picture is made, and the material to which the story line gives occasion.

The story of the three animal characters is done either in straight animation or a mixture of cartoon and photography. . . . In Coonskin [Bakshi uses it] purposefully. Here it can be seen as the old con's fantasticated story, in cartoon, poised against the real world as he imagines it to be—shown sometimes in photography.

Bakshi only rarely uses real and animated characters in the same shot; usually, when he mixes, he puts animated characters against photographed backgrounds that have been altered or juxtaposed to fine effect. When the three animals decide to go North, we cut to our first view of Harlem, live: a wintry street at night with a lone bareheaded black man playing a trumpet in the middle of it; a "squeezed" shot—that is, a very wide-screen shot shown through a regular lens so that we get a compressed and elongated El Greco touch. Bakshi uses this effect again behind animation from time to time. (pp. 166-67)

Many of the cartoon characters are drawn with wild wit, especially a hippo-like black religious leader and the Godfather (white, of course)—not a Brando caricature but a puffy, incredibly ravaged old face with an obscenely dyed mustache. One usage is startling. Some of the young black women are drawn with faces like snouts—not just snout noses, the whole face from the hairline forward looks like the end of an elephant's trunk. But Bakshi, unsentimental, refuses to spare the people he likes: they, too, have to pass through the channel of his wit.

The flood of pictures—ingenious, bitter, funny, beautiful, lewd, touching—cascades across the screen. Although the script sags, the pictorial inventiveness never does. Oppression of blacks, black crime, black anger, black silliness, black resilience—all the elements of black life that are the center of the film—are not editorial matters to Bakshi, they are artistic matters. He is no Stanley Kramer of animation, inflated with a Good Cause, then plunking it onto film somehow. As in all good art, the way he works is part of why he works. Bakshi has been finding his style through his first two pictures, fairly firmly in the second. Now he has it. What he sees—what he saw before he started—is, first and finally, what the picture is about, what he has to "say."

But I've omitted an important element of his style: the sound track. Bakshi has ears as well as eyes. First there is fine music by Chico Hamilton. Second, those voices, those black speaking voices. It's not a matter of yuk-yuk har-har chocolate gargles. It's a matter of richness, orchestration of timbres, the humor and pathos of inflection, the acute interplay. Bakshi's animated sequences have one of the best sound tracks I can remember in animation, immediate and warm. (pp. 167-68)

The only scene that stands out as extraneous is one between a live white couple and cartooned blacks that is just warmed-over Lenny Bruce. Most of the rest—the Godfather and his blatantly homosexual sons, the devil-angel who flits around the Mafia (a fantastically good touch), the "God-fearing" black brothel where the preacher marries couples at night and divorces them in the morning, dozens of other sharp scenes—is digested into a flashing acid stream. Bakshi has even found a way to work in a Jewish caricature, as if he had looked over the film when finished, had found that his blistered New York contained no Jews, and mended the lack by putting in a Jew as Mafia crony.

But, from the wry joke of the title on, this film is not against groups—it's against snarling, short-sighted, scrabbling, egocentric, murderous American city life, particularly as it beats up on blacks. Progressively through his three films Bakshi, who is white, has staked his territory—the American city as hell, racially torn hell, engulfing people who are learning how to live in hell. *Coonskin* is a flawed but fierce little work of art, done at a high level of imaginative energy and with some touches of brilliance. (p. 168)

Stanley Kauffmann, in his review of ''Coonskin'' (originally published in The New Republic, *Vol. 173, No. 11, September 13, 1975), in his* Before My Eyes: Film Criticism and Comment *(copyright © 1975 by Stanley Kauffmann; abridged by permission of Harper & Row, Publishers, Inc.),* Harper & Row, *1980, pp. 165-68.*

JOHN SIMON

Ralph Bakshi's new animated feature, **Wizards,** tries to be a fresh departure but looks more like a late arrival. Even though we are in a fairytale future, there is still much uninteresting contemporary street lingo, the plotting is still weak, the idea still hackneyed. The quality of the drawing is not bad, though lacking in intense originality, and the simplistic tale of good, sloppy pacifism winning out over wicked, hyperefficient militarism is not couched in terms that could be considered arresting.

As usual with Bakshi, there is an inadequate musical score . . . , and, again as usual, only worse here, the dragging in of poorly integrated live action. The only one ever to get away with this kind of cinematic miscegenation was the fine Czech animator, Karel Zeman, and even he only intermittently. What makes it so offensive here is that scenes from Nazi newsreels, *The Triumph of the Will,* and *Alexander Nevsky* juxtaposed with Bakshi's elves, fairies, and wizards make Bakshi look pretentious and his inventions puny. The strategy also cheapens the great horrors of history, not to mention Eisenstein's art. Were the brush of a Leonardo at work here, it could not paint over the coarseness of the imagination. (pp. 73-4)

John Simon, ''Well-Intentioned, Ill-Conceived,'' in New York *Magazine (copyright © 1977 by News Group Publications, Inc.; reprinted with the permission of* New York *Magazine), Vol. 10, No. 19, May 9, 1977, pp. 70, 72-4.**

ALEXANDER STUART

Sadly short on magic, *Wizards* is an interesting, unsuccessful try by animator Ralph Bakshi. . . . With a rather naïve, very late-1960s story about two wizards, one good, one bad, and their tussle for the kind of world each wants, the film is a stylistic mishmash that relies on far too many animation shortcuts to tell its tale.

Decidedly too much of the story is communicated through lengthy sequences of still sketches with narration over the top. These parts of the movie are the kind of thing Disney animators might produce just for themselves to get an impression of the feel of the thing they're working on—*not* the type of work you expect to end up in a finished feature film.

When *Wizards* does leap into animation one of the most instantly noticeable losses is in design. The sketches have a kind of sophistry: they seem to be aiming for the visual fantasy explored by artists like Roger Dean and Bruce Pennington in their album sleeves and posters. The backgrounds for the animation retain something of this, but the character design is pure Betty Boop, and the two really don't gel.

Then there are the tricksy sequences mixing animated foreground action with live action abstract backdrops; these seem only to accentuate the flatness of much of the artwork and its relative crudity. Worked into the storyline is a helping of Nazi rally footage, a nice idea but again the fusion between live action and animation is none too successful. The battle sequences use a different trick: stock footage, apparently from some viking movie; put through a solarisation-like optical process and given animated embellishments—some of the horsemen have batwings, for example. Again, nothing fits together very well. (p. 33)

Wizards looks like it was made in record time and on a record low budget—but where's the point in doing things that way if it shows? (p. 34)

Alexander Stuart, in his review of ''Wizards'' (© copyright Alexander Stuart 1978; reprinted with permission), in Films and Filming, *Vol. 24, No. 4, January, 1978, pp. 33-4.*

VINCENT CANBY

''The Lord of the Rings'' is both numbing and impressive.

Yet it would be difficult to recommend this movie to anyone not wholly absorbed by the uses of motion-picture animation or to anyone not familiar with Tolkien's home-made mythology, which borrows liberally from various Norse myths, the Eddas, the Nibelungs and maybe even Beatrix Potter. In the way of grand opera sung in Urdu, **''The Lord of the Rings''** is likely to be total confusion to someone who doesn't speak the language. . . .

The major fault of the screenplay by Chris Conkling and Peter S. Beagle is that the film attempts to cover too much ground too quickly, packing in more incomprehensible exposition in the first 15 minutes than you'd get in a year of ''All My Children.'' I know one 12-year-old Tolkien scholar, who otherwise thoroughly approved of the movie, who was disappointed because a lot of the events of the books had been ''simplified'' in the movie. This comment prompted a certain amount of awe among a small group of adults who'd had difficulty following the simplified material. . . .

As in all his films, Mr. Bakshi attempts to go beyond the limits of movie animation as we know it. Before he and his staff began the actual animation, he shot most of his script with live actors in Spain (where else?) and used this material as a guide for the animators. Some of this original material appears to have been incorporated into the finished production, though it has the look of video tape that has been electronically altered to give it an unworldly, unfilmlike quality. Sometimes this is most effective: at other times it simply looks like badly developed film stock. Still, the film is visually compelling even when murk overtakes the narrative.

If Tolkien was not above quoting the mythology of others, Mr. Bakshi appears to have had his own fun quoting such films as ''2001,'' ''Ivan the Terrible,'''''Henry V'' and ''Snow White and the Seven Dwarfs.'' His hobbits look very much like Disney dwarfs, though somewhat more introspective, and not once does anyone waste time wishing on a star. The War of the

Ring is serious business, and the movie seldom makes light of it, which is something parents should keep in mind.

Vincent Canby, ''Film: 'Lord of Rings' from Ralph Bakshi,'' in The New York Times (© 1978 by The New York Times Company; reprinted by permission), November 15, 1978, p. C21.

TOM ALLEN

The Lord of the Rings has been made almost exclusively for Tolkien devotees. In adapting the long, unwieldy saga, the filmmakers have settled for *The Song of Bernadette* axiom: ''To those who believe, no explanation is necessary; to those who do not believe, no explanation is possible.'' When I saw the film, the audience cheered each introduction of the books' stars as if it were the opening night of *Gone with the Wind*. They were celebrating their own fond literary memories, not the characters materializing on screen. Yet their reaction seems to have been anticipated in the special care given such favorites as the Uriah Heepish Gollum, the Sancho Panchoesque Samwise, and the highly theatrical Gandalf the Wizard; and the audience seemed not to mind the strategy of speeding over the highlights of the book's dense plotting.

I have no idea whether *The Lord of the Rings* will be intelligible to the uninitiated. The film never gets around to introducing adequately the villian of the first major battle, not to mention the heavy of the climactic, yet-to-be-filmed fall of Mordor. It picks up most of the characters on the run, so to speak, and for a cartoon feature is extraordinarily short on establishing shots, voiceover narration, and title plates. Tolkien's maps, the sections of the book most dogeared by readers anxious to follow a complex odyssey through overlapping kingdoms, are not referred to on the screen. Either Bakshi has miscalculated here, or is presuming again on the reader's acquaintance. I suspect a mixture of both as well as a last-minute draconian editing in order to get the film out to the winter-holiday crowds. At present, *Lord of the Rings* is down to 133 minutes, but that is still an exhausting length for animation, the richest, most demanding form of film. . . .

The intimate interplay among the hobbit heroes, between Frodo and Samwise, for instance, or between Frodo and Bilbo, is expressive in a way never before attained by cartoon characters. They contribute a new heart to the work, a firm base on which Bakshi may yet create a great film.

The crowd scenes are a more mixed blessing. When the simulation of humans is realistic, as in the inn at Bree, it's like watching pop-up cardboard figures behind a wavy glass. The scenes of groups running or fighting, on the other hand, are a strikingly powerful form of animated locomotion. Bakshi, unfortunately, has diverted too much of his resources to large-scale battle scenes, the least developmental parts of the story. Besides, the dark army of orcs, even when animated, still come across as human extras with cheap papier-mache face masks, not that different from one of the schlockiest horror films ever made, *She Demons*.

So, wherein does the promise of *Lord of the Rings* lie? As the film stands now, it is already the most mature, most sober, and potentially the most sweeping showcase of animation yet fashioned in America. Beside it, Bakshi's earlier works—including the X-rated *Fritz the Cat*—are child's play under dollops of sophomoric scatology and racist virulence. The public is being offered a truncated, flawed *Lord of the Rings,* but not

a castrated one. If this preemptive, rough-hewn work earns a nest egg and Bakshi gets a stronger fix on the outlines of the odyssey saga, then a master work is in the making.

Tom Allen, ''An Ent Too Far'' (reprinted by permission of The Village Voice and the author; copyright © The Village Voice, Inc., 1978), in The Village Voice, Vol. XXIII, No. 47, November 20, 1978, p. 62.

WILLIAM WOLF

Ralph Bakshi, the mad genius of animation, has outdone himself. To meet the heady challenge of bringing J.R.R. Tolkien's fantasy world to the screen, he took the revolutionary, expensive step of first shooting [*The Lord of the Rings*] with actors. Then his vast staff of animators used the footage as models for the drawings. The result is amazing, particularly in the battlefield clashes.

And yet . . . I suppose much depends on how you react to Tolkien's Middle Earth world of hobbits, elves, orcs, men, or on how much entertainment and/or significance you find in this turbulent saga of good versus evil. Although some 20 million copies of Tolkien's trilogy have been sold, on screen the material seems too limited to sustain such a complex animation effort, however innovative.

But visually it's a helluva trip. . . . The spectacular epic scenes have the quality of paintings come to life. Little of this is kid's stuff; there is an abundance of violence, and even a bloodspurting killing à la [Sam] Peckinpah. Leonard Rosenman's thumping score makes an imposing accompaniment.

I much prefer Bakshi's use of animation for controversial social comment, as in *Heavy Traffic* and *Coonskin,* but *The Lord of the Rings* is the work of a master who has taken animation a long way from Mickey Mouse. (pp. 11-12)

William Wolf, in his review of ''The Lord of the Rings,'' in Cue (copyright © Cue Publications, Inc., 1978; reprinted by permission of News Group Publications, Inc.), Vol. 47, No. 24, December 8, 1978, pp. 11-12.

CHERYL FORBES

If you read the critics, you might not suspect that J.R.R. Tolkien's *Lord of the Rings,* the first true epic to come along since Milton revitalized Homer's and Virgil's genre, was a monumental work. That its followers, as with Abraham's seed, are as numerous as the sands. That there are people who meet each week to play Middle-earth games. That maps, calendars, pictures, puzzles, and deluxe editions of the trilogy sell in the millions year after year. I suspect that the critics and the audiences of Ralph Bakshi's animated version of *The Lord of the Rings* . . . will be just as far apart.

With few exceptions, the critics find it a bad film. The audiences don't. . . . Bakshi, the director, hasn't created a flawless film; here is no *Star Wars;* neither is it *Billy Jack.* But considering the sprawl and scope of Tolkien's story, Bakshi in a somewhat long 131 minutes captures well the atmosphere of an earlier and easier time.

The most compelling aspect of the film comes at the beginning with the recitation of the ring poem and the explanation of how the ring came to Frodo. Black silhouettes against a blood-red background set the tone and put the plot in motion. Those critics who found the film difficult to follow have watched too much television. They could do with a course in Shakespeare, whose popular plots are notoriously complex. . . .

Some straight lines were necessary. The beginning is as good a place as any to remove Tolkien's curves, though I wish the battle of Weathertop hadn't been so underplayed. Bakshi opted for the more subtle aspects of book one and he gave more time to the later battle scenes. But since he already had an unusually long film, why add a scene that doesn't occur in Tolkien: Saruman giving his orcs a pep talk before the big battle.

Several animation techniques seem distracting at first. The director, to achieve as much realism as he could, staged the action live, and produced his animation from that. No cartoon character has ever used so many facial expressions or talked with so mobile a mouth as does a Bakshi hobbit. Once you get over the surprise, the technique aids your belief that these are real characters. That also goes for the animals. His horses must have been a labor of love. Galloping, eating, sniffing— they move as realistically as any horse John Wayne ever rode.

The director's hand was less sure when it came to characterization. Here all Tolkien fans will disagree with him—and with each other. Who doesn't have his mental picture of Frodo, Gandalf, Strider, or Treebeard?

I thought that Frodo and Bilbo were approximately in the right spirit. Certainly Gandalf was as wizardly a wizard as Tolkien intended. Strider's first appearance was as foul as in the original, though once he removed his hood he resembled a Cherokee or a Navajo more than half-man, half-elf. Gollum looked all that he should—gray, slimy, and all stretched out, though his voice did not evoke the same impression. Most animators rely on good voices to make the characters live. Not so with Bakshi. If he had matched good actors with his superb animation techniques, the result would have been unforgettable.

With Sam Gamgee we have a complete misunderstanding of the hobbit Tolkien intended. Bakshi's Sam is a silly, simpering pudge of a character. Tolkien began with an unsophisticated, though intelligent, gardener, who grew into the ruler of the shire. I realize that Bakshi filmed only the first half of the story, but with such an unfortunate start, how can Sam become what he ought? For much of the original adventure, Sam carries Frodo (emotionally, and, at times, physically). All the animated Sam could carry is his girth. (p. 32)

I wish that Bakshi had emphasized the cosmic nature of the struggle between the allies of the Dark Lord. Without a strong sense of who controls Middle-earth and why Sauron needs to be resisted, the point of the plot gets lost in the superfluity of characters. Tolkien gives us that throughout the story. Bakshi cut most of the dialogue that indicates the religious nature of the conflict. This is no simple war story. The direction should have reinforced that.

Despite all these drawbacks, and I admit there seem to be a great many, the overall impact of the film is a credit to the story (it's also an entertaining film). An epic, with its overblown language and stock descriptions, almost inevitably fares ill under close scrutiny. The language and structure look sloppy. But relax and take in the atmosphere. The impression will change.

Tolkien created a sweeping history—almost, you might say, a new mythology. He has helped many younger Christians bring new meaning to the phrase "created in the image of God," as well as to imagination, even to history. Bakshi's film will bring

that tale to people who haven't read the trilogy. For those who have, it should send them back to the original. It did for me. (p. 33)

Cheryl Forbes, "Round One with the Ring," in Christianity Today (© *1979 by Christianity Today, Inc.), Vol. XXIII, No. 7, January 5, 1979, pp. 32-3.*

JAMES CRAIG HOLTE

American Pop is not a *Hester Street* nor a *Mean Streets,* films which deliberately develop ethnic themes and settings as their central focus. On the contrary, it is a film which incorporates ethnic material in a subplot, but the subplot of the melting pot and the call of the American Dream is so essential to the history of American popular music that the subject actually provides the narrative core for the entire film. . . . *American Pop* is more than music; it is about nothing less than the Great American Dream. All of Bakshi's films in fact, with the exception of his two voyages into fantasy, *Wizards* and *The Lord of the Rings,* are about the American Dream in one form or another. . . . (pp. 105-06)

Aside from his two fantasy films, all of Bakshi's work dramatizes the cultural diversity of American urban life. In *Fritz the Cat* (1972), *Heavy Traffic* (1973), and *Coonskin* (1975), Bakshi satirized various forms of the American Dream, that vision rooted in the past and projected into the future which promises the good life for those who follow the advice of the Dream's godfather, Benjamin Franklin, and diligently work to rise from poverty and obscurity to success and celebrity.

These three early films are full of violence, sex, drugs, and stereotypes; they are also very moving and very funny. They were attacked vehemently for Bakshi's inclusion of scenes of drug use, as well as for the openly sexual and often violent nature of his characters. Of course, self-proclaimed defenders of the public morality rise to attack any realistic portrayal of life which does not at least implicitly condemn drug use, violence, and open sexuality, and Bakshi's treating of such taboo subjects in a "children's medium" brought forth the double wrath of the moral critics. Critics of "serious literature" accept the fact that realistic satire of modern urban life cannot ignore these subjects, but, again, there was a feeling that the subjects were not suitable for animated film.

Bakshi's use of ethnic stereotypes raises more serious questions. Ethnic stereotypes are dangerous, and many people were offended by Bakshi's use of them in his early films. Watching these films is, at times, uncomfortable, but social satire exists within a framework of exaggeration and stereotype; the objects of the satire must be easily recognized by a fairly wide audience. And often, as is the case in Bakshi's films, the stereotyping is as much an object of satire as the satirist's other targets. Bakshi has not been discriminatory in his use of stereotypes; nothing escaped his ridicule in these early films. All of his characters—Blacks, Jews, Italians, Irish, Wasps, hippies, straights, politicians, cops—were exaggerations drawn from the popular imagination. And like all good satirists, Bakshi's intention was to make all of us laugh at ourselves and our eccentricities.

Fritz the Cat made Bakshi a hero of the counter-culture and offended everyone else. He adapted R. Crumb's hip and sassy cat from Zap Comics and turned him loose in theaters across the country. Fritz, with his bad mouth and bad attitude, was the perfect character to attack comfortable middle class assumptions about sexuality and the work ethic. The ideology of the American Dream preaches sexual fidelity and hard work as *the* way to happiness and success, but in *Fritz the Cat* Bakshi told the story of happiness from the other side. Fritz and his friends took drugs, never worked or studied, and pursued sex as if it were the Holy Grail; they also enjoyed themselves, appeared to prosper, and never felt retribution. The solid citizens in the film—the policemen, businessmen, and politicians—were boring, stupid, and unhappy. Bakshi's message came straight from the pages of Zap Comics and the spirit of the late Sixties, and even though *Fritz the Cat* is the least serious of his non-fantasy films, the hip message Bakshi delivered challenged comfortable beliefs.

He turned to more serious issues in *Heavy Traffic.* Most reviewers who bothered to write about the film at all saw it as another *Fritz the Cat,* a pornographic cartoon. But while the language and sexuality looked back to his first film, the subject matter was different. *Heavy Traffic* is a story of urban life. Unlike *Fritz the Cat,* which used an urban setting but did little with it, Bakshi's second film is all about life in the city. (pp. 107-08)

In *Heavy Traffic* Bakshi launched his first direct attack on the idea of the melting pot. In this film he drew upon his own background in Brooklyn. . . . Set in the Fifties, *Heavy Traffic* tells the story of a young, virginal cartoonist whose father, a small-time mafiosi, ignores his wife, a stereotypical smothering Jewish mother. The cartoonist falls in love with a Black barmaid and follows her to Harlem. Along the cartoonist's trail Bakshi provides images of the racism, poverty, drug abuse, crime, and empty lives that make up a large part of city life. Much like Stephen Crane's naturalistic novel *Maggie: A Girl of the Streets, Heavy Traffic* documents the underside of ethnic life in New York City; it shows not how far the members of the various ethnic groups have come, but rather how far they still have to go. (p. 108)

American Pop is Bakshi's most ambitious and carefully made film. In it he avoids the excesses which at times distracted from his serious satires before, and by grounding his critique of the American Dream in a story of popular music he creates a far wider audience for his most sustained attack upon comfortable assumptions. The style is less abrasive, but the subject is still deadly serious. (p. 110)

The controlling themes in the film are the development of American popular music, the assimilation of the family into the culture, and the frantic pursuit of success. The history of popular music gives the film its title and is the vehicle by which the various family members move into the culture, especially the lucrative musical subculture. The musical selections, ranging from "The Maple Leaf Rag" and "Swanee" to "I Got Rhythm," "Take Five," and "Don't Think Twice It's All Right," provide an overview of the century's hit parade, documenting the changing nature of popular music and the fascination it held for Bakshi's representational characters.

While the music becomes a metaphor for the dream of success and excitement which the characters chase with the intensity of Jay Gatsby's pursuit of the green light at the end of Daisy Buchanan's dock, the real story of *American Pop* is more serious. Bakshi uses the image of the melting pot, first popularized by Israel Zangwell's play, *The Melting Pot,* to describe how successive members of the family "make it." Bakshi's characters continually throw off old forms of behavior and take

on new ones as they prosper in America and become Americans. For his characters the process of assimilation is not a matter of choice for any single individual; it is a process which takes all of four generations. Bakshi is no romantic; he documents the cost, a loss of identity and community, as well as the successes. The way to wealth and acceptance, according to Bakshi, is fraught with losses. (p. 111)

In a sense, *American Pop* is a cartoon. Complex processes are simplified, and story and character are developed only in outline. In this particular cartoon, however, serious ideas are presented. The image of America as a land of plenty and opportunity, part of our cultural heritage since William Bradford's *Of Plymouth Plantation,* the suggestion of a rise to worth, and the idea of a melting pot provide the theoretical foundation for the story of an immigrant family. This is the subject of serious art, and this has been the subject of most of Bakshi's work. Bakshi asks us to examine some of our most fundamental assumptions about our country and our optimistic visions. Just as ethnic scholars are debating these very questions in traditional literary works, *American Pop* demonstrates that they are embedded as well in the popular arts. (p. 112)

> *James Craig Holte, "Ethnicity and the Popular Imagination: Ralph Bakshi and the American Dream," in MELUS (copyright, MELUS, The Society for the Study of Multi-Ethnic Literature of the United States, 1981), Vol. 8, No. 4, Winter, 1981, pp. 105-13.*

MIKE GRECO

American Pop is the product of a mature Bakshi. The anger, frustration, and intensity of *Traffic* and *Coonskin* are more controlled and focused. Bakshi's vision of America, while still ambivalent, reflects the changes that have occurred in both the filmmaker and his society in the last decade. Bakshi equates his personal and fantasy life with the recent American experience, synthesizing the two in this dramatic history of four generations of an immigrant family trying to make it in America. He understands both the creative and destructive power of the American Dream as only someone who has believed in it and has been disillusioned can. *American Pop* is in the tradition of *The Great Gatsby*: a brilliant indictment of the American Dream of Success.

American Pop follows a poor Jewish family from turn-of-the-century Russia, where a pogrom forces them to immigrate to America, to Los Angeles in the Eighties, where the great grandson descendant of this displaced Old World family realizes the American Dream by becoming a rock star. (pp. 18-19)

The theme of *American Pop,* the irony of the American Dream, and the broad sweep of its story, encompassing eighty years of the American experience, make it a modern American epic. This film is also a cinematic epic because of its synthesis of images and music, character and cultural milieu, story and *mise en scène. American Pop* is the first animated film ever to approach the potential of the medium. . . .

Music is an integral part of *American Pop* because it plays such an important role in the lives of all four generations of the film's immigrant family. It is not only the vehicle for their quest for the American Dream, it also represents their inmost selves. Bakshi believes that "the values of a generation are reflected in its popular music. Music is part of our times. Popular songs remind you of different periods more effectively than anything else can. I've attempted to select songs for *Pop* that evoke a sense of time and place."

Music is not the only element Bakshi employs to evoke a "sense of time and place." The style and form of different scenes in *American Pop* reflect the time period, geographical location, emotional tone, and character of each scene's protagonists. Bakshi adapted the style of the artists he thought epitomized the art of each generation. (p. 19)

Few filmmakers ever tap the power of popular music to affect their audiences. Fewer still have fully exploited film's potential for manipulating the viewer's senses, utilizing symbols that have an impact on both the conscious and subliminal levels, or integrating story, character, imagery, sound, and symbolism in a way that affects both the intellectual and visceral response the viewer has to a movie. How many times have you left a theater having experienced film in a new way—knowing more about yourself and your society? *American Pop* provides such an experience. . . .

The irony of *American Pop* is the irony of the American Dream. Bakshi is trying to tell us we spend all our lives chasing a sham and in the process lose our real opportunities for happy and meaningful lives. By extension, America is losing its opportunity to fulfill its promise—to make the American Dream a reality instead of a religion based on avarice and lust for fame.

The family member who finally wins fame and fortune, Pete, knows nothing about his family or their traditions. He is a bastard without friends, family, or a sense of belonging to a community. . . .

What had they gained, after eighty years, this immigrant family questing after the American Dream? They won a platinum LP and lost their souls. It's no wonder that Bakshi is controversial. He is holding up a mirror we don't want to look in. (p. 20)

> *Mike Greco, "Bakshi's American Dream," in* Film Comment *(copyright © 1981 by Mike Greco; reprinted by permission of the Film Society of Lincoln Center), Vol. 17, No. 1, January-February, 1981, pp. 18-20.*

VINCENT CANBY

["American Pop"] is a Pop vision of American life since the turn of the century, seen in the stories of four generations of one family of would-be American musicmakers. Though the film is animated, it makes free use also of old newsreels, still photographs and pencil sketches, as well as work in the manner of dozens of recognizable artists from George Grosz and Reginald Hopper to Andy Warhol, with passing references to Edward Hopper, Rockwell Kent and Norman Rockwell, among others. . . .

"American Pop" looks like no other animated film ever made, except for Mr. Bakshi's earlier works, nor does it sound like any other. It's rough and violent and occasionally very moving, as well as cruelly funny. It begins with the story of Zalmie, a Russian Jewish boy who, following a pogrom, comes to America with his widowed mother in 1900. Young Zalmie wants desperately to succeed and seeks fame and fortune in burlesque, where he meets and eventually marries a stripper who can sing.

Zalmie's son, Benny, is a middling-to-good pianist and songwriter, whose music reflects the 30's and 40's. Benny, before going overseas in World War II, marries the daughter of a Mafia chief and leaves, on his death, a disenchanted son. This boy, Tony, raised in suburban splendor on Long Island, breaks with the family to become, first, a beat poet and then songwriter-in-residence to a Janis Joplin kind of star of the 60's.

When Tony dies, a junkie and a bum, the line should stop there, but he, too, leaves an heir who, at long last, climbs to the top as a punk-rock star. . . .

The soundtrack is dense with popular music that need not be catalogued here. Though there were times when I wasn't at all sure that the particular music being heard belonged to a particular period, the music is terrifically effective—invigorating, ironic and not for a minute sentimental. If anything, "American Pop" tries too hard to avoid a kind of sentiment that the look of the picture occasionally seems to ask for. . . .

[Mr. Bakshi] makes witty use of the cliches of the American musical-film genre, both by putting them into the film straight and by turning them inside out. There were times when "American Pop" reminded me of "Alexander's Ragtime Band," one of those Darryl F. Zanuck-20th Century-Fox musicals of the 40's, but one that had somehow been wickedly tampered with.

Mr. Bakshi tried to cover a lot of ground. How many other films have you seen recently that managed to include World Wars I and II, the Korean War, Vietnam, the Triangle Shirtwaist Factory fire, Kent State, Frank Sinatra, Eva Tanguay, the Sex Pistols, Allen Ginsberg, Benny Goodman and the Prohibition gang wars (though not necessarily in that order)?

His is a talent that won't be stopped.

> *Vincent Canby, "Screen: 'American Pop,' Grown-Up Animation," in* The New York Times, Section 3 *(© 1981 by The New York Times Company; reprinted by permission), February 13, 1981, p. 5.*

COLIN L. WESTERBECK, JR.

Because his style *does* have to be styleless—flat, simple, unelaborated for the most part—Bakshi has stuck to naturalistic stories with human characters and *bildungsroman* plots. If you use today's abbreviated animation techniques on animals, you get something about as affecting as *Crusader Rabbit*. The animals constantly remind the viewer that this is a cartoon he's watching, and as a consequence he remains aware of the art work. With human characters, the viewer more readily sees a cartoon the way he does a live-action movie, as if it were real life. This makes him oblivious to the cartoonishness of it. It also keeps him from asking himself why this movie should have been made as a cartoon in the first place. The whole aesthetic of the cartoon is so extraneous to *American Pop* that Bakshi actually had his sketch men work from photographs of live models acting out the script, posing for each shot to be drawn.

So far as I can see, the only reason to make *American Pop* as a cartoon is that it would have been too expensive to make as a live feature. The film is a *Godfather*-like saga of four generations of a single family involved, one way or another, in pop music. Doing this story as an animation not only allows its innumerable, far-flung locations and period scenes to be handled cheaply, it allows a certain amount of ellipsis in the narrative. It permits the film to have an illustrative quality which would seem stilted and jumpy with real characters and situations. Again, Bakshi's talent, both economically and artistically, is for the short-cut.

The result is a peculiarly amorphous, purposeless movie. On the one hand, it's not really about pop music (only one or two songs are even performed in their entirety) so much as it's about the history of organized crime and the sub-culture of drugs in America. On the other hand, its attention to history is pretty random, too, as when it mixes up Woody Guthrie with Jack Kerouac and has the third generation of its family, Tony, doing some thirties-style hoboing during the fifties. As one monochromatic historical setting replaces another, the only area where Bakshi tries to render some detail and keep the action alive is in his characters' facial expressions, which he likes to show in close-up. But even the faces are bizarrely flaccid and inexpressive. Each of them moves like a waterbed on which somebody has just lain down. In fact, you might say Bakshi's whole film moves that way. (pp. 209-10)

Colin L. Westerbeck, Jr., "Too Pooped to Pop: Ralph Bakshi's Animation," in Commonweal *(copyright © 1981 Commonweal Publishing Co., Inc.; reprinted by permission of Commonweal Publishing Co., Inc.), Vol. CVIII, No. 7, April 10, 1981, pp. 209-10.*

Walter Becker
1950-

Donald Fagen
1948-

Photograph by Susan Singleton; reproduced by permission of Melody Maker

American songwriters.

Becker and Fagen write and record songs for the group Steely Dan. Because of their use of satire and complex imagery, their writing style has been compared to that of William Burroughs, from whose novel *Naked Lunch* the name Steely Dan derives. In their songs, Becker and Fagen comment on failed romances, drugs, revelations, and character transformations. Many critics feel that the songs of Becker and Fagen are self-consciously intellectual and that their style is the antithesis of the simple lyrics and elaborate stage shows prevalent in 1970s rock and roll.

Steely Dan's debut album, *Can't Buy a Thrill*, includes the hit songs "Do It Again" and "Reelin' in the Years." Their next

few albums are characterized by rueful irony and increasingly obscure lyrics. With *The Royal Scam*, however, Becker and Fagen's lyrics became easier to understand. The songs are about ordinary people trapped by crime and sexual passion, and the album has been referred to by Kenneth Tucker as "the ultimate 'outlaw' album." The songs on *Aja* use relatively few words to say as much as possible. They deal with relationships and breakdowns in communication between the narrator and numerous women.

Becker and Fagen describe Steely Dan as "more a concept than rock band" because they do not perform in concert or record with a specific group of musicians. Even so, their distinctively polished sound and elusive lyrics have gained for them a wide following among the pop music audience.

CHUCK MITCHELL

Steely Dan may be too good for its own good. The rock audience seems rather content lately to stagnate in its own shallow pool of pompous British art-rockers, somnabulistic middle-class folk-poets, and infantile southern boogie bands, while it waits lethargically with glitter on its eyelashes for the Beatles to regroup. Into this mess springs Steely Dan, with its short, lucid, offbeat melodies and literate, semi-obscure but meaningful lyrics. They're bound to either take off completely or become cult heroes. . . .

[There] is much to be reckoned with on *Pretzel Logic*, all of it smooth, elegant, and unacceptable only to those with the most neanderthal of commercial ears. . . .

[The] lyrical style of the band is cynically, sarcastically appropriate to the '70s. While not totally opaque, the words demand careful attention and some thought. More often than not, the visions they project are jaundiced and bleak. But the lyrics are also well-written; they use the language intelligently, which is all too rare these days.

Pretzel Logic presents us with a band that has much to say, and they say it with grace, wit, intelligence, and economy. Hopefully, the album has the power to place Steely Dan once again in that rare group whose work has artistic resonance, subtlety, and depth, as well as the ability to appeal to a vast audience.

> *Chuck Mitchell, in his review of "Pretzel Logic,"* in down beat *(copyright 1974; reprinted with permission of* down beat*), Vol. 41, No. 10, May 23, 1974, p. 18.*

BUD SCOPPA

Steely Dan is the most improbable hit-singles band to emerge in ages. On its three albums, the group has developed an impressionistic approach to rock & roll that all but abandons many musical conventions and literal lyrics for an unpredictable, free-roving style. . . . *Pretzel Logic* is an attempt to make complete musical statements within the narrow borders of the three-minute pop-song format. . . .

This band is never conventional, never bland.

And neither is its material. Despite the almost arrogant impenetrability of the lyrics . . . , the words create an emotionally charged atmosphere, and the best are quite affecting. While it's disconcerting to be stirred by language that resists comprehension, it's still difficult not to admire the open-ended ambiguity of the lyrics.

But along with *Pretzel Logic*'s private-joke obscurities (like the made-up jargon on **"Any Major Dude Will Tell You"** and **"Through With Buzz"**), there are concessions to the literal: **"Rikki Don't Lose That Number"** makes sense as a conventional lover's plea, while **"Barrytown"** takes a satirical look at class prejudice. But each has an emotional cutting edge that can't be attributed directly to its viewpoint or story. As writers, Fagen and Becker may be calculating, but they aren't cold.

> *Bud Scoppa, "Stainless Steely Band," in* Rolling Stone *(by Straight Arrow Publishers, Inc. © 1974; all rights reserved; reprinted by permission), Issue 161, May 23, 1974, p. 73.*

RICHARD CROMELIN

Steely Dan is about, among other things, connection. It's the 3,000-mile live wire buzzing between 60s New England school days and 70s Laurel Canyon Showbiz, steel handcuffs linking jazz with pop, the Archies with William Burroughs, a shifting patchwork of vindictiveness and tenderness. Connection on all levels, deliberate and wildly accidental. . . .

There are more, and shorter, songs [on *Pretzel Logic*] than on *Countdown to Ecstasy,* and while those maddening, fascinating references to private people, places and events still crop up, the overall feeling of the lyrics is significantly less obscure. The Dan evokes and suggests, yet the songs always feel complete and direct. . . . They seem confident that whatever you create out of what they suggest is going to hit the intended targets. The lushness of the music is tempered by their incomparable dry wit.

Though there's an uncharacteristic lack of import in some of the tunes (**"Parker's Band," "With a Gun"**) and unexpected mellowness in others (**"Any Major Dude Will Tell You," "Rikki Don't Lose That Number"**), it's the moments in which Walter Becker and Donald Fagen lash out from quicksand insecurity that remain the metallic heart of Steely Dan. **"Through with Buzz"** is one of the best. . . .

Another peak is **"Charlie Freak,"** the story of a down-and-out denizen of the streets who sells his precious ring to our hero, then ODs on the drugs he buys with the windfall. . . . The singer rushes to the morgue and returns the ring to the cold finger. . . . Go back, Jack, do it again. Connection. . . .

Steely Dan is the best band in America. . . . *Pretzel Logic* is great. Connect.

> *Richard Cromelin, in his review of "Pretzel Logic,"* in Creem *(© copyright 1974 by Creem Magazine, Inc.), Vol. 6, No. 2, July, 1974, p. 62.*

GEOFF BROWN

Often, at first, [Steely Dan's] music has to be approached through a mist of murky alienation (many of their lyrical themes are negative statements) and foggy intent which gradually disperses with the warmth of repetition and recognition.

Nevertheless it's a satisfying experience for the "cleverness" of the combo is never in question yet when pure talent applies and expresses itself obliquely the results are bound to need a shade more assimilation than the normal brainless, bone-crunching rock.

The heart of Steely Dan, writers Walter Becker and Donald Fagen, draw a thin veil across their purpose, expressing lyrics vaguely, not telling the whole story. . . . They are toying with inaccessibility but their grasp of attractive rock is sure as the list of US hit singles—**"Reeling In The Years," "Do It Again," "Rikki Don't Lose That Number"**—illustrates. . . .

"Katy Lied" doesn't have the heady impact of [**"Can't Buy A Thrill"**] and falls short of the masterful [**"Pretzel Logic"**], but like a slow unfolding tale, the album grows in stature by the play. . . .

"Daddy Don't Live In That New York City No More" is a hoot. Sugar daddy stops messing round in Big Apple and quits. A simple, witty song. . . .

"**Everyone's Gone To The Movies,**" a song from 1972, is, like "**Daddy,**" blessed by Dan's characteristic black humour. . . . "**Any World**" continues the theme of disenchantment, Dan's sure melodic touch belies the subject matter. It does on "**World**" and it does on the cynical "**Throw Back The Little Ones,**" which is testament to Fagen-Becker's understanding of the hustler on the city streets.

"**Katy Lied**" doesn't boast the welter of grand songs which set 1974's "**Pretzel Logic**" apart from the pack but in the coming year few albums will confound, intrigue and finally charm the listener as sneakily as Steely Dan's latest.

> *Geoff Brown, in his review of "Katy Lied," in* Melody Maker *(© IPC Business Press Ltd.), April 5, 1975, p. 24.*

JOHN MENDELSOHN

Steely Dan sound like a million dollars not only next to at least 26 of their coresidents of the Boss 30 when they're in it, but also in comparison to three-quarters of the stuff with which they share FM needletime. . . .

The words, while frequently not easy to get the definite drift of, are almost always intriguing and often witty. . . .

Why, then, do I—without the slightest intention of undermining anyone else's enthusiasm for it—find myself not caring if I ever again hear any of Steely Dan's music up to and including *Katy Lied*?

It has to do primarily with the fact that, however immaculately tasteful and intelligent it all may be, I *personally* am able to detect not the slightest suggestion of real passion in any of it. . . .

When it comes to the words . . . , I feel all too frequently as though I must choose between concluding that I'm a thickhead and suspecting that the Dan lyricist either is too lazy to make his stuff penetrable or else is oblique simply to conceal the fact that, however facilely he may string together unusual and interesting images, he really hasn't much to say through them. . . . I can make only the wildest guess as to what Messrs. Becker and/or Fagen wanted to tell me about their perception of the world. . . .

Steely Dan's music continues to strike me essentially as exemplarily well-crafted and uncommonly intelligent schlock.

> *John Mendelsohn, in his review of "Katy Lied," in* Rolling Stone *(by Straight Arrow Publishers, Inc. © 1975; all rights reserved; reprinted by permission), Issue 186, May 8, 1975, p. 66.*

MELODY MAKER

[Only the real Steely Dan fans listen hard enough to] know that "**Reelin' In The Years**" is as venomous as [Bob Dylan's] "Positively Fourth Street," or that "**Do It Again**" is a very black little tale about a born loser, or that "**King Of The World**" is, in fact, about the end of civilisation.

These are dark, even bitter, themes, and it's the special irony of this, the most ironic of rock groups, that their glossy musicianship should be a lick of paint upon a nest of Chinese boxes, in which moves intact a world so enigmatic and different in mood from the sunny image of hit-makers. Surely the disparity between their intentions and their reception by an au-

dience is quietly enjoyed by Steely Dan's principals and co-songwriters, Donald Fagen and Walter Becker, for this world of theirs is as cynical as it's brilliantly observed, a world in which they can sing, on "**Black Friday,**" a song about a stock market crash, . . . or, in "**With A Gun,**" outrageously set a jaunty, Beatlesque tune to a lyric about a psychopath.

Fagen and Becker show remarkable nerve and intelligence in their writing, which has a literary quality of coolness and detachment quite unusual in rock bands, but whose low-profile has also turned off or eluded some critics who, as American writer Robert Christgau once perceived, feel that art is dictated by Self-Expression and autobiographical imperatives. Steely Dan, on the contrary, have revealed practically nothing about themselves. . . .

It's tempting to speculate that the paradoxes in their work have been influenced by the fact that they are from the East Coast but now resident in California. . . . It might also be conjectured that their music has something of the West Coast bounce, while their lyrics retain the intellectual approach of an East Coast upbringing; their second album, in fact, "**Countdown To Ecstasy,**" was rooted in their adolescent experiences at Bard College in New York.

I believe for sure, however, that Steely Dan have made more consistently interesting records than any other rock group in the past four years, although this approval is not unstinted. Occasionally their lyrics have been so self-contained as to be disingenuous—mere private references that might work for the Dylan, say, of "Blonde On Blonde"/"Highway 61 Revisited", where the author positively invites the unbridled fantasies of his listeners, but which seem spurious within a body of work so generally controlled and economical. Yet riddles and mind-games are so obviously, and tantalisingly, a part of their writing that one eventually becomes a willing accomplice in the pursuit of their meaning, even when, one suspects in some cases, there is nothing definite. . . .

On "**The Royal Scam,**" therefore, it's hardly surprising that questions should be posed right from the cover, which shows a drawing of a man in an overcoat asleep on the top of a radiator as he dreams of tall skyscrapers surmounted by the giant heads of a lizard, a puma, a bat and some prehistoric animal. He's not quite a tramp, because there's a crease in his trousers and his shirt-cuffs are recognisable, and yet there's a large hole in one shoe. Someone well-to-do now down on his luck, no doubt, and oppressed in his dreams by the ferocity of the City—an interpretation partly supported by the title track itself, with its mysterious tale of foreigners from some unnamed country arriving in New York, and their eventual descent "to the bottom of a bad town amid the ruins." The measured, martial music keeps in step with the ominous inevitability of their fortunes, just as the pay-off in the chorus line ("see the glory of the Royal Scam" . . .) ironically suggests that they are the victims of some duplicity. But Fagen and Becker resist being more specific, and the album, which is closed by this track, leaves us suspended and fascinated by its great enigma.

Most of "**The Royal Scam,**" however, has relatively straightforward, if ingenious, lyrics. . . .

Title song to the contrary, "**The Royal Scam**" is, if anything, more lyrically accessible than "**Katy Lied,**" their previous record, which is the least melodically distinguished of all Steely Dan albums (though it contains two of their greatest songs in "**Black Friday**" and "**Doctor Wu**"). I wouldn't wish to say whether it's better than the other four. That's not a relevant question for me. Steely Dan records don't compete with each other, they co-exist. But I will say that I'm playing it to death.

And, of course, the listener doesn't have to delve into the lyrics. You can just tap your foot.

M.W., in a review of "Royal Scam," in Melody Maker *(© IPC Business Press Ltd.), May 8, 1976, p. 24 [the excerpt from Walter Becker's and Donald Fagen's lyrics used here was taken from "The Royal Scam" (© copyright 1976, 1978 by Duchess Music Corporation, New York, NY: used by permission; all rights reserved)].*

MICHAEL WATTS

[The first part of this excerpt contains criticism by Michael Watts; the second part is from an interview by Michael Watts with Walter Becker and Donald Fagen.]

Donald Fagen and Walter Becker are living proof that intelligence is still regarded with suspicion in rock and roll. I confess it annoys me that they are more persistently categorised as "oddballs" and "smartasses" rather than considerable songwriters, which is what they are, because rock music and literary qualities are still held to be incompatible even by those who write about rock. Or so it seems.

Yet I suppose that, ultimately, Fagen and Becker, progenitors of Steely Dan, have only themselves to blame for insisting upon erudition and references drawn from jazz, Latin and classical music, as well as pop, whilst concealing it all beneath shiny music that can demand very little beyond an acquiescent toe unless one wishes it; for the supreme irony of Steely Dan, with whom irony as a device is second-nature, is the apparent equanimity with which they go about being most things to all men and everything to a few. . . .

[Their] concerns are the most wide-ranging within rock writing, and have become the subjects for more interpretations than songs by any other artist since the Dylan of the period leading up to "John Wesley Harding." Not usually very specific—the most recent album, **"The Royal Scam,"** is the least difficult of the five—they range from the typically black little tale of a compulsive loser (**"Do It Again,"** the hit single from the first album, **"Can't Buy A Thrill"**) to the grandly worked title track of **"Royal Scam,"** which in three verses encapsulates an epic story of Puerto Rican settlement in New York. . . .

Nothing if not carefully constructed, their writing does not flow along with Dylan's stream-of-images; it relies upon nuance, upon literary style and the suggestion of atmosphere in a novelistic manner far removed from the traditional workings of the pop song.

In lyric terms, very few writers in rock—perhaps Randy Newman, Robbie Robertson, Joni Mitchell—are working as consciously towards the aesthetic experience; for a start, there is nothing in the whole of Becker-Fagen's output that is overtly autobiographical, which, because there's nothing except for the songs themselves to which the audience can relate, helps explain why Steely Dan seems so faceless.

Eng. Lit . . . looms large in the Steely Dan canon.

Of course, the name itself is an obscure term taken from William Burroughs' Naked Lunch.

But their literary influences range from the American black humorists (Vonnegut, Terry Southern, Nathanael West) through

to their (possibly) English counterpart, Evelyn Waugh, and on to such diverse writers as Beckett, Aldous Huxley, Voltaire, Nabokov, Borges and even Joseph Conrad.

Only their big interest in science fiction short stories, evident on another song from **"Scam," "Sign In Stranger,"** seems familiar from conversations with other rock performers. . . .

[They] are saved from any pretentiousness by a very bloody sense of humour that's employed both in their songs and on a personal level. (p. 24)

• • • • •

Do you see a specific mood for each album? . . .

Becker: We do try to put together a programme of songs that somehow hangs together.

Fagen: But mostly that's things like tempo.

Becker: Yeah, not in terms of themes, really. . . .

[Fagen:] You know, if there is a lyrical unity to each album it's simply because most of the songs on each album are written in a certain time period, and naturally a certain phase of our personalities would be prominent while the songs were written, and that would give it a lyrical unity, certainly. . . .

Let me ask you about individual songs, beginning with those on **"The Royal Scam."** . . .

"Kid Charlemagne," *for instance—could that be about a Leary or a Manson? Am I in the right direction?*

Fagen: You're on the right track. I think it would probably be about a person who's less of a celebrity than those people. . . .

"Sign In Stranger"—*that's almost like a school for gangsters?*

Fagen: That's true. Of course, it does take place on another planet. We sort of borrowed the Sin City/Pleasure Planet idea that's in a lotta science fiction novels, and made a song out of it. But, indeed, you're right. . . .

Is **"The Royal Scam"** *about Puerto Ricans trying to settle in New York?*

Fagen: Because the interpretation is so accurate I wouldn't even want to comment any further.

Becker: In other words, you already know more than is good for you.

Fagen: To tell you the truth, we tend to refrain from discussing specifics as far as lyrics go, because it is a matter of subjective interpretation, and there are some things that are better that man does not know. You are on the right track, and whatever you make of it will suffice. Really.

You leave yourself open to the interpretation of playing guessing games with your audience.

Becker: Well, hopefully the idea is that there won't be any guessing games. You see, you have a fairly precise picture in your mind of what is in that song, I can see, but when we write the songs we hope that a listener hearing that song who does not translate St. John into San Juan would still be able to enjoy the song without being too worried about what it means.

In other words, it should work for somebody who doesn't get nearly that far.

Yes, but it would work for him if he understood it, wouldn't it?

Becker: Well, maybe so, but I would hope it will work for him even if he considers it a complete fairy tale.

On some songs you are quite specific. **"Don't Take Me Alive"** *is a very specific song. I don't think people would have any problems understanding that.*

Becker: I shouldn't think so.

So why do you intend some songs to be very mystifying?

Becker: Well, it's not that it came out to be mystifying. We did decide to write that song in a kind of . . .

Fagen: Allegorical.

Becker: We were trying to imitate the inflection of a King James bible just a bit, so that made it vague necessarily.

Fagen: It's kind of like The Trinity, you know. We think we'd probably destroy the spell if we laid it on the line, you know what I mean? There's a certain mystique that that song depends upon for it to be effective.

Becker: We're not topical songwriters. We're trying always not to write the same lyric, but to write lyrics that have to do with something interesting; and so, when we get an idea on the lines of that one, we don't want it to sound like a Phil Ochs song . . .—may he rest in peace.

We don't want its political or social overtones to be so specific that someone who hasn't lived in New York would have no use for the song.

But one of the great virtues of your writing is that it's not autobiographical—or, at least, overtly.

Becker: That's another thing.

And neither is it hog-tied to a particular mood of the times, as is the case with so many rock writers.

Fagen: That's true. I guess one of the great cornerstones of what rock and roll is supposed to be is that it's somehow supposed to reflect now, the time we're living in, and not reflect back; and, in fact, there is very little reflection in rock and roll.

Becker: It's generally the cry of an anguished teenage soul. And we're not doing that too much anymore. . . .

Fagen: As far as specifics like that, our audience will have to trust our sincerity, just trust us in not just laying down some bulls—. When they think they don't understand something it's certainly not a random lyric.

It's been suggested that your writing is after the image of your own world, in the sense that you create a private world and your themes and lyrics relate more to that than the actual world outside it. Do you take the point?

Fagen: Well, I think it's more a way of viewing the actual world through our eyes. I think probably in our earlier works we were fantasising more than we do now. I think now we're synthesising what we see.

Becker: Nevertheless, it may be right in saying that the world crystallised through our eyes bears very little resemblance to anyone else's world, even though we think we're recording it as we see it.

We may be so bent that it's unrecognisable. I would like to think so. That would certainly make it more interesting. (p. 25)

What would you say were your main themes as writers?

Becker: Well, of course, we have all the usual ones. Unrequited love, destructive love, er . . .

Fagen: Self-destruction.

Becker: The erotic.

Fagen: Violence . . . Oh, we can write about anything. In fact, we were recently thinking of writing something about the Congress of Vienna, which is actually part of the reason I visited the Museum at Monaco, to get a little atmosphere.

We think the Congress of Vienna because it was a turning-point in European affairs, and we see certain parallels between that and what's going on now.

But that's yet to come. We haven't quite crystallised it yet, but we're thinking about it.

Becker: It will work out. If you can do that kind of thing without making it pretentious, that's the secret, because then you're dealing with really interesting and unusual subject matter, and still making it into a pop song that doesn't sound like a, er . . . Frank Zappa epic, or a Kinks musical comedy number.

Fagen: You see, we use that more as a starting-point to write a song which may, when it's finished, not suggest to anyone what we had in mind. The song that we wrote about the bierhalle putsch, for instance, no one ever had to think about the bierhalle putsch to think about that song. That's our method of writing a song: to have something in mind that may not actually be in the song. . . .

There's a feeling that underneath all your themes there's a pervasive tone of cynicism.

Becker: That's an accusation to which we are not unfamiliar.

Fagen: Well, we like to keep a certain distance from the protagonist.

Might not your music, therefore, be generally symptomatic of the times?

Becker: In terms of cynicism? Oh, I dunno. I don't think these are particularly cynical times. You just wait to see what's coming up! I'm inclined to think that things are going to become far more pessimistic. . . .

Would you say pessimism is a more accurate description for what you do?

Becker: No, I wouldn't say that. I suppose we are cynical by comparison to the people who are sincere, but musically I wouldn't have it any other way.

A song like **"Charlie Freak"** *is unusually tender when set beside most of your writing.*

Becker: Well, I think so, and hopefully those little glimmers of tenderness are all the more effective in the context they are in rather than a constant syrup being poured over our audience.

Fagen: In other words, without putting emotional limitations on what you're doing, tenderness is just sentiment rather than a true glimmer of affirmation, or whatever you wanna call it. . . .

I should tell you, though—sometimes, when we play an album back to sequence the songs, sometimes I get the feeling that we *are* hitting a little hard, that it's too *down*.

But it's getting back to what I was saying before: there's so much distance from what is actually happening to the protagonist of each song, to use a literary word.

In other words, when I sing a song I just take the role of narrator; I'm sort of acting out a part. It's really quite impersonal, although the music in me, and the words themselves, can be very personal—like **"Don't Take Me Alive"**, **"Kid Charlemagne"**.

Becker: I think we probably are conspicuous in our thematic concerns in rock and roll. But if we were novelists dealing with the subject matters of our songs it would not stick out as much, because in the literary field what we are writing about are more the traditional concerns than in rock and roll. (p. 26)

> *Michael Watts, "Steely Dan: Art for Art's Sake . . . ,"* in Melody Maker *(© IPC Business Press Ltd.), June 19, 1976, pp. 24-6.*

KENNETH TUCKER

With each successive album, Steely Dan's popular success and appeal become more obscured by sundry admirers' claims of abstruseness and complexity. To some it seems inevitable that the Dan will eventually produce the *Finnegans Wake* of rock. . . . Walter Becker and Donald Fagen bow to no one in the matter of composing immaculate, catchy cul-de-sacs, but it is that same immaculateness, the way the words, as impenetrable as they may appear, fit with metrical seamlessness into the melodies that makes their impenetrability of little importance to any casual listener caught up in the sound of the entire song.

That said, one must immediately note that their latest, *The Royal Scam,* is the Dan's most atypical record, possessing neither obvious AM material nor seductive lyrical mysteriousness. . . .

[On *The Royal Scam* there] is little of the self-confident gentleness that dotted *Pretzel Logic,* less still of the omniscience that suffused *Katy Lied. The Royal Scam* is a transitional album for Steely Dan; melody dominates lyric in the sense that the former pushes into new rhythmic areas for the group . . . while the verbal content is clearer, even mundane, by previous Dan standards.

While *Scam* is certainly not a concept album, every song—with the possible exception of **"The Fez"**—concerns a narrator's escape from a crime or sin recently committed. Becker and Fagen have really written the ultimate "outlaw" album here, something that eludes myriad Southern bands because their concept of the outlaw is so limited. Rather than just, say, robbing banks (**"Don't Take Me Alive,"** in which the robber is a "bookkeeper's son"), Becker and Fagen's various protagonists are also solipsistic jewel thieves (**"Green Earrings"**), spendthrift divorcees (**"Haitian Divorce"**) and murderously jealous lovers (**"Everything You Did"**).

But the Dan's outlaws are also moral ones, guilt-ridden over comparatively minor sins. . . . **"Kid Charlemagne"** is a selfish egotist, and suffers for it. **"The Fez,"** a sort of Dan-esque answer to Randy Newman's "You Can Leave Your Hat On," concerns a rather pathetic, if kinky, megalomaniac. At their best, these songs yield up concise surrealist introspection; at their worst, they suggest a paranoid death wish that is very

amusing, if a bit unnerving. The lyrics are also pretty histrionic, and perhaps should not be scrutinized too solemnly.

In any event, I doubt that Steely Dan will ever become merely precious or insular; through five albums they have consistently circumvented their complexity with passionate snazziness and fluky, cynical wit. (p. 66)

> *Kenneth Tucker, in his review of "The Royal Scam,"* in Rolling Stone *(by Straight Arrow Publishers, Inc. ©1976; all rights reserved; reprinted by permission), Issue 216, July 1, 1976, pp. 66-7.*

PETE MATTHEWS

[*The Royal Scam*] has wormed its way into my subconscious far faster than its slightly less sharply focused precursor, *Katy Lied.* . . .

Most so-called artists working in rock are reduced to self-parody after five albums, but [Becker and Fagen] refine and develop their terminally depressive vision like the true masters they are. The melodies are sharper than ever on this collection, and the lyrics somehow more direct. I've never supported the notion that they were deliberately misleading in the past, because their sub-obsession with the passage of time and its effect on relationships lend itself to the aural equivalent of, say, *Last Year in Marienbad.* . . .

Here, the preoccupations are mostly contemporary, not too wide-ranging if in the future or the past, and neatly signposted: *Haitian Divorce* allows the stage whispered "Now we dolly back, Now we fade to black" to set the scene for a cunningly unfaithful spouse to return home; a mind-bending Californian chemist from the 1960s finds himself transmuted into obsolescence; cave paintings silently scream a message across recorded history; the fetishist pleads "Don't make me do it without the fez on" to a disco beat; a sexual victim is seduced for a pair of earrings—and, in a stately musical setting, *The Royal Scam* itself comes into view: a biblically phrased allegory chronicling the waves of immigrants who poured into the land of milk and honey from the land of cows and bees without checking the price tag on the goodies. For me, at any rate, this is seventies rock at its most incisive—and, as such, is indispensable.

> *Pete Matthews, in his review of "The Royal Scam" (© copyright Pete Matthews 1976; reprinted with permission),* in Records and Recording, *Vol. 19, No. 11, August, 1976, p. 78 [the excerpt of Walter Becker's and Donald Fagen's lyrics used here was taken from "Haitian Divorce" (© copyright 1976, 1978 by Duchess Music Corporation, New York, NY; used by permission; all rights reserved); the excerpt of Walter Becker's, Donald Fagen's and Paul L. Griffin's lyrics used here was taken from "The Fez" (© copyright 1976 by Duchess Music Corporation, New York, NY; used by permission; all rights reserved)].*

MICHAEL WATTS

"Aja" sounds graceful, rounded, *complete.* But it is also a little dry, as if from constant refinement. The reason lies not in the familiar usurpation of technique, but in the exacting ambitions of Becker and Fagen, forever trying to integrate their jazz affections with pop appeal. For all its brilliant polish and acute sensibilities, **"Aja"** has less surface attraction than any other Steely Dan album.

However, although the ambience may strike some as cerebral, Steely Dan continue to work within a recognisable format of song. There is much here that I find memorable, and most of all **"Deacon Blues,"** a relatively straightforward ballad—"languid and bitter-sweet," to borrow one of its own lines—that seems to be about the night-club musician as a kind of existentialist figure.

The mood is film noir. . . . And the chorus . . . is just about the most haunting they have written, with its images of roulette wheels spinning and Scotch tossed back while the saxophonist plays his own lonesome song.

Their lyrics, indeed, remain as allusive and elusive as ever. They still invite guessing games, and I would say if anything that the songs on **"Aja"** are about relationships, or lack of them, with women. **"Black Cow"** . . . is a put-down of a swinger or hooker. **"Josie"** is about the good-natured local lay. **"Peg"** has a sarcastic lyric about a model.

And **"I Got The News"** features a very clever dialogue with a rich girl whom the author is at that moment screwing! . . . Even **"Deacon Blues,"** in true Bogey fashion, has the "hero" kissing his girl goodbye and walking away.

Finally, **"Home At Last,"** which is a kind of up-date of the Homeric tale of Odysseus and Penelope, recounts the sailor's traditional fickleness with women; while **"Aja,"** which perhaps has the most specific lyric, is about a girl (Oriental) to whom the narrator always returns.

Throughout the album Steely Dan exemplify the art, little understood in pop music, of saying as much as possible in as few words. And no-one better appreciates the literary technique of irony.

> *Michael Watts, "Steely Dan: More Enigma Variations," in* Melody Maker *(© IPC Business Press Ltd.), September 17, 1977, p. 18.*

MICHAEL DUFFY

The title cut is the one song on *Aja* that shows real growth in Becker's and Fagen's songwriting capabilities and departs from their previous work. It is the longest song they've recorded, but it fragilely holds our attention with vaguely Oriental instrumental flourishes and lyric references interwoven with an opiated jazz flux. **"Aja"** may prove to be the farthest Becker and Fagen can take certain elements of their musical ambition.

Lyrically, these guys still seem to savor the role they must have acquired as stoned-out, hyperintelligent pariahs at a small Jewish college on the Hudson. Their imagery can become unintelligibly weird (Frank Zappa calls it "downer surrealism"); it's occasionally accessible but more often (as on the title song) it elicits a sort of déjà vu tease that becomes hopelessly nonsensical the more you think about it. Focus your attention on the imagery of a specific phrase, then let it fade out. . . .

The last album, *The Royal Scam,* was the closest thing to a "concept" album Steely Dan has done, an attempt to return musically to New York City, with . . . a fascination with grim social realism. The farthest *Aja* strays from the minor joys and tribulations of the good life in L.A. are the dreamy title cut and **"Josie,"** which hints ominously about a friendly welcome-home gang-bang. The melodramatic **"Black Cow"** is about love replaced by repulsion for a woman who starts getting too strung out on downers and messing around with other men. **"Deacon Blues"** (a thematic continuation of **"Fire in the Hole"**

and **"Any World"**) exemplifies this album's mood: resignation to the L.A. musician's lifestyle. . . . (p. 76)

More than any of Steely Dan's previous albums (with the possible exception of *Katy Lied*), *Aja* exhibits a carefully manipulated isolation from its audience, with no pretense of embracing it. What underlies Steely Dan's music—and may, with this album, be showing its limitations—is its extreme intellectual self-consciousness, both in music and lyrics. Given the nature of these times, this may be precisely the quality that makes Walter Becker and Donald Fagen the perfect musical antiheroes for the Seventies. (pp. 76-7)

> *Michael Duffy, "Dazed at the Dude Ranch," in* Rolling Stone *(by Straight Arrow Publishers, Inc. © 1977; all rights reserved; reprinted by permission), Issue 253, December 1, 1977, pp. 74, 76-7.*

JON PARELES

They all look alike. The casings are always bland. The sauce, however tasty, is an afterthought. What matters is what's inside, and by the time you know if it's any good, the dumpling is gone.

Steely Dan—Walter Becker and Donald Fagen—do nothing unself-consciously. So it's entirely likely that in **"Glamour Profession"** on their new album, *Gaucho*, the coke dealer chooses Szechuan dumplings as celebratory chow in an offhand metaphor for Becker and Fagen's songwriting. With *Gaucho*'s seven songs—which, in the first few plays but not thereafter, tend to sound alike—the casings are the adult-contemporary arrangements, the sauce is the piquant solos and horn charts, and the meat—wait a minute. Is there meat in any pop song?

I think so, although one listener's meat is another's Twinkie. Sometimes popmakers know what the meat of a song is, sometimes not. My operational definition: it's the part that drives your friends crazy, because every time you hear it, you sing along. It can be, but isn't always, a hook; it can be an isolated moment (the scream in [The Rolling Stones's] "Gimme Shelter"), a gimmick (the auto ignition in [Roxy Music's] "Love Is the Drug"), a rhythm (the intro to [Talking Heads's] "Artists Only"), a quirk (Dylan's pauses in "Memphis Blues Again"), a lyric ("and this loneliness won't leave me alone"), and especially the combinations.

Steely Dan's catalogue offers all of the above, in abundance. Yet Becker and Fagen apparently disdain such easy pleasures. As far as they're concerned, their dumplings are packed with songwriterly subtleties like unusual forms, tip-of-the-iceberg lyrics, polytonality, extended melodies. Ideally, what pulls you into their songs isn't identification, but curiosity—sometimes overtly analytic, sometimes just a vague sense that something strange is going on. With each successive album, Becker and Fagen have cut down on anything that might distract from the songs themselves, banishing flash, flippancy, loose ends, and nonstructural surprises. . . . [The] emphasis on smoothness also has a lot to do with Becker and Fagen's continuing mission: to push pop as far as it will go.

Not to destroy it, or even undermine it. *Gaucho* includes some of the oddest, densest Steely Dan songs yet. . . .

The real break with the rest of Steely Dan's repertoire is in the lyrics. The irony is muted (but still there, as "Living hard will take its toll" is undercut by the rest of **"Glamour Profession"**), the humor damped down, but there's a perverse optimism. On their last few albums, the songs have been about outsiders—trapped, exiled, about to get stomped—while on **"Gaucho,"** the outsiders have the upper hand as the normals grumble. The coke dealer, the gaucho, the rival, the 19-year-old, and the guru (in **"Time Out of Mind"**) are all smiling and jolly, while the narrators of **"My Rival," "Babylon Sisters," "Gaucho,"** and **"Hey Nineteen"** contemplate existential crises. Maybe Becker and Fagen are telling themselves that they can vacate the middle of the road—they don't have to crawl like vipers through suburban streets, they can buy the ranch (house). *Gaucho* is as subtle as they'll ever have to be.

Jon Pareles, "Steely Dan's Szechuan Dumplings" (reprinted by permission of The Village Voice *and the author; copyright © News Group Publications, Inc., 1980), in* The Village Voice, *Vol. XXV, No. 49, December 3-9, 1980, p. 85.*

ARIEL SWARTLEY

The thing you begin to notice, listening to Steely Dan's songs, is that no one ever answers anyone. For all the talk—and their latest album, *Gaucho,* is as compulsively chatty as dinnertime on death row—there's no conversation. Whoever keeps asking, "Who is that gaucho, amigo?" might as well be talking to the wall. (p. 41)

Naturally, the guy gets a little hysterical as the game goes on, but not so much so that he can't remember details—such as everything that freaky gaucho was wearing. To Steely Dan's constantly talking heads, surfaces seem very clear. It's only people who are indistinct: shadow figures, possibly hallucinations, always unknown quantities.

But sometimes that's a godsend. In **"Hey Nineteen,"** the satire is straightforward enough. Between a thirty-five-year-old's nostalgia and a nineteen-year-old's nonchalance, there's not a lot of rapport. . . . Yet the composition ends in a blessedly fuzzy epiphany, with the generation gap bridged by Cuervo Gold and fine Columbian. The labels are important—Steely Dan's characters seem to know the world exclusively through brand names. These characters are the true "heads": solitarily

confined intelligences who've had to order all their experience from a catalog. But oh, with the right blurring agents, not knowing can be a beautiful thing.

It's always been a problem with Steely Dan to figure out who's being ironic about whom: Walter Becker and Donald Fagen's cynicism blasts pretty indiscriminately. (pp. 41, 52)

[The] metamorphosis that began with *The Royal Scam* is complete. Steely Dan have perfected the aesthetic of the tease. Their sound is as slippery as their irony. Are those the trumpets of angels near the end of the title tune? Could that slouching gaucho, the one denied a room in the singer's high-rise inn, be the new messiah? On *Gaucho,* the melodies are questions, too—long-winded, probing, unresolved.

There are people who will tell you that that's not enough. That Steely Dan have fallen into the dread imitative fallacy, making a record as desolate as the self-absorbed paranoids they describe. But I don't think so. For all their sneering sendups of the superficial, the current and the hip—their name-dropping characters, those Szechuan dumplings at Mr. Chow's—they take a sensualist's delight in names and surfaces. Donald Fagen's tongue slithers over a phrase like "Brut and charisma," tasting the syllables, appreciating the copywriter's wit in the civilized machismo of the continental spelling. That appreciation of, and absorption in, detail lends substance to Steely Dan's obsession with surfaces. And, accuracy being satire's cutting edge, it also makes their songs funnier than their characters realize.

Yet *Gaucho* is more than a good laugh or a twinge of recognition. If you leave a question hanging long enough, it becomes practically metaphysical. (Are you with me, Dr. Wu?) And that's a loophole big enough to let the angels in. If, like Steely Dan's characters, you're not quite sure about what's real, then you have no way of knowing what's out of the question either. (pp. 52, 54)

Ariel Swartley, "'Gaucho': The Art of Aesthetic Tease," in Rolling Stone *(by Straight Arrow Publishers, Inc. © 1981; all rights reserved; reprinted by permission), Issue 336, February 5, 1981, pp. 41, 52, 54.*

Gunnel Beckman

1910-

Swedish novelist and editor.

Beckman explores social themes as they relate to young adults. Her compassionate and realistic depictions of maturing characters suddenly faced with monumental concerns have earned the respect of both critics and readers.

Among the problems Beckman's young protagonists must deal with are death, the loneliness of living on one's own, and the various consequences, both emotional and physical, that arise from being sexually active. One of Beckman's most outstanding protagonists, Mia, of *Mia Alone* and *That Early Spring*, must make complex decisions as she faces pregnancy and an agonizing loneliness. *That Early Spring* has been commended for the sensitive, mutually beneficial relationship that develops between Mia and her aged grandmother.

Although some of the conflicts presented in Beckman's novels have been called melodramatic, the responses of her characters are considered refreshingly unique and believable. The credibility of her characters and their situations is not accidental; Beckman has based many of them on her experiences as a probation officer in her hometown of Solna.

(See also *Contemporary Authors*, Vols. 33-36, rev. ed. and *Something about the Author*, Vol. 6.)

Courtesy of Gunnel Beckman

KIRKUS REVIEWS

[*Admission to the Feast* presents stream] of consciousness meditations on her 19 year life and imminent death typed out in anguish by Annika Hallin after learning—accidentally—that she has leukemia. What begins as random expressions of disbelieving grief, opinions on the state of the world . . . , and remembered lines of poetry, soon coalesces into a memoir of her recently deceased alcoholic father. Rejecting the available bottle of sleeping pills, Annika soon begins to long in spite of herself for comfort from her boyfriend Jacob—whose intellectual dominance she'd only begun to resist. The final suggestion that Jacob may need her help (did he try to cross the thin ice of the lake on his way to her isolated cabin?) is somehow a less than satisfactory way of demonstrating her commitment to the days of life still ahead. . . . Annika is not profound enough to come to a real accommodation with death, but her gropings toward understanding and acceptance have a universal validity. Her reactions could be anyone's given the circumstances—there lie the story's limitations, and also its undeniable fascination.

> A review of "Admission to the Feast," in Kirkus Reviews (copyright © 1972 The Kirkus Service, Inc.), Vol. XL, No. 18, September 15, 1972, p. 1106.

ANITA SILVEY

[In *Admission to the Feast* Annika Gerd Maria Hallin] confronts her own death from leukemia. . . . After learning about her plight, Annika flees to her family's summer cottage to face solitarily becoming "nothing, nothing in the infinity of in-

finity." In a letter to a friend, written like a stream-of-consciousness narrative, Annika pours out her heightened sensations about the beauty of the world around her, her struggle to find an identity of her own making, the events of her reconciliation a few months earlier with the father she had not seen for years, and—as the days go on—her awareness of her growing ability to confront death with dignity. By the end of the story, she anticipates seeing her fiancé Jacob and will face with him what she has worked out alone. . . . Grim and stark and powerful, the book explores emotions rarely touched upon in children's literature—and does so honestly and frankly. A haunting story which blends Annika's desperate situation with a fragmented, urgent writing style.

> Anita Silvey, in her review of "Admission to the Feast," in The Horn Book Magazine (copyright © 1972 by The Horn Book, Inc., Boston), Vol. XLVIII, No. 5, October, 1972, p. 474.

MARGARET A. DORSEY

Through a letter written to a friend, 19-year-old Annika Hallin tells most effectively of her discovery of and reaction to having leukemia [in *Admission to the Feast*]. . . . In the letter, written over a 48-hour period, she recounts the events of the recent past—her love affair with Jacob, her unexpected reconciliation with her long-absent father and his subsequent death, her relationship with her mother, her summer job as an aide in an old people's home, observations of the early spring countryside—and reminiscences about childhood memories. The ending is stunning in its ambiguity: the possibility that Jacob may have been killed accidentally in his hurry to reach the cottage; that Annika might commit suicide; that everything might turn out happily. The avoidance of a neat wrap up is the capstone to a well-controlled story with fresh, balanced characterizations. Teenage girls will find it easy to identify with Annika's conflicting feelings about Jacob and her own identity and appreciate the well-handled treatment of an admittedly melodramatic situation. The author has resisted the many obvious opportunities to preach on subjects ranging from individual happiness to social justice, allowing the fully-developed character of Annika to speak for herself. (pp. 63-4)

> *Margaret A. Dorsey, in her review of "Admission to the Feast," in* School Library Journal, *an appendix to* Library Journal *(reprinted from the December, 1972 issue of* School Library Journal, *published by R. R. Bowker Co./A Xerox Corporation; copyright © 1972), Vol. 19, No. 4, December, 1972, pp. 63-4.*

ZENA SUTHERLAND

She cannot write to the people who love her most, her fiance and her mother, because what Annika [in ***Admission to the Feast***] has to say would shock them too much. She writes to an old friend, and her story is grim and pathetic, yet not morbid. Due to a young doctor's careless remark, Annika has just discovered that she has incurable cancer. . . . In her long letter, she describes a meeting with her father, whom she had met the year before after not seeing him (divorce) since she was a very small child, she tells her friend Helen about her love affair, she describes the agony she feels and her adjustment to the fact that she is going to die. Translated from the Swedish title ***Tilltråde Till Festen,*** the story may be found depressing by some readers, but it is strong and candid, remarkably varied and well-paced for a monologue, and certainly unusual in its theme.

> *Zena Sutherland, in her review of "Admission to the Feast," in* Bulletin of the Center for Children's Books *(reprinted by permission of The University of Chicago Press; © 1973 by The University of Chicago), Vol. 26, No. 8, April, 1973, p. 118.*

SISTER MARY COLUMBA OFFERMAN

[***A Room of His Own***] is a candid account of the confusions, problems, apprehensions, and anguish of today's young people. The author does not give answers regarding politics, sex, war, or pornography.

Anders, the main character, goes to the city to school. He is homesick, finds it hard to make friends, cannot adjust to situations and people. His apprehensions sap the energy needed to enjoy school life. He is tempted to return to his small, home town to work in his father's grocery store and disregard his many dreams for the future. Monica Tornquist, a teenage girl who lives upstairs in the same building, is a concern of Anders. She is always in trouble of one kind or other—with the police, her mother, motorcycle gangs, etc. His every effort to befriend her meets with defeat. Anders finally concludes that, like himself, Monica has to make her own decision about what she is to do with her life.

> *Sister Mary Columba Offerman, in her review of "A Room of His Own," in* Best Sellers *(copyright 1974, by the University of Scranton), Vol. 34, No. 6, June 15, 1974, p. 148.*

DALE CARSON

Very little is coherent about ["**A Room of His Own,**" the] story of a boy on his own for the first time in a big city. His feelings about himself are muddled, his feelings about the family he left behind are muddled, his relationship to the girl who lives in his building is muddled. There is no plot to speak of, no story to tell, no discovery, no resolution. The outpouring of adolescent ruminations is depressingly unrevealing.

Anders, a young Swedish boy who has left his home town to go to school in Stockholm, has taken his own room in a boarding house. His major problems are homesickness, loneliness and guilt at leaving his family to their problems. In the same boarding house lives a young girl, Monica, who can't stay out of trouble—fast friends, drugs, difficulties with her mother. Anders becomes briefly involved with her troubles. That's the story.

Possibly part of the problem with the book is the translation from Swedish [by Joan Tate]. But I don't think so. As the prose is insufficient, so is the plot, the characterization, the conception. It's just a muddled, dull story about another teenager struggling through his adolescence, with little insight, insignificant relationships and little meaning.

> *Dale Carson, in a review of "A Room of His Own," in* The New York Times Book Review *(© 1974 by The New York Times Company; reprinted by permission), June 23, 1974, p. 8.*

PEGGY SULLIVAN

Several plot strands are inexpertly threaded through [***A Room of His Own***]. . . . Anders' parents' health and economic problems, the conflict between a rebellious girl and her mother who live upstairs, and Anders' growing need for identity and sexual maturity are superficially treated. Needless profanity and stylistic awkwardness further detract from the novel. Though there are a couple of interesting characters and entertaining incidents (e.g., flashbacks of Anders' relationships with his grandfather and an elderly neighbor in Stockholm) they do not compensate for the book's weaknesses.

> *Peggy Sullivan, in her review of "A Room of His Own," in* School Library Journal, *an appendix to* Library Journal *(reprinted from the September, 1974 issue of* School Library Journal, *published by R. R. Bowker Co./A Xerox Corporation; copyright © 1974), Vol. 21, No. 1, September, 1974, p. 97.*

THE TIMES LITERARY SUPPLEMENT

Gunnel Beckman's new book [***Mia,*** published in the United States as ***Mia Alone,***] is outstanding less for its nuances and artistry, though these are present, than for its willingness to look fearlessly and with compassion at the terrible moral problems with which liberal thinking on sexual freedom can confront the young. Like Mrs Beckman's earlier books (***Admission to the Feast*** and ***A Room of his Own***) ***Mia*** is very far from being a documentary novel of the dry conventional kind; everything she writes is informed not only with fact but with abundant feeling. Here her heart is with Mia, a sixteen-year-old who has slept with her boyfriend and who discovers to her horror that her period is long overdue. Lesser writers than Mrs Beckman might have allowed Mia's self-absorption with her physical state and its practical as well as emotional problems to obscure the picture of the family of which Mia herself is a treasured part. But this is a portrait of a Swedish family, itself on the brink of collapse—so that, in sorting out her own problems (one of which is concerned simply with getting enough money to have a pregnancy test), Mia must also cope with the distress of her mother and father over their failing marriage and decide whether she can add her anxiety to theirs. Mia's anguish over the moral dilemma of abortion, and her agonizing over the decision whether to go through with pregnancy and an over-early marriage, pregnancy and single parenthood, or pregnancy and adoption are always painful and thought-provoking. It may all look easy in *Nova* and *Cosmopolitan,* but anyone who reads Mia's story and suffers with her will emerge saddened, exhausted and closer to the truth.

"Teenage Problems," in The Times Literary Supplement *(© Times Newspapers Ltd. (London) 1974; reproduced from The Times Literary Supplement by permission), No. 3785, September 20, 1974, p. 1003.* *

PAMELA D. POLLACK

Suspense is meant to mount [in *Mia Alone*] as Mia Järeberg marks time awaiting results of her pregnancy test, but there's no need for nail biting since the scare is just that. Mia gets "the curse" (a surprising Victorianism for a modern-day story set in sexually free Sweden) and Beckman gets an easy way out of the not-so-simple issues raised: Mother had to get married before abortion on demand and where would Mia be if . . . ; boyfriend Jan opposes the operation . . . ; Mia's option to choose abortion means accepting responsibility for her own body; etc. Lacking any concrete action, the story becomes a bloodless marathon talk fest. Still, Beckman keeps a lid on moralizing and melodrama, and the absence of some of the genre's creakier conventions—one-shot pregnancies (here it's five times); Neanderthal parents (though in the throes of divorce, Mr. Järeberg is a model supportive father); bad-guy boyfriends (well-meaning Jan offers marriage)—makes this a mild improvement over run-of-the-abortion-mill tracts. . . .

Pamela D. Pollack, in her review of "Mia Alone," in School Library Journal *(reprinted from the January, 1975 issue of* School Library Journal, *published by R. R. Bowker Co./A Xerox Corporation; copyright © 1975), Vol. 21, No. 5, January, 1975, p. 52.*

PUBLISHERS WEEKLY

[In **"Mia Alone,"** Mia] is sure she's pregnant but unsure about the morality of abortion. Her lover, Jan, is dead against abortion and wants them to marry. But Mia, who knows to her sorrow that her parents married only because her birth was imminent, feels that such a union would be wrong. The book is candid; the girl arouses sympathy. Young readers will be keen to know how she resolves her difficulties, but annoyed by the author, who fudges the issue and the ending.

A review of "Mia Alone" in Publishers Weekly *(reprinted from the March 10, 1975 issue of* Publishers Weekly, *published by R. R. Bowker Company, a*

Xerox company; copyright © 1975 by Xerox Corporation), Vol. 207, No. 10, March 10, 1975, p. 57.

MARGERY FISHER

The Loneliness of Mia [published in the United States as *That Early Spring*] does at least broaden the terms of reference which, in the earlier *Mia,* seemed painfully narrow. Mia's concern is not now exclusively with her own body and she shows herself capable of responding with some emotional strength to the troubles that now beset her—her parents' separation and the loss of her boy friend Jan. As an outlet for her feelings she turns to Martin, a music student who has no intention of treating her as anything but a pastime and a pleasant companion. Far more rewarding, in fact, is the confidence the girl places in her grandmother, who is able to help her to some sense of proportion, especially in regard to the Women's Liberation movement which Mia and her school friends endlessly discuss. Here the stylistic rigidity of the book is most in evidence. Conversations, especially in a group of young people, are neither naturally consistent nor orderly. . . . In *The Loneliness of Mia* we hear the sound of a debating society, not of an informal group talking naturally about what truly concerns them. The result is not—could never be—good fiction. (p. 2644)

Margery Fisher, "Family Ties," in her Growing Point, *Vol. 14, No. 1, May, 1975, pp. 2642-45.* *

JONATHAN KEATES

[Gunnel Beckman] appears to have laboured under the popular misconception that anyone with enough common sense can write fiction. The success of her *Mia* . . . was due far more to its careful analysis of adolescent sexual dilemma than to nice points of art. Two years later [in *The Loneliness of Mia*] the heroine has ditched Jan in favour of Martin, a smoothie with a neat line in unbuttoning blouses, and has become an enthusiastic member of a women's group. Superior kitsch though much of the writing is, we are never left in doubt as to the piety of the author's aims and the breadth of her understanding.

Jonathan Keates, "Occult," in New Statesman *(© 1975 The Statesman & Nation Publishing Co. Ltd.), Vol. 89, No. 2304, May 16, 1975, p. 668.* *

MARY HOBBS

[In *The Loneliness of Mia*] Mia has broken with her boyfriend, who has not been at all changed by all they have gone through. She has the idea of bringing her father's mother from an old people's home to live with them. The brave old woman is prepared to risk shortening her own life in order to be useful, and feel wanted by her son and grand-daughter. She gives Mia the benefit of her wise experience, not only on relationships, but on Women's Lib. Swedish feminist problems have been different from ours, but the principles remain the same. It is not a dramatic subject, and the weakest part of the book is the non-debate in Mia's flat with Grandma, a mere excuse for crusading quotations, in preparation for a class discussion on the emancipation of women. Though we become closely involved with the family, and teenage loneliness and death are most sensitively and understandingly presented, not all parents, teachers or librarians will feel happy about putting before older girls such matter-of-fact acceptance by the adults, from Grandma and the author onwards, of pre-marital sex, providing one is on the pill. (pp. 208-09)

> *Mary Hobbs, in her review of "The Loneliness of Mia," in* The Junior Bookshelf, *Vol. 39, No. 3, June, 1975, pp. 208-09.*

HILDAGARDE GRAY

Topics come and go as surely as the seasons—remember a few years ago when every other juvenile fiction was student rebellion, or black-white problems, then drugs, then divorce and runaways—now abortion/pre-marital sex is in. . . .

Mia Alone is on the abortion bandwagon. It gives no solutions, no sound advice, no pattern to follow. But it offers what many others have not—the barren feeling of loneliness that is the common denominator for all deeds falling outside social structure; the leader and the renegade alike share this, the young and the old, the male and the female.

While trying to decide on abortion as an answer to possible pregnancy, Mia learns that ultimately we are all alone—and much strength is needed to face this fact and carry on. There should be no hesitation in placing this book in either religious or public school, since no stand is taken. The hell of decision is the same everywhere.

> *Hildagarde Gray, in her review of "Mia Alone," in* Best Sellers *(copyright © 1975 Helen Dwight Reid Educational Foundation), Vol. 35, No. 4, July, 1975, p. 95.*

KIRKUS REVIEWS

The solitude of *Mia Alone* . . . ends fortuitously [in *That Early Spring*] when Gram comes from the old age home to share the lonely apartment Mia and her Dad have inhabited since Mother and sister Lillian moved to the country. Gram's reminiscences of a time when her husband was also her legal guardian and her confession that "the last time I slept with your grandfather, he was 72" are the foundation of an affectionate solidarity, unlike any Mia has shared with her reserved, preoccupied parents. Yet Gram's confidences also make Mia uncomfortably aware of the gulf between the earnest discussions of sex roles in her school study group and her passive, romantic crush on Martin, an "older" man of 21 who introduces her to liberated sex. Mia eventually summons the courage to announce to Martin that "freedom isn't just for *men* . . . I don't want to be a sex machine." . . . Mia's equation of personal and societal ills and the schoolgirl seriousness with which she attacks both simultaneously may be peculiarly Scandinavian, yet the characters of Gram (a major presence here and never merely a

colorful oldster) and of Martin, the likably ingenuous sexist, have dimensions that go beyond the issues they represent.

> *A review of "That Early Spring," in* Kirkus Reviews *(copyright © 1977 The Kirkus Service, Inc.), Vol. XLV, No. 3, February 1, 1977, p. 97.*

ALLEEN PACE NILSEN

Today there is a lot of talk about the negative or non-existent portrayal of old people in books for young readers. *That Early Spring* can serve as a counterbalance. The main focus of this sequel to *Mia Alone* is the productive and satisfying relationship that develops between Mia and her grandmother during the last months of her grandmother's life. . . .

[In some ways *That Early Spring*] is less promising than either *Mia Alone* or the earlier *Admission to the Feast*. In one part there is a discussion group meeting at Mia's apartment in which the grandmother participates. The discussion of feminist views which ensues seems didactic rather than a natural outgrowth of the story. Nevertheless, the characterization of Mia is excellent and the reader shares her fears, uncertainties, and annoyance at herself because she can't quite match her feminist views with her romantic feelings.

> *Alleen Pace Nilsen, in her review of "That Early Spring" (copyright © 1977 by the National Council of Teachers of English; reprinted by permission of the publisher and the author), in* English Journal, *Vol. 66, No. 6, September, 1977, p. 86.*

BOB DIXON

Mia and *The Loneliness of Mia* are less outstanding as works of literature [than some young adult novels], I would say, but then they are on a smaller scale. For young people of about thirteen and over, they deal in an outspoken way with sexual questions teenagers have to come to terms with. However, this is all within a context of relationships. Mia, her parents and her grandmother—and even another generation has to be taken into account while Mia is possibly pregnant—all these are linked by questions of love and responsibility, one generation to another. In the first book, especially, powerful emotions are handled with understanding and realism. . . . It seems to me that Beckman tries to deal with too many very serious problems at once and therefore the overall structure of her work suffers. Her clear-sightedness and honesty, however, compel attention. Here is a writer dealing with the world of today. (p. 39)

> *Bob Dixon, "Sexism: Birds in Gilded Cages," in his* Catching Them Young 1: Sex, Race and Class in Children's Fiction *(copyright © Pluto Press 1977), Pluto Press, 1977, pp. 1-41.**

Sue Ellen Bridgers

1942-

American novelist and short story writer.

In her work, Bridgers draws from her roots as a small town Southerner and reveals her fascination with family relationships. She has been generally praised for her vivid characterizations; her female characters are particularly outstanding, showing strength in their personal convictions and their ability to support and assist those around them.

In her highly acclaimed first novel, *Home Before Dark*, Bridgers relates the plight of a migrant family in the changing rural South through the eyes of a fourteen-year-old female protagonist. A teenage girl is also the main character in Bridgers's second novel, *All Together Now*, which explores the themes of loyalty and communication among various groups of people. Bridgers's recent novel *Notes for Another Life* focuses on a teenage brother and sister who have been abandoned by their parents.

Most critics agree that Bridgers's work demonstrates pervasive optimism without lapsing into sentimentality. Her characters, whether central or peripheral, are skillfully drawn and their problems and solutions are consistently believable.

(See also *Contemporary Authors*, Vols. 65-68 and *Something about the Author*, Vol. 22.)

Photograph by Ben Bridgers; courtesy of Sue Ellen Bridgers

BARBARA HELFGOTT

Reading a first novel is like meeting a stranger—one has no idea what to expect. We come prepared to accept the mildest of diversions, though we long for much more. We want to be stirred, involved and enlightened.

The home of ["**Home Before Dark**"] is a tobacco farm in Montreet County, N.C., to which James Earl Willis returns after an absence of 16 years. Those years have given him a wife, four children and a life of endless wandering as a migrant worker. Acting from some dimly realized compulsion to return to the world of his childhood, he brings his family to live in an old cabin on the family property, which now belongs to his brother.

The homecoming is experienced by each member of the Willis family in a different way. For James Earl, it represents a chance for self-renewal. . . . For the children, it offers the chance to explore a world they've fleetingly glimpsed from the back seat of a car. And for 14-year-old Stella Willis it means everything: "A place to store the secret Stella and draw her longings out slowly, carefully, one by one, and keep them safe."

Stella's longings, for all her road-wise knowledge, are not so different from those of other girls her age, and by the time the book ends, she is well on her way to fulfillment. She has learned a little about love and friendship, about keeping and letting go—about growing up.

No summary can convey the tremendous integrity of a book like "**Home Before Dark.**" The author speaks with a voice that is intensely lyrical yet wholly un-selfconscious. Character

and theme have been developed with such painstaking attention that each episode seems inevitable and right.

> *Barbara Helfgott, in her review of "Home Before Dark," in* The New York Times Book Review *(© 1976 by The New York Times Company; reprinted by permission), November 14, 1976, p. 40.*

SALLY HOLMES HOLTZE

[*Home Before Dark* is an] outstanding first novel. . . . The events are engrossing, to be sure, but the plot is secondary to the style. [Bridgers's] unique insights are expressed in profound metaphors, and she creates haunting images. Stella sleeps on a fancy mattress that is bloodstained from the day her grandmother shot herself; her father gave it to her because Stella had "'never seen a mattress with flowers on it.'" The character studies are thorough and concise; the author records equally well the emotions of a middle-aged man and a teen-aged girl, and she is able to explore the innermost thoughts of her characters within the confines of a few pages. Perceptive, masterful writing for mature readers. (pp. 165-66)

> *Sally Holmes Holtze, in her review of "Home Before Dark," in* The Horn Book Magazine *(copyright © 1977 by the Horn Book, Inc., Boston), Vol. LIII, No. 2, April, 1977, pp. 165-66.*

JEAN McINTYRE

I have recently seen [*Home Before Dark*] for sale on a rack of adult fiction, which is where it belongs even if its author intended it for children. Its story entwines two problems, the Migrant Willis family's conflicts as the father attempts to settle again on his brothers' North Carolina farm, and sex as it embroils all the main characters from the aging spinster Maggie Grover to the barely adolescent Toby Brown. Though this story centers on fourteen-year-old Stella Willis, it is not so much about her as about the social and personal conflicts that come first as her mother Mae's obsessive urge to keep moving on fails to budge daughter and husband (until she actually appears to summon down the lightning strike which kills her), then as the impact of father and daughter unsettles two generations of neighbors. Stella provokes premature sexual love from Toby Brown and delayed sexual urges in Rodney Biggers, until Rodney's jealousy issues in violence against Toby and his own total human failure. . . . The main events take second place to the background commentary of Toby's parents, settled in an unobtrusive domestic resignation, of Anne Willis, whose marriage with Newton and subsequent life with him have come about by cool planning, of Jean Biggers, typically sure that love is mere sex and the sure path to ruin. Its focus on the sexual, its dominant interest in adult emotions (even as felt by those little more than children), and its shifting viewpoints as it moves from one mind to another make *Home Before Dark* a book for readers too mature to be called children. (pp. 94-5)

> *Jean McIntyre, in her review of "Home Before Dark,"* in The World of Children's Books (© 1978 Jon C. Stott), Vol. III, No. 1, Spring, 1978, pp. 94-5.

KATE M. FLANAGAN

[As portrayed in Sue Ellen Bridgers's novel *All Together Now,* the] summer twelve-year-old Casey Flanagan spends at her grandparents'—while her mother is working and her father is fighting in the Korean War—is a time of growing self-awareness. A shy, sensitive girl, she is at first apprehensive about the arrangement but cheers up she meets Dwayne Pickens—a retarded man who was once a boyhood friend of her father's. Dwayne dislikes girls, but he easily mistakes Casey, with her short hair and jeans, for a boy. Anxious to have him as a friend, the girl convinces her family to keep her secret, and though she sometimes feels guilty about deceiving Dwayne, the two become inseparable. The narrative winds through a summer of family dinners, fishing trips, and outings to the track where Uncle Taylor races stock cars. Casey . . . is enfolded into the loving circle of family and friends, and in the course of the summer her refreshingly innocent personality touches them all. The thoughts and feelings of each character are revealed through shifting viewpoints as each in his own time learns that love must be based on truth and acceptance. . . . The characters—from good-natured, honest Dwayne to bumbling Hazard Whittaker—are remarkably individualized. The book is exceptional not only for its superb writing and skillful portrayal of human relationships but for its depiction of a small southern town, where everyone knows everyone and neighbors care enough to rally in times of trouble. (pp. 197-98)

> *Kate M. Flanagan, in her review of "All Together Now,"* in The Horn Book Magazine (copyright © 1979 by The Horn Book, Inc., Boston), Vol. LV, No. 2, April, 1979, pp. 197-98.

SARA MILLER

[*All Together Now* is] a warm, well-written if overly sentimental narrative with slices of each character's feeling and motives, and a touchingly tentative romance between a never-married couple in their 50s. Seeing through so many eyes, readers lose Casey herself too often, and more important—lose a sense of dramatic tension. The summer experience becomes a kaleidoscope of emotional responses with heavy doses of a likable but undiluted philosophy of love.

> *Sara Miller, in her review of "All Together Now,"* in School Library Journal (reprinted from the May, 1979 issue of School Library Journal, published by R. R. Bowker Co./A Xerox Corporation; copyright © 1979), Vol. 25, No. 9, May, 1979, p. 70.

DANA G. CLINTON

The title of Sue Ellen Bridgers' newest novel, **"All Together Now"** is the final touch of perfection to an exceptional story. . . . It sets in motion the musical strains of emotion and memory which harmonize our lives just as they do this novel of a group of people in a small North Carolina town who grow together during a summer in the 1950s. Long after the story ends, the haunting force of harmony stays with the reader and attests to the power of the tale and the mastery of its teller.

Our major interest is in Casey, a tomboyish, curious and sensitive youngster sent to spend her 12th summer with her grandparents. Throughout the story we see Casey grappling with problems old and new. . . .

The panoply of characters which grow around Casey fills out the tale and creates a world vibrant with the love and hope necessary to balance out the pains of living. . . .

It is the delicacy with which Bridgers weaves together the various strains of her story that creates the beauty of the book. There are no caricatures among the people and nothing artificial in the telling. . . . [The] whole is a smooth rendition of emotions captured by just the right phrase or revealed through a single important observation. The comingling of love at all levels of life stands out as the lesson Casey learns. "These shadowy forms that she knew held such a tenacious grip on her 12th summer." **"All Together Now"** is the deceivingly effortless writing of an artist at work.

> *Dana G. Clinton, "Summer Witness to Forces of Love" (reprinted by permission of the author), in* The Christian Science Monitor, May 14, 1979, p. B6.

KIRKUS REVIEWS

[*All Together Now* is a] superior novel about a twelve-year-old's summer friendship with a 33-year-old man whose mind is that of a boy of twelve . . . and about her allowing him to believe that she's a boy because she knows he can't stand girls. It sounds like another of those worthy and sensitive problem stories, with a neat moral dilemma worked in. But this is different from the start. Duane Pickins is a real person, someone you can love and laugh at. Casey, too, is a real person, who might make you think of yourself at twelve even if you weren't a bit like her. And the other characters are far more than a supporting cast. . . . [This] is a real novel, recognizably a juvenile for its general good feeling and individual happy endings, but remarkably full and genuinely empathic in its projection of the characters and their relationships.

A review of "All Together Now," in Kirkus Reviews (copyright © 1979 The Kirkus Service, Inc.), Vol. XLVII, No. 10, May 15, 1979, p. 579.

DICK ABRAHAMSON

Home Before Dark and **All Together Now** quickly established Bridgers' reputation in the YA field and *Notes for Another Life* puts her at the head of the pack. In this latest novel, Bridgers introduces us to thirteen-year-old Wren and her older brother, Kevin. They live with their grandparents because their father is in and out of the state mental hospital. Their mother, after years of living with the ups and downs of a mentally ill husband, has chosen a career of high fashion and city life over Wren and Kevin.

Once again it is Bridgers' fine sense of characterization that makes her book work so well. The reader watches Kevin and Wren struggle with developmental tasks made more complicated by mental illness in the family and absent parents.

The author beautifully balances the father's retreat from reality with what appears to be a similar journey by Kevin. Kevin's moodiness, his lack of friends, and his perceived rejection by his mother and his girlfriend push him to a suicide attempt. The family comes together to help Kevin and to deal, this time successfully, with yet another tragedy.

Running through this finely crafted novel is the theme of the soothing power of music, which is an ointment to ease the pain, an escape, and an old friend to lean on for help and strength. It is music that provides notes for another life. Because *Notes* is not as demanding as [Judith Guest's] *Ordinary People* nor as simplistic as [John Neufeld's] *Lisa, Bright and Dark*, this fine novel will get a bigger share of teenage readers.

Dick Abrahamson, in his review of "Notes for Another Life" (copyright © 1981 by the National Council of Teachers of English; reprinted by permission of the publisher), in English Journal, Vol. 70, No. 5, September, 1981, p. 75.

JANET FRENCH

The blurb suggests that [*Notes for Another Life*] is "a family chronicle for all ages." It would have been more accurate to describe it as a propaganda vehicle for female domesticity. Good women subordinate their talents and yearnings to the home and their children; all other paths lead to havoc. For a riveting story of four deserted children, lead readers instead to Cynthia Voight's marvelous, upbeat *Homecoming*. . . .

Janet French, in her review of "Notes for Another Life," in School Library Journal (reprinted from the September, 1981 issue of School Library Journal, published by R. R. Bowker Co./A Xerox Corporation; copyright © 1981), Vol. 28, No. 1, September, 1981, p. 133.

JOAN L. ATKINSON

[*Notes for Another Life*] is superbly written, with every word manipulated to count. Topics of contemporary interest—suicide, mental illness, divorce, living with loss—are placed in the context of family living so skillfully that they appear as universal rather than contemporary themes. There is genius in the development of so many rounded characters in a medium length novel. Sue Ellen Bridgers continues a pattern developed in **Home Before Dark** and **All Together Now** of portraying incredibly strong women, young and old. . . . Male characters, while less complex as a whole, are given individuality and effectiveness. Bill and Sam are sensitive and staunch support-givers; the minister is capable of understanding Kevin and leading him toward self insight. The novel's guardedly positive ending leaves one pondering and wanting to return to the book again. Its picture of an adolescent brother and sister deeply concerned for and never failing each other is hard to find in literature and is entirely believable.

Joan L. Atkinson, in her review of "Notes for Another Life," in Voice of Youth Advocates (copyrighted 1981 by Voice of Youth Advocates), Vol. 4, No. 4, October, 1981, p. 20.

DIANE C. DONOVAN

The devastating impact of mental illness upon family relationships is intimately explored in [*Notes for Another Life*]. (p. 317)

In focusing intimately upon each family member's personal struggles with [the father's] mental illness, the book moves away from the current spate of young adult novels which concentrate on the afflicted patient's inner struggles. It encompasses the lives and thoughts of one family so powerfully that readers are made aware of the special problems teenagers encounter when confronted with a family member's disability.

The author has succeeded in painting a portrait of mental illness that, for once, is not overburdened with melodrama and journalistic self-examination. It's intimate without being confessional, and it presents the points of view of each family member so successfully that, by the novel's conclusion, all characters are fully developed and easily understandable. No easy answers or conclusions are drawn—the book is just an excellent portrait of life's varied influences upon one family, among them mental illness. (pp. 317-18)

Diane C. Donovan, in her review of "Notes for Another Life," in Best Sellers (copyright © 1981 Helen Dwight Reid Educational Foundation), Vol. 41, No. 8, November, 1981, pp. 317-18.

JOAN L. ATKINSON

Your reviewer's treatment of Sue Ellen Bridgers' **Notes for Another Life** [see excerpt above by Janet French] . . . so simplified a complex work that it makes the book sound like an issues novel. Far from being a "propaganda vehicle for female domesticity," *Notes* . . . says that family life is multi-faceted—a mix of love and loss, of responsibilities accepted and rejected, of forces controllable and out of hand, of disappointment and support. Kevin and Wren's mother, Karen, wants both emotional and physical distance from her children; apparently their father does too, though his mental illness obscures the distinction between what is willed on his part and what is fated by heredity. The novel does not assign blame to either parent or grandparent. It makes a case for learning to live with whatever losses can't be recouped.

Kevin at one point opts for giving up, for suicide. He sheds tears—isn't it OK for a boy to cry in anger over his helplessness? His sister Wren is the stronger sibling. While Kevin wonders what to believe in, Wren believes in music, in love and in herself. Her characterization belies the reviewer's statement that "Good women subordinate their talents and yearnings to the home and their children." In the book's terms, Wren is a "good" woman who's going to develop her talent. . . . To me the book says that both men and women struggle to find that delicate balance between self-actualization and care for the meaningful others in their lives. But its more important message is that people need inner resources, stamina and will to live fully.

Joan L. Atkinson, "Mote in the Eye," in School Library Journal *(reprinted from the January, 1982 issue of* School Library Journal, *published by R. R. Bowker Co./A Xerox Corporation; copyright © 1982), Vol. 28, No. 5, January, 1982, p. 57.*

JOSEPH O. MILNER

[*All Together Now*] seems clearly out-of-step with most of the books of our day. The presence of the family, as it extends itself vertically and horizontally, and of the larger community run deep in the account of Casey's summer with her grandparents. In contrast, much of today's children's fiction reports the family as extinct or, if alive, merely meddling. As a part of this difference, Bridgers pays homage to powerful adults and attends to them sufficiently to allow her reader to feel both their silliness and their wisdom. Although she focuses on Casey and her relationship to the quick-spirited, but slow-minded, Dwayne Pickens, Bridgers's omniscient point of view carries her into the minds of folk who are placed all along the chronological path of life. She deftly slips into the thoughts of most of her characters and renders a less rarified, more complete assessment of life than is found in much of children's literature. Multiple interior responses to Dwayne's threatened institutionalization by his prideful brother Alva—to the misfire honeymoon and subsequent estrangement of the middle-aged Pansy and Hazard, to the quiet solidity of the elder Flanagan's relationship, and to the on-and-off courtship of Uncle Taylor and the candy-counter girl Gwyn, make the book less parochial and more real than the typical single-issue, youth ghetto books of our time. Furthermore, although Casey's summer includes a good bit of pain and foolishness, Bridgers persistently affirms life at its core; without being a Pollyanna she departs from the current norm of despair by championing brotherhood and love. (p. 176)

Joseph O. Milner, "The Emergence of Awe in Recent Children's Literature," in Children's Literature: Annual of the Modern Language Association Group on Children's Literature and the Children's Literature Association, Vol. 10, *edited by Francelia Butler (copyright © by Children's Literature An International Journal, Inc.), Yale University Press, 1982, pp. 169-77.**

David Byrne

1953?-

American songwriter.

Byrne is one of the most prominent songwriters to come out of the New Wave movement of the late 1970s. He writes mostly for the group Talking Heads, although he has also collaborated with avant-garde musician Brian Eno and dancer Twyla Tharp. Byrne's songs are intensely private explorations of human emotions and personal observations of commonplace events. Probably the most important theme running through his songs is his despairing view of contemporary American society. Byrne has been criticized for the triteness of some of his lyrics. However, he is less concerned with expressing complex thoughts than with composing lyrics that are strictly logical. John Picarella has written of Byrne's songs, "Perceptions and sensations are experienced systematically, almost as if they're on a graph."

***Talking Heads: 77* is considered a triumphant debut album. It introduces the major topics of Byrne's songs: love, fear, and violence. Byrne's staccato-punctuated singing style in songs like "Psycho Killer" heightens the urgency and impact of his lyrics. The songs on *More Songs about Buildings and Food* center on the need to be in control of one's emotions and the unpleasant result of distancing oneself from emotional involvement. *Remain in Light* and *Speaking in Tongues* indicate that Byrne is becoming interested in unusual rhythm structures and is moving from individual concerns to more universal ones.**

Lynn Goldsmith/LGI © 1980

MARK STEVENS

Mr. Byrne's lyrical approach, with his thick, involved poetic style, serves up the element which most distinguishes Talking Heads from other rock groups. His main topic (and he makes no attempt to disguise it) is love.

He couches his thoughts in abstract images—space, distance, time—and he delivers them in a uniquely disjointed manner that has become a Talking Heads trademark. Like an overstuffed suitcase, Mr. Byrne's lyrics are hard to unpack. . . .

Mr. Byrne's lyrics are open to any number of interpretations. But, like Bob Dylan lyrics, sometimes accused of the same "fault," they may manage to outlive such criticism.

> *Mark Stevens, "Two Fresh Rock Groups on the Way Up," in* The Christian Science Monitor *(reprinted by permission from* The Christian Science Monitor; *© 1977 The Christian Science Publishing Society; all rights reserved), April 25, 1977, p. 27.**

CHRIS BRAZIER

I fully expected to be floored . . . by Talking Heads' first album ["**Talking Heads: 77**"]. . . . Unfortunately, I haven't been. Trouble is, I don't know quite what the album does do for me.

Maybe I shouldn't have expected so much. For instance, "**Psycho Killer, qu'est-ce que c'est**" always seemed a fascinating

song-title—I imagined some eerie midnight lurking classic—but, while this is okay, it does no justice to the potential of the idea, even incorporating the inevitably self-conscious use of French. . . .

There's so much to praise, not least the quality of some of the songs. The single, "**Uh-Oh, Love Comes To Town**," for example, is beautifully eccentric, simultaneously challenging and appealing. . . . On the other hand a couple of the pieces—"**Who Is It?**" and "**Carefree**" are dispensable, and the quirky stop-go style which pervades the album tends to push me away. . . .

My uncertain reaction to the work is quite appropriate because indecision seems to be the key to Byrne's lyrics. In "**Tentative Decisions**" the world is so confused that all decision-making, even distinguishing between male and female characteristics, becomes impossible.

One way of escaping decision is to retreat into a cosy private universe ("**Don't Worry About The Government**," a dead ringer for early 10cc), another is to hand over power to a stronger figure ("**Pulled Up**"), but both are rightly ridiculed as inadequate here. But that leaves Byrne stranded "In a world where people have problems / In a world where decisions are a way of life."

Most of the album sees him taking another escape-route—that of submission to the "mystery" of love. Thus the questions of **"Who Is It?"** give way to simple affirmations of love, and, in **"Happy Day,"** where his initial desire to "talk like I read before I decide what to do" is swept away by his heart, which has a will of its own, and the subsequent abandonment to love brings about an ecstatic "summer."

Which is all very good, but the lyrical message isn't conveyed quite as well as I've perhaps made it appear. For a start, the words are often cutesy and obscure, and sometimes simplistic, seldom achieving an ideal balance. And then, despite the general bounciness, the music throughout is very self-contained, its clever but cold formality suggesting rational control, but unbridled emotion.

And that rather contrived atmosphere (the inherent failing of all art-rock?) is what makes me point to **"No Compassion"** as the heart of the album. Here a magnificent flowing intro with acoustic slide overlay leads into a song which sees selfishness as necessary if one is to make the decisions which Byrne seems to see as the essence of life. . . . The song even sees people as *functioning*, as if to confirm the absence of real human warmth—note that Byrne is always concerned with his own feeling and never with the person inducing the feeling (not characterised at all).

I reckon the group name is significant—this cerebral attack is entirely divorced from the gut-thrust of rock 'n' roll. Despite the concern with love there's some *feeling* missing here. . . .

It's all very clever, and some of it's great, but I'm afraid they leave me rather cold. And I did so want to be warmed.

> *Chris Brazier, "Heads or Tails?: 'Talking Heads: 77'," in* Melody Maker *(© IPC Business Press Ltd.), October 1, 1977, p. 24.*

SCOTT ISLER

[David Byrne's] songs are childishly simple, employing straightforward declarative lyrics and repetitious rhythmic motifs. . . .

Talking Heads: 77 is distinctly more listenable than the group in person. . . . The vocals themselves are clearly recorded, allowing one to appreciate Byrne's involuted imagery. Few songwriters would attempt setting psychiatric advice to music, but Byrne (on **"No Compassion"**) makes it sound natural. **"The Book I Read"** . . . is a joyous celebration of love which even transcends words after awhile. . . .

In common with Jonathan Richman, David Byrne is taking almost a zen approach to rock; the Heads aren't likely to trade in their amplifiers, however. This album will test your capacity for wonder.

> *Scott Isler, in his review of "Talking Heads: 77," in* Trouser Press *(copyright © 1977 by Trans-Oceanic Trouser Press, Inc.), Vol. 4, No. 9, November, 1977, p. 37.*

STEPHEN DEMOREST

[Talking Heads' debut album, *Talking Heads '77*, is an absolute triumph.] (p. 98)

"The Book I Read," like so many of their songs, burbles with excitement, a feeling of expansion overcoming restraint. **"Pulled Up"** is the real champ, though, a fiercely exhilarating rush of aural amyl nitrate. . . .

Exploring the logic and disorientation of love, decision making, ambition and the need for selfishness, [Byrne] gropes for articulation like a metaphysician having difficulty computing emotions.

Given his relatively unlyrical nature, Byrne's burgeoning persona is not in the least tentative. **"No Compassion"** asserts all the impatience of Lou Reed in a bad mood, while **"Psycho Killer"** pulses with vehemence. . . .

Not only is this a great album, it's also one of the definitive records of the decade. (p. 101)

> *Stephen Demorest, "Talking Heads' Stunning Debut," in* Rolling Stone *(by Straight Arrow Publishers, Inc. © 1977; all rights reserved; reprinted by permission), Issue 251, November 3, 1977, pp. 98, 101.*

FRANK ROSE

[*Talking Heads: 77*] comes in on an artfully oblique plane. . . .

[What] do you make of a band that delivers lines like "My building has every convenience / It's going to make life easy for me" with the same fervor the Who always reserved for "My Generation"? Those lines are from **"Don't Worry About the Government,"** by far the strangest song on this album. The other tunes are mostly about love and problems and decision-making (heavy emphasis on decision-making), or else they seem like fractured images from some kind of drug experience. **"Don't Worry About the Government"** is about two things that don't have to do with any of this. It's about how nice it is to move into a new building with all the modern conveniences, and how nice all the civil servants are in Washington, D.C. Somehow the two become confused, and at the end you hear Byrne singing "Don't you worry 'bout ME!" in a way that suggests "me" and the government are identical.

There's something reminiscent of the '50s about this song in particular and *Talking Heads: 77* in general: a faith in know-how and the basic rightness of things that's as characteristically American as it is naive. Yet somehow it doesn't come out very American with Talking Heads; theirs is a romantic, lyrical faith—an intellectual glorification, and an artistic rendering, of innocence that seems both simple-minded and complex and is never quite what it seems.

> *Frank Rose, "Babytalking Heads" (reprinted by permission of* The Village Voice *and the author; copyright © The Village Voice, Inc., 1977), in* The Village Voice, *Vol. XXII, No. 45, November 7, 1977, p. 53 [the excerpt from David Byrne's lyrics used here was taken from "Don't Worry About the Government" (© 1977 Bleu Disque Music Co., Inc. & Index Music, Inc.; all rights reserved; used by permission of Warner Bros. Music)].*

IAN BIRCH

I can hardly believe ["**More Songs about Buildings and Food**" is] THIS good. On a law of averages, we've almost exceeded our current quota of 24-carat albums.

Dylan has returned to Olympian form, the Stones and Springsteen have shown they are alive and creatively kicking, while

Magazine has lived up to all those Great Expectations. Now we have the second Talking Heads album and it's superb. . . .

It touches all the vital parts at one and the same time. The songs are intelligent and provocative without being condescending or too obtruse. That must satisfy the *head*. If the words at first seem indecipherable, just persevere. You'll be rewarded.

David Byrne . . . has the ability to conjure up unsettling perspectives. They are like a series of short stories which startle through their use of shorn words in bizarre combinations. As he economises so efficiency *and* mystery multiplies. I know this may sound horribly pretentious but before you howl, LISTEN. . . .

"The Good Thing" is constructed along near-perfect lines and sports a lyric about the search for a sort of ideal state of mind which is nowhere near as daunting as it might first appear.

Another fascinating piece of scaffolding is **"I'm Not In Love"** which alternates space with thunderous attack to wonderful effect.

My current fave rave, though, has to be **"The Big Country."** Over a rolling gait and translucent guitar, Byrne comes up with an aerial view of the complacent American Way. The duplex in Marlboro country. His persona is the sadly disillusioned traveller who sees it all but finally decides he wants no part of it.

It really *IS* this good.

Ian Birch, "Heads, Eno Wins . . . ," in Melody Maker *(© IPC Business Press Ltd.), July 15, 1978, p. 23.*

JOHN PICCARELLA

On the cover of [Talking Heads'] new album, ***More Songs About Buildings and Food,*** a life-sized group portrait is created from hundreds of extreme close-up Polaroids; the composite is sectioned into squares, the way a photorealist would reproduce a photograph on canvas. The resulting photomosaic, though composed of clear photographic images, is more like a painting—distorted, fascinating, and unreal.

Talking Heads' songs are similarly dissociated, blindly passionate while rigidly logical, naively logical though twisted by passion. Perceptions and sensations are experienced systematically, almost as if they're on a graph. . . .

The Talking Heads program for living in a mechanical world is to assimilate systemization with the rigor of religion. Byrne is forever asserting his faith in himself, making decisions, reasoning, and getting organized; but he is just as often losing control, threatening, angry, distracted by sensation, vision, buildings, or food. Delusions and paranoid structures create a network of snapshot perceptions organized by geometry. This may be ultimately hysterical, but it's . . . efficiently arbitrary. . . .

The two recent songs that close each side are more substantial and coherent lyrically than any of the band's previous material. . . . [These] are the Heads' longest songs, and they are well sustained. **"Found a Job"** is a narrative about a couple quarreling over television who take David's advice and are "Happy as can be / Making up their own shows / Putting them on TV." This serves as Byrne's example of getting everything together, including family and friends, in a life-style where

work is a pleasure. The final song, **"The Big Country,"** is even more expansive, presenting a panoramic view of America in images right out of elementary geography lessons. . . . Here, as in **"Found a Job,"** Byrne is an observer, an organizer of images, further removed than in the self-distanced first-person confusions of his hysterical strategems. Having proposed the most infinite American image system—television—as a successful career strategy, he paradoxically rejects the whole big country. "I wouldn't live there if you paid me . . ." he says. But he does, rearranging its images, like Gertrude Stein, to make up an American space, precise juxtapositions of buildings and food, as real as . . . a map.

John Piccarella, "Talking Heads' Polaroid Vision" (reprinted by permission of The Village Voice *and the author; copyright © The Village Voice, Inc., 1978), in* The Village Voice, *Vol. XXIII, No. 30, July 24, 1978, p. 43 [the first excerpt of David Byrne's lyrics used here was taken from "Found a Job" (© 1978 Bleu Disque Music Co., Inc. & Index Music, Inc.; all rights reserved; used by permission of Warner Bros. Music); the second excerpt was taken from "The Big Country" (© 1978 Bleu Disque Music Co., Inc. & Index Music, Inc.; all rights reserved; used by permission of Warner Bros. Music)].*

JON PARELES

[On ***More Songs About Buildings and Food,*** David Byrne gazes] wide-eyed at the universe, absorbing and accepting. Byrne is determinedly childlike; he picks up pieces but either refuses to assemble them or applies his own para-rational analyses. In **"The Good Thing,"** he hints at some weird combination of messianism and futurism. . . .

Distance—the distance of a bewildered child—seems to have become the major fact of the Heads' world. On their first album, they were "happy," "carefree," optimistic; now, they're only separate. . . . Byrne doesn't seem upset by it, though; at least, he's no more upset than he is in general. It's just one more thing he finely observes. **"The Girls Want to Be with the Girls"** could almost be a [Jean] Piaget cognitive-development treatise: The first verse is all one-syllable words, the second allows two-syllable words ("common sense"), the third goes into "intuitive leap." The tinker-toy music on the verses reinforces the pediatric feeling. . . .

Talking Heads have gotten odder than ever with ***More Songs About Buildings and Food,*** which is just fine with me. **"Warning Sign"** is completely wacked out. . . . David Byrne sums it up in **"Artists Only"** when he sings, "I don't have to prove that I am creative," as crazily as he can. True to form, he sings it twice.

Jon Pareles, "I Am a Child," in Crawdaddy *(copyright © 1978 by Crawdaddy Publishing Co., Inc.; all rights reserved; reprinted by permission), September, 1978, p. 75 [the excerpt from David Byrne's lyrics used here was taken from "Artists Only" (© 1978 Bleu Disque Music Co., Inc. & Index Music, Inc.; all rights reserved; used by permission of Warner Bros. Music)].*

KEN TUCKER

[On **"More Songs about Buildings and Food,"** *The Girls Want to Be with the Girls*], with its unstated but inevitable political implications, is exceptional to the Heads' style, which most often piles up vapid declarative sentences with idiot's repetition. But set within the context of the glowingly astute music, the repetition becomes everything *but* idiotic: the multiply allusive words serve both as hooks and quietly ironic jokes. So it is with the very title of the album. . . . Byrne uses as models not other rock & rollers . . . , but the young poets loosely referred to as the New York School—Tom Clark, Ron Padgett, and Anne Waldman. Byrne . . . shares with them an aesthetic/geographic sensibility in which New York is the locus of a cool, distanced, but funny approach to art. (p. 164)

For these poets, the banality of an accumulation of quotidian comments becomes, at its best, whimsically witty; at its worst, it becomes merely coy and cute. For the Heads the banal is kept on its toes since it must compete with the beat. This is certainly true of Byrne's masterpiece *The Big Country*, in which a startling bit of detail is added here and there or a deadpan zinger is tacked onto the end of a verse.

This grounding in the everyday, the placid ordinariness of the words and Byrne's voice, keeps the Heads honest, even earthy. . . . **"More Songs"** achieves a rock & roll rarity: It is gentle-spirited but never sentimental—a delicate, precise record that rocks hard. (pp. 164-65)

Ken Tucker, "Buildings, Food, Clothes, Landscapes, and Talking Heads," in High Fidelity *(copyright © by ABC Leisure Magazine, Inc.; all rights reserved; excerpted by permission), Vol. 28, No. 10, October, 1978, pp. 164-65.*

KEN EMERSON

[On *More Songs about Buildings and Food*], Byrne's lyrics obsessively juxtapose the irreconcilable, nonnegotiable demands of the head and the heart. . . .

If, in one song, Byrne chides the girls for ignoring the boys . . . , in most of the others, Byrne himself seems frantically to be staving off amorous involvement: "I've got to get to work now" (the traditional male equivalent of "Not tonight, honey—I've got a headache"). Indeed, the word *work* recurs throughout the record as the singer both pushes and parodies the Protestant ethic. . . . Love wreaks havoc on the rational, workaday world, and David Byrne's comic cold shoulder recalls the more strenuous resistance of Joni Mitchell, so many of whose songs have expressed a similar fear that love will deflect her artistic career.

Love *and* work, of course, is what Freud said all of us need, but on *More Songs about Buildings and Food*, Byrne appears able to imagine the proper equilibrium only in **"Found a Job,"** wherein a bickering couple's relationship improves while collaborating on television scripts. He sings about this improvement with considerable sarcasm, though, and elsewhere on the LP, love and logic are at loggerheads. The tension between the two, like the similar tension Bryan Ferry creates between sentimentality and sophistication, is excruciating, and when it snaps in the album's final song, **"The Big Country"** . . . , Byrne is bounced into the void. Flying over the United States, he looks down with regret and revulsion at life below. . . . Yet, at the same time, he's "tired of traveling" and wants "to be somewhere." Like a hijacked airplane that no nation will permit to land, the singer seems doomed to fly until his fuel is exhausted and he plummets to a fiery death.

Sound gloomy? Well it would be if Byrne didn't see hilarity in tight-assed hysteria and laugh at his Puritan pratfalls. . . .

The eclecticism of *More Songs about Buildings and Food*—its witty distillations of disco and reggae rhythms, its reconciliation of "art" and punk rock—is masterful. The music represents a triumph over diversity, while the words spell out defeat by disparities between mind and body, head and heart.

This, presumably, is why Talking Heads make music—and superb music at that. Because talk is cheap. (p. 89)

Ken Emerson, "Talking Heads: Preppie but Potent," in Rolling Stone *(by Straight Arrow Publishers, Inc. © 1978; all rights reserved; reprinted by permission), Issue 276, October 19, 1978, pp. 89-90.*

LESTER BANGS

Fear of Music provides Heads'/Byrne's most explicit blueprint yet for survival in the face of paranoias—real or imagined, makes no difference. . . . [The] songs have a flow that makes it more immediately accessible. Byrne's a kind of Everyneurotic, wandering through the world encountering ouch-producers every step and breath he takes, relaying them back to us filtered through his sense of humor. . . . *Fear of Music* might as well have been called *Fear of Everything*. Show me an item extant sentient or otherwise in the world we share and I'll show you a clinically certified list of reasons why proximity to said item should be considered risky if not downright lethal. . . .

In this album Dr. Byrne examines various popularly proposed panaceas [for the disease called life] with dissecting knife and discards them one by one.

Socialized day-to-day living in this imminent nullkreig is outlined in **"Life During Wartime."** . . . When there is no firm ground, the only sensible thing to do is keep on the move, ergo on their third album the first example of what might qualify as the Heads' version of "road" songs—the other one is **"Cities."** . . .

"Drugs" is a hilariously solemn recitation of the usual chemical comicstrips, and **"Animals"** puts away all those maudlin mabels like Robinson Jeffers and Euell Gibbons who belabor us with man's odiousness behaviorwise when stacked up against our noble ancestors dwelling next door in the wilds or more properly zoos. But the bottom line is that "They're setting a bad example." The truth, as Byrne points out, is that animals, besides having no intelligence beyond brute fear reflex, are a bunch of smug little bastards who are *laughing* at us just because we keep drawing diagrams across a universe they knew was chaotic in the first place.

Which brings us to David Byrne's basic philosophy of existence: To feel anxiety is to be blessed by the full wash of life in its ripest chancre—everything else is wax museums. Having rejected drugs, animal husbandry, jogging not to mention breathing itself, towns, cities and whole continents in his search for some little nook where he can relax for even one instant, Byrne finally lays it on the line: "Heaven is a place where nothing ever happens." . . .

The implicit answer in all these songs is that, given the hopelessness of the situation, we should also recognize how hysterically funny it is. In the Middle Ages the population of Europe felt so haunted and tainted by the Devil, so hopelessly damned, that they developed a predilection, as manifested in the paintings of Bosch, for taking all this damnation and redemption stuff as a kind of huge joke, with God, Satan and the demons as cartoon characters. The closer you get to whatever you're terrified of, the more it and your dread begin to seem like old friends, ergo terror decreases. David Byrne seems to be a sort of dowzer's wand for neuroses and trauma, and as darkness looms over all of us, he strolls down its maw, placid, bemused, humming little tunes to himself. Sometimes I think *Fear of Music* is one of the best comedy albums I've ever heard. Which doesn't mean the fear isn't real. Byrne just reminds you that it's something you're going to have to live with, so you might as well get a kick out of it while you can.

Lester Bangs, "David Byrne Says 'Boo!'" (reprinted by permission of The Village Voice *and the author; copyright © News Group Publications, Inc., 1979), in* The Village Voice, *Vol. XXIV, No. 34, August 20, 1979, p. 65.*

ROBOT A. HULL

[*Fear of Music*] is the inevitable consequence of toying with psychosis. It's a work that is built, and also feeds, upon the paranoia of Fritz Lang's cinema, the violence of *The Friends of Eddie Coyle* and the terrorization of *Mission: Impossible*. This album lacks, and constantly avoids, the patriotism, sense of community and bubble gum-disco-psychedelic playfulness that make Talking Heads' first two albums such warm, albeit odd, friends. Like Randy Newman, Byrne has mastered the ironic backhand (i.e., **"The Big Country"**, **"Don't Worry About the Government"**), but on *Fear,* songs like **"Animals"** and **"Electric Guitar"** are ironically banal. . . .

The beauty of *More Songs About Buildings and Food* is that one can never figure out what the songs are exactly *about* (about aboutness, perhaps). The disappointment of *Fear of Music* is that one can immediately decode its aboutness: inertia, the no-blink of the no wave, Eno Brain, artsy skool, obtoooose conceptualism. It isn't the forced, disjointed music on the album that bothers me . . . , but the whole frightening motivation behind it; that, at any moment, the words "helter skelter" could be carved into one's flesh, the overwhelming fear of every lurking shadow.

On a rock album, to put it simply, this is no fun. Perhaps a key to part of the record's difficulties can be heard on **"Heaven,"** . . . in which heaven is celebrated as empty existence, white-on-white, an idle void while the music (paradoxically?) transports the listener beyond the stratosphere to "A place where nothing ever happens." But as any real rock 'n' roller knows, heaven is a place where *everything* happens—*Death Race 2000*—with "White Light/White Heat" blasting full volume, pure ACTION, the kind that crazy-eyed Byrne perhaps only dreams about.

Robot A. Hull, "When Paranoia Strikes Deep," in Creem *(© copyright 1979 by Creem Magazine, Inc.), Vol. 11, No. 6, November, 1979, p. 51.*

JON PARELES

David Byrne's lyrics on Talking Heads' *Fear of Music* are paralogical visions stated with almost childlike directness: he thinks that air hits him in the face, that animals want to change his life, that "someone controls electric guitar." By itself, this perspective makes Byrne's songs fascinating. (p. 67)

Byrne has drastically shifted his verbal approach for *Fear of Music*. In his lyrics for earlier records, he let himself be self-conscious: he'd observe, analyze and make judgments. His

new lyrics virtually eliminate abstraction—he doesn't consider, he *feels*. There's very little past and no future, just a jumble of sensations, as if it's all he can do to handle *right now*. The songs are invariably in the first person and mention very few outside characters: the singer's inner world is his last refuge.

This way lies solipsism perhaps. But David Byrne's private, paranoid universe is dangerously close to yours and mine. (p. 68)

Jon Pareles, "How to Live with 'Fear'," in Rolling Stone *(by Straight Arrow Publishers, Inc. © 1979; all rights reserved; reprinted by permission), Issue 304, November 15, 1979, pp. 67-8.*

MITCHELL COHEN

Talking Heads have always—from their seven-inch start, **"Love→A Building On Fire,"** a chain of logical emotionalism in which that arrow implied all—reminded me of the Bronx High School Of Science, which is probably why I've approached them with a mixture of attraction and wariness. Give a guy like Byrne a box of tinker toys and he'll build you a metropolis with a working sewer system; then, with colored pencils, he'll chart the links between the chamber of commerce and the red light district. A dangerous boy. On *Remain In Light* he's like a whizkid stoned on a whiff of the Famous Flames, caught in his own beat, mumbling disconnected phrases . . . on the stairwell. Not since Love's Arthur Lee has mulatto-rock sounded like it was concocted on a bunsen burner. . . .

The more "contemplative" tunes on *Remain In Light* lack the propulsive persuasiveness of [the] side-one rave-ups but are not without their own concrete jungle swing and sway. The terrorist who "plants devices in the free trade zone" in **"Listening Wind,"** accompanied by deceptive calm, **"Seen And Not Seen"**'s character . . . who meditates on the malleability of facial structure, the twilight zone domestic situation of **"Once In A Lifetime"** (with the eerie chant "same as it ever was"): all are real, and realized, subjective reaches. Only **"The Overload,"** an overlong, over-obscure stretch . . . , dims the project. . . .

It's all-hook, or anti-hook, depending on how you look at it. It's music that sounds cornered and liberated at the same time, and quirky beyond comprehension. *Remain In Light* is to these ears the first time that an album by Talking Heads is as likeable as the theory of Talking Heads is intriguing. The band is chasing something that may ultimately be out of reach, but at this juncture I wouldn't bet against them.

Mitchell Cohen, "Play That Funky Music White Boy," in Creem *(© copyright 1981 by Creem Magazine, Inc.), Vol. 12, No. 8, January, 1981, p. 52.*

SCOTT ISLER

Not to denigrate Talking Heads' well-deserved popularity, but as *Remain in Light* goes zooming up the record charts one is forced to ask: Just what are its purchasers going to do with it? Will it be taken as dance music with a college education, the spearhead (probably no pun intended) of an Africa-chic movement? Or will the consumer, stumbling over the enclosed lyric sheet, be caught up in David Byrne's metaphysical challenges? . . .

Rhythmic complexity, both vocal and instrumental, suffuses the songs. . . . Byrne doesn't write throwaway lyrics, though, and the tension between a funky groove and agonizing words is part of the Heads' unique formula. . . .

Not all of *Remain in Light* adheres to the new musical rulebook. **"Seen and Not Seen"** is less a song than a Borges-like tale read matter-of-factly by Byrne over a syncopated beat. . . .

While *Remain in Light* can be appreciated as sheer sound . . . , its most powerful moments blend words and music. **"Once in a Lifetime"** questions reality and illusion in the verses, and a chorus employing plaintive thirds introduces a water motif—one of the most powerful images in the poet's arsenal. Byrne is certainly a poet, if poetry can be considered the juggling of language for expressive purposes. This album taps a primeval vein in the subconscious: You'll tap your toes but you won't be able to shut out what these songs mean. Like the inverted A's in its name on the cover, Talking Heads has stood the dance concept on its head. Their music gains in meaning with each listen.

> *Scott Isler, in his review of "Remain in Light," in* Trouser Press *(copyright © 1981 by Trans-Oceanic Trouser Press, Inc.), Vol. 7, No. 12, January, 1981, p. 42.*

ERIC SALZMAN

Byrne writes classic arty/surreal rock lyrics. *The Catherine Wheel* . . . apparently had something to do with the life and death of the American family, and Byrne's words hover menacingly around this topic. I recently described commercial television as being concerned with "stories of extreme violence and danger performed in an elliptical, laconic, laid-back style with heavy, threatening rhythmic undertones and a clipped, stylized surface." Except for the fact that there is no story, that is an accurate description of what's on this disc. Not only is there no literary, dramatic, or narrative content, there is no musical story either. No tune. These are rhythmic *outlines* for music with a ghastly emptiness inside—tight, heavy, even powerful structures that, frighteningly, contain . . . nothing. (pp. 93-4)

> *Eric Salzman, in his review of "The Catherine Wheel," in* Stereo Review *(copyright © 1982 by Ziff-Davis Publishing Company), Vol. 47, No. 6, June, 1982, pp. 93-4.*

DAVID FRICKE

Speaking in Tongues, Talking Heads' first studio release in three years, is the album that finally obliterates the thin line separating arty white pop music and deep black funk. Picking up where their 1980 Afro-punk fusion *Remain in Light* left off, this LP consummates the Heads' marriage of art-school intellect and dance-floor soul. . . . *Speaking in Tongues* gives new meaning to the word *crossover.* (p. 53)

The Heads have never cut the funk into finer, more fluent pieces. Nor have they ever displayed such a sense of purpose and playfulness. . . . (pp. 53-4)

[It] is David Byrne's propulsive score for Twyla Tharp's 1981 dance piece *The Catherine Wheel* that may be the most important influence on *Speaking in Tongues.* The severe constraints of matching music to movement—of making music inspire expressive movement—forced Byrne to write and arrange his *Catherine Wheel* score with both crisp dramatic precision and provocative imagistic flair.

The nine songs on *Speaking in Tongues* . . . demonstrate that same percision and flair in remarkable combinations. On the surface, **"Girlfriend Is Better"** is a brassy, straightforward bump number sparked by Byrne's animated bragging . . . and by the kind of rapid, zigzagging synth squeals so common on rap and funk records. But the edgy paranoia smoldering underneath . . . is colorfully articulated by guitar and percussion figures that burble along in a fatback echo, sounding like a sink backing up.

"I Get Wild/Wild Gravity," Byrne's unsettling account of isolation and disorientation, alludes to the funky voodoo reggae of Grace Jones and is heightened by arty dub intrusions and electronic handclaps. . . .

But the complexity of these songs doesn't keep any of them from being great dance tracks. They are all rooted in a shrewd yet elastic sense of rhythm, thereby avoiding the brittle, plastic feel of such glorified disco troupes as the Thompson Twins or Spandau Ballet. And unlike, say, *My Life in the Bush of Ghosts,* Byrne's academic safari with Brian Eno, *Speaking in Tongues* is an art-rock album that doesn't flaunt its cleverness; it's obvious enough in the alluring hooks, deviant rhythms and captivating mix of reliable funk gimmicks and intellectual daring.

The real art here is the incorporation of disparate elements from pop, punk and R&B into a coherent, celebratory dance ethic that dissolves notions of color and genre in smiles and sweat. A new model for great party albums to come, *Speaking in Tongues* is likely to leave you doing just that. (p. 54)

> *David Fricke, "Talking Heads' Arty Party," in* Rolling Stone *(by Straight Arrow Publishers, Inc. © 1983; all rights reserved; reprinted by permission), Issue 397, June 9, 1983, pp. 53-4.*

Lois Duncan (Steinmetz Arquette)

1934-

(Also wrote as Lois Kerry) American novelist, short story writer, and journalist.

Duncan's plots and characters vary, but her books always contain a good deal of suspense. In her works, Duncan has dealt with the murder of a high school teacher, witches, kidnapping, a group of sadistic feminists, and treason. Most notably, Duncan's love of suspense has found expression in her novels about the supernatural.

Her first book of this type, *A Gift of Magic,* relates a young girl's awakening to her extrasensory perception. *Down the Dark Hall* is the story of a boarding school for girls with ESP. In this Gothic mystery, Duncan spiced the plot with ghosts, an evil headmistress, and a handsome hero. *Stranger with My Face* is the story of Laurie and Lia, twins who were separated at birth. After a series of inexplicable events, Laurie finds out that Lia is using astral projection in an attempt to take over Laurie's body. Following several twists in the plots of her novels, Duncan consistently ensures that good triumphs over evil.

Although some critics accuse Duncan of being melodramatic, she has found an eager audience of young adults. Through her use of action, deft characterization, and other-worldly elements, Duncan weaves stories that capture the reader's attention. She has said that her primary goal is to entertain: "My own most successful books have been those that were high in entertainment value. . . . The most valuable thing an author can do for today's teenagers is to help them to realize that it's as much fun to read a book as to turn on the television."

(See also *Contemporary Authors,* Vols. 1-4, rev. ed.; *Contemporary Authors New Revision Series,* Vol. 2; and *Something about the Author,* Vol. 1.)

Courtesy of Lois Duncan

THE CHRISTIAN SCIENCE MONITOR

Lynn Chambers [protagonist of **"Debutante Hill"**], pretty and popular high school senior, declines to join the Rivertown debutante group because her father thinks the idea undemocratic. Thus cut off from the social life of her normal circle of friends, and lonely for Paul Kingsley, her "steady," who has gone away to college, Lynn finds herself pushed toward a new series of experiences. Some of them are good, some are bad, but from all of them Lynn learns a lot. The end of the winter season finds her a much wiser and happier girl. Miss Duncan writes exceptionally well, and has the happy ability to make a reader care what happens to her characters. A few places are weak in plausibility, notably Paul's involvement in his first date with Brenda. It makes him more of a spineless wonder than the author has prepared us to believe.

S.B.B., "Widening Horizons: 'Debutante Hill'," in The Christian Science Monitor (reprinted by permission from The Christian Science Monitor; © 1959 The Christian Science Publishing Society; all rights reserved), February 5, 1959, p. 11.

RUTH HILL VIGUERS

[*The Middle Sister* is the] story of a girl's discovery that although she could not follow in the footsteps of her older sister, she was a person in her own right with her own beauty, talent, and integrity. The characters are alive and also very pleasant to know, and while the outcome of events is never surprising, the old theme is handled so exceptionally well that interest never lags.

Ruth Hill Viguers, in her review of "The Middle Sister," in The Horn Book Magazine (copyright, 1960, by the Horn Book, Inc., Boston), Vol. XXXVI, No. 5, October, 1960, p. 408.

BEST SELLERS

[*Season of the Two-Heart*] delicately handles racial prejudice and the lack of understanding of both the Indian and American cultures. The characters bring out the fact that, if there is an honest effort and a willingness to try, the prejudice will melt into the background and personal worth will come to the forefront. A well-written story with evidence of much research in Indian customs present. Characters are life-like. (p. 289)

A review of "Season of the Two-Heart," in Best Sellers (copyright 1964, by the University of Scran-

100

ton), Vol. 24, No. 14, October 15, 1964, pp. 288-89.

ETHNA SHEEHAN

[In *Season of the Two-Heart*] Martha Weekoty takes her first step away from her Pueblo Indian environment by attending high school in Albuquerque. Now she can evaluate the loving but lackadaisical ways of the Pueblo. She sizes up the white family with whom she is living—the self-centered girl, the club-conscious mother, the lovable small boys, the kindly father. Above all, she weighs her love for the white boy Alan, who wants to marry her. The author does not provide a pat answer for Martha's dilemma concerning her future, but leaves the reader to ponder things from all angles as Martha will have to do. An absorbing story with serious undertones.

> *Ethna Sheehan, in her review of "Season of the Two-Heart," in* America *(reprinted with permission of America Press, Inc.; © 1964; all rights reserved), Vol. 111, No. 21, November 21, 1964, p. 670.*

RUTH HILL VIGUERS

Even though the adjustment of young people from various American Indian cultures to the white man's world is an old theme, the story of Martha Weekoty in her alien setting [*Season of the Two-Heart*] compels interest. At once proud of her Pueblo Indian heritage and impatient with the indifference of her family to new ways that would serve the well-being of her people, Martha hoped to reconcile the two ways of life. . . . [She soon realizes] that she would never serve her people by renouncing her chances for a university education and following the pattern her parents expected of her. Sharply contrasted with her own home, in which attention to the children's diets may have been lacking but attention to their emotional needs was abundant, was her home with the Boyntons in Albuquerque, where she lived and worked during her last year of high school. Much as Martha loved little Daniel Boynton she resented giving him the care he should have received from his mother. The several threads of plot are woven together in a convincing and moving climax.

> *Ruth Hill Viguers, in her review of "Season of the Two-Heart," in* The Horn Book Magazine *(copyright © 1965, by The Horn Book, Inc., Boston), Vol. XLI, No. 1, February, 1965, p. 59.*

DOROTHY M. BRODERICK

["**Ransom**" deserves] mention for its portrait of the thoroughly amoral, egocentric Glenn Kirtland, a character unique in children's books, though not in life. Glenn, the high-school wonder boy, is one of the five teen-agers kidnapped because they live in wealthy Valley Gardens. The other four have conventional problems: shyness, divorce in the family, physical handicap and lack of self-confidence. As each reacts in his own way to being held captive atop an Arizona mountain, the predictable growth takes place—except in Glenn. It is this consistency of Glenn's personality that sets the book apart and makes it something more than another good mystery.

> *Dorothy M. Broderick, in her review of "Ransom," in* The New York Times Book Review *(© 1966 by The New York Times Company; reprinted by permission), June 5, 1966, p. 42.*

ZENA SUTHERLAND

[*Ransom* is a] dramatic story of a kidnapping, suspenseful despite the fact that the number of characters, character sketches, and sub-plots crowds the background; the plot is less emphatic than it would be in a setting more sparse. Three criminals seclude the kidnapped young people in a mountain cabin, having shanghaied the school bus. Each of the five has his own problem; each reacts to the tension of the situation, and there are some interesting interactions among the five.

> *Zena Sutherland, in her review of "Ransom," in* Bulletin of the Center for Children's Books *(reprinted by permission of The University of Chicago Press; copyright 1967 by The University of Chicago), Vol. 20, No. 7, March, 1967, p. 107.*

KIRKUS REVIEWS

Selfish, smooth-dressing, pot-pushing Larry [protagonist of *They Never Came Home*], balking at discipline from Dad, decides that he can vanish (presumed dead) with the $2000 he's embezzled from his dope ring by pushing handy Dan off a cliff during their camping trip. Dan is sturdy (in spirit and body) and survives the fall with only a case of amnesia. . . . [Masterminded] by Larry, the two (as brothers Lance and Dave) reach the California coast where recuperating "Dave" works six days a week while "Lance" makes hay with pot. When Dan learns who he is and how he's been had, his revulsion and refusal to play along cause Larry to lunge at him, but this time it's Larry who goes over the balcony rail. . . . There'll be no embarrassing questions: in terms of the story, Larry's an enemy of society, fair game for extermination. Shallow, slick, sick.

> *A review of "They Never Came Home," in* Kirkus Reviews *(copyright © 1969 The Kirkus Service, Inc.), Vol. XXXVII, No. 5, March 1, 1969, p. 245.*

PEGGY SULLIVAN

Effective characterizations, dialogue, and transitions from one set of characters to another can't redeem [*They Never Came Home,* a] melodrama in which a corkscrew plot curls around coincidences and contrivances. . . . An unlikely story from an author whose competence with main elements of fiction promises more and better storytelling to come.

> *Peggy Sullivan, in her review of "They Never Came Home," in* School Library Journal, *an appendix to* Library Journal *(reprinted from the April, 1969 issue of* School Library Journal, *published by R. R. Bowker Co./A Xerox Corporation; copyright © 1969), Vol. 15, No. 8, April, 1969, p. 126.*

ZENA SUTHERLAND

[In *They Never Came Home* the] doubts about Larry's character are skilfully developed, so that it comes as little surprise to the reader to find that he had arranged to disappear, taking advantage of an accident that left Dan an amnesia victim. Save for that contrivance, the plot is deft; the story has action and suspense, and a compelling dénouement. (p. 157)

> *Zena Sutherland, in her review of "They Never Came Home," in* Bulletin of the Center for Children's Books *(reprinted by permission of The University of Chi-*

cago Press; © 1969 by The University of Chicago),
Vol. 22, No. 10, June, 1969, pp. 156-57.

RICHARD F. SHEPARD

["**They Never Came Home**"] follows its leads to a crackling
finale that makes the novel live up to its billing as "psychological suspense."

Lois Duncan writes well and simply on mature situations. She
gives her readers comprehensible, yet not oversensational descriptions of a mother's nervous breakdown; of a plain girl
discovering beauty in herself; of a younger brother learning
not to live in the reflected glory of an older one; of a mentally
deranged boy who has cut himself off from the love his family
wanted to give him. "**They Never Came Home**" is a well-
paced action story, with a full quota of heroes and villains,
and a series of narrative hooks guaranteed to hold any reader.

> *Richard F. Shepard, in his review of "They Never
> Came Home," in* The New York Times Book Review
> *(© 1969 by The New York Times Company; reprinted
> by permission), June 8, 1969, p. 42.*

KIRKUS REVIEWS

John Andre was the British Army man who negotiated with
Benedict Arnold at West Point, missed the boat to camp and
was discovered a few miles from his own base in civilian
disguise, the incriminating papers concealed in his sock. A
romantic figure of his time and in [the pages of *Major Andre:
Brave Enemy*], he was convicted of spying and hanged, both
armies noting his courageous posture. His inner thoughts from
boyhood on are imputed, a technique which tends to overdra-
matize a dramatic personality and force each gesture into significance. And the "spy" episode is quite brief, so readers
looking for that kind of excitement will be disappointed to find
so much more about his relationships with women.

> *A review of "Major Andre: Brave Enemy," in* Kirkus
> Reviews *(copyright © 1969 The Kirkus Service, Inc.),
> Vol. XXXVII, No. 12, June 15, 1969, p. 633.*

MURIEL KOLB

The story of the infamous treason plot between General Mathew Arnold and Major André is told in [*Major André: Brave
Enemy,* an] admiring biography of the dashing young British
officer-spy. Some detail on Arnold is omitted, and there is a
little fictionalization, though no distortion of facts. However,
the book is more interesting and smoothly written than the very
similar, recent biography by [Adele] Nathan, *Major John André
. . .* which, though listed as an adult title by the publishers,
is not too difficult for good junior high school readers; it has
more historical detail, but is far from being comprehensive or
scholarly. (p. 136)

> *Muriel Kolb, in her review of "Major André: Brave
> Enemy," in* School Library Journal, *an appendix to*
> Library Journal *(reprinted from the March, 1970 is-
> sue of* School Library Journal, *published by R. R.
> Bowker Co./A Xerox Corporation; copyright © 1970),
> Vol. 16, No. 7, March, 1970, pp. 135-36.*

KIRKUS REVIEWS

Titillation, exploitation, anything but history: [*Peggy* is] the
cattiest first-person portrait of a vixen, Peggy Shippen, the girl
who becomes Mrs. Benedict Arnold. The girl who sulks,
screams, cries, faints (and reports it all proudly) when Father
moves out of Philadelphia. . . . The girl who marries Arnold
after stealing someone else's beau; who masterminds the grand
betrayal; who despises the unborn infant sullying her perfect
figure; who declares about the baby that its "'Mama' (she
herself) was ready to put a pillow over his head and sit on it
and might actually have done so if Major Franks had not been
there." Cloaked with spiteful dagger thrashing out in all directions—unconscionable even as fiction.

> *A review of "Peggy," in* Kirkus Reviews *(copyright
> © 1970 The Kirkus Service, Inc.), Vol. XXXVIII, No.
> 18, September 15, 1970, p. 1047.*

MARY M. BURNS

[Peggy Shippen] is an intriguing and controversial historical
figure, for the exact extent of her influence over Arnold's
attempt to betray his command at West Point is, according to
at least one source, a disputed issue. The point of view that
Peggy was aware of, approved of, and was indeed implicated
in Arnold's treachery is the basic assumption underlying [*Peggy*,
a] presentation of a pivotal event in American history. Peggy
as narrator of her story from June, 1776, to September, 1780,
is revealed as a self-centered yet fascinating, high-spirited girl
whose ability to bend men to her desires finds its match in the
equally self-serving Benedict Arnold. . . . Chosen as go-be-
tween because of his affections for Peggy during the British
occupation of Philadelphia in 1778, the unfortunate Major André
is presented as a gentlemanly, artistic, and sensitive officer—
an obvious contrast to Arnold—unable to see Peggy's feminine
wiles as anything but innocent, womanly charm. The conversational tone of the narrative gives a sense of immediacy to a
fictionalized biography of a remarkable anti-heroine, whose
unswerving devotion to self is reminiscent of two other famous,
although fictional, coquettes Becky Sharp and Scarlett O'Hara.
(pp. 622-23)

> *Mary M. Burns, in her review of "Peggy," in* The
> Horn Book Magazine *(copyright © 1970 by The Horn
> Book, Inc., Boston), Vol. XLVI, No. 6, December,
> 1970, pp. 622-23.*

PEGGY SULLIVAN

[In *A Gift of Magic* each] of the three Garrett children has a
distinctive personality and talent. The older sister, Kirby, is
determined to be a dancer, and little brother Brendon is a
phenomenal pianist, although he has little real interest in music.
But this above-average story centers on middle-child Nancy's
gift of extrasensory perception and on the responsibilities, problems (in school, with her siblings), and advantages it gives
her. It is an understanding high school counselor in love with
her divorced mother who convinces Nancy of the values of her
gift, and of the need to use it without trying to manage the
lives of others (e.g., sister Kirby and her mother, whom Nancy
had wanted to stay with her father). Background on extrasensory perception is well woven into the story, and current interest
in the occult and psychic phenomena will widen the audience
for the book.

*Peggy Sullivan, in her review of "A Gift of Magic,"
in* School Library Journal, *an appendix to* Library
Journal *(reprinted from the November, 1971 issue of*
School Library Journal, *published by R. R. Bowker
Co./A Xerox Corporation; copyright © 1971), Vol.
18, No. 3, November, 1971, p. 122.*

KIRKUS REVIEWS

In the same mail as Julie's acceptance to Smith College comes an anonymous note with the menacing reminder: I KNOW WHAT YOU DID LAST SUMMER. Though the weight on Julie's conscience seems to have left her more apathetic than anguished, the note sends her into a frenzy because what Julie—and her former boyfriend Ray, and his friends Helen and Barry—did was no harmless frolic; in a moment of panic they left the scene of an accident in which they had killed a 10 year-old boy. Even after Barry is lured to an empty athletic field and critically wounded he refuses to release his friends from their vow of secrecy. But both he and Helen (a narcissistic TV weathergirl) are so vacuous that one hardly cares whether they get murdered or not. Still, the madman murderer is cleverly concealed among a bevy of red herrings and as he zeroes in for his revenge [*I Know What You Did Last Summer*] turns into a high velocity chiller with a double identity twist.

*A review of "I Know What You Did Last Summer,"
in* Kirkus Reviews *(copyright © 1973 The Kirkus
Service, Inc.), Vol. XLI, No. 17, September 1, 1973,
p. 972.*

ZENA SUTHERLAND

Almost a year had passed since Julie and the others had made a pact of silence, and now this message had come, anonymously, in the mail. Who could have known? Barry had been driving when they hit the boy on the bicycle, had persuaded the others to drive off, and had convinced them that reporting their involvement could do no good. They did report seeing the boy—but help came too late. He had died. With taut suspense [*I Know What You Did Last Summer*] builds as each of the four miscreants is taunted or attacked (Barry is shot) and they fear that the mysterious avenger is bent on killing them all. The pressure of events affects other factors of their lives in a book that has vivid characterization, good balance, and the boding sense of impending danger that adds excitement to the best mystery stories.

*Zena Sutherland, in her review of "I Know What
You Did Last Summer," in* Bulletin of the Center for
Children's Books *(reprinted by permission of The
University of Chicago Press; © 1974 by The University of Chicago), Vol. 27, No. 6, February, 1974,
p. 93.*

LINDA SILVER

[*I Know What You Did Last Summer* is a] slick whodunit, pedestrian in style, mediocre in characterization, but suspenseful to the end. Four teenagers—friends who have drifted apart since they were involved in a hit-and-run accident—are jolted by a series of ominous notes and phone calls from someone who is on to their crime. . . . False leads and several suspicious characters will keep readers guessing the identity of the vengeful enemy and may even divert some from the regrettable fact

that the four protagonists are too vapid to merit any real concern.

*Linda Silver, in her review of "I Know What You
Did Last Summer," in* School Library Journal, *an
appendix to* Library Journal *(reprinted from the April,
1974 issue of* School Library Journal, *published by
R. R. Bowker Co./A Xerox Corporation; copyright
© 1974), Vol. 20, No. 8, April, 1974, p. 64.*

KIRKUS REVIEWS

When Kit and the other three high ESP-quotient pupils [in *Down a Dark Hall*] who have been chosen for Mme. Duret's new boarding school get their first sight of isolated Blackwood manor only one word comes to their minds—evil. But you don't have to be psychic to anticipate some fishy goings on— what with the locked gates, unmailed letters home and those nightly dream visitors who inspire the girls to discover hitherto non-existent artistic talents. When the spirit guides, including Emily Bronte, Schubert and landscapist Thomas Cole, start using the increasingly weary girls as a channel for delivering their posthumous masterpieces to Mme. Duret (who will use them for financial gain) only resolute Kit has the will to resist openly. Stranger still, Mme. Duret's honest and irresistibly handsome son Jules considers the whole undertaking a noble experiment—until he learns the fate of his mother's previous pupils and sees the nasty creations of some dirty-minded deceased artists who have been insinuating their way into the nocturnal dictation sessions. We aren't let in on the unpleasant details, but of course by this time it's too late anyway. . . . Blackwoods goes up in flames and Kit is rescued from a fiery death by the ghost of her own departed Dad. This last (especially?) is on the slick side, but Lois Duncan (*A Gift of Magic* . . .) is a practiced medium and manages to summon up the chilling specter without dwelling overmuch on its distinguishing features.

A review of "Down a Dark Hall," in Kirkus Reviews
*(copyright © 1974 The Kirkus Service, Inc.), Vol.
XLII, No. 18, September 15, 1974, p. 1012.*

GLORIA LEVITAS

Two gothic novels, Lois Duncan's **"Down A Dark Hall"** . . . and David Severn's **"The Girl in the Grove"** . . . are on the whole, more interesting than many that flood the adult market. Perhaps teenagers more credibly embody, than do women in their twenties, the uncertainties and mild hysteria of gothic personality. At any rate, both books are suitably equipped with bright, attractive heroines, brooding mansions and brooding young men, and the requisite ghosts from the past. David Severn's book is crisply written, although its cloying plot and the heroine's inexplicable attachment to a boorish young man will put it high on feminist lists as a book to avoid. By contrast, Lois Duncan's off-hand treatment of romance allows her to focus on the intelligence and rationality of her heroine. The result is highly original; a gothic novel that is more a commentary on the dangers of education than on the perils of unrequited love. (p. 10)

Gloria Levitas, "Haunts and Hunts," in The New
York Times Book Review *(© 1974 by The New York
Times Company; reprinted by permission), November 10, 1974, pp. 8, 10.**

SARAH LAW KENNERLY

When 14-year-old Kit arrives at Blackwood, a new and exclusive school for girls run by Madame Duret, she is frightened by an unsettling atmosphere of evil. . . . The climax of terror [in *Down a Dark Hall*] comes when Kit discovers what happened to the pupils Madame had exploited in previous schools. What first appears to be a juvenile Gothic romance turns into a disturbing fantasy about the invasion of a sensitive human mind by an alien intelligence.

> *Sarah Law Kennerly, in her review of "Down a Dark Hall," in* School Library Journal, *an appendix to* Library Journal *(reprinted from the December, 1974 issue of* School Library Journal, *published by R. R. Bowker Co./A Xerox Corporation; copyright © 1974), Vol. 21, No. 4, December, 1974, p. 50.*

KIRKUS REVIEWS

Long before she suspects orphaned cousin Julia of being a ringer, Rae [protagonist of *Summer of Fear*] is convinced that the new member of the family is a witch—and when the awkward Ozarks teenager promptly turns into a femme fatale to steal Rae's best dress and best boyfriend, all the while making eyes at Rae's dad, she shows herself to be the kind of villainess who'd make any red-blooded girl spitting mad. Rae finds evidence of supernatural doings—a wax doll, a mutilated photograph, the smell of sulphur . . . even the body of the family dog, felled by Julia's curse. But Duncan doesn't rely overmuch on conventional props; her speciality is high-gloss malice and murder (*I Know What You Did Last Summer* . . .) and Rae, isolated as much by her uncontrollable jealousy as by Julia's plotting, might just convince even those who swore they'd never taste another witch's brew recipe.

> *A review of "Summer of Fear," in* Kirkus Reviews *(copyright © 1976 The Kirkus Service, Inc.), Vol. XLIV, No. 12, June 15, 1976, p. 691.*

SARAH LAW KENNERLY

When Rachel's orphaned cousin comes to live with the Bryants, 17-year-old Julia, whom the family had never seen before, charms everybody: Rachel's parents, her brothers, her best friend, and worst of all, her steady boyfriend. But for Rachel, Julia's arrival signals a *Summer of Fear*. . . . Sweet, lovely Julia, it turns out, is a witch: how Rachel finally uncovers the truth and saves her family from the ruthless sorceress makes for a sensational climax that may cause even young cynics to suspend their disbelief in black powers.

> *Sarah Law Kennerly, in her review of "Summer of Fear," in* School Library Journal *(reprinted from the December, 1976 issue of* School Library Journal, *published by R. R. Bowker Co./A Xerox Corporation; copyright © 1976), Vol. 23, No. 4, December, 1976, p. 69.*

JULIA WHEDON

["**Summer of Fear**"] is the story of a very square Southwestern community invaded by a sorceress in lithesome teen-age form. Julia is orphaned by sudden tragedy and taken in by trusting relatives. Rachel—the narrator and resident teen-age daughter in that household—watches in helpless horror as cousin Julia steals her boyfriend, takes over her best friend, and displaces her in the affections of her own family. Rachel surmises this chick has a lot going for her besides looks and personality. She's not just a bitch—but a witch! Killing the family dog with voodoo, putting her curse on those who suspect her (a near homicide), and finally plotting a fatal accident for Mom, she is found out only at last, and almost too late.

Though the characters are the usual Mom, Pop, Sis and Junior cut-outs, the story is well paced and decently suspenseful. Lois Duncan is a pro. Good practice for young readers getting ready for Eric Ambler.

> *Julia Whedon, "Witches and Werewolves," in* The New York Times Book Review *(© 1977 by The New York Times Company; reprinted by permission), March 6, 1977, p. 29.**

ETHEL L. HEINS

Vigorous characterization, a neatly tailored plot, and a sense of foreboding that rises with the accelerating pace of the storytelling—all these are the hallmarks of a successful thriller. Rachel [protagonist of *Summer of Fear*], almost sixteen that June, was totally at peace with her responsive, loving family and with her boy-next-door romance. A long, happy summer stretched ahead. Then came the news that an aunt and an uncle had been killed in a mysterious single-car accident and that her seventeen-year-old cousin Julia—whom she didn't know—was coming to live with them. From a remote part of the Ozarks she came, a curiously mature-looking, ungrieving, inscrutable girl who immediately seemed to cast a spell over almost everyone. . . . Kindly old Professor Jarvis, an authority on the folklore of witchcraft, became [Rachel's] refuge; seriously he told her that the magic of modern witches was the "'the utilization of the mind force to make things happen as they are desired.'" Finally, when the professor, without warning, suffered a stroke, Rachel was certain that Julia was evil incarnate; and in a fearsome climax she managed to head off total disaster.

> *Ethel L. Heins, in her review of "Summer of Fear," in* The Horn Book Magazine *(copyright © 1977 by the Horn Book, Inc., Boston), Vol. LIII, No. 2, April, 1977, p. 167.*

RICHARD PECK

Contrary to certain opinion, the new wave of novels for adolescents hasn't explored every sensational topic after all; mainly because the adult author doesn't live in a world as corrosively conformist or as criminally cruel as that of the teenager. Breathy novels about drugs, sexual liberation and sub-proletariat gang warfare let off scot-free the majority of young readers, who are virtually all middle-class, who deny drugs are a problem, and who are amazingly prudish about other people's sex lives.

Lois Duncan breaks some new ground in ["**Killing Mr. Griffin**"], a novel without sex, drugs or black leather jackets. But the taboo she tampers with is far more potent and pervasive: the unleashed fury of the permissively reared against any assault on their egos and authority. A group of high-school seniors kill an English teacher who dares trouble them with grades, homework and standards.

Before all this is smiled nervously away as a sick fantasy, let's meet the perpetrators, familiar figures all. There's Jeff, the jock, who suspects his teacher, Mr. Griffin, of lying awake nights "trying to think of questions that don't have answers."

Jeff is never likely to learn that this is a central point of education.

There's Betsy, "the all-American girl—head cheerleader—homecoming queen" who has eliminated enemies before, without violence, and is in complete possession of a mother who assures her that her cuteness will last.

There's Mark, who would not like me for failing to list him first. He's been crossed even less often than Betsy. There's madness in his eyes, and in his psychiatric history. But his charisma and talent for delegating authority will make him the most familiar figure to young readers. This is a book for people who've learned in the schoolyard where nice guys finish.

The nice guy is David, senior-class president, quietly sincere, thoughtful, fond of a challenge, and political enough to know that Mark's malevolence takes precedence over Robert's Rules of Order. The novel is of two minds about who the central figure is. It's either David, or Susan—"a little creep with glasses"—early conscripted as a decoy in an asexual seduction by The Group. When she receives this brief acceptance, her parents are thrilled.

We've even come far enough from the 1960's to see the victim clearly. Mr. Griffin is a professor who's given up trying to teach the classics to college freshmen who can't pronounce the words. . . .

His students dislike his punctuality, his necktie, his irony. They're triggered by his assignment of homework on a basketball night. They plan to kidnap and terrorize him into a sort of pedagogical impotence, so he'll be like the rest of the faculty. But the book's title has reached the reader before this plan does. And the scheme becomes feasible to the schemers for the most airtight of reasons: They remind one another that legally they are minors. Not only are they untouchable, they're not *guilty*.

You don't stop reading at this point, though you well might. The value of the book lies in the twisted logic of the teen-agers and how easily they can justify anything. But then the plot descends into unadulterated melodrama. One murder leads to another. And a murder attempt at the end is evidently meant to establish the comparative innocence of one character at the expense of the others. The book becomes "an easy read" when it shouldn't. But there's veracity unto the end: the parents are the last to lose their innocence.

Will this book give the impressionable unspeakable ideas? I doubt it. They already have them. The impulse toward crime is surely to be found nearer than a book: the paranoia of the permissively handled and the unlikelihood of punishment for anything. Adolescents have witnessed far more graphic scenes of teacher humiliation and brutalization in their own schools, in terms more immediate than this book.

And besides, who will read it? Teen-agers won't choose to identify with these meticulously unflattering portrayals, though they'll see their friends in them. Parents won't go near the book. Nor will school administrators, who spend increasing time, not in dealing with school crime, but in keeping it out of the newspapers. Perhaps it's a book for teachers.

Richard Peck, "Teaching Teacher a Lesson," in The New York Times Book Review *(© 1978 by The New York Times Company; reprinted by permission), April 30, 1978, p. 54.*

DREW STEVENSON

The latest thriller by Lois Duncan, *Killing Mr. Griffin* . . . , unfolds as a gag to scare a hated English teacher erupts into a nightmare for a group of high school students in New Mexico. . . . As in the author's *Down a Dark Hall* . . . , skillful plotting builds layers of tension that draw readers into the eye of the conflict. The ending is nicely handled in a manner which provides relief without removing any of the chilling implications.

Drew Stevenson, in his review of "Killing Mr. Griffin," in School Library Journal *(reprinted from the May, 1978 issue of* School Library Journal, *published by R. R. Bowker Co./A Xerox Corporation; copyright © 1978), Vol. 24, No. 9, May, 1978, p. 86.*

KIRKUS REVIEWS

[In *Killing Mr. Griffin*], a portrait of group guilt that recalls Duncan's *I Know What You Did Last Summer* . . . , five members of demanding Mr. Griffin's senior English class decide to teach him a lesson by kidnapping him from the high school parking lot and leaving him bound and gagged in a lonely spot out of town—where, before the students return to free him, the teacher dies. (Unknown to the kidnappers, he has been under medication for angina.) The prank is engineered by the stereotypically disturbed and evil Mark. . . . Shifting viewpoints among the five, their families, and the teacher's wife, Duncan allots the most attention to Susan, the least involved, and she lets her off most easily in the end. It's all a bit too easy, but well-greased as ever—another of Duncan's nonstop thrillers, with as cunning a hold on its readers as Mark has on his confederates.

A review of "Killing Mr. Griffin," in Kirkus Reviews *(copyright © 1978 The Kirkus Service, Inc.), Vol. XLVI, No. 9, May 1, 1978, p. 500.*

HILDAGARDE GRAY

Seldom has a book left me more apprehensive as to its merits than *Killing Mr. Griffin*. Good mysteries are always welcome, and today's young reader enjoys a psychological twist. After all, his favorite geography is that of the inner "me." Points in favor of the book include: fairly decent language, the bad guys get their just desserts, and families work out their problems. The teacher's (Mr. Griffin's) philosophy—"students should be challenged to do their best"—is viewed first from the side of the student and then, in a most perceptive chapter, from the teacher's side—"by the time they're in college it's too late to teach them to study . . . they expect to be entertained not educated. [As a high-school teacher] I wouldn't baby them or play games with them. I'd push each one into doing the best work of which he or she was capable. . . ."

This very dedicated thinking leads into the plot. A handful of students are led by a psychopathic fellow student into kidnapping their perfectionist literature teacher, whose bad heart turns the "prank" into murder. An innocent girl, who joined the ranks out of a desperate need of acceptance, begins to crumble. . . . The story is exciting, loaded with suspense and terror, moves rapidly, and falls into the easy-to-read class, all factors that assure the book's constant circulation.

All these assets, however, are nullified by a story that absolutely invites the borderline delinquent to branch out into areas of rebellion that horrify when their potential is considered. Spin-offs—pranks to tease or harrass teachers—would be encouraged by the ease with which such events are presented here. Granted, the killers are caught and sentenced, but their reaction and fate are glossed over in the last page or two. I have become suspicious of books that tend to "blueprint" antisocial behavior for a generation that is surrounded by such information, via TV, movies, and current periodicals. Our obligation to the future must begin somewhere. Where better than in a child's recreational pursuits? (pp. 154-55)

> *Hildagarde Gray, in her review of "Killing Mr. Griffin," in* Best Sellers *(copyright © 1978 Helen Dwight Reid Educational Foundation), Vol. 38, No. 5, August, 1978, pp. 154-55.*

THE BOOKLIST

[In *Daughters of Eve,* Duncan] distorts feminist principles into weapons of vengeance. A bitter, disturbed teacher turns her malleable high school charges into a confused, misanthropic group of girls who, beneath the facade of a small school-sponsored service club called the Daughters of Eve, use the physical and psychological strength of their numbers to punish traitorous men. Acts of defiance against their families and school, which include violence against a male classmate who takes advantage of the loneliness and sexual naiveté of one of the girls and vandalism perpetrated against an instructor thought to have been unfair, culminate in murder when one of the less stable of the group is threatened by her brutal father and kills him. A postscript hints at the success of the club's new ideology and portends chilling horrors for the future. One-dimensional characterizations and an episodic plot strain credulity, and there will likely be objections to the twisted use of the feminist theme, but Duncan has successfully created a disturbing climate of latent evil—couched within the familiarity of teen-age life—where vicious acts go unpunished and villains triumph and, as in the past, has manipulated everything for maximum effect.

> *A review of "Daughters of Eve," in* Booklist *(reprinted by permission of the American Library Association; copyright © 1979 by the American Library Association), Vol. 75, No. 22, July 15, 1979, p. 1618.*

CYRISSE JAFFEE

[*Daughters of Eve* is a] slick, scary occult novel with a stereotypical "women's libber" (bitter, frustrated, ultimately revealed as mentally disturbed) as the force of evil. Irene Stark, the new faculty advisor of the Daughters of Eve, an exclusive social club for girls at a suburban Michigan high school, encourages the members to become more socially conscious and assertive. . . . The only doubter is Tammy Carncross, whose ESP (an artificial device) warns her that something is wrong. She is, of course, correct. Ms. Stark has been manipulating the girls and channeling their anger into a vicious hatred of men. . . . The inevitable denouement is a cold-blooded murder. . . . Though some may object to the violence, most YAs will be drawn by the ease with which this popular author builds suspense. But none of the characters are more than stick figures and the implication that sisterhood is not only powerful but downright dangerous is hardly a progressive message.

> *Cyrisse Jaffee, in her review of "Daughters of Eve," in* School Library Journal *(reprinted from the September, 1979 issue of* School Library Journal, *pub-*

lished by R. R. Bowker Co./A Xerox Corporation; copyright © 1979), Vol. 26, No. 1, September, 1979, p. 155.

KIRKUS REVIEWS

In last year's *Killing Mr. Griffin,* a disturbed and evil high school student led four classmates in kidnapping and inadvertently killing a strict teacher. [In *Daughters of Eve*] the mad instigator is a new teacher and adviser to the selective, nationally affiliated service club Daughters of Eve; and the instruments of her revenge against males are the club's ten members, whose small Michigan town seems to have been by-passed by the winds of women's liberation. . . . Despite slickness and stereotypes, *Killing Mr. Griffin*—and another of Duncan's group-guilt numbers, *I Know What You Did Last Summer* . . . —had a good share of seductive suspense; this is just manipulated melodrama. Duncan takes care to maintain an ideological balance with her offending males and her twisted feminist, but both sides are too heavily drawn to hold up.

> *A review of "Daughters of Eve," in* Kirkus Reviews *(copyright © 1979 The Kirkus Service, Inc.), Vol. XLVII, No. 19, October 1, 1979, p. 1149.*

ZENA SUTHERLAND

Restricted to a membership of ten, the Daughters of Eve is the most exclusive club at Modesta High School; it is with an invitation to join the group that [*Daughters of Eve*] begins. . . . Although the story focuses on . . . three new members, it includes material about the other girls, about the influence of the bitter teacher who is sponsor for the [strongly feminist] group, about relationships among them, and about the meetings at which they discuss their problems as a group and as individuals. The style and characterization are competent, but the book is weakened by the amount of material and number of characters it covers and it has an embittered tone of hatred that colors the characterization to the extent that few of the parents or the males of any age have commendable facets to their personalitites. (pp. 92-3)

> *Zena Sutherland, in her review of "Daughters of Eve," in* Bulletin of the Center for Children's Books *(reprinted by permission of The University of Chicago Press; © 1980 by The University of Chicago), Vol. 33, No. 5, January, 1980, pp. 92-3.*

NATALIE BABBITT

[*Daughters of Eve*] is a savage novel full of troubled, angry characters. At first it appears that the author has identified completely with Irene Stark, advisor to an exclusive high-school girls' club called "Daughters of Eve" and is speaking to us all when Irene urges the club's 10 members toward action against male chauvinism.

Soon, however, as Irene's paranoia reveals itself, the reader begins to see that Lois Duncan has instead chosen the Movement only as a setting, and is detached enough to use it with great effectiveness. I was reminded of William Golding's "Lord of the Flies"—the horror of Lois Duncan's novel erupts just as violently at the end. Still, **"Daughters of Eve"** seems less real than "Lord of the Flies," for all of that work's phantasmagoria. Perhaps this is because the Golding novel is set on a desert island where anything might happen, whereas "Eve" takes place down the street.

What *is* vivid, though, is the female rage that Lois Duncan portrays—any open-minded reader is bound to recognize much of it—and the story itself is finely constructed and told. Also—how refreshing!—there are no lessons. Instead, this novel enables us to see ourselves as the barely civilized creatures we truly are, and it is strongly evenhanded, for it lets us see that women can be as bloodthirsty as men ever were. We haven't had much of that since Madame Defarge.

> *Natalie Babbitt, in her review of "Daughters of Eve,"*
> *in* The New York Times Book Review *(© 1980 by*
> *The New York Times Company; reprinted by per-*
> *mission), January 27, 1980, p. 24.*

JAN M. GOODMAN

Daughters of Eve is a suspenseful novel that invalidates legitimate problems by presenting misdirected solutions. The author raises such feminist issues as wife-beating, inequality on the job, unfairness in high school athletics and the sexist dimension of male/female relationships, but the violence of her solutions implies that it may be dangerous to even recognize the issues.

Daughters of Eve is an elite high school group; its ten members are dedicated to sisterhood and sworn to secrecy. The book chronicles the lives of the young women and their new advisor, Irene Stark. (p. 17)

Irene encourages the club members to assert themselves and fight their oppression. At first, the Daughters' actions are reasonable. . . . However, as the novel progresses, Irene stands by as the Daughters get angrier and their solutions become more violent. . . . When Fran's [science] project is rejected in favor of a male student's, the Daughters destroy the science lab, after Irene symbolically provides the key. . . .

The book implies that the Daughters have gone too far and that Irene's personal bitterness has caused her to misrepresent matters and incited the violence. For example, after the science lab is destroyed, it is revealed that Fran's project was rejected not because she was female but because her experiment violated state rules. The author clearly places a harsh value judgment on violent solutions, and because she provides no alternative solutions, she leaves the impression that fighting for women's rights leads to uncontrollable anger and senseless destruction.

In addition, the book contains many negative stereotypes. It is anti-fat in its description of Laura, who is too "ugly" to "get a man" and is loved only by her mother who overlooks her daughter's "weight problem" because she is overweight herself! The club is elitist in that only the "choicest of the choice" can join. An anti-gay reference is made by Ruth's father, who refuses to let his sons do household work because he's afraid they'll turn into "fags."

The book suggests that Irene is an angry woman, not because she is justified, but because she is "empty" (note the symbolism of her last name, *Stark*). The book also implies that Irene is not a complete, or "normal" woman—she has an "unappetizing" appearance, a low voice, a harsh face and a trace of a mustache! The author subtly distorts Irene's potentially strong feminist character into that of a vindictive fanatic who manipulates and co-opts vulnerable young minds to achieve her sick revenge.

In summary, the book's deceptive interpretation of feminism plus its dangerous stereotypes make it a harmful distortion of reality. However, the book could be sensitively used to raise feminist issues as they affect the lives of adolescents. But the issues must be presented as real to women everywhere, and not as obsessions of fanatics like Irene Stark. If the book is used, it must be followed by a discussion of alternate solutions to violence, all the while stressing the validity of oppressed peoples' anger and frustration. Readers must be asked to consider what they would do when all "rational" solutions to their problems don't work. (p. 18)

> *Jan M. Goodman, in her review of "Daughters of*
> *Eve," in* Interracial Books for Children Bulletin *(re-*
> *printed by permission of* Interracial Books for Chil-
> dren Bulletin, *1841 Broadway, New York, N.Y.*
> *10023), Vol. 11, No. 6, 1980, pp. 17-18.*

HOLLY SANDHUBER

The element of the supernatural is so gradually and deftly introduced into [*Stranger with My Face*] that its presence seems natural and believable and, hence, more menacing. While some of the author's attempts at "symbolism" are a bit obvious, and some of the minor characters are sketchily portrayed, most readers will not mind. They will be completely caught up in this suspenseful, gripping book. The ironic surprise ending is one more asset in a finely crafted story.

> *Holly Sandhuber, in her review of "Stranger with*
> *My Face," in* School Library Journal *(reprinted from*
> *the November, 1981 issue of* School Library Journal,
> *published by R. R. Bowker Co./A Xerox Corporation;*
> *copyright © 1981), Vol. 28, No. 3, November, 1981,*
> *p. 103.*

KIRKUS REVIEWS

[*Stranger with My Face*] is one of Duncan's sleazier supernatural thrillers, which doesn't mean that it won't find its shiver-seeking readers. It's told, with appropriate shudders and foreshadowing, by 17-year-old Laurie Stratton, whose senior year of high school on a remote New England island is haunted by (she learns midway) a twin sister left behind when Laurie was adopted as an infant. First, others report seeing Laurie where she wasn't—a boyfriend breaks with her because of the assumed deceit—and at last twin Lia, identical except for those evil, malevolent eyes, reveals herself to Laurie. Laurie's parents confirm the adoption, the twin, and the fact that the girls are half Navaho; and Helen, a new school friend from the west, explains to Laurie about astral projection—a talent more common among the Navaho, who can leave their bodies to travel at will. Laurie masters the technique herself and learns, in her out-of-body travels, of her sister's vicious and terrible past. Helen is seriously and mysteriously injured; a new boyfriend, Jeff, and then Laurie herself, are lured to an almost fatal accident on the rocks; and in one of Duncan's ingenious climactic twists, Laurie must fight her twin for her own real body, which she regains only through her little sister's perspicacity, Jeff's fast action, and Helen's earlier gift of a Navaho turquoise fetish. Professionally orchestrated suspense for the willingly susceptible.

> *A review of "Stranger with My Face," in* Kirkus
> Reviews *(copyright © 1982 The Kirkus Service, Inc.),*
> *Vol. L, No. 1, January 1, 1982, p. 11.*

ANN A. FLOWERS

[In Duncan's *Stranger with My Face*, protagonist Laurie Stratton] eventually discovered that she was an adopted child, one of a pair of identical twins of an American Indian mother and a white father; she was both fascinated and repelled by her twin, Lia, who became more and more visible and began to exert great influence. But Lia was an envious, malevolent person with a secret aim to inhabit Laurie's body. After several near-tragedies, Lia did take over her twin, and only the quick-witted action of Laurie's sister Megan saved Laurie from roaming forever as a disembodied spirit. The ghostly Lia is deliciously evil; the idea of astral projection—Lia's method of travel—is novel; the island setting is vivid; and the relationships among the young people are realistic in the smoothly written supernatural tale.

> Ann A. Flowers, in her review of "Stranger with My Face," in The Horn Book Magazine (copyright © 1982 by The Horn Book, Inc., Boston), Vol. LVIII, No. 1, February, 1982, p. 51.

TERRY LAWHEAD

[*Chapters: My Growth As a Writer*] is an autobiography of Lois Duncan, and should be classified strictly as such; by no stretch of the imagination should it be regarded as containing information having to do with the craft of writing. We get tales from her teens and before on love and life; we get the chance to read short rejected poems and stories she wrote before making it to the big time. It reads easily, like one of her novels; she has a good hold on her adolescence and one would swear she is indeed 14 years old. She always wanted to write, and it seems she has never had to invent much in the way of plot for her novels: her life is one long teen novel.

> Terry Lawhead, in his review of "Chapters: My Growth As a Writer," in School Library Journal (reprinted from the March, 1982 issue of School Library Journal, published by R. R. Bowker Co./A Xerox Corporation; copyright © 1982), Vol. 28, No. 7, March, 1982, p. 156.

STEPHANIE ZVIRIN

[In *Chapters: My Growth As a Writer*, Duncan] displays an intriguing, very different side of herself as she traces her evolution as a writer from its roots in an eager 10-year-old penner of short stories and poetry to her recognition as a full-fledged professional. Filled with her original stories and poems—many written during her teenage years and published in such popular magazines as *Seventeen* and *American Girl*—her writer's guide cum autobiographical sketch clearly shows how she used material from her own experiences in her work. She eschews in-depth analysis of her writings and includes disappointingly little about the juvenile novels she is more recognized for today, but she does indeed illustrate her coming of age as a writer and, at the same time, provides a highly entertaining collection of vigorous, candid, often sentimental pieces that express the ups and downs of childhood and adolescence as perhaps only a teenager can really see them. (pp. 853-54)

> Stephanie Zvirin, in her review of "Chapters: My Growth As a Writer," in Booklist (reprinted by permission of the American Library Association; copyright © 1982 by the American Library Association), Vol. 78, No. 13, March 1, 1982, pp. 853-54.

JENNIFER MOODY

Lois Duncan, who lives, works and sets her novels in Albuquerque, New Mexico, is a recent but immediately successful arrival on the British scene. Popular as she is, not only with the soft underbelly of the literary world, the children's book reviewers, but with its most hardened carapace, the teenage library book borrower, her novel of 1973, *I Know What You Did Last Summer* has now been published in England. . . .

The story takes place on several levels. As a simple thriller, the mystery of who is responsible for the letters, the threats and the violence, is handled with skill and panache, and, as we have come to expect from Miss Duncan, with a rare gift for suspense. She makes illuminating use of the contrasts between the relationships of Julie and Ray on the one hand and Helen and Barry on the other. Miss Duncan also airs the moral conflict between personal responsibility and obedience to group decisions made democratically. Despite all these positive qualitites, it must be said that this novel has dated badly. Set against a background of campus riots and the Vietnam War, the attitudes and the slang are now remote from the present age and may be quite meaningless to its intended readers. They are in no way intrinsic to the plot, and it would be a shame if this novel failed to find the audience that would appreciate its perception and maturity.

> Jennifer Moody, "The Onset of Maturity," in The Times Literary Supplement (© Times Newspapers Ltd. (London) 1982; reproduced from The Times Literary Supplement by permission), No. 4121, March 26, 1982, p. 343.

LEIGH DEAN

Avid readers of Duncan's YA novels who are accustomed to unconventional characters, and situations steeped in danger, magic, and intrigue will be hard-pressed to recognize or to relate to the Duncan found in the pages of [*Chapters: My Growth As a Writer*]. For the person we meet in her published short stories (circa 1949-62), poems, and the connective autobiographical narrative is as conventional, predictable, and comfortably dull as baked beans and apple pie. True, Lois Duncan was a most intuitive and precocious writer, but there is not a glimmer of the person and author she has become. So great is the split between her early "chapters" and her present novels that I think this book may serve to alienate rather than to enlighten and win her new fans. For those who persevere, scattered along the way are some fine kernels of practical advice to hopeful authors.

> Leigh Dean, in her review of "Chapters: My Growth As a Writer," in Children's Book Review Service (copyright © 1982 Children's Book Review Service, Inc.), Vol. 10, No. 12, Spring, 1982, p. 116.

ZENA SUTHERLAND

Laurie [narrator of *Stranger with My Face*] is seventeen. Oldest of three children, she lives a happy and uneventful life on an island off the New England coast, attending school on the mainland, enjoying her friends and her artistic and pleasantly off-beat parents. At first Laurie is puzzled when people say they've seen her in places she hasn't been. Then she sees her doppelgänger—and the book smoothly moves into the occult plane as Laurie learns that the "stranger with her face" is a twin sister who has learned astral projection. . . . One must, of course, suspend disbelief to accept the story, but Duncan makes it possible and palatable by a deft twining of fantasy and reality, by giving depth to characters and relationships, and by writing with perception and vitality about other, universal aspects of adolescent life as well as the more dramatic core of the story, a core that includes Laurie's discovery that she is adopted—a fact she stumbles on as she tries to learn about her malevolent twin.

Zena Sutherland, in her review of "Stranger with My Face," in Bulletin of the Center for Children's Books *(reprinted by permission of The University of chicago Press; © 1982 by The University of Chicago), Vol. 35, No. 8, April, 1982, p. 146.*

Robert (Lee) Frost

1874-1963

American poet.

Frost is recognized as one of the foremost American poets of the twentieth century. Because his settings and subjects are usually the landscapes and folk of New England, Frost was once considered a simple farmer-poet. However, critical re-evaluation has centered on the complex themes and profound philosophic issues beneath the deliberately rustic surface of his poems. Frost's best work explores fundamental questions of existence, depicting with chilling starkness the loneliness of the individual in an indifferent universe.

Although Frost was forced to seek publication for his first poems in England, he became a public literary figure, almost an artistic institution, in America. While critical opinion concerning the importance of his poetry has varied, most critics agree that Frost's poems can be read and enjoyed on many levels. Frost received many honorary degrees and numerous awards, including four Pulitzer Prizes in poetry.

(See also *CLC*, Vols. 1, 3, 4, 9, 10, 13, 15; *Contemporary Authors*, Vols. 89-92; and *Something about the Author*, Vol. 14.)

© Rollie McKenna

T. K. WHIPPLE

In the title-poem of *New Hampshire,* Robert Frost demurs at being thought a local poet; he says that his books are "against the world in general," and that to apply them more narrowly is to restrict his meaning.

This assertion Frost's readers outside New England are inclined to question. True, he is not local in the derogatory sense; he is not provincial. But to say that Frost is not a New England poet would be like saying that [Robert] Burns is not Scottish or that [John Millington] Synge is not Irish. For good and for evil his work is the distilled essence of New England, and from this fact spring both his marked limitations and his unique value. Frost himself, with his belief that "all poetry is the reproduction of the tones of actual speech," must admit that his language is local, that his diction and his rhythms bear much the same relation to the talk of New Hampshire farmers that Synge's bear to the talk of West Irish fisherfolk. But Frost's localism does not stop there: his characters and their life as he pictures it, the natural setting in which they live, the poet himself in his point of view and habit of mind, are all peculiarly local, for better and for worse. Only in so far as New England is not entirely unlike other regions and Yankees are not entirely inhuman, and in so far as poetry of marked excellence appeals to every one, can Frost claim to write for "the world in general."

Frost's district does not cover all New England even; it is confined to the inland, to the hilly farm country. And needless to say, he concerns himself only with the present, not with the New England of witches, Jamaica rum, the slave trade, reform crusades, and elevated philosophizing. His is the New England which most of us know only from the verandas of summer hotels, a land of great natural loveliness, with a sprinkling of uncomfortably quaint natives, . . . strange fragments of for-

gotten peoples, somehow more remote from us than the Poles and other immigrants who are settling the abandoned farms. (pp. 94-5)

Frost himself, by saying that he writes "against the world in general," intimates that he considers his characters not essentially different from the normal, average run of humanity; but west of the Hudson he will find few to agree with him. To the rest of us, they look like very queer fish indeed. In brief, what ails them is their ingrowing dispositions. Not merely the famous New England reserve: it is a positive lack of frankness, an innate love of indirectness and concealment, which leads them not only to hide their own thoughts and feelings and motives, but to assume, naturally, that others do the same. Out of this tendency grows a suspiciousness, a tortuous habit of mind, which is a constant source of surprise to the more credulous and easy-going alien. To them, an act of kindness which other folk would think the sheerest matter of course seems so unnatural, so momentous, that it must be sedulously concealed. Even more striking is the meanness and the pettiness of these people. Not that they are unfeeling or frigid; on the contrary, they attach an excessive, often a morbid, intensity of feeling to the merest trifles. This makes them touchy, always with a chip on their shoulder, often close to hysterics. Most of them show an extraordinary capacity for dislike, hatred, and contempt—which may explain why New England has been the nursery of so many great reformers.

A good example of this exaggerated emotionalism is found in **"The Code"**: a farmer tells his hired man, who is unloading hay, "Let her come," and the farmhand, injured in his dignity by the order, dumps the whole load on his employer. A more startling instance is **"The Vanishing Red"**: a miller, because he does not like an Indian's tone of voice, proceeds to drown the Indian. Evidently, what at most would make a normal man swear, makes a Frost character commit murder. The most terrible and tragic illustration of this morbid excess, though here the cause is not trivial, is **"Home Burial,"** the story of a woman so sunk in her grief for her child, so deliberately and purposely sunk in it, that she has contracted a violent hatred of her husband and is all but outright insane. In much of Frost's work, particularly in *North of Boston*, his harshest book, he emphasizes the dark background of life in rural New England, with its degeneration sinking too often into total madness.

Frost apparently regards the woman in **"Home Burial"** as abnormal, but he seems to approve the hired man's "independence" in **"The Code"** and to find nothing out of the way in the miller's murder of the Indian in **"The Vanishing Red."** The explanation is not far to seek. These folk look normal to Frost because his own turn of mind is similar to theirs; his is the Yankee mind transmuted, raised to a higher level. Indirectness and suspiciousness are transformed in him into an extraordinary subtlety, which shows itself in his narratives as subtlety of analysis and portrayal of character, in his lyrics as subtlety of thought, feeling, and imagination. Similarly, he has all the Yankee intensity; but this keenness, instead of manifesting itself as meanness and pettiness, undergoes a metamorphosis and weights details with feeling and significance. Because he feels details so sharply, he is unexcelled for minute and exact observation. No less is Frost Yankee in his restraint. He surprises us, to alter [John] Keats' saying, by a fine deficiency—perhaps omission or suppression would be the better word. He never whips up his emotion or strives for a spurious effect. His flashes of intensity, when they come, are the more effective because his manner is uniformly easy and unforced. Even at his climaxes the language and the rhythm remain colloquial; his method is to build up a dramatic situation and then, in the same even tone of voice, to condense the whole into one touch. . . . (pp. 98-100)

To many tastes [Frost's] peculiar virtues may not appeal, but not his harshest critic would charge him with pretense. By the side of his genuineness most poetry of the day looks more than a little forced. He carries sincerity, indeed, to the point of absolute naturalness. It is a triumph of art to be so natural as Frost; only an expert artist could manage the feat. His is the *ars celare artem* with a difference: it is not merely that he attains the apparent ease which Horace had in mind, the classical simplicity, but that his poems seem spoken impromptu, not written at all, as if we overheard him speaking aloud. In part, of course, this is an amazing gift for mimicry, but it is more than that: to the mimetic skill is added a gift for condensation and selection and an exquisite sense of form, which give his work not only verisimilitude but also the typical and essential quality of high art. (pp. 100-01)

Frost's love of reality is so pronounced as to constitute a danger, though so far eluded, the danger to which [Henry David] Thoreau succumbed, of coming to feel that any fact, however insignificant, was important. None of his lines is more characteristic than the early "The fact is the sweetest dream that

labor knows." . . . Similarly he carves his poetry out of experience, merely educing what is already implicit. And yet—here we approach the inmost secret of his poetry—he values the fact because to him it is more than mere fact. He is reported to have said that "sight and insight" are the whole business of the poet, and the second term is even more important than the first. As [Louis] Untermeyer has observed, Frost's writing possesses "the double force of observation and implication"; in it are sounded "spiritual overtones above the actual theme." Frost, in short, has not a little of the transcendentalist in his make-up. Sometimes his feeling as to the significance of the fact is worked out into overt and explicit symbolism and even allegory, as in **"Mending Wall," "Birches," "Wild Grapes," "Two Look at Two,"** but in his most characteristic and appealing work the feeling of mystery is left merely as a mood of strangeness and not developed intellectually. (pp. 101-02)

Apparently, Frost is not so constituted that his reaction to a sense-impression is simple and direct, and in proportion to the force of the impression. His reaction bears no obvious and calculable relation to the stimulus; on the contrary, the relation of cause to effect is unpredictable, perhaps incomprehensible. It is a relation as incommensurate and arbitrary as that between pushing a button and turning on an electric light or ringing a bell. With him it is not only—not, I think, chiefly—sensuous pleasure that counts, but a subtle train of emotion and thought which the perception rouses in his mind. He is devoted to the fact, true—but because the fact is necessary to light the fuses of suggestion in his mind. A birch tree is to him not primarily an arabesque in black and white: it is fraught with hidden import. Conversely, he may be greatly moved by something quite devoid of sensuous appeal—a grindstone or axe-helve or woodpile—because to him it is tinged with hints of meaning that impart a feeling of the mysterious and the wonderful. And this is especially true if the perception is such as to excite the buried savage who sleeps within the most sophisticated of us. Consequently, in such a man's account of what he sees and hears we get sounds and sights not simply as they are, but on the one hand almost denuded of their physical beauty, on the other so transfigured that we see and hear them as it were through the shimmering veil of the more or less vague ideas and feelings which they have served to liberate. (pp. 103-04)

[In] spite of his close observation and minute detail, [Frost] is not a markedly sensuous poet; in fact, he is markedly ascetic. . . . Though Frost deals by preference in the concrete, though his writing abounds in images that are sharp and specific, he does not luxuriate in sensuous gratification, in a frank relish for savor and color and sound. A mere reference to Keats and [Algernon Charles] Swinburne is enough to illustrate this point: there is no "purple-stained mouth," no "cloth of woven crimson, gold, and jet," no "lisp of leaves and ripple of rain" in Frost. Or perhaps the sensuous austerity is more in the expression than in the image itself. He all but eschews the appeal of musical sound, preferring the effect of talk to that of song; such lines as "The slow smokeless burning of decay" are conspicuous by their rarity. In his treatment of feeling also, . . . he is ascetic; his language seldom swells or rises; the emotion is conveyed by implication only, by economy and elimination. Consequently, a reader less abstemious by nature than Frost may make the mistake of thinking him severe and stark, even bleak and bare and cold. (p. 105)

[Frost] tells us little of his philosophy, for he is as chary with his reflection as he is with his feeling, preferring hints and implication to forthright statement. But he tells enough to show that his is a philosophy of attachment, of realization, of intuitive apprehension, of what [Walt] Whitman unpleasantly called "adhesiveness." . . . There can be no doubt of Frost's passion for experience; he calls himself "Slave to a springtime passion for the earth"; and he returns to the theme again and again— at the end of "**Birches**," of "**Wild Grapes**," and in his striking lines called "**To Earthward.**" . . . He cannot take actuality for granted; he shows an almost bloodthirsty clinging to people and things. He never knows repletion; he is like a hungry man who never gets enough to eat.

How shall this paradox of Frost's asceticism and of his craving for experience be resolved? Would it be too fanciful to liken him to a newsboy gazing into a confectioner's window at Christmas time? Frost sees all the beauties of the world spread before him, but some mysterious agency prevents him from getting at them and absorbing them. . . . Perhaps it is the old transcendental streak which keeps him from a simple, naïve, unreflecting enjoyment of things, which suggests that a bird is not merely a song and a splash of color, but something mysteriously tinged with meaning, and which always sets up an inner experience to vie with, if not to outdo, the outer. . . . Whoever it was told Frost he always saw himself was a discerning critic, though I think it is more accurate to say that he sees the world, not himself, but the world only as reflected in his own temperament, and that, if he could, he would turn from reflections altogether and deal direct with actuality. But in spite of his wishes, the New England reserve, the New England tensity, will no more permit him to abandon himself freely to the world than to pour out his heart in unpremeditated verse. Always in his attitude there is a check or rigor which he cannot let go or relax; he cannot lose himself and be absorbed wholly by experience.

Yet, in trying to account for the vein of austerity which is always in Frost, apparently in spite of himself, I do not wish to overstress it. There is nothing gaunt or famished about him. Rather the reverse: his work, as contemporary American poetry goes, is remarkable for its solidity and completeness. He has come to better terms than most of our poets with his environment, and has had a better environment to come to terms with, and has profited by both circumstances. That may explain why . . . , though the tragedy of frustration is by no means absent from his writing, it is not set forth as the whole or even the norm of human life. Whatever may be Frost's limitations, he gives the impression of a wider and sounder and more many-sided development than that of any other living American poet. (pp. 107-09)

Robert Frost's is preëminently a farmer's poetry. His familiarity with nature and with objects is not, for all his deservedly famous observation, that of the observer or spectator, but that of the man who has worked with them and used them. His acquaintance with them is more intimate and more intuitive than that of the onlooker. A grindstone to him is not a quaint object with rustic associations, but something which has made him groan and sweat; a scythe does not remind him of Theocritus but of the feel of the implement as he has swung it. Blueberries and apples are less connected in his mind with their color or their taste than with the process of picking them. . . . [As a poet] he is still the craftsman and the husbandman; he judges a poem by the same standards which he would apply to an axe or a hoe or a spade: it must be solid, strong, honest. And his own poetry meets the test, severe though it is. (pp. 110-11)

[Frost's] work, to be sure, is severly restricted by the bonds of his own nature and by the lacks of his subject-matter. His

is a poetry of exclusions, of limitations not only in area and in localism, but equally in temperament. . . . He has given us poetry with little music, little delight for the senses, little glow of warm feeling. He has introduced us to a world not rich in color, sound, taste, and smell, a world mainly black and white and gray, etched in with acid in deep shadow and fine lines and sharp edges, lighted with a fitful white radiance as of starlight. His predilection, among natural phenomena, for stars and snow is symptomatic. Even his people are etchings, or woodcuts—droll, bizarre, sometimes pathetic: when we see them crumple up, we know how they can suffer. But somewhere among their ancestors there was a snow man, and his essence runs in their veins, a sharper, keener fluid than common blood, burning and biting like snow water. Yet, like the etchings of the older masters and like the best of modern woodcuts, this poetic world of his has a good three-dimensional solidity. One cannot put one's finger through it.

And it has an even more valuable quality. Frost's poetry is among those useless, uncommercial products of New England which constitute her tenacious charm. It belongs with the silver birches and the bayberry, and it shares their uniqueness. It has the edged loveliness and the acrid relish and fragrance of every growth native to New England earth and air. It is the last flowering of the seeds blown to the Massachusetts coast by the storms of 1620. For it has about it the quality of the final and ultimate; it is an epitome. As perfect in its way as blueberries or wintergreen, what it lacks in nutriment and profusion it atones for like them in flavor. We may look elsewhere for our bread and meat; but nowhere else can we find in all its pungency that piquant aromatic raciness which is New England. (pp. 113-14)

T. K. Whipple, "Robert Frost," in his Spokesmen: Modern Writers and American Life *(copyright— 1928—by D. Appleton and Company), Appleton, 1928, pp. 94-114.*

HARRIET MONROE

Perhaps no poet in our history has put the best of the Yankee spirit into a book so completely, so happily, as Robert Frost. [Ralph Waldo] Emerson, greatest of the early New England group, was a citizen of the world—or shall we say of the other world. [John Greenleaf] Whittier was a Quaker, with something of the Yankee thrift of tongue. [Henry Wadsworth] Longfellow was a Boston scholar, untouched by Yankee humor. [James Russell] Lowell had some of the humor, but he condescended to it, lived above it. Edwin Arlington Robinson came from New England, but his spirit did not stay there and his poetry escapes its boundaries. . . . But none of these is so completely the real Yankee, and so content to confess it in his poetry, as this "plain New Hampshire farmer." . . . (p. 59)

There are three or four facets of this local tang in Mr. Frost's art. One is the rural background—landscape, farms, animals. We have this more or less in all the poems, and specifically in a number—*Birches, The Woodpile, The Mountain, The Cow in Apple-time, The Runaway* and others. And close to these are the poems of farm life, showing the human reaction to nature's processes—*Mowing, Mending Wall, The Axe-helve, After Apple-picking, Putting in the Seed* and others. Then there are the narratives or dialogues presenting aspects of human character: some of them dryly satirical, with a keen but always sympathetic humor, like *The Code;* others, *Snow* for example, broadly humane and philosophic; a few lit with tragic beauty—*The*

Death of the Hired Man, the agonizing *Home Burial,* the exalted and half-mystical *Hill Wife.* And lastly we have the more personal poems, never brief confessional lyrics of emotion such as most poets give us—here Mr. Frost guards his reserves—but reflective bits like *Storm Fear, Bond and Free, Flower-gathering,* or meditative monologues quaintly, keenly, sympathetically humorous, the humor veiling a peering questing wisdom. . . . (p. 60)

The poems of nature and of farm life all express delight, and some are ecstatic. The poet knows what he is talking about, and loves the country and the life. . . . His touch upon these subjects is sure and individual, the loving touch of a specialist. . . . And in the character pieces we feel just as sure of him. (pp. 60-1)

When it comes to personal confession—to autobiography, so to speak—Mr. Frost refuses to take himself seriously. He has to laugh—or rather, he has to smile in that whimsical observant side-long way of his. This mood greets us most characteristically in *New Hampshire,* the long poem which, in painting a portrait, so to speak, of his state, establishes a sympathetic relation with himself, and paints, more or less consciously, his own portrait. That is, he presents a spare, self-niggardly, self-respecting, determined, uncompromising member of the sisterhood of states. . . . (p. 61)

New Hampshire and her poet both have character, as well as a penetrating, humorous and sympathetic quality of genius. They face the half-glance of the world, and the huge laughter of destiny, with pride and grit, and without egotism. (p. 62)

> Harriet Monroe, "Robert Frost," in her Poets and Their Art (© 1926 and 1932 by Macmillan Publishing Company; reprinted by permission of the Literary Estate of Harriet Monroe), revised edition, Macmillan, 1932, pp. 56-62.

RICHARD CHURCH

I am tempted to look upon [Robert Frost] as a major poet. A major poet is one who brings into a language and its poetry a new element of thought and experience, and a new twist of phraseology. (p. 29)

What is this new element which Frost has brought? It is difficult to define, because it is a quality of the man, of his whole personality and outlook on life. It is also something which is *local,* belonging to the people, the stock from which he springs. It is a characteristic of New England Puritanism, and its source may thus be traced back a long way until we find it originating in the Home Country, amongst the Quakers and Wesleyans of the eighteenth century. It is a complicated element (if that is not a contradiction in terms). It is a combination of quietism, piety with its underlying enthusiasm, suspicion of this world and especially of the world of man, self-restraint with its ever-imminent abandonment, humility with its threat of arrogance. There is a negativeness about these forces. They have a sort of dove-grey colour, like the cloak of a Quakeress. But how restful that colour is, how tender, how evocative of the latent beauty of all other hues with which it comes into contact! They represent a whole period of English history. It is that period which included the break away of the American branch, and established a community in New England more emphatic of the same power than the trunk from which it sprang.

Many sociologists to-day believe that this quality of quietism, of exerting authority by means of understatement, is doomed to extinction beneath the flood of barbaric noise brought in by the machine, the radio, and the dictator. I don't believe it. The United States, which is supposed to be the pioneer of latter-day hustle and go-getting, is saturated in this spirit of allusiveness, of understatement, of quiet emphasis. Examine the pages of the *New Yorker,* that hard-boiled humorous journal, and you will find that its technique has much in common with that which Robert Frost accentuated in English poetry thirty-five years ago. It is a native technique; that of the laconic Yankee. . . . Robert Frost is thus a spokesman of his own people. He is probably a more representative American than Walt Whitman. That is why his fame has not been a temporary one. His work needed only to be pointed out to the self-distrustful Americans, and they at once recognized it as something near home, something expressing their own habits, their own point of view, their own reaction to the society which they were still building, and the wild nature which they were still only beginning to subdue and to appreciate.

We all need to get things outside ourselves before we can see them and appreciate them. Robert Frost thus did his people as well as himself a service by leaving home and settling for a decade in Europe. Further, the scenery and the folk of England stirred something ancestral in him, waking his instincts to a fuller consciousness. He strengthened those instincts by means of a fine detachment, which enabled him to objectify the material from which his verse was made, and to give the result a universality without spoiling its local flavour. (pp. 31-3)

[Simplicity] is the quality which most marks him. He has practised it until he can make it convey the most subtle ideas and emotions. . . . It is another aspect of his inherited puritanism; and the other outstanding feature of his work, its marvellous utilization of the laconic, is only another development of this same quality. And the discipline necessary for the constant refining down of a poetic nature to this purpose has added something else to that nature; a gift of humour; a humour wry, dry, sharp, but an eager participant in the process of unifying a personality.

That personality I have always found very much to my liking. There is no other poet to whom he can be compared. . . . Frost seems, for one thing, always to choose the disappearances of human life and of wild nature as symbols to fit his moods. His is the genius of shyness, and its abbreviated gestures may be overlooked by the reader who expects to find the fine exaggerations so common to poetry. (pp. 34-5)

[There is, too, laughter] lurking in this poet's work. It is a serious laughter, folded over tenderness and love, ringing through his poems, toning down the high lights, lifting up the shadows, and intensifying that laconic monotone, at first strange to the ear, which becomes dearer and more entrancing by familiarity. And with this laughter, there trembles a note of passion, and deep understanding of the conflict of mind with heart, of man with woman, of humanity with the forces of life and death. (pp. 37-8)

Laughter denotes detachment, and detachment denotes dramatic sense. Frost has that sense, and he uses it as [Robert] Browning did in a collection of narrative poems, each of which deals with a tense situation that he solves with humour, but sardonic humour that delights in revealing the subtlety of false endings, inconclusive endings, irrelevancies; devices which real life abounds in, but literature is shy of. But Frost loves such implicit criticism of human and natural affairs. (pp. 38-9)

[His philosophy is: reject] nothing; but minimize it, in order to see it more roundly, and to locate it in its place in the chain of endless eventuality. So though his work is so quiet, it is not static. He pretends to step aside, as observer, from the universal mobility. But he also makes poetry out of that pretence. Indeed, it is the source of his laughter. (p. 39)

Richard Church, "Robert Frost," in his Eight for Immortality *(copyright 1941 Richard Church; reprinted by permission of Laurence Pollinger, Ltd. and the Literary Estate of Richard Church), J. M. Dent & Sons Ltd., 1941 (and reprinted by Books for Libraries Press, 1969), pp. 27-40.*

PETER VIERECK

Robert Frost's name is rarely heard among the exquisites of *avant-garde.* His poems are like those plants that flourish in the earth of the broad plains and valleys but will not strike root in more rarefied atmospheres. The fact remains that he is one of the world's greatest living poets. Frost, W. H. Auden, Wallace Stevens, and William Carlos Williams are the contemporary poets in America whose styles are most intensely original, most unmistakably their own. Of the four, Frost is the only one to be widely read in terms of general circulation and the only one who has never been adequately subjected to the Higher Criticism of the *doctores subtiles* of the Little Magazines.

On first reading, Frost seems easier than he really is. This helps account both for the enormous number of his readers, some of whom like him for wrong or irrelevant reasons, and for the indifference of the coteries, who become almost resentful when they can find no double-crostics to solve. Frost's cheerfulness is often mistaken as smug, folksy, Rotarian. This fact, plus his reputation for a solid New England conservatism, frightens away rebel youth and "advanced" professors.

In truth, his cheerfulness is the direct opposite of Mr. Babbitt's or even of Mr. Pickwick's. It is a Greek cheerfulness. And the apparent blandness of the Greeks was, as [Friedrich] Nietzsche showed in his *Birth of Tragedy,* the result of their having looked so deeply into life's tragic meaning that they had to protect themselves by cultivating a deliberately superficial jolliness in order to bear the unbearable. Frost's benign calm, the comic mask of a whittling rustic, is designed for gazing—without dizziness—into a tragic abyss of desperation. This is the same eternal abyss that gaped not only for the Hellenes but for such moderns as [Blaise Pascal, Sören Kierkegaard, Nietzsche, Charles Baudelaire, Franz Kafka]. . . . In the case of this great New England tragic poet, the desperation is no less real for being a quiet one, as befits a master of overwhelming understatements. His almost too smooth quietness is a booby trap to spring the ruthless doubt of the following typical Frostian quatrain:—

It was the drought of deserts. Earth would soon
Be uninhabitable as the moon.
What for that matter had it ever been?
Who advised man to come and live therein?

(pp. 67-8)

Let those who consider Frost obvious or superficial brood a bit upon the last line of **"Never Again Would Birds' Song Be the Same."** Consisting only of simple monosyllables yet subtly musical and full of "the shock of recognition," that concluding sentence is perhaps the most beautiful single line in American literature, a needed touchstone for all poets writing today. . . .

A word about his metrics and his diction. Frost is one of the few poets today who dare use contractions like "as 'twere" and "e'er." I don't care for this sort of thing, especially in a poet who makes a point of catching the idiom of everyday speech. But I don't let this annoying anachronism spoil my enjoyment of him. Equally old-fashioned, but this time in a better sense of the word, is the fact that his meters scan with a beat-by-beat regularity, usually in the form of rhymed iambic pentameters. In this connection, do not overlook his thoughtful preface [to **Complete Poems of Robert Frost**] on poetic techniques and meters.

Frost's stubborn conventionality of form makes many young poets and readers think his is also a conventionality of meaning. On the contrary, he is one of the most original writers of our time. It is the self-conscious *avant-garde* rebels who follow the really rigid and tiresome conventions. (p. 68)

Peter Viereck, "Parnassus Divided," in The Atlantic Monthly *(copyright © 1949, by The Atlantic Monthly Company, Boston, Mass.; reprinted with permission), Vol. 184, No. 4, October, 1949, pp. 67-70.**

ROBERT PENN WARREN

A large body of criticism has been written on the poetry of Robert Frost, and we know the labels which have been used: nature poet, New England Yankee, symbolist, humanist, skeptic, synecdochist, anti-Platonist, and many others. These labels have their utility, true or half true as they may be. They point to something in our author. But the important thing about a poet is the kind of poetry he writes. (p. 118)

In any case, I do not want to begin by quarreling with the particular labels. Instead, I want to begin with some poems and try to see how their particular truths are operative within the poems themselves. (p. 119)

As a starting point I am taking one of Frost's best-known and most widely anthologized pieces, **"Stopping by Woods on a Snowy Evening."** . . . It will lead us to the other poems because it represents but one manifestation of an impulse very common in Frost's poetry. (p. 120)

The poem does, in fact, look simple. A man driving by a dark woods stops to admire the scene, to watch the snow falling into the special darkness. He remembers the name of the man who owns the woods and knows that the man, snug in his house in the village, cannot begrudge him a look. He is not trespassing. The little horse is restive and shakes the harness bells. The man decides to drive on, because, as he says, he has promises to keep—he has to get home to deliver the groceries for supper—and he has miles to go before he can afford to stop, before he can sleep.

At the literal level that is all the poem has to say. But if we read it at that level, we shall say, and quite rightly, that it is the silliest stuff we ever saw. (p. 121)

With [the] first stanza we have a simple contrast, the contrast between the man in the village, snug at his hearthside, and the man who stops by the woods. The sane, practical man has shut himself up against the weather; certainly he would not stop in the middle of the weather for no reason at all. But, being a practical man, he does not mind if some fool stops by his woods so long as the fool merely looks and does not do any practical damage, does not steal firewood or break down fences. With this stanza we seem to have a contrast between the sensitive and the insensitive man, the man who uses the world and the man who contemplates the world. And the contrast seems to be in favor of the gazer and not the owner—for the purposes of the poem at least. In fact, we may even have the question: Who is the owner, the man who is miles away or the man who can really see the woods? (p. 122)

[In the second stanza] we have the horse-man contrast. The horse is practical too. He can see no good reason for stopping, not a farmhouse near, no oats available. The horse becomes an extension, as it were, of the man in the village—both at the practical level, the level of the beast which cannot understand why a man would stop, on the darkest evening of the year, to stare into the darker darkness of the snowy woods. In other words, the act of stopping is the specially human act, the thing that differentiates the man from the beast. The same contrast is continued into the third stanza—the contrast between the impatient shake of the harness bells and the soothing whish of easy wind and downy flake.

To this point we would have a poem all right, but not much of a poem. It would set up the essential contrast between, shall we say, action and contemplation, but it would not be very satisfying because it would fail to indicate much concerning the implications of the contrast. It would be a rather too complacent poem, too much at ease in the Zion of contemplation.

But in the poem the poet actually wrote, the fourth and last stanza brings a very definite turn, a refusal to accept either term of the contrast developed to this point. (pp. 122-23)

The first line proclaims the beauty, the attraction of the scene. . . . But with this statement concerning the attraction—the statement merely gives us what we have already dramatically arrived at by the fact of the stopping—we find the repudiation of the attraction. The beauty, the peace, is a sinister beauty, a sinister peace. It is the beauty and peace of surrender—the repudiation of action and obligation. The darkness of the woods is delicious—but treacherous. The beauty which cuts itself off from action is sterile; the peace which is a peace of escape is a meaningless and, therefore, a suicidal peace. There will be beauty and peace at the end of the journey, in the terms of the fulfillment of the promises, but that will be an earned beauty stemming from action.

In other words, we have a new contrast here. The fact of the capacity to stop by the roadside and contemplate the woods sets man off from the beast, but in so far as such contemplation involves a repudiation of the world of action and obligation it cancels the definition of man which it had seemed to establish. So the poem leaves us with that paradox, and that problem. . . . We must find a definition of our humanity which will transcend both terms.

This theme is one which appears over and over in Frost's poems—the relation, to state the issue a little differently, between the fact and the dream. In another poem, **"Mowing,"** he puts it this way, "The fact is the sweetest dream that labor knows." That is, the action and the reward cannot be defined separately, man must fulfill himself, in action, and the dream must not violate the real. But the solution is not to sink into the brute—to act like the little horse who knows that the farmhouses mean oats—to sink into nature, into appetite. But at the same time, to accept the other term of the original contrast in our poem, to surrender to the pull of the delicious blackness of the woods, is to forfeit the human definition, to sink into nature by another way, a dangerous way which only the human can achieve. So our poem, which is supposed to celebrate

nature, may really be a poem about man defining himself by resisting the pull into nature. There are many poems on this subject in Frost's work. (pp. 123-24)

[But let] us leave the dark-wood symbol and turn to a poem which, with other materials, treats Frost's basic theme. This is **"After Apple-Picking,"** the poem which I am inclined to think is Frost's masterpiece, it is so poised, so subtle, so poetically coherent in detail. (p. 127)

The items [in this poem]—ladder in apple tree, the orchard, drinking trough, pane of ice, woodchuck—all have their perfectly literal meanings—the echo of their meaning in actuality. And the poem, for a while anyway, seems to be commenting on that actual existence those items have. Now, some poems make a pretense of living only in terms of that actuality. For instance, **"Stopping by Woods on a Snowy Evening"** is perfectly consistent at the level of actuality—a man stops by the woods, looks into the woods, which he finds lovely, dark and deep, and then goes on, for he has promises to keep. It can be left at that level, if we happen to be that literal-minded, and it will make a sort of sense.

However, **"After Apple-Picking"** is scarcely consistent at the level of actuality. It starts off with a kind of consistency, but something happens. The hero of the poem says that he is drowsing off—and in broad daylight, too. He says that he has a strangeness in his sight which he drew from the drinking trough. So the literal world dissolves into a kind of dream world—the literal world and the dream world overlapping, as it were, like the two sets of elements in a superimposed photograph. (pp. 128-29)

The dream will relive the world of effort, even to the ache of the instep arch where the ladder rung was pressed. But is this a cause for regret or for self-congratulation? Is it a good dream or a bad dream? (p. 130)

[We] must look for the answer in the temper of the description he gives of the dream—the apples, stem end and blossom end, and every fleck of russet showing clear. The richness and beauty of the harvest—magnified now—is what is dwelt upon. In the dream world every detail is bigger than life, and richer, and can be contemplated in its fullness. And the accent here is on the word contemplated. Further, even as the apple picker recalls the details of labor which made him overtired, he does so in a way which denies the very statement that the recapitulation in dream will "trouble" him. For instance, we have the delicious rhythm of the line,

I feel the ladder sway as the boughs bend.

It is not the rhythm of nightmare, but of the good dream. . . . So even though we find the poet saying that his sleep will be troubled, the word *troubled* comes to us colored by the whole temper of the passage, ironically qualified by that temper. For he would not have it otherwise than troubled, in this sense. (p. 131)

[What] does the woodchuck have to do with it? . . . His sleep is contrasted with "just some human sleep." The contrast, we see, is on the basis of the dream. The woodchuck's sleep will be dreamless and untroubled. The woodchuck is simply in the nature from which man is set apart. The animal's sleep is the sleep of oblivion. But man has a dream which distinguishes him from the woodchuck. But how is this dream related to the literal world, the world of the woodchuck and apple harvests and daily experience? It is not a dream which is cut off from that literal world of effort—a heaven of ease and perpetual rewards, in the sense of rewards as coming after and in consequence of effort. No, the dream, the heaven, will simply be a reliving of the effort—magnified apples, stem end and blossom end, and every fleck, every aspect of experience, showing clear. (pp. 131-32)

[It] may be well to ask ourselves if the poet is really talking about immortality and heaven—if he is really trying to define the heaven he wants and expects after this mortal life. No, he is only using that as an image for his meaning, a way to define his attitude. And that attitude is an attitude toward the here and now, toward man's conduct of his life in the literal world. (p. 132)

What would be some of the implied applications [of such an attitude]? First, let us take it in reference to the question of any sort of ideal which man sets up for himself, in reference to his dream. By this application the valid ideal would be that which stems from and involves the literal world, which is arrived at in terms of the literal world and not by violation of man's nature as an inhabitant of that literal world. Second, let us take it in reference to man's reward in this literal world. By this application we would arrive at a statement like this: Man must seek his reward in his fulfillment through effort and must not expect reward as something coming at the end of effort, like the oats for the dray horse in the trough at the end of the day's pull. He must cherish each thing in his hand. Third, let us take it in reference to poetry, or the arts. By this application, which is really a variant of the first, we would find that art must stem from the literal world, from the common body of experience, and must be a magnified "dream" of that experience as it has achieved meaning, and not a thing set apart, a mere decoration.

These examples, chosen from among many, are intended merely to point us back into the poem—to the central impulse of the poem itself. But they are all summed up in this line from **"Mowing,"** another of Frost's poems: "The fact is the sweetest dream that labor knows." (pp. 132-33)

The process [Frost] has employed in all of these poems, but most fully and subtly I think in **"After Apple-Picking,"** is to order his literal materials so that, in looking back upon them as the poem proceeds, the reader suddenly realizes that they have been transmuted. . . . [In] these poems, Frost is trying to indicate, as it were, the very process of the transmutation, of the interpenetration. That, and what that implies as an attitude toward all our activities, is the very center of these poems, and of many others among his work. (pp. 135-36)

Robert Penn Warren, "The Themes of Robert Frost" (1947), in his Selected Essays *(copyright © 1958 by Robert Penn Warren; reprinted by permission of Random House, Inc.), Random House, 1958, pp. 118-36.*

JOHN T. OGILVIE

Together with **"Birches," "Mending Wall," "The Road Not Taken," "After Apple-Picking,"** and a dozen or so other familiar descriptive pieces, **"Stopping by Woods on a Snowy Evening"** is one of Robert Frost's most admired poems. The beginning poetry student in particular is likely to take to it, for quite understandable reasons: its diction is unpretentious and subtly musical; it presents an engaging picture and hints at a "story" without too much taxing the imagination; it is short and seemingly unambiguous. And the teacher, from his side, likewise welcomes the opportunity to present a poem that can

be enjoyed purely for its visual and verbal interest without having to be subjected to a rigorous search for "hidden meanings." But, as experienced readers of this poem know, **"Stopping by Woods"** has a disconcerting way of deepening in dimension as one looks at it, of darkening in tone, until it emerges as a full-blown critical and pedagogical problem. One comes to feel that there *is* more in the poem than is given to the senses alone. But how is one to treat a poem which has so simple and clear a descriptive surface, yet which somehow implies a complex emotional attitude? (p. 64)

"Stopping by Woods," I believe, represents one of those junctures where the critic must enlarge on his findings through searching comparisons with other of the author's productions. Taken in isolation, **"Stopping by Woods"** gives only a partial view (and for some readers possibly a misleading view) of what is actually an absorbing and central concern in Frost's poetry. The collaboration of a number of related poems is required to reveal this preoccupation in its entirety.

The visible sign of the poet's preoccupation—the word is not too strong—is the recurrent image, particularly in his earlier work, of dark woods and trees. Often, as in the lyric with which we have begun, the world of the woods. . . , a world offering perfect quiet and solitude, exists side by side with the realization that there is also another world, a world of people and social obligations. Both worlds have claims on the poet. He stops by woods on this "darkest evening of the year" to watch them "fill up with snow," and lingers so long that his "little horse" shakes his harness bells "to ask if there is some mistake." The poet is put in mind of the "promises" he has to keep, of the miles he still must travel. We are not told, however, that the call of social responsibility proves stronger than the attraction of the woods, which are "lovely" as well as "dark and deep"; the poet and his horse have not moved on at the poem's end. The dichotomy of the poet's obligations both to the woods and to a world of "promises"—the latter filtering like a barely heard echo through the almost hypnotic state induced by the woods and falling snow—is what gives this poem its singular interest. . . . The artfulness of **"Stopping by Woods"** consists in the way the two worlds are established and balanced. The poet is aware that the woods by which he is stopping belong to someone in the village; they are owned by the world of men. But at the same time they are *his,* the poet's woods, too, by virtue of what they mean to him in terms of emotion and private signification.

In Frost's first book, *A Boy's Will* (1913), we find a dark-woods imagery used repeatedly. It is not too much to say that the quiet drama of youthful love portrayed in the subjective lyrics of this volume takes place within the constant shadow of surrounding trees. That the trees are themselves part of this drama, and not simply descriptive background, is evident from such pieces as **"Going for Water"** and **"A Dream Pang,"** in which the act of withdrawing into "forest" and "wood" becomes the very subject of the poem and is endowed with an undefined, almost ritualistic significance. In the first poem, husband and wife enter a wood together on a moonlit autumn evening to get water from a brook. In the second, the poet dreams that he has "withdrawn in forest," his song "swallowed up in leaves. . . ." He watches his wife, who comes to the edge of the forest in search of him, "behind low boughs the trees let down outside," but does not call to her, though it costs him a "sweet pang" not to do so. The overtones here may be too "romantic" for most readers, but the psychological pattern symbolized is of considerable interest in a total view of Frost's poetry. (pp. 65-6)

[In the opening lyric of *A Boy's Will*, "**Into My Own**," the] wished-for freedom to retreat into the "vastness" of "those dark trees," where the poet will not encounter the exposed, man-made world of open land and highways, is identified with coming "into his own": for this he is willing to forsake even those he holds dear—they must seek him out. The pattern is the same as in "**A Dream Pang**." In another revealing lyric of this volume, "**The Vantage Point**," the poet pictures himself occupying a strategic position, a "slope," between the world of nature and the world of human society. (p. 67)

[It is] typical of Frost, as in "**Stopping by Woods**" and "**The Vantage Point**," to counter the emotional drift toward "woods" with the realistic knowledge that, as a human being, he is implicated in the affairs of men and cannot justifiably disclaim them. The necessity for participating in both worlds, the worlds of self-in-society and self-in-seclusion, sets up a rhythm of continual advance and retreat which informs Frost's entire poetic expression. "Trees" and "mankind" are alternately sought and avoided as circumstances direct. . . . There must be periodic withdrawals from the world "of considerations," but not a permanent withdrawal. . . . The double set of obligations enforces a partial compromise. Frost's characteristic attitude, as the title of a later poem indicates, is "not quite social." But on the whole, the balance between society and solitude in his poetry is successfully maintained: the poet presents two full sides to his experience—the "neighborly" and the introspective. One feels, however, that the neighborly Frost, being the more accessible Frost, is much better known, while the poet of the dark trees, the poet who is "acquainted with the night," remains furtive and ambiguous for most readers. Yet there are reasons for thinking, I believe, that the latter image is closer to being the essential Frost.

To begin with, the creative impulse itself, in at least two poems ("**Pan With Us**" and "**The Demiurge's Laugh**," both from *A Boy's Will*), is identified in a quite intriguing way with the dark woods. In the first, Pan (the god of forests and pastures and also a musician), gray of skin, hair, and eyes, comes out of the woods one day and stands in the sun above an uninhabited wooded valley. Although he is pleased with the solitude of the scene, he tosses away his pipes. They are "too hard to teach a new-world song"; he lets nature speak instead. . . . Pan (the poet) is in love with his woodland solitude; yet having no audience, his impulse toward expression tends to dwindle away into fruitless self-interrogation. In the second poem, the poet pictures himself pursuing "the Demon," the Demiurge (again the creative impulse) "far in the sameness of the wood." He follows the trail "with joy," though aware that his quarry is "no true god." Then suddenly he hears [laughter behind him]. . . . The mocking laugh from somewhere in the dim woods is the mockery of the poet's search, the mockery of self-expression in the middle of such a solitude. The loneliness of the dark woods gives rise to poetry, but that same loneliness ultimately defeats its meaning and pleasure. (pp. 67-9)

The imagery of dark woods, woven so indelibly into the texture of these early poems, persists in succeeding collections. "**The Road Not Taken**," introductory to *Mountain Interval* (1916), can be read as a further commentary on the price of the poet's dedication. The two roads that "diverged in a yellow wood" represent a critical choice between two ways of life. The poet takes "the one less traveled by," the lonelier road, which, we can presume, leads deeper into the wood. . . . The dark woods, though they hold a salutary privacy, impose a stern isolation, an isolation endured not without cost. In the poem "**An En-

counter**," the poet pictures himself "half boring through, half climbing through a swamp of cedar," weary and overheated, and sorry he had ever left the road he knew. While resting, he looks skyward and sees above him "a barkless specter," a telegraph pole "dragging yellow strands of wire with something in it from men to men.". . . The poet's quest, in contrast to the unswerving telegraph lines, appears to lack direction and purpose. The poet is alone, in communication only with himself.

In the lyrics of *A Boy's Will*, woods and trees foster a mood of youthful yearning and romantic furtiveness. In later poems, however, the mood perceptibly darkens. In "**The Sound of Trees**" and "**Misgiving**," for example, trees and leaves are associated with thwarted desire. As they are swayed by the wind, their sound and motion suggest to the poet a longing to get away; but "a sleep oppresses them as they go" and they end by remaining, vaguely stirred, where they are. The poet himself desires the freedom to make "the reckless choice," to "set forth for somewhere," but by association we are led to believe that he will not do so. Though they are less congenial to him now, he will stay with the trees. (pp. 69-70)

[In several of Frost's] poems, the imagery of woods, trees, and leaves is so intimately and persistently identified with certain psychological states as to assume a symbolic significance. The dark woods represent the privacy of the self, the sacred domain where poetry is made. Their area is the area of the poet's introspective life, his subjective experience. The pattern of feelings established by this recurrent imagery is fluctuating and ambivalent. The poet guards and cherishes the woods as his own, but there are times when he must close his windows against them and turn outward toward the larger world of social intercourse. There is lurking terror in his woods as well as keen pleasure, numbing loneliness as well as quiet satisfaction; one can as much lose himself there as find himself. This becomes more apparent as the poet grows older and his introspective life deepens. In "**Leaves Compared with Flowers**" (*A Further Range*) he confesses that "leaves are all my darker mood," and finally he reaches a point when he cannot be enticed into the dark woods at all.

When viewed as part of this pattern, such a poem as "**Stopping by Woods**" is put into meaningful perspective. What appears to be "simple" is shown to be not *really* simple, what appears to be innocent not *really* innocent. . . . The poet is fascinated and lulled by the empty wastes of white and black. The repetition of "sleep" in the final two lines suggests that he may succumb to the influences that are at work. There is no reason to suppose that these influences are benignant. It is, after all, "the darkest evening of the year," and the poet is alone "between the woods and frozen lake." His one bond with the security and warmth of the "outer" world, the "little horse" who wants to be about his errand, is an unsure one. The ascription of "lovely" to this scene of desolate woods, effacing snow, and black night complicates rather than alleviates the mood when we consider how pervasive are the connotations of dangerous isolation and menacing death. (pp. 72-3)

When reading through the *Complete Poems* (1949), one can see that at some undefined point in Frost's mid-career—roughly with *West-Running Brook* (1928) and *A Further Range* (1936)— his orientation begins to shift. He becomes more the "neighborly" poet who chats at length with his readers about the issues of the day, and less the objective dramatist and self-exploring lyricist of the earlier books. He becomes more outspoken about himself and about the world of men. He projects himself into the "further ranges" of politics, science, philosophy, education, and theology. "Ideas" as such become more important to him than the individual persons and objects of nature, the "specimens" of concrete life, so lovingly collected in *North of Boston* and *Mountain Interval*. The very manner of voice changes. Metaphorical indirection gives way to explicit generalizations. The forms of satirical discourse and epigram are introduced to convey his opinions more directly. The poet's old game of hide-and-seek is still evident but now is carried on more by means of a bantering verbal irony. . . . (pp. 73-4)

The drift in Frost's poetry from an empirically operative intuitiveness toward an insistent didacticism is reflected, interestingly enough, by a shift in imagery pattern. Woods, symbolic of the introspective life, are gradually displaced by the heavenly bodies of outer space, symbolic of more impersonal, intellectual considerations. . . . As loneliness and grief more and more fill those woods where youth and love once delighted, the poet turns his attention upward toward the abstract questions framed by the stars. (See, for examples, such later productions as **"Canis Major," "On Looking Up by Chance at the Constellations," "Lost in Heaven," "All Revelation," "A Loose Mountain [Telescopic]," "The Literate Farmer and the Planet Venus," "An Unstamped Letter in Our Rural Letter Box," "Bravado," "On Making Certain Anything Has Happened," "Astrometaphysical," "Skeptic,"** and **"Two Leading Lights."**) (p. 74)

The passage from woods to stars that we have been tracing in Frost's poetry is poignantly recorded in one late lyric (*A Witness Tree*, 1942) called **"Come In."** . . . [In this poem, the] poet refuses to re-enter the dark woods; he will not answer that beautiful voice (his own deepest poetic impulse?) that bids him come and lament. He is a stranger to the woods now. He is "out for stars," and will stay out. . . . The empty spaces above are preferred to the empty spaces within. . . . It is not so much a different Frost speaking in the later poems as it is the same Frost who, like the people portrayed in *North of Boston*, has had to make adjustments in the face of life's "shocks and changes" in order to survive. Though there is less of the true poetic vision in the later work, the courage and the intelligence are steadfast:

They would not find me changed from him they knew—
Only more sure of all I thought was true.

(pp. 75-6)

John T. Ogilvie, "From Woods to Stars: A Pattern of Imagery in Robert Frost's Poetry," in South Atlantic Quarterly *(reprinted by permission of the Publisher; copyright © 1959 by Duke University Press, Durham, North Carolina), Vol. LVIII, No. 1, Winter, 1959, pp. 64-76 [the excerpts of Robert Frost's poetry used here were originally published in* The Complete Poems of Robert Frost, *edited by Edward Connery Lathem (copyright © 1916, 1923, 1928, 1934; © 1969 by Holt, Rinehart and Winston; copyright 1936, 1942, 1944, 1951; © 1956, 1962 by Robert Frost; copyright © 1964, 1970 by Lesley Frost Ballantine; reprinted by permission of Holt, Rinehart and Winston, Publishers), Holt, Rinehart and Winston, 1969].*

JAMES M. COX

Frost has established himself securely in the position which Mark Twain created in the closing years of the last century—

the position of American literary man as public entertainer. Frost brings to his rôle the grave face, the regional turn of phrase, the pithy generalization, and the salty experience which Twain before him brought to his listeners. He is the homespun farmer who assures his audiences that he was made in America before the advent of the assembly line, and he presides over his following with what is at once casual ease and lonely austerity.

Because the popularity surrounding Frost the public figure and hovering about his poetry has become the halo under which admirers enshrine his work, to many serious critics bent on assessing the value of the poetry this halo becomes a sinister mist clouding the genuine achievement. (pp. 73-4)

Yet Frost's success as a public figure, rather than being a calculated addition to his poetic career, is a natural extension of it, and one way to approach his poetry is to see that the character who moves in the poems anticipates the one who occupies the platform. They are in all essentials the same character—a dramatization of the farmer poet come out of his New England landscape bringing with him the poems he plays a rôle in. To observe this insistent regional stance is to realize that Frost has done, and is still doing, for American poetry what [William] Faulkner has more recently accomplished in American fiction. They both have made their worlds in the image of their particular regions, and, moving within these self-contained and self-made microcosms, they have given their provincial centers universal significance. But while Faulkner has concerned himself with establishing the legendary Yoknapatawpha county and its mythical components, Frost has, from the very first poem of **"A Boy's Will,"** been engaged in creating the myth of Robert Frost, [the one Randall Jarrell calls, "The Only Genuine Robert Frost in Captivity"]. It is a myth with a hero and a drama.

The hero is the New England farmer who wears the mask, or better, the anti-mask of the traditional poet. But it is not a literal mask concealing the poet who lurks behind it; rather, it is a mode of being which releases the poetic personality in the person of a character who lives and moves. (p. 74)

It is Frost's ability to *be* a farmer poet which distinguishes him most sharply from [William] Wordsworth, with whom he is often compared. Wordsworth played the part of the Poet concerned with common man, but Frost has persistently cast himself in the rôle of the common man concerned with poetry. Such a strategy, while it cuts him off from the philosophically autobiographical poetry which Wordsworth built toward, opens up avenues of irony, wit, comedy, and dramatic narrative largely closed to Wordsworth. (p. 75)

[Instead] of direct revelation through autobiography and confession, Frost has from the start pursued the more indirect but equally effective mode of dramatizing and characterizing himself. Even the lyrics of **"A Boy's Will"** lean toward narrative and monologue, and the peculiar Frost idiom, so integral a part of the Frost character who eventually emerges, is evident in remarkable maturity in such early poems as **"Into My Own," "Mowing," "A Tuft of Flowers,"** and **"In Hardwood Groves."** The dramatic monologues and dialogues of **"North of Boston,"** which have impressed many critics as a wide departure from Frost's lyric vein, constitute a full discovery and perfection of that idiom. Moreover, Frost himself emerges prominently as a member of the volume's *dramatis personae*, playing an important rôle in nine of the sixteen poems. As a matter of fact, **"Mending Wall,"** the first poem in the volume, marks the full-dress entrance of the farmer poet. Possessed of all the characteristics by which we have come to know him, this figure is full of sly observations as he assumes a slightly comic poise with eye asquint—already poetry is "his kind of fooling." He goes to great length to disarm his audience with colloquial familiarity and whimsical parentheses. Then, after an agile imaginative leap in the grand style, he returns to earth as if he feared being caught off guard.

This cautious refusal to declaim too far or too soon, while it may leave too much unsaid or enclose the issue in a blurred dual vision which accepts both sides, is often one of Frost's most effective modes of self awareness. (pp. 75-6)

Beyond this playfully ironic self portrayal so characteristic of Frost, there is also the tragic self-awareness which enabled him to create the great dramatic monologues. In such poems as **"The Fear," "Home Burial,"** and **"A Servant to Servants,"** for example, sensitive wives are so caught between the lonely natural world and the rigid proverbs of their husbands that, locked in an unutterable loneliness, they disintegrate into hysteria or slump into depression. Those husbands bear enough similarity to the figure of the farmer poet to indicate how much Frost realizes, for all his willingness to exploit the poetic possibilities of aphorism—how blind and hard a proverb quoter can be. (pp. 76-7)

Like his great New England antecedents, Emerson and Thoreau, he casts his own shadow upon the landscape he surveys. Skeptical in his cast of mind, Frost inclines away from their tendency to abstract doctrine, but he retains much of the method and many of the attitudes they left behind them. . . . (p. 77)

Seeing the nature of his task, one can understand why he contended in **"The Constant Symbol"** that every poem is "an epitome of the great predicament; a figure of the will braving alien entanglements." . . . [The] drama he sees the poet playing recalls Emerson's insistence that a man must be self-reliant, "obeying the Almighty Effort and advancing on Chaos and the dark." But even as he accepts the antagonists of the Emersonian drama, Frost, lacking Emerson's evangelical temperament, recognizes a larger chaos and sees the drama of existence as man's willingness to risk himself before the spell of the dark woods. For him self-reliance becomes self-possession, and the victory lies not in the march forward into the wilderness but in the freedom he feels while patroling the boundary of consciousness. (p. 80)

Unlike Emerson, [Frost] is deeply concerned with his past—not the past of organized tradition so much as the disorganized past he himself has strewn behind. . . . In repossessing [familiar rural New England artifacts], Frost is turning back upon himself to reclaim the fragments of his personal past—fragments which apparently meant nothing when they were current but which come to constitute the primary medium of exchange in the economy of reorganization. (pp. 80-1)

In addition to the remnants of abandoned farms, there are also the living victims who linger in stunned confusion along the border. . . . Above all, there is the poet himself, who feels the terror of loneliness. . . . [Occasionally, Frost's] entire landscape becomes a haunting reflection of psychic desolation. (pp. 81-2)

The haunting rhythms of **"Stopping by Woods on a Snowy Evening"** express the powerful fascination the woods have upon the lonely traveler, who, in the face of a long journey, descending night, and falling snow, pauses in the gathering gloom of the "darkest evening of the year," transfixed by the compelling invitation of the forest. . . . The poem is *about* the spell of the woods—the traveler's own woods, we want to say, but they are alien enough and belong to someone else enough for him to sense the trespass of his intent gaze into them at the same time he recognizes their sway over him. His heightened awareness projects his concern for himself back to the representatives of civilization, the unseen owner of the woods and the horse in harness. Thus, the indifferent animal becomes, in his master's alerted imagination, the guardian who sounds the alarm which rings above the whispered invitation.

The poem *is* the counter-spell against the invitation, the act by which the traveler regains dominion of his will. . . . The logic of the rhyme scheme, in which the divergent third line of one stanza becomes the organizing principle of the next, is an expression of the growing control and determination described in the syntax. Thus, the first line of the last quatrain finally *names* the nature of the spell and also provides the term which is answered in rhyme by the poet's decision to refuse the invitation.

Seen in this light, the poem reveals what Frost means when he says that "every poem written regular is a symbol small or great of the way the will has to pitch into the commitments deeper and deeper to a rounded conclusion. . . ." . . . The poem in its totality is the image of the will in action, and the poet's spirit and courage convert words into deeds. (pp. 82-4)

Frost, like the Paul Bunyan in **"Paul's Wife,"** is a terrible possessor; indeed, the action of that poem recapitulates Frost's own process of creation. . . . Frost too has gone back into the desolation of a world abandoned to seize his own particular kind of beauty.

Of course, he has shared it with the world, but he clings fiercely to his poems as his private property, and even the titles of his several volumes describe the progress of his endeavor to lay claim to his world. From **"A Boy's Will"** he went on to define his province, **"North of Boston,"** and in **"Mountain Interval,"** **"New Hampshire,"** and **"West Running Brook,"** he established enough landmarks within the region to open what he calls **"A Further Range."** (pp. 84-5)

Frost's long career of returning into his own to enlarge his province has been a continual thrust of both will and memory, and he quite logically defines the initial delight of making a poem as the "surprise of remembering something I didn't know I knew." If there are times when his poetry fails, as in the editorializing poems which have been increasing in ratio until they fairly dot **"Steeple Bush,"** he fails because he is remembering something he knew all the time, and his poetry hardens into provincial cynicism. Although critics have lamented this departure from the earlier lyric and dramatic vein, Frost's penchant for bald statement followed as necessarily from his earlier poems as self-assurance follows self-possession. Moreover, out of this almost brash assurance comes **"Directive,"** surely one of Frost's highest achievements.

Here the poet is not the listener or the narrator, but the confident guide leading his reader back into a "time made simple by the loss of detail," to discover among the ruins of a vacant farm the broken goblet the guide has hidden under a cedar tree against the day of his return. The broken goblet, originally cast aside by the adults as a mere toy for the children's playhouse and again abandoned when everyone departed, becomes the all important detail which the poet has seized to save from the ruins of the past. It is for Frost an image of the charmed grail itself, a talisman not carried like a spear of grass but stored away in a secret niche and displayed only to the right persons who, following the poet along the intricate pathways toward the heart of his property, are lost enough to find themselves. (pp. 85-6)

Yet Frost maintains a sharp comic detachment from the central association he exploits, the allusion to the grail quest. His poem is not a recapitulation or variation of the legend but a masque, a performance staged for his audience's benefit by the knowing god who owns the salvaged grail. His whimsy . . . is actually an aspect of his comic delicacy. . . . (p. 86)

"Directive" rehearses the course Frost has pursued as a poet and is thus a survey of the ground he has possessed. But it also points toward what is to come, toward the masques and beyond to his latest poem, **"Kitty Hawk,"** in which, while commemorating the Wright brothers' famous flight, he seizes the chance to celebrate his own first flight into poetry with his sacred muse—an event which considerably anticipated the first propeller-driven flight.

Finally, **"Directive"** is a performance by the same "character" who so often commands the central stage as lecturer and whose public performances imitate to a remarkable degree the structure of his poems. For Frost's primal subject is always poetry and the poet—*his* poetry and himself the poet. . . . Even in [the poem's] introductory movement, Frost is already retreating from his audience toward himself, and the conversational idiom functions as an invitation, never as an appeal.

When he reaches the poems he is to "say," as he puts it, Frost has gained a presence of remote loneliness. His manner of "saying" them is neither recitative, declamatory, nor bardic; rather he seems to be remembering each poem as he moves through it, and even when he forgets his way he usually chooses to find himself without benefit of text. There is a manifest anticipation both in speaker and audience as the remembering proceeds, a kind of wonder and suspense as the tenuous thread of the poem is pursued; and when the end is grasped there is a distinct sense of discovery *and* relief. (pp. 87-8)

To know Frost's poems and then to watch his mind close tenderly about them is to see again that they are his triumphs in form wrought out of the chaos he has lived through. (p. 88)

James M. Cox, "Robert Frost and the Edge of the Clearing," in The Virginia Quarterly Review *(copyright, 1959, by* The Virginia Quarterly Review, *The University of Virginia), Vol. 35, No. 1 (Winter, 1959), pp. 73-88.*

ROY HARVEY PEARCE

Frost allies himself with Emerson, not Whitman, thereby demonstrating that he has resisted the temptation (so fatal because so self assuring) to take a way of poetry that only a person as tremendous as Whitman could take without losing his identity as poet. Even better than Emerson, Frost knows the dangers of too much inwardness. For this is clearly an Emersonian sentiment, and yet not quite the sort entertained by those readers of Frost who would make him "easier" than he is—a celebrant of hard-headed self-reliance, village style, a "sound" poet because somehow "traditional." Moreover, in the poems themselves, even this authentic Emersonianism *is* qualified, qualified by being projected always out of situations which are not quite "modern.". . . Frost has no interest in being a specifically "contemporary" poet—which is what Emerson felt

he had to be, or perish. Moreover, in his poems Frost is master of all he surveys in a way that Emerson would never allow himself to be. Frost knows himself as person so well, he can record the knowledge in such exacting detail, that he never has occasion to celebrate the more general and inclusive concept of self which is everywhere the efficient cause of Emerson's poetry.

The gain is one of objectivity and precision. Unlike his prose (of which there is precious little), his poetry is not at all slippery. The loss is one of that inclusiveness and sense of ever-widening possibility, characteristic of Emerson's poetry at its best. . . . At the heart of Frost's achievement lies his ability to consolidate the Emersonian mode, to adopt it on his own terms, and so make it a means whereby a certain stability and certitude, however limited, might be achieved. From his position of strength, he bids others depart—and leave him behind. As poet, he will not be a leader. The farthest thing from his mind is the desire to be a culture hero. For good and for bad, this has been the heart's desire of most of his predecessors and contemporaries. Herein his work marks a pause—a series of moments in which confusion is stayed, perhaps comprehended—in the continuity of American poetry. Frost is our greatest stock-taker.

The major tradition of American poetry before his time serves Frost as a limiting condition for the making of poems. He has come to be a large poet (in a way, our most "complete" poet), because he knows how small man is when he acknowledges the limitations within which he labors. Frost has been able to perfect his work as have none of his contemporaries. Maybe we refer to this sort of thing when we are tempted to speak of him as a "minor poet." We mean perhaps that in his work he portrays a world, and himself in it, that is not as readily available to us as is that of some of his contemporaries. In any case, he has known quite clearly what he has been doing. (pp. 272-73)

The conditions which circumscribe Frost's poems are those of a world not yet dominated by urban, industrialized, bureaucratized culture—the very world which, seeing its inevitable coming, Emerson and his kind strove to confront and save for man before it would be too late. Frost glances at this world, only to turn to one he knows better. In that world the proper life style—which in turn generates the literary style—is that of Frost's characteristic protagonists: individuals who again and again are made to face up to the fact of their individualism as such; who can believe that a community is no more than the sum of the individuals who make it up; who are situated so as to have only a dim sense, even that resisted mightily, of the transformations which the individual might have to undergo if he is to live fully in the modern world and still retain his identity as an individual. But, of course, Frost's protagonists refuse to live fully in the modern world and will have little or nothing to do with such transformations. Frost's work is in the end a series of expressions of that refusal and assessments of its cost. The cost is great, and is acknowledged unflinchingly. Reading Frost, many of us—finding ourselves in the end unable to go along with him and deny the world in which we live—must deny the world of a poet who will not live in ours with us. It is not so much that he does not speak our language, but that we do not, cannot, speak his. Perhaps he means us to deny his world, so that we will be forced to live in our own, all the while knowing just how much we must pay in order to do so. This indeed would be freedom, but a dreadful freedom, generating none of the confidence in the future toward which Emerson pointed his poems. (pp. 273-74)

Even if we cannot speak his language, we yet know what he means. We listen to him as we would listen to a sage, not daring to interrupt him because not knowing how. . . . His individualism, as it comes out in his poems, is of a self which is emphatically not free to sound its barbaric yawp over the rooftops of the world. Its freedom is a freedom to decide not what it will do unto others but rather what it will allow others to do unto it. (p. 274)

[Frost] puts the Emersonian doctrine of freedom to his own special use. For Emerson, and his great contemporaries too, conceived of the "free" person as, by internal necessity, one who had to break through and away from substantial concerns—the life of the workaday world, the life of the older order—so as to *transform* himself in the breaking. . . . Emerson broke from the past in order to look forward. Frost does so in order to look at the here and now, and thereby is by far more loyal to the past than Emerson could bear to be.

For Frost there is a new order, to be sure; but it is the product of a recovery and reconstitution, rather than of a reinvention and transformation, of the old. For the great nineteenth-century poets, life consisted of an infinite series of willed, self-generated transformations forward; the opportunity for each transformation was only that—an opportunity, its possibilities exhausted as soon as the transformation had occurred. . . . Thus, in the deepest sense, the "opportunism" of their poetry. In Frost, however, this conception of the transformative opportunity has been stabilized to a point where it is not a means of advancing, but of withdrawing and consolidating. . . . The freedom, he might say, allows him to define, not unleash himself. To be sure, Frost has called freedom "departure." But, as he departs, he looks backward, not forward. He would have us enjoy our going hence because he knows so well whence we have come hither.

Frost's best poems demonstrate . . . his certainty that he is one kind of man moving down one kind of road. The most telling of the poems are the monologues and dialogues which begin in *North of Boston,* early in his career. Again and again the subject is the failure of communication, a failure which shows just how small and delimited the effective community can be. As often as not it comes to be a community of one—a community which can be called such only because its existence is, as it were, authorized by the fact that all men of high sensibility who live in it will quite readily come to recognize that in the end they can communicate only the fact that they cannot communicate, that they can but find the rather limited terms in which they can communicate this fact. The terms—deriving from Frost's abiding sense of farm, mountain, and village life—are sharp enough to cut off cleanly from his fellows him who lives by them.

Moreover, Frost is honest and clear-headed enough to admit that they cut off from one another even those who would *together* live by them. This sentiment is at the heart of most of the monologues and dialogues. . . . (pp. 276-77)

Always in Frost there is the desire (or a temptation so strong as to be a desire) to "go behind" something. Almost always there is the failure to do so, and then the triumph in living with the failure and discovering that it is a condition of strength—the strength in discovering oneself as a person, limited by the conditions which can be made clearly to define oneself as a person. This is the subject which "shall be fulfilled." In the dramatic poems it is difficult to find precise points where this is fully realized, because the realization is not the protagonist's,

but rather the poet's—as a result of the total effect of the poem. For Frost (and this is an aspect of the achievement of such poems) the failure infuses what he makes out to be a whole experience. Here, one might say, Frost is almost a novelist, because the meaning of his poems depends so much upon a minute attendance to the conditions in which particular failures must be portrayed. There are moments of pure, unmediated realization, however—epiphanies. Such moments are by definition private and are accordingly rendered in first-person lyrics—**"Tree at My Window," "Desert Places," "The Tuft of Flowers," "The Road Not Taken," "Bereft," "Once by the Pacific," "Stopping by Woods . . ."** and so many more. To name them is to recall a series of instants of awareness whose abounding clarity is gained at the expense of a certain willed irrelevance to many of the conditions in modern life. This is, one is forced to conclude, a failure which Frost wills so that he can understand it and proceed to build positively out from it. (p. 278)

What finally gives the best poems their tremendous effectiveness is a sense of local detail so sharp, so fully controlled, so wholly the poet's own, as to make us know once and forever the gulf between his world and all others. Above all, Frost can call up a sense of place and of the working of an individual sensibility when limited by and therefore complementary to it. . . . (p. 279)

Frost has long well known where and who he is. But more and more he has chosen to speak only to himself, albeit in public. We listen, we are delighted, we are moved and enlightened; but we are on the outside looking in at a poet who remains resolutely on the inside looking out, telling us what we are not by telling us what he and his special kind are. . . . In his work the nineteenth-century faith in the ultimate equivalence of the "I" and the "we" has been renounced. He has no need for the after-the-fact transcendentalism toward which such a faith drove Emerson and Whitman. What is gained is a sense of the concrete, particular, bounded "I," anticipated only in the work of Emily Dickinson. Yet Frost lacks even her variety—the product of a mind which dares to be more capacious than his. That is what is lost, the expense of Frost's greatness: variety and capaciousness. Frost manages in his poems to create nothing less than an orthodoxy—as against Emerson's heterodoxy—of the self. (p. 283)

Roy Harvey Pearce, "The Old Poetry and the New," in his The Continuity of American Poetry *(copyright © 1961 by Princeton University Press; excerpts reprinted by permission of Princeton University Press), Princeton University Press, 1961, pp. 253-92.**

ROBERT GRAVES

Frost was the first American who could be honestly reckoned a master-poet by world standards. [Edgar Allan] Poe, Longfellow, Whittier, and many more of his American predecessors had written good provincial verse; and Whitman, a homespun eccentric, had fallen short of the master-poet title only through failing to realize how much more was required of him. Frost has won the title fairly, not by turning his back on ancient European tradition, nor by imitating its successes, but by developing it in a way that at last matches the American climate and the American language. (p. ix)

Frost has always respected metre. When, during the *Vers Libre* period of the Nineteen Twenties and Thirties his poems were disdained as old-fashioned, he remarked disdainfully that writing free verse was like playing tennis without a net. The *Vers Librists,* it should be explained, had rebelled against a degenerate sort of poetry in which nothing mattered except getting the ball neatly over the net. Few games are so wearisome to watch as a methodical ping-pong, ping-pong tennis match in which each player allows his opponent an easy forehand return from the same court. The *Vers Librists,* therefore, abandoned the tennis-net of metre altogether, and concentrated on rhythm. But though metre is boring without rhythm, the reverse is equally true. A rhythmic manipulation of metre means—in this tennis metaphor—so placing your shots that you force the other fellow to dart all round his territory, using backhand, forehand, volley or half-volley as the play demands. Only the 'strain of rhythm upon metre' (Frost's own phrase), makes a poem worth reading, or a long rally in tennis worth watching. That you can't achieve much in poetry without, so to speak, a taut net and straight whitewashed lines, is shown by the difficulty of memorizing free verse; it does not fix itself firmly enough in the imagination.

Frost farmed for ten years among the well-wooded hills of Vermont. The four natural objects most proper to poems are, by common consent, the moon, water, hills and trees; with sun, birds, beasts and flowers as useful subsidiaries. It is remarkable that, among the ancient Irish, Highland Scots and Welsh, from whose tradition (though at second or third hand) English poetry derives most of its strange magic—the Muse was a Moon, Mountain and Water-goddess, and the word for poetic literature was always 'trees'. Bardic schools were built in forests, not in towns; and every letter of the alphabet had a tree name. Frost's most haunting poems, such as *The Wood-Pile, Birches, An Encounter, Stopping by Woods on a Snowy Evening,* are set in woods. The moon floats above, and water rushes down from every hill. The farmhouse in the clearing—unless it is staging one of those poignant country dramas which are his specialty—provides him with a convenient centre from which to saunter out and commune in thought with the birches, maples, hickories, pines, or wild apples. . . . Among trees, you are usually alone, but seldom lonely: they are companionable presences for those in love and, although Frost seldom uses the word 'love', all his poems are instinct with it.

He reminds us that poems, like love, begin in surprise, delight and tears, and end in wisdom. Whereas scholars follow projected lines of logic, he collects his knowledge undeliberately, he says, like burrs that stick to your legs when you walk through a field. Surprise always clings to a real poem, however often it is read; but must come naturally, cannot be achieved by the cunning formula of a short story or detective thriller. (pp. xi-xiii)

One good way of judging a particular poem . . . is to ask yourself whether the package contains anything irrelevant to its declared contents, and whether anything essential has been left out. I admit that even Frost lapses at times into literary references, philosophy, political argument and idle play with words; yet has any other man now alive written more poems that stand up to this packaging test? His chief preoccupation is freedom: freedom to be himself, to make discoveries, to work, to love, and not to be limited by any power except personal conscience or common sense. (p. xiii)

Though Frost owns to the growing materialism of the United States, which stultifies the Founding Fathers' prayer for courage and self-control among those destined to occupy the land, he refuses to lament bygone times. The land, the tools, and the language are all still available, and he has himself proved

how nobly they can be used. . . . A great part of the countryside has been scheduled for industrialization and, as everyone tells me, this is a critical, rather than a creative, age. But give thanks, at least, that you still have Frost's poems; and when you feel the need of solitude, retreat to the companionship of moon, waters, hills and trees. Retreat, he reminds us, should not be confused with escape. (p. xiv)

> *Robert Graves, "Introduction" (copyright © 1963 by Robert Graves; reprinted by permission of the author), in* Selected Poems of Robert Frost *by Robert Frost, Holt, Rinehart and Winston, 1963, pp. ix-xiv.*

ISADORE TRASCHEN

Robert Frost wrote some of the finest verse of our time. He created his own extraordinarily flat, "unpoetic" variant of the conversational idiom which has become the medium of most modern poetry. He restricted himself to the homeliest diction, to words largely of one or two syllables, a remarkable feat. And he countered this simplicity with a highly sophisticated rhetoric, with the devious twistings of the poem's development, with the irony of simple word and subtle thought. His diction was just right for the rural scene he chose in the face of the intimidating international subjects of [T. S.] Eliot and Pound, and just right, too, for its simple particulars. He was no doubt our master of the realistic particular. Things magnified at his touch; they seemed to live. His themes were familiar to most, and appealed—though in widely varying degrees—to everyone: the exhaustion of living, the sense of imminent danger . . . , personal isolation, the need for community, etc. Frost is so good, so much pleasure to read that you wonder why he needs to be defended so often. . . . Is there some really critical defect in him, one that might explain why Frost never had the passionate following Eliot had? Why didn't Frost so affect us, so transform us that we had no choice but to be his?

What I want to do is to develop an aspect of Frost's poems which I feel represents such a defect. . . . My principal argument is that Frost never risked his life, his whole being; he was never really lost, like the Eliot of *The Waste Land.* He remained in control, in possession of himself. He did this by keeping himself from the *deepest* experiences, the kind you stake your life on. And this is reflected in various ways, all of which point to a central division in Frost's experience, in himself. He has been represented, by himself as well as by others, as one able to integrate his life. . . . But when we read his poetry we encounter division of several kinds.

To begin with, it has been pointed out that though Frost looks at nature closely, and renders it faithfully, he often fails to fuse his idea of it with his feeling. Thus poems like **"Tuft of Flowers," "Two Tramps in Mud Time,"** and **"Hyla Brook"** divide in two: the things described, the pure existent, free of any abstraction, and the abstract comment, the moral or philosophical lesson in the tradition of Longfellow and Emerson, whom he admired. (pp. 57-8)

Frost does not resolve his identification with particulars and his separation from them by laying on a general meaning. His poetry reveals a division between the imagist and the commentator, between the man who is involved and the man who observes, between the naturalist and the rationalist. In some remarks on Edwin Arlington Robinson, Frost says, "I am not the Platonist Robinson was. By Platonist I mean one who believes what we have here is an imperfect copy of what is in heaven.'' But the structure of many of his poems, an ascent from matter to idea, is Platonic. I do not mean to imply that Frost thought matter inferior to the idea; he is frequently skeptical about the mind's way of knowing. . . . Still, it is fair to say that the structure of his poems often gives the impression that matter, or, more generally, existence is an illustration of an idea.

The dramatic narratives (''**The Death of the Hired Man,**'' ''**A Servant of Servants,**'' etc.) are exceptions to Frost's Platonic structure. Because of the form, probably, the action is sustained all the way; no formulation is tagged on; these poems are memorable in themselves, free of abstract wisdom. Of course this fusion of image and idea happens on occasion in the lyrics . . . and with fine effect. . . . But this fusion is not characteristic. Generally there is a division between subject matter and idea, and the poem suffers. (pp. 59-60)

This division in Frost is reflected in the frequent disjunction between his subject matter and his verse rhythms. The meter is varied from poem to poem; the iambic measure has a human voice, a quiet one which secures a tension between the dramatic substance and its own effortlessness. Yet as we read a number of poems at a stretch, another effect emerges, one of monotony—especially, as Yvor Winters points out, in those in blank verse [see *CLC*, Vol. 10]. . . . You get the same rhythm in a poem of rural manners like ''**Mending Wall,**'' with its theme of community, as you do in a quasi-tragic piece like ''**An Old Man's Winter Night,**'' with its theme of isolation. The poems call for different intensities of feeling, but there is little evidence of this in the rhythms. . . . Frost rarely breaks up [the flow of his rhythms]; rarely staggers under the burden of his subject; his tone is level even when the theme is disintegration. The effect of his rhythms is generally one of understatement—all to the good in the modern canon. But continual understatement acts as an anodyne, beguiling us into what we like to believe is the quiet voice of wisdom. This may have been all right in more contemplative times; but I would think our age is more authentically expressed through pain, through the pure, simple scream it would have been so *pleasant* to hear at times in Frost's poems. Frost's level tone works well in poems of trance-like surrender, as in ''**After Apple-Picking**'' or ''**Stopping by Woods on a Snowy Evening**''; here there is a happy conjunction of rhythm and subject matter. Frost's ''monotony'' may be connected with his philosophic attitude, an even-tempered skeptical rationalism which has been the dominant tradition in Western culture since Plato and Aristotle. It has little in common with another tradition, that of the great howlers who risked everything: the Old Testament prophets, Job . . . , the Greek tragic playwrights and Shakespeare, or romantics like [William] Blake and [Arthur] Rimbaud.

Frost's incapacity for the tragic howl is of a piece, I believe, with the sentimentality which marks a further division in him, the separation of fact and feeling. . . . [In ''**The Road Not Taken**''] Frost acknowledges that life has limits . . . , yet he indulges himself in the sentimental notion that we could be really different from what we have become. He treats this romantic cliché on the level of the cliché; hence the appeal of the poem for many. But after having grown up, who still wants to be that glamorous movie star or ball player of our adolescent daydreams? In ''The Jolly Corner'' James saw the other road leading to corruption, the fate of those who deny themselves, who suffer a division of the self.

These divisions in Frost may help us see what is unsatisfactory about a finely wrought poem like ''**The Onset.**'' . . . [In this poem] Frost is again divided in his response. He resists winter and welcomes spring; he welcomes life but does not see that death is organic to it. . . . But Frost largely flirted with the dark woods that appear with some frequency in his poems; he was not lost in them so deeply . . . for them to transform him. Instead, he made a ''strategic retreat.''

If Frost's resistance to death is unnatural, his sense of spring in ''**The Onset**'' is incomplete. It lacks the organic singleness of spring and winter of Dylan Thomas' ''The force that through the green fuse drives the flower / Drives my green age; that blasts the roots of trees / Is my destroyer.'' What is also lacking is the pain of birth, as in [D. H.] Lawrence's ''Tortoise Shout.'' . . . For Frost spring is simply another occasion for his even-tempered reassurance, compounded in the idyllic image of houses and church worthy of Rockwell Kent. . . . The village church is pretty to look at, but too often filled with people divided in their own ways: loving mankind but fearing if not hating Catholics, Jews, and Negroes, not to speak of foreigners. (pp. 60-3)

Now ''**The Onset**'' hints at difficulties, but these are overlooked or forgotten in the interests of the pleasant solution. The speaker says he is like one who ''lets death descend / Upon him where he is, with nothing done / To evil, no important triumph won, / More than if life had never been begun.'' This is a characterization of the Laodicean temper comparable to [William Butler] Yeats' ''The best lack all conviction,'' or Eliot's ''We who were living are now dying / With a little patience.'' But Frost does not draw the conclusions Yeats and Eliot do. . . . April's slender rill will still return as life-giving as ever, untouched by Laodicean lifelessness; April will not be the cruelest month, bringing a rebirth we do not want and cannot stand. Frost's Chaucerian response to spring is simply no longer possible, even before the fallout, except to one who has seriously isolated himself from our times. . . . (p. 63)

Frost generally separates himself from nature, as when he speaks with an oddly exploitative élan of our increasing ''hold on the planet''; unlike Wordsworth, who identifies with nature as his spirit is ''Rolled round in earth's diurnal course, / With rocks, and stones, and trees.'' Now there is a sense of fully meeting nature in ''**After Apple-Picking,**'' but usually, as in ''**Come In**'' or ''**Stopping by Woods,**'' the poet only seems to give himself, while actually withdrawing. Robert Penn Warren explains the withdrawal in ''**Stopping by Woods**'' as ''man defining himself by resisting the pull of nature'' [see excerpt above]. No doubt we must *distinguish* ourselves from the rest of nature, but we cut ourselves off from a critical part of our existence if we do this by *resisting*. . . . Sometimes, as in the beautiful ''**Oven Bird,**'' Frost seems to identify with nature, but even here he is really personifying the bird, imposing his philosophical mood of the moment: ''The question that he [the bird] frames in all but words / Is what to make of a diminished thing.''

The difference between Frost and Lawrence and Thomas is critical. Lawrence defines his humanness in a mutual encounter with nature, Frost by resisting it. . . . Both [Thomas and Lawrence] become more profoundly human by surrendering, or at least immersing themselves in nature. They *grow* out of their relation to it; Frost does not because he is curiously divided from it, observing it to introduce his own ideas. He does not sink to come up new; he cannot lose himself, follow his own advice and surrender himself; he will not let go of himself, allow nature to work on him and change him. As a skeptic, the poet of the middle way, not committing himself to extremes—passional or intellectual—Frost remains separate from the objects he looks at, unchanged. There is no mutual penetration which transforms subject and object. Instead, Frost puts on his armor of ideas to confront nature with; perhaps, strangely, to protect him from it. Two impulses work against each other, the naturalistic and the civilized, and the latter prevails. Despite all the suggestions of disaster in his poetry Frost does not really disturb us. He is all too frequently prepared to reach some reasonable agreement. Problems—yes; but solutions too.

What all this comes to is a detachment which in its cultural context is a poetry of isolationism. This is obviously appealing to an American audience. The title of his first volume, *A Boy's Will,* alludes to the favorite American poet of the nineteenth century, Longfellow, and to the poem which appeals to our nostalgia as well as our Edenic impulse. Succeeding titles—*North of Boston, Mountain Interval, New Hampshire, West-running Brook*—all reassure us of the importance, the validity, the worth not merely of our country, but of that part where we began and where our virtues were seeded and flourished. Nor do the images which trouble that scene—the hired man, the servant of servants, and the others—trouble Frost's audience; on the contrary, the harsh realism validates its nostalgia. Rural America is offered as the theatre of this world, appealing to anyone who would like to forget the world.

Delmore Schwartz once called T. S. Eliot our international hero; Frost is our national, isolationist hero, withdrawn as Americans generally are from the dialogue of ideas which give form to living not only in our time but at least as far back as the Old Testament days. (pp. 63-5)

Intellectual heat has tempered most of us; but Frost "is able," as Robert Langbaum says, "to shrug off those conflicts between man and nature, thought and reality, head and heart, science and religion, which since the romantic period have torn other poets apart." As a consequence, many of his poems which seem to bear upon our crises do not really confront them. . . . Frost paralyzes us with merely passive or stunned responses to modern terror, as in **"Design," "Bereft,"** or **"Once By the Pacific"**; he does not take up the arms of the intellect against our sea of troubles. Failing to be involved, he falls back on eternal commonplaces. (p. 66)

When Frost confronts our civilization in its totality—the encounter that defines our great moderns, as Stephen Spender has pointed out—he is inadequate; all he can muster is a commonplace. Perhaps he is prone to aphorisms in a poem dealing with the modern scene because he does not see it. He talks about it, but is incapable of creating its personae, like Eliot's carbuncular clerk. Having committed himself to by-road, rural figures not shaped by central modern concerns, he falls into archness or waspishness when dealing with features of our world—and not least, incidentally, its representative literature. In the later, rightly admired **"Directive,"** he advises us to retreat from "all this now too much for us" back to a "time made simple by the loss / of detail." Here once more is the refusal to confront the particulars of our world; after a journey which Frost invites us to compare with that of a Grail knight, yet with only a hint of the Grail trials, we will be saved, "be whole again beyond confusion" by drinking the cup of the past, the simple time. . . . Langbaum comments that Frost's poetry is the kind "that delivers us from the poignancy of the historical moment to place us in contact with a survival-making eternal folk wisdom. We can live by Frost's poetry as we could not by Yeats's or Pound's." On the contrary. The poetry that disturbs us most strengthens us most, much the way the tragic

hero affirms himself by acknowledging the last truth. Eternal wisdom is comic to those conscious of the awful fact of *this* historic moment. Divided from our time, Frost, our wisdom-poet, has so little of the kind of wisdom appropriate to our time, the hellish, existential wisdom of Kafka and [Albert] Camus, or the biological wisdom of Lawrence.

In his famous speech celebrating Frost's eighty-fifth birthday Lionel Trilling links Frost with the tragic poets. He makes this assertion with an unusual rhetorical violence: "when ever have people been so isolated, so lightning-blasted, so tried down and calcined by life, so reduced, each in his own way, to some last irreducible core of being." . . . He cites **"Design"** as an example of Frost's tragic sense. . . . Its argument is that the universe is a "design of darkness." But the tragic sense involves something more. It requires a belief in or a coherent vision of the design of life, traditional as with Eliot or private as with Yeats and Kafka; it requires this together with the feeling that the design is breaking down. It implies more than mere ruin. The tragic sense requires a person highly developed in spirit and mind who, broken by the imminent failure of his sense of things, is moved to probe and question—apocalyptically, or humorously, but always passionately, not with the mild, wry, even-tempered humor of Frost.

The great moderns have thought steadily about our age; from this has come intense commitments taking the form of those consistent visions of modern life which have shaped our imagination. . . . Frost writes in a historical vacuum, with almost nothing to say to us about the modern content of our alienation and fragmentation. His efforts here yield little that has not been more passionately and tragically said by many others. . . . No one seems to be more solidly planted in the world, yet no one of Frost's stature tells us less about our world.

It is the absence of a modern texture which in one way gives Frost his special appeal to moderns. As a poet of particulars, especially of nature, Frost has an effect on the city person something like that Wordsworth had for John Stuart Mill. For such a person—especially a bookish one—Frost brings a momentary salvation. He restores the *things* that our organized way of living and our abstract way of seeing have obliterated. . . . And in making us see these things he saturates us with the texture of American life, the life of its beginnings. This too is good for the intellectual who for many reasons . . . often feels like an outsider in his own country. Frost has reminded us of all that cannot be spoiled by the politician or the brassy patriot. For this we are grateful. Blueberries, ax-helves, birches, oven birds—these are stable vantage points, solid stations—but not enough. They are the moving particulars common to any time, not the disturbing particulars of our own. Neither his images nor his scenes are modern; his isolation provides him only with situations out of another era. . . . Frost is contemporary rather than modern. He lives in our time but at bottom is not affected, disturbed, shaken, transformed by it. Everyone rightly praises **"An Old Man's Winter Night,"** but [Eliot's] "Gerontion," drawing on fewer particulars of old age, disturbs us more, for it is a portrait of old age in our age, and so becomes a portrait of our age.

The division in much of Frost's poetry between image and idea, matter and rhythm, the naturalist and the rationalist is reflected in Frost's withholding himself from nature, and this in turn we see is a reflection of the division between his subject matter and that of the age. This was fatal to his full development, preventing the kind of growth and transformations that marked Yeats and Eliot. His simplicity and homeliness probably contributed to this fate. He took these qualities too seriously, as though they were the heart of truth. He became his own imitator, beguiling himself enough to keep himself out of the complexities and contentions of our time, out of the political, moral, religious, and philosophical crises which might have led to a passionate commitment. Even if wrongheaded, this at least would have opened hell to him. (pp. 67-70)

Isadore Traschen, "Robert Frost: Some Divisions in a Whole Man," in The Yale Review *(© 1965 by Yale University; reprinted by permission of the editors), Vol. LV, No. 1, Autumn, 1965, pp. 57-70.*

ELAINE BARRY

Frost was not a systematic thinker. He was against systems on principle. . . . Part of his suspiciousness toward "structure" lay in the fact that "wisdom" could so easily lose itself in questions of political or ideological debate, in "grievances" rather than "griefs." . . . But essentially he would have been suspicious of anything that implied a single answer. He was born too late to be reassured by Emerson's cheerful monism.

If the subjects of Frost's meditative poems tend to be disparate and inconclusive, simply "momentary stays against confusion," they at least deal with complex and important issues. Exploratory and speculative, they represent a lonely pondering on the central problems of existence: man's identity and freedom, his relation to the natural world and the flux of time, his defenses against an engulfing chaos, the place of human suffering and the possibility of salvation. His poems are torn, as his life was, between affirmation and negation, and if the resolution of this conflict seems at best tenuous, that tenuousness is deliberate. Essentially a pragmatist, Frost was less concerned with chronicling the spirit of his age, as Eliot was, or with forging his insights into a philosophical system, as Wallace Stevens was, than with working out a practical *modus vivendi*, a way of making something out of the facts that life presented him with.

One extremity of the philosophical spectrum that Frost's mind sought to encompass finds expression in the poems of terror that Lionel Trilling referred to. This is the pull of the annihilating dark, the fear of his "own desert places." The personal tragedies in his life added poignancy to the basic question of whether "all the soul-and-body scars / Were not too much to pay for birth." Intellectually he had even taken the step beyond the romantic awareness of personal despair to contemplate the possibility of cosmic meaninglessness. **"Design"** and **"Neither Out Far Nor in Deep"** give us a glimpse of absurd and absolute blankness, just as [Herman] Melville's "Bartleby" does. But, unlike Melville, Frost never steps into this blankness to explore its bleak reality, and his poetry thus lacks that dimension of intellectual daring. He does not even create a positive metaphor for it. Perhaps Frost could not afford to risk his precarious sanity. (pp. 100-02)

Very few of Frost's poems are as unequivocally affirmative as **"Bereft"** or **"Acquainted with the Night"** are unequivocally negative. In most of them a sense of affirmation is hard won, with a realistic awareness of its opposite clearly present in the poem. It is rarely simplistic or moralistic. . . . If Frost's poetry on the whole is positive in its attitude to life, the affirmation is scarcely exuberant.

Yet his overall attitude is positive, despite a temperamental bias toward negation, and it is won through a conscious and

tough-minded pragmatism. Pragmatism is the general philosophical premise behind most of Frost's poetry. . . . If his refusal to follow his intuitions of meaninglessness through to an intellectual conclusion denied his poetry the tragic intensity of Melville, this was partly due to a courageous awareness that life has to be lived on its own terms. (pp. 102-03)

[Frost's] attitude in this was reinforced by the contemporary philosopher and psychologist, William James. . . . (p. 103)

James based his commitment to living on the practical grounds of creating one's own human meaning and value rather than on orthodox Christian attitudes to faith. . . . Unlike Emerson, James was skeptical, doubting, yet determined to use his doubts in a positive way. His "self-reliance" is far more tentative and courageous than that of Emerson; it is what Frost meant later by "falling forward in the dark." (pp. 103-04)

There were many things about James's philosophy that appealed to Frost. Frost was agnostic enough to need a philosophy that would justify itself in purely human terms and yet would satisfy the spiritual and intuitive in him; James's emphasis on self-realization did that. Perhaps more importantly, Frost was temperamentally receptive to the moral commitments that James demanded—the courage, will, effort, that were needed to choose life and to propel the "maybes" into positive action. All through Frost's writing we find such ideas reoccurring, the Jamesian vocabulary unchanged—words such as courage . . . , [will, effort, hero]; words such as "risk," "tussle," "threat." . . .

The basic premise, then, is a conscious, pragmatic acceptance of life as it is. . . . With a certain self-righteousness he poured scorn on T. S. Eliot and other prophets of doom who saw the 1920s as fragmented and sterile, the worst of all possible ages. (p. 105)

As part of [his] tough, pragmatic acceptance of life as it is, Frost accepts the limitations of human knowledge and capacity. Commenting on the folly of bringing a peach tree too far north into New England for it to have a fair chance of survival, the speaker of **"There Are Roughly Zones"** recognizes that "There are roughly zones whose laws must be obeyed," though he has a sneaking admiration for "this limitless trait in the hearts of men" that will gamble on defying the "zones." (p. 107)

Heroic will, conscious choice, self-definition through suffering: these are the concepts through which Frost tried to find an intellectual rationale for his pragmatism, his acceptance of life as it is. At a time when naturalism, with its philosophy of pessimistic determinism, had a strong foothold in American literature, Frost refused to admit that men's fate might be determined by such factors as heredity or environment. His concepts of individualism and self-reliance were as strong as Emerson's, though more existential, more grounded in the idea that man not only improves himself but actually creates himself, defines himself, through taking on a "trial."

These ideas of will, choice, and trial are basic to Frost's thinking. . . . But **"The Trial by Existence"** is not a convincing poem—partly because this argument for an affirmative attitude to life is intrinsically implausible, and partly because it is presented in too didactic a way. In his later meditative poems Frost overcame both these drawbacks. In such poems as **"Mending Wall," "Birches,"** and **"West-Running Brook"** the ideas are presented through the richer and subtler techniques of metaphor and symbol rather than through simple didactic exposition. And the ideas themselves are less abstract and moralistic. That sense of conflicting tensions that Frost was all too aware of in his life, and to which his pragmatism was a conscious answer, is explored in terms that are more human and practical.

In **"Mending Wall"** (1914) the central symbol of the wall acts as a focus for two conflicting attitudes. Economically, it thus concentrates the poem's theme. The poem describes how each spring two farmers—the narrator and an older neighbor—meet at their property boundary to repair their common stone wall after the ravages of winter. The narrator questions the need for a wall at all, since he has an apple orchard and his neighbor pine trees. . . . To this rationalizing, the old man simply retorts: "Good fences make good neighbors," and they go on constructing the barrier between them.

The balance of sympathy in the poem seems to rest with the narrator, and an inattentive reader might be led to assume that the poem simply advocates the abolition of walls. The narrator's argument is practical and sensible, his voice easygoing and tolerant. (pp. 109-10)

All reasonableness is on the narrator's side. Yet it is not ultimately convincing. Despite his good-humored condescension toward the old man, he continues with the job. In fact, it was he who initiated the wall mending. . . . Ultimately the poem would seem to be not so much about a simple conflict of attitude as about the different modes of thinking that inform both attitudes. Each of these modes—the purely empirical and the purely traditional—is found wanting. The conflict is deliberately unresolved, and the total effect of the poem is, ironically, more thoughtful and subtle, more true to human experience, than the effect of **"Trial by Existence,"** in which Frost tried to justify the general conflicts of life by a simplistic account of their origin.

The equivocation in **"Mending Wall"** reflects Frost's own feeling. Whatever compunction he might have had at times, he would on the whole have opted for the principle of maintaining walls. . . . He had no time for any philosophy that assumed that absolute harmony was possible or even desirable. . . . The consciousness of individuality, the constructive tension between disparate elements, and the instinctual, intuitive interaction that he called "passionate preference"—these, for Frost, were the only viable premises for human action and creative thought. The function of a wall as a symbol then, lies not in the fact that it shuts people off from each other ("Good fences make good neighbors") or that it may be rationally unnecessary ("Before I built a wall I'd ask to know / What I was walling in or walling out"), but that it focuses the constant tension of opposing elements, which Frost saw as the essence of the human condition. (pp. 111-12)

Finally, let us look at a poem that is in many ways the pinnacle of Frost's achievement as a poet—**"Directive"** (1946). It is perhaps the most fully realized of all his poems. It is one in which theme is inseparable from symbol, tone, rhythm, and structure, and one in which so many of the Frostian themes reach a kind of culmination: the existential loneliness, the self-defining resistance to the engulfing flow of existence, the individual salvation that is partly given . . . and partly earned. . . . Yet it is a poem that has been largely overlooked. . . .

[**"Directive"**] is a journey back up the "universal cataract of death," a step beyond that stoic point where human identity bravely holds its own, "not gaining but not losing," against the annihilating tide; a step beyond the tension of contrariety to an original source. It is Frost's only attempt at some rec-

onciliation of that conscious ambivalence that he maintained so deliberately in so many of his poems. (p. 120)

"Directive" describes a journey that begins in a world of confusion and decay, and progresses, through various "serial ordeals" that echo the quests of Arthurian romance and the paradoxes of the Christian mystics, to a state "beyond confusion." (p. 121)

The present world which is the starting point of the poem is not "too much with us" but "too much for us." How subtly Frost modifies and extends the Wordsworthian echo here. His phrasing, after what we have already noted in his themes about the creative value of some tension of contrariety, implies a flabby lack of challenge—the world is too much *for* us. At the same time, its colloquial sense—as in "It's all too much for me"—reinforces the impression of spiritual defeatism.

The journey is "back . . . back": past individual life . . . ; past a Whitmanesque identification with others who have lived on the same earth . . . ; past the "upstart" reclamation of one's human traces by Nature, which has overgrown the apple orchards that man had long ago won from her; past even the marks of geological change in which the "road" is described as following a "ledge" that was "the chisel work of an enormous Glacier / That braced his feet against the Arctic Pole''; and back beyond the anthropomorphic world of myth. . . . (pp. 122-23)

The speaker maintains an assured colloquiality. He addresses most of the poem to "you," but the "you" slips so easily into "I" at the end that it is obvious the two are integral. The "you" form makes the total effect less personal perhaps, but more importantly it establishes an easy colloquial tone. . . . The only other "character" in the poem is a "guide"—if you'll let him direct you—who also blends so easily into the "you" and the "I" that he may be seen as a kind of alter ego of both the reader and the poet.

The journey is fraught with the paradoxes that beleaguer most quest myths. The guide "only has at heart your getting lost." The apparent destination—"There is a house"—is immediately negated—"that is no more a house." And just when the "height of the adventure" is reached—a high place where two village cultures once faded into each other—we are deflated by the statement that "Both of them are lost." But the resolution of all this paradox is not the orthodox salvation-through-surrender idea, losing one's life in order to save it; that would be too clichéd altogether for this highly individualized poem. (pp. 123-24)

Ultimately, any attempt to explain the "meaning" of this poem belittles it. Its real power is emotional, drawn from the rich resonance of its sparse narrative. The Arthurian echoes combine with a certain fairy-tale incantation ("There is a house that is no more a house / Upon a farm that is no more a farm") to give it the dimension of myth. At the same time the colloquial voice of the guide ("pull in your ladder road behind you . . . make yourself at home") anchors it to the realities of individual experience. Indeed, the sureness with which all the literary echoes in the poem—biblical, Arthurian, Wordsworthian—are interwoven shows that Frost could match Eliot in the business of ironic analogy. In **"Directive,"** Frost achieves a poetic integration of theme and form that makes it one of his finest poems.

Throughout this brief examination of some of Frost's major themes, we have seen that, despite his reputation as a nature poet, his concerns are essentially human ones. In a very real sense he is a philosophical poet. Nature simply provided him with a constant metaphor—the "fact" with which his imagination could work. Certainly it provided no haven for him; Frost's characters move in a terrible loneliness. (pp. 127-28)

Frost has his limitations as a thinker. Even in his definition of a poem as a "momentary stay against confusion," there is an implication that whatever meaning can be thus won is accidental and transitory. His intellectual preoccupations are disparate, not welded into any coherent structure. His moral values—concerned with consciously maintaining a perpetual cold war between affirmation and negation—make for an unglamorous stability rather than a tragic grandeur, for adjustment rather than confrontation.

In spite of all this, there is something reassuringly sane and unpretentious about Frost's thematic concerns. If he fails to explore the heart of darkness it is because he has come close enough to it to be wary of entering in. His acceptance of life on its own terms represents an affirmation that was won at the cost of bitter personal negations, and it rarely becomes complacent. There is an intellectual rigor behind the often whimsical irresolution of its expression. Frost held his irresolution deliberately. To say this is not to make it automatically a viable philosophical position. It *may* be "spiritual drifting" [as Yvor Winters charged (see *CLC*, Vol. 10)]. But, bearing in mind the consistency of such ideas in Frost's poetry, their hardheaded practicality, and the stern discipline of metaphor and symbol through which they are examined, this seems too glib a charge. (p. 129)

> Elaine Barry, in her Robert Frost *(copyright © 1973 by Frederick Ungar Publishing Co., Inc.), Ungar, 1973, 145 p. [the excerpts of Robert Frost's poetry used here were originally published in* The Poetry of Robert Frost, *edited by Edward Connery Lathem (copyright © 1930, 1939, 1947; © 1969 by Holt, Rinehart and Winston; copyright 1936, 1942; © 1958, 1960, 1962 by Robert Frost; copyright © 1964, 1967, 1970, 1975 by Lesley Frost Ballantine; reprinted by permission of Holt, Rinehart and Winston, Publishers), Holt, Rinehart and Winston, 1969].*

DONALD J. GREINER

[What Frost did] to American poetry was to insist that a poem must have definite form, be dramatic, and use voice tones to vary the "te tum" effect of traditional iambic meter. Although all three prescriptions reflect his belief that poetry should include the intonation of the speaking voice, his concern with form has philosophical implications as well. Frost writes about confusion, about the universal "cataract of death" that spins away to nothingness. Yet while he faces the chasm, he refuses to accede to its lure. Confusion is a universal state to be acknowledged as a kind of boundary against which man can act by creating form. No form is permanent, as Frost suggests in his famous phrase "a momentary stay against confusion," but man may delight in chaos because it provides the opportunity for form. (p. 5)

When Frost applies his ideas about form to the art of poetry, he shifts his concern with universal chaos to the "wildness" of the creative impulse. The tension generated by the union of the untamed impulse and the countering restrictions of traditional meter and stanza forms reflects some of Frost's philosophical concerns as well as adds to the appeal of his poems.

To abandon poetic form is to court chaos. One can thus understand his averson to free verse.

Frost also suggests that the absence of traditional form in poetry diminishes the dramatic element, a quality he prized. Calling on poets to show "a dramatic necessity" in their art, he explains that the intonations of the speaking voice are the best means for creating a sense of drama. . . . Frost believes that sentences in poetry cannot hold the reader's attention unless they are dramatic and that only the entanglement of the "speaking tones of voice" in the words will supply drama.

His comments reflect his concern for what he calls "sentence sounds," his favorite topic when discussing prosody. Briefly, Frost tries to unite the free-ranging rhythms and tones of actual speech which do not necessarily have iambic pentameter and its variations. This union was primarily responsible for the bewilderment experienced by the first reviewers of *North of Boston,* for while Frost seemed to be writing in traditional forms, his lines did not scan in the traditional way. (pp. 5-6)

In short, the three elements of form, drama, and sentence sounds gives Frost's poetry what Lawrance Thompson calls "a fresh vitality without recourse to the fads and limitations of modern experimental techniques." (p. 6)

Frost looked for *old* ways to be new. No matter how bewildering his blank verse appeared to the first readers of *North of Boston,* he always stressed the necessity for traditional form and coherent content. His variations with standard meter and rhyme were designed not to cast away the heritage of American poetry but to renew it. Frost showed how recognizable voice tones encourage natural departure from the iambic rhythm even though the predominate poetic foot of the entire poem remains iambic. In his best poems, . . . he unites three levels of sound: the primary rhythm of the line, the pronunciation of words and phrases, and the sentence sounds communicated by inflections of tones of voice. One problem facing the uninitiated reader is not to let his feeling for the predominately iambic rhythm violate the pronunciation of the words and phrases. The enduring vitality of **"Mending Wall"** and **"The Death of the Hired Man"** results from the tension between the opposite pulls of the freer voice tones and the stricter poetic meter all within the restrictions of traditional verse forms. (p. 7)

[An] impressive example of Frost's prosody is the first line from **"The Death of the Hired Man"**: "Mary sat musing on the lamp-flame at the table . . ." Despite the efforts of early reviewers to read it as free verse, **"The Death of the Hired Man"** is a blank verse poem. The reader's sense of puzzlement results from the conversational tone, prosaic vocabulary, the trochee "Mary," the spondee "lamp-flame," the anapest "at the table," and the thirteen syllables instead of the traditional ten. Frost not only varies the sound from the "te tum" effect of standard blank verse, but he also links the unusual rhythm with theme. Realizing that a close proximity of trochee, spondee, anapest, and additional syllables forces a slow reading of the line, the reader turns to the next line and notes that the first word is "waiting": "Waiting for Warren. When she heard his step . . ." Although Frost again begins with a trochee, he assigns this line the ten syllables normally expected in blank verse. In addition to the opening trochee, he includes alliteration and a caesura which once more slow the reader to reenforce the sense of waiting before the rush of sound in "When she heard his step."

The reader who compares the virtuosity of these lines to the relatively colorless blank verse of **"Waiting—Afield at Dusk,"** published just a year before **"The Death of the Hired Man,"** will marvel at the confidence Frost shows in so much of his poetry after *A Boy's Will.* He learned to avoid the jerkiness and rigidity present in poems of five-stress lines which rely too much on metrical regularity and too many end-stopped lines. . . . After Frost realized the possibilities for uniting dramatic speech tones with traditional meter, he used run-on lines, feminine endings, and the variations of trochaic and anapestic feet to illustrate the old way to be new. (pp. 7-8)

When Frost is at his lyrical best, the speech rhythms and variations determine even the position of rhymes. **"After Apple-Picking"** and **"The Rabbit-Hunter,"** for example, are rhymed in spite of Frost's refusal to supply a traditional scheme to govern rhyme placement. The natural rhythm of the spoken phrases dictates both metrical variations and the unscheduled rhymes. At first reading, **"After Apple-Picking"** looks like free verse or even untraditional blank verse because of the surprising metrical irregularity which results in some lines of iambic dimeter. But when the poem is heard, the reader notes that it can be neither free verse nor blank verse because of the insistent sound of the iambic stresses and the gracefully placed rhymes. (p. 13)

In many of Frost's later lyrics, as opposed to the dramatic narratives, his genius with metrical variations and substitutions encourages the reader to ignore the central rhythmical pattern. Only by a deliberate notation of syllable count, poetic feet, and accent can the reader define the basic rhythm. Clearly, the more Frost wrote, the more confident and sophisticated he became with prosody. Even a lyric as short as the fifteen-line **"November"** has anapests, feminine endings to suggest uncertainty, unscheduled rhymes, and repetition of syntax. Yet the general cadence throughout is rhymed iambic trimeter.

Frost continued to experiment with versification during his long career. How mistaken are those readers who even today insist that he was too conservative with technique to be honored with the great modern poets of his time. His successful innovations with the traditional forms and rhythms of poetry confirm his goal to discover old ways to be new. . . . Surely it is fair to say that Frost's experiments with prosody rejuvenated the traditional rhythms, meters, and patterns of rhyme which readers have always associated with poetry. (p. 14)

> *Donald J. Greiner, "The Difference Made for Prosody," in* Robert Frost: Studies of the Poetry, *edited by Kathryn Gibbs Harris (copyright © 1979 by Kathryn Gibbs Harris), G. K. Hall & Co., 1979, pp. 1-16.*

W. J. KEITH

[Let us consider Frost's] relation to his material. . . . [There are] some poems in which no narrator is specified, and others in which the centre of attention has been 'I,' 'he,' 'they,' and even 'we.' Frost has always been conscious of the artistic possibilities of such variation, and one reason for the narrative variety clearly lies in the poet's reluctance to be identified too closely with the speaker of his poems. . . . The angle of narration depends not on the reflection in subject-matter of autobiographical experience but, as in poets from whom he learned his trade, on the artistic needs of individual poems.

One has only to alter the pronoun in the first line of **'The Most of It'** and read,

> I thought I kept the universe alone,

to begin to realize what is at stake. Although we tend to assume that the first person gives greater vividness and immediacy, and that vividness and immediacy are unquestionably desirable qualities, Frost's effect in this poem . . . clearly depends upon impersonality and detachment. We need to look down on the solitary human being by the side of the lake and watch the great buck blundering past him. So far as I am aware, there is no evidence that the poem was based on any autobiographical experience, but even if it were, Frost's point is not 'This is how I feel in relation to the natural world,' but 'This is every man's situation when ultimately faced with what is apparently the brute indifference of nature.' (pp. 134-35)

The well-known **'Mending Wall'** offers a more complicated instance. Here, true to what is obviously a favourite Frostian pattern, one looks at one over a separating barrier. In this case, however, the 'I' is a participant, and this has caused some readers to assume (illegitimately, I think) that in the friendly disagreement that is the subject of the poem we are to take sides with the speaker against his more traditional and conservative neighbour. But although the speaker maintains that the tradition is kept up at the insistence of the neighbour, he initiates the ritual himself: 'I let my neighbour know beyond the hill.' One suspects that both men enjoy the annual duty, that the give-and-take of neighbourly argument is cherished on both sides. Even the two catch-phrases, 'Something there is that doesn't love a wall' and 'Good fences make good neighbors,' both occur twice in the poem and so help to maintain a balance. **'Mending Wall,'** we might say, is poised between these two mutually exclusive 'right' attitudes.

But should we equate the 'I' of the poem with Frost? Surely not. . . . Just as the symbolic application of the wall needs to be kept flexible if the poem is to have the maximum effect, so the limitation that any specifically personal reference would imply needs to be avoided. Besides, Frost offered a valuable clue to the tensions behind **'Mending Wall'** when he remarked during an interview: 'Maybe I was both fellows in the poem.' . . . Though **'Mending Wall'** has been the subject of numerous critical commentaries, the possibility of Frost's deliberately dividing his allegiance between the two speakers has not yet been given the attention it deserves. Yet much of the poem's appeal may be explained by the way in which this conflict of attitudes which intrigued the poet is carried over to his readers. The poem's universality derives from the split sympathy that the vast majority of us feel between the respective claims of 'traditionalism' and 'progress.'

'The Road Not Taken' presents even greater complexities. Although countless readers have taken it at its face value, although it stands as opening poem in *Mountain Interval* and in one of Frost's recordings (suggesting that the poet saw it as a direct introductory statement), and although Elizabeth Sergeant has pointed to an autobiographical origin in an incident when Frost sensed that he was going to meet his double at an intersection in the woods, a strong case can be made for its not being about Frost at all. Frost claimed it to be a playful parody of Edward Thomas, whose hesitant indecision Frost found both amusing and appealing, and on different occasions he gave varying accounts of the poem's development and of Thomas's attitude towards it.

It is perfectly justifiable, however, to see the poem as about both Frost and Thomas. Indeed, the incident in the woods . . . may well have become associated in Frost's mind with Thomas's poems 'The Sign-Post' and 'The Other.' Both these were written while Frost was in England and he most probably read them quite soon after they were completed. The former is about choosing which direction to take, the latter about an *alter ego* who seems to dog Thomas's path. Frost, I suspect, saw in Thomas exaggerated manifestations of his own traits, and by the same token the poem appeals to a wide audience because it deals with the problem of choice in terms that are universally applicable. Once again, too much individualizing . . . would have limited the scope of the poem; as it is, the reader, faced with a poem that demands to be approached dramatically, has little difficulty in blending the 'I' with himself. (pp. 135-37)

> *W. J. Keith, ''Robert Frost,'' in his* The Poetry of
> Nature: Rural Perspectives in Poetry from Words-
> worth to the Present *(© University of Toronto Press
> 1980), University of Toronto Press, 1980, pp. 119-
> 40.*

Marvin (Penze) Gaye

1939-

Black American songwriter.

Gaye is one of many songwriters credited with expanding the scope of contemporary black music, which had become dormant during the late 1960s and early 1970s. As a member of Motown Records's huge company of performers, Gaye was Motown's top male vocalist and teenage heartthrob. His collaborations with Tammi Terrell were especially praised. Their success as a duo ended when Terrell died after a long illness. Shaken by her death, Gaye went into seclusion, surfacing in 1971 with the album *What's Going On.*

What's Going On is recognized as the first rhythm and blues "concept album," a collection of songs that center on one theme. Many reviewers considered *What's Going On* a milestone for Gaye as well as for the black popular music industry, which previously had produced mostly superficial love songs. Gaye wrote of the powerlessness of urban blacks in "Inner City Blues (Make Me Wanna Holler)," the threat of nuclear war in "Save the Children," and environmental concerns in "Mercy, Mercy Me (The Ecology)." He acknowledges the seriousness of this work, citing Terrell's death as an inspiration and stating that he "felt moved to [write songs] . . . that dealt with real issues and true feelings."

Let's Get It On and *I Want You* contain songs that are sexually oriented. On both albums, Gaye's lyrics are passionate, yet subtle, reminiscent of those of Smokey Robinson. *Here, My Dear,* Gaye's most controversial album, generated the most critical attention. It tells the story of Gaye's marriage and divorce from Anna Gordy. Many reviewers believed that this album was an incoherent effort on Gaye's part, while others voiced their disapproval and disappointment over his candidness. In 1982 Gaye emerged from another self-imposed retreat with *Midnight Love,* whose single "Sexual Healing" won the Grammy Award in 1983 for best rhythm and blues single.

VINCE ALETTI

[Marvin Gaye has designed *What's Going On*] as one many-faceted statement on conditions in the world today, made nearly seamless by careful transitions between the cuts. A simple, subdued tone is held throughout, pillowed by a densely-textured instrumental and vocal backing.

At first this sameness in sound persisting from one song to the next is boring, but gradually the concept of the album takes shape and its wholeness becomes very affecting. The style is set in the first cut, **"What's Going On."** . . . As they are throughout, the lyrics here are hardly brilliant, but without overreaching they capture a certain aching dissatisfaction that is part of the album's mood.

"What's Happening Brother" picks up from **"What's Going On,"** strengthening its impact by making its situation more specific: a brother returning from Vietnam and trying to get his bearings on the block again, shifting between questions about old hang-outs and fears that there's no work anywhere. . . . **"Mercy, Mercy Me"** is one of the most bearable

Chris Walter/Retna Ltd.

ecology songs, a genre that doesn't seem to inspire especially subtle or intelligent lyrics; Gaye's are inoffensive and the song itself is lovely. Considerably changed from the version that had backed the 45 of **"What's Going On,"** **"God Is Love"** still has a strange attraction. It begins, "Don't go and talk about my father / God is my friend," and kinda grows on you.

"Inner City Blues (Make Me Wanna Holler)" ends the album and is one of its finest cuts. Again, an effective combination of latin drumming and strings with multi-tracked vocals make the most of direct lyrics. . . . Taking the album full circle, **"Inner City Blues"** blends back into **"What's Going On,"** confirming itself nicely.

One or two other cuts don't hold together quite as well (**"Right On,"** the longest number, misses) but the album as a whole takes precedence, absorbing its own flaws. There are very few performers who could carry a project like this off. I've always admired Marvin Gaye, but I didn't expect that he would be one of them. Guess I seriously underestimated him. It won't happen again. (pp. 43-4)

Vince Aletti, in his review of "What's Going On," in Rolling Stone *(by Straight Arrow Publishers, Inc. © 1971; all rights reserved; reprinted by permission), Issue 88, August 5, 1971, pp. 43-4.*

TIME

After listening to the Motown album *What's Going On,* the Rev. Jesse Jackson informed its creator, Soul Crooner Marvin Gaye, that he was as much a minister as any man in any pulpit. Gaye does not see himself in quite that way, though he does admit to a certain "in" with the Almighty. . . . While such words would sound intolerably conceited from any other pop star, they come inoffensively from Gaye. Part mystic, part pentecostal fundamentalist, part socially aware ghetto graduate, this particular Motown superstar simply happens to believe that he speaks to God and vice versa.

The most prominant musical result these days is black beatitudes of sorts called *What's Going On.* The LP laments war, pollution, heroin and the miseries of ghetto life. It also praises God and Jesus, blesses peace, love, children and the poor. Musically it is a far cry from the gospel or blues styles a black singer-composer might normally apply to such subjects. Instead Gaye weaves a vast, melodically deft symphonic pop suite in which Latin beats, soft soul and white pop, and occasionally scat and Hollywood schmalz, yield effortlessly to each other. The overall style of the album is so lush and becalming that the words—which in themselves are often merely simplistic— come at the listener like dots from a Seurat landscape. They are innocent individually but meaningful en masse.

> *"Motown Beatitudes," in* Time *(copyright 1971 Time Inc.; all rights reserved; reprinted by permission from* Time*), Vol. 98, No. 15, October 11, 1971, p. 69.*

ALAN LEWIS

Mercy, mercy, me . . . if only one could be sure. Is ["**What's Going On**"] a heartfelt personal statement by a brilliant singer who has at last been given the chance to express his true self? Or is it that Motown are determined not to be caught with their social consciences down when people like Curtis Mayfield have done so well out of displaying theirs? Like the other black labels, Motown have realised that in order to sell albums by black artists to the general (i.e., young, white) audience, it is necessary to present them as being "important," "serious" and "relevant." Out goes Funk, in comes Ecology. Thus this album contains printed lyrics (about war, pollution, poverty, drugs, God, inequality, etc), an earnest sleevenote and pictures of Gaye standing against a slum background in the rain, looking suitably concerned. About all that's missing is a lapel badge saying "I CARE." And yet, despite such cynical doubts, it has to be said that this is an impressive album, and that Gaye does emerge as a man of integrity with a deep love of life and God. Politically, the lyrics aren't going to scare anybody, but coming from a man who has spent the past ten years singing other people's songs, they are surprisingly sharp. . . . [The] album improves with every hearing. Gaye produced and cowrote all the songs, and plays piano. So here's a whole new dimension to a man, who, perhaps more than any other (remembering his beautifully spare and precise vocal lines on songs like "Grapevine" and "I'll Be Doggone") has always avoided excess and indulgence in his work.

> *Alan Lewis, "Gaye Liberation: 'What's Going On',"* in Melody Maker *(© IPC Business Press Ltd.), October 16, 1971, p. 54.*

VINCE ALETTI

Even when a movie soundtrack isn't so awful you'd just as soon throw it down the stairs, it very rarely achieves anything beyond a sort of banal, predictable mood music; a little suspense, a little drama, an ooze of romance, maybe a brisk driving-in-the-car-to-possible danger track counterpointed with a lighter, romantic-leads-take-a-walk sequence—all compressed, like a week's worth of garbage, for one tight, bright under-the credits Main Theme. Altogether, it's about as creative as an hour of elevator muzak and only slightly more bearable. . . .

Marvin Gaye's work for *Trouble Man* (yet another *Shaft*-style black film, this one dropped from sight soon after its release) falls somewhere between that of [Isaac Hayes for *Shaft* and Curtis Mayfield for *Superfly*]. He lacks the Hayes double-punch but avoids his heavy-handedness. While there's no attempt to make a song-score like that of *Superfly*—"**Trouble Man,**" the title song, is practically the only cut with lyrics and even these are spare—Gaye, like Mayfield, has created a score strong enough to be completely independent of the film. It's not a lot of fluff wrapped around some slick images and obvious themes; mostly, it's sweet and churning jazz that abstracts the action rather than decorating or interpreting it.

Gaye's first album since his surprising and innovative *What's Goin' On* more than a year ago, *Trouble Man* doesn't take his music a whole lot further and certainly sidesteps the problem of how to follow up a sweeping life statement—aha! Just take this movie assignment and make no personal statement at all. Yet it's no throwaway. Most of the music carries on in a similar vein from *What's Goin' On,* although here it's a little more hard-edged . . . and at times self-consciously dramatic. The "**Main Theme**" is handsome if slightly overdrawn; I wouldn't miss the strings if they were cut from the arrangement, however. "'**T' Plays It Cool**" is more successful and gripping. . . .

Much of the other material is moody and more reminiscent of Gaye's "**Mercy, Mercy Me**" or "**Save The Children.**" . . . *Trouble Man* is surely one of the most attractive and listenable of the recent picture soundtracks, but it only stalls the question of what Marvin Gaye will do after *What's Goin' On.* A stylish way of stalling, yes, but it's still your move, Marvin.

> *Vince Aletti, in his review of "Trouble Man," in* Rolling Stone *(by Straight Arrow Publishers, Inc. © 1973; all rights reserved; reprinted by permission), Issue 129, March 1, 1973, p. 63.*

JON LANDAU

[On *Let's Get It On*] Gaye uses his voice (in both lead and background) to create a dreamlike quality only slightly less surreal than he did on *What's Goin' On,* his very best record to date. But while on the earlier work he sang of the difference between his vision of God's will and man's life, he is currently preoccupied with matters purely secular—love and sex.

And yet he continues to transmit that same degree of intensity, sending out near cosmic overtones while eloquently phrasing the sometimes simplistic lyrics. But then that should come as no surprise from the man who sang "She makes my day a little brighter / My load a little bit lighter / She's a wonderful one," in a way that made it difficult to remember whether he was singing about God or woman—and whether he felt there was any difference. . . .

Let's Get It On is as personal as *What's Goin' On* but lacks that album's series of highpoints. Instead, it ebbs and flows, occasionally threatening to spend itself on an insufficiency of ideas, but always retrieved, just in time, by Gaye's performance. From first note to last, he keeps pushing and shoving, and if he sometimes takes one step back for every two ahead, he gets there just the same—and with style and spirit to spare. (p. 74)

> *Jon Landau, in his review of "Let's Get It On," in* Rolling Stone *(by Straight Arrow Publishers, Inc. © 1973; all rights reserved; reprinted by permission), Issue 149, December 6, 1973, pp. 74, 76.*

JOEL VANCE

Marvin Gaye was one of the original Motown stable of artists. Like Stevie Wonder, he has declared his artistic independence, and his recordings avoid the shrewd, assembly-line "Motown Sound." . . . A few years ago he cut an album, **"What's Goin' On,"** which seemed to be entirely made up of one ethereal melody to which he set different lyrics dealing with the conditions of life on the planet. Out of this album came *Inner City Blues,* which said more in five minutes about the black experience than Curtis Mayfield has been able to say in three years.

Gaye has never been sanctimonious or preachy (though he can preach); his recent efforts have shown him to be a fellow of good will and common sense, as well as being a highly skilled entertainer. [On **"Let's Get It On"**] he turns to the joys of sex. Fifteen years ago this would have been called a "mood music" album, and that's what it really is. Gaye is honest without being blunt. None of the tunes are memorable, but the point of a mood music album is to create an effect no matter what the qualities of the material might be. And here the effect is right. The album is a happy development. Put it on and enjoy.

> *Joel Vance, in his review of "Let's Get It On," in* Stereo Review *(copyright © 1974 by Ziff-Davis Publishing Company), Vol. 32, No. 2, February, 1974, p. 90.*

GEOFF BROWN

Three points. First, if you liked **"Let's Get It On,"** Marvin Gaye's last studio album, you'll love **"I Want You."** Second, it will not convert the unbelievers. Third, it is the sort of album that Barry White and his grunt 'n' groan cronies would dearly love to produce, but can't. . . . Marvin still looks to sex for direct inspiration. If anything, he's now even more explicit. The title **"I Want You"** need absolutely no explanation. And much of the remaining music here is likewise straight down the middle: **"Come Live With Me Angel," "Feel All My Love Inside," "Since I Had You"** and **"Soon I'll Be Loving You Again"** say most, if not all, in their titles. The important consideration, however, is that **"I Want You"** is not a series of tracks but a complete, flowing, luxurious mood based on the desire of a man for a woman. Marvin deals with age-old themes and makes passionate truths of standard soul cliches ("hey sugar", "oh darlin'") while the musicianship is beautifully deft. It's a thick-textured album and the deeper one dips into it, the more one finds. . . . [Marvin's] still as high, pure, warm, light and soothing as ever. He is a singer who needs only to hint at the first syllable of a word and you know the whole sentence. His emotional panache, his ethereal, husky delivery come together on **"After The Dance"** as he blends the lyric and melodic themes of "I want you / You want me" with the satisfied physical exhaustion of a dancer whose prime

drive is to impress his partner. The album is a fine melt of Gaye's personal expression with the current, general themes of black experience in America. Folks, he suggests, know the hardship and austerity of yesterday, but also know there's better to come, whether it is given or they take it. Through it all, however, says Marvin, love is strong and love drives. **"I Want You"** is highly recommended.

> *Geoff Brown, in his review of "I Want You," in* Melody Maker *(© IPC Business Press Ltd.), May 1, 1976, p. 29.*

VINCE ALETTI

With Barry White on the wane, Marvin Gaye seems determined to take over as soul's master philosopher in the bedroom, a position that requires little but an affectation of constant, rather jaded horniness. The pose has already been established in *Let's Get It On* . . . , on which Gaye was hot, tender, aggressive, soothing and casually raunchy—the modern lover with all his contradictions.

I Want You continues in the same vein but with only the faintest traces of the robust passion that shot through and sustained the earlier album. . . . As pillow talk this is entirely too limp, and in spite of the presence on several tracks of a woman's delighted sighs and moans (such a common effect these days that one is surprised not to find a background orgasm credit), the action here isn't much more than attractive but unenthusiastic foreplay. Gaye pleads and cajoles—"Baby please let me do it to you"—but too often he ends up sounding like a little boy whining for candy.

All of this might have been more acceptable—or less disappointing—from a lesser performer than Gaye, but after a landmark album like *What's Goin' On* one expects a little more substance and spirit. But there's no fire here, only a well-concealed pilot light.

> *Vince Aletti, in his review of "I Want You," in* Rolling Stone *(by Straight Arrow Publishers, Inc. © 1976; all rights reserved; reprinted by permission), Issue 214, June 3, 1976, p. 69.*

BILL ADLER

Marvin's latest attempts to scale new heights in sexual immediacy unfortunately fail, since they are delivered in the bogus, overblown manner of Barry White. Like the epochal *What's Goin' On* and *Let's Get It On,* [*I Want You*] has a dreamy, watery feel that is sustained throughout. However, what was unified before sounds homogenized now.

Marvin continues to multi-track his voice, each track in constant call-and-response counterpoint to the others, the arrangements swamped by a veritable ocean of strings, horns, and percussion. Things are rhythmically kept in a tight, if gentle, groove (especially on the title cut and *All The Way*), but there isn't a distinctive *composition* within earshot or anything remotely resembling a provocative lyric. The problem is that this slush for disco-dancers has almost nothing to do with the funk and vitality of the magnificent dance scene portrayed on the album's cover, or for that matter, any of the now-classic hits Marvin has recorded during the last 15 years.

> *Bill Adler, in his review of "I Want You," in* down beat *(copyright 1976; reprinted with permission of* down beat*), Vol. 43, No. 13, July 15, 1976, p. 26.*

CONTEMPORARY LITERARY CRITICISM, Vol. 26   **GAYE**

RICHARD MORTIFOGLIO

If you didn't know about Marvin Gaye's divorce, one look at the cover of *Here, My Dear* would be enough to guess the plot of this home-movie soap. Fake Rodin love sculptures litter a Greco-Roman courtyard bounded by two plaques, one inscribed "Love and Marriage," the other "Pain and Divorce." In front stands Marvin himself, a bogus Socrates gone toga party, inviting us to drink from his own very bitter cup. Pretentious is too good a word for this clutter. What happened to the sharp eye responsible for the exhilarating blur—Gaye's red knit cap as soul icon—of the *Let's Get It On* cover?

Gaye is no stranger to bad taste—remember the "sex voices" in "**You Sure Love To Ball**" or the mercury-tunafish line in "**Mercy, Mercy Me**"? But *Here, My Dear* goes somewhat beyond or below these small outrages. The spoken intro makes it clear that this record is not only dedicated to Anna Gaye but given to her as well, literally, as alimony. And the songs' excessive length and, in one case, repetition in "versions," lead one to suspect Gaye of padding his material to double-album length for double-album prices.

Fortunately the music isn't as shoddy as the packaging or the "concept." It finds a gentle groove early on and rarely deviates except for an excursion in light swing called "**Sparrow**," which wavers nicely into a choral overdub at the end, the record's tastiest moment. Otherwise, this material is so nondescript that after more than a dozen listens, I still have trouble recalling any lyrics or more than a few melodic lines.

And even these few hooks seem no more than tired remakes cloned from Gaye's earlier hits anyway. The vaguely pretty "**I Met a Little Girl**," a five-minute chronology of the Gayes' courtship and marriage, resembles "**Distant Lover**" (on *Let's Get It On*) but lacks distinguishing features, such as the latter's subliminal pulsating wah-wah. "**Anna's Song**," a light blue-moody chant, is a ghost of "**Trouble Man**." Still, this is Gaye's most sincere performance on the album, as might be expected. The meandering convolutions of "**When Did You Stop Loving Me, When Did I Stop Loving You**" might seem inventive if Gaye's singing wasn't so depressed. . . .

As for the subject matter, public airing of this sort of dirty laundry is not unheard of in pop. Leonard Cohen has made a career of it. Lou Reed's seminal *Berlin* is a blunt, despairing narrative of a dying marriage. But these two have the courage of some ruthless self-dissection. by turns apologetic and accusatory, self-pitying and self-congratulatory, Gaye is too involved in justifications to tell us anything real about marriage. This is especially distressing because *Let's Get It On* is one of the best (one of the only!) albums about "pure" sex ever made. . . .

Gaye's ambitions—and he is very ambitious; he once compared his music to Beethoven's—are mostly musical anyway. Heir to the smooth style of Sam Cooke, Gaye also sings with enough hard gospel grit to make him something more enduring than the entertainer he was born to be. . . . It would be hard to deny that he has sold at least part of his soul to the devil though, what with the rip-off *Trouble Man*, the execrable *I Want You*, and this latest inflated teardrop.

So Marvin Gaye is a man of contradictions—the best kind, usually. And he has carried these contradictions to the heart of his great music. While *What's Going On* gave slick class to social realism, *Let's Get It On*, the modern make-out manual, can be rough going for the casual listener. From the grating "ugly" opening to the sweet, string quartet severity of "**Just To Keep You Satisfied**," Gaye demonstrated uncompromising good taste along with the occasional bad as an independent composer and producer.

Here, My Dear notwithstanding, Gaye is too valuable and too shrewd (for all his aggressive innocence) to write off. . . . If next time he moves like he means it too, don't be surprised—born-again is second nature for an old soul.

> *Richard Mortifoglio, "Marvin Gaye Gives Something Up" (reprinted by permission of* The Village Voice *and the author; copyright © The Village Voice, Inc., 1979), in* The Village Voice, *Vol. XXIV, No. 5, January 29, 1979, p. 53.*

STEPHEN HOLDEN

A two-record concept album about conjugal love, "**Here, My Dear**" is a fascinating failure, as flawed as it is ambitious. In some respects it seems almost designed to be off-putting. (p. 122)

In the scope of its ambition and the lavishness of its production, "**Here, My Dear**" bears many resemblances to Gaye's 1971 masterpiece, "**What's Goin' On**," possibly the most eloquent evocation of social upheaval to come out of the Motown era. In that album, Gaye introduced a moody aural collage in which the brooding inner voices threatened to burst out of the production; the result was ominous, tense, exhilarating. "**Here, My Dear**" struts the same sort of echoy melange, thick with strings, horns, and chorus. The atmosphere is even more ruminative, the rhythms lighter.

But when turned to soap opera, as opposed to social drama, these textures become repetitive, even pretentious. True, there are some lovely moments. . . . But the narrator too frequently adopts a conversational singing style that lacks dramatic punch, so the details of the marriage (the album covers the union from courtship through divorce settlement) become the stuff of soap opera: realism without art. Most serious of all, the material is not tuneful enough to sustain four sides—a difficulty compounded by the sound's laidback dynamic evenness. Had Gaye edited all this into a single disc, it might have come together. (p. 124)

> *Stephen Holden, in his review of "Here, My Dear," in* High Fidelity *(copyright © by ABC Leisure Magazine, Inc.; all rights reserved; excerpted by permission), Vol. 29, No. 4, April, 1979, pp. 122, 124.*

LARS GABEL

While most soul music already relies on a very direct relationship between life and artistic expression, Marvin Gaye may well be the first singer to subscribe to the current trend of confessional art. Presumably, inspiration is where you find it, and out of something as prosaic and antithetical to the creative process as his recent divorce case, Marvin Gaye has produced the proverbial silk purse: *Here, My Dear* is an exciting and personal work—his best since the towering *What's Going On*. . . .

Starting on a bitter you asked-for-it note to Anna ". . . I guess I'll have to say this album is dedicated to you . . . although it may not make you happy, this is what you wanted . . .", Gaye gives the listener the impression that he or she is about to watch an embarrassing family quarrel, an airing of dirty laundry. Such fears and the chill of the dedication are quickly dispelled as Gaye glides into the title cut on a choral backdrop of his own overdubbed shrieks and moans so haunting and heartfelt that one is forced again to go back to *What's Going On* for similar emotional penetration. Gaye's naked, evidently pained yet vividly inspired performance renders the unadorned, private words unforgettable, true and touching. I cannot imagine any other contemporary pop artist in a like situation intone ". . . one thing I can't do without is the boy that God gave to both of us . . . I'm so happy for the son of mine . . ." and get away with it, but here, transcended by Gaye's luminous voice, such moments simply become very moving. (p. 27)

I Met A Little Girl is the one fond memory of Anna that Gaye allows himself. A slow meandering ballad affectionately set in a '50s doo-wop style, beautifully sung and arranged, *I Met A Little Girl* is the album's high point, free of the sadness and occasional outbursts of recalcitrance which, with the album's progression, cumulatively begins to bear down on the listener, leaving him with a notion, after all, of the grueling experience of a divorce. The lift and courage of *What's Going On* is missing here.

This conclusion, however, does not detract from the fact that several songs such as *When Did You Stop Loving Me, Sparrow* and *Anna's Song* individually provide Marvin Gaye with an opportunity to invoke his shimmering, magical harmonies and to draw on his gift for holding together his fragmentedly composed songs, which are a far and advanced cry from the mainstream patterns of A/B structures.

Also, in more concrete terms, the double-album runs out of steam: *When Did You Stop Loving Me* is repeated twice with no artistic gain; *A Funky Space Reincarnation* is funk filler while *You Can Leave* is plain filler. A serious threat to the integrity of the album is posed by *Falling In Love Again,* where Gaye does an about-face and jubilantly tells us of his already having found a new love. This odd, ill-placed prancing is the single instance when one is left cold and with a sense of listening to a self-centered person's private affairs. We feel sorry for Anna.

It remains to be said that *Here, My Dear* represents Marvin Gaye at the full height of his vocal power. While all titles are written or co-written by him, he more than ever proves to be an interpreter/improviser rather than a melodist. With his soaring, suddenly shifting technique, with his ability to somehow register peaks at every voice level, then lift, stretch and undulate these peaks, Marvin Gaye reminds us that he is still a truly unique, truly exciting soul singer. On *Here, My Dear* he further perfects his innovative blend of lead voice and his own dubbed background vocals, deriving overtones from both contrapuntal and unison interplays so seamlessly that one has come to accept this highly contrived and prepared sound as the final Marvin\Gaye instrument. (p. 28)

Lars Gabel, "Marvin Gaye," in down beat *(copyright 1979; reprinted with permission of* down beat*), Vol. 46, No. 10, May 17, 1979, pp. 27-8.*

STANLEY CROUCH

Since *What's Going On* in 1971, Marvin Gaye has proven himself the most brilliant and complex thinker in contemporary black popular music. He's succeeded at bringing ideas beyond the novel to a form from which we expect wonderfully sung but simple passions, and the successes have expanded the music itself. The result has been the development of a personal language at ease with gospel quartet crooning, despairing gutteral

moans that slide back into the delta, the purple-hearted street-corner falsetto, and the silken sound of elegant erotic ambition.

His is a talent for which the studio must have been invented. Through overdubbing, Gaye imparted lyric, rhythmic, and emotional counterpoint to his material. The result was a swirling stream-of-consciousness that enabled him to protest, show allegiance, love, hate, dismiss, and desire in one proverbial fell swoop. In his way, what Gaye did was reiterate electronically the polyrhythmic African underpinnings of black American music and reassess the domestic polyphony which is its linear extension. Much of this probably has to do with his early experience as a Motown drummer, for the arrangements he wrote or supervised staggered off percussion voices and instruments with almost peerless precision. The upshot of his genius was the ease and power with which he could pivot from a superficially simple but virtuosic use of rests and accents to a multilinear layered density. In fact, if one were to say that James Brown could be the Fletcher Henderson and Count Basie of rhythm and blues, then Marvin Gaye is obviously its [Duke] Ellington and Miles Davis. He seeks an urbanity and sophistication, an intricacy and subtlety that challenge the adolescent sentimentality at the core of the idiom without abandoning the dancing and seductive inclinations of the tradition. Perhaps, as with Davis, his strength developed from his knowledge of his own limitations. . . .

Not all of his records after *What's Going On* have been pleasing, partly because one doesn't produce a masterwork every time out but also because his primary concerns changed from social comment to sorting out his own experience. Sometimes to the consternation of his listeners, he produced recordings for a few years that seemed to reach for a more narrow satisfaction, an erotic and romantic one in flight from the notorious burden of consciousness. Even so, there was often a spiritual anguish at the back of the dance hall, a mosquito net of sorrow the sleeping Don Juan would have to meet upon awakening.

The boil of bile was lanced by *Here, My Dear,* the controversial double album, inspired by his divorce, which made many feel they were listening to pus running from their speakers. Its emotional range was too great, its bitterness too close to the surface, its despair and self-revelation perhaps too heavy and intricate for both his audience and the form. . . . Many women hated it because they thought Gaye was dropping the responsibility on the woman and letting himself off easy (they didn't hear the revelations about his own unfaithfulness and short-sightedness, his own irrational stubbornness and self-inflation). Most importantly, however, the musical ambition was extraordinary. It was [Duke Ellington's] *Black, Brown, and Beige* of rhythm and blues, with arrangements that mapped a territory stretching from street-corner doowop simplicity to the final selection, "**Falling in Love Again**," which began with Fela-like harmonies and phrasing, then developed its statement with a bold use of overdubbed backup voices and styles. A flawed popular masterpiece, his most ambitious album since *What's Going On.*

Now Marvin Gaye has turned it around again with *In Our Lifetime,* a recording on which lust and mysticism are braided like some plait of secular and religious passion strung across a contemporary dance band. . . .

Though one of his best dance records, this album is simpler in certain ways than what he does at his most adventurous. But the mastery of the idiom and the continued development of his arranging skills give it strength. Though the emotion sloshes back and forth between desire for both salvation and flesh, it is made clear that the latter, while easier to obtain, is never enough. At one point he sings, "Lots of ladies love me but it's still a lonesome time."

Gaye has a superb sense of how to develop his songs chorus by chorus. He usually starts a song singly over the rhythm, adding other instruments, vocals, and occasional improvised instrumental solos or saxophone obbligatos. When he's not developing counterpoint he will sing a line in unison with one of the rhythm instruments or add a sung note to a chord played by the horns to extend the harmony. Gaye's accents are rarely less than brilliant; he likes to float over the tempos and the rhythms as he italicizes beats that find unexpected spaces in the arrangements. **"Far Cry"** is a perfect example of his rhythmic invention, while **"Love Me Now or Love Me Later"** is the high point of his powers of synthesis. In that song, Gaye tells the tale of Creation, speaking of God and the Devil as the composition perfectly combines gospel, blues, and jazz elements. The lyrics, alas, are not very strong, but none of the others are either. Yet Gaye transcends his own lyrics just as jazz singers have transcended those of Tin Pan Alley. That, it seems to me is the problem at the center of Gaye's work, one which we will probably hear him do battle with for the rest of his career. After all, a man's greatness is often measured by the personal limitations he must overcome. And when Marvin Gaye triumphs, as he does through most of the second side especially, it is pleasing indeed.

Stanley Crouch, "Marvin Gaye's Interconnections" (reprinted by permission of The Village Voice *and the author; copyright © News Group Publications, Inc., 1981), in* The Village Voice, *Vol. XXVI, No. 11, March 11-17, 1981, p. 59.*

DAVE MARSH

As a comeback album, Marvin Gaye's *Midnight Love* is remarkably arrogant: it simply picks up from 1973's *Let's Get It On* as if only ten minutes, and not a confusing ten years, had elapsed since Gaye hit his commercial peak. But make no mistake: this record, which has become the biggest crossover hit of the singer's career, is a comeback for Gaye, whose last couple of albums, despite their funkster defenders, committed the unpardonable sin of tedium.

Midnight Love is anything but boring. It has the rhythmic tension, melodic delicacy and erotic resilience of Gaye's greatest music, and it extends those attributes by applying contemporary synthesizer gimmickry judiciously and soulfully. . . . And everything here, including the ribald greeting-card verse of the lyrics, underscores the relentless erotic obsession that's at the core of Gaye's concerns.

But *Midnight Love* isn't as truly ambitious a record as Gaye's greatest album, *What's Going On* (1971), was. In the disintegration of his marriage and his eventual divorce, Gaye seems also to have experienced a separation from the social concerns that fueled that music, and as a result, his themes have narrowed: eroticism, on the one hand (**"Sexual Healing"** is a sort of polemic for the power of rampant humping, which is strange, since Gaye claims to have abstained for the past three years), and an obligatory, somewhat desperate nod to Jesus (in the liner notes and the dedication that opens the final track).

On the other hand, *Midnight Love* is a consequential record, a fact that has something to do with another kind of ambition. In a period when most performers are content to stake out a narrow corner of the marketplace, Marvin Gaye demands center stage and is determined to hold it. That Gaye not only commands our attention so forcefully but that he commands it so effortlessly should remind us that he has been one of our most underrated musical forces for a long time. . . .

Dave Marsh, in his review of "Midnight Love," in Rolling Stone *(by Straight Arrow Publishers, Inc. © 1983; all rights reserved; reprinted by permission), Issue 387, January 20, 1983, pp. 48, 50.*

PHYL GARLAND

[On **"Midnight Love"**] Gaye concentrates on music that, he admits, is intended to be superficial and commercial. The lyrics are obviously trite and at times downright abominable; all of the worn-out sexual references are expressed in the unimaginative terms that have branded commercial funk as an aggressively anti-intellectual medium. But Gaye as an artist could not fail to produce an album that tingles with musical excitement. *Sexual Healing,* the first single released from this set, engagingly fuses reggae rhythms with soul references. *Midnight Lady* has contrived, campy lyrics yet reverberates to off-beat rhythm patterns and unexpected chord changes. Some tracks have no redeeming qualities—*Rockin' After Midnight* and *Joy* are so thuddingly banal as to be take-offs on the usual funk fare—but Gaye's artistry shines through. He plays most of the instruments and does all the singing, and, if the content isn't all that we would like to hear from him after a prolonged silence, it is enough to reassure us that he has not lost his basic appeal. After all, it hasn't been just *what* Marvin Gaye has said that has drawn us to him, it's also been the way he says it.

Phyl Garland, in her review of "Midnight Love," in Stereo Review *(copyright © 1983 by Ziff-Davis Publishing Company), Vol. 48, No. 3, March, 1983, p. 99.*

Sol Gordon

1923-

American nonfiction writer, psychologist, editor, and teacher.

Gordon is a clinical psychologist who writes books for young adults and younger children in which he candidly discusses the physical aspects of sex and the sexual roles of young people. Gordon often defines and explains four-letter words in his books, reasoning that young people who understand the words will be less likely to include them in their everyday speech. Gordon's frankness has alienated some critics, who contend that he is trying to conceal a basic lack of direction in his books. Others, however, find Gordon's approach fresh and attractive to young adults.

Facts about Sex: A Basic Guide (retitled *Facts about Sex for Today's Youth*) is probably Gordon's most widely read book. In it he tries to clear up the confusion that many young people have toward their sexuality by discussing sympathetically and without condescension premarital sex, homosexuality, contraception, and venereal disease. *You!*, which has been revised as *The Teenage Survival Book*, continues along the same lines. Written with Roger Conant, it includes drawings and cartoons to lighten the mood, yet still offers helpful information. *You Would If You Loved Me* comprises a list of seductive phrases used by boys and advice to help girls cope with such sexual advances.

(See also *Contemporary Authors*, Vols. 53-56; *Contemporary Authors New Revision Series*, Vol. 4; and *Something about the Author*, Vol. 11.)

Courtesy of Sol Gordon

EDA J. LeSHAN

[A] book for teen-agers—older ones—"**Facts about Sex**" . . . by Sol Gordon, has me somewhat stumped. Dr. Gordon . . . felt it would be helpful to have a book that openly and frankly acknowledged language of the streets, what he calls "the vulgar or so-called dirty words." I cannot imagine that there are many school systems experimental or adventurous enough to try such an approach, and so the book will have limited usefulness. I also question whether it is the better part of wisdom to confuse our roles with young people, who really want us to act like grownups and serve as models. . . . There is, however, a sensible and honest candor about the book that might be especially useful with young people who feel quite alienated from adults and have had little or no opportunity to communicate with them about sexual matters.

> *Eda J. LeShan, in her review of "Facts about Sex,"* in The New York Times Book Review *(© 1970 by The New York Times Company; reprinted by permission), August 2, 1970, p. 18.*

SCIENCE BOOKS

Many books have been written for children of all ages on the subject of sex education, but [*Facts about Sex: A Basic Guide*] is the first one for adolescents that faces the fact squarely that most of them get their sex information and misinformation through conversations with their peers. But many of them don't

get their facts straight and have consequent feelings of guilt and uncertainty. Dr. Gordon . . . believes that it is important for young people to know and understand sex and the language associated with it, including the so-called dirty words. His book is brief, to the point, has listed and explained the vulgar or taboo terms either in the text or in footnotes. He hopes that parents will accept his book and be willing to talk with their young people about it. If not, he suggests that they leave the book where they can find it, when and if they are interested, and can have opportunities to read it in private. . . . The book does well what it sets out to do—to deal with the physical processes and realities of sex and sex relations. The moral and ethical aspects of sex are obtainable from other books or sources.

> *A review of "Facts about Sex: A Basic Guide,"* in Science Books *(copyright © 1970 by the American Association for the Advancement of Science), Vol. 6, No. 2, September, 1970, p. 156.*

DIANE FARRELL

[*Facts About Sex: A Basic Guide* is a] slim volume that should do much to dispel adolescent confusion about sex and the language associated with sex, specifically the obscenities, dirty jokes, and graffiti that are part of the media of the teen subculture. . . . What distinguishes this presentation is that all the vulgar or "dirty" words are defined together with the acceptable colloquial expressions and the correct medical terms. The author's premise is that once young people understand the correct meaning of the vulgar words, they cease to be anxious about them and seldom use them to anger, shock, or annoy adults. . . . An enormously useful book, it imparts both physical information and emotional reassurance, putting the whole subject into a wholesome, sane, psychologically sound perspective. (pp. 65-6)

> *Diane Farrell, in her review of "Facts about Sex: A Basic Guide," in* The Horn Book Magazine *(copyright © 1971 by The Horn Book, Inc., Boston), Vol. XLVII, No. 1, February, 1971, pp. 65-6.*

KIRKUS REVIEWS

[*Facts about Sex for Today's Youth,* a revised edition of *Facts about Sex: A Basic Guide,* is] hardly substantial enough to merit reprinting. The insufficiency of detail is indicated by the suggestion that "Girls who want to know more about menstruation should write for free literature . . ." and the limits of Gordon's frankness are reached when he says that "ball, jump, go down and screw are also used as impolite ways of referring to sexual intercourse" without ever alluding to that most popular impolite word of all.

> *A review of "Facts about Sex for Today's Youth," in* Kirkus Reviews *(copyright © 1973 The Kirkus Service, Inc.), Vol. XLI, No. 8, April 15, 1973, p. 467.*

KIRKUS REVIEWS

[*Facts about Venereal Disease for Today's Youth*] has the merits of brevity and simplicity and will be a [good choice] . . . for anyone who wants to obtain the facts necessary for self-protection without reading a full-length book. In addition to a description of symptoms Gordon lists some do's and don'ts for those undergoing treatment which a doctor might neglect to mention . . . and includes illustrated instructions for the use of condoms. Inessential information on prevalent "myths" about VD and the diseases' histories are relegated to later chapters where they can be skipped over, and though Gordon's recommendation that condoms always be used (even by women on the Pill) seems somewhat impractical, his attitude is generally commonsensical. . . .

> *A review of "Facts about Venereal Disease for Today's Youth," in* Kirkus Reviews *(copyright © 1973 The Kirkus Service, Inc.), Vol. XLI, No. 16, August 15, 1973, p. 890.*

KIRKUS REVIEWS

[*Girls are Girls and Boys are Boys: So What's the Difference?* involves some] random poking around at various levels of sex and sex-role education, beginning with the interchangeable play and career preferences that were more effectively celebrated in [Eve] Merriam's *Boys & Girls, Girls & Boys.* Then there's a perfunctory investigation of where babies come from, and finally a swift glance at wet dreams, masturbation, and menstruation, the sort of topics [Wardell B.] Pomeroy covers at length. . . . [The] grab bag explanations cover questions asked at different developmental levels—and better answered in many other places.

> *A review of "Girls are Girls and Boys are Boys: So What's the Difference?" in* Kirkus Reviews *(copyright © 1974 The Kirkus Service, Inc.), Vol. XLII, No. 21, November 1, 1974, p. 1154.*

ZENA SUTHERLAND

[In *Girls are Girls and Boys are Boys; So What's the Difference?*] Gordon moves from a debunking of sexist ideas about the characters and roles of boys and girls to the area of sex education, describing sexual intercourse, menstruation, nocturnal emission, and masturbation. The writing is direct, informal, and candid; the author makes no judgments, pulls no punches, and he concludes with the fact that all human beings are of equal value and should have equal opportunities—pointing out that both boys and girls can have many interests. This doesn't explore either physical differences or social attitudes very deeply but it serves well as an introduction.

> *Zena Sutherland, in her review of "Girls are Girls and Boys are Boys; So What's the Difference?" in* Bulletin of the Center for Children's Books *(reprinted by permission of The University of Chicago Press; © 1975 by The University of Chicago), Vol. 28, No. 7, March, 1975, p. 113.*

LEAH DELAND STENSON

Teens who have the good fortune to read Gordon's self-help and how-to guide will learn ways to mitigate adolescent angst [in *You!: the Psychology of Surviving and Enhancing Your Social Life, Love Life, Sex Life, School Life, Home Life, Work Life, Emotional Life, Creative Life, Spiritual Life, Style of Life, Life*]. Covering numerous aspects of interpersonal relations and behavior—sex and love (hetero- and homosexual), drugs, depression, marriage, death, etc.—Gordon offers noncondescending advice and insightful analyses of common problem situations. . . . Appealing to browsers, the book has an eclectic, free-form format: bold chapter headings, photographs and drawings (including some nudity), poems, lists, text set off in boxes for emphasis, cartoon asides, and colored comic book inserts—e.g., **"Ten Heavy Facts About Sex"**—which, though lighthearted, don't pull any punches. The comics are explicit . . . while the accompanying text gives the hard facts. . . . One of the best books offering psychological help for teens to date, this doesn't insult readers by suggesting simple solutions or glibly telling them the "right" way to behave.

> *Leah Deland Stenson, in her review of "You!: The Psychology of Surviving and Enhancing Your Social Life, Love Life, Sex Life, School Life, Home Life, Work Life, Emotional Life, Creative Life, Spiritual Life, Style of Life, Life," in* School Library Journal *(reprinted from the February, 1976 issue of* School Library Journal, *published by R. R. Bowker Co./A Xerox Corporation; copyright © 1976), Vol. 22, No. 6, February, 1976, p. 52.*

GARY BOGART

One doesn't read a book [like *You*] so much as experience it. And believe me, there are experiences here too numerous to count. Basically the book is a potpourri of comments on the various subjects mentioned in the title, all surrounding a core of six comic books. . . . If my antennae are any good at all, I can safely predict that YAs will flip over this book. I can also predict that many adults will squirm at its frankness in dealing with certain subjects often deemed taboo for teenagers. To be sure, some of the material is in questionable taste; I sometimes felt that [Sol Gordon and Roger Conant] were trying very hard to shock. But much of the material is excellent—the comic book on V.D., for example, is both informative and clever. Furthermore, the authors manage to speak to young people without condescension, offering sound advice for a terribly traumatic period of life. (p. 641)

> *Gary Bogart, in his review of "You: The Psychology of Surviving and Enhancing Your Social Life, Love Life, Sex Life, School Life, Home Life, Work Life, Emotional Life, Creative Life, Spiritual Life, Style of Life, Life," in* Wilson Library Bulletin *(copyright © 1976 by the H. W. Wilson Company), Vol. 50, No. 8, April, 1976, pp. 641, 655.*

WEST COAST REVIEW OF BOOKS

The attempt is greater than the overall effect [in *You*]. . . . The book supposedly is aimed at our "young people" but somebody ought to tell Gordon and Roger Conant, who assisted, that one has to be able to read a book comfortably in order for one to use it, eh? Here we have the most garish layouts these eyes have ever seen. The cartoons, the art work, knock you down before the text gives you the message. And when you get the message, you find the trip wasn't worth it.

> *A review of "You," in* West Coast Review of Books *(copyright 1977 by Rapport Publishing Co., Inc.), Vol. 3, No. 2, March, 1977, p. 43.*

JOAN SCHERER BREWER

[The readings in *Sexuality Today—and Tomorrow: contemporary issues in human sexuality*] are intended to supplement a basic text in college and university human sexuality courses. [Coeditors Gordon and Roger W. Libby] believe that information about alternative lifestyles provides a basis necessary for intelligent decision making, and emphasize a morality based on responsible relationships rather than dogma. In five sections, each introduced by an essay, they cover changing sex roles and sexual behaviors, the politics of sociosexual issues, variations in sexual expression, social ethics and personal morals, and future sexuality. . . . Most of the articles are competent and thought provoking; however, few of the contributors are adequately identified. The book omits consideration of black sexuality included in other works of this kind, but covers such often neglected topics as prostitution, transsexualism, and bisexuality.

> *Joan Scherer Brewer, in her review of "Sexuality Today—and Tomorrow: Contemporary Issues in Human Sexuality," in* Library Journal *(reprinted from* Library Journal, *April 1, 1977; published by R. R. Bowker Co. (a Xerox company); copyright © 1977 by Xerox Corporation), Vol. 102, No. 7, April 1, 1977, p. 824.*

PUBLISHERS WEEKLY

[In *You Would if You Loved Me* Gordon] has collected a pride of lines, used more or less successfully by hot-blooded youths trying to warm up cool young women. For the most part, the "invitations" are crude and markedly offensive, many followed by no more edifying examples of riposte that only quick-thinking maidens would fire back. An introduction cites woeful statistics on betrayed and pregnant young women who certainly need all the help they can get against the importunities of love-them-and-leave-them types. Perhaps this book, clumsy and slapdash though it is, will give ignorant teenaged females some life-saving ammunition.

> *A review of "You Would If You Loved Me," in* Publishers Weekly *(reprinted from the July 31, 1978 issue of* Publishers Weekly, *published by R. R. Bowker Company, a Xerox company; copyright © 1978 by Xerox Corporation), Vol. 214, No. 5, July 31, 1978, p. 99.*

PATTY CAMPBELL

In his latest effort, **You Would if You Loved Me,** [Sol Gordon] has collected a noxious nosegay of one-liners ostensibly used by boys bent on seduction. Oldies but not goodies, they range from the oily . . . to the crude. . . . In some cases Gordon has supplied snappy comebacks for girls ("He: I've been admiring your rear end for weeks. She: Admiring will get you nowhere!").

Far from discouraging the male, this approach is provocative and makes the female a player in the game. An honest "Sorry, I'm not interested" is far kinder. But most of these remarks don't deserve kindness; many are so insulting . . . that a self-respecting girl could only respond by immediately walking away. (pp. 83, 93)

The author's rationale for perpetrating this witless, repetitive, and grossly sexist collection is that forewarned is forearmed. Although this is a simplistic solution to the problem of teenage pregnancy, it may be true that inexperienced girls might benefit by first encountering these ancient lines in a book rather than in the dark. (p. 93)

> *Patty Campbell, in her review of "You Would If You Loved Me," in* Wilson Library Bulletin *(copyright © 1978 by the H. W. Wilson Company), Vol. 53, No. 1, September, 1978, pp. 82-3, 93.**

SALLY C. ESTES and STEPHANIE ZVIRIN

[In *You Would if You Loved Me*] Gordon has assembled dozens of [seduction lines] in a clever, yet serious attempt to "wise up the naive and vulnerable" teenage girl and help her recognize some of the verbal advances that may lead to physical sex. The lines (many with appropriate replies) have been collected by Gordon over the past 10 years and are grouped roughly into categories (lines to cry by, inside lines, lines to make you drowsy, etc.) that parody the emotion or situation the line reflects. Although the author occasionally breaks the continuity by intruding with advice, he speaks frankly to teens with appealing informality. Despite the fact that some teenage boys may use this as a treasury of new hustle material, girls will find Gordon's approach eye-opening, and the glib and humorously phrased repartees he offers a real help in coping with awkward, high-pressure situations.

> *Sally C. Estes and Stephanie Zvirin, in their review of "You Would If You Loved Me," in* Booklist *(reprinted by permission of the American Library Association; copyright © 1978 by the American Library Association), Vol. 75, No. 26, November, 1978, p. 537.*

KLIATT YOUNG ADULT PAPERBACK BOOK GUIDE

In his introduction [to *You Would if You Loved Me*], Gordon deplores the double standard which has in fact encouraged the male in our culture in his role as seducer. He states once again the appalling number of teenage pregnancies in the U.S. and his aim is to protect young women from being pressured to have sex before they are ready. He says frankly that some critics might feel that this book will provide males with more ideas for seduction techniques; however, as one reads the lines with their suggested rebuttals and as one giggles at the cartoons, the message is clear that females should be alert to recognize a "line" for what it is, and learn to counter with an assertive negative, or at least with a witty refusal. A particularly poignant section, amidst the predominantly humorous ones, is a list of successful lines volunteered by out-of-wedlock—and abandoned—pregnant teenagers.

> *A review of "You Would If You Loved Me," in* Kliatt Young Adult Paperback Book Guide *(copyright © by Kliatt Paperback Book Guide), Vol. XIII, No. 1, Winter, 1979, p. 36.*

PATTY CAMPBELL

Facts About Sex for Today's Youth by Sol Gordon has been the best simple book on the subject since 1969, when it was first published. Its straightforward, primer-easy text makes it useful with unskilled or unwilling readers, but its honesty and lack of condescension and the joyful, handsome illustrations give it appeal to all sexual beginners. In this revision (the third) there are a number of minor changes. . . . Herpes is now included in the section on venereal disease, and Gordon claims that all states now permit VD treatment without parental consent. Girls are warned against seductive "lines" (an echo of the author's *You Would If You Loved Me*). . . .

The major change, which makes it obligatory to discard the previous edition, has to do with the section headed **"Sex Differences"** (previously **"Sex Problems and Differences"**). This has been rewritten to clarify that homosexuality is neither a disorder nor a disease. The slang terms (except for "gay" and "lesbian") have been labeled pejorative, and other "different" but acceptable life choices mentioned are celibacy, bisexuality, and the sexually active single life. (p. 712)

> *Patty Campbell, in her review of "Facts about Sex for Today's Youth," in* Wilson Library Bulletin *(copyright © 1979 by the H. W. Wilson Company), Vol. 53, No. 10, June, 1979, pp. 712-13.**

PATTY CAMPBELL

Sol Gordon's *Facts about VD,* like his *Facts about Sex,* is designed for older teens who may be experienced but not knowledgeable, and who are not readers by inclination or ability. Without wasting a single word, he lays out the basics about understanding and preventing the transmission of the love diseases. In this edition there is an expanded description of herpes, a new emphasis on oral and anal VD, some new pictures, a few updated statistics . . . , and new resource lists. Gordon has also added a page strongly advising teens to seek medical help every time they have sex without a condom. (p. 327)

> *Patty Campbell, in her review of "Facts about VD," in* Wilson Library Bulletin *(copyright © 1980 by the H. W. Wilson Company), Vol. 54, No. 5, January, 1980, pp. 326-27, 350.**

PATTY CAMPBELL

[*The Teenage Survival Book*] is a new edition of *You,* the self-consciously super-hang-loose sex and life manual that came out of the author's belated sixties consciousness (in 1975). Little is changed here, although at first glance it might seem that the inside is as new as the title because the author has scrambled the contents around. Gordon has also dropped much of the most valuable part of the original: those raunchy straight-ahead comics. . . . The leftover space is filled in with a lot of Gordon's own embarrassingly bad poetry, a long piece on Margaret Sanger by Toby Clinch, an inappropriate article titled **"Toward a Successful Marriage,"** and some updated book lists. What seemed like so much fun six years ago now looks like sloppy and egocentric pseudowisdom caught in a time-warp. (p. 371)

> *Patty Campbell, in her review of "The Teenage Survival Book," in* Wilson Library Bulletin *(copyright © 1982 by the H. W. Wilson Company), Vol. 56, No. 5, January, 1982, pp. 370-71.**

JORJA PERKINS DAVIS

I must begin by saying I am not Gordon's staunchest fan and supporter. I find his style too smug. In comparing [*Teenage Survival Book* with *You!*], however, I find that his changes are generally positive, his additions so-so, his deletions disappointing and some things he left as they stood, I wished he'd revised. He has made some steps toward making this edition less objectionable by leaving out the picture of nude teens and many of his off-color jokes and cartoons. Gordon has updated some of his essential reading bibliographies, but his lists of recommended fiction and nonfiction for general reading reflect his adult interests and not the young teen to whom the book itself is directed. His statistics on sex were updated, but the one on life-time earnings was not. He has updated the flavor of the text by changes in catch words (sexual orientation for sexual preference, etc.): at times, by revising his slant (He has dropped the statement that people can choose their sexual orientation); and adding sections on disabilities (advice for having or approaching those with) and his smugly liberated views on and reaction to the Moral Majority. He has added new poetry and rather than his general statements on moving out of boredom, he gives a list of things to do by yourself. . . . The section on VD is not updated to include Herpes. He has maintained the workbook browsing style of *You!* decreasing further its usefulness in a library setting.

> *Jorja Perkins Davis, in her review of "Teenage Survival Book," in* Voice of Youth Advocates *(copyright 1982 by Voice of Youth Advocates), Vol. 5, No. 2, June, 1982, p. 44.*

Rosa (Cuthbert) Guy
1928-

West Indian-born American novelist, short story writer, playwright, and editor.

Guy writes with sensitivity and compassion about black youths, often drawing upon her West Indian heritage and her experiences as a transplanted youth in Harlem. While portraying teenagers who mature by resolving conflicts, Guy also pursues special problems of black ghetto youths as they attempt to transcend the roles society has traditionally ascribed to them.

Guy's realistic depiction of ghetto life and the adversity facing black youths comes through especially well in her first novel, *Bird at My Window*, in which a brilliant black youth is destroyed both by exploitation from whites and by the subservient attitudes of his own community. *The Friends*, generally acknowledged as Guy's finest novel, explores the themes of friendship and family relationships. Following *The Friends* with two companion volumes, *Ruby* and *Edith Jackson*, Guy completed a compelling trilogy that perceptively reflects the struggles of youth.

Guy is respected by readers and critics for portraying contemporary conflicts. She has been especially commended for creating black heroines with whom readers can identify. In doing so, she has helped to fill a significant void in young adult literature.

(See also *Contemporary Authors*, Vols. 17-20, rev. ed. and *Something about the Author*, Vol. 14.)

Courtesy of Dell Publishing Company, Inc.

Glendy Culligan, ''Seeds for Thought,'' in Book Week—New York Herald Tribune (© 1966, The Washington Post), January 9, 1966, p. 16.

GLENDY CULLIGAN

Sincerity, compassion, and the all too evident authenticity of her material offset the merely routine technical competence of [*Bird At My Window* by Rosa Guy] who has survived the indignities of growing up in Harlem without the crippling effects of anger.

Her hero, Wade Williams, has all the reasons for rage that have been chronicled by James Baldwin but none of the saving techniques for putting them to use.

The reader first meets Wade in the psychopathic ward of a New York City hospital, where he has been committed after beating his sister Faith during a drunken brawl that he can't remember. Unfolding bleakly backward as well as forward in time, the novel explores the mystery of Wade's brutality toward the only person he trusts. The frustrations of the childhood that he and Faith shared, leading so inevitably to the sterile violence of maturity, are detailed with a precision all the more painful for the author's lack of rhetorical pyrotechnics.

Her final indictment does, however, contain an element of surprise when it points the finger of blame not only at the white exploiters but at failure of value judgment within the Negro culture. Like novelist William Kelley, Miss Guy suggests that even in a world where the whites are proven villains, Negroes can never be heroes so long as they think of themselves as puppets.

THOMAS L. VINCE

When first encountered [in "**Bird at My Window**"], Wade Williams is recovering in the psychopathic ward of a New York hospital. . . . Unlike the bird at his window, thirty-eight-year-old Wade has never been free and, as the novel unfolds, one is given a stunning insight into the forces that hampered his freedom, discouraged his talent, and crushed his spirit. . . .

All the frustrations of the Harlem Negro are sounded clearly through Wade's experiences. Family problems are foremost, especially those posed by the matriarchal system which is willing to settle for respectability alone; and which is deplored for what it can do to break a man. The inevitable racial clashes both in New York and in France where Wade is sent during World War II are movingly portrayed, and the perennial problems of sex, fundamentalism, and alcohol are carefully, but never sensationally, explored. What is achieved is a balanced portrait of a man who might have been, but who either wilfully missed his opportunities or was denied them by an unsympathetic society. . . .

This is Rosa Guy's first novel, but considering the intensity and power it evokes, we can expect more from such promising talent. Her demonstrative skills in character portrayal and in the etching of crucial incidents are certain to keep the reader absorbed. Some of the language and a few of the scenes may upset the prudish, but there is none of the garish prurience or repetitious vulgarity so common in modern fiction. **"Bird at My Window"** may even become a commercial success; but, whatever its fate, it deserves critical attention for being, perhaps, the most significant novel about the Harlem Negro since James Baldwin's "Go Tell It on the Mountain."

> *Thomas L. Vince, in his review of "Bird at My Window," in* Best Sellers *(copyright 1966, by the University of Scranton), Vol. 25, No. 20, January 15, 1966, p. 403.*

MILES M. JACKSON

[*Bird At My Window*] is about ghetto life in Harlem and the relationship between young Wade Williams and members of his family. Wade, sensitive and intelligent, has very little choice in his life because of a domineering mother who places on him the responsibilities normally reserved for the father of a family. But there is no father in the Williams family and very little money. As a youth, Wade encounters all of the harshness of Harlem and an overseas tour of duty with the Army leaves him as a disillusioned misanthrope. . . . What happens to Wade Williams in Harlem is a story we should all be familiar with by now. The devastating effects of life in Harlem as a subject in fiction runs the risk of becoming overworked, perhaps to some it *has* already been overworked and by now tiring. But to this reviewer there is always room for another well-written novel that uses ghetto life in Harlem as a subject. At times this work comes off very well, especially those sections showing the conflicts between mother and son; but all in all, this is a borderline novel. There are too many parts in the book that smack of the sociological treatise.

> *Miles M. Jackson, in his review of "Bird at My Window," in* Library Journal *(reprinted from* Library Journal, *February 1, 1966; published by R. R. Bowker Co. (a Xerox company); copyright © 1966 by Xerox Corporation), Vol. 91, No. 3, February 1, 1966, pp. 713-14.*

VICTOR P. HASS

[Rosa Guy knows Harlem's] hopes and its desperations, its ugliness and its bits of beauty, its reeking squalor, sights, sounds, drunks, drifters, and the occasional patches of happiness sewn on the garment of its over-all awfulness. All of these things are woven into the fabric of her punishing first novel ["**Bird at My Window**"].

She makes Wade Williams, the tragic anti-hero of her story, as real as a toothache. . . .

Wade's tragedy was that he was born with the IQ of a genius but, for all the chance in life he had, he might as well have been born an idiot. Once, just once, Wade was given a chance "to make something of himself" but thru fear and inexperience he fumbled it and no other chance presented itself. . . .

Society did need him for World War II and it found the black rages to which he was subject made him an appallingly efficient killer in uniform. But after the shooting stopped, society lacked the patience and understanding to unmake its machine of destruction. It sent its de-uniformed killer back to Harlem. . . .

It can be argued, of course, that other remarkably efficient killers made the transition from war to peace without too much difficulty but what Mrs. Guy seems to be saying is that they perhaps didn't have to cope with doors slammed in their faces, racial prejudice, lack of opportunities, and ghetto life.

It would be idle to suggest that you can enjoy **"Bird at My Window"** in any acceptable definition of that word but it is possible, nevertheless, to admire the way she has translated into living terms [Henry David] Thoreau's inspired phrase "quiet desperation." This is her triumph and it is by no means a small one.

> *Victor P. Hass, "A Case of Quiet Desperation" (reprinted by permission of the author), in* Books Today, *Vol. II, No. 7, February 20, 1966, p. 6.*

ALICE WALKER

I feel especially blessed when reading the books of Virginia Hamilton, Toni Cade Bambara, Lucille Clifton, June Jordan, Louise Merriweather, Toni Morrison and other fine *engagé* black women writers; for I am thinking of a young black girl who spent the first 20 years of her life without seeing a single book in which the heroine was a person like herself. . . .

[Now, with books like] Rosa Guy's heart-slammer, **"The Friends,"** I relive those wretched, hungry-for-heroines years and am helped to verify the existence and previous condition of myself. . . .

[The] struggle that is the heart of this very important book [is] the fight to gain perception of one's own real character; the grim struggle for self-knowledge and the almost killing internal upheaval that brings the necessary growth of compassion and humility *and courage*, so that friendship (of any kind, but especially between those of notable economic and social differences) can exist.

This book is called a "juvenile." So be a juvenile while you read it. Rosa Guy will give you back a large part of the memory of those years that you've been missing.

> *Alice Walker, in her review of "The Friends," in* The New York Times Book Review *(© 1973 by The New York Times Company; reprinted by permission), November 4, 1973, p. 26.*

ETHEL L. HEINS

[*The Friends*] is a penetrating story of considerable emotional depth. Two teenaged girls—Phyllisia and her older sister Ruby—come to New York from the West Indies to join their *émigré* parents in "this trap of asphalt and stone called Harlem." Phyllisia's strangeness draws the fury of her classmates, and she is persecuted for her unfamiliar accent, her well-tended clothes, and her knowledgeable answers to the teacher's belligerent, sarcastic questions. The only amiable girl is Edith, poor and scruffy, whose cheerful assurances of friendship are accepted by Phyll with resentment and humiliation. To complicate matters, Phyll feels bitterness and defiance towards her father, Calvin, a big, boastful man, overbearing and even brutal—but hard-working and pathetically ambitious. Worse yet, her beautiful, intelligent mother is dying of cancer; and the family who adores her is gripped by helpless agony. Meanwhile, Edith too is the victim of catastrophe: Orphaned and existing in abject poverty, she wages and loses a battle against hunger and disease to keep her younger sisters with her. Then one day, Calvin is enraged to find the "ragamuffin" Edith visiting his ill wife; and Phyll, ashamed of her friend and mortified by her shame, hides behind her own fraudulent pride. In a passionate scene, her mother speaks out to her about love, cruelty, responsibility, and death. A strong, honest story—often tragic but ultimately hopeful—of complex, fully-realized characters and of the ambivalence and conflicts in human nature.

> *Ethel L. Heins, in her review of "The Friends," in* The Horn Book Magazine *(copyright © 1974 by the Horn Book, Inc., Boston), Vol. L, No. 2, April, 1974, p. 152.*

THE TIMES LITERARY SUPPLEMENT

There is affection . . . in Rosa Guy's short novel, *The Friends,* but also a hard core of toughness, which goes with its New York setting. . . .

Rosa Guy's evocation of the hot, steamy city, the subways, the coolness of air-conditioned shops after the sweltering street, the oasis of Central Park, the narrow restaurant where Phyllisia's father works, aproned and sweating, alongside his employees, make this a vigorous and unusual book. Nor is the New York scene so alien as to be incomprehensible, perhaps because the heroine is herself an outsider and so views it all through foreign, critical eyes. And if the details of the plot smack slightly of the Dickensian—Edith's father vanished, her brother shot by the police, her little sister dead of meningitis and herself consigned to an orphanage—the feelings are very true to life.

> *"Lives against the Odds," in* The Times Literary Supplement *(© Times Newspapers Ltd. (London) 1974; reproduced from* The Times Literary Supplement *by permission), No. 3785, September 20, 1974, p. 1006.**

M. R. HEWITT

Neither friend [in *The Friends*] is very endearing; one a rather priggish girl from a proud West Indian family, the other a sluttish, thieving but ever loyal and loving drudge struggling to keep her parentless family together. Set in Harlem against a background of prejudice (between the varying strata of coloured families) and violence, the girls are growing to maturity with the usual problems of adolescence magnified by the difficulties of the society in which they live. The style of writing is idiomatic and rather difficult in its unfamiliarity, the setting and life style is alien—one is conscious of being an outsider to the Harlem community—and this leads to difficulty in identifying with the characters despite—perhaps even because—of the author's very real sympathy with them.

> *M. R. Hewitt, in a review of "The Friends," in* The Junior Bookshelf, *Vol. 38, No. 6, December, 1974, p. 378.*

MICHAEL H. MILLER

[In *The Friends*] Rosa Guy has written a real novel about real people in a real world. The characters' problems arise naturally from their background, circumstances, personalities and rela-

tionships; they are not problems imposed by an author who wants to write about problems. The story is full of incident; the life of Harlem is ever-present, though rarely obtrusive; the writing is alive, with extra richness in the West Indian speech. Highly recommended.

> *Michael H. Miller, in his review of "The Friends," in* Children's Book Review *(© 1975 Five Owls Press Ltd.; all rights reserved), Vol. IV, No. 4, Winter, 1974-75, p. 152.*

PUBLISHERS WEEKLY

["**Ruby**" is] an intensely committed novel talking directly to teenagers, black, white, particularly those who are uncertain and scared of what their loneliness may involve them in. This is a very sensitive novel in which adolescent homosexuality is viewed as nothing so frightening, but perhaps just a way-step towards maturity. Ruby is desperately unhappy, unfairly labeled as an "Uncle Tom" in her school. She becomes drawn to Daphne, a strong, dramatic black girl, who, we will learn, has her own secret fears and family problems. Ruby's father is a lost, lonely widower. Her younger sister is spunky, a reader finding release in books. If Rosa Guy had taken a camera and put it down in 1970 (the year of her novel) on a completely believable black middle class family situation in any big city in America, she could not have achieved a more riveting picture of basically decent people, floundering because of the generation gap. Neatest of all, she has a sense of humor and hope for the future. (pp. 80-1)

> *A review of "Ruby," in* Publishers Weekly *(reprinted from the April 19, 1976 issue of* Publishers Weekly, *published by R. R. Bowker Company, a Xerox company; copyright © 1976 by Xerox Corporation), Vol. 209, No. 16, April 19, 1976, pp. 80-1.*

ZENA SUTHERLAND

[*Ruby*] has some strong qualities and some weaknesses: the characters are vividly real and distinct, the relationships (especially those within the family of the stern father and the two motherless girls) are perceptively seen, the affair between Daphne and Ruby treated with dignity; on the other hand, the first physical encounter is followed by a rhapsodical paragraph that includes such florid writing as, "Love was orange. A blinding orange pulling the world out of darkness, tinging the air with gold . . . orange that opened the sense into exquisite, inexpressible joy. Love was gray . . . the gray of Daphne's eyes. . . . Love was red. . . ." Such prose halts the story, as do the unconvincing sparring dialogues between Daphne and one of the teachers.

> *Zena Sutherland, in her review of "Ruby," in* Bulletin of the Center for Children's Books *(reprinted by permission of The University of Chicago Press; © 1976 by The University of Chicago), Vol. 30, No. 3, November, 1976, p. 42.*

THE HORN BOOK MAGAZINE

[*Ruby*] is essentially a teenage novel: rich, full-bodied, and true in its portrayal of the world of the Black teenager. . . . Ruby, deeply sensitive and lonely, finds love in a secret homosexual relationship with Daphne, a beautiful, arrogant Black classmate. Their experience fills a desperate need at a crucial time in the lives of both girls, affording them an early insight into the depths and complexities of human relations and emotions. The author writes gracefully in the West Indian idiom as she analyzes perceptively the problems of young Blacks facing up to the emotional, political, social, and educational responsibilities of their own lives.

> *A review of "Ruby: A Novel," in* The Horn Book Magazine *(copyright © 1976 by the Horn Book, Inc., Boston), Vol. LII, No. 6, December, 1976, p. 652.*

REGINA WILLIAMS

Author Guy has drawn her characters broadly [in *Ruby*]: Calvin Cathy is a strict, hard-working head of household who feels the loss of his wife deeply and is somewhat terrified by the task of raising two daughters alone. Daphne is an arrogant, domineering person who seeks to exercise absolute control over the elements of her environment, including and especially over the people to whom she is exposed. Disinclined to accommodate other people's needs and desires, she is strikingly authoritarian and power-oriented. Ruby, being unsure of herself and of her identity, is passive, submissive and dependent—a perfect foil for the superiority syndrome out of which Daphne operates.

Instead of the two young women engaging in a relationship of equality, mutual support and exchange, Daphne manipulates Ruby and enjoys their relationship wholly on her own terms. There is little evidence that Daphne cares for Ruby. Indeed, Daphne seems to lack warmth or deep affection for anyone.

Basically, Ruby's personality problems come off as being the story's central element, yet they remain unresolved. In the end, father Calvin promotes the rekindling of a relationship between Ruby and a neighborhood boy whom Calvin had previously spurned as a suitor for his daughter. In the absence of any evidence that Ruby has grown in the course of the story's events, the implication is that she will once again neurotically seek fulfillment through another person—this time a male.

Sexism is reflected both in the aggressive/passive relationship between Ruby and Daphne and in the implications of the book's conclusion. Another component of the story's sex-role stereotyping is the Daphne characterization itself, which recalls the pervasive image of lesbians as being universally "mannish" in their behavior. The story is further marred by a general unevenness in the writing. Attitudes and actions are assigned to people that would have been more characteristic of the 1940's or 1950's than the story's 1960's setting, and occasional passages of "purple prose" are cloying. In the case of Daphne, her super-intellectual manner of speech and ultra-sophisticated behavior are unrealistic.

Anti-Semitism taints the portrait of the racist teacher, who is named Miss Gottlieb. Given the extremely negative qualities that are assigned to this character (she is disabled, ugly and seems to possess no redeeming virtues), her clearly ethnic name automatically evokes negative images of the cultural group with which the name is associated. Unfortunate also is the author's choice of words in describing Daphne's mother as "fair, much fairer than Daphne (Ruby is "bronze" with light brown eyes). To describe light-skinned Black persons as "fair" in 1976 is both anachronistic and reinforces the concept that lightness—in skin, hair, eyes—is a more desirable state of being.

Due to its mixed messages and murky style, *Ruby* fails as a novel for young adults. (pp. 14-15)

> *Regina Williams, in her review of "Ruby," in* Interracial Books for Children Bulletin *(reprinted by permission of* Interracial Books for Children Bulletin, *1841 Broadway, New York, N.Y. 10023), Vol. 8, No. 2, 1977, pp. 14-15.*

PAMELA D. POLLACK

Edith Jackson's hard luck story started in Guy's *The Friends*. . . . On her own [in *Edith Jackson*], after rejecting a Reverend with roving hands as a foster father, Edith hooks up for hit-and-run sex with a street person who telegraphs his undesirability at every turn. . . . At the end, Edith is awaiting an abortion—pathetically, her one and only act of self-determination. Edith is no statistic—there's complexity in Guy's portrait of one so stunted she can't even make it as a martyr—but the impact is diminished by overwrought writing and the author's short cut of cataloging characters' feelings ("Crying, hysterical. Going crazy.") instead of conveying them.

> *Pamela D. Pollack, in her review of "Edith Jackson," in* School Library Journal *(reprinted from the April, 1978 issue of* School Library Journal, *published by R. R. Bowker Co./A Xerox Corporation; copyright © 1978), Vol. 24, No. 8, April, 1978, p. 93.*

PAUL HEINS

Completing a trilogy about contemporary Black life, which includes *The Friends* . . . and *Ruby,* [*Edith Jackson*] explores the experiences of Phyllisia's poverty-stricken friend Edith Jackson. In a first-person account, occasionally colloquial and only infrequently coarse, the seventeen-year-old orphan tells of her efforts to keep her young sisters—Bessie, Suzy, and Minnie—together as a family. . . . The novel, written in a naturalistic vein, is powerful in its depiction of character and creates scenes memorable for their psychological truth; and so well integrated are theme, character, and situation that they redeem whatever is superficially sordid in the story.

> *Paul Heins, in his review of "Edith Jackson," in* The Horn Book Magazine *(copyright © 1978 by The Horn Book, Inc., Boston), Vol. LV, No. 5, October, 1978, p. 524.*

BERYLE BANFIELD

On one level, [*Edith Jackson*] is a skillfully written account of [a] seventeen-year-old hero's determination to assume full responsibility for her three orphaned sisters, "her family," as soon as she reaches eighteen. But in 187 pages of tight, dramatic writing, Ms. Guy manages to address several critical social issues and to bring into sharp focus those special problems that are encountered by women of varying ages.

There is a devastating indictment of the residential care bureaucracy, referred to in the novel as "The Institution." Exposed are the gross insensitivity to the needs of children, the damaging effect of the constant shunting of children from one foster home to another, and the physical and mental retardation that can result from emotional starvation and physical neglect. The sexuality and sexual problems of women of varying ages and their male relationships are explored with great sensitivity and honesty. Running through the entire book is the theme of the special vulnerability of women and that special strength which enables so many to survive.

It is impossible not to become emotionally involved while reading this book. Ms. Guy deserves high praise for her remarkable achievement.

> *Beryle Banfield, in her review of "Edith Jackson," in* Interracial Books for Children Bulletin *(reprinted by permission of* Interracial Books for Children Bulletin, *1841 Broadway, New York, N.Y. 10023), Vol. 9, No. 6, 1978, p. 15.*

ZENA SUTHERLAND

[In *Edith Jackson*] Edith, who appeared in the author's *The Friends,* is now seventeen; although she and her three younger sisters live with a foster mother, it is Edith who feels responsible for the others, who vows that when she is of age she will work and provide a home for them. . . . [When the story ends] what is left unsaid (and is clear) is that Edith has admitted to herself that the encouragement Mrs. Bates has offered, and her help, will be accepted. Proud and strong, Edith had been insisting on getting a job and holding the family together—which meant accepting the role of mother to her sisters—and now she can admit that she can change her life if she will focus on her own needs. The characterization is excellent, the writing style smooth, and the depiction of an adolescent torn between her need for independence and achievement and her feeling of responsibility (which has pushed her into protecting the sisters who don't want protection) strong and perceptive. (pp. 117-18)

> *Zena Sutherland, in her review of "Edith Jackson," in* Bulletin of the Center for Children's Books *(reprinted by permission of The University of Chicago Press; © 1979 by The University of Chicago), Vol. 32, No. 7, March, 1979, pp. 116-17.*

JERRIE NORRIS

"The Disappearance," Rosa Guy's fourth novel, is a compelling and suspenseful story. The reader is immediately captured by the characters, who are so sharply defined, so clearly who they are. Dora Belle could only by a quirky, middle-aged West Indian and only Ann Aimsley, as Guy draws her, could be the queen of her dust-free, plastic-covered home. It is as if Guy excised whole chunks of life and brought her characters up whole. Juxtaposing characters and details of their lives, Guy outlines a picture. She paints a picture of images built up and arduously maintained to mask those common human frailties—fear, loneliness and insecurity—which touch people wherever they live. And so we see those frailties as they move an Ann Aimsley in Brooklyn or Imamu's mother in Harlem and set off events that march steadily toward tragedy.

And it is tragedy and victims that we find here, victims—intended or unintended—of false images. The victimizers are here as well. But there are no happy endings. What we are offered, and I think more realistically, is characters who are "willing to move from where they are," to use their experiences as a basis for growth. In Imamu, Guy gives us such a character, a victim who turns adversity to his benefit, one who dares to find some advantage in his disadvantaged life style.

"The Disappearance" will be no disappointment to readers of Guy's previous work or to young adults and adults newly discovering her. It is a suspenseful and readable novel that treats thought-provoking and complex issues.

> *Jerrie Norris, "Urban Strife on Suburban Streets" (reprinted by permission of the author), in* The Christian Science Monitor, *October 15, 1979, p. B4.*

ROBERT UNSWORTH

[*The Disappearance*] is a combination of a Black "street boy's" reluctant acceptance into a Black middle-class family's life and the suspense of an eight-year-old girl's disappearance. . . . There are some soft points: surely the police spend more time and effort searching for lost Black girls than is indicated here, and the Aimsley family seems to accept Perk's disappearance a bit too readily. Some readers might have difficulty with the Black and West Indian speech; others may not appreciate the "down" ending. But, by story's close, each character has touched us and the fine delineation of all of them stands out as Guy's greatest strength.

> *Robert Unsworth, in his review of "The Disappearance," in* School Library Journal *(reprinted from the November, 1979 issue of* School Library Journal, *published by R. R. Bowker Co./A Xerox Corporation; copyright © 1979), Vol. 26, No. 3, November, 1979, p. 88.*

JEAN FRITZ

[In "The Disappearance"] Rosa Guy has taken a plot and turned the people inside out to give us both a cliff-hanger and a shrewd commentary on human nature. . . .

The question is bound to be asked: Is this book, with its overtones of violence and sex, really intended for young readers 12 and up? In a way, the answer is the book's theme. Innocence is not beautiful, Miss Guy says. Behind lace curtains on pretty streets, ugly things happen, just as they do in Harlem. And perhaps the so-called disadvantaged have the advantage after all, for they already understand that. Certainly all readers will be riveted by the suspense in this story, but it may be that only those older than 12 will understand the message.

> *Jean Fritz, in her review of "The Disappearance," in* The New York Times Book Review *(© 1979 by The New York Times Company; reprinted by permission), December 2, 1979, p. 40.*

ETHEL L. HEINS

[*The Friends* established Rosa Guy] as a major novelist concerned with "the grotesque in life and character." Now she has written a raw and powerful work that centers on a sixteen-year-old boy from the streets of Harlem. . . . The second half of the book is a shocking, suspenseful whodunit; but all of the book, transcending race and environment, is a remarkably mature exposure—as clean and penetrating as surgery—of fear and loneliness, desperation and suffering, deception and pride. (pp. 62-3)

> *Ethel L. Heins, in her review of "The Disappearance," in* The Horn Book Magazine *(copyright © 1980 by The Horn Book, Inc., Boston), Vol. LVI, No. 1, February, 1980, pp. 62-3.*

GEOFF FOX

There is little gentleness in [Rosa Guy's] Harlem. Within a few lines [of *The Disappearance*], we are stumbling among empty wine bottles and cockroaches with Imamu, a sixteen year old black Muslim recently returned from a detention centre and looking for his mother, an alcoholic widowed by Vietnam. Imamu has been offered the chance of better things with the Aimley family in Brooklyn. . . . [The] plot becomes a skilfully told, absorbing thriller as Imamu is suspected of being implicated in the disappearance of the Aimleys' young daughter. Only 10 years ago, Leon Garfield could say to an approving audience that a children's book must end optimistically—here, the first glimpse of the lost child is of a decomposing fist, "stretching up out of the shallow grave" under fresh concrete in the murderer's basement. A harsh, relentless and exciting tale of the streets, whose truth to life I am unable to judge (through cultural ignorance) but in which I completely believed.

Geoff Fox, "Songs of Innocence and Experience," in The Times Educational Supplement *(© Times Newspapers Ltd. (London) 1980; reproduced from* The Times Educational Supplement *by permission), No. 3338, June 6, 1980, p. 27.**

DAVID REES

[*The Disappearance* is] particularly good in its ability to evoke a sense of place—the contrasts between middle-class black New York (Brooklyn) and the crime-ridden ghetto of Harlem. Imamu, a teenager in trouble with the police, is fostered by a kindly, fairly well-to-do family, whose attitudes to him change for the worse when their younger daughter, Perk, disappears. It is interesting to see how black liberal modes of thinking crumble; how the tensions within the family turn to ugly hysteria when the smooth easy-going surface of their lives is destroyed.

The characters are credible; they develop and grow, not always in the way the reader expects. But the book is marred by absurdly improbable twists in the plot—Perk is killed by her Aunt Dora and buried in wet cement when she discovers that Dora's beautiful hair is a wig. No one of any age is going to accept that very easily. It reflects the author's uncertain feelings about writing for adolescents—that somehow subtly changing relationships are not enough; that, to hold the reader's attention, a grisly crime story has to be tagged on to what is otherwise a persuasive portrayal of real life.

David Rees, "Approaching Adulthood," in The Times Literary Supplement *(© Times Newspapers Ltd. (London) 1980; reproduced from* The Times Literary Supplement *by permission), No. 4034, July 18, 1980, p. 807.**

KENNETH L. DONELSON AND ALLEEN PACE NILSEN

The confusion and disagreement regarding sex roles is not just an adult problem that youth does not have to think about. On the contrary, it is probably more important to them than to most adults whose lifestyles and obligations are already so established that all they can comfortably do is play the game out to its conclusion. In light of this, the best of the current writers are presenting honest portrayals of all kinds of relationships and roles and then hoping that young readers can observe and make choices that will best fit their own personalities and needs.

Rosa Guy's trilogy, *The Friends, Ruby,* and *Edith Jackson,* exemplifies one of these alternative explorations that would

not have been presented to young readers a generation ago. The first book in the group treats an unlikely but believable friendship between Phyllisia and Edith who are both rejects in the social structure of their Harlem neighborhood. . . . One unusual thing about the book is that it treats the friendship of two girls with the same kind of serious respect with which boys' friendships have traditionally been written about. In most earlier books, girls' friendships always broke up as soon as boys appeared on the scene.

The second book in Guy's trilogy, *Ruby,* focuses on Phyllisia's sister who is two years older than Edith and Phyll. It includes the story of a lesbian relationship between Ruby and a beautiful classmate. . . . In *Edith Jackson,* the protagonist is looking forward to her eighteenth birthday when she hopes to be free of foster homes and The Institution so that she can try again to set up a home for her sisters. But, by the end of the book, the girls are scattered, and Edith realizes that it is her own life she must plan. She has had a brief love affair with a handsome Harlem playboy almost twice her age and is excited at finding herself pregnant. But in the end of the book, she has decided that the mature thing to do is to have an abortion.

A difficulty inherent in the problem novel is that it looks at life from a basically negative stance and in many ways presents an unbalanced set of options. For example, critics ask, how can young readers get insights into the kinds of men and women they want to be and into preparing for marriage and family life when most of the parents in these books are so unsuccessful? The lack of positive role models, particularly adult males and females in family roles, is definitely a problem with the new realism. Writers have presented a much wider range of successful role models who are themselves young adults. (pp. 195-96)

Kenneth L. Donelson and Alleen Pace Nilsen, "The New Realism: Of Life and Other Sad Songs," in their Literature for Today's Young Adults *(copyright © 1980 Scott, Foresman and Company; reprinted by permission), Scott, Foresman, 1980, pp. 181-204.**

ZENA SUTHERLAND

Although Guy writes fairly well, she is an uneven unwriter; [*Mirror of Her Own*] is marred by oddly constructed passages like "Gloria, leaned back and stretched out, sinking in her waistline," or, referring to a clock, "The ticking . . . emphasized the stillness . . . rubbing against Mary's sensitized nerves," and by a repeated and awkward attempt to reproduce phonetically Mary's nervous stuttering. The greater weakness, however, is in the diffusion of the story line; the author uses the book as a vehicle for expressing her ideas about race relations and class differences and the story remains a showcase rather than a narrative. (pp. 171-72)

Zena Sutherland, in her review of "Mirror of Her Own," in Bulletin of the Center for Children's Books *(reprinted by permission of The University of Chicago Press; © 1981 by The University of Chicago), Vol. 34, No. 9, May, 1981, pp. 171-72.*

LILLIAN L. SHAPIRO

[The protagonist of *Mirror of Her Own*]—Mary Abbot, 17, is shy and plain and stutters. Her efforts to find acceptance within her high-school crowd are handicapped not only by her unfortunate friendship with abrasive and prejudiced Gloria but also by the contrast between Mary and her beautiful, talented 22-year-old sister Roxanne, the object of attention from the very eligible John Drysdale. . . . The main theme is Mary's unrequited "love" for John, obviously unworthy, unrequited only until too much wine, pot and cocaine bring about the outcome for which Mary has yearned. It is, however, clearly a case of exploitation on the part of John, and Mary's flight through a swampy wood after her escapade is made to seem like a purgatorial punishment. The empty values of the white characters, as exemplified by their conspicuous consumption of clothes, homes, yachts, liquor and drugs, are contrasted with those of a few Black characters, who are proud, dignified and financially secure, and by a patronizingly superior African visitor. Though this purports, on the book jacket blurb, to be "a strong and perceptive novel of a young woman's search for an end to a life lived in the shadow of an older sister," it delivers a cliché-laden moralistic story about cardboard figures.

Lillian L. Shapiro, in her review of "Mirror of Her Own," in School Library Journal *(reprinted from the May, 1981 issue of* School Library Journal, *published by R. R. Bowker Co./A Xerox Corporation; copyright © 1981), Vol. 27, No. 9, May, 1981, p. 73.*

KIRKUS REVIEWS

["**Mirror of Her Own**" is a] vehement, bluntly cast portrayal of an upper-crust community called Oak Bluff and a timid, drab family that reflects its values and dynamics. Shy, stuttering Mary Abbot, 17, has always been slighted in favor of her beautiful blond older sister Roxanne. . . . The events, centering on frivolous teenage society (some characters are in their twenties, but no more mature), take place the summer Roxanne is going with John Drysdale, the playboy son of rich and powerful neighbors who have illegally appropriated some of the Abbots' land. Mary has had a crush on John for years, and the novel climaxes when she goes to a big Oak Bluff party, gets high, and goes off to bed with John. Next morning, alone in "the family wilderness," a melodramatic morass of vines and quickslime and mosquitos and "the coils at the center of her own mind," Mary comes to some realizations about her family, Oak Bluff, and the world at large. Other characters whose roles relate to these conclusions include Mary's vicious, racist, unpopular friend Gloria; a proud black family relatively new to Oak Bluff; and a visiting African prince who comments from an unruffled height on American faults and foibles. It's all strident and heavy-handed, but at least Guy's own emotional intensity gives it some life.

A review of "Mirror of Her Own," in Kirkus Reviews *(copyright © 1981 The Kirkus Service, Inc.), Vol. XLIX, No. 11, June 1, 1981, p. 682.*

FRANCIS GOSKOWSKI

It is impossible to respond to [*Mirror of Her Own*] with pleasure or to write about it without scorn. In *Mirror of Her Own* no one except foreigners behaves well; no one is honest, brave, or sincere; no one has the sense to reject the slobs and cruel little misses who inhabit the Abbots' world. The novel has no

center, no moral compass. When Mary turns away from the Drysdales of this world, she retreats into herself. But what kind of solution is this? Emulating her narcissistic sister will not bring this profoundly confused adolescent any improvement in virtue or strength of character. At the end of the book she is just as pathetic as she was before. Ditto her parents, her sister, and her friends.

The literary style does not help. Ms. Guy specializes in pomposity: "Drizzle, mist, gloom, permeated her spirits"; "the stench of their awful capabilities, their spoiled friendship, had already become a casualty"; "she fell, and her face dug into the smell of rotten leaves." Young people interested in writing can only pick up bad habits from *Mirror of Her Own*.

Where are you, Jane Austen, when we need you?

Francis Goskowski, in his review of "Mirror of Her Own," in Best Sellers *(copyright © 1981 Helen Dwight Reid Educational Foundation), Vol. 41, No. 6, September, 1981, p. 238.*

JUDITH N. MITCHELL

Rosa Guy's *Ruby* hints at its quality through its title. It's a multi-faceted jewel of a novel, especially memorable for the unerring accuracy of its recreation of adolescent loneliness and commitment, and for the bitter-sweet quality of its resolution. The two girls who fall in love—Ruby, gentle, yielding, but with an inexorable impulse toward helping, and Daphne, bright, realistic, utterly pragmatic and more than occasionally unsympathetic, are complex, richly-detailed characters.

Bludgeoned by the loss of her mother and her father's absorption into his work, Ruby seeks in Daphne a solution to intolerable pain. Once she and Daphne have retreated, literally and figuratively to the sanctuary of Daphne's room with its warning red light, Ruby finds Daphne every bit as demanding as Calvin, her father. Under Daphne's tutelage, Ruby develops academic self-confidence, while managing to drive Daphne to irritation and beyond by her unflagging compassion. It is this friction which lies at the heart of the relationship and labels it most clearly as risk-prone, lacking in the very security which Ruby seeks. Neither girl seems, perhaps as a result, to be permanently and irretrievably lesbian in orientation. When Daphne cold-bloodedly ends their affair, she says she'll go straight. And, desolate after Daphne's withdrawal and exhausted by a scene of extraordinary cathartic power with Calvin, Ruby nevertheless beings to evince some resurgence of interest in Orlando, a boy whom she had found attractive at the beginning of the story.

If one had to sum up Guy's attitude toward homosexuality from this story, one would conclude from the internal evidence that she believes the need to love and be loved is paramount. To assuage that hunger, young people may fall in love within or outside of their own gender. What determines the success or failure of the relationship may have more to do with personality than with being male or female; a male Daphne would have moved beyond Ruby's sphere in precisely the same way. (p. 32)

Judith N. Mitchell, "Loving Girls," in The ALAN Review, *Vol. 10, No. 1, Fall, 1982, pp. 32, 34.**

Virginia (Edith) Hamilton

1936-

American novelist, biographer, critic, and editor.

Hamilton has won acclaim for her daring and imaginative fiction in which she explores a variety of themes. She blends such elements as mystery, dreams, legend, and folklore, using an intensive prose style rich in symbolism. Hamilton has helped raise the level of sophistication in young adult literature. Her protagonists are black adolescents who face problems relevant to all human beings, reflecting her belief that "the experience of a people must come to mean the experience of humankind."

Hamilton's characters often display a wildly fertile imagination. Her early works *Zeely* and *The Planet of Junior Brown* feature protagonists whose worlds of fancy become more real to them than reality. These protagonists are helped back to a more balanced view of life through sympathetic friends. The same theme is explored again in the Justice Cycle trilogy, where unchecked mental and physical powers result in disaster and a "unit" of psychic characters survives only by helping each other.

Hamilton's most celebrated work, *M. C. Higgins, the Great*, follows a poor boy's growing awareness of himself and his surroundings. M. C. thinks little of what he has, preferring to sit atop a pole and dream. But when his home is threatened, M. C. stops dreaming. He learns to take pride in his heritage and to be responsible for himself and others. *M. C. Higgins, the Great* won the Newbery Medal and the National Book Award, both in 1975. Hamilton has received numerous other awards, including the Edgar Allan Poe Award in 1968 for best juvenile mystery with *The House of Dies Drear*.

(See also *Children's Literature Review*, Vol. 1; *Contemporary Authors*, Vols. 25-28, rev. ed.; and *Something about the Author*, Vol. 4.)

Photograph by Cox Studios; courtesy of Virginia Hamilton

ELINORE STANDARD

At the start of Virginia Hamilton's *Zeely,* Miss Elizabeth and Master John Perry are traveling by train to Uncle Ross' farm for the summer. New holiday names are quickly minted— Elizabeth is Geeder and John is Toeboy.

Miss Hamilton tells with perfect, nostalgic descriptions of the uncle's old farmhouse, of country days and doings, good country things to eat, and of summer nights slept in the dewy outdoors, of moonlight tricks and exchanged whispers in the dark. Best of all, this is the story of Geeder and Zeely.

Zeely Tayber was more than six and a half feet tall, thin and deeply dark as a pole of ebony. . . .

> She had very high cheekbones and her eyes seemed to turn inward on themselves. Geeder couldn't say what expression she saw on Zeely's face. She only knew that it was calm, that it had pride in it, and that the face was the most beautiful she had ever seen.

Geeder listens while Zeely tells a haunting story of her own origins and of her people. The tale has a moral and one from which Geeder profits.

Zeely is a fresh, sensitive story, with a lingering, serene, misty quality about it which the reader can save and savor.

Elinore Standard, "Weaving Spells," in Book Week— The Washington Post (© 1967, The Washington Post), June 25, 1967, p. 12.*

VIRGINIA HAVILAND

The author of *Zeely* has surpassed her earlier excellent achievement by dramatizing the history of an Underground Railroad Station in Ohio [in *The House of Dies Drear*], viewed from its extraordinary present-day milieu. . . . In depicting Pluto, the bizarre ancient caretaker of the place, and the macabre play-acting devised by his son to scare off the greedy neighbors, Miss Hamilton establishes an almost Gothic atmosphere. Successful in presenting the seemingly occult, she does well, too, with the plain and everyday—the realistic details of household management and the service in the little African Methodist church. Satisfying every demand of the mystery story, the tale far more importantly deals with a boy's searching spirit and the history of a great cause. Thomas's responsiveness to the people in his life, including his twin baby brothers, reveals him to be an unusually sensitive child.

> *Virginia Haviland, in her review of "The House of Dies Drear," in* The Horn Book Magazine *(copyright © 1968 by The Horn Book, Inc., Boston), Vol. XLIV, No. 5, October, 1968, p. 563.*

DOROTHY STERLING

The last few years have seen a slow trickle of children's stories with Negro characters. For the most part these "integrated" books have been the work of white writers who too often have substituted sentimentality and good will for authenticity and depth of feeling. In **"The House of Dies Drear"** we have a story about black people, written by a black writer, Virginia Hamilton, whose first book, **"Zeely,"** won a prize for promoting interracial understanding.

Above all, Miss Hamilton tells a corking good story. Thomas Small's father, a history professor in a college in Ohio, rents the century-old house that abolitionist Dies Drear built as a station on the Underground Railroad. The night the Smalls move in, things begin to happen. Ghosts walk. Walls slide back to reveal secret passageways. A labyrinth of tunnels leads to a cave under the ground. Thomas and his father explore, investigate and find treasure concealed behind a stalactite curtain. Simultaneously, the boy gains new insights into the history of his people which still, too often, remains stored in academic caves. No matter if the plot unravels too easily. Youngsters, black and white, will gulp the story in a single suspenseful sitting.

"The House of Dies Drear" is written with poetic precision. Miss Hamilton polishes her sentences with care, develops her characters with imagination and love. Thomas is a sensitive boy, self-sufficient, sometimes lonely, his relationship with his father like nothing dreamed of in the [Moynihan Report of 1965, which cited the number of black absentee husbands in proportion to white absentee husbands to support its contention that "the Negro family in the urban ghettos is crumbling"].

> *Dorothy Sterling, in her review of "The House of Dies Drear," in* The New York Times Book Review *(© 1968 by The New York Times Company; reprinted by permission), October 13, 1968, p. 26.*

JULIA G. RUSSELL

[*The House of Dies Drear* is an] unusual, highly intriguing story skillfully incorporating Civil War history. Thirteen-year-old Thomas Small, his father (a Civil War historian), his mother and brothers arrive at their new home in a small Ohio town. . . . Thomas is both fascinated and frightened by the legends of escaped slaves, the eccentric old caretaker Pluto; the uncharted passageways of the house, unnerving noises, vandalism intended to frighten the Smalls away, forbidding neighbors with threatening sons, and an unpredictable, mysterious little girl. The ending is an anticlimax in view of the preceding tension, but it does serve to tie up loose ends in revealing the treasure of Dies Drear and the mystery surrounding old Pluto. . . . [The deft lack of emphasis on the family's race] puts the story's interest where it belongs—on the mystery. The fact that the main characters are Negro neither adds to nor detracts from the suspense, but does provide an unobtrusive and convincing point of view for Thomas's discussion of the community with his father. This is a superior mystery with well-sustained sus-

pense and an unself-conscious story of a boy who gains a new appreciation of his heritage. (pp. 53-4)

> *Julia G. Russell, in her review of "The House of Dies Drear," in* School Library Journal, *an appendix to* Library Journal *(reprinted from the December, 1968 issue of* School Library Journal, *published by R. R. Bowker Co./A Xerox Corporation; copyright © 1968), Vol. 15, No. 4, December, 1968, pp. 53-4.*

MICHAEL CART

A stunningly good, absolutely compelling, weird and unique book, Virginia Hamilton's [*The Planet of Junior Brown*] is the story of three outsiders in New York City: Junior Brown and Buddy Clark, both in their early teens, and Mr. Pool, a one-time teacher and now school custodian. While all three are black, what they suffer at the hands of an uncaring, unfeeling world might be suffered by anybody, anytime, anywhere. Buddy, parentless and on his own, lives by his wits in deserted building where he is the self-appointed guardian of two younger boys. Junior, luckier in material terms, lives comfortably with his overprotective mother, but he is grotesquely fat, withdrawn and, perhaps, mentally ill. Mr. Pool, who had quit teaching 15 years before, stifled by the lack of freedom in an over-structured educational system, is the two boys' companion during the days which they spend together hidden in a secret room he has constructed in the basement of the school. Through the story of the three, *The Planet of Junior Brown* presents an unforgettable evocation of madness—madness in the individual (overwhelming, generalized fear resulting from unrelieved spiritual/emotional/physical solitude) enforced by the madness of society which is indifference (the indifference which rejects Junior's need, while walking, "to touch a profile here and a full face there . . . [his] seeing and longing for the faces."). Readers see advances, probably unalterable madness in old Miss Peebs, a concert pianist whom Junior visits, and progressive madness in Junior himself. Junior's hope lies in the fact that he has the love and support of Buddy and Mr. Pool, who have learned that if they are truly to survive they must live for each other. This is the message expressed in the book's dedication—"For. . . the Race To Come," and the meaning of the title: the planet of Junior Brown refers not only to the model solar system Mr. Pool has constructed for the boys in the school basement, not only to the incredibly dynamic world contained in Junior's head, but to the new world that will be born from enclaves of mutually responsible people such as the one Buddy oversees (and to which he takes Junior and Mr. Pool to live). . . . The book is like a perfectly executed piece of music; the author doesn't strike a single false note.

> *Michael Cart, in his review of "The Planet of Junior Brown," in* School Library Journal, *an appendix to* Library Journal *(reprinted from the September, 1971 issue of* School Library Journal, *published by R. R. Bowker/A Xerox Corporation; copyright © 1971), Vol. 18, No. 1, September, 1971, p. 126.*

ALICE WALKER

Junior Brown [the protagonist of **"The Planet of Junior Brown"**] is a fat, black, hopeless boy, a 300-pound musical prodigy whose mother has untied the wires of the family piano. He sweats profusely, talks to himself, reaches out on the street to touch the faces of passing strangers and beats out his music lesson on the back of a chair. He looks like Buddha and eats like Paul Bunyan.

Into his miserable life come two friends: the janitor, Mr. Pool, once a teacher but now custodian of the high-school broom closet, and Buddy Clark, a tall, quiet, Robin Hood type. Buddy is the surrogate parent of a "planet" of homeless children, a "Tomorrow Billy" (because he always returns "tomorrow" with the food and clothing his dependents desperately need), and much of the story focuses on his attempt to be responsible for all the lost and unloved people he meets. When Junior Brown cracks up, following the lead of his already lunatic piano teacher, Miss Peebs, Buddy talks Mr. Pool out of sending him to a mental institution and with love and patience they try to help Junior Brown overcome the delusion that he carries Miss Peebs's relative, "a frightening monster with dirty, smelly socks," around with him. . . .

There are interesting ideas in **"The Planet of Junior Brown,"** but the book itself is surprisingly dull. Virginia Hamilton's characters and the situations she places them in are inventive but not inspired. Nothing *lives*. Episode follows episode with the spontaneity of something dragged in chains. Unlike the warm and memorable exchange between Geeder and Zeely in Miss Hamilton's finely woven tale, **"Zeely,"** the exchanges between Junior Brown and Buddy Clark are oddly stilted, studied and false. This causes the book to move so slowly that impatience with the tedious stringing together of events soon obscures the sharpness of Miss Hamilton's occasionally impressive perception.

> Alice Walker, in her review of "The Planet of Junior Brown," in The New York Times Book Review (© 1971 by The New York Times Company; reprinted by permission), October 24, 1971, p. 8.

MARILYN GARDNER

"The problem of the twentieth century is the problem of the color line," W.E.B. DuBois wrote prophetically in 1903. Virginia Hamilton's excellent biography, **W.E.B. DuBois** . . . , is a tribute to the lifetime he spent trying to solve that problem.

Her book follows him through his years with the NAACP, which he helped found. It outlines the great struggles which threatened the civil rights movement from without—whites vs. black—and from within—DuBois vs. Booker T. Washington, for example. It also attempts to set the record straight on Dr. DuBois' later years—to show how and why he was maligned, misunderstood, and ignored because of alleged pro-Communist sympathies.

Mrs. Hamilton's work is meticulously annotated, comprehensive, and generally objective—too detailed for pre-teens, perhaps, but extremely good for slightly older readers.

> Marilyn Gardner, "Rebels Black and White," in The Christian Science Monitor (reprinted by permission from The Christian Science Monitor; © 1972 The Christian Science Publishing Society; all rights reserved), May 4, 1972, p. B5.*

ZENA SUTHERLAND

[Carefully] researched and documented, sympathetic toward the subject yet candid about his failings, [**W.E.B. Du Bois: A Biography**] is a sober record of the long career of William Du Bois. The biography concentrates on his adult life, giving a detailed account of the teacher, writer, and political activist and very little about his personal life. This lacks the warmth that characterizes Virginia Hamilton's fiction, but it makes a particular contribution in placing the events of Du Bois' life not just in the stream of black history but against the background of what was happening in the United States and how it inevitably affected what was happening to William Du Bois.

> Zena Sutherland, in her review of "W.E.B. Du Bois: A Biography," in Bulletin of the Center for Children's Books (reprinted by permission of The University of Chicago Press; © 1972 by The University of Chicago), Vol. 26, No. 1, September, 1972, p. 8.

SHERYL B. ANDREWS

William Edward Burghardt Du Bois struggled for ninety-five years as educator, writer, intellectual, and poet against prejudice and fear, so that black people throughout the world could claim their blackness with pride, their humanity with honor. There is no easy definition for such a man; perhaps the most honest approach is simply to chronicle his achievements and let them speak for themselves. [Virginia Hamilton in **W.E.B. Du Bois: A Biography**] has done just that. With grace and dignity she has recounted the story of W.E.B. Du Bois, quoting from his many works, detailing his very full life. . . . The book is an affirmation of Du Bois' life, and a fascinating historical document of the Black Movement in America. Comprehensive Notes, Bibliography, and Index complete a fine, scholarly work. Unfortunately, there are often more facts than characterization, and a young reader may find it, at times, a little dry and difficult. Still, this is unequivocally the best of all the biographies of Du Bois for young people—and clearly conveys the sense of his intellectual struggle, frustration, and search.

> Sheryl B. Andrews, in her review of "W.E.B. Du Bois: A Biography," in The Horn Book Magazine (copyright © 1972 by The Horn Book, Inc., Boston), Vol. XLVIII, No. 5, October, 1972, p. 476.

NIKKI GIOVANNI

They say the pity of youth is that it's wasted on the young. Since we're well into our thirties and because we love the stories of Virginia Hamilton we must agree. Before motherhood descended upon us we could curl up in a corner with **"Zeely"** or **"The Planet of Junior Brown"** and cry all alone remembering . . . wishing . . . hoping about a childhood of our dreams. Now we gather child, dog, and gerbils (after we have extracted their promise not to chew the book) around us on the couch, under the quilt, with a big bowl of popcorn and share **"M. C. Higgins, the Great."** Actually we're proud to share Virginia Hamilton with our family. They should know the good things.

M. C. Higgins is a very nice dude. He's just beginning to recognize girls as different from boys and basically worthy of kissing. But M. C. also has come into a recognition of responsibility. His family lives on Sarah's Mountain which, because of strip mining, is in danger of being deluged by the waste. M. C. doesn't quite understand that strip mining will forever change the countryside he has grown so used to but he does know his way of life is in danger. He dreams and ultimately plans a way to save his mountain. . . .

Into M. C.'s and [his best friend] Ben's life comes Lurhetta, a girl who works all year during school so that she can roam the countryside in the summer. She is, as neither Ben nor M. C. are even likely to know, free. But with freedom comes always a price. The ability to take care of yourself, to follow your own wishes also compels you to travel alone. M. C. can leave Sarah's Mountain, can leave his stubborn father, can be free from watching his younger brothers and sisters but he will also be without roots. His great-grandmother Sarah had traveled to this mountain with a baby on her hip and the hounds of the slavemaster at her heels some hundred years ago. Could he, should he really turn that land over to those who only see the coal beneath . . . not the love . . . the sacrifice . . . the history the hill represents? . . . Mayo Cornelius Higgins makes the only decision a truly great person could make.

Once again Virginia Hamilton creates a world and invites us in. **"M. C. Higgins, the Great"** is not an adorable book, not a lived-happily-ever-after kind of story. It is warm, humane and hopeful and does what every book should do—creates characters with whom we can identify and for whom we care. . . . Virginia Hamilton has joined the forces of hope with the forces of dreams to forge a powerful story. We're glad Miss Hamilton is a writer. It makes the world just a little bit richer and our lives just a little bit warmer.

Nikki Giovanni, in her review of "M. C. Higgins, the Great," in The New York Times Book Review *(© 1974 by The New York Times Company; reprinted by permission), September 22, 1974, p. 8.*

BERYL ROBINSON

The richly detailed story of the Appalachian Hills [**M. C. Higgins the Great,**] tells of a few important days in the life of thirteen-year-old M. C. Higgins, self-styled "The Great." . . . Much of the story is devoted to the effect that two strangers had on M. C. One was a dude from the city, who was going through the hills making tape recordings of singers and their old songs. (M. C. was certain that when the dude heard his mother's magnificent voice, he would get her started on the way to becoming a great star.) The other stranger was a restless girl who walked fearlessly through the woods and camped briefly beside a lake. She was impatient with the local superstitions and stimulated M. C. to a wider acceptance and richer experience than he had thought possible. All of the characters have vitality and credibility as well as a unique quality that makes them unforgettable. Particularly charming are the scenes in which M. C.'s mother, Banina, climbing the hill after a day of housework in the town, sings antiphonally with her waiting family, or, seated on the floor at home, leads them in old ring songs. Visual images are strong and vivid; and many passages are poetic in their beauty. M. C., however, is aware of a continuing note of sadness in the hills; for pervading the entire story is his dread that the huge pile of subsoil and trees bulldozed together and left behind by strip miners would begin to slide and suddenly crash down upon his home. All of the themes are handled contrapuntally to create a memorable picture of a young boy's growing awareness of himself and of his surroundings. (pp. 143-44)

Beryl Robinson, in her review of "M. C. Higgins, the Great," in The Horn Book Magazine *(copyright © 1974 by The Horn Book, Inc., Boston), Vol. L, No. 5, October, 1974, pp. 143-44.*

ELAINE LANDAU

[Until] recently it was rare to find an American under 18 who knew who Paul Robeson is. However, within less than a year, several of his old films have been revived, black students at Rutgers named their student center for him, and a three part series on Robeson, sponsored by National Educational Television, won an Emmy.

Now Robeson's renaissance is further enhanced by Virginia Hamilton's outstanding biography [**Paul Robeson: The Life and Times of a Free Black Man**]. In a lively narrative style, she recounts Robeson's life from the warmth of his closely knit family, through his professional and political growth, to his persecution during the McCarthy witch-hunt and its final resolution. Virginia Hamilton actually tells two stories, so skillfully interwoven they are indivisible—Robeson as the black singer and actor refusing to play "darkie" parts, and Robeson as the humanist and political activist whose determination to free black America eventually stripped him of his career and wealth.

The story is told in a rich historical context; Miss Hamilton's readable explanation of political ideologies prevalent during the Second World War and McCarthy era enables young readers to identify with Robeson's actions, as well as grasp the complexities of the times. Unlike most young-adult biographies, the text remains unfictionalized and acquires chilling authenticity as each incident is fully documented by Senate testimony, newspaper and magazine quotes, Robeson's autobiography or texts by his wife and close friends. Yet Virginia Hamilton's magical ability to conjure up vivid images is still present in parts of the book, especially in her portrayal of Robeson's near-lynching in Berlin. . . .

[Virginia Hamilton's] book is far more than a compelling story of a banished black; it is a vivid chronicle of dignity and determination with which all young people can identify.

Elaine Landau, "A Brave Man, a Baby Gorilla, a Poisoned Planet," in The New York Times Book Review *(© 1974 by The New York Times Company; reprinted by permission), December 22, 1974, p. 8.**

LOUIS D. MITCHELL

Virginia Hamilton is a craftsman, often good at being just that and nothing more. Biographical artist she is not, in [**Paul Robeson: The Life and Times of a Free Black Man**], perhaps because of her lack of range and her deficient sympathy in capturing, even for children, the protean character of Paul Robeson. She merely suggests and, given the stature of Robeson, one ought to expect and receive more depth, more insight from a biographer. Perhaps this biography has merit in being pitched to a youthful reader's level—if one is to consider the very young as less intelligent, less worthy of art, less lucid in perception.

Robeson has suffered greatly for his opinions but he stands immensely above and beyond those who tried to destroy him, to abuse him, to rid the world of his vast talents and influence. But, as he so proudly put it, "The problem of Othello is the problem of my own people. It is a tragedy of racial conflict, a tragedy of honor rather than of jealousy." Unfortunately, Miss Hamilton does not capture this spirit, this outlook. (pp. 474-75)

Louis D. Mitchell, in his review of "Paul Robeson: The Life and Times of a Free Black Man," in Best Sellers *(copyright 1975, by the University of Scran-*

ton), Vol. 34, No. 20, January 15, 1975, pp. 474-75.

NICHOLAS TUCKER

American award-winning children's literature has sometimes been on the over-earnest side; it seems more difficult to win prizes for writing a funny, even irreverent book. What can one expect, therefore, from Virginia Hamilton's **M. C. Higgins, The Great,** which has scooped this year's pool by landing the National Book Award, the Newbery Medal and the Boston Globe award? Is it three times as good, or merely three times more earnest than previous winners?

Perhaps a bit of both; Virginia Hamilton writes in heavy but compelling prose. Characters lumber rather than leap from the page, but once in focus they make their mark. . . .

Certainly, this is a sincere and highly original work. An English audience may have occasional trouble with the vocabulary—it is worth discovering what exactly a "dude" might be before starting—but generally the story has enough force to keep most adult readers going. But not, surely, most young readers: the opening of the book is almost impenetrable, little use for any child accustomed to giving up after the first difficult page, let alone a whole chapter. For those that stay, there are rewards but some punishment. Emotion sometimes slides into over-intensity. There is an absence of the casual; everything from cooking meals to swimming takes on large significance. Silences between characters usually contain as many arguments as anything they happen to say. Like adolescence itself, so well described in this book, continual excess of feeling, although authentic, is sometimes hard to live with. While I admire Virginia Hamilton's achievement, honesty compels me to add that I was relieved as well as sorry to finish this strongly imagined story.

Nicholas Tucker, "Earnest Endeavour," in The Times Literary Supplement *(© Times Newspapers Ltd. (London) 1975; reproduced from* The Times Literary Supplement *by permission), No. 3826, July 11, 1975, p. 766.*

CAROL VASSALLO

[*M. C. Higgins, the Great* is] a composite of rich interwoven themes, strengthened by vivid characterization and a deep sense of place. (p. 194)

Much of the story revolves around M. C.'s emotional tension as his love for the mountain conflicts with his belief that the family must leave its home. Further, his friendship with Ben Killburn is thwarted by his family's superstitious dread of the Killburns, whom they consider "witchy." In the end M. C. saves his home by building a wall to stem the onslaught of the threatening "spoil heap." The wall is made of dirt, reinforced by rusty fenders and other car parts and, finally, by the very burial stones of his ancestors, with their markings still visible. And it is an itinerant young girl who helps him to see the folly of the local superstitions and gives him a larger vision of the world. She tells him to "find out what there's to see. What there's to know, just to be knowing."

There is magic in this book. Virginia Hamilton's style is mesmerizing, a combination of such poetic expressions as the description of a sunrise as "a brilliant gash ripped across the summit of Hall Mountain" and of such quaint mountain ex-

pressions as the remark Banina, M. C.'s lovely mother, makes about the mountain. She says it "must be what Sunday people call God Almighty. . . . High enough for heaven and older than anybody ever lived."

The symbols this author uses are also unique. M. C.'s forty-foot steel pole, his prize for swimming the Ohio River (the feat which he thinks gives him the right to the title "M. C. Higgins, the Great"), is unusual and significant, but its purpose is not quite clear. When M. C. climbs the pole and makes it move in "a slow, sweeping arc," he seems to have visionary glimpses of the past: . . . Again, the pole seems to be the pivot around which the whole story turns. Banina calls it "the marker for all of the dead," and, indeed, the bones of the ancestors are actually buried around the pole. Finally, it is the gravestones themselves, encased in the wall, that seem to be the cement that connects the living present to the past.

It is impossible to do justice to this many-faceted book. The beauty of the writing, the poetic imagery, the characters, each unique yet completely believable, and the original themes all make the reading of this book an unforgettable experience, and mark Virginia Hamilton as one of the most important of today's writers for children. (pp. 194-95)

Carol Vassallo, in her review of "M. C. Higgins, the Great," in Children's Literature: Annual of The Modern Language Association Seminar on Children's Literature and The Children's Literature Association, *Vol. 4, edited by Francelia Butler (© 1975 by Francelia Butler; reprinted by permission of Francelia Butler),* Temple University Press, 1975, pp. 194-95.

JANE LANGTON

Virginia Hamilton likes dangerous edges. She tries things that might not work. Her books are experimental, different, strange. She runs bravely along the edges of cliffs.

Her characters also exist on the edges of things. Often they cross the border into adolescence, teeming out of childhood into the chancy independence of maturity with a bursting strength that sometimes brims over into violence. They are black, but their color is not what is most important about them. At Virginia Hamilton's best, her characters transcend race and youth, and grow larger until they are towering images of dignity and power.

In **"Arilla Sun Down"** the muscular young presence is Arilla's big brother Jack Sun Run. Sun skirts dangerous precipices. Bare-chested, splendid as an Indian warrior, he rears his horse, defying white policemen. And Arilla, too, bumps up against hostile boundaries. There is the bruising rivalry with her overpowering brother and the grinding chafe between black and red in the mixed inheritance of her family. . . .

Writers brave enough to take risks sometimes fail. **"Arilla Sun Down"** is not one grand ascending curve like Hamilton's **"M. C. Higgins, the Great."** Perhaps too many things are piled too precariously on too many edges. There is too much talking, too much explaining and forced Indian imagery.

And there are things this reader couldn't quite believe. Arilla remembers her Indian origins by thinking back to her early childhood with a kind of feel-speech: "Late in the big night and snow has no end. Taking me a long kind of time going to the hill." So far, so good. But her memory also includes exact adult language, like the monologue of an old Indian woman:

"And women, Hōhé, tough and poor. They talk tribal politics, you know, baby? . . . Tribal and individual." Nor do I believe rebellious Jack Sun Run is an A-student. The contrast between the Indian reminiscences and the daily facts of contemporary suburban life is sometimes more grotesque than it is haunting and sad. It is hard to focus into one vision Jack Sun Run standing at attention in his war bonnet in his mother's dance studio and his mother performing as a mime in leotards.

But amid all this confusion two things are unforgettable, the stature of Jack Sun Run and Arilla's painful sense of insignificance beside him. "Here comes Jack Sun Run and the day just sucks its breath, then breezes in place around him." In the end she becomes his equal. After Sun falls disastrously from his horse, she bravely rescues him. Secretly, then, she abandons the Indian name of her childhood, Little Moon (the moon shines only by reflecting the sun), and gives herself the name which is the title of this book. . . .

This book is some trouble, but it's not ordinary and it's not dull. Virginia Hamilton's failed tries are more interesting than other people's tidy successes.

> *Jane Langton, in her review of "Arilla Sun Down,"*
> *in* The New York Times Book Review *(©1976 by*
> *The New York Times Company; reprinted by per-*
> *mission), October 31, 1976, p. 39.*

KRISTIN HUNTER

Virginia Hamilton's ["**Arilla Sun Down**"] delicately explores one of the most ignored facts of American society: that a great many "vanishing Americans" did not really vanish, but were absorbed instead into the relatively friendly black community. The evidence is everywhere for those who are willing to see it: Plains and Cherokee features appear startlingly at the windows of many sharecroppers' shacks and ghetto tenements, as well as in newspaper and magazine pictures of black achievers. And there are less obvious traces of this oddly hidden heritage, habits of mind and deeply rooted beliefs neither Afro nor Anglo in origin.

Imparting these last, subtlest parts of the Native American heritage through the consciousness of a 12-year-old girl is the difficult task that Hamilton has set for herself. Mystical ideas and experiences are not supposed to be communicable in words. But Hamilton, a communicator of rare ability, succeeds. For this reason, and because she has dared to break the mysterious taboo against mentioning the Native American ancestry of many blacks, this is a valuable book—not just for young readers but, to quote the author's dedication, "For all who remember twelve."

> *Kristin Hunter, "The Secret Strength of Names," in*
> Book World—The Washington Post *(© 1976, The*
> Washington Post*), November 7, 1976, p. G7.*

ROSEMARY STONES

"Never before has black creative intelligence coincided so opportunely with the development of black pride, the advancement of political-cultural awareness, independence, and style to affect black art" wrote Virginia Hamilton in a 1975 article "**High John Is Risen Again**" . . . Nowhere is this "black creative intelligence" so evident as in Virginia Hamilton's own writing, first in *M. C. Higgins The Great,* and now in her latest book . . . *Arilla Sun Down*.

Virginia Hamilton, herself a descendant of slaves, is concerned with black identity. In *M. C. Higgins The Great* this concern is subtly explored in the history of the Higgins family. In *Arilla Sun Down* the concern is continued and deepened in the author's sophisticated treatment of intra-family relationships, the conflicts of adolescent choice, and sibling rivalry. Here the "interracial" Adams family is split between those who identify exclusively with one cultural component of their heritage against those who accept a shared collective interracial past.

The narrator is twelve-year-old Arilla Adams. Her mother is black, her father part-black, part-Indian. Her sixteen-year-old brother Jack Sun Run plays at being more Indian, more of "The People" than the native Americans themselves. For Jack, "if the day didn't naturally evolve round him, then it couldn't happen". But in spite of her self-possessed, glamorous brother, Arilla manages to grow. . . . [She becomes] independent, her interracial identity confirmed.

An equally strong theme of *Arilla Sun Down* is the ethnic identity of the family as a whole. This identity breaks through the narrative in Arilla's disjointed infant memories and in snatches of half-remembered conversations which all merge as the book progresses into an acceptance of the family's shared interracial character. The conflicts and compromises of this splendid family portrait fit alongside each individual member's pride in and growing awareness of their need for each other and of their common heritage.

Virginia Hamilton is an important chronicler of the black experience. She writes in an intense, understated narrative, interspersed with evocative flashbacks, the whole richly reflecting the different levels of this complex and powerful story. And, coming from a direction that is new and unfamiliar to most of us, *Arilla Sun Down* is a little culture shock all on its own: here there are no "ghetto" signposts, no bland apologia for the liberal conscience. In describing so perceptively this particular interracial family struggling with the choices thrown up by their heritage and the pressures of the movement, Virginia Hamilton has achieved a universal statement about people and their roots.

> *Rosemary Stones, "Pressures of the Past," in* The
> Times Literary Supplement *(© Times Newspapers*
> *Ltd. (London) 1977; reproduced from* The Times
> Literary Supplement *by permission), No. 3915, March*
> *25, 1977, p. 359.*

KAREN RITTER

[In *Justice and Her Brothers*, with] school out for the summer and their parents gone for most of the day, 11-year-old Justice is left in the company of her twin brothers, Thomas and Levi, two years older and as different in personality as they are identical in appearance. . . . The surface action involves Justice's attempts to keep up with her brothers and their gang in such average-kid activities as riding bicycles and catching snakes, but the subtle, sometimes confusing psychic power-struggle underneath has vivid and terrifying effects and is the source of the carefully created tension in the story. Many rich details— heat, dust, smells, patterns of sound, etc. are skillfully woven into a complex plot all the more chilling for being so firmly grounded in reality. The suspense is slow in building although very strong; the characters all have considerable depth; the exploration of the relationship between the twins is fascinating; and the parents exhibit realistic problems, worries, flashes of humor and affection. The ending, though satisfying, leaves a lot of dangling ends that would seem to indicate a sequel. A compelling and expertly written book, of particular interest to those with a taste for fantasies involving supranormal powers of the mind.

Karen Ritter, in her review of "Justice and Her Brothers," in School Library Journal (reprinted from the December, 1978 issue of School Library Journal, published by R. R. Bowker Co./A Xerox Corporation; copyright © 1978), Vol. 25, No. 4, December, 1978, p. 60.

JEAN FRITZ

Reading Virginia Hamilton is like being shot out of a cannon into the Milky Way. Sometimes just a phrase sends you off, an image or a scene, but invariably at the end of a book you marvel: look how high I've been *just on words!* Indeed such is the extraordinary quality of Miss Hamilton's imagination that her characters seem to have to go faster than other fictional characters just to keep up with her. They speed past, splintering time: M. C. Higgins (in the award-winning book of that name) swimming as if he were made of quicksilver; Arilla Sundown (in the book of the same title) guiding her sled at breakneck pace to the very edge of a precipice. And now [in *Justice and Her Brothers*] we have Justice on her bicycle, hurtling down Quinella Hill, faster and faster to the flat place at the bottom. . . .

Justice is practicing to impress her twin borthers ("identicals," the family calls them) especially Thomas, the mean one who exercises some kind of secret power over Levi, the other identical. She's also practicing the art of catching garter snakes for The Great Snake Race that Thomas has called for the neighborhood boys. . . . But on the day of the race, Justice blows it—not only her bicycle performance but her snake catch. Although she has bagged the largest snake, it turns out the point of the contest is simply to catch the most snakes.

Here is Miss Hamilton at her best, plunging her characters into unique situations in order to work out the ambivalence and antagonisms of family relationships which she understands so well. She reaches over the precipice and risks even more than usual when she gives the identicals the power of telepathic communication with each other. It is only when, towards the middle of the book, she extends (and even magnifies) this power to include Justice, her strange neighbor, Mrs. Jefferson, and her son, Dorian, that we wonder if this time the author may not have risked too much. The idea is a dazzling one— these five born in the wrong age, the first unit of a new people with new powers; the difficulty is that we see Miss Hamilton manipulating and maneuvering to get the idea across. The book is like an expertly crafted, highly original painting over which a surrealistic film has been tacked. The author has given herself a hard assignment, but even in the Milky Way, a reader doesn't want to see an author at work.

Jean Fritz, in her review of "Justice and Her Brothers," in The New York Times Book Review (© 1978 by The New York Times Company; reprinted by permission), December 17, 1978, p. 27.

JOHN ROWE TOWNSEND

Clearly Virginia Hamilton is concerned as a writer with the black, or non-white, experience. To the best of my recollection, no fictional character in any of her work up to the time of writing is white. But there is no taint of racism in her books; as she said herself in [her article **"High John is Risen Again"**] 'the experience of a people must come to mean the experience of humankind.' All through her work runs an awareness of black history, and particularly of black history in America. And there is a difference in the furniture of her writing mind from that of most of her white contemporaries: dream, myth, legend and ancient story can be sensed again and again in the background of naturalistically-described present-day events.

Her first book, *Zeely*. . . , exemplifies this and other Hamilton qualities. Elizabeth, who is calling herself Geeder by way of make-believe while on holiday in the country, sees the beautiful, regal, immensely-tall Zeely first as a night-traveller (a phrase which of course connotes escape from slavery) and then, obsessively, as a Watutsi queen. At the end of the story, when for the first and only time she actually talks to Zeely, she faces the truth that Zeely is a very tall girl who looks after hogs. Zeely has accepted herself as what she is, and with the aid of a parable of seeking and finding she helps Geeder to do the same. She is not a queen; and perhaps there is an implication that for black Americans to look back towards supposed long-lost glories in Africa is unfruitful. Yet the story manages at the same time to hold within itself a different truth, almost a contradiction. There is a sense in which Geeder's illusions have not been illusions at all; in which the figure of Zeely does embody that of the night-traveller, who, according to Geeder's Uncle Ross, 'must be somebody who wants to walk tall . . . it is the free spirit in any of us breaking loose'; in which, as Geeder says at the end, Zeely truly is a queen as well as a hog-keeper. If there is a simple message here for younger children (and I do not think Virginia Hamilton would scorn to offer a simple message to young children) it can be summed up in those two words 'walk tall'; but it is a simplicity that has profound resonances.

The House of Dies Drear . . . , with its crowded action and melodramatic trappings, is in many ways at the opposite fictional pole from *Zeely*. Thomas is the eldest child of a black historian's family which moves into a great rambling old house, once a station on the Underground Railroad, supposedly-haunted home of a murdered abolitionist, and now guarded by 'that massive, black and bearded man some souls called Pluto'. Thomas and his father penetrate the labyrinthine complexities of the house, discovering at last the extraordinary treasure which is its ultimate secret; and they drive off those who have threatened it. Here is a tale of mystery and excitement; of all Miss Hamilton's novels it is the one with the most obvious attractions to the child reading for the story. Indeed, an adult reader may feel she has been rather too free with the Gothic embellishments. . . . The hidden buttons, sliding panels and secret passages can too easily suggest a commercially-inspired Haunted House from a superior fairground: at the same time gruesome and giggly. And the play-acting with which 'our' side frightens off superstitious intruders at the end is not really worthy of this author. One has initial doubts, too, about the marvellously-preserved treasure cave of Dies Drear, with its magnificent tapestries, carpets, glassware, Indian craft work and so on. Is it appropriate to the story that there should be a tangible, financially-valuable treasure, and anyway is it the right kind of thing for a dedicated abolitionist to have and to hide?

Here however one must recall Virginia Hamilton's comment on the tendency of the people and properties in her books to turn into emblems. It is a reasonable supposition that the treasure represents a cultural inheritance, of which Mr Pluto is the guardian or some kind of guardian spirit. The whole book has a strong, almost tangible sense of the presence of the past. It is a dramatic and at the same time a rather rambling piece of work, with something in it of the character of the house itself: much of it is below the surface, passages open out of the story in all directions, some are explored and some are only glanced into. It is highly interesting, highly readable, but it does not quite succeed in being both an exciting adventure story and a satisfying work of art.

The mysteries of *The Planet of Junior Brown* . . . are of a different order from those of *Dies Drear*: more akin to those of *Zeely* and of the later novels. *Junior Brown* is not fantasy, as the word is commonly understood: the laws of nature are never broken, and occasionally, as in the description of Junior's mother's asthmatic attack, there is an insistent, almost cruel realism. Yet there is much in the book that requires a different kind of assent from that which we give to an account of everyday events. The ex-teacher janitor who has a large rotating model of the solar system erected in the hidden basement room to which his truant friends come; the 'planets' of homeless boys dotted around the big city, each with its 'Tomorrow Billy' as leader; the lowering of 262-pound Junior Brown into the basement of a deserted building by means of a specially-rigged hoist: these carry a conviction which has more to do with the character and atmosphere of the story, the hypnotic power of the author to compel belief, than with literal probability. (pp. 100-03)

A planet in this story is a person's refuge, and perhaps also his sphere of action. There is an analogy between the huge uncaring city and the vast indifference of space by which planets are surrounded. The school from which Junior Brown and Buddy are alienated, but in which they find a temporary home in the janitor's room, expresses the same analogy on a smaller scale. Buddy, coping and compassionate, instinctual and imaginative, 'swinging wild and cool through city streets', is a forerunner, a leader into the future, a kind of saint of the streets. Too good to be true? Too good to be literally true, I think; it is hard to suppose that a homeless street lad could be so noble, so uncorrupted by hardship and by the company of those already corrupted. But when Buddy affirms on the last page that 'the highest law is for us to live for one another', he surely speaks not as Buddy Clark but as Tomorrow Billy, a mythological figure, conceivably related to the High John de Conquer who was the hero and inspiration of slaves in the last century. (pp. 103-04)

M. C. [of *M. C. Higgins the Great*] is the early-teenage black boy who sits on [a] pole, which was his reward from his father for swimming the Ohio River, and which he has equipped with a bicycle saddle, pedals and a pair of wheels that enable him to move the pole in a slow, sweeping arc. The title 'the Great' is self-awarded, a joke, but by the time the book is read the reader is likely to feel it justified; for M. C. *is* great, he *does* ride high; though he is poor and presumably uneducated he has wisdom, competence, determination. At the end he is building a wall which he hopes will hold back the spoilheap that threatens his home; he will inherit and defend the family territory. Unlike Buddy Clark, though, he is not a saint or an inspirational figure; he is human, makes mistakes, has his inadequacies. (p. 104)

Events in *M. C. Higgins the Great* either define the people and their situation or else, by apparently small redirections (like points on a rail track) change the courses of people's lives.

The most important event happens inside M. C.: his acceptance of his own rootedness in Sarah's Mountain and his determination to stop that spoilheap.

Roots, more than anything else, are what this novel is about: roots in place and also the roots of ancestry. After telling M. C. how Great-grandmother Sarah came to the mountain, his father, Jones Higgins, sings some words from a song she used to sing. The words have been passed down through succeeding generations, but Jones doesn't know what they mean: 'I guess even Great-grandmother Sarah never knew. Just a piece of her language she remembered.' Both Jones and M. C. occasionally have a sense of the presence of Sarah on the mountain. (pp. 104-05)

It may be noted that M. C.'s wisdom is itself rooted in the earth and does not move away from it; he is hopelessly naïve about the visiting dude and about Mama's prospects of stardom. Two more small but significant events may be noted at the very end of the story: Jones accepts, albeit reluctantly, the presence of Ben Killburn on his property, helping M. C. to build the wall, and he gives the boys a gravestone to build into it. . . . It is the reinforcement, once more, of the present by the past.

The Adams family in *Arilla Sun Down* are interracial. Arilla's mother is a light-skinned black woman, beautiful, and a teacher of dancing. Her father is part-black, part American Indian; and her older brother Jack Sun Run, though neither more nor less Indian than Arilla, asserts himself to be 'a blood'. Arilla feels overshadowed; doesn't know who or what she is.

Jack Sun Run—handsome, flamboyant, a brilliant horseman—is the dominant figure in this novel; but he is a more subtly ambiguous creation than any in Virginia Hamilton's earlier books. There's a sense in which he is a phoney: 'playing the brave warrior', as his mother unkindly says, and, for instance, showing off shamelessly at Arilla's birthday party. . . . Yet the phoney and the genuine are not entirely incompatible. There is something in Jack Sun Run's blood and background, and in his father's, that will come out and that will always be strange to Mother, who doesn't share it. And it is there in Arilla, too. In flashbacks to her earlier childhood, Arilla recalls half-forgotten experiences and encounters with the People: especially her friend, mentor, storyteller and source of wisdom, an old man called James False Face. Arilla receives—reluctantly, as a birthday present—a horse; she learns to ride well, and saves Jack Sun Run's life after an accident while out riding in fearful conditions. That is how she earns the name of Arilla Sun Down, becomes able to see Jack as human rather than as a being of sunlike power and brilliance, and also puts herself level with him, since he saved her life as a small child.

But in the end it is through her father that Arilla comes into a share of the Indian inheritance. Every year Dad, who is a supervisor in a college dining hall, disappears for a while, and Jack has to go and bring him back. Now, with Jack in hospital, the duty falls on Arilla. She finds Dad where he is known to be, up in the country of his people; and he has gone sledding— flying wild and free over the snow. Arilla sleds with him, as she did when a small child. Sledding, riding, even roller-skating: these are important, she needs the movement for the nomad that is in her. There is something of the experience, the transmitted wisdom of the People in her, too. All this is more real than the earlier posturings of Jack Sun Run.

Lastly there is the thing that is Arilla's own, the gift that is individually hers, that comes out in her urge to write. It goes with the name that old James has given her, along with his stories: her secret name. It is there in the book, at a key moment, a moment remembered by Arilla from years before. In this memory James has just died; Arilla is feverish and she seems to hear him speaking to her of life and death, and concluding:

> 'Wordkeeper?'
> 'I hear you.'
> 'Remember who you are.'

In its movement back and forth in time, and its shifts of style, *Arilla Sun Down* may make one think occasionally of the [William] Faulkner of *The Sound and the Fury*. But it is an original work, and a poetic one. Among many memorable lyric passages are Arilla's childhood recollection of sledding with Father, and, in her 'present-day' narrative, a parallel pages-long account of roller-skating, both capturing to an astonishing degree the poetry of motion. (pp. 105-07)

[*Arilla Sun Down*] is a book that takes risks. It is not for casual, easy reading, and among young people (or adults) it is likely to be appreciated only by a minority, and perhaps fully understood by none. The read book is always a collaboration between writer and reader, and this one requires that the reader should willingly contribute his or her own imaginative effort. It offers in return the high delight of sharing in an achieved work of art. (p. 108)

> *John Rowe Townsend, "Virginia Hamilton," in his*
> A Sounding of Storytellers: New and Revised Essays
> on Contemporary Writers for Children *(copyright ©*
> *1971, 1979 by John Rowe Townsend; reprinted by*
> *permission of Harper & Row, Publishers, Inc.; in*
> *Canada by Penguin Books Ltd), J. B. Lippincott,*
> *1979, pp. 97-110.*

JEAN FRITZ

No one can claim that "**Dustland**," the second book in Virginia Hamilton's trilogy, can stand alone. Nothing is meant to be resolved, and I confess that it's hard to wait for the last and decisive volume. It's not simply that I'm impatient at the interruption of narrative; I want to know what Virginia Hamilton *thinks*. Is there a future for mankind? That's the kind of question she's leading up to and that's what I want to know. And I won't know until the last sparks have fallen.

In the first book, "**Justice and Her Brothers**," she introduces her characters: Justice, the 11-year-old heroine, her identical-twin brothers, Tom and Levi, mirror images of good and evil, and Dorian, their strange friend. Although the group lives in today's real world, there is a growing extrasensory power at work that finally binds them together and enables them to enter the future as a unit that promises a new evolutionary step for mankind.

"**Dustland**" is the future which the unit enters in the second book. A barren place of boundless dust, it is the result (and this is barely suggested) of a chemical disaster. But it is not uninhabited. Fleshy little Dawips are there, finger-like worimas, three-legged Slakers, and most important to the plot, Miacis, a friendly dog-like creature who breathes through ear pouches and mind-reads with the children. Although the personalities of the characters are maintained, they become somewhat abstract as each assumes a specific role in the unit on which survival depends. The plot centers around the terror that

Tom causes when he breaks the unit and runs away. (pp. 26, 28)

Although we find few answers at the end of this volume, we are thoroughly involved with the quest and know at least that there is more to the future than Dustland. What else? Is it reachable? Perhaps there can never be definite answers. But from Virginia Hamilton we can count on wisdom. The final book will be worth waiting for. (p. 28)

> *Jean Fritz, in her review of "Dustland," in* The New
> York Times Book Review *(© 1980 by The New York*
> *Times Company; reprinted by permission), May 4,*
> *1980, pp. 26, 28.*

BETTY LEVIN

Virginia Hamilton is a writer of rare depth and range. Her subjects, her stories, her style, continue to press forward and away from what she has written before. "**Dustland**" is an exception only because it follows "**Justice and Her Brothers**" and ought to be read as part of the Justice cycle.

Dustland is a place—or is it simply the future?—to which Justice and her twin brothers and their friend travel in their minds. The four children, each endowed with extrasensory power, can only move as a unit from home and the present to Dustland. Their mutual need is a blessing and a burden—as are all intense relationships, all commitments.

In Dustland, nothing the children have previously known appears applicable to the strange life forms they encounter. The arid, choking, nearly featureless world means nothing if the four children cannot bring to it, along with their uncanny intelligence, a capacity to feel and care.

Dustland's inhabitants are few: the almost human Slakers, whose tortured thirst and perpetual quest for the end of Dustland are the basic conditions of their existence; and Miacis, a doglike creature who discovers through Justice the gift of language. Thomas, the illusionist who can create such compelling images that the others actually feel them, carries in his nature and powers the terrible flaw of power unchecked and unrelated.

The struggle between Thomas and Justice, the recurring questions about the nature of reality, and the moral limits to which any individual may apply his or her unique powers, create a narrative tension in which character and idea become indivisible.

Young readers may be so spellbound with this book that they will taste the grit of Dustland for hours or days after the book is finished, but no one can close the book without a sense of being lifted, like the Slaker, beyond the dust into Hamilton's "enormous world of light."

> *Betty Levin, "Fantasy Journey for All Ages" (re-*
> *printed by permission of the author), in* The Christian
> Science Monitor, *May 12, 1980, p. B9.*

HOLLY ELEY

The four children who make up ["the unit" in *Dustland*], Thomas, Levi, Justice and Dorian, and who in their encounter with "the future" sometimes lose "psychic chunks", are so scantily drawn as to evade the imagination. However assiduously we follow up clues and try to interpret allegories (even with recourse to *The New Testament*, Tolkien, or *Psychic News*), without a picture of the children, only available in *Dustland's* precursor, *Justice and her Brothers* or towards the end of *Dustland* itself, we risk bewilderment and boredom. This is a great pity for if the two books had been combined the Dustland episode would have been absorbed into an intriguing whole.

In the earlier book we gradually become aware of the extrasensory powers of a family of three American, small-town, lower middle class children and their friend Dorian. The unlikelihood of ESP, which is skilfully inserted into the main narrative, is acceptable to the sceptic and enhances rather than detracts from a delicate and adventurous story of sibling rivalry. It is easy to believe in the telepathic "identicals" (twins, Thomas and Levi), and Dorian who has healing powers and whose slovenly down-South mother, "the Sensitive", shows the heroine, "singleton" Justice how to come to terms with her extra dimension of perception. Parental attempts to understand their children's abnormal powers and adolescent quarrels, with the aid of common sense, folk adage and adult-education-class science, help keep the story on a knife edge of reality; at the same time we are prepared for the improbable.

Perhaps Miss Hamilton's original intention was one book. Perhaps her publishers may yet reissue *Justice and her Brothers* and *Dustland* under a single title. Such is the strength of her first book that if this should happen we would be in possession of a minor American classic. The Douglass children's ancestors are Huck Finn and Tom Sawyer. It is not just that they live in the same part of America, but they respond to life with the same verve and their cameraderie and pranks are reminiscent of some of the best of Twain's invention. Desegregation and the Space Age are opportunities for new kinds of adventures.

It should be mentioned that Miss Hamilton is a black writer, writing about, and surely to a certain extent for, black children. She can hardly fail to have absorbed the works of black writers such as Toni Morrison, yet at no point in *Justice and her Brothers* or *Dustland* does she allow racial issues to obtrude and her writing is the more powerful for this restraint. This is yet another reason to hope that the soft centre of *Dustland* may one day be encased in its appropriate shell.

> Holly Eley, "Future Darkness," in The Times Literary Supplement (© Times Newspapers Ltd. (London) 1980; reproduced from The Times Literary Supplement by permission), No. 4042, September 19, 1980, p. 1024.

BARBARA H. BASKIN AND KAREN H. HARRIS

[*The Planet of Junior Brown,* a] powerful, haunting, troubling book, contrasts sanity and madness, endorsement and rejection of life, commitment to others and absorption with self. Characters are at once individual and deeply symbolic. They are complex and act in ways that are often inconsistent, inimical to their own interests, and totally irrational, yet their behavior is haunting and disquieting and echoes with broader meaning. The treatment of Junior Brown's withdrawal from reality is paradoxical. It is a response to an oppressive, uncaring world, and yet it embodies a surprising innocence. Mrs. Peebs surrounds herself with objects, trying to compensate for a life of losses. Her barely manageable fantasy life substitutes for a totally unmanageable real one. Mrs. Brown is victim and victimizer; her asthma and loneliness (her husband is perpetually due home, but never manages to arrive) trap her and are simultaneously the devices she uses to control her son. Hamilton chronicles the inexorable progress and contagion of emotional stress. Buddy's characterization makes an assertive statement,

presenting a caring, loving alternative to social trauma and a metaphor for a hopeful future. A well-constructed plot, superb characterizations, fine, tight, compelling style, and a unique concept are blended in this exceptional story. (pp. 146-47)

> Barbara H. Baskin and Karen H. Harris, "A Selected Guide to Intellectually Demanding Books: 'The Planet of Junior Brown'," in their Books for the Gifted Child (reprinted with permission of the R. R. Bowker Company; copyright © 1980 by Xerox Corporation), Bowker, 1980, pp. 146-47.

JOYCE MILTON

"**The Gathering**" is the third volume of a trilogy about time travel that might conveniently be called science fiction but is more accurately described as a poet's flight into the future, in the same vein as Marge Piercy's "Woman on the Edge of Time" though unfortunately not as successful. . . .

In volume one of this series ("**Justice and Her Brothers**" . . .) "Ticey," her twin brothers and their friend Dorian discover that they share a telepathic bond and a special mission, which will eventually draw them out of their own time. The scenes where the youngsters first test their extrasensory powers work well, mainly because the author manages to inject a bit of magic into the proceedings. In volume two ["**Dustland**"] when Tom Douglass wants to demonstrate his telekinetic powers, he does so by summoning up a gigantic astral projection of—what else?—McDonald's golden arches.

Now, having followed Justice and company into the final stage of their wanderings, one arrives in the distant future expecting something more exotic than a McDonald's logo, but the rewards just aren't there. In volume three Justice hardly exists as an independent character; for much of the story she and her companions take the form of a disembodied mind-set called the "unit." Escaping the arid waste known as Dustland, the children finally make their way to something called a "domity"—a domed city in the desert run by a godlike super-computer, Colossus, and its cyborg-archangel, Celester. Through Colossus we finally learn how this strange world came to be, but the explanation is extremely perfunctory—no more than a sketchy summary of how Earth as we know it was finally exhausted by greed, pollution and nuclear warfare and then abandoned by the genetically superior humans remaining on it, who sailed for distant stars and left the Colossus machine behind to clean up the mess.

This grim vision might be more impressive if only we could see what it means to Justice. Supposedly she has come into the future to deliver to Colossus a spiritual gift that will enable the machine to introduce an element of freedom into the cloned, drug-sedated kingdom it rules over. However, it's never clear how the gift will change things or what it costs Justice to give it.

Virginia Hamilton is basically such an intelligent writer that she manages to pull her readers along even when there's no clear destination, and for all I know there are youngsters out there who will see their way through those murky passages that seemed so opaque to me. Nevertheless, getting through the last two-thirds of this story is a bit like listening to a recitation of the fascinating things that happened on someone's acid trip. You'd have to have been there to appreciate how meaningful it was.

156

Joyce Milton, in her review of "The Gathering," in The New York Times Book Review *(© 1981 by The New York Times Company; reprinted by permission), September 27, 1981, p. 36.*

HOLLY ELEY

The Gathering, volume three of Virginia Hamilton's alluring but incohesive trilogy, is an innovative book; likely to engender a spate of analysis from Black Studies Departments, it is difficult to understand and not easy to read. . . .

Justice, Thomas, Levi and Dorian (transformed in a time warp into "the unit") have returned to Dustland (a country akin to the dust storm-plagued mid-west prairies of the 1930s) in order to guide the decrepit three-legged Slaker mutants to freedom. But once there, they encounter, empathize with and decide to help the half-child leggens, smooth keeps and youngens who, grouped in "packens" of threes, are inching their way towards a Celestial City in the face of threats from other species of marauding mutants and the omnipotent Mal. They join forces and the vicissitudes of their progress to what proves to be a dystopian illusion provide straightforward adventure and the most intelligible section of *The Gathering.*

[H. G. Wells's *The Time Machine,* George Orwell's *1984,* and Aldous Huxley's *Brave New World* are all] accounts of the hazards of a future in which man's obsession with scientific advancement has superseded his concern for humanity . . . [that are] more accessible than *The Gathering.* But Virginia Hamilton's Colossus, the crippled computer which controls Domity with its smooth-running transport system, clement climate and tranquil, because drugged, inhabitants is not complacent. Its robotic interpreter, Celester remembers the satisfactions of self-determination and the Colossus continues to hope that it may regain contact with the few starters (or superior twentieth-century humans) who escaped to another planet after their relentless pursuit of technology and nuclear power had destroyed the world and reduced the less gifted survivors to wanderers in Dustland.

Hope that the reconstruction of a free world may be possible is indicated by Justice's willingness to give her particularly sensitive psychic power to the Colossus, even though in so doing she may be marooned forever in the Crossover. With her power the Colossus may be able to contact the Starters and together they will rebuild a humanitarian, if imperfect, planet. More interestingly, the youthful packens, who have never wholly lost their independence, decide to return to and make the best of purgatorial Dustland.

[Hamilton's] depiction of the aftermath of holocaust is, once one has worked out how to follow the narrative, predictable; though the possibility of an optimistic solution, however distant and for however few, is refreshing. Oblique allusion to black folklore, traditional American children's books such as Frank Baum's *Wizard of Oz,* comics and junior science fiction annuals will not be easily followed by British children and one is often tempted to treat *The Gathering* as a treasure hunt. The arbitrary use of lower case personal pronouns and dated hip-phraseology ("Be tight, you . . . be tight me") are irritating red herrings rather than welcome clues.

But it is not easy to deal with the complicated genre of science-fictional allegory for children while at the same time encouraging black confidence. Among Virginia Hamilton's more inventive devices are the children's abolitionist and humanist

surnames of Douglass and Jefferson—a clear encouragement to young blacks, though also possibly a warning against losing touch with their roots and becoming the strongest of Starters.

Holly Eley, "Building New Worlds," in The Times Literary Supplement *(© Times Newspapers Ltd. (London) 1981; reproduced from* The Times Literary Supplement *by permission), No. 4103, November 20, 1981, p. 1362.*

BETSY HEARNE

The author of award-winning *M. C. Higgins the Great* . . . and other imaginative works has ventured again into new ways of exploring the human spirit—literally, in [the case of *Sweet Whispers, Brother Rush*]; one of the three principal characters is a ghost. . . . The story is minutely and vividly developed, with no jarring of continuity between scenes of present time and past. Each character takes shape both from current behavior and influential factors of his or her background. This interplay of past on present is one of the most skillful aspects of the book, another being the emotional portraiture of several distinctive, empathetic individuals unbared by crisis. The language is a blend of occasionally lilting black dialogue and the author's own peculiarly musical style. This will require thoughtful reading and will be well worth it.

Betsy Hearne, in her review of "Sweet Whispers, Brother Rush," in Booklist *(reprinted by permission of the American Library Association; copyright © 1982 by the American Library Association), Vol. 78, No. 22, August, 1982, p. 1525.*

ETHEL L. HEINS

Few writers of fiction for young people are as daring, inventive, and challenging to read—or to review—as Virgina Hamilton. Frankly making demands on her readers, she nevertheless expresses herself in a style essentially simple and concise—though often given to outbursts of intense feeling. And meeting those demands, the reader not only forgives but learns to enjoy her small lapses into obscurity, which a less subtle writer would find intolerable.

Not quite fifteen, Tree (short for Teresa) [the protagonist in *Sweet Whispers, Brother Rush*] was bright and self-reliant; every day she came home from school promptly, her whole existence centered on looking after Dab, her retarded older brother, whom she adored. Ever since she could remember, they had had no father and were mysteriously devoid of other relatives—except for their mother, Viola, "whom they called Muh Vy. Muh Vy, spoken M'Vy. . . . [But M'Vy] was absent weeks at a time, working as a practical nurse, coming home occasionally on a Saturday to leave some money and lay in groceries. Sharing her profound aloneness with the sad, simple seventeen-year-old boy, Tree knew "quiet for years, the way other children knew noise and lots of laughter."

Tree had learned to accept the fact that Dab often suffered incomprehensible pain; and at the time when his vague misery suddenly sharpened into terrifying illness, there began to appear to the girl a splendid-looking young man dressed in finery. Arriving in an uncanny light, the "cold miracle of him" made her realize with fear and fascination that he was a ghost; and eventually she came to know that he was Brother Rush, M'Vy's youngest brother, who had died—as had all her brothers—from an obscure disease. Through a small bright space that Brother

Rush brought with him, like a mirror in his hand, Tree was able to penetrate the forgotten world of her early childhood—a world peopled with M'Vy's extensive family. Gradually, the past unreeled before the girl; and as her experience deepened, so did her understanding. Predictably, the author has not written a conventional ghost story, however, for Brother Rush—the ghost—is the literary device that makes the flashbacks both possible and plausible.

Not until about one-third of the story has been told does M'Vy, a vibrant figure, make her dramatic appearance—soon to be followed by that of her "'man friend,'" the sensitive, wonderfully gentle Sylvester Wiley D. Smith, nicknamed Silversmith. By this time Tree had discovered, to her horror, that the melancholy Dab had been a severely abused child; and when his agonizing illness ended in death, the story rises to a passionate peak as Tree vented her fury and her frustrated love—before she could be calmed by reconciliation and the prospect of a less isolated, more natural life.

The characters are as complex, contradictory, and ambivalent as is life itself: sometimes weak, sometimes attractive, always fiercely human. (pp. 505-06)

Ethel L. Heins, in her review of "Sweet Whispers, Brother Rush," in The Horn Book Magazine *(copyright © 1982 by The Horn Book, Inc., Boston), Vol. LVIII, No. 5, October, 1982, pp. 505-06.*

DAVID GUY

Tree—short for Teresa—is a black girl with a world of problems. She has never known a father. Her mother is a nurse and stays away for weeks at a time. School means little to Tree. Not only must she cook and keep house, but she has to take care of her older brother Dab, who is marginally retarded and also exhibits symptoms of another illness; he cringes from light, grows absent-minded and distracted, sometimes experiences severe pain. Tree and her brother are extremely close; in the small apartment where they live, he has been her whole world. At the age of 14, she seems ready to expand her horizons.

Such facts are not unusual in a novel for young people, which characteristically loads its protagonist down with a host of problems as if to gather as many sympathetic readers as possible. Where these books seem contrived they are often just being didactic, teaching their readers the lessons that the characters learn. In the case of *Sweet Whispers, Brother Rush,* since Tree justifiably resents her mother's absence, we would expect the book to explain why her mother—M'Vy, as Tree calls her—is so often gone. M'Vy has always been distant from Dab, and Tree must come to understand that distance too. Tree has suddenly realized she knows nothing about her father, or her mother's family. She is beginning to long for a larger world, for a real family, for some respect as a person, for a little romance. . . .

Tree finds these things, but the way in which she finds them is extraordinary. She is visited by a ghost—Brother Rush, her mother's brother. . . . He holds up a piece of her drawing paper, and in an oval "like a mirror" on the paper, Tree sees scenes from the past. She sees M'Vy as a young mother, with a darling girl child and a much more difficult son. She sees a scene in which Brother Rush exhibits the same symptoms Dab has. She sees her father with Brother Rush, and witnesses Brother's death. She not only sees these experiences, but is

able to live them, both as herself as a child and as an unseen participant.

These are not the hallucinations of a lonely and burdened girl. Dab also sees the ghost, as does an elderly cleaning woman, and M'Vy is able to feel its presence without actually seeing it. The ghost is an accepted part of Tree's experience, as real as cleaning up after Dab. M'Vy simply explains that her daughter has "seen the mystery," and her man friend Silversmith also takes it in stride: "Ain't nothing to it. It just our way. Black folks is gifted."

Thus in reading *Sweet Whispers, Brother Rush,* I felt an unusual tension. At times it seemed simply a very well-written young adult novel, in which a young person's problems are bravely faced and explained. When Brother Rush was on the scene, however, I felt in the presence of another kind of imagination altogether, that of a poetic visionary who, for instance, could see two black men riding off into eternity in a fancy car smelling of alcohol and cigars. The book could vaguely bore me and utterly astound me within the space of a single chapter.

Virginia Hamilton is obviously an author who is willing to take chances, not only with her story but also in her use of language; much of her novel is told in black slang and dialect that were not easy for this white reader to follow. Her dialogue seems accurate, however, and her descriptive writing is vivid and succinct. . . . I can't help wishing, however, that she would release her remarkable imagination from the contrived situations of the conventional young adult novel. I would love to see where such an imagination might lead her.

David Guy, "Escaping from a World of Troubles," in Book World—The Washington Post *(© 1982, The Washington Post), November 7, 1982, p. 14.*

KATHERINE PATERSON

There are those who say that Virginia Hamilton is a great writer but that her books are hard to get into. [*Sweet Whispers, Brother Rush*] is not. It fairly reaches off the first page to grab you, and once it's got you, it sets you spinning deeper and deeper into its story. Needless to say, this is not a conventional ghost story. In fact, the function of the ghost in this book is to provide 14-year-old Tree Pratt with a place from which to view her world. (p. 41)

Through the space of [the ghost of] Brother Rush, Tree mystically learns the tragic history of her mother's people. But why does she need to know these things? Why has Brother Rush come? What are his whispers—the message—that he will not give directly but that Tree must discover for herself? In the end it seems that Brother's red Buick is the sweet chariot of death come to carry her brother home and leave Tree behind in a strange, wide world where she must learn to accept help and to offer forgiveness.

The supernatural, the search for identity, the need to belong to a family and the pain of belonging, the encounter with death—Miss Hamilton has taken ideas that occur repeatedly in books for the young and bathed them in her unique black light. Her readers have come to expect stories peopled with almost mythic black characters, but in this book everyone we meet, including the ghost, is wonderfully human: Tree, in the depths of her grief, takes secret delight in the attentions of a young man; her mother, Vy, who, when young, abused her strange little boy, is able as a woman to care for him with efficiency and love but still cannot call him by his name; and Miss Cenithia Pricherd, in her pageboy wig, is the prickliest, most lovable bag lady you'd ever want to know. The language too is of Miss Hamilton's own special kind, which uses the speech forms of the young to enhance rather than restrict the music of the book.

There is no need for me to say anything to those fierce Hamilton fans who will leap joyfully into anything she writes. But to the more timid reader, young or old, who may feel inadequate to Miss Hamilton's always demanding fiction, I say: Just read the first page, just the first paragraph, of **"Sweep Whispers, Brother Rush."** Then stop—if you can. (p. 56)

Katherine Paterson, "Family Visions," in The New York Times Book Review *(© 1982 by The New York Times Company; reprinted by permission), November 14, 1982, pp. 41, 56.*

Robert A(nson) Heinlein

1907-

(Also wrote under the pseudonyms Anson MacDonald, Lyle Monroe, John Riverside, and Caleb Saunders) American novelist, short story writer, nonfiction writer, and scriptwriter.

Heinlein has played a long and significant role in the evolution of science fiction into a more sophisticated genre. He began writing in the post-Depression science fiction magazine era when simplistic plots and farfetched gadgets were the norm. Heinlein's witty style and his use of social themes and realistic technology helped give rise to speculative science fiction, which emphasizes probable technological and societal developments projected into future worlds.

After World War II Heinlein wrote a series of novels aimed at juvenile audiences which some critics consider his best work. These books feature naive protagonists who, in the course of wild adventures, learn to be "competent" human beings. Like all his works, these novels advocate "survival of the most competent." Heinlein's reliance on social Darwinism has been a constant source of controversy among critics of his work. Heinlein's survivors are those who adopt a military-like discipline and outlook, and some novels, like *Starship Troopers*, glorify militaristic society. Although some critics find fault with Heinlein's rigid logic, almost all agree that his bold exploration of social themes actively challenges a reader's view of society and has helped elevate science fiction above escapist entertainment.

Heinlein is considered "the dean of science fiction writers." His *Stranger in a Strange Land* has maintained a cultlike popularity, and his recent works are still greeted with anticipation. Heinlein has won four Hugo Awards for his novels and a Grandmaster Award for overall achievement.

(See also *Contemporary Literary Criticism*, Vols. 1, 3, 8, 14; *Contemporary Authors*, Vols. 1-4, rev. ed.; *Contemporary Authors New Revision Series*, Vol. 1; *Something about the Author*, Vol. 9; and *Dictionary of Literary Biography*, Vol. 8.)

Photograph by Jay Kay Klein

Mr. Heinlein is so straightforward and matter of fact in recounting all this that it's pretty hard not to believe every word of it.

Creighton Peet, "Martian Adventure," in The New York Times Book Review (© 1949 by The New York Times Company; reprinted by permission), October 23, 1949, p. 50.

CREIGHTON PEET

In Mr. Heinlein's cosmos, interplanetary rocket travel is old stuff. Earlier books got his characters to the moon and to stations parked in space. [In **"Red Planet"**] he describes colonial life on Mars some years after men from the earth have settled there. He even throws in a desperate revolt against dishonest agents of the operating company back on earth.

When Jim and Frank, sons of colonials go to boarding school they take Willis, a Martian called a bouncer, about the size and shape of a volley ball. A charming, friendly creature, Willis can record and play back long stretches of conversation. It is Willis who records the plotting of the crooked agents and thus starts the revolt. Before justice triumphs, the boys have many terrifying experiences skating endless miles down a Martian canal. They visit mysterious Martian cities deep underground and talk with even more mysterious natives.

IRIS VINTON

["**The Star Beast**" tells the story of] an octopod, six-ton, talking creature who was the very special pet of John Thomas Stuart XI of Westville, Planet Earth. One day, waiting for John and his friend Betty to fly home from school, Lummie began eating the neighbor's rosebushes. Mrs. Donahue drove him away with a broom and thereby started him on an innocently destructive tour of the town. . . .

The small town clash . . . soon reached interstellar proportions, full of surprises.

Mr. Heinlein's name on a book of science fiction is sure to make young space-eaters reach for it, and this one, written with his usual deftness and fine sense of humor, will not disappoint them.

Iris Vinton, "Visitor From Outer Space," in The New York Times Book Review, Part II (© 1954 by The New York Times Company; reprinted by permission), November 14, 1954, p. 10.

H. H. HOLMES

Regularly every year Robert A. Heinlein produces the best juvenile science fiction novel—and in so doing creates a work more maturely satisfying than 90 per cent of "adult" science fiction. **"The Star Beast"** . . . equals any of his previous books in lively adventure, and perhaps surpasses them in charm and in fullness of characterization (human and alien). The story of a boy and his pet always attracts readers; here the pet is a titanic but lovable monster from outer space, and the politics and even the future existence of Earth comes to hinge upon its identity and origin. The future civilization is developed with all the meticulous ingenuity one expects of Heinlein, but the emphasis is on individuals.

H. H. Holmes, in his review of "The Star Beast," in New York Herald Tribune Book Review *(© I.H.T. Corporation), November 28, 1954, p. 16.*

H. H. HOLMES

"In science-fiction circles," says Willy Ley on the jacket of Robert A. Heinlein's **Tunnel in the Sky** . . . "it has become customary to use Robert A. Heinlein as the standard; unfortunately for most writers, that standard is too high." I agree wholeheartedly—with the addendum that the standard is sometimes a smidgin high for the Old Master himself. This story of high school students who are, for a senior seminar in Advanced Survival, translated to an unknown planet to survive on their own resources is, by the Heinlein Standard, a rambling and not compelling tale, particularly weak on character-creation; but its detailed plausibility and careful thinking set it, of course, well above the run of teen-age science fiction.

H. H. Holmes, "Space in Fact and Fiction," in New York Herald Tribune Book Review, *Part II (© I.H.T. Corporation; reprinted by permission), November 13, 1955, p. 14.*

H. H. HOLMES

The nominally "teen-age" science-fiction novels of Robert A. Heinlein stand so far apart from even their best competitors as to deserve a separate classification. These are no easy, adventurous, first-steps-to-space boys' books, but mature and complex novels, far above the level of most adult science fiction both in characterization and in scientific thought. **Time for the Stars** . . . is one of the best—and possibly the most difficult for the novice. This story of the first exploration outside the solar system combines humor and adventure with pretty intensive speculation on the mathematics and philosophy of time and relativity, the unused reaches of the human mind, and even a skilful touch of psychoanalysis. This may be too meaty for some young readers; but those who have relished the other Heinlein novels (and how adroitly he has brought his readers along from the relative simplicity of **"Space Cadet"!**) should find it stimulating.

H. H. Holmes, "Journey into Outer Space," in New York Herald Tribune Book Review, *Part II, (© I.H.T. Corporation; reprinted by permission), November 18, 1956, pp. 3-4.*

VILLIERS GERSON

In Robert A. Heinlein's latest science fiction novel [**"Citizen of the Galaxy"**] a young boy searches the world of the future for the family he has never had. Thorby at first attaches himself to Baslim the Cripple, the ancient beggar on Jubbul, capital of the Nine Worlds; Baslim had bought Thorby out of slavery and was Earth's master spy. When Baslim's disguise is penetrated and he dies, Thorby finds another family among the space-hopping Traders. Then, while serving in the Hegemonic Guard, Thorby discovers his identity and embarks upon his last search amid treachery and intrigue.

Mr. Heinlein's ending is unfortunately weak and inconclusive; it was a mistake to compartment each of Thorby's adventures into a length in which none has the chance to develop as it should. But even with these faults, a Heinlein book is still better than 99 per cent of the science-fiction adventures produced every year.

Villiers Gerson, "Into the Wild Blue Yonder," in The New York Times Book Review *(© 1957 by The New York Times Company; reprinted by permission), December 29, 1957, p. 16.**

ROBERT BERKVIST

Robert A. Heinlein wears imagination as though it were his private suit of clothes. What makes his work so rich is that he combines his lively creative sense with an approach that is at once literate, informed and exciting. **"Have Space Suit—Will Travel"** . . . carries the reader into the universe in the company of Kip (Clifford) Russell, a lad whose ambition is to go to the moon, and his unexpected traveling companion, Peewee (Patricia) Reisfeld, a terrifying 10-year-old genius whose penchant for getting into trouble is at least equal to her IQ. When the two team up with a lovable, fuzzy creature of vast capabilities, called simply Mother Thing, against some ghastly intruders dubbed Wormfaces, the reader is propelled into a yeasty—and often sobering—fantasy.

Robert Berkvist, "Teen-Age Space Cadets," in The New York Times Book Review *(© 1958 by The New York Times Company; reprinted by permission), December 14, 1958, p. 18.*

R. A. JELLIFFE

[Heinlein's] own statement of his intent in writing [**Stranger in a Strange Land**] may well be noted; but it is not necessarily the reader's best guide in his perusal of it. "My purpose in this book," the author says, "was to examine every major axiom of the western culture, to question each axiom, throw doubt on it—and, if possible, to make the antithesis of each axiom appear a possible and perhaps desirable thing—rather than unthinkable."

An ambitious and comprehensive undertaking, surely. "Western culture," even tho restricted to its major axioms—and who is to determine which they are?—is a complex of multiple concepts and behavior patterns. To stand each one of them upside down, with the avowed objective of discovering whether they may thereby appear more acceptable, is to subject each axiom to the warped mirror of ruthless reflection. Such a quixotic venture might well seem foredoomed to disaster.

But the author calls to his aid the helpful technique of science fiction, to lend a trace of plausibility to the preposterous. An experienced and expert practitioner in that occult craft, he launches his social critique by virtue of the rocket propulsion of this device. . . .

[*Stranger in a Strange Land*] is an excellent yarn, creating its own atmosphere of fantasy and fascination as it proceeds. It is Alice in Wonderland for grownups of the space age. Disturbing vestiges of human actions and reactions in the characters who play their topsy turvy roles in this extravaganza project a mirage of veracity that lures us on and on.

In the quaint vernacular of our everyday world, a man from Mars . . .—becomes the protagonist of the fable. It is he who justifies the title, as well as the author's avowed intention in writing the book in the first place. It is he who reveals our mores and our morals to ourselves. He forces us to see ourselves as others see us—some god has given us, thru him, the gift to do so.

Even so, the earthbound reader may well be excused if he disregards this elaborate examination of our culture, except in passing, and finds his chief enjoyment, instead, in the wide ranging fantasy of the story for its own sake.

R. A. Jelliffe, "Alice in Wonderland Tale for Space Age Grownups," in Chicago Tribune, *Part 4 (© 1961 Chicago Tribune), August 6, 1961, p. 5*

THE TIMES LITERARY SUPPLEMENT

The besetting sin of most SF is its humourlessness; there is precious little gaiety in space. Robert Heinlein is the exception. He is so completely the master of his medium that he can afford to make fun of it. *Space Family Stone* [published in the United States as *The Rolling Stones*] is, for the most part, an agreeable send-up of the spaceways. The Stones wisecrack their way from planet to planet, doing a little trade here and there, tending the sick (Mrs. Stone is a doctor) but mainly enjoying themselves. Grandmother Hazel, who is "the only juvenile delinquent old enough for a geriatrics clinic", justifies her decision to go on to Titan: "The dull ones stay home—and the bright ones stir around and see what trouble they can dig up. It's the human pattern." Grandmother is beyond question one of the bright ones, and so is the baby, Buster, who has all the youngest's tiresomeness and who is a chess genius. So are the twins, who try to sell second-hand bicycles on Mars, and Father, who sometimes seems a buffoon but is not. Behind the knockabout fun, beyond the quiet heroism, there is a sense of adventure and—rarest of all ingredients in SF—a feeling of wonder. Notwithstanding the bureaucracy which bedevils the planets, the Stones believe that there are fine things yet to see, and they take with them, carefully dieted to control its alarming fertility, one of the compulsively loving and lovable flat-cats of Mars.

"Rewards for the New Age," in The Times Literary Supplement *(© Times Newspaper Ltd. (London) 1969; reproduced from* The Times Literary Supplement *by permission), No. 3529, October 16, 1969, p. 1202.*

THE TIMES LITERARY SUPPLEMENT

That old master of SF, Robert Heinlein, knows [science fiction] well enough to make fun of it. Kip, his engaging hero [in *Have Space Suit—Will Travel*], saves the world from an invasion of bug-eyed monsters—or their equivalent—and then goes back to his part-time job as soda-jerk in a drugstore. Kip has a nice line in wise-cracking; he also has great courage and deep hu-

manity—it is his humanity which responds to the wisdom and tenderness of the Mother Thing. The M.T. is a Vegan, small, graceful and feline, and above all comforting. . . . As the complex, powerful story develops, the M.T. changes and becomes infinitely more formidable, but her vast compassion grows proportionately and she becomes no less lovable.

A few other writers manage the science in SF almost as well as Mr. Heinlein; no one else has his lightness of touch, the gaiety which in no way diminishes his fundamental seriousness. No one else draws so well the American Boy—the Girl, too, for Kip is accompanied into remotest space by Peewee who is ten and a genius. Peewee, who carries a dirty rag doll called Madame Pompadour through a series of appallingly perilous adventures, is one of Mr. Heinlein's best creations. In her maddening sophistication, her dreadful temper, her aggressive prejudices, her vulnerability, he is always entirely convincing, totally human. She deserves the father who, of all adults, is able to believe the story of their adventures and who knows all the right strings to pull. Professor Reisfeld is almost as good as Kip's father, who pays his taxes in cash (tied in a bundle) once a year and gives his occupation, on the official returns, as "Unemployed Spy".

Like all the best SF writers, Mr. Heinlein makes the most fantastic of adventures acceptable by relating them to the everyday world. His relaxed, throwaway style, precisely geared to the first person narrative pushes the story on briskly to a good-humoured conclusion.

"New Worlds," in The Times Literary Supplement *(© Times Newspapers Ltd. (London) 1970; reproduced from* The Times Literary Supplement *by permission), No. 3589, December 11, 1970, p. 1460.**

THE TIMES LITERARY SUPPLEMENT

Starman Jones first published in America in 1953, is the story of a poor farm boy who longs to be an "astrogater", makes his way on to the space ship *Asgard*, duly gets his chance, and finishes the voyage as acting captain. The scope for wishful self-identification on the reader's part is obviously enormous. The tour de force of this novel is the hero's initiation into the mysteries of the ship's control room; so assured and absorbing are the author's descriptions that even the least technically minded reader receives the illusion of experiencing the perils of long-distance space navigation.

"Stars in their Eyes," in The Times Literary Supplement *(© Times Newspapers Ltd. (London) 1971; reproduced from* The Times Literary Supplement *by permission), No. 3605, April 2, 1971, p. 383.**

BRIAN W. ALDISS

In 1941, Heinlein revealed the plans of his scheme for a Future History series, while [Isaac] Asimov began his long series of stories about robots with positronic brains whose behaviour is guided by three laws of robotics which prevent them from harming men.

In this respect, Heinlein and Asimov brought literary law and order into magazine science fiction. . . .

Both Asimov and Heinlein brought intelligence and wide knowledge to their storytelling. Heinlein's preoccupation with power was sometimes to express itself disastrously, as in his novel *Starship Troopers*. But that was later; in the early forties, he could do no wrong. In 1941 alone, [the magazine] *Astounding* published three of his novellas which can still be read with pleasure, *Logic of Empire,* set on Venus, *Universe,* set on a gigantic interstellar ship, and *By His Bootstraps,* a time-paradox story which still delights by its ingenuity, as well as several excellent short stories.

It seemed that the cosmos was his oyster, so diverse was his talent. But no author has more than one secret central theme, or needs it; *Logic* is about resistance to authority; *Universe* is about what happens when authority breaks down; and *Bootstraps* is a good-humoured demonstration of the trouble that can come when the father-figure is removed.

The Golden Age [of science fiction magazines] was in full swing. (p. 229)

Heinlein's transition from magazine writer to novelist is dramatic. His great and rare virtue is that he has never been content to repeat a winner or rely on a formula. . . . (p. 269)

He is very much a pulp writer made good, sometimes with his strong power drives half-rationalised into a right-wing political philosophy, as in *Starship Troopers*. . . , a sentimental view of what it is like to train and fight as an infantryman in a future war. Anyone who has trained and fought in a past war will recognise the way Heinlein prettifies his picture. But realism is not Heinlein's vein, although he has an adroit way of dropping in a telling detail when needed, sometimes giving the illusion of realism. This technique is notably effective in his boys' novels, such as *Starman Jones*. . . , where close analysis of character and motive is not demanded.

For my taste, Heinlein's most enjoyable novel is *Double Star,* which first ran as a serial in *Astounding* in 1956. *Double Star* is a hymn to behaviourism. For once Heinlein begins with a "little" man, . . . a pathetic failed actor, Lawrence Smith, who liked to style himself Lorenzo the Great.

Because of his chance resemblance to Bonforte, one of the leading politicans of the solar system, Lorenzo is forced to impersonate the politician and take on his powers, until he eventually becomes the man himself, clad in his personality and office. People in other Heinlein novels often have to fit into unaccustomed roles, become revolutionaries, become space troopers, wear slugs on their backs, or—like Smith in *I Will Fear No Evil*—live in a woman's body.

Heinlein's grasp of politics has always been remarkably frail, and the political issues concerning liberty which lie close to the heart of *Double Star* are absurdly falsified by the coarsely impractical methods the politicians employ. Thus, Lorenzo is shanghaied into playing his role, while Bonforte is kidnapped by the opposing party, the Humanists. This Chicago gangsterism is rendered the more silly because an effort is made to model political procedures on British parliamentary method: Bonforte is a Right Honourable, and "leader of the loyal opposition."

Despite this monstrous drawback, *Double Star* survives somehow because at its centre is the process whereby Lorenzo becomes Bonforte, and Heinlein handles this with a clarity he is rarely able to sustain in his other adult novels. The scene on Mars where Lorenzo as Bonforte goes to be adopted into a Martian Nest (rare honour for Earthmen) is effective. There are parallels between this novel and [Anthony] Hope's *Prisoner of Zenda.*

In a juvenile novel, *Red Planet*. . . , Heinlein presents another effective picture of Mars. Heinlein is obscurely moved by Mars. As a thinker, he is primitive; perhaps this is the source of his appeal. . . . Although it is true that several of his novels are about revolution and wars, this does not make of Heinlein a Zapata. The dark and blood-red planet shines only in the complex universe of his own mind; his ideas of liberty boil down to what a man can grasp for himself.

More nonsense has been written about Heinlein than about any other sf writer. He is not a particularly good storyteller, his characters are often indistinguishable, his style is banal, and to compare him with [Rudyard] Kipling is absurd. A better comparison is with Nevil Shute, who also loved machines and added mysticism to his formulae; but Shute is more readable.

Shute, however, is not as interesting as a character. The interest in Heinlein's writing lies in the complexity of Heinlein's character as revealed through the long autobiography of his novels. He is a particular case of that magic-inducing not-growing-up which marks so many sf writers.

And this is best exemplified in his best novel, *Stranger in a Strange Land*. . . . Though it is a faulty book, Heinlein's energy and audacity are turned to full volume. It also is an ambitious book and that, too, one respects.

Mars hangs just below the horizon again.

The central figure of *Stranger in a Strange Land* is Valentine Michael Smith, twenty-five years old and a distant relation of Tarzan; he was born on Mars and brought up by Martians. Back on Earth, his strange Martian ways threaten political stability. He is even better equipped than Tarzan, materially and mentally—materially because oddities of his birth have left him heir to several considerable fortunes and have possibly made him owner of Mars as well; mentally, because he has picked up all sorts of psi powers, learnt from his Martian parents.

Although the novel is by no means "a searing indictment of Western Civilization," as the blurb on one edition would have it, it does pitch in heartily against many of our idiocies, just as the early Tarzan books did.

But the odd attraction of *Stranger* is that it mixes the [Edgar Rice] Burroughs tradition with the [Thomas Love] Peacock-Aldous Huxley tradtion. It is full of discussions of religion and morals and free love. For Smith comes under the protection of Jubal Harshaw, a rich old eccentric know-all, who holds forth about everything under the Sun. (pp. 269-72)

All the characters talk a great deal, their verbosity only exceeded by the characters in *I Will Fear No Evil*. (p. 272)

Stranger in a Strange Land has an odd fascination, despite its faults; it reminds one of Huxley's *Island* in its attempt to offer a schema for better living, but one imagines that Huxley would have been horrified by its barely concealed power fantasy. . . . *Stranger* in fact represents the apotheosis of [magazine science fiction], and so of the long pulp tradition. (p. 273)

Before leaving Heinlein, one more thing remains to be said. Old-time fans still think of him as hardware specialist. In fact, he moved over very early to writing a different kind of sf, and one, I believe, much more in tune with the sixties and seventies—a variant which we may call Life-Style Sf; that is to say, a fiction which places the emphasis on experimental modes of living more in accord with, or forced on us by, pressures of modern living. (p. 274)

*Brian W. Aldiss, "'The Future on a Chipped Plate':
The World of John W. Campbell's 'Astounding'"
and "'After the Impossible Happened': The Fifties
and Onwards, and Upwards,'' in his* Billion Year
Spree: The True History of Science Fiction *(copyright © 1973 by Brian W. Aldiss; reprinted by permission of Doubleday & Company, Inc.; in Canada
by Wallace & Sheil Agency, Inc.), Doubleday, 1973
(and reprinted by Schocken Books, 1974), pp. 215-
43, 244-84.**

DAVID N. SAMUELSON

[The] frontier metaphor has been basic to Heinlein's writing.
Only eight of his . . . novels take place primarily on Earth,
and four of them concern relations between humans and intelligent extraterrestrial beings, while a fifth concludes on the
Moon. This outward spatial movement, coupled with a forward
temporal movement, places Heinlein's characters in situations
of extremity, facing the unknown and having to learn to understand it, in order just to survive. Whether they are in spaceships or on alien worlds, exploring or settling or righting
wrongs—fighting off other species or learning to live with
them, their situations parallel those of the American pioneers,
for all that they are equipped with advanced technology, "scientific" thinking, and the benefits of historical hindsight. Even
in a utopian situation, even in the present or near future here
on Earth, even where mental or "psi" powers are involved,
a kind of frontier ethic is invoked in order to make possible a
free exercise of individual initiative, or to justify pragmatically
certain measures that in more structured situations, such as
those of the society we actually live in, would have to be
considered extreme. On the frontier, Heinlein's heroes can be
free *from* anything that technology and good will can overcome,
such as physical slavery, mental bondage, the "prisons" of a
single planet and the human body, the limitations of distance
and even of death. They can be free *to* roam, explore, discover,
earn fame and success, learn things that are useful for the
individual or the race, or to achieve self-actualization.

That these freedoms are primarily available to those who can
best profit by them—i.e., that they represent what [Alexei]
Panshin calls a "wolfish" sort of freedom for "the Heinlein
individual"—should not be too surprising, since this is a logical extension of the adolescent dream, especially its American
versions. American literature and history are full of famous
"wolfish" individuals who pioneered land, technology, and
money matters in a society which encouraged everyone to seek,
and enabled a few to achieve, their wildest dreams, believing
the losses they brought to some were outweighed by the benefits
they brought to all. That Heinlein is from a generation and a
region which valued those achievements more than many people do today who take them for granted is surely relevant, but
so is the fact that in any situation, certain people are more
likely to succeed than others. In changing situations, such as
the last five centuries of Western Civilization and the various
futures Heinlein extrapolates from them, those who succeed
are likely to be adaptable, even opportunistic. And Heinlein
does not treat freedom, for the most part, as a simple escape.
To be sure, some of his works contain large amounts of good-
vs.-evil melodrama and lengthy sermons generalizing from inadequate particulars, while most of his work is pitched to the
level of a reader of modest intellectual achievement. More often
than not, however, the melodrama is subsidiary, the sermons
are in character, and freedom is a complex issue, involving

both power and responsibility and requiring various kinds of
trade-offs.

By using analogies with situations familiar from history, legend, and personal experience, by anchoring the unfamiliar in
specific detail generated by these analogies, Heinlein manages
to make his frontier worlds seem real, however weak he may
be in plot construction, however limited his range of characters
and emotions, however objectionable some of his tics of style,
especially in dialogue. (pp. 107-09)

The background chart for Heinlein's **"Future History"** series
. . . places up to twenty-seven stories in relationship to an
assumed time-line stretching from about 1950 to approximately
2600 A.D., suggesting lines of political, scientific, and technological continuity which are only sketchily apparent in the
stories themselves. . . . Progress is assumed in both technology (transportation, power sources) and society . . . with some
cross-over (psychometrics, semantics), but not as a straight-
line projection. Heinlein takes it for granted that power will
be abused by some and that severe setbacks will occur, with
a pendulum-like swing between freedom and enslavement (in
psychological, as well as physical terms). Against this large-
scale movement, individual human dramas will be played out
which may support or contradict the slow cultural rise and fall;
the "Future History" concept does not imply a *novel manqué*
(like [Clifford] Simak's *City* or [Ray] Bradbury's *The Martian
Chronicles*), but rather a general set of assumptions about the
history behind the individual stories. (pp. 101-10)

Using teen-agers as protagonists allowed [Heinlein] to combine
the two plots with which he was most comfortable, "the Little
Tailor''—or the success story—and "the man who learned
better,'' while suppressing the third plot that he recognizes,
"boy meets girl.'' Romance is handled just as gingerly as it
was in his pre-war magazine stories, whereas the success story
keeps most of his books upbeat, however somber their tone
may be. Since it is tied to the hero's education, this kind of
story gives Heinlein's didacticism a free rein. Far from being
hampered by formulaic constrictions, Heinlein seems to have
thrived on them; new frontiers, the need for change, the proper
tools with which to face the future, all these could be emphasized again and again in different contexts, each of which is
at least related to the grand design of the Future History. Necessary to avoid stagnation, expansionism would require survival traits, some of which are given only lip service in American schools and society. These traits are rewarded, and their
opposites denigrated in this series of books which emphasizes
not characters (most are indistinguishable) or plot (most are
episodic), but ordinary details of living in exotic settings. (pp.
121-22)

[The] novels labelled "juvenile" are not necessarily childish.
They may be quite serious in their extrapolation and exploration
of technological and social problems and, indeed, five of Heinlein's fourteen "juveniles" were published first in "adult"
science fiction magazines. The innocence, energy, and willingness to please of the youthful protagonists is often endearing, if sometimes quaint, but allows for only limited distinctions between the heroes of different novels. Other debilitating
problems include the apparent formulaic need for something
eventful to happen in every chapter and the perennial Heinlein
problem with endings. . . . [The] general effect of focusing
on a single character in a lengthy narrative is to involve the
reader in the development of that character, and in the effect
on him of adapting to the changing world around him. Since
Heinlein's heroes are survivor-types, their personal stories have

happy endings, however somber the background or the theme of the novel may be. But if Heinlein could have taken the same care in developing those characters that he did on their backgrounds, I could agree more easily with Panshin's assessment of the "juveniles" as Heinlein's best. Seen as a whole, the series provide a kind of transparent overlay of other adventures taking place against the same general background as that sketched out for the Future History. Seen as a sequence, the series shows the same growing seriousness of tone, the same growing seriousness of characters' social and personal insecurity, that is reflected in Heinlein's other works. (pp. 131-32)

Certainly Heinlein shares with his whole society, including the makers of science fiction, a positive attitude toward the frontier, toward adolescent potential, and toward the proper use of gadgetry. The frontier, with its challenge of the unknown, inviting expansion of man's territory and his knowledge, and often threatening his survival, is a staple of Western literature and philosophy. So is youth, with its romantic dreams, and the volition and potential to learn in order to achieve them. And the ambivalence of man toward science and technology, his fascination with gadgets coupled with his justifiable fear of their progressive disruption of his way of life, is a key theme continuing through at least the last two centuries in Western civilization. The settings against which themes are sounded, and to a large extent the manner in which they are presented, Heinlein shares with many other writers of science fiction. Space and the future, instant wisdom and quick technological fixes recur functionally in almost all of his writings, providing the typical science fictional perspective on the present which, it is pretended, allows us to see it whole. Given a single human species, planet, and period in time, differences in race, religion, even sex, and life-style, become relatively unimportant. And any single-minded assertion of supremacy, of sex or nation, race or religion, and almost any intolerant attitude (except perhaps one's own) becomes fair game for satire. (pp. 147-48)

From the first, [Heinlein had a] sense of realism, of ordinary actions in daily life, or the detailed texture of a limited range of experience, of the continuity between future and current behavior. Then there was his caring about the larger canvas, the Future History so many readers, and other writers, took to heart, only to have a younger generation rebel against it. Having fitted these to the adventure-story formulas that sustained the science fiction magazines, Heinlein then adapted them to the formulas of the mass magazine and juvenile novel markets, selling all the time to the sf magazines as well. Finally, as other writers, more competent with words, more careful with design, surpassed him, and gradually did away with the need to follow formulas so faithfully, Heinlein tried to keep up. The results were highly individual, but far from unqualified successes, since Heinlein, shifting more and more from pulp adventure toward philosophical dialogue, did not have the necessary resources of style to fall back on.

Although his latest work shows belated influences of the great "modernist" writers of the earlier part of the century, Heinlein's attitude toward style and manner which was not, like his, lucid, transparent, ostensibly objective, generally has been, if not antagonistic, at least indifferent; in that too, he reflects the attitude of most sf writers of his generation. . . . His very mastery of formulas was, in a sense, his downfall, for it obviated the need to create distinctive characters, to explore more than a very narrow emotional range, even to complete the plots and constructs he had begun. Having been successful, too,

under formulaic limitations, at suggesting a philosophy rather than spelling it out, he was either unwilling or unable to support his positions more fully in his talky later novels, where no taboos or limits on length were operative. And the authoritative insider manner, replete with wisecracks and homey sayings, which he affected in the early 1940's, has become dated, while the garrulousness of the 1950's and 1970's has not been an adequate replacement.

Generally a competent craftsman, if nothing else, Heinlein stood out among his contemporaries before the War, and again as a writer of "juvenile" novels, and his level of consistency over all is probably unmatched except by H. G. Wells. . . . The "juveniles" stand up as an overall achievement, but none of them really stands out, though my personal preference is for *Citizen of the Galaxy* and *Starship Troopers,* despite my reservations about their philosophical-political underpinnings (i.e., the inevitability and acceptability of slavery and war), over such rollicking jaunts as *The Rolling Stones* and *Have Space Suit—Will Travel.* But Heinlein's best—such stories as "'It's Great to be Back,'" "They," and "'All You Zombies'"; such novels as *Double Star* and *The Door Into Summer*—do not seem to me to match the best single novels of a dozen or more other writers, even limiting the list to those whose fame lies mainly in the science fiction field. And his worst, such as "Elsewhen," "Gulf," "Searchlight," *Rocket Ship Galileo,* and *I Will Fear No Evil* are as bad as anything ever used to show science fiction up as inept and infantile.

Today, Heinlein is known to many, thanks to paperback advertising techniques at least, as the "Dean" of science fiction writers, not so much because of his length of service as because of his relationship to the corporate body of science fiction. He is "historically" important as a pioneer in realistic and extrapolative science fiction, and as a representative writer whose craftsmanship and technical knowledge-ability were generally quite high. But he may also be a victim, in a sense, of another basic lesson of the frontier: the earliest settlers, laying the groundwork, making possible further developments and greater accomplishments, may be indispensable, but frequently they are remembered, if at all, only for being there first. (pp. 150-52)

David N. Samuelson, "The Frontier Worlds of Robert A. Heinlein," in Voices for the Future: Essays on Major Science Fiction Writers, Vol. 1, *edited by Thomas D. Clareson (copyright © 1976 by The Popular Press), Bowling Green University Popular Press, 1976, pp. 104-52.*

ALEX de JONGE

If one is going to republish Heinlein I would have thought it ought to be something like *Glory Road,* but *Rocketship Galileo* . . . was an inspired choice. This is pure nostalgia, from the world of *Mecanix Illustrated* and *Authentic Science Fiction.* It is the story of three bright young high school kids and their brainy scientist uncle who just get together and build a moon rocket. An air-force general was once asked what he expected to find on the moon and he replied 'Russians'. Ross, Maurice, Art and uncle Donald Cargreaves go one better; they find the Fourth Reich. A bunch of fanatical Nazis are about to use the moon as a base to drop atom bombs on the earth. Our lot thwart them just in time. Lovely.

Alex de Jonge, in his review of "Rocketship Galileo," in The Spectator *(© 1977 by The Spectator;*

reprinted by permission of The Spectator*)*, Vol. 239, No. 7778, July 30, 1977, p. 22.

ROBERT SCHOLES AND ERIC S. RABKIN

[Robert A. Heinlein] has been a vivid and controversial figure for three decades. His values have been called everything from fascistic to anarchistic, and as a writer he has been described as both a "natural storyteller" [see excerpt by Alexei Panshin in *CLC*, Vol. 3] and "not a particularly good story-teller" [see excerpt above by Brian Aldiss]. There is disagreement about which of his works are the best and which the worst, and about the value of his work as a whole. The fans have agreed for some time that he is their favorite writer, but the only thing that most critics agree about is the fact that he is *there*, he is important, he must be dealt with. And the first thing that must be dealt with is the fact that his immense popularity is based on something very real—his immense readability. When a reader picks up a Heinlein he knows that he is likely to get his money's worth of entertainment. That is, he will be engaged by the characters in the work, moved by their situations, and concerned about the outcome of the events in which they are involved. And he will sense this has been accomplished in a natural and apparently effortless way. How, in fact, is it done?

It is done, first of all, through a kind of psychological and social knowhow. Heinlein, who was trained as an engineer at the U.S. Naval Academy, and continued his career until invalided out of service by tuberculosis in 1934, knows how a lot of things work. He also knows how to present unworkable things in such a way as to convince us that they do work. And he knows a good deal about how people work in social situations, how animals work, and how society itself works. What he knows is quite similar to what the best American writers of detective stories have known—people like Raymond Chandler, Ross MacDonald, and John D. MacDonald. And his style is something like theirs. It is not fancy, but it is very workmanlike. The conversation is lively and has an authentic ring, the narration is brisk, the description pointed. As in most popular forms of fiction the good guys and the bad are clearly distinguishable—and the good guys always win.

Heinlein's values are close to those of Ayn Rand and the ideology associated with her. He believes in a freedom which will allow the "best" people to rise to the top. He is, as Panshin has argued, an elitist who believes in an elite of competence. In many respects he is a "social Darwinist," who feels that life should be a struggle for survival of the fittest and that the unfit should go to the wall. These views, which are far from "liberal," are more or less the views of many Americans. In some respects Heinlein is the most typically American writer in all the ranks of science fiction. He is energetic, optimistic, and broadly knowledgeable about technology and human behavior. He is skeptical of noble ideals and highly dubious of democratic process. But he clearly believes in life, liberty, and the pursuit of happiness. For him, freedom to trade, to wheel and deal, to gain position, money, and power—this is very important. . . . Man is an animal, in his view, and a dangerous one, who must fight. He can unite and cooperate only when he has a common enemy. Thus military organizations are ideal models for human society. They are run by those who have proved themselves competent and courageous; they offer a hierarchy open to the talented, where all compete on an equal basis; and they can be cooperative because their aggressive behaviour is directed outward, at a common enemy. For Heinlein the idea that society can be based on equality and coop-

eration is founded on a misconception about human nature. Mankind is incapable of true communism—and of true democracy. The world is too complicated for "the people" to govern it themselves. They must be led by those among them who are best fitted for leadership. Many of these ideas are unpalatable to most critics. But they clearly strike a responsive chord in a wide readership. (pp. 55-6)

Heinlein loves a story of individuals triumphing over a system, of small groups defeating large bureaucracies, of freedom winning over control. And, ranging over the future, he can pick his spots so as to treat just this kind of situation. His world is open, unfinished, and therefore amenable to an ethic of development. Closed systems with limited resources do not appeal to him. His social ideal is a tightly organized hierarchy, like the space-ship society in *Citizen of the Galaxy* . . . , which survives by trading with other societies less fortunate in their social and political structures—or like the military organization of *Starship Troopers,* in which rights of citizenship are earned by government service. But his ideal individual is a totally free man, which means that his heroes fit awkwardly into his ideal societies. He is shrewdly realistic about a certain level of human motivation and group behavior—but he is not realistic enough to look into all the dark corners of existence. Which is why he is a superb entertainer but a dangerous guide for conduct.

Heinlein's greatest commercial success came with *Stranger in a Strange Land,* which first appeared in 1961. . . . Like the rock opera *Jesus Christ Superstar,* it blends contemporary materials with the story of Christ. But where the opera projects modern elements back into the biblical setting, *Stranger* reenacts the story in the near future. Valentine Smith, an earthman trained on Mars, comes to earth and performs miracles of extrasensory perception, telepathy, and psychokinesis. He founds a cult and teaches others how to use the same powers. Above all, he teaches his faithful to "grok" things—to understand them by harmonizing with their essences. His followers enjoy great sexual freedom, and great communal rapport. When he is "crucified," they drink broth made from his remains, "savoring it, praising and cherishing and grokking their donor." . . . (p. 57)

The values of the sixties could hardly have found a more congenial expression. Valentine Smith is a combination of Captain Marvel and Christ—a Jesus Christ Superman who builds a commune into a great religious cult. Heinlein's Smith is as American as the Mormon Joseph Smith, and Heinlein knows it. The values of Ayn Rand and the hippie communes of the late sixties manage a precarious combination in this book, so as to tell a lot of different readers what they want to hear. But Heinlein's own voice speaks clearly through the character of "Jubal E. Harshaw, LL.B., M.D., Sc.D., bon vivant, gourmet, sybarite, popular author extraordinary, and neo-pessimist philosopher." . . . Too much of this voice, in fact too much talking altogether, is a fault in several of Heinlein's later works. The books have become longer, much longer, and most of that length is the result of talk. When he talks too much, Heinlein becomes a village social scientist—shrewd and amusing at first, then cranky, then repetitive, and finally repellent. It is this, and his coy and clumsy attempts at being sexually up to date, that make a book like *I Will Fear No Evil* . . . seem like an inflated monster alongside the fluid fiction of his earlier years. But his whole body of work, almost twenty volumes of adult fiction and a number of juveniles, stretching from the Golden Age to the seventies, is a remarkable performance. His adult entertainment has been just that—both adult and entertaining—

for a long time, and he has had as much to do with the maturing of American science fiction as anyone. Students of American culture and values will do well to consider him, for his contradictions and confusions are very much our own—as is his energy and the optimism that lies below his "neo-pessimistic" facade. (pp. 57-8)

Robert Scholes and Eric S. Rabkin, "The 'Golden Age' and After," in their Science Fiction: History, Science, Vision (copyright © 1977 by Oxford University Press, Inc.; used by permission), Oxford University Press, New York, 1977, pp. 51-70.*

DAVID N. SAMUELSON

In a Heinlein juvenile, a young boy typically (one was a girl) grows to maturity, in the process of living through and effecting events projected into our next century, by means of making decisions that involve his intelligence and mold his character. (p. 144)

[The vision Heinlein gave teenagers] was like Horatio Alger's in some ways, not only because it gave its readers a sense of their own potential, but also because it made clear that this potential could be limited as well as enhanced by scientific, technological, social, and psychological factors. Since Heinlein's juveniles are still popular in libraries, and are never out of print, millions by now must have been introduced by them to the concepts of science fiction, to science fiction as myth, and to science fiction as literature.

It was not until the Sixties, however . . . that he became a really popular writer for "adult" audiences, known to large numbers of people outside the science fiction subculture. . . . The growth in Heinlein's sales and reputation was gradual, centering on one book, which shared with Frank Herbert's *Dune* (1965) the dubious blessing of becoming an "underground classic." *Stranger in a Strange Land* (1961) sold well over a million copies, improved the market for the sale and revival of his other books, and made it possible for his two long, rambling, ostensibly sexy and philosophical novels of the Seventies to become best-sellers virtually on publication. (p. 145)

Stranger in a Strange Land did a number of other things . . . that made it in some ways emblematic of the Sixties. As a work presumed to be science fiction—though the connection was not emphasized in promotion—it suggested to the public that the genre had possibilities for objects other than adventures in outer space and cautionary tales of horrific futures. It fit the iconoclastic mood of the times, attacking human folly under several guises, especially in the person or persons of the Establishment: government, the military, organized religion. By many of its readers, too, it was taken to advocate a religion of love, and of incalculable power, which could revolutionize human affairs and bring about an apocalyptic change, presumably for the better.

The ugly side of this reading was illustrated by the strange case of Charles Manson, self-appointed Messiah of Southern California, who apparently found in this book, as in the Beatles' song, "Helter Skelter," a cornerstone of his own religion of love *and* hate that culminated in the Tate-La Bianca murders of 1969. . . . I have heard elsewhere that [cults in Southern California] use *Stranger* and some of Heinlein's other works practically as sacred texts, for their "water-sharing" and sexual rituals, and their mystical outlook on life.

The Manson publicity and the "water-brotherhood" cults may give us pause in trying to evaluate this curious book. . . . But it may be impossible, except in the most sterile and clinical terms, to judge this book solely on intrinsic grounds, such as matters of form and style, plot and character, artistry and craftsmanship. With any "popular" work, matters extrinsic to the text are of signal importance, too. The artist and his audience are in a symbiotic relationship; they must be ready for him, and he must validate their view of the world. I do not pretend to know to what extent *Stranger in a Strange Land* was cause or effect of the social patterns it reflects, but I am certain its popularity has not been due simply to literary excellence. Its importance as a social document, as a representative artifact of a stage of Heinlein's career, and as a harbinger of the phenomenal popularity of science fiction and related art in the late Seventies, far outweigh whatever merits or demerits I claim for it as a work of "speculative fiction," a term preferred by Heinlein.

Before examining these other aspects, however, it may be well to examine just how it does function as literary art. In its simplest form, *Stranger in a Strange Land* pretends to answer the question, "What would happen if a Man from Mars were to come to Earth?" Formally, it combines some elements of the science fiction thriller with two conventions popular in the eighteenth century as vehicles for holding up society to ridicule or admiration. In the first case, a visitor from an exotic land . . . tries to understand the customs of the writer's world; or, like [Jonathan] Swift's Gulliver and [Daniel] Defoe's Crusoe, the emissary of our civilization brings his customs with him when visiting someone else.

In the second case, the *Bildungsroman* or "novel of education or development," the writer traces the personal growth and education of a young man (usually), from childhood to maturity, dropping him before he does the presumably great things for which he is destined. This pattern is familiar from Heinlein's juveniles, but here it is extended back to more primitive roots in the tragic hero, or more precisely, the dying and resurrected god whose sacrifice implies immortality for all his followers.

In other words, the Man from Mars, if he came to Earth, would see what a sham our society is, but would become educated in it to the extent that he could combine Earth and Mars realities, attempting to bring the combination to others. Since Earth is not ready for such changes, however, he would be "punished," although the punishment would be in vain, since he is immortal and so is his legacy.

Setting this frame in the near future, Heinlein draws on the resources of science fiction to help make his story plausible. (pp. 145-47)

How important the story is for the book may be a matter of controversy. Heinlein himself maintains that with *Stranger* he realized that his readers really wanted to hear more philosophy from him, that the story was simply a frame on which to hang his observations . . . . And philosophizing there is in *Stranger*, in good measure, filling out the outline not simply in the satirical perceptions of the Man from Mars, and his elder alter ego, Jubal Harshaw, but also in the development of the mingled Earth-Mars religion that the "visitor" establishes. But the meaning of all this talk is very dependent on what happens, both to the Man from Mars, and his mentor, who stand in for Christ and the "doubting" apostle, Thomas; if their opinions have any meaning at all, it must be supported by their actions and reactions in a story with heavily mythical reverberations. (p. 148)

Its choppy structure, unrealistic characters, talky presentation, frequently banal style and inconsistent tone immediately mark [*Stranger*] unsatisfactory by most literary criteria. But the plausibility of its science fictions, the isolated effectiveness of some of its scenes, the coherence of Mike's world-view and the logic of its unifying symbols suggest that something other than realistic criteria may legitimately be invoked.

At the center of the story are Mike's martyrdom and Jubal's apostolic succession, Heinlein's ambivalence toward which is responsible for the uncertain, hybrid manner in which the tale is told. (p. 155)

[The] novel is uneven at best to a critical reading, which values the shape and style of a book, its consistency both internal and with the world outside. . . . Idiosyncratic manipulation of point-of-view is perhaps the most blatant example, but it reveals an inconsistency of focus and other discontinuities of style and approach. (pp. 155-56)

Given this arbitrary jumping back and forth and around, a reader is unsure of what to focus on. Mike is in the background, then the foreground, then the background; Jubal is a filter, then Ben is a filter for Jubal. On the outskirts of the action, the omniscient narrator sometimes exposes us to the general follies of mankind, the millennial meditations of the Martians, and the uninspired horseplay of the supposedly comic angels. (p. 156)

Although one seldom knows what Heinlein's characters look like in any of his books, where they go and what they do are usually clearly visualized. But Mars, this time around, is a shadow of its former self in *Red Planet*.

The characters are a mixed lot, none of them substantial from a realistic standpoint. (p. 157)

The only characters approaching depth or consistency are Mike and Jubal, though they take some abrupt turns, too, and are in some ways different versions of the same person. . . . Even more than the others, they are predominantly talk, especially Jubal. One of his functions, of course, is just that, to talk, to act as a mouthpiece for Heinlein's observations, some of them scathing, on the contemporary (1960) scene. . . . But he can't stop talking, about anything and everything, even if he contradicts himself, or violates the good sense he is also supposed to represent in contrast to the dictates of custom. (pp. 158-59)

Nowhere, perhaps, is Heinlein's inconsistency more irritating than in his refusal to establish a position from which the whole farrago can be viewed. . . . The deepening tone as the story goes on suggests taking Mike and his Church seriously, but the makings of his religion are preposterous—and are so labeled within the book—and his own immortality removes any tragic sting from his death.

It is as if Heinlein had been seized by a story with its own inexorable logic, then sought to undercut its effectiveness by devices that might absolve him of responsibility for the story's message. . . . The commitment in this story was to nothing less than martyrdom, the myth of the dying god whose demise liberates his followers; but being forced into the position of offering that lesson to his readers seems to have been unacceptable to Heinlein's better judgment.

For all that it fails to work as a realistic novel, however, *Stranger* is not totally removed from the plane of the plausible, and it does have a symbolic coherence. (pp. 159-60)

The internal contradictions of the book center on the symbiotic but contradictory relationship between Mike and Jubal, who are both versions of the Heinleinian "competent man." Both are puppet masters, manipulating others as if they had no wills of their own, paying no real attention to anyone except each other. If Jubal is Mike's teacher at the beginning, the roles are soon reversed; since there is not room for two puppet masters in the story, one must give way. The structure of the story dictates that Mike's commitment must win out over Jubal's skepticism, but not without a struggle. The problems of point-of-view and ground level of reality are among the evidences that the fight is incompletely resolved.

The story is about Mike, if we can believe the titles of the five parts, each of which represents a stage in the development of a hero. As a young man, Mike seems to have something in common with the protagonists of Heinlein's juveniles; their characters are in the process of formation, as they learn how to survive in the big world, survival being the prime virtue for a Heinlein hero. Unlike the juvenile heroes, however, Mike does not have to learn how to put up with limitations; superior in every way, he does not so much develop as reveal himself in all his glory. . . . He is not so much a character as the story itself; his function is to happen.

If we see him as a person at all, it is as a perpetual innocent. . . . He is untouched by his learning, except that he discovers better how to cope; he does not form his character by compromise as Heinlein's earlier adolescent heroes did. Sex and pity do not corrupt his innocence, as neither involves his really interacting with anyone else; in fact, his disciples either are, or become, equally innocent, or holy. Perhaps only innocents could live up to the angelic commitment of their faith, a commitment that in Mike's case will lead not to survival in the usual sense, but rather to martyrdom. Heinlein undercuts that ending, of course, but at a cost; Jubal must become apostle to the risen god, after playing Thomas to Mike's Messiah.

This is an ill-fitting role for Jubal to play, not only in the context of the book, but also in the niche Jubal occupies among Heinlein's creations. . . . [He] is predominantly skeptical and uncommitted, pragmatic about what works but amoral about the values he knows so well how to manipulate. A manipulator of people as well, he is only slightly more respectful of them, and never awed, except for his conversion to faith in Mike.

But there is another side to Jubal as well, some of which is coincident with this characterization, some of which comes out mainly in his apostolic function late in the book. Skeptical, he does not necessarily reject commitment as a matter of principle. He seems to revel in his own contradictions, but he is also world-weary. As an intellectual in a society he can manipulate, he is to some extent a victim of *anomie:* rootless, lacking social norms and values. Jill calls him cynical, which implies a disillusioned idealism; he wants to believe in something, but can't.

When Mike gives him something to believe in, Truth, which his senses can not deny, Jubal capitulates, but he resists all the way. (pp. 166-67)

Jubal's changeability is also evident in his opinions, of which there are a myriad. This aspect of his character is the primary vehicle of Heinlein's satire, but in a number of cases, the satirist is inconsistent, either recanting what he said earlier, or acting contrary to an expressed belief. (p. 168)

Jubal is parallel to Heinlein not only in profession, his avowed commercialism, but also in some of his opinions and their inconsistency, in his individualism and general crotchetiness, in his all-around experience and competence, even in age (i.e., Jubal must have been born around 1907 to be his apparent age around the turn of the next century). And Jubal is the major viewpoint character of the book, not acting so much as reacting, primarily to the Man from Mars. His consistency, such as it is, is all we have to go on, inside the book, in judging or evaluating Mike and his behavior. What Mike does, Jubal explains, rationalizing away his own rationality at times. Thus he acts as a surrogate for the reader. If this skeptic can become a believer, this individualist can become part of a self-effacing movement, this critic of man's folly can learn to love his neighbor, how long can we be expected to hold out . . .? (pp. 169-70)

Charting Heinlein's self-consciousness has been the thankless, self-appointed task of Alexei Panshin, who is convinced that underneath the extroverted, commercial exterior there is indeed an excited and terrified interior man. For Panshin, the key to the real Heinlein, the "private language" as it were, is the author's fascination with solipsism, the belief that no one, perhaps nothing, exists except oneself, that all is illusion produced by one's imagination. (pp. 170-71)

In *Stranger in a Strange Land,* solipsism is implicit in the manipulations of Mike and Jubal, especially in Mike's mental power over inanimate and animate matter. (p. 171)

The true solipsist of the piece, however, is Heinlein himself, like any author willing his creations into existence. For all his claims, in various places, to want people to live by "the scientific method," his imagined societies work—on paper, despite the carpings of critics—because he wills them to. According to the dust jacket of *Stranger,* his admittedly unreachable "purpose in writing this novel was to examine every major axiom of Western culture, to question every axiom, throw doubt on it—and, if possible—to make the antithesis of each axiom appear a possible and perhaps a desirable thing—rather than unthinkable." This grandiose scheme seems conceivable only to an author who takes it for granted that he can create the real and unreal alike, and make his audience sit still for it. Like Jubal, he may be "fooling around," but for serious purposes.

One of them—as Panshin insists—is a concern for what life is worth living for; why else would he throw in all those passages in which Jubal opines about creation, life and death, art and religion? Heinlein's perennial answer is survival for its own sake; thus Jubal, like Lazarus Long in *Methuselah's Children* and *Time Enough for Love,* seems destined to live forever. But Jubal is also a creator—of commercial art, and of Mike, who repays the compliment by calling him "father," making him a "patron saint," and waiting for his blessing before he accepts his martyrdom. As a creator—the original solipsist—Jubal/Heinlein knows that none of this exists except in his imagination, but his creation is troublesome. Mike is invincibly innocent, as Jubal/Heinlein is not, though he may have nostalgic longings for that state. His creation nourishes him—literally in the story, as a broth—forcing him to feed off himself. If Jubal is a mirror, as he tells Ben, in which Mike sees what he wants to see, Mike is the same, for Jubal/Heinlein and for many readers. Mike, however, has the Martian sense of appreciating life as a rounded whole; he seems to know what life is worth living—and dying—for. (p. 172)

The book's confusion, then, stems in part from the contradiction between an exemplary tale of men like gods and a solip-

sistic sense that it's all make-believe. The sophisticated reader may see this as confusion, rejecting both fantasies as adolescent wish-fulfillment. But the more naive audience might more easily accept what it wants to, from the satirical denigration of common knowledge and established tradition to the assumption of godlike powers. The audience in the Sixties, I suspect, has the latter reaction. . . . College students, and other members of the "counterculture" that grew in the wake of the loss of John Kennedy's dream of Camelot, and in shared opposition to a technocratic society that had no use for them except as cannon fodder, devoured *Stranger in a Strange Land* and handed it on. Its reputation grew by word of mouth, as a "book of wisdom" for our time, an "underground classic."

Heinlein was regarded as a sage, a guru, unafraid to give direction, when more conventional teachers feared to advocate anything but tolerance. (p. 173)

Criticism of the book for bad taste in style or contents would hardly have been welcome, except as evidence of the critic's defense of the Establishment. Besides, old-fashioned ideas of taste were part of what the book attacked. In addition, it offered, with impenetrably confusing irony, a new program to establish utopia on Earth in which everyone who believed would love and share. It even seemed to be preaching revolution, at the cost of martyrdom if necessary. And the decade bore these supposed teachings out, in abortive form, from the Flower Children to the Weathermen. Even the most "shocking" aspects of *Stranger* seem pale against the background of the last seventeen years, and its solipsism fits right in to today's "laid-back" hedonism, in which everyone is trying to find—or create the "real me."

As the book's popularity grew throughout the decade, Heinlein would have been a fool not to see where the growing audience was. The three novels he wrote during this period were more conventional, though studded with social commentary. But by the Seventies the lesson took hold and his most recent books, disliked intensely in the science fiction community but snapped up by the public at large, are primarily novels of sex and opinions. The world as it is they virtually condemn out of hand, while they indulge in wish-fulfillment fantasies with hardly a glance back at plausibility.

The rest of the science fiction community—not to mention Hollywood—were not slow to catch on, either. . . . The vast majority of "science fiction" marketed in the seventies . . . seems totally divorced from any real world of scientific, technological, social, and psychological limits. (pp. 173-74)

Heinlein did not create that market, any more than he created Charles Manson. But he was among the first in the postwar era to exploit it, and to confirm his reputation, if not as a forger of new trails, at least as a barometer of public taste. An intensely personal book, *Stranger in a Strange Land* also implied a great deal about the state of society, past and future, in spite of its dearth of futuristic trappings. The makings of a significant work of art may be buried in it, in a welter of story and symbol and correspondences between art and sex and religion. But a better book might have defeated its purpose. The problem of what to do with one's life was at the root of the Sixties' social unrest, just as it is today in the "Me" Decade. A better book would not have spoken to that ferment in the same way, and could never have had as great an effect. (p. 175)

David N. Samuelson, " 'Stranger' in the Sixties: Model or Mirror?'' in Critical Encounters: Writers and Themes in Science Fiction, *edited by Dick Riley (copyright © 1978 by Frederick Ungar Publishing Co., Inc.), Ungar, 1978, pp. 144-75.*

JOSEPH D. OLANDER AND MARTIN HARRY GREENBERG

Robert A. Heinlein is an outstanding figure in modern American science fiction. He has published voluminously, his science fiction sells well, and his work continues to be in print. His *Stranger in a Strange Land* and *Starship Troopers* have sold in the millions, especially in college bookstores. He has been described as one of the "fathers" of modern science fiction. He is also one of the few science fiction writers who have helped in making science fiction well known in "mainstream" literary circles.

But Heinlein is also a writer whose fiction and ideas often lead to strong feelings and reactions. Throughout his work, Heinlein appears to adopt positions favored by the American political right. . . . He is enthusiastic about what he considers the importance of military-style discipline to hold a community together. He exhibits a strong respect for custom in his work, although he makes it clear that custom must not stand in the way of societal change. When his heroes are in control of society, Heinlein resists criticism with "love it or leave it"; when they are out of power, he becomes a strong advocate of the right of revolution.

To dwell on the content of his advocacy, however, is to miss the opportunity to take advantage of the insights of his science fiction. Among them are perspectives and issues which relate to some of the perennial concerns of philosophy, such as the best form of government, whether and to what extent political utopias are possible, and the dimensions of power, liberty, equality, justice, and order. Sexuality, family, love, and immortality are also major themes in his fiction. The quality of his style certainly comes in for severe criticism, but the treatment of his subject is frequently insightful.

Plots usually center around a protagonist—the famous "Heinlein hero"—who is always tough, just, relatively fearless when it counts, and endowed with extraordinary skills and physical prowess. The protagonist's most noteworthy characteristic—whether male or female—is "competence." Heinlein defines competence partially as success, partially as ability (in fields like mathematics or engineering), partially as capability for fighting—but, most important, as the capacity to survive. For Heinlein, individual or collective survival is the criterion which seems to shape the structure and thematic apparatus of his fiction. Through it, major political, ethical, and moral questions can be examined. (pp. 7-8)

While Heinlein is concerned with the survival of the group and of the race, his emphasis is on the survival of those individuals within society with the talent and the courage to ensure racial survival—the competent. The view that the survival of the fittest equals the survival of the best finds contemporary expression in his science fiction. Survival for the competent is a prerequisite for the survival of the rest, and from this perspective flows his attitude toward morality.

But one should not be misguided by this simplification, for Heinlein often forces us to recognize basic questions: What kind of political order do we ourselves live in? Does it affirm, reaffirm, or deny our own good qualities as human beings? What instruments, purposes, and values does our own political order serve? What will it serve in the future, and what will it mean in terms of our survival as a species and as individuals?

We may be surprised to learn that Heinlein's fiction points less to the importance of technological tools to help us confront the future and more to our need to reexamine ourselves. (pp. 8-9)

Joseph D. Olander and Martin Harry Greenberg, in their introduction to Robert A. Heinlein, *edited by Joseph D. Olander and Martin Harry Greenberg (copyright © 1978 by Joseph D. Olander and Martin Harry Greenberg; published by Taplinger Publishing Co., Inc., New York; reprinted by permission), Taplinger, 1978, pp. 7-11.*

JACK WILLIAMSON

I suspect that [Heinlein's] most enduring work will turn out to be the dozen juvenile novels he wrote for Scribner's after the war.

Juvenile science fiction, as a labeled category, begins with Heinlein—though in fact most of the earlier magazine science fiction had been written for youthful readers and censored of anything likely to give offense. There had been new inventions, too, in Tom Swift and the dime novels, but no real futurology. The Heinlein series was a pioneer effort, quickly imitated. . . .

Based on solidly logical extrapolations of future technology and future human history, [the novels] are cleanly constructed and deftly written, without the digressions and the preaching that often weaken the drama in his later work.

What I most admire about them is Heinlein's dogged faith in us and our destiny. No blind optimist, he is very much aware of evil days to come. His future worlds are often oppressively misruled, pinched by hunger, and wasted by war. Yet his heroes are always using science and reason to solve problems, to escape the prison Earth, to seek and build better worlds. (p. 15)

Heinlein never writes down. His main characters are young, the plots move fast, and the style is limpidly clear; but he never insults the reader's intelligence. (p. 16)

Heinlein's heroes are pretty much alike—all competent people. The protagonists of the juvenile novels are born bright, and we see them learning how to do everything. They mature into the all-around experts of his adult fiction and finally mellow into such extraordinary oldsters as Jubal Harshaw and Lazarus Long.

These efficient folk reflect Heinlein himself. [Jonathan] Swift wrote *Gulliver's Travels* to satirize man's self-important faith in his own reason. Heinlein clearly belongs to the satirized camp, and his people embody the attitudes of the self-confident, reasonable man, the scientist who yearns to know all about the universe and the technologist who toils to control it.

I suspect that this independent individualism can explain Heinlein's often-puzzling bits of irrational mysticism, for example the interludes in heaven in *Stranger in a Strange Land* and the climactic scene in *Starman Jones* when Max has a sense of the dead astrogator standing behind his chair to help him guide the lost ship back through the anomaly. Lacking any rational basis for belief in personal immortality, Heinlein and his heroes must either face the inevitability of death or somehow evade it. The long life of Lazarus Long appears to be an evasion, and the flashes of mysticism must be wishful escapes from the rational universe that neither the writer nor his people can finally master.

Actually, I think the supercompetent characters serve Heinlein well. He is no Tolstoy, recording known life. His major motif has always been future technology, treated with some degree of optimism. The theme itself implies people who invent, build, use, and enjoy machines. Technological man has to be rational and competent.

Yet there's a conflict here that I don't think Heinlein has ever fully resolved. As evolving technologies become more and more complex, so does the teamwork needed to support them. Heinlein seems completely aware of this when he is carrying his young protagonists through their education and their rites of initiation, yet he often seems unhappy with the sacrifice of personal freedom that a technological culture seems to require. In **The Rolling Stones**, for instance, his competent people are in full flight from their mechanized environment. (pp. 16-17)

[In Heinlein's first juvenile novel **Rocket Ship Galileo** (1947) the] plot is often trite, and the characters are generally thin stereotypes, with none of the colorful human beings and charming aliens soon to follow. Too, the book has dated badly. Anticipating the first flights to the Moon, it's a poor prediction. The rocket builders work almost alone, on a tiny budget, with no seeming need for the vast NASA organization. The villains are Nazis, an idea perhaps not so badly worn in 1947 as it seems today. The spacecraft land horizontally, like airplanes, rather than on their tails. The action stops for science lectures not related to the story. Yet the book is still readable, with Heinlein's familiar themes already emerging. (p. 17)

Space Cadet, published in 1948, is a long step forward. The characters are stronger, and they use more of the wisecracking dialogue that gradually became a Heinlein hallmark. The background is carefully built, original, and convincing, the story suspenseful enough. Set a century after **Rocket Ship Galileo**, it has few of the discrepancies with history that date the first book. . . .

Here he is already perfecting the *Bildungsroman* form that shapes the whole series. His heroes are learning, maturing, discovering their social roles. The rite-of-passage pattern shows most clearly when Matt goes home from the Space Academy to find himself alienated from his own past. (p. 18)

Heinlein's intellectual kinship with H. G. Wells appears in the theme of the novel: the idea that common men must be guided and guarded by a competent elite. Like Wells, he is something of a classicist; rejecting the romantic notion that society corrupts, he assumes instead that we need social training to save us. I suppose this feeling was fostered by his own military training. Though stated with most force in **Starship Troopers**, it appears in such early stories as "**The Roads Must Roll**," and it becomes a basic premise for the *Bildungsroman* pattern of the juveniles—a premise often in conflict with Heinlein's own deep sense of romantic individualism. (pp. 18-19)

With **Red Planet**, published in 1940, Heinlein found his true direction for the series. The Martian setting is logically constructed and rich in convincing detail. . . . The characters are engaging and the action develops naturally. Here, for the first time, Heinlein is making the most of his aliens. Willis, the young Martian nymph, is completely real and completely delightful. The whole tone of the book is set by the contrasts between the selfish human bureaucrats who exploit the settlers and the courteous and benign Martians who save them.

The aliens and robots of science fiction are commonly interesting only as symbols of human traits and feelings, and Hein-lein makes his extraterrestrials an important part of the symbolic structure. Sometimes they are antagonists; those in **Starman Jones** and **Time for the Stars** can stand for the hostility of untamed nature. But more commonly they are neutral or friendly, and they often serve as teachers for the maturing heroes.

The essential action of the *Bildungsroman* is the process of conflict and growth that replaces native animal traits with social behavior. In **Red Planet,** the Company and its minions stand for the primitive self, the Martians for society. Like society itself, they are old but timeless, wise, bound by custom and tradition. Some of them are ghosts, transcending individual death as society does. (p. 19)

Farmer in the Sky, published in 1950, is a hymn to the pioneer. The sky frontier is on Ganymede, Jupiter's largest moon, but the plot parallels the familiar history of the colonization of America—the torch ship that carries the settlers from Earth is named the *Mayflower*.

As a novel of education, the book shows the creation of a rugged individualist. Heinlein uses point of view of unified action that covers half a billion miles of space and a good deal of time, letting Bill Lermer tell his own story in a relaxed, conversational style. Bill is a Scout—the novel was serialized in *Boy's Life*—and Scout training helps to build his competent self-reliance. The contrasting characters are the incompetent misfits who expect society to solve their problems.

The story has a harsh realism unusual for a juvenile. The migrants leave the overpopulated Earth to escape hunger and the threat of war. They struggle to survive on a world never meant for men. More than half are killed by a destructive quake. They meet no friendly aliens, though, near the end, Bill and his friend discover a cache of machines left long ago by a mysterious space visitor. Not very important in the story, this incident does give the reader a welcome break from the grimly hostile setting. (p. 20)

Between Planets, published in 1951, moves the series still further from its juvenile origins toward grown-up concerns. Though we meet the space-born hero while he is still a schoolboy in New Mexico, at the end of the novel he is a combat-tested fighting man with marriage in view. (p. 21)

Though some of the action is pretty traditional space opera, the characters are ably drawn and Heinlein closes the novel with a vigorous statement of his unhappiness with "the historical imperative of the last two centuries, the withering away of individual freedom under larger and [ever] more pervasive organizations, both governmental and quasi-governmental." (pp. 21-2)

The Rolling Stones, published in 1952, displays an inevitable craftsmanship. The narrative is episodic and nearly plotless, a fact that Heinlein emphasizes with the contrast between the lives of his protagonists and the events of the melodramatic adventure serial they are writing about the Galactic Overlord. Discarding most of the standard devices for suspense, he is still able to compel the reader's interest in his lively people and their almost aimless wanderings from Luna City to Mars and the Asteroids and on toward Saturn . . . and "the ends of the Universe."

They are the Stone family, ranging in age from the apparently immortal Grandmother Hazel, through the teenaged "unheavenly twins," Castor and Pollux, down to Lowell, the infant genius who can already beat his grandmother at chess. (p. 22)

The Stones leave Luna City in a secondhand spaceship, with no motives except an impatience with social restraints and an itch to see the universe. With the father in command, as captain of the ship, the family becomes once more the fully independent social unit.

Here, I believe, Heinlein is dramatizing a personal concern that is also a dilemma of our technological world. Advancing technology not only asks competent people to master special skills, but it also asks for smooth cooperation. The increasingly complex division of labor requires a social discipline strong enough to prevent sabotage and acts of terrorism, to restrain the power grabs of narrow selfish interests, to unite workers and managers, to fuse the elite and the mass. The protection of the world machines requires a painful sacrifice of personal freedom which I think Heinlein is reluctant to accept.

But *The Rolling Stones,* unlike such later works as *Farnham's Freehold,* carries its thematic burden lightly. It is a delightful romp through space, brightened with such terms as the Martian flat cats, which multiply like the guinea pigs in Ellis Parker Butler's famous funny story (''Pigs is Pigs''), until the money-minded twins find a market for them in the meteor-mining colony.

Much of the effect comes as usual from the sense of an accurately extrapolated future background, with all the new technologies given an air of commonplace reality. The used spaceship, for example, is bought from ''Dealer Dan, the Spaceship Man,'' who is drawn after today's used-car salesmen. Though the meteor miners use radar and rocket scooters, they live like forty-niners. (p. 23)

Starman Jones, published in 1953, is a classic example of the *Bildungsroman* pattern and perhaps my own favorite of the series. Max Jones is a poor, hill farm boy faced with the hard problem of finding the place he wants in a closed society. With Heinlein's reasonably consistent future history moving on, the old torch ship *Einstein* has become the starship *Asgard,* now equipped with Horst-Conrad impellers that can drive her at the speed of light and beyond, to jump her across the light-years through the congruences of a folded universe. Max wants to be a starman, but his way is barred by a rigid guild system that has no room for him.

Good science fiction mixes the known and the new—in more formal terms, it recognizes that we can perceive and respond to those items that can somehow attach to the mental structures we already possess. Heinlein gives us exciting novelties enough in Max's universe, but not without his usual deft preparation. We see Max slopping the hogs and feeding the chickens before he runs away from an intolerable ''step-stepmother'' and her insufferable new husband to look for his way to the stars.

For all his social handicaps, he has several things going for him: a genius for math, an eidetic memory, a friend named Sam. . . . Sam is an older man, a figure who neatly complements Max in the role-finding pattern of the novel. Once an Imperial Marine, he has lost his social place because he lacks Max's moral strength. Now a colorful conniver, whose entertaining speech tag is his habit of mixing familiar proverbs, he gives his life at the end of the book in full atonement for his social faults. (pp. 23-4)

Aboard the *Asgard* with forged papers provided by Sam, [Max] is always in a precarious position, his social status always in jeopardy, yet he learns to make the most of social opportunity. At the end, when all the other qualified astrogators are dead

and the tech manuals and tables are missing, it is Max alone who can take command and pilot the ship through the new congruity, back to galactic civilization.

With its bold symbolism, the book makes a universal appeal. We are all born lonely individualists; we must all make the same struggle, often hard and painful, for a foothold in society. Though there is unlikely coincidence and occasional melodrama in Max's story, such faults don't matter. The novel is a fine juvenile, but also something more. It reflects hopes and fears we all have known.

Star Beast, published in 1954, is vastly different from *Starman Jones* but equally outstanding. (pp. 24-5)

[*Star Beast*] is a wildly delightful comedy grown from Heinlein's continual concern with the able individual in conflict with incompetent pretenders. Most of the fun comes from our anarchistic joy in the successful defiance of rigid social norms and the stupid people who attempt to enforce them. The victims of this satiric exposure range from the Westville city officials to the bumbling politician who is Mr. Kiku's nominal superior. (p. 25)

[The] devastating shots at society and its leaders imply the same reservations about popular rule that H. G. Wells often expressed. Near the end of the book, Mr. Kiku says that the government ''is not now a real democracy and it can't be.'' Majority rule might be good, ''But it's rarely that easy. We find ourselves oftener the pilots of a ship in a life-and-death emergency. Is it the pilot's duty to hold powwows with the passengers? Or is it his job to use his skill and experience to bring them safely home?''

But the book is no sermon. Though this familiar theme is stated with force enough, it isn't allowed to spoil the fun. . . . (pp. 25-6)

Tunnel in the Sky, published in 1955, lacks the mad fascination of *Star Beast,* though it is built on a wonderful story idea. Life has now become lean on the crowded future Earth, but the star gates are opening on new planets all across the galaxy. Since some of these are dangerous, the schools teach survival. Rod Walker is a high school senior who is dropped with his classmates on an unfriendly new world for a survival test. When a nova explosion disables their gate, the young people are left on their own.

Though the situation is much like that in [William] Golding's *Lord of the Flies,* the development is vastly different. In Golding's book, we watch civilization dissolve into savagery; Heinlein's heroes, before they are rescued, have begun to plant a vigorous new civilization. Golding is a classicist, I think, distrusting the human animal; Heinlein, though half a classicist in making the social adaptation of the naive individual the subject of the whole series, is still I think somehow a romanticist at heart, rejoicing in competent individualism and conceding no more than he must to society.

Another novel of education, *Tunnel in the Sky* begins with both Rod and his teacher uncertain that he is ready for the survival test. On his upward way to leadership in the accidental colony, he must learn to cope with human rivals as well as with an unkind environment. Yet, though the book sometimes seems to have been planned as a parable of man and society, the theme is blurred. The ending strikes me as arbitrary; with the star gate reopened, the young people simply abandon their social experiment.

The problem, I suspect, is another unresolved conflict between Heinlein's romantic individualism and his awareness of the social discipline required by a technological culture. The best writing is in the first half of the book, in which Rod's competence for survival is being developed in conflicts with savage nature and savage-seeming human beings. The latter chapters, in which he is establishing social relationships within the new culture, seem oddly flat and hollow. He avoids sex relationships in a hardly normal way—though his behavior here may have been only Heinlein's concession to his juvenile editors.

In any case, the book simply fails to live up to its initial promises. We are told in the opening that man, "the two-legged brute," is the most dangerous animal in the universe, "which goes double for the female of the species." The first half of the book supports that assumption, but then the human menace fades, leaving only the wilderness planet with its less-than-human threats.

Yet the book is far from bad. The setting, as always, is solidly done. We feel the pinch of want on the overpopulated Earth and we understand the history and the working of the planetary gates that have made migration an alternative to war. (pp. 26-7)

In *Time for the Stars,* published in 1956, Heinlein drops back in history to an age when the torch ships are first venturing beyond the solar system to find room for teeming humanity on new planets. Traveling at less than light-speed, the explorer ships take many years for each crossing between stars, and few of them return.

The plot builds from the idea that telepathy, existing most often between twins, can cross interstellar distances with no time lag. Often in science fiction psionics becomes a wild card allowed to wreck all story logic, but here Heinlein limits and explores it in a completely believable way. (p. 27)

Citizen of the Galaxy, published in 1957, is a sort of epilogue to the whole Scribner's series. The other books, taken together, tell an epic story of the expansion of mankind across the planets of our own Sun and the stars beyond. All that is now past history. The plot action begins off the Earth, in the tyrannic Empire of the Nine Worlds, and carries us on a grand tour of galactic cultures already long established. (p. 28)

As the story of a young man's education and self-discovery, this clearly fits the classic juvenile pattern. . . . The opening is gripping; the old beggar and the slave boy compel our sympathy; the several settings are detailed with Heinlein's usual captivating skill; the whole novel still reads well.

Yet, for all its ambitious scope, it has major faults. The jumps from one setting to another break it almost into a series of novelettes. . . . Too, I miss the new technologies that add so much genuine wonder to the other books. With the conquest of space already complete, however, I see no real need for new inventions here, and I suppose Heinlein's interests were already shifting from the physical to the social sciences, from gadgets to cultures—the culture of the Free Traders is certainly an anthropologist's delight. In the next novel, anyhow, he comes back to physical science, with one last completely fascinating gadget.

Have Space Suit—Will Travel, published in 1958, brings the series to a highly satisfying climax. The novel opens on a near-future, very familiar Earth. The hero is Kip, another bright and likable boy, who tells his own story in his own breezy style. He wants to go to the Moon, and things begin when he

tries for a free trip offered in an advertising giveaway and wins a badly used space suit.

Again we have the rite-of-passage pattern, but done with unusual love and verve. Kip's world is convincingly familiar: he reads *National Geographic* and attends Centerville High and works after school as a soda jerk. His story moves fast. Though he packs it with simplified scientific fact and with philosophic ideas picked up from his individualistic father, he never stops to preach.

The space suit is the essential gadget. It's worthless junk when Kip receives it from the satirized sellers of soap, but he rebuilds it in time to become involved, along with an eleven-year-old girl genius, in a melodramatic space adventure. The girl, Peewee Reisfeld, has been caught by a gang of evil, worm-faced aliens who have also captured the Mother Thing, a furry and appealing creature who is a sort of galactic cop. There is a good deal of routine space opera in the plot action that carries us stage by stage to the Moon, to Pluto, to the Mother Thing's home on Vega V, out to the capital of the Three Galaxies in the Lesser Magellanic Cloud, and finally back again to Earth. With Heinlein's zest and his fine detail, however, the stereotypes are well disguised. Peewee and the Mother Thing are likable people, and the story still holds me.

At the crisis, Kip and Peewee find themselves the spokesmen for the human race before a high court that has already exterminated the worm-faced villains and now charges humanity with being too savage and too intelligent, therefore too dangerous to be left alive. The trial becomes a test of Heinlein's symbolic competent character, perhaps of his own philosophy. (pp. 28-30)

The happy outcome, after an appeal from the compassionate Mother Thing, is that humanity is placed on probation and Kip and Peewee are returned to Earth. Kip is a soda jerk once more, but now with the nerve to toss a chocolate malt into the face of a boy who has bullied him. . . . The series couldn't have had a finer conclusion.

Following the same story-of-education pattern, [*Starship Troopers*] traces the making of a starship soldier. In contrast to *Have Space Suit—Will Travel,* however, it is a dark, disturbing novel, set in a time of vicious space war and devoted to glorification of the fighting man. (p. 30)

Considering the Scribner's books as a group, we can claim for them a major role in the evolution of modern science fiction. Certainly they gave many thousand young readers, and thousands not so young, a delightful introduction to the genre. Built on sound futurology, they still make a fine primer for the new reader. The best of them are splendid models of literary craftsmanship, with more discipline and finish than most of Heinlein's other work. Revealing significant conflicts and shifts of thought, they are relevant to any survey of his whole career.

If their generally optimistic vision of space conquest is not so popular now as it once was, one reason is that we have almost abandoned our real space programs, giving up our grand designs to probe too often into festering "inner space." Our loss of faith in our future and our science and ourselves will surely become a global tragedy if it is not recovered. These books have a spirit too great to be forgotten. They need to be read again. (pp. 30-1)

Jack Williamson, "Youth Against Space: Heinlein's
Juveniles Revisited," in Robert A. Heinlein, edited
by Joseph D. Olander and Martin Harry Greenberg

(copyright © 1978 by Joseph D. Olander and Martin Harry Greenberg; published by Taplinger Publishing Co., Inc., New York; reprinted by permission), Taplinger, 1978, pp. 15-31.

GERALD JONAS

It is often said that Robert Heinlein was one of the handful of writers (John W. Campbell Jr. and Isaac Asimov are others usually mentioned) who created modern science fiction. This may explain the strain of hubris in his most recent novel [*The Number of the Beast*] in which he seems bound to destroy his own brainchild, or at least reduce it to a figment of his imagination, together with the entire known universe and a number of other universes as well. Since this is a Heinlein novel, and not the product of some imprecise unscience-fiction writer, we know the exact number of universes the author has in mind: "Six raised to its sixth power, and the result in turn raised to its sixth power. That number is *this*: 1.03144+ x 10^{28}—or written in full, 10,314,424,798,490,535,546,171,949,056—or more than ten million sextillion universes in our group."

This gives a fair sample of Mr. Heinlein's style, or I should say one of his styles. His characters, two men and two women who go gallivanting through the cosmos in a "continua craft" that one of them has invented, are not merely super-intelligent: They are also super-brave, super-knowledgeable and super-sexy. . . . Here is what the older woman says: "I refuse to be the campus widow who seduces younger men. Save for minor exceptions close to my age, I have always bedded older men. When I was your age, I tripped several three times my age. Educational." That qualifying phrase—"Save for minor exceptions"—is purest Heinlein, combining his passion for accuracy with his conviction, expressed more and more boldly in his most recent novels, that women and men and computers talk alike, think alike and function pretty much alike, except in what one character calls the "methods and mores of sexual copulation."

I have discussed style before plot because this novel consists almost entirely of dialogue in which it is impossible to tell who is speaking. This makes it difficult to follow the plot. But such difficulties, like everything else in the book, dissolve at the end into a long solipsistic set-piece in which Mr. Heinlein makes fun of science-fiction conventions, science-fiction readers, other science-fiction writers and his own penchant for solipsistic fiction—as expressed, for example, in his much-anthologized short story **"All You Zombies,"** which took a philosophical conundrum—"How do I know anyone else is real?—and pressed it to its logical conclusion. **"The Number of the Beast"** fails because it plays with ideas that it ultimately fails to respect.

In a multiplex cosmos where everything is possible, the concepts of "fact" and "fiction" lose their meaning. The people in this book suffer a similar fate; their poses and pedantries—which Mr. Heinlein so meticulously recounts—are reduced to mere verbiage in a totally arbitrary setting. The author apparently wants it both ways: He wants to awe us with the implications of a cosmos where "everything is possible," and at the same time he wants to lecture us on his philosophy of life, which comes down to a string of aphorisms: "One must accept death, learn not to fear it, then never worry about it." "Cops and courts no longer protect citizens, so citizens must protect themselves." "*Every* major shortcoming of our native planet

could be traced to one cause: too many people, not enough planet."

Mr. Heinlein writes best about people struggling to overcome constraints, whether natural or man-made. In such books as **"Stranger in a Strange Land"** he achieved the goal of most science-fiction writers: a larger audience beyond the confines of the s.-f. genre. But like the characters in his latest novel, he doesn't seem to know what to do with his newfound freedom.

Gerald Jonas, "Other Worlds," in The New York Times Book Review *(© 1980 by The New York Times Company; reprinted by permission), September 14, 1980, pp. 12, 38.**

ALGIS BUDRYS

There are two ways to review Robert A. Heinlein's work since *Stranger in a Strange Land,* excepting . . . *The Moon is a Harsh Mistress.* With that exception, there is a pre-1961 Heinlein and then there is this "new" fellow. . . .

The old Heinlein was a crisp, slick wordsmith of uncommon intelligence and subtlety. His gift for characterization was sharp within its narrow limits, and those limits were fortuitously placed to include the archetypical science fiction hero. . . . All his people talked alike. You could tell the stupid and villainous from the worthy and heroic only by their choices of subject matter. But his dialogue worked; its purpose was to propel the story, and it served quite well. (p. 55)

The Number of the Beast reflects the quintessence of the "new" Heinlein. Where the pre-1961 writer clung to the old pulp tenets—Tell your story quickly, clearly, basing the resolution on physical action emerging from inner growth, and for God's sake never give the reader a chance to realize there's a writer involved—the new one repudiates them, deliberately.

The new Heinlein hero is perfect to begin with. The world is best served by acknowledging his perfection and acting in accordance as quickly as possible. The plot thread is a rambling one, strung with incidents whose one common purpose is to give the world, and the reader, time and evidence required to work out details of the hero's perfection. The nature of the incidents is not organic to the story. They do not grow out of the hero's explorations of his problem. They can't—he has no problems, only transient difficulties, and this is obvious from the first paragraphs.

Therefore, the incidents can take place anywhere, anytime, and must be attractive in themselves. They are not successively unlocked rooms in an unknown structure, through which the hero must pass to find the ideal egress. They are way-stations on a circular tour of the hero's nature, and they must be furnished to engage the reader's interest as a reader, rather than as an involved rider in the searching hero's head.

That results in a kind of game, with Heinlein visibly his own hero. At times he invents new-ish settings which are actually recalls of typical Heinlein settings. At other times he directly borrows settings—E. E. Smith's Lensman universe, the Land of Oz, and the universe of Lazarus Long. In every case, the reference is to the relationship between conscious author and reader, not between hero and the reader's subconscious role-playing as a hero-surrogate. There can be no doubt on either side that at all times there is a book involved. The magic of forgetting that the reader is actually sitting in a quiet room surrounded by creature comforts—that special magic which is what reading does for most of us—cannot occur. *The Number of The Beast* is a book for critics; for the reader as critic, not as participant. It can be impressive. It has cut itself off, by first intention, from any attempt to be compelling. (p. 56)

Algis Budrys, in his review of "The Number of the Beast" (reprinted by permission of the author), in The Magazine of Fantasy and Science Fiction, *Vol. 59, No. 4, October, 1980, pp. 55-6.*

H. BRUCE FRANKLIN

From 1947 through 1958, Robert Heinlein was primarily an author of science fiction aimed at the "juvenile" market, specifically at teenaged boys. Besides two minor novellas serialized in *Boys' Life,* the magazine of the Boy Scouts of America, there were twelve dazzlingly successful novels published as a juvenile series by Scribner's. These dozen novels have proved to be as popular and influential as anything Heinlein ever wrote, all going into continual mass-market reprintings, with several transposed into movie, television, and comic-strip versions. (p. 73)

[These works] form a coherent epic, the story of the conquest of space. Like the tales and sketches Heinlein was publishing in general-circulation magazines, these longer works are optimistic, expansionary, romantic, pulsing with missionary zeal for a colossal human endeavor and also throbbing with a fever to escape from the urbanized, complex, supposedly routinized and imprisoning experience of Earth. The central figures are always boys making their passage into becoming men, emblems of a human race attaining what Heinlein construes to be its maturity in the solar system, the galaxy, and beyond. (pp. 73-4)

The movement is outward bound. The first novel describes the first trip to the moon, the next five are set on and around Venus, Mars, the asteroids, and Jupiter; the ensuing five all involve voyages between Earth and parts of our galaxy beyond this solar system; and the final one climaxes someplace in the Lesser Magellanic Cloud, where our race is judged by the composite mind of the Three Galaxies. (p. 74)

The point-of-view character is usually a teenaged boy attempting to enter the adult world and often trying to relate to what he perceives as the even stranger world of females, who sometimes seem to him more alien than the strangest extraterrestrial life forms. The central subject, however, is space travel.

Space travel provides some ideal settings for an author who believes in the primacy of individual or small-group achievements and who wishes to indulge fantasies of escape from the late industrial world. Small heroic groups or individuals may be placed in dramatic situations alone in spaceships or on other planets, where their actions may have great consequences. There is, however, a contradiction, for space travel is the product of an entire highly industrialized, complexly organized society. Unaware of this, early science fiction could ignore it. Hence there was often the spectacle, amusingly archaic to us, of some lone genius inventing and building a spaceship in his workshop and launching it from his backyard. Later, a single industrial corporation could be imagined as the sole creator of a spaceship, of course through the genius of one or two scientists or engineers. By the close of World War II, however, it was fairly obvious that space travel would take the kind of vast, highly

socialized efforts that had developed the Nazi V-1 and V-2 rocket bombs or the U.S. atomic bombs. (pp. 74-5)

Many of the boys' books consist of extended tests of endurance, loyalty, courage, intelligence, integrity, and fortitude. They dramatize a personal ethic and pervasive social Darwinism, displaying how and why "fit" types survive while the "unfit"—the sulkers, the weaklings, the whiners, the lazy, the self-centered, the vicious—are eliminated. The first of these books is *Space Cadet* . . . , the story of how a boy from Des Moines, Iowa, becomes an officer in the Interplanetary Patrol. (pp. 76-7)

Most of the novel is a detailed account of the training program for Cadets—with emphasis on how the unfit are eliminated. Then comes the big adventure that shows the Patrol in action.

One of the Cadets eliminated as unfit is the son of a big capitalist, Chairman of the Board of Reactors, Ltd. He has his father make him captain of a merchant rocketship that is "transferred to the family corporation 'System Enterprises'" . . . , and he promptly attacks the peaceful, aquatic Venerians in an ill-fated attempt to exploit precious metals found in a taboo swamp. Our youthful hero and fellow Cadets find themselves having to rescue this greedy antithesis of their own values and establish peaceful relations with the Venerians, "the Little People."

The Venerians introduce what is soon to be a characteristic feature of these boys' books—charming, endearing, delightful space creatures, who often turn out to be at least as intelligent as the Terrans. Until their appearance in *Space Cadet,* the novel presents an almost purely masculine world, like the unrelieved male world of *Rocket Ship Galileo.* But all the Little People encountered by the Terrans, including the Venerian rulers and scientists, are female. This encounter with the feminine in an alien form gives a special psychological twist to this book written for adolescent boys.

In *Red Planet* . . . , the endearing creature is Willis, a bouncy and affectionate little pet who turns out to be a Martian in its first stage. Willis is attached to James Madison Marlow, Jr., who lives with his family on Mars in the South Colony, "a frontier society." . . . (pp. 77-8)

The novel is about growing up. Jim becomes a man. Willis prepares to metamorphose into a mature Martian. The colony issues a Proclamation of Autonomy modeled on the Declaration of Independence. Human society itself seems youthful compared with that of the Martians, who outgrew space travel millions of years ago. The general relevance of the theme of growing up is enunciated by a character found in many of Heinlein's novels, a warm-hearted old curmudgeon serving as the author's mouthpiece (and probably deriving from young Robert's memories of his grandfather, Dr. Lyle), in this case a grizzled doctor acting as Jim's true mentor. . . . (p. 78)

[The novella] **"Nothing Ever Happens on the Moon"** . . . [focuses] on the heroism, self-sacrifice, and resourcefulness of people conquering the new frontier of space. Here the two heroes are Boy Scouts, one from Earth and the other from the moon, trapped in a lunar cave, sharing their last cylinder of air, and persevering to survive. (p. 79)

[In *Farmer in the Sky*] the new frontier theme [becomes] the whole story.

These pioneers embark on spaceships named the *Mayflower* and the *Covered Wagon* to convert Ganymede, one of Jupiter's moons, into a world fit for terrestrials. Bill, the young narrator, and his family do not tarry long in the "frontier town" . . . , but move to become "homesteaders" . . . on the virgin soil, or rather virgin rock that they must convert to soil.

Heinlein, who began life as a boy in rural Missouri, here projects an imaginary future that resurrects one of the most cherished symbols of the American past, the family farm, with its combination, at least in the ideal, of cooperation and independence. "You can't do it alone" and "Pioneers need good neighbors" . . . are mottoes of these people, but the symbol of Bill's manhood is becoming "a property owner, paying my own way." . . . (pp. 79-80)

[*Between Planets*] was published first as a serial in an adult magazine . . . demonstrating that there is no clear demarcation of Heinlein's "juvenile" fiction. The novel's youthful protagonist, Don Harvey, embodies the next stage in the outward-bound movement of this space epic. Born in space, his parents both scientists who move from planet to planet, Don proudly claims, "'I'm a citizen of the System'." . . . Swept up in an interplanetary struggle, he moves toward a discovery of his true identity, one that makes homesteading on Ganymede as humdrum as life in the corn belt, for he is the true spaceman:

> He knew now where he belonged—in space,
> where he was born. Any planet was merely a
> hotel to him; space was his home.
>
> (pp. 80-1)

In lurid contrast to this soaring freedom spins the decadent planet Earth. As the story opens, Earth is on the verge of the war predicted toward the end of *Farmer in the Sky*. New Chicago is "a modern Babylon," a "Sodom and Gomorrah" displayed in a chapter entitled "Mene, Mene, Tekel, Upharsin" (the biblical handwriting on the wall). . . .

The Terran Federation itself has become the instrument of interplanetary colonialism and exploitation. . . . This generates, as in *Red Planet* and, later, *The Moon Is a Harsh Mistress*, an anti-colonial revolution modeled on the original American Revolution. (p. 81)

The last of the series kept within the confines of the solar system is *The Rolling Stones* . . . a novel glorifying the outward-bound Stone family, "a crew of rugged individualists" . . . , all geniuses . . . . Tiring of life on the moon, the Stones buy their own used spaceship and zip off for a two-year voyage of sightseeing and commerce to Mars and the asteroids, slipping in and out of scrapes all the way.

The episodes are structured like a serial, and seem intended to contrast with the science-fiction TV serial [the Stones] write collectively as they wander along. Heinlein has achieved one of the main objectives of the first half of his juvenile space epic: making the moon, Mars, and the asteroids as familiar and ordinary as Missouri. The TV series, *The Scourge of the Spaceways*, moving of course toward an inevitable confrontation with the Galactic Overlord, is thus a parody of the kind of science fiction Heinlein himself is pointedly not writing, at least not at this time. Yet the last paragraph of *The Rolling Stones* shows this domesticized spaceship, like its creators, preparing to move out from the tamed frontiers near Earth toward the ends of the solar system and beyond. . . . (pp. 82-3)

Starman Jones . . . is the story of a midwestern farm boy who becomes an astrogator. The young hero moves from the wretched loneliness of an orphan trapped on a dismal Earth to the glorious loneliness of guiding ships through space. . . .

Earth, now the center of an interstellar empire, has become a prison without hope, a rigidly structured society made up of three classes—the rich, a labor aristocracy organized into feudal guilds, and a semislave proletariat transported to the colonies as contract labor, "convicts and paupers." . . . (p. 83)

Only two alternatives to all these rigid structures are suggested. One is Heinlein's lost world of the frontier and the unspoiled American wilderness to be found on the planet Nova Terra, whose "comfortable looseness" seems like "anarchy" to Max, as Sam [a roguish, but heroic, picaro] describes it. . . . (p. 84)

The other alternative appears first as Sam is painting this idyllic picture, when Max interrupts to say, "'I don't want to get married.'" Sam responds. "'That's your problem.'" The girl who woos Max for half the book, concealing her own intelligence so as not to scare him off, ends up marrying another after Max rejects her. At the end, Max has chosen the lone, loveless, unfree, heroic life of the starman.

The Star Beast . . . is the only novel in the Scribner's series that takes place entirely on Earth. The action revolves around a creature from remote space, an eight-legged, brontosaurus-sized, fully omnivorous, lovable monster known as Lummox, the backyard pet of John Thomas Stuart XI, a teenager in a small Colorado town. (pp. 84-5)

As in *Red Planet*, there is a parallel between the growing up of the endearing space creature—in this case Lummox begins to sprout arms—and the growing up of the teenaged male protagonist. (p. 85)

In *Tunnel in the Sky* . . . an overpopulated Earth sends streams of colonists through special time-space gates directly to thousands of new planets. (p. 86)

Leaders are necessary to guide the way into these new environments where the race must "kill or be killed, eat or be eaten." . . . The final examination for these future leaders is to be sent alone on a survival test to "ANY planet, ANY climate, ANY terrain" with "NO rules, ALL weapons, ANY equipment." . . . This fantasy of the individual overcoming a strange natural environment through his own ingenuity and fortitude is not some aberration peculiar to Robert A. Heinlein; it is a fantasy central to the bourgeois historical epoch, recurring insistently in the novel from its classic form in [Daniel Defoe's] *Robinson Crusoe* through its most incisive parody, J. G. Ballard's *Concrete Island*.

In *Tunnel in the Sky*, Heinlein attempts to reconcile this vision of extreme individualism with his belief in social cooperation. Here too he is working with myths familiar to bourgeois society, for he is dramatizing the fantasy of free individuals, "naked against nature," coming together of their own volition to form human society. The youths placed on a strange planet for their final test in survival are stranded there when a supernova disrupts the gate through which they are supposed to return to Earth. Gradually they come together, creating a society formed by individuals capable of survival but needing the interrelations necessary for authentic human development. By the time Earth has re-established links with the planet, these young people have established the complete pioneer colony—including square dances.

Heinlein's ideology sharply contrasts with that of a book published the previous year, William Golding's *Lord of the Flies*.

Golding, considered a ''liberal,'' shows a group of proper English boys who, stranded on an island, quickly degenerate into savage, sadistic, warring beasts, supposedly demonstrating that war and all other evils of the human race are just an expression of our essential nature. In *Tunnel in the Sky,* the few uncooperative bullies get their lumps and are exiled from society; Heinlein, in these books written for boys during this period, projects an underlying faith in the potential of the human race and in the inherent qualities of individuals, at least those in his interchangeable categories of ''leader'' and ''survivor.''

The young protagonist, Rod Walker, the first leader of the pioneer society and later its trailblazer, embodies the extreme form of the outward-bound man. . . . He is oblivious to the advances made by all girls, ranging from the rugged Zulu to the petite French lass whom he mistakes for a boy during the days the two live together in a cave. At the very end, we see him astride his horse, dressed in fringed buckskins, leading a pioneer wagon train, now as ''Captain Walker headed out on his long road.''

The self-denying psychology of the spaceman is the central focus of *Time for the Stars* . . . , which purports to be an autobiographical narrative written as psychotherapy under the advice of a starship's psychiatrist. The narrator, Thomas Paine Leonardo da Vinci Bartlett, communicates telepathically and instantaneously over the rapidly growing distances of space and time with his identical twin brother back on Earth, Patrick Henry Michelangelo Bartlett. Pat, a cocky, brash, cheerful go-getter who bosses and bullies his twin, had seemed the better candidate for going into space, and he had originally gotten himself selected over the moody, introspective, self-defeating Tom. . . . As the twins grow apart from one another in all ways, Tom gradually becomes aware of his own identity and the peculiarly self-effacing psychology Heinlein projects as an essential tool in the conquest of space.

Once again we receive a heavy lecture on the sanctity of authority and the dangers of democracy, summed up in the motto, ''The Captain is right even when he is wrong.'' . . . As we saw in *The Star Beast,* this message applies to nations and planets just as much as it does to spaceships. So Tom discovers that ''it was more important to back up the Captain and respect his authority than anything else'' . . . , a message wildly contradictory to Heinlein's professed love of near-anarchic ''looseness'' and freedom. (pp. 86-8)

The central theme of *Citizen of the Galaxy* . . . is slavery and freedom. The novel moves inward from a remote part of the galaxy toward Earth and upward through many social classes. These tours take place through the experiences of Thorby, a boy maturing into a man, seeking his roots, his identity, and his family, as he completes a rags-to-riches saga that takes him from the very lowest role in the galaxy to the very highest. (p. 90)

Thorby is . . . adopted into the extended matriarchal family of a ''Free Trader'' spaceship, which gives us a fine tour through different civilizations as well as Heinlein's most incisive exploration of the contradictory nature of bourgeois freedom. Dr. Margaret Mader, an anthropologist studying the structured tribal society of the Free Traders, who call themselves ''the People'' and refer to everybody else as subhuman ''fraki,'' explains to Thorby that when he was adopted into the spaceship's extended family he thereby became another kind of slave. She admits that they ''enjoy the highest average

wealth in history'' because ''the profits of your trading are fantastic.'' . . . The freedom she concedes they have is the ideal freedom implicit in the bourgeois quest—and in Heinlein's fiction. . . .

> The People are free to roam the stars, never rooted to any soil. So free that each ship is a sovereign state, asking nothing of anyone, going anywhere, fighting against any odds, asking no quarter, not even cooperating except as it suits them. Oh, the People are free: this old Galaxy has never seen such freedom. . . .

But the price of this '''unparalleled freedom . . . is freedom itself,''' for the Free Traders must submit themselves to a code of customs, rules, and hierarchical order '''more stringent than any prison,''' telling them precisely what they can and cannot do within the metal bounds of their free spaceships. (pp. 90-1)

[The novella **''Tenderfoot in Space''**] suggests that Heinlein is nearing the end of his engagement with boys' stories. In this truly juvenile tale of a Boy Scout who moves with his dog to Venus, the dog turns out to be the hero and the only competent scout.

Have Space Suit—Will Travel . . . , the twelfth and final novel in the Scribner's series, soars through and beyond our galaxy to a trial of the human race, conducted by a million-year-old composite mind, to determine whether we should be annihilated as a threat to the survival of wiser and more mature races. Contrasted to this cosmic drama, but playing a crucial role within it, is the life of Kip Russell, a high-school senior from Centerville, who works in the local drugstore, yearns to go to the moon, and narrates his breathtaking travels. (pp. 91-2)

[Kip] teams up with an eleven-year-old girl genius, who demands that he '''quit being big and male and gallantly stupid''' . . . , and ''the Mother Thing,'' an intergalactic policewoman from a race of superbeings. The Mother Thing—''around her you felt happy and safe and warm'' . . .—is the ultimate embodiment of maternal protection, cherishing our young hero and heroine and interceding at the intergalactic trial to save our youthful race.

The trial is the climax of the novel and the Scribner's series. Our race is represented by a Neanderthal man, ultimately determined to be a ''cousin'' rather than an ancestor, a brutal Roman legionnaire whom Kip, unlike the judge, admires as a ''tough old sergeant'' who ''had courage, human dignity, and a basic gallantry,'' and the two youngsters. The court condemns human history as unmitigated evidence of inherent ferocity. . . . The Mother Thing offers two defenses. She argues that no race can '''survive without a willingness to fight.''' But her main argument is that we are mere children, both as a race and because we are short-lived '''ephemerals''' who '''all must die in early childhood.''' Since we '''all are so very young,''' we should be given '''time to learn''': '''Toward evil we have no mercy. But the mistakes of a child we treat with loving forbearance.''' Through this vision we see that the entire juvenile space epic is Heinlein's version of the human epic, the story of the childhood of a race, best symbolized in the lives of children becoming adults as they grow into a role in the galaxy. (pp. 92-3)

In 1959, Heinlein's fabulously successful career as a juvenile author came to an abrupt end. . . . [*Starship Troopers*], perhaps his most controversial book . . ., marks the end of this period in his career. (p. 110)

Starship Troopers displays the superelite force designed to fight the permanent wars necessary to fulfill Earth's manifest destiny in the galaxy. And the Terran Federation, the society employing this force, is ruled entirely by veterans of this elite military machine and its non-combatant auxiliaries.

Recently there has been some debate about whether *Starship Troopers* is as militaristic as it seems, and Heinlein himself disclaims any militaristic intentions. But to argue about whether or not *Starship Troopers* glorifies militarism would be as silly as arguing about whether or not "My Country 'Tis of Thee" glorifies America. Militarism shapes the speech and sets the tone of all the characters, including the narrator-hero; militarism animates every page; militarism—together will imperialism—is the novel's explicit message. What we must probe is not the quantity of militarism in *Starship Troopers* but its special quality. For *Starship Troopers* expresses its own time, and gives a striking vision of times to come. (pp. 111-12)

Starship Troopers imagines and applauds a future in which the imperialism of Earth has become virtually cosmic. (p. 112)

In *Starship Troopers*, the social organization created and ruled by service veterans has proved to be the most efficient of all forms of human society, allowing a unification of the peoples of Earth and an extension of the Terran Federation deep into the galaxy. But at the time of the action, this powerful state built upon a combination of voluntary self-sacrifice and co-operation has met what may be its match—"the Bugs," a hive-like society of arachnids, every bit as tough and just as expansionary as Heinlein's humans. Like the slugs of *The Puppet Masters,* the Bugs of *Starship Troopers* are obviously extrapolations from Heinlein's conception of twentieth-century communism. They embody "a total communism." . . . , "they are communal entities, the ultimate dictatorship of the hive.". . . So the society of cooperating individuals is now locked in struggle with the communist hive for total control of the galaxy.

Heinlein makes explicit connections between this vision of a struggle for galactic control and his vision of the twentieth-century struggle for global control. . . . And just as Heinlein imagines . . . the Russians, joining in an alliance against the utmost in human communism, the Chinese hordes, he projects another humanoid race, "the Skinnies," more communistic than humans but less communistic than Bugs, who switch from being allies of the Bugs to become our allies in the final showdown. (pp. 117-18)

The deepest emotional experiences in *Starship Troopers* all have to do with the relationships among the men in the Mobile Infantry. The psychological climax comes in the concluding passage of the novel. Throbbing with intensity, this passage reveals a new human order, as the female Captain of the ship prepares to deliver a father and son who have switched places, leaping to sow death and destruction to the words and tune of a song from World War II. . . . (pp. 119-20)

If we were to continue beyond [the conclusion] in the same direction we would arrive at a man who is both his own father and his own mother, whose mission in life is to recruit himself into military service, and who can love only himself because he is the only real being in the world. And this summarizes that other work published by Robert Heinlein in 1959, at the end of this period in his career, "All You Zombies—."

"All You Zombies—" is Heinlein's most ingenious short story, and, I think, his finest. . . . A fitting climax to Heinlein's mastery of the short-story genre, "All You Zombies—" recapitulates and integrates many of his most significant themes and leaves us with a brilliant vision into the tangled contradictions at the heart of his achievement. (p. 120)

[There are] some deep similarities and differences between *Starship Troopers* and "All You Zombies—." Just as the novel glorifies militarism, the short story exposes its hollow core. Just as the novel revels in death and destruction, the short story seeks to evade and escape the horrors of war and the history that Heinlein perceives in the future. (pp. 122-23)

Instead of the "freedom" of voluntary self-sacrifice and co-operation presented by *Starship Troopers,* "All You Zombies—" presents a deterministic maze that leads nowhere but to a series of holes in a dike constructed to hold back the flood of history. Instead of the intense passion that binds the Troopers of the Mobile Infantry to each other, to their mission, and to their glorious history and future, "All You Zombies—" offers us the loveless solipsism of the ultimate narcissist, the self-created individual spinning out webs of fiction in which he wanders alone, not even believing in the existence of his audience.

In 1959, the New Frontiers of Robert Heinlein's juvenile space epic seem to have become lost. He leaves us to choose between a hymn to a corps of elite destroyers and the inverted agony of a lonely officer of a Bureau designed to save us from our time. (pp. 123-24)

> *H. Bruce Franklin, in his* Robert A. Heinlein: America As Science Fiction *(copyright © 1980 by Oxford University Press, Inc.; used by permission), Oxford University Press, New York, 1980, 232 p.*

THEODORE STURGEON

Robert Heinlein's following was ardent and instant with the appearance of his first short story in Astounding Science Fiction magazine more than 40 years ago, and it has multiplied with each of his publications. His series of "juveniles" had a great deal to do with raising that category from childish to what is now called YA—"Young adult." His influence on science fiction has been immense; his knowledge of the hard sciences and his gift for logical extrapolation inspired many beginning writers—and a good many already established hands—to knit fact and conjecture with a little more care and a great deal more literary quality than previously. The net effect over the years has been to erode the snobbery placed on science fiction. [Vladimir] Nabokov, [Doris] Lessing, [Kurt] Vonnegut, [Jorge Luis] Borges and other luminaries have found it a worthy metier with full awareness that it is, after all, not all zap-guns and special effects. And throughout this swift and steady evolution can, almost always, be seen the Heinlein influence.

Heinlein's . . . most recent books have been largely didactic, interior, sometimes pedantic, though each has its good measure of action. Some of his idolators mourned the lack of the Heinlein of the decisive hero, the blinding pace, the magnificent sweep of very possible near-future developments; above all, that element of capital-S Story.

Well, "**Friday**" has it all. Friday herself is a delight. She is as strong and resourceful and decisive as any Heinlein hero; in addition she is loving (oh, yes) and tender and very, very female. She also has an evolved ethos—the ability to discard past hatreds and dislikes and so to meet people, day by day, in terms of what they now are, and not to judge them by what they have been.

Heinlein's gift for invention—we owe him the remote manipulator that scientists call "waldoes" after a Heinlein story, and another gave us the waterbed—moves pretty far out from time to time. In this book he describes a completely Balkanized North America, complete with his typical meticulous analysis of its currencies, customs and political forms, its border guards and variegated moralities. . . . This, like so many of Heinlein's works (particularly the earlier ones), is as joyous to read as it is provocative.

> *Theodore Sturgeon, "Heinlein with a Capital S for Story" (reprinted by permission of the author), in* Los Angeles Times Book Review, *June 20, 1982, p. 4.*

H. BRUCE FRANKLIN

You have to admit this about Robert A. Heinlein: He provokes strong reactions. Whether or not he is still the most popular and influential living author of science fiction, as he has probably been for four decades, Mr. Heinlein remains the most controversial, with hordes of fans and foes. **"Friday"** will convert few from one camp to the other.

One of Mr. Heinlein's self-images is that of a lone genius in the role of a carnival showman, providing fun for the masses, money for himself and deep truths for the select few who penetrate his disguise. So **"Friday"** is meant to have something for everyone: laughs and tears, thrilling adventures, titillating sex, delicious fantasies of power, and profound messages.

Like most of Mr. Heinlein's heroes, Friday is a superbeing. Engineered from the finest genes, and trained to be a secret courier in a future world of chaotic ferocity and intrigue, she can think better, fight better and make love better than any of the normal people around her. The Earth she inhabits has become a nightmare in which some 400 "territorial states," including the tyrannical Chicago Imperium, the madcap California Confederacy and the Mexican Revolutionary Kingdom, endlessly struggle for the power actually held by the "corporate states," gigantic multi-national conglomerates that are all secretly controlled by one interlocking interstellar cartel, originally founded by "the most American of myth-heroes," a "basement inventor." The best values the world has ever known—being, of course, the values of Midwestern farming communities at the time of Mr. Heinlein's childhood in the early 20th century—have been overwhelmed by the evils already dominant in the late 20th century: too much government and too many people, bureaucracy, alienation, welfare, cities, religious cults, socialism, monopoly cpaitalism and, worst of all, mediocrity and incompetence. As usual, the highest virtue is supreme competence. . . .

The bulk of the novel describes Friday's amours. Unfortunately, Mr. Heinlein has a knack for the difficult task of making sex boring. Neither Friday's sexual partners (as in effective romance) nor the details of her sex life (as in effective pornography) are of interest. Her numerous partners, male and female, are all interchangeable, and the details are coyly vague, unlike the precise descriptions of her sexy clothes, elegant meals and artful fighting techniques. Some readers may decide to skip the sex to get to the good parts.

But the espionage plot is also disappointing, being a mere contrivance to get Friday from one liaison to another as she moves toward her ultimate goal. This goal, as always in recent Heinlein, is escape from the world of the future or developing present to the world of the middle-American mythic past—pioneering, rural or small-town. For Friday, this means abandoning her supposedly exciting job and the adventure plot, along with the Earth. She finally finds happiness as a "colonial housewife" in a group marriage on a faraway planet, where she can have her fill of sex while writing a cookbook and working in the local town council, girl-scout troop and P.T.A.

Mr. Heinlein's latest apocalypse goes beyond all those practical best sellers telling us how to survive and prosper amid the developing doom. For him, the only place to hide is in a fantasy of the mythic past on a faraway planet. His increasingly monotonic message is: Stop the world, I want to get off.

> *H. Bruce Franklin, "Genius and Supergenius," in* The New York Times Book Review *(© 1982 by The New York Times Company; reprinted by permission), July 4, 1982, p. 8.*

Nat(han Irving) Hentoff

1925-

American novelist, critic, journalist, and editor.

Hentoff's nonfiction and young adult fiction reflect his passions for jazz, literature, and civil rights. Hentoff is a critic and historian of jazz and often uses jazz-related backgrounds and characters in his fiction. Topical social themes also appear in Hentoff's fiction, noted for representations of teenagers who are more socially and politically aware than traditionally portrayed.

Hentoff's studies of civil rights, both as historical analysis in *The First Freedom: The Tumultuous History of Free Speech in America* and as discussion of developments since the civil rights movements of the 1960s in *The New Equality*, have been praised for their treatment of conflicting viewpoints. They are strongly recommended for young adult readers. Social issues also challenge the young protagonists in Hentoff's fiction. *I'm Really Dragged but Nothing Gets Me Down* relates the story of seventeen-year-old Jeremy Wolf, who is willing to serve his country but refuses to register for the draft; *In the Country of Ourselves* analyzes relations between people of different races; and *The Day They Came to Arrest the Book* explores freedom of expression and the issue of censorship. In addition to the social problems that challenge his young protagonists, Hentoff also examines more personal concerns, such as the relationships between young people and their peers, parents, and authority figures.

Hentoff has been cited for his ability to "get inside" the life and thoughts of modern teenagers. The ardent concern and sympathy with which he writes has earned him respect from readers of all ages.

(See also *Children's Literature Review*, Vol. 1; *Contemporary Authors*, Vols. 1-4, rev. ed.; *Contemporary Authors New Revision Series*, Vol. 5; and *Something about the Author*, Vol. 27.)

MARTIN B. DUBERMAN

In the current deluge of "civil rights" literature, this excellent book [*The New Equality*] is unlikely to get the wide reading it deserves. Which is too bad, for it is one of the few to put "the movement" in a broader context, to deal in recommendations as well as jeremiads, and to adopt a radical as opposed to a liberal stance (that is, dealing in essentials rather than palliatives).

The book has faults, largely organizational. Since they are not significant when weighed against the suggestive contents, it is better to list them now and be done. First, the argument does not "build"; it is episodic rather than cumulative. The chapters are more a series of self-contained essays than well-related units of a whole. Second, too much space is given to summarizing and rebutting the views of others. Some of this is necessary and some of it is brilliant (the devastating but not vindictive critique of [Norman] Mailer), but there is too much rehashing of the obvious (the defective arguments of John Fischer).

Against these minor faults, *The New Equality* has major virtues. The radical approach is what gives the book its special flavor and importance. This is not one more panegyric to the "American genius for compromise," nor yet another bit of self-congratulation on the "slow but sure" progress in this best of all possible countries. Our large failures are writ large and their gruesome human toll bluntly counted.

None of this is shrieked. The defects of tone we sometimes associate with a radical stance are absent. There is no claim here on a monopoly of truth, no attempt to blueprint the One Way to Salvation, no trumpet calls to the righteous for a cleansing and a violent rebirth. Hentoff is dispassionate and detached. He thus makes his hard-nosed analysis the more persuasive, and his message the more urgent.

Actually he has three interrelated messages. The first concerns the widening chasm between the white "moderate" and the Negro "activist." . . . The argument between moderate and activist represents contrasting attachments to order and justice. The moderate, who already shares in some of the "good things" of life, prefers to believe that social justice can be achieved without "unduly" disturbing social order. The activist, who sees little in that order worth preserving, believes that considerable tension and conflict are concomitants of meaningful change. . . .

Aside from being "too little, too late," the moderate position suffers from the optimistic defect of placing too much faith in man's "conscience." Here is Hentoff's second theme. An appeal to morality, he argues, a reliance on the white man's guilt, is in itself an insufficient guarantee of reform. Conscience has brought some improvement in the Negro's status, but only some. If fundamental change is to come—and nothing less will do—"the movement" must organize and demonstrate its power. The hostile or apathetic white majority will not surrender its privileges unless frightened or forced into doing so: the dictum that "power only respects power" is as true of our domestic as of our foreign Cold War.

In this sense the activists are tough-minded realists. Their refusal to place entire faith in an appeal to conscience, or in the benevolent workings of time, separates them from the genteel main stream of the American reform tradition. That tradition has always been grounded in a double optimism—that the world can be made better, and that this can be done through an appeal to "right reason" rather than force and fear. The activists share the belief that the world can be made a better place, but they put their faith for change in power, not good will. To this degree, they are more in the tradition of European radicalism than American reform.

The civil rights struggle is growing more radical in ends as well as means. Hentoff's third and most far-reaching theme is that the struggle must increasingly orient itself toward larger goals—not merely an ending to segregation, but the restructuring of our society. Hentoff reflects the growing view among civil rights leaders that merely trying to win full partnership in American life is not enough. The view has two sources, one "intellectual" and one tactical. The first, represented by James Baldwin and Lorraine Hansberry, is that partnership may not be desirable because the firm is corrupt. The root fear of the Baldwins, in part based on a romanticization of Negro-hipster-slum life, is that the Negro might exchange whatever uniqueness his sufferings have given him for a mess of middle-class white complacencies; he might surrender spontaneity and sensuality for the desiccated rituals of bourgeois life.

A second source of protest against aiming the civil rights movement solely at assimilation comes from tactical rather than ideological considerations. The view here is that although full participation in American life may be desirable, it will not materialize unless the basic assumptions of our society are first challenged. The Negro will never be fully accepted until the value structure which has so long denied him is itself overhauled. Until then, he will be given partial concessions only, just enough semblance of good faith to pacify the gullible—or the tired.

Both these sources—the intellectual and the tactical—are moving the Negro protest into a deeper form of social criticism, one which sees racism as one symptom rather than the entire embodiment of our social rot. . . . The problem of poverty underlies the problem of civil rights; the inequalities of American life are phenomena of class as well as color. And it is essential, Hentoff argues, for the underprivileged and poor of all colors and backgrounds to recognize their kinship. In his view, a new neo-Populist alliance is called for—one which would unite the American underclasses in a concerted drive to acquire power in the name of making fundamental changes in our society.

The possibility of such an alliance, as Hentoff himself shows, is highly uncertain. Low-status whites are often those most hostile to Negroes. Their prejudice is part of their essential protective equipment; it could be surrendered only if a new scapegoat could be found for their frustrations—possibly the wealthy and privileged. The Negro poor, on their side, "are far too preoccupied with survival and the particular afflictions of being black to think in terms of a potential alliance between them and the white poor." . . . [The] obstacles to a coalition of the poor are formidable. Not only the specific obstacle of color prejudice, but the inhibiting effect of our middle-class value structure (not confined to the middle-class) with its emphasis on what is safe and secure, and our reform tradition of piecemeal adjustment.

Hentoff's argument, then, can be summarized as follows: There are fundamental inequities in American life which call for fundamental reforms; these reforms require the full weight and support of the Federal government behind them; the government cannot be brought to exercise its weight unless "encouraged" to do so through political pressure from below; the best way to exert such pressure is through an alliance of the poor, a coalition transcending the civil rights issue.

It is this last leg of the argument which is the most wobbly. Hentoff does not pretend that the alliance can come about easily, but he does see it as the only real hope for revitalizing the country. Many will agree, which makes the unlikeliness of the alliance all the more depressing.

> *Martin B. Duberman, "Wrongs That Can't Be Civilrighted," in* Book Week—The Washington Post *(© 1964, The Washington Post), August 9, 1964, p. 5.*

EDWARD T. CHASE

Mr. Hentoff's book [*The New Equality*] is the most sophisticated gloss of the [Civil Rights] Movement to date. So keen is his sensibility, so evident his intimacy with what's going on, and, most important, so pertinent are his suggestions for social action that *The New Equality,* for all its brevity, stands almost alone . . . among the flood of recent books on the subject. One has confidence that Hentoff really understands what Negroes are feeling.

But a further distinction is that his account traces the intellectual evolution of the Movement's leadership and the concurrent criticism of "outside" observers. Hentoff's style is to counterpunch. He makes his points by scoring off the inadequacies of such commentators as Norman Mailer, Norman Podhoretz of *Commentary* and John Fischer of *Harper's.* Sometimes he misreads Fischer. Yet his pinpointed charges of naïveté and condescension are mostly telling.

Hentoff is not satisfied with mere reportage. The most ambitious aspect of his book is his prescription of where the Movement now must go—namely into a drive for structural changes of the social order, preeminently in education, employment and economic opportunity. Sensitively and logically the reader is led into a confrontation with a rationale for social revolution, the peaceful variety. The revolution he outlines may strike you as mild or not so mild. That will depend on where you stand—and not where you stand on Negroes' rights so much as on your assessment of the equity of American life in general. For Hentoff is suggesting that the victimization of the Negro is, among other things, only the most extreme instance of the cruelties in a competitive, market-dominated society insufficiently imbued with concern for social justice. (p. 29)

Hentoff's resources are a highly intelligent empathy combined with experience of Negro life. He can deftly make a point with a quotation such as Miles Davis's "Every Negro over fifty should get a medal for putting up with all that crap"; or by deftly marshalling the most pertinent evidence from the new findings of sociology and psychology. Whatever Hentoff may lack in system is compensated for by his astonishing range and the relish with which he brings his own mind to reflect upon it as an amateur, in the best sense of that word. (p. 30)

Edward T. Chase, "Faces of the Racial Revolution," in The New Republic *(reprinted by permission of* The New Republic*; © 1965 The New Republic, Inc.), Vol. 152, No. 4, January 23, 1965, pp. 29-30, 32.**

ROBERT COLES

Jazz Country is a novel directed at young people struggling to realize themselves; it is also a gem of a book that talks rare sense about the ambiguities of race, the difficulties of a child's growth, and the ironies of artistic life.

Tom, son of a New York corporation lawyer, plays the trumpet with near single-minded devotion. He is finishing high school and wondering whether to enter college or make a try at being a professional jazz musician. To do the latter means leaving white, middle-class territory for "jazz country," where creativity lives exceptionally close to tragedy and where racial stereotypes dissolve or harden as a profession now comes to terms with whites rather than Negroes. The boy meets up with himself by learning about lives differently lived. He begins to see that he cannot flee his past, even as he does not wish to be confined by its values. Eventually he will at least start at Amherst instead of working full-time in a band; by the time he makes that decision he (and the reader) have seen arrogance unmasked in many places, doubt and suffering revealed in many forms. No race or class has a corner on either virtue or evil.

The writing is clear and direct. Jazz talk is delicately worked into everyday language. The author will settle for none of the handy postures so fashionable today: racism of one sort or another; foul language as a substitute for art and thought alike; the latest social and cultural snobbery, that turns everything inside out, with each success in our nation considered a measure of our failure, and every accomplishment in a person held either a drawback or evidence of wrongdoing: and finally, that misty sentiment so common to portrayals of growing youth and jazz alike. Indeed, Tom's fight to be his own man is placed alongside the struggle of others whose racial identity has cursed them, yet also set the stage for their music, compelling, stunning, devastating—and enviable.

Mr. Hentoff has chosen not so much to compare or contrast lives as to let them be, separately and together. Such restraint, enabling a touching and real story, deserves our surprised, grateful recognition.

Robert Coles, in his review of "Jazz Country," in Book Week—The Sunday Herald Tribune *(© 1965, The Washington Post), May 9, 1965, p. 5.*

CAROLYN HEILBRUN

["**Jazz Country**"] is the best of the teen-age books I have read. Not only does it render the experience of jazz with passion, with what strikes an uninformed reader as veracity; it presents

its Negro characters with honesty and dignity, capturing well the white boy's longing to partake of the Negro experience in order, as he thinks, to produce great jazz. Yet it is precisely in so far as it is tailored for teen-agers that the book fails. Its teen-age hero is cardboard, its plot an outrageous tissue of coincidences which do not, as coincidences should, mirror inner compulsions of the characters. The setting is New York, but the hero keeps tripping over people he knows as though he were strolling around a town of 500 people.

Carolyn Heilbrun, "Life in Safe Doses," in The New York Times Book Review, *Part II (© 1965 by The New York Times Company; reprinted by permission), May 9, 1965, pp. 3, 26.**

THE TIMES LITERARY SUPPLEMENT

By any standard—and surely these days books for the 14-year-old upwards ought to stand up as adult fare—[*Jazz Country*] is an excellent novel. Not only does Nat Hentoff show with great perception the development of one boy's understanding of other people, but without any strain, without recourse to either hip jargon or learned explanations, he opens for the uninitiated the significance of the world of jazz. . . .

Tom is a nice guy, making good grades at school and with the kind of calm, sympathetic parents every teenager must long to have. The narrative comes clearly and straightforwardly from his lips. "Your life has been too easy for you to be making it as a jazz musician", the Negro bass player in the great Moses Godfrey's band tells him after hearing his talented but heartless trumpet playing. "And too white", adds his militant wife, Mary. By the end of the book Tom knows a lot more about life and how difficult it is to be both a jazz musician and black. The race relations material in *Jazz Country* is not a crude emotional appeal for togetherness because we all like music. We see the white cops beating up the black man for no better reason than because he is black, but we are also made to visualize the dilemma of the educated Negro whose sole desire is to live his own life as an individual but who constantly feels guilty that he is not a champion of his race at its time of destiny.

"Top of the Pops," in The Times Literary Supplement *(© Times Newspapers Ltd. (London) 1966; reproduced from* The Times Literary Supplement *by permission), No. 3351, May 19, 1966, p. 442.**

TIME

Horatio Alger's Ragged Dick, Tattered Tom and Ben the Luggage Boy—those brave little ragamuffins of a century ago—have long since petrified into pillars of the community. Sweet were their uses of adversity, as they parlayed pants patches into stock certificates. . . . [Today, one hundred years after Alger, rags] have become the symbol of riches. Youthful outcries against the system, the Establishment and middle-class consuming have become so persistent and eloquent that moral outrage itself threatens to become a lucrative commodity.

The new triumph over adversity, as Nat Hentoff programs it in *I'm Really Dragged but Nothing Gets Me Down,* is going from resentment to resistance. The book is an attempt to put a little chest hair on that artificial category of literature known as "young-adult novels." Hentoff injects such themes as Viet Nam, racism, generation gap, civil rights, drugs, black rage, white guilt and, for old times' sake, a touch of anti-Semitism.

Sex is still a no-no, although the vocabulary is raunched up with such words as ''bastard,'' ''damn it,'' and ''hard-on.''

Specifically, [*I'm Really Dragged but Nothing Gets Me Down*] is about 17-year-old Jeremy Wolf's decision to enter antiwar work. Should he break the law by refusing to register for the draft? Lacking the true instinct for martyrdom, he decides to become a draft counselor and turns his house into ''an underground station on the freedom road to Canada.'' His dad— having feared the worst—is much relieved.

Hentoff, a jazz authority and wide-ranging social critic, is one of the most visible freelance writers in circulation. In this slight assignment he overcomes his modest talents for fiction with competence, concern and sympathy. But to what worthwhile end? Surely today's ''young adults'' do not need such pallid dramatizations of their problems when Simon and Garfunkel and the Beatles do it so much better.

> *''From Rags to Rages,'' in* Time *(copyright 1968 Time Inc.; all rights reserved; reprinted by permission from* Time*), Vol. 92, No. 15, October 11, 1968, p. 109.*

DIANE G. STAVN

[*I'm Really Dragged but Nothing Gets Me Down* is an] episodic story in which believable, sincere, intelligent and philosophically opposed characters discuss their differences, don't resolve them, and are left with nagging frustration and a sense of solitude. High school senior Jeremy Wolf wishes he were sufficiently emancipated to smoke pot, sufficiently courageous and zealous to resist the draft, and enough of a soul brother to be able to get through to a kid in a tutorial program. While despising himself for his inability to live up to his image of the totally committed man, he scorns his father for his materialistic, don't-rock-the-boat concerns. Sam Wolf, contemplating his possibly forthcoming prosperous man's heart attack, recalls his own youthful revolutionary activities and secretly admires his son's spunk while worrying about the impractical decisions he might make. Though they glower at each other across the generation gap, father and son are closer than they realize: Jeremy finally chooses draft counseling over jail and Sam flails out against the Vietnamese war, to the chagrin of his firmly Establishment brother-in-law. . . . [The] extensive dialogues constitute confrontations between young and old, black and white, dove and hawk, head and straight opinion in America today. This relevance gives the book its value and at the same time flaws it—for readers may easily find themselves being persuaded from side to side in a series of editorials and losing track of the minimal plot and story.

> *Diane G. Stavn, in her review of ''I'm Really Dragged but Nothing Gets Me Down,'' in* School Library Journal, *an appendix to* Library Journal *(reprinted from the November, 1968 issue of* School Library Journal, *published by R. R. Bowker Co./A Xerox Corporation; copyright © 1968), Vol. 15, No. 3, November, 1968, p. 96.*

JOHN WESTON

Nat Hentoff's **''I'm Really Dragged But Nothing Gets Me Down''** treats an important dilemma: how best can a young man serve his country and himself and retain his sense of morality? Jeremy Wolf, 18, and his friends must face the issues of the draft. Refusing to register means a prison sentence, a

loss of five years out of life; accepting a draft card, in their view, means accepting a sellout to murder; capitalizing on their opportunity for deferment by attending college means that the dumb and the poor must take their places. Mr. Hentoff attempts to present all sides of the question, concluding with the only unarguable decision—that, through education (in this case, draft counseling) each potential draftee must make his own peace and that a larger peace begins at the one-to-one human level.

Although timely and important in theme, the book falls short as a novel for basic reasons. It lacks driving power; it becomes, instead of a story that moves the reader, a philippic that instructs. The welding of a moral and philosophic discussion to a dramatic form is never easy to do but done well that is precisely what makes great books great. Because the surface of this one remains so flat, the characters so blurred, the arguments so objective, the impact of Mr. Hentoff's theme is largely ineffective. (pp. 2, 66)

> *John Weston, ''Hang-ups Do Happen,'' in* The New York Times Book Review, *Part II (© 1968 by The New York Times Company; reprinted by permission), November 3, 1968, pp. 2, 66.**

BENJAMIN DeMOTT

Mr. Hentoff's [**''In the Country of Ourselves''**] focuses on three urban high school activists—Josh, Schwartz and Jane— in course of telling the story of a student uprising that's violently put down by cops. Josh is the head of a Revolutionary High School Collective and bent on major acts of violence— to awaken classmates to the truth that they are in ''a state of false consciousness . . . unfree . . . channelled into roles in the society that would . . . make them instruments of everyone else's oppression.'' Schwartz is briefly a member of the Collective, but rebels at his initiation assignment—to ''get into the principal's office, find the senior class records, tear them up, flush them down the toilet''—and is moving toward apoliticality. Jane represents a middle stance: an activist in issues of school governance, she sternly rejects the policies and actions of the Collective, which she sees as an attempt to ''play God.''

Implicit in the positions and behavior of each student is a question or issue that could quickly open a way to clarification of some major quandries facing politicized teen-agers. Is the culture of slots so rigid and life-despoiling that all energy must be directed toward its destruction? Is a turn toward violence so inevitable among activists as to make commitment an inferior moral option—less worthy than neutrality or apathy? Is the decision to concern yourself primarily with ''local issues''—school governance and the like—a copout or a realistic coming-to-terms with the relative powerlessness of adolescence?

None of these matters is trivial, and none is, for newly political youth, closed or resolved—yet each is shrugged off in the pages of this book, mentioned only to be abruptly dropped. The author's account of differences among his trio treats of tics of personality (Josh is a tyrant, Schwartz is a softie, Jane is naive), not of issues: the reality of the latter is distanced by condescending, adult political disillusionment; and the primary perspective is that of an elder who, while ''still caring,'' is no longer in imaginative touch with the excited confusion, the energy, the generosity of youthful political commitment.

Readers of Nat Hentoff's columns know that disillusionment is by no means this writer's single note. **"In the Country of Ourselves,"** moreover, has several pointed and "relevant" intentions—the most notable is a cynically manipulative radical teacher who shamefully exploits his students. And it's possible that the absence of healthy, unmocked political intensity from this story merely testifies that a murderous metropolitan knowingness is now wholly pervasive even among children. But whatever the explanation, the impression left by the book as a whole—namely that politics is boring—is under-nourishing and false.

> *Benjamin DeMott, in his review of "In the Country of Ourselves," in* The New York Times Book Review, Part II *(© 1971 by The New York Times Company; reprinted by permission), November 7, 1971, p. 3.*

JACK FORMAN

In the Country of Ourselves [like *Jazz Country* and *I'm Really Dragged But Nothing Gets Me Down* is] about being in high school today, but it displays even more of an awareness of the complexities of this situation than did the two earlier novels. Here, mutually suspicious black and white radical students, with the aid of a concerned teacher and an apparent New Left sympathizer in the local police force, attempt to disrupt order in the high school they attend. Opposing them is a stubborn, authoritarian, yet concerned and dedicated principal. Unfortunately, some of the episodes are a bit strained, and the responses of the characters are occasionally overdrawn in an attempt to make the philosophies they espouse clear. Nevertheless, most of the kids behave believably—and, thankfully, not always predictably—and the book is very wittily written. All in all, it's one of the fairest and most entertaining titles available about politically aware young teens today.

> *Jack Forman, in his review of "In the Country of Ourselves," in* School Library Journal, *an appendix to* Library Journal *(reprinted from the December, 1971 issue of* School Library Journal, *published by R. R. Bowker Co./A Xerox Corporation; copyright © 1971), Vol. 18, No. 4, December, 1971, p. 64.*

ELEANOR CAMERON

Nat Hentoff has written two novels for teenagers: one good, *Jazz Country* . . . ; and one, to my mind, a failure, *I'm really dragged but nothing gets me down*. . . . In his essay **"Fiction for Teenagers,"** Hentoff says, "Is it possible, then, to reach these children of McLuhan in that old-time medium, the novel? I believe it is, because their primary concerns are only partially explored in the messages they get from their music and are diverted rather than probed on television. If a book is relevant to those concerns, not didactically but in creating textures of experience which teenagers can recognize as germane to their own, it can merit their attention."

What troubles me is that, in Hentoff's intense concern to reach teenagers, the difference between bibliotherapy and literature is lost sight of. I'm sure Hentoff knows the difference between the two: that literature was never written with the purpose of providing a tool or a release for the desperate. It is written because someone must make palpable and seen and understood his private vision of the universe. What we call literature gives the reader an intensified sense of existence, a revelation, gives him people with idiosyncrasies and habits and beliefs, people with histories and possible futures which the reader cannot help dwelling upon when the last page is turned. People, I should think, at the opposite pole to those faceless ones, the message carriers (most of them depressingly, boringly alike in their involvements and rebellions and obsessions) presented us by the writers of the catering and problem type of teenage novel. Reading a stack of them becomes tedious beyond endurance, especially when they are written in the first person, purportedly by a teenager.

And yet Hentoff, desiring, I am sure, to write an admirable novel, one with quality, has given us exactly what he speaks against—didacticism, an arrangement of ideas already well-known to teenagers—but has not given us what he created in *Jazz Country,* a texture of experience. This, it would seem to me, ought of necessity, given the nature of the human body, to include Flannery O'Connor's all important eye. Yet very rarely does *I'm really dragged* give us the look either of human beings or of places; we are not, strangely enough, made aware of any particular place. And in losing the particularity of place, we lose somehow the sense of reality, and I mean an intense sense of reality. We are all but blind—like the chambered mole. Nor do we feel the surfaces of solid objects; they seem scarcely to exist. We never smell anything. As readers, we seem stripped of all senses except hearing, and remember McLuhan's saying, "For the eye has none of the delicacy of the ear."

I'm really dragged is like a play, with the characters coming through to us only in their speeches about subjects of interest to contemporary teenagers. You experience Hentoff's people as you do those in a play, only the strictly pertinent core of them rather than the accomplished novelist's exploration of facets of personality. And you can go through the short chapters and assign a title to each just by running an eye down the dialogue: Chapter One, the draft and blacks vs. whites; Chapter Two, father vs. son; Chapter Three, drugs, to smoke pot or not to smoke it; Chapter Four, father vs. son; Chapter Five, blacks vs. whites; Chapter Six, father vs. son; Chapter Seven, the generation gap; Chapter Eight, parents and school; and so on. Is *this* what Hentoff calls "textures of experience"? But surely that texture we call "the novel" gives us, at its most treasurable, a passionate, sometimes rapturous meeting between the artist's private vision and the haunting, ambiguous, paradoxical world of feelings and objects—all interlaced. And these interlacings open up for us intimations about ourselves and the world we had not guessed at before, or had not seen, nor been able to put into words for ourselves. (pp. 111-13)

> *Eleanor Cameron, "McLuhan, Youth, and Literature" (copyright © 1972, 1973 by Eleanor Cameron; reprinted by permission of the author), in* The Horn Book Magazine, *Vol. XLVIII, Nos. 5 and 6 and Vol. XLIX, No. 1, October and December, 1972 and February, 1973 (and reprinted in* Crosscurrents of Criticism: Horn Book Essays, 1968-1977, *edited by Paul Heins, The Horn Book, Incorporated, 1977, pp. 98-120.)**

ZENA SUTHERLAND

Sam Davidson [the protagonist of *This School Is Driving Me Crazy*] is a bright, energetic boy with a Big Problem: he doesn't want to attend the school of which his father is headmaster. Father insists. Sam, always in some minor scrape or up to some mischief, is his teachers' despair. When a smaller boy, lying, accuses Sam of being the bully who forced him to steal, matters come to a head; the trio of real bullies is unmasked and expelled, the attitudes of teachers are exposed, and the relationship between Sam and his father improves—with Sam's impending transfer decided on by the end of the story. Sam is an engaging character, and the writing style—in particular the dialogue—is pungent. And a good thing, too, because the messages almost overbalance the narrative. Hentoff is concerned not only about the relationships between father and son, but about the role of the school, the responsibility of the teacher, and relationships between students and teachers. To make his points, he has overdrawn some characters, such as the adamantly hostile teacher Kozodoy or the glib, mendacious brother of one of the three expelled. Yet the issues affect all children in school, public or private, and the minor imbalances of the book are more than compensated for by humor, action, and setting.

> *Zena Sutherland, in her review of "This School Is Driving Me Crazy," in* Bulletin of the Center for Children's Books *(reprinted by permission of The University of Chicago Press; © 1976 by The University of Chicago), Vol. 29, No. 5, January, 1976, p. 78.*

RODERICK NORDELL

Two centuries after Shakespeare, not to mention ten times as many after Homer, people still did not know what "poetry is." . . .

So it is hardly surprising that, after the mere 75 years in the history of jazz, this latter-day art form still tempts the definers. In **"Jazz Is"** a long-time social critic and heart-on-sleeve jazz specialist throws the latest lifeline to a laity left floundering by such wry semi-truths as the one attributed to jazz's Shakespeare, Louis Armstrong: "If you have to ask what jazz is, you'll never know."

Nat Hentoff is a kind of prototype of the white kid who hung around the dancehall door and never got over the sounds of the black musicians and their musical descendants, now of every color. Today he's in that middle-aged generation which can still look around and find what he calls "survivors of every one of the campaigns" waged by "thousands of fiercely individualistic players" during the dramatic changes from ancient New Orleans to modern international (yes, even "third-world") jazz. Mr. Hentoff is particularly, and searchingly, responsive to those occasions when the generations meet and swing together; when the elder statesman recognizes a link to the raucous newcomer and vice versa; when an individual, such as "mainstream" saxophonist Gerry Mulligan, seems to have absorbed everything and can play the right thing at the right time with any generation. . . .

Objections might be made to Mr. Hentoff's own sometimes inflated prose. How many uses of the word "nonpareil" can one book take? But he does masterfully convey a sense of jazz in its broad human and artistic context.

> *Roderick Nordell, " 'Jazz Is': Insiders' Definitions," in* The Christian Science Monitor *(reprinted by permission from* The Christian Science Monitor; *© 1976 The Christian Science Publishing Society; all rights reserved), October 1, 1976, p. 23.*

PETER FANNING

[Despite] a forthright title *This School is Driving Me Crazy* proves something of a disappointment. Deep in the heart of

the Blackboard Jungle, where protection rackets flourish and honour rides high, Nat Hentoff's anti-hero plays an unpleasant double-act as petulant pupil and headmaster's son. The text makes heavy weather of a fine central theme. Furious bursts of capital letters and italics highlight parental psychology; interest lapses after the villains' cover is blown and the final pages totter into comic strip tedium.

Mr Hentoff makes a believable creation of Sam, the Nogood Boyo, who receives paternal guidance in the form of official memoranda. But otherwise both setting and characters are of a predictable kind. They range from the jackbooted child-hating teacher to cringing bullies and their teeny-tiny victims.

> *Peter Fanning, "Tooth and Claw," in* The Times Educational Supplement *(©* Times Newspapers Ltd. (London) 1978; reproduced from *The Times Educational Supplement by permission), No. 3267, January 20, 1978, p. 23.**

DOROTHY M. BRODERICK

[Nat Hentoff's *The First Freedom: The Tumultuous History of Free Speech in America*] is the first truly popular history of the First Amendment, making it accessible to senior high students and non-scholarly minded adults. . . . [Hentoff provides] the background for understanding why the framers of the Constitution's Bill of Rights felt that it was necessary to spell out the restrictions the Constitution was placing on government. This background information is followed by discussion of numerous events in American history where the First Amendment was at issue. Sometimes free speech carried the day; sometimes it lost. The complexities are here, but there is no question where Hentoff stands—he is a free speech purist. He is also eloquent in defense of his view and this very fine book deserves a wide reading by both young adults and all Americans, particularly those who can't tell the pollsters what the First Amendment is or means.

> *Dorothy M. Broderick, in her review of "The First Freedom: The Tumultuous History of Free Speech in America," in* Voice of Youth Advocates *(copyrighted 1980 by Voice of Youth Advocates), Vol. 3, No. 3, August, 1980, p. 40.*

JACK FORMAN

Fresh from Hentoff's *This School Is Driving Me Crazy* . . . , [in *Does This School Have Capital Punishment?*], Sam Davidson enrolls in Burr Academy, noted for its discipline and fairness. Sam's rebelliousness and carelessness, however, soon get him into trouble—he's caught with the circumstantial evidence after Jeremiah Saddlefield had thrown half-smoked joints at Sam and his friend Rob and run out of the locker room. The headmaster places Sam and Rob on probation until he can get the truth. In the meantime, Sam confides in Major Kelley, an old jazz trumpeter he is interviewing for a class assignment. Kelley travels to Chicago to track down information about Jeremiah's father (a newspaper magnate), whom the boy fears, and during a lecture to Sam's class, Kelley interests Jeremiah in jazz. Eventually, he convinces Jeremiah to confess the truth and confront his powerful father. The jazz sensibility is effectively and movingly described, and Hentoff's attempt to deal with the complexities of justice and fairness is appealing. But the story is full of unlikely contrivances and didactic messages.

Jack Forman, in his review of "Does This School
Have Capital Punishment?" in School Library Jour-
nal (reprinted from the May, 1981 issue of School
Library Journal, published by R. R. Bowker Co./A
Xerox Corporation; copyright © 1981), Vol. 27, No.
9, May, 1981, p. 74.

ANNIE GOTTLIEB

["**Does This School Have Capital Punishment?**" is] a sentimental fantasy, complete with good guys who need to learn
compassion, bad guys who turn out to have soft hearts and a
fairy godfather in the form of a great old black jazz musician.

It is improbable, to say the least, that a renowned trumpeter
named Major Kelley would travel from New York to Chicago
to help a bright, smart-alecky white kid beat an unfair accusation of marijuana possession—and then buy a cake inscribed
"INNOCENT" to celebrate the victory for the boy. . . . But
then almost everything in this book is a little unreal. Both kids
and teachers at tough, exclusive Burr Academy are impossibly
clever; Major Kelley is often impossibly oracular; and any
character can in an instant become a mouthpiece for a mini-
lecture (thoroughly worthy, mind you) on why jazz should be
taught in the schools or why it *feels* better to tell the truth. The
creepy kid who pins the bum rap on Sam is impossibly victimized by a newspaper-tycoon father who's a moustache-twirl-
ing capitalist villain . . . and so on.

The whole mix might appeal only to urban preppies were it
not for Mr. Hentoff's virtuoso writing on jazz, which soars
out of its silly setting like a silver phoenix. This book is worth
reading just to meet a clarinetist with a "sound like hot spice,"
to learn that jazz can "bring you back from the dead" and to
hear about an era in the Kansas City of the 1930's when "the
air, the air itself, moved in jazz time." And Major Kelley and
his ancient father are grand characters, despite the mawkish
roles they are made to play vis à vis Sam and friends.

Annie Gottlieb, in her review of "Does This School
Have Capital Punishment?" in The New York Times
Book Review (© 1981 by The New York Times Company; reprinted by permission), July 26, 1981, p.
13.

HOLLY WILLETT

Without using an over-abundance of slang [in **Does This School
Have Capital Punishment?**, Nat Hentoff] creates believable
teenage dialogue. Sam is both funny and earnest in his ironic
observations; conversation reveals the character of the adults,
too. The contemptuous school director and Jeremiah's callous
father are antagonists, and—realistically—neither of them is
completely vanquished at the conclusion. The relationships
between the fathers and the sons are central to the plot, yet
none are explored to a satisfying depth. Most of the personalities are vivid and distinctive, but they need more room in
which to interact. Jazz is described so lyrically the reader regrets that Major Kelley is merely a fictitious character. Contemporary and entertaining, the novel offers humor and a bridge
over the generation gap. (p. 433)

Holly Willett, in her review of "Does This School
Have Capital Punishment?" in The Horn Book Magazine (copyright © 1981 by The Horn Book, Inc.,
Boston), Vol. LVII, No. 4, August, 1981, pp. 432-
33.

JOHN A. NELSON

Hentoff's ability to speak both passionately and objectively
makes **The First Freedom** a success. Readers are left with two
valuable insights, each essential to a healthy tolerance for the
role of free expression in our society. The first is that the First
Amendment has never been static. The wording seems simple
enough ("Congress shall make no law . . .") but the interpretation and application of those words to changing circumstances has been one of the great challenges to our society. It
follows, then, that there will never be a time when answers to
questions involving the First Amendment are easy. It is, rather,
as Thomas Paine suggested over two hundred years ago, ". . .
those who expect to reap the blessings of freedom must . . .
undergo the fatigue of supporting it." **The First Freedom** makes
us aware that we should not expect an end to the fatigue.

The second insight is that the history of free speech, and the
advancement of ideas in our society, has been a history of
unpopular people with controversial ideas. The theme developed early in the book, and supported by example throughout,
is that it is in times of greatest danger to our system that the
right to speak and print dissenting views is most seriously
threatened. People who have expressed minority views during
times of crisis have done so at great personal risk. They may
not have lived to see their views vindicated. Sometimes, as in
the recent Nazi march case in Skokie, Illinois, their views have
been repulsive.

In making these points in a book of over three hundred pages,
Nat Hentoff chose a format and a style that make the lessons
accessible to high school students as well as graduate students.
The case study format presents issues of importance to the
history of the First Amendment in the context of the time and
the people who raised them. Since several of the examples are
about students in schools, Hentoff's book is particularly relevant to anyone in education.

Legal issues surrounding free expression are raised through
Tinker v. Des Moines, a Viet Nam era case remembered for
the utterance of Supreme Court Justice Abe Fortas that "students in school as well as out of school are 'persons' under
our Constitution." The story is worth study by students and
teachers, for it raises central questions about the right to express
unpopular views.

In *Tinker*, and all the cases that follow, Hentoff helps us know
the people, as well as the legal questions, in the controversies.
Before going back to the beginning chapters of the history of
free speech, **The First Freedom** continues with modern examples involving library censorship and academic freedom in
public schools. By the time we are introduced to John Peter
Zenger and the other early figures in American free speech,
we are caught up in the format and style of Hentoff's book.
(p. 71)

Of course, the First Amendment was designed to protect more
than expression. Specific prohibitions in the amendment are
designed to prevent governmental intrusions in the practice of
religion. The words *establishment* and *free exercise* were used
by the authors of the amendment, and their application to very
puzzling situations has become the job of courts. Again, Hentoff chooses cases of interest to students when he addresses
the subject of religious freedom. The school prayer decisions
of the early 1960s were among the most emotional and controversial ever issued by the United States Supreme Court. **The
First Freedom** sets forth the legal rationale of those cases, an

understanding essential for those who continue to debate the questions they raise.

Finally, the terribly complex questions of the 1970s and 1980s are raised. The ''Pentagon Papers'' case was the most celebrated of those recent cases testing the power of a government to prevent publication of matters that, in the view of those in power, threaten the security of the nation. In another case, contrasted to the ''Pentagon Papers,'' the government temporarily prevented *The Progressive* from publishing information on the construction of a hydrogen bomb.

Hentoff introduces readers to new trends in the constant evolution of the First Amendment. In the *Progressive* case, for example, government lawyers argued that there is a difference between ''political'' and ''technical'' speech, the latter being excluded from protection by the Constitution. Only after months of litigation and censorship, when it was pointed out that the material being suppressed was available to the public on the Los Alamos library shelves, was the case against the *Progressive* abandoned.

In the highly emotional area of obscenity, new trends may also be found. The Supreme Court now appears ready to distinguish between ''serious'' speech and speech of no ''redeeming social importance.''

Of particular interest to students of journalism are cases involving a reporter's right to protect sources and the recent ''shield law'' disputes. Nowhere is the balance of interests more difficult than in these cases. Two closely held sets of interests, those of a free press and those of defendants in criminal trials, are at odds. Hentoff appears to side with the reporters, but he provides sufficient insight into the merits of both sides to provide readers with materials to reach informed conclusions of their own.

We should be aware of trends in First Amendment interpretation. We should know the history of free expression in America. Nat Hentoff's book ably puts into perspective the evolutionary process that is our First Amendment. *The First Freedom* is about the free exchange of ideas, a subject of considerable importance to teachers and students. It should be read by everyone. (p. 72)

> *John A. Nelson, ''Too Good To Miss'' (copyright ©*
> *1982 by the National Council of Teachers of English;*
> *reprinted by permission of the publisher and the author), in* English Journal, *Vol. 71, No. 4, April, 1982,*
> *pp. 71-2.*

GEOFF FOX

The American boys' private school has had a bad press in recent times. John Knowles's *A Separate Peace* and Robert Cormier's *The Chocolate War* uncovered tensions and animosities of peculiar cruelty. Nat Hentoff's Alcott School [in **This School Is Driving Me Crazy**] is seen from a more comic standpoint, but the plot still turns upon bullying and extortion in the corridors and cloakrooms.

Sam Davidson is amusingly scatter-brained, highly articulate, given to thoughtless horsing around and basically a good kid; as is the way of many post-[Paul] Zindel heroes in American novels. . . .

Nat Hentoff's dialogue is particularly lively and the scenes between [Sam and his friends] are thoroughly entertaining. The headmaster's problems about Sam (to the despair of his wife,

he is unable to show his supportive love to his son) might seem implausible to the layman. In practice, headmastering regularly throws up circumstances where the public mask sits uncomfortably, threatening to mould the features beneath.

Sam is the target for criticism from other members of staff, and it is here that the book is least convincing. Teachers, absorbed in their community, may indeed lose a sense of perspective, but the personal animosity which drives Mr. Kodozoy to try to destroy Sam and weaken the head's influence is difficult to credit; as indeed is Mr. Davidson's vindictive pleasure in determining to increase Kodozoy's teaching load next year as retribution.

Very many readers will find the underworld of school, flourishing beyond the knowledge of the staff, all too believable, and the text's energy and hilarity should sweep readers along. Mr. Hentoff does not exactly tell it like it is, but he has that nicely judged sense of the slightly larger than it is, so satisfying to the inmates of the institutions he describes.

> *Geoff Fox, in his review of ''This School Is Driving*
> *Me Crazy,'' in* Children's literature in education *(©*
> *1982, Agathon Press, Inc.; reprinted by permission*
> *of the publisher), Vol. 13, No. 2 (Summer), 1982,*
> *p. 57.*

PUBLISHERS WEEKLY

''Fiction can be more real than fact, can tell you more about what ordinary people were like,'' according to a student at the high school where Hentoff sets [**''The Day They Came to Arrest the Book''**]. The statement implies the reason for the fictional treatment of real and widely aired demands for book censorship. The format works well, thanks to the author's striking use of dialogue, individualizing a large cast of opposing characters. . . . Adding fuel to incendiary debates [about whether or not Mark Twain's ''The Adventures of Huckleberry Finn'' is racist] are Kate, a feminist student who damns the Twain classic's portrayal of women, along with an avowed champion of the right to ban all writing that he and his advocates decide are antireligious and/or antimoral. The battle is joined and rages on in the engrossing story. It is an outstanding work, given added value by the author's honest, comprehensive coverage of all sides of the argument over ''dangerous freedoms.''

> *A review of ''The Day They Came to Arrest the Book,''*
> *in* Publishers Weekly *(reprinted from the September*
> *10, 1982 issue of* Publishers Weekly, *published by*
> *R. R. Bowker Company; copyright © 1982 by R. R.*
> *Bowker Company), Vol. 222, No. 11, September 10,*
> *1982, p. 76.*

STEPHANIE ZVIRIN

[*The Day They Came to Arrest the Book* is an] undisguised but timely and articulate issue book with a number of artfully developed stereotypes. . . . New librarian Dierdre Fitzgerald finds herself smack in the middle of [a censorship] controversy when a student, objecting to Twain's portrayal of blacks and his use of the word ''nigger'' in [**Huckleberry Finn**] . . . , complains to his father, who petitions the principal (the most odious character in the book) for the novel's withdrawal from classroom use and from the high school library. Using a number of staged debates, among them a volatile book-review-committee meeting, Hentoff makes his own views clear while he presents principal arguments involved in book censorship and a crystalline statement of the freedoms at stake. He closes with a chilling little scenario that points to the false sense of security that comes from winning one battle while the war rages on. A smattering of realistic language fits in perfectly with the highly charged issues Hentoff brings to the fore, and while his characters remain static and one-dimensional, he presents the issue at hand with zeal and perception.

Stephanie Zvirin, in her review of "The Day They Came to Arrest the Book," in Booklist *(reprinted by permission of the American Library Association; copyright © 1982 by the American Library Association), Vol. 79, No. 2, September 15, 1982, p. 105.*

KIRKUS REVIEWS

[*The Day They Came to Arrest the Book* is a] fictionalized airing of the book censorship issue, set in a high school with a weak, oily principal, a strong and principled English teacher, and a new librarian. . . . Hentoff avoids the predictable alliances by making the complainant a black parent who objects to the use of "nigger" in *Huckleberry Finn*. Before the book issue emerges, Hentoff sets the stage with a guest debate, for an American history class, between an articulate conservative and an equally articulate if less smooth young ACLU lawyer. Later the conservative sides with the black father, as does Kate, an aggressive feminist student who objects to Mark Twain's treatment of women. They are joined by the usual guardians of morality shocked by Huck and Jim's nudity and the message that "a child ought to decide for himself what's right and wrong." Hentoff allows both sides persuasive arguments at the school board hearing that results in the book being restricted but not removed altogether, and again at the second meeting where a black student testifies to his ability to "tell when the word nigger is directed at me." This time the review committee reconsiders and lifts the restrictions. What the anti-censorship forces learn is that it's best to bring such conflicts into the open. There are other twists to this conflict: the principal schemes behind the scenes in the interest of his own career; the school paper editor backs down on an editorial attacking the principal, but later publishes a more damning interview. Hentoff, however, stages no inner agonizing, sticks in no personal subplots, and doesn't bother to pass off the various mouthpieces as characters or personalities. Even more than his other novels, this issue "novel" is all issue, without pretense or apology. As such it's accessibly well-reasoned, timely once more despite the ancient heritage of all the arguments, and probably better off without the extracurricular padding.

A review of "The Day They Came to Arrest the Book," in Kirkus Reviews *(copyright © 1982 The Kirkus Service, Inc.), Vol. L, No. 18, September 15, 1982, p. 1060.*

SAUL MALOFF

[At the end of **"The Day They Came to Arrest the Book"**], George Mason High School and the community have just emerged from bloody struggle between the forces of darkness seeking to censor "Huckleberry Finn" and the forces of light. By a dramatic last-minute shift the latter have won a precarious victory, and Moore [the high school principal] is already plotting to unleash another assault when the balance on the school board is tipped.

The new members include a black "activist" for whom the great novel comes down to that single unspeakable six-letter epithet, a right-wing zealot and moralizer who wants God established and sin cast out and others of his persuasion gathered together in such organizations as Save Our Children From Atheist Secular Humanism (SOCASH). Against them stand an attractive, intelligent, principled librarian, the teacher passionately committed to democratic rights who assigned the book for reading alongside [Alexis de] Tocqueville, and other admirable people and good kids.

Nat Hentoff, himself well known for his devotion to the First Amendment, makes honorable efforts to give the most unsavory characters their due, such as it is. He is also fairly merciless in his portraiture. The black parent is obsessional, dogmatic, pompous; the mealy-mouthed white ultrist is wily, slithery, unctuous; Moore has further distinguished himself by excising from the school Bible some of the more awkward episodes (see II Samuel 13 and Judges 19).

Mr. Hentoff takes such scrupulous care that in places he almost makes it seem that there are indeed two rational positions on the novel from which we are all descended, and that is no small achievement, especially considering his own uncompromising partisanship. If the book is less a novel than a morality play, the arguments are lucidly and forcefully laid out—though we are never in doubt that Mr. Hentoff is steadfastly on the side of the seraphim.

Saul Maloff, in his review of "The Day They Came to Arrest the Book," in The New York Times Book Review *(© 1983 by The New York Times Company; reprinted by permission), March 6, 1983, p. 30.*

Thor Heyerdahl

1914-

Norwegian writer on travel, anthropology, and archaeology.

Heyerdahl, an anthropologist, is best known for his accounts of the exciting journeys he undertook to prove his scientific theories. He has long contended that the early settlers of the Polynesian Islands were Indians from South America, not Asians, as was generally believed. To demonstrate that ancient Peruvians could have completed a trip to Polynesia on balsa rafts, he himself accomplished the feat. *Kon-Tiki* describes his voyage. Continuing the argument in *Aku-Aku* and *The Art of Easter Island*, he explores similarities between the cultures of pre-Inca Peru and that of Easter Island. In further adventures, he tests his theories that Egyptians could have settled in Mexico (*The Ra Expeditions*) and that the Sumerians could have built ocean-going ships, thereby extending their contact with other civilizations (*The Tigris Expedition*).

Heyerdahl relates his experiences in a way that captures the interest of both experts and the general reader. His books are informative without being dry and scholarly and contain enough humor to mitigate the actual dangers encountered. Although the majority of Heyerdahl's colleagues do not feel he has sufficiently proved his hypotheses, they agree that his questions provide new insight into anthropological study.

(See also *Contemporary Authors*, Vols. 5-8, rev. ed. and *Something about the Author*, Vol. 2.)

ALFRED STANFORD

It is the deep connection with nature and a tremendous simplicity that makes ["**Kon-Tiki: Across the Pacific by Raft**"] great as few books of our time are great. . . . [It has quickly spread through the world] with the speed of a small classic being born and the suggestion that it contains a strong medicine for modern man.

The book records the straight-forward chronicle of a 4,300-mile passage across the Pacific by six naked men on a raft. Its pages reflect a minimum of philosophical overtones. But on every page there is a perceptiveness of the sea and the sky that has delicacy and sureness. Through it all runs the awareness that ancient man ventured here before. . . .

It is in the record of daily life, so close to the water as to be virtually a part of it for the 101 days of the passage, that the best writing occurs. (p. 1)

There is no mention of monotony or boredom. Every day was full of its own events, the sky, the stars, the marine life and the clouds. The story of these days and nights creates picture after picture. . . .

The final landing at the Raroia barrier reef that should have wrecked a normal craft and crushed normal men unprotected by pre-Inca legends is told with great skill and excitement, as are the days that followed in exploration and meeting with the Polynesian inhabitants. (p. 10)

Alfred Stanford, "They Floated across the Pacific on a Vine-Tied Raft," in New York Herald Tribune

Book Review (© *I.H.T. Corporation*), September 3, 1950, pp. 1, 10.

HARRY GILROY

[The saga of "**Kon-Tiki**"] is a revelation of how exciting science can become when it inspires a man with the heart of Leif Ericsson and the merry story-telling gift of an Ernie Pyle. . . .

[The six men on the raft came to learn that] whether it was 1947 A.D. or B.C. was of no significance. "We realized that life had been full for men before the technical age also—in fact, fuller and richer in many ways than the life of modern man."

Here is the heart of the powerful appeal of this book. . . . These are cultivated modern men, scientists, artists, technicians. They have a particular quality, which is that an idea can have such value to them that they are willing to stake their lives upon its validity. . . .

[They] have this quality and they arm the reader with it as he goes along on the unpretentiously daring escapades, the low comedy and high philosophizing of the voyage. The thought of six intelligent men putting out to sea on a raft held together with a few ropes—practically guaranteeing the sharks a fat meal—is utterly absurd. Yet the absurdity fades in the face of the realization that the expedition proved, and proved in the only possible way, exactly how the races of men spread across the seas of the world.

Harry Gilroy, "Six Who Dared to Live a Legend," in The New York Times Book Review (© 1950 by The New York Times Company; reprinted by permission), September 3, 1950, p. 1.

ROLAND SAWYER

[*Kon-Tiki*] is a mystery story—although there is no crime beyond the polite defiance of "sound advice," no plot except a problem of long-distance transport by raft, no solution to an ethnological question that has intrigued men since Magellan, Querios, and Cook explored the Pacific Ocean. Here, too, is an adventure story—for it is an extraordinary record of men drifting 4,000 miles on the sea amidst unforeseen perils, under a world of stars. And here is fine descriptive writing.

Thor Heyerdahl sought evidence to support a theory. That seeking brought about as remarkable a journey as the 20th century has witnessed. It will be a rare reader who will be able to put the book down once he has read beyond the first page. For the author opens his exciting narrative midway through the 101-day odyssey of six men on a raft in the Pacific. And once aboard that raft, even for a few safe paragraphs, the reader can no more get off than could Heyerdahl and his companions, from the moment they were set adrift off the Peruvian coast until they were flung, raft and men, over the Raroia reef to safety in Polynesia. . . .

Heyerdahl and his men were fortunate from beginning to end—but they deserved to be, as the log of the Kon-Tiki, the name given to the raft from a pre-Columbian sun-god, shows. It is from the log that this book is largely written, and while this is not the first time that a log has been turned into literature, it has seldom been done so superbly.

The book is cast in terms of men-against-the-sea, which gives it a general rather than particular appeal. . . . Not being a specialist, this reviewer cannot attempt to discuss the thesis itself—that aboriginal Americans, not Asiatics, settled Polynesia. Heyerdahl's seamanship proves this could have been done, and his archaeological deductions would seem to leave a challenger in a difficult position. Certainly the book will impel renewed research into the mystery of the origin of the people of the many islands, Polynesians.

It will do so not only because of the feat it records, but because Heyerdahl is both a fascinating and a philosophical narrator. Here is an epic of our own time, at least the equal of Bligh's journey by open boat in the 18th century. When that statement is measured against the famous sailing feats of the Polynesians themselves, no more can be said.

Roland Sawyer, "An Epic for Our Time," in The Christian Science Monitor (reprinted by permission from The Christian Science Monitor; © 1950 The Christian Science Publishing Society; all rights reserved), September 7, 1950, p. 22.

WENDELL C. BENNETT

[The] daring and dramatic journey [of the Kon-Tiki and her six crewmen] demonstrated beyond any doubt that the pre-European inhabitants of South America could have reached Polynesia.

The possibility is one thing, the probability another. In ["**American Indians in the Pacific: The Theory Behind the Kon-Tiki Expedition**"], Mr. Heyerdahl presents his arguments for the reality of such migrations. His thesis, to state it briefly, is that the earlier Polynesians came from Peru via Easter Island, and that the later migrants came from the northwest coast of North America, traditional home of the totem-pole Indians, via the Hawaiian Islands. . . .

To support this thesis, Mr. Heyerdahl has assembled an impressive array of evidence and arguments, covering a vast bibliography and many fields of knowledge. He deals with the ethnography of Oceania and the Northwest Coast, geography, ocean currents, botany, archeology, physical anthropology and linguistics. No author could have equal competence in all of these fields, but the approach is commendable.

The Northwest Coast argument is based on the known seamanship of these Indians, the ocean currents which drift pine logs to Hawaii, and the striking similarities in plank houses, totem poles, single and double canoes, and many artifacts. Furthermore, Mr. Heyerdahl believes that the Polynesians refer to the Hawaiian Islands as their traditional homeland, "Hawaiki."

The greatest part of the book is devoted to the Kon-Tiki thesis, namely the Peruvian migrations. . . .

The quantity and quality of the materials which Mr. Heyerdahl has assembled are too great to be ignored. Henceforth, American contributions to the Polynesian cultures will have to be considered. However, there are still serious objections to attributing total Polynesian origins to the New World. One is physical, namely how a distinctive Polynesian racial type could be derived from two basically Mongoloid Indian stocks. Mr. Heyerdahl argues at length that there was a "Caucasoid" strain in the early Indian populations, but the data are far from adequate.

A second is linguistic. The Polynesian languages are noted for their simple phonetics, analytic structure and positional syntax. The languages of Peru and the Northwest Coast are phonetically complex and extremely poly-synthetic in their extensive use of affixes. These differences cannot be dismissed with what Mr. Heyerdahl calls a "softening" process. Instead, the affiliations of Polynesia are with the Malayan languages.

A third is archeological. The ancient Peruvian civilizations long before 450 A.D. placed great emphasis on weaving, ceramics, metalwork and domesticated maize. All of these are absent in Polynesia, although there existed suitable clays, native cotton and an intensive agricultural pattern.

Mr. Heyerdahl has, perhaps deliberately, overstated his case. In spite of his voluminous arguments, he has not yet resolved the question of Polynesian origins, but he has at least introduced a new chapter.

Wendell C. Bennett "Behind the Bold Kon-Tiki Voyage," in The New York Times Book Review (© 1953 by The New York Times Company; reprinted by permission), August 9, 1953, p. 1.

KENT BUSH

[In "**American Indians in the Pacific**"] Heyerdahl marshals exceedingly convincing visual evidence of pre-Columbian

American Indian influences in the Pacific. In no other single book can there be found an equally rich collection of that data—scientific, cultural, historical—so necessary for the development of a reasoned theory of the colonization of Polynesia. Without taking into account these facts and their interpretation—many of them published for the first time in this volume—no scholar can speak with accuracy on the problem. This book will be required reading for all students of American and Pacific culture, history, and pre-history.

Any scholar who necessarily deals with the findings in a dozen or more sciences will come under attack from the siege guns of specialization. The central question in evaluating an effort to synthesize broadly in any scholarly field is: has the factual evidence been handled with respect on its own merits and has all available evidence been presented and brought to bear on resulting conclusions? I can find no mark of Heyerdahl's failing in this scholarly trust.

But don't accept the notion that this is only a scientific document. For anyone who has sailed the enormous distance between the major Polynesian island systems—distances known to have been navigated in canoes, and possibly rafts, by Stone-Age migrants—in fact, all travelers will gain from Heyerdahl's account a new appreciation of the intelligence and vigor of Neolithic man. **"American Indians in the Pacific"** is as stirring a tribute to ancient man as **"Kon-Tiki"** is to modern. . . .

The exhaustive treatment makes the book bulky and the presentation occasionally tortuous. It may be that a desk dictionary will have to be used now and then, although the context usually provides operational definitions. But even so, most readers will find in the reading of it straightforward enjoyment.

[It] will be clear that the conclusions are based on first-hand observation and first-rate scholarship. It will be clear that the excitement of unraveling an ethnographic "detective thriller" is a delightful way to enjoy and appreciate a scholarly theory and dissertation in this important field of study.

> *Kent Bush, "Solving Some of the Problems of Pacific Pre-history," in* The Christian Science Monitor *(reprinted by permission from* The Christian Science Monitor; *© 1953 The Christian Science Publishing Society; all rights reserved), August 13, 1953, p. 11.*

THE TIMES LITERARY SUPPLEMENT

[Thor Heyerdahl] wrote a book about a raft which will not soon be forgotten. It is unreasonable to expect an equal success when the same gifts are employed in the same way on a subject involving, much more than mere adventure, a difficult and intricate scientific experiment. [*Aku-Aku*] brings home a brilliant outline of Easter Island and its present inhabitants. It closes with a whimsical dialogue between the author and his aku-aku [guardian spirit], concerning the relation between archaeological fact and speculation, which admits in effect some weakness in his treatment in these pages of his central problem. There is little doubt that he made some important discoveries. It is time for him to throw away his glowing colours and report in black and white exactly what they amount to.

> *"Island of the Stone Men," in* The Times Literary Supplement *(© Times Newspapers Ltd. (London) 1958; reproduced from* The Times Literary Supplement *by permission), No. 2929, April 18, 1958, p. 211.*

GLYN DANIEL

Thor Heyerdahl, whose *Kon-Tiki* expedition captured the young imagination of the world, visited Easter Island in the last few years and with a party of arachæologists and anthropologists made his own investigations. . . . He claims that as a result he has solved the mystery of Easter Island, that it was first settled about AD 400 by people from central and south America, that the great statues (which he places in his second period of occupation, say between the tenth and fifteenth centuries AD) get later as one travels westwards, and that the statue-building people were massacred by the ancestors of the present inhabitants of the island who came in canoes from Polynesia.

All this may be right, but it is impossible to accept his case, or even to understand it clearly, on the basis of the present book [*Aku-Aku: The Secret of Easter Island*], which is a highly garnished and overdramatised account of his visit to Easter Island. But behind its façade of personal encounter and adventure, its publicity and colour, it is clear that Heyerdahl has done a great deal of interesting work particularly on the technique of cutting and moving the statues. *The Kon-Tiki Expedition* was followed by a learned statement of case, *American Indians in the Pacific,* and in due course *Aku-Aku* will be followed by a learned account of Heyerdahl's investigations on Easter Island; we must await that full statement before we evaluate his views in relations to those of Métraux and others. But there is this difference between *Kon-Tiki* and *Aku-Aku*. Scholars said that it was impossible for men to sail in balsa-rafts from the west coast of America to Polynesia; Heyerdahl demonstrated that the impossible was practicable for bold, buccaneering twentieth-century Vikings. He demonstrated that it was possible that the culture of Polynesia *could* have come from America, and no one can gainsay that. But now he argues that the culture of Easter Island certainly *did* come from America, and while we admit the possibility, we await proofs of the certainty, and will wish to study them in relation to the adduced proofs of the Asian origin of Polynesian culture. Meanwhile, *Aku-Aku* will hold all kinds of men and women from the chimney corner.

> *Glyn Daniel, "Telling Secrets," in* The Spectator *(©1958 by* The Spectator; *reprinted by permission of* The Spectator*), Vol. 200, No. 6776, May 9, 1958, p. 599.*

JOHN M. CONNOLE

Heyerdahl's latest book, **"Sea Routes to Polynesia,"** is a collection of papers and addresses from the years 1951-1964, most of which were delivered before international scientific societies throughout the world. For the most part, they either amplify, or give further evidence in support of, the conclusions reached in [**"Kon-Tiki"** and **"Aku-Aku"**]. Thus their interest for the general reader will depend upon how enthusiastically he felt about these books. (p. 42)

> *John M. Connole, in his review of "Sea Routes to Polynesia," in* The New York Times Book Review *(© 1968 by The New York Times Company; reprinted by permission), December 8, 1968, pp. 42, 46.*

PHILIP MORRISON

Thor Heyerdahl made his voyage on the balsa raft in defense of a theory, the theory of the Pacific as a highway by which Peruvian men and ideas came to Polynesia. [*Sea Routes to*

Polynesia is] a set of nine of his papers, mostly written in the 1960's, expounding and elaborating on this theme. His work on the curious multiple centerboards of the Incas that make balsa rafts such as *Kon-Tiki* capable of tacking and sailing into the wind, and his understanding of long sea voyages under plausible early circumstances, are fully convincing. . . . Heyerdahl argues that, whereas there are no good sea routes out of America across the Atlantic, there are plausible routes, one equatorial and one southerly, out of America toward Asia, and one ''natural passage'' from Indonesia north of Hawaii to Mexico, found by Spanish shipmasters in 1565. Much less compelling is the evidence that by such routes Polynesia was settled, or that cotton, gourds, sweet potatoes and yams were taken to Asia. (p. 138)

> *Philip Morrison, ''How Man and His Domesticated Plants Crossed the Oceans, and Other Matters,'' in* Scientific American *(copyright © 1969 by Scientific American, Inc.; all rights reserved), Vol. 220, No. 6, June, 1969, pp. 138-40, 42.**

CHRISTOPHER WORDSWORTH

Thor Heyerdahl's latest feat is to have reconstructed a papyrus ship from Egyptian tomb-reliefs and crossed the Atlantic in it with a polyglot crew, a stirring enough enterprise in itself, related with his own brand of visionary robustness [in *The Ra Expeditions*]. But those who know their man will not need telling that his primary motive was not to get from A to B. By demonstrating the unguessed sea-going capabilities of papyrus he has exposed a chink in one of the strong points of an argument that rules out all possibility of early contact between the Mediterranean civilisations of antiquity and the New World. (p. 638)

Kon-Tiki had a specific theory, scientific evidence and a logical conclusion: *Ra* admits to chronological snags and inexplicable contradictions in its general drift. We knew that Egyptians and Phoenicians rounded the shoulder of Africa; it is reasonable to suppose that some vessels were carried off-course by the Canary current; now we have seen it proved that papyrus could have stood the Atlantic passage. Has Heyerdahl succeeded in putting another cat among the ethno-anthropological pigeons? It is pleasant to picture that gurgling hamper of reeds bearing down on the pundits like Columbus's doom-burdened caravels. But somehow, this time, one doubts it. (p. 639)

> *Christopher Wordsworth, ''Straws in the Wind,'' in* New Statesman *(© 1971 The Statesman & Nation Publishing Co. Ltd.), Vol. 81, No. 2094, May 7, 1971, pp. 638-39.*

THE TIMES LITERARY SUPPLEMENT

The voyages of Thor Heyerdahl across the Atlantic provide instructive examples of adventures undertaken ostensibly in search of knowledge. In *The Ra Expeditions* the story is told of how, in pursuit of an idea, if not of a theory, Mr Heyerdahl at a second attempt succeeded in crossing the Atlantic from Morocco to Barbados in a craft made of papyrus stems lashed together with ropes. . . .

The account of the [first attempt and the second successful voyage] can do nothing but arouse admiration for the temerity and determination of the two crews—amateur in every respect—driven to epic achievement by the obsession of Thor Heyerdahl. . . . He is very careful not to claim too much, but

the implication of the whole book is that Egyptians colonized America, probably by chance, and that they did it by means of papyrus craft.

It is as an adventure story that *The Ra Expeditions* must be judged, not as an account of a serious scientific experiment. The principal reason why this is so is that the basic premise of Mr Heyerdahl's thinking does not stand up to close examination. Did the Egyptians in fact use papyrus vessels for sea voyages? There is not a scrap of good evidence to support the idea. On the contrary, there is much evidence to show that the sea-going ships of the Egyptians were built of wood. . . .

[Possibilities] are not enough to satisfy the serious student. Mr Heyerdahl has shown that it is possible to travel from Africa to America by papyrus craft. He has not demonstrated that the Egyptians used papyrus for large vessels or that they undertook sea voyages in such craft. . . .

To the prosaic scholar the idea of voyaging to America in a papyrus craft is unacceptable, not because of the danger, but because of its implausibility in the face of the ancient evidence. Happily for the watching world and the reading public Mr Heyerdahl chose to follow his own instincts. If he had considered the evidence more closely, he might never have built Ra I and Ra II, and the history of adventure would have been much the poorer.

> *''Unepistemological Expedition,'' in* The Times Literary Supplement *(© Times Newspapers Ltd. (London) 1971; reproduced from* The Times Literary Supplement *by permission), No. 3617, June 25, 1971, p. 745.**

GEOFFREY BIBBY

Let it be said immediately that Thor Heyerdahl has pulled it off again. He has written a superb adventure-book [''**The Ra Expeditions**''] about a superb adventure. . . .

Heyerdahl has lost none of his magic of phrase, and the translation renders faithfully the laconic playing-down of real danger and hard work which comes almost naturally to Norwegians. We are introduced most thoroughly to the reed boat as still existing—in Peru, Mexico, Central Africa and Ethiopia—and this section, a third of the whole book, might be tedious, were it not for the superb color illustrations, and for the circumstance that such fact-finding preliminaries are in real life necessary to the setting-up of experiments, and deserve recording by the author and attention from the reader.

Once the construction of Ra I is underway, the pace is fast enough, and the book is compelling reading as the vessel gradually approaches America and gradually falls more and more to pieces. Nor is the Ra II voyage, which ends the book, anticlimactical. On the contrary, it takes the same story onward to the final triumph as, escorted by 50 vessels of all types, Ra sailed into Bridgetown harbor.

But what does the experiment prove? Thor Heyerdahl is modest. ''I still don't known,'' he writes. . . . Yet his book leaves little doubt that he firmly believes that the ''bearded white men'' recorded as bringing civilization to Central America came from the Mediterranean. . . .

> *Geoffrey Bibby, in his review of ''The Ra Expeditions,'' in* The New York Times Book Review *(© 1971 by The New York Times Company; reprinted by permission), August 22, 1971, p. 21.*

TIMOTHY SEVERIN

[In *The Ra Expeditions* Heyerdahl's] narrative—and some of his more provocative theories as well—unfold with deceptive ease. The book is an effortless read and has an old-fashioned adventure story quality that sweeps it along as inexorably as the ocean currents which Heyerdahl believes were the conveyor belts of world culture. Anyone who enjoyed the vicarious thrill of riding them in a balsa raft, will take nostalgic pleasure in this papyrus venture, the cruise of the ''paper boat.'' (p. 9)

> *Timothy Severin, ''Place Your Trust in a Broken Reed,'' in* Book World—Chicago Tribune *(© 1971 Postrib Corp.; reprinted by permission of* Chicago Tribune *and* The Washington Post*), October 3, 1971, pp. 7, 9.*

PHILIP SNOW

Two unique voyages, three ponderous books of scientific probings: what more can Heyerdahl do? He can continue to produce entertaining books.

Fatu-Hiva is of the same quality as his three popular classics, *The Kon-Tiki Expedition, The Ra Expeditions* and *Aku-Aku*. But it appears to be a reissue (for the first time in English) of a 1938 Oslo publication, and retains some inevitable naivety. . . .

It was on Fatu-Hiva, the first Polynesian island seen by Europeans nearly 400 years ago, that Heyerdahl came to believe in the likelihood of Polynesia being inhabited from the direction of America. His search for links with ancient South America is indefatigable, but may still leave gaps (fairly, he has always acknowledged a shortage of linguistic affinities).

In *Fatu-Hiva* he is graphic and forceful throughout. It is not surprising to anyone having experiences of life close to nature, even as it is in the South Seas, that his wife and he would not elect to live there for ever. Disease, deprivation, discomfort overwhelmed them. Very soon he was to give further proof of his intrepidity in the Norwegian Resistance movement. But he had previously recorded this fine account of the realities of escapism. . . .

> *Philip Snow, ''Polynesian Bliss,'' in* The Times Literary Supplement *(© Times Newspapers Ltd. (London) 1975; reproduced from* The Times Literary Supplement *by permission), No. 3822, June 6, 1975, p. 632.*

FREDERICK H. GUIDRY

[''*Fatu-Hiva*''] indefatigably records the details of [Liv and Thor Heyerdahl's] semi-informed leap into another way of life. The account is buoyed by the author's persistent enthusiasm for the project, despite obvious privations, bouts with disease, and incidents of danger.

The journey itself, and not surprisingly the book about it, carries an undertone of hippie-like defiance of modern-day conveniences and customary ways of looking at life and purpose. The reader races ahead to the conclusion that, yes, it is possible to ''tear ourselves away from our artificial life,'' but to what end? Most people do not need to go through such a grueling experience to arrive at such simple knowledge that ''we have nowhere to retreat to, no choice but to help one another to build a durable civilization in harmony with whatever natural environment we have left.''

But for readers who enjoy a survival story told from the standpoint of youthful idealism, ''*Fatu-Hiva*'' has much to offer by way of adventure and discovery, capped by a satisfying glad-to-be-back finale.

> *Frederick H. Guidry, ''The Kon-Tiki Man Describes How His Career Began,'' in* The Christian Science Monitor *(reprinted by permission from* The Christian Science Monitor; *© 1975 The Christian Science Publishing Society; all rights reserved), August 20, 1975, p. 27.*

ROBERT TRUMBULL

[''*Fatu-Hiva*''] is an attention-riveting escape book as well as a revealing, if unnecessarily preachy, essay on what white men have done to a once happy South Sea island, and how the island retaliated against a white couple attempting to settle there. Although scarcely the literary equal of some of the work of other authors [such as Robert Louis Stevenson, James Michener, and Herman Melville], or Heyerdahl's own best seller, ''**Kon-Tiki**,'' it is a valuable contribution to the knowledge of Polynesia and, especially, of Heyerdahl himself and his persuasive, if disputed, theory that the islands were peopled by Western migration from South America. (pp. 10, 12)

[It was on Fatu-Hiva] that Heyerdahl became convinced that Polynesians are the descendants of prehistoric voyagers from South America, rather than from a migration from Southeast Asia. The evidence he adduces in support of his theory—countless cultural similarities, including the practice of trepanning, common in the Pacific Islands and ancient Peru but unknown in East and Southeast Asia in the same period—is fascinating and convincing. This was the beginning, on remote, lonely Fatu-Hiva, of the Kon-Tiki saga. (p. 12)

> *Robert Trumbull, ''Following a Dream,'' in* The New York Times Book Review *(© 1975 by The New York Times Company; reprinted by permission), September 21, 1975, pp. 10, 12.*

ADRIENNE KAEPPLER

[Thor Heyerdahl's] ability to write for the general reader and to capture the imagination of all who have hidden desires to discover lost information about exotic peoples has endeared him to a public not overly concerned with scientific facts. After all, what could be more exciting than sailing on a raft from South America to Polynesia or dangerous rope descents to secret storage caves to discover small stone sculptures unknown to all who had gone before? These sculptures are the focus of Heyerdahl's new book *The Art of Easter Island*. The book's title, impressive size, and extensive illustrations excite one's hope that there might be a dispassionate analysis of art from an island that has always been shrouded in mystery. . . . How disappointing, then, to find that the book is not an analysis of these remarkable objects. Instead, it is a presentation yet again of his evidence in support of his view that Easter Island had direct contact from South America and that Polynesians came to Easter Island only in the final period of the island's history. . . .

[Many] of the hypotheses which he presents here as facts have been challenged by archaeologists using Heyerdahl's own evidence, from Jack Golson in 1965 (in *Oceania*) to Kenneth Emory in 1972 (in the *Journal of the Polynesian Society*). These and the works of others, which demonstrate that Heyerdahl's prehistoric sequences can be turned upside down and that Easter Island script is equally likely to be post-European, undermine the whole theoretical basis of Heyerdahl's argument and render many of the conclusions in this new book suspect. . . .

The most exciting section of the book is the long chapter on cave disclosures. Here Heyerdahl is at his best relating exciting tales of entering secret caves at midnight after chicken sacrifices and the recitation of sacred ritual formulae. . . . From such writing comes Heyerdahl's justly deserved reputation as an outstanding singer of tales. If only he would stop there and let us make our own inferences. But no, he goes on to draw endless parallels with South America and includes numerous plates and drawings calculated to convince. He does not, however, include examples from Polynesia, but states, often erroneously, that such do not exist. One is left with the uncomfortable feeling that he has not done his homework. . . .

One is surprised by his dichotomy between "genuine art" ending at 1886 and "commercial art" after that time, which completely disregards European influence during 164 years; by the seeming arbitrariness with which he assigns undatable specimens to one of his early middle, or late periods; or by such things as his attribution of a Hawaiian stone image to Easter Island because it looks as though it comes from Easter Island. . . . And could not the Easter Islanders invent or evolve anything themselves—must it have all come from somewhere? Quoting outdated source material makes it all sound so logical but nearly every page will be challenged by Polynesianists.

But, more seriously, where is his analysis of art? A study of art does not lie in relating stories of finding stone images or in their dubious parallels with related or not so related peoples. If it is impossible to reconstruct native categories or concepts of art, one might at least expect a structural analysis of the artistic forms, the relationships of the art forms to each other, or an analysis of motifs. . . . Can it be that Heyerdahl is not really interested in art—but rather in proving his theories with art objects? In the end one does not have a deeper understanding of the art of Easter Island, but the book is nevertheless a valuable source for further study of that art.

Adrienne Kaeppler, "Cave Caches," in The Times Literary Supplement *(© Times Newspapers Ltd. (London) 1976; reproduced from* The Times Literary Supplement *by permission), No. 3877, July 2, 1976, p. 830.*

JO-ANN D. SULEIMAN

[In *Early Man and the Ocean: A Search for the Beginnings of Navigation and Seaborne Civilizations*], one of the last of the world's great explorers synthesizes and discusses the implications of his combined studies and travels supporting the diffusionist perspective of the global spread of early man. Drawing on the Ra and Kon-Tiki experiences and on his vast knowledge of early civilization and oceanography, Heyerdahl hypothesizes on such topics as the early settlers of South and Central America and the Pacific Islands and the "paths through the seas" of Columbus, the Vikings, and the Spanish conquistadores. Much of this material has been previously published, and there are no startling revelations or departures. However, the book is a good summation of a brilliant life's work.

Jo-Ann D. Suleiman, in her review of "Early Man and the Ocean: A Search for the Beginnings of Navigation and Seaborne Civilizations," in Library Journal *(reprinted from* Library Journal, *February 15,*

1979; published by R. R. Bowker Co. (a Xerox company); copyright © 1979 by Xerox Corporation), Vol. 104, No. 4, February 15, 1979, p. 491.

TOBA KORENBLUM

Much of the credit for establishing early man's rightful foothold in history goes to author-adventurer Thor Heyerdahl, who popularized his theory of the evolution of navigation and civilization in his Kon-Tiki (Pacific) and Ra (Atlantic) expeditions. This slightly repetitive and highly detailed collection of essays [*Early Man and the Ocean*] bolsters the Norwegian's contention that "invisible marine conveyors"—tides and currents—not only dictated the flow of ancient oceanic traffic, but also determined the diffusion of culture.

More compelling is Heyerdahl's understated, secondary theme, that historical evidence can be manipulated and perverted by scientific bias or ethnocentrism. . . . For the sake of simplicity, if not greed, it was quietly overlooked that European explorers were drawing on the expertise of Inca informants, Phoenician merchant colonizers, West Coast Haida Indians and other "primitives," who, generations earlier, carved routes through the same waters. (pp. 56-7)

That same narrow-mindedness gripped 19th- and 20th-century scientists who misconstrued botanical, zoological and cultural parallels between civilizations because they could not recognize that aborigines were capable of extended sea travel in brilliantly constructed crafts—well before the European pilgrimages. Cultural cartographer Heyerdahl takes the reader to Vancouver Island, the Galápagos Islands, Greenland and Easter Island in search of his mentors. Ironically, *Early Man and the Ocean* obliquely illustrates that even as we race into space we have a limited insight into those who came before us. (p. 57)

Toba Korenblum, "Adrift on the Sea of Time," in Maclean's Magazine *(© 1979 by Maclean's Magazine; reprinted by permission), Vol. 92, No. 11, March 12, 1979, pp. 56-7.*

JOHN HEMMING

[In *The Tigris Expedition* Heyerdahl goes to] the very cradle of Western civilization for the most impressive of all his craft and the most satisfying of his theories.

This new venture, the building of a reed boat in Mesopotamia, started with few preconceived theories. Thor Heyerdahl simply wished to prove that the Sumerians were capable of building ocean-going boats from the berdi reeds that grow in such profusion in the Tigris marshes. But as the voyage progressed and the reed boat Tigris proved triumphantly seaworthy, Heyerdahl almost stumbled upon convincing answers to a series of archeological problems. The result is an excellent mix of mariner's yarn and historical detective work. . . .

With his ship still proudly afloat after five months at sea, Thor Heyerdahl disproved the theories of Armas Salonen, the Finnish authority on Mesopotamian watercraft, who had been sure that reed boats could not sail beyond the rivers. By venturing forth so boldly, Heyerdahl gave the lie to another accepted wisdom [that voyages were possible only so long as the navigator could hug a mainland coast]. Tigris was often in danger of being smashed or grounded on hostile coasts; her crew could relax only when they were far out to sea in their unsinkable boat. . . .

A fitting last leg for Tigris would have been to reach Egypt. This was frustrated by political upheavals around the Horn of Africa. A constant theme of this book is the contrast between ancient harmony and modern folly. . . . At times, Tigris was alone in oceans teeming with fish; at other times she was in danger of being rammed by speeding tankers, rotted by industrial effluents, or buzzed by aircraft of the superpowers. Trapped in Djibouti by political barriers, Tigris's crew burned their beloved vessel as an act of protest. But their gallant voyage yielded practical solutions to various archaeological questions. It also led to this delightful book, exciting, informative and challenging in the true Heyerdahl tradition.

John Hemming, "The Sea, Sumerian-style," in The Times Literary Supplement *(© Times Newspapers Ltd. (London) 1980; reproduced from* The Times Literary Supplement *by permission), No. 4046, October 17, 1980, p. 1176.*

George Roy Hill

1922-

American film director.

Hill's most successful films characteristically exhibit a playful, robust brand of American adventurism where male camaraderie is central to tone and plot. The main characters in many of Hill's movies are eccentric or socially reprehensible individuals who challenge accepted values and standards, often using considerable style and humor to accomplish their questionable activities.

Hill directed two of the biggest box office attractions of all time, *Butch Cassidy and the Sundance Kid* and *The Sting*. The films present the escapades of outlaws, in the former, and con men, in the latter, in such an endearing fashion that they recruit the audience wholeheartedly into the "bad guys" camp. Hill won the Academy Award for Best Director for *The Sting*. Hill has displayed a penchant for directing films of nostalgic eras, such as the "roaring twenties" in *Thoroughly Modern Millie* and *The Great Waldo Pepper*, but he has also demonstrated his ability to manage such contemporary subjects as violence in professional sports in his controversial film *Slap Shot*.

Hill has directed film adaptations of two contemporary novels which many critics believed were not good candidates for the screen. His version of Kurt Vonnegut's *Slaughterhouse-Five* won the special jury prize at the Cannes Film Festival in 1972. *The World According to Garp,* based on the popular John Irving novel, has received mixed reviews.

© Sygma

RICHARD WHITEHALL

[*Period of Adjustment*] is a fine example of the schizophrenic cinema, teetering uneasily between cinema and television, the forerunner of a completely new *genre* perhaps (the tele-cinema?). It could just be that George Roy Hill has not shaken off his television influences, but this feature looks exactly as if he were trying to please two separate audiences—the cinema audience now, and the box watchers when at some future date the 1963 film catalogue is sold to the TV channels. It will, I think, look more at home on the small screen than it does on the large one. There have been a number of notable recruits from the television to the film studios but, on the available evidence, George Roy Hill isn't one of them.

The small-sized compositions cramped in the centre of the screen fit uneasily into the larger playing area; there is too much inter-cutting of static close-ups; it's all too studied, somehow, all too telegenic. Sometimes, it is true, Hill gets bitten by the movement bug and we have two men standing at either end of a room passing a football between them as they talk, with the camera following the movement of the ball. This isn't what Sergei [Eisenstein] thought cinema should be, nor [Jean] Renoir either and, visually, I found the film a constant irritant like a mote of dust under the eyelid.

> *Richard Whitehall, in his review of "Period of Adjustment" (© copyright Richard Whitehall 1963; reprinted with permission), in* Films and Filming, *Vol. 9, No. 6, March, 1963, p. 38.*

STEPHEN FARBER

Richard Morris's script [for ***Thoroughly Modern Millie***] . . . is clever enough, though it merely strings together jokes on flat-chested rich girls, Harold Lloyd movies, innocents in the big city, Victorian melodrama. Somebody spent a lot of time researching all of the expressions from the twenties that sound ever so cute now, but nobody worried much about wit. . . . In its parody of old-fashioned movie Romance ***Millie*** is especially delightful, and promising. . . . But this is only one target of the movie's burlesque, and not all of them are so rewarding. As musical spectacle the film disappoints. The songs themselves—mostly retrieved from the period and nicely lampooned—are pleasant, but the choreography is insipid, and both the color photography and settings are thoroughly ordinary. George Roy Hill's direction is consistently unimaginative. (pp. 61-2)

> *Stephen Farber, in his review of "Thoroughly Modern Millie," in* Film Quarterly *(© 1967 by The Regents of the University of California: reprinted by permission of the Regents), Vol. XXI, No. 1, Fall, 1967, pp. 61-2.*

JUDITH CRIST

'I never met a soul more affable than you, Butch, or faster than the Kid,' a friendly sheriff notes [in ***Butch Cassidy and*** the Sundance Kid], 'but you're still nothing but a couple of two-bit outlaws on the dodge'. . . . The dodging is beautiful under George Roy Hill's direction. The man who made youthful poetry out of the New York scene in *The World of Henry Orient* turns a potent camera eye on the awesome vastnesses of the West, catches a quick tourist's view of New York and Coney Island and a voyage to Bolivia in wonderfully giddy rotogravure montages and—wonder of wonders these 'blood ballet' days—uses his past mastery of slow motion to absolutely stunning effect. Where the slow-motioning of death has been used with purely blood-wallow profusion in an abomination like [Sam Peckinpah's] *The Wild Bunch*, Mr. Hill uses it brilliantly on one occasion, when Butch kills for the first time—and we experience the slow death and drawn-out scream with his eye and ear. Sundance shoots and his victims drop like figures in a shooting gallery; for Butch there is the horrifying initial moment—and it signals the turn of the tide, the surfacing of the malaise that has been beneath the fun of the game. . . . But in the hands of [Paul] Newman and [Robert] Redford . . . and [screenwriter William] Goldman and Hill, it's a glorious game, an affectionate one—and one made meaningful. (p. 339)

> Judith Crist, in her review of *"Butch Cassidy and the Sundance Kid"* (reprinted by permission of the author), in New York *Magazine, Vol. 2, No. 39, September 29, 1969 (and reprinted in* Filmfacts, *Vol. XII, No. 15, 1969, pp. 338-39*).

TOM MILNE

[*Butch Cassidy and the Sundance Kid*] is a feast of self-indulgence. . . . [The film] is so anxious to present its characters as characters, and to let the spectator get an eyeful of their scenic surroundings, that the image of . . . desolation which lies behind [it] tends to become obscured.

'What happened to the old bank? It was beautiful.' These are the first words one hears from Butch Cassidy as he cases the joint for robbery, only to find it a veritable barrage of locks, bolts and shutters; and a moment later, intervening in a gambling quarrel, he warns the Sundance Kid, 'I'm over the hill—it can happen to you. Every day you get older, that's a law.' He means it as a joke, of course, but as in *The Wild Bunch* times are changing, the fences are closing in, and Butch Cassidy and his Hole in the Wall gang are finding it more and more difficult to live. Prepare to meet thy doom runs like a refrain behind the film, occasionally brought out into the open ('It's over and you're both gonna die bloody, and all you can do is choose where'), but mostly ignored by Butch and Sundance. They (legitimately) and the audience (less legitimately) are having so much fun that the message is never delivered.

Like Bonnie and Clyde, Butch and Sundance pursue their life of crime without malice or forethought, and there is an irresistible insolence in the way they assume that friendship is its own protection. They also see themselves as doing what comes naturally, as much for the fun of it as anything else . . . , but where Penn gradually withdrew the fantasy to prepare for the reality of the bullets at the end, *Butch Cassidy* simply keeps going. Even in their last stand in Bolivia, they bungle a robbery because they don't know enough Spanish to ask the victims to put their hands up, they bungle a guard job by looking for bandits *before* the payroll has been collected, and they die with their minds fixed optimistically on rich new pickings in Australia. Arguably, of course, Butch and Sundance should die, as they lived, in fantasy; but it does mean that one is neither

moved nor horrified by the last shot, which freezes them under a hail of bullets.

With all faults, and these include somewhat slavish nods to *Bonnie and Clyde,* [François Truffaut's] *Jules and Jim* and the inevitable slow-motion death scene, *Butch Cassidy and the Sundance Kid* is an enormously likeable entertainment which is as likely to be underrated as overrated for its fashionable derivation. George Roy Hill, one remembers, has always been at his happiest as a director of actors. . . . Here, although Conrad Hall provides some wonderful, glowing landscapes, one is always focused on the wryly eccentric characters. . . . William Goldman's beautifully literate script is always attempting to define and enlarge on even the least of its characters by playing on their private preoccupations. [Etta Place], for instance, . . . gets one key speech which not only makes complete sense of her character but suddenly irradiates the film with an explanation of her otherwise unlikely involvement with the gang: 'I'm twenty-six, and I'm single, and I teach school, and that's the bottom of the pit. And the only excitement I've ever known is sitting in the room with me now. So I'll go with you, and I won't whine, and I'll sew your socks and stitch you when you're wounded, and anything you ask of me I'll do, except one thing: I won't watch you die.' The pity of it is the film's similar refusal to watch its heroes die in a way that might mean something. (p. 102)

> Tom Milne, "'Butch Cassidy and the Sundance Kid' and 'Tell Them Willie Boy Is Here'," *in* Sight and Sound *(copyright © 1970 by The British Film Institute), Vol. 39, No. 2, Spring, 1970, pp. 101-02.*

STEVE DIMEO

Occasionally the film version of a novel is successful enough to make a comparison between the two helpful in understanding the strengths of both. . . . [Such is the case for] George Roy Hill's adaption of Kurt Vonnegut, Jr.'s *Slaughterhouse-Five*.

While [screenwriter Stephen] Geller has imposed a sense of order to improve the visual adaptation, director George Roy Hill . . . has wisely chosen to eschew any sense of sensationalism in what could have been misconstrued by some as nothing more than another, if somewhat bizarre, science-fiction film. The movie has a fluttering circle of white light grow out of the skies and pause outside Billy's bedroom window; then he is promptly pixilated off the screen. In the book Vonnegut describes the abduction as involving a saucer one hundred feet in diameter, complete with an imprisoning cone of purple light and zap gun as well. The Tralfamadorians in the movie are conveniently invisible because they exist in the fourth dimension. . . . Even the rifle that kills Billy is only a rifle in the movie, not the laser-gun Lazzaro aims in the book. Aside from obviously saving money on the special effects . . . avoiding the spectacle of real saucers. . . , which would have satisfied sci-fi buffs looking for visual tricks à la Douglas Trumbull or Ray Harryhausen, keeps our attention riveted without distraction on the more important story of Billy Pilgrim's pilgrimage in character. (p. 4)

Billy Pilgrim's character, of course, is the most important feature in both the film and the book, and Hill's interpretation . . . seems to be as just as it could be. The only danger is that in Billy's obvious passivity to the uncontrollable events that befall him he comes off as a bit too simple, at least compared to Vonnegut's treatment. (p. 5)

The movie may also oversimplify the underlying symbolism of the reason he is abducted to Tralfamadore late in 1967. The saucer comes for the second time after his wife dies from the exhaust of her Cadillac when she hurries in melodramatic mawkishness to the hospital where Billy is recovering from the plane accident. The chronological placement of his abduction suggests that his need for the consolation of life on another planet with the movie star Montana Wildhack . . . stems from his wife's death. But it is rather doubtful he could be grieving much for her when he admits later that what he misses most about his wife is her pancakes. The grief has a much broader base than the broad base of his wife. (pp. 6-7)

Significantly, when Billy's asked if he's happy on Tralfamadore, Vonnegut records, "'About as happy as I was on Earth,' said Billy Pilgrim, which was true." . . . But the Tralfamadorians and his strange family life with the naked Montana in the human zoo there give him the wherewithal to accept his life in its entirety. His mother's question in the old people's home asked only in the novel "How did I get so old?" . . . compares in a way with Billy's own remark later in the book— "Where have all the years gone?" . . . These are standard questions we all ask ourselves at one time or another, but the difference here is that Billy has been able to put time in a new perspective, whether the experience on Tralfamadore be interpreted as dream, symbol, or actuality. . . . [In] a way *Slaughterhouse-Five* is an exorcism of adverse experiences; Vonnegut implies as much when he confesses in the first chapter and once in the context of the story that he is Billy Pilgrim and actually underwent most of the same experiences. It is noteworthy that the novel ends with a symbolic scene in springtime. . . . [Images] of spring intertwined with death imply rebirth, and the movie, without resorting to the symbolism of Vonnegut's conclusion, communicates that sense when it leaves us with Montana nursing the baby in the cell with Billy while the invisible Tralfamadorians rejoice outside.

The other characters extracted from the book are, for the sake of humor, necessarily flat and one-dimensional, though Valerie Perrine's interpretation of Montana Wildhack—as *Playboy* has perceptively noted—obviously offers more ample proportions than one might expect for such a restrictive dimension. . . . [Actually] the proportion that Miss Perrine gives to Montana's character is not all physical. Despite even her taste for macrobiotic foods and the greater amount of dialogue between her and Billy that Geller adds, she is still ultimately stereotyped as the starlet who readily serves Billy even in her confusion over the sudden abduction. But especially after Billy's obvious infatuation with Montana on the movie screen at a drive-in with his family (in the book it's in a peep show in the back of an "adults only" store, a detail that in this film might have associated prurience rather than perfection with her nudity), Miss Perrine's angelic face and voice enhance the Edenic escapism implicit in Billy's trip to Tralfamadore. When Vonnegut has Billy look at Montana's body and recall the "fantastic architecture in Dresden, before it is bombed," . . . it is obvious that he means her to represent some kind of return to beauty unviolated by the vicissitudes of time. The serene beauty and biological naturalness of the cinematic Montana adequately convey that message.

The movie, not quite as perfect as Billy's distant but finally tangible dream girl, does have its weaknesses but they are relatively minor. Billy remains the main character throughout, but there is an inexplicable and unnecessary shift in the point of view when the camera centers on Valencia in an admittedly

funny slapstick sequence as she hurtles her Cadillac towards the hospital, and again when Billy's daughter, Barbara, learns of her mother's death out of earshot of her father. Neither is the tone of both those scenes consistent with the successful deadpan humor that dominates most of the other scenes. . . . Of course, Hill's design throughout the movie is to mine the black humor by playing the scenes straight, but here the seriousness tips too far because the screenplay falters in its wit. There is no apparent reason that white titles indicating the day to be February 13, 1945, should be super-imposed on the screen or that three different times during the day the Allies bombed a city that was without military significance in the war should be shown. The titles probably were inserted for the sake of clarity in a movie fraught with time shifts, but the viewer should be able to tell from the close-ups of the common people and the chronology of the war sequence up to this point that this is the day Dresden was destroyed. The titles are a documentary affectation which is glaringly out of place in a subtle and ironic satire. (pp. 7-9)

As is often the case, the movie has to omit aspects of the novel and in those omissions shows up not necessarily its weaknesses but certainly the strengths of the book itself. The movie tries as much as possible to imitate the dry wit of Vonnegut. Naturally because it is a different medium there is no real way it can echo the phrase which Vonnegut uses like an incremental refrain—"So it goes"—which he says after reporting anyone or anything's death, including champagne. It's that kind of comprehensiveness, incidentally, that reduces so many elements in the book to the absurd. Even the description of Billy's suffering is reduced to that level by relying on incongruity or understatement, all in a deliberately primer-sounding prose. (pp. 9-10)

For the sake of simplicity again, some of Vonnegut's images are left out. When Billy sees a film of the bombing of Dresden in reverse, the theme of death/rebirth is epitomized. Billy himself takes the reversal to its limit when he adds that if life were like the film, we would not only become children again but ultimately Adam and Eve. Even the science-fiction writer Kilgore Trout's analogy, comparing Billy's reaction to seeing through a "time window" to a dog standing on a mirror and thinking it stands on thin air, becomes significant in the light of Billy's journey towards resignation and self-acceptance. (pp. 10-11)

Probably the most obvious omission is the character of Kilgore Trout himself. Since he is significant only in that his absurd science fiction novels have had a great influence on Billy, it's easy to see why he had to be left out of the movie; there would be no effective way of summarizing the plots which Vonnegut can do more readily in prose. (p. 11)

None of this is to say, of course, that the movie, already acknowledged for its excellence at the Cannes Film Festival if not by *Time* and *Newsweek*, is any less successful because it can't draw on all the resources Vonnegut has brought to bear in this 1971 Pulitzer Prize nominee. But in its design and execution Hill's *Slaughterhouse-Five*, even in resorting at times to the more conventional, still lifts itself like the novel above jaded tales that tell us aliens alienate, be they human or extraterrestrial. In blending reality and fantasy in the absurdist tradition, they both escape tradition in depicting, beyond the Hemingwayesque limitations of such a theme, a Celinean dance with death, a reconciliation with the forces of change and time. (pp. 11-12)

Steve Dimeo, "Reconciliation: 'Slaughterhouse-Five'—the Film and the Novel," in Film Heritage *(copyright 1973 by F. A. Macklin), Vol. 8, No. 2, Winter, 1972-1973, pp. 1-12.*

LEE ATWELL

The recent George Roy Hill-Paul Monash production of *Slaughterhouse-Five* impressed me as one of the most advanced and systematic achievements in deployment of Space-Time and recalled especially the theme and style of [Alain] Resnais's last film, *Je t'aime, je t'aime* (1968). Although Hill confirmed to me that he has never seen the Resnais film . . . the formal treatment of the story is structurally and thematically close to the earlier Resnais work. (p. 3)

Anyone familiar with the nuances of Resnais's filmic expression will be prepared for *Je t'aime* and its constant detours in time. But to encounter a similar, integrated development of Space-Time in an American commercial film, by an established Hollywood director, is an aesthetic shock of the first order. When George Roy Hill read the galleys of Kurt Vonnegut, Jr.'s *Slaughterhouse-Five*—still at work on *Butch Cassidy and the Sundance Kid*—his immediate reaction was positive, yet he viewed the time structure of the novel as insurmountable filmically. Hill was still thinking in terms of traditional norms, and it was not until he later read a first-draft screen version by Stephen Geller that he was able to grasp an "emotional thread" that would provide a central focus and make the fractured time concept viable.

Vonnegut's story was inspired by his searing memory of the firebombing of Dresden in World War II, and in order to comment on the present, he uses as his central character, Billy Pilgrim, a man who has, in his words, become "unstuck in time," having survived the Dresden holocaust during his youth. Vonnegut, however, tells the story as an omniscient observer in the third person, explaining in detail Billy's personal history and thus providing a rationale for Billy's time-tripping. The main body of the novel is flanked by two chapters in which Vonnegut explains his personal reasons for the narrative and creates an ironic contrast with the present bombing of Vietnam. While remaining true to the tone and spirit of Vonnegut, Geller and Hill have eliminated the author and the descriptive mode, restructuring the entire work, building up sketchy details, and making Billy the central consciousness of the film. As a result, virtually all the expository scenes in the novel are gone to make way for a direct yet startlingly elliptical dramatic development and a very flexible use of filmic Space-Time as we move through the disordered landscape of Billy's memory and fantasy life, with occasional stopovers in the "real" world. Thus our sense of a "free-fall" in time is much the same as in *Je t'aime;* but at least in one respect the Resnais film appears almost classic by comparison.

In *Je t'aime,* the idea of time-tripping is set up in no uncertain terms by the opening scenes, detailing the experiment, and though there is progressing ambiguity in the flow of consciousness, the rules of the game are established: there is a beginning, middle, and end, in that order. In *Slaughterhouse-Five,* however, our bearings from a narrative viewpoint are initially less certain, and the logic of the structure is suggested but never directly stated in the film.

The opening shots of the film, set in the present, immediately connote dislocation in perspective as the camera peers through the windows of Billy's suburban house to his daughter and her husband on the exterior, trying to locate Billy. When we finally see him, Billy is well past middle age and is engrossed in typing a response to his local newspaper, detailing his experience of being "unstuck in time," which he has recently revealed. Between paragraphs, Billy time-trips back to his youth on the snow-covered battlefield somewhere in Germany, where he is fiercely accosted by three GI's who suspect him to be an enemy agent. . . . The image-logic signals a "flashback," but an abrupt and unexpected cut to a shot of Montana Wildhack . . . to whom we are later introduced—thumbing through a magazine and responding, "Time-tripping again, Billy?" breaks up the connection. When we return to a shot of Billy at his typewriter 25 years later, then back to Germany, thence to Billy's wedding night after the war, an elliptical, achronological pattern establishes itself as part of a *mental continuum,* reflecting inner experience.

Just as in the Resnais film, the stylistic "playing with time," aside from its critical distancing of the spectator and its purely aesthetic appeal, expresses an existential portrait. . . . Because time in *Slaughterhouse-Five* is levelled off into relatively broad dramatic scenes, we can perceive Billy's situation, not only in terms of his private fantasy life, but in his alienated behavior, which the film is rich in detailing. (pp. 6-7)

Even more daring is the way Hill juxtaposes two sequences in exactly their reverse chronological order, like the musical effect of dropping from a *sfortzando* to *pianissimo* passage with exposition following development. Billy is the sole survivor of a plane crash in which he is critically injured and mumbles the address recited to him by a German officer in Dresden years earlier: "Schlachthof-funf, Schlachthof-funf." In a sequence of hair-raising intensity that could have been inspired by a Mack Sennett chase, Valencia hysterically flies from their home screaming, "Billy, I'm coming!" She tail-ends another car, rockets the wrong direction up a freeway exit, careens across hills and lanes to avoid police, in an absurd, frantic dash to the hospital, reducing the Cadillac to a pile of rubble as she crashes into the emergency entrance, ironically her final resting place. From the hospital, where Billy is undergoing surgery, Hill cuts to the morning of Valencia's previous birthday as Billy awakens her with a stretch of ribbon that she gleefully follows to the front lawn and her dream-come-true—the gleaming new El Dorado we have just seen demolished.

The climactic development of the film is centered around two themes: the tragic destruction of Dresden, and Billy's increasing regression into fantasy. The entrance to Dresden is a kind of travelogue extravaganza as seen by Billy; a "land of Oz" as he calls it, casting a spell of enchantment in its sculptured trellises and baroque architectural detail, as well as its smiling inhabitants still unscarred by the war. . . . This paradise with its happy atmosphere is soon transformed into a fiery hell which Hill and his cameraman Miroslav Ondricek capture in beautifully executed tracking shots, moving from the figure of a young German soldier traversing the landscape in an anguished attempt to find his family. The irony here, is that Billy's emotions are already so shattered at the time that he can only comprehend the horror of the event through memory, prompted by an arrogant military historian (who sees Dresden as a mere "tactical error" compared with Hiroshima) with a stoical resistance to moral assessment.

As Billy moves closer to an adult realization of this past experience, he becomes more detached from it, retreating more often into his fantasy of Tralfamadore and his idyllic life there with the sexy starlet Montana Wildhack. Vonnegut has to go to great pains in his book to establish the background of this fantasy, rooting it in the imagination of a science-fiction novelist Billy has read. The film, however, more satisfactorily establishes it through visual iconography. At one point, Billy discovers his son with a girlie magazine, cautions him against it, then smiles knowingly over a nude fold-out of Montana. At a drive-in movie, Valencia explodes into rage when Billy and her son greedily absorb the vision of Montana's exposed breasts on the silver screen. When we finally see Billy transported to the geodesic dome on Tralfamadore, along with Montana, surrounded by the luxury trappings of Sears Roebuck, the fantasy becomes an apotheosis.

Billy's time-tripping becomes a form of enslavement rather than liberation because, for him, fantasy becomes the only viable reality. He tries to explain (in the opening sequence, which is continued near the end of the film) to his daughter his life in the fourth dimension of time—just like the Tralfamadorians—but naturally Earthlings cannot understand and think him insane. He sees life as "a series of moments in random order," . . . a concept which the Tralfamadorians use to describe their books, in Vonnegut's novel, as "brief clumps of symbols." (pp. 8-9)

Some people see Billy's fantasy-images in the film as inspired and poetic; in a sense, they *are*, but what they represent is something else. Although he is presented as a lovable sad sack, Billy's imaginative resources are very limited; they are shaped, more than anything, by the idealism of popular literature and films. . . . [In] the final shots of Tralfamadore, against a background of fireworks and grandiose organ accompaniment, Billy and Montana acknowledge the applause of Tralfamadore after the birth of their son—a supreme parody of the sentimental Hollywood finale. Audiences automatically cheer at this "happy ending," but there is a critical dimension built in by the filmmakers, by concluding on this fantasy. Billy's inspiration is only a hiatus, and existentially a sad one; he has transcended the real world but he is still the same placid, ineffectual self as in reality. He has failed to achieve any growth or self-identity.

When I mentioned the striking similarity in theme and style between this film and that of Resnais, George Roy Hill replied, "I don't want you to think I haven't been influenced by Resnais . . . but I wasn't interested in making an experimental film . . . that's not my bag." At the same time, he is greatly pleased with the film and is quite surprised that the distribution has been handled so well with enthusiastic reception, unusual for a film that boasts no celebrities and only Vonnegut's name and the jury prize at Cannes as selling points. Equally significant is the fact that Hill and writer Stephen Geller have successfully reorchestrated Vonnegut's material into a unique filmic structure . . . that questions most of the traditions of Space-Time adhered to in commercial cinema, and challenge the spectator to an effective participation in the experience at a time when Hollywood seems to be returning to traditional formulas and nostalgia for success. When most of the films of the seventies have become passé, *Slaughterhouse-Five* will, I think, remain durable and achieve its rank as an American masterpiece. (p. 9)

Lee Atwell, "Two Studies in Space-Time," in Film Quarterly *(© 1973 by The Regents of the University of California; reprinted by permission of The Regents), Vol. XXVI, No. 2, Winter, 1972-73, pp. 2-9.**

GORDON GOW

George Roy Hill, who directed the coy long-windedness of *Thoroughly Modern Millie* as well as regaling us with such a jubilant tone poem as *Butch Cassidy and the Sundance Kid*, hovers here between the funny and the touching and the glum. *Slaughterhouse-Five*, based on the novel by Kurt Vonnegut Jr. is like a simplified Resnais film. Almost from the outset we are informed that the non-hero Billy Pilgrim has 'come unstuck in time' and keeps jolting back and forth among his past and future experiences. When he was a very young prisoner during the Second World war, the fire bombing of Dresden had a traumatic effect upon him. Peacetime brought surburban conformity in the States, with a plump and witless wife, material success, and a pet dog for real company. Moreover, beyond this earth looms the planet Trafalmadore, where the unseen powers decide to transport a pair of earth creatures for zoological study: Billy is chosen, arbitrarily it would seem, along with a near-nude Hollywood starlet whose image he has ogled dreamfully at his local drive-in.

Quite an assortment of things, to be sure. These places and periods are rapidly interwoven in a serviceable psychological sequence, and in moods that range a bit startlingly through satire to slapstick with a hopeful drop of pathos every now and then. It is hardly surprising that the film works only in fits and starts, being sometimes entertaining and at other times embarrassing, but never as profound as it has a right to be in view of the topics it raises. . . .

The wartime passages are the most plentiful. Sometimes the inhumanity is pointed up against certain backgrounds of virgin whiteness, making an effect that is strong in irony: there is a snowfield for violence in Belgium, and a benign mist hovers beyond the first glimpses of Dresden. On the other hand, the futuristic scenes carry a sort of comic-strip ambiance which is inadequate, and there is little to take the eye in the design of the transparent dome to which Billy and the starlet are confined on Tralfamadore. The day after tomorrow is indicated more credibly in a short episode in a lecture hall, a square auditorium towering in tiers above the platform where Billy gives a lecture and is murdered in the course of it.

Death is stressed repeatedly. Billy's wife meets her end by dangerous driving while emotionally distressed, and this is the sequence that Hill presents as slapstick—with surprising success, doubtless because the deliberately fractured structure of the screenplay is a big aid to the switches of style. (p. 50)

Oddly, after [considerable] emphasis on violence and death, the film closes with a sort of affirmation of life. On the alien planet, the starlet has presented Billy with a baby, and the populace is roaring approval while the sky glows in the pallid hues of a Tralfamadore fireworks display. This comes dangerously close to being twee, even though one is bound to assume that it is intended as another of life's perpetual ironies. In fact, quite a few of the sequences are on the tacky side—too much is sentimental, and not enough is sharp. It is a film of mixed qualities, some of them virtuous. (p. 51)

Gordon Gow, in his review of "Slaughterhouse-Five" (© copyright Gordon Gow 1973; reprinted with permission), in Films and Filming, *Vol. 19, No. 4, January, 1973, pp. 50-1.*

NEIL D. ISAACS

Peace, free will, and art are . . . the essence of Vonnegut's *Slaughterhouse-Five;* but George Roy Hill's movie of the same name is redolent of different juices entirely. Hill's burden was heavy: he not only had to reconceive the story according to his own filmic lights, he had to reverence the details of the fiction as so many cult objects for his projected audience. And his artifices do not suffice to carry the load.

His failure is similar to that of Mike Nichols with *Catch 22*. [Joseph] Heller's text was so cluttered with cult objects that Nichols' reconception of the story in film form, with abundant optical and structural gimmickry, was topweighted with the demands of the literary paraphernalia. Hill never even tried, as Nichols clearly did, to integrate the obligatory items into the movie's story. The appearances of Wild Bob from Cody, Wyoming, and of Eliot Rosewater in a Lake Placid mental hospital, for example, serve no purpose whatsoever in the movie except to remind viewers, perhaps, of significances lost from the book. Rosewater's main function is to introduce Kilgore Trout to Billy Pilgrim, but neither Trout nor his science fiction appears in the movie. Still, Trout is not the major character lost from the text—that is the narrator, Kurt Vonnegut, Jr. of Indianapolis and Barnstable.

This novel adapts itself to reduction to statements of essence better than most, though there are three separate statements, like the voices of a fugue, in a tripartite essence and structure. First and foremost, it is an anti-war document, conceived in anguish for firebomb-destroyed Dresden and dedicated to the propositions that war is an absurd assertion of man's will, that it must be revealed in all its absurdity, and that all men must see the futility and desperate irony in all the manifestations of war, past, present and future. . . . *Slaughterhouse-Five* is a denunciation of war, written compulsively to denounce war, designed to denounce war, and fulfilled by the litany of that denunciation. This is the element that has won a large audience among the peace-seeking young.

Second, it is a science fiction that deals with the topic of free will versus fatalism and a related philosophical issue of the nature of time. If the self-assertiveness of humanity inevitably leads to war, the alternative is a kind of sublime acceptance of everything. This is the fatalistic message from Tralfamadore brought to earth by Billy Pilgrim. The Tralfamadorian response to death and destruction, however violent, pointless, mindless, brutal, or unnecessary, is, "So it goes." (pp. 127, 129)

Third, *Slaughterhouse-Five* is a book about the writing of the book. The whole first section is a kind of foreword in which Vonnegut, in propria persona, talks about the conception of the book, the history of its composition, some of the research involved, the incident that supplied the subtitle, and the personal significance of the whole project. Then, throughout the narration, there are frequent interjections like "I was there" or "That was me, the author of this book" to remind us to distinguish the voices and to keep this element in mind. (pp. 129-30)

Hill's *Slaughterhouse-Five* resembles its source only superficially, sometimes translating to the screen textural details that are pointless in their new context. The sci-fi time concept seems perfectly suited to cinematic structure. Indeed Bily's time travel (called "time-tripping" in the now dialogue of the movie) becomes the editing rationale of the whole film. Good idea, poor execution. In practice, what we get is an elaborate exercise in the kind of "thematic cut" that was so popular in the late Fifties.

Of the tripartite essence of the book, a complete transformation has taken place. Instead of a compulsive anti-war statement, there is an anti-establishment theme that slightly alters the base of audience support. The anti-war element remains implicit,

as in the blank faces of the Russian prisoners in the German camp, but it supplies material for some splendid snow shots in the opening sequence and the broad satiric scene of the British prisoners welcoming the Yanks. We don't even see any of the Dresden bombing, just Billy's gawking tour of the lovely city (Prague) before and the rather unconvincing sets of rubble after.

Instead of Vonnegut's bitter irony of fatalistic acceptance, Hill presents a comedy based on destruction and distortion. The biggest laugh-getter is the sequence of Valencia's drive to the hospital, a zany highway bit that features the demolition of her Cadillac and incidental casualties to many others, climaxed in her hornblaring, crashing death by carbon monoxide poisoning outside the emergency entrance. So it goes: and note, again, the disparity of tones. The sound track is leaned heavily upon for laughs, but it is a very frail support, at times insupportable itself as it attempts to make fun of social patterns and institutions. The overwhelmingly impressive sound of the *Clockwork Orange* experience may get in the way here, but the sound in *Slaughterhouse-Five* seems by turns shrill, blatant, gross, and gauche, undercutting whatever satiric or comedic effectiveness it was intended to have. This element may have audience appeal, too, but to my subjective ear a comparable theater crowd enjoyed its laughs at *What's Up, Doc?* much more.

Finally, instead of the writing of the book . . . we get a new theme—the natural versus the mechanical. And this is what really gets the audience with it. When Billy and Montana Wildhack successfully mate, we rejoice with the invisible Tralfamadorians, and when Montana nurses the infant in the film's final, triumphant gesture, we necessarily join in the Tralfamadorian applause. It is a winning—and winsome—device, and we depart in a kind of mindless chuckle at what feels good.

But where have all the powers gone? A potentially potent property has become as slight as Billy Pilgrim's person. Vonnegut's ironic point about pornographic pictures, even, has faded into the naive non-prurience of the zoo-goers. The Tralfamadorians have disappeared. They have become invisible, disembodied voices. . . . [The] life has gone out of the story with its essence, despite undeniable innate appeal, certain charm, and an intelligent structural concept. Hill's failure is far from complete, rather on the order of Arthur Penn's with *Little Big Man*. . . . What both Hill and Penn gained by shooting and playing for laughs and gut responses, they lost in the weakening of overall content or—not to be mealymouthed about it—integrity. Listen: *Slaughterhouse-Five* has come unstuck in itself. (pp. 130-31)

*Neil D. Isaacs, "Unstuck in Time: 'Clockwork Orange' and 'Slaughterhouse-Five'," in Literature/ Film Quarterly (© copyright 1973 Salisbury State College), Vol 1, No. 2, April, 1973, pp. 122-31.**

JOHN COLEMAN

He may never make the *auteur* circuit (something devoutly to be wished), but George Roy Hill is a director to be reckoned with, a clever fellow capable of fluffing up the thinnest stuff into a plausible tangle, a kind of cinematic back-combing, for amusement—***Period of Adjustment*** (1963), ***Thoroughly Modern Millie*** (1967)—and, better yet, totally alert to the potential of a really useful script. His ***Butch Cassidy and the Sundance Kid*** latched on to the mostly excellent words of William Goldman: his ***The Sting*** neatly repays its debt to a script of unusual brevity, wit and purpose by David S. Ward. You could say that Mr Hill has gone **Butch** again, engaging the same charmers—Paul Newman and Robert Redford—to enlist our sympathies on the side of criminals. The period this time is post-Depression, 1936 the year, and nostalgia an ally. The affair draws on our notorious affection for baddies who are not all bad, hardly hurt anyone physically, and are funny with it: one might call it the Great-Train-Robbery syndrome. It relies on the emotional callousness that relishes a good swindle from afar. It is about a couple of con-men who take a big New York crook, Doyle Lonnegan . . . , for a financially depleting ride. . . .

The publicists for this film have seen fit to furnish reviewers with a small but summoning booklet, detailing some of the activities of such cheats and providing a glossary of their lingo. Glamour's in: 'Confidence men are the aristocracy of the underworld.' And Mr Hill sets out to substantiate the dubious claim. I think one can detect the chill, shadowed, hunched artistic world of Edward Hopper behind a good deal of Robert Surtees's superb photography, his flash and seedy images in this case quite properly supported by a whole laboratory paraphernalia of wipes, unfurled pages, irises in and out, together with the newer revival of interest in chapter-headings, culminating in 'The Sting' or monetary kill. The film steadily looks good, has good actors not only among its principals but in minor roles, is partly—in fact—about acting. Its twists and turns coil in places round the setting-up of a false gambling parlour, for which men are recruited as for a road-show. That big-time Lonnegan should be fooled (surely someone on his payroll would have twigged this was a set-up?) is a rough reflection of what the occasion does to us. It may not bear thinking about, but it cunningly passes the smaller immediate test of viewing.

John Coleman, "Big Con," in New Statesman (© *1974 The Statesman & Nation Publishing Co. Ltd.), Vol. 87, No. 2233, January 4, 1974, p. 26.**

JON LANDAU

[**The Sting**] is intended to form the basis for "pure entertainment," but Hill, Redford and Newman's idea of a fun picture is to skirt any form of moral, intellectual or human dilemma, focusing our attention instead on the mechanics of their scheme and the good-natured but unexplained camaraderie infusing their relationship. In that light, Hill's preoccupation with production values winds up serving as a smoke screen for his own lack of viewpoint. (p. 56)

It's hard to understand why Hill concentrates on the mechanics of the con to the exclusion of other considerations when he so obviously lacks the one skill essential for that kind of directing: the ability to break an action down into its component parts. When con gang member Ray Walston . . . masterminds a phony betting operation, we're never convinced that [Robert] Shaw, despite his vanity, could so easily be deceived.

But then Hill intuitively understood that the story wouldn't be enough and, although he doesn't develop a theme, he has come up with a gimmick. Each segment of the movie has a title, among them "The Hook," "The Wire" and "The Setup." By the time he gets to the latter, it's obvious that Robert Shaw isn't the only one being set up. For **The Sting** is in many ways a movie about its own audience, and it is we who are to be stung by its insultingly arbitrary conclusion.

Especially in the Redford character, [Johnny Hooker, David S.] Ward's script does raise human issues. In fact, the conclusion of the story at first seems to hinge on Redford having to choose between loyalty to Newman [as Henry Gondorff] and duty to his black friend's widow. The movie's contrived ending elminates the need for his making that choice, also eliminating in the process Hill's need to show us what kind of man Redford really is.

As a further irritant, Hill and Ward set up this bogus copout by withholding the true identity of a major character. Thus, we have a cheat of an ending based on a cheat in the storytelling. No wonder the most likely reaction to the conclusion is a quick laugh at the sudden shock of it (providing you haven't already sussed it out) that curdles as we realize we've been as badly conned as Robert Shaw, and turns to outright disgust at the film's gratuitously sentimental closing shot, which asks us to show more concern for the film's heroes than its makers have.

The Sting remains sufficiently entertaining to be genuinely frustrating. Ward's story was in some ways a director's dream, sufficiently open-ended so that anyone with a strong personality could have molded it to his own style. Billy Wilder could have made it a screwball comedy . . . ; Howard Hawks could have played down the caper in favor of Newman and Redford's relationship (which seldom rises above the level of plot convention). He would also have thrown in some women, because he likes them. Robert Aldrich could have made a *Dirty Dozen* crime extravaganza and shown the con men to have been no more or less lovable than their sordid opponents. And, of course, in Don Siegel's version, Redford and Newman would have spent more time figuring out how they were going to screw each other than Robert Shaw.

But George Roy Hill has brought nothing of himself to the story except a flair for opulence and a compulsion to avoid dramatic issues. Not content to rest at that, he makes a joke out of his own shortcomings and us the butt of it by inviting our interest in his characters and then laughing at us for taking them more seriously than he does. If you ask me, that's what hurts most about **The Sting**. (pp. 56-7)

Jon Landau, "Now for the Bad News," in Rolling Stone (by Straight Arrow Publishers, Inc. © 1974; *all rights reserved; reprinted by permission), Issue 152, January 17, 1974, pp. 56-7.**

STANLEY KAUFFMANN

About an hour into **The Sting** I began to understand it. Not the plot, which is clear enough, but the raison d'être. This Paul Newman-Robert Redford vehicle is set in the thirties, and I couldn't really understand why. Unlike (say) *Bonnie and Clyde,* the story isn't tied to the period. Why do it that way? . . . Audiences, I guess, aren't as nostalgic for the decade itself—most of them are too young to have known it—as they are for films of the decade. This isn't a film about the thirties as much as it's an attempt to make a thirties film. It's the Antiques Made to Order business. (p. 252)

Recurrently, to the point of galloping tedium, articles appear telling us how American films have lost the Golden Glow of the high Hollywood days . . . and how pictures may now be more mature and more serious and candid, but what happened to all the fun? When these articles don't make me yawn, they make me laugh. First, there's the implication that our film world is just bursting with maturity; second, there's the curious belief that "they don't make them like that anymore." The biggest hit last year, says *Variety*, was *The Poseidon Adventure*—$40 million in domestic rentals alone for mildewed corn. When the Hollywood-regret articles go on long enough, I stop yawning and get sick. If there's anything worse than bad "serious" pictures it's condescension by people who feel they can save their brains and taste for something other than films.

The Sting probably won't make those people happy enough because it lacks romance in two senses. Girls play almost no part in the story, and myth-making glamour—star as Star—doesn't figure much, either. Everyone has compared the picture with **Butch Cassidy and the Sundance Kid,** with the same leads and the same director, George Roy Hill; but I would bet that the people involved also saw *Borsalino* (1970), with Jean-Paul Belmondo and Alain Delon, directed by Jacques Deray, an engaging French attempt to manufacture a Hollywood crook picture of the thirties. Those pictures were probably more what the buffs like; still *The Sting* may carry them back to the Bijou balcony again. (pp. 252-53)

The original script by David S. Ward has pretty good dialogue, but besides the fact that some of the surprises are phony, the weight is thrown largely on the mechanics of the complicated swindle that the two men set up to fool the wily racketeer. So much time is given to these details that the characters of the three leading men are thin, with occasional spoonfuls of "depth" ladled over. There's a lot of *bonhomie,* on the movie principle that criminals who don't hurt or kill are Good Guys. . . . It's more than two hours long, but if you can edit out about twenty minutes in your mind as you watch, it's passably entertaining. . . .

Hill, the director, is mildly competent but has no style or flavor. (And is overly addicted to cute thirties tricks like iris-outs and "wipes" and to following feet or elevators as a way of bringing us into places.) Robert Surtees, the vastly experienced cinematographer, gets more out of the pictures than the director knows how to use; and Henry Bumstead, the art director, has given Surtees some good stuff to work with. (p. 253)

> *Stanley Kauffmann, in his review of "The Sting" (originally published in* The New Republic, *Vol. 170, No. 5, February 2, 1974), in his* Living Images: Film Comment and Criticism *(reprinted by permission of Brandt & Brandt Literary Agents, Inc.; copyright © 1970, 1971, 1972, 1973, 1974, 1975 by Stanley Kauffmann),* Harper & Row, Publishers, 1975, pp. 252-53.

JOHN SIMON

The Sting works endearingly without a single hitch. George Roy Hill's film concerns conmanship in Chicago in the thirties, and the exploits of a few independent confidence men banding together against a big gang boss and his henchmen. This is one of those precarious movies in which murder must look absurd or funny—except in one case, where it has been taken seriously—and it is to Hill's and his scenarist's, David S. Ward's, credit that they just about carry off this colossally queasy task. It must be said right away that certain plot elements in these cinematic rodomontades are bound to be unbelievable; the question is merely to what extent the filmmakers, con artists in their own right, can carry off the caper without allowing us time to unsuspend our disbelief. The main tools at their disposal are surprise, wit, credibility in trappings

and details, fast pacing, and good performances. *The Sting* possesses them all.

Sets, costumes, and locations could not look more authentic. . . . The plot has more twists to it than a boa constrictor taking its constitutional, and even if you guess something correctly, you are made to abandon your hypothesis only to have it prove right after all, and so have been had, anyhow. There are funny lines and situations throughout, and no pretensions whatsoever. Well integrated subplots fill in the gaps of the main plot, and Hill has a good sense of camera placement for getting bustle or moodiness into a shot. (p. 134)

> *John Simon, "Cops, Crooks, and Cryogenics" (originally published in* Esquire, *Vol. LXXXI, No. 3, March, 1974), in his* Reverse Angle: A Decade of American Film *(copyright © 1973, 1974, 1975, 1977, 1978, 1979, 1980, 1981, 1982 by John Simon; used by permission of Crown Publishers, Inc.),* Clarkson N. Potter, Inc./Publishers, 1982, pp. 131-35.*

ANDREW SARRIS

[One] cannot begin to talk about **"The Great Waldo Pepper"** without dragging in the previous outings of George Roy Hill (directorial analysis), Robert Redford (star iconography), male-oriented movies (feminist sociology), airplane movies (genre analysis), and for Richard Corliss perhaps even a study of William Goldman's screenwriting stylistics, not to mention Henry Mancini's rainbowish melodies, and the sterling cinematography of Robert Surtees. After all this and more, it is not hard to see why some critics seem to be playing three-dimensional chess while their readers are still engrossed in checkers.

What to do? Nothing really. . . . It is too early . . . for me to make a final judgment on George Roy Hill when I am still in the process of reevaluating [William] Wellman and [John] Huston and [Stanley] Kubrick and [William] Wyler.

Still, I must admit that **"The Great Waldo Pepper"** struck me as a somewhat better movie than I had anticipated in advance. (p. 67)

This is the movie that is supposed to have pulled [Hill] out of the collaborative cocoon of relative anonymity, and transformed him into a butterfly with the brightly colored wings of art and aspiration. It can be said that **"The Great Waldo Pepper"** has gotten off the ground. It flies, but somehow it doesn't soar.

The picture opens from the bright-eyed vantage point of a little boy in Nebraska in the '20s. The Great Waldo Pepper (Robert Redford) comes swooping down out of the sky with such vivid authenticity that we intuit the literal meaning of "barnstorming." . . . [The] way the little boy . . . looks at Redford, we get a kind of Icarus-Shane tremor though without the Homeric sobriety of "Shane." Hill hedges his bets from the beginning by intimating that his bird man is something of a con man. Still, he milks the audience by having Pepper tell the boy to run errands for him in return for a ride on the plane. When Pepper pretends to renege on his promise, the little boy's face clouds with an expression of sadness Norman Rockwell might have contributed to a Saturday Evening Post cover. Then the patented Redford grin from ear to ear, and the little boy and his little dog are next seen high in the sky in the cockpit behind Waldo Pepper's. Too much. It is not a question here of sentimentality, but of structure. The emotional transaction between the child and the man is excessive as mere exposition, particularly since we are never going to see the child again. By blowing up the simplest scenes into dreamy soap bubbles, Hill hardly qualifies for his self-appointed role as the master of narrative cinema. Ever since the Vigoesque slow-motion leaps of [the young girls] in **"The World of Henry Orient,"** Hill has specialized less in narrative flow than in a kind of glossy lyricism through which his more privileged characters display their superior sensitivity. . . .

Because of his recent collaborations with Redford and Newman, Hill may indeed seem more sexist than he is. His distinction is not so much between men and women, as between dreamy poetic characters and the drab prose figures who surround them. (p. 68)

"The Great Waldo Pepper" is completely a man's show, not because Hill hates women necessarily, but because there is no place for the female in Hill's cockpit. Even so, . . . Mary Beth is one of the most degraded characters ever conceived in any genre. . . . [She] turns out to be the stupid victim of her own flightiness when she gets out on the wing, her grotesque period underwear flapping in the wind, and hangs on for dear life. Since we see her mostly from the unflattering angle and uninvolving distance of the male cockpit, she becomes a figure of ridicule. She embodies all the fear of flying, but none of the ecstacy of elevation. The latter is reserved for Waldo Pepper and the Red Baron and people like that. Worse still, Mary Beth is not even remotely sexy during her agony on the wing. . . . Perhaps Hill has decided that genuine sexiness doesn't pay in today's PG sweepstakes. Certainly, his accountant would not argue with him.

Ultimately, nothing less becomes Mary Beth than the way she dies. She does not so much fall from the plane with all the excitement such an experience would entail. . . . We are not really prepared for Mary Beth's death (or for anyone else's) at this point because Hill has directed the first half of the film in a mood of slapstick facetiousness. People play pranks on each other, and cause hilarious accidents with quick cuts to casts and crutches. In this world of sadistic slapstick, nobody ever dies. It is virtually a genre convention. Then suddenly we get not one death, but two, the second straining for an anti-crowd comment with its spectacle of rubbernecking rubes gawking at a man pinned in the cockpit of his crashed plane, and slowly being burned alive. Waldo Pepper goes berserk at this point, partly because the victim was his business partner and the brother of his girl friend . . . , partly because of his own frustration over being grounded, and partly because he suddenly sees the mass of humanity as a malignancy. This last point was made more cogently by Howard Hawks in "The Crowd Roars" in 1932, and he made it in the opening credits. Hill flings it in from left field on the fly with no advance warning.

After the two deaths have banished facetiousness forever, **"The Great Waldo Pepper"** turns somber and romantic in the twilight of solo flying. . . . Hill has not worked nearly hard enough to create the proper mood of weary fatalism. . . . Perhaps, Hill has tried to jam too much into one picture. Certainly, one cannot question his sincerity and dedication. As it happens, I admire the film's vulnerability as much as I despise its facility. But if Hill were more vulnerable and less facile he might well be unemployed. Nonetheless if Hill feels nostalgia for a period in American life when individual initiative was more feasible than it is today, I feel nostalgia for a period in American Cinema when the virtues of orderly, coherent storytelling were taken for granted and not trumpeted as the products of transcendent genius. (pp. 68-9)

Andrew Sarris, "Butch Pepper and the Sundance Sting, or Wherefore Art Thou Waldo?" (reprinted by permission of The Village Voice and the author; copyright © The Village Voice, Inc., 1975), in The Village Voice, Vol. XX, No. 14, April 7, 1975, pp. 67-9.

GORDON GOW

We know that George Roy Hill has a versatile directorial range: *Toys in the Attic, Thoroughly Modern Millie, Butch Cassidy and the Sundance Kid* and *The Sting* have been richly varied. So maybe the news that in his personal life he has been hooked since childhood on aerobatics, and that he has been not only a wartime pilot but a peacetime barnstormer, ought not to come as a surprise. Yet somehow it does. And so does his latest film [*The Great Waldo Pepper*], which has obviously been made with true affection and pays tribute to the idols of his youth, as well as to such venerable aviation films as *Wings* (William Wellman, 1927) and *Hell's Angels* (Howard Hughes, 1930). Solemnly and quaintly, the little white monoplane circles the globe in the oldest of the Universal trade marks—and we're off on a spree where process trickery is eschewed and stunt men, as well as the star (Robert Redford) in certain shots, take daringly to the skies and venture some breathtaking wing-walks at considerable heights, or fly perilously low along the length of a town street.

Waldo Pepper is fictitious. . . . But disbelief is easily suspended, and one warms very quickly to both character and actor. At the beginning it's all fun. Henry Mancini provides carnival music for aerial antics which indicate the kicks derived by fliers who had grown so fond of their reckless 'duties' in the First World War that they simply couldn't turn off afterwards. Barnstorming for a pittance in America's Middle West of the 1920s, Waldo is capable of roguery: he loosens the wheels of a rival's plane and causes him to crash-land in a pond. . . . And how wryly unrepentant he remains when a mishap reduces him for a while to an ambulant invalid, waddling around with plaster casts on limbs that look as if they belong to a jokey statue!

Yet, very lightly for a time, the merriment is underscored by desperation. A certain alarming absurdity reaches its peak when a girl is added to the act. Her required feat is to walk out on the wing in mid-air, clad in loosely-stitched garments that will blow off her body as the plane flies low for the delectation of the crowd. The ensuing sequence is remarkable, changing the film's mood on the instant from wild exhilaration to heartsickening drama.

Then by swift and shrewd degrees, Waldo Pepper's resilience brings us out of our thoughtful gloom, never to regain that earlier rapture, but nevertheless to understand the peculiar craving of such a guy. He submits himself to knockabout perils as a Hollywood stuntman, in fragments of action which build towards the film's very curious final phase, wherein Waldo is employed by a director to help to enact a dogfight in which the other plane is piloted by a real wartime ace from Germany. This is a man long admired by Waldo on account of his exploits, and their rapport is ironically sentimental, allied to the somewhat weird compatibility that is known to have existed between certain opponents in wars, who behaved respectfully to one another as though they were sportsmen engaged in a challenging game.

For the German, indeed, life is only rewarding when he is airborne. . . . Poor daredevil Waldo reveres this ageing glamour boy, and by unspoken consent they disobey the film director's cautions and proceed to turn their 'act' into a combat fought with the relish of men who enjoyed the war and yearn to be back in it. George Roy Hill controls our responses so well as to keep us simultaneously enthralled and aghast as this kinky climax is played out in aerial images of appropriately haunting poetry. (pp. 39-40)

> *Gordon Gow, in his review of "The Great Waldo Pepper" (copyright Gordon Gow 1975; reprinted with permission), in* Films and Filming, *Vol. 21, No. 8, May, 1975, pp. 39-40.*

TOM MILNE

When *The Great Waldo Pepper* opens with the now obligatory nostalgia of an evocative montage of period photographs, it looks as though one is in for another no-holds-barred assault on the box-office. As it turns out, George Roy Hill keeps his penchant for whimsy well under control, only once, and quite acceptably—the winning smile near the beginning which tells us that Waldo won't really be so mean-spirited as to fail to keep his promise of a free ride to the boy who has laboured all afternoon on his behalf—fringing the cuteness which marred *Butch Cassidy* and *The Sting*. [Roger] Corman's *The Red Baron*, of course, dug much deeper into the mystique of daredevilry and deathwish associated with World War One aces; but in this third exploration of shrinking frontiers, which is really a homage from one dream factory to another closed long ago by the encroachments of civil aviation and safety regulations, Hill acknowledges quite early on . . . that his movie is only a movie, and rooted in the early days of innocence and adventure somewhere betwen *The Perils of Pauline* (the rivetingly funny and exciting scene of Mary Beth's only and disastrous effort at wing-walking) and *Hell's Angels* (the romantically heroic final sequence of the gallant self-sacrifice of two aces). One can't really complain, as one could in *Butch Cassidy,* that serious perspectives are opened up only to be ignored; nor has one to mutter, as with *The Sting,* that the absence of any real content at all had to be papered over by decorative exotica from any number of ill-assorted periods. Here the marvellously rackety old monoplanes and biplanes, dispensing the heady aroma of speed and grace with a poetic sureness never even approached by the most streamlined jet, tell their own sad story of how the men who flew them, having once found a way out of the strait-laced paths of commercial flying by cheerfully daring death to conquer space, time and gravity with the air circuses, were once more forced down to earth and sobriety. Wisely the film rarely departs for too long from its aircraft, and benefits by ensuring . . . that they remain the stars in the limelight. . . . Some of the scenes are mordantly funny, like the rehearsal for the ladder-from-car-to-plane stunt, with Waldo crashing bodily into a shack which inconveniently materialises in the way; some are nakedly exciting, like Kessler's attempt to achieve ten successive loops, or Ezra's three doomed tries at the outside loop; and some are charged with enthralling balletic precision, like the final dogfight. Put together, they ensure that *The Great Waldo Pepper* is the least pretentious, most enjoyable of the three entries to date in this series.

> *Tom Milne, in his review of "The Great Waldo Pepper," in* Monthly Film Bulletin *(copyright © The*

British Film Institute, 1975), Vol. 42, No. 496, May, 1975, p. 108.

VINCENT CANBY

George Roy Hill's unruly, funny new comedy, **"Slap Shot,"** . . . dramatizes the age-old contest between good and evil as clean vs. dirty, and it's dirty that wins, hands (and pants) down.

"Slap Shot," which follows the fortunes of the [Charlestown] Chiefs through their last, dizzy season, was written by Nancy Dowd. . . . She's a young woman who appears to know more about the content and rhythm of locker-room talk than most men. . . .

I don't know enough about professional hockey to judge how accurate a picture **"Slap Shot"** is, but it does seem a stretch of the imagination to ask us to believe in this day and age, that neither the Chiefs' manager nor coach would have known that a dirty, violent game, accompanied by a lot of publicity hoopla, would bring in the crowds. Which is pretty much what happens to the Chiefs, first by accident, then on purpose, as the team goes onward and upward to the top of the league.

The film's point of view also appears to be ambiguous, for though it seems to want to be on the side of the clean, old-fashioned game, played by the rules, **"Slap Shot"** itself, like the Chiefs, largely triumphs by exploiting—sometimes uproariously—the brutality of the game and the protective vulgarity of the players.

Mr. Hill, a director of real sensibility, is certainly aware that people as thick-headed and slow-witted as are most of these characters aren't very interesting when seen in close-up for very long. Seen as a collective spectacle in a long-shot, though, they make a sometimes bitterly comic comment on one aspect of the industry that is professsional American sports.

The performances—which have a lot to do with the right casting, particularly in the smaller roles—are impeccable. . . .

[**"Slap Shot"**] has a kind of vitality to it that overwhelms most of the questions relating to consistency of character and point of view. Much in the manner of [Sidney Lumet's] "Network," you know that it's an original and that it's alive, whether you like it or not.

> *Vincent Canby, "Hot Time on Ice, Newman's 'Slap Shot'," in* The New York Times *(© 1977 by The New York Times Company; reprinted by permission), February 26, 1977, p. 11.*

PAULINE KAEL

Nothing in movies is surefire anymore, yet George Roy Hill, who directed . . . two of the ten biggest money-makers of all time, will probably have a third with his new *Slap Shot*. The picture is set in the world of minor-league ice hockey, and the theme is that the public no longer cares about the sport—it wants goonish vaudeville and mayhem. Hill's last picture, *The Great Waldo Pepper*—a box-office failure—was bright and clear; it had the coolness of a schoolboy reverie. This time, he's heated up his technique. *Slap Shot* is darker-colored and grainier; it's faster, noisier, more profane, and more brutal than previous Hill productions. . . . *Slap Shot* never slows down. You're aware of the seams and joins, but you can admire their proficiency; Hill directs with dispatch. (p. 273)

Hill's attitudes are elusive; he's making a comic hymn to violence, and yet you can sense his own reserve, his qualms. *Slap Shot* might be the work of a coldly sensitive man who has seen [Martin] Scorsese's films and can't decide if their heat is great or just cheap and nasty; he simulates it ambivalently. The simulation works, but it's also unsettling; it's rough on the surface but slick underneath—like machine-made graffiti. The flag is defaced at the start by running the credits on it; a hockey player is nudged by another during the play of "The Star-Spangled Banner" and says, "I'm listening to the ******* song"; a busload of players and another busload of their boosters arrive in a town, are greeted by hecklers, and make moons out the bus windows. Hill is shooting the works. You feel as if he were telling himself what the picture says about ice hockey: that there's no longer any way to play the game except as a dirty, violent joke. Expletives are sprinkled around like manure to give the film a funky seasoning—the stink of reality. But they're plastic turds—you're conscious of every dirty word. The director has thrown up his hands; he's like the character Ned Braden . . . , the one college-educated member of the Charlestown Chiefs, who at first refuses to play the thug's game of his teammates but finally gives up—he goes out on the ice and does a striptease, to the delight of the fans. Much of the script dates back to the movie era in which a college education made a man an intellectual and imbued him with principles; Braden broods and looks dissatisfied—a gentleman-jock Hamlet. When he strips, he retains his jockstrap. The meaning of his act is left in doubt: Has Braden degraded himself or has he joined the human race? It may be that the director isn't convinced there's a difference. Hill has technique, but he lacks the conviction or the temperament to hold *Slap Shot* together. What holds it together is the warmth supplied by Paul Newman. As Reggie, the player-coach of the Chiefs, he gives the performance of his life—to date. (pp. 273-74)

The story premise is that the steel mill in the mythical town of Charlestown . . . is closing, and the Chiefs, a third-rate team, dependent on the support of the local workers, are going to fold at the end of the season. Reggie, who has nowhere else to turn and nothing else he knows how to do, convinces himself that if the team has a winning streak a buyer may be found, and in order to improve morale he bluffs the men into believing that a Florida syndicate is interested. They begin to play dirty and to draw crowds, and Reggie deliberately provokes fights with their opponents to raise the bloodshed level. Shabby as the team is, it would mean a lot to the decaying town, but we don't get to see this or feel it. The director skims the material, as if he were directing from a low-flying helicopter. (pp. 275-76)

The plot of *Slap Shot* and its asserted theme never get together. The purpose of the plot is simply to provide for bone-crunch humor, like that in Robert Aldrich's farce *The Longest Yard*. . . . We're told that the fans only want blood and gore. Yet toward the end, when Reggie inspires his men to go out and play "old-time hockey," they don't get the chance to play, and we never find out whether the fans would actually reject a good fast game. The film is too buffoonish to care about its own theme. *Slap Shot* is *The Longest Yard* on ice, but with much sharper timing. The bruisers bash each other more dexterously—you laugh without groaning—and the locker-room scenes, and the glimpses of the Chiefs on the road or in their home city, are comicked up with throwaway humor, in the manner of [Robert Altman's] *M*A*S*H* and *California Split*. Hill, however, uses this manner for archaic running gags, such as one teammate's grinning lecherousness and a pompous sportscaster with a tou-

pee that's more of a doormat than a rug—you wait for it to be knocked off. (p. 276)

The film lavishes condescension on the players' wives; they wear their cheapness like a costume. Hill isn't strong on male-female attachments—the ones here are so kitschy that they're still part of the old movies they came out of.

The modernizing element is the Hill-Dowd ribaldry—the constant derisiveness about homosexual practices and the outright baiting. In the ugliest scene in the picture, Reggie goes to see the owner of the team and discovers that the owner is a woman—a young widow. When she tells Reggie that she *could* sell the team but is going to fold it instead, for a tax write-off, he's defeated—but not quite. He has the laugh: he tells her that her little son is going to be a faggot if she doesn't get herself a man and loosen up. That's the worst fate he can promise her. This scene could have been directed so that it exposed Reggie's narrowness. . . . But we're goaded to laugh; it's not only Reggie who's telling her off—*we're* telling her off. It's obvious that the owner has been made a woman just for this thrust; she's been set up, like the man with the toupee, the busloads of mooners, and the rest of the incidents. (p. 277)

There's a lot of ugliness in this movie, yet Hill sanitizes things even when he tries to be tough. That's probably why this film will be a huge hit. The profanity is dirty but meaningless—Broadway blue. The use of hockey as a metaphor for what has been going on in movies—the greater intensity of effects—is self-serving. Hill is a technician, not an artist. Yet he's not just putting down the bums who use shock effects—he's putting down the artists who use violence organically. Scorsese gets in there and digs around and makes you feel it; the relentlessness of *Taxi Driver* isn't just rhythm and pacing. Hill is like a big-money Broadway-blue playwright complaining of the crude tastes of the avant-garde while ripping them off. His crudeness here is livelier than anything he's done before, but I don't know that I've ever seen a picture so completely geared to giving the public "what it wants" with such an antagonistic feeling behind it. Hill gets you laughing, all right, but he's so grimly determined to ram entertainment down your throat that you feel like a Strasbourg goose. (pp. 277-78)

Pauline Kael, "Hill's Pâté" (originally published in The New Yorker, *Vol. LIII, No. 3, March 7, 1977), in her* When the Lights Go Down *(copyright © 1975, 1976, 1977, 1978, 1979, 1980 by Pauline Kael; reprinted by permission of Holt, Rinehart and Winston, Publishers), Holt, Rinehart and Winston, 1980, pp. 273-78.*

ANDREW SARRIS

First, the good news: *Slap Shot* is the funniest hockey movie since Walt Disney's *Hockey Homicide* with Goofy at his meanest and most murderous. For a change, the female leads . . . are given parts with zing and feeling, and men hunger after them. A marvelous trio of moronic zanies . . . come on like the Marx Brothers, though mostly Chico, and the production zips along with unflagging pace. So far, so good. Why then do I remain uneasy enough to keep all my critical options open? Perhaps I find something fundamentally hypocritical in the way that director George Roy Hill and scenarist Nancy Dowd poke fun at hockey macho in a movie that is itself raunchy and violent, which is to say that Hill and Dowd are not above taking a few cheap shots of their own at such easy establishment figures as a tax-loss club-owning heiress and a pompous, small-town sports announcer.

Perhaps a warning signal went off in my skull when I read an interview in which Hill described *Slap Shot* as a "metaphor" for certain tendencies in American life. I have been wary of the word "metaphor" in show-biz conversations ever since an eerie encounter with Raquel Welch at Gaylord's about two years ago. She had just seen *A Chorus Line* in previews, and I asked her how she liked it. "Very interesting as a metaphor," she replied. Of course, the theatre has been virtually all metaphor for a long time, and, now particularly, old B-movies can be revamped for the stage as metaphors for the shoddiness and shabbiness of the American Dream. . . .

Fortunately, the cinema still clings to its curious tradition of magical naturalism. Each image is endowed with its own expressive integrity, and so it remains difficult to assemble clusters of images into a coherent argument. Far more systematic directors than George Roy Hill have found themselves confounded by the thematic drift of their material. Still, *Slap Shot* seems to go out of its way to contradict its ultimate intentions with its intermediate effects. One of the problems may be that Paul Newman seems to preside over the action without ever plunging into it, and thus one is never sure whether the character he plays is a Brechtian commentator or a brawling combatant. The uncertainty between distancing and involvement carries over to the minor-league hockey team in a New England mill town. Hill and Dowd go through the motions of rooting for the team without ever seeming to care about the actual outcome of its games.

Hockey is a long way from being one of my favorite sports, but I wouldn't have minded a loving evocation of its tactical maneuvers and physical exploits. Instead, we are treated to an unadulterated goon show, complete with a male striptease right out of [Jerry Schatzberg's] *Scarecrow*. By not choreographing hockey as the visually intricate game that it is, Hill creates a situation in which the sudden onset of unbridled violence on the ice serves as welcome comic relief. That audiences roar with laughter at the very excesses the movie is supposedly condemning must strike the most disinterested observer as decidedly opportunistic. The answer, of course, is not to eliminate the violence but, rather, to eliminate all traces of moralistic rhetoric about violence. All slapstick comedy, after all, is irresponsibly violent. How many parents would really want their children to imitate the Marx Brothers, particularly by hitting people over the head with wooden mallets?

For all its mayhem, however, *Slap Shot* may turn out to be more a woman's picture than a man's picture. Associated in the past with such buddy-buddy bonanzas as *Butch Cassidy and the Sundance Kid*, *The Sting*, and *Waldo Pepper*, Hill seems to have gone out of his way to give his female characters more stature and significance than ever before. . . . There is something tough and knowing about all the women in the movie, something that keeps the male camaraderie in check. It may be nothing more than the woman's point of view in the script. Nancy Dowd reportedly utilized her own brother's experiences as a small-time hockey player and went so far as to hide a tape recorder in the locker room to get the undiluted macho lingo with which we are now regaled.

Here again there may be some confusion as to what is actually intended by this verbal striptease. We all laughed in the beginning at the unguarded profanity on the White House tapes. The cream of the jest was the public piety of Nixon and his

cohorts, but upon reflection, some of us realized that a tape recorder hidden in the editorial conference rooms of *The Washington Post*, *The New York Times*, or *The Village Voice* might have proven to be equally embarrassing. Certainly, at this point in time, it is difficult to determine if the laughter at locker-room expletives is aroused by condescension or complicity. Is the dialogue gleaned from Dowd's hidden tape recorder a step forward in the screen's march toward truth, or a step backward as a consequence of her snooping into a self-conscious tribal ritual and thereby distorting incantation into information? Through the '60s and '70s, the thin line between liberation and license has been completely obscured as audiences have become increasingly fragmented. I have tried to occupy the middle ground by insisting upon wit as a chaperon for profanity, and I must say that in *Slap Shot* the funny redeems the filthy on the sound track a great deal of the time.

Yet, I am still bothered by the film's notion that hockey teams and hockey players must make a Faustian decision whether to win by playing dirty or lose by playing clean. I think that speed and strength and talent come into play more forcefully than Hill, Dowd, and Company would indicate. Also, goons start out being goons very early in their careers, and they are usually neutralized by other goons. Again, the view of hockey in *Slap Shot* seems to be almost exclusively from outside. It strikes me that only a woman would conceive of a male hockey player doing a striptease on the ice to show his disgust for all the violent shenanigans. The point made is too neatly and symmetrically antimacho. . . .

[In *Slap Shot*] the violence seems to bring the community closer together in a kind of M*A*S*H-like impudence. When the team bus roars into a hostile town, the outstretched legs of the team groupies taunting the townspeople, and a few male assholes exposed for good measure, seem to suggest modish defiance of a conformist community. I confess that I am confused, which is to say that there is much more in *Slap Shot* to recommend as a movie, than as a metaphor.

> *Andrew Sarris, "SlapStick 'Slap Shot'" (reprinted by permission of* The Village Voice *and the author; copyright © The Village Voice, Inc., 1977), in* The Village Voice, *Vol. XXII, No. 11, March 14, 1977, p. 41.*

VINCENT CANBY

Paris in the spring. A beautiful, brilliant, American student named Lauren meets and falls in love with Daniel, who is French and as brilliant as Lauren. They both read [Martin] Heidegger and share a fondness for American films, especially those, like **"Butch Cassidy and the Sundance Kid"** and **"The Sting,"** that were directed by George Roy Hill. Though they act as if they were sophisticated, they are naïve at heart. When Daniel takes Lauren to see her first porn film, she runs out in tears. She hadn't expected it to be "like that." "That," says Daniel, "isn't love." . . .

Lauren and Daniel are, I think, meant to be comic and appealing in their mixture of innocence and worldliness. Yet Mr. Hill's **"A Little Romance"** . . . recalls most vividly the arch manner in which the Our Gang comedies worked—by having their child actors ape not the behavior of children but of grownups.

"A Little Romance" is a movie that seems to have melted the minds of everyone of any stature connected with it. Fifteen years ago, Mr. Hill made one of his first big splashes in movies with that still-charming comedy, **"The World of Henry Ori-**

ent,'' after which he went on to do **"Butch Cassidy," "The Sting," "Slaughterhouse Five"** and **"The Great Waldo Pepper."** That's an impressive record in terms of art and commerce. Yet **"A Little Romance"** is so ponderous it seems almost mean spirited. It's been a long time since I've seen a movie about boorish American tourists and felt sorry for the tourists—which is one of Mr. Hill's achievements here.

I'm sure nothing mean-spirited was intended, but such is the film's effect. This may be the main hazard when one sets out to make a film so relentlessly sweet-tempered that it winds up—like Pollyanna—alienating everyone not similarly affected.

> Vincent Canby, "Movie: George Roy Hill Offers 'A Little Romance','' in The New York Times (© 1979 by The New York Times Company; reprinted by permission), April 27, 1979, p. C16.

ROBERT ASAHINA

[*A Little Romance*] is a downright simple-minded adult's fantasy of young love. . . .

Three things redeem [its] foolishness. The first, surprisingly, is Hill's direction, which never condescends to the material. Somehow, he manages to maintain just the right note of romantic humor that had virtually disappeared with the musical comedies (like [Vincente Minnelli's] *Gigi*) of the '50s. Hill's single lapse is his fondness for showing clips from his previous works.

The second is the acting of [Thelonious] Bernard and [Laurence] Olivier. Both have difficult roles; perhaps only a loveable old curmudgeon is harder to portray than a loveably obnoxious kid. Since the script is so silly and the director is better known for his engineering of pleasant entertainments than his talented handling of performers, I'm inclined to believe that Bernard could have a future in this business. Olivier, of course, could have played the part in his sleep.

Finally, [Diane] Lane is simply the most charming young actress to appear in a generation. . . . To watch her in *A Little Romance* is to witness the birth of a star. (p. 22)

> Robert Asahina, "Young Love,'' in The New Leader (©1979 by the American Labor Conference on International Affairs, Inc.), Vol. 63, No. 10, May 7, 1979, pp. 21-2.*

ANDREW SARRIS

George Roy Hill's *A Little Romance* seems to be an international remake of *The World of Henry Orient*, a slightly underrated mixture of lyrical adolescence and extramarital hi-jinks. Here, Diane Lane and Thelonious Bernard play two young lovers with high IQs who combine puppy love under the Bridge of Sighs with conversations about Heidegger. . . . Bernard is not merely a young lover; he is also an avid movie buff with a particular passion for George Roy Hill's works, several of which are excerpted in *A Little Romance*. . . . *A Little Romance* abounds with heavy-handed caricatures lumbering around its two elfin sprites. George Roy Hill and scenarist Allan Burns may simply have lost their deftness with peripheral characters under the strain of being funny and charming within American, French, and Italian contexts. There are moments when the movie is exuberantly elitist, and that is all to the good, but for the most part, *A Little Romance* is disconcertingly soft and

fatuous. Nonetheless, Hill does display bursts of taste and energy even in this misfired project.

> Andrew Sarris, "Captains Courageous'' (reprinted by permission of The Village Voice and the author; copyright © News Group Publications, Inc., 1979), in The Village Voice, Vol. XXIV, No. 18, May 7, 1979, p. 49.*

DAVID ANSEN

As any reader of John Irving's popular novel knows, a lot happens in "The World According to Garp''—assassinations, attempted assassinations, grotesque mutilations, grotesque self-mutilations, a dog biting a man, a man biting a dog, rape, marital infidelity . . . . A high percentage of these bizarre events has been preserved in George Roy Hill's ambitious attempt to bring "Garp'' to the screen, but what the movie cannot do is supply the glue that binds them together—Irving's jaunty, muscular narrative presence, which goes to the mat against life's absurdities to emerge bloodied but unbowed.

A lot of people felt that "Garp'' couldn't be made into a movie. A lot of people were right. Take away the prose, and one is left with a concatenation of events that seems increasingly—and distastefully—gratuitous. Even when the artist's theme is the randomness of fate, it's his challenge to make that randomness cohere. What happens in Steve Tesich's screenplay seems willed by literary fiat. When anything can happen at any given moment no matter what—a sniper busting up a feminist rally one instant, a plane crashing into a house the next—the audience begins to feel like puppets on a string. Anyone unfamiliar with Irving's book will have precious little notion of where the story is leading, of why he is on this particular journey with a man named Garp. Tesich and director Hill have tried to compensate for the book's picaresque, stop-start form by loading it down with thematic and visual symmetry—repeated images of flying and heavy foreshadowings of death. . . . But these fancy cosmetic touches can't disguise that old problem: how do you make a writer's internal struggles dramatic? . . .

What **"The World According to Garp"** fails to create is a coherent, believable world. It's a movie of bits and pieces, fits and starts. Many of those pieces do indeed sparkle. (p. 77)

For all its isolated lovely touches—there's a wonderful moment of repose while Garp listens to Nat King Cole on his car radio—the movie leaves a cold, sour aftertaste. Some of this can be attributed to the uncertain tone of Hill's direction—overly broad here, too remote there—but much of it goes back to Irving. Behind **"Garp"**'s sentimental salute to hearth and home lurks the rancid whiff of misogyny and a willful zest for violence. Because Garp assumes traditional female roles as a husband, he has been hailed as a feminist hero, yet Irving's real rage is reserved for the fanatical feminists he invents—the Ellen Jamesians, who have cut out their tongues to protest the rape and disfigurement of a little girl. One is meant to be appalled by their perversion of feminism, but their appearance on screen boomerangs: I was more appalled by the imagination that conceived them, that gleefully dreamed up the relentless horrors that befall everyone thereafter. Some may call this a tragicomic vision; to others it will seem like pulling the wings off flies. (p. 79)

> David Ansen, "T. S. Garp Rides Again,'' in Newsweek (copyright 1982, by Newsweek, Inc.; all rights

reserved; reprinted by permission), Vol. C, No. 4, July 26, 1982, pp. 77, 79.

printed by permission), Issue 376, August 19, 1982, pp. 33-4.

MICHAEL SRAGOW

[With his film version of *The World According to Garp*, director George Roy Hill] hasn't created a movie as potent as the original literary myth—that is, he hasn't done what Milos Forman did with *One Flew over the Cuckoo's Nest*. But he hasn't trashed the novel, either, as Forman did *Ragtime*. Indeed, he's retained enough of the book's vitality and humor to make this film far more enjoyable than most other prestige literary adaptations, including [John Fowles's] *The French Lieutenant's Woman*. The big difference is that if Garp sees life "as an X-rated soap opera," George Roy Hill sees it as a soft R.

There will be two audiences for this movie—those who've read the book and those who haven't. I've seen it twice, once before reading the book and once after. The first time, I found it an unusually compelling, if uneven, slapstick tragedy about a man's struggle to protect his family from the emotional and political fluctuations of the moment and the dark undertow of fate. There were gaping holes, but there was also enough surprise and verve to keep me engrossed. The second time, I was equally entertained, but I realized that Hill and Tesich had pruned Irving's novel without inventing enough new material to support their own cozier vision. (p. 33)

To my mind, what the book is about most of all is a wrestler-writer creating a vision of the world that contains its random violence as well as all its "normal" human failings, without succumbing to hopelessness. Garp battles for the sanctity of individual feeling, whether it's against urban thugs or single-minded political activists. . . . Garp runs the gamut of advanced sexual exploraton and confusion, becoming a house-husband for his college-teacher wife. . . , a common adulterer, a wife-swapper and a cuckold. His best friend is a transsexual, and one of his major preoccupations, in both his literary and real life is rape—the ultimate horror.

Since Hill and Tesich have chosen not to grapple with Garp's world view, it's understandable that they've deemphasized the book's carnage and Garp's literary obsessions. They sift Irving's protean novel for material that coincides with their message: family life is precious and must be preserved with constant wariness. For roughly the first hour, they move with confidence and grace, creating a sort of dark, mock-Mickey Rooney movie. . . . But as the film progresses, the moviemakers' partial surgery starts to come apart at the stitches. In the book, both Garp and his wife, Helen, who marry young, deal with Garp's fleeting lust and overweening literary ambition, and Helen's need to seek solace elsewhere when he becomes oblivious to everything except his children. But in the movie, infidelity alone seems the cause, not the symptom, of the marriage's shattering.

Partly because of the semisatiric, semisentimental banality of the movie's style, Garp often comes across less as a wrestler with fate than as its victim. . . .

Irving's exuberant vision proves to be unsinkable; it can't help but sneak into Hill and Tesich's confining format. This is one square movie with delightfully flaky edges. (p. 34)

Michael Sragow, "The World of 'Garp,' According to Hollywood," in Rolling Stone (by Straight Arrow Publishers, Inc. © 1982; all rights reserved; re-*

STANLEY KAUFFMANN

[*The World According to Garp*] begins with the infant son of the dead tail-gunner being tossed into the sky; it ends with the grown Garp dying in the sky, in an ambulance helicopter, and then there's a repeat of the opening infant shot.

This is one of several attempts by Hill and his colleague Tesich to evolve patterns from the novel and to underscore ones that already exist in the book. Examples: Garp's college girl friend, Helen, sees another girl practicing fellatio on him; later, years after Helen and Garp are married, his car accidentally rams another car in which she is practicing fellatio on a student of hers. Early in the film, a sniper is shot out of a tree before he can shoot Garp's mother at a public meeting; later, another sniper gets her; still later, Garp is shot—by the vindictive sister of the first girl who fellated Garp.

Hill clings very hard to these patterns. The ones that he took from the novel he highlights as Irving didn't need to. Because the acute Hill was aware of the problems he faced in filming *Garp,* he apparently thought that this emphasis on designs might bind the picture together. I respect his fore-knowledge of the problems and his refusal to be deterred: I wish I could add that he overcame the problems, but he has only demonstrated again an aesthetic difference between novels—some novels, anyway—and films.

I'm not about to make a checklist of the differences between Irving's book and this film. . . . Hill's basic trouble was not that he was dealing with a first-class novel—I don't think Irving's book is anything like first class—but that, if Irving achieved anything, it was the creation of his novel *in its prose*. And that prose is deliberately paradoxical: it uses brisk, vigorous, good humor to deal with lives that entail the grotesque and horrible. In the book, those horrors influence the hero's cheer as little as they do the prose he lives in. That paradoxical prose gives the book its tone, a combination of a civilian *Catch-22* with a macabre *Candide*. And it's that prose, that nearly literal *body* of the work, for which Hill has not found a cinematic equivalent. In his film, the materials he has taken from the book are like several kinds of fish, which were lively and colorful in a huge tank, hauled out and plunked into a small aquarium where they have difficulty in moving, even surviving.

Or, to change figures, it's as if Hill had filmed bits of an opera libretto, omitting the score. Without the score, the bits are unfulfilled and disconnected. (p. 26)

The result is that we never quite know how to react to the film. Some sequences are well directed—such as the courtship scenes in the empty college bleachers or the interweavings of reminiscence and fantasy—and some roles are well acted. But we never know who Garp himself is, in relation to us. With Irving, it was the novel *itself* that we reacted to; with the film, we need a vicar, and Garp doesn't satisfy. *Is* he a doomed Candide? Or a symbol of human resistance to reality? Or an instance of the capriciousness of fate?. . . . All of these things, and more, can be true of any one life, of course, which may be part of Irving's point—to contain life's errancies in a constancy, his consistent prose. In the film, all we can do is laugh at the funny stuff, be moved by the family stuff, be shocked by the horrible stuff, one discrete bit after another. (pp. 26-7)

*Stanley Kauffmann, "Garp's World and Others"
(reprinted by permission of Brandt & Brandt Literary
Agents, Inc.; copyright © 1982 by Stanley Kauffmann), in* The New Republic, *Vol. 187, No. 9, August 30, 1982, pp. 26-8.**

JOHN SIMON

The Germans have a word for it: *Edelkitsch,* noble trash. Some
recent fictional examples of it are [Erica Jong's] *Fear of Flying,*
[D. M. Thomas's] *The White Hotel,* and [John Irving's] *The
World According to Garp. . . .* The movie of **Garp,** written
by Steve Tesich and directed by George Roy Hill, seems to
me both more simple-minded and better than the novel. If this
sounds like faint praise, it is meant so. Still, as movies go
these days, it may not be all that faint after all.

Garp . . . concerns well-born Jenny Fields, a nurse and fierce
feminist, who wants a child but no husband, and so, during
World War II, conceives by a dying ball-turret gunner, Technical Sergeant Garp, a child she names T. S. Garp. (p. 1096)

As you must further know, Jenny will write her autobiography
as a "sexual suspect" and become a great guru for embattled
feminists, including the Ellen Jamesians, who cut out their
tongues to show their solidarity with Ellen James, a girl who
was raped and had her tongue cut out to prevent her from
betraying her violator. As you must also know, Garp, who,
just like John Irving, turns into both a fine wrestler and a noted
writer, is not so successful as his charismatically best-selling
mother, but does well enough to marry nice Helen Holm, who
becomes a professor of English. They have nice children whom
they adore. . . . And yet they somehow start cheating on each
other, and. . . .

But why am I telling you all this? If you already know it, you
surely want to forget it; if you don't and decide to see the
movie, which greatly depends on oddball twists, you're better
off if you're kept guessing. The novel's complicated plot and
subplots have been considerably pared down. This makes the
film less tricky and cloyingly sentimental than the book, and
also less sadistic: the mutilations in which Irving revels have
been omitted or toned down. On the other hand, certain absurdist elements that fit into the fabric of the book are doubly
bothersome in the film. First, because film, unable to circum-
vent the real world, is intrinsically less hospitable to absurdism;
and, second, because the screenplay winnows out so many
absurdist elements that those left in stick out more jarringly.

Even so, one cannot but admire the talent for compression and
suggestion that both Hill and Tesich exhibit. Take the very
title sequence: to the accompaniment of the Beatles singing
"Will you still love me when I'm 64?" an angelically smiling
yet slightly befuddled baby keeps bouncing skyward. We do
not see the cause of his soarings: is baby Garp being tossed
up by his mother, or is he already on the great trampoline of
life, treading air before even walking the earth?. . . Tesich
and Hill keep moving things along: if you don't like [a par-
ticular] scene, never mind, there'll be another one along in a
jiffy.

Certain elements are handled more suavely than in the book,
without, however, being shirked, e.g., the inadvertent emasculation by fellatio during the car crash. A potentially sticky
character, such as Robert/Roberta, the transsexual football player,
emerges charming. . . . Even young Garp's fantasy about his
aeronautical father's epic demise, done as a cartoon sequence
partly drawn and partly dreamed by the child, comes off with

flying colors. And though there are countless clever children
pullulating throughout the movie, they do not, individually or
collectively, sour us on their sweetness.

There are, however, less pleasant aspects. Garp, the delectable
wrestler, writer, cook, and clown, is played by Robin Williams
merely adequately. . . . (pp. 1096-97)

Most of the supporting roles are well handled, and Irving himself makes a congenial cameo appearance as a wrestling ref-
eree. Miroslav Ondriček's unassumingly authoritative cinematography makes the most of some extremely well-chosen
locations. And, as I said, the film moves right along. But, as
I also said, it is *Edelkitsch* or, *anglice,* garpage. (p. 1097)

John Simon, "An Intellectual Suspect," in National
Review *(© National Review, Inc., 1982; 150 East
35th St., New York, NY 10016), Vol. XXXIV, No.
17, September 3, 1982, pp. 1096-97.**

EDWARD SHORES

Hill's films can be seen as a continuing critique of the ideas
which have shaped and still support the American culture. He
questions such traditional concepts as the nobility of individual
heroism, the role and nature of the family, and the American
obsession with success. These concepts are a small part of a
core of ideas that can be termed "conventional morality,"
wisdom that, whatever its origins, comes to be accepted as
given by the members of a culture. The configuration of this
morality is ambiguous, but a suggestive and subjective outline
can be drawn. The conventional wisdom with which Hill's
films deal holds that the forces of good invariably triumph over
the forces of evil; that righteousness is rewarded while wrongdoing is punished; that the universe is providentially and be-
nevolently ruled; that the family is a strong force for good;
that violence, if channeled in socially approved directions, is
acceptable; that union with society is a person's most important
goal; that the development of the individual spirit is a person's
most important goal; that acts of heroism are meaningful and
add to a person's stature; that marriage is the ideal relationship
between two people; that success marks the individual; and
that material success is secondary to emotional happiness. The
list could be extended, but this at least suggests what is meant
by conventional morality. (pp. 8-9)

[Hill] challenges these still prevailing concepts of conventional
morality. His films tell us that these trusted ideas are antiquated; the simple truths they espouse are inconsistent with the
more complex modern world. Identification with and acceptance of the concepts does not bring happiness, for an orderly
and comprehensible world does not exist. For Hill, these concepts are lenses that distort perception and lead the individual
into limiting, enervating, and occasionally self-destructive actions. In contrast, Hill presents a world where ambiguity, not
clarity, is quintessential and where happiness is not inevitable.
He disavows or dispassionately examines the cultural conventions, asking that we understand as well as accept them, and,
if necessary, reject them. He calls, in essence, for a new independence, a personal determination of one's attitudes, aims,
and understanding. His films, like those of most critically acclaimed new directors, stand as a challenge to the old ways of
seeing and defining self.

Hill's films contravert conventional thought through *irony.* He
weaves variations on the stereotypical characters and plots in
with the conventional action to give his stories more substance

and depth. The contrast between the familiar genre story and the variations creates an ambiguity that prevents the easy identification common to most genre films. Hill emotionally distances the audience from the characters, and makes possible a critical evaluation of them and their actions. (pp. 9-10)

All Hill's works belong to the category of commercial movies, films which, despite their variety, have remarkably similar characters, structures, and morality. In these films, representative characters resolve problems or achieve happiness by voluntarily accepting and practicing the tenets of conventional morality. The characters may begin outside society . . . , and then move to a reconciliation with society, or remain outside society but essentially endorse its values. Or the character may begin as a member of society and then reaffirm its power by using its values and resources to defeat an enemy. Whatever the case, the characters usually move through a series of trials, eventually finding happiness through acceptance of conventional morality. The films thus become implicit or explicit advocates of the American culture; entertainments, but nonetheless assertions of the fundamental validity of certain values.

Although Hill's films seem produced from this mold, they are more accurately variations of it. Ideally . . . , the central characters, no matter what their limitations, ultimately embody a number of virtues with which the audience can identify and toward which it can feel sympathetic. Loyalty, courage, integrity, friendship, moral character are emphasized or, more often, emerge as the character undergoes a series of trials: town drunks reform, failures succeed, refugees from love become romantic, uncommitted figures turn patriotic, cowards gain courage, and sinners repent. The protagonists draw us into the world of the film, allowing us to experience vicariously the emotions around which the film is structured, and tacitly teaching us the moral lessons of our culture. Hill's characters, like all genre figures, have attractive qualities which draw us to them, and their problems—conflict with an increasingly bureaucratic or technological world, or a dispirited or materialistic one—engage our sympathy. But complicating the familiar frame are flaws that prevent total identification. Eventually the protagonists demonstrate some weakness, insensitivity, or failing that negates their hold on our feelings, drawing instead our wonder or disapprobation. We begin to question the characters, and in that questioning move away from the unthinking stock response. In addition, these flaws, unlike those of traditional characters, are never truly overcome; they stay with the characters throughout and, by virtue of their presence, contribute to our sense of ambiguity. The weaknesses are sometimes well-hidden, as in *The Sting,* or obvious, as in *Waldo Pepper,* but are always an integral part of the film.

The outlaw heroes of *Butch Cassidy* are lovable, charming, attractive figures whose stereotypical strengths are counterpointed by their seemingly limitless capacity for bad judgment. As the film progresses, their inability to see the hopelessness of their situation becomes a mark of their limitation, not their charm. Any sympathetic judgment is qualified by recognition that their independence is as much stumbled into as chosen; they do not understand the consequences of their actions. (pp. 11-13)

Billy Pilgrim [of *Slaughterhouse-Five*] is an engaging, but impotent naif who accepts prisons, such as life in Ilium, with a perseverance that borders on masochism. He lacks the ability or initiative to solve his problems, and accordingly his "triumph" on Tralfamadore is more accidental and fantastic than earned. Despite our sympathy for him, he never becomes competent

or strong enough to draw our identification. Hooker and Gondorff [of *The Sting*] are roguishly charming con men, but no charm can hide the fact that "the sting" is performed as much for self-gratification as for revenge. At the end of the film, they deny that justice, the motive that has sanctioned their actions and made them more sympathetic than Lonnegan, is attainable or even worthwhile. This last minute reversal mutes some of our strong feelings for them and negates an unthinking emotional response to them.

While Waldo Pepper emerges victorious over Kessler, his road to that victory seems accidental, not earned. In addition, his lie about the fight with Kessler, his inability to learn from the experiences of his friends, and his failure in the attempted rescue of Mary Beth are qualities inconsistent with those usually associated with heroes. Once again the complete identification customary in commercial film is lacking. Reggie Dunlop of *Slapshot* demonstrates few of the virtues we expect to find in a conventional protagonist. There is no sensitivity or understanding hidden beneath his rough exterior; the crudity is the man. The championship cannot disguise the fact that Dunlop has manipulated the emotions of his players, ruined his own marriage, and almost destroyed the neurotic Lily Braden.

Daniel and Lauren, the teenage protagonists of *A Little Romance,* are among Hill's most engaging characters. They have a sensitivity and an ingenuous love that sharply contrasts to their parents' world. Yet they are also dominated by cultural ideas about romance, particularly Daniel, who attempts to fulfill the ideal of manhood that he sees set forth in films. By paying such close attention to that concept, he comes close to losing Lauren.

The variations in character, which suggest an additional dimension to the films, are adumbrated and buttressed by the variations in structure. In conventional films, the character moves from a state of tension or estrangement to one of harmony and order through acquiescence to the conventional morality. Whatever problems the characters encounter are eventually resolved by an appeal to the precepts of traditional wisdom. They (and we) learn the "proper" way to act and think, and the world becomes clearer and less threatening. (pp. 13-14)

In Hill's films, this basic structure is reversed. The characters have problems *because they accept the dictates of conventional wisdom,* not because they have cut themselves off from it. They begin as firm adherents to some quintessentially American belief and untypically move to a state of estrangement or tension because of their adherence to that belief. Such a basic reversal of structure alters the thematic thrust of Hill's films. Conventional morality hinders, not aids the comprehension of the world, and consequently, its validity is undercut.

In *Butch Cassidy,* for example, the outlaws are prime examples of American individuality. They reject the closed technological society and insist on their right to lead their own lives. Ordinarily such an attitude would be supported or shown as a source of strength, but Hill shows their blind adherence as a weakness leading to death. Their inability to see that the concept of unfettered individualism is no longer valid destroys them. Waldo Pepper and Reggie Dunlop are typically American in their pursuit of excellence and success. Identification with them is easy because their desire has been bred into most Americans through schools and social institutions. But, unlike the traditional heroes, their desire for success leads to troublesome dilemmas, and their "triumphs" are of such an ambiguous nature that we question, rather than applaud, their achievements. Billy Pilgrim starts with an unshakable belief in the sanctity of the American family, an institution long dear to social and religious leaders. But Billy finds only unhappiness with his families; the strength that should theoretically support him is inadequate or nonexistent. Even his rescue by Tralfamadore, because fantastic, underscores his failures with his earth families. The characters in *The Sting* begin with the traditional belief that there should be equal justice for all, even those who are seemingly beyond the law. But that attitude causes serious problems, and the two con men end up rejecting the validity of the traditional notion to assert that self-gratification is equally important. Lauren and Daniel first embrace certain established concepts of romance. Lauren is captured by the ideas of Elizabeth Barrett Browning, and places her hopes for happiness in an old "legend" associated with the poetess; Daniel faithfully imitates the attitudes of his favorite film heroes, aping them to the point that his personality is submerged. Dedicated to their own particular ideals, the adolescents pursue separate goals until it is almost too late to save their relationship.

Once we recognize that Hill's films are not crass imitations of traditional works, we can perceive the outline of the world present in his films. In his universe the individual has become burdened with cultural misconceptions. The culture has shaped his attitudes in such a way that he or she can conceive of discovering meaning and attaining happiness only through the attainment of certain preordained goals. For the character, prescribed rituals, such as the performance of a heroic action, lead to the prescribed results of respect and reward. The cultural concepts are so dominating that the individual cannot conceive of alternatives, and thus the concepts occasionally become more valuable than life itself. Further, Hill argues, the concepts are antiquated, describing fixed relationships that no longer apply to a fluid, changing world, and, at their worst, they absorb the individual. (pp. 15-16)

Characters so dominated by a concept lose their individuality; they play the role society expects and repress natural feelings in order to maintain a particular image. The outlaws become courteous, chivalrous, and gallant despite the incongruity of their profession with such virtues, and maintain this facade even in times of danger. (pp. 19-20)

Once the difference in character and motivation are seen, the dynamics of Hill's counter story become clearer. As noted earlier, the characters begin as adherents of conventional American beliefs and move, because of their fidelity to those beliefs, to ambiguous resolutions of their problems. Such a filmic structure suggests the inadequacy of conventional views, for they cannot account for the changed, occasionally insensitive, sometimes threatening world the characters encounter. The conventional morality, accepted unthinkingly, is shown to be spiritually bankrupt; the roles it prescribes for individuals are now irrelevant, and it has no reserve resources to sustain its adherents.

Hill's films, then, juxtapose two understandings of the world. On the one hand there are the familiar genre narratives with their conventional metaphysics. The extraordinary success of his films indicates that the genre conventions have maintained their potency. The audience still finds American vitality, ingenuity, and skill attractive, and sees the qualities as tools that enable one to deal with the world. The characters seem familiar heroes, models whom we can safely emulate. But the films also show a world where conventional morality is false and inaccurate, hindering rather than helping the individual deal with the world. Characters who accept the fraudulent conventions dissipate their strengths in pursuit of illusory goals. Integrity, loyalty, skill, and courage are wasted in service to outworn ideals, and the individual, trapped by a system of unrealistic beliefs, is doomed to slow disintegration.

The two narratives, seen together, yield more than the naive optimism of the genre story or the cynicism of the genre variations. The second narrative reveals an ugly side of the first, forcing us to question conventional assumptions often taken for granted. We are asked to see that the frame of reference, the genre conventions, is no longer valid, and that a more complex understanding of the world must be arrived at.

Thus the films usually end on a negative note (*A Little Romance* is an exception), showing the disparity between the ideal (conventional assumptions) and the depressing reality in which individualism is impossible and characters are doomed by antiquated cultural beliefs. The films can be seen solely as a negative criticism of the culture for they do not suggest an alternative to the traditional understanding of the world. The majority of characters fail to come to terms with their problems or discover any potential solutions. But it is also possible to see the films as implicitly asserting the need for a new independence. The shock of recognition, the realization that Hill's criticisms are correct, may motivate some viewers to action. Instead of blindly accepting the dictates of others, the individual, in order to avoid the fate of Hill's characters, must learn to see with his own eyes, rely on his own judgments, and be willing to change. (pp. 21-2)

Edward Shores, in his George Roy Hill *(copyright © 1983 by Twayne Publishers; reprinted with the permission of Twayne Publishers, a Division of G. K. Hall & Co., Boston), Twayne, 1983, 163 p.*

Billy Joel

1949-

(Born William Martin Joel) American songwriter.

Joel is best known for his songs about urban/suburban life. His first hit single, "Piano Man," is based on his experiences as a lounge singer in Los Angeles. The song is noted for its stirring characterizations of the "losers" who patronize such bars, searching to fulfill their unrealized dreams.

Joel's vision is often despairing, although an ironic sense of humor is sometimes evident in his lyrics. His socially acute vignettes are frequently laced with anger, especially when he urges his listeners to grow up and face the strangers within themselves and loved ones or to come together and support each other. Joel gained mass popularity with his 1977 album *The Stranger*. The songs deal mostly with leaving home, and critics praised Joel's honest commentary on everyday life. The tone of Joel's work sometimes seems hypocritical, but even his detractors agree that he is able to depict people as he sees them without condescension.

On *The Nylon Curtain* Joel went farther afield than the streets of suburbia for his subject matter. "Goodnight Saigon," about the Vietnam war, and "Allentown," about the demise of the once-prosperous Pennsylvania steel town, are considered the outstanding cuts on the album. Joel's songs about the working class succeed because he presents his stories without sentimentality or melodrama.

(See also *Contemporary Authors*, Vol. 108.)

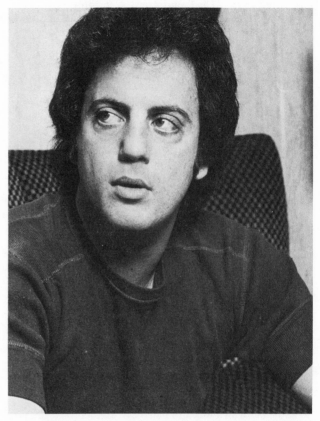

JACK BRESCHARD

[Billy Joel's] *Piano Man* reflects a new seriousness and musical flexibility. . . .

Joel's best efforts speak to the point about people around him. His sense of detail fleshes out his B-movie characters. "**Somewhere Along the Line**" holds the album's most concise observations, waxing philosophical without wallowing in pretentious drivel. . . .

Despite Joel's facility at portraying others, he seems unable to come to terms with himself. The title tune tries to reflect the piano man through his patrons, but Joel fails to illuminate his own character. At other times, like in "**The Ballad of Billy the Kid**," the singer's bristling ego mocks his supposedly objective point of view. (p. 62)

Billy Joel's enthusiasm and musical straightforwardness keep everything together and moving briskly along. (p. 63)

Jack Breschard, in his review of "Piano Man," in Rolling Stone *(by Straight Arrow Publishers, Inc. © 1974; all rights reserved; reprinted by permission), Issue 156, March 14, 1974, pp. 62-3.*

PETER REILLY

Composer-performer Billy Joel's new album ["**Piano Man**"] has several striking bands, among them the title number, a really brilliant piece of work. *Piano Man* is a highly dramatic song, beautifully constructed and performed, about the patrons of an O'Neill-type bar, each sunk in dreams of glory about his future: the piano man himself, who hopes to be a movie star; the insurance man convinced that he is a novelist; and many others caught in the web of self-delusion. It's very strong stuff. . . . Nothing else here comes up to that song or performance, but there are moments in *Captain Jack* and in *Ain't No Crime* that pulsate with the same intensity.

At the moment Joel has two problems: the similarity of approach in performance and orchestration from band to band, and an occasional inability to pare down the central thought of his lyrics. However, this is an album that certainly deserves attention, if only for the superb *Piano Man* track.

Peter Reilly, in his review of "Piano Man," in Stereo Review *(copyright © 1974 by Ziff-Davis Publishing Company), Vol. 32, No. 6, June, 1974, p. 94.*

STEPHEN HOLDEN

Billy Joel's pop schmaltz occupies a stylistic no man's land where musical and lyric truisms borrowed from disparate sources are forced together. . . . [Joel's lyrics seem Harry] Chapin-influenced in their appeal to Middle American sentimentality. "**Piano Man**" and "**Captain Jack**," the centerpieces of [*Piano*

Man], compelled attention for their despairing portraits of urban fringe life, despite their underlying shallowness. By contrast, *Streetlife Serenade* is desiccated of ideas. The opening cut, "**Streetlife Serenader**," fails to develop a melody or lyrical theme. "**Los Angelenos**" presents a hackneyed picture postcard of L.A. as sexual wasteland. "**The Great Suburban Showdown**" seems even more dated than its apparent inspiration, *The Graduate*. In "**The Entertainer**," a spinoff from Chapin's "**WOLD**," Joel screams homilies about the callousness of the music business. . . . [He] has nothing to say as a writer at present.

> *Stephen Holden, in his review of "Streetlife Serenade," in* Rolling Stone *(by Straight Arrow Publishers, Inc. © 1974; all rights reserved; reprinted by permission), Issue 175, December 5, 1974, p. 77.*

FRED DeVAN

Billy Joel may be a new face and not exactly the most experienced performer around, but when he does something right, he does it very right. [The song] *Piano Man* . . . might well stand the test of time and vagaries of rockdom to become a true classic. The other cuts on the *Piano Man* album seem pale in comparison and may be the weakness of that album. Its strong lead is so strong it makes you expect too much of this one. . . . Billy Joel had a lot of middle-weight material vying with a blockbuster. The temptation to bypass much of his material may lead one past the quality that is there. (p. 74)

Streetlife Serenade sets out to overcome this difficulty; it succeeds. True, the blockbusters are there, but this time out they do not seem bigger than life. They are in proportion. . . . As the piano player has matured, so have his words and themes.

Billy Joel is able to write sensitively about almost ordinary things without becoming maudlin. He writes about love without resorting to Paul Williams style of omnipresent tragedy as he did on *Piano Man*. Joel writes about an entertainer (himself?) honestly and with a touch of bitterness. He, too, is feeling the crush of staying alive and healthy in today's music world, and his life is pretty much where most of this album comes from.

It may be unfair to compare him to Elton John, but much of what he does is what Elton would do if he stopped to reflect on himself during those few hours between record albums. Billy Joel pulls off this . . . album with far more maturity than I expected when I first saw it. *Weekend Song* is the only cut that I would exchange for another. *The Entertainer* is the star of the album, but *Souvenir, Roberta, The Mexican Connection*, and *Streetlife Serenade* all are strong contenders for top billing. The textures of this record change and flow from song to song, and serve to make it complete. A good album—well done and interesting. (pp. 74-5)

> *Fred DeVan, in his review of "Streetlife Serenade," in* Audio *(© 1975, CBS Publications, The Consumer Publishing Division of CBS Inc.), Vol. 59, February, 1975, pp. 74-5.*

PETER REILLY

It was obvious from last year's "**Piano Man**" that Billy Joel was very good, but . . . "**Streetlife Serenade**" runs well beyond the high expectations set up by the first, achieving what I shall have to call a dark brilliance. In it he casts an eye as cold as that of novelist Nathanael West (try *Miss Lonelyhearts*)

on the contemporary scene in a series of wry, occasionally savage, and often funny songs that nevertheless betray a certain compassion and even fondness for their targets.

It has been apparent for some time that what we need right now is a gifted eccentric to set us straight, someone who can cancel out with a fine, ripe raspberry the dull thud of yet another commercial sausage dropping off the end of the pop assembly line and the shrieks of robotic exhibitionists who are as uniform in their outrageousness as anything Karel Čapek ever dreamed up.

Joel has all the sound, basic credentials that an eccentric (perhaps more than anyone else) needs if he expects to get a hearing. . . . But first of all, most of all, there are the songs, each of them ringing with real, if slightly lopsided, truth.

Further description would be as pointless as trying to describe W. C. Fields' walk, Barbra Streisand's giggle, or Paul Lynde's simper. You'll simply have to listen to Billy Joel's new album to hear what I mean. Once you do, your head ought to be changed around *quite* a bit. (pp. 84-5)

> *Peter Reilly, "'Streetlife Serenade': The Cold Eye and Warm Heart of Billy Joel," in* Stereo Review *(copyright © 1975 by Ziff-Davis Publishing Company), Vol. 34, No. 2, February, 1975, pp. 84-5.*

COLIN IRWIN

Ooh, the agony . . . the heartache . . . the self-sacrifice is killing. Yep, here we have another young man pouring his soul out while his heart bleeds. Singer-songwriters as a breed seem exceptionally prone to over-acting and self-pity, placing their own heads on the guillotine. Having made a fair impact with "**Piano Man**," Joel offers his head to the block, withdrawing it with some creditable moments during the course of ["**Streetlife Serenade**"], but basically creating the impression of a verbose uncle boring everyone with stories of his own problems and experiences. . . . His singing lifts a record that too often drifts into a dirge-like moroseness. Seems he's struggled for many years and wants to get revenge on us all by telling us about it, while the dourness of the arrangements don't help at all. There are really just two outstanding songs, "**Streetlife Serenader**" and "**The Entertainer**." . . . Both concern the wandering musicians and their struggles . . . and have strong enough structures to make them stand when the rest of the record crumbles. Elsewhere there is little of the compelling ingredients which made "**Piano Man**" such a fine record.

> *Colin Irwin, in his review of "Streetlife Serenade," in* Melody Maker *(© IPC Business Press Ltd.), September 20, 1975, p. 42.*

ROBERT COWAN

Last year Billy Joel was some kind of American Elton John; this year he's a piano-playing Bruce Springsteen, returning from the West Coast to New York, presumably—judging from two of the better tracks [on "**Turnstiles**,"] "**Say Goodbye To Hollywood**" and "**New York State Of Mind**"—to re-mine his roots. . . . [The switch] certainly puts a mite more muscle behind his music. The songs have more bite, yet they invite instant comparison with Springsteen, and, alongside the works of the Asbury Park Kid, Joel's seem sadly dull, the vibrant urgency of the former becoming mere freneticism. The basic fault is in the lyrics: both the writing and the singing of them.

Joel's constructions are often needlessly clumsy; good ideas are stripped of their cutting edge and made worse by an often flat singing style that tends to shake off any initial interest in what the man is trying to say. . . . The one track that really does stand out is **"New York State Of Mind,"** a moody, slow blues with liberal quotes from "Nobody Knows You When You're Down And Out." Much more than the surrogate-Springsteen numbers, it conjures up all those archetypal images of New York: dirty streets, grey river, Broadway lights, bars, etc. . . . Superb. Perhaps with a little more thought the rest of the album could have matched it. The potential is certainly there.

> Robert Cowan, "School of Art: 'Turnstiles'," in
> Melody Maker (© IPC Business Press Ltd.), August
> 21, 1976, p. 18.

PAM BROWN

More like a preacher than an entertainer, [Joel] continues to sing real-life soap opera ballads that rarely show any signs of imagination. . . . I'm tired of hearing stories about the pains of the lonely and the strife endured by angry young men, and about how rough it is to be a musician and have to play the piano in bars where horny divorcees come to diddle with their gin and tonics. . . .

He does have a natural talent for writing good, poetic lyrics but he never puts enough guts into them, mostly because he's so pessimistic and spends a lot of time feeling sorry and apologizing for himself. . . .

"I've Loved These Days" is the most boringly regretful cut on [*Turnstiles*]. . . .

Turnstiles does have a bit of musical variety. . . . ["**All You Wanna Do Is Dance"**] is a great rocker but the lyrics contradict that because they're actually about his disdain for rock music. . . .

He's trying to be some sort of rock star and at the same time he's saying it's all over, he's grown up, that's not where it's at anymore. . . .

"Miami 2017" is one fantasy tale on the album, and it's pretentious, futuristic shit about the fall and sinking of Manhattan. He should worry more about the sinking of his own artistic and commercial potentials.

> Pam Brown, in her review of "Turnstiles," in Creem
> (© copyright 1976 by Creem Magazine, Inc.), Vol.
> 8, No. 4, September, 1976, p. 60.

PETER REILLY

"Turnstiles" is an intelligent, perceptive airing of young middle-class values and attitudes in 1976, though there's not nearly as much sentiment or drama here as in Billy Joel's earlier work. The pervading mood is one of exhausted malaise. *All You Wanna Do Is Dance* is a deftly aimed shot at the Beatles generation, baffled and resentful at the party's end; *James* is the male equivalent of the girls Janis Ian was talking about in *At Seventeen* (play by Their Rules and you still end up loser); *I've Loved These Days* is a sour paean to Life at the Top; and *Miami 2017* is a description of a future time when New York has long since been dismantled completely, we are all living in Florida, and "the Mafia took over Mexico." . . . *Angry Young Man* is the toughest, best, most mordant piece here. The lyrics have

a bitter wisdom that contrasts sharply with so much of the complaint, no matter how trenchant, that has gone on before. . . .

Joel's tunes are just that, tunes, but they serve him well enough as a setting for his ideas. **"Turnstiles"** is a mildly depressing but, I think, valid glimpse into under-thirty thinking today. Unfortunately, it's probably too tough-minded for the audience that it's aimed at, yet not shrill enough to entice the older I-told-you-so contingent who, no matter what their age, remain as anti-youth as ever. And there is, too, something rather Dylanesque about it all—not an imitation, of course, but more of an updating, different strokes for different folks, different rhymes for different times. Billy Joel therefore still bears close watching.

> Peter Reilly, "Billy Joel: Too Tough-Minded?" in
> Stereo Review (copyright © 1976 by Ziff-Davis Pub-
> lishing Company), Vol. 37, No. 4, October, 1976,
> p. 91.

RAY COLEMAN

This man is a venomous poet. . . .

[With **"The Stranger,"** Billy Joel] is now turning out albums showing an originality, bite, determination and poetic strength rarely matched by his contemporaries. . . .

We have no smiling romantic here, instead a razor-sharp commentator on many aspects of society. In **"Scenes From An Italian Restaurant,"** the separation of husband and wife, and the inevitability of divorce, is observed with a fine eye for detail. On **"Movin' Out (Anthony's Song)"** Joel tells of the desperation that afflicts every teenager who thinks there's no future in working hard to achieve the suburban material values of his elders.

"Everybody Has A Dream" is a near-perfect fantasy song, as the title implies. It's the attitude, the inquiring mind, of Billy Joel that clinches his strength. There's a touch of arrogance in his lyrics as he assumes his opinions about worldly situations to be beyond reproach, but he's never less than interesting, and usually fearlessly abrasive. A singer-songwriter of exceptional talent.

> Ray Coleman, in his review of "The Stranger," in
> Melody Maker (© IPC Business Press Ltd.), No-
> vember 26, 1977, p. 23.

SUSAN ELLIOTT

It's time to find a new tag for Billy Joel. His first and biggest hit of three years ago, *Piano Man,* has left him with a reputation as the small, power-packed, yet sensitive rocker behind the great big concert grand. Lyrically, the album of the same name and its two successors contained a few potent references to life in the suburbs (e.g. *Captain Jack*). That seemed pretty unusual for a commercial recording artist these days. Thus was born tag No. 2, "suburban."

It should all change with **"The Stranger."** While the album is by no means a radical departure, Joel's continued stylistic expansion comes to a new peak here. . . . *Scenes from an Italian Restaurant*—the whatever-happened-to tale of Brenda and Eddie, the queen and king of the prom—is the only song that can even remotely be called suburban.

So what's the new tag? Alas, there isn't one. **"The Stranger"** defies easy classification. . . . The onomatopoeic lyric of *Movin' Out (Anthony's Song)* enables him to acidly spit out the lower East Side workingman's gripe while a teasing, driving six-teenth-note ostinato effectively sets off the monotony and frustration of it all.

There are good times here too. . . . ["The Stranger" is] one of Joel's most thoroughly realized efforts to date. (pp. 135-36)

Susan Elliott, in her review of "The Stranger," in High Fidelity (copyright © by ABC Leisure Magazine, Inc.; all rights reserved; excerpted by permission), Vol. 27, No. 12, December, 1977, pp. 135-36.

PETER REILLY

The title of Billy Joel's newest release, **"The Stranger,"** may echo the Albert Camus novel, but once into it you soon discover that it is much more like a *Remembrance of Things Pasta*, an Italian-American nostalgia trip. True, it has a directness that Proust would probably have found appalling, but it gives the listener a unique opportunity to get into the head and feelings of a now grown-up ex-greaser through a group of songs that are at once a love letter and a farewell to youth, by turns touching, mordant, funny, gross (new sense), melodramatic, and naïve. . . .

"The Stranger" works because Joel knows his territory first-hand. Beginning with *Movin' Out (Anthony's Song)*, you know that the testimony you are about to hear is the truth, the whole truth, and nothing but. . . .

Another closely observed vignette is *Only the Good Die Young*, in which the tensions of sexual urge and sexual guilt are beautifully sketched. A young Casanova half cajoles, half pleads with a girl to let him ease her off her virgin pedestal with a technique as timeworn as it is dishonorable, pretended hurt feelings, pious illogic, and all. What really gets him is that her mother has warned her about him. . . . It is such accurate little touches that make Joel's work a delight.

Scenes from an Italian Restaurant is a lot moodier but no less candid. It is an eight-minute monologue about running into a buddy from the old neighborhood and catching up on what's happened to everybody—mostly to Brenda and Eddie who were, to the narrator, the Scott and the Zelda, the golden kids of the hang-out set. . . . Much of the impact of the song comes from the tone of resigned acceptance (that's the way things turn out) in which he sings it, the kind of sarcastic wisdom with which a man looks at the boy he was.

There are a couple of things here that don't work in the way they were probably intended, but they still carry weight because of Joel's performing intensity. The most ambitious is the title song, a thoroughly respectable failure that attempts the almost impossible—describing the stranger within us who knows all our secrets, shares all our lies, and tries to hide us from ourselves and from other people. It is a rather too abstractly presented attempt to ape the log-cabin philosophizing of a Harry Chapin or an Elliot Murphy. Joel's best work is too real and too wise for him to bother with such solemn chit-chat.

A world apart from this kind of introspection is the melodramatic *She's Always a Woman*, about one of those five-and-dime Loreleis who can do an honest man in with the flick of a beaded eyelash. It gets fairly silly before it cranks down to its mas-

ochistic end, but then even greasers must have *some* myths to live by. . . .

"The Stranger" isn't a particularly showy or innovative album, but it is bone-honest, filled with a very privileged kind of insight, and as gritty as life.

The next time a young greaser sideswipes your car, gives you the finger, and roars off into the sunset, remember that he is probably one of those Anthonys cursed with the strong premonition that his personal sunset will begin promptly at the end of his teens. Billy Joel seems to be about the only artist who is pointing out what this sad little sociological footnote means in human terms, and that, I think, is important.

Peter Reilly, "Billy Joel: Looking Back," in Stereo Review (copyright © 1978 by Ziff-Davis Publishing Company), Vol. 40, No. 1, January, 1978, p. 114.

DON SHEWEY

Joel has always been an easy target for his arrogance, pretentiousness, hypocrisy, and on *52nd Street* he's still showing them off. He talks tough to get the Warren Zevon fans (**"Big Shot"**) and acts out his laughable misogyny (**"Stiletto"**), but he also wants to sweet-talk the teen-screamers (**"Honesty"**). And here he pretends to be this street-hip cat in with all the jazz players—"I've got a tab at Zanzibar," he boasts—but the all-important love interest intrudes—seems he's interested in the waitress. . . . No, you can't dig in too deeply. Whatever illusion there is of truth, beauty or significance, underneath it's only product.

But good, sometimes great product. There's nothing on *52nd Street* as silly as **"Angry Young Man"** or boring as **"Scenes from an Italian Restaurant"** or hokey as **"She's Always a Woman"** (but never a gerbil to me?). . . . [On] the whole, the friction from Joel's pretensions clashing with his accomplishments makes for more excitement than the smooth surfaces of the likes of Stephen Bishop. It also produces **"Until the Night."** . . . Like a cross between the Righteous Brothers' "You've Lost That Lovin' Feeling" and Springsteen's "Incident on 57th Street," it is a majestic confrontation between heart-rending passion and inevitable tragedy, 6:39 of thrilling emotional turbulence!

That something as powerfully moving as **"Until the Night"** can come from an artist as essentially shallow as Billy Joel doesn't conflict with the notion that such heavy-duty pop stars are mere imposters fashioning trinkets to sell. In fact, it explains why we keep buying.

Don Shewey, "Billy & Bish: Love or Money?" in Feature (copyright © 1979 Feature Publishing Co., Inc.; all rights reserved; reprinted by permission), No. 92, January, 1979, p. 63.*

SUSAN ELLIOTT

[How] does **"52nd Street"** sound? In a word, seasoned. There are a number of factors at play on this album, all of which seem to stem from Joel's own sense of artistic confidence. With that has come a new freedom of musical exploration, which, combined with the unshakable craft of producer Phil Ramone, has yielded a creative richness of the most thoroughly realized kind. . . .

The material on **"52nd Street"** is a typical Joel potpourri, with this singer/songwriter emerging once again as one of the few whose output can be covered by any number of stylistically diverse artists. There are three ballads—*Honesty, Until the Night,* and *Rosalinda's Eyes*—and each seems to come from a different musical place. . . . Initially, his claim that he writes his melodies first seems to follow. But the lyric fits so beautifully and makes so much sense that it seems an impossible afterthought. Like *She's Always a Woman* and *Just the Way You Are, Honesty* reveals a capacity for rare insight and perception, not to mention for outright sincerity of delivery. . . .

[Typical] is the album's opener, *Big Shot,* whose lyric combines elements of mafioso humor with references to contemporary New York City chic. (p. 122)

My Life, similar in subject matter to *Movin' Out* (from **"The Stranger"**), has one of the catchiest instrumental hooks you'll ever hear. Though the message is basically "leave me alone," this time it appears to come more from strength than bitterness. . . .

Ramone remarked that Joel was "on a high roll" when they recorded **"The Stranger"** together, but to these ears **"52nd Street"** sounds even better. That must put him somewhere in the vicinity of the ionosphere. (p. 123)

> Susan Elliott, "Billy Joel, Rock Star," in High Fidelity *(copyright © by ABC Leisure Magazine, Inc.; all rights reserved; excerpted by permission), Vol. 29, No. 1, January, 1979, pp. 122-23.*

PETER REILLY

Blue-collar, lower-middle-class sociology found its seminal literary expression in Hubert Selby's *Last Exit to Brooklyn* almost two decades ago. The book's influence on a whole generation of creative talent is probably most clearly demonstrated in the work of three current superstars of the entertainment media: Martin Scorsese in films (*Mean Streets, Taxi Driver,* and *New York, New York*), Richard Price in fiction (*The Wanderers* and *Bloodbrothers*), and Billy Joel in pop music (**"The Stranger"** and his latest . . . album, **"52nd Street"**).

Selby's book is a brutal, jarring, nightmarish cityscape littered with the contemporary equivalents of figures from an Hieronymous Bosch painting—the monstrous, the diabolical, and the grotesque. Scorsese's films have concentrated, as have Price's books, on the sickness-of-it-all, laying it out in all its fetid, phosphorent glory for the fascination/revulsion of the beholder. Billy Joel, on the other hand, is paradoxically able to find in this same social framework a heartening amount of humanity, lots of hope (remember *Anthony's Song* from **"The Stranger"**?), and a kinetic, high-spirited humor about people and the situations they find themselves in.

His new **"52nd Street"** is about being grown-up and making your first few attempts at adult responsibility, just as **"The Stranger"** was about the trauma of leaving home. There is no internal evidence to explain why he has chosen 52nd Street as a symbol. . . . The title song itself may be a good enough, if rather arbitrary, reason: it's short on meaning and inventiveness for a Joel effort, but it *is* fun to listen to. So's the rest of the album, the work of the same warm, sensitive, and ironically funny songwriting talent who first plugged into the big time with **"Piano Man."** . . .

Well, enough about the roots and on to the flowers. Let's take *Half a Mile Away* for starters. It's about a housebound romantic who, once the lights are out, creeps out and joins his friend Little Geo on the corner where they split a bottle of wine. . . . There is a certain amount of heartache, but there's also a lot of wry humor and sardonic wisdom in this saga of a guy who'd like to fit into a class stereotype. . . . Then there is *Zanzibar,* which seems to be a kind of parody of a typical Selby/Scorsese/Price scenario: the squalid, dingy Zanzibar Club where Anything Can Happen. . . .

My Life is again about a man who wants to escape from a cliché life. He takes off for California (which for Joel characters seems to have the same promise of mystery and excitement India did a hundred years ago for the English working classes) and discovers the joys of making it on his own. He's talking to his buddy from back east, telling him that L.A. may not be all he wanted, but it's more than he used to have. . . . Strong stuff, beautifully performed.

There is even stronger stuff in *Stiletto,* deep into blood-and-gore territory, and the rage-filled *Big Shot,* a man's abusive tirade against a woman who has hogged the spotlight on a gala evening. They are powerful songs, but they are also ugly and angry and abusive. Joel's greatest strength in comparison with his contemporaries is his ability to show people as they are without lapsing into the condescending kitsch of *All in the Family* or the spasmed frenzy of a Scorsese Grand Guignol. The thinking here seems to me to be coming from somewhere outside, something along the lines of "Hey, look, you wanna stay in fashion, right?" No, not really. Not if you have talent with the breadth and depth of Billy Joel's; with that you make your own fashion. Despite these two inauthentic lapses, **"52nd Street"** is another fine piece of work from a fine composer/performer, an album that belongs in any serious collection of the young pop masters.

> Peter Reilly, "Billy Joel: Strong Stuff," in Stereo Review *(copyright © 1979 by Ziff-Davis Publishing Company), Vol. 42, No. 1, January, 1979, p. 131.*

PETER GAMBACCINI

Cold Spring Harbor is of value chiefly because it presents the performing and composing genius of Billy Joel in its fledgling stages. . . . [There] are intermittent flashes of brilliance, musical foreshadowings of things to come, and hints of the influences that were to shape the man's grander accomplishments. (p. 17)

"She's Got A Way" is very unexceptional. It's a typical romantic tune, with rhymes that are extremely obvious from beginning to end. . . .

The fast-paced **"Everybody Loves You Now"** is quite a bit better and might even be worth resurrecting in the current Joel repertoire. It is far less of a paean than the first two tunes [on the album]; it is the first example we'd yet heard of the very telling Joel sardonicism. . . .

[The] lyric is smug and accusatory. . . .

The attitude is mature, and likewise there is an inkling of a maturing talent at work here. (p. 19)

[**"Falling Of The Rain"**] gets to be a very lyrically ambitious parable; the two characters come to stand for Billy and a girl he's pursuing. His efforts appear unsuccessful, and she goes away. "The falling of the rain" would seem to represent the natural passage of time, real life in essence. He can't seem to acknowledge it, and that's where he's beaten.

No one has talked much about Billy Joel as a symbolist, and maybe there is no reason to take such a discussion very far. There is symbolism in **"Falling Of The Rain,"** however. The fantastic imagery of the first verses is far more gripping than the real-life situation he later introduces. A potentially interesting tale becomes one about which we are likely to remark "Oh, is that all?" (pp. 19-20)

As he was to do frequently in his career with Columbia [Records], Billy ends his album on a quiet note with a song that suggests a need for temporary solitude, a sense of direction, and general rebirth. The soft **"Got To Begin Again"** is eerily prophetic. A fledgling talent has come to the end of his first album, a good experience and a nice introduction to the business, but one that was not about to make him a household word. (pp. 21-2)

"Piano Man" [the title cut of his second album] draws much of its inspiration from Billy's days as a Los Angeles lounge entertainer. . . . The cast of characters drawn in **"Piano Man"** includes many representative types whose real-life counterparts probably spent a lot of time slumped over Joel's keyboard in the L.A. bar. The piano man's locale seems to be a less than cheery one, and the pianist plays the role of psychiatrist to a larger extent than the proverbial bartender. (p. 26)

"Piano Man" shows early on that Joel has great strength as a teller of tales, that he vividly brings characters and situations to life. Microcosmic as the world of the **"Piano Man"** might be, the anguish and dissatisfaction in that piano bar are universal. In this song, Billy creates a kind of stationary *Ship of Fools*. . . .

[**"You're My Home"**] is the song which started Joel's reputation as a romantic, even though that is only one portion of his nature. . . .

The basis of the song is an endearing if old romantic cliché. Billy, the boy with wanderlust and perhaps even no fixed address, has at least one place he can call home, and that place is his woman. (p. 27)

With its very simple instrumentation and hardly new premise, **"You're My Home"** might just be sappy stuff if it weren't for some clever literary references . . . and clear indications that these are flesh-and-blood humans that do a lot more than just pine for each other and get misty-eyed. . . . This is an adult love story about real people; there's no ludicrous "oh come now" idealism. It's not an ivory tower relationship; it's street-people stuff.

The closing piece on side one, **"The Ballad of Billy The Kid,"** is absolutely terrific. . . .

In a superb lyric worthy of any old Ned Buntline dime-novel myth, Joel tells the step-by-step saga of the young and small fellow whose "daring life of crime made him a legend in his time." . . .

Joel the storyteller has a good sense of detail, making us appreciate Billy the Kid as a loner and a man who was capable of generating some weird form of respect. His inevitable downfall assumes some dimension of tragedy, and the hopeless misfit finally finds a home [in a Boot Hill grave]. . . . (p. 29)

Joel has a deft sense of timing and drama. And his fascination with the late William Bonney (Billy the Kid) becomes expli-

cable. Before the last notes of The Kid's saga can be heard, almost as soon as he is nestling into that Boot Hill grave, this becomes the ballad of Billy Joel. . . . (pp. 29-30)

The Bonney-Joel analogy comes suddenly and without warning but seems not at all out of place; it is very striking. . . .

"The Ballad of Billy The Kid" is a stunner; who could ask for anything more? Its sound is completely fresh, not a retread or derivative of too familiar material. Joel's saga is strong, evocative, and gripping. (p. 30)

"If I Only Had The Words" is very bland from a musical standpoint and all too obvious and mundane from a lyrical one. . . . [The lyrics] are hardly groundbreaking, and hardly worthy of a man who has shown himself to be a sharp wordsmith many times on this album. Detractors could point to this song to say that Billy Joel is nothing special. What they should do is just skip this song and advance to his better material. (pp. 31, 34)

The capper on the *Piano Man* album is **"Captain Jack."** . . .

Much of Joel's reputation for sardonicism and biting social commentary, often directed at suburban lifestyles, found its origins in **"Captain Jack."** It is unrelenting and pretty nasty. As he sings **"Captain Jack,"** disdain seems to be Billy Joel's major motivator. . . .

Billy, as he often does with his lyrics, quickly establishes the place, the time, the character, and the mood. . . .

It's boring suburbia, where the kid's only escape is to . . . voyeuristically view the freaks. What might be a dream for some—split-level life on the outer fringes of the metropolis—is, in **"Captain Jack,"** painted as the most dismal, bleak, and useless of existences. (p. 34)

It is never made [clear] exactly who or what Captain Jack is, but that's not important. Indeed, it is better that he/it remain undefined and therefore universally applicable. Captain Jack is whoever or whatever this twenty-one-year-old needs to get him to the state of consciousness that will at least temporarily blot out his miseries. Clearly, the possibility that it is a drug is very much there, but it needn't necessarily be that. As a salve to all sorts of youthful anxieties, Captain Jack is a seventies counterpart to Mr. Tambourine Man. . . .

Joel's distaste for suburban blandness is well publicized and quite justifiable for a songwriter who has experienced Levittown firsthand. As far as spitting on its subject is concerned, **"Captain Jack"** is right up there with Bob Dylan's "Ballad of a Thin Man" and John Lennon's "Working Class Hero." **"Captain Jack"** *is* electrifying. A direct frontal assault lyrically and an epic musically, it is intended to startle and it does. (p. 35)

Streetlife Serenade is quite clearly his weakest Columbia album. Still and all, it is *not* a bad album. . . . There are problems with [**"Streetlife Serenader"**]. Most of the lyrics are not grammatical sentences but a string of adjective-noun combinations. . . . Despite these gobs of information, we miss an overall picture—like, for instance, what is the real point of this song? We know that this streetlife serenader performs to his utmost and barely scratches out a living—that's in there somewhere—but the actual thesis here seems to be absent. (p. 41)

[**"The Great Suburban Showdown"**] is obviously an addition to Billy's portfolio as suburban chronicler, but the approach here is quite different from that of, say, **"Captain Jack."** That song was an out-and-out attack; no empathy was shared. On **"The Great Suburban Showdown,"** however, the protagonist is feeling the pain of re-encountering wretched blandness, and he is expressing it in such a wide-open manner as to invite plenty of "you ain't kidding, that's just how it is" responses. Here, Billy Joel gets a response from way down deep; that's certainly a measure of success. (p. 42)

"Roberta" is the kind of song one might let slip by without a close listen. But it is really remarkable. It is the only seventies popular song that comes to mind about a man's devotion to a particular prostitute, and certainly the only one that is offered up in such a hallowed framework. . . . Billy's dedication to Roberta is almost religious. Juxtaposed with so secular a subject, the sacred treatment is quite amusing. This isn't exactly subtlety, but **"Roberta"** shows that Billy Joel is capable of marvelous irony, something we hadn't previously seen a great deal of in his compositions. . . .

Joel's aggressive stance on **"The Entertainer"** is that of a man who in his profession can state, "I know just where I stand." The road from **"Piano Man"** to **"The Entertainer"** has been a rocky one, with plenty of lessons learned along the way.

This may be the strongest lyric on *Streetlife Serenade.* Considering how quickly the song moves along, and how many truisms he tries to pack into the verses, it is amazing how Billy has managed to fit his message so masterfully into a regular metric scheme. (p. 43)

A truer picture of the dark side of pop stardom probably hasn't been written, although in the years since there have been many such attempts. . . . Billy Joel is never vague; he always takes a definite point of view. Here, with **"The Entertainer,"** he has come up with the definitive song on the subject. (p. 46)

[On] side two, we begin to get indications that first-rate material for *Streetlife Serenade* was in short supply. . . .

"Souvenir" features a sadly reflective Billy at the piano, chronicling the tangible reminiscences of someone's past—the post cards, the programs, the photographs. Not a joyful theme here—the notion is that life "slowly fades away." (p. 47)

Billy has tackled a number of subjects on *Streetlife Serenade,* so why not try mortality, even if it doesn't seem to fit into the overall scheme (is there one?). **"Souvenir"** is a mere tidbit, inoffensive, a lyrical denouement to the album (although one instrumental track follows). Bidding us soft adieu is okay, but it would have been better if heftier material were etched in our memories. . . .

[While] *Streetlife Serenade* is nothing to get angry about, most of it is quite forgettable. (p. 48)

Turnstiles is such an enormous improvement over *Streetlife Serenade* that one would almost imagine Joel had emerged from some prolonged semi-comatose state. It is still primarily a songwriter's album; the emphasis is chiefly on words and basic melody, not the fully developed sound that would be heard on later albums.

That approach is fine, however, because the material Joel put together for *Turnstiles* is truly topnotch. Some of these songs are well on their way to becoming contemporary standards. . . .

Turnstiles in part chronicles Billy's exodus from California and his return to his native New York. His impressions of both

places, and the reasons for his move, provide the substance of many of the Joel compositions here. (p. 52)

["New York State Of Mind" is] a theme song for everyone who has any reason at all to love New York; so many specific glories of the place are itemized that there's a line in here for just about anyone. . . .

"New York State Of Mind" is understandably a celebration of coming home. It is also true Tin Pan Alley stuff; skillfully composed and fresh as it may be, it still has a totally timeless quality. It wouldn't be a surprise if one were to hear that **"New York State Of Mind"** were written in the thirties or forties, when virtually all American popular music (the mainstream stuff, not cowboy songs, gospel, or Dixieland) was being written on the island of Manhattan. (p. 54)

There have been plenty of love songs written to the biggest city in the U.S.A., but not too many recently. **"New York State Of Mind"** is definitely the best one to come out of the seventies; the fact that so many Gothamites have taken it to heart is not surprising. But its significance goes beyond such local considerations; it is a classic composition about coming home, about touching base with the things by which one can measure oneself. *That* has a meaning for folks in Paducah, Peoria, Provo, and Pawtucket as well. (p. 56)

Generally, *Turnstiles* is more sympathetic than earlier Joel albums, reflecting perhaps some feeling of inner peace. **"Angry Young Man"** is the one reminder here of exactly how acerbic Billy can be. Still, it is nowhere near as scathing as, say, **"Captain Jack."** There is something in Billy's approach that suggests this **"Angry Young Man"** should be pitied a little. . . .

[His] greatest joy seems to come from being known as what he is—an angry young man.

And how does Billy Joel feel about all this? We don't have to guess; he tells us straight out . . . :

> I believe I've passed the age of consciousness and
>   righteous rage,
> I found that just surviving was a noble fight.
> I once believed in causes too,
> I had my pointless point of view,
> And life went on no matter who was wrong or right.

Those sentiments are common seventies postradical fallout, but expressed far better than most folks have been able to verbalize them. The angry young man, who seems to be operating with blinders on, cannot perceive certain realities, certain changes in time and situation. Events have no impact on him; they do not change his mind. And although Billy Joel can half-heartedly salute the angry one's honor, courage, fairness, and truth, the upshot of it is that this fellow is exceedingly tedious and will "go to the grave as an angry old man." (p. 58)

"Angry Young Man" ends quite suddenly and segues into **"I've Loved These Days,"** to which its relationship is like day and night. **"I've Loved These Days"** is sedate, contemplative, and reflective, a looking back on the recent past. . . .

"I've Loved These Days" is about living high—and ultimately empty. The singer and his woman are Cole Porter or Noel Coward types updated for the seventies. They haven't a care in the world . . . , their life is silk, chandeliers, champagne, cocaine, and caviar, all described in jaded detail by Billy. Such good fortune may be temporary and short-lived . . . , and increasing sloth, sleep, and body weight do dictate a change, but Joel can fondly state without regret, "I've loved these days."

"I've Loved These Days" has an exquisite set of lyrics; the life detailed here seems to be a dreamlike state. It is probably a mixture of fact and fantasy. . . .

["**I've Loved These Days**"] possesses a unique kind of foggy beauty, merely a trace of sadness, and mainly a promise to begin again. It's a very accessible song.

The final track on *Turnstiles* is "**Miami 2017 (Seen The Lights Go Out On Broadway),**" which may be Billy Joel's only piece of recorded science-fiction. . . . [It] takes a few moments to glean exactly what he's telling us. The result is a colorful and vivid glimpse of life as it could be forty years or so down the line. (p. 59)

"**Miami 2017**" details the destruction of New York; however, it is a mystery yarn which leaves questions unanswered. For one, who are "They," the force that is orchestrating the devastation? And why are "They" doing it? . . .

The reasons behind all this remain cryptic, but that is the author's prerogative; he has still painted a fascinating scenario. . . .

"**Miami 2017**" wraps up *Turnstiles*. Eight songs might not seem like enough, but one of the reasons you're left wanting more is because none of them have been clinkers. From the munificent "**New York State Of Mind**" to the frivolous "**All You Wanna Do Is Dance**" to the reflective "**I've Loved These Days,**" Joel has tackled the widest scope of subjects and moods yet on any of his first three . . . albums. He was maturing artistically and personally. If his songwriting impressed a bit more than his musical execution—well, the difference is slight. The raw materials were there to be honed. . . . (p. 60)

There is no evidence of complacency on *52nd Street;* there is no playing it safe. Joel confronts his material with the same freshness and fervor that got him his stardom in the first place. It is not uncommon for a superstar, right after he gets to that lofty pinnacle, to more or less tread water or run in place for another album or two—to regurgitate the same stuff that has proved popular in the past. Such a cop-out doesn't suit Billy Joel; he has got new things to say and new ways to say them. (p. 91)

"**Big Shot**" is a song of unbridled anger. . . . Joel's disdain for the kind of life led by this big shot could not be more strongly expressed, unless he were to go a step too far and suggest she slash her wrists. He doesn't do that, but "**Big Shot**" is a powerful commentary about young folks who attain sudden money and notoriety. Joel is part of that class, but clearly he does not subscribe to all of its pasttimes. (p. 94)

"**Stiletto,**" which launches side two, is about a most deadly woman, a kind of Jackie the Ripper. Her cutting, described in gruesome detail by Billy, is purely metaphorical. No actual blood is shed, but her effect is probably just as devastating. . . .

The knife-wielding metaphor continues throughout the entire song. Here's a woman who does serious, deep damage—more spiritual and emotional than physical—but is such a skillful manipulator that she always comes back and has little trouble reestablishing things *status quo ante bellum.* . . .

"**Stiletto**" is a thoroughly realized undertaking; music and lyric work hand in hand to make Joel's theme as vivid as possible. Always interested in relationships, he is a frequent commen-

tator on their dark side. And "**Stiletto**" seems to suggest that the one who allows his partner to perform such acts of mental cruelty is as much to blame as the one who is cruel. (p. 96)

The epic of *52nd Street* is . . . "**Until The Night.**" For some tastes, this track alone is worth the price of the record. (p. 100)

This may be his finest recorded song; it is certainly the one that best demonstrates the high level and variety of his musical abilities. (p. 105)

> *Peter Gambaccini, in his* Billy Joel: A Personal File *(reprinted by permission of Perigee Books; copyright © 1980 by Quick Fox), Quick Fox, 1979, 128 p. [the excerpt from Billy Joel's lyrics used here was taken from "Angry Young Man" (© 1976, 1978 Blackwood Music Inc. (BMI), words and music by Billy Joel; reprinted by permission)].*

COLIN IRWIN

The aggression [on "**Glass Houses**"] is just too deliberately calculating; and aren't the scenarios—so vividly portrayed— just a little self-consciously conceived? When in doubt, Joel does seem overly intent on sending his verses into grubby bars and desperate crises of loneliness with interesting accessories like "brandy eyes" and "sweating bullets". . . .

I'm not sure I can *believe* Joel on "**Glass Houses**".

The album spends much of its time meditating on insecurity, and Joel is most effective when he freely parades his own frailties in this direction, via self-mockery. There's one glorious track, "**I Don't Want To Be Alone,**" in which he sketches a reprobate character repeatedly wronging his partner and constantly being wracked with self-recrimination as a result. Its strength is the undercurrent of humour (the absurd vision he creates of the hero) which is his most potent weapon, yet one that's often deferred in preference to the moody macho image, doing his wronging without the saving grace of being a clown too.

Another honourable exception is "**It's Still Rock 'n' Roll To Me**," in which he cheerfully chides the fickleness of fashion. . . . Elsewhere, though, there's an unhealthy abundance of self-seriousness—"**Sleeping With The Television On**" has a double-edged moral (again, the subject's insecurity) but while "**Close To The Borderline**" comes on like a raging rocker, it's jammed with an almost maudlin theme concerning the pressures of life (yawn).

A generous smattering of schmaltz doesn't help. "**C'était Toi**" smacks of "Michelle", right down to the outburst of French; and "**Through The Long Night**" is rescued only by a perverse vocal style that has him sounding like Wreckless Eric on tranquillisers. Bizarre tangents like this are amusing, but they don't alleviate the frustration of *knowing* what he's capable of and hearing him opt instead for the tried and predictable. . . .

Joel's philosophising is made accessible by the quality of the decoration, and his hook-lines are determined and deadly—it's fun picking out the ones that'll see you pleasantly through tomorrow's coffee-break and the ones that'll drive you to distraction. I suspect the latter will prevail.

> *Colin Irwin, "Schmaltz House," in* Melody Maker *(© IPC Business Press Ltd.), March 8, 1980, p. 24.*

DON SHEWEY

[The] model for *Glass Houses* is the Beatles (circa 1965, with stylistic updates), and it is probably the best Beatles album since *Abbey Road* and certainly the best Billy Joel album ever. . . . The songs on *Glass Houses* are so distinct and catchy individually, and they fall together so cohesively, that you just want to play the record over and over to learn the songs and then play it over and over to sing along.

Now, I don't feel that way about too many albums, especially Billy Joel albums. Joel is some people's pet peeve; they consider him a pushy poseur. That's never bothered me—if anything, it puts him in the company of most rock giants (Jagger and Dylan, to name two). My beef was always that his records weren't good enough. For every catchy pop song or ballad I liked (**"Until the Night," "Just the Way You Are," "Movin' Out"**), there was something whiny or obnoxious (**"The Stranger," "Stiletto," "Big Shot"**), so I couldn't bear to listen to an album all the way through. . . .

[What's] different about *Glass Houses* [is]—it's *fun*. Living out his rock-star fantasy frees Joel emotionally, vocally, musically. His idea of rock'n'roll is strictly back-to-basics, and the album gives him the chance to do his impressions of all the rock greats (from Presley to Springsteen) within the context of his own songs. Sure, it's derivative, but Joel steals his way through the history of rock'n'roll with the craft of a composer and the passion of a fan, compiling his own museum of hooks. . . . **"You May Be Right,"** which kicks off the album, combines "Chantilly Lace" with "I Feel Fine" and "19th Nervous Breakdown" in the Faces' best slapdash party-rock style; **"Sometimes a Fantasy"** . . . mates "Be Bop a Lula" with "I Think We're Alone Now"; **"Don't Ask Me Why"** is pure McCartney. Stuff like that. . . .

Glass Houses isn't perfect. There is an awful line in **"C'Etait Toi"** about "Here I am again in this smoky bar with my brandy eyes." And I suspect that **"Still Rock and Roll"** wants to make some grand statement championing timeless rock over musical fads, but it's pretty confused. At least Joel doesn't think you have to play dumb to rock'n'roll; the new songs are among his most mature and sympathetic. Whereas *52nd Street*'s **"Stiletto"** presented Joel's typical poor-me-victimized-by-women complaints, *Glass Houses*'s best song, **"Sleeping with the Television On,"** identifies with both parties; a singles-bar cruiser who mentally criticizes an aloof woman . . . eventually admits his own emotional hang-ups. . . . And there's nothing on the new album that's a deathless classic like **"Just the Way You Are";** I hope when Joel gets this Rock Star out of his system he'll revive his genuine talent for ballads. But this album deserves to be taken on its own terms. It's not aimed at the "Death or Glory" school of rock'n'roll; *Glass Houses* is strictly fun, fun, fun. I know, it's only Billy Joel, but I like it.

Don Shewey, "Billy Joel Knows How to Pose" (reprinted by permission of The Village Voice *and the author; copyright © News Group Publications, Inc., 1980), in* The Village Voice, *Vol. XXV, No. 15, April 14, 1980, p. 57.*

PAUL NELSON

[Unless] you consider [*Glass Houses*] one bland and endless bad joke—as I do—there aren't any real howlers. Just fake this and fake that. (p. 51)

What's most annoying about Joel is his holier-than-thou sneakiness, his insistence to have it both ways. In **"You May Be Right,"** the singer strikes one of the silliest tough-guy poses ever . . . , in general behaves like a perfect asshole, blames his girl for his actions when she points out that he's nuts, and then sums up everything with the logic of an egomaniac. . . .

I guess what Joel's trying to do here is picture himself as a lovable loony, a teddy bear with a zip gun, but this brand of madness is snug enough—and smug enough—to make someone like Art Garfunkel look like Iggy Pop. . . .

[It's] obvious that this Long Islander regards rock & roll as a braggart's game in which the blowzy, blustering good guy—i.e. himself—can lord it over everybody else and crow to his heart's content without taking any responsibility for his actions. Real kid stuff. The spoiled-brat special.

Billy Joel loves to play the bully. He's always laying down terms, drawing lines in the dirt that he dares you to cross. Especially if you're a woman: . . . [**"It's Still Rock and Roll to Me"** is] the L.P.'s two-pronged philosophical bummer. On one level, the song depicts a battle of the sexes; on another, it's about rock & roll. **"It's Still Rock and Roll to Me"** is structured as a give-and-take dialogue in which the woman talks back in a futile attempt to get the man to shape up. The singer resists, of course, and tries to paint his female friend as a flighty harpy. In Joel's eyes, his reluctance makes him a no-bullshit hero, yet this grandstand play for independence is just another way to put down what he can't be part of and to give himself a pat on the back while he's doing it.

If that sounds like a contortionist's trick, so does the whole album. *Glass Houses* was apparently intended to be loose, raucous and less "well made" than its slick predecessors, but it comes out sounding twisted and confused. In **"It's Still Rock and Roll to Me,"** Billy Joel's so screwed up that he sees himself championing good old rock & roll against what he considers the newfangled fads. . . .

Maybe Joel just ought to 'fess up, forget about being a rock & roller and settle down in the middle of the road. . . . [What] many of his defenders say is true; his material's catchy. But then, so's the flu. (p. 52)

Paul Nelson, "Billy Joel's Songs for Swingin' Lovers," in Rolling Stone *(by Straight Arrow Publishers, Inc. © 1980; all rights reserved; reprinted by permission), Issue 316, May 1, 1980, pp. 51-2.*

PETER REILLY

"Glass Houses" lives up to absolutely no preconceptions, expectations, generalities, or genres other than those Billy Joel himself has chosen to establish. There isn't one instance in which he's coasting, or repeating himself, or taking a second (easy) shot at a favorite subject or theme. This album is a continuation of the kind of work he began to show he was capable of with **"The Stranger"** and after that with . . . **"52nd Street."** . . . The ten songs here are uniquely Joel: sharp, immediate, often harshly funny vignettes about the way things are *now* with his characters, about their genuine emotional impulses, not their coy philosophizing or maudlin poeticizing about them. . . .

Interestingly, a new, wryly charming facet of Joel's talent is beginning to move front and center here. *It's Still Rock and Roll to Me* is one example: it manages to be simultaneously satirical, endearing, and hilarious. . . . *Sleeping with the Television On* is another. It has the kind of droll but unregretted sadness of lived experience that one might expect more from a French *chansonnier* than from a kid from Long Island, but it works beautifully. . . .

But you mustn't take only my word for any of this; get **"Glass Houses"** and hear for yourself. I can't give guarantees, but I can give you odds that you'll be regularly amused, often touched, and continuously entertained by an album you'll be playing again and again. (p. 75)

[Billy Joel's] secure and able talent places him among the best American songwriter/performers now working. . . . **"Glass Houses"** proves that it is all there: the music is there, the ideas are there, and the ability to execute both superbly is there. Billy Joel has reached an exciting and singular moment in his career: the first big crest. But there are going to be more of those—just as there were for, shall we say, Irving Berlin? (p. 76)

> Peter Reilly, ''Billy Joel's 'Glass Houses': Beyond Category,'' in Stereo Review (copyright © 1980 by Ziff-Davis Publishing Company), Vol. 44, No. 6, June, 1980, pp. 75-6.

TIMOTHY WHITE

Joel's *Songs in the Attic* is a very careful edit of his scuffling days. These cuts are gimcracks from a catalog that didn't catch fire until the release of *The Stranger* in 1977, and Joel, very much aware that they show his development from intent greenhorn to creator of standards, plays them with self-absorbed vigor.

It's precisely this vigor, along with Joel's canny pugnaciousness, that lifts *Songs in the Attic* above the level of a pop-rock rummage sale. At his best, Billy Joel is an angry, defensive wiseacre of a songwriter, so angry about his own suburban *angst* that he storms with exquisite impatience from typewriter to piano, scarcely noticing the shift in keyboards as he skillfully sketches his all-American rage. . . . [He] grew up to simultaneously mock and admire the fierce follies of the middle-class dream, turning out car-radio singles that forged a neat link between Barry Manilow and Paul McCartney. This is especially true of his sweet but sturdy ballads, yet you have to be in the mood for the uptempo stuff, because it's sometimes spiced with a venom that smells like piss and tastes like vinegar.

While I'm not a fan of everything that Joel cranks out, I love his ballsiness. . . . **"Miami 2017 (Seen the Lights Go Out on Broadway)"** . . . is one chauvinistic New Yorker's reaction to the famous *Daily News* default-era headline, FORD TO NEW YORK—DROP DEAD, and the composer's elaborate fantasy-farce about the apocalyptic destruction of the city is as take-it-or-leave-it defiant as the front page that inspired it. (p. 67)

Songs in the Attic is a reprise of miniatures and night moves made by Joel on the way to tempering the best of the music he hears in his head. As such, these revised versions of his seminal works may not be especially significant (though the bitchy dynamism of the frenetic **"Everybody Loves You Now"** flirts with real inspiration), yet they're frequently a lot of fun. And, hell, it's commendable that this talented eccentric still has the nerve to be his own surly self. (p. 69)

> Timothy White, ''Billy Joel Retraces His Halting Early Steps'' (reprinted by permission of William Morris

Agency, as agents for the author), in Rolling Stone, Issue 356, November 12, 1981, pp. 67, 69.

STEPHEN HOLDEN

"Goodnight Saigon," the turning point of Billy Joel's ambitious new album [*The Nylon Curtain*], may well be remembered as the ultimate pop-music epitaph to the Vietnam War. (p. 71)

While **"Goodnight Saigon"** is *The Nylon Curtain*'s stunner, there are other songs in which Joel's blue-collar smarts, Broadway theatricality and rock attitude blend perfectly. **"Allentown,"** his portrait of a crumbling Pennsylvania mining city in which the American dream has died hard, could be a scene from *The Deer Hunter* put to music. Like **"Goodnight Saigon,"** its tune, language and singing are all brazenly direct. And that directness is presumably what the album title refers to. For in one way or another, the songs on this LP are concerned with the tearing away of protective emotional filters to reveal naked truths.

But for every starkly descriptive song like **"Goodnight Saigon,"** there's another that teases with ambiguous images and aural finery. While Billy Joel has long admitted to idolizing Paul McCartney, *The Nylon Curtain*'s mixture of brutal directness and tantalizing ambiguity suggests the late-Sixties John Lennon more than McCartney. . . .

Coming after the frolicsome but forgettable *Glass Houses, The Nylon Curtain* finds Billy Joel on higher artistic ground than ever before. Until this album, Joel's socially acute songs have been set mostly on his own home turf; **"Captain Jack," "Piano Man"** and **"Scenes from an Italian Restaurant"** defined the New York suburban milieu in bold, if occasionally awkward, strokes. On *The Nylon Curtain*, **"Goodnight Saigon"** and **"Allentown"** find Joel tackling subjects farther from home and larger than his own neighborhood, and they bring out the painterly side of him that has always identified with that master of American light, Edward Hopper.

Instead of inspiring Joel's scorn, the way suburbia has done, they've challenged his eye and stirred his compassion. (p. 72)

> Stephen Holden, ''Billy Joel's Brutally Frank, Aurally Ambitious Pop Masterpiece,'' in Rolling Stone (by Straight Arrow Publishers, Inc. © 1980; all rights reserved; reprinted by permission), Issue 380, October 14, 1982, pp. 71-2.

JOHN MILWARD

"The Nylon Curtain" is Billy Joel's ''Magical Mystery Tour.'' (p. 85)

Allentown is the album at its high point, with Joel's chunky piano rhythm complemented by assembly-line sound effects that conjure a cartoon factory where a whistle sticks fingers in its own mouth to call the troops to work. The scene, however, isn't comic, for this is a plant that is wilting, and a town that's dying while its young people ask, ''What happened?'' There's empathy in this tune—Joel might not have lost a factory gig, but he knows about chances washed away in America. The same can't be said for *Goodnight Saigon*. Though delicately beautiful, . . . it's an ambitious but misguided attempt to capture an alien experience. Collecting images from *Apocalypse Now* does not an authentic testimonial make.

Pressure puts these outward struggles in the realm of the personal, and the tough syncopation snaps all the right synapses. Joel's love songs are a mixed bag, as he spits out tired venom on *Laura* ([a] Lennon ringer) and welcomes her home with a familiar but rocking beat on *She's Right on Time.* The wooing winner, though, is the jaunty *A Room of Our Own,* which lists the reconcilable differences . . . of a couple of hapless homemakers.

Though the album closes with the schlocky *Where's the Orchestra?,* . . . the festivities really end with *Scandinavian Skies,* a psychedelic European travelog that substitutes a plane for a magic bus. Swaddled in echoes, Joel's voice drifts alongside the lyric, and it's precisely this meeting of studio craft and sturdy songs that gives **"The Nylon Curtain"** its winning pop texture. (p. 86)

John Milward, in his review of "The Nylon Curtain," in High Fidelity (copyright © by ABC Leisure Magazine, Inc.; all rights reserved; excerpted by permission), Vol. 32, No. 12, December, 1982, pp. 85-6.

STEVEN SIMELS

Billy Joel's late-Seventies records have revealed a songwriter with a fair amount of wit, a tough, unsentimental view of generational and class concerns. . . . [It] should be obvious that, compared with his commercial competition—the Styxs, REO Speedwagons, and Journeys that glut our airwaves and pretty much define mainstream above-ground rock—the guy comes off as a genius. Or at least an honest, respectable craftsman.

That said, Joel's new . . . album, **"The Nylon Curtain,"** feels like something of a throwback to his earlier, dismissable work. (The songs that made his initial reputation—*Piano Man* and the like—seem overheated and faintly embarrassing now.) The admirable Long Island bar-band rocker who had emerged in his recent work is strangely muted here, as is the social diarist, and in their place at times seems to be just another cabaret artist. The songs, when they're not weighted down with shameless and inexplicable references to the Beatles' "Sgt. Pepper,"

are vague and far too personal. They're not annoyingly confessional in the usual manner of the nakedly emotional singer/songwriter; they're simply cryptic. Instead of sketching specific incidents and letting them stand as metaphors for experiences we've all had, they pile on so many specific, seemingly unconnected details that they become unintentionally surreal. *Scandanavian Skies,* for example, is basically just another band-on-the-road song, but Joel has tricked it up to the point where I defy anybody who wasn't along for the ride to know what the hell he's talking about.

Other songs that might have worked are scuttled by their length. *Laura,* a potentially interesting portrait of a desperately unhappy girl of a type we have probably all known, goes on longer than *War and Peace* (well, perhaps it just seems to). And some are simply overambitious. *Goodnight Saigon,* for example, tries for a large-scale statement about the horror of the Vietnam War but collapses in a confused welter of irony and secondhand period scene-setting that suggests its author OD'd on home viewings of *Apocalypse Now.*

There are two marvelous exceptions, however. *Pressure* is a satisfyingly spiteful put-down song in the great tradition (an upwardly mobile *Like a Rolling Stone,* perhaps) in which the singer sneers at a young woman whose world view seems limited to college psychology courses and *Time* magazine. . . . Even better is *Allentown.* . . . Joel recounts a story as contemporary as the morning paper, a story of broken promises and fading dreams in America's industrial heartland. It rings utterly true, evoking a genuine mood of contemporary despair without once lapsing into mawkishness or cheapjack cynicism. It's a grand song—and the most overtly rock-and-roll cut on the record, which may not be coincidental.

While **"The Nylon Curtain"** is not a great album, or even a topflight Billy Joel album, it has to be accounted a partial success for these two songs. Their presence is all the more laudable in an era when the musical mainstream is deliberately bland and the "avant-garde" is recycling devices from fifty-year-old Dada manifestos.

Steven Simels, "Billy Joel," in Stereo Review (copyright © 1982 by Ziff-Davis Publishing Company), Vol. 47, No. 12, December, 1982, p. 82.

Diana Wynne Jones

1934-

English novelist and playwright.

Jones weaves contemporary themes into fantastic worlds, often creating a universe which seems familiar but also detached because of magical qualities. Like J.R.R. Tolkien, Jones is praised for her ability to make imagined worlds seem as real as the world outside one's own window.

Jones's protagonists are generally youngsters living in confused family or societal situations who discover and utilize magic to relieve tense conditions. The way in which a character responds to magic reflects that character's personality, and magic often becomes a means to self-discovery and maturity. Jones's medieval-like fantasy worlds, Dalemark and Caprona, are filled with enchanted animals, witches, legendary gods, or fairy people, as well as magical instruments or magic coats. Though her worlds are somewhat obscure, Jones always manages to say something relevant about contemporary life.

Although some critics feel that the use of magic in Jones's stories provides too easy an escape for her troubled protagonists, most critics agree that her works are entertaining and effectively project positive values. Critics praise her use of comic action which allows her to avoid the problems that plague other fantasy writers, such as excessive gimmickry, symbolizing, mythologizing, or moralizing. In 1977 Jones won the Guardian Award for *Charmed Life*.

(See also *Contemporary Authors*, Vols. 49-52; *Contemporary Authors New Revision Series*, Vol. 4; and *Something about the Author*, Vol. 9.)

Courtesy of Diana Wynne Jones

CATHY S. COYLE

Desperately in need of money, Frank and Jess form a neighborhood revenge service [in *Witch's Business*, published in Britain as *Wilkin's Tooth*]. However, instead of paying off their debts, they become involved with Biddy Iremonger, a bona fide witch who has a vendetta going for all of mankind. With help from the local bully and his gang, the children finally destroy the witch. . . . Although the English setting is interesting and the confrontations with the witch properly frightening, the "Puss and Boots" plan for her destruction is too obvious so there is little suspense as the trap develops. Moreover, the bully's references to a Black character as "nig" are offensive, and the substitution of colors or "blankety-blank" for the kids' frequent swearing is distracting.

> *Cathy S. Coyle, in her review of "Witch's Business," in* School Library Journal, *an appendix to* Library Journal *(reprinted from the April, 1974 issue of* School Library Journal, *published by R. R. Bowker Co./A Xerox Corporation; copyright © 1974), Vol. 20, No. 8, April, 1974, p. 58.*

MARGERY FISHER

The ogre downstairs will be wasted if it is not accorded the widest possible readership—not that young readers won't ap-preciate it but their elders should not miss it either. Like E. Nesbit, Diana Wynne Jones uses magical events as a way of revealing character; by the way people react to extraordinary happenings you see what they are like and how they change. Here are two families faced with the need to unite and fiercely resenting it. When Mrs. Brent married Jack Macintyre, her children—Caspar, Gwinny and Johnny—found his sons Douglas and Malcolm unutterably stiff and stuck up, while the Macintyre boys thought the Brents noisy and uncivilised. Something had to be done, but the dour martinet whom his stepchildren thought entirely worthy of the title of Ogre was as bewildered as their mother, who had been used to treating her children in a relaxed way. Magic saved the day—a layer of ingredients at the bottom of the two apparently harmless chemistry sets which the Ogre, as a gesture of good will, gave to Malcolm and Johnny. Labels like *Misc.pulv.*, *Petr.Philos.* and *Dens drac.* meant nothing to the children until experiments revealed their peculiar properties; and with each surprising chemical reaction the hostile offspring drew a little nearer to understanding one another. To carry off this idea without being either silly or didactic would have been beyond many writers but Diana Wynne Jones, with the brilliantly successful *Wilkin's Tooth* behind her, is quite equal to making us believe her new fantasy. (p. 2399)

Margery Fisher, "Enterprise," in her Growing Point, *Vol. 13, No. 1, May, 1974, pp. 2396-99.*

CHRISTOPHER DAVIS

["**Witch's Business**"] is typical of a kind of TV story style—two-dimensional, linear, endlessly this-happened-then-that-happened. Talk, events, background, acquire no reality. . . . There is a claim here for the actuality of evil, and I am not persuaded. However, the way in which a child's total world is conveyed is impressive: its obliviousness to adult ways and solutions. No authority but the child's own is ever recognized and adults are never appealed to, no matter how serious the trouble or great the need, as if such an appeal must be useless. When an adult does speak, it is as though a large empty building had uttered sensible sounds. The old "Our Gang" movies suggested the same sealed mini- or parallel world. Here it is frightening rather than comic, and that's good. (p. 22)

Christopher Davis, "There's the Devil to Pay," in The New York Times Book Review *(© 1974 by The New York Times Company; reprinted by permission), May 5, 1974, pp. 22, 24, 26.**

JOHN FULLER

[Folk-magic] is tricky to set up. In *The Ogre Downstairs* . . . Diana Wynne Jones goes to town on something far more practical: a magic chemistry set. Caspar, Johnny and Gwinny feel oppressed by their new stepbrothers and irritable stepfather: the magic experiments at once liberate them and bring them further into opposition (the stepbrothers have a magic set, too). This may not sound like anything very much, but the adventures are beautifully propelled and sustained by Mrs Wynne Jones's imagination, working much on the level of [H. G.] Wells's Magic Shop. Who could resist animated toffee bars that seek the warmth of a radiator and melt, eat sweaters and can't easily be drowned? The children fly, shrink and change colour, but none of this seems overdone: the physical consequences of each experiment are described in ingenious detail, and the last episode involving Dragon's Teeth warriors in the shape of crash-helmeted toughs who mushroom up from the ground talking joke-Greek ('Λετμι αττεμ') is a fine stroke. Having found the fantasy in her first book [*Wilkin's Tooth*] a little breathless and uncontrolled, I am happy to report that *The Ogre Downstairs* is an unqualified success. (p. 738)

John Fuller, "Schemers," in New Statesman *(© 1974 The Statesman & Nation Publishing Co. Ltd.), Vol. 87, No. 2253, May 24, 1974, pp. 738-39.**

MARGERY FISHER

By now we can trust Diana Wynne Jones to sustain daylight magic with aplomb, humour and total logic. Like *The Ogre downstairs,* her new story, *Eight days of Luke,* is based on the intrusion of mythological figures into a tense, confused family situation. David suffers from a plethora of unprepossessing and unfeeling relatives—a great-aunt and great-uncle, their son and daughter-in-law, who, after grudgingly offering him a home, ignore him as far as they can. At the beginning of the summer holidays, when arrangements are in a muddle and tempers decidedly frayed, David gets rid of his accumulated misery by reciting a resounding curse against his relations. He is on the compost heap at the time and the result is sudden and surprising—the wall falls down, fire flares up, snakes wriggle out

of the ground, and while he is bashing them with a spade a strange boy appears from nowhere to help him. Luke—not quite a friend, too unexpected to be an altogether effective ally—is in flight from strange, raven-supported enemies. In spite of his wayward behaviour he commands David's regard and respect, and they find unexpected help from Astrid, wife to smug Cousin Ronald, who at last allows herself to express her own distaste for the mean, bullying Allards. Astrid's name proves to be significant, for Luke and his pursuers (Mr. and Mrs. Fry, Mr. Chew and Mr. Wedding) have materialised out of Norse mythology, and the Hammer of Thor is the most important of many symbols that guide the reader through the convolutions of the plot. Wit and humour are employed to carry through a bold, intriguing invention, in which human frailties and idiosyncracies are unerringly related to the distantly reverberant sounds of myth-psychology. (p. 2601)

Margery Fisher, "A Tangential View of Everyday," in her Growing Point, *Vol. 13, No. 9, April, 1975, pp. 2597-2601.**

LESLEY CROOME

Diana Wynne Jones, who showed her talent for exploiting the tensions that exist between adults and children to create hilarious situations in *The Ogre Downstairs,* has now gone one step further and woven a mythological dimension into the plot of [*Eight Days of Luke*]. . . .

The book is shot through with the most delightful humour, the effect of which is both immediate and rewardingly cumulative. All the loose ends are tied up in the final chapter when it becomes clear that, in helping Luke, David has also been extricated from the toils of his relatives. Diana Wynne Jones clarifies the identity of Luke's pursuers and their link with Norse mythology on which the plot has been built, and in doing so defends herself against the charge of wilful obscurity which has been levelled at some writers of fantasy. While admiring the ingenuity of her puzzle, I admit to being more interested by the gloriously comic superstructure that has been erected upon it: an immensely enjoyable and dramatic story which should not be missed.

Lesley Croome, "Dangerous Wishes," in The Times Literary Supplement *(© Times Newspapers Ltd. (London) 1975; reproduced from* The Times Literary Supplement *by permission), No. 3813, April 4, 1975, p. 365.**

JILL PATON WALSH

The making of large imaginary worlds, whole kingdoms with their landscape, their peoples and their politics (usually medieval, these, with barons, and kings good and bad) is a recurrent form of story. *Cart and Cwidder* is just such a story. North and south are at loggerheads; vile tyranny crushes the south. Clennan, the travelling singer with his cart, journeys between the two. He and his children are just entertainers, busking in one town after another for their bread—or so the children think, but Clennan is not only what he seems.

A fantasy adventure, especially one that culminates in the gathering of armies, epic fashion, invites comparison with [J.R.R. Tolkien's] *The Hobbit;* but this is not another derivative book, for Diana Wynne Jones has a subject of her own to involve us in. Not the eternal war of good and evil, as in Tolkien, but the mysterious power of song is at the heart of her story. For one of the instruments in Clennan's cart is a huge old cwidder, that once belonged to one of the heroes of his songs, and if played with passion enough this instrument does strange things. The book tells us not only how Clennan's children escaped their enemies, and brought home the true heir to his kingdom, but also how Moril learnt about the power of the cwidder, and the use and abuse to which it could be put by such as he. This deeper strand, though handled with a light touch, gives subtlety and thoughtfulness to a story that is otherwise full of such sunny charm that only the villainous Tholian is hard to believe in.

> *Jill Paton Walsh, "Epic Ventures," in* The Times Literary Supplement *(© Times Newspapers Ltd. (London) 1975; reproduced from* The Times Literary Supplement *by permission), No. 3826, July 11, 1975, p. 764.*

ZENA SUTHERLAND

Adroitly blended realism and fantasy, [*The Ogre Downstairs*] . . . uses the results of magic potions to further compatibility. Caspar, Gwinny, and Johnny detest their new stepfather, the Ogre, and he is indeed detestable: an impatient, self-centered bully; they dislike almost as much his two sons, Douglas and Malcolm. . . . Sharing troubles and the wrath of the Ogre produces more understanding, and when an angry mother decamps, all unite in an effort to improve the family situation. The Ogre's conversion to comparative sweetness and light isn't quite convincing, but this weakness is outweighed by the strengths of the story: action, variety, humor, strong characterization, and sprightly, polished writing style.

> *Zena Sutherland, in her review of "The Ogre Downstairs," in* Bulletin of the Center for Children's Books *(reprinted by permission of The University of Chicago Press; © 1975 by The University of Chicago), Vol. 28, No. 11, July-August, 1975, p. 179.*

MARGERY FISHER

Classic adventure is seldom hampered by social morality. In a treasure hunt the seeker is, by prescriptive right, the hero: the holder—dragon or man—is in the wrong. Since [Robert Louis Stevenson's] *Treasure Island* this has been one of the strongest conventions of the adventure story. The ethics of aggression have been in the past accorded a similar ambiguity; a certain concept of honour, differing in its nature from country to country or from period to period, has been considered reason enough for one antagonist to be accounted hero and another, villain. Today political and social sensitiveness is making its mark on children's stories, not only in the kind of adventure . . . with a topical, contemporary setting, but also in fantasy and space adventure. The change is particularly interesting in regard to *Cart and Cwidder,* for here the old chivalric idea of honour and a modern liberal attitude are interwoven. The villains—as so often in adventure stories nowadays—are those who curtail freedom (everybody's bogy, in fact). They are the corrupt, totalitarian earls of the South, in an unnamed country, engaged in a protracted Cold War with the North, where people can be themselves. . . . This slow-moving, allusive, enigmatic tale has a chivalric atmosphere, conveyed in details of costume, in slightly archaic idiom, in the rustic settings and medieval-type settlements and in the moral attitudes of Clennen and of Moril; the modern concern for liberty has been given almost an Arthurian gloss. (pp. 2708-09)

> *Margery Fisher, "The Noble Ends of Adventure," in her* Growing Point, *Vol. 14, No. 4, October, 1975, pp. 2708-11.*

MARGERY FISHER

Dogsbody has as its point of departure dissension among the Heavenly Bodies, during which the Dog Star, falsely accused of murder and the loss of a Zoi [a symbol and agent of power], is condemned to be born on earth as a pup so that he may search for the sacred object, which has fallen as a meteorite. . . . [The pup, Sirius,] is rescued by Kathleen, a waif from Ireland taken in unwillingly by stony-hearted Mrs. Duffield who sees in this relative of her husband's a useful domestic slave. Child and dog endure blows and insults, and Sirius suffers a persecution from the heavens which he only understands after he has remembered, piece-meal, his own origin. Like all Diana Wynne Jones's fantasies, this is a confident, intricate interweaving of contemporary family tensions and alliances with flashes of extra-human activity, as stars and planets join in the search for the Zoi and make their several contributions to the final unravelling of plot and counter-plot. The parallel between Duffie's cruelty to Kathleen and the ruthless actions of Sirius's Companion is significant. The conflict is not a moral so much as a psychological one, and the fantasy, with its constant emphasis on light and darkness, is there to make a point about human behaviour. (pp. 2771-72)

> *Margery Fisher, "Darkness Against Light," in her* Growing Point, *Vol. 14, No. 6, December, 1975, pp. 2769-73.*

PENELOPE FARMER

Diana Wynne Jones has a remarkable ability to grasp the basic elements of myth or fairytale, twist them sharply, then fit them without undue strain into patterns of her own making. In *Power of Three,* her most ambitious book yet, she has marched onto that dangerous, old, but not very straight Celtic track along which so many others have strayed recently. Still, if she has not quite avoided all the pitfalls her version is highly distinctive, funny, exciting and with one marvellous twist. It is about the peoples who mythologically and historically have displaced each other within the British Isles. Her heroes—and so for this book, the norm—are three children of the Mound People (the little folk to us) who help to bring their own people together with their traditional enemies. . . . The surprise comes when we realize that what appears to have been an imaginary country is in fact our own; and that the Giants with their mysterious magics and even more mysterious habits are actually our human selves.

This book tackles large themes, from ecology to international and racial understanding, taking in the individual's struggle to understand and use his particular gifts on the way. Some of it is brilliant; but ultimately it is perhaps too neatly resolved to be wholly satisfactory or even believable. Still, if in her refusal to leave her audience enough uncertainties Mrs Wynne Jones is the victim of her own intelligence let us be grateful for it. In this kind of book such observation and such wit are rare.

> *Penelope Farmer, "Self-Examination," in* The Times Literary Supplement *(© Times Newspapers Ltd. (London) 1976; reproduced from* The Times Literary Supplement *by permission), No. 3864, April 2, 1976, p. 383.*

GRAHAM HAMMOND

Dogsbody is about Sirius, the hot-tempered star, framed and found guilty of the murder of a young luminary by striking him with a Zoi which is lost in the process. He is banished to the body of a creature in the sphere where the missing Zoi is thought to have fallen. Sirius will be reinstated if he retrieves the Zoi during the life span of the creature; if not, he will simply die when it dies. . . .

The idea is quite ingenious and gives Diana Wynne Jones scope for her invention, but some important things elude her, such as convincing human dialogue and moments of pathos. Confusing shifts of tone from serious to comic put the dramatic tension at risk, and the attempt to combine so many strands—stellar, canine, human, and the troubles in Ireland—over-taxes the author, even though in the end she neatly resolves the dichotomy of Sirius and Kathleen moving in their respective but interacting spheres.

> Graham Hammond, "Death Duties," in The Times Literary Supplement (© Times Newspapers Ltd. (London) 1976; reproduced from The Times Literary Supplement by permission), No. 3864, April 2, 1976, p. 383.*

JULIA BRIGGS

To the reviewer's jaded palate, stories set in invented other worlds, involving magical apprenticeships and witchcraft contests, are scarcely more welcome than yesterday's cold fillet of a fenny snake, so it is a pleasant surprise to come across a really enjoyable example, one that avoids portentous moralizing or mythologizing in favour of a rapid and remarkably sustained comic action. Diana Wynne Jones's *Charmed Life,* in spite of touches of Joan Aiken and, in the final chapters, C. S. Lewis, is an outstandingly inventive and entertaining novel, which never for a moment loses its characteristic pace and verve. Its setting is a world whose culture has evolved through magic rather than technology, where taxpayers subsidize research into spells and warlocks appeal to their MPs when deprived of their powers. There are some splendid set pieces of witchery, such as the havoc caused during a dull sermon when the sober figures in the stained glass windows run riot, and a stone crusader thumbs his nose at the vicar. The comic invention is at once prolific yet well-disciplined, and the presentation of a parallel scheme of things is much strengthened by the introduction of a heroine from our own world, who finds the Edwardian garters, petticoats and bootbuttons all too much for her. The plot combines real surprise with psychological and fictional consistency—you must wait till the very end for the opening mysteries to be explained. Altogether a delightful book. . . .

> Julia Briggs, "Spells of Power," in The Times Literary Supplement (© Times Newspapers Ltd. (London) 1977; reproduced from The Times Literary Supplement by permission), No. 3915, March 25, 1977, p. 348.

JULIA ECCLESHARE

[*Charmed Life* offers a light but] satisfying picture of a world where magic prevails. It is a brilliantly funny story which, with its seemingly Edwardian setting, is deceptively straightforward until the frightful Gwendolen's wild misuse of her magical powers reveals all the characters to be part of a formidable hierarchy, stretching from the dreaded Enchanters at the top of the scale to the mere witches and warlocks, who, for everyday purposes, are disguised as housekeepers, butlers or small-time charmers. With such a cast the magic and trickery are nonstop, but all is perfectly controlled, and while laughing at the everyday, small-scale, joke-shop display of supernatural powers, one is gradually drawn towards a more serious moral skirmish.

> Julia Eccleshare, "As If by Magic," in New Statesman (© 1977 The Statesman & Nation Publishing Co. Ltd.), Vol. 93, No. 2409, May 20, 1977, p. 686.*

KIRKUS REVIEWS

[*Power of Three* is a] fantasy about events on the Moor after brash Orban kills a Dorig for its golden collar. The delicate balance among the local races—Lyman, Dorig (mound- and water-dwelling fairies), and Giant—is upset when the collar brings a vague but powerful curse down upon all three peoples: the Moor, it seems, will soon be covered with water. Lyman and Dorig blame each other, and all-out war impends until three Lyman youngsters stumble into a friendship with Gerald and Brenda, two Giant children. Enlisting the help of a Dorig prince, the young folk envision a bright new day when their peoples will realize that "we're all the same underneath." . . . Jones paints lively portraits of her Moor folk and displays an amused humor toward their world, one in which Giants steal children because, as one character says wryly, "they seem to think they can bring them up better"; and the Lymen have an engaging medieval/middle-class approach to their magic. But—horrors!—this isn't MiddleEarth, it's the 1970s. Gerald and Brenda are human kids . . . and the Moor is being flooded to provide a reservoir for the people of London. The story never recovers from the shock.

> A review of "Power of Three," in Kirkus Reviews (copyright © 1977 The Kirkus Service, Inc.), Vol. XLV, No. 15, August 1, 1977, p. 790.

RALPH LAVENDER

[*Drowned Ammet*] takes place in the same land of Dalemark as the author's earlier *Cart and Cwidder,* where the southern earls are forever bickering while the north is united and the Holy Isles are in between. It cannot be said that this is a powerfully imagined country, like [C. S. Lewis's] Narnia or [J.R.R. Tolkien's] Mordor: it simply *is,* and is with utter consistency. The hero, Mitt, is a free soul who at the beginning has a mighty childhood vision of a place "just beyond somewhere", from which he learns that where he lives is not the same as home. . . . He enjoys a laughing childhood, but things turn grey when his father is lost through revolutionary activity. By the taste of it, the story is about late medieval; but even then, there were political revolutionaries, and so Mitt follows in his father's footsteps. He tries to blow up the earl with a bomb. Like many revolutionary acts, he bungles it. He escapes by sea, and there is a fine description of a storm; later he and his shipmates collect a castaway, and eventually they reach the Holy Isles.

About this point in the story, an extraordinary thing happens. It takes place so quietly, like a breath from [Joseph] Conrad, that you can almost miss it, and then you have to go back to the last plain-sailing point in the story to check up on what it is (which is, of course, how every reader goes about his business). And from here on, the soft light of vision steals back over the narrative, together with a new ritual form of language. Mitt has discovered his home, as well as most of the other important things about himself.

It is rare to find a book which relates to the theory of modern revolutionary politics through dealing with an imagined past, while at the same time keeping alive the great dream of Utopia—which all politicians and revolutionaries ought to have in their hearts.

Ralph Lavender, "Sea Scapes," in The Times Educational Supplement *(© Times Newspapers Ltd. (London) 1977; reproduced from* The Times Educational Supplement *by permission), No. 3258, November 18, 1977, p. 40.**

KIRKUS REVIEWS

Younger brother of a talented witch, Cat [the protagonist of **Charmed Life**] seems to be the only guy on the block—and, later, the only resident of the strange castle to which the two orphaned children are transported—who can't do magic. For a while after their move, Sister Gwendolen raises all sorts of supernatural hell in protest against her less-than-fawning treatment at the hands of Chrestomanci, the aristocratic lord of the castle. . . . [After] Gwendolen's disappearance, Cat learns that he is one of a very rare breed of nine-lived enchanters, that his special gifts have marked him as a future Chrestomanci, and that Gwendolen has been using *his* powers all along to perform *her* wicked tricks. Jones' talents are slighted in a synopsis, for she writes with exceptional finesse—whether establishing the atmosphere of the castle, orchestrating large confrontations, or filling in the domestic scene with vital incidentals. But the framing ideas are weak. The notion of alternate worlds with duplicate populations is commonplace, if functional, and not worth all her meticulous, anticlimactic unraveling. And the revelation that the enigmatic Chrestomanci is a "government employee," charged with keeping other witches in check so they don't muck up the world (this in a world where only the rich have cars), is both disappointingly tame and disturbingly paternalistic.

A review of "Charmed Life," in Kirkus Reviews *(copyright © 1978 The Kirkus Service, Inc.), Vol. XLVI, No. 4, February 15, 1978, p. 177.*

MARGERY FISHER

[In **"Drowned Ammet"** set in] the southern part of Dalemark (a country first described in **"Cart and Cwidder"**), a boy grows up with one idea in his mind, that his duty is to avenge his father's betrayal by fellow revolutionaries; he discovers when it is almost too late that his father was the villain all the time and that not all the members of the ruling family against whom the Holanders were plotting are tyrannical. . . . Turbulent, superstition-ruled Holand, somewhat between Nursery-land and Ruritania in atmosphere, has in this book, as in the earlier one, an extraordinary reality that comes from an alternation of precise domestic detail and deliberately enigmatic utterances. The author uncovers people's feelings in the anonymous, unmoral and beguiling way of folk-tale.

Margery Fisher, in her review of "Drowned Ammet," in her Growing Point, *Vol. 16, No. 8, March, 1978, p. 3279.*

EILEEN A. ARCHER

[**Power of Three**] is inventive, exciting and immensely pictorial. These words, used to praise, could however be the basis of a criticism of the book. It appears, on reading the book, that the author sees every scene as in a film, and she transfers the image on to the written page most vividly and successfully. The trouble arises when the action becomes peopled with too many characters, and in order to paint them in she has to litter the book with proper names, Gair, Ayna, Ceri, Garholt, Dorig, Otmounders, Adara, Gest etc, etc, sometimes as many as forty or fifty to a page, and so the narrative becomes stilted and disjointed as the words intrude on the wonderful story she weaves. Oh, for the film of the book, when the creatures of the marsh would rise in the mist, when the Giants would make their surprising entrance, and when the dwellers on the Moor could be seen with their beautifully worked golden collars and all the other fascinating inventions of Diana Wynne Jones.

Eileen A. Archer, in her review of "Power of Three," in Book Window *(© 1978 S.C.B.A. and contributors), Vol. 5, No. 2, Spring, 1978, p. 31.*

RUTH NICHOLS

The vocabulary of fantasy has become familiar to the contemporary reader who will find in [**Cart and Cwidder**] nothing new. North and South of an imaginary kingdom are at war; the names are vaguely Nordic, the setting vaguely medieval. (p. 69)

Ms. Jones's work is highly derivative. This is particularly unfortunate with regard to her style. One of the surest marks of second-rate fantasy is the presence of formal speech-patterns ineptly handled and apparently only half-understood by the author. Ms. Jones interrupts her "high" speech with frequent modern slang, apparently without any suspicion of incongruity.

This lack of linguistic sensitivity is paralleled by what I can only call a lack of emotional authenticity. Even the hangings and murders, of which the story has quite a few, have a passionless air about them: that is, their violence is taken disturbingly for granted and arouses no convincing depth either of sympathy or of revulsion in the characters. The moral problem of violence is thus in essence avoided: violence becomes merely a counter in the plot. The fantasy kingdom is too ill-realized to make us care about its affairs, although this need not be the case even in a small-scale fantasy: witness the marvellously realized landscapes and people in Peter Beagle's *The Last Unicorn*. Ms. Jones's characters have a mechanical, derivative quality. One cannot escape a suspicion that even the "magic" element of the ancient cwidder is included because magic is a stock ingredient in the fantasy formula. I have never read an author whose style and story were so empty of real magic.

A reviewer appears graceless when he finds nothing in a book to praise, but I must accept this unsavory responsibility. *Real* fantasy can nourish a child's imagination on so high a level, can awaken him to beauty, to grief, to moral passion. One searches in vain for these excellences here. **Cart and Cwidder** is a sort of fantasy paint-by-numbers set. (p. 70)

Ruth Nichols, in her review of "Cart and Cwidder," in The World of Children's Books *(© 1978 Jon C. Stott), Vol. III, No. 1, Spring, 1978, pp. 69-70.*

CHUCK SCHACHT

The setting [of *Drowned Ammet*], a different section of the same imagined group of late medieval earldoms as [*Cart and Cwidder*], is interesting, and the main characters—the strong, active girl, Hildy, and the Oliver-like, street-wise Mitt, who appealingly represents the deserving but downtrodden poor—are generally well portrayed. However, the story falls victim to its author's excesses. For example, Mitt's concern for social justice is admirable, but when, as a six- or seven-year-old, Jones gives him lines like "Can't the poor people get together and tell the rich ones where to get off?" it all starts to sound unlikely. And, in the last third of the book, when the old gods get almost hyperactive and demonstrate a truly impressive array of tricks (e.g., instant island raising) the plot goes beyond credulity. Although *Drowned Ammet* has it's appealing moments, Jones has not been able to shape them into a satisfying whole; both Ursula Le Guin's *Earthsea* trilogy . . . and Lloyd Alexander's Prydain series . . . are better crafted examples of historical fantasy.

Chuck Schacht, in his review of "Drowned Ammet," in School Library Journal *(reprinted from the April, 1978 issue of* School Library Journal, *published by R. R. Bowker Co./A Xerox Corporation; copyright © 1978), Vol. 24, No. 8, April, 1978, p. 85.*

PENELOPE FARMER

She is a clever and witty writer, Diana Wynne Jones—too clever in some of her books; you admire the means, ultimately not so much the ends. Not so, however, with her latest book *Drowned Ammet*, set like the earlier *Cart and Cwidder* in the mythical country of Dalemark. . . . Escaping plot and counter-plot, the three [protagonists] sail away to the Holy Islands, assisted during storms by the two gods whose worship is centred there, and who, in the undignified guise of poor Old Ammet and Libby Beer, are carried through Holland in effigy during the annual sea festival and thrown into the harbour.

The origins of this are anthropological rather than mythological perhaps, some familiar enough but all properly rooted in a living and integrated plot. The evoking of magical powers is strong, idiosyncratic and interesting. With water the prevailing image, I am reminded of Dannie Abse's dictum on poetry, that like a stream it should be clear right down to the depths, yet leave you in the end not quite able to touch bottom. For this is clear water all right; you can see what the author is doing, follow the progression and recognize the sources of her ideas. None the less you do find yourself floating sometimes; there is enough that is whispered and hinted at, that you can almost hear and see and yet not quite. Perhaps the mythical setting helps give to it its integrity—even if there is less scope for fireworks, it does mean that the author does not have to strain to connect sceptical age and impossible event. Nor is any humour sacrificed in the process. There is no whimsy in her invented land; this book is as sharp about people as her others, sharper in some respects.

Diana Wynne Jones has always been an exceptionally inventive writer, but the invention here seems particularly unforced. I especially like villainous, yet not quite villainous Al and his somewhat ambiguous demise; and also Mitt's longed-for country which he recognizes by smell as much as sight or sound—though the description of this is nearer poetry than invention.

Penelope Farmer, "Dalemark Festivities," in The Times Literary Supplement *(© Times Newspapers*

Ltd. (London) 1978; reproduced from The Times Literary Supplement *by permission), No. 3966, April 7, 1978, p. 377.*

DENNIS HAMLEY

Watching a novelist really getting it all together is one of the great pleasures of life. This is why I so hugely enjoyed Diana Wynne Jones's [*Drowned Ammet*]—itself surely ranking as one of the best examples of 'sub-creation' of recent years. . . . [Magic] is not used arbitrarily but to further the developing insights of the main characters. Humour and near-farce intermingle with vivid danger and action; relationships and responsibilities are portrayed squarely and unsentimentally. There are echoes towards the end of [John] Masefield and [Ursula K.] Le Guin—nevertheless, the whole brew is unique. It is a story which illustrates perfectly Jill Paton Walsh's image of 'the rainbow surface'—for here indeed is a brilliant outside with real pressure behind it.

Dennis Hamley, in his review of "Drowned Ammet," in The School Librarian, *Vol. 26, No. 2, June, 1978, p. 161.*

MARCUS CROUCH

Diana Wynne Jones has already written twice about the country of Dalemark. In this new, and remarkable, book [*The Spellcoats*] she explores some of its prehistory, the archaeological evidence for which consists of two woven coats into which a narrative had been worked. *The Spellcoats* is the story of that weaving and of the weaver.

Stories of imagined worlds are acceptable only so far as they present inhabitants with whom we can feel some bond of sympathy. Miss Wynne Jones captures our interest and concern from the first page. Here is a united and reasonably happy family, father and three boys, two girls, living in a small and mainly hostile community, the village of Shelling. This stands on the bank of [a] river, and the river dominates their lives and puts a bound to their experience. War comes to the country, and father and the eldest son go off to fight for the King. (pp. 221-22)

In the adventures which follow, supernatural forces and dark magic are skilfully balanced against the everyday quarrels, affections and fun of family life. These are seen through the eyes of Tanaqui, the weaver, a girl of character whose role is to be the intermediary between the living and the dead. She, for all her impatience and quick temper, has the gift of seeing both sides of the story, and through her the fortunes of natives and Heathen are united against a common enemy.

There are some spine-chilling moments and a fine climax, and a conclusion which is not too tidy, leaving the imagination many loose ends to work upon. In fact this is one of those books which goes on in the mind long after the last page has been scanned. If such are to your taste, you have to thank Miss Wynne Jones' philosophy as much as her knowledge of character and her skill in narrative. It is a big book, long and continuously demanding of attention and a degree of surrender. (p. 222)

Marcus Crouch, in his review of "The Spellcoats," in The Junior Bookshelf, *Vol. 43, No. 4, August, 1979, pp. 221-22.*

NEIL PHILIP

As the fantasy genre fastens its grip on children's writing its landscapes seem to be growing more shadowy and indistinct. The detailed, concrete worlds of Tolkien and le Guin, in which topography, social, economic, religious and political structure, language, flora and fauna slowly and painstakingly given the solidity of the pavement outside the reader's front door, have given way to a sort of generalized other country with pseudo-medieval village or tribal communities, stark ranges of mountains, enclosed valleys, decadent cities, sinister priesthoods and wars and rumours of wars.

Diana Wynne Jones' Dalemark, for instance, seems insubstantial, at the service of her stories rather than served by them. I found **The Spellcoats**, in which five supernaturally gifted children foil the attempt of the evil mage Kankredin to destroy the river, "the soul of the land", and thus come to power, somewhat flimsy. The central symbol of the river is a strong one, and is skilfully kept at the forefront of the book; but the characters are bland and uninteresting, their human qualities dwarfed by their magical ones.

Diana Wynne Jones's best work, **Charmed Life, Dogsbody** and **Eight Days of Luke,** has had a quirky humour which the short, flat sentences of **The Spellcoats** cannot convey, and a subtlety which here turns to cleverness. The magic confuses rather than clarifies.

> Neil Philip, "Stark Mountains, Haunted Valleys," *in* The Times Educational Supplement (© *Times Newspapers Ltd. (London) 1979; reproduced from* The Times Educational Supplement *by permission*), *No. 3312, November 30, 1979, p. 25.**

NEIL PHILIP

[**The Magicians of Caprona**] is a sprightly, pleasant, ingenious book, but it is neither as strong nor as multi-layered as **Charmed Life;** the author seems here, as in her other recent work, to be marking time. . . .

Neither the rivalry between the families nor the threat of defeat generate much tension. Only in the fifth chapter, when Tonino and Angelica, captives of an evil enchantress, are forced to act out a degrading Punch and Judy show for their captor's sadistic amusement, does the action rise to any pitch of excitement or suspense. Otherwise, it is light-hearted fun, played out against a rather ready-made, stagey background, written with flair but without penetration.

> Neil Philip, "To Combat the Forces of Evil," *in* The Times Educational Supplement (© *Times Newspapers Ltd. (London) 1980; reproduced from* The Times Educational Supplement *by permission*), *No. 3332, April 18, 1980, p. 25.**

MARY M. BURNS

Like Joan Aiken, [Diana Wynne Jones] has a remarkable talent for creating a time which never was yet which seems believably familiar. The fantasy [**The Magicians of Caprona**] is set in the imaginary duchy of Caprona, located in the vicinity of Siena, Pisa, and Florence. It has its own history and geography, fluctuating in consonance with the squabbling neighboring city-states. . . . The enchanter Chrestomanci, the enigmatic and fascinating personality developed in **Charmed Life** . . . , plays a less dominant role in the Capronian capers, yet his presence

serves as a necessary element in the resolution of the problems. A gorgeous concoction of humor, suspense, and romance, the narrative has the gusto and pace of a commedia dell'arte production. (pp. 407-08)

> Mary M. Burns, in her review of "The Magicians of Caprona," in The Horn Book Magazine (copyright © 1980 by The Horn Book, Inc., Boston), Vol. LVI, No. 4, August, 1980, pp. 407-08.

MARCUS CROUCH

What a brilliant and talented writer this is! [In **The Magicians of Caprona** Diana Wynne Jones] breaks all the usual rules of fantasy with impunity, secure in her own virtuosity.

We are in Italy. Caprona is a Renaissance City State, ruled by its Duke and threatened by enemies with familiar names like Siena and Florence. But how strange; while some people travel by coach others have motor cars. It appears that we are not in a conventional Italy after all but in one parallel to our world, in a world where magic is a respected and indeed indispensable trade. In Caprona magic is traditionally the business of two families, the Montana and the Petrocchi, and also by what seems to be a long tradition the Montana and the Petrocchi are enemies. As if spell-making was not hard enough you—if you are a Montana—have always to be worrying about what the Petrocchi may be up to.

Then life becomes even more complicated because a foreign enchanter seems to be at work, one who is bent on the destruction of Caprona. (p. 192)

I must say no more about the plot, because full enjoyment of its delights depends on a degree of surprise. Miss Wynne Jones tells a magnificent story for all it is worth, but she is far more than a master narrator. She has created a whole world, consistent in all its details, and peopled it with living and fascinating beings, clever and perverse, comic and eccentric. There are some wonderful moments, the best perhaps being a terrifying Punch and Judy show, although the State visit of the Montana and the Petrocchi to the Ducal palace runs it close, but these are not isolated inventions; they spring from the natural reactions of people and events and places.

Funny and frightening and profoundly exciting as this story is, it demands of the reader total surrender. It is not an easy book. Casual and lazy readers will give up early. For those who persist, children and adults alike, the rewards are very great. Miss Wynne Jones has set a standard for 1980 which will take some beating. (pp. 192-93)

> Marcus Crouch, in his review of "The Magicians of Caprona," in The Junior Bookshelf, Vol. 44, No. 4, August, 1980, pp. 192-93.

JUDITH ELKIN

The Homeward Bounders is a fantasy novel with elements of science fiction, in which Diana Wynne Jones develops the idea of war gaming by playing with live characters in an infinite number of different worlds. As in her previous novels, her apparently inexhaustible imagination takes in many moods and themes. The book contains terror, humour, adventure, everyday problems of survival and references to mythical characters.

The story begins in our own world in 1879 when thirteen-year-old Jamie stumbles unknowingly into forbidden territory and witnesses "Them" (faceless grey-cloaked figures) playing a mysterious game involving minute worlds, huge dice and complicated machines. This is the "Real Place" from which They control what goes on in different worlds, having previously absorbed the reality of those worlds. The details of this are only revealed later, but Jamie has already seen too much and must be "discarded" to the "Bounds" between the worlds. There are, of course, certain rules: he may not "enter play" in any world and every time a move ends in his field of play, he will be transferred remorselessly on to another field of play. He is allowed to return home—if he can find home—and only then can he re-enter play. He has become a "Homeward Bounder". The full horror of the implications of this, is only gradually revealed to the reader, as Jamie relates his experiences in a pleasantly chatty, intimate style which subtly emphasizes his terror, loneliness and his longing for home. . . .

[Jamie meets] numerous vividly drawn characters: Helen with the magical Hand of Uquar, Joris, the demon-hunter, the mythical Titan chained endlessly to his rock, Ahasuerus, the Wandering Jew and The Flying Dutchman.

It is a complex story with many different threads running through it. The early allusions to characters and situations in the latter part of the story may well be missed on a first reading. The recurrence of the anchor symbol, references to mythology and the emphasis on Hope, are important elements in the understanding of the story. "Hope is an anchor" Ahasuerus states prophetically: "If you cast hope aside . . . all evil is cast out with it". . . .

It is not an easy book to read and many of the ideas may be difficult for all but the most dedicated reader to grasp. But for that reader, the story is strangely compelling—rather like a monster jigsaw puzzle in which the reader can become totally and intensely absorbed.

Judith Elkin, "Walking the Bounds," in The Times Literary Supplement *(© Times Newspapers Ltd. (London) 1981; reproduced from* The Times Literary Supplement *by permission), No. 4069, March 27, 1981, p. 339.*

MARGERY FISHER

Good and evil are in opposition on a cosmic and a local scale at the same time in *The Homeward Bounders.* The extraordinary power of this narrative is the result of strong feeling combined with brilliant technique. The author does not lay down her theme or her plot bluntly but allows the shape and point of the story to come to the reader clue by clue, as events are suffered, and assessed, by the victims of 'Them' and most of all by young Jamie, central among the Homeward Bounders. The idea that 'They' are playing an enormous, multi-part war-game with whole worlds is chillingly real because of Jamie's words and actions, as he slowly realises the penalties of being a random piece on the board, gathering information from the people he meets—dark, enigmatic Helen and the acquiescent slave Joris among them—and using intellect and emotion in judging the enemy's weakness and deciding on his special duty for the future. At times Jamie seems, simply, the questing, questioning spirit of Man, and this is confirmed by his bitterly real dealings with the Promethean sufferer who encourages his independence of mind: at other times he is a boy driven by gigantic, inexplicable forces. This is not a book that could have an 'ending' as such, but it has a conclusion, and one that sums up the elusive hints and emotional tides of a book precise and

perceptive in details and immensely powerful as a whole. (p. 3882)

Margery Fisher, "Ventures in Magic," in her Growing Point, *Vol. 20, No. 1, May, 1981, pp. 3880-83.**

MARCUS CROUCH

The central theme [of *The Homeward Bounders*] is appallingly probable. What better explanation of the mess we are all in than to have it the result of the dispassionate manipulation of *Them.* [Edward Lear and Thomas Hardy] had their own words for it, and now Diana Wynne Jones enters the big league with a story of cosmic proportions. It is some measure of her success that she is believable, humane and humorous. What is more, she contrives a kind of happy ending, but denies happiness to her own hero. When *They* have been defeated, Jamie is left alone on his travels, as the anchor who holds all the worlds in place. It could be worse. He has friends in many worlds, but wandering is a lonely business.

As you may gather, there are difficulties in this book. Reading it is not to be undertaken lightly. It demands concentration and total suspension of disbelief. The rewards are a magnificent story, lots of good humour, shrewd characterisation, and a deeply disturbing theme presented with deep wisdom and rich understanding. Miss Wynne Jones' biggest book to date and probably her best, too. Fortunate those children, and adults, who can meet its challenge. (p. 213)

Marcus Crouch, in his review of "The Homeward Bounders," in The Junior Bookshelf, *Vol. 45, No. 5, October, 1981, pp. 212-13.*

ELAINE MOSS

Diana Wynne Jones is a prolific novelist of enormous range who can raise hairs on the back of the neck one minute, belly laughs the next. A certain untidyness and self-indulgent prolixty have characterized many of her novels to date, especially the group set in an imaginary medieval period. But she also writes about modern children, witty, abrasive, articulate, often neglected, always resilient: they need to be resilient if they are to cope with the emanations of the paranormal that threaten their lives.

Diana Wynne Jones's new novel, *The Time of the Ghost,* is one of her modern stories. The title is instantly forgettable one may think as one picks up this book but as, three hours later and in a state of bewildered admiration one lays it down again, realization dawns: the title pinpoints the theme exactly. Mrs. Wynne Jones is skilfully exploring time—and the ghost.

In the conventional literary ghost story it is the ghost of past happenings that rises, walks, haunts the present demanding retribution. Diana Wynne Jones defies this convention; for here it is from the present that a ghost returns to a period seven years past, desperate to avert a catastrophe in its own "now". . . .

Not since K. M. Briggs, that great folklorist and author of *Kate Crackernuts,* has the supernatural been so firmly and convincingly handled. But here the horror of dealing with evil spirits, the blood rites, the elemental disturbances lie cheek-by-jowl with a richly humorous story in which three schoolgirls, determined to catch the attention of their over-busy parents for once, send off the fourth sister to see whether "Himself" and Phyllis will notice Sally is missing. *The Time of the*

Ghost is a great feat of imaginative writing. It will be a thousand pities if, like the ghost of Sally, it fails to float over the artificial barriers of the adolescents' world to attract the attention of adults.

> Elaine Moss, "Ghostly Forms," in The Times Literary Supplement (© Times Newspapers Ltd. (London) 1981; reproduced from The Times Literary Supplement by permission), No. 4103, November 20, 1981, p. 1354.*

MARGERY FISHER

Atmosphere is all, in true ghost stories. Motive and situation may be infinitely plausible, characters carefully shown to be vulnerable, but the thrill, the conviction of ghostliness, depends on less detectable, less tangible elements, on appropriate combinations of words and rhythms and on such *selected* details of place and circumstance as will strike at the senses. Too little atmosphere and the story will fall flat: too much, and it will turn into farce. In *The Time of the Ghost* Diana Wynne Jones shows impeccable control of her material. In particular, she uses description scrupulously so that we get to know just as much of the school buildings and the surrounding country as we need, and no more. Emotion and atmosphere grow out of these settings. In the school house four sisters, ferociously individual and frustrated, decide to punish their parents, whose attention is turned from them to the boys in their care. They plan that thirteen-year-old Sally shall go away on a visit; then the older Charlotte, the younger Imogen and Fenella, will see how long it is before their parents notice she is absent. They do not realise that Sally has been experimenting in Black Magic with a precocious schoolboy and has invoked a spirit which, by a fateful semantic accident, has lodged in an old doll used by all the sisters in the past in vaguely sinister and shiversome games. The situation comes to the reader slowly, after an electrifying first chapter in which one of the four, a ghost, wanders the gardens and house trying to decide which sister she is. The doll-spirit Monigan exercises her power for seven years: at the end of it, the sisters and two staunch friends work out a way to defeat her. The turmoil of humans close in birth and rearing, passionately different in temperament, at once dictates and is dictated by the ghost-element in the story, whose complexities tease the mind and harry the heart while weird, flickering humour eases the tension. This unorthodox 'ghost story' has more real supernatural terror in it than hundreds of more usual hauntings. (p. 3992)

> Margery Fisher, "Ghostly Matters," in her Growing Point, Vol. 20, No. 5, January, 1982, pp. 3991-94.*

A. R. WILLIAMS

[Although *The Time of the Ghost*] is told by a ghost, the ghost is puzzled rather than tortured; at least, the ghost is tortured only to the extent that she does not quite know who she is. The four Melford sisters (one of whom she *might* be) have parents who are so preoccupied with the running of their private school that one of the sisters absents herself without being missed by anyone. It would be improper to reveal the rest of the plot but apart from the personalities of the girls the book's charm lies in its weirdly hilarious vignettes of the school and its boys, the family life of the girls, and often and just as entertainingly in the combination of both. A sinister thread does come to the surface occasionally but one never knows how seriously to regard it and perhaps the readers may feel

cheated at the end, but not many will mind. Miss Wynne Jones has broken the rules of fantasy before and got away with it. If single adjectives are required, there is a choice of whacky, grotty or kooky, but certainly not grotesque, mind-boggling or quaint. (p. 34)

> A. R. Williams, in a review of "The Time of the Ghost," in The Junior Bookshelf, Vol. 46, No. 1, February, 1982, pp. 33-4.

MARGERY FISHER

Comic witches are fashionable just now—likewise comic ghosts and familiars of various kinds. Fortunately, for every facetious tale centred on a broomstick-version of the banana-skin joke, there is one which uses humour as a way to set the anarchic impulses of youth in a new light. Like the necromantic academies described in recent years by Barbara Willard and Jill Murphy, Larwood House School is plagued by magic going awry but in *Witch Week* the magic is not a curriculum subject but a secret and forbidden undercurrent. This is one of those fantasies which describe in familiar and concrete terms an alternative world, one which diverged from our own back in the past when legislation against witches had to take into account the persistence of a genetic freak. . . . Diana Wynne Jones takes everyday incidents (lost running-shoes, illicit night-expeditions, water-fights) and gives them an edge of weird improbability, while the familiar rivalries and alliances of schooldays are made strangely urgent by the impending investigations from staff and outsiders. There seems no limit to this author's inventive energy; ingenious in plot, with a mock-casual twist at the end, her new book offers one more rollicking and provocative study of human behaviour. (p. 3984)

> Margery Fisher, "Hauntings," in her Growing Point, Vol. 21, No. 4, November, 1982, pp. 3983-86.*

MARCUS CROUCH

Among the post-war generation of children's writers none is more individual and more unpredictable than Diana Wynne Jones. Of her next book all one can be sure of is that it will be exciting, amusing and unlike the last. For one who treads the tricky paths of fantasy that is saying quite a lot.

In some ways the society shown in *Witch Week* is not unlike that of present-day England. Larwood House School is, in a nasty way, similar to other boarding schools. The pupils are not much more horrid than others; the teachers are odd, but then some of them are in real life. But something is wrong, as if we were looking at reality through a distorting glass. There is this preoccupation with witchcraft. And in an apparently civilized society witches, of all ages and both sexes, are burnt. With the Inquisitor ready to move in at a moment's notice, no wonder that witches and their probable fate occupy more than a fair share of the children's thoughts. (p. 231)

Miss Wynne Jones' favourite necromancer Chrestomanci comes to the rescue . . . , but not before we have had some pleasurable scares. The solution involves some explanations that belong to science-fiction more than fantasy.

Adults, who often find it more difficult than children to accept incongruities, may be bothered that so revolting a subject as death by burning can be treated in a funny way. I must admit that one or two things in this story stuck in my throat; on the other hand I also found myself laughing aloud, and that doesn't often happen. The invention, of character and incident (and the two are interlinked), is brilliant, the writing, and especially the dialogue, beautifully controlled. An offbeat masterpiece. (p. 232)

Marcus Crouch, in his review of "Witch Week," in
        The Junior Bookshelf, *Vol. 46, No. 6, December,*
        1982, pp. 231-32.

DOROTHY NIMMO

Someone some day had to write a story about a boarding school without romanticism or self-pity, and this could have been it. The children [of *Witch Week*] fill familiar roles: Nan is unpopular, Estelle is pliant, Theresa is a bully, Charles a loner, Brian a victim, Simon a born leader. But they are living in a world in which witchcraft is dreadfully alive, where Guy Fawkes succeeded in blowing up the Houses of Parliament, and history developed differently. By a tremendous effort of witchcraft the two worlds are wrenched together again, and everyone comes to themselves in an ordinary comprehensive. It doesn't actually end 'So it was all a dream', but there is something of the same let-down that Diana Wynne Jones should have found a way of conveying the stifling conformity of a closed community and the crooked subterfuges the children develop to preserve their identity, and then refused to take her creation quite seriously. But it's still a good story.

        Dorothy Nimmo, in her review of "Witch Week," in
        The School Librarian, *Vol. 30, No. 4, December,*
        1982, p. 359.

Stephen King

1947-

American novelist, short story writer, and scriptwriter.

King is primarily known for his modern Gothic novels in which supernatural events reflect psychological disturbances or moral problems. Critics praise King's ability to present aspects of American culture and vernacular. However, some feel that he is derivative in a field that too easily lends itself to imitation and cliché. King's work is a hybridization of the traditional horror tale, as written by Edgar Allan Poe, and the modern thriller, which capitalizes on trendy concerns such as parapsychology, telekinesis, and ESP.

King wrote his first novel, the popular culture classic *Carrie*, in 1974. Since then he has produced seven novels, two collections of short stories, an autobiography, and a screenplay. Among his recent novels is *The Dead Zone*, a thriller dealing with paranormal psychology. *Different Seasons*, a collection of four novellas, is King's bid for recognition as a more serious writer. Another recent addition to the King canon is the novel *Christine*, a tale of horror about a boy and his vintage car.

(See also *CLC*, Vol. 12; *Contemporary Authors*, Vols. 61-64; *Something about the Author*, Vol. 9; and *Dictionary of Literary Biography Yearbook: 1980*.)

JOHN GAULT

[The] arrival of a new Stephen King novel is something of an event: a minor event, perhaps, but still an event. And even when that novel is less than totally satisfying, as is the case with *The Dead Zone*, it is only slightly less.

King, who explored psychokinesis in *Carrie*, vampirism in *Salem's Lot*, mediumship and places of evil in *The Shining*, applies his considerable writing skills to psychometry (not the science, but the paranormal phenomena) in *The Dead Zone*. His hero, John Smith—a name choice more playful than profound—awakes from a 4½-year coma with the ability to fully "know" people's present and future circumstances just by touching them or an object they have touched. This skill, in the hands—literally—of good, decent and affable Smith, becomes progressively more curse than blessing, and leads to a final confrontation with a corrupt and dangerous politician whose future Smith knows and deeply fears.

There are two fundamental problems with *The Dead Zone*: the first is that it is really a meshing (or perhaps overlapping) of two novellas, suggesting that King did not have enough material for one full-length hard-cover novel. Too much of this book is spent demonstrating Smith's strange ability and agonizing over it. The second is that we have come to expect more from Stephen King; if this is unfair, so be it, but the fact remains that his earlier work is still his best work. And he is, after all, the acknowledged contemporary master of the horror/supernatural genre. It follows then that each new novel be judged accordingly.

In defence of *The Dead Zone* and King, it is a good read; in fact, it is a very good read, not impossible to put down, but putting it down is not something one does willingly. It more

© *Jerry Bauer*

than meets the two criteria that King set forth for his kind of book in *The New York Times Book Review* a couple of years ago: it is "accessible" and it is rendered with "honest intent."

John Gault, "Not Quite Fright," *in* Maclean's Magazine (© 1979 by Maclean's Magazine; *reprinted by permission*), *Vol. 93, No. 39, September 24, 1979, p. 56.*

ALEX E. ALEXANDER

To be sure, [*Carrie*] is a special kind of fairy tale: it is an adult fairy tale explicit in matters of sex, killing and revenge, and if the young appreciate it, it may be because their tastes have grown ahead of their chronological age. But *Carrie* is nevertheless a fairy tale: *rites de passage*, supernatural powers, magic and rites of sacrifice. Since fairy tales feed on such themes, the folktale opus is quite similar the world over. But *Carrie*, made into a highly popular movie, and thus rendered into a series of images, largely does away with the one unshakable source of ethnicity in folklore, namely the language of the people. The film medium as well as the inexpensive translations into many languages made by the industry of successful paperbacks assure *Carrie* of a wide, international diffusion and turn it into the new universal fairy tale.

The German romantic poet Friedrich Schiller (1759-1805), once said: "deeper meaning lies in the fairy tale of my childhood than in the truth that is taught by life." (p. 282)

The fairy tale . . . suggests, implies, hints about significant problems facing the child, and does so through imagery rather than discourse. In Brothers Grimm's "Little Snow White," we read:

> (The Queen) whilst she was sewing and looking out the window, at the snow, she pricked her finger with the needle, and three drops of blood fell upon the snow. . . . Soon thereafter she had a little girl, who was as white as snow, and as red as blood, and her hair was as black as ebony; the child was therefore called Little Snow White. And when the child was born the Queen died.

What follows is the appearance of the cruel stepmother and the conflict between the two. . . . The stepmother looks into the mirror and says, "Mirror, mirror on the wall, who is the fairest of them all?" only to discover that now Snow White outshines her in beauty. She decides to destroy the rival. But are we not dealing in this fairy tale with a deeper meaning covertly presented as magic? Could not the drop of blood in the snow be menstrual blood signifying Snow White's coming of age and thus leading to mother-daughter rivalry? In the child's mind the mother in her role of a rival becomes an evil stepmother. In another fairy tale from the Grimm collection, "The Goose-Girl," the blood and a girl's sexual maturation are tied together even closer. In this tale a queen sends her daughter to her betrothed, "to a prince who lived a great distance." Along with many objects which would seem to fit a dowry, the mother gives her daughter something rather curious: a blood stained handkerchief. . . . (pp. 282-83)

Unless we are willing to seek a deeper meaning in this story, "The Goose-Girl" becomes rather senseless. On a rational plane, the gift of a handkerchief with three drops of blood has precious little meaning. But the blood-stained piece of cloth clearly suggests maturation demonstrated by the menstrual cycle; this is all the more obvious since the girl having received the blood-stained handkerchief departs to marry. But the goose-girl refuses to grow up. She drops the handkerchief. Still, with the help of the old king, a father figure, she reaches maturity and is ready for marriage.

Thus the fairy tale imagery catalyzes fantasies about social and sexual anxieties. By identifying with the fairy tale hero, the child meets these anxieties head on, lives through them. At the end of the fairy tale, the child experiences not only moral edification, but also a sense of catharsis for having lived through an often frightful experience. . . . Hence the mass appeal of the fairy tale: it is edifying, it is entertaining and it is consoling—one needs not be overly fearful, things will always turn all right; the fairy tale answers the child's psychic needs.

Stephen King too reserves a deeper, subtextual meaning for *Carrie,* when he states on the very first page of his novel: "Nobody was really surprised when it happened, not really, not at the subconscious level, where savage things grow." (p. 283)

Carrie begins with Carrie White's first period. Unlike the fairy tale, the flow of menses is made here quite explicit. The opening scene of the book takes place in the school shower room. There, Carrie's schoolmates in a "hoarse, uninhibited abandon" shout "Period, Period!" and "Plug it up!", as Carrie

White is experiencing her first menstrual cycle: "The blood was dark, and flowing with terrible heaviness. Both of Carrie's legs were smeared and splattered with it, as though she had waded through a river of blood."

[Sigmund] Freud once observed that ever since the menstrual flow ceased to function as an olfactory attraction between the male and female of the species . . . , the menstrual cycle became an activity both feared and abhorred. Anthropological studies well complement Freud in this respect. Joseph Campbell notes, for example, that among the primitive tribes girls in their first period are placed in isolated huts where they remain secluded for the duration of the menstrual flow. This, one should think, to impress upon them the significance of the rite of passage from girlhood to womanhood, and also to stress the privacy of the act. Carrie, therefore, is guilty of breaking a taboo by displaying her menses in public. But her schoolmates are guilty too. For it is the duty of those who know to instruct those who are coming of age. It must be noted that Carrie has her first period at sixteen; thus unusually late. All her classmates are, therefore, well initiated into womanhood. But rather than help, they merely give vent to their disgust and abhorrence. Only one girl in the group, Susan Snell, assumes the role of an older and wiser member of the community who will lead Carrie through the difficult rite of passage. . . .

But Carrie does not listen. In a sense, like the goose-girl, she refuses to grow up. Later on in the novel Sue Snell will try to help again and at the end she will be the only person present at Carrie White's death.

A child cannot cope with the idea of a mother that is both good and bad: a mother that on the one hand brings the child into the world, feeds it, tends to its many needs and on the other is angry, scolds the infant, indulges in sexual rivalry (often imaginary) with the child. Whence in "Little Snow White," (as in many other fairy tales), the mother, having given birth to the child, conveniently dies, while it is the stepmother who wants to repress Snow White's budding sexuality, because she wishes her own to blossom.

In Stephen King's novel the fairy tale stepmother finds her counterpart in Carrie White's own mother who wishes to repress her daughter's sexuality. The good mother on the other hand is Susan Snell.

In *Carrie,* Carrie White's first period, or in other words her passage from childhood to womanhood, is followed by the School Spring Prom. Only girls invited by boys can attend. Carrie has no boyfriend, but Sue Snell does—Tommy Ross—and she convinces him that he should ask Carrie to the Prom while she, Sue, will simply stay at home. Carrie goes to the Prom with Tommy disregarding her mother's violent objections:

> "Red," Momma murmured. (Referring to Carrie's dress she made herself for the Prom).
>
> "I might have known it would be red."
>
> "I can see your dirty pillows. Everyone will. They will be looking at your body. The Book says—"
>
> "Those are my breasts, Momma. Every woman has them."
>
> "Take off that dress," Momma said.

"No." "Take it off, Carrie. We'll go down and burn it in the incinerator together, and then pray for forgiveness.

We'll do penance . . . "

"No, Momma."

Momma screamed. She made her right hand a fist and struck herself in the mouth, bringing blood.

She dabbled her fingers in it, looked at it dreamily, and daubed a spot on the cover of the bible.

Carrie's mother flaunts religion as a substitute for human growth due to her own sexual inadequacy. (pp. 283-85)

But if Carrie's natural mother, like the fairy tale stepmother, tries to repress the girl's budding sexuality, Susan Snell, assuming the role of a fairy tale natural parent, gives Carrie Tommy Ross and at the Prom, significantly called the Spring Prom, Carrie White blossoms in her womanly beauty. . . . And finally, Tommy and Carrie are elected the first couple of the ball. . . . And then came the blood. Just as Carrie White, unmindful of the age-old taboo, displayed her menses in public, so now the vengeful crowd composed of school kids, at the moment of Carrie's greatest triumph on her path of passage from childhood to maturity, repays her by showering both her and Tommy with buckets of pig's blood.

Spring and pig's blood are significant concepts. Carrie, through her awakened sexuality, becomes the Queen of the Spring Ball. Does she not imitate Persephone, who too rises each year in the spring with the awakened nature? But, as [Sir James George] Frazer points out [in *The Golden Bough*], Persephone may have been worshipped in the figure of the pig, with pigs sacrificed in her honor. . . .

Since Thesmophoria [an ancient Greek agricultural festival dedicated to Demeter and her daughter Persephone] was celebrated in November and the rites with the swine concern Persephone's descent into the underworld, isn't the drenching with pig's blood a kind of mock sacrifice aiming to render the rising spring goddess Persephone-Carrie, into a goddess descending into the earthly abyss with the onset of winter?

In the aftermath of this mock sacrificial rite to Carrie-Persephone, the heroine of Stephen King's novel does indeed grow into a kind of divinity of winter's death, rather than spring's renewal, who imparts her will and thoughts to others, and whom others, albeit total strangers, *know* with that special kind of mythical knowledge. To investigate this aspect of Carrie's development, however, it is necessary to step back to the beginning of the novel.

In folk *lore*, it is a commonly accepted tenet that sexual maturation should be accompanied by the acquisition of special kind of wisdom hitherto not possessed by the novice. Rites of passage, or initiation rites are the major theme of fairy tales, and are usually depicted as a quest. At the end of the quest, after many trials, a young boy or girl emerges safe and whole to be sure, much wiser, and usually with a spouse. (pp. 285-86)

Thus in the framework of folklore it is quite natural that Carrie White should develop a special kind of knowledge upon reaching sexual maturity. For Carrie this knowledge is telekinesis, or the ability to move objects at will, by the power of one's will. . . . (p. 286)

Splashed, drenched in pig's blood at the point where she was selected the Queen of the Spring Prom and thus cruelly mocked at the climactic point in her short and unhappy life, Carrie puts her telekinetic powers to awesome use of destructive vengeance which she hurls upon the people and property of Chamberlain, Mass. . . . At the end of the novel Carrie dies from wounds inflicted by her own mother whom she in turn kills by telekinetically stopping her heart from beating. But like Persephone, the dying and born again goddess of spring renewal, Carrie too has her resurrection in the little girl Annie, about whom we read on the last page of King's novel. The little girl, only two years old, is endowed, like Carrie, with the telekinetic potential.

Knifed by her own mother, Carrie staggers from the house and dies some distance from her home. Susan Snell is with her in her last dying moments. Susan simply knew, with that special kind of unexplainable knowledge where Carrie was, what she felt. . . . (pp. 286-87)

In her death Carrie clearly merges the image of Susan with that of her mother. Susan Snell, to be sure, is the good parent who helps in the child's development and growth. Susan is central to the concepts of consolation and moral instruction that are an integral part of the fairy tale and are present, as well, in Stephen King's *Carrie*. Susan Snell is the only person from Carrie's school not to have fallen prey to Carrie's telekinetic ire—hence the consolation and also the moral lesson: good people live, bad die. Susan is a good mother and she lives; Carrie too lives on in Annie.

It is important to note that the film prefers Gothic horror to this important aspect of folklore tradition, namely consolation and moral edification. In the film *Carrie*, at the very end, Susan has a dream . . . in which she goes to Carrie's grave only to be threatened suddenly and most unexpectedly by a horrid, bloody hand reaching for her from Carrie's grave. This scene is most effectively horrifying, alas at the expense of very important aspects of folklore tradition: moral edification and consolation.

Carrie then is folklore. It is a fairy tale and like the fairy tales of the Brothers Grimm and Afanas'ev in Russia, it feeds on universal myths, magic, ancient ways and the narrator's rich imagination. But Carrie's narrator is far more sophisticated than the story tellers of the Grimms or Afanas'ev, and so is his audience. The narrator has evolved into a writer and the mode of transmission to a *literate* audience is no longer oral: it is "the million copy bestseller" paperback easily translatable into many languages, and the film largely reducing the story to its image content. *Carrie* then is a universal fairy tale, folklore of the last quarter of the twentieth century. And *Carrie* enjoys the popularity of folklore, updated to be sure through the explicit treatment of sex and violence. It responds to deeply rooted sexual and social anxieties. It also offers consolation and moral edification; but alas, it would seem that there exists an inverted ratio between explicit sex and violence on the one hand and consolation and morality on the other: the greater the one, the lesser the other. (p. 287)

Alex E. Alexander, "Stephen King's 'Carrie'—A Universal Fairytale," in Journal of Popular Culture *(copyright © 1979 by Ray B. Browne), Vol. XIII, No. 2, Fall, 1979, pp. 282-87.*

JOHN BROSNAHAN

A master of psychic terror returns with [*Firestarter*], yet another study of strange phenomena guaranteed to enthrall his audience. Two college students sign up as paid guinea pigs for a secret and unknowingly dangerous government experiment in telekinesis. . . . When the subjects marry and have a baby, however, their child develops not only telekinesis but pyrokinesis as well; in short, the tot can not only push things with her mind, but set them ablaze as well. The government's plan to use the girl as a human weapon set King's plot into action, and an extended chase ensues with the expected havoc wreaked in vivid detail. King's highly visual style, almost akin to Hollywood special effects, sends the blood splattering, the flesh ripping, and the bodies flying in particularly gruesome fashion.

> *John Brosnahan, in his review of ''Firestarter,'' in* Booklist *(reprinted by permission of the American Library Association; copyright © 1980 by the American Library Association), Vol. 76, No. 20, June 15, 1980, p. 1464.*

KIRKUS REVIEWS

[*Firestarter* is an] improvement over *The Dead Zone,* with King returning to his most tried-and-true blueprint. As in *The Shining,* the psi-carrier is a child, an eight-year-old girl named Charlie; but instead of foresight or hindsight, Charlie has fire-starting powers. . . . Dumb, *very,* and still a far cry from the excitement of *The Shining* or *Salem's Lot*—but King keeps the story moving with his lively fire-gimmick and fewer pages of cotton padding than in his recent, sluggish efforts. The built-in readership will not be disappointed.

> *A review of ''Firestarter,'' in* Kirkus Reviews *(copyright © 1980 The Kirkus Service, Inc.), Vol. XLVIII, No. 14, July 15, 1980, p. 930.*

PAUL STUEWE

[*Firestarter* is another] smasheroo from a writer whose books haunt bestseller lists as well as impressionable imaginations. This is your advanced post-Watergate cynical American thriller with some eerie parapsychological twists, and it's been done so distinctively well that we'd better talk about genius rather than genre. Complex characterizations, credible dialogue and a no-nonsense prose style are among the uncommon virtues King brings to popular fiction, and his novels will be read long after this year's Prix Limburger winner has gone the way of all big cheeses for a season. As scary as *Carrie.*

> *Paul Stuewe, ''American Thrillers: 'Firestarter', 'Brass Diamonds', 'Brain 2000','' in* Quill and Quire *(reprinted by permission of* Quill and Quire*), Vol. 46, No. 10, October, 1980, pp. 40-1.**

MICHELE SLUNG

H. P. Lovecraft once called Nathaniel Hawthorne's *The House of the Seven Gables* ''New England's greatest contribution to weird literature.'' *Pace* Hawthorne scholars, there's a new contender, out of Maine, for the title. At least booksellers today would be unanimous in citing Stephen King, author of *Carrie, The Shining, Salem's Lot, The Stand, The Dead Zone,* and now *Firestarter,* best sellers all, as the northeast's preeminent scribe of the spooky.

King has not been taken very seriously, if at all, by the critical establishment. Unfortunately for him, it's all too easy to take cheap shots at his material by lifting bits of it out of context;

what is ghastly when the mood has been set can be risible when the lights are up, so to speak. (p. 38)

But King's real stigma—the reason he is not perceived as being in competition with *real* writers—is that he has chosen to write about ghoulies and ghosties, about things that go bump in the night. Rats and vampires, necromancers and mind-readers, deadly plagues and telekinetic children: it may sound silly but, as King is well aware . . . , there's a long, as the saying goes, and honorable tradition.

It's a familiar list, these distinguished folk who've been intrigued with what Lovecraft termed ''the overtones of strangeness in ordinary things'': Dickens, Henry James, Kipling, Walter de la Mare, de Maupassant. And there are many best known for their work in the horror genre alone: J. Sheridan Le Fanu, Bram Stoker, Arthur Machen, Algernon Blackwood, M. R. James. References to these greats . . . are dotted throughout the King oeuvre. It is apparent that he has read widely and appreciatively in SF, fantasy, and supernatural literature.

King began by borrowing freely. In his collection of short stories, *Night Shift* . . . , two tales in particular call to mind earlier classics: **''Jerusalem's Lot''** (which sets the scene for the novel *Salem's Lot*) resembles Lovecraft's ''The Case of Charles Dexter Ward'' and **''Gray Matter''** seems to owe a bit too much to Arthur Machen's ''The Novel of the White Powder.'' But overall, King has been moving in the direction of admirable originality; it is no mean trick to make the here-and-now creepy, without recourse to gothic ruins or the Carpathian Mountains.

Firestarter is dedicated to Shirley Jackson and takes its epigraph from Ray Bradbury, another writer whom King often calls to mind, specifically when he elegizes small-town America. . . . *Firestarter* is [as Henry James would say] ''an excursion into chaos,'' much as was *Carrie,* another novel in which a young female mind could upend the fixed laws of nature.

This time, however, the child is a grade-schooler, not a sexually strait-jacketed adolescent: Charlene Roberta McGee, a precocious seven-year-old when the story begins, is on the lam with her father, Andy, running from minions of ''the Shop.'' (pp. 38-9)

Flashbacks reveal that Andy and Vicky, the woman who became his wife, had volunteered as guinea pigs in a drug-testing experiment back when they were seniors in college. Their encounter with ''di-lysergic triune acid''—administered by a faculty member, yet secretly controlled by the Shop—is an episode of unsettling gruesomeness that doesn't really end when the effects ostensibly have worn off. Not only do Andy and Vicky find themselves afflicted with low-grade psychic powers, but their genes are somehow affected as well. They realize the extent of the problem when the infant Charlene shows herself to be capable, if annoyed, of sizzling up the hairs on her teddy bear. . . .

The bulk of [*Firestarter*'s scenario] is King's characteristic long-windedness; the rest is pursuit-and-flight . . . and the anticipation of those moments when Charlie shows herself to be ''capable of manufacturing hell, or a reasonable facsimile.'' Yet the whole is greater than the sum of the parts, and once again King has given the supernatural epic a good name, for those not afraid to meet it on its own terms. Though an inelegant writer . . . King impresses, finally, by virtue of his enthusiasm and self-confidence, his faith in his own imaginative powers.

Some may object that King's writing is too enthusiastic, or, at least, too energetic. A true son of the 1960s, King in all his books makes the music coming out of the era one of his touchstones for decency and sensitivity. . . . Even his love of parentheses, to indicate thought or menace or to heighten a mood, could be considered writing stereophonically. Sometimes a King novel or story is a veritable lightshow of italics, ellipses, and parentheses; one imagines him drumming it out on an electric typewriter with rock music blaring behind and the occasional blown fuse.

King also has a well-known predilection for brand-name products: Hush-Puppies, Adolph's Meat Tenderizer, Pledge, Woolco, Sara Lee, Cheez Doodles, Cremora, Hefty Bags, Shakey's Pizza, etc. Certainly these items were missing from Castle Dracula, as were such favorite King expressions as "pissant," "doodly-squat," and "shitcan." King also does very well with making modern appliances and machinery, like lawnmowers and trucks, ominous, even predatory: perhaps he will one day give us a killer Cuisinart.

Stephen King, in short, is not the kind of occult writer who would have gone out and joined a satanic society; brushed by the counterculture, he's still much more likely to be a pillar of the local Kiwanis. But his Sears catalogue horror can be appealing, as it taps everyone from Edgar Allan Poe to Chuck Berry. Moreover, King's fiction fulfills, in its own way, Henry James's dictum that "a good ghost-story . . . be connected at a hundred points with the common objects of life." James might have fastidiously recoiled from King's lumbering prose but he would have understood what he was about. (p. 39)

> Michele Slung, "A Master of the Macabre," in The New Republic (reprinted by permission of The New Republic; © 1981 The New Republic, Inc.), Vol. 184, No. 8, February 21, 1981, pp. 38-9.

TOM EASTON

I defend [Stephen King as a SF writer] now because I have a good excuse: *The Dead Zone.* (p. 164)

Technology doesn't enter into this tale. The occult does, however, for Johnny's talent *is* occult. It is of the light, though, not the dark; and he uses it to fight for the good. And here is the key to King's choice of themes. He writes of good versus evil, putting a usually shaded white up against the blackest black. He uses the occult, I suspect, solely because it lends itself to tales of horror, and perhaps because it makes good and evil seem more akin. Yet he treats it as rationally as he can, given its nature. It is a source of power, but one with limits that restrict his heroes. And, at least in *The Dead Zone,* it is not quite the sort of occult beloved of the masses. On that silliness [King] heaps scorn. Johnny's mother goes all out for flying saucers, interstellar and subpolar True Christians, and all the other goodies in the cosmic fruitcake. An occult-oriented tabloid seeks Johnny as a "house psychic" and gets the bum's rush. Fans are avoided like the ten plagues of Israel.

Does Steve King write science fiction? It's a fair question, for to most people he is a horror writer, a fantasist. But his premises that the occult (especially ESP) is real and evil can be personified are hardly foreign to our field. And he is as much a rationalist, free-will advocate, and moral reactionary ("absolutist," as opposed to "relativist"; he does not believe that society makes evil, even though he does use background to

flesh out his evil characters) as that demigod of SF, Robert A. Heinlein.

King's works have their fantasy components, sometimes more strongly than others, but at least his latest are indeed SF. *The Stand* and *The Dead Zone* are both examples. And they are both ripping good stories. For all their length, I enjoyed both tremendously. . . . (p. 165)

> Tom Easton, in his review of "The Dead Zone" (reprinted by permission of the author), in Analog Science Fiction/Science Fact, Vol. CI, No. 4, March 30, 1981, pp. 164-65.

PUBLISHERS WEEKLY

With a master's sure feel for the power of the plausible to terrify as much or more than the uncanny, [in *Cujo*] King builds a riveting novel out of the lives of some very ordinary and believable people in a small Maine town, and an unfortunate 200 lb. St. Bernard. . . . [There is] a succession of bloody deaths and, the main event, the nerve-stretching siege of a woman and her four-year-old son, trapped in a small car by the mad dog for two broiling days and endless nights. King's work is so powerful because he troubles to give his characters' lives dimension beyond the minimal needs of the situation. His expert use of colloquial language in both dialogue and narration augments the impact of the extraordinary events he describes. These qualities and his remarkable instinct for pacing have you turning pages effortlessly from the start, and then with increasing urgency as the tension builds. This is a biting novel of gut-twisting terror and suspense. More tightly written and perhaps therefore superior to King's last couple of books, it is likely to equal or surpass their popularity.

> A review of "Cujo," in Publishers Weekly (reprinted from the July 17, 1981 issue of Publishers Weekly, published by R. R. Bowker Company, a Xerox company; copyright © 1981 by Xerox Corporation), Vol. 220, No. 3, July 17, 1981, p. 80.

MICHAEL BISHOP

Stephen King has written a dog story?

Well, yes and no. Mostly no, but it takes 30 or 40 pages to find out for certain. (p. 1)

[*Cujo*'s] eponymous canine—a Saint Bernard belonging to the family of an aggressively uncouth auto mechanic by the name of Joe Camber—contracts rabies and turns from a gentle giant into an indefatigable engine of madness and death. Although Camber's garage lies in the boondocks well beyond Castle Rock, Maine, Donna Trenton and her 4-year-old son Tad drive out there to see about her malfunctioning Pinto. Her husband Vic, meanwhile, has flown to Boston with his partner to try to dissuade their tiny ad agency's most lucrative client from dumping them. When Cujo lays murderous siege to the stalled Pinto, and when Vic's long-distance calls to home go unanswered, the reader soon realizes that King's dog story owes more to Alfred Hitchcock than to Albert Payson Terhune.

Deft characterization and rigorous plotting, a la Hitchcock, inform the best of King's bravura experiments in the horror genre. A conscious awareness of this fact—elsewhere King has confessed especial admiration for the methods of Jack Finney, in whose work the alien and the bizarre often casually emerge from the mundane—has enabled him to develop a useful storytelling formula. By introducing believable middle- and lower-middle-class Americans into situations that defy conventional logic, King subjects the reader to a harrowing tour of the lives of characters who must attempt to defeat the irrational—whether prejudice, plague, vampires, or the cumulative evil accruing to a particular site—in order to restore a modicum of sanity to their world.

Cujo is carefully cut to this formula, but its supernatural element—a rabid dog's possession by the spirit of a psychotic killer from *The Dead Zone,* a previous King novel—strikes me as obtrusive and phony. Why go mucking up a good, if somewhat overlong, dog story with such drivel? Does King lack the confidence to forgo this nod to previous successes, or does he hope to justify Cujo's insane pertinacity and stamina by imputing to the dog the free-floating force of cosmic evil? The latter, I feel sure. The worm at the heart of *Cujo,* then, probably uncoils from the author's fear that no mortal animal, healthy or otherwise, could behave as does his doggy Rasputin. This fear, I think, is unfounded, and I wish King had been content to write a thriller without these annoying curtsies to the great grinning idol of the commercial horror novel.

Despite this objection and the inordinate number of pages devoted to Cujo's siege, King's ability to draw character and to marshal a complex series of forward-moving scenes redeems the book. By easy and justifiable reference to dozens of contemporary American icons—Darth Vader, Tupperware, Count Chocula, *Where the Wild Things Are,* Travis McGee, etc.—he skillfully evokes the here-and-now reality of his characters. . . . (pp. 1-2)

To resort to hackneyed terminology, we *identify* with King's characters. He has made it impossible for us not to. This feat, accomplished with such apparent offhandedness, deserves notice and praise. It suggests that King's talent could easily lend itself to the writing of fiction of a decidedly more "literary" order.

But I am fairly happy with what he has given us. Nineteenth-century England had Wilkie Collins for literate, headlong melodrama; we have Stephen King. Both tend to pile up the words along with the suspense, and excessive length is not really necessary for a dog story incorporating implicit observations about the nature of evil. (See Stephen Crane's "A Small Brown Dog" or Jack London's "Batard.") *Cujo,* however, is a dog story in which human beings dominate our concern. As an adult, I appreciate this fact and do not begrudge King the space he needs to bring them to life. He does it well. (p. 2)

> *Michael Bishop, "Mad Dogs . . . and Englishmen,"*
> in Book World—The Washington Post *(© 1981, The*
> Washington Post*), August 23, 1981, pp. 1-2.*

SYLVIA PASCAL

[In *Cujo,* victims of the mad dog's] violence are two families—that of his owner, backwoods auto mechanic Joe Camber, and of Vic Trenton, an ad man struggling to keep an important account while "dealing" with his wife's infidelity and his four year old's fears. Counterpoint to the ad campaign's folksy slogan and the writer's lush reveries are nightmarish vigils in stalled Pintos where one awaits deadly assault and relentless visions of heat and horror. Beyond the façades of modern life, the ordinary world of creaky closets and baseball bats, coloring books and toy trucks, Slim Jims and shabby affairs, lies the potential for savagery unwitting and otherwise . . . , the men-

ace that Aldous Huxley has termed "the imminent maniac." It is King's style of "bringing it all back home" that leads one effortlessly, if gratuitously, to the bloody denouement.

> *Sylvia Pascal, in her review of "Cujo," in* School
> Library Journal *(reprinted from the October, 1981
> issue of* School Library Journal, *published by R. R.
> Bowker Co./A Xerox Corporation; copyright © 1981),
> Vol. 28, No. 2, October, 1981, p. 162.*

DOROTHY M. BRODERICK

While the usual aura of the supernatural, of which King is master, hangs over [*Cujo*], the real terror is its reality. Given the right circumstances, anyone of us could find ourselves held captive in a small automobile on a blazing hot day by a rabid dog, driven to rage by his pain. . . . Cujo has already killed [his owner] Camber and his drinking buddy and he will kill again before the book ends.

Younger King fans may not find this quite as appealing as earlier titles since it places great emphasis on the marriage relationship of Vic and Donna Trenton as well as Vic's struggle to save the ad agency in which he is a partner. It also offers considerable insight into how women like Mrs. Camber find themselves trapped in a marriage in which poverty is the major jailer. One additional problem is the overkill of profanity that occurs early in the book and then fades away. None of this, of course, will keep King fans away; the only question is whether you will want to let them sneak it from adult or risk putting YA on its spine.

> *Dorothy M. Broderick, in her review of "Cujo," in*
> Voice of Youth Advocates *(copyrighted 1981 by* Voice
> of Youth Advocates*), Vol. 4, No. 4, October, 1981,
> p. 34.*

RON HANSEN

The movie is *Creepshow* [directed by George A. Romero] and the script is by Stephen King, whose novels *Carrie* and *The Shining* became stunning films by Brian De Palma and Stanley Kubrick, and whose second novel, *Salem's Lot,* was a CBS mini series. That's the connection between King and Romero: a studio executive saw Romero's 1977 vampire movie, *Martin,* at a Utah film festival and asked him to direct *Salem's Lot,* a project from which Romero eventually removed himself.

Nevertheless, Romero and King remained in contact, for the match of talents was irresistible. "What Stephen King and George Romero have in common is a lack of inhibitions," says Kirby McCauley, an agent who specializes in science fiction and fantasy. "Other writers and filmmakers dance around horror—those two plow right into it." (p. 72)

[It took King two months to write] *Creepshow,* a conscious and affectionate imitation of William M. Gaines's horror comics of the Fifties, screamers like *Weird Science* and *Tales from the Crypt,* of which King was an avid reader as a child. Like them, *Creepshow* consists of five short stories interleaved with advertisements for *Grit* newspapers, Joy Buzzers, X-ray glasses, and novelties to "Amuse and Amaze Your Friends."

Wrapped around these five stories is a sixth, situated on Maple Street, in Centerville, U.S.A. A boy named Billy . . . is in his room at night reading a comic book called *Creepshow.* When Billy's cruel father discovers his son's secret vice, he slaps the boy, snatches the comic book, and stuffs it into a garbage can in the street. Lightning flickers as the camera seeks out the book in the can. The cover is blown over, and we see Crayola-colored artwork: a family in a sitting room beneath the title, "Father's Day." Then the lettering vanishes, the splash page becomes a freeze frame, the actors move, and *Creepshow* the comic becomes *Creepshow* the $8 million film.

The situations in the stories are classic: an autocratic father returns from the grave after seven years to chasten his errant daughter; a shirttail farmer . . . unearths a meteor that seeds his land and his face with weeds; a janitor and a student are both slaughtered by a ravenous monster inside a cobwebbed crate. Says King, "The comic-book form allowed us to pare the motivations and characterizations down to a bare minimum and let us just go for scares."

The texture and mood of a creepy comic is likewise being imitated with the camera work and production design. Scrolled borders indicate flashbacks, scrims behind an actress make the camera frame flare with her scream, titles indicate time passage: "Soon," "Later," "Meanwhile." (pp. 72-3)

Romero's are the sort of movies that some critics execrate, but they've earned him a cult following. For Michael Gornick, director of photography on *Creepshow,* as well as on Romero's *Dawn of the Dead* and *Knightriders,* only the script has changed; the ironic treatment of fantasy material was there ever since *Night of the Living Dead.* (pp. 73, 76)

And then too there is that recovered sense of childhood's certainties, of what's good and what's evil and of just desserts. producer [Richard P.] Rubinstein concurs. "I think George has always regarded fantasy and horror as basically allegorical, and that's something he has in common even with Grimm's fairy tales. He says it's a way of doing morality plays and still remaining commercial. You look at these stories in *Creepshow,* and it's sin and retribution in almost every case." . . .

Creepshow isn't like one of those hackabout horror films currently making the rounds. Romero's scenes are mitigated by what Rubinstein calls "violence so stylized that the audience can't forget they're watching a movie." (p. 76)

> Ron Hansen, "'Creepshow': The Dawn of a Living Horror Comedy" (reprinted by permission of the author), in Esquire, Vol. 97, No. 1, January, 1982, pp. 72-3, 76.

KIRKUS REVIEWS

It will take all of King's monumental byline-insurance to drum up an audience for [*Different Seasons,* a] bottom-of-the-trunk collection: four overpadded novellas, in non-horror genres—without the gripping situations needed to transcend King's notoriously clumsy writing. Best of the lot is *Rita Hayworth and Shawshank Redemption.* . . . The climax is feeble (especially after such a long build-up), the redemption theme is murky—but the close observation of prison life offers some engaging details. . . . [Throughout *Different Seasons,* we find thin] gimmicks, weighed down with King's weak characters and weaker prose (unlike his crisp short stories)—but the fans may come around yet again, despite the clear evidence that King needs the supernatural to distract from his awesome limitations as a mainstream storyteller.

> A review of "Different Seasons," in Kirkus Reviews (copyright © 1982 The Kirkus Service, Inc.), Vol. L, No. 12, June 15, 1982, p. 693.

BILL OTT

Readers who are drawn to what Stephen King calls the "gooshy parts" of his books—arms mangled by garbage disposals, etc.—may find themselves a little disappointed by these four novellas. The title of the collection [*Different Seasons*] is meant to suggest a foray into something a bit closer to mainstream fiction, but three of the four stories still rely heavily on elements of the macabre. One of these, **"Apt Pupil,"** is a disjointed tale of a teenager and the parasitic relationship he falls into with an ex-Nazi. The tone of this novella goes somehow wrong, as if King, looking for a way to exploit his characteristic combination of humor and terror, can't find anything to laugh at. The last two stories in the collection are much more successful: **"The Body"** describes four 10-year-olds and their first encounter with death, while **"The Breathing Method"** concerns a group of elderly gentlemen who sip brandy and tell horror stories, one involving a woman's bizarre application of a Lamaze-like birth technique. King is guilty of some self-indulgence here . . . , but there is no denying his narrative drive.

> Bill Ott, in his review of "Different Seasons," in Booklist (reprinted by permission of the American Library Association; copyright © 1982 by the American Library Association), Vol. 78, No. 21, July, 1982, p. 1394.

THOMAS GIFFORD

It's not often that a single individual puts you in mind of both J. B. Priestley and Yogi Berra, but when someone does you might as well pay attention. An extraordinary occurrence. But then Stephen King, who managed this paradoxical feat, is not an ordinary writer. Though, to further confuse the issue, it is precisely King's remarkable ordinariness that makes him what he is, one of the world's best-selling authors. . . . Before I further complicate my observations on King and his new collection of novellas, *Different Seasons,* let me get back to Priestley for a moment.

Priestley, in his working prime, which spanned 40-odd years, seemed all but unable to stop the flow of words from his pen. Most of the words were particularly well chosen, and as the cataract poured forth he built remarkably detailed, realistic worlds, novel after novel, play after play, however fanciful the themes. We were chatting about this enormous output one snowy spring day in his comfortable study and he fixed me with what must always have been intended by the expression "a gimlet eye" and said: "Gifford, the important thing is to do the work, keep writing, whether you feel like it or not. Just keep it coming, let nothing get in your way."

I was reminded of this stricture recently as I regarded the apparently bottomless well of Stephen King's word supply. Like clockwork they come, *The Stand, The Shining, Cujo,* on and on, richly observed, full of the particular ordinariness of our lives and times—and worlds are built within each work, built and then dismantled in spasms of horror which have become his trademark. A Lovecraft for our times. Ozzie and Harriet and Beaver and Wally with brain tumors, and things that eat people held back by fraying ropes in damp cellars.

Now with *Different Seasons,* works written at different times following the completion of one novel or another, he's doing a kind of Yogi Berra, showing he can hit the off-speed curve, the change-up well off the plate, and still drive a fastball to the opposite field. Let me explain. Berra used to say he could hit it if he could reach it. King has done some reaching . . .

and drilled some liners off the green monster of his own particular muse.

Each of the novellas herein reflects a slightly different tone, thus the "seasons" of the title, but the devoted will not be disappointed: each has a decidedly macabre quality. The first, and best, **"Rita Hayworth and Shawshank Redemption,"** has some really lovely things in it—the story of two men in prison for a very long time, one unjustly convicted of murder and the other who has long ago paid for the murder he committed. How they deal with their lives, their friendship, and the quirky fate life has chosen for them makes for the kind of story that sticks in your mind.

The second story, **"Apt Pupil,"** is the most overtly startling of the four: a nightmare in which a teen-aged all-American lad discovers a Nazi relic, a war criminal, living in his idyllic California village. The symbiosis which develops between them is not subtle, not psychologically sophisticated, but utterly pathological. And it does make a hell of a story. The other two stories don't require description; they are more King. Which is sort of dumb sounding, but there is a crucial point about King.

He is obsessed by the piling up of words, incident, a cliche locked in time, values which represent a year unlike the years on each side of it, the rubbing of personalities upon one another—all the values of the traditional storyteller. His art lies in his artlessness. His prose style is utterly conversational: he is literally telling you the story. The constant references to pop culture, which might irritate in another writer, don't irritate here because King *is* pop culture, an artifact himself. He speaks the vernacular, the patois, and it informs his thought.

What can I say to make this point clearly? Try this: he is the storyteller his readers would want to be if they were indeed storytellers. In *A Man's a Man*, Bertolt Brecht says of Jeriah Jip, his Everyman hero, "He is one of us!" which explains everything, all the appeal. The important thing to acknowledge in King's immense popularity, and in the Niagara of words he produces, is the simple fact that he can write. He can write without cheapening or trivializing himself or his audience. You may or may not enjoy these stories but you won't feel cheated or demeaned by them. They will entertain; they may disturb you only slightly, superficially. You will feel as if you've just stepped into a time warp and seen a new episode of TV's *Alfred Hitchcock Presents* or *The Twilight Zone* or *The Outer Limits*. I am convinced that King is aiming roughly at that response.

Wait. Let me try again. I think I've got it. Think of Stephen King and Steven Spielberg; work on that simple equation. One with words, the other with images. Elemental story values; broad strokes. You begin to grasp an explanation of both phenomena. *E.T., Poltergeist, Close Encounters, Jaws,* **Carrie, The Shining, Firestarter, Cujo** . . . *Raiders of the Lost Ark,* **Different Seasons.**

Such popular phenomena represent accomplishments and impulses our culture has no need to be ashamed of. And these days that is cause for rejoicing. (pp. 1-2)

> *Thomas Gifford, "Stephen King's Quartet," in* Book World —The Washington Post *(© 1982, The Washington Post), August 22, 1982, pp. 1-2.*

KENNETH ATCHITY

In the afterword to [*Different Seasons*], Stephen King calls his "stuff" "fairly plain, not very literary, and sometimes (although it hurts like hell to admit it) downright clumsy." He summarizes a career of horror novels as "plain fiction for plain folks, the literary equivalent of a Big Mac and a large fries from McDonald's."

To find the secret of his success, you have to compare King to [Mark] Twain, [Edgar Allan] Poe—with a generous dash of Philip Roth and Will Rogers thrown in for added popular measure. King's stories tap the roots of myth buried in all our minds. . . .

King's visionary flights in these four novellas show us the natural shape of the human soul—a shape even more horrifying, for its protean masks, than the ghouls he has conjured up in the novels. His productivity is based on his awareness that audience psychology responds to the simple elements of fiction, presented directly. . . .

In **"Rita Hayworth and Shawshank Redemption,"** he hooks us blatantly with the narrator's predicted triumph. Within a page or so, he can admit the falseness of the hook—and we don't care. For King, the art is to reveal the art. We adore the special effects. . . .

In **"The Body,"** King shows his skill at assuming a youngster's character, at the same time expressing how Americans sound not at their best but in their everyday voices. . . .

The most chilling story in the collection, perhaps the most horrifying King has published to date, is **"Apt Pupil,"** subtitled "Summer of Corruption." . . .

The repulsion of the all-American newsboy extorting from the dying Nazi the chilling details of his role in the war is bad enough, but what evokes the infernal depths of human nature is the transfer of evil and inhumanity from one to the other by story's end. The boy is innocent no longer, and the reader recognizes his own face in King's mirror:

> "Todd smiled at him. And incredibly—certainly not because he wanted to—Dussander found himself smiling back."

King's afterword describes his conversations with editor Bill Thompson concerning his career. Thompson was afraid King might be typed as a horror writer. . . . King allowed that things could be worse: "I could, for example, be an 'important' writer like Joseph Heller and publish a novel every seven years or so, or a 'brilliant' writer like John Gardner and write obscure books for bright academics who eat macrobiotic foods and drive old Saabs with faded but still legible Gene McCarthy for President stickers on the rear bumpers."

Whatever King and his editors decide about his image, our appetite for his McDonald's shows no signs of abating.

> *Kenneth Atchity, "Stephen King: Making Burgers with the Best" (reprinted by permission of the author), in* Los Angeles Times Book Review, *August 29, 1982, p. 7.*

ALAN CHEUSE

Over the last decade Mr. King has certainly not wanted for ears; he is one of the most popular writers of our era. But unlike other vulgar—in the root sense of speaking in the voice of and to the average person—best-selling authors, Mr. King seems to have remained unsatisfied by mere popularity. . . .

[The] author of some of the best horror stories since those of Ambrose Bierce and H. P. Lovecraft may want [understanding as well as acceptance]. And it's precisely this quest for understanding, the drive to make his vision not only well known but deeply felt, that appears to have led him to publish ["**Different Seasons**," an] uneven, though often surprising, volume.

The first surprise comes early: The opening prison narrative titled "**Rita Hayworth and Shawshank Redemption**" shows us that the creator of such studies of the criminal mind as "**The Shining**" and "**The Dead Zone**" can effectively treat innocence as well as guilt. Set in a fictional state penitentiary in the author's home state of Maine, the tale is told in the first person by Red, a prisoner and entrepreneur who has as one of his best customers a former banker and convicted murderer, Andy Dufresne. Dufresne stands out among the lifers in the yard long before Red discovers his real story; the man is a cultivated type who, even as he's fighting off the brutal sexual advances of Shawshank's population of "sisters," apparently spends his time alone shaping and polishing pieces of quartz from the yard. This dedication to an art form of sorts impresses Red, who thought he had seen it all. . . .

It's difficult to imagine any reader feeling a sense of awe at the way Mr. King bullies his way through this tough-guy novella . . . , but the piece does give off a certain warmth. And if it's not "pretty," it is still an admirable departure from the genre that made the author famous.

"**Apt Pupil**," the second and longest narrative in the volume, also stands as the most disappointing. It is a psychological study of the tandem corruption of Todd Bowden, a Southern California high-school student, and Kurt Dussander, the Nazi war criminal he discovers in his own hometown. The story links the sunny present of America with the nightmare past of death camps and all of what Todd calls their "gooshy" atrocities. Big theme here—but in execution the piece comes off as somewhat silly, with the tone wavering between that of cartoon images from horror comic books and the worst variety of pulp fiction. . . . (p. 10)

But if Mr. King stumbles in "**Apt Pupil**," he picks himself up again and continues at a fast clip with "**The Body**," which is narrated by his doppelgänger, Gordie Lachance. In this supposed memoir we return to the scene of a number of crimes from Mr. King's earlier fiction—Castle Rock, Me., the setting of "**The Dead Zone**" and "**Cujo**"—but the style here is once again in the psychological rather than the supernatural mode. Narrator Lachance takes us back to the initiation rite that may have formed him as a successful writer—the overnight trek into the Maine woods he took with three other working-class friends in search of another teen-ager's rotting corpse. . . . There's some pretentiousness to Lachance's tale, especially in the inclusion of two stories that he published in little magazines early in his career, some swipes at writers such as John Gardner . . . , praise of Ralph Ellison, and some Mailerlike conceit. . . . But there's a lot to admire in this recollection of dead and dead-end kids—and a scene in which the boys attempt to cross a railroad trestle as the tracks begin to hum may induce a permanent fear of hiking.

Readers who fear that Mr. King may have hiked permanently out of the territory in which they love to see him travel will be reassured to learn that in "**The Breathing Method**," the final novella in this collection, he returns to the horror story as a conquering hero. . . . The natural narrative force that previously has helped Mr. King overcome his often clumsy prose and sophomoric philosophizing churns through these pages stronger than ever before; and yet he's never written anything that seems so polished and finished.

As a collection "**Different Seasons**" is flawed and out of balance, but that shouldn't deter anyone with a taste for interesting popular fiction. Each of the first three novellas has its hypnotic moments, and the last one is a horrifying little gem. (p. 17)

Alan Cheuse, "Horror Writer's Holiday," in The New York Times Book Review (© 1982 by The New York Times Company; reprinted by permission), August 29, 1982, pp. 10, 17.

PAUL GRAY

Those who have already rushed out to buy *Different Seasons* . . . may be a trifle shocked by what they have brought home: a collection of four novellas, only one of which offers the chills that have become King's trademark. *The Breathing Method* is an eerie account of a terribly unnatural childbirth. But the other three, though sporadically gruesome, come without King's customary trimmings. Gone are varieties of telekinesis (*Carrie, Firestarter*) and precognition (*The Shining, The Dead Zone*). There are no vampires (*Salem's Lot*), apocalyptic plagues (*The Stand*) or satanically rabid Saint Bernards (*Cujo*). The only reader likely to find these long tales truly frightening is an old-fashioned book lover: they are spooky examples of what can be called postliterate prose.

The genre is new, its methods still in the formative stage, but King is its popular master. *Different Seasons* offers a dazzling display of how writing can appeal to people who do not ordinarily like to read. King uses language the same way the baseball fan seated behind the home-team dugout uses placards: to remind those present of what they have already seen. In *Apt Pupil*, for example, a 13-year-old boy tracks down a Nazi war criminal hiding out in his own Southern California suburb. When he confronts the fugitive, the youth is disappointed by the old man's accent: "It didn't sound . . . well, authentic. Colonel Klink on *Hogan's Heroes* sounded more like a Nazi than Dussander did." Perhaps a teen-ager might find a TV sitcom more vividly real than a phenomenon that predated his birth. But members of his immediate family are judged in the same way: "Dick Bowden, Todd's father, looked remarkably like a movie and TV actor named Lloyd Bochner." When Todd finds himself in a dilemma, he mentally goes to the movies: "He thought of a cartoon character with an anvil suspended over its head."

Such perceptions spare readers the task of puzzling them out. They short-circuit thought, plugging directly into prefabricated images. And they are by no means limited to young characters. . . .

Even King's elderly characters talk as if they had spent their lives at Saturday kiddie matinees. In *The Breathing Method*, an old physician sits in an exclusive Manhattan club, spinning a long-ago yarn. He recalls the terror he once saw on the face of an ambulance driver. "His eyes widening until it seemed they must slip from their orbits and simply dangle from their optic nerves like grotesque seeing yo-yos." In postliterate prose, reality is at its most intense when it can be expressed as an animated drawing.

King is not the first to turn his fiction over to the echo chamber of pop culture. Writers as dissimilar as Thomas Pynchon and Donald Barthelme have toyed for years with the mass-produced icons that have invaded the communal memory. But King takes them dead seriously, and so, evidently, do his millions of readers. . . .

[King] is both pleased by the popular response to his writing and irked by charges that he is cynically exploiting a lucrative market: "I'm as serious as I know how to be when I sit down to the typewriter." *Different Seasons* is, in fact, his bid to be recognized as something other than a writer in a fright wig. . . . The book may not win him critical respect, but it does suggest that horror, after all, has been incidental to his stunning success. For every scare he has given his readers, he has provided more than enough reassurance. Life is stock footage: ancient history means *The Flintstones.*

> *Paul Gray, "Master of Postliterate Prose," in* Time *(copyright 1982 Time Inc.; all rights reserved; reprinted by permission from* Time*), Vol. 120, No. 9, August 30, 1982, p. 87.*

DAVID ANSEN

Revenge—the more horrible the better—is a favorite adolescent fantasy, and it is the subject of four of the five tales of horror that comprise *Creepshow,* an unashamedly adolescent spectacle dreamed up by director George Romero and writer Stephen King. A murdered patriarch bursts from his grave to take revenge on his family. A cuckolded husband . . . buries his wife and her lover up to their necks in the sand and forces them to watch each other drown on closed-circuit TV. The appearance of an ancient, very abominable snowman on a college campus gives a henpecked professor . . . a novel chance to do away with his shrewish wife. . . . And in the final story, destined to be the gross-out favorite at grammar schools, a malicious millionaire . . . gets his cosmic comeuppance at the hands of millions of carnivorous cockroaches.

Creepshow is conceived as an E. C. Comic come to life, complete with panels, balloons and the lurid colorings of an old issue of "Tales From the Crypt." Romero and King want to be as unsophisticated as possible, while maintaining a sense of humor, and they succeed all too well. The characters, story lines and images are studiously one-dimensional. For anyone over 12 there's not much pleasure to be had watching two masters of horror deliberately working beneath themselves. *Creepshow* is a *faux naif* horror film: too arch to be truly scary, too elemental to succeed as satire.

> *David Ansen, "The Roaches Did It," in* Newsweek *(copyright 1982, by Newsweek, Inc.; all rights reserved; reprinted by permission), Vol. C, No. 21, November 22, 1982, p. 118A.*

RICHARD CORLISS

In the past, Novelist Stephen King . . . and Director George A. Romero . . . have shown that they know how to scare people through the poetry of pulp. . . . In *Creepshow* they have aimed lower, and hit the mark. The film is an elaborate tribute to *Tales from the Crypt* and other horror comic books of the early '50s. Five tales play with the theme of moral revenge taken on corrupt humankind by nature, alien forces or the Undead. But the treatment manages to be both perfunctory and languid; the jolts can be predicted by any ten-year-old with a stop watch. Only the story in which [the] Evil Plutocrat . . . is eaten alive by cockroaches mixes giggles and grue in the right measure.

> *Richard Corliss, "Jolly Contempt," in* Time *(copyright 1982 Time Inc.; all rights reserved; reprinted by permission from* Time*), Vol. 120, No. 21, November 22, 1982, p. 110.**

MICHAEL SRAGOW

Despite King's plodding prose and facile characters, he's managed to concoct plots multilayered enough to sustain the length, and sometimes the scrutiny, a feature film demands. At his best, he puts everyone in touch with the nightmare anxieties of youth. . . .

[*Creepshow*] is a salute to the cult-beloved EC horror comic books of the early Fifties. As a movie, *Creepshow* is negligible, but as a cultural indicator, it's terrific—a big clue to what even the most skillful and likable schlock-horror purveyors have been up to in all those years since 1957's *I Was a Teenage Werewolf.* They want to make an enormous catharsis for hundreds of thousands of slobs and to make slobs out of nonslobs. To them, the lowest common denominator isn't a term of derision but an admirable goal.

In the only relatively benign episode of *Creepshow,* "The Lonesome Death of Jordy Verrill," King makes the most revealing acting appearance by a writer since his literary peer, Mickey Spillane, played Mike Hammer in *The Girl Hunters.* . . . King plays the title character, a Down East hick and screw-up who thinks his life problems can be solved when a meteorite lands in his yard. Dreaming of making a killing by selling it to the "Department of Meteors" in a local college, Verrill throws a bucket of water on the meteor to cool it off, only to end up catalyzing a weedlike growth that attaches itself to his grass, his house, his fingers, his cheeks—and, as he realizes in the bathroom—to just about everything.

What's fascinating is that King wrote and plays the character as a drooling, slovenly arrested-infant moron. Perhaps Jordy Verrill is King's own worst self-image nightmare. As Jordy Verrill, King's turned his Everyman persona into the Great American Slob. (p. 48)

The EC publications have long been revered for the unbridled brio of their artwork and the uninhibited savagery of their story lines. Indeed, in King's book-long analysis of horror, *Danse Macabre,* King admitted that, for him, the EC comic books are "the epitome of horror." To King, "terror" is the most refined of fearsome emotions because it centers on largely unseen forces. "Horror," according to King, "also invites a physical reaction by showing us something which is physically wrong." And King discerned a *third,* even cruder, level of fear in the EC comic books: "the gag reflex of revulsion," like the infamous comic-book story in which an evil minor-league ballplayer is punished by dismemberment—his body parts used as the bases, bats and ball.

What disturbed me in King's analysis, especially after seeing *Creepshow,* is King's frank admission that, though he tries to *terrorize* the reader, "if I find I cannot terrify him/her, I will try to horrify; and if I find I cannot horrify, I'll go for the gross-out. I'm not proud."

In *Creepshow* . . . he and Romero consistently go for the gross-out. Their five episodes contain three walking corpses, one suicidal living weed, a Tasmanian devil who sinks her teeth into three victims, a few vivid deaths by drowning . . . and one death by cockroaches. Both Romero and King seem to be taking their quasi-comic-book formula simply as an excuse to be as broad as possible in their comedy and fear effects. The best comic moments are reminiscent of *Airplane!* no less—parodies of theatrical, movie and TV clichés . . . pushed to the outer limits of hysteria. The most effective horrific moments work mostly because of their undiluted viciousness—we're invited to share in the sadistic satisfaction that a henpecked husband takes in seeing his shrewish wife clawed and chomped to death.

Romero and King have created a rogue's gallery that looks like the hit list of a crazy, mixed-up kid: the heirs of a country-gentry fortune, college professors, a TV executive, a vaguely Howard Hughes-like tycoon. Along the way, there are some piquant touches—for example, the college professors seem to be teaching at Who's-Afraid-of-Virginia Woolf University. . . . But the movie doesn't have a pulp vision, only a snickering attitude. It's all in the spirit of the young boy in the framing story . . . who says he hopes his comic-book-hating father rots in hell.

Romero and King seem to feel that the purpose of horror is to bring out the crazy mixed-up kid in all of us. . . . (pp. 48, 54)

I'm not enough of a paranoid moralist to suggest that films as silly as *Creepshow* help encourage deviant behavior or lynch mobs, but I *am* enough of an aesthete to feel that the way these moviemakers transform an audience into a Pavlovian mob endangers the art of movies. The only way to enjoy movies like *Creepshow* is to get into the howling and screaming, and that turns movies from dramatic forms into audience-participation shows (*The Slice Is Right*, perhaps, or *Name That Fright!*). They want to prove that underneath our civilized veneer lie frightened cave children. They want to turn us all, for a time, into dumb clucks—Jordy Verrills. (p. 54)

Michael Sragow, "Stephen King's 'Creepshow': The Aesthetics of Gross-Out," in Rolling Stone *(by Straight Arrow Publishers, Inc. © 1982; all rights reserved; reprinted by permission), Issue 383, November 25, 1982, pp. 48, 54.*

PUBLISHERS WEEKLY

In ["**Christine**"], King drives back to familiar terror-territory in a haunted car named Christine—and there will no doubt be truckloads of readers thumbing their way through his 500-odd pages. Arnie Cunningham—a teenager who has never fit in—buys a dilapidated 1958 Plymouth Fury from an equally broken-down Army veteran, Roland LeBay. But Christine—and the soon-dead LeBay—have mysterious regenerative powers; Christine's odometer runs backwards and the car repairs itself. Arnie becomes obsessed by the car and possessed by its previous owner. . . . At times genuinely frightening, but at 500 pages a bit long, "**Christine**" contains some of the best writing King has ever done; his teenage characters are superbly drawn and their dilemma is truly gripping. However, Christine, we soon realize, is just a car, a finally inanimate machine that does not quite live up to the expectations King's human characterizations have engendered.

A review of "Christine," in Publishers Weekly *(reprinted from the February 25, 1983 issue of* Publishers Weekly, *published by R. R. Bowker Company, a Xerox company; copyright © 1983 by Xerox Corporation), Vol. 223, No. 8, February 25, 1983, p. 80.*

John Knowles

1926-

American novelist, short story writer, and essayist.

Fascinated by the era affected by World War II, Knowles often places his fiction during that period. He writes of young heroes facing the tests of modern life. His young male protagonists arrive at a painful awakening, the realization of the evil in society and in themselves. Knowles perceives this realization as their major step toward manhood.

Knowles's most famous novel, *A Separate Peace*, is characteristic of his greatest concerns. This fictional account of a young man's moral and emotional maturation has been consistently popular with young adults since its publication in 1960. Like most of Knowles's other works, *A Separate Peace* portrays two protagonists who battle with the love/hate relationship that evolves out of their strikingly different views of life. Gene and Phineas exemplify Knowles's use of doubles to portray the dichotomy in the American personality, which Knowles characterizes as "a careful Protestant with a savage stirring in his insides."

Following *A Separate Peace*, almost universally considered a classic, beautifully wrought novel, Knowles wrote several works which failed to attain the critical acclaim of this first novel. Even his recent *Peace Breaks Out*, which shares the elite prep school setting and a similar theme with *A Separate Peace*, does not fulfill its promise.

(See also *CLC*, Vols. 1, 4, 10; *Contemporary Authors*, Vols. 17-20, rev. ed.; *Something about the Author*, Vol. 8; and *Dictionary of Literary Biography*, Vol. 6.)

SIMON RAVEN

[*A Separate Peace*], modest as it is in tone, is likely to leave you thinking. The misuse of science now makes it necessary to articulate a new and purely practical form of Pacifism, a Pacifism which, free of crankiness and owing nothing to religious sensitivity, depends entirely on simple common sense. From now on, people must say, war will mean not only a shortage of cakes and ale but the end of everything. It is this form of protest, of personal withdrawal from political folly which, among other things, makes such pleasant reading of John Knowles's *A Separate Peace*. It is the story of two friends at a smart American preparatory school (for 'preparatory' read 'public' in this country) at the time when America first joined the Second World War. In the beginning the younger boys are more or less ignored while their elders are hurriedly prepared for the blood bath; but as time goes on the whole school is efficiently geared to the conditioning of cannon-fodder, and every aspect of work and play comes to be valued, by masters who are themselves too old to fight, only in so far as it is a preparation for the trial to come. . . . Gene, the intellectually inclined narrator, has a fit of insane resentment and causes his athletic friend, Phineas, to break his leg. Phineas, so badly crippled that he will be out of the war in any case, broods over the separate peace thus forced upon him and eventually decides that the war is entirely spurious, that the whole thing has been thought up by Roosevelt, Churchill and the authorities in general simply because they are old men jealous of youth and pleasure. . . .

Phineas, of course, is in part rationalising his annoyance at being out of something; but the more sensitive Gene accepts what he says as an important truth. So privately and together they resist the war and all it implies until reality makes itself felt—sickeningly so—in its own good time. . . . In emphasising the wider theme of this book, I have done less than justice to other matters—the quietly told story of the boys' relationship and its crises, the sweat and hopeless melancholy which pervades the whole. But then the real importance of Mr. Knowles's novel does indeed lie in its account of the attempt, made by two powerless individuals, to dissociate themselves from *them* and the follies for which *they* are responsible. It is an attempt strictly in accord with the principles of the 'commonsense' pacifism I described above—but an attempt doomed to painful failure unless *everyone* makes it. How silly the Generals on both sides, how silly *they* would look then. But Mr. Knowles makes it plain enough (if we hadn't guessed already) that quiet common sense is a feeble match for reality and the Generals: *they* are sure of the last word.

Simon Raven, "No Time for War," in The Spectator (© 1959 by The Spectator; reprinted by permission of The Spectator), Vol. 202, No. 6827, May 1, 1959, p. 630.*

THE TIMES LITERARY SUPPLEMENT

[*A Separate Peace*] is, indeed, a novel of altogether exceptional power and distinction. [Mr. Knowles] writes of a New England preparatory school—what over here would be called a public school—and of two sixteen-year-olds in particular, Finny and Gene, the narrator, who looks back on his wartime schooldays from the standpoint of his present adulthood.

It would be easy to say that Finny is the brilliant, outward-looking athlete, Gene the first-class brain and subtle self-analyser, and that from the element of latent, hardly formulated antagonism which is present in their close friendship springs the tragedy which causes Gene the man to write: "I did not cry then or ever about Finny. I did not cry even when I stood watching him being lowered into his family's strait-laced burial ground outside of Boston. I could not escape a feeling that this was my own funeral, and you do not cry in that case."

It would be easy, but it would be an over-simplification. Mr. Knowles's world is the real world where black-and-white character-contrasts rarely lie conveniently to hand. Gene and Finny can slip in and out of each other's roles and yet remain entirely themselves while doing so. Their relationship has that subtle elusiveness which is entirely human and which novelists, with good reason, find desperately difficult to convey.

The other characters—masters and boys—are all given life and individuality. The school itself, gradually losing something of its relaxed, patrician manner as the war draws closer, is described with precision and economy. There is no gush. There is no smut. If this is Mr. Knowles's first novel it shows an astonishingly firm grasp of the right end of the stick.

> *"School Reports," in* The Times Literary Supplement *(© Times Newspapers Ltd. (London) 1959; reproduced from* The Times Literary Supplement *by permission), No. 2983, May 1, 1959, p. 262.**

MAURICE RICHARDSON

A Separate Peace is a short, thoughtful, ambitious American study of a fatal relationship between two upper-class schoolboys in late adolescence during the war. . . . There are several abrupt and pleasing variations from conventional American attitudes, including a pretence that the war does not exist. Mr Knowles has clearly worked hard on this novel, modelling it carefully on the best neo-Forsterian, Trillingesque lines. Yet somehow it just fails to convince. The school background exerts none of the fascination that generally belongs to these most compelling of institutional frameworks. Gene and Finney seem to be performing their odd psychological warfare in a vacuum. Gene is particularly unsatisfactory; he has almost none of the ego-sense that you expect in a first-person narrator and it makes him difficult to identify with.

> *Maurice Richardson, in his review of "A Separate Peace," in* New Statesman *(© 1959 The Statesman & Nation Publishing Co. Ltd.), Vol. LVII, No. 1468, May 2, 1959, p. 618.*

HARDING LEMAY

"A Separate Peace," John Knowles' first novel, is a consistently admirable exercise in the craft of fiction—disciplined, precise, witty and always completely conscious of intention and effect—and yet, in spite of these rare assets (or perhaps because of them), the novel's final effect is one of remoteness and aridity. The theme, that of the corroding flaw in friendship between young males, has engaged the talents of such disparate writers as Thomas Mann, William Maxwell and Scott Fitzgerald. Having chosen a theme which echoes in every sensitive man's experience, Mr. Knowles chooses further to isolate it from the mainstream of life, almost as if he were examining one case of a disease which rages in an epidemic throughout the rest of the world. All that intelligence and industry, tact and talent can bring to his novel are here, but its virtues breed its defects as the story unfolds. . . .

The force and grief which might have charged "A Separate Peace" with an electric depth are diluted by the restrictions the author has chosen to impose upon his story (especially the deliberate exclusion of parents and backgrounds, as if boys arrive at school from a vacuum) and a somewhat cautious approach which insists upon gazing from a distance upon the seething cauldron of adolescent nature. The sorrows, the guilts, the uncertainties and the exuberance of youth pass in shadow here, sketched with irony and conscious artistry, but it is we the readers who must provide the substance from our response to personal experience in similar relationships.

> *Harding Lemay, "Two Boys and a War Within," in* New York Herald Tribune Book Review *(© I.H.T. Corporation; reprinted by permission), March 6, 1960, p. 6.*

TIME

[*A Separate Peace*, Knowles's] excellent first novel, is remarkable not only for the virtues it possesses but for the faults it lacks. There is little of the melodrama customary in books about adolescence. There is no Wolfeian confluence of the literary and the pituitary—the youthful poet growing an inch a month on a diet of a book a day. The author is no more sentimental or romantic about his hero than Stephen Crane was about the protagonist of *The Red Badge of Courage*. The books are similar in kind and (to a considerable extent) in quality: Author Crane's young soldier had to endure the discovery of fear, and Author Knowles's schoolboy must face the discovery of hatred—a bitter and homicidal knot of hatred in himself. (p. 96)

To insist on a single explication for a book as subtle and brilliant as Author Knowles's would be idle. But one of the things the novelist seems to be saying is that the enemy Gene killed, and loved, is the one every man must kill: his own youth, the innocence that burns too hotly to be endured. (p. 98)

> *"The Leap," in* Time *(copyright 1960 Time Inc.; all rights reserved; reprinted by permission from* Time*), Vol. 75, No. 14, April 4, 1960, pp. 96, 98.*

JAY L. HALIO

[It is] heartening to see a few like John Knowles who, taking his cue from [Ernest Hemingway's] *The Sun Also Rises* rather than from [Hemingway's] *For Whom the Bell Tolls*, has brought back to recent fiction some of the clear craftsmanship and careful handling of form that characterizes our earlier and best fiction in this century. (p. 107)

[Before] man can be redeemed back into social life, he must first come to terms with himself, he must first—as has been said so often of American writers—discover who and what he is. That we must look inward and learn to face honestly what we see there and then move onwards or anyway outwards is necessary if in the long run we are to salvage any part of our humanity—if, indeed, humanity is in the future to have any meaning or value. This is the enterprise carried forward in contemporary literature by such novelists as Angus Wilson in England and Saul Bellow at home; and alongside their novels John Knowles has now placed two brilliant pieces of fiction, *A Separate Peace* (1960) and *Morning in Antibes* (1962 . . .). His gift is different from theirs as theirs is different from each other, for he speaks with a voice that is at once personal and lyrical in a mode that, with the possible exception of Bellow's *The Victim*, neither of the others has as yet attempted. In his first novel, moreover, Knowles achieves a remarkable success in writing about adolescent life at a large boys' school without falling into any of the smart-wise idiom made fashionable by *The Catcher in the Rye* and ludicrously overworked by its many imitators.

A Separate Peace is the story of a small group of boys growing up at an old New England prep school called Devon during the early years of World War II. The principal characters are the narrator, Gene Forrester, and his roommate, Phineas, or "Finny," who has no surname. As yet but remotely aware of the war in Europe or the Pacific, the boys give themselves up during Devon's first summer session to sports and breaking school rules under the instigations of the indefatigable Finny. It is the last brief experience of carefree life they will know, for most of them will graduate the following June. But within this experience, another kind of war subtly emerges, a struggle between Gene, who is a good student and an able competitor in sports, and Finny, who is the school's champion athlete but poor at studying. Believing Finny's instigations aim at ruining his chances to become valedictorian of their class—and so upset the delicate balance of their respective achievements—Gene awakens to a mistaken sense of deadly enmity between them. (Anyone who has attended such schools will immediately recognize this conflict between intellectual and athletic glory.) Impulsively, Gene causes his roommate to fall from a tree during one of their more spectacular games, and cripples him. This is the central episode of the novel, and the fear which lies behind such destructive hatred is its major theme.

How Gene eventually loses this fear, and so is able to enter that other war without hatred, without the need to kill, is the business of the succeeding episodes. Confession by Gene of deliberate viciousness is alone insufficient release; indeed, far from bringing release, it causes deeper injury to Finny and to himself because of its basic half-truth. Freedom comes only after an honest confrontation of both his own nature and that extension of it represented by Finny, whose loss at the end of the novel he must somehow accept and endure. For if, as the book shows, Finny is unfit for war, and hence unfit for a world engaged in a chronic condition of war, it is because of his fundamental innocence or idealism—his regard for the world not as it is, but as it should be—that renders him unfit. Under Finny's influence, most of the summer of 1942 was, for Gene, just such a world; and it is briefly restored during the following winter when, after convalescing, Phineas returns to Devon. But the existence of this world, and the separate peace this world provides, is doomed. In Finny's fall from the tree Gene has violated, or rather surrendered, his innocence, and he learns that any attempt to regain it, to "become a part of Phineas," . . . is at best a transient experience, at worst a gesture of despair. Nor will either of the twin expedients, escape or evasion, serve him. Escape, as it presents itself to Gene after Finny's second fall, the final crisis in the novel, is rejected as

"not so much criminal as meaningless, a lapse into nothing, an escape into nowhere." . . . And evasion—any recourse into the various dodges of sentimentality, such as aggressive arrogance, insensitive factionalism, or self-protective vagueness as variously portrayed by other boys at Devon—such evasion, Gene comes to realize, is only a mask behind which one does not so much seek reality, as hide from it, for it is a mask to cover fear. "Only Phineas never was afraid, only Phineas never hated anyone," the book concludes. The essential harmony of his nature could not allow such emotions, and his "choreography of peace" in a world he alone could create and sustain, as for example during Devon's first, only, and illegal "Winter Carnival," is not the dance of this world. His death, coming as it does on the eve of graduation, is, then, for Gene a kind of necessary sacrifice before he can take the next step. And his forgiveness is Gene's way of forgiving himself for what he at last recognizes is "something ignorant in the human heart," . . . the impersonal, blind impulse that caused Finny's fall and that causes war. It is an acceptance, too, the acceptance (as [T. S.] Eliot shows in *Four Quartets*) of a reality which includes ignorance and prepares for humility, without which the next step remains frozen in mid-air.

In *Morning in Antibes*, Knowles prepares to take the next step—or to complete the first—the step that leads to the possibility of human encounter, of real and fruitful meetings with others. But before actually taking this step, he repeats much of what he has already presented in *A Separate Peace*. Perhaps this repetition is necessary for the shape of the novel, which ostensibly is not a continuation of the first (as part of a trilogy, for example) and must tell its own story. But to readers of Knowles's first book, *Morning in Antibes* unavoidably appears as a retelling, in part, of what he has already demonstrated; and so it drags a bit, if only just slightly. The novel opens with the separation of a young couple, Nicholas and Liliane Bodine, after a brief and unhappy marriage. Nick has left Liliane in Paris for the pleasures and transparent lures of the Riviera and for the love he mistakenly hopes to find there; but his unfaithful wife, now deeply troubled and wanting to reconcile, follows him to Juan-les-Pins. It is the summer of 1958, and reflected against this portrait of impending marital dissolution is the mounting struggle of Algeria to free itself from France during the last days of the Fourth Republic: as in *A Separate Peace*, the private and the public war are clearly related. Before reconciliation is possible, however, or even desirable, both Nick and Lili must suffer an agonizing inward look, recognize their self-limitations with neither exaggeration nor minimizing, and with this knowledge of both good and evil in the human heart, discover the means and the will to forgive, and to love. (pp. 107-10)

[Significantly, a character] enters Nick's life, a young man called Jeannot, whom Nick at first distrusts implicitly: he is an Algerian and all Algerians in France are naturally suspect. But Nick's distrust gradually gives way before Jeannot's gentleness and his profound need to be treated as a human being, even though he is an unemployed Algerian in France during her most stressful period since the War. Nicholas learns a great deal from Jeannot during Liliane's absence, much of it having to do with Jeannot's love for the country which has misprised and misused him. (p. 110)

For it is through Jeannot as much as by his wife's absence—to go on a prolonged cruise with a cynical, degenerate French nobleman—that Nicholas begins to understand what love means and what it demands. Through Jeannot, Nick learns that love begins by valuing (or loving) ourselves justly; only then can we take others at their own just evaluation. Love prevents either party from imposing false valuations upon themselves. In this way Nick's relationship with Jeannot grows and flourishes. (p. 111)

As a second novel, *Morning in Antibes* stands up well against *A Separate Peace,* although readers will doubtless recognize the superior achievement of Knowles's first book. Finny's fall from the tree, while it makes use of old and familiar symbolism, loses none of its power but gains instead by its complete integration within a realistic design. By contrast, Nick's skin-diving episode just before Liliane returns to Juan-les-Pins, though it draws upon equally ancient symbols, parallels too closely Jake Barnes' deep dives off San Sebastian in *The Sun Also Rises.* Here, as in other places, such as a few clipped passages of dialogue, or some detailed descriptions of French cuisine, a purely literary recollection intervenes, detracting from the reader's experience of the presentation and robbing it of some of its felt reality. Nevertheless, in his second novel Knowles retains much of the individual voice mentioned earlier; despite the occasional ventriloquism, it is still there. Moreover, he demonstrates an important development of his theme, and we may well wait for what he has to say next with aroused expectations. (p. 112)

Jay L. Halio, "John Knowles's Short Novels," in Studies in Short Fiction *(copyright 1964 by Newberry College), Vol. 1, No. 2, Winter, 1964, pp. 107-12.*

JAMES ELLIS

To read *A Separate Peace* is to discover a novel which is completely satisfactory and yet so provocative that the reader wishes immediately to return to it. John Knowles' achievement is due, I believe, to his having successfully imbued his characters and setting with a symbolism that while informative is never oppressive. Because of this the characters and the setting retain both the vitality of verisimilitude and the psychological tension of symbolism.

What happens in the novel is that Gene Forrester and Phineas, denying the existence of the Second World War as they enjoy the summer peace of Devon School, move gradually to a realization of an uglier adult world—mirrored in the winter and the Naguamsett River—whose central fact is the war. This moving from innocence to adulthood is contained within three sets of interconnected symbols. These three—summer and winter; the Devon River and the Naguamsett River; and peace and war—serve as a backdrop against which the novel is developed, the first of each pair dominating the early novel and giving way to the second only after Gene has discovered the evil of his own heart.

The reader is introduced to the novel by a Gene Forrester who has returned to Devon after an absence of fifteen years, his intention being to visit the two sites which have influenced his life—the tree, from which he shook Finny to the earth, and the First Academy Building, in which Finny was made to realize Gene's act. (p. 313)

Described as ". . . tremendous, an irate, steely black steeple," the tree is a part of the senior class obstacle course in their preparation for war and is the focal center of the first part of the novel. As the Biblical tree of knowledge it is the means by which Gene will renounce the Eden-like summer peace of Devon and, in so doing, both fall from innocence and at the

same time prepare himself for the second world war. (pp. 313-14)

What Finny represents . . . is the pure spirit of man (mirrored in the boy Finny) answering its need to share the experience of life and innocent love. For Finny the war and the tree, which represents a training ground for the war, are only boyish delights. The reality of war is lost upon him because he is constitutionally pure and incapable of malice. . . .

The tragedy of the novel ultimately is that Gene is not capable of maintaining the spiritual purity that distinguishes Phineas and so must as he discovers his own savagery betray Phineas. . . .

Incapable of the spiritual purity of Phineas, Gene finds himself jealous of Finny's ability to flout Devon rules in his quest to enjoy an "unregulated friendliness" with the adult world. (p. 314)

It is during a bicycle trip to the beach on the morning of the day on which Gene will push Finny from the tree that Finny confides to Gene that he is his best friend. Gene, however, cannot respond. He says: "I nearly did. But something held me back. Perhaps I was stopped by that level of feeling, deeper than thought, which contains the truth." . . . The effect of this trip is to cause Gene to fail a trigonometry test and thereby to bring his hatred of Finny into the open. . . .

Later, just before he will shake Finny from the tree, Gene confronts Phineas with his suspicions. Finny's surprise at the charge is such that Gene realizes its falsity. Confronted with the evident truth of Finny's denial, Gene understands his inferiority to Phineas and his own moral ugliness, made the more so when juxtaposed to Finny's innocence. It is this realization that prompts his conscious shaking of the tree, which casts Phineas to the earth and which serves as Gene's initiation into the ignorance and moral blackness of the human heart.

Returning to the fall session without Phineas, Gene finds that peace has deserted Devon. And replacing the freedom of his careless summer are the rules of Devon, to which Gene now gives his allegiance.

Unable to take part in the boyish activities and sports of Devon because of his guilt, Gene attempts to find anonymity in a dead-end job as assistant crew manager. But here, confronted with the arrogance of Cliff Quackenbush (about whom there is an aura of undefined ugliness which separates him from the other boys), Gene is forced to defend Phineas from a slighting remark. This fight between Gene and Quackenbush concludes with their tumbling into the Naguamsett River.

Both the Naguamsett and the Devon flow through the grounds of the school; but it had been into the Devon, a familiar and bucolic river suggestive of Eden, that Finny and Gene had jumped from the tree. But after his fall from innocence, Gene experiences a baptism of a different sort as he plunges into the Naguamsett—a saline, marshy, ugly river "governed by unimaginable factors like the Gulf Stream, the Polar Ice Cap, and the moon." (p. 315)

The return of Phineas to Devon signals the rejuvenation and regeneration of Gene. Immediately prior to Finny's return, Gene had discovered in Brinker's announcement of his intention to enlist a chance to close the door on the pain that has haunted him since his crime against Finny. . . . But with Phineas' return and Gene's realization that Phineas needs him to help him maintain his integrity, Gene finds moral purpose and determines to live out his life at Devon with Finny. . . . With Gene's resolution, peace returns to Devon and the war is forgotten.

For Phineas, who had even before his fall denied the American bombing of Central Europe, the war is a make-believe—a rumor started by various villains who wish to keep the pure spirit of youth enslaved. (p. 316)

What is important in Finny's theory is that it makes of the war an adult device which curtails the enjoyment of youth and its gifts. To accept the war is for Finny to accept a fallen world. So persuasive is his own illusion and his own magnetic power that Gene is momentarily caught up in it and can deny the war, the denial, however, being occasioned not so much by Finny's explanation as it is by Gene's "own happiness" in having momentarily evaded the ugliness of the war.

The Phineas-inspired Devon Winter Carnival is the occasion during which Gene is to be paraded in all his Olympic glory, signifying that he, through consecrating himself to Finny's tutelage, has become like Phineas. About this winter carnival and his brilliant decathlon performance, Gene says:

> It wasn't the cider which made me surpass myself, it was this liberation we had torn from the gray encroachments of 1943, the escape we had concocted, this afternoon of momentary, illusory, special and separate peace. . . .

Yet even as this illusion is achieved, a telegram arrives from Leper, an "escapee" from the war, come back to destroy Gene's illusion of withdrawing from the war.

At Leper's home in Vermont, Gene finds himself accused of having been responsible for Finny's fall. Later, after the heat of the accusation has passed, the two boys walk in the snow-covered fields while Leper reveals the horror of the military. As he talks, Gene hears the "frigid trees . . . cracking with the cold." To his ears they sound "like rifles being fired in the distance." This paralleling of the trees (the scene of Gene's fall in particular and nature in general) with the war (and hence the ignorance of the human heart, which is responsible for both war and private evil) is given reverberation at Gene's inquisition when Leper describes Gene and Finny as they stood in the tree just before Finny's fall. To Leper they looked "black as death with this fire [the sun] burning all around them; and the rays of the sun were shooting past them, millions of rays shooting past them like—like golden machine-gun fire." . . . Nature then is presented as both damned and damning, with man's death and fall insured by nautre's deadly fire and by his own inability to escape the savage within himself.

For Gene, as he listens to Leper, the ugliness of the war finally becomes so forcefui that he must run. . . .

What Gene wants is to return to the world of the winter carnival and his training for the Olympics, his and Phineas' withdrawal from the ugliness of the world. (p. 317)

The reconciliation of Gene and Finny after Finny's refusal to accept Brinker's "f——ing facts" and his fall provides the culmination of the novel. Questioned by Finny, Gene denies that his pushing of Phineas was personal. Beginning to understand himself, Gene says: "It was just some ignorance inside me, some crazy thing inside me, something blind, that's all.". . . And joined with this realization is Gene's admission that war, despite Phineas, does exist and that it grows out of the ignorance of the human heart. In rejecting Brinker's thesis

that wars can be laid to one's parents and their generation, Gene says: ". . . It seemed clear that wars were not made by generations and their special stupidities, but that wars were made instead by something ignorant in the human heart.". . . Gene has discovered that his private evil, which caused him to hurt Phineas, is the same evil—only magnified—that results in war.

Finny alone, Gene now knows, was incapable of malice. (pp. 317-18)

Because of his ability to admit only so much of the ugliness of life as he could assimilate, Phineas was unique. Gene says:

> No one else I have ever met could do this. All others at some point found something in themselves pitted violently against something in the world around them. With those of my year this point often came when they grasped the fact of the war. When they began to feel that there was this overwhelmingly hostile thing in the world with them, then the simplicity and unity of their characters broke and they were not the same again.
>
> Phineas alone had escaped this. He possessed an extra vigor, a heightened confidence in himself, a serene capacity for affection which saved him. Nothing as he was growing up at home, nothing at Devon, nothing even about the war had broken his harmonious and natural unity. So at last I had. . . .

It is because of his having known and loved Phineas that Gene can recognize that hatred springs from a greater evil that is within. It is the realization of this that releases him from the hysteria of the war, which now moves from its controlling position off-stage onto the campus of Devon in the form of the parachute riggers.

Unlike his friends who had sought through some building of defenses to ward off the inevitability of evil, Gene has come to see that this enemy never comes from without, but always from within. He knows, moreover, that there is no defense to be built, only an acceptance and purification of oneself through love. Such a love did he share with Phineas in a private gypsy summer. And it is because of the purity of this love that he is able to survive his fall from innocence. (p. 318)

James Ellis, "'A Separate Peace': The Fall from Innocence," in English Journal *(copyright © 1964 by the National Council of Teachers of English; reprinted by permission of the publisher), Vol. LIII, No. 5, May, 1964, pp. 313-18.*

RONALD WEBER

Professor Halio's recent appreciation of the two short novels of John Knowles [see excerpt above] was especially welcome. Knowles's work, and in particular his fine first novel, *A Separate Peace,* has not yet received the close attention it merits. In a time that has seen high praise for fat, awkwardly-managed novels, he stands out as a precise and economical craftsman. For this alone he demands serious consideration.

Although Professor Halio calls attention to this technical achievement—Knowles, he writes, "has brought back to recent fiction some of the clear craftsmanship and careful handling of form that characterizes our earlier and best fiction in this century'' . . .—he is not concerned to illustrate it. He is more interested in examining what he sees as Knowles's second strong point: a thematic concern with the individual's efforts to come to terms with himself as a prior condition to his coming to terms with his society. A reversal of this emphasis—focusing on technique and the relationship of technique to theme—can, I believe, add something to an understanding of Knowles's work. (p. 63)

[A] comparison of *A Separate Peace* with [*The Catcher in the Rye*]—especially a comparison of the way narrative method relates to theme—offers a useful approach to Knowles's novel.

In both books the narrative is presented from a first-person point of view; both Holden Caulfield and Gene Forrester tell their own stories, stories in which they serve not only as observers but as narrator-agents who stand at the center of the action. Generally, first-person narration gives the reader a heightened sense of immediacy, a sense of close involvement with the life of the novel. This surely is one of the charms of *Catcher* and one of the reasons for its immense popularity. The reader, particularly the young reader, is easily caught up in the narrative and held fast by a voice and an emotional experience he finds intensely familiar. With Knowles's novel, however, this is not the case. While the reader may greatly admire the book, it does not engage him quite as directly or perhaps even as deeply as *Catcher;* throughout it he remains somewhat outside the action and detached from the narrator, observing the life of the novel rather than submerged in it. This difference in reader response, taking place as it does within the framework of first-person, narrator-as-protagonist telling, is, I believe, a highly-calculated effect on Knowles's part. It indicates a sharply different thematic intention, and one that is rooted in a skillful alteration of the conventional method of first-person telling.

Holden Caulfield never comes to an understanding of his experience. He never quite knows what it means; he only feels certain things about it. . . . Gene Forrester, on the other hand, arrives at a clear understanding—a deeply felt knowledge—of the experience he narrates. At the end of the novel he knows, unlike Holden, precisely what he thinks about it.

Understanding demands a measure of distance. We can seldom understand an experience, truly know it, until we are clearly removed from it—removed in time and removed in attitude. Holden achieves such distance only slightly, hence his understanding is slight at best. He tells his story at only a short remove in time from the actual experience of it. It all took place, the reader learns at the start, ''around last Christmas.'' . . . Just as there has been some lapse of time between the experience and the telling, there has also been some shift in Holden's attitude. At the end of the novel, when we again return to the opening perspective, the recuperating Holden now thinks he will apply himself when he returns to school, just as he now sort of misses the people he has told about. In both cases, however, Holden is not sufficiently separated from his experience, either in time or attitude, to admit any real mastery of it.

Holden's relation to the experience of the novel illustrates a major problem of first-person telling. Although the method, by narrowing the sense of distance separating reader, narrator, and fictional experience, gains a quality of immediacy and freshness, it tends for the same reason to prohibit insight or understanding. . . . Understanding exists in *Catcher,* but not self-understanding for Holden. Because of the intense method

of narration, narrowing rather than enlarging the sense of distance in the novel, understanding exists only for the reader, and then only by implication. This situation, as we shall see, is wholly congenial to Salinger's thematic intention; Knowles, however, seeks a different end, and therefore he must somehow modify the effect of his narrative method.

Unlike Holden, Gene Forrester is separated by a broad passage of time from the experience he relates. ''I went back to the Devon School not long ago,'' Gene says in the novel's opening sentence, ''and found it looking oddly newer than when I was a student there fifteen years before.'' . . . That this lapse in time between the experience and the telling has brought understanding is also established early. . . . Although Knowles quickly leaves the distant perspective and turns to immediate scene, he keeps the reader aware that Gene is looking back on the experience with a mature vision. At one point, for example, the distant perspective suddenly opens up at the end of a scene when Gene says: ''But in a week I had forgotten that, and I have never since forgotten the dazed look on Finny's face when he thought that on the first day of his return to Devon I was going to desert him.'' . . . (pp. 64-6)

The distant point of the narration allows a detachment that permits Gene the mastery of his experience. Even when Knowles gives over the narrative wholly to immediate scene the reader is reminded, sometimes with a phrase, at other times with an entire passage, of the perspective. The war, in addition, serves to create an increased sense of distance, a removal in attitude, within the story. Although the war touches Devon School only slightly—one of the joys of the summer session is that it seems totally removed from the world of war—it cannot be forgotten or ignored for long; it exists not only as an event that stands between the experience of the novel and Gene's telling, but as an event that, at the very moment of the experience, dominates the life of each character. ''The war,'' Gene says in retrospect, ''was and is reality for me. I still instinctively live and think in its atmosphere.'' . . . The anticipation of war forces Gene and his companions into a slight yet significant detachment from their life at Devon—a life that, at times, seems unimportant and even unreal—and towards an unusual amount of serious, if carefully guarded, reflection. The relation between the fact of war and the atmosphere of detachment or removal in the novel—removal, again, necessary for understanding—can be seen in Phineas' disclosure that, despite his humorous disavowal of the existence of the war, he has been trying for some time to enlist. . . . (p. 66)

Gene comes to self-understanding only gradually through a series of dramatic episodes, as we shall see; the final extent of his understanding can, however, be indicated by a passage from the concluding chapter. ''I was ready for the war,'' he says, thinking ahead to his entry into the army, ''now that I no longer had any hatred to contribute to it. My fury was gone, I felt it gone, dried up at the source, withered and lifeless.'' . . . This final awareness contrasts sharply with Holden Caulfield's lack of self-understanding at the end of *Catcher.* While Holden, looking back on his experience, thinks he may be somewhat changed, Gene is certain he is a radically different person. This differing response of the characters to the experience they relate is additionally underscored for the reader by the tone of their narration. In each case, Holden and Gene indicate their relation to their experience as much by how they speak as by what they say and when they say it. Holden's voice, uncertain at times and dogmatic at others, is always exuberant and emotional; it is a voice vividly responsive to the experience of the novel but one that suggests little mastery of it. Gene's voice, on the other hand, is dispassionate, reflective, and controlled; it is, in his own words, a voice from which fury is gone, dried up at its source long before the telling begins. If Holden's voice is that of the restless adolescent groping for an uncertain maturity, Gene's is a voice looking back on adolescence after the hard passage to maturity has been won.

It is clear that Knowles, to return to Professor Halio's phrase, does not fall into the "smart-wise idiom made fashionable" by Salinger's novel. He does not follow in Salinger's wake because of the important variation he works on the method of first-person narration used in *Catcher*. By attempting to maintain a sense of distance within a narrative method that naturally tends to narrow distance, he sacrifices some of the method's freshness to gain depth and insight. In *Catcher* the reader, with Holden, tends to respond to the experience with feeling rather than knowledge; understanding exists for him in the novel only by implication. In *A Separate Peace* the reader, with Gene, remains partially detached from the experience, able to examine and reflect upon it; and understanding can finally take the form of direct statement.

At this point we can begin to see some connection between Knowles's narrative method and his thematic concern. Again, comparison with *Catcher* is useful. Both novels, in a broad and very basic sense, are concerned with the response of the central character to an awareness of evil in the world; they are narratives in which the characters confront, during a concentrated period, part of the reality of life. In face of this reality Holden Caulfield suffers a severe physical and mental breakdown. At the end of the novel, when Holden admits he misses the people he has told about—the assorted phonies who represent the world—the reader is to understand that he now has begun to make some beginning accommodation with that world. Holden of course does not understand this change; it is, as we have said, merely a new feeling, a feeling of missing people he previously despised. Although it is clear that some change has taken place in Holden, it is important to see that it is explained in terms of other people; what must in fact be an inner change—Holden arriving at some peace within himself—is communicated in exterior terms.

In the course of his maturing process, Gene Forrester likewise must confront the fact of evil in the world. But in this case the location of that evil is quite different. At the very beginning of the novel, . . . Gene, looking back fifteen years, says he can see with great clarity the "fear" he had lived in at Devon School and that he has succeeded in making his "escape" from. Even now, he adds, he can feel "fear's echo," and this in turn leads him back to the direct experience of the story. . . . The meaning of this experience is to be found in the development of the words *fear* and *escape*—in Gene's growing realization of what they mean as well as what they do not mean. (pp. 67-9)

[Gene] comes to the conclusion that Phineas, the school's finest athlete, envies him his academic success. This knowledge instantly shatters any notions he has had of "affection and partnership and sticking by someone and relying on someone absolutely in the jungle of a boys' school." . . . He now sees that he has been envious of Phineas too—envious to the point of complete enmity. (p. 69)

When Phineas, in a moment of seriousness, urges him to stick with his studies rather than come along on a campus diversion,

Gene suddenly sees he has been wrong—Phineas has never envied him. During a scene immediately following, in which he and Phineas perch in a tree waiting to leap into a river below, Gene is overwhelmed by the implications of this new insight:

> Any fear I had ever had of the tree was nothing beside this. It wasn't my neck, but my understanding which was menaced. He had never been jealous of me for a second. Now I knew that there never was and never could have been any rivalry between us. I was not of the same quality as he. I couldn't stand this. . . .

It is at this moment that he causes Phineas to fall from the tree, an "accident" that cripples him and ends his athletic career. After watching Phineas crash through the branches of the tree and hit the bank, Gene jumps confidently into the river, "every trace of my fear of this forgotten." . . . (p. 70)

It is Phineas' innocence that Gene cannot endure. As long as he can believe Phineas shares his enmity, he can find relief; but with this assurance gone, he stands condemned before himself and must strike out against his tormentor. *Fear,* again, is the key word. Fear in this instance is the emotional response to the discovery of hate, the vast depths of enmity that exist within the human heart. Gene loses his fear and achieves his separate, personal peace only when he acknowledges this fundamental truth. It is a truth that he must first recognize and then accept; he can neither avoid it, as he tries to do in his first encounter with Phineas after the accident . . . , nor flee from it, as he again seeks to do when Leper charges that he always has been a "savage underneath." . . . He can find escape from fear only in the acceptance of its true source and the location of that source. Gene must come to see and endure the truth, as he finally does in a climactic scene just before Phineas dies from a second fall, that his fear is the product not of rivalry nor of circumstance but of "some ignorance inside me, some crazy thing inside me, something blind." (pp. 70-1)

None of Gene's companions at Devon could bring themselves to face this inner source of their fear. When they began to feel this "overwhelmingly hostile thing in the world with them," . . . they looked beyond themselves and felt themselves violently pitted against something in the outer world. When they experienced this "fearful shock" of the "sighting of the enemy," they began an "obsessive labor of defense" and began to parry the menace they thought they saw facing them. They all

> constructed at infinite cost to themselves these Maginot Lines against this enemy they thought they saw across the frontier, this enemy who never attacked that way—if he ever attacked at all; if he was indeed the enemy. . . .

The infinite cost in this case is the loss of self-knowledge. Only Phineas is an exception; only Phineas "never was afraid" because only he "never hated anyone." . . . Phineas alone is free of the awareness of that hostile thing that is to be found not across any battlefield but within the fortress itself. As the archetypal innocent, he must serve as the sacrifice to Gene's maturity. (p. 71)

Gene Forrester comes to learn that his war, the essential war, is fought out on the battlefield within. Peace comes only when he faces up to this fact. The only escape, the price of peace, is self-awareness. One finds the resolution of Holden Caulfield's war, on the other hand, beyond him, in his relation to society. As Holden flees a corrupt world he is driven increasingly in upon himself, but towards collapse rather than awareness. Salinger presents the hope that is finally raised for him not in terms of self-knowledge but in the ability to move out of himself. It is not, then, awareness that is offered for him so much as a kind of accommodation; he must somehow learn to live, as Mr. Antolini tells him, with what is sickening and corrupt in human behavior. Although this implies facing up to what is corrupt in his own nature, this is not Salinger's emphasis. He seeks to focus the novel outside Holden rather than within him; and for this the conventional method of first-person narration with its tendency to narrow and intensify the story, eliminating the sense of distance vital for the narrator's self-understanding, is admirably suited. Knowles, using a similar but skillfully altered narrative method, develops a very different theme—that awareness, to put it baldly, must precede accommodation, that to look without before having first searched within is tragically to confuse the human condition. To convey his theme Knowles modifies the first-person narrative to create for both narrator and reader an atmosphere of detachment that permits the novel to be focused within Gene, where, he shows, a basic truth of life is to be found.

While the reader may come to feel the experience of *A Separate Peace* somewhat less than that of *Catcher*, he eventually knows it more. While Salinger may give him a stronger sense of life, Knowles provides a clearer statement about life. Although the two novels work towards different ends with different means, they help finally to illustrate, in their separate ways, the close functional relation of meaning and method of telling in carefully-wrought fiction. (pp. 71-2)

Ronald Weber, "Narrative Method in 'A Separate Peace'," in Studies in Short Fiction *(copyright 1965 by Newberry College), Vol. III, No. 1, Fall, 1965, pp. 63-72.*

PAUL WITHERINGTON

The development and resolution of tensions between Gene and Finny provide the well-balanced structure of *A Separate Peace,* as several critics have noted. What has not been appreciated, however, is the ambiguity of the boys' conflict in its several phases, an ambiguity expressed in both character and symbol. The story is not a simple allegory of man's fortunate or unfortunate fall from innocence, or even an extension of that theological debate to the process of growing up, though both of these arguments are in the novel. Rather, Knowles is investigating patterns of society as a whole, patterns consisting of ambiguous tensions between rigidity and flexibility, involvement and isolation, and magic and art. To understand the necessity of a broader interpretation of the novel than has been generally given, one must see that for Knowles opposite emotions and forces often only seem to face or move in contrary directions.

The relationship between Finny and Gene is said to be one of primitive innocence confronted with and eventually destroyed by the necessities of civilization. Natural, noble Finny, another of the durable procession of American Adams, is maimed and hounded out of Eden by the hatred he is finally forced to see in his best friend, Gene. On the other hand, Gene's emerging recognition of his guilt in Finny's fall from the tree signals his passage from childhood's innocent play to the responsible eth-

ical concerns of adulthood. Phrased socially rather than theologically, there is a movement toward acceptance of the outside world—that of World War II—and corresponding acceptance of the fact that wars occur not only between nations but between individuals, sometimes even friends, and that the blame in either case can be traced to lack of understanding, an ignorance in the human heart. (p. 795)

Knowles resists defining innocence and evil and their interaction in simplified, allegoric terms. If there are parallels to Eden, they must surely be ironic, for Finny falls physically without sin whereas Gene falls spiritually without any recognizable physical discomfort. Finny's fall (he falls twice, actually, once from the tree and once on the steps at Devon) seems to represent an awareness of evil that is incompatible with his basic assumptions about unity and goodness; his gradual acceptance of Gene's hostility is accompanied by a physical decline which is strongest at the moments of greatest disillusion. But this awareness of evil remains merely physical in Finny. When asked how he knows that World War II is not real, he says, "Because I've suffered." It appears that nothing is learned after all, that Finny never really understands the world around him; his fall is sad, but nothing more. Gene, on the other hand, seems to endure and even to thrive on his knowledge of evil. His metaphysical fall is, after all, painless, for unlike Claggart in [Herman] Melville's allegory of good and evil, *Billy Budd,* Gene is untouched by the thrust of mistreated innocence; his moments of mental anguish seem strangely inadequate when compared to those of his classmate, Leper. Greek drama develops in Western literature the notion of suffering as a means to understanding, and American literature is full of innocents who fall from purity only to gain a much more valuable wisdom, but the irony in Knowles is that the sufferer does not understand the nature or purpose of his suffering, and the one who does not suffer both understands and prospers. (pp. 795-96)

Apparently complicating matters still further is Finny's announcement near the end of the novel that he has really known there was a war all the time, that his pretending otherwise was his defense against being unable to go to war with his friends. Knowles may have gotten himself into a structural dilemma here; what seems at first in Finny a genuine misconception of human character, a metaphysical innocence, has become a rationalization, the suppression of an unpleasant fact; illusion becomes delusion, and the reader may conclude that Knowles has lost control of his character, that what started as a semi-abstract personification of innocence has come to life as a fully realized character who says that, after all, the grapes really were sour.

The answer to these problems is that Finny is no more of a spiritually pure being than Gene is a spiritually depraved being. Both boys project their inadequacies onto others; Gene's transfer of his own hostility onto Finny is balanced by Finny's notion that wars are contrived by "fat old men" who profit from wartime economy. Moreover, Finny is a breaker of rules, not incidentally but systematically. . . . Finny's anarchy, however, gives rise to a set of rules just as rigid as the school's and just as imperative. . . . Finny's effort to entice Gene from his studies appears just as conscious as Gene's movement of the tree limb causing Finny's fall.

There is something almost diabolical about Finny's "innocence." His power over people is uncanny; Gene describes it as hypnotic, and it consists of inducing others temporarily to suspend their practical, logical systems of belief to follow his non-logical argument, acted out either verbally or on the playing fields. The answers he gives in class are "often not right but could rarely be branded as wrong," . . . for they presuppose a world in which ordinary standards of judgment are impossible. Finny's pranks themselves—skipping classes and meals, wearing the school tie as a belt, playing poker in the dorm—are actually serious offenses only within the disciplinary framework of a prep school. The audacity is his defense of them which is always disconcerting because it is never relevant, or sometimes too relevant, as when he is being frank about a normally touchy subject. Finny's simplicity, by its very rarity, tends to shock and to threaten the established order of things, to throw ordinary people off balance.

Further ambiguity exists in the imagery of flow which Knowles uses to describe Finny's harmony with others and with his environment. Friendship to Finny is a harmony of equal tensions and movements. Like his idea that everybody always wins at sports, this notion of reciprocal benevolence naively presupposes a level of human interaction superior not only to individual selfishness but also to pressures and events of the actual world. . . . Finny cannot understand why people build walls between what they feel and what they let others know they feel; his benevolence, a two-way avenue between friends, is his reason for being. His walk, his play and even his body itself are described as a flow, a harmony within and without, a primitive attunement to natural cycles. The world of graduation, the draft, and adult necessity is oriented differently, however, and Finny's rhythm is broken in his fall into the civilized world. . . . After Finny's second fall, on the stairs, he dies when bone marrow gets in the bloodstream and stops his heart.

Yet Knowles is careful not to oversimplify nor to sentimentalize Finny's stopped flow, the heart ruptured by a violent world. Like the Devon River, that clear, innocent center of summer fun in which the boys play their last summer of childhood, Finny is shut off from natural progress, dammed into isolation and perpetual youth. . . . There is irony in the fact that Gene's rigid, West Point stride endures, whereas Finny's graceful body breaks so easily; of course Finny risks much more, for his position is supported precariously by shaky illusions. . . . Finny's flawed flow steadily becomes worse with each new awareness of the hate around him.

Finally, love and hate are themselves ambiguous in *A Separate Peace*, from Gene's first suspicions of an undercurrent of rivalry till the time in the army when he wonders if the "enemy" he killed at Devon was really an enemy at all. Gene is never sure of his relationship with Finny because he—like the reader who sees the action through Gene's eyes—is never sure what Finny represents, whether he is a well-meaning friend who simply resists growing up, a pernicious fraud acting out of spite, or a neurotic who builds protective illusions.

Ambiguity, then, seems to be Knowles' method of showing that people and their emotions must be treated as complex rather than as simple. Good and evil, love and hatred, involvement and isolation, self and selflessness are not always clearly defined nor their values constant. Part of growing up is the recognition that the human condition is a dappled one, that the wrong we feel in things is often only some pattern erected by fear and ignorance, some rigidity that divides life into lifeless compartments. It remains to show how these patterns are fashioned in the novel and what their effects are on the central characters. (pp. 796-97)

The major patterns, of course, are those described in Finny and Gene, ways of approaching the problems posed by growing up and adjusting to civilization, patterns for the two boys respectively of magic and naturalism.

For Finny, life is a continuous effort to control reality by creating comfortable myths about it. War is only make-believe on the fields and rivers of Devon: a game resembling football and soccer is invented and named, for its speed and devastating unpredictability, "blitzball;" snowball fights are staged as military operations; the tree hanging over the Devon River is a torpedoed ship that must be evacuated. But these games which at first seem to have the practical function of preparing boys mentally and physically for war actually become shields against reality, ways of sugarcoating the externals of war by making its participants invulnerable, like playful Olympian deities. . . . [The] real basis for Finny's notion that everybody always wins at sports is his idea that the game consists in finding a proper method of play which then makes its outcome irrelevant. His rigidity in this respect is most apparent in a game he plays badly, poker. Following a plan that ought to win, Finny ignores the fact that he actually never does, even when the game is his own weird invention, like a child who asks and keeps asking a question, learning the language by which to frame it and seeming not to hear the answer that is given.

Finny appears essential to Devon's organized defense against war, not only because he directs the boys' last peaceful summer of play and infuses it with ideals of love and equal interaction, but because he seems to have the power to sustain this idyllic atmosphere beyond its natural limits. Described by Gene, Finny is a primitive, god-like priest celebrating the essential unity and indestructibility of man and nature and mediating between the two. . . . Even after he falls from the tree, Finny preserves this function as priest. His broken body makes winter seem inevitable but only temporary, and his creation of the winter carnival by fiat . . . is an act of magic designed to recreate the harmony of summer. The ritual is begun by burning [Homer's] *Iliad,* not so much as a protest against war as a magical attempt to destroy war by destroying an early, typical account of it. Standing on a table at the ceremonies, hopping about on his one good leg in protest against war and deformity, Finny tries to represent life as he feels it should be; the others, intoxicated with their desire for earlier, less demanding forms of existence, allow Finny to lead them in this "choreography of peace," . . . suggesting Hart Crane's line in *The Bridge:* "Lie to us—dance us back the tribal morn."

In Finny's universe all things are possible as long as the bulwark of illusion holds; as long as Finny can believe each morning, for example, that his leg has overnight been miraculously healed, there is evidence for all magic, not only his but that of a sympathetic universe. When reality does not meet his expectations, though, he is gradually forced into a defensive position. At Gene's "trial" by fellow students, Finny testifies that he believed the tree itself shook him out and tumbled him to the ground. This is more than a defense of Gene, just as the "trial" is more than Gene's; it is Finny's defense of himself, of his notions of reciprocal benevolence and of the inner harmony of all things, and of that supernatural world which sustains these illusions. The evidence convicts him as well as Gene, but— as his second fall shows—Finny cannot adapt to the fact of a Darwinian universe, a world where there are no absolute principles, but only the reality met in experience. . . . The fall comes—as in so many movie cartoons—not when one does the impossible, but when one realizes that he is doing what in fact is impossible. Finny dies when he realizes he has had no magic, that he can no longer, as Knowles puts it, exist "primarily in space.". . . The other boys are propelled forward into the real world by the force of Finny's violent death, for spring inexorably comes in spite of his physical decay, and the correspondence between the priest and the object of his religion is broken.

Finny's imagination moves always from war to play, first grasping the game as a simile for war and then—when the thought of training for something which he cannot use becomes unendurable—playing the game as a substitute for war. The imaginations of the other boys move in opposite directions, from play to war, for that is the way of growing up, recognizing that the patterns of childhood are masks behind which stand the real patterns of life. One day at Devon these different imaginations, facing opposite directions, reach a high moment of dramatic tension in a mock snow war that prefigures Finny's death. . . . [Gene] has for some time had conscious premonitions about things to come, about a turned-inside-out situation where games become real wars: "I didn't trust myself in them, and I didn't trust anyone else. It was as though football players were really bent on crushing the life out of each other, as though boxers were in combat to the death, as though even a tennis ball might turn into a bullet.". . . This is a prelude to the awareness that world wars are but expansions of individual hatred and ignorance and therefore anticlimactic to the anguish of growing up. For Gene the war with Germany and Japan is a simile for his experiences at Devon, less intense because less personal.

The ability to see patterns between world wars and personal wars and between friendly and hostile conflict is to see at once the horrible depravity and the irony of the world where varying and even conflicting experiences often take on the same form. This consciousness of ambiguity, this appreciation of the variety and relativity of human experience, is what Gene learns. His movement, in short, is not toward the primitive, magical effort to control reality in the sense of making it fit preconceived ideas but toward the naturalistic effort to understand reality by relating it to forms of personal experience. As the patterns of experience are realized, they take on meaning, and this meaning itself is a kind of control, not that of the magician but of the artist who finds order and harmony in the structure of things rather than in categorical moral imperatives.

Rejecting Finny's magical view promotes in Gene a new awareness of self and a new self-responsibility. As the compulsive rituals of Finny give way to Gene's nonprescriptive view, and myth is conceived as serving experience rather than dictating it, Gene separates himself from his environment and recognizes in himself the capabilities for idealism and hatred he had formerly projected on the outside world. This emancipation is represented symbolically in Gene's changing relationship with Finny. At first he thinks of himself, rather guiltily, as an extension of Finny, but after becoming an athlete in his own right he sees Finny as smaller, both relatively and absolutely, like memories from childhood, like the tree at Devon which seemed "high as a beanstalk" and yet is scarcely recognizable years later. Finally Gene thinks of himself as including Finny ("Phineas-filled"), and this indicates his maturity: preserving the myth associated with Finny but only so it can serve him as it serves the artist, as a metaphor for experience.

Finny tries to construct a separate peace by explaining away the war as a fraud or by ignoring its content of violence, and

Knowles' message is, of course, that this is impossible. Much as Finny's ideal world of changelessness, irresponsibility, and illusion is desirable—and Knowles does present it as desirable—one must eventually abandon it for the world of possibility. Gene's final comment, made on his return to Devon years after the major action of the novel, is the key to what he has learned from the tragedy of Finny: "Nothing endures, not a tree, not love, not even a death by violence. Changed, I headed back through the mud. I was drenched; anybody could see it was time to come in out of the rain.". . . Gene frees himself from fear not by hiding from war and the ambiguities of the human heart, not by building barriers between youth and age, but by accepting the inevitability of change and loss. The act of coming in out of the rain, that ancient criterion distinguishing the idealist from the realist, represents the peace Gene finds, the treaty established between what the world should be and what it really is. (pp. 798-800)

Paul Witherington, "'A Separate Peace': A Study in Structural Ambiguity," in English Journal *(copyright © 1965 by the National Council of Teachers of English; reprinted by permission of the publisher), Vol. 54, No. 9, December, 1965, pp. 795-800.*

GRANVILLE HICKS

Indian Summer is a selection of the Literary Guild, and in the Guild's bulletin for August, Knowles says that the book "came about through the collision in my mind of two things: a strange little town I knew in Connecticut, and the friendships I have formed with people who later turned out to be very rich." This, however, was not the whole story: "But in essence what I tried for in *Indian Summer* was neither a novel of place nor a novel about great wealth. I wished instead to express the plight, and the wide dreams, of a certain kind of young American, one who has had to come *down* in the world."

It is with the young American, Cleet Kinsolving, that the novel begins—on the day in 1946 on which he was discharged from the Army Air Force. Although he didn't know exactly what he wanted to do, he was full of optimism. . . .

Not much of a mixer, Cleet has had one close boyhood friend, Neil Reardon, heir to a large fortune, and that is how the rich come into the story. Neil, who has come out of the service with political ambitions, lectures at a nearby college and Cleet goes to see him. Immediately Cleet is seized upon by the Reardons, and the next thing he knows he is back in Wetherford, Connecticut.

Knowles does fairly well with Wetherford. . . . Although it still looks like an old New England town, most of the old families have vanished, and their houses are inhabited by newcomers. It is the kind of town that can help a *nouveau riche* family such as the Reardons to believe that it has roots. We can see the town clearly enough and even make a guess at the identity of the place Knowles has in mind.

At first he seems to be doing rather well with the Reardons, too. He describes their huge house, High Farms, with its haphazard enlargements and incongruous adornments and innumerable servants. But the more he tells us about the Reardons, the less we understand them. In the end about all he has to report concerning the rich is that, as Hemingway said to Fitzgerald a long time ago, they have more money than the rest of us. It does seem to me that the Reardons aren't very bright, but that is true of a lot of people who aren't rich.

In any case the only Reardon who particularly concerns us is Neil, who is somewhat more comprehensible than his parents. He has recently married a girl of proletarian tastes, as he puts it, and at the moment he is satisfied with her because she is pregnant and is, he is sure, about to bear him a son. The girl, Georgia, is somewhat interesting, and so are her parents, who appear in the latter part of the story. But I find it hard to believe that Neil would have married such a girl as Georgia. In fact, Neil puzzles me in many ways. For the sake of his political career he advocates a welfare state, but, it seems clear to Cleet at any rate, he doesn't believe what he is saying and writing. The idea of a millionaire demagogue might have been worth developing, but Knowles does little with it.

What Knowles does work at is the relationship between Neil and Cleet, which is a little like the relationship between Gene and Finney in *A Separate Peace*. Through their boyhood Neil "had no friends except his peculiar, unlettered, shrewd, erratic, dreaming, lifelong pal, Cleet." Like Finney, Cleet is a spontaneous person, a true individual, and that is why Neil looks up to him but at the same time has to try to dominate him.

I can understand after a fashion what Neil sees in Cleet, but I cannot understand why Cleet is attracted to Neil. In fact, Cleet is a mystery whatever way I look at him. In the passage I have quoted, Knowles speaks of Cleet as "one who has had to come down in the world." But coming down doesn't seem to me the point at all. Cleet is simply an old-fashioned rugged individualist who finds himself out of place in the modern world. (p. 23)

Much is also made of another trait that may or may not be part of Cleet's Indian heritage: "When it came to understanding people he had a peculiar kind of talent." Something of the sort is said three or four times, and I suppose Knowles believes it's true; whereas the story seems to me to demonstrate that all along Cleet has been mistaken in his judgments of the Reardons, especially Neil.

I assume that *Indian Summer* is intended to be light fiction—vacation reading, so-called—but I found it heavy going. Having just read two novels that in different ways make tremendous demands on the reader—John Barth's *Giles Goat-Boy* . . . and Bernard Malamud's *The Fixer*, . . . I may have less patience than usual with books such as Knowles's. Both Barth and Malamud have made imaginative efforts of the highest order, and if they ask a lot from the reader, they give a lot. *Indian Summer,* on the other hand, seems something that Knowles just tossed off—and might better have tossed away. (p. 24)

Granville Hicks, "Blandishments of Wealth," in Saturday Review (© 1966 Saturday Review Magazine Co.; reprinted by permission), Vol. XLIX, No. 33, August 13, 1966, pp. 23-4.

JAMES L. McDONALD

It may be too early to attempt more than a tentative appraisal of the overall achievement of John Knowles. Certainly one can say that he ranks among the most promising young American novelists; and one can recognize the obvious fact that *A Separate Peace* . . . has become a small classic among college students and seems likely to last for some time. His other novels, however, have only been noticed in passing: *Morning in Antibes* and *Indian Summer* have not really been analyzed and evaluated. Nor is there any substantial critical commentary on Knowles's work as a whole.

I would like to begin such a commentary; and I propose to do so by placing Knowles, as it were—by relating him to the American literary tradition which I see him working within. He is writing what Lionel Trilling has called "the novel of manners"; and it seems to me that there are affinities between his aesthetic preoccupations and those of Henry James and F. Scott Fitzgerald. An examination of his subjects, themes, and techniques should show this affinity; and I hope that it will also provide a basis for a reasonably sound estimate of Knowles's stature as a novelist.

From the beginning of his career, Knowles—like James and Fitzgerald—has written about manners, about what Trilling defines as "a culture's hum and buzz of implication . . . the whole evanescent context in which its explicit statements are made." In Knowles's first novel, *A Separate Peace*. . . , the "explicit statements" are the Second World War and its moral effect on American society; the "context" is made up of the precarious situation of American prep-school students who will soon be combatants, and of the moral responses that they, their teachers, and their parents make to this situation.

As many critics have noted, *A Separate Peace* can be viewed as a war novel, drawing its title from Frederic Henry's personal declaration of personal armistice in [Ernest Hemingway's] *A Farewell to Arms*. Knowles's concern, however, is not with the direct confrontation of the obvious realities of the battlefield; rather, it is with the impact of war on the minds and sensibilities of individuals who are not, as yet, immmediately involved. The novel examines the cultural upheaval created by the war, and shows how the resulting moral climate affects the thoughts, feelings, attitudes, and actions of Gene Forrester, Phineas, Leper, Brinker, and the others. The novel deals, then, with culture, and with the sensibility of the individual as it is formed by a particular culture: like James and Fitzgerald, Knowles draws the reader's attention to the individual's efforts to adjust to cultural change, and to the quality of his moral responses as he attempts to cope with the disruption of his formerly stable world.

Particularly Jamesian in this novel is Knowles's use of point of view. The narrator, the principal character, is Gene Forrester. On the surface, it appears that he is telling his story honestly, attempting to grapple with his past and forthrightly informing the reader of its significance. Yet, like the narrators of James's "The Liar" or *The Aspern Papers,* for example, Forrester frequently seems either unaware of or deliberately unwilling to acknowledge the moral nature and consequences of his attitudes and actions. There is, then, a discrepancy between Forrester's judgments and the actions and attitudes he is judging. The reader's awareness of this discrepancy is enforced by the dramatic statements of other characters in the novel, especially by the comments of Leper.

Thus the reader's judgments are not always the same as the narrator's; and so the reader is led to question the narrator's motives and interpretations. Should Forrester be taken at his own evaluation? Or is really, as Leper charges, "a savage underneath" his pose of refined, dispassionate, reflective survivor and recounter of the ordeal? (pp. 335-36)

The complexity—or the ambiguity—of the novel is precisely here, and so is Knowles's debt to James. Neither novelist merely uses his narrator to direct the narrative. Both, instead, use the narrative as the scene and occasion of a complex, dramatic confrontation between the narrator and his past which the reader participates in. For James and Knowles, the aesthetic effect of this type of novel depends on a dramatic interplay between the narrator's judgments and the reader's; and, in this sense, the narrator *is* the story.

The locale of Knowles's second novel, *Morning in Antibes* . . . , naturally leads the reader to think of F. Scott Fitzgerald. Knowles's sleek, sparkling Riviera reminds one of the destructive playground evoked in *Tender Is the Night*. The similarity extends to the quality of observation: Dick Diver himself might have described the "very young couple" that Nick Bodine sees early in Knowles's novel: " . . . the girl angelically lovely, tanned and formed for love, the boy like a nearly naked matador." . . . Knowles's concentration on manners also is akin to Fitzgerald's. Both writers keenly perceive "tone, gesture, emphasis, or rhythm . . . the arts of dress or decoration" as signs of cultural trends; and they use these signs to indicate the moral implications of cultural norms and fashions. . . . (p. 337)

The actual situation and themes of the novel, however, are closer to those of James than to Fitzgerald's. *Morning in Antibes* offers the classic Jamesian situation of the innocent American encountering the complexities of European culture. The thematic lines of the novel follow James's typical pattern: a conflict between American innocence and European experience is drawn. The naïveté and vitality of the Americans, Nick and his wife Liliane, are juxtaposed to the worldliness and moral sterility of the Europeans, Marc de la Croie and his sister Constance.

The narrative line of the novel revolves around the struggle between these two worlds for the soul of Liliane; and the struggle is drawn in terms of a sharply defined political situation: the rise of De Gaulle in opposition to French Fascism during the Algerian crisis. But the "evanescent context" of manners is all-important in this novel. Liliane's rejection of Marc de la Croie is, of course, a stand against his decadent Fascism: she realizes that he has been "dead for fifteen years," and that in him "nothing survives except the wish to kill." . . . But she is also repudiating the affluent, corrupt cultural norms and attitudes that he represents. (pp. 337-38)

Politically, the novel, then, raises the question "who will rule France?" But it also asks what moral positions are involved in this struggle for power; and Knowles tries to define the cultural attitudes which are desirable and necessary if the individual is to survive and maintain his integrity. It seems to me that Knowles has advanced beyond the achievement of *A Separate Peace*. The issues are drawn more precisely; his subject has a greater range; and his evaluation of the material is much more clear than it was in his first novel.

Knowles's latest book, *Indian Summer* . . . , is his most ambitious attempt to establish himself as a novelist of genuine stature. In it, he takes up the theme which has obsessed so many major American writers—"the American Dream." And, in dealing with this theme, he seems deliberately to force the reader to think of F. Scott Fitzgerald and *The Great Gatsby*.

Certain affinities between Cleet Kinsolving, the hero of *Indian Summer,* and Fitzgerald's Nick Carraway are immediately discernible. Both encounter the world of the rih, the wealth and luxury, the success and the good life to which so many Americans aspire. Both act as stewards to the rich: Nick to Gatsby and the Buchanans, Cleet to the Reardon family. (pp. 338-39)

The narrative of *Indian Summer* is constructed on a series of gradual discoveries about the disintegration of the American

Dream. Cleet and Georgia, Neil Reardon's wife, slowly come to an understanding of the cultural and moral realities of wealth; they learn what money and privilege have done to the rich. Their discovery is remarkably close to Nick Carraway's realization that the Buchanans were "careless people" who "smashed up things and creatures and then retreated back into their money or their vast carelessness . . . and let other people clean up the mess they had made." Cleet encounters the same carelessness, the same ruthlessness. So does Georgia. (p. 339)

It is a case of wealth hideously and dangerously misused. Success has been attained; but the Reardons, like the Buchanans, have lost the American Dream of greatness, the vision of the ideal, which inspired it. . . .

The American Dream now exists only as a memory of what once might have been. . . . The American Dream has vanished, and now, "as America started into the second half of the twentieth century," Georgia knows that there is no dream worthy of the dreamer, that "the world had become too mechanized for his [Cleet's] kind of nature, he asked too much of life. . . . What a pity, what a waste, what a tragedy. . . . He was like a beautifully armored warrior facing a tank." . . . (p. 340)

Knowles, however, adds another dimension to Cleet Kinsolving. As Georgia realizes, Cleet is "one of the few remaining heirs to a far older tragedy" than the unfulfilled promise of the American Dream. His face, expression, and impassivity exhibit "the last vestiges and relics of his Indian blood . . . that persistent strain in his nature making him sometimes utterly bewildered by this America today . . . " (pp. 340-41)

As such, then, Cleet is an embodiment of the "Adamic Myth" which so many critics have seen as characteristic of American literature. And, as such, he can be related to the "bound and affronted" heroes of Henry James, struggling honorably for life amidst those forces which stifle it. He stands with Christopher Newman, Isabel Archer, Adam Verver, and Milly Theale. . . . (p. 341)

Clearly, *Indian Summer* is another step forward for Knowles. He has dared to treat a theme which has been dealt with by some of the masters of American fiction—[James Fenimore Cooper, Herman Melville, Mark Twain, Henry James, Theodore Dreiser, F. Scott Fitzgerald, and William Faulkner], for example. Few contemporary novelists would be willing to risk the obvious comparisons.

It would be foolish, of course, to claim that Knowles belongs in the select company of Fitzgerald and James, to contend that *Morning in Antibes* and *Indian Summer* are comparable in quality to *Tender Is the Night* and [James's] *The Ambassadors*. But I think that he is an enormously promising novelist, and that he has already achieved a genuine stature. He has exhibited the courage to tackle large subjects and significant themes; and he has treated them with taste, understanding, and considerable technical skill. He certainly deserves more attention than he has received up until now. (pp. 341-42)

James L. McDonald, "The Novels of John Knowles," in Arizona Quarterly *(copyright © 1967 by the Arizona Quarterly), Vol. 23, No. 4, Winter, 1967, pp. 335-42.*

FRANZISKA LYNNE GREILING

The topic of this article will be not innocence but freedom, the Greek theme of *A Separate Peace*. (p. 1269)

Knowles is concerned with the implications of certain Greek ideas: the necessity and effects of freedom, and its corollary ideal of arete: the individual's fulfillment of his own excellences—moral, physical, intellectual, and political. In the first half, Phineas reflects these concerns.

Phineas has a love of excellence and fulfills his ability in the discipline of athletics. When Finny understands that Gene must study to satisfy his ability as a scholar, he says:

> We kid around a lot and everything, but you have to be serious sometime, about something. If you're really good at something, I mean if there's nobody or hardly anybody, who's as good as you are, then you've got to be serious about that. Don't mess around, for God's sake. . . .

Phineas represents Greek ideas more than Christian in another way. One of the basic contrasts between the two philosophies is that the Christians trust in God while the Greeks believed in man. In John 14:6, Jesus says: "I am the way, the truth, and the life; no man cometh unto the father but by me." Hippocrates, who took medicine from the care of the gods to scientific study by man, said: "Life is short, art is long, the occasion instant, experiment perilous, decision difficult." The contrast emphasizes the Greek awareness of the limitations and the greatness of man. Finny represents Greek more than Christian ideas when he respects the individual, not inviolable rules. He trusts too much, however. Finny lacks Hippocrates' mature awareness that while there is much to respect in man, he is vulnerable to time and ignorance.

Phineas' respect for others is one of the reasons he lives successfully outside the rules. Finny loves freedom because in it, he can create "a flow of simple, unregulated friendliness . . . and such flows were one of Finny's reasons for living." . . . Finny's charm and his delight in giving pleasure to others allow him to lead other people to break the rules. . . . Finny himself does not need rules to keep him good; he has an inner harmony, a humanity which allows him to respond with affection and generosity to even the rule-givers who must punish him. Phineas assumes that others would be his equals if only they would ignore the rules. He cannot understand that rules protect individuals from their own and others' weaknesses. He does not comprehend fear, envy, rage at one's own moral ugliness, nor the desire for revenge; so he uneasily ignores these in the individual and in their public manifestation—the war. In Phineas is an idealism and innocence which protect him from seeing life as it is, but these also cause him to try to create around him his ideal world. In the novel, the best and last example of this special ability is Finny's Winter Carnival. Here, Finny's denial of war, of evil really, is most successful, and the festival has risen to anarchy and inspiration. . . . Appropriate to his defensive innocence, Phineas begins the games by burning *The Iliad*. And here is his flaw, Phineas does not fulfill one of the most prized Greek virtues—intellectual excellence. To Phineas, "freedom" is not the opportunity to "Know thyself."

Perhaps his imperfection makes him all the more Greek. Yet Phineas does partake of the combination of moral and physical beauty that Plato described in *The Republic*. . . . Phineas' physical beauty and personal harmony remind one of two fifth-century Greek sculptures: Myron's Discobolus and Polyclitus' Doryphorus. The body of the Discus Thrower is slender and competent, the face is serene, revealing an inner calm. The agony of violent effort is absent in this disciplined athlete. The Doryphorus depicts an athlete after performance who, like the Discus Thrower, is unmarked by effort. He walks with a unified, flowing movement, and his face reveals a quiet, inner fulfillment. Both statues reflect a Greek idealism and both express a Greek poise: pride without egotism and self-confidence without complacency. Phineas' poise, like that of fifth-century Greece, is vulnerable. As the Greeks feared, the weakness was in man's inadequate knowledge of himself and his world. During the decline of Greece, the resulting loss of confidence is evident in sculpture. In the Laocoon, heavily muscled figures struggle against inevitable defeat. These subjects have no harmonious relationship with the cosmos. In *A Separate Peace*, Gene destroys Phineas' unity by committing an act which Phineas cannot assimilate into his view of life. . . . Like the figures of the Laocoon, Phineas is unable to survive when he is betrayed. Gene's is the agonized struggle.

At the beginning, Gene thought of himself as Phineas' equal, first in excellence, then in enmity. Discovering Phineas incapable of hatred, Gene has to face his own moral ugliness and then strikes down Phineas for inadvertently revealing it to him. Rules are unnecessary and restricting for Phineas, but Gene has need of the rules, for he lacks the humanity to make the generous response to others. Gene fails the high demands of freedom, accepts himself as evil, and retreats to the rules. (pp. 1269-71)

But there is more goodness in Gene than he knows. Phineas, in his need, gives Gene the opportunity to do good and unknowingly gives Gene the self-confidence to be free once more. For Gene's act had damaged Phineas' athletic excellence and, worse, threatened the basis for Phineas' humanity; and Phineas uses his remaining strength to deny this loss. He proceeds to recreate his world through Gene's friendship and athletic development. In this experience, Gene, freed now of envy and despair, understands himself and Phineas.

In fulfilling this second gift of freedom Gene achieves a tragic victory. He is the only one in the book to know himself. . . .

It is Gene, the scholar, who understands that his sin against Phineas was due to an ignorance of his own nature and that war is a manifestation of a general defensive ignorance in mankind. . . . Gene redeems his guilt with understanding. So, at the end of the book, Gene more than Phineas embodies the Greek ideal. He has arete; he has unity. Gene has penetrated the appearances which deceive others and made a harmony of his own that is more profound and more stable than Phineas'.

> As pain that cannot forget falls drop by drop upon the heart and in our despite, against our will, comes wisdom to us from the awful grace of God.
>
>   Aeschylus
>
>   (p. 1272)

Franziska Lynne Greiling, "The Theme of Freedom in 'A Separate Peace'," in English Journal *(copyright © 1967 by the National Council of Teachers of English; reprinted by permission of the publisher), Vol. 56, No. 9, December, 1967, pp. 1269-72.*

ROBERT H. DONAHUGH

Youth is dominant in five of the six stories comprising this distinguished collection [*Phineas and Other Stories*]. The title story and "**A Turn With the Sun**" are set in a boy's boarding school. In both Mr. Knowles gives a nostalgic view of memorable boys and the educational system. "**The Peeping Tom**" is a painfully personal drama of a young man's meaningless life. While "**Martin the Fisherman**" is little more than a vignette, "**The Reading of the Will**" is a suspenseful story of a father's bequest, a sealed envelope, and two brothers who inherit different things. This collection of superior stories by one of America's most appealing writers should be welcomed by adult readers and by young adults.

Robert H. Donahugh, in his review of "Phineas and Other Stories," in Library Journal *(reprinted from* Library Journal, *September 15, 1968; published by R. R. Bowker Co. (a Xerox company); copyright © 1968 by Xerox Corporation), Vol. 93, No. 16, September 15, 1968, p. 3156.*

SALLY KEMPTON

John Knowles's first book, "**A Separate Peace**," was one of those legendary adolescent novels, passed hand to hand around the dormitories at Groton, buoyed into successive paperback editions by that most valuable of commercial assets, an underground reputation. It was a very special book, about a special type of Eastern prep-school kid, and it was notable for two qualities: a complete absence of humor and a curious air of self-seriousness, as if it had been composed in the service of a 16-year-old boy's romantic self-image. "**A Separate Peace**" was a schoolboy tragedy seen entirely in schoolboy's terms. Its protagonist was the classic prep-school hero, a sort of eccentric Hobie Baker, innocent, straight, the victim of someone else's destructive complexity. For all its tragedy and blood-guilt, Knowles's first novel was squarely in the tradition of Dink Stover and the Boys Own Paper. Like many cult books, its success derived from a perfect coincidence between an author's preoccupation and that of his audience.

Knowles subsequently published two novels and a travel book ["**Double Vision**"]. The novels were as humorless and as self-important as "**A Separate Peace**"; neither had its mystique, and certainly neither had its success. His new book ["**Phineas**"], a collection of six stories which one hopes was put together at his publisher's insistence, exhibits the same weaknesses as well as a certain sense of reprise.

The title story is actually an old sketch from which "**A Separate Peace**" was ultimately developed, outlining the themes of the novel and its initial action, but stopping short of the final confrontation and tragedy. And there is another Devon School story, a sidelong glance at another schoolboy tragedy, which has virtually the same plot as Fitzgerald's "The Freshest Boy" except that in Knowles's version the young misfit dies.

The rest of the collection deals with what I suppose might be called the author's central theme, personal insecurity and the fear of displacement. . . . All of them are accurately, if conventionally motivated and oddly, though unobtrusively, self-important. None of them is memorable.

The difficulty is not that Knowles writes badly; it is that he is essentially a writer of sub-New Yorker stories who once wrote a novel that found a response. That novel was not especially contemporary, although it could be called timeless. . . . But the people who read it grew up and found other preoccupations, while Knowles's preoccupations remained the same. The adolescent's sense of his own significance cannot be expected to serve a great many situations.

Sally Kempton, "De Vries, Auchincloss, Knowles, O'Hara, All Doing Their Thing," in The New York Times Book Review *(© 1968 by The New York Times Company; reprinted by permission), November 24, 1968, p. 4.*

JAMES P. DEGNAN

[*Phineas* is] concerned mainly with the psychological problems of American male adolescents. Admirers of Mr. Knowles's well-known novel, *A Separate Peace*, will recognize in the title story, as well as in "**A Turn in the Sun**," much of the source material for *A Separate Peace*. Competent, sophisticated, and a master of place description, Mr. Knowles also dramatizes as well as anyone I know the torments—especially the torments of ostracism—suffered by the sensitive and intelligent male adolescent. But when he gets off this subject he seems lost. In "**The Peeping Tom**," for example, he seems desperately and unsuccessfully to be searching for a subject worthy of his ambition and talent. (pp. 275-76)

James P. Degnan, "Sex Ex Machina and Other Problems," in The Kenyon Review *(copyright 1969 by Kenyon College), Vol. 31, No. 2, 1969, pp. 272-77.*

PETER WOLFE

John Knowles's concern with morality colors all his books. This preoccupation finds its most general expression in a question asked in *Double Vision* . . . , an informal travel journal: "Can man prevail against the bestiality he himself has struggled out of by a supreme effort?" Knowles's novels, instead of attacking the question head-on, go about it indirectly. They ask, first, whether a person can detach himself from his background—his society, his tradition, and the primitive energies that shaped his life.

The question is important because Knowles sees all of modern life shot through with malevolence. (p. 189)

[It is Knowles's major premise] that the condition of life is war. *A Separate Peace* describes the private battles of a prep school coterie boiling into the public fury of World War II. The individual and society are both at war again in Knowles's second novel, *Morning in Antibes* . . . , where the Algerian-French War invades the chic Riviera resort, Côte d'Azur. *Indian Summer* . . . not only presents the World War II period and its aftermath as a single conflict-ridden epoch; it also describes civilian life as more dangerous than combat.

The Knowles hero, rather than tearing himself from his background, submerges himself in it. According to Knowles, man can only know himself through action; he learns about life by acting on it, not by thinking about it. The action is never collective, and it always involves treachery and physical risk.

A full life to Knowles is one lived on the margins of disaster. Brinker Hadley in *A Separate Peace* and Neil Reardon in *Indian Summer* are both actionists, but since their lives are governed by prudence and not feeling they can never probe the quick of being. In order to touch the spontaneous, irrational core of selfhood, man must act unaided. At this point Knowles's ontology runs into the roadblock of original sin. Whereas the characters in his books who shrink from a bone-to-bone contact with life are labelled either escapists or cowards, the ones who lunge headlong into reality are usually crushed by the reality they discover. That all of Knowles's leading characters smash their closest friendship and also fall sick conveys the danger of a highly charged encounter with life.

This danger increases because of the way they go about the problem of self-being. Instead of struggling out of bestiality, to use Knowles's metaphor from *Double Vision,* they sink back into it. The Knowles hero moves forward by moving backward. (pp. 189-90)

[Prime being] is both sensory and prereflective, a tremor of uncensored energy. By obeying this dark urgency we can unleash a wildness that cuts down everything in its path. . . .

A Separate Peace shapes the problem of man's inherent savagery to American culture. In contrast to the characters of D. H. Lawrence, those of Knowles do not discharge their deepest impulses sexually. Instead they retrace the familiar American fictional pattern of immersing themselves in the past. . . . [Gene Forrester] sounds the uncharted seas of our common humanity and in so doing both undoes the work of civilization and reawakens the wild meaninglessness of primitive man.

The novel's setting gives Gene's problem an American emphasis. In *Double Vision,* Knowles discusses the primitive barbarism underlying American life: "The American character is unintegrated, unresolved, a careful Protestant with a savage stirring in his insides, a germ of American wildness thickening in his throat." (p. 190)

[And as] he does with the smiling, boyish soldiers who appear in the last chapter of the novel, Knowles uses a prep school setting to show that even innocence and beauty cannot escape the corrosive ooze of evil. (Devon's Field House is called suggestively "The Cage," indicating that bestiality is already in force at the school.) Contributing to the irony established by the disjuncture of cause and effect, or setting and event, is Knowles's quiet, understated style. That violence should leap so suddenly out of Knowles's offhand, conversational cadences sharpens the horror of the violence. (pp. 190-91)

The first chapter of *A Separate Peace* shows Gene Forrester returning to Devon fifteen years after the key incident of his life—that of shaking his best friend Phineas out of a tree and shattering his leg. Mingling memory and fear, Gene is not only the archetypal criminal who returns to the scene of his crime or the American fictional hero who retreats into a private past. His return to Devon is purposive, even compulsive. His neglecting to mention his job, his family, or his home suggests that he has none of these things, even though he is past the age of thirty. He relives his act of treachery and the events surrounding it in the hope of recovering the separate peace of the summer of 1942.

Gene interests us chiefly because of his moral ambiguity: whereas he accepts his malevolence, he also resists indulging it at the expense of others. Fear of unleashing his inherent wickedness explains his inertia since Devon's 1942-43 academic year. It also explains his psychological bloc. His first-person narration is laced with self-abuse, special pleading, flawed logic, and evasiveness. As has been suggested, self-exploration is dangerous work, and Gene cannot be blamed if he sometimes cracks under the strain. Out of joint with both himself and his time, he subjects to reason an area of being which is neither rational nor reducible to rational formulas. Although the sum will not add, he has no choice but to try to add the sum if he wants to re-enter the human community.

Like the novel's memoir technique, Gene Forrester's name certifies that *A Separate Peace* is his book. Of the forest, Gene

is a primitive, bloodthirsty woodlander; his occasional self-disclosures spell out the urgency of his deathpull: "I was used to finding something deadly in things that attracted me; there was always something deadly lurking in anything I wanted, anything I loved. And if it wasn't there . . . I put it there myself." (p. 191)

Devon represents the last outpost of civilization to Gene. It wards off the primitive madness encroaching from the great northern forests, and it shields its students from the organized madness of World War II. Devon's 1942 summer term, the first in its history, is giving Gene and Phineas their last reprieve from a war-racked world. At sixteen, the boys and their classmates are the oldest students at Devon excused from taking both military subjects and preinduction physical exams.

In contrast to this freedom, winter brings loss, unreason, and hardness of heart. Nor is the heartless irrationality equated with Gene's forest background uncommon. His first name universalizes his glacial cruelty. While Phineas is a sport (who happens to excel in sports), Gene is generic, his barbarism deriving from his North American forebears. And the fact that he is a southerner shows how deeply this northern madness has bitten into American life.

The first object of Gene's return visit to Devon is the tree he ousted Phineas from fifteen years before. James Ellis places the tree in a Christian context by calling it "the Biblical tree of knowledge" [see excerpt above]. (pp. 191-92)

Yet Christian myth fails to exhaust the tree's meaning. Its rootedness in the earth, its riverbank location, and its overarching branches suggest organic life. Lacking a single meaning, the tree stands for reality itself. Knowles develops this powerful inclusiveness by projecting the tree to several levels of being. For the tree not only exists forcibly at more than one dimension; it also brings together different aspects of reality. Over the spectrum of Gene's life, it is by turns an occasion for danger, friendship, betrayal and regret. (p. 192)

[The] tree combines metaphorically with both the War and the aboriginal northern frost to create a strong impression of lostness. The tree's combining power, in fact, is as great as its power to halt or cut short. For while it marks the end of the gipsy summer of 1942, it also yokes Gene's past and present lives.

The victim of the tree incident, Phineas, is best summarized by a phrase Knowles uses in *Double Vision* to describe modern Greeks—"a full life lived naturally." Nor is the classical parallel askew. Phineas's name resembles phonetically that of Phidias, who helped set the standard of all-around excellence that marked the golden age of Pericles. . . . Finny stands under five feet nine and weighs only a hundred and fifty pounds. His athletic prowess stems not from brawn but from his superb coordination and vitality.

Interestingly, the trophies he wins are for gentlemanly conduct. Finny's mastery goes beyond sports. His great gift is the ability to respond clearly and fully: his "unthinking unity of movement" . . . and his favorite expressions, "naturally" and "perfectly okay," express the harmony and interrelatedness of his life. . . . Finny's commitment to life overrides the requirements of reason and law, but not out of innate lawlessness. His responses strike so deeply that, while they sometimes make nonsense of conventional morality, they create their own scale of values.

Finny's organicism also sets the style and tempo of the free, unclassifiable summer of 1942. It must be noted that the separate peace Finny and Gene carve out is no idyllic escape from reality. By founding the Super Suicide Society of the Summer Session, membership in which requires a dangerous leap into the Devon River, the boys admit both danger and death into their golden gipsy days. Accordingly, the game of Blitzball, which Finny invents the same summer, includes the bellicosity and treachery that perhaps count as humanity's worst features: "Since we're all enemies, we can and will turn on each other all the time." . . . Nevertheless, the boys rejoice in Blitzball and, while they sustain a fierce level of competition, they manage to avoid injuries.

For opponents do not inflict pain in the world of *A Separate Peace;* the worst menaces dwell not in rivalry but in friendship. Gene and Phineas become best friends, but Gene cannot live with Finny's goodness. Finny's helping Gene overcome fear and his opening his friend to bracing new adventures rouses Gene's worst traits. Man is a hating rather than a loving animal. (pp. 192-93)

Of all modern psychoanalytical theories, perhaps [Alfred] Adler's doctrine of masculine protest best explains Gene's malignancy. But even Adler falls short; Gene's cruelty is unconscious and it brings him no prizes. Nothing so simple as worldly success is at stake in the tree incident. For Gene is one of Devon's best students, and he knows that his gifts, although less spectacular than Finny's, are more durable.

Besides having time in his favor, Gene is already Finny's equal: "I was more and more certainly becoming the best student in the school; Phineas was without question the best athlete, so in that way we were even. But while he was a very poor student, I was a pretty good athlete, and when everything was thrown into the scales they would in the end tilt definitely toward me." . . . (pp. 193-94)

By shaking his friend out of the tree, Gene obeys an urge deeper than reason or wounded vanity. But his act of aboriginal madness is empty. The things that happen to him after his treachery demonstrates the pointless waste of violence.

But they do not draw the sting of his violent tendencies. Gene's first reaction to Finny's shattered leg is complex. Since Finny's vitality diminishes Gene, he is glad to be rid of his friend. Finny's confinement in the Infirmary lets Gene become Finny. He calls Finny "noble" . . . and in the next paragraph, after putting on his friend's clothes, says that he feels "like some nobleman." . . . Even the relaxed, supple style in which he writes his memoir fits with his desire to merge with his male ideal.

Ironically, Finny is just as eager as Gene to switch identities. Rather than accusing him of treachery or languishing in self-pity, he tries to recover some of his lost splendor through his friend. Knowles says at one point in the book that a broken bone, once healed, is strongest in the place where the break occurred. The statement applies to Finny's recuperative powers. His athletic career ended, Finny acquires new skills and learns to exist on a new plane while preserving his high standard of personal loyalty. . . .

The two boys institute a routine based on their best gifts: while Finny coaches Gene on the cinderpath and in the gym, Gene helps Finny with his studies. (p. 194)

Gene ends this regimen because he cannot forgive Phineas for submitting to his brutality. He determines to make his cruelty

a counterforce to Phineas's loyalty and courage. After Phineas breaks his leg falling on the slick marble steps of the First Academy Building, Gene follows him to the Infirmary. But instead of showing compassion for his stricken friend, his thoughts turn inward. Astonishingly, his attitude is one of cool self-acceptance. "I couldn't escape a confusing sense of living through all of this before—Phineas in the Infirmary, and myself responsible. I seemed to be less shocked by it now than I had been the first time last August." . . . (pp. 194-95)

Gene's detachment imparts the final horror to his actions. Yet Phineas can take his worst thrusts. Although he can no longer control his muscular reactions, his mind stays whole. His body breaks before his spirit; he accepts Gene's treachery, and when he dies he has transcended it. Nobody in the book can come near enough to him to kill him. He dies as he had lived—untouched by human baseness. While his broken leg is being set, some of the bone-marrow escapes into his bloodstream and lodges in his heart. In that bone-marrow produces the body's life-giving red corpuscles, Phineas dies from an overplus and a richness of animal vigor.

Gene's barbarism finds another outlet in Elwin "Leper" Lepellier. Although Leper is not so well perceived as Finny, he serves structurally as Finny's foil. Whereas Finny attracts people, Leper is an outsider; and Leper matches Finny's physical breakdown by cracking psychologically. A solitary at school, he is crushed by the tighter discipline and organization practiced by the Army. But the organized madness of the Army, while wrecking his sanity, sharpens his insight. He tells Gene, "You always were a savage underneath," . . . and later in the book he describes the tree episode with a poetic accuracy that lays bare the core of Gene's treachery.

Yet none of Leper's hearers can understand him. Finny, on the other hand, communicates by bodily movements and is always perfectly understood. Leper's oppositeness to Finny reveals two important things about Gene's savagery: its all-inclusive sweep and its static nature. Although Finny and Leper both grow, Gene is hunkered in his wickedness. In the same way that primitive societies are the least free, he can neither explain nor change himself once he gives in to his primitive drives. . . .

The Leper-Finny doubling motif is but one example of Knowles's fondness for sharp contrast as a structural principle. The author also plays the carefree summer of 1942 against the winter term that follows. He manages his contrast by means of the various associations created by the intervening season, fall.

Finny's fall from the tree by the river, in ending the boys' summer, draws the warmth and light from Devon. (p. 195)

The daily character of life at Devon also expresses the darkening shift from summer to winter. The change in mood is observable the first day of winter term: "We had been an idiosyncratic, leaderless band in the summer . . . Now the official class leaders and politicians could be seen taking charge." . . . Gene's murder of the "simple, unregulated friendliness" . . . marking the summer term validates the need for restricting man's freedom. Like that of [Nathaniel] Hawthorne, Knowles's attitude toward the law is complex. If civilization is to survive, then man's intrinsic savagery must be bridled. Yet any formal legal system will prove unreliable. The members of the older generation described in the book cannot claim any natural or acquired superiority over their sons. They stand to blame for the War and also for the congressional investigating committees the novel attacks indirectly.

Rules and restrictions turn out to be just as poor a standard of civilized conduct as feelings. Knowles introduces the character of Brinker Hadley—a classmate of Finny, Leper, and Gene—to point up the murderous cruelty of the law. Significantly, Brinker does not enter the book until the 1942-43 winter term. He makes the distressing point that man tends to use the law not as a check to man's aggressiveness, but as an outlet. Legalistic, rule-bound, and calculating, Brinker only invokes the law in order to frustrate or to punish. . . .

But he also reminds us that although Justice balances the scales of human conduct, she is also blindfolded. Brinker's blind spot is the life of feeling, his fact-ridden life having ruled out compassion. Brinker, who has a large posterior, or butt, presides from the Butt Room, a cellar which is both the dreariest and the lowest site on the Devon campus. Because Gene could not rise to the example set by Phineas, he must pass muster with Brinker's Butt-Room morality. . . .

The structure of *A Separate Peace* includes . . . tensions, stresses, and balances. Chapter Seven, the middle chapter of the novel, is dominated by snow, a common symbol for death. Suitably, the big snowfall of Chapter Seven, like the tree incident of Chapter Four, occurs out of season. Chapter Seven also introduces Brinker Hadley and restores Phineas to Devon. As the chapter advances, the thickening snows envelop Gene; by the end of the chapter, they obstruct all of life. (p. 196)

Gene's visit to Finny's home in Boston in Chapter Five and his visit to Leper's in Chapter Ten contain enough striking similarities and differences to stand as mutually explanatory. In Chapter Ten Leper, painfully disoriented after his abortive tour of military service, accuses Gene of having deliberately knocked Phineas out of the tree the previous summer. Gene hotly denies the charge and goes on to abuse and then desert Leper during his crisis: "I was the closest person in the world to him now." . . . Chapter Five, curiously, shows Gene confessing the same treachery and Finny defending him to himself.

The two chapters mirror each other nearly perfectly: Gene reverses field completely, and Finny's self-command balances Leper's mental collapse. But Gene's shift in roles from self-accuser to self-defender is flawed. He shows Leper none of the kindness extended by Finny in Chapter Five, even though his moral situation in Chapter Ten is less difficult than Finny's was.

Gene's failure is one of moral escapism. When Leper reveals himself as a misfit in a world where nothing fits with anything else, Gene flees. Leper's description of the ugliness and disjointedness underlying life strikes Gene so hard that he must deny it in order to keep peace with himself: "I didn't want to hear any more of it. Not now or ever. I didn't care because it had nothing to do with me." (p. 197)

The technique of the last chapter tallies well with both the events and the morality it describes. Knowles violates the unity of time by leaping ahead several months to June 1943; he also breaks a basic rule of fictional art by introducing an important character in his last chapter. These discordancies are intentional: a novel about disjointedness should have its components out of joint with each other. Accordingly, *A Separate Peace* extends a chapter after Phineas's death and funeral.

But instead of joining its dramatic and thematic climaxes, the last chapter has a scattering effect. Gene's class at Devon has just been graduated, and the boys are shipping out to various branches of the military. The new character, Brinker Hadley's father, is a World War I veteran whose lofty code of patriotism and service means little to the younger generation.

Mr. Hadley cannot, however, be dismissed as a stale anachronism. His argument implies that he knows something the boys have not yet learned. Combat duty is important to him, not as an immediate goal but as a topic to reminisce about in future years. Could Mr. Hadley be suggesting that maturity contains few pleasures and that only a heroic youth can make up for this emptiness? That the boys overlook this implication means little. The chapter is full of communication failures, including the generation rift Mr. Hadley introduces by visiting Devon.

Another new presence at Devon is the U.S. Army. Devon has donated part of its grounds to a Parachute Riggers' school. Appropriately, the sector of the campus used by the soldiers is the Northern Common. But Knowles pulls a stunning reversal by overturning this fine narrative stroke. For although the Army as the collective embodiment of man's aggressiveness invades Devon from the icy North, man's aggressiveness has already established a stronghold at Devon. Likewise, the convoy of jeeps driving through campus stirs no warlike fervor. The boyish troops are "not very bellicose-looking," . . . and the jeeps do not contain weapons but sewing machines.

The logic of the novel makes eminent sense of this unlikely freight: the sewing machines, which will service parachutes, allude to the novel's central metaphor of falling, and the young soldiers will lunge headlong into violence in the same way as Devon's Class of 1943. By the end of the book, the malevolence uncoiling from man's fallen nature has engulfed all.

Except, strangely, for Gene. His savagery already spent, he has no aggressiveness left for the Navy. Although his country is at war, he is at peace. Yet the armistice is false. A man so askew with his environment enjoys no peace. Gene's lack of purpose not only divides him from his country; it separates him from himself. Divided and subdivided, he is fighting a war just as dangerous as his country's. He has not killed his enemy, as he insists. . . . (pp. 197-98)

His return to Devon in his early thirties and his memoir of Devon's 1942-43 academic year prove that his private struggle has outlasted the public holocaust of World War II. Just as the anvil can break the hammer, the tree incident hurts Gene more than it does Finny. The novel turns on the irony that the separate peace mentioned in its title excludes its most vivid presence—its narrator. Gene's fall 1957 visit to Devon fixes the limits of his fallen life. His self-inventory is either a preparation for life or a statement of withdrawal. But the question of whether he can convert his apartness into a new start goes beyond the boundaries of the novel. (p. 198)

Peter Wolfe, "The Impact of Knowles's 'A Separate Peace'" (copyright 1970 The Curators of the University of Missouri; reprinted by permission of the author), in University Review, *Vol. 36, No. 3, March, 1970, pp. 189-98.*

WEBSTER SCHOTT

John Knowles has written a beautiful, funny, moving novel about a young man in trouble. If **"The Paragon"** is flawed—and I think it is—the cracks may shorten its life but they won't seriously impair the pleasure of reading it. Knowles, who got his medals for **"A Separate Peace,"** is an intelligent man telling us things we need to know about ourselves. He tells them well.

The title is important. It's not "A Paragon." It's **"The Paragon."** And Knowles's model or pattern of perfection for youth and manhood is a seeking, nonconforming, erratically brilliant and socially maladjusted college student. For Knowles the perfect model must be less than perfect. Not an irony. A moral position.

"I think readers should work more . . . a novel should be an experience," Knowles once said in the pages of this review. Experiencing the character of Lou Colfax, Knowles's paragon human being, is the joy and trial of the novel. Lou's screwy behavior is also muddy. No matter how hard we work beside Knowles, we can't see clearly to the depths of Lou Colfax. . . .

The important episodes in the novel—important in exploring the character of Knowles's confused paragon, important for lovely language—have to do with Lou's relationship with his relatives, and with Lou's love affair with Charlotte, an English actress.

Knowles commands language to feel. This is Charlotte the night she thinks she is conceiving Lou's child: "She felt this act between them as wondrously new, limitlessly meaningful and so as though carried out in slow motion, that all its profound movements and their meanings and clamoring excitements might be clear, its stages so fully expressed that they could be carved in stone for—yes, for future generations. . . . She slept as though wrapped in soft gauze, layer on layer."

Lou's mother dies. His father suffers a debilitating stroke. They've been bad for his psyche. Lou's other relatives—a cheap politician, a bad actress, a stupid minister—have left scars on him. But Knowles can't make us—me, at least—sense the consequences of these scars because he doesn't show scars happening. In Knowles's imagination Lou's awful childhood somehow prevents his giving Charlotte a child and leads to his mad kidnapping of her baby after she has married. I don't think Knowles knows how Lou got the way he is—and he may not especially care. The family business is melodramatic scenery. What Knowles does care about is the richness of Lou's bizarre personality and his dilemmas of commitment.

Here lies the present relevancy of **"The Paragon."** Knowles shows us a young man confused by choice. The choices are real: to love and fulfill love or to run from its risks; to kick a no-good past or to live programmed for catastrophe; to play with knowledge or to convert it to effect; to be Lou Colfax or someone society requires.

Lou makes his choices. They come out a draw. We believe him. We recognize his state because it's our own. A magnificent fiction would show all the tendrils leading to Lou Colfax's condition. An intelligent novel would make Lou's condition credible. **"The Paragon"** is intelligent.

Webster Schott, "The Surface of Lou Colfax, Complete with Scars," in The New York Times Book Review (© 1971 by The New York Times Company; reprinted by permission), January 31, 1971, p. 6.

THE BOOKLIST

[In *The Paragon* Knowles] again shows empathy with young people. With considerable freewheeling humor and light irony he depicts the Yale University scene and Louis Colfax, a decided original in spirit and behavior, as he seeks to express his assorted doubts and talents and strives to surmount the strangeness and failure that he considers inescapable in his family heritage. Characterization often slips into caricature, less so with Louis himself and young Charlotte—whom he loses because he feels unready to give her the child she desires—than in the case of Louis' wealthy, haughty, insensitive roommate, the roommate's glamorous, earthy, outspoken former stepmother, and Louis' radical Afro-Brazilian friend.

A review of "The Paragon: A Novel," in The Booklist (reprinted by permission of the American Library Association; copyright © 1971 by the American Library Association), Vol. 67, No. 15, April 1, 1971, p. 641.

LARRY GRAY

A Separate Peace proves that John Knowles is a good writer. *Spreading Fires* does not. It begins like a travelogue (the setting is Cannes, a town that lends itself to the picturesque), changes into a psychological study, and ends up a thriller. The main character, Brendan; his sister, Miriam; their mother, Marietta; and Miriam's lover, Xavier make up a villa-full of flawed personalities trying to cope with a psychotic servant, Neville. They cope badly, supposedly highlighting their own problems. It doesn't come off. There are too many vibrations trying to become subplots and never quite making it. Perhaps the characters simply need more time, more space to develop. The reader is left with loose ends, questions—not those a skillful writer imbeds in an inquiring mind, but those left when a novelist simply doesn't do his job.

Larry Gray, in his review of "Spreading Fires," in Library Journal (reprinted from Library Journal, June 1, 1974; published by R. R. Bowker Co. (a Xerox company); copyright © 1974 by Xerox Corporation), Vol. 99, No. 11, June 1, 1974, p. 1564.

CHRISTOPHER LEHMANN-HAUPT

Did you admire John Knowles's first novel, **"A Separate Peace"**? After floundering somewhat in his three subsequent novels (**"Morning in Antibes," "Phineas"** and **"The Paragon"**), Mr. Knowles seems to be in firm control again in **"Spreading Fires."** At least for a while, he does. A lot of tension builds on the surface of this story about a strange cook named Neville who comes with a villa in the South of France that Brendan Lucas has rented for the summer. As long as Brendan stays alone at the villa, Neville is merely compulsively neat and industrious; but when Brendan's sister and fiancé arrive, Neville starts venting rage and paranoia; and when Brendan's overdomineering mother arrives, Neville starts fondling his butcher knife and meat cleaver. Tension builds beneath the surface too, as Mr. Knowles skillfully mirrors in the Mediterranean landscape the smoldering homosexual fires that spread among the villa's occupants.

But midway through the novel something goes wrong. Superficially, Mr. Knowles plays his trump card too soon: Neville the cook goes berserk around page 100, and the last third of the plot is dissipated in the incredible mechanics of Neville's comings and goings between a local mental hospital and the villa. But beneath the surface, Mr. Knowles plays his hand too reluctantly: he never goes beyond signifying that Neville is Brendan's doppelgänger, acting out Brendan's unresolved Oedipal rage at his mother and approaching a commitment of homosexuality. Surface and subsurface seem out of phase with each other. The murderer stalks too soon to kill anyone, while the fire spreads too slowly to burn anything. We are left with the frustrated wish that Mr. Knowles had either stuck to writing a straight thriller about a cook who gradually goes insane or gone further in exploring the homosexual passions that burn beneath his abortive thriller.

> Christopher Lehmann-Haupt, "Scalpels and a Gay Blade," in The New York Times (© 1974 by The New York Times Company; reprinted by permission), June 11, 1974, p. 39.*

AGNES C. RINGER

West Virginia in the boom days of the coal industry is the locale for [A Vein of Riches, a] rather pedestrian novel which opens in 1909 when coal has made Middleburg a "city of a hundred millionaires," among them the Catherwood family. Clarkson, the husband and father, head of one of the larger companies, is too engrossed in business affairs to pay much attention to his son, Lyle, an only child, or Minnie, his wife, who finds escape in a "born again" religious experience. . . . A romance of sorts between Lyle and the widow of one of his father's assistants does little to enliven a novel whose characters are basically uninteresting people and whose pace is lethargic.

> Agnes C. Ringer, in her review of "A Vein of Riches," in Library Journal (reprinted from Library Journal, February 15, 1978; published by R. R. Bowker Co. (a Xerox company); copyright © 1978 by Xerox Corporation), Vol. 103, No. 4, February 15, 1978, p. 482.

JACK SULLIVAN

John Knowles, author of the highly acclaimed A Separate Peace, has now written a soap operatic historical novel about a coal baron's family in West Virginia that loses its money but discovers "things that really mean a lot more." That A Vein of Riches refers not just to the novel's coal boom setting but also to these newly plumbed human feelings and values is a point Knowles wants very badly for us not to miss. . . .

By relentlessly spelling everything out, Knowles demonstrates little confidence in his own or in his readers' imagination. If he thinks we may miss a symbol, he identifies it for us: "Clarkson surveyed the scene, a formidable figure in his vested navy blue suit with high stiff collar, watch chain, all the symbols of business power." When waxing allegorical, Knowles not only perpetrates clichés but sometimes capitalizes them: "It seemed to him that a door, the one opening on a room known as Good Clean Fun, was closing in his life." And he even labels epiphanies: "These words broke over him with the force of an epiphany."

When reading the first few pages of a novel as trite as this, one has a perverse feeling of comfort, a sensation that at least our sensibilities are not going to be taxed. After a while though, the experience becomes embarrassing and a bit depressing.

> Jack Sullivan, in his review of "A Vein of Riches," in Saturday Review (© 1978 Saturday Review Magazine Co.; reprinted by permission), Vol. 5, No. 10, February 18, 1978, p. 33.

DIANE J. SWANBROW

Coal mining has yielded literary riches for several generations, and John Knowles strikes yet another solid vein in this tale of his native West Virginia [A Vein of Riches]. Knowles exercises masterful discrimination, both in his choice of characters and in his selection of the details to portray those characters, making the novel richly readable. The Catherwoods are the wealthiest and most influential family in Middleburg, West Virginia, depicted at the height of their power—during the coal boom of 1910-1920. Forming a kaleidoscopic backdrop for the family, the turbulence of the First World War, the scandal of the Harding administration, and the bloody fight for unionization in the mines all contribute to the tale, while never dwarfing the personal crises of the Catherwoods.

Clarkson, the head of the Catherwood family, is a smugly satisfied businessman. . . . Minnie, his nervous, ineffectual wife, faces the glittering world through an opiate haze, dressing only in white to convey a spiritual aura to her son. But in the dark days to come, it is Minnie who draws upon inner reserves, coping with the grim realities of economic ruin strongly and courageously. Lyle, the only child, grows into manhood with the burden of his father's wealth pressing heavily upon him. . . . A readable book, vividly recreating a time that is no more.

> Diane J. Swanbrow, in her review of "A Vein of Riches," in West Coast Review of Books (copyright 1978 by Rapport Publishing Co., Inc.), Vol. 4, No. 2, March, 1978, p. 27.

PUBLISHERS WEEKLY

[In "Peace Breaks Out"] Pete Hallam—class of '37—returning to the Devon School in New Hampshire in the fall of 1945 as a teacher, hopes to recover there from wartime traumas. But the boys in the class of '46 are an edgy bunch, frustrated and guilty because they won't be graduating from the prep school to the armed forces like the classes before them. There's a simmering air of violence among them during the long winter as Pete in his low-keyed way tries to help them cross the threshold to adulthood. The students include the familiar types . . . but Knowles makes each one a unique and vulnerable character. This may not be the virtuoso performance that "A Separate Peace" was, but it's a sympathetic and nostalgic recreating of a vanished academic oasis.

> A review of "Peace Breaks Out," in Publishers Weekly (reprinted from the February 6, 1981 issue of Publishers Weekly, published by R. R. Bowker Company, a Xerox company; copyright © 1981 by Xerox Corporation), Vol. 219, No. 6, February 6, 1981, p. 368.

PAUL PIAZZA

In Peace Breaks Out, John Knowles revisits Devon School, the New Hampshire prep school that provided the setting for his 1950s best seller, A Separate Peace. Perceptively and sensitively written, A Separate Peace movingly chronicled the struggle between two adolescents who, too young to enlist, discover the enemy not in Europe or in the Pacific, but in themselves. Unfortunately, Knowles' new novel lacks the power and tightly wrought structure of his earlier work.

The time of Peace Breaks Out is September 1945; the war has ended, and veteran Pete Hallam returns to his alma mater to teach American history. From the beginning the book disappoints. As a veteran, Pete must of necessity reflect on his experiences at the front, but those reflections are gratuitous, vague and literary. His anguish is reported and cursorily analyzed rather than felt.

Knowles' intentions are lofty. Like W. H. Auden, Christopher Isherwood, C. Day Lewis and other British writers who just missed the Great War, Knowles hopes to dissect the fear and loathing of a new lost generation, those for whom the second Great War ended too soon. But Knowles' adolescents strike the reader as neither lost nor alienated, but quite normal. Rowdy, well-fed, friendly, deceitful, charming, they cut sports, detest *The Scarlet Letter*, affect sophistication, and cruelly bait one another.

The irony of Knowles' title is that in the post-war era peace does not exist. Like the adolescents of *A Separate Peace*, and the youngsters of William Golding's *Lord of the Flies*, Knowles' characters find that the battlefield is within. Wexford, a precocious, manipulative and indulged Devon senior, declares war on the scholarly, Germanic Hochschwender, who in Pete's first class proclaims his abhorrence of America. At once Hochschwender is labeled a Nazi sympathizer, and both students and reader await the inevitable explosion.

Instead of breaking into open conflict, the novel smolders interminably. Knowles takes the reader through two extraneous ski trips, Wexford's superfluous jaunt to New York (vaguely reminiscent of Holden Caulfield's sojourn), several issues of the school newspaper that any right-minded headmaster in the '40s would have instantly and justifiably scotched, and a number of vapid dialogues between students and between students and teachers. Finally a climax nears as Wexford spearheads a drive to raise funds for a window in honor of Devonians slain in World War II. . . .

Why does *Peace Breaks Out* fail? There is of course no pat answer. Knowles' descriptions of the New England countryside are at times inspired. His vision of moral ambiguity—the uncertainty with which we live—is valid. However, the return to Devon may have been unwise; successor novels seldom live up to expectations. Perhaps Knowles' biggest problem is with viewpoint. Through Gene, the narrator of *A Separate Peace*, Knowles imprinted upon the reader an unforgettable vision of adolescent life during World War II. Irony was always within reach as Gene labored to justify his actions by self-deceptive rationalizations. The narrative technique in *Peace Breaks Out*, shifting so frequently from character to character, lacks tension and subtlety. Too often Knowles loosely reports and informs when he should dramatize.

Paul Piazza, "A School for Scandal," in Book World—The Washington Post *(© 1981, The Washington Post), March 15, 1981, p. 8.*

JULIAN MOYNAHAN

The continuing appeal of **"A Separate Peace"** has little to do with its wartime atmosphere, though that is well handled. Rather, the attraction is its central character, Phineas, the 16-year-old epitome of "schoolboy glamour" who is done to death over the course of a school year. Phineas, with his gift for fantasy, capacity for affection and sheer physical grace, must stand somewhere between [F. Scott Fitzgerald's] Gatsby and [John Irving's] Garp in the spectrum of American white middle-class culture heroes. Tragically, as the force of Phineas's natural superiority impinges on his impressionable roommate, Gene, Gene reacts with panic and an unconscious need to play the part of Judas in Phineas's life. Gene, the narrator of **"A Separate Peace,"** tells the story of his betrayal of his friend with Calvinist conscientiousness, connecting his discovery of the destructive potential in himself with the greater destructiveness of the world conflict.

No wonder the book is a teen classic. Moved by the desire to be like Phineas and the fear of turning out like Gene, the young reader is ravaged; and it's no secret we love best the books that ravage us, particularly in adolescence.

The even more slender **"Peace Breaks Out"** also takes place at the Devon School, this time in 1946. Again the focus is on the senior class, and again a boy dies when accidental factors combine with the destructive impulses of a classmate. And once again there is a distressing suggestion that herd behavior, so often a part of student life at isolated, sexually segregated schools, contributes to the tragedy. (p. 3)

The story quickly comes to focus on the feuding of two boys—both clever, neither well liked by their classmates—who have clashed from the time of their first encounter in Pete's American history class. Hochschwender, from Wisconsin, professes pro-German sympathies and describes America as "a mongrel country getting bigger and bigger and winning wars because the land they've got is so rich in resources that they can defeat superior countries." This is pretty offensive stuff, but only the self-described "Anglo-Irish" Wexford takes it personally; the rest of the students at least dimly surmise that Hochschwender—who courts their dislike after a weak heart bars him from athletics, the only sure route to popularity at Devon—is likely to grow less obnoxious in time.

But Wexford, who is editor of the school paper, carries his dislike of Hochschwender fatally far. Something of a monster of opportunism and manipulation, Wexford makes the harrying of Hochschwender his principal senior activity and stops at nothing to bring him down, finally desecrating the school chapel and making it appear that it was Hochschwender who smashed the new stained-glass War Memorial window. Of course the intended irony, which works quite convincingly, is that the two boys have a lot in common. Each is an outsider who will never be invited into the inner circle of Devon sports heroes and top boys.

Where the book goes rather askew is in the portrayal of Wexford. He is limned with something like hate; John Knowles dwells obsessively on his physical quirks (such as the way he works his mouth), on his many vices, his dishonesty, his wealthy, cynical, Roosevelt-hating father. . . . In short, the school editor is presented as too loathsome a hypocrite. Beyond a certain point, we're tempted to cry, "C'mon now! The kid is only 17."

But for John Knowles, Wexford is much more than a creepy schoolboy. With his flair for self-advertisement, his compulsion to manipulate other people, his lack of moral scruples, his utter unlovableness, and, in consequence, his tendency to make dangerous mischief, Wexford may represent one face of the American future. The career of troublemaking begun at Devon in 1946 may well proceed and develop until by the '70s or '80s, the same Wexford, hollowest of hollow men, stalks the corridors of power, putting his awful mouth to the ear of the mighty. Maybe. Yet showing what rotten kids the Wexfords of this world were at school seems something of an exercise in futility. (pp. 3, 37)

There are many good things in **"Peace Breaks Out,"** among them the spare prose and the skillful plotting, which blends the routine and the remarkable to persuade us that a whole year of school has been lived through before Graduation Day. (p. 37)

Julian Moynahan, "More Trouble at Devon School,"
in The New York Times Book Review (© 1981 by
The New York Times Company; reprinted by permission), March 22, 1981, pp. 3, 37.

PETER S. PRESCOTT

Despite several virtues—some good writing and good observations about how boys live at school—"**Peace Breaks Out**"
suffers from its author having told such a similar story so much
better before [in "**A Separate Peace**"]. A moral mystery of
this kind requires, if not the first-person narration of the earlier
version, then at least a unified point of view. I suspect Knowles
once meant to provide one in the person of his teacher and at
some point sensed that his teacher is too dull to sustain it.
Worse, his story requires that the culprit go free—which means
in this case that neither police nor coroner may take an interest
in the victim. The particular strength of "**A Separate Peace**"
lay in Knowles's inspired conception of his characters: of a
victim who in no way resembles a victim and a murderer who
does not know he is one until after the event. By contrast, in
this recension the boys are neither likable nor believable. Going
back to your old school is always a risky business: the old
pranks you used to play will never work again. (p. 92J)

Peter S. Prescott, in his review of "Peace Breaks
Out," in Newsweek (copyright 1981, by Newsweek,
Inc.; all rights reserved; reprinted by permission),
Vol. XCVII, No. 16, April 20, 1981, pp. 92H, 92J.

DICK ABRAHAMSON

It has been twenty years since Knowles' classic *A Separate
Peace* first appeared. Now the author returns to Devon, that
same New Hampshire boys' school, for his latest novel, *Peace
Breaks Out*. While World War II provided the background for
the Gene and Phineas story, in the new novel the war is over
and a Devon graduate, Pete Hallam, returns from the war to
teach history at the school. Devon serves as a place for Pete
to rest and halt time a bit as he tries to sort out a broken
marriage and the horror of the war. What Pete meets at Devon
is a new group of teenagers who have been brought up with
the war but now seem confused, upset, bewildered, and short-
changed because the war has ended and questions about their
future are no longer clear-cut. . . .

As in *A Separate Peace*, an accidental death occurs, and the
elite sports heroes of Devon are enveloped in a cloud of guilt.
There's the same kind of follow-the-leader corruption that appears in Robert Cormier's *The Chocolate War*.

The writing in *Peace Breaks Out* is superb. The book does not
depend on *A Separate Peace*, but lives on its own. It will take
its place alongside the earlier book as a fine novel. (p. 75)

Dick Abrahamson, "Old Friends with New Titles,"
in English Journal (copyright © 1981 by the National
Council of Teachers of English; reprinted by permission of the publisher), Vol. 70, No. 5, September,
1981, pp. 75-7.*

M. JEAN GREENLAW

Twenty-one years of real time have passed since John Knowles
wrote his classic, *A Separate Peace*. Three years of novel time
have passed with the emergence of the companion book *Peace
Breaks Out*. It is 1945, the war is over, and Pete Hallam returns
to Devon as an instructor. He needs to regain his perspective
on life and recover from the war, his wounds, and a broken
marriage. Hallam's attempt at a retreat is thwarted when two
students clash in his first class in American history, and a
power struggle is begun within the school. The ensuing violence is carefully and masterfully developed and is reflective
of the horror that can occur when a talented leader misuses
his/her ability and manipulates others. The book is carefully
called a companion piece and not a sequel, and should be
judged on its own merit. The story is strong and compelling
and will be appreciatively read by high school students.

M. Jean Greenlaw, in her review of "Peace Breaks
Out" (copyright 1981 by the International Reading
Association, Inc.; reprinted with permission of the
International Reading Association and M. Jean
Greenlaw), in Journal of Reading, Vol. 25, No. 3,
December, 1981, p. 286.

THE VIRGINIA QUARTERLY REVIEW

Knowles surely has been urged many times over the years to
write a sequel to his most successful novel, the much admired
A Separate Peace, set at the Exeter-like academy called Devon
School. [*Peace Breaks Out*] is that sequel. Devon alumnus Pete
Hallam has returned to his alma mater to teach, having survived
the Second World War—just starting in the first book—in a
prisoner-of-war camp. Knowles knows Devon's turf thoroughly, and, as in the earlier book, his keen eye for examining
the ambitions and motivations of his student foils gives more
than average interest to his tale. Yet his heart clearly isn't in
this project, the attractive economical prose style of *A Separate
Peace* here reduced to almost a shorthand, as if there were a
pressing need to finish and be done with it.

A review of "Peace Breaks Out," in The Virginia
Quarterly Review (copyright, 1982, by The Virginia
Quarterly Review, The University of Virginia), Vol.
58, No. 1 (Winter, 1982), p. 20.

Kris Kristofferson

1936-

American songwriter and actor.

Kristofferson is credited with broadening the range of country music in the early 1970s. In contrast to the simple emotions expressed in many country songs, Kristofferson's sensitive, autobiographical lyrics touch "the more tender aspects of the human condition," according to Laura Cunningham. Kristofferson's songs have a literary quality rare in country music, for he utilizes uncommon metaphors and unique rhyme schemes in his bittersweet portrayals of love and life. The emotional depth of his songwriting has gained Kristofferson a following in the pop music world as well.

Kristofferson became successful as a songwriter before he began his recording career. His first album, *Kristofferson* (1970), featured several songs recorded previously by other artists. Although many critics feel that his writing had already peaked by the time this album was released, Kristofferson won the Country Music Association's Song of the Year award in 1970 for "Sunday Mornin' Comin' Down."

***Spooky Lady's Sideshow* (1974) is considered by some critics to be Kristofferson's most ambitious album. The songs examine the themes of personal and social alienation and reveal a strain of irony that some believe is deliberate self-parody. Although he still records albums and performs concerts, Kristofferson has also pursued an acting career that has overshadowed many of his recent songwriting efforts.**

(See also *Contemporary Authors*, Vol. 104.)

Michael Putland/Retna Ltd.

RAY REZOS

It's been a good long while since an old folkie like Kris Kristofferson has come along. Kristofferson embodies the folksinger's tradition. He sings simple songs that speak eloquently of experiences—spending a night in a small-town jailhouse, hitching a ride to New Orleans, paying a call on an old-time used-to-be. He is always totally believable; you know Kris has paid some dues. . . .

Kristofferson is a superb album. Kris shows plenty of versatility—from a rousing gospel chant, **"Blame It on the Stones"** . . . , to tender mellow things like **"Casey's Last Ride"** and **"For the Good Times,"** to rockin' country stuff like **"Best of All Possible Worlds."** His lyrics are always right; he can be bitter, cynical when he has to be, then turn around and be poetically pretty without being saccharine. . . .

As a songwriter, [Kristofferson] is both versatile and original. He is going to go a long way, and soon.

> *Ray Rezos, in his review of "Kristofferson," in* Rolling Stone *(by Straight Arrow Publishers, Inc. © 1970; all rights reserved; reprinted by permission), Issue 70, November 12, 1970, p. 38.*

NOEL COPPAGE

[Kristofferson's] songs deal with how it is to feel inadequate. The world is a mess, all right, he concludes, but then so am

I. The hero winds up in jail only partly because of his life style and politics—there also was the matter of his being roaring drunk and raising hell. The South, being so conservative, has always been a tough place for rebels, and Kristofferson has been able to construct a stable of Southern characters—mostly shades of himself—to personify actions and reactions that anyone anywhere can identify. Hank Williams, his boyhood hero, knew what it was like to be poor and scrambling in the South (which is pretty much like what it's like anywhere else, only more so) and it got into his songs, too. Like Williams, Kristofferson looks at it with a mixture of sympathy, objectivity, and hope. . . .

[*Sunday Mornin' Comin' Down* on **"Kristofferson"**] is his ultimate statement to date about loneliness, and Kris has made a lot of statements about loneliness. The lament for lost or never-had companions or loves dogs his songs with the quiet efficiency of a small-town bookkeeper. Many songs also mention being broke and hung over. . . .

Kristofferson tosses out a better-than-average adage occasionally. . . . But his lyrics don't have the gloss of self-conscious surrealism that so many other songwriters picked up by listening to Bob Dylan. Kristofferson's lyrics are straightforward and, in their way, generally graceful. Compare his songs with those of writers ten years his junior, those who are trying to say the same things, and you can see how experience—and even an Oxford education—can be helpful.

Kristofferson says he wants to affect people emotionally rather than intellectually—but any songwriter interested in survival wants to do that. The thing is that in order to write well for the viscera, one must have his own cerebrum in order, otherwise he won't know how thick to pour it on. Kristofferson, in this album, poured it on just about right.

Noel Coppage, "The Sound of Kristofferson," in Stereo Review *(copyright © 1971 by Ziff-Davis Publishing Company), Vol. 26, No. 4, April, 1971, p. 61.*

ALEC DUBRO

[Kristofferson is] a romantic, and unashamedly so. Not too different from the Kerouac vision of the Fifties, with a reverence for the "real" America and an unfortunate case of city sophistication. It's a feeling most of us have felt, but Kristofferson has pulled it off in his life and made some really fine music in the process.

Kristofferson's biggest hit in rock circles has been **"Me and Bobby McGee,"** an undiluted piece of romance, and to some extent, an epitome of a Kristofferson ballad. On [*The Silver Tongued Devil and I*] there is a song that is even more sentimental, to some people cloyingly so, but which I think is just a real pretty country song. **"Jody and the Kid"** is that, a neat kind of circle song. It begins with a little girl following Jody around, with folks saying "Looky yonder . . . there goes Jody and the kid." In the second verse she grows up and they get hitched. And it ends with another little girl, their daughter, following Jody down to the levee, just like her mama did.

"Jody and the Kid" is a perfect example of one of Kristofferson's contradictions, and of his ability to charm. It's the contrast between the crying-sweet lyrics and Kris' gravelly-deep macho voice, which is just arresting. . . .

It is as lyricist that Kristofferson excels. His melodies are good, but without his poetry they wouldn't be much. In another **"Bobby McGee"** type of song, **"When I Loved Her,"** Kris sings some deceptively simple lines that make people listen. . . .

There is, undoubtedly, nothing harder to bring off than simplicity and directness. It is, truly, a measure of the artist as a person. Kristofferson is direct in a way that few can make a go of. Johnny Cash is another, and so was Otis Redding. It's a case where the overwhelming personality animates a relatively simple artistic framework. Kristofferson hasn't reached the level of either of those artists, but he clearly shows the potential as a singer and a songwriter. . . .

If his style puts him in a class apart from most folk singers, then his contemporary vision, his compassion, separate him from the more simplistic variety of country singer. Country music is developing a sense of the complexities of moral issues, and Kris Kristofferson writes about the new world.

"Billy Dee" is Kristofferson's song about a needle-freak friend who was just overwhelmed by the world. His picture lacks the moralistic tone that most songs have when they attempt to deal with hard dope. . . .

Kris Kristofferson is a very talented man. He's worked hard and waited long, and it looks like his time is here. *The Silver Tongued Devil and I* is one of the better albums to be released

this bleak year, and one that has the capability of reaching an awful lot of people.

Alec Dubro, in his review of "The Silver Tongued Devil and I," in Rolling Stone *(by Straight Arrow Publishers, Inc. © 1971; all rights reserved; reprinted by permission), Issue 91, September 16, 1971, p. 42.*

BEN GERSON

[Kristofferson is best] known as a lyricist, and so any consideration of his latest album, *Border Lord* . . . , ought to begin there. At regular intervals, I was confronted with lines ranging from [confusion to inanity to hyperbole to the kind of pseudopoeticizing which should have gone out with Bob Lind and the Electric Prunes]. . . .

Kris' celebrations of *machismo* are his most patently stupid entries. When [Mick] Jagger works with the form, it's endearing because basically Jagger's assertiveness is compensating for failure. With Kris, it's sheer one-dimensional braggodocio. . . .

"Smokey," "Border Lord" . . . and **"Gettin' By High and Strange"** . . . are the "love" songs least ambiguous in their intent. But when Kris attempts to shade in the emotional side of his affairs, he really steps in it. In **"Little Girl Lost,"** for example, the stanzas alternate between objective consideration of his "little girl," bitterness at the way he was treated by her, and a melting forgiveness addressed to a third party who is about to "take her." The transitions are abrupt and irrational.

Kris is equally indigestible when he waxes reflective. . . . On **"Burden of Freedom,"** Kris plays his namesake, Christ . . . but proves his obtuseness and egocentricity in the last stanza when he "cleverly" turns the tables. . . . Asking for forgiveness of your enemies is indeed Christ-like; to ask for forgiveness of your own transgressions, with the implications that the person who would refuse it is morally unenlightened, is grossly self-indulgent.

Kris has a fondness for dualities—"the bitter for the sweet," "the laughter and the tears"—which includes a backwoods Calvinist sense of right and wrong. He also has a taste for cheap irony . . . as well as the ability to make the tautological sound striking. . . . His sentences are very long clauses and prepositional phrases Latinately balanced, and betray this country and western singer's Oxford education. . . .

Kris may or may not be a poet, a picker, a prophet, a pusher, a pilgrim, and a preacher, as his song **"The Pilgrim—Chapter 33"** enumerates, but he certainly is "a walking contradiction." By appealing to the more cosmopolitan urges among C&W listeners, as well as the more provincial yearnings among the rock audience, Kris has won a sizable following in both camps. But what makes him commercial condemns him artistically. He has neither the intensity and originality of vision of the solo artist (Neil Young or Joni Mitchell), nor the simple integrity and force of personality of the more restricted country and western artist (*e.g.*, his mentor, Johnny Cash). What is left is a strange hybrid: a C&W Jim Morrison, or a Bobby Goldsboro with sex appeal. . . .

In the final analysis, Kris is no more a good old boy from Nashville than Neil Young is a rancher, George Harrison a mystic, or Frank Zappa a freak. He's just as rootless as the rest of us, creating his identity not out of family, work, religion, geography, but wishes, fantasies and the need for a sense of place.

Ben Gerson, "Kristofferson: Goin' Down Slow," in Rolling Stone (by Straight Arrow Publishers, Inc. © 1972; all rights reserved; reprinted by permission), Issue 107, April 27, 1972, p. 50.

CHET FLIPPO

[*Jesus Was A Capricorn*] is a satisfying album, though in a more mellow, quiet way than would have been expected. Most conspicuous by its absence is [Kristofferson's] earlier despair, although the other themes that have sustained him appear less and in muted forms.

The obvious comparisons are to such albums as [Bob Dylan's] *John Wesley Harding* and [Leon Russell's] *Carney*. Works that mark a certain maturity as well as signifying a breathing spell; a time for the artist to answer critics, to tend to loose ends, and to try out one or two new things. In short, a request that he be at last judged on realistic terms. In that light, he's mostly successful.

The critics get a gentle blast in the title cut, the message of which is "everybody's gotta have somebody to look down on." . . .

There is little of the old Kristofferson here: only one road song (**"Out of Mind, Out of Sight"**) and the only thing that would qualify as an outlaw song (**"Jesse Younger"**) is strangely substanceless. The varying love songs—**"It Sure Was (Love),"** **"Enough for You,"** and **"Give It Time to Be Tender"**—are quiescent and almost passive. It's as if they were dealing with emotions at arm's length, on a second-hand basis. . . . They also suggest that he is a man who isn't a hungry writer any more and is no longer hurting and is now accepting life on different terms.

Chet Flippo, in his review of "Jesus Was a Capricorn" (reprinted by permission of the author), in Rolling Stone, Issue 125, January 4, 1973, p. 66.

STEPHEN HOLDEN

[John] Prine and Kristofferson have much in common: naturalistic singing styles that owe a lot to the early Dylan and to Johnny Cash, respectively, and lyric themes that evoke rural and/or working-class sensibilities. . . .

Unlike Prine, Kris Kristofferson seldom plays the role of social commentator. He came into prominence as the author of **"Me and Bobbie McGee."** . . . With its memorable catch phrase, "Freedom's just another word for nothin' left to lose," this great song generated expectations that Kristofferson has not lived up to. *Jesus Was a Capricorn* is his fourth and weakest album.

Prior to *Jesus,* Kristofferson's self-made image was that of a hard-drinking, hard-loving man-of-the-road, a rustic cosmopolite and earthy philosopher of romantic disillusionment. While *Jesus* belies that image, it offers little to replace it. . . . The best song is the title cut, a blunt comment on tolerance. . . .

The several long songs on *Jesus* are uncharacteristically tentative and gentle for Kristofferson. **"Give It Time to Be Tender"** (coauthored with Donnie Frith) is the first Kristofferson song ever to express fear of love. Another ballad, **"Enough for You,"** contradicts Kristofferson's established *macho* image with

its expression of personal inadequacy and vulnerability in a relationship. . . .

For all their faults, Prine and Kristofferson are better-than-average singer/songwriters. Kristofferson is the more tuneful; Prine, though not the facile phrase-maker that Kristofferson is, probes more deeply into his subjects to unearth a socially rooted *Angst.* In the long run, neither Prine nor Kristofferson shows the capacity to transmute sorrow into rage or resignation into love as Dylan has done so often and so well. (p. 55)

Stephen Holden, "Prine, Kristofferson, Green, and Wonder," in Saturday Review of the Arts (© 1973 Saturday Review Magazine Co.; reprinted by permission), Vol. 1, No. 2, February 3, 1973, pp. 55-6.*

COLIN IRWIN

This album [**"Spooky Lady's Sideshow"**] is one of depressing dullness. I always thought Leonard Cohen took the prize for monotonous vocals and James Taylor for pretentious word games, but K.K. reaches a new low in dismal music. He established his reputation basically on one good song (**"Me And Bobbie McGee"**) and apart from looking pretty and turning on housewives with his gruff voice, he's never done anything of comparable quality. A hip Johnny Cash, he wallows in romanticism and highbrow philosophy which is at best plain uninteresting and at worst pretentious and patronising. He uses clever phrases and grand words, but doesn't come out of it at all convincing while the treatment of the songs follows a predictable uninspiring pattern. . . . There's a plentiful supply of superficial "heavy" lyrics which are little more than an irritating bore. Then there's **"Same Old Song"**, which is a tedious reflection on the struggle to the top—party girls, cheap hotels, good-time band and the "I don't regret a bit of it" anthem. Horrible. At least that evoked some sort of positive reaction, which is more than can be said for most of the rest of the material on this album. **"Rescue Mission"**, a tale of the sea, is the only track with any real substance, and even then it's spoiled by dirge-like vocals. "Do I look like a loser?" he asks in **"Rock and Roll Time."** Quite frankly, on this showing, Kris—yes.

Colin Irwin, in his review of "Spooky Lady's Sideshow," in Melody Maker (© IPC Business Press Ltd.), July 6, 1974, p. 46.*

ELLEN WOLFF

Imagine a few friendly drunks, arms linked to bolster their balance while they sway to the downbeat songs of a rasping crooner singing into his beer. The soundtrack for this scenario could easily be Kris Kristofferson's *Spooky Lady's Sideshow,* the perfect mood music for malt liquor melancholics. Despite the provocative promise of the peepshow title, the songs exhibited here offer a bevy of down and outers like he's shown us before.

Sideshow begins on a resigned note, with **"Same Old Song,"** a mellow motel blues that's been hanging around Kris' repertoire for a while. It bears his droll, understated trademark, summarizing success as "just a few more friends that you'll be losing when you drop." (p. 73)

Kris further slows the pace by following up with a loser's lament, **"Broken Freedom Song."** . . . Simple images of suffering sketch sensitive vignettes that evoke understanding as well as pity. The low-key arrangement is just right, a subtle complement to the sparse, poignant lyric. . . .

["**Shandy**" is] a highly recognizable Kristofferson lyric, balancing on the thin line between cleverness and contrivance. . . .

The poetry in "**Shandy**" is more suggestive than explicitly narrative, which leaves more to the imagination than most of the album. It's highlighted by an archetypal Kristofferson chorus, the best in this collection. . . .

On side two the pace is lightened by "**Rescue Mission.**" . . . Though it's almost a 'novelty' song, standing in marked contrast to the rest of the album, its colorful imagery and bawdy humor make it an enjoyable oddity. It also points out that *Sideshow* provides only the perspective of the itinerant musician; self-analysis instead of tangible events peopled with someone other than the First Person. The narrowness of the "I'm alone on the road" genre is a problem, in Kris' case especially, since his poetry is his main drawing card. . . .

Country and western purists may find that Kris has simply settled into a comfortable groove. But for the rest of us, who've been waiting for song poems with the appeal of "**The Pilgrim**" and "**Bobby McGee,**" *Sideshow* displays a monochrome portfolio. Kristofferson's becoming a polished performer, world wiser and wearier, too. Somehow, he seemed more intriguing when he was still a smartass outcast. (p. 74)

> *Ellen Wolff, in her review of "Spooky Lady's Sideshow," in* Crawdaddy *(copyright © 1974 by Crawdaddy Publishing Co., Inc.; all rights reserved; reprinted by permission), August, 1974, pp. 73-4.*

PETER REILLY

[Kristofferson] uses a personalized c-&-w form as his mode, but the brains and wit apparent in his songs are as far removed from Nashville as Balliol. *Star Spangled Bummer (Whores Die Hard)* is probably the most ambitious track [on "**Spooky Lady's Sideshow**"]; an allegory about the current American predicament, it is unsuccessful because of Kristofferson's habit of burying meaning in a welter of symbols and images so complex that it would take a cryptographer to figure them out—and all this in that hokey down-home accent yet! Much to be preferred are his performances of such material as *I May Smoke Too Much,* the story of a Mr. Clean who slowly realizes that the smokers and drinkers and Casanovas are having all the fun and finally decides to join them, or his comment on his own life and career in the subtly defiant *Rock and Roll Time.* In these songs the use of a specific patois actually enhances the ideas in a solid American literary (Joel Chandler Harris, Arthur Kober) and musical (Stephen Foster, Charles Ives) tradition.

> *Peter Reilly, in his review of "Spooky Lady's Sideshow," in* Stereo Review *(copyright © 1974 by Ziff-Davis Publishing Company), Vol. 33, No. 3, September, 1974, p. 95.*

DAVID McGEE

It's been a long time since a Kristofferson album didn't sound like an afterthought to his movie career and *Who's to Bless and Who's to Blame* is no exception. . . . His decline as a songwriter is shocking only in its rapidity; all of those "shadows" lurking in and around his early compositions were tip-offs that the decline was inevitable. His most fully realized work, *The*

Silver-Tongued Devil and I, came in 1971 and subsequent albums have only given rise to the question of whether he'll ever be able to pull himself up again. This album leaves the question unanswered.

Kristofferson isn't even rewriting his best songs anymore; he's just falling flat on his face trying to write one song that might say something, anything.

> *David McGee, in his review of "Who's to Bless and Who's to Blame," in* Rolling Stone *(by Straight Arrow Publishers, Inc. © 1976; all rights reserved; reprinted by permission), Issue 205, January 29, 1976, p. 52.*

JON PARELES

Ah, the truth is revealed. These past few years, I, deceived like so many others, believed Kristofferson was a good-turning-mediocre songwriter who hated critics for reasons you'd expect. They'd keep pointing out his sloppy lyrics . . . , his repeated tunes, his Dylan cops . . . , his homogenized production. They'd even neglect decent songs like "**The Golden Idol**" in the rush to proclaim his wasted potential. *Surreal Thing*'s long-rumored revenge number, "**Eddie The Eunuch,**" dedicated to critics, tries to reinforce this mistaken impression with sexual cheap-shots and downright lies. . . .

The fact is that Kristofferson is actually jealous because he longs to *join* the critical ranks. He makes his first attempt in "**If You Don't Like Hank Williams,**" and—I hate to be the one to say this, Kris old buddy—sentences like "Hearin' Joni Mitchell is as good as smokin' grass" just aren't up to the high editorial standards of today's rock rags. Better brush up on the songwriting.

> *Jon Pareles, in his review of "Surreal Thing," in* Crawdaddy *(copyright © 1976 by Crawdaddy Publishing Co., Inc.; all rights reserved; reprinted by permission), October, 1976, p. 80.*

RICHARD HOGAN

Easter Island's boxing imagery suits Kristofferson better than the repetitious exercises in bedside manner which filled his previous seven solo discs. Fans began to harbor serious doubts about who would raise the kids if Kris' squaw wised up to all the furtive trysts her husband's songs boasted. But new songs such as "**Risky Bizness**" and "**The Fighter,**" which liken an entertainer's career to a boxer's, aren't so self-destructive as "**The Stranger**" and reflect Kristofferson's peculiar fascination with winning in public. . . .

[Though "**The Fighter**"] is executed in the standard, poky Kristofferson/Prine style that makes much of their output intolerable, "**Easter Island**" has enough rock strength to lift it above the level of a mere chordal backdrop for the writer's teasing, thoughtful lyric. The song's heartfelt spirituality makes Kristofferson's more familiar persona seem a narcissistic sham. For once Kristofferson is so eloquent that he sounds tipsy with his own sobriety.

One unanswered identity problem faces this champion-in-training. Kristofferson still mixes his prize-ring parables with the myth of the Sam Peckinpah man, that martyred, coonskin-capped messiah who rides with the Wild Bunch but ends up inside the Alamo vainly dodging bayonets. A talent of Kristofferson's stature shouldn't need a romanticized frontier definition of masculinity any more than his liver needs cirrhosis.

Richard Hogan, "Kris' Craft," in Crawdaddy *(copyright © 1978 by Crawdaddy Publishing Co., Inc.; all rights reserved; reprinted by permission), July, 1978, p. 68.*

ROBIN GRAYDEN

Kristofferson's got a fixation about the devil—he called a previous album "The Silver Tongued Devil And I"—and he could be Old Nick himself for all I care, as long as he produces albums like this. . . . [While "Shake Hands With The Devil"] may not carry such masterpieces as "Sunday Morning Coming Down" or "Casey's Last Ride," for example, the songs linger in the memory; they're "sleepers" rather than instant hits. . . .

The title track is a powerful rocker about a lustful lover. . . . Love comes in different guises, and Kristofferson exploits them with a variety of approaches—"Killer Barracuda" starts as an allegory; he's the predator in search of female prey. Then in "Whiskey, Whiskey" he's a failed lover getting solace from the bottle.

The soft approach to the subject is represented by "Prove It To You One More Time Again", a strong pop-country ballad with plenty of punch; and the hard approach by "Once More With Feeling". . . .

Kristofferson may have had problems in the past, but this album shows that he's lost none of his prowess as both a writer and an entertainer.

Robin Grayden, in his review of "Shake Hands with the Devil," in Melody Maker *(© IPC Business Press Ltd.), November 31, 1979, p. 28.*

NOEL COPPAGE

Kris Kristofferson, like most of us, writes better when something's bothering him; unfortunately, he doesn't *sing* any better. ["To the Bone"], apparently designed to work off some of the feelings attending his split with Rita Coolidge (at least it will be taken that way), has some poignant and well-crafted songs in it, but Kris' vocals are so limited in range and emotional expressiveness that the listener has to do a lot of imaginative reconstruction to appreciate them. *Daddy's Song* . . . , a sort of *Jody and the Kid* revisited, walks a fine line between pathos and bathos, alternating between the guilt and agony a father feels when he can't live with his child and a "rational" viewpoint. . . . Something similar is true of *The Last Time,* a song whose economy and near-perfect mating of words and melody recall the glory days of the *Bobby McGee* era. The shock of hitting the bottom of the barrel and bouncing up slightly with a "to hell with it" attitude is deftly planted in *Nobody Loves Anybody Anymore,* co-written with Billy Swan. . . . *Magdalene* (a soft and third-person way of saying "she's going to be sorry I'm gone") . . . is the most impressive cut without being the most impressive song. I tend to value good songs more than good singing . . . up to a point. Kristofferson seems to be writing so much beyond his vocal equipment that most of this album is beyond that point. (pp. 101-02)

Noel Coppage, in his review of "To the Bone," in Stereo Review *(copyright © 1981 by Ziff-Davis Publishing Company), Vol. 46, No. 5, May, 1981, pp. 101-02.*

John Landis

1950-

American film director and screenwriter.

Landis is noted for zany comedies that poke fun at contemporary culture. Containing a combination of slapstick, sight gags, and satire, Landis's films effectively convey his sense of the absurd. Landis first gained critical attention as a director for *The Kentucky Fried Movie.* This film, similar to Ken Shapiro's *The Groove Tube,* consists of fast-paced vignettes that parody commercial television, sex education courses, and such film genres as the martial arts and the Blaxploitation movies produced during the early 1970s.

National Lampoon's Animal House was an enormously popular film that greatly advanced Landis's career. Primarily a satire on collegiate life, *Animal House* is a direct assault on authority and self-imposed stratification of social fraternities. Landis's next film, *The Blues Brothers,* which he wrote with comedian Dan Aykroyd, is a rhythm-and-blues musical whose epic structure has been compared to the MGM musicals of the Depression era. *An American Werewolf in London* is a spoof of the werewolf films popular during the 1930s and 1940s. Although this film contains many of the same comic elements used in Landis's earlier work, it is noted also for its realistic special effects.

Because of the tone of his films, Landis's work is considered buffoonery by some critics. However, Landis insists that his work contains serious social commentary, claiming that "all movies are political, no matter how silly they are."

© Jerry Bauer

LAWRENCE VAN GELDER

Anyone interested in the condition of humor and wit in the United States stands likely to come away depressed from "The Kentucky Fried Movie." . . . "The Kentucky Fried Movie" is in the tradition of "The Groove Tube" and "Tunnelvision." The range of its satire and comedy, as displayed in 22 segments running from a minute or two up to 30 minutes, is fairly narrow.

Television is both an inspiration and a preoccupation, with commercials, news shows, early morning talk-news shows, talk shows and 50's-style courtroom dramas all serving as targets.

Movies come next. "Cleopatra Schwartz," dealing with the love of a black superwoman and a Hasidic rabbi, is this movie's comment on black exploitation films.

Disaster movies, soft-core pornographic movies and martial-arts films are also the focus of a mordancy that gives the impression—particularly in the 30-minute martial-arts segment—of being undercut by the maker's affection for the original genre. Sex records and charity appeals are also inspirations for efforts at humor in this 86-minute film, which seems at least twice as long. . . .

Television is at once this movie's nourishment and onus. The caliber of television wit and humor has never been uniformly high, and comedy derived from it is likely to have difficulty surmounting such humble origins. It is little wonder, then, that

"The Kentucky Fried Movie," being freed from the restraints of television, though not from its inherent defects, occasionally descends into juvenile tastelessness (a dignified woman using four-letter words; a board game built around the assassination of President Kennedy; a charity appeal involving a child's corpse). . . .

Lots of people will probably like "The Kentucky Fried Movie," just as they like Kentucky Fried Chicken and McDonald's hamburgers. But popularity is still no reason for deifying mediocrity.

Lawrence Van Gelder, "'Kentucky Fried' a Yolky Film," in The New York Times *(© 1977 by The New York Times Company; reprinted by permission), August 11, 1977, p. C14.*

RICHARD SCHICKEL

The Kentucky Fried Movie is a sort of *National Lampoon* that talks and moves. It offers a compilation of very broad show-business parodies aimed at sophomoric sensibilities (and those permanently arrested in those realms). The picture is indelicate, obvious, often less funny than it thinks it is, but lively and sufficiently on-target to reward casual attention.

Most of the film satirizes television commercials and movie trailers. Since such bits and pieces cannot, in the nature of things, exceed the length of the material being sent up, the misfires do not detain, and are quickly forgotten. Among those most likely to be remembered—at least for a day or two—are a beer commercial in which those seeking gusto from the suds are a group of Hare Krishna sect members coming in after a hard day's chanting and leaflet peddling, and an institutional plug from an oil company experimentally reclaiming oil from greasy containers cast off by fast-food restaurants.

There is also a public service message . . . informing the world of death's danger signals and advising what to do when the end arrives (don't attempt to operate heavy machinery). Finally there are previews of coming attractions, the products of the fevered imagination of a mythical movie producer, Samuel L. Bronkowitz, offering foretastes of epics like *That's Armageddon.*

Bronkowitz is also producer of record of the movie's longest, most carefully worked-out and best sequence, a bargain-basement Kung Fu adventure called *A Fistful of Yen.* The hero has a lisp. The villain uses a gong instead of a beep to tell callers when to start talking into his answering machine and speaks in a dubbed voice that in a masterly manner sends up all the dubbed voices one has ever suffered through while watching imported pictures.

It would be nice to report that everything in **Kentucky Fried** reaches the level of this segment, but many of its subjects are themselves self-parodying and scarcely worth even the class-day skit efforts expended on them here. Still, the film avoids the scatological depths of *Groove Tube,* its most obvious forebear, while offering the hope that television is not bending to the breaking point all the young minds exposed to it. To be sure, a moment or two of genuine outrage might have enlivened **Kentucky Fried,** but there is a lot of good sense and humor in its assaults on television and the movies' sillier realms.

Richard Schickel, "Lightly Browned," in Time *(copyright 1977 Time Inc.; all rights reserved; reprinted by permission from* Time*), Vol. 110, No. 9, August 29, 1977, p. 76.*

DAVID DENBY

Fraternity-house pranks, which depend on humiliating your rivals and yourself at the same time, may be the lowest of all forms of humor, but they have a necessity that anyone can see: They are probably the only form of rebellion available to square college boys. (Hip kids tend not to join fraternities, i.e., they get laid off campus.) In a few years those boys will be doctors, lawyers, businessmen, but at nineteen they can make outrageously cruel and infantile jokes and no one will give them too hard a time. At college I halfheartedly admired the guys who tore themselves apart on Saturday night, but I never wanted to join their revels. *National Lampoon's Animal House,* which is a genial, uneven, occasionally hilarious celebration of frat-house anarchy, doesn't give you the chance to stand back: The movie says that anyone who won't join the fun is a prig. . . .

Animal House was written by three *National Lampoon* contributors (Harold Ramis, Douglas Kenney, and Chris Miller) as a continuation of that magazine's nonstop guerrilla war against respectful attitudes toward culture, women, blacks, animals, etc. The year is 1962 at Faber College, one of the less rigorous West Coast institutions. The place is in a state of war. On the

one side is Delta House, a sorry collection of fatties, geeks, near-criminal misfits, and outrageous make-out artists (our heroes). On the other side are the embattled dean . . . and his obsequious student allies in Omega House, an even sorrier collection of murderously ambitious John Dean types with prom-queen girl friends who are all hot and bothered underneath their colorless, waxy lipstick. The war is fought in the frat houses, in bed, and in the dean's office, where such genuine atrocities as shooting the ROTC commander's horse are regularly committed.

Director John Landis (**Kentucky Fried Movie**) doesn't have what you would call a light touch, but he's good at keeping the frenetic action clear, and he uses the large cast well. . . . In this movie women are definitely seen as prey, but they have their own feelings, too. Or at least their own desires: Sex is the one thing the *National Lampoon* can't bring itself to ridicule. The sexiness, even tender sexiness, that gently breaks through the scabrous surface is the redeeming sign of grace in what could have been a very rancid show. (p. 65)

David Denby, "Man without a Country," in New York *Magazine (copyright © 1978 by News Group Publications, Inc.; reprinted with the permission of* New York *Magazine), Vol. 11, No. 31, July 31, 1978, pp. 64-5.*

PENELOPE GILLIATT

"**National Lampoon's Animal House,**" directed by John Landis, is set in a college called Faber in 1962. But it is not by backdating comedy that one gets away with bad comedy. This comic-book frat-house farce goes WHAM! EECH!! at the expense of a system that self-evidently fosters invaluable intelligences. The picture gives us much facetiousness about a fat undergraduate who steals food (ZOWIE!!) and a professor who apologizes because "Paradise Lost" is a long read (SPLAT!!!!). . . . One's ribs are nudged until they ache. The witty hard truths about American college education in the early sixties scarcely inhere in guffaws about beer-drinking and about rather Germanic pranks and about the taking of "diet pills" during exams. Some of us—a lot of us—were there at the time, and the pith of any good lampooning would surely lie in showing the straits of a privileged class of young people with a feeling of thwarted morality. A point could be made of the fact that there are virtually no blacks in the student cast, but the film ignores it. Nor does the picture, in its roll call of stereotypes, give any attention to the intellectually underendowed. The status of being intentionally funny is awarded exclusively to the good-looking and the successfully flirtatious. If one didn't know something about education here, one would think it hermetic from the rest of the world to the point of hygienic refrigeration; if one didn't know the unique rapidity and self-criticism of humor here, one would think wit an absent ingredient. The film tells social untruths that go beyond the excuse of presenting the sort of humor called "undergraduate." "**Animal House**" depicts a university life that is deeply anti-academic, an undergraduate life that is as blind as a pit pony, and an almost criminally false idea of the national sense of the comedic. The inhabitants of this country, including its undergraduates, surely proffered in the sixties some of the bravest jokes in its history. (pp. 53-4)

Penelope Gilliatt, "Glazed," in The New Yorker *(© 1978 by The New Yorker Magazine, Inc.), Vol. LIV, No. 26, August 14, 1978, pp. 53-4.*

VINCENT CANBY

"Animal House" is cinematically sloppy—I've now seen the film twice and I still can't separate some of the people. There always seem to be two characters who look much alike to represent a single type. It's full of supposedly comic scenes that have no adequate punch lines to end them, and some of the cross-cutting seems to have been done during a blackout. Yet the movie's fondness for sloth, mess, vulgarity, non-conformism (circa 1962, of course), as demonstrated by the members of an epically disorganized college fraternity, is frequently very, very funny.

The targets of its humor (gung-ho fraternities, neatness, Nixon, chastity, sobriety, Vietnam, patriotism, ceramics) are not exactly sacred at this point, but the gusto of the movie is undeniably appealing. So too are the performers. . . .

The success of "**Animal House**" . . . is rather easier understood after the fact than before. Among other things, "**Animal House**" calls attention to a sentimentality not previously acknowledged in a movie like "American Graffitti." I suspect too that some portion of the movie-going public is a lot more bored with orderliness—with the formulas—of conventional comedies and dramas in theaters and on television than has been recognized heretofore. ["Animal House" manages] to suggest the sublime, if sometimes infantile, joys of chaos and disorder without seriously questioning the system that contains them.

> *Vincent Canby, "What's So Funny about Potheads and Toga Parties?" in* The New York Times, *Section 2 (© 1978 by The New York Times Company; reprinted by permission), November 19, 1978, p. 17.**

IAN HAMILTON

[There are many laughs] in the *National Lampoon's Animal House*: the decor, the uniforms, and many of the attitudes come to us straight from early Presley campus idylls, or even from *Rebel Without a Cause,* and at least some of the chirpy delinquencies derive from Sergeant Bilko, but the film's animating spirit is blisteringly up to date. More than just a comic fantasy about going back to school to punch some loathed teacher in the mouth, it's essentially a mean-eyed dream of vengeance against what Teacher, in that bygone epoch, used to get away with teaching.

The setting is an Ivy-Leagueish American college in the early days of the Vietnam conscription, and the characters are sliced into two camps. There are the Omegas: the ultra-clean-limbed fraternity, button-downed, forever sucking up, but also—as we learn from the way they handle their initiation rites and from their attachment to the college military corps—sadistic, cowardly and crooked. Publicly moralistic, privately corrupt: the all-American good boy, we are meant to feel. Pitting against the goodies are the inhabitants of the Delta fraternity—a marvellous collection of scruffs and villains, but comradely, adventurous and free of bullshit. The Deltas booze and screw, cheat in their exams (or vaguely try to), play the new rock records, and tirelessly dedicate themselves to what they describe as 'pointless' acts of self-fulfilment. The Deltas may be pointless, but they are as resourceful as Hollywood commandos when it comes to protecting their own lack of interests. The Dean of the college . . . is busy planning a college parade in the local town (and he's been heavily warned by the local Italian mayor that he'd better make sure it's a really nice parade) and he recuits the Omega leaders in a plan to get rid of the Deltas

before the great day. The Deltas, to whom all parades are rather like exams, fight back, and this is the film's main point of contest. (The showdown, I should say, is disappointingly tame and chaotic.)

Main contests aside, though, most of the film's fun is situation-fun. . . . There are a dozen . . . genuinely funny individual sketches and, for belly laughs alone, *Animal House* should certainly be seen. But there's also an affecting incongruity, between that period and this treatment, which makes the whole atmosphere of the thing likely to last even longer than its individual jokes. (pp. 263-64)

> *Ian Hamilton, "Delta Plus," in* New Statesman *(© 1979 The Statesman & Nation Publishing Co. Ltd.), Vol. 97, No. 2501, February 23, 1979, pp. 263-64.**

ERIC BRAUN

[Landis] shows firm control of the satirical content of [*Animal House*] so that every jab strikes home and very few gags go on too long, unlike his *Kentucky Fried Movie* where almost every sequence lingers until the initial laugh turns to a yawn. His bad-taste buds have been tightened, too, so that the killing of the bully-boy officer's adored horse by the idiot freshmen trying to prove themselves as 'mad, bad and dangerous' as their peers, stops short of actually wanting to make one throw up and produces instead a smile of relief—but only just. . . .

This is a painfully funny movie, which may offend as many as it amuses, but, to quote Gloria Swanson: 'It's not the fault of films today that they are ugly: it is their business to mirror life, and that has become ugly, so they're only doing what they are supposed to do'. (p. 32)

> *Eric Braun, "'National Lampoon's Animal House'" (© copyright Eric Baun 1979; reprinted with permission), in* Films and Filming, *Vol. 25, No. 7, April, 1979, pp. 31-2.*

MARTYN AUTY

The self-conscious irony of equating a junk movie with junk food suggests exactly what is wrong with *The Kentucky Fried Movie*: its knowing comedy is so disposable as to be almost non-existent. Parody follows parody, each one half-baked and then half-digested. Here and there a trace of humour suggests an idea that might profitably have been developed (the trailer for CATHOLIC HIGH SCHOOL GIRLS IN TROUBLE, or the straight black comedy that follows Henry Gibson's lugubrious "United Appeal for the Dead"), but the problem is essentially the same one that defeated *The Groove Tube* (an inauspicious antecedent). Parody has no existence beyond its object, leads nowhere, is not sharp enough to amount to satire nor sufficiently indulgent to be enjoyable simply as slapstick: *Kentucky Fried Movie* is precisely half-witted comedy. . . . More limiting still is director John Landis' dependence on *Monty Python*-type jokes: a patient in the headache clinic is repeatedly hit over the head with a brick; a lone cinema patron is perfunctorily touched up by an usher at a "Feel-A-Round" movie show. (Landis, of course, has since struck a richer vein of more indigenous comedy with *National Lampoon's Animal House*.) Laboured in this way, Python-esque humour very quickly goes cold. And it is in this form—though always with a smile—that the Kentucky Fried people serve up their movie.

> *Martyn Auty, in his review of "The Kentucky Fried Movie," in* Monthly Film Bulletin *(copyright © The*

British Film Institute, 1979), Vol. 46, No. 543, April, 1979, p. 73.

JANET MASLIN

There isn't a moment of "The Blues Brothers" that wouldn't have been more enjoyable if it had been mounted on a simpler scale. This essentially modest movie is reported to have cost about $30 million, and what did all that money buy? Scores of car crashes. Too many extras. Overstaged dance numbers. And a hollowness that certainly didn't come cheap. A film that moved faster and called less attention to its indulgences might never convey, as "The Blues Brothers" does in all but its jolliest moments, such unqualified despair. . . .

["The Blues Brothers" features] two very deadpan white men whose love of black culture forms the story's main, perhaps only thread. This aspect of the movie, potentially its most interesting and original aspect, goes largely neglected. Though the story leads Jake and Elwood Blues of Chicago to a number of wonderful soul or blues performers—among them Aretha Franklin, James Brown, Ray Charles and Cab Calloway—it uses the musicians in cameo roles and devotes itself otherwise to a conventional, poorly rendered plot. The whole movie supposedly hinges on Jake and Elwood Blues's efforts to raise money to pay taxes on a church orphanage. Had the orphanage been tax exempt, there would be no story at all. . . .

In the movie's only show-stopping episode, they walk into a Chicago luncheonette, and there, behind the counter, is Aretha Franklin, playing a waitress. Her husband is a former member of their band, and they want him. Miss Franklin wants him too, and lets him know it by singing "Think" with all her formidable might. It's quite a song, and she offers quite a rendition. Even this, the best scene here, is furiously ill-directed, with cutting that really hampers the rhythm of the music. One of the musicians is directed to stand on the luncheonette counter, although that means the camera will lop off his head.

John Landis, who also directed "Animal House," manages to fill "The Blues Brothers" with senseless extra shots, distracting editing, views of virtually everything from too many angles. This is part of the movie's exhausting overkill, and it also means that when the brothers drive a car into a shopping mall, they will crash into every last plate glass window. And it means that when the brothers perform before an audience, the crowd will rise to its feet in unison, or clap so enthusiastically that their behavior seems entirely pre-fab. There are parts of "The Blues Brothers" that would have played infinitely better with a knock-about feeling, a sloppiness like that of "Animal House." As it is, the movie is airless. The stakes needn't have been so suffocating high.

Janet Maslin, "Movie: 'Blues Brothers'—Belushi and Aykroyd," in The New York Times *(© 1980 by The New York Times Company; reprinted by permission), June 20, 1980, p. C 16.*

LAWRENCE O'TOOLE

There's no denying that certain scenes in *The Blues Brothers* have a wild, off-the-hip humor, and that the great Aretha Franklin sings a sizzling *Think* and that the stunt work is spectacular. But this cop-chase-car-crash-let's-be-as-crass-as-we-can farce, where everything in sight is smashed with infantile pleasure, has a rankling edge of desperation to it. That desperation re-

flects the sorry state of movie comedy right now, which began with the anarchic *Animal House* and left a trail of forced funnies—*Meatballs, 1941, Where the Buffalo Roam, Roadie, Wholly Moses* et al. Crude comedy used to release us from our complacencies; now the vulgarity has lost its charm—it has become, ironically, too common. Being irreverent has no bite because young directors feel they have to be irreverent about everything: they don't have a focus, or reason, for their anarchy, and so they begin with a single idea and just toss it to the winds.

The Blues Brothers is a single idea out of control. . . .

The cutting of the chase scenes and the musical numbers is so frantic you get the feeling that Landis . . . just kept shooting footage, piling the jokes and the cars on top of one another as a last, rash resort. When he parodies other movies (*Close Encounters, The French Connection, The Sugarland Express*), the scenes have some zest—we know where they're coming from. When Landis stages a demolition derby through a shopping mall, it's nihilistic in the most juvenile way—a kind of baby's rage over not being able to do anything better. *The Blues Brothers* doesn't have a plot; it strings gags together by connecting them to the chase. The moviemakers probably assume that audiences will laugh so that they won't feel square, and the moviemakers are probably right. Current comedies don't stop to relax and crack a good, honest joke—they're too busy bullying.

Lawrence O'Toole, "The Animals Go to a Demolition Derby," in Maclean's Magazine *(© 1980 by Maclean's Magazine; reprinted by permission), Vol. 93, No. 26, June 30, 1980, p. 53.*

DAVID DENBY

The Blues Brothers is a monstrous $30 million expansion of a ramshackle old Hollywood musical revue (like *The Big Broadcast of 1938*)—the kind of movie that used to be made for a few hundred thousand dollars. Those vaudeville musicals, their unrelated musical numbers stitched together with comedy routines, often featured jazz musicians, or black singers and dancers who would never get the chance to star in a movie of their own. Racism was built into the form. Well, things haven't changed all that much in 45 years. . . . Hectic, exhausting, often gross and stupid, *The Blues Brothers* nonetheless makes a tiny purchase on immortality when Aretha Franklin opens her mouth to sing.

People who love soul music and blues may have a little trouble accepting Aykroyd and Belushi as great performers in a movie that consigns the authentic greats to backup roles. Ever since the two comics started doing it a few years ago on *Saturday Night Live*, the Blues Brothers routine has inhabited an uneasy region between parody and put-on. . . .

Belushi and Aykroyd doubtless intended to pay homage to the great black performers who have inspired them, but the homage often comes close to insult and outright ripoff. Some of the performers are treated shabbily. Spotted in front of a soul-food store, the great John Lee Hooker gets a minute or so of screen time. Aretha Franklin, as a hash-house waitress attached to a member of the band, does a tremendous number, "Think," and then she's dropped out of the movie. Aretha Franklin left behind to wait tables! In their own way director John Landis, Belushi, and Aykroyd recolonize the black performers. The great old Cab Calloway, his smile as brilliantly insinuating as ever, sings "Minnie the Moocher" in white tie and tails in front of a huge audience, killing time for the impatient crowd while the boys are being chased by the police. Calloway's smile—the seal of a great entertainer's joy in giving pleasure—shows up Aykroyd and Belushi's sullen "cool" for the sophomoric thing it is. Yet what an insulting context for Calloway's triumph—as a fill-in! From this movie, today's kids might think that Calloway, Franklin, and Ray Charles were important because they led to the emergence of the Blues Brothers. (p. 52)

John Landis makes a movie the way General Westmoreland made war—he piles on the technology and the destruction. It's not enough for cars to chase each other all over Chicago and leap across open drawbridges: they must also demolish a huge shopping mall and skid into each other in monumental pileups. Landis repeats every gag five times without ever achieving a formal style; visually, the movie is cluttered and graceless and cold—the dominant colors are iron gray and blue. And Landis destroys some moments that might have been great if done more simply. When James Brown, as a singing preacher, begins to let loose, and fantastic black dancers leap ecstatically across the church aisle, Landis cuts back and forth from one camera angle to another in time to the music. Once again, a hot-shot director has turned a potentially great dance number into an editing-table tour de force, ruining our pleasure. *The Blues Brothers* leaves us feeling dazed, grateful, and frustrated all at once. (pp. 52-3)

> *David Denby, "Two-Faced Blues," in* New York Magazine *(copyright © 1980 by News Group Publications, Inc.; reprinted with the permission of* New York Magazine*), Vol. 13, No. 26, June 30, 1980, pp. 52-4.**

PAULINE KAEL

It has taken all these years for Aretha Franklin to reach the screen—and then she's on for only one number! Getting her into **"The Blues Brothers"** was the smartest thing that the director, John Landis, did; letting her get away after that number was the dumbest. (p. 95)

This musical slapstick farce, set in Chicago, is good-natured, in a sentimental, folk-bop way, but its big joke is how overscaled everything in it is, and that one sequence that's really alive is relatively small-scale. John Landis has a lot of comic invention and isn't afraid of silliness, but in terms of slapstick craft he's still an amateur. This showed in **"Animal House,"** but it didn't seem to matter as much there: the sloppiness was part of the film's infantile gross-out charm. Here he's working with such a lavish hand that the miscalculations in timing are experienced by the audience as a form of waste. There are funny moments. . . . The script, by Aykroyd and Landis, keeps the jokes coming, and maybe it wouldn't matter much when they miss if almost all the musical numbers weren't staged so disappointingly. And maybe the jokes missing *and* the musical number fizzling wouldn't matter *too* much if only Aykroyd and Belushi really clicked together, in the slightly hallucinated way you expect them to. But the fun has gone out of their hipster-musicians act. Possibly it was only good for a few skits. There's nothing going on between them, and the taciturn style doesn't allow them to show enough personality for a full-length movie. (pp. 96-7)

Does the film traduce the great black rhythm-and-blues musicians in the cast? Only inadvertently, by not knowing how to use them. Since Aretha Franklin transcends the film's in-

competence, one can perhaps forgive Landis (who is still in his twenties) for the somewhat patronizing casting of the black performers. No doubt he would do something comparable with Benny Goodman and Hoagy Carmichael and Gene Krupa. (Amateurism crosses color lines.) A chief ingredient of the film is noisy car crashes, pileups, and demolition scenes: the Blues Brothers antagonize so many individuals and organizations in the course of rounding up their old band that thousands of vehicles chase them and converge on unlucky streets and plazas. [**"The Blues Brothers"**] is probably more fun for people who drive than for people like me. Even when I laugh at car stunts, I'm not having a good time—I'm just giving in. I blot them out instantaneously, the way one forgets pain. (p. 97)

> *Pauline Kael, in her review of "The Blues Brothers" (© 1980 by Pauline Kael), in* The New Yorker, *Vol. LVI, No. 20, July 7, 1980, pp. 90, 93-7.**

ANDREW SARRIS

Like so many other contemporary movies, including the anticlimactic *The Empire Strikes Back,* the overproduced **The Blues Brothers** could have been better rendered as an animated cartoon. The uncomically surreal car smashes belong in a *Roadrunner* series, and Belushi and Aykroyd are infinitely more effective in motion than in conversation. As for the great black musical performers—Aretha Franklin, Cab Calloway, Ray Charles, and James Brown—they might just as well be featured in vaudeville shorts for all the dramatic or narrative impact they have. For example, Aretha Franklin literally stops the show with her soulfully feminist rendition of "Think" when her man is tempted to leave the kitchen of their tiny diner for a precarious life on tour with the Blues Brothers. What happens? Her man leaves even more defiantly than before. The song has changed nothing, meant nothing. Even the three girl back-up singers, supportive during the number, end up snickering at the hopeless quandary of the Franklin character.

I hate to keep bringing up the old-fashioned critical criterion of coherence at a time when movie patrons seem to have an even shorter attention span than they used to. Certainly, **The Blues Brothers** is not as much of a mess structurally as **Animal House** or **Meatballs** or **The Jerk,** to name three broadly anarchic surprise hits. The trouble is that **The Blues Brothers** makes even less sense than any of its three predecessors.

I do not buy the line of one reviewer that **The Blues Brothers** is hip-racist in the way that the movie exploits traditional stereotypes of blacks (as opposed to the naive racism of King Vidor's 1929 *Hallelulah!*). I do believe, however, that there is some conflict between the affectionately enlightened attitude of the Blues Brothers as characters. It is one thing to conceive of Rocky as a Capraesque hero by downplaying the mob connections. But Sylvester Stallone would never have allowed Rocky to hold up a gas station even for the noblest motives as Belushi's Joliet Jake is said to have done for the good of the band. Joliet Jake is introduced to us as a convict being released by a slightly ridiculous prison system. I say "slightly" because Landis has staged many of the scenes as if he were dabbling in an honest-to-goodness film noir. The audience titters expectantly waiting for some **Animal House** anarchy. Instead, *The Bells of St. Mary's* motif is introduced laboriously with the meanest nun . . . in Christendom. From then on, the movie becomes mystical and mythological as the Blues Brothers pursue their holy quest for 5000 honest dollars to save an orphanage from foreclosure. Cab Calloway, the elderly watchman at the orphanage, adds a sympathetic dimension to the mission for God that the nasty nun cannot. . . .

For *The Blues Brothers,* God serves as an excuse both for a series of bullying skits in which Belushi and Aykroyd can act as hoods, and for their seemingly miraculous invulnerability to the assaults of all the policemen in Illinois, the American Nazi Party, a troupe of country and western singers and a vengeful ex-girl friend abandoned at the altar. During the interminable chases, my frame of reference was not Buster Keaton's *Cops* but Stanley Kramer's *It's a Mad, Mad, Mad Mad World.* Destruction for the sake of destruction, without wit, grace, or humor. Significantly, *The Blues Brothers* took an R [rating] simply to allow Belushi and Aykroyd to garner easy laughs from the small fry with gratuitously foul language. . . . The writing of this film is so faint-hearted, however, that one cannot get involved enough to be offended. All the "energy" has gone into the car crashes, and all the talent has gone into the musical numbers. The rest is undeveloped drivel.

> Andrew Sarris, "Can't Stop the Blues Brothers" (reprinted by permission of The Village Voice and the author; copyright © News Group Publications, Inc., 1980), in The Village Voice, Vol. XXV, No. 27, July 2-8, 1980, p. 33.*

JANET MASLIN

Imagine a college boy from Great Neck, L. I., carrying a knapsack and wearing a down parka, wandering very, very incongruously across the English moors. Now imagine two such innocents abroad, to the musical accompaniment of "Blue Moon." As the song suggests, the sun will be going down soon, and the moon will be coming up, and those deserted moors will prove to be not so empty after all. **"An American Werewolf in London"** begins on a note that's equally balanced between comedy and horror, and that also has a fine touch of restraint. It gets off to a wonderful start.

John Landis, who also directed **"Animal House"** and **"The Blues Brothers,"** has the makings here of a much better movie than either of those. He's serious about the hipness of his two leading characters, who behave, even after one has been killed by a werewolf and the other maimed, as if this were all part of a fraternity hazing. Mr. Landis is also serious about making this a horror film that packs a wallop. For a while, he is able to fit both of these seemingly irreconcilable ingredients into the same movie, the offhand humor and the terror, too.

When the movie backfires, which it finally does, it's because too much grisly footage has been used too lightly. Mr. Landis's comic detachment, which has been fascinating throughout much of the movie, is something he holds on to even when a deeper response is needed. Eventually it becomes less comic than callow. . . .

[David and Jack] are attacked by a monster early in the movie, and it's hard to say who fares worse of the two. Jack is mauled and relegated to the ranks of the undead, which in a movie like this hardly means he won't be heard from again. David is due to become a monster every month, which is something Mr. Landis signals by playing Van Morrison's "Moondance," Creedence Clearwater's "Bad Moon Rising" and two more versions of "Blue Moon" on the soundtrack. How Warren Zevon's "Werewolves of London" escaped him is the movie's one big mystery. . . .

The werewolf gimmickry, though it is plenty scary, is only part of what Mr. Landis offers in the way of horror. The movie can't fail to catch its audience off guard, because many of David's savagely violent fantasies begin as harmless, realistic-looking conventional scenes.

The biggest jolts come with these moments of the unexpected, but there is another brand of horror here, too. Jack keeps coming back, in worse and worse states of decomposition, to chat with his friend. "I realize I don't look so hot, David, but I thought you'd be glad to see me," he chides the first time. David isn't, and you won't be either—though the camera lingers on Jack and his ghoulish makeup for a very long time. . . .

In addition to Jack's various visits and David's worries about the full moon, the movie has a love-story subplot. . . . The romance does not mix well with anything else in the movie, and Mr. Landis's including it is a measure of his occasional indiscriminateness. By the end of the film, he has graduated to car crashes à la **"The Blues Brothers,"** with the dubious new ingredient of bodies to be crushed between the cars.

The last part of the story cries out for some emotion over David's fate, since werewolfhood is not a condition for which the director has a cure. All Mr. Landis offers in the way of sentiment are some dented fenders.

> Janet Maslin, "Film: 'American Werewolf,' Horror Plus Laughs," in The New York Times (© 1981 by The New York Times Company; reprinted by permission), August 21, 1981, p. C12.

JACK KROLL

John Landis (**"National Lampoon's Animal House," "The Blues Brothers"**) is a member of the wise-guy generation of movie directors. The wise guys include major talents like Steven Spielberg and George Lucas and lesser talents like Landis and others. What they have in common is their neo-hip attitude. "I am a movie camera," the wise guys might say, and what they see through that camera is not so much the real world as other movies, which they parody, put on, take off and otherwise play with like the brilliant kids they are. Landis has now come up with *An American Werewolf in London,* a nearly perfect specimen of the wise-guy movie.

This film is a spoof of the old wolfman horror classics starring beloved cornballs like Lon Chaney Jr. Landis's heroes aren't corny, they're college smoothies. . . .

The wise-guy essence of the film is its blend of gory horror and cute cool, sort of like The Fonz Meets Frankenstein. When the undead [Jack] returns to shoot the breeze with [David], his face is seen close up in an advanced state of putrefaction, liquefaction and general yukkification while he tells his buddy about non-life in lupine limbo. "Have you ever talked with a corpse?" he asks. "It's *boring.*" The movie mocks the creaking romantic mysticism of the old horror flicks while being infinitely more horrific than they ever were. . . .

[Connoisseurs] of monstrous metamorphosis will be thrilled out of their Adidases by the scene in which [David] is transformed into a werewolf. None of your hoary 1940s lapdissolves here: you actually see and hear [his] face convulse, bones cracking, features erupting into a snout, ears sharpening to points, claws popping from fingers, follicles sprouting into the hairy hide of a snarling carnivore.

This is state-of-the-art stuff, and clearly Landis is as proud of it as those kid prodigies who build computers out of Q-Tips. Landis also out-palms Brian De Palma, not only giving you nightmares about massacres but double nightmares that go on to meta-massacres just when you think they're over. But despite all of this super-sophistication . . . [*An American Werewolf in London*] is finally just as silly as the old horror pictures it ambiguously kids. There's nothing like a rotting, wisecracking corpse to embody the bubble-gum nihilism of the Wise-Guy Wave.

Jack Kroll, "Cool Ghoul," in Newsweek *(copyright 1981, by Newsweek , Inc.; all rights reserved; reprinted by permission), Vol. XCVIII, No. 10, September 7, 1981, p. 82.*

JOHN PYM

Sophomore humour appeals, if at all, simply because it is sophomoric; thus, there was no dickering with 'sophistication' in the John Landis team's *Animal House*. [In *An American Werewolf in London*], however, the material calls for a much lighter tread, so often has the ground been covered by filmmakers in hobnail boots. Landis ends *An American Werewolf in London* with a title card congratulating the Prince and Princess of Wales on their marriage; and hovering above the preceding action is a feeling that it is taking place in a cinematic country of the imagination not far removed from tourist Britain. Trafalgar Square, Tower Bridge, the Zoo and Piccadilly Circus are all used, and all perceptibly draw attention to themselves. What is refreshing, however, about the film's ambience is that these British clichés are neither extended nor dwelt on. The Eros cinema in Piccadilly where the climactic transformation occurs is showing an authentic (though specially made) piece of homegrown tat titled *See You Next Wednesday;* the pub on the moors, filled with catatonic locals, has a sort of four-square reality, despite the pentangle scratched on the wall flanked by two immense prop-shop candles; the hospital employs an Indian porter, who is inevitably parodied but not, thankfully, in the usual oh-by-golly fashion. It takes perhaps a percipient outsider to bring off such a cockeyed view of Britain's national monuments. Nurse [Alex Price] is also something of a surprise, sustaining herself through the watches of the night (in what might have been a tiresome literary plant, but isn't) with Mark Twain, and displaying both pity and love for the luckless David which just hints, intriguingly, at a deeper tragedy. John Landis' other achievement is to have successfully grafted on elements from his previous work. The young Americans are straight out of *Animal House*'s Faber College, at heart sublimely self-concerned and enthusiastically naive. Entering the Slaughtered Lamb, East Procter's pub, they settle for a pot of tea when coldly informed that there isn't anything to eat and cocoa isn't served. Furthermore, this open quality . . . is carefully integrated with the plot. Jack returns, ashen, with half his neck missing (at each appearance his putrefaction has advanced), and addresses David in his customary sing-song voice as if nothing really untoward has occurred: his death is a misfortune of the same order as his scuppered chances of bedding the girl he has been pursuing. The film is enhanced by uniformly careful casting in the secondary roles . . . and no one is allowed to run away with his tempting part.

John Pym, in his review of "An American Werewolf in London," in Monthly Film Bulletin *(copyright © The British Film Institute, 1981), Vol. 48, No. 574, November, 1981, p. 215.*

Gordon (Meredith) Lightfoot
1938-

Canadian songwriter.

Lightfoot is one of the few songwriters who emerged during the folk music revival of the early 1960s and is still successful. Critics attribute his enduring popularity to his ability to elevate ordinary subjects into meaningful lyrics. Lightfoot's best works are ballads about the history and natural splendor of Canada, and his travel songs are described as compassionate, eloquent, and honest. His recent albums also include songs of bittersweet love affairs, possibly reflecting his troubled private life.

Lightfoot was a major figure in Canadian folk music several years before he became well known in the United States. He first gained attention for his compositions "For Lovin' Me" and "Early Morning Rain," which were recorded by Peter, Paul, and Mary and became popular successes. Lightfoot gained international recognition with the release of "If You Could Read My Mind" in 1970, but his most important popular breakthrough came in 1974 with the success of *Sundown*. The songs on this album explore social, sexual, and spiritual topics, and the imagery has been described as evocative and graphic. Although Lightfoot has yet to match the commercial success of *Sundown*, his graceful, honest lyrics continue to touch the emotions of his ever-growing following.

Ken Regan/Camera 5

PETE WELDING

One of the handsomest, most perfectly conceived and executed albums I've heard in recent months is *Did She Mention My Name?* . . . Lightfoot is a romantic, to be sure, but he is a clear-eyed realist at the same time; the combination results in songs that are lyrical, full of tenderness and compassion, but above all real, honest, and totally without artifice. The whole album is a gas, but especially memorable are the lovely *Pussy-willows, Cat-tails; The Last Time I Saw Her; The Mountain and Maryann*, and the title song, *Did She Mention My Name?* Unqualifiedly recommended. This is in every respect an essential set.

> Pete Welding, in his review of "Did She Mention My Name?" in down beat (copyright 1969; reprinted with permission of down beat), Vol. 36, No. 5, March 6, 1969, p. 29.

JANET MASLIN

Gordon Lightfoot may never seem to be doing anything all that unusual—his melodies tend to be simple, his subjects seldom original, his voice is nice enough but rarely lends itself to anything fancy, and in fact the whole genre he works in is anything but new. But Lightfoot, unlike virtually all other folk artists who started out successful in the early Sixties, has managed to mellow so gracefully (and without any need for a current comeback, or any gratuitous shots at rock and roll) that he's at his absolute strongest right now, as *Don Quixote* and the album before it [*Summer Side of Life*] bear witness. Even though—or perhaps because—what he does isn't nearly as unusual as the fact that he does it so well. . . .

[Part] of his appeal must certainly stem from his considerable gift for songwriting, which is easy to underrate. He combines the kind of voice that never seems to do his material justice with deceptive simplicity, a highly sophisticated ear for clever rhyme structures, and a unique knack for elevating subjects that could easily have been mundane. And, prolific as he's been over the past ten years, Lightfoot has never degenerated into hackdom. His writing, like the rest of what goes into his recordings, has improved steadily with age. . . .

Certain structural strains from the past two albums [*If You Could Read My Mind* and *Summer Side of Life*] tend to repeat themselves here, such as his use of the opening cut to present the album's dominant image of a romantic, mysterious traveler (here he's Don Quixote, last time the hitchhiking minstrel of **"Ten Degrees And Getting Colder"**), and the long, ambitious conclusion (**"The Patriot's Dream"**). In between, he seems to have shifted away from the straight storytelling he handles so well, using more mood pieces than usual (up for **"Alberta Bound,"** down in **"Looking At The Rain,"** and somewhere in between with the slow, dreamy **"Christian Island"**). (p. 49)

[**"Second Cup of Coffee"** indirectly tells] a story of broken marriage with a typically clever refrain about reaching for the bottle versus reaching for the phone. It's the kind of song that sounds so immediate and familiar that you're certain you must have heard it before, the only question being where. But still it's as original as everything else he does, fresh and unique behind a familiar-sounding facade. I just don't know how he does it.

The fact is I can't quite figure out how he does any of it, really, but I do know that his material never wears out, just gets more interesting all the time. Gordon himself keeps getting better and better, and that's one knack I hope he never loses. (pp. 49-50)

> *Janet Maslin, in her review of "Don Quixote," in* Rolling Stone *(by Straight Arrow Publishers, Inc. © 1972; all rights reserved; reprinted by permission), Issue 107, April 27, 1972, pp. 49-50.*

THE CANADIAN COMPOSER

Don Quixote, from beginning to end, is a superb album—certainly the best Lightfoot has ever put together. . . .

The songs themselves are among his best—the title song is certainly the equal of **Early Morning Rain** . . . , **Alberta Bound** is a piece of superb Canadiana, and **Christian Island** is a hymn to a northern Ontario summer.

A magazine like this one is certainly no place to comment on the personal lives of composers—but it is hard to avoid doing so in the context of this particular album, because so many of the songs relate directly to Lightfoot's unhappy home life. **Looking at the Rain, Ordinary Man** and, particularly, **Second Cup of Coffee,** are all songs about lost love and loneliness—songs of pain, sung with feeling and with the warmth of past memories.

Lightfoot is, on the showing of this record, Canada's finest songwriter. And it seems a pity that so much personal turmoil has to be experienced to write such perfect songs.

> *A review of "Don Quixote," in* The Canadian Composer, *No. 70, May, 1972, p. 20.*

LORAINE ALTERMAN

It seems so easy when Gordon Lightfoot does it—writes songs that just flow out in his warm, mellow tones. Yet, it's the rare talent who can approach Lightfoot's class and a rarer one who achieves the taste that marks every one of Lightfoot's recordings. You know that Lightfoot's effortless style comes from hard work: here is a mind that can sort out the feelings all of us share and convey them in music that is perfectly expressive of their meaning.

[On **"Old Dan's Records"**] Lightfoot isn't singing and writing about the loves of boys and girls but of men and women. **"Can't Depend on Love"** is the wry realization of an adult human being. **"Farewell to Annabel"** is about another love that didn't last, but again it's presented from a mature point of view, asking the former lover to remain friends.

Of course, Lightfoot isn't just a writer of love songs. The title tune is a rollicking ditty about how much fun it would be to dance to the old-time tunes. You can almost see people tapping their toes and swinging their partners. Lightfoot brings on a smile of recognition on **"Easy Morning,"** a song which everyone who longs for Sundays will love. **"Hi-Way Songs"** is his own testament to the love-hate relationship performers have with being on tour. . . .

Let's hope this Canadian singer never changes and continues to provide us with treasures like **"Old Dan's Records."**

> *Loraine Alterman, in her review of "Old Dan's Records," in* The New York Times *(© 1972 by The New York Times Company; reprinted by permission), December 10, 1972, p. 38D.*

NOEL COPPAGE

[**"Old Dan's Records"**] is] rather a daring album, representing considerable growth, with no accompanying loss of taste or of any of Lightfoot's other virtues. True, one of the most satisfying cuts is **It's Worth Believin',** the kind of tightly paced ballad—in the tradition of **Early Morning Rain** and **Second Cup of Coffee**—that Lightfoot does better than anyone, but most of the rest of this album is not so easily hooked up with preconceptions about what Lightfoot's music is.

My Pony Won't Go is a near-blues thing, with lyrics that metaphorically broach a subject that I don't think pop music has tackled before (no, I won't spoil it for you). **Lazy Mornin'** has Lightfoot, in the manner of Randy Newman, assuming a viewpoint he does not agree with, that of a complacent suburbanite. **That Same Old Obsession** draws a subtle unstated parallel with an old hymn that also uses a garden allegorically, and it amounts to a melody that is mildly surprising for Lightfoot and a verse that probes the depths in two directions at once—I can see all sorts of political applications of it, for one thing. (pp. 94, 96)

The obvious clinker is the title song, and there are a few other indications that Lightfoot is feeling his way—but, cowabunga! is he advancing! It's all right to go on believing Lightfoot is the consummate troubadour—an informed, properly biased, sympathetic but moralizing and perceptive voice in a figure of earnestness and strength, with just a touch of swagger—it's all right, but don't let it lead you to underestimate his depth. (p. 96)

> *Noel Coppage, in his review of "Old Dan's Records," in* Stereo Review *(copyright © 1973 by Ziff-Davis Publishing Company), Vol. 30, No. 3, March, 1973, pp. 94, 96.*

STEPHEN HOLDEN

Gordon Lightfoot's ninth album [**Old Dan's Records**] . . . is more and better of same: middle-of-the-road, homogenized folk rock that is sumptuously pleasant, but lacking the indelible stamp of emotional veracity that would make it irresistible. Lightfoot is certainly an important talent, whose prolific output of good songs is continuously impressive. Yet the overall impression he conveys is one of glibness. . . .

Lightfoot clearly wants to be all things to all people—rustic folkie, cosmopolite, social commentator, and above all, the apostle of romantic love. Despite the remarkable facility and fine craftsmanship of his writing, these roles tend to overlap, resulting in work that too often is stylistically bland. . . .

[**Old Dan's Records**] contains ten songs, all Lightfoot originals that display his characteristic lyrical competence and strong melodic sense.

> *Stephen Holden, in his review of "Old Dan's Records," in* Rolling Stone *(by Straight Arrow Publishers, Inc. © 1973; all rights reserved; reprinted by permission), Issue 131, March 29, 1973, p. 56.*

NOEL COPPAGE

Gordon Lightfoot is an absolute must for anyone who would learn about Canada by listening. His preoccupation with the images of summer is a Northern predilection. His songs such as **Love and Maple Syrup** and **Redwood Hill** are specifically concerned with both Northern and country folk hardware. Outdoor imagery . . . predominates in his lyrics, and his melodies are purified and refined country melodies. His perspective is reminiscent of that of rural people in the States twenty years ago—a bit defensively testy when any country-*vs.*-city comparisons come up, and always putting in a plug for the country when they don't. . . . (p. 74)

> *Noel Coppage, "I Hear Canada Singing," in* Stereo Review *(copyright © 1973 by Ziff-Davis Publishing Company), Vol. 31, No. 2, August, 1973, pp. 72-4.**

STEPHEN HOLDEN

Sundown is a fine album which weaves conventional folk and pop strands into a whole that is greater than the sum of its parts. The polish of Lightfoot's singing has tended in the past to undermine the seriousness of his songs, inviting the listener to appreciate his records mainly as aural artifacts rather than explore their contents. But most of **Sundown**'s 12 songs are so evocative that they prohibit such easy perusal. . . .

Lightfoot's reflections are those of a mature man, capable of strong romantic and political emotions, tempered by a suave sexuality and an elegiac mysticism. "**Somewhere U.S.A.**" is a lovely evocation of romantic complications experienced during the daze of travel. "**High And Dry**" also celebrates travel and uses the image of a ship and its different skippers to affirm continuities. The six-minute "**Seven Island Suite**" is the album's most ambitious cut, and presents an elusive apocalyptic vision. More incisive are "**Sundown**," an ominous assertion of sexual jealousy, and "**Circle Of Steel**," a protest song about the antagonisms of welfare and poverty.

The album's last and most powerful cut, "**Too Late for Prayin'**" is perhaps Lightfoot's finest creation. A modified hymn, somewhat reminiscent of Paul Simon's "American Tune," "**Too Late**" is both a prayer for our spiritual restoration and a lament for its absence. It is the work of a master craftsman. . . .

> *Stephen Holden, in his review of "Sundown," in* Rolling Stone *(by Straight Arrow Publishers, Inc. © 1974; all rights reserved; reprinted by permission), Issue 156, March 14, 1974, p. 61.*

NOEL COPPAGE

In the old days of popular music, men were men and women were—it says in some of those recent analyses of old songs—abused. Now, though, David Bowie and other painted persons are happy to be asexual, bisexual, polysexual, pansexual, whatever works, and many of the pop stars who are still interested in music (you remember music) are phasing out the Me-Tarzan-You-Jane (or vice versa) slant in favor of a commitment more, ah, *aware* politically.

Against that background then, one is likely to notice all the more that two powerful new albums from America's best Canadian songwriters, Joni Mitchell and Gordon Lightfoot, have the flavor of yesterday's heterosexuality about them, and seem, too, rather luxuriously traditional in their romanticism. The

Canadian upbringing no doubt is a factor, as is the long view both artists are able to take. Lightfoot's "**Sundown**" . . . is a scrumptious summation of what else he has done; compared to what several *other* troubadours are doing, it's notably broad-shouldered, wide-brimmed, lean-hipped and outdoorsy. (pp. 75-6)

Lightfoot takes a direct (manly?), no-nonsense approach to instrumentation. His songs don't need anything getting in their way, anyhow, and these particular ones have quite a way about them; one after another, they are remarkable.

Too Late for Prayin', an embarrassment of riches in itself, demonstrates how *quietly* remarkable they can be, but give yourself time and it will also demonstrate Lightfoot's uncanny ability to invent beautiful melodies and keep them simple, to say his piece in verses so graceful and economical that you can enjoy the flow of the syllables as many times as you like before settling down to what the words mean. **Circle of Steel** is another such demonstration, and my other special favorite is **Somewhere USA**, which has that long-legged pace that Lightfoot practically owns. The title song is perhaps *too* simple, but its refrain—which will stay in your head for a month, and you have no choice in the matter—has three different wordings. . . .

Lightfoot puts images, mostly with outdoor settings, into your head; Mitchell puts you in parties, trains, social situations, and thinking situations. It isn't quite a purely objective-subjective contrast you'll find in their approaches, but no one can blame you if you do a little broad-brush (no pun intended) thinking about male-female questions when listening to two albums so different, so similar, and so fine. (p. 76)

> *Noel Coppage, "Mitchell and Lightfoot: The He and the She of It," in* Stereo Review *(copyright © 1974 by Ziff-Davis Publishing Company), Vol. 32, No. 5, May, 1974, pp. 75-6.**

STEVE LAKE

When it comes down to cracker-barrel philosophising, only Cat Stevens has Canada's Gordon Lightfoot beat. ["**Cold on the Shoulder**"] is the successor to the best-selling "**Sundown**" album, and contains roughly the same proportion of lovesick ballads and homespun sophistry. . . . The problem, basically speaking, is that Lightfoot doesn't know what he's talking about. Granted, when relating personal experience, Gordon writes a mean love song . . . , but as for metaphysics, well, John Donne he isn't. His imagery simply doesn't work for him. It's at its most laboured in "**Rainbow Trout**," . . . forever trying to provide analogies between stock country singer/songwriter cliches and something deeper. It's a dangerous approach, and one that consistently backfires. But not to be totally negative, even at his most gibberishly ineffective, Lightfoot still sounds attractive. . . .

> *Steve Lake, in his review of "Cold on the Shoulder," in* Melody Maker *(© IPC Business Press Ltd.), May 10, 1975, p. 33.*

NOEL COPPAGE

Few words of intriguing implication—words, say, sporting a positive and colorful mantle of romanticism—fit a performer better than *troubadour* fits Gordon Lightfoot. Time has shown him to be *the* troubadour of this modern bunch, and his new

"Cold on the Shoulder" album . . . —in addition to adding evidence that quality will surface and be recognized—shows how gracefully the consummate troubadour goes about the business of traveling, writing, and singing songs.

It is a mellow album that rocks when the mood arrives, and some of it is just about timeless. It is also much more varied than it at first appears; *Rainy Day People* is one type of song, and an almost classically elegant example of that type, and *Bells of the Evening,* without fussing over its own individuality, is a fine example of an entirely different sort. There's a magnificent children's song, *Fine as Fine Can Be,* that Lightfoot wrote for his eight-year-old daughter. . . . *All the Lovely Ladies* suggests a round; Lightfoot *knows* music inside out, you see. *Rainbow Trout* puts the emphasis on lyrics . . . to offer a glimpse of the whimsey in Lightfoot's sense of humor. And the detail work everywhere is as fine as fine can be. (pp. 81-2)

[Brace] yourself, America, for one of those infrequent jolts of that thing grandparents lament when the handles of new station wagons come off in their hands. Quality, they call it. (p. 82)

> *Noel Coppage, in his review of "Cold on the Shoulder," in* Stereo Review *(copyright © 1975 by Ziff-Davis Publishing Company), Vol. 34, No. 6, June, 1975, pp. 81-2.*

BART TESTA

It may be an anomaly that no one has become more cliched than the "singer-songwriter." With only him/herself to talk about, the singer-songwriter has either to transcend personal perspective or repeat him/herself to the point of dry exhaustion. Most singer-songwriters, protected by the screen of high income and cult worshippers, choose dry exhaustion. The exceptions—Elton John, Loudon Wainwright and, lately, Bruce Springsteen and Bob Dylan—have returned to folkie/rock 'n roll eccentric topicality. This exceptional group came full circle, back to where the folkie thing left off (*i.e.,* Bob Dylan rejoins Joan Baez), or back to rock 'n roll (*Born To Run* and "Philadelphia Freedom").

But Gordon Lightfoot is special. He is the only songwriter to have gone the whole route without even slightly changing his style of writing or performance. Well, there is another exception but John Denver is an unforgivable abomination, Gordon Lightfoot is nothing if not forgivable. . . . Lightfoot still gets away pretending that he is part Indian and all wandering minstrel. Even Neil Young gave that up years ago. But Lightfoot's secret is that he has managed *not* to develop, even slightly, in over a decade. On *Gord's Gold,* he redoes his "classics." The most notable thing about the record is that, aside from a few slight changes in production, the songs sound exactly the same as they did when Lightfoot originally recorded them. But, for all his sameness, Lightfoot is still not tiresome. A little standardized maybe, but only as befits a national—that is, a Canadian—institution. (p. 69)

> *Bart Testa, "Royal Canadians," in* Crawdaddy *(copyright © 1976 by Crawdaddy Publishing Co., Inc.; all rights reserved; reprinted by permission), June, 1976, pp. 69-71.**

COLIN IRWIN

Not much to tell those familiar with Lightfoot's previous work— you can take it ["**Summertime Dream**"] is very much on par for the course. The guy's long established a formula of agreeable tunes and undemanding lyrics that's been amazingly successful for him, and he ain't gonna change it now, despite surely being second only to John Denver as the artist critics hate the most. Now and again he comes up with a particularly catchy song which grabs the imagination, or a lyric that delves beyond the usual commentary on personal relationships. . . . Not as strong as his best work, **"Sit Down Young Stranger"** (later re-titled **"If You Could Read My Mind"**), but far superior to the dull **"Sundown."** . . . Lightfoot has two explorations into deeper-than-usual waters here with **"Protocol,"** which is brimming with bitterness—ten years ago it would have been called a protest song along the lines of [Buffy Sainte-Marie's] "Universal Soldier"; and the other one is **"The Wreck Of The Edmund Fitzgerald,"** which describes a shipping disaster.

> *Colin Irwin, in his review of "Summertime Dream," in* Melody Maker *(© IPC Business Press Ltd.), July 31, 1976, p. 21.*

NOEL COPPAGE

There is a *literati* in popular music, a group of people with refined musical taste, education, and judgment, and my contention that Gordon Lightfoot is at the head of it just keeps getting more plausible with every record he makes. Lightfoot imposes increasingly tougher standards upon himself, and his albums consistently add poetry to the mostly commercial form in which he works. In short, he keeps adding songs to that precious five or so per cent of everything new that is worth keeping.

Technically, his work is excellent; he's every bit the craftsman the old boys were before rock-and-roll made amateurish writing and performing the most profitable kind. Yet he is a *folk* artist in the sense that he works down among the people instead of in an ivory tower overlooking Broadway and Twenty-eighth Street (Tin Pan Alley, that is). He's relevant, accessible, and all that, working . . . in verses that deal with what really happens rather than what's supposed to in idealized boy-meets-girl fairy tales. And so his new **"Summertime Dream"** . . . is a remarkably direct, trimmed-down, person-to-person album, and it is running over with poetry.

Not the least of its achievements is that it manages—according to my grasp of the whole of it—to wish the other person well, to realize how *complicated* it is for all of us (most of us?) to confer more dignity, wish less guilt, lend a little encouragement. That's extremely hard to do without fawning or sounding stuffy; it's much easier to cheer our side and boo theirs. The songs have a variety of interior messages of their own, of course, and so many of them are superb that I hate to single out any. *Never Too Close,* though, with its sense of what to remember about a so-called "failed" relationship—"That is all right / We meant no one no harm"—and with the nice surprises in the way it is constructed, is hard to beat. Most of the songs talk in common language edited in that expert, subtle way that makes it elegant. . . . A man like Lightfoot, and an album like this, can cut through the cynicism we've understandably fortified ourselves with and show us the popular song can actually amount to something.

> *Noel Coppage, "Gordon Lightfoot's 'Summertime Dream': Running Over with Poetry," in* Stereo Review *(copyright © 1976 by Ziff-Davis Publishing Company), Vol. 37, No. 4, October, 1976, p. 87.*

COLIN IRWIN

[Though the songs on Lightfoot's "**Endless Wire**"] are firmly in the rather narrow poppy side of folk in which the man specialises, there is certainly more aggression and bite here than the man's ever displayed on record before. . . .

By his standards, this is quite a bold album . . . but it still doesn't go far enough to be hailed a true breakthrough.

Tepid, instantly hummable songs of introspection like "**Sometimes I Don't Mind**" and "**Dreamland**," or the trivia of "**Songs The Minstrel Sang**" suggest Gordie's keeping his options open and attempting to maintain the affections of middle America's pseudo-trendies on the one hand while branching out more ambitiously on the other with tracks like "**If There's A Reason**" (an outstanding song with an unexpectedly bluesy feel) and the commendable honesty of "**Hangdog Hotel Room.**" . . . The self-portrayal of a directionless drifter in "**Endless Wire**" compounds the view of him as insecure and unfulfilled.

However, it's always a fight with the formula mechanics of his songs to sort out the true substance. Two tracks of particular merit, nevertheless, are "**If Children Had Wings**," a beautiful song which transcends all preconceptions and individual markets, and "**The Circle Is Small.**" . . .

Colin Irwin, in his review of "Endless Wire," in Melody Maker *(© IPC Business Press Ltd.), April 29, 1978, p. 13.*

DAVID MIX

Lightfoot's well-crafted songs match appealing, folkish melodies to simple, sometimes appallingly simple, lyrics. These he sings with such authority that every word takes on a certain dignity. . . .

Slowly, however, the substance has been leaking out of his songs, to be replaced by puffery and posturing. On *Endless Wire,* few of the lyrics deserve the richly textured support provided by Lenny Waronker's production (in association with Lightfoot). . . .

Two songs seem to describe women, but abdicate that responsibility. "**Daylight Katy**" might as well be a cat, a lush backup makes it into likeable fluff. "**Sweet Guinevere**" tells a West Virginia miner's daughter . . . [not to go to coal town], but never explains why—the ambiguity is pointless. . . .

Lightfoot is at his best on a one-to-one level, at his worst when he tries to be mythic. There's a thin line between the simple and the banal; Lightfoot shouldn't have to keep crossing that line to stay popular.

David Mix, "Heavy-Handed Lightfoot," in Crawdaddy *(copyright © 1978 by Crawdaddy Publishing Co., Inc.; all rights reserved; reprinted by permission), May, 1978, p. 70.*

NOEL COPPAGE

"**Endless Wire**" is a departure of sorts, but only to about the same degree that "**Old Dan's Records**" was in its time. The new one, quantitatively measured—by the amplification of instruments and the nature of such songs as *I Don't Mind, If There's a Reason,* and the verse (but not the chorus) of *Endless Wire*—is [Lightfoot's] rockingest album yet. But it is really no more Rock than his Nashville one, "**Summer Side of Life,**" was Country.

Lightfoot's other abiding interests, including his feel for the working class and working-class settings, his fondness for narratives, and his preoccupation with the loved one who got away, are all in this one too. His songwriting is everywhere crafty and in spots exceptionally bright. *Daylight Katy* is a wonder, actually two seemingly unrelated kinds of song successfully combined, and the title song's chorus snares your mind from the straight-ahead rock mode of the verse and gives it a little snap. *The Circle Is Small,* which I believe he's had around for a while, is the kind of song you hear and then say, "Now why wasn't that written ages ago?" It's a natural, as if it's been hanging there in the air for years and Lightfoot was the first one smart enough to pluck it.

Overall, the album is "different," but . . . it's a gradual and graceful difference. . . . It makes everyone involved, especially the listener, feel a little more secure about any more changes that might be on the way.

Noel Coppage, "'Endless Wire', Gordon Lightfoot's 'Different' Album, Is His Rockingest Yet," in Stereo Review *(copyright © 1978 by Ziff-Davis Publishing Company), Vol. 40, No. 5, May, 1978, p. 91.*

NOEL COPPAGE

Gordon Lightfoot takes a turn for the quiet in "**Dream Street Rose,**" a subtle album that at first seems oddly impersonal coming from Lightfoot, a private man who, as private men sometimes do, tends to make his work intensely personal. And at first it seems regressive; the songs sound (superficially) like some he was writing ten years ago. . . . A casual first impression might be that it is some kind of retreat from the experimentation of ["**Endless Wire**"].

That impression would be wrong. . . . In fact, it represents a refinement of the lyrical aspect of his lyrics. The words of *Sea of Tranquility,* which at first seem so ignorably casual, gradually ingratiate themselves because they have an easy rhythm reminiscent of one of our better poets. . . . *Sea* is a fantasy, if, on the surface, a still-obtainable one—a place of otters and frogs and spotted groundhogs—but the song's language is both literal and symbolic at once. *Make Way* purports to be off-handedly autobiographical while it points out one of the ways (practice!). But it, too, is symbolic; it uses a bluesy tune to keep its optimism under control, and there's an under-the-surface tension in it. *Mister Rock of Ages* is a sort of prayer Lightfoot does now and then (*Too Late for Praying* is a prime example), and it is also talkative between the lines. It shows that Lightfoot has distanced himself more than the usual amount from this type of material. It is nonlinear the way the blues can be, a series of couplets that don't seem to need to be in any particular order.

That song and several others, including *Hey You* . . . , also represent refinements in Lightfoot's way of lifting clichés out of everyday language (or, in the case of *Whisper My Name,* everyday tunes), mixing them up into his own special blend, and giving them another dimension of meaning. This, of course, is what the fine arts have always done with the folk arts. One of the ways Lightfoot shows that he's more artist than journalist is pretty much to ignore the transitory cliché (his language is never super whatchacall *hip*) in favor of the long-term one: "bless my soul," "sad repair," "time on your hands," even "beneath the halo'd moon"—stuff the old folks *and* the young folks can understand. Not to mention the future folks.

Noel Coppage, "Digital Lightfoot," in Stereo Review *(copyright © 1980 by Ziff-Davis Publishing Company), Vol. 44, No. 6, June, 1980, p. 88.*

NOEL COPPAGE

Is Gordon Lightfoot the best songwriter of modern times? He has written and recorded upwards of one hundred and fifty songs, of which at least ninety are not only "keepers" but demonstrably superior, in one way or another, to most of their contemporaries. I know of no one else who has lately produced such quality in such quantity. He's at it again in his just-released "Shadows" with eleven new ones, and ten of them are beauties as engrossing as they are elegantly structured.

What makes Lightfoot great, I think, is his believability. . . . [He is one of the few pop stars] with such command of the English language that he can use word play as an end in itself. And so he writes with the folkie's sense of what is real even as he writes with the trained musician's awareness of the many possible ways of expressing it.

Of course, he's also inordinately gifted. His melodies are so natural-sounding you find yourself thinking there's no excuse for their not having existed before. . . .

["Shadows" is full of] songs for which there *are* precedents—but only in the earlier work of Lightfoot himself. *Heaven Help the Devil,* whose forerunners include *Too Late for Praying,* is the kind of generalized, generally pessimistic social commentary Lightfoot occasionally writes. . . . Lightfoot's two other approaches to making social comments, both as nonspecific in their own ways, involve work songs such as *Cotton Jenny* or what he calls "topical" songs such as *Circle of Steel* or *Cherokee Bend.* Similarly, the title song here is a throwback to another, softer kind of song Lightfoot has written before. But each new invocation of any of these composing modes has its own sound and its own special qualities. *Shadows,* while fitted with quite an active melody, has a whole slew of seven-syllable lines followed by an eleven-syllable "resolution" that paradoxically leaves things still about halfway up in the air.

But I don't have to go into detail to show you there's a rare craftsman at work here; you'll hear that right away. . . . [*Triangle*] is about the Bermuda Triangle, and the words are the imaginings of a sailor who's about to sail through it. It isn't quite as striking as its recent precedent, *Ghosts of Cape Horn,* but it is much more infectious.

I'll Do Anything is almost as strong, although the sentiment it expresses strikes me as uncomfortably close to masochism. (p. 68)

"Shadows" doesn't rank at the *very* top of his work, but ten keepers out of eleven is still semi-remarkable, and you have to consider how high that top is. So, to get back to the question at the beginning: "*Is* Gordon Lightfoot the best songwriter of modern times?" As his compatriot Ian Tyson might put it, "Hell, yes!" (p. 70)

Noel Coppage, "Gordon Lightfoot's 'Shadows': A Rare Craftsman at Work," in Stereo Review *(copyright © 1982 by Ziff-Davis Publishing Company), Vol. 47, No. 6, June, 1982, pp. 68, 70.*

Kevin Major

1949-

Canadian novelist and editor.

With his first two novels, *Hold Fast* and *Far from Shore*, Major emerged as a highly regarded novelist for young adults. His use of local color, the dialect and way of life in Newfoundland, and his depiction of the often confusing state of life between childhood and adulthood are considered particularly noteworthy.

***Hold Fast* describes the struggles of an unsure young man who faces changes in his life and must make some important decisions. This allows Major to explore the conflict between "big city" values and those of the isolated "outport" culture of Newfoundland. The novel won immediate acclaim, including the Canadian Library Association Book of the Year for Children award and the Canada Council Award for Children's Literature, both in 1979.**

Although Major's second novel, *Far from Shore*, met with less enthusiastic response, it was generally well regarded, winning the Canadian Young Adult Book Award in 1980. More experimental than his first book, *Far from Shore* depicts a family disrupted by unemployment and rivalry and explores the role of economic determinism versus personal reponsibility in shaping one's life. In both works, Major displays keen awareness of the concerns of young adults and the ability to communicate the struggles of adolescence.

(See also *Contemporary Authors*, Vols. 97-100 and *Something about the Author*, Vol. 32.)

Photograph by Tony Parsons; courtesy of Kevin Major

R. G. MOYLES

It is, I suppose, decidedly unfair to compare the first novel of a young new writer with the acclaimed classic of a master storyteller, but Kevin Major's *Hold Fast* brought me so often into remembered contact with Mark Twain's *Huckleberry Finn* that a comparison (or at least a referential glossing) became unavoidable. Such a comparison, in fact, tells us much about Major's technique and purpose and, lest the reader be apprehensive on this point, does nothing to devalue this young Newfoundland author's achievement.

Anyone who has read *Huckleberry Finn* cannot, for example, fail to see just how much alike Huck Finn and Michael (Major's protagonist) are. Both are physical and spiritual orphans treading the hard road to self-awareness; Michael, like Huck, is unsure of himself, stubborn ("pig-headed" Michael calls it), given to lying and to fits of self-pity and remorse; and even when a degree of self-awareness is attained there is always that shadow of doubt. How similar they are, and how close Major comes to achieving Twain's poignancy through his first-person naive narrator can be seen in a juxtaposition of the key (climactic) passages in the novels. Huck Finn, in that famous bout with his conscience [when he debates whether or not to do the "right thing" and alert the owner of Jim as to where the runaway slave can be found], comes to grips with his lying. . . . Michael, after having hitched a ride with an old man (in a

chapter which is both amusing and forceful), and having deceived him outrageously, states: . . .

> See, I can certainly screw up things for myself. I made a vow then and there that if there was any more lies that I'd have to tell then they'd only be enough to get us off the hook. That was all. Not a word more.

"They'd only be enough to get us off the hook"; how typically Huck Finn that is.

Apart from the thematic similarity, other Twainian characteristics abound: Michael's cousin Curtis is a perfect foil, another Tom Sawyer; the first-person narrative (especially the employment of a naive narrator) is full of subtle ironies; Major's use of Newfoundland dialect, like Twain's innovative use of the southern dialect, offers a sense of immediacy and a control of tone. Major, in fact, is at his best in his execution of dialect and dialogue.

Now, all this does not mean that *Hold Fast* is a derivative novel, that Major has simply imitated Twain. Far from it. Indeed, the comparison serves to show that the major theme of *Huckleberry Finn* is not sacrosanct, that it can be restated with fresh insights, that a new environment and age reveals new problems and new solutions, that the picaresque novel can still provide an exciting experience. The fact that *Hold Fast*, even though it reminds me so forcibly of *Huckleberry Finn*, absorbs my interest and abounds with originality means that it does succeed in its own right. (pp. 56-8)

[*Hold Fast*] has a multi-dimensional appeal: those who are not impressed by or interested in my Twainian-thematic approach may read it for its insights into youthful grief, modern-day rebellion, confused teenage values, adult-child conflicts, Newfoundland dialect and ways of life; or Major's frankness may be your interest—certainly his description of Michael's wet dream (a very controlled and realistic bit of writing) will give rise to discussion, even denunciation. Surely a novel which offers such a variety of issues should not be overlooked. Especially since, though not a masterpiece, *Hold Fast* is such a well-written novel. (p. 58)

R. G. Moyles, in his review of "Hold Fast," in The World of Children's Books *(© 1978 Jon C. Stott), Vol. III, No. 2, Fall, 1978, pp. 56-9.*

ROBERT FULFORD

There aren't many novels that connect a commercial American style and the special qualities of a Canadian region, but Kevin Major's first book, *Hold Fast* . . . , does just that. It brings together the current mode of "young adult" novel as developed in the United States and the longings of Newfoundlanders for their past. In this sense it's a unique product of recent Canadian literature. . . .

Newfoundlanders realize that, spiritually, all that they possess is the tradition their ancestors left them: the tradition of the intimate and isolated fishing villages, the seal hunt, the special language that is so different from the English most of us speak. At the same time, they know that forces they can't control (including forces within themselves) are drawing them away from that tradition, into urbanization and a closer contact with mainland Canada.

This is an odd subject for a juvenile novel, but it is one of the subjects of *Hold Fast.* Major's hero and narrator, Michael, is a fourteen-year-old outport boy whose parents die in an automobile accident. As a result he must leave his outport and move to a "big" (in Newfoundland terms) city, which is almost as drastic a step for an outport boy as moving to Toronto. There he finds himself repressed by both a tyrannical uncle and a school system that has no real place for him. Major stresses the contrasts between the authenticity of outport life—its close relation to nature, particularly in hunting and fishing—and the artificiality of the city. It's a romantic view, but one that everyone who knows Newfoundland, even slightly, will understand immediately.

Major also uses a written version of Newfoundland dialect to give his book regional atmosphere. Sometimes he expects too much of mainland readers: when he refers to people watching "the story" on TV he assumes we'll know that by this Newfoundlanders mean U.S. soap opera (many of us won't know). Most of the time, though, the dialect is both right and comprehensible. . . .

Hold Fast isn't entirely a tale of boyish innocence. The hero defies his elders, breaks the law, and even has a sex life. This is partly because Major has absorbed the lessons of the American "young adult" novels of the last decade or so. (p. 14)

Michael contains a bit of Holden Caulfield and a bit of Huckleberry Finn, but there is also something authentically Newfoundland about him. *Hold Fast* isn't in any sense a sophisticated novel, but it speaks honestly from a regional consciousness. (pp. 14-15)

Robert Fulford, "Capturing Newfoundland Before It Goes Away" (copyright © 1978 by Saturday Night; *reprinted by permission of the author), in* Saturday Night, *Vol. 93, No. 8, October, 1978, pp. 14-15.*

GARY H. PATERSON

Hold Fast is a novel surrounded by death. It begins with the burial of Michael's parents, who have been killed in a car crash involving a drunken driver, and ends with his grandfather's death in sickness and old age. In between, we have the struggle of a fourteen-year-old boy to maintain his identity in a world of harshness, ignorance, and insensitivity. (p. 81)

Hold Fast is divided into three sections, each of which contains the motif of escape and return to reality by the hero. The first escape is simply a brief but meaningful run to the seashore during the burial of his parents; the second, also brief, is a running away from the circumstances concerning Michael's fight with a classmate. The third escape, more elaborate and adventurous, is a kind of initiation rite into young manhood and an assertion of pride in his heritage when he "borrows" a car and survives by his wits for two wintry days in the washroom of a deserted campsite. These three escapes have considerable character-building power and when Michael is faced with his grandfather's death, there is no running away: "In the cemetery I watched the casket go into the ground, and never once did I move from the spot where I stood."

Probably what one notices most readily about this novel is the style of the hero-narrator. His colourful, earthy, rhythmic idiom may jar at first, but then it settles into warm, colloquial undulation. . . . The diction is salted with four-letter words too well known to fourteen-year-olds but there is an occasional arresting phrase which rolls out of the narrator just as naturally: "Downstairs, me and Brent walked in on a kitchenful of miserable silence." One wishes there were more of these.

A definite weakness in the novel is Kevin Major's delineation of adults. Admittedly, there is always a difficulty in portraying adults in children's books. Either they come off as weak, flat characters as in E. Nesbit's *The Treasure Seekers* or they are merely absent for the better part of the action as in Arthur Ransome's *We Didn't Mean to Go to Sea*. Quite obviously, Mr. Major sees adults in *Hold Fast* as symbolic destroyers of freedom and naturalness in human relations—qualities of life that are so precious to Michael. Whether it is the busdriver, the official at the airport, the principal or Uncle Ted, Michael must face a world of repression and red tape totally foreign to his upbringing. The only adult who can communicate with Michael is his grandfather, but they share only brief memories before being separated at the beginning. Yet, it is surely a falsification of reality—in this most realistic of novels—to view adults as a predictable series of Uncle Teds.

In spite of this stereotyping, the novel does work—and work admirably. Kevin Major, according to the note on the dust jacket, would have us believe that his novel "is a plea for us Newfoundlanders to be like certain of the species of seaweed that inhabit our shores, which, when faced with the threat of being destroyed by forces they cannot control, evolve an appendage to hold them to the rocks, a holdfast.''

The message is not just for Newfoundlanders. The values emphasized here are some of the most significant and universal: pride in oneself and one's heritage, courage to express and hold to one's opinions, the necessity to find a balance between emotion and reason and to cultivate a fine sensitivity for others and absolute honesty in assessing social relations.

Hold Fast may be a novel surrounded by death, but it pulses with an unbounded love of life which is attractive and meaningful. (pp. 82-3)

> Gary H. Paterson, "Learning to Hold Fast," in Canadian Children's Literature: A Journal of Criticism and Review (Box 335, Guelph, Ontario, Canada N1H6K5), No. 14, 1979, pp. 81-3.

KIRKUS REVIEWS

[In *Hold Fast,* fourteen-year-old] Michael, orphaned along with his seven-year-old brother Brent when his parents are killed by a drunken driver, tries to grapple with the changes in his life. The Newfoundland idiom [in which he speaks] soon becomes as natural as Michael himself as he recounts his move from Marten, his fishing village, to live with relatives in distant St. Albert. While Michael's relationship with straight-arrow cousin Curtis slowly solidifies, he is hard put to accept his uncle's dictatorial, arbitrary rules; and despite new friends and a girl at school, there are teasings and fights, which eventually lead to his expulsion. Overwhelmed, Michael runs away, with Curtis joining him in the latter's first defiant act ever; after a "borrowed" car caper and a few days spent in a national park closed for the winter, they arrive at Marten to find Michael's beloved grandfather dying. . . . A classic innocent who sometimes sounds like a sort of Newfoundland Holden Caulfield, Michael is more than redeemed as a character by the directness and strength of his emotions. And first novelist Major projects all the action as Michael experiences it, with the same directness and vigor.

> A review of "Hold Fast," in Kirkus Reviews (copyright © 1980 The Kirkus Service, Inc.), Vol. XLVIII, No. 10, May 15, 1980, p. 651.

CAROLYN S. LEMBECK

At 14 kids need to look outside the small world of home and family to fix their bearings on their own independence and individuality. Literature can provide such a reading. Adolescents recognize in their fictional counterparts the same irretrievable loss of childhood, the inevitability of adulthood, and the paradox of being in both places at one time. Sometimes it is enough to "hold fast," a discovery made by Michael, a young Canadian from the fishing village of Marten, Newfoundland, in [*Hold Fast*]. . . .

Pushed by family and social pressures to the point of losing his grip, Michael takes his young life into his own hands. . . . Michael's courage inspires his intimidated cousin, Curtis, to join him in his adventure. After a few days of "running away from home" the two boys are bored enough to face the job of growing up on their own terms. Curtis returns to St. Albert and his troubled family; Michael makes his claim to his parental home just as a second loss is demanded of him, the death of his best friend, Grandfather. Now no stranger to sorrow and

rage, Michael accepts the tragedy as part of an imperfect world in which he now directs his own course. It is a long way to have come in one year.

Very few young people will find themselves in Michael's unhappy situation; yet they will recognize his struggles as their own. A good book does more, however, than offer the consolation of not being alone. It instructs and inspires. *Hold Fast* does both.

> Carolyn S. Lembeck, in her review of "Hold Fast," in Best Sellers (copyright © 1980 Helen Dwight Reid Educational Foundation), Vol. 40, No. 3, June, 1980, p. 118.

LINDA GRANFIELD

Kevin Major's *Far From Shore* is a commendable example of writing pared to the essentials in character development, dialogue, plot and interpretation. The narrative technique and the skilful description of Newfoundlanders are equally praiseworthy.

As he did in his award-winning *Hold Fast* . . . , Major depicts not only a Newfoundland adolescent, but also the universal adolescent, the strength and fragility of youth caught up in the immediacy of life.

The emotional side of 15-year-old Chris Slade is perceptively and finely drawn. His scenes with the lonely Morrison, capturing the turmoil and love within, are moving and haunt the reader throughout the book. While the characters toil amidst broken hearts and broken homes, they also show a spirited and often humorous display of optimism, a *joie de vivre* that Major has engagingly captured on paper.

> Linda Granfield, in her review of "Far from Shore," in Quill and Quire (reprinted by permission of Quill and Quire), Vol. 46, No. 11, November, 1980, p. 41.

JANET LUNN

Far from Shore is the story of what happens to a family when the work gives out. It's also the story of Chris, who, despite his strong Newfoundland speech, could be a teen-aged boy anywhere yearning for the security of a solid home, awkwardly pursuing the excitement of sex, stabbing at the adventure and responsibility of manhood. It begins on Christmas Eve when Father stumbles home drunk and crashes into the Christmas tree. (p. 21)

Over the next couple of months things get worse until finally Father takes off for Alberta to find work. Mother gets a job in a fast-food restaurant—and more than a friend in the affectionate, lonely widower who owns it. Jennifer immerses herself in her last year at school. And Chris begins to cave in.

Growing angry and morose, he loses his girlfriend, he fails his year and decides not to go back to school and he picks up with a crowd of older boys who have a car, lots of beer, and dope. The morning the cop comes to charge him with smashing windows in a nearby school he is too hung-over to remember whether he did it or not.

To the rescue comes Rev. Wheaton to offer a job as a junior counsellor at the church camp. Chris's first responsibility there is to cheer up a despondent boy named Morrison. He does a good job of it because he likes the kid. But one night he succumbs to the temptation to smoke up with his room-mate and, early the next morning, tired and still a bit stoned, he takes Morrison out in the canoe too far from shore and nearly drowns them both.

It's a chastened and more thoughtful Chris, and a chastened and more thoughtful mother and father, who face the judge when Chris's case comes up for trial. The book ends with the mother and father reconciled, Jennifer at university and Chris back at school. Father doesn't swear off drink completely, Jennifer doesn't become a sugar-sweet sister, and Chris sees no blinding light to turn his life around. But it's clear that the Slades are going to go on as a family and that Chris is ready to face the next crisis with a bit more wisdom than he faced this one with.

The book has flaws. For one thing its structure is awkward and often confusing. It's told from the points of view of all the major characters. The result is choppy. It's like the kind of television interview show that leaps from subject to subject until you get knots of frustration in your stomach trying to keep everyone straight.

And Major's strength is not story-telling. His plot is trite and the story doesn't flow. There are, in fact, a couple of abrupt shifts that really jar. The most serious one comes when Chris goes off to camp after his big binge. Like the *deus ex machina* of the Greek dramas Rev. Wheaton appears, plucks Chris out of his tight spot and drops him into a new milieu—and it might be a whole new story. Neither plot nor character development follow from what has gone before. It's almost as though the author had two plots in mind, couldn't decide which to use, and so used both.

But the weaknesses of plot do not destroy the book. This isn't just another fashionably slick tale of sex, violence, and drugs among young adults. It's an honest and deeply felt story. Kevin Major, himself a Newfoundland high-school teacher, cares so much about his characters that you find yourself at the edge of tears even while you're laughing or shaking your fist in frustration or outrage. And he writes well. His picture of life in Newfoundland is bright and sharp. . . . His portrait is a gutsy view of people you could really know (and want to). And Chris Slade is one of the most engaging young men you're apt to meet in modern fiction for the young. (pp. 21-3)

Far from Shore is a more ambitious book [than Major's first novel, *Hold Fast*]. Major tries to explore more fully the relationships in a family. He fails because this is so much Chris's story that we get both too much and too little of the other characters. But even the failure is interesting in that the attempt provides a richness and a roundness not often found in books about kids in high school. Major understands people; he really knows kids. There are times when the teacher in him shows through too clearly but he puts his finger on the raw, heart-breaking quality of the adolescent so perfectly, so delicately, and so without that sense of the adult watching that too often mars work for the young, that young people are bound to respond to him with thanksgiving. (p. 23)

Janet Lunn, "Huck Finn in Newfoundland," in Books in Canada, *Vol. 9, No. 10, December, 1980, pp. 21-3.*

ANN JOHNSTON

For those who like to think that family life is still more or less as it was on *Leave It to Beaver*, **Far From Shore** hits hard and low. For others, weary of the sensationalism of juvenile novels, Kevin Major's story is a brave look at how a tough period can harden a boy like a nut. The pressures on the Slade family are like a vise gripping a migraine. Some (as in Major's last novel, **Hold Fast**) come from the frustrations of life in a small Newfoundland outport—boredom, unemployment, a general yearning to be anyplace but home. But more often they are the pressures of a family that isn't sure it's a unit any longer, and the one who flounders most is 15-year-old Chris. A cocky, wisecracking kid—when Jennifer snarls, he considers tossing her "a chunk of raw meat to quiet her down"—he is snared by the dissatisfaction around him, and becomes angry and confused. As a counsellor at summer camp, he agrees to take a boy who can't swim on a secret canoe ride, and is as baffled as everyone else when they almost drown.

Brilliantly, Major tackles his story in five voices—the four Slades, plus Rev. Wheaton, the camp director. They pass their story along like a hot potato, contradicting, misunderstanding and forgiving, until voices reverberate from the four corners of the house. When they finally come together, it's like the end of any family argument: you're pummelled and drained, and you can't remember whose side you first took. Major has pulled powerfully at unwilling chords, making sense of the most confusing battleground there is. (p. 57)

Ann Johnston, in her review of "Far from Shore," in Maclean's Magazine *(© 1980 by Maclean's Magazine; reprinted by permission), Vol. 93, No. 50, December 15, 1980, pp. 56-7.*

KLIATT YOUNG ADULT PAPERBACK BOOK GUIDE

[The critically acclaimed novel **Hold Fast**] is set in Newfoundland where the author lives. The dialect of the main characters, the details of life in a small fishing village, the path of the runaways—all these factors place the story solidly there. This in itself makes the novel unusual, certainly attractive to Canadians and to others interested in Newfoundland.

The fact that the story is exciting and in every way appealing, particularly to teenagers, should cause it to be received by a very wide audience. It is a counterpoint to the numerous suburban-city stories about teens. . . . Being the new kid and different from everyone else is a theme to which many teens can relate. . . .

The story is told in the first person by Michael, whose emotions and restless action drive the narrative forward; outsiders will be able to adjust to the dialect easily. (pp.4-5)

A review of "Hold Fast," in Kliatt Young Adult Paperback Book Guide *(copyright © by Kliatt Paperback Book Guide), Vol. XV, No. 8, November, 1981, pp. 4-5.*

KIRKUS REVIEWS

Set in Newfoundland like last year's **Hold Fast,** this weaker novel [**Far From Shore**] also deals with a basically likable but undisciplined kid in trouble. In a family where his unemployed father has become a surly drunk and his high-achieving sister, bound for University, is forever "at" her Dad—till he hauls off and hits her one on a disastrous Christmas—Chris flunks ninth grade, starts hanging out with a no-good older crowd, and gets in trouble with police over an episode of gang vandalism he's too drunk to remember. . . . By the end of the story Dad has returned, Chris (who had considered dropping out) is back in school, and the family is back together, thanks partly to the intercession of the camp head who is also their local minister. This is told mostly from Chris' viewpoint but Major also switches among the other principals' thoughts—most of which could be almost entirely skipped because they are such predictable projections of the concerned minister, the long-suffering mother, the self-excusing father, or whatever. Despite his bad ways, other characters comment on Chris' good nature, and this, along with all his crossroads choices (will he be a dope and smoke the second joint? lunge at the girl? take the canoe out on the rough lake?), may well strike a sympathetic chord in young readers too. Another plus is the true sense of teenage life on a depressed island, where there's little to do but drink and make out. But [*Far From Shore*] . . . is a come-down from the young author's *Hold Fast,* not the advance one might have hoped for. (pp. 1467-68)

> *A review of "Far from Shore," in* Kirkus Reviews *(copyright © 1981 The Kirkus Service, Inc.), Vol. XLIX, No. 23, December 1, 1981, pp. 1467-68.*

MURIEL WHITAKER

The strength of *Far From Shore* lies in the author's ability to present each of the major characters sympathetically in spite of their shortcomings. Through the device of interior mono-logue, actions and attitudes are provided with an emotional frame of reference that makes them comprehensible. (p. 52)

Major's use of dialogue is particularly admirable both as a means of projecting character and as a device for conveying regional flavour. He catches the rhythms of Newfoundland speech without the peppering of apostrophes that has annoyed me in dialect stories ever since I encountered "Brer Rabbit and the Tar Baby" at an early age. Chris's language is also enlivened by the profanity that Salinger's *Catcher in the Rye* established as a means of expressing teenage turmoil. The deterioration of the boy's social relationships is marked by a corresponding increase in his use of four-letter words. . . .

Kevin Major should also be commended for the fine balance which he strikes between social and economic determinism, on the one hand, and personal responsibility, on the other. It is not Chris's fault that he chooses to waste his time in bad company. Having drifted far from shore, both literally and figuratively, his recognition that "Come right down to it and it was all my own friggin' fault" indicates his new-found maturity. Major's social realism is essentially optimistic. Each of the characters has the opportunity of starting over. (p. 53)

> *Muriel Whitaker, "Getting Loused Up in Newfound-land," in* Canadian Children's Literature: A Journal of Criticism and Review *(Box 335, Guelph, Ontario, Canada N1H6K5), No. 22, 1981, pp. 50-3.*

JON C. STOTT

When Kevin Major's *Hold Fast* was published three years ago, it was rightly hailed as a milestone in Canadian children's book publishing. Major captured in stark, vivid, detail the violent, troubled life of a Newfoundland teenager. (p. 29)

We approached [Major's second novel, *Far From Shore*] with some trepidation, knowing that second novels can often be disappointing. However, we were not disappointed. *Far From Shore* is in many ways similar to *Hold Fast*. Set in Newfoundland, it is the story of a troubled teenager. Chris Slade is failing in high school, he is drinking too much beer and smoking too much pot. And he finds his girlfriend in the backseat of some-one else's car. At home, things are not good: Chris' father, unemployed and often drunk, decides to leave for Alberta to find work; his mother, not completely happy in her marriage, becomes emotionally involved with her employer; his sister shames him with her high grades at school.

While the novel focuses on Chris—his unhappiness with himself, his troubles with the police, and his nearly fatal error as a camp counsellor—it is not exclusively his story. Showing a daring not often found in young novelists, Major has decided to tell *Far From Shore* from multiple points of view. Thus we see the reactions of each member of the family not only to the events that most concern them individually, but also to those touching each other. The reader thus becomes aware of rela-tivity; no man, or woman, is an island.

Far From Shore belongs to the type of fiction known as social realism, the type of story which deals with the troubles ex-perienced by children and adolescents growing up in the com-plex modern world. Too often, social realism can fall into mere didacticism or into a kind of clinical case study. And often, there are happy endings which seem forced: the central figure has faced his problems and mastered them and is ready to enter into a meaningful relationship with society.

Now *Far From Shore* does have a happy ending, of sorts. . . . However, the author does not allow either the readers or the characters to believe that everything will be perfect from now on. (pp. 29-30)

Major has written a good second novel. It isn't perfect: some of the swearing seems gratuitous, although not offensive; and the relationship between father and son might have been more fully developed. We await with great interest his third novel; it should give a fairly clear indication of whether or not Major will fully develop the considerable talent that we find in his first two books. (p. 30)

> *Jon C. Stott, in his review of "Far from Shore," in* The World of Children's Books *(© 1981 Jon C. Stott), Vol. VI, 1981, pp. 29-30.*

Norma Fox Mazer

1931-

American novelist and short story writer.

In her fiction, Mazer presents people of all ages, socioeconomic classes, and family backgrounds grappling with common dilemmas and emotional conflicts. She strives to give her readers an accurate representation of the world in which they live, but her view is neither bleakly pessimistic nor unduly optimistic. Mazer's stance is one of confident humanism, which is reflected in her characters' heightened awareness and control over their lives.

In her early novel, *A Figure of Speech*, which won the Lewis Carroll Shelf Award in 1973, Mazer portrays an adolescent girl's sympathy and respect for her grandfather's desire to preserve his independence and dignity. Mazer has been especially praised for her short stories. *Dear Bill, Remember Me?* and *Summer Girls, Love Boys, and Other Short Stories* are both considered outstanding collections.

(See also *Contemporary Authors*, Vols. 69-72 and *Something about the Author*, Vol. 24.)

HILDAGARDE GRAY

[In *A Figure of Speech*, fine], strong affection based on a mutual need presents a plea for our reconsideration of today's old people. Jenny has felt an unwanted child all her thirteen years. When her "thoroughly middle-class" family starts a campaign along lines of what's best for eighty-three-year-old Grandpa, Jenny is personally wounded. She has shared most of her hours with the old man, who was alert, interested in life, and no trouble to anyone.

Details of the story are unimportant here; the point driven home with tremendous force is a painful, but proven, one—when we feel we are no longer needed, we begin to atrophy, physically and emotionally—a theory shown to be fact, repeatedly, in institutions and "old folks homes."

A pitiable attempt to regain dignity and youthful independence leads Grandpa and Jenny on a chase to recapture a bygone day—one best left to be re-lived in his strong mind, not to be attempted by the worn-out flesh.

Very good—moving without becoming maudlin—and deserving of a place in non-fiction sections because it speaks the truth about our contemporary selfishness and ingratitude.

> *Hildagarde Gray, in her review of "A Figure of Speech," in* Best Sellers *(copyright 1973, by the University of Scranton), Vol. 33, No. 16, November 15, 1973, p. 382.*

JILL PATON WALSH

In "**A Figure of Speech**" Jenny Pennoyer loves her Grandpa, and finds it tough to get along with the rest of her family. This is hardly surprising, considering what a selfish lot they are. Grandpa lives in the basement, which is damp, but at least it keeps him out of the way. Only Jenny visits with him. . . .

[And] she is horrified at [her family's] fussy and humiliating attitude toward him.

The crisis comes when Jenny's brother drops out of college and comes home with a young wife, and the couple look covetously at Grandpa's basement apartment. . . . [They] move him upstairs to share a bedroom with Jenny's teen-age brother—where Grandpa is even more in the way.

When the old man asserts himself by running away, back to his remembered past, Jenny goes with him to share the last days of his life. "Didn't suffer a bit," say her parents, talking about his death. "A real comfort to us that he went so easily." But then they have a cozy figure of speech to cover up the truth about anything. . . .

["**A Figure of Speech**"], written in a quiet, remorselessly realistic style, [is] . . . infused with a deeply felt compassion and humanity. And yet [it does not quite rise] . . . to the importance of its subject. Death is always a mystery; when it comes it is a cataclysmic finality. Rightly perhaps, [Norma Mazer concentrates] . . . on those aspects of aging that can be avoided. . . . "If we'd thought of it in time, we might have saved him," says Jenny's mother. But the truth is that no one can be saved from death—either his own, or another's. Children, too, must face this; it is one of the conditions of life. . . .

[Yet] **"A Figure of Speech"** comes [close] to the heart of things. . . . [The book] offers us an image of death itself: an old man lying in the attitude of sleep on the wet grass under an apple tree.

> *Jill Paton Walsh, in her review of "A Figure of Speech," in* The New York Times Book Review *(© 1974 by The New York Times Company; reprinted by permission), March 17, 1974, p. 8.*

MARY M. BURNS

[In *A Figure of Speech*] the euphemisms which cloak the attitudes of the middle-aged and the young toward the elderly are presented as a series of shabby self-deceptions. . . . [The book's narrator, Jenny,] has always felt alienated from her short-sighted, thoroughly middle-class family. Her one bulwark is her grandfather, who came to live with the family the year Jenny was born and, feeling as unwanted as she, virtually raised her to adolescence. Shifting the focus between Jenny and her grandfather, the narrative chronicles the climactic weeks in the crowded Pennoyer household following the elder son's arrival with his new bride. His indulgent parents plan to move the old man into a nursing home so that the young couple can have the basement apartment. The denouement is tragic, not simply because the old man dies but because Jenny cannot reconcile her family's post-mortem commentaries with their actions toward the man who had once lived with them. The subordinate characters are seen primarily from Jenny's and the grandfather's points of view; they are one-dimensional types, hypocritical and unlikeable. . . . Yet, the tendency toward melodramatic oversimplification is offset by the significance of the situation and by the crusty personality of grandfather, who refuses to "go gentle into that good night." (pp. 152-53)

> *Mary M. Burns, in her review of "A Figure of Speech," in* The Horn Book Magazine *(copyright © 1974 by The Horn Book, Inc., Boston), Vol. L, No. 2, April, 1974, pp. 152-53.*

BARBARA WERSBA

Consider for a moment this plot: a 14-year-old girl who lives in a crowded city is by accident swept back into the primeval past. A world of cave men. At first horrified, she gradually learns to become one of them, discovers the joys and sorrows of primitive life and finds that she has bridged a metaphysical river where past, present and future are one. Suddenly she is returned to the modern world, but no one believes in her journey. . . . She is sent to a psychologist and learns to behave like a "normal" person. But the memory of an earlier, more beautiful life haunts her, and she prays never to forget, never to become ordinary. . . . Her story ends on a note of pain.

In synopsis, I find this idea fascinating. But in Norma Fox Mazer's rendition something has gone wrong. It is not only that [**"Saturday, the Twelfth of October"**] is too long . . . , but that the mechanics which make it work are not dramatic. All science fiction and fantasy demand a crisis through which a human being can journey from one world to another. But our young heroine's dilemma is no more crucial than the fact that her brother and his friends have read her diary (a document fraught with the fear of menstruation). Enraged by this, she flees to a nearby park, leans against an ancient boulder—and is transported back to a world of innocence.

The premise does not succeed, and no one is sorrier than I, for Mrs. Mazer is a dazzling writer and brings to her work a literacy that would be admirable in any type of fiction. Her sense of character and place are expert, her use of suspense masterly and her descriptive powers superb. But one wonders why menstruation looms so largely in the plot, why it has been chosen as a device to show the innocence of the cave people and the frozen sophistication of the girl. One also wonders why—over and again—biological realism is forced upon stories that do not need it. (pp. 12, 14)

> *Barbara Wersba, in her review of "Saturday, the Twelfth of October," in* The New York Times Book Review *(© 1975 by The New York Times Company; reprinted by permission), October 19, 1975, pp. 12, 14.*

JACK FORMAN

To escape [from the anxieties of modern life, Zan, the heroine in *Saturday, the Twelfth of October*,] fantasizes a world in the Stone Age, complete with a new language and primitive culture. Zan gradually becomes accustomed to her new life in this primitive world, and the adventures which emerge from this unexplained time jump provide a fascinating and completely believable story within a story. Mazer never lets readers know for sure whether Zan's experience is real or schizophrenic escape, and the characters are developed with skill and understanding in both the primitive society and Zan's everyday world. An intriguing and compelling mixture of science fiction and fantasy.

> *Jack Forman, in his review of "Saturday, the Twelfth of October," in* School Library Journal *(reprinted from the November, 1975 issue of* School Library Journal, *published by R. R. Bowker Co./A Xerox Corporation; copyright © 1975), Vol. 22, No. 3, November, 1975, p. 93.*

TOM HEFFERNAN

The fine definition of all characters, the plausibility of the situations and the variety of realistic insights into motivation make [*A Figure of Speech*] almost too good to be true. There is no point at which it passes into an area of depiction or explanation that would exceed the experience of a young adolescent. But there is also no point at which the psychological perceptiveness and narrative control would disappoint an adult reader.

It is hard to say whether the story would be more poignant to a young or old reader. The child may read with a strong identification with Jenny as victim; the adult will probably read with appreciation of the exposure of the stupid, attritive family conflicts. The vindication of the old man, which entails Jenny's vindication also, is one of the most pleasing Justice Triumphs plots that could be devised. (p. 207)

> *Tom Heffernan, in his review of "A Figure of Speech," in* Children's Literature: Annual of The Modern Language Association Seminar on Children's Literature and The Children's Literature Association, *Vol. 4, edited by Francelia Butler (© 1975 by Francelia Butler; reprinted by permission of Francelia Butler),* Temple University Press, 1975, pp. 206-07.

ALLEEN PACE NILSEN, JANE COY, AND MIKEN OLSEN

[A] fantasy that makes for exciting reading is *Saturday the Twelfth of October*. Zan Ford is a fourteen-year-old growing up in today's New York City complete with muggings, family squabbles, and impersonal relationships. Through an unexplained time warp, Zan is removed from Mechanix Park and set down in the same spot during the Stone Age. She is in almost a Garden of Eden. There is laughter, honesty, and people touching and relating to each other. When tempers flair, a hollering match is held to relieve tension and solve the problem. But as the story unfolds, violence and selfishness are introduced through a shiny knife that Zan happened to have in her pocket when she went through the time warp. Whether or not the people's lives will ever be the same after Zan returns to the present could be the basis for an exciting class discussion.

> *Alleen Pace Nilsen, Jane Coy, and Miken Olsen, in their review of "Saturday the Twelfth of October" (copyright © 1976 by the National Council of Teachers of English; reprinted by permission of the publisher and the author), in* English Journal, *Vol. 65, No. 7, October, 1976, p. 88.*

PAMELA D. POLLACK

["**Dear Bill, Remember Me?" and Other Stories** contains eight] stories that turn on small moments of defiance or determination. Mazer is at her best dissecting all-female families—in "**Peter in the Park**," an intense tale of breaking out of maternal bondage, or in the splendidly ironic "**Guess Whose Loving Hands**," in which an uncosmeticized cancer victim is cheated of an honest acknowledgement of her impending death by her ministering mother and sister. The women are drawn with every nuance and even a smothering mother is not without sympathy. Unfortunately, the men have a limited range, tending to be jellyfish, skunks, or dark horses, e.g., the men in "**Chocolate Pudding**" are spineless wino Dad and a reverse snob who's turned on by the heroine's poverty; "**Mimi the Fish**" is menaced by her beefy butcher father and romanced by a dreamboat who is as much an unknown quantity to her as to readers. Death, alcoholism, divorce are unremarkable facts of life in these stories which defy the self-help problem-solution mold and, though boy-girl interest is always there, are anything but romantic confessionals. Quiet and unaffected, these are fiercely felt renderings of misplaced love and search for selfhood.

> *Pamela D. Pollack, in her review of "Dear Bill, Remember Me? and Other Stories," in* School Library Journal *(reprinted from the October, 1976 issue of* School Library Journal, *published by R. R. Bowker Co./A Xerox Corporation; copyright © 1976), Vol. 23, No. 2, October, 1976, p. 119.*

KIRKUS REVIEWS

Short story collections at this level are scarce, and when a good one . . . does appear on a YA list it often seems to have wound up there by default. . . . [Mazer's stories in *Dear Bill, Remember Me?*] are clearly broadcast on a young teenager's wavelength, with the signal unobtrusively amplified as in good YA novels; and just as clearly, Mazer appreciates the short story form, with its narrow focus and spotlit moments, where others might do up the same material as diluted novels. Except for "**Zelzah**," a resilient immigrant of "long ago," these are sympathetic views of ordinary, contemporary girls and their relationships with mothers and new boyfriends. In the funniest,

and shrewdest, a socially insecure girl ends up carrying limburger cheese all through her first date. . . . Elsewhere a thirteen-year-old breaks free of the loving protection of her mother, aunt, and grandmother; a working class teenager discovers her bouncy, light-hearted mother's affair; a dying eighteen-year-old pleads with her smiling mother and sister to acknowledge the truth; and there are some happy pairings as when the loner who lives in a trailer with a drunken father and uncle finds a boy who shares her enthusiasm for chocolate pudding. The modesty of the characters' social backgrounds and intellectual horizons, not to mention the brevity of the pieces, adds to the stories' appeal as sturdy rungs on a gently sloping reading ladder. (pp. 1101-02)

> *A review of "Dear Bill, Remember Me? and Other Stories," in* Kirkus Reviews *(copyright © 1976 The Kirkus Service, Inc.), Vol. XLIV, No. 19, October 1, 1976, pp. 1101-02.*

ANN A. FLOWERS

In [*Dear Bill, Remember Me? and Other Stories*] the heroines are all young girls, each passing through a crisis in search of her own particular freedom. A certain similarity among the stories is noticeable; many of the mothers are rather protective and most of the girls are fatherless or have ineffectual or unfeeling fathers. Individually, however, each girl's struggle to reach her goal is realistic in the presentation of the options now open to young people. Zoe in "**Peter in the Park**" is almost suffocated by the excessive love and understanding of her grandmother, her mother, and her aunt; her mild rebellion in the form of a late-night walk in the park brings her a sense of satisfaction. . . . Tart and amusing Jessie in "**Up on Fong Mountain**" strives to be accepted as a person rather than as the appendage of her overbearing boy friend. In "**Guess Whose Friendly Hands**" eighteen-year-old Louise knows she is dying of cancer and simply wishes her mother and sister to acknowledge it, so that they will all be relieved of the insupportable burden of pretense. And the admirable last story, "**Zelzah: A Tale from Long Ago**," concerns a quiet and determined immigrant girl who breaks away from the conventional peasant role of wife and mother to become a teacher—alone and by her own efforts. A somewhat uneven, but varied and thought-provoking collection with a theme of timely and universal interest. (pp. 58-9)

> *Ann A. Flowers, in her review of "Dear Bill, Remember Me? and Other Stories," in* The Horn Book Magazine *(copyright © 1977 by the Horn Book, Inc., Boston), Vol. LIII, No. 1, February, 1977, pp. 58-9.*

JOYCE MILTON

The best that can be said about *The Solid Gold Kid* is that the authors have hit on a plot with 14-carat potential. The mass kidnapping of five teenagers, previously strangers, is a premise that's virtually guaranteed to keep youngsters turning pages.

The solid gold kid himself is Derek Chapman, the lonely, insecure son of a self-made millionaire. While waiting for a bus outside the gates of his private school, Derek unsuspectingly hitches a ride with Pearl and Bogie, a self-styled Bonnie and Clyde who have been planning to kidnap him for a cool half-million in ransom. Just as innocently, Derek invites five townies who happen to be standing at the bus stop to share the back of the van with him. Thus Pearl and Bogie, luckless as they are desperate, are stuck with four accidental hostages.

Our introduction to the five victims is the first hint of heavy going ahead. This supposedly random bunch is as calculatedly balanced as the cast of a singing Pepsi commercial. In addition to Derek, there is Jeff, a nattily dressed black whose drive to be realistic about their predicament verges on cynicism, and Eddie, a working-class ethnic type who passes remarks about "boogies" and tends to identify with his captors. And there are two girls: Pam is blonde, idealistic and outspoken; and Wendy is Jewish, asthmatic and apparently the weakest member of the group.

Pearl and Bogie's plans go wrong from the outset, and the kids are carted around, bound and half-starved, from one hideaway to the next. Their attempts to escape provide some solid suspense. . . . By the time Derek is rescued six days later, he is under the impression that all his fellow victims are dead.

Unfortunately, the Mazers aren't content to spin a straight action adventure. They gum up the works trying to make serious statements. Often, these teenagers sound less like crime victims than self-conscious participants in a weekend encounter group. Especially annoying is the attempt to deal with Derek's guilt over being disgustingly rich. . . .

On [one] occasion, Derek muses lugubriously, "It was fate, I told myself, and I thought of fate like a giant hand scooping up the five of us, squeezing us together in this unbearable, hateful intimacy." Actually, young readers know as well as the Mazers do the difference between fate and contrivance. They may well be satisfied with the latter, and as a thriller this is passable fair. Too bad it tries so hard to be more.

> Joyce Milton, "A Kid's Ransom," in Book World— The Washington Post (© 1977, The Washington Post), July 10, 1977, p. H10.

ETHEL L. HEINS

[*The Solid Gold Kid* is] a skillfully written and credibly plotted suspense story with fascinating psychological overtones. . . . At the mercy of a vicious, sadistic couple, . . . five young people—three boys and two girls—endure days of agonizing imprisonment and live through unspeakable physical and mental torture. Several times they nearly escape, and once they come within a hairsbreadth of being cremated alive; one of the girls is shot and severely wounded, and the other risks her life in a perilous but vain attempt to free the captives. The teenagers, from diverse racial and social backgrounds, are incisively individualized characters; closely confined and under the pressure of constant terror, their attitudes toward one another alternate between genuine solicitude and snarling hostility. The appalling events reach a climax with a breathtaking police chase; but more significantly, the reader feels that the story is essentially concerned with the human capacity for survival and with the futility of violence and hatred. (pp. 451-52)

> Ethel L. Heins, in her review of "The Solid Gold Kid," in The Horn Book Magazine (copyright © 1977 by the Horn Book, Inc., Boston), Vol. LIII, No. 4, August, 1977, pp. 451-52.

PATTY CAMPBELL

Not since [Maureen Daly's] *Seventeenth Summer* have the agonies and yearnings of sexual avoidance been presented so vividly

as in *Up in Seth's Room*. . . . [The relationship of Seth and Finn] soon develops into a grotesque battle over whether she is willing to let him—as they used to say in the sex manuals— achieve penetration. She accepts every other form of intimacy with cheerful enthusiasm, but protects her technical virginity with hysterical zeal. This medieval attitude has evidently been absorbed from Finn's parents, who regard her older sister's cohabitation as a terrible tragedy. In the end, Finn and Seth go off into the sunset, after working out a method of satisfaction for him. (It doesn't seem to occur to anybody that she has needs too.) Mazer presents all this with approval and sympathy for the prohibiting parents. (pp. 123, 139)

> Patty Campbell, in her review of "Up in Seth's Room," in Wilson Library Bulletin (copyright © 1979 by the H. W. Wilson Company), Vol. 54, No. 1, October, 1979, pp. 123, 139.

BOOKLIST

[In *Up in Seth's Room*, fifteen year old Finn] feels confident that she wants to remain a virgin despite pressure to "go all the way". . . . [It] is not until Finn meets handsome Seth . . . that her attitude is put to the test. Ignoring prohibitions from her disapproving family . . . , Finn begins to see Seth in secret and the two develop real feelings for each other. Their sexual relationship is limited to kissing and petting until Seth finds his own apartment when matters rapidly change. After an encounter that stops just short of force, the pair realizes that Seth has interpreted Finn's resistance as a challenge to his masculinity. The knowledge affects them both, forcing Finn to weigh her romantic attachment to Seth with her right to govern her own desires and helping Seth reevaluate his ideas about relationships between men and women. While sexual encounters are explicit, Mazer focuses on the emotions they engender rather than the acts themselves, and an obvious message to teenagers is softened considerably by the use of natural dialogue and well-rounded characters.

> A review of "Up in Seth's Room," in Booklist (reprinted by permission of the American Library Association; copyright © 1979 by the American Library Association), Vol. 76, No. 5, November 1, 1979, p. 440.

KIRKUS REVIEWS

[*Up in Seth's Room* presents a] cliché situation, with some goopy descriptions of sexual bliss and what might well be seen as a ludicrous solution in these days when technical virginity has pretty much lost its cachet. But one can imagine other girls becoming involved in Finn's lonely battles (defying her parents, disagreeing with Vida, resisting Seth). And the fact that different readers can come out of this taking different sides— Finn's, Seth's, even the parents'—attests to Mazer's skill in giving the single-issue story some human contours.

> A review of "Up in Seth's Room," in Kirkus Reviews (copyright © 1979 The Kirkus Service, Inc.), Vol. XLVII, No. 23, December, 1979, p. 1380.

KAREL ROSE

[*A Figure of Speech* is] a tragic novel about the continuing deterioration of a "senior citizen" and the family's plan to move him into an "old folks" home. Living in a basement apartment in his son's house, the old grandfather refuses to submit to the arrangements that are being made for his life. His confidante and dear friend is his granddaughter Jenny, and the very thought of her dispels his self pity. "Of course he had a reason to get out of bed every morning. Jenny. She was his reason."

The language interchanges in the book are exciting. The old man always fights for what is real in language and life, rejecting the euphemisms applied to him. He refuses, for example, to be categorized as a "senior citizen" and as he writes in one note, he will not be "passing away" but will die. Nevertheless, day by day, individual members of the family grow impatient with grandpa's habits and routines. Furthermore, his apartment, though in the basement, would provide the necessary accommodations for Jenny's older brother and his new wife. The handwriting is on the wall and even grandpa's son says, "The day I get too old or too lazy to hold my own toothbrush and swish it back and forth on my teeth a few times you can take me to the old people's home and leave me there. Amelia, you got that: The old folks' home." . . . And that is indeed where the family plans to send the old man. Apprised of this by his granddaughter Jenny, grandpa plans to run away. (pp. 68-9)

[The] nursing home in this story has nothing to recommend it. More important than the lack of basic comforts which are carefully described is the clear implication that the old man will continue to receive the same insensitive treatment that he has received at home. Jenny reacts violently when she visits Castle Haven. "The back of Jenny's neck went cold. She felt sick, sick. She hated this place and pitied every old person here. . . . She didn't want to . . . hear Mrs. Burr McCarthy going on in her calm, sensible way about the 'lovely' residents." . . .

Despite his acerbity, grandfather comes through as a real character—brave, stubborn, independent to the end, determining his own fate even to the point of succeeding in taking his life. Professionals and parents before recommending this book will have to decide whether the emotional resilience of this courageous "old codger" justified the grim, detailed representation of this very real situation. (p. 69)

Karel Rose, "The Young Learn About the Old: Aging and Children's Literature," in The Lion and the Unicorn *(copyright © 1980 The Lion and the Unicorn), Vol. 3, No. 2, Winter, 1979-80, pp. 64-75.**

JEAN FRITZ

[*Up in Seth's Room*] is strictly for teenagers, although the under-12 Judy Blume crowd will probably sniff it out.

The questions we follow relentlessly from beginning to end are the perennial ones of adolescence: Will she or won't she? And what's it like? Fifteen-year-old Finn says she won't. It's too soon, she's too young, and she's not ready. . . . Seth, who is 19 (old enough and definitely ready) is the brother of the man that Finn's older sister is living with. "Living in sin," as far as the parents are concerned.

Well, to make a long story short, everyone should be pleased with the outcome. Finn sticks to her guns, although the fact that she "doesn't" is hardly more than a technicality. There are enough explicit scenes to give young readers who don't know a good idea of "what it's like."

Although Seth finally lets up on the pressure, he almost immediately moves away. A perfect ending for first love: no more temptation, parents relieved, girl's principles intact, and a goodbye forever scene that justifies a nice cry. If the characters are less fully developed than those Mrs. Mazer has given us before, young readers probably won't notice. They'll be too busy turning the pages.

Jean Fritz, in her review of "Up in Seth's Room," in The New York Times Book Review (© 1980 by The New York Times Company; reprinted by permission), January 20, 1980, p. 30.*

LAURA GERINGER

[*Mrs. Fish, Ape, and Me, the Dump Queen*] is told from the point of view of Joyce, orphaned ward of her uncle Ape Man, the town trash collector. Mocked and ostracized by other children for her association with rubbish . . . , she lives a sheltered routine with her surly, diamond-in-the-rough guardian. . . . But when the sturdy isolationist has a stroke, the girl enlists the aid of fat Mrs. Fish, the cleaning lady at school. . . . In the ailing giant's rude behavior, the lonely custodian sees buried gallantry. . . . The trio become an odd family in the end and the young heroine . . . is finally able to share her Swiss cheese sandwich with a new friend. The tone here is self-conscious and contrived. People fly into rages, sing manic songs, do dances, and fling taunts for no visible reason. And a tedious series of lists, e.g., the contents ad infinitum of the junkyard, substitutes for true detail.

Laura Geringer, in her review of "Mrs. Fish, Ape, and Me, the Dump Queen," in School Library Journal *(reprinted from the April, 1980 issue of* School Library Journal, *published by R. R. Bowker Co./A Xerox Corporation; copyright © 1980), Vol. 26, No. 8, April, 1980, p. 114.*

RUTH M. STEIN

Dumps seem to be popping up frequently in juvenile literature this year. [The one in *Mrs. Fish, Ape, and Me, The Dump Queen*] is the Queenship Town Dump, whose smells and sights come alive under Mazer's deft pen. "Ape" is what people call Old Dad, Joyce's uncle in charge of the dump. Mrs. Fish is the temporary custodian in Joyce's school who befriends the lonely girl. How life becomes more bearable for all is the ordinary theme made extraordinary by well-delineated characters and the proper mixture of laughter and tears.

Ruth M. Stein, in her review of "Mrs. Fish, Ape, and Me, The Dump Queen" (copyright © 1981 by the National Council of Teachers of English; reprinted by permission of the publisher and the author), in Language Arts, Vol. 58, No. 2, February, 1981, p. 185.*

LEONORE GORDON

Steadfastly maintaining self-respect in spite of their derogation by others, the three protagonists [of *Mrs. Fish, Ape, and Me, the Dump Queen*]—Joyce, "Ole Dad" and Mrs. Fish—have a great deal to teach readers of any age.

Joyce, the central character who tells the story, lives with her uncle, Ole Dad, in a garbage dump, of which he is the caretaker. Together, they recycle old garbage into useful forms, critically eyeing the materialism and wastefulness of others.

Ole Dad is a positive, nurturing single male parent, still a rarity in children's books.

Each of the three central characters must face the challenge of enduring the age-old sport of name-calling, and children who have experienced this indignity for any reason will find new strength from this story. Due to his short frame, large head and long arms, Ole Dad is tauntingly referred to as "Ape Man" by town residents. Joyce herself is rejected and harassed by classmates for living in a dump. Other children call her "Dump Queen" and "Cootie Queen"; chants are created about her, and at one point, students stuff vile-smelling garbage into her desk. . . .

What is remarkable about Joyce is her ability to remain proud and uncompromised, in spite of her loneliness. This loneliness is eased, however, with the arrival of Mrs. Fish, a temporary custodial worker at the school. This large, loving, somewhat eccentric woman creates a shelter for Joyce in her small basement office, and offers her both strength and humor.

Like the other two protagonists, Fish is stigmatized by classist and bigoted attitudes. . . . Her response to name-calling is a consistent one: "Tush on them all!" Joyce responds to her with great admiration. . . .

Ultimately, Mrs. Fish meets Ole Dad, who is initially belligerent and suspicious of strangers and seems jealous of Joyce's undisguised love for her new surrogate parent. When he has a stroke, however, he is forced to spend time with Mrs. Fish, who begins to spend weekends at the dump, helping Joyce to maintain and sort the garbage. The relationship that eventually develops between Ole Dad and Mrs. Fish constitutes a moving subplot; the struggle Ole Dad has in overcoming his insecurities and lack of trust in order to experience a growing love is especially touching.

The heart of the story lies in the process of these three individuals beginning to work as a unit, drawing deeply on each other's goodness and individuality, with the mutual understanding that their relationships are far more important than validation from an unsympathetic outer world. . . . The author tackles the problem of being different with tremendous success, and gives her characters the ego-strength and values to be invulnerable to others' judgements.

> *Leonore Gordon, in her review of "Mrs. Fish, Ape, and Me, the Dump Queen," in* Interracial Books for Children Bulletin *(reprinted by permission of Interracial Books for Children Bulletin, 1841 Broadway, New York, N.Y. 10023), Vol. 12, Nos. 7 & 8, 1981, p. 17.*

KAREN RITTER

Considering all the recent publicity about divorced parents who kidnap their own children, there was certain to be a juvenile novel on the subject sooner or later. And [*Taking Terri Mueller*] is a good one, not just capitalizing on that gimmick—in fact, readers don't learn until halfway through the book what has actually happened—but developing strong characters and a plot that involves the kidnapping angle as a basic element. Terri has always been told that her mother died when she was four years old, and since her father has effectively cut off all contact with most of their relatives . . . , Terri has no sources of information on her family. Terri and her father apparently have a warm, loving, open relationship; he explains their frequent moves from one city to another by his "Restless Feet." But

during her 13th year, Terri begins to wonder about the gaps in her knowledge of the past and, to her great distress, she learns the truth. She does manage to contact her mother, over her father's emotional objections, and eventually re-establishes a relationship with her and with the grandparents she has all but forgotten. All the characters are very human. Both parents are portrayed sympathetically; while the author does not excuse or approve of the father's actions, it is clear that he acted out of love.

> *Karen Ritter, in her review of "Taking Terri Mueller," in* School Library Journal *(reprinted from the December, 1981 issue of* School Library Journal, *published by R. R. Bowker Co./A Xerox Corporation; copyright © 1981), Vol. 28, No. 4, December, 1981, p. 67.*

ILENE COOPER

[In *Taking Terri Mueller*,] thirteen-year-old Terri and her father, Phil, have an almost idyllic relationship. . . . Terri has no reason to doubt what her father has told her about her mother's death in an auto accident nine years before. . . . Through snooping and pressuring her father, she learns the truth—that when her mother planned to remarry and move abroad, Phil kidnapped Terri. The ramifications of that disclosure and Terri's eventual reunion with her mother comprise the rest of this well-written, fast-paced story. For a book that begins so benignly, amazing emotional depths are reached. Strong characterizations on all sides make Terri's eventual decision about who she will live with realistically difficult.

> *Ilene Cooper, in her review of "Taking Terri Mueller," in* Booklist *(reprinted by permission of the American Library Association; copyright © 1981 by the American Library Association), Vol. 78, No. 7, December 1, 1981, p. 500.*

KLIATT YOUNG ADULT PAPERBACK BOOK GUIDE

Mazer became interested in writing a novel about children who have been kidnapped after divorce when she learned that about 25,000 children each year are stolen from one parent by the other parent. [In *Taking Terri Mueller*] Terri Mueller is just such a child. For eight years she has believed that her mother died in a car crash. Now that she is thirteen, she begins to notice certain discrepancies in her father's story, and she asks questions. At times, it appears that she has opened up a Pandora's box—her knowledge causes even more suffering and division. Mazer has looked at the issue from all angles and successfully conveys the overwhelming emotional impact inherent in the situation. Readers will readily sympathize with Terri, a level-headed, sensitive girl, whose joy at finding her mother who has loved her and longed for her each day of the eight-year separation, is immeasurable.

> *A review of "Taking Terri Mueller," in* Kliatt Young Adult Paperback Book Guide *(copyright © by Kliatt Paperback Book Guide), Vol. XVI, No. 1, January, 1982, p. 13.*

DICK ABRAHAMSON

[*Taking Terri Mueller*] is one of Norma Mazer's best. Terri moves from town to town with her father. Their relationship is one of mutual love and friendship. As Terri grows older, she begins to question the secrecy and frequency of their moves across the country. . . .

Terri eavesdrops on a conversation between her father and her aunt and finds out that her mother is not dead as she'd been told. She also finds that her father kidnapped her after her mother was granted child custody. Mazer does a fine job of taking Terri through the emotional ups and downs caused by her discovery. She wants to contact her mother, but she's afraid her father will be jailed. She's mad at him for denying her a permanent home and an extended family, but she loves him for the sacrifices he's made to keep her. Against her father's wishes, Terri goes to visit her mother. Again, the awkwardness and the tension of the mother/daughter meeting is well done. Terri ultimately faces the decision of whether or not she lives with her mother or goes back to her father. The book is timely and well written.

> *Dick Abrahamson, in his review of "Taking Terri Mueller," in* The ALAN Review, *Vol. 9, No. 3, Spring, 1982, p. 15.*

KIRKUS REVIEWS

If the title [of *Summer Girls, Love Boys and Other Short Stories*] turns you off, the first story, cast as a series of unsent letters to a boy the girl writer is stuck on, will confirm the worst. It's pure teen-romance drivel. The title story is tuned to the same wave-length, though less sappy and possessed of more elements: 15-year-old Mary's doting older parents, her weak stab at independence, a charming boy who gives her rides on his motorcycle but openly admits his love for another girl, the boy's attractive father who eventually shocks Mary by kissing her, and her aching, on her sadder-because-wiser sixteenth birthday, "to still be fifteen—oh! To still be fifteen!" The other entries are so obvious and one dimensional that capsule summaries [would] miss no nuances. . . . [The stories in this collection] make their points with . . . unmodulated banality. Mazer's earlier short story collection, *Dear Bill, Remember Me?,* was about ordinary people's ordinary relationships. These are ordinary in the most limiting sense.

> *A review of "Summer Girls, Love Boys," in* Kirkus Reviews *(copyright © 1982 The Kirkus Service, Inc.), Vol. L, No. 18, September 15, 1982, p. 1061.*

STEPHANIE ZVIRIN

[*Summer Girls, Love Boys and Other Short Stories* is a] satisfying collection of nine short stories sandwiched together between two poems reflecting on parent/teen relationships also written by Mazer. Featuring female protagonists, the stories mix the bitter and the sweet of life while encompassing a variety of narrative techniques, settings, themes, and tones. For example, in **"Avie Loves Ric Forever,"** Mazer uses letters, a device she employed in the title story of her last collection, *Dear Bill, Remember Me?* . . . , to record the ache of a teenager's unrequited love; in **"Do You Really Think It's Fair?"** she writes a kind of extended monologue to depict a teenager verbalizing her feelings about her sister's death to a silent therapist; and in **"Carmella, Adelina, and Florry,"** she vividly re-creates a 1940s sweatshop in an effort to expose what things were frequently like for nonunionized women workers during the first part of the century. The remaining six pieces are equally diverse, with characters ranging from a dreamy-eyed 15-year-old and an eccentric who talks to herself and loves

monopoly to an old woman afraid to put her past in proper perspective. Woven in are some memorable moments, and Mazer writes honestly and provocatively of human emotion and circumstances while she demonstrates her versatility as a writer. (pp. 198-99)

> *Stephanie Zvirin, in her review of "Summer Girls, Love Boys and Other Short Stories," in* Booklist *(reprinted by permission of the American Library Association; copyright © 1982 by the American Library Association), Vol. 79, No. 3, October 1, 1982, pp. 198-99.*

C. NORDHIELM WOOLDRIDGE

[The stories in *Summer Girls, Love Boys and Other Short Stories*] are bound by locale, Greene Street; but with one peripheral exception the characters do not cross the boundaries of their individual stories. Four center on a first love. . . . Three protagonists face or cause crises. . . . The spotlight that swings through this neighborhood sympathetically catches women of all ages at various junctures in life and gives equal time to puppy love, marriage and death because all carry equal significance at the moment they occur. If there is an overall message here it is that Mazer can really write a short story.

> *C. Nordhielm Wooldridge, in his review of "Summer Girls, Love Boys and Other Short Stories," in* School Library Journal *(reprinted from the November, 1982 issue of School Library Journal, published by R. R. Bowker Co./A Xerox Corporation; copyright © 1982), Vol. 29, No. 3, November, 1982, p. 102.*

KIRKUS REVIEWS

Jenny and Rob: as Jenny's friend Rhoda points out, their initials are the same as Romeo and Juliet's. Their situation [in *When We First Met*] is similar too. Jenny Pennoyer and Rob Montana are drawn to each other on first sight, then realize that Rob's mother was the driver who hit and killed Jenny's sister Gail two years earlier. Knowing how her mother nurses her grief and her grudge against Mrs. Montana . . . , Jenny resists Rob's overtures. Eventually however they fall in love. At first Jenny keeps the relationship from her family, and she breaks with Rob later when it seems too much for the Pennoyers. But finally, after Mrs. Montana attempts suicide and Rob is seen with another girl, Jenny decides that she must live her own life, and that Rob is a part of it. Though the relationships and the characters are less contoured than those in *Up in Seth's Room,* Mazer's ability to take her teenage characters' relationships as seriously as they do themselves gives this something of that same soap-opera appeal.

> *A review of "When We First Met," in* Kirkus Reviews *(copyright © 1982 The Kirkus Service, Inc.), Vol. L, No. 22, November 15, 1982, p. 1241.*

ETHEL R. TWICHELL

A single neighborhood is apparently the setting for [*Summer Girls, Love Boys and Other Short Stories,* a collection of] nine short stories that are otherwise unrelated and are uneven in quality. Among the best of them is **"How I Run Away and Make My Mother Toe the Line,"** in which a young girl—big, mouthy, and prickly about her rights—runs away from her weary, bossy mother, only to realize on her return a grudging respect and love for Mom. In the story the author has successfully used the rhythms and cadences of street talk to reveal character and plot. Another good tale, **"Down Here on Greene Street,"** again shows the author using specific speech patterns and details of food, dress, and furniture with a sure hand, as a middle-aged widow reaches a decision to remain alone in her own home rather than move to Florida with a man she is genuinely fond of. Other stories, however, are not as successful because of a certain slickness in style and because the reader feels less concern for the central characters. All of the stories revolve around girls or women and deal with the discovery each one makes about herself or others, opening the way for growth or at least for an enlightened acceptance of life. Some of the narratives lack the dramatic impact of good short stories, but throughout the book the author skillfully articulates the speech and emotions of believable people. (pp. 660-61)

Ethel R. Twichell, in her review of "Summer Girls, Love Boys and Other Short Stories," in The Horn Book Magazine *(copyright © 1982 by The Horn Book, Inc., Boston), Vol. LVIII, No. 6, December, 1982, pp. 660-61.*

PUBLISHERS WEEKLY

[*When We First Met*] is plotted on a situation that a less sure hand would reduce to a soap opera. But the award-winning author invests the ordinary people in her story with realism and draws readers into lives tragically altered when Nell Montana is convicted of drunken driving and fatally injuring Gail Pennoyer. Two years later, Gail's sister Jenny, 16, and Rob Montana meet and fall in love, despite their shock at realizing his mother is the object of the Pennoyer family's implacable hatred. Jenny and Rob meet secretly for a time, until he persuades her to introduce him to her parents, an occurrence with shattering results. Mazer adroitly handles ensuing developments and earns one's admiration for making each person's viewpoint understandable and the suffering of all deeply affecting.

A review of "When We First Met," in Publishers Weekly *(reprinted from the December 17, 1982 issue of Publishers Weekly, published by R. R. Bowker Company, a Xerox company; copyright © 1982 by Xerox Corporation), Vol. 222, No. 24, December 17, 1982, p. 75.*

GARY H. PATERSON

Credibility of plot is essential [in a realistic novel]. In Norma Fox Mazer's depiction of old age in *A Figure of Speech* . . . , Jenny tries to protect her grandfather from being sent off to a nursing home. The actual portrayal of the home is a fine caricature of the stereotype of efficiency at the cost of personal identity that persists even to-day, but caricature is not realism. Quite obviously, the plot depends upon saving grandfather from the nightmarish nursing home, so the novelist's solution is to create an inappropriate one. To me, this is an example of realism cheating. (p. 30)

Gary H. Paterson, "Perspectives on the New Realism in Children's Literature," in Canadian Children's Literature: A Journal of Criticism and Review *(Box 335, Guelph, Ontario, Canada N1H6K5), No. 25, 1982, pp. 26-32.*

SUZANNE FREEMAN

It's not hard to see why Norma Fox Mazer has found a place among the most popular writers for young adults these days. At her best, Mazer can cut right to the bone of teenage troubles and then show us how the wounds will heal. She can set down the everyday scenes of her characters' lives in images that are scalpel-sharp. In Mazer's books, we find lovers who cheat and fathers who cry. We find elephant jokes and pink champagne. We find college students who live in apartments which smell of cats and we find high school kids who walk through corridors which smell of "lysol, oregano (pizza for lunch again) and cigarette smoke." What's apparent throughout all of this is that Mazer has taken great care to get to know the world she writes about. She delves into the very heart of it with a sure and practiced hand. . . .

In *Someone to Love,* Mazer deals with the subject of living together ("L.T." in college lingo). Nina Bloom, a college sophomore meets and falls in love with Mitch Beers, a house painter and college dropout. In relatively short order, the couple decides to live together and Nina moves her clothing and her cat into Mitch's apartment.

For a while, they exult in their new intimacy. Nina learns to eat breakfast to please Mitch. Mitch puts up with Emmett, the cat, for Nina's sake. "If the heat went off they got into bed. Nothing bothered them. If they ran out of bread or Band-Aids or bath powder, they bundled up and went out together to shop." . . .

Mazer gets all these cozy details just right. And, as the honeymoon ends and things get less than cozy between Mitch and Nina, the details are just as true to life. There are the fights over silly little things—shoelaces and sugar in the coffee. There are the kiss-and-make-up episodes which grow few and far-between. And, finally, there are big issues which become the big problems—Nina's attraction to her handsome English professor and Mitch's obvious interest in Lynell, Nina's former roommate.

The pieces of this story fit together neatly. The only trouble is that it's all a bit *too* neat. We are left with the feeling that the cards were stacked against Nina and Mitch from the start, that they were set up to fall apart before our eyes so that we could learn from their experience. The ending of their story is predictable, but they carry it off with the good grace and show of strength that is typical of Mazer's characters.

In its sharpest moments, Norma Fox Mazer's writing can etch a place in our hearts. In the passages that are perhaps not so well-honed, her people and their stories still manage to make us care. And that is no small achievement.

Suzanne Freeman, "The Truth about the Teens," in Book World—The Washington Post *(© 1983, The Washington Post), April 10, 1983, p. 10.*

Milton Meltzer

1915-

American historian, biographer, critic, editor, and novelist.

Meltzer's histories and biographies reflect his concern for past and present injustices and point to the need for the protection of human rights and the preservation of human dignity. He writes for young adults with the hope that his books, in addition to presenting pertinent historical facts, will move his readers to question themselves and society, in order to recognize injustice and help effect social change.

Meltzer is best known for portraying the struggles of minorities. His histories have helped fill a gap in high school and college textbooks that briefly mention or ignore the uglier aspects of minority problems in the United States and elsewhere. Critics have applauded Meltzer's books for shedding new light on the racism and oppression faced by American blacks, Jews, Indians, Chinese, and Hispanics.

Meltzer's biographies, particularly his *Langston Hughes* (Hughes was his personal friend and collaborator) and his *Dorothea Lange: A Photographer's Life*, are considered of special value. Meltzer feels that biographies can show young adults how individual men and women have aspired to and accomplished great things in spite of countless obstacles. Widely read and acclaimed by many critics, Meltzer is considered a committed and challenging writer.

(See also *Contemporary Authors*, Vols. 13-16, rev. ed. and *Something about the Author*, Vol. 1.)

Photograph by Janet Fletcher; courtesy of Milton Meltzer

SOPHIA B. MEHRER

[In *Tongue of Flame: The Life of Lydia Maria Child,* Milton Meltzer] has provided teenagers with an outstanding biography of a little-known nineteenth-century woman writer, founder and editor of the first children's magazine, *Juvenile Miscellany,* and a fiery and tireless crusader for the abolition of slavery. In describing her activities as friend, co-worker, and advisor to many of the outstanding social reform figures of the time, Mr. Meltzer gives his readers a history of the period and the turbulent movements in which Maria Child took part. Read in the context of today's civil rights movement, this is a timely and exciting biography.

> Sophia B. Mehrer, in her review of "Tongue of Flame: The Life of Lydia Maria Child," in School Library Journal, an appendix to Library Journal (reprinted from the May, 1965 issue of School Library Journal, published by R. R. Bowker Co./A Xerox Corporation; copyright © 1965), Vol. 11, No. 9, May, 1965, p. 117.

JEAN FRITZ

Maria Child served so many causes and served them so zealously, a biographer less skillful than Milton Meltzer might easily depict her as one of those shrill women reformers who strode so militantly across the American scene in the middle of the 19th century. [In **"Tongue of Flame: The Life of Lydia Maria Child"**], Mr. Meltzer falls into no such trap. Mrs. Child

emerges as a gifted many-sided person who could commit herself totally and passionately to a movement without losing her independent view of it. And it is this view that, thanks to Mr. Meltzer, is so illuminating to the modern reader. Indeed, there could hardly be a better way to experience the cumulative effect of the slavery conflict, incident by incident.

"I sweep dead leaves out of paths and dust mirrors," Mrs. Child once said. Milton Meltzer has also dusted a mirror and he has done it well.

> Jean Fritz, in her review of "Tongue of Flame: The Life of Lydia Maria Child," in The New York Times Book Review (©1965 by The New York Times Company; reprinted by permission), July 18, 1965, p. 22.

PUBLISHERS WEEKLY

[*Time of Trial, Time of Hope: The Negro in America, 1919-1941*] begins with the return of Negro soldiers from World War I and ends with the threatened march on Washington in 1941 that culminated in the first Fair Employment Practices Commission fought for by A. Philip Randolph. It's the rare book of history that points out the problems of American Negroes in those years: problems of economic survival, court injustice, lynchings. Here are the bare facts, presented clearly and objectively without mincing of words.

> *A review of "Time of Trial, Time of Hope: The Negro in America, 1919-1941," in* Publishers Weekly *(reprinted from the August 22, 1966 issue of* Publishers Weekly, *published by R. R. Bowker Company; copyright © 1966 by R. R. Bowker Company), Vol. 190, No. 8, August 22, 1966, p. 106.*

ZENA SUTHERLAND

[*Time of Trial, Time of Hope: The Negro in America, 1919-1941, by Milton Meltzer and August Meier is a]* quite good description of the many problems and the few victories of the Negro people in the United States in the years between the first and second world wars. The authors write with authority and sympathy in a straightforward style. . . . The book considers political, economic, cultural, agricultural, educational, and other problems; the sections on the depression and on the organization of the CIO are particularly good. . . . (pp. 112-13)

> *Zena Sutherland, in her review of "Time of Trial, Time of Hope: The Negro in America, 1919-1941," in* Bulletin of the Center for Children's Books *(reprinted by permission of The University of Chicago Press; copyright 1967 by The University of Chicago), Vol. 20, No. 7, March, 1967, pp. 112-13.*

MARILYN GOLDSTEIN

[*Thaddeus Stevens and the Fight for Negro Rights* is a] timely, authoritative account of the career of a fanatical anti-slavery Congressman. . . . Stevens' intolerance and acid wit are presented sympathetically yet objectively. The documentary style is enlivened by quotations from leading political figures of the day. . . . A welcome book on a much neglected early "civil rights" crusader.

> *Marilyn Goldstein, in her review of "Thaddeus Stevens and the Fight for Negro Rights," in* School Library Journal, *an appendix to* Library Journal *(reprinted from the March, 1967 issue of* School Library Journal, *published by R. R. Bowker Co./A Xerox Corporation; copyright © 1967), Vol. 13, No. 7, March, 1967, p. 138.*

JOSEPH H. TAYLOR

[In *Thaddeus Stevens and the Fight for Negro Rights*] Milton Meltzer has given us a readable little account of Thaddeus Stevens' career. He has also weaved in much of the history of the period of Stevens' political activity. Although the author quotes extensively from the sources and from secondary works, the reader is not "plagued" by footnotes or references to notes at the back of the book. *Thaddeus Stevens and the Fight for Negro Rights* will probably fail to meet the test of rigid historical scholarship, but the average reader will be able to gain an appreciation of the life and works of one of the greatest precursors of "The Negro Revolution."

> *Joseph H. Taylor, in his review of "Thaddeus Stevens and the Fight for Negro Rights," in* The Negro History Bulletin *(reprinted by permission of The Association for the Study of Afro-American Life and History, Inc.), Vol. 30, No. 6, October, 1967, p. 23.*

ROBERT COLES

[A] lot has happened in this country in the last century, as Milton Meltzer has shown in *Bread—and Roses*. The title comes from a poem by James Oppenheim, who saw mill girls in Lawrence, Massachusetts, picketing for higher wages and better working conditions. Their signs said, "We want bread and roses." They wanted the money their labor deserved, and the sense of dignity, too. Mr. Meltzer's book shows how hard and long American workers have struggled to achieve the power some of their unions now have. He relies heavily on quotations from both rich men and poor men. He is unsparing in the political and economic details he brings forth—so that at least those youths who read his book will know some of the less pleasant facts of the American labor movement's early history.

> *Robert Coles, in his review of "Bread—and Roses: The Struggle of American Labor, 1865-1915," in* Book World—Chicago Tribune *(© 1968 Postrib Corp.; reprinted by permission of the* Chicago Tribune *and* The Washington Post*), January 21, 1968, p. 12.*

A. H. RASKIN

["**Bread—and Roses: The Struggle of American Labor, 1865-1915"**] is a one-dimensional story of battle by an infant labor movement against the forces of corporate greed in a period when all the institutions of government and polite society were on the side of the employer. The very fact that the book is episodic and often overdrawn adds to its usefulness in supplying a new generation of readers with some illumination on the atavistic hatreds and insecurities behind many of the seemingly irrational things unions do now that they enjoy large membership, huge treasuries and economic power sufficient to paralyze entire communities. . . .

Mr. Meltzer's pages, prickly with eyewitness accounts of unionism's birthpains in the sweatshops, the factories, the railroads and the mines, are a goad to revitalized activity in defense of industrial democracy and higher economic standards for those who remain on the outskirts of American affluence. . . .

Many will feel, with considerable validity, that Mr. Meltzer's book is oversimplified history—that none of the epic labor struggles he recounts could possibly have involved such a monopoly of guilt as emerges from page after page of workers' laments about the villainy of their employers. Still others may argue that, in any event, such an unrelieved picture of industrial oppression has scant relevance to this day when labor is often the aggressor and shows autocratic unconcern about the hardship its abuses of power inflict on the public.

But those who put forth such demurrers will find it hard to explain why other pillars of the community, through all the period of which Mr. Meltzer writes, were invariably certain that labor was ruining the country by its arbitrariness and its contempt for lawful process. No present executive of a giant corporation looks back with pride on what happened at Homestead or Ludlow; the fashion now is shamefaced dismissal of such episodes as skeletons to be buried with the vanished "robber baron" phase of capitalist expansionism. . . .

Mr. Meltzer's book will not tell young people all they need to know about labor. But it will give them a better understanding of the reasons for labor's undiminished belief that its unity is its only dependable source of strength, the rock on which rest both its material success and its capacity for survival.

A. H. Raskin, in his review of "Bread—and Roses: The Struggle of American Labor, 1865-1915," in The New York Times Book Review *(© 1968 by The New York Times Company; reprinted by permission), January 28, 1968, p. 26.*

ALMONT LINDSEY

[*Bread—and Roses: The Struggle of American Labor, 1865-1915*] provides a somewhat kaleidoscopic view of the plight of the worker and the more dramatic episodes that have characterized his struggle for a better life. . . . The most exciting chapters are devoted to such conflicts as the Railroad Strike of 1877, the Haymarket Affair, the Homestead Strike, the Pullman Strike, the Textile Strike at Lawrence and the Ludlow Massacre. Drawing on carefully selected eyewitness accounts and skillfully weaving them into the narrative, the author makes everything come alive with telling effect.

Meltzer is an impassioned writer and he gives the impression of being very angry over the callousness and greed of management and the glaring injustices that confronted the worker. The author, who approaches the subject almost exclusively from the viewpoint of the embattled worker, has chosen his material judiciously and has marshalled it effectively. For the most part he lets the facts speak for themselves and they do carry a powerful message.

The absence of specific source citations, the very limited bibliography and the brevity of treatment (almost too sketchy in places) are blemishes in an otherwise excellent book. The dictionary of labor terms is helpful . . . and the author does achieve his purpose in producing a highly readable and fast moving account of the American worker as he lived and fought in an era when the odds were seldom in his favor.

Almont Lindsey, in his review of "Bread—and Roses: The Struggle of American Labor, 1865-1915" (reprinted by permission of the author), in The Social Studies, *Vol. LIX, No. 6, November, 1968, p. 289.*

BRUCE L. MACDUFFIE

[*Langston Hughes: A Biography* is] acceptable only by default, as there is little material in libraries on this most important Black writer. . . . Accurate as far as it goes, this covers most of Hughes' work and includes bibliographies both of it and of studies on the author. But Hughes deserves better than the informal but plodding style which characterizes this pedestrian portrayal of him.

Bruce L. MacDuffie, in his review of "Langston Hughes: A Biography," in School Library Journal, *an appendix to* Library Journal *(reprinted from the January, 1969 issue of* School Library Journal, *published by R. R. Bowker Co./A Xerox Corporation; copyright © 1969), Vol. 15, No. 5, January, 1969, p. 85.*

HOYT W. FULLER

In *Langston Hughes,* the impressive new biography of the poet by Milton Meltzer, emphasis rightly is placed on the apparent simplicity of the man. The poet's countless friends and acquaintances knew him as an unassuming, unfailingly good-humored fellow, entirely without pretense, and his acts of kindness and generosity to aspiring young writers are legendary.

The enigma of Langston Hughes (for there remains one) is not raised for the speculation of the reader. From the always interesting events of the poet's life as recorded in this very readable book, one can move without nagging questions to the varied pleasures of the poet's works.

Hoyt W. Fuller, in his review of "Langston Hughes: A Biography," in Book World—The Washington Post *(© 1969 Postrib Corp.; reprinted by permission of* Chicago Tribune *and* The Washington Post*), February 2, 1969, p. 12.*

CAROLINE BIRD

Robert Goldston's "The Great Depression" summarizes the politics of [the] era from Hoover to Willkie in the terms Roosevelt liberals used to describe them at the time. Milton Meltzer's **"Brother, Can You Spare a Dime?"** . . . aspires to tell "what happened to auto workers and wheat farmers, to sales clerks and secretaries, to teachers and doctors, to miners and sharecroppers, to old folks and children, to white and black" between the Crash and the inauguration of Roosevelt. Both draw on the emerging photo-journalism of the day for illustration, but Meltzer relies heavily on eye-witness accounts of the time, while Goldston describes and interprets trends as if he were writing a newspaper feature story. . . .

[The] Meltzer book is much better reading, and why shouldn't it be? Not only does it quote liberally from such masters as John Dos Passos, Edmund Wilson, Louis Adamic, Erskine Caldwell, John Steinbeck, but from scores of reporters and witnesses whose conviction made them momentarily eloquent. The selection is expert and wide-ranging. The most suspicious teen-ager cannot but recognize that (whatever has happened to these people since) they were speaking from the heart. Explanations are brief, clear, and free of journalistic jargon.

Caroline Bird, in her review of "Brother, Can You Spare a Dime?" in The New York Times Book Review *(© 1969 by The New York Times Company; reprinted by permission), March 23, 1969, p. 26.*

PAUL M. ANGLE

[In **"Brother, Can You Spare a Dime?: The Great Depression 1929-1933"**], Mr. Meltzer is concerned primarily with the crash of 1929 and its effect, in the next four years, on the people most directly concerned: farmers, workingmen, miners, Negroes and small merchants. . . . The book has a directness and an immediacy beyond [Mr. Robert Goldston's "The Great Depression: The United States in the Thirties"], although one man writes as well as the other. And that is very well indeed. . . .

Both are supposed to have been written for young people, but neither is beneath the notice of adults.

Paul M. Angle, "The Crash, and After," in Book World—Chicago Tribune *(© 1969 Postrib Corp.; reprinted by permission of* Chicago Tribune *and* The Washington Post*), May 4, 1969, p. 22.**

KIRKUS REVIEWS

The one solid, unassailable accomplishment of [*Freedom Comes to Mississippi: The Story of Reconstruction*] is to set forth the achievements of the black-supported Republican state government and black office holders on the state and local levels between 1870 and 1873; as a history of Reconstruction, however, it is emotional and partisan, fuller of blame than of sober, discriminating assessment. Omitted from the impressionistic tableau are the very limitations to the Emancipation Proclamation that the Thirteenth Amendment rectified and the absolute necessity for Congress to give the blacks votes to gain ratification of the Fourteenth Amendment; much that was specifically motivated becomes a matter of amorphous pressures. Neither do even the most sympathetic studies of the period substantiate the claims made for black militance . . . or slave transformation. . . . That socially and economically life changed very little for the majority is thereby obscured. Obscured also, in a quote, is the revolutionary nature of the expansion of government services beyond their prewar level. On the one hand more is made of Reconstruction than the facts justify; on the other hand, less. And the concentration on oppression, injustice and terror, inarguable per se, overshadows what explanations are offered for both the inception and termination of Reconstruction.

A review of "Freedom Comes to Mississippi: The Story of Reconstruction," in Kirkus Reviews *(copyright © 1970 The Kirkus Service, Inc.), Vol. XXXVIII, No. 19, October 1, 1970, p. 1114.*

FRANCIS D. LAZENBY

A great deal has been written about slavery in the ancient world, but, unfortunately, some of the information is hidden away in scholarly books and journals often inaccessible. The merit of this short, but authoritative work [*Slavery: From the Rise of Western Civilization to the Renaissance*] is that it makes available to the general reader many of the findings of scholars intent on their own special interests. Meltzer, widely known for numerous works on black history and social reform, writes directly and without sentimentality, making visible the entire pattern of slavery in human history, and in a manner which never fails to point up man's inhumanity to man. What emerges with especially graphic force is the life, the hopes and fears, of the slaves themselves.

Francis D. Lazenby, in his review of "Slavery: From the Rise of Western Civilization to the Renaissance," in Library Journal *(reprinted from* Library Journal, *May 15, 1971; published by R. R. Bowker Co. (a Xerox company); copyright © 1971 by Xerox Corporation), Vol. 96, No. 10, May 15, 1971, p. 1709.*

JANET G. POLACHECK

[In *Slavery: From the Rise of Western Civilization to the Renaissance,* the] economic and political basis of slavery is developed and forms an excellent introduction for those readers concerned with the more recent racial basis of the "peculiar" institution. . . . Mr. Meltzer has contributed a basic work in an area where almost no material exists on the junior-senior high school level, making this an essential item.

Janet G. Polacheck, in her review of "Slavery: From the Rise of Western Civilization to the Renaissance," in Library Journal *(reprinted from* Library Journal, *July, 1971; published by R. R. Bowker Co. (a Xerox company); copyright © 1971 by Xerox Corporation), Vol. 96, No. 13, July, 1971, p. 2370.*

JOHN K. BETTERSWORTH

Milton Meltzer, one of our best writers in the field of black history, handles the Reconstruction story in ["**Freedom Comes to Mississippi**"] with the spit and polish of a man with a message and the craftsmanship to get it told with dramatic impact. Instead of relating the story in the entire South, he concentrates upon what happened "when freedom came to Mississippi." From that, we may draw our conclusions about what happened to the South as a whole. The reader is introduced to a minimum number of people and events—but the point emerges, loud and clear: A century ago, freedom came to the black man, who experienced it for a few years—until the political bargain of 1877 between Republicans and Democrats left the whole business to be done over again a century later as the Second Reconstruction.

John K. Bettersworth, "After the War Was Over," in The New York Times Book Review *(© 1971 by The New York Times Company; reprinted by permission), July 25, 1971, p. 8.*

KIRKUS REVIEWS

[The second volume of Meltzer's study of slavery, *Slavery II: From the Renaissance to Today,*] encompasses slavery as it existed, and in some cases still exists, in Africa, Arabia, China and under the Nazis, and also [gives] a remarkably detailed picture of the everyday existence of slaves in the Americas. As always, Meltzer is a careful historian who looks for the documentable truth behind prevalent generalizations—he gives the lineage of his statistics, citing Curtin's revised estimates of the volume of the Atlantic slave trade and, on such controversial topics as the extent of resistance among American slaves, he presents the opposing views of prominent historians. (Meltzer himself concludes that there is a good deal of evidence of widespread rebellion, both passive and active, but shows that there is room to doubt the scope of some of the more famous conspiracies, such as the Vesey uprising.) The attention given to cultural and economic differentials—the higher frequency of manumission in Cuba and South America, the practice of hiring out and, in some cases, of "breeding" slaves, the difficulty of eradicating the institution in countries where starvation may be the only alternative—and the generous use of quotations from primary sources make the narrative both more interesting and more illuminating than the ambitious scope might indicate. First rate.

A review of "Slavery II: From the Renaissance to Today," in Kirkus Reviews *(copyright © 1972 The Kirkus Service, Inc.), Vol. 40, No. 12, June 15, 1972, p. 681.*

KIRKUS REVIEWS

[*The Right to Remain Silent* is a] passionate, far ranging defense of the Fifth Amendment protection of the right to remain silent which goes back to the origins of its systematic violation during the inquisition . . . and its gradual establishment as a principle of English common law through the struggles of political prisoners such as leveler John Lilbourne. Meltzer extends his examination of the right on through the nonpolitical applications of the Miranda and Esposito decisions, defending it as logical and necessary . . . against the desire of the police to obtain a confession. Many will be surprised to learn that the much lauded Thomas More was a proponent of the inquisition, and Meltzer's defense of the rights of accused criminals strikes a note of welcome sanity. . . . Meltzer presents the historical evidence and often relies on his readers to draw the correct conclusions from excerpted testimony; still he covers a lot of ground and those who are able to keep up with him should be well rewarded.

> *A review of "The Right to Remain Silent," in* Kirkus Reviews *(copyright © 1972 The Kirkus Service, Inc.), Vol. XL, No. 16, August 15, 1972, p. 954.*

BERYL ROBINSON

"'I have been hunted like a wolf and now I am being sent away like a dog,'" uttered [Henry Wager] Halleck, one of the last leaders of the Seminole resistance, after he had been captured. The destruction of his small band was among the final decisive acts of the U.S. Government in its struggle to conquer the Seminole people during a war that lasted from 1835 to 1842, "America's longest, bloodiest and most costly Indian war." [In Milton Meltzer's **Hunted Like a Wolf,** the] period of exploitation and conquest that was preface to Halleck's capture forms the bulk of the sober account beginning with the arrival of Columbus. . . . The story of the Seminoles' eventual subjugation is a sorry one, akin to similar stories from all parts of the country. Well-documented, it reveals how they were destroyed by greed, trickery, and the superior strength of a powerful government which completely disregarded their status as human beings. . . . [This book is a] substantial addition to the author's excellent examinations of social history in the United States. (pp. 606-07)

> *Beryl Robinson, in a review of "Hunted Like a Wolf: The Story of the Seminole War," in* The Horn Book Magazine *(copyright © 1972 by The Horn Book, Inc., Boston), Vol. XLVIII, No. 6, December, 1972, pp. 606-07.*

ALICE MILLER BREGMAN

[**Slavery II: from the Renaissance to Today,** a] sequel to Meltzer's commendable **Slavery: from the Rise of Western Civilization to the Renaissance** . . . completes his comprehensive study of the institution of slavery throughout the world and its history. Volume I covered the practice from primitive times to the Renaissance; volume II covers the remaining portion of recorded history to the present. Meltzer's purpose "is to help the general reader to see the whole pattern of slavery in human history and how it has shaped the lives we are leading." He has admirably succeeded in reaching his goal. . . . [Meltzer's] conclusion that slavery is essential to the world's economy holds forth little hope for its abolition, though almost every country in the world has laws preventing it. This is well documented. . . . An excellent overview of a distressing pattern in world culture which cannot be ignored.

> *Alice Miller Bregman, in her review of "Slavery II: From the Renaissance to Today," in* School Library Journal, *an appendix to* Library Journal *(reprinted from the December, 1972 issue of* School Library Journal, *published by R. R. Bowker Co./A Xerox Corporation; copyright © 1972), Vol. 19, No. 4, December, 1972, p. 68.*

PUBLISHERS WEEKLY

The reader of this excellent and searching book [**The Right to Remain Silent**] will have a thorough understanding of the constitutional right that insures due process of law in trying the accused. Discussing actual cases of people persecuted because they claimed their privilege under the Fifth Amendment, the author shows how dangerous it is to take this stand as an admission of guilt. He reaches far back into ancient times as well to show how necessary it is to respect the right of the accused to remain silent.

> *A review of "The Right to Remain Silent," in* Publishers Weekly *(reprinted from the January 15, 1973 issue of* Publishers Weekly, *published by R. R. Bowker Company, a Xerox company; copyright © 1973 by Xerox Corporation), Vol. 203, No. 3, January 15, 1973, p. 65.*

BARBARA RITCHIE

Adolescents and young adult readers of **"Underground Man"** may perceive that they have already experienced young Josh Bowen's America of the 1830's, through participating (if only via TV newscasts) in the social and civic disorders of the 1960's. In writing an absorbing story of a young Yank's adventures as a "nigger stealer" for the Underground Railroad, Milton Meltzer has written a contemporary novel. The cultural, political, moral and ethical issues that troubled young Joshua Bowen are those troubling today's youth. We hear them say so.

The familiar generation gap is dramatized in the opening chapters. It is not the expected brouhaha between a rebellious kid and his mean old man. Nowhere in the novel does Meltzer deal in stereotypes or resort to cliché situations. . . .

After serving a term in a Kentucky jail for "nigger stealing" Josh returns to New England and becomes an effective and popular speaker at Abolitionist rallies—but, once again, he finds that what he is doing does not fit what he is. He goes back to his "criminal" activity along the Ohio.

For a second time, Josh lands in a Kentucky jail; the jailer tells him that this time "it will take a whole army of nigger stealers to get you outa here." At first glance, this seems a most dismaying finale. But to turn the page and read the short Afterword is to learn the historic necessity for the "unhappy" ending. The author based his novel on the fragmentary, forgotten memoirs of a young man of another name, who was indeed set free—after 17 long years—by "nigger stealers" wearing the uniform of the Union Army.

Meltzer, historian of the Civil War era, moves through those times, and among those people, with authority and ease. There is satisfaction in **"Underground Man"** for those who read for "story" and an extra measure for the thoughtful who read between the lines. A fine novel.

> *Barbara Ritchie, in her review of "Underground Man," in* The New York Times Book Review *(© 1973 by The New York Times Company; reprinted by permission), March 18, 1973, p. 12.*

ROSALIND K. GODDARD

Slavery and the abolitionist movement provide the background for this stiff historical novel [**Underground Man**]. . . . Meltzer's nonfiction accounts of black history are much richer and tighter in their illumination of time and place. There is an absence of depth and intensity here due to his failure to develop the black characters fully as people instead of as types.

Rosalind K. Goddard, in her review of "Underground Man," in School Library Journal, *an appendix to* Library Journal *(reprinted from the April, 1973 issue of* School Library Journal, *published by R. R. Bowker Co./A Xerox Corporation; copyright © 1973), Vol. 19, No. 8, April, 1973, p. 77.*

JANET P. SARRATT

[In *Hunted Like a Wolf: The Story of the Seminole War*], Meltzer reveals how the Americans took advantage of the Seminoles' innocence and drove them from their homeland with greed, doubletalk, and treachery. The facts are presented in a clear, straightforward manner, showing each aspect of the war from the causes to the lasting effects. This well-written account will appeal to an older audience than would read [Henrietta] Buckmaster's *Seminole Wars*.

Janet P. Sarratt, in her review of "Hunted Like a Wolf: The Story of the Seminole War," in Library Journal *(reprinted from* Library Journal, *June 15, 1973; published by R. R. Bowker Co. (a Xerox company); copyright © 1973 by Xerox Corporation), Vol. 98, No. 12, June 15, 1973, p. 2012.*

ZENA SUTHERLAND

Although fictionalized, the life story of Joshua Bowen . . . [in *Underground Man*] is based on fact: the sources cited in the author's postscript are evidence that Milton Meltzer has done the thorough research that distinguishes his nonfiction titles. . . . Spare in construction, the book has historical interest, dramatic appeal, and an aura of suspense and danger that emanates from the events rather than by the declaration of the author.

Zena Sutherland, in her review of "Underground Man," in Bulletin of the Center for Children's Books *(reprinted by permission of The University of Chicago Press; © 1973 by The University of Chicago), Vol. 27, No. 1, September, 1973, p. 14.*

KIRKUS REVIEWS

[*Bound for the Rio Grande: The Mexican Struggle, 1845-1850*] is not another history from the Mexican or Mexican-American viewpoint, but a study of how the war with Mexico grew out of the spirit of Manifest Destiny and the conflict between anti- and pro-slavery forces. . . . Meltzer devotes some attention to the very fluid political situation in Mexico and to Santa Anna's overconfident strategy, but the primary sources principally reveal the American soldier's disillusionment with the violence, cruelty and bungling of this "most abominable war." In one especially interesting chapter, Meltzer reports on widespread desertion from the American army and on the formation of the San Patricio Battalion, composed of former soldiers (many of them Irish Catholic immigrants) who fought for the Mexican cause in a number of important battles. . . . And Meltzer draws together a number of critical issues—including slavery, expansionism and the Presidential conduct of foreign policy—which converge to make the Mexican War such an important period in the American past.

A review of "Bound for the Rio Grande: The Mexican Struggle, 1845-1850," in Kirkus Reviews *(copyright © 1974 The Kirkus Service, Inc.), Vol. XLII, No. 9, May 1, 1974, p. 493.*

SANFORD SCHWARTZ

Reading ["**The Eye of Conscience: Photographers and Social Change**" by Milton Meltzer and Bernard Cole] is a little like those times in school when you went in for a session with the guidance counselor: the man meant well, but the points he made, even about important things, were so predictable, and the terms he used were so solemn, and he repeated himself so much, that you were never sure, by the end, whether you were more bored or more annoyed with him. Like the guidance counselor's, the language in "**The Eye of Conscience**" isn't the kind that's geared for having fresh perceptions, or even for presenting old perceptions in a lively way. It's a shame everything is so smothered, because the book presents good subjects for its audience: how photography helps affect social change, or mirrors social problems, and how the camera, when used daily and continually, is an instrument that tells us about our instincts and feelings.

The main focus in the book is on 10 photographers and their involvement with social problems. . . . The main trouble with the biographies is that the authors don't relate the individual photographer's character and motives to his pictures; the pictures just dangle alongside, like evidence. Social commitment is hammered in as the only thing to keep in mind. That commitment is important but, taken by itself, it's not why some people make memorable photographs. . . .

[Meltzer] and Cole's assumption is that, if a career is noble and committed, the photographs automatically will be moving and important. They should have proved this—which isn't always the case here. . . .

[The] book's implied meaning, that socially oriented photography is the kind that will most stimulate the young, is also questionable. Distinctive social photography takes more than sympathy. . . . Anyway, the best art made by children, whether in photography or painting, rarely shows sympathetic awareness of people and their problems; children's art is private, it's derived more from spontaneous, instinctive reactions, usually to family and friends, and it's often close to fantasy. Meltzer and Cole, because they never clearly differentiate their Social Photography theme from their Be-a-Photographer theme, and because of the way they describe their subjects' lives, make it seem as if they want art to be the product of altruism. That's wishful thinking.

Sanford Schwartz, in his review of "The Eye of Conscience," in The New York Times Book Review *(© 1974 by The New York Times Company; reprinted by permission), August 25, 1974, p. 8.*

PUBLISHERS WEEKLY

In the foreword to this special trip into a particular past [*World of Our Fathers: The Jews of Eastern Europe*], Milton Meltzer articulates what must be an almost universal experience: He tells us that, as a child and as a youth, he expressed no interest in where his immigrant parents had come from or what their life was like. Later, he began to search for his own roots as he became involved in writing history. What he has to tell young readers should fascinate them, no matter what their color or religion, because modern teenagers don't merely accept the present and take the past for granted. The rich and the poor Jews of 19th century Europe come to sturdy life in these pages; the author's research is thorough and his style is compelling. . . .

A review of "World of Our Fathers: The Jews of Eastern Europe," in Publishers Weekly (reprinted from the January 13, 1975 issue of Publishers Weekly, published by R. R. Bowker Company, a Xerox company; copyright © 1975 by Xerox Corporation), Vol. 207, No. 2, January 13, 1975, p. 60.

PAUL HEINS

In his frankly autobiographical Foreword [to **World of Our Fathers: The Jews of Eastern Europe**], the author has poignantly stated what impelled him to write this book: "I had too little knowledge of my past." In part a history of the Jews during the Christian era, the account is chiefly concerned with the life and fate of Eastern European Jews before and after the partition of Poland and especially under the restrictive and repressive rule of the Russian Czarist government. Pointing out the Eastern European Jewish social distinction between those who worked with their hands and those who didn't—between the scholars and businessmen and the mass of artisans, unskilled laborers, and factory workers—the author conveys a sense of daily life as well as of the fundamental cultural conflicts among the Eastern European Jews during the 18th, 19th, and 20th centuries. Conventional Orthodoxy and Hasidism; the Enlightenment, socialism, and Zionism; the creation of two bodies of literature (one in Hebrew and one in Yiddish)—all are explored and clarified. Many quotations from first-hand accounts give existential reality to the historical and cultural topics of the book.

Paul Heins, in his review of "World of Our Fathers: The Jews of Eastern Europe," in The Horn Book Magazine (copyright © 1975 by the Horn Book, Inc., Boston), Vol. LI, No. 1, February, 1975, p. 60.

ANITA SILVEY

[Milton Meltzer's] previous works of nonfiction have already established him as one of the finest American historians for young readers. [**Bound for the Rio Grande: The Mexican Struggle**] demonstrates once again his skill at combining readable and enjoyable prose with an excellent choice and handling of original historical material. . . . The numerous illustrations, the interspersed songs and poetry, the colorfulness of the first-hand historical accounts—all add to a superb analysis of the "most disgraceful war."

Anita Silvey, in her review of "Bound for the Rio Grande: The Mexican Struggle 1845-1850," in The Horn Book Magazine (copyright © 1975 by the Horn Book, Inc., Boston), Vol. LI, No. 2, April, 1975, p. 160.

SAUL MALOFF

Milton Meltzer's [**"Never to Forget: The Jews of the Holocaust"**] is an act of desperation—an act of piety and pity, wrath and love, despair and homage; but the motive force, the terrible sense of urgency which drives and animates it, is desperation. In an afterword, he notes that an authoritative study of American high school history textbooks, conducted nearly 30 years after World War II, revealed that "their treatment of Nazism was brief, bland, superficial, and misleading," that "racism, anti-Semitism, and the Holocaust were ignored or dismissed in a few lines," and that textbooks designed for colleges and universities were "not substantially better."

"Darkness," said the historian Golo Mann, "hides the vilest crime ever perpetrated by man against man." . . .

Into this infinite void Meltzer sends his book levelling it without distinction—for none should or need be made—at teen-agers and young adults who came along after the fact, and at their elders who may have repressed or chosen to forget it. Within its small compass, he undertakes a task of intimidating scale: to convey some compelling sense of the experience of European Jewry in the Hitler years, culminating, of course, in the unprecedented slaughter of six million Jews. Not much more than a sketch is possible in a small book, yet what a full and resonant sketch it is. ("Definitive" studies, of course, abound, and are listed in a bibliography. Meltzer's intention is far more modest though it is uncompromising: he strives for a hard clarity of style and presentation that will span the divide between generations, and an unwavering concentration on essences unobstructed by the cumbersome and discouraging apparatus of scholarship.)

The progression is inexorable, unrelenting, beginning with the millennia-long historical background of anti-Semitism throughout Christendom and particularly in the Czar's Pale of Settlement in Eastern Europe and in pre-Hitler Germany. . . .

Six million massacred—men, women, children, babies straight from the womb. The imagination cannot encompass or fathom the horror; nor can the intelligence assimilate the magnitude and human meaning of those inert statistics. So Meltzer, with an intuitive eye for the illuminating image, event, moment, quickens and deepens his chronicle of catastrophe by brief, telling, heartbreaking and sometimes exhilarating passages from the records of survivors and of the dead; makes human what would otherwise be remote, stupendous, overpowering. (p. 25)

Nothing is evaded or scanted in this extraordinarily fine and moving book: not the vexed question of "why" the Jews "allowed" themselves to be destroyed . . . , nor the abysmal existence of the sometimes brutal Jewish ghetto police and concentration camp trustees, nor the tormenting issue of the complicit role of some members of some of the Jewish Councils. Meltzer does not equivocate and he does not relent; he does not patronize or condescend or indulge—he respects his readers, whatever their age, and is therefore free to make moral and intellectual demands of them; he tells harsh truths harshly, and noble ones (the Warsaw Ghetto Uprising, the camp revolts, the magnificent Jewish partisans and resistance forces) proudly. He is never sentimental, bombastic, falsely romantic or heroic. His deeply felt and trenchantly written book is an act of mourning and a call to remember. For our own souls' sake it is indispensable. (p. 42)

Saul Maloff, in his review of "Never to Forget: The Jews of the Holocaust," in The New York Times Book Review (© 1976 by The New York Times Company; reprinted by permission), May 2, 1976, pp. 25, 42.

ANITA SILVEY

The Holocaust is a difficult subject to present to children; for although the tendency to protect young readers from harsh reality has been somewhat abandoned in the last decade, an author could scarcely enjoy describing barbarity and cruelty to young people. Yet the understandable impulse to soften the impact and horror of such events would be intolerable in discussing the Third Reich's extermination of the Jews. Facing this difficult problem, the author [of **Never to Forget: The Jews** *of the Holocaust*] has managed to present a powerful and over-whelming picture of the Final Solution. By carefully choosing eyewitness accounts, by excellent use of sources such as Raul Hilberg's *The Destruction of the European Jews . . .* , he has managed to convey the tragic slaughter of the Jewish people— in pogroms, in ghettoes, in work camps, and finally in death camps. Given the complexity of the subject, it is not surprising that the book's presentation is flawed. There are statements one would have to question, such as "Germany is the country where modern anti-Semitism of the racist kind began"; the tone sometimes gets a bit overemotional; and a subtle but consistent anti-German prejudice pervades the writing. But few writers of history for children could record such an unflinching and impassioned account of the grimmest chapter in human history.

> *Anita Silvey, in her review of "Never to Forget: The Jews of the Holocaust," in* The Horn Book Magazine *(copyright ©1976 by the Horn Book, Inc., Boston), Vol. LII, No. 3, June, 1976, p. 298.*

LYLA HOFFMAN

The mass murder of six million Jews by the Nazis during World War II is the subject of this compelling history ["**Never to Forget: The Jews of the Holocaust**"]. Interweaving background information, chilling statistics, individual accounts and newspaper reports, it provides an excellent introduction to its subject for American young people, whose lack of knowledge about the war and/or about anti-Semitism continually amazes people like the reviewer who lived through those times.

Scapegoating a minority group to gain and consolidate political power was not a device originated by Adolf Hitler, but it was used by him with outstanding success. Meltzer documents just how and why this happened, and how Hitler retained mass support even though "wages sank while profits rose." The one deficiency of this background information is that readers are given the impression that Hitler controlled everything in Germany, including big business. It is much more likely that Hitler was encouraged by big business because, in addition to killing Jews, he also suppressed all labor union activity and all political opposition. (p. 16)

In relating information about the infamous German leaders and presenting first-person tales by anonymous victims, Meltzer exposes the myth of Jewish non-resistance. He says this myth developed because "historians based themselves largely on the captured Nazi documents, which gave only a one-sided version of what happened". . . . Using recently discovered documents and the accounts of concentration camp survivors, Meltzer gives a stirring and important description of active and passive resistance that was marked by courage, confusion over tactics and passionate struggle for survival.

In his "**Never to Forget**" wrap-up chapter, the author makes it clear that the Holocaust must never be regarded merely as an aberration. . . . He not only shows that "it can happen here" but that it *has* happened everywhere both before and after Hitler. He cites the many places where genocide has been practiced and explains that such horrors are always possible when people believe in the superiority of one group over another. He also makes it clear that all humanity was responsible—individuals, churches, governments, along with the Germans who actually committed the murders—by not acting to prevent the Holocaust.

Readers will gain a greater understanding of history, of racism and of individual responsiblity from this excellent book—and hopefully, neutrality will be impossible. (pp. 16-17)

> *Lyla Hoffman, in her review of "Never to Forget: The Jews of the Holocaust," in* Interracial Books for Children Bulletin *(reprinted by permission of* Interracial Books for Children Bulletin, *1841 Broadway, New York, N.Y. 10023), Vol. 7, No. 6, 1976, pp. 16-17.*

NANCY AGHAZARIAN

Statistics alone cannot convey the extent of death and human misery suffered by the Jews of the holocaust. . . . [In *Never to Forget: The Jews of the Holocaust*] Milton Meltzer tries to give meaning to these statistics by relating the fates of many individuals and having others tell their own stories through memoirs, poems, letters and songs. While no book can convey the Jewish suffering in its true dimensions, *Never to Forget* makes an excellent attempt. Written on a subject about which everyone should be knowledgeable, the book compels the reader to turn the pages until its conclusion. Meltzer includes short histories of anti-semitism and Hitler's rise to power. The bulk of the text, however, is devoted to the systematic rounding up of the Jews into ghettos, their deportation to the concentration camps and finally Jewish efforts at resistance. While the author acknowledges that some sympathetic Gentiles did exist, he plays this point down (much to the detriment of the book) and prefers to let it appear that the Jews were universally disliked and left completely alone. In no way does this book exaggerate the horrors of the holocaust. In fact, it practically ignores the 'medical experimentation' done on human subjects in the concentration camps. Still, *Never to Forget* will make the reader very uncomfortable and could conceivably cause nightmares. Recommended for older young adults only.

> *Nancy Aghazarian, in her review of "Never to Forget: The Jews of the Holocaust," in* Young Adult Cooperative Book Review Group of Massachusetts, *Vol. 13, No. 1, October, 1976, p. 22.*

GILBERT MILLSTEIN

I think of "**Violins and Shovels**" as a *salutary* book. It is intended for young readers—but I think it could be read profitably by older ones who have neither the time nor the inclination to plow through the records [of the W.P.A. Arts Projects] in great detail. All will learn that, for a time, anyway, no government in history ever did what the Roosevelt Administration did: Make it possible for artists to live—neither well nor ill but in reasonable comfort, so that they might tend their arts and bring them to flower.

Readers will learn once more of the fundamental hostility toward the arts of legislatures and businesses. . . . And they will learn exactly how little is required for an artist to survive and work.

It is Meltzer's belief—I share it with him—that what Federal One did was to insure the survival of an entire generation of talented people. . . .

> *Gilbert Millstein, in his review of "Violins and Shovels: The WPA Arts Projects," in* The New York Times Book Review *(© 1976 by The New York Times Company; reprinted by permission), November 14, 1976, p. 42.*

ELIZABETH McCORKLE

[*Violin and Shovels: The WPA Art Projects, a New Deal for America's Hungry Artists of the 1930's* is a] first-rate piece of reporting on the outlet the New Deal Works Progress Administration (WPA) provided for writers, musicians, actors, directors, and artists of the Depression period. The text is dotted with vivid thumbnail sketches of famous figures from the art/theatre/music world (e.g., Nikolai Sokoloff, Henry Alsberg, Hallie Flanagan, Jackson Pollock, Olive Stanton) and with brief accounts of fascinating incidents from this little-known phase of our artistic history. Written in the same flowing style and with the same accuracy that characterizes Meltzer's histories, this is the only indepth treatment of the subject available for [a young adult] audience. The fact that Meltzer worked in the New York WPA project and relates his personal experiences is an added bonus. (pp. 61-2)

> *Elizabeth McCorkle, in her review of "Violins & Shovels: The WPA Arts Projects, a New Deal for America's Hungry Artists of the 1930's," in* School Library Journal *(reprinted from the December, 1976 issue of* School Library Journal, *published by R. R. Bowker Co./A Xerox Corporation; copyright © 1976), Vol. 23, No. 4, December, 1976, pp. 61-2.*

DAVID E. SCHERMAN

It is one of the glories of Milton Meltzer's superb life of Lange ["**Dorothea Lange: A Photographer's Life**"], perhaps an unintended one (but more about unconscious art in a minute), that his innate reporting skill and honesty forbade him to gloss over the complexities and conflicts despite which his subject managed to become a legendary figure in recent American social history and even, to many critics and somewhat fewer photographers, a great photographer. There are other fortuitous reasons why it is a good book. Mr. Meltzer is a historian himself, with a special expertise on the Depression ("**Brother, Can You Spare a Dime**"), which produced a Dorothea Lange, and Government subsidy to the arts ("**Violins and Shovels**"), which enabled Lange to work effectively. . . .

Lange was a great unconscious artist. . . . She had a clear understanding, and Mr. Meltzer reminds us of this simple fact, that subject matter, not technique, not equipment, not even a sense of timing, is what distinguishes a professional from an amateur. . . .

Lange's subject of consequence was to document the breakdown of the American ideal exemplified by the Homestead Act of 1862—that our land shall be farmed by working owners. . . . She made a memorable picture of a dislocated [Depression Era] American ("White Angel Bread Line"), the first of thousands she was to see, and discovered that she could no longer *arrange* her subjects—she had to learn how to *select* them, the crucial difference in the making of a photographer.

Both Lange and her biographer are quick to point out that she did not invent documentary photography—what she has come to epitomize and what this book is all about. Lewis Hine, Jacob Riis, even Mathew Brady, to name a few, had preceded her. . . .

The most touching passages describe how in her old age she marshaled about her the children and grandchildren whom she felt she had neglected in her single-minded urge to record the misconditions of history. . . . Her dramatic final race, with death, to put together a lifetime retrospective for the Museum of Modern Art, is a surprising cliffhanger. But that episode is really characteristic of any committed photographer.

Milton Meltzer's handsome book is worth reading not just because it meticulously chronicles the life of one rather mad genius, but because it gives insight into a whole mad profession.

> *David E. Scherman, "Pictures of Things As They Are," in* The New York Times Book Review (© *1978 by The New York Times Company; reprinted by permission), August 6, 1978, p. 9.*

GEORGE P. ELLIOTT

[Though] Dorothea Lange's genius for seeing with a camera is what makes her important in the world and also intensifies the reader's interest in her, it is not that genius in itself which makes her a good subject for a biography. For that purpose, it matters much more that she talks well about herself and her work. Unlike many artists, she does not cover her traces as a creator. Reading [Milton Meltzer's *Dorothea Lange: A Photographer's Life*], one does not just contemplate the end result of her striving to make images that, to her mind, are beautiful only if they are true; one can follow her as she strives, because in the book she talks intelligently about this process, in letters and notebooks, through the memories of friends and disciples, from tape in an extensive oral history interview made when she was sixty-five, five years before her death. (pp. 109-10)

Meltzer has done his legwork, following leads no one else followed; he has not distorted story or character in any significant way that I am aware of; he has an overview which orders the facts coherently; nevertheless, the story he tells, while good, is not quite right. There are, I believe, two reasons for this: haste and psychologizing.

Haste is evident in many small errors which polishing and double-checking would have eliminated. . . . Many more ill-identified or even unidentified names of people appear than narrative clarity and ease of understanding permit. The prose sometimes descends from standard English to the irrelevantly colloquial, for instance in the frequent use of incomplete sentences. There are some needless repetitions. There are minor errors of fact. . . . [The] inaccuracy about how the family learned of Dorothea's original name does not matter very much, and one by one the other inaccuracies in the book matter even less. But, accumulated, these and the other evidences of haste do matter, enough to prevent the book, thorough and interesting though it is, from being as good as it could have been.

The other unfortunate element in the book is its chronic psychologizing. A typical example . . . : "It seems to have been a name she wanted desperately to forget." Such a sentence is not just superfluous, it interferes; in any kind of narrative, to spell out the obvious in motivation is to do some of the reader's imaginative activity for him, and so deprive him of just that much of his vital enjoyment. In occasional small doses, over-explanation does little harm; but as a steady thing it not only vitiates the experience of reading a story, it tells you what to think, limiting and stultifying that play of speculation which is one of the high goods of narrative. . . . Indeed, in those shaded, ambiguous areas of the self to which story is drawn by its very nature, especially when the protagonist is as subtle as Dorothea Lange, interpreting an anecdote limits its imaginative truth.

But, though psychologizing makes the book gummy, especially toward the end, it does not prevent the essential story. And happily, Meltzer, who clearly is not knowledgeable about photography, does not intrude in respect of her work but by and large lets her and her colleagues and students speak about it in nonpsychological language. The core of this crucial theme, her photography, is to be found in the opening paragraphs of chapter 18. For example, one student in the first seminar she taught recalls:

> She paused often, aware of what a pause can mean. Every statement seemed a commitment. "The good photograph," she kept repeating, "is not the object. The consequences of that photograph are the object. And I'm not speaking of social consequences. I mean the kind of thing where people will not say to you, how did you do it, or where did you get this, but *that such things could be!*"

This is the sort of thing biography cannot have too much of.

Psychology is far better equipped, in theory, vocabulary, and popular acceptance, to talk about family relationships than about artistic creation. In this biography, Meltzer lets the materials for understanding the photographer as documenter and as artist speak for themselves, leaving the mystery intact; but, though the materials for presenting the wife and mother are also abundant and also capable of speaking for themselves, he psychologizes them, obfuscating their mystery. However, he does not overexplain or overmoralize the connection between the elements at war in her personality, so that the structure of the story emerges clearly—an imperfect and excessive narrative, yes, but also potent and coherent. Her flawed grandeur is not lost. (pp. 114-16)

> *George P. Elliott, "A Genius for Seeing" (copyright ©1978 by George P. Elliott; reprinted by permission of Mary J. Elliott), in* The American Scholar, *Vol. 48, No. 1, Winter, 1978-79, pp. 109-10, 112, 115-16, 118.*

ROBERT DAVID TUROFF

It is not clear why Milton Meltzer wrote [*Dorothea Lange: A Photographer's Life*]. She was a fine photographer, but that is not reason enough for a biography; she suffered misfortune—polio and a long and painful illness before death—but that, without illuminating insight into its meaning, is also not reason enough for a biography; and neither in a preface nor in the body of the text is sufficient reason for the work shown, either explicitly or implicitly.

This is a straight narrative that begins by detailing Lange's family background—nothing unusual there; her childhood—polio, the departure of her father—fully linked to her photographic work later on; and then a chronological narrative of her life—hardly gripping. Most biographies, in fact, are written as straight narratives, often successfully—a recent, superb example is Ronald Clark's biography of [Albert] Einstein. But Meltzer's work falls far short of this standard.

Meltzer accompanies his narrative with photographs. Most of them are by Lange; some, by others, are of her and her associates. Although enough of her photographs are included that one might regard them as an overview of her work, the collection has formidable omissions. As her health deteriorated, in the late fifties and early sixties, Lange traveled to Asia and the Middle East. Photographs made on these journeys appeared in the posthumous exhibition of her work at the Museum of Modern Art and in the exhibition catalog. Not one of these, among her most notable achievements, appears in the biography. Indeed, Meltzer's treatment of these journeys is tedious. In narrating one event after the other, he appears interested only in putting down every fact on his index cards. The style is strongly reminiscent of Babar the Elephant.

Meltzer does illuminate some aspects of Lange's personality, most of them negative but treated sympathetically. One might not find this information in other sources; otherwise there is little of importance in the book not published elsewhere.

> *Robert David Turoff, in his review of "Dorothea Lange: A Photographer's Life," in* The Antioch Review *(copyright ©1979 by the Antioch Review Inc.; reprinted by permission of the Editors), Vol. 37, No. 1, Winter, 1979, p. 121.*

LYLA HOFFMAN

Meltzer has made another timely contribution to the collection of nonfiction works on topics not sufficiently emphasized in schools. *The Human Rights Book* begins with a short . . . , thoughtful introduction to the subject of human rights at home and abroad. The remaining pages offer a bibliography, names and addresses of organizations working in the field, and documents issued by the United Nations and others dealing with human rights. . . .

Meltzer describes some of the torture methods used and discusses a few of the countries with the worst records—Iran, Philippines, Argentina, South Africa, the Soviet Union and others. There is a chapter on U.S. violations of political freedom by the FBI and the CIA and about U.S. political prisoners such as the Wilmington Ten, although Meltzer does not deal with the cruel treatment (including torture by isolation and many forms of degradation) routinely accorded to thousands of ordinary prisoners in U.S. jails. He does introduce differences in conceptions of what "human rights" means, including the different perspectives of socialist and capitalist nations. And he does point out that among the worst offenders using torture throughout the world are those who are "client" nations of the U.S. and dependent upon our official assistance.

This book belongs on all high school library shelves and would be a fine gift for any thoughtful young person.

> *Lyla Hoffman, in her review of "The Human Rights Book," in* Interracial Books for Children Bulletin *(reprinted by permission of* Interracial Books for Children Bulletin, *1841 Broadway, New York, N.Y. 10023), Vol. 10, No. 6, 1979, p. 18.*

KEITH B. COOPER

[In *The Human Rights Book*] Meltzer seeks to determine the condition of human rights since the adoption of the Universal Declaration of Human Rights in 1948. He offers a brief history of the human rights movement, a variety of examples of human rights violations worldwide, and a useful bibliography and appendix of related documents. For these reasons alone, his book is valuable. Further, while one might question anyone's ability to survey this topic in a single volume, Meltzer has provided a concise and clear outline of an issue so broad and complex that many find it overwhelming. The greatest value of the book may be as an entry point for more concentrated study. Such tools are rare in this field.

Keith B. Cooper, in his review of "The Human Rights Book," in Library Journal (reprinted from Library Journal, December 15, 1979; published by R. R. Bowker Co. (a Xerox company); copyright © 1979 by Xerox Corporation), Vol. 104, No. 22, December 15, 1979, p. 2638.

KIRKUS REVIEWS

[In *All Times, All People: A World History of Slavery*] Meltzer surveys the history of slavery from ancient times, pointing out that it has existed on all continents (in Africa before Europeans got involved) but in most societies was considered a matter of poor luck rather than inferior birth. He sees racism here developing as an excuse for slavery among free people dedicated to the rights of man. He tells readers that slavery exists today in some underdeveloped parts of the world "where people are hungry, ignorant, and without a voice in government." However, his discussion of how we can get rid of slavery emphasizes laws against it and mentions that richer nations helping poorer nations "could make a difference too"—which doesn't come close to addressing the issues. As a history, though, this younger, easier summary clearly benefits from the author's having researched and thought out the subject for his substantial two-volume *Slavery*. . . . Here that information is neither condensed nor skimmed, but assimilated into a strong introduction that makes its points unemotionally with descriptions and examples.

A review of "All Times, All People: A World History of Slavery," in Kirkus Reviews (copyright © 1980 The Kirkus Service, Inc.), Vol. XLVIII, No. 20, October 15, 1980, p. 1358.

ZENA SUTHERLAND

[*All Times, All Peoples: A World History of Slavery* is] serious prose, dry but inherently dramatic. . . . Although Meltzer makes an occasional broad statement ("It was Christopher Columbus who started the American slave trade") that may seem inadequately clarified, he writes for the most part with scrupulous attention to facts, his attitude as objective as it is possible to be when describing the bondage of human beings.

Zena Sutherland, in her review of "All Times, All Peoples: A World History of Slavery," in Bulletin of the Center for Children's Books (reprinted by permission of The University of Chicago Press; © 1980 by The University of Chicago), Vol. 34, No. 4, December, 1980, p. 75.

KIRKUS REVIEWS

The next thing to slave labor, Chinese workers were imported by the thousands to build the Western end of the transcontinental railroad. They were paid less than whites and worked longer hours (twelve a day), were forcibly prevented from leaving and exposed to avalanches, explosives, and other dangers which killed 1200 (ten percent) of them during the project. . . . [In *The Chinese Americans*] Meltzer reveals all this with proper force. . . . Meltzer's own memories of childhood rhymes (of the "chinky chinky chinaman" variety) occasions a patient lecture on racial stereotypes in very simple terms before he takes Chinese American history up to today's sweat-

shops and tongs and the need, again, for alliance with others working for equality. Written for easy assimilation, but with no loss of impact and a contained indignation that gives it an edge over other entries at this level. (pp. 80-1)

A review of "The Chinese Americans," in Kirkus Reviews (copyright © 1981 The Kirkus Service, Inc.), Vol. XLIX, No. 2, January 15, 1981, pp. 80-1.

JOHN TCHEN

When I received **The Chinese Americans,** my conditioned initial reaction was that it would probably be another poorly researched, poorly thought out and uncritical book about the history of Chinese in the U.S. To my pleasant surprise, I found the book quite good and thoroughly engaging.

Meltzer is not only a competent social historian with an impressive number of books to his name; he is also a very good writer who presents material in a way that is far from dry and boring. Instead of giving the usual chronology—*i.e.*, the immigration, what the Chinese did first, what they did second, and so on—Meltzer begins with the only bit of knowledge most non-Chinese Americans know about this neglected history. What did the Chinese build? Of course: The Chinese built the railroads. By dealing with the obvious Meltzer draws his readers into a fascinating reconstruction of this monumental project. The reader then quickly realizes, "Gee, I didn't know that." Meltzer goes on to discuss Chinese miners, farmers, fishermen and a number of other "I-didn't-know-that" occupations.

One chapter deals with where Chinese immigrants came from by discussing the history of relations between the West and China. Meltzer displays a fair knowledge of the difficult conditions within China which prompted much immigration, and he discusses the imposition of Western imperial powers upon the weak Manchu dynasty. Throughout, China is treated with understanding and respect.

The book's most effective chapter, "Pictures in the Air," examines the very difficult problem of cultural stereotypes of Chinese and Chinese Americans. Meltzer talks about his own childhood images and misunderstandings of Chinese and he writes frankly about learning the chant, "Chink, Chink, Chinaman sitting on a rail / Along comes a white man and cuts off his tail. . . ." He discusses how he came to realize that stereotypes distorted his understanding. Instead of moralizing about racism, the author carefully shows how stereotypes are all around us in the media, in jokes, in stories passed down for generations. This gives the reader concrete examples of racism in U.S. culture.

Two things bothered me. The first is relatively minor, but worth raising. A photograph shows a Chinese woman dressed in ornate holiday attire walking on a sidewalk. (Although it is not mentioned, the photograph was taken by Arnold Genthe in San Francisco before the 1906 earthquake.) The caption states that this woman had bound feet in "accordance to Chinese custom." First of all, the woman's feet are *not* bound, as evidenced by the type of shoes she is wearing and the fact that she is walking about unaided by an attendant. Secondly, Chinese custom did not dictate that all Chinese women have their feet bound. . . . A more significant reservation I have is Meltzer's overuse of the word Chinese. It is difficult in such condensed histories to include the names of individual Chinese people. Nevertheless, constant referrals to a monolithic Chinese people do not help the reader to identify with individuals; they also encourage blanket statements about a whole people, such as "All Chinese are hard working." I have often been guilty of this same tendency when I want to make a general point; the solution is to be specific and give examples of actual situations. In order to give names to the people, a great deal of additional historical research in the field of Asian American studies is necessary.

It isn't often that a book for young readers is as well researched as this one. Meltzer manages to combine informed historical knowledge with a great deal of sensitivity for his readers and for Chinese Americans. The end product is a book with intelligence and feeling. It should be noted that this is a state-of-the-art book: it offers some of the best current scholarship, but it also means that current scholarship is far from where it should be, and a great deal more primary, nitty-gritty research is necessary to give names to the many faces and statistics that can now only be described as "the Chinese."

John Tchen, in his review of "The Chinese Americans," in Interracial Books for Children Bulletin *(reprinted by permission of* Interracial Books for Children Bulletin, *1841 Broadway, New York, N.Y. 10023), Vol. 12, No. 1, 1981, p. 17.*

KIRKUS REVIEWS

[In his **The Hispanic Americans**], Meltzer gives us the most forthright treatment yet of the force behind Hispanic-American immigration: namely, the devastating effect on the Mexican, Cuban, and Puerto Rican economies of European colonialism and later US government and business practices. . . . Except for the relatively prosperous first-wave Cubans, Hispanic Americans find themselves "at the bottom of the job ladder" and have received a "dismal" education here. . . . Meltzer describes the wretched conditions of farm workers, somewhat alleviated by the union movement, that are better known to YA readers, and the effective slave labor system that traps illegals. He emphasizes that the Hispanic-American experience is not uniform: In New York, Hispanic-Americans have revitalized Jackson Heights, where newsstands sell papers from Bogota, Buenos Aires, Guayaquil, and Santo Domingo; yet in Spanish Harlem, an older Puerto Rican community, "the people live poorly." Their very numbers make their problems urgent: one in four New Yorkers is of Hispanic origin, as is 28 percent of the Los Angeles population and 40 percent of Miami's; and this group is growing nearly four times as fast as that of all others in the nation. To these facts and descriptions Meltzer adds an earnest chapter, similar to that in his **Chinese Americans** . . . , on the folly and evils of racial stereotypes and discrimination. He ends with the example of San Antonio's Chicano mayor, elected in 1981, and the hope that Hispanic-Americans can overcome the obstacles to organizing for political action. Essential.

A review of "The Hispanic-Americans," in Kirkus Reviews *(copyright © 1982 The Kirkus Service, Inc.), Vol. L, No. 6, March 15, 1982, p. 351.*

PAUL HEINS

[Milton Meltzer, the] author of many books about the various ethnic groups living in the United States feels that the "story of the Hispanic Americans has been neglected or hidden. Yet that history, that life in the past, has shaped our present, no matter what ethnic group we ourselves may belong to." First

reminding us of the part played by the Spaniards in exploring and colonizing the Western Hemisphere, [Meltzer, in **The Hispanic Americans,**] considers in detail the three main streams of Hispanics who have become part of American life: the Puerto Ricans, the Chicanos in the Southwest, and the political émigrés from Cuba. He explores the development of their legal, economic, political, and cultural status in the United States and informs us that "Hispanic people will replace blacks as the country's biggest minority by the end of the 1980s." The sympathetic narrative, which stresses the tenacity of the Spanish way of life, frequently relies upon references to specific individuals and quotes their statements verbatim. In keeping with the author's strong sense of justice, one chapter discusses the evils and the stereotypes nurtured by racism, while the documentary photographs concentrate on the environment and on the daily activities of contemporary Hispanic Americans.

Paul Heins, in his review of "The Hispanic Americans," in The Horn Book Magazine *(copyright © 1982 by The Horn Book, Inc., Boston), Vol. LVIII, No. 4, August, 1982, p. 424.*

ETHEL R. TWICHELL

[**The Jewish Americans** is] a thoughtful and well-researched book [that] presents the history of the Jews in America through their own letters, diaries, and recollections. From a soldier's account of a skirmish with the British in 1776 to a description of an American Jew's life on a contemporary kibbutz in Israel, a wide spectrum of experience is reflected, both American and specifically Jewish. A Jewish slave trader ordering his captain to be particularly "'careful of your vessel and slaves, and be as frugal as possible'" is counterbalanced by a rebel who joined John Brown's anti-slavery forces. In the 1880s the great immigrations began; there were high expectations and the reality of wretched jobs. Jews report of service in both world wars and share the nightmare of the Holocaust. Almost every passage resounds with a will to survive, a passion for education, and a shrewd and ready wit. One finds greed and arrogance but also intense loyalty to causes—labor unions, women's rights or, above all, the retention of a Jewish identity. [Milton Meltzer] provides enough historical background to orient his readers, but it is the lively immediacy of his examples which will remain, as he wisely lets his witnesses speak for themselves. (pp. 531-32)

Ethel R. Twichell, in her review of "The Jewish Americans: A History in Their Own Words," in The Horn Book Magazine *(copyright © 1982 by The Horn Book, Inc., Boston), Vol. LVIII, No. 5, October, 1982, pp. 531-32.*

KIRKUS REVIEWS

[**The Jewish Americans: A History in Their Own Words** offers some] documentary material reflecting aspects of American Jewish history—but, as an entity, [is] less coherent or substantial than Meltzer's various earlier books on the subject. A handful of selections show Jews confronting historical anti-Semitism: Asser Levy's appeal to the New Amsterdam authorities for the Jews' "burgher rights"; the protest of three Paducah, Ky., Jews, to Lincoln, against Grant's order expelling Jews from the Tennessee district; a rabbi's memoir of bucking Klan agitation in 1920s Indiana. A considerable number, especially of early date, attest to Jewish participation in mainstream American events—the Revolution (a patriot, a Tory), the Mexican War, Western settlement, the Gold Rush. Also of this ilk are Ernestine Rose's 1832 feminist speech and August Bondi's recollection of John Brown. A very few derive, without Meltzer's precisely saying so, from particularly Jewish union or radical activity (Rose Schneiderman's Triangle Fire speech, Emma Goldman's protest against deportation). The largest number, however, are snippets of Jewish life. . . . These are classics of immigrant autobiography—and so is Maurice Hindus' awe at "the decorative and juice-soaked tomato," and other things American, or Charles Angoff's memory of his father's disdain for just such American things. The chronicles of more recent times mainly commemorate salient experiences (a Jewish G.I. at Buchenwald, an Auschwitz survivor, an American kibbutznik) and have little individual flavor. Not an especially auspicious group, then, or in any single way outstanding—except for some of those vivid and affecting immigrant impressions. (pp. 1002-03)

> *A review of "The Jewish Americans: A History in Their Own Words," in* Kirkus Reviews *(copyright © 1982 The Kirkus Service, Inc.), Vol. L, No. 17, September 1, 1982, pp. 1002-03.*

TERRY LAWHEAD

The story of the Ku Klux Klan is a nightmare, and [*The Truth About the Ku Klux Klan*] does a very fine job of examining and demystifying the bizarre history of a strange and dangerous cult. . . . Meltzer is one of the best social historians writing for children, and he somehow manages to maintain an admirable objectivity while listing in detail the atrocities done in the name of white supremacy. A final chapter on what can be done and a bibliography remind readers that the final challenge is left up to each individual. What we know about can't truly hurt us.

> *Terry Lawhead, in his review of "The Truth about the Ku Klux Klan," in* School Library Journal *(reprinted from the November, 1982 issue of* School Library Journal, *published by R. R. Bowker Co./A Xerox Corporation; copyright © 1982), Vol. 29, No. 3, November, 1982, p. 102.*

Arthur Miller

1915-

American dramatist, essayist, novelist, short story writer, and scriptwriter.

Miller's fame as a dramatist derives from his four plays first produced between 1947 and 1955: *All My Sons, Death of a Salesman, The Crucible,* and *A View from the Bridge.* These dramas have been praised for their examinations of individual and social commitment, and have earned Miller the reputation of a moralist.

Family conflicts, particularly between fathers and sons, appear throughout Miller's early work. In *All My Sons,* Joe Keller chooses to sell inferior airplane parts during World War II in order to save his business. At the end of the play, Keller is forced by his idealistic son Chris to take responsibility for his partner's imprisonment and for the deaths of American pilots. *Death of a Salesman,* Miller's most famous play, is a critique of America's preoccupation with materialism after World War II. Originally titled *Inside of His Head, Death of a Salesman* depicts the mental deterioration of Willy Loman, a salesman whose superficial doctrine for success turns into tragedy when he realizes that he is no longer wanted by his company.

The Crucible sparked much controversy. Based on the seventeenth-century Salem witch trials, many critics believed *The Crucible* was a thinly-disguised attack on Senator Joseph McCarthy and the House Committee on Un-American Activities, before which Miller was called to testify in 1956. He was charged with contempt of Congress for his refusal to identify writers seen at Communist-sponsored meetings that he himself had attended. Despite the topical tone of the play, John Gassner remarked that *The Crucible* "will remain alive long after every carping criticism directed at its political implications has been forgotten." Gassner's prediction has proven correct; *The Crucible* is still widely read and produced today.

Miller has won numerous awards for his work. In 1947 he received the New York Drama Critics Circle Award and the Antoinette Perry (Tony) award for *All My Sons. Death of a Salesman* won the New York Drama Critics Circle Award, the Tony, and the Pulitzer Prize in drama in 1949. Miller also received a Tony in 1953 for *The Crucible* and an Emmy in 1967 for *Death of a Salesman.*

(See also *CLC,* Vols. 1, 2, 6, 10, 15; *Contemporary Authors,* Vols. 1-4, rev. ed.; *Contemporary Authors New Revision Series,* Vol. 2; and *Dictionary of Literary Biography,* Vol. 7.)

JOHN GASSNER

[Arthur Miller's **'Death of a Salesman'**] is not quite the masterpiece of dramatic literature that the enthusiasts would have us believe. It is well written but is not sustained by incandescent or memorable language except in two or three short passages. Moreover, its hero, the desperate salesman Willy Loman, is too much the loud-mouthed dolt and emotional babe-in-the-woods to wear all the trappings of high tragedy with which he has been invested. It is, indeed, a feature of the play's rather

trite orientation that Willy, whose ideals are so banal and whose strivings are so commonplace, is sent to his death in a catafalque as if he were worthy of [Ludwig van] Beethoven's Eroica symphony. For writers of the stamp of Molière and [George Bernard] Shaw, Willy would have been an object of satirical penetration rather than mournful tenderness and lachrymose elegy. By contrast with even contemporary dramatists of a fine grain like [Eugene O'Neill, Tennessee Williams, and Sherwood Anderson], Mr. Miller has written his story on the level of *drame bourgeois.* Although his intellect denies assent to the main character's fatuous outlook, some commonplaceness attends the sentiments of the writing, the overvaluation of Willy as a hero, and the selection of a bumptiously kind-hearted bourgeois, Charley, as the proper foil for the unsuccessful salesman. Charley is the model of right living because he was practical-minded and made a success of his business, and because his son Bernard married and became a lawyer who is now on his way to Washington to argue a case and takes his tennis rackets along, presumably to hobnob with successful people. No one in the play stands for values that would not gain the full approval of Mr. Bruce Barton, Mr. Dale Carnegie, and the anonymous editors of the Gideon bible. The Promethean soul is inconspicuous in **'Death of a Salesman.'** The mind and the spirit that manifest themselves in it are rather earthbound and not in themselves interesting.

Once these reservations are made, however, one cannot deny that the play has singular merits, that it is often moving and even gripping, that it is penetrative both in characterization and in social implication. It expresses a viewpoint of considerable importance when it exposes the delusions of 'go-getting,' 'contacts'—inebriated philistinism by reducing it to the muddle of Willy's life, which is surely not an isolated case.

Miller has written a play remarkably apposite to an aspect of American life, and the audiences that are held by it and the many playgoers who are moved to tears pay him the tribute of recognition. Their interest and sympathy are engaged by the pathos of a man who gave all his life to a business only to be thrown on the scrap-heap, a householder whose pattern of life was interwoven with instalment plans with which he could hardly catch up, a doting father disappointed in his children, and an American *naïf* bemused by the worship of uncreative success and hollow assumptions that 'personality' is the *summum bonum*.

A notable feature of the effectiveness of **'Death of a Salesman'** is that the author's judgments are not delivered down to the playgoer from some intellectual eminence but stem almost entirely from close identification with the outlook and thought-processes of the characters. This probably explains all that I find intrinsically commonplace in this otherwise powerful play. The playwright is not 'outside looking in' but 'inside looking out,' and at least for the purposes of immediate effect it is less pertinent that he is not looking very far out than that he is so convincingly and sensitively inside his subject. Largely for this reason, too, Miller has also given the American theatre of social criticism its most unqualified success, for that theatre, ever since the nineteen-thirties when it became a distinct mode of playwriting, has tended to be argumentative and hortatory. . . . Instead of debating issues or denouncing Willy's and his society's errors, Miller simply demonstrates these in the life of his characters. He confines himself, moreover, to the particulars of normal behavior and environment, and nothing that Willy or his family does or says betrays the playwright as the inventor of special complications for the purpose of social agitation. The play does not even set up a conflict between two distinctly different sets of values, which . . . is in some respects a limitation of the work, as well as a merit. Even the life of Charley which is contrasted to Willy's is only a sensible counterpart of it (it is merely a sensible materialism), and no challenging conversion by a character leads us out of the middle-class world. Willy's son Biff surmounts his father's attitude only in acquiring self-knowledge and resigning himself to being just an ordinary, dollar-an-hour citizen. Arthur Miller, in short, has accomplished the feat of writing a drama critical of wrong values that virtually every member of our middle-class can accept as valid. It stabs itself into a playgoer's consciousness to a degree that may well lead him to review his own life and the lives of those who are closest to him. The conviction of the writing is, besides, strengthened by a quality of compassion rarely experienced in our theatre. One must be either extraordinarily sharp or exceptionally obtuse to stand aloof from the play. (pp. 89-91)

> *John Gassner, "Aspects of the Broadway Theatre,"*
> *in* The Quarterly Journal of Speech *(copyright 1949*
> *by the Speech Communication Association), Vol.*
> *XXXV, No. 3, October, 1949, pp. 289-96.**

SIGHLE KENNEDY

The questions of whether or not *Death of a Salesman* is a great dramatic structure, or whether or not its writing is splendid or only roughly adequate, can hold but secondary importance in any discussion of the play. Above them one fact shines: Willy Loman, egotistical, greedy, affectionate, lonely, has risen up as a modern Everyman.

But the very way in which Willy speaks so immediately to so many people has brought his problems into sharp and varied scrutiny. . . . [The play] speaks not only to, and for the problems of, an American audience but to countries whose insecurity is even more obvious than that of the U.S. represented by Willy—countries which often look toward the U.S. as an easy and automatic way out of their troubles. To them, as to Americans, the self-destroyed Willy rises up in warning.

So powerfully projected and personally received has been this story of Willy Loman that a not-surprising doubt has risen up about it. People see in it an accurate picture of their own mental stresses and feel defensive about Willy. Many of them wonder: was Willy really responsible for his death, or was he, as Luke Carroll in the *Herald Tribune* put it, "a pathetic little man caught in an undertow that's much too strong for him"? (pp. 110-11)

Was Willy the victim of brute economics? or of an unbounded, irrational desire for success? or of the thoughtless ingratitude of his sons? These questions and many others have remained with the *Salesman*'s audience long after the final curtain has gone down.

Perhaps the largest single group that thinks of Willy as a helpless "little man" is made up of those who see economics as the all-powerful factor in the play. They make the most of the epitaph spoken by Willy's friend, Charley: "Nobody dast blame this man. For a salesman there is no rock-bottom to the life. He don't put a bolt to a nut, he don't tell you the law or give you medicine. . . . A salesman is got to dream, boy. It comes with the territory." The territory, they say (and have said all along) is to blame. Willy had no chance against the capitalistic system.

The other half of the group is at the opposite extreme of belief. They also feel that economics is the determining power in the play, but they believe that Miller, in criticizing "the territory" is trying to undermine democracy. . . .

Such a group contends that Miller has stacked the cards against Willy and used his single tragedy to point an unjustifiable finger at salesmanship itself. If Willy died, they say in effect, Arthur Miller killed him. (p. 111)

Far from painting a one-sided economic picture, Miller is almost painfully scrupulous in showing that Willy's tragedy must not be set at the door of his particular type of work (symbolic though that surely is). Willy's braggadocio, his confidence that he and his sons, by divine right of personality, are above the laws that bind ordinary men, put his acts in the realm of universal moral censure—not in the cubbyhole of an ideology. (p. 112)

The very multiplicity of problems which confront Willy must put us on our guard against placing too much stress on any one of them. Yet, if no single cause compelled Willy's suicide, was it perhaps the sum of all of them? Two facts seem to answer this last question. The first is the action of the play itself. Miller has shown Willy, through the years, letting his vanity and pretensions undermine his sense of right and wrong. He repays those who try to help him only with contempt. At the end of the play he has swollen to the dreadful traditional figure of tragedy—destroyed by a single cancerous fault.

The second fact (if this first is not sufficient) is the testimony of Miller himself. In several very earnest articles he has made clear his belief that a play based on pathos—"pity for a helpless victim"—presents an essentially false view of life. The contrast to pathos is tragedy, he says, "which must illustrate a principle of life. . . ." . . . (p. 114)

In theory as in dramatic practice, Miller shows the same brave and deliberate effort to meet problems "in head-on collision"—and take the consequences. His stated aims not only show him well worth a thoughtful hearing, but they set a very high standard for judgment of his work. He believes that "tragedy brings not only sadness . . . but knowledge. What sort of knowledge? In the largest sense of the word it is knowledge pertaining to the right way of living in the world. Tragedy . . . makes us aware of what the character might have been. But to say . . . what a man might have been requires of the author a soundly based, completely believed vision of man's great possibilities."

Does *Death of a Salesman* "make us aware of what Willy Loman might have been"? (pp. 114-15)

Certainly, Biff, if anyone, should be the one to demonstrate what Willy "might have been" and what the "right way of living" is which might have saved him. What does Biff say? He says—"I'm nothing"—at least the beginning of wisdom. He further implies that his value will consist in doing the outdoor physical work he is best fitted for.

At Willy's grave, he thinks of what his father has thrown away—"There were a lot of nice days. When he'd come from a trip; or on Sundays, making the stoop. . . . You know something, Charley, there's more of him in that front stoop than in all the sales he ever made." Charley agrees: "He was a happy man with a batch of cement."

True and touching as these reminiscences are, they seem on another level entirely from the dreams, the furies ("all, all, wrong") that are shown at work in Willy. These driving forces, which all of us have felt pressing on our lives from one direction or other indeed seem to call for a "weightier counterbalance" than these words of Biff provide.

From the character of Charley, too, we might expect some statement of vision, but Charley never seems able to illuminate the principle that underlies his good deeds. This lack appears in terrible relief when, after being fired, the disillusioned Willy says to him: "After all the highways, and the trains, and the appointments, and the years, you end up worth more dead than alive." Charley's answer is not only negative, but a double negative. "Willy," he says, "nobody's worth nothing dead." How very little light that sheds on the right way of living!

At Willy's grave Charley shows more insight. When Linda wonders that Willy should choose death when "he only needed a little salary," Charley replies: "No man only needs a little salary." (A reply which manages to strike at the root of all economic materialisms.)

What might Willy Loman have been? What can Biff Loman become? These great possibilities are left for each person in the audience to answer for himself. . . . If no man's satisfaction can be found in a "little salary," can it really rest—ultimately —in a little "cement"?

In spite of the fact, however, that *Death of a Salesman* ends so—with a question rather than an answer, Arthur Miller has performed in its creation an act of truly heroic stature. His far-reaching, sympathetic and insistent formulation of Willy's question has made millions of Willys in his audience care deeply about the answer—the best way, surely, of spurring them to find it. (pp. 115-16)

Sighle Kennedy, "Who Killed the Salesman?" in Catholic World *(copyright 1950 by The Missionary Society of St. Paul the Apostle in the State of New York; used by permission), Vol. 171, May, 1950, pp. 110-16.*

ROBERT WARSHOW

One of the things that have been said of *The Crucible,* Arthur Miller's new play about the Salem witchcraft trials, is that we must not be misled by its obvious contemporary relevance: it is a drama of universal significance. This statement, which has usually a somewhat apologetic tone, seems to be made most often by those who do not fail to place great stress on the play's "timeliness." I believe it means something very different from what it appears to say, almost the contrary, in fact, and yet not quite the contrary either. It means: do not be misled by the play's historical theme into forgetting the main point, which is that "witch trials" are always with us, and especially today; but on the other hand do not hold Mr. Miller responsible either for the inadequacies of his presentation of the Salem trials or for the many undeniable and important differences between those trials and the "witch trials" that are going on now. It is quite true, nevertheless, that the play is, at least in one sense, of "universal significance." Only we must ask what this phrase has come to mean, and whether the quality it denotes is a virtue. (p. 189)

The "universality" of Mr. Miller's play belongs neither to literature nor to history, but to that journalism of limp erudition which assumes that events are to be understood by referring them to categories, and which is therefore never at a loss for a comment. Just as in *Death of a Salesman* Mr. Miller sought to present "the American" by eliminating so far as possible the "non-essential" facts which might have made his protagonist a particular American, so in *The Crucible* he reveals at every turn his almost contemptuous lack of interest in the particularities—which is to say, the reality—of the Salem trials. The character and motives of all the actors in this drama are for him both simple and clear. The girls who raised the accusation of witchcraft were merely trying to cover up their own misbehavior. The Reverend Samuel Parris found in the investigation of witchcraft a convenient means of consolidating his shaky position in a parish that was murmuring against his "undemocratic" conduct of the church. The Reverend John Hale, a conscientious and troubled minister who, given the premises, must have represented something like the best that Puritan New England had to offer, and whose agonies of doubt might have been expected to call forth the highest talents of a serious playwright, appears in *The Crucible* as a kind of idiotic "liberal" scoutmaster, at first cheerfully confident of his ability to cope with the Devil's wiles and in the last act babbling hysterically in an almost comic contrast to the assured dignity of the main characters. Deputy Governor Danforth, presented as the virtual embodiment of early New England, never becomes more than a pompous, unimaginative politician of the better sort.

As for the victims themselves, the most significant fact is Miller's choice of John Proctor for his leading character. . . . It is all too easy to make Proctor into the "common man"—and then, of course, we know where we are: Proctor wavers a good deal, fails to understand what is happening, wants only to be left alone with his wife and his farm, considers making a false confession, but in the end goes to his death for reasons that he finds a little hard to define but that are clearly good reasons—mainly, it seems, he does not want to implicate others. You will never learn from this John Proctor that Salem was a religious community, quite as ready to hang a Quaker as a witch. The saintly Rebecca Nurse is also there, to be sure, sketched in rapidly in the background, a quiet figure whose mere presence—there is little more of her than that—reminds us how far the dramatist has fallen short.

Nor has Mr. Miller hesitated to alter the facts to fit his constricted field of vision. Abigail Williams, one of the chief accusers in the trials, was about eleven years old in 1692; Miller makes her a young woman of eighteen or nineteen and invents an adulterous relation between her and John Proctor in order to motivate her denunciation of John and his wife Elizabeth. The point is not that this falsifies the facts of Proctor's life (though one remembers uneasily that he himself was willing to be hanged rather than confess to what was not true), but that it destroys the play, offering an easy theatrical motive that even in theatrical terms explains nothing, and deliberately casting away the element of religious and psychological complexity which gives the Salem trials their dramatic interest in the first place. In a similar way, Miller risks the whole point of *Death of a Salesman* by making his plot turn on the irrelevant discovery of Willy Loman's adultery. And in both plays the fact of adultery itself is slighted: it is brought in not as a human problem, but as a mere theatrical device, like the dropping of a letter; one cannot take an interest in Willy Loman's philandering, or believe in Abigail Williams' passion despite the barnyard analogies with which the playwright tries to make it "elemental."

Mr. Miller's steadfast, one might almost say selfless, refusal of complexity, the assured simplicity of his view of human behavior, may be the chief source of his ability to captivate the educated audience. He is an oddly depersonalized writer; one tries in vain to define his special quality, only to discover that it is perhaps not a quality at all, but something like a method, and even as a method strangely bare: his plays are as neatly put together and essentially as empty as that skeleton of a house which made *Death of a Salesman* so impressively confusing. He is the playwright of an audience that believes the frightening complexities of history and experience are to be met with a few ideas, and yet does not even possess these ideas any longer but can only point significantly at the place where they were last seen and where it is hoped they might still be found to exist. What this audience demands of its artists above all is an intelligent narrowness of mind and vision and a generalized tone of affirmation, offering not any particular insights or any particular truths, but simply the assurance that insight and truth as qualities, the things in themselves, reside somehow in the various signals by which the artist and the audience have learned to recognize each other. For indeed very little remains except this recognition; the marriage of the liberal theater and the liberal audience has been for some time a marriage in name only, held together by habit and mutual interest, partly by sentimental memory, most of all by the fear of loneliness and the outside world; and yet the movements of love are still kept up—for the sake of the children, perhaps.

The hero of this audience is Clifford Odets. Among those who shouted "Bravo!" at the end of *The Crucible*—an exclamation, awkward on American lips, that is reserved for cultural

achievements of the greatest importance—there must surely have been some who had stood up to shout "Strike!" at the end of *Waiting for Lefty*. But it is hard to believe that a second Odets, if that were possible, or the old Odets restored to youth, would be greeted with such enthusiasm as Arthur Miller calls forth. Odets's talent was too rich—in my opinion the richest ever to appear in the American theater—and his poetry and invention were constantly more important than what he conceived himself to be saying. In those days it didn't matter: the "message" at the end of the third act was so much taken for granted that there was room for Odets's exuberance, and he himself was never forced to learn how much his talent was superior to his "affirmations" (if he had learned, perhaps the talent might have survived the "affirmations"). Arthur Miller is the dramatist of a later time, when the "message" isn't there at all, but it has been agreed to pretend that it is. This pretense can be maintained only by the most rigid control, for there is no telling what small element of dramatic *élan* or simple reality may destroy the delicate rapport of a theater and an audience that have not yet acknowledged they have no more to say to each other. Arthur Miller is Odets without the poetry. Worst of all, one feels sometimes that he has suppressed the poetry deliberately, making himself by choice the anonymous dramatist of a fossilized audience. In *Death of a Salesman,* certainly, there were moments when reality seemed to force its way momentarily to the surface. And even at *The Crucible*— though here it was not Miller's suppressed talent that broke through, but the suppressed facts of the outside world—the thread that tied the audience to its dramatist must have been now and then under some strain. . . . (pp. 192-96)

Mr. Miller has nothing to say about the Salem trials and makes only the flimsiest pretense that he has. *The Crucible* was written to say something about Alger Hiss and Owen Lattimore, Julius and Ethel Rosenberg, Senator [Joseph] McCarthy, the actors who have lost their jobs on radio and television, in short the whole complex that is spoken of, with a certain lowering of the voice, as the "present atmosphere." And yet not to say anything about that either, but only to suggest that a great deal might be said, oh an infinitely great deal, if it were not that— what? Well, perhaps if it were not that the "present atmosphere" itself makes such plain speaking impossible. As it is, there is nothing for it but to write plays of "universal significance"—and, after all, that's what a serious dramatist is supposed to do anyway.

What, then, *is* Mr. Miller trying to say to us? It's hard to tell. In *The Crucible* innocent people are accused and convicted of witchcraft on the most absurd testimony—in fact, the testimony of those who themselves have meddled in witchcraft and are therefore doubly to be distrusted. Decent citizens who sign petitions attesting to the good character of their accused friends and neighbors are thrown into prison as suspects. Anyone who tries to introduce into court the voice of reason is likely to be held in contempt. One of the accused refuses to plead and is pressed to death. No one is acquitted; the only way out for the accused is to make false confessions and themselves join the accusers. Seeing all this on the stage, we are free to reflect that something very like these trials has been going on in recent years in the United States. How much like? Mr. Miller does not say. But *very* like, allowing of course for some superficial differences: no one has been pressed to death in recent years, for instance. Still, people have lost their jobs for refusing to say under oath whether or not they are Communists. The essential pattern is the same, isn't it? And when we speak of "universal significance," we mean sticking to the essential pattern, don't we? Mr. Miller is under no obligation to tell us whether he thinks the trial of Alger Hiss, let us say, was a "witch trial"; he is writing about the Salem trials. (pp. 196-97)

But if Mr. Miller isn't saying anything about the Salem trials, and can't be caught saying anything about anything else, what did the audience think he was saying? That too is hard to tell. A couple of the newspaper critics wrote about how timely the play was, and then took it back in the Sunday editions, putting a little more weight on the "universal significance"; but perhaps they didn't quite take it back as much as they seemed to want to: the final verdict appeared to be merely that *The Crucible* is not so great a play as *Death of a Salesman.* As for the rest of the audience, it was clear that they felt themselves to be participating in an event of great meaning: that is what is meant by "Bravo!" Does "Bravo!" mean anything else? I think it means: we agree with Arthur Miller; he has set forth brilliantly and courageously what has been weighing on all our minds; at last someone has had the courage to answer Senator McCarthy.

I don't believe this audience was likely to ask itself what it was agreeing to. Enough that someone had said something, anything, to dispel for a couple of hours that undefined but very real sense of frustration which oppresses these "liberals"—who believe in their innermost being that salvation comes from saying something, and who yet find themselves somehow without anything very relevant to say. They tell themselves, of course, that Senator McCarthy has made it "impossible" to speak; but one can hardly believe they are satisfied with this explanation. Where are the heroic voices that will refuse to be stilled?

Well, last season there was [James Thurber's] *The Male Animal,* a play written twelve or thirteen years ago about a college professor who gets in trouble for reading one of Vanzetti's letters to his English composition class. In the audience at that play one felt also the sense of communal excitement; it was a little like a secret meeting of early Christians—or even, one might say, witches—where everything had an extra dimension of meaning experienced only by the communicants. And this year there has been a revival of [Lillian Hellman's] *The Children's Hour,* a play of even more universal significance than *The Crucible* since it doesn't have anything to do with any trials but just shows how people can be hurt by having lies told about them. But these were old plays, the voices of an older generation. It remained for Arthur Miller to write a new play that really speaks out.

What does he say when he speaks out?

Never mind. He speaks out. (pp. 198-99)

> Robert Warshow, "The Liberal Conscience in 'The Crucible'" (originally published in Commentary, *Vol. XV, March, 1953), in his* The Immediate Experience: Movies, Comics, Theatre & Other Aspects of Popular Culture *(reprinted by permission of Paul Warshow), Doubleday, 1962, pp. 189-203.*

GEORGE JEAN NATHAN

As [August] Strindberg was the most positive influence on O'Neill so [Henrik] Ibsen is the most positive on Arthur Miller. O'Neill as a consequence was primarily interested in analyzing the grinding emotions of man and woman that often lie below the calmer surface emotions. Miller as a consequence is pri-

marily interested in man's sociological aspects. Above all, O'Neill as a dramatist was concerned with character, whereas Miller seems in large part to be concerned with theme and with character only incidentally. . . . [In] *The Crucible,* his latest play, we find all theme and no character. His people are spokesmen for him, not for themselves. They possess humanity, when they possess it at all, only in the distant sense that a phonograph recording of it does. They speak and act at an obvious turning of his crank. And the result is a play of large thematic force whose warmth, even heat, remains on the other side of the footlights and is not communicated, save in cold, intellectual terms, to its audience. It is impressive, as a lecture may be impressive, but for the major part it is equally remote from the listener's heart and feeling.

As heretofore, Miller shows himself to be a thoroughly honest and thoroughly sincere dramatist who, unlike the great majority of our present American playwrights, has nothing of the box-office today in his composition, and all credit to him on that score. But he also and at the same time here shows himself as one whose conscious indifference to the box-office seems to be accompanied by an unconscious indifference to any kind of theatrical audience, even one of the higher grade. It may be, of course, that he thought he had worked out his theme in terms of character and so would insinuate it into such an audience's emotion. That I can not tell. But if he did, he has failed. And if, on the other hand, he believed that the sheer vitality of his theme would satisfactorily infiltrate itself in his audience independent of any recognizable and pulsing character to assist it, he has not yet sufficiently educated himself in dramatic eccentricity.

That theme, centered on the historical Salem witch hunts and witch trials in the last years of the seventeenth century, is the mass hysteria born of superstition, ignorance, fear and bigotry and the tragedy it can bear for the guiltless. The play, which unfortunately veers toward extended documentation, seeks to crystallize the thesis in the persons of a man and wife who fall victims to the witch hunt but they too unfortunately are more mere documentary mouthpieces of the author than human beings with any real life, and their tragedy accordingly has the distant air of a dramatic recitation rather than of any personal suffering. Though Miller has written some scenes with his customary energetic pen, though there is a certain eloquence in them and though here and there contagious drama threatens to issue forth, it is this lack of character convincingly and warmly to project the whole into an audience's emotions that enfeebles the play. There is, in addition, such a repetitive flavor to it—it seems at times that the author is saying exactly the same thing over and over again—that the whole gives the effect of being on a treadmill and that, while there is an appearance of motion, it is really static.

The scene in the second act wherein the young women in the grip of hysteria proclaim again their certainty of the operation of evil spirits and overwhelm another of their number who has been cozened into denial is the play's closest approach to infectious drama. The prologue, in which the seeds of the witch mania are sewn, also has promise but, except for the subsequent scene noted, the promise is never realized and what we get is largely only discourse, sometimes interesting in itself, that does not succeed in ridding itself of its dialectic chill and in resolving itself, for all its fury, into even the mild fever of affecting drama.

That Miller had contemporary parallels in mind is obvious. He has, indeed, had them so closely in mind that he has not been able to put them out of it when a momentary forgetfulness of them would have profited his play. Though he does not at any point emphasize them and in this respect remains the dramatic artist, they somehow persist in indicating their hold upon him, and a wayward sense of propaganda, that enemy of dramatic art, forces its way into his auditors' consciousness. There is, let it be repeated, power in his play and not only power but intellectual purpose. Yet the power is that of an impersonal machine and the intellectual purpose that of a historical analyst, with a dramatist late in arriving on the scene and, when he does arrive, too deeply impressed and overcome by his materials to guide them into dramatic life. (pp. 24-5)

The Crucible, in sum, is an honorable sermon on a vital theme that misses because the sting implicit in it has been disinfected with an editorial tincture and because, though it contains the potential deep vibrations of life, it reduces them to mere superficial tremors. (pp. 25-6)

> *George Jean Nathan, "Henrik Miller" (reprinted by permission of Associated University Press, Inc., for the Estate of George Jean Nathan), in* Theatre Arts, *Vol. XXXVII, No. 4, April, 1953, pp. 24-6.*

BROOKS ATKINSON

"A View from the Bridge" has power and substance. It is based on a story that Mr. Miller once heard in the Brooklyn neighborhood where he lives. Eddie, an ordinary longshoreman, is unconsciously in love with his niece—the daughter of his wife's dead sister. Early in the play two of his wife's Italian relatives are smuggled in and start to live furtively in Eddie's apartment. Catherine, the niece, falls in love with the younger Italian brother and proposes to marry him.

Eddie does not understand why he opposes the marriage so violently, nor do any of the other people who are involved. Searching around for a plausible reason, Eddie convinces himself that the young Italian is a homosexual whose only motive in marrying Catherine is a chance to legitimize his citizenship in America. But Eddie's real motive is the undeclared, unrecognized, unappeased hunger he has for her himself. Like the heroes of Greek tragedy, he topples the whole house down on himself in the final catastrophe of a haunted play.

Mr. Miller understands the full tragic significance of this stark drama. Although he scrupulously underwrites the narrative, he introduces a neighborhood lawyer in a pool of light on one side of the stage to serve as chorus and commentator. . . . [The] lawyer analyzes Eddie's malady and puts it into human perspective. He also introduces a poetic strain by relating the Italian immigrants to the heroes of Roman history and the great myths of classical literature. . . .

[The] dimensions of **"A View from the Bridge"** are those of imaginative drama. Mr. Miller is straining for all the altitudes he can reach, and he is an uncommonly tall man.

The story is vivid. He meets it head-on. His intimate knowledge of the people—their living habits, their principles, their idiom—is solid. What he has to say about life in Italy today makes an illuminating contrast that all the characters like to conjure with. Everything about **"A View from the Bridge"** rings true.

Yet something inhibits it from expressing the fullness of tragedy that the theme promises. And this is the place where Mr. Miller's principle of underwriting may have been ill-advised.

If tragedy is to purge and terrify the audience, in the classical phrase, the characters must have size. Their fate must have spiritual significance. Aristotle limited tragic heroes to kings and queens and people renowned in other respects. If the modern world limited tragedy to such people, we would have very little to write about.

Eddie's deficiency as a tragic character is not a matter of social inferiority. It is simpler than that: Mr. Miller has not told us enough about him. Since the play begins in the middle of a tumultous story, his background is dim and vague. On the basis of what we are told about him, Eddie is not an admirable person. He is mean. He is vicious toward the end, and he gets just about what he deserves. It is difficult to believe that fate has struck a decent human being a staggering blow that enlightens him about himself.

Nor are his wife and niece better portrayed. Their roots are shallow, too. The two Italian immigrants are the only well-defined characters in the central play. When Mr. Miller introduces them in the midst of a story that is already in motion, he is under the necessity of telling us who they are, where they come from and why. They are the only characters whom we can fully understand. . . .

"A View from the Bridge" needs flesh, not only because the characters are working people, but because Mr. Miller has written his play sparingly. Working in a mood of artistic austerity he has eliminated himself from both of these dramas. Many of us would be very happy to have as much of him as he can give.

> *Brooks Atkinson, in his review of "A View from the Bridge," in* The New York Times, *Section 2 (© 1955 by The New York Times Company; reprinted by permission), October 9, 1955, p. 1.*

RICHARD J. FOSTER

Sooner or later most discussions of the merits of Arthur Miller's *Death of a Salesman* turn to the question of the possibility of modern tragedy. Given the conditions of the modern world, the question runs, is it possible to write true tragedy in our time? Of course the very asking of the question sounds the negative. But there are likely to be answerers around who will invoke the names of certain moderns—Ibsen, or Strindberg, or O'Neill, or [Sean] O'Casey, or even Arthur Miller—who are alleged to have made tragedies out of the common materials of modern life. And Miller himself, in response to commentators who have denied that *Salesman* is a tragedy, has vigorously affirmed, in an essay called **"Tragedy and the Common Man,"** the right of his play, and the matter it is made of, to the epithet *tragic*. (p. 82)

To put the matter very simply, Arthur Miller has a very general or very loose and vague theory of tragedy, or perhaps no clear theory at all, while the critics have a fairly definite one derived from a couple of thousand years of literary tradition. The traditional view of tragedy, founded very largely upon the principles of Aristotle and the practice of Sophocles and Shakespeare, assumes at least two prior essentials to be inherent in the materials of any tragic action. First, the hero must have "stature": this means that while he must in some way represent the general human condition, he must also be larger and grander than the norm—certainly in the inherent fineness and depth and energy of his mind and character, and perhaps also in his exterior societal role—so that his fall will have deep emotional consequence for the audience. Second, the world in which the tragic hero acts must be sensed as bounded or permeated by some meaningful and larger-than human order—call it a Moral Order, or the Natural Law, or Providence, or even Fate—which he in some way challenges or violates and which correspondingly exacts, but not without some sense of ultimate justice in the exaction, the tragic hero's life in consequence of that violation. The first part of this formula, the requirement of "stature" in the tragic hero, Miller's play obviously fails to live up to. Willy Loman is a childish and stupid human being, and his societal role of salesman is of only very minor consequence. And since one of the thematic intentions of the play is to present the picture of a world in which there can be no moral appeal to an order more profound than those of commerce and the machine, *Salesman* obviously cannot meet the second requirement either.

So by the test of tradition, *Death of a Salesman,* whatever else it may be, is no tragedy. But wait, Miller seems to say in **"Tragedy and the Common Man,"** by the test of *feeling* it *is* tragedy. "The tragic feeling," he writes, "is evoked when we are in the presence of a character who is ready to lay down his life, if need be, to secure one thing—his sense of personal dignity." . . . Miller is affirming, then, a continuity in tragedy that is not dependent upon historical accidents: what counts is the tragic *sense,* not the mechanical details of an abstract formula for the tragic. In spite of history, Miller is saying, in *felt* significance **Death of a Salesman** is just as much a tragedy as Sophocles' *Electra* or Shakespeare's *Hamlet.* Putting aside formulas and abstractions, let us examine it on its own grounds— not only in the light of the *kind* of play it is ("bourgeois tragedy," with a pretty weighty tradition of its own behind it from Ibsen to Clifford Odets), but also in the more universal light of the truth and depth and integrity that we expect from any piece of real literature, regardless of its time or type.

Two things will strike us when we consider Miller's focal character, Willy Loman, and both of them are in Miller's favor. First, we cannot miss the force of Willy's imagination, the energy of his language, the ferocity of his hope and rage. . . . We *know* that Willy is a pathetic fool, but we nevertheless *feel* him vividly as a vital human being. He may be mediocre, even barbaric, but he is not dull. And second, we cannot miss Willy's failure always to translate imagination and feeling into effective action. His continual inconsistencies, for example: Biff is both a "lazy bum" and "hard worker" to Willy in Act I, and in Act II Willy's advice to Biff on conducting his interview with Bill Oliver is that he should both "talk as little as possible" and "start off with a couple of . . . good stories to lighten things up." Willy says of himself at one point, and all in one breath, "I'm very well liked in Hartford. You know, the trouble is, Linda, people just don't seem to take to me." Willy's great intensity provides a recognizable touch, at least, of something like "stature." And perhaps his incoherence of mind and will resembles the "flaw" of nature or judgment usually borne by the traditional tragic hero. Like Hamlet—or at least the Hamlet that some of the critics think they see—Willy's personal tragedy is that he is inherently unable to bring himself to take the rational action necessary to save himself and put his world in order. But unlike Hamlet, Willy seems to have suffered his tragedy all his life. With reflections of the past playing continually over the present, Miller's play focuses on the end of that life when, ironically, the last opportunity for creative action remaining to Willy is the opportunity to destroy himself.

Death of a Salesman is a play remarkably lacking in action— which is not to say that it is a bad play for that reason. This lack of action, this continual dispersion of motive in Willy, is of course part of the play's theme. Intensity of feeling plus confusion of intellect yields paralysis of will. Willy's inability to act in any coherent way, an inability that the flashbacks show us is not confined only to Willy's old age, seems to be related directly to his inability to see the truth, or to his inability to distinguish between illusion and actuality, or to harmonize his dreams with his responsibilities. Charlie says to Willy, after Willy has been in effect fired by Howard, "The only thing you got in this world is what you can sell. And the funny thing is that you're a salesman, and you don't know that." Charley means that Willy is suffering because he is looking for a deeply human fulfillment in an activity which is conditioned not by what is human, but by goods and cash. (pp. 82-4)

Biff, who functions in the play as an amplification or reflection of Willy's problems, has been nurtured on Willy's dreams too. But he has been forced to see the truth. And it is the truth— his father's cheap philandering—in its impact on a nature already weakened by a diet of illusion that in turn paralyzes him. Biff and Willy are two versions of the idealist, or "dreamer" may be a better word, paralyzed by reality: Biff by the effects of disillusionment, Willy by the effects of the illusions themselves. This is how they sum themselves up at the end of the play, just before Willy's suicide: "Pop!" Biff cries, "I'm a dime a dozen, and so are you!" "I am not a dime a dozen!" Willy answers in rage. "I am Willy Loman, and you are Biff Loman!" And the tragedy—if it *is* tragedy—is that they are both right.

But why is it that Willy and Biff, both of them meant by Miller to be taken as men of potential, must be paralyzed and defeated? It seems to be a matter partly of psychological accident. Willy never had a real father, and his hard predatory older brother became his father-substitute. "Never fight fair with a stranger" was Ben's wisdom. And his faith—"When I was seventeen I walked into the jungle, and when I was twenty-one I walked out. And by God I was rich!" It seems also to be a matter partly of historical accident: times have changed. If ever there were days when essentially human values and loyalties prevailed in the world of selling, those days passed with old Dave Singleman and Willy's former boss. The business world is now run by cold young materialists like Howard, and though a wise realist like Charley may survive, there is no place in it for the all-too human dreamer and vulgarian, Willy Loman.

Psychology, history—these lead us to the third and most important cause of Willy's suffering, the great evil, the great villain of most modern writing in the realist vein—Society. Keeping in mind traditional tragedy and how it brings the audience's attention to bear on the relation between the tragic hero and the moral order implied in the background of his action, we see that Willy, unlike the traditional tragic hero, is meant to be seen as greater and better, at least in potential, than the world that destroys him. . . . Willy Loman is potentially better than his world in that he has at least incipient values that are better than the world's values. Society's guilt, as it is projected in **Death of a Salesman,** lies in its not making available ways and means for a man like Willy to implement and realize those values, and in dooming him thus to frustration, paralysis, and ultimately destruction as a human being.

The values that seem to be represented in Willy, the "good" values that function in the play as implicit criticisms of society's "bad" values, are the familiar romantic ones: nature, freedom, and the body; free self-expression and self-realization; individualism and the simple life. . . . Willy's memories of the wistaria and elms around the house when the boys were young, his vague dream of having a farm in his old age, his symbolic attempts to plant seeds in the night, and Biff's rhapsodies about the bare-chested life and young colts and the western plains, are all overshadowed and threatened by the encroaching bulwarks of apartment houses and the costly and complicated machines that sap one's resources and won't perform their functions. Willy's life is a continuum of futile worry, and his garden is a shadowed and sterile plot where the life-giving sun can no longer get in. Though Biff was a "young god" and Willy a spokesman for toughness, Society seems to have stifled these goods too: Willy has become soft and fat: Biff and Happy, inhabitants of a world where "getting ahead of the next fella" is the prime goal, find their strength and energy turning into bullying; and all of them display a mistaken and self-defeating contempt for the mind.

Another category of value against which society militates has to do with the feelings, with love, with deep and full and natural human relationship. The real capacities for love of both Willy and his boys disperses itself in meaningless and trivial philanderings. Biff and Happy yearn fruitlessly to run a ranch or a business together—the *together* is what is important—and to marry decent girls with, as they put it, "substance," just as Willy dreams of a happy old age with his children and his children's children thriving happily around him. But sterility and disharmony obtain: the boys, growing older, do not marry, and Willy's hopes for his family explode with finality in the chaos of the terrible restaurant scene in Act II. The enemy of love, of course, is society's principle of "success"—getting ahead by competition, which is the impersonal opposite of love. It is significant that Willy's vision of fulfillment is made up of characters who stand alone—Willy's father, Brother Ben, Biff as a public hero, Dave Singleman—characters who have succeeded, who stand not with but above and beyond the rest of humanity, and who do not give love but receive it, and at an impersonal distance, from cheering crowds or from faceless respectful voices at the other ends of telephone lines. This vision, created and enforced by the norms of the competitive, success-centered society that Willy lives in, is a denial of the deeply personal and human capacities for love that are inherent in Willy's nature.

A final set of values implicit in Willy's character, and defeated by the circumstances in which he finds himself, are his unformed impulses toward two of the original American virtues— self-reliance and individualism of spirit. These virtues, implying basic self-sufficiency and personal creativity, *not* domination of others, are perhaps the pure forms underlying the corrupt and destructive societal imperatives of success and getting ahead. Willy has the self-reliant skills of the artisan: he is "good at things," from polishing a car to building a front porch, and we hear of his beloved tools and his dream of using them some day to build a guest house on his dreamed-of farm for his boys and their families to stay in. But self-reliance has collapsed, the tools rust, and Willy has become the futile and pathetic victim of a machine culture. . . . If, then, the leading character and world of the play are made to interact in such a way as to engage our conviction, can we agree with Arthur Miller that, whatever the formula, the *feeling* evoked by *Death of a Salesman* succeeds in being "tragic"? I think we are likely to have to answer, No. All formulas for the tragic aside, when we say a play is tragic we are ascribing perhaps the highest literary value to it. We are saying that it is an instance of the most serious form of literature, and that it engages not only the emotions but also the intellect and the moral sense in their

fullest and most profound state of awareness. This, I think, is what *Death of a Salesman* is not able to do. For to read it as literature betrays in it a softness, a damp sentimentality, an intellectual and moral confusion that destroys the effectiveness both of its moral themes and its central character. As I have said, in portraying the victimization by society of one of its members, *Death of a Salesman* functions as both a negative criticism of society and a positive assertion of counter-values. But one simply cannot look too closely at the values implied by the play without feeling real doubt as to what they amount to, nor at certain of the characters that embody them without feeling confusion, embarrassment, possibly even boredom. (pp. 84-6)

The theme of Success, while it undergoes criticism in the play, seems always to be before us—the idea of the romance of selling, for example, is articulated by solid Charley as well as by Willy—in some desirable, even worthy manifestation. In fact, the bourgeois religion of Success haunts *Death of a Salesman* throughout, and in the end pretty well defeats the values that all along Miller had seemingly wished to pit against it.

There are many fine elements in the play, of course, perhaps the finest of them Willy himself. In Willy, the pathetic bourgeois barbarian, Miller has made an intense and true character, perhaps a nearly great one, surely a greater one than Sinclair Lewis's mythic but rather flat Babbitt. Just as Willy is a humanly great character, there are humanly great scenes, too— like the powerful and devastating restaurant scene, which corresponds to the "catastrophe" of traditional tragedy. And while Miller is surely no poet of the theatre, there are moments even of real expressive power. Though the writing is consistently bad—dull, cliché-ridden, vacuously corny—around Biff and what he stands for, Willy's talk always has great energy and validity; and his cry, "The woods are burning!", the emblem of his personal tragedy, is poetry, and as that it is memorable.

Willy's requiem, a kind of ritual elegy or coda in which, each in his own way, those who loved Willy pay tribute to him in death, is a graceful completing touch. Biff, having learned from his father's sacrifice, proclaims the mistakenness of Willy's ambitions, and will head west again; Happy, as if in duty to Willy's memory, will stay behind in the hope—probably futile—of licking the system on its own terms; Charley rhapsodizes the meaning and value that survives the defeat ("A salesman is got to dream, boy. It comes with the territory."); and Linda utters the simple human grief of one who, without thought, loved. A graceful touch structurally and tonally—that is it would have been so, a fitting recognition of the whole range of relevant human response to Willy's destruction, had the play that it completes and depends on for its significance been the intellectually coherent one it ought to have been. But appended to *Death of a Salesman* as it stands, the requiem lacks meaning; it is *only* a touch, a sentimental flourish, an exercise of dramatist's technique for its own sake.

Death of a Salesman's failure, then, lies in the failure of its intellectual content and order. So when the traditionalist critics protest that the play is not a tragedy they are right, but I think for the wrong reasons. And when Miller says it is tragedy because it creates tragic feeling, I think he is wrong, unless the audience he has in mind is an intellectually inadequate one. For the play fails simply because it is sentimental: and by that I mean that if we read it with the full awareness and intelligence that we try to bring to a great playwright like Shakespeare or a great novelist like [William] Faulkner—or even to a good non-tragic dramatist like Shaw—we discover that Miller is relying not on ideas but on a frequently self-contradictory and often quite arbitrary melange of social and moral clichés and the stock emotional responses attached to them. (pp. 87-8)

Richard J. Foster, "Confusion and Tragedy: The Failure of Miller's 'Salesman'" (reprinted by permission of the Literary Estate of Richard J. Foster; originally a lecture delivered at the University of Minnesota in 1959), in Two Modern American Tragedies: Reviews and Criticism of "Death of a Salesman" and "A Streetcar Named Desire", *edited by John D. Hurrell, Charles Scribner's Sons, 1961, pp. 82-8.*

RICHARD A. DUPREY

In the accents of ordinary speech, in the idiom of the mundane, the conventional, the everyday, Arthur Miller has pitted his not inconsequential talents as a playwright against the difficult, if not absolutely impossible, problem of fashioning a tragic hero out of the common clay of contemporary man. With **Death of A Salesman** many thought he had achieved that self-set goal and largely as a result of that play, having never really found a true success since, Miller attained something close to first rank status among American playwrights.

Arthur Miller is, in a certain sense, Henrik Ibsen warmed over for a contemporary audience. Like O'Neill, he would be a new Sophocles and like O'Neill he falls markedly short. There is too much of Ibsen in him—too much thundering, too much the pointed contemporary image, too much the topical issue. Though Miller's aseptic language has a bite that O'Neill could never have matched, it is in his didacticism, his moralizing, his constant reiteration, and his choice of character that Miller falls short. Most of these things we might forgive and it's just possible that Miller might be the one to write a contemporary tragedy, if it can be done at all in this day when we worship commonness. The common man and the tragic hero are truly contradictions in terms and we can hardly blame Miller for missing the unattainable, for failing to achieve the unachievable. (pp. 137-38)

Society will accept with no hesitation the sufferings of one of its rank and file members. There is no "catharsis" to use the technical, Aristotelian term, in seeing one's equal suffer. We are a bit relieved that we are not the victim and then we mutter, "What is all this to me? I'm sorry for the guy, but what can I do?" We say it not without callousness and then we go away. It is only in the fall of one who means something to all of us— one whose fate ritualistically or even in fact touches us all that the full truth of tragedy can be driven home to us. I don't suppose it's any accident that the word "tragedy" is derived from *tragos,* the Greek word for goat. The tragic hero becomes the sacrificial goat for all of us. He suffers for all of us, for he is somehow linked to us—he is our "super alter-ego." In a redemptive way he is led to the slaughter for all of us.

How can a stupid, virtually will-less Willie Loman be our scapegoat? Who of us can let the wistful Willie represent us? Willie's only will is in his name. Willie the insensate slob who is to be pitied as a confused wretch, not as a proxy for man. Why, there isn't even a realization, on the part of Miller's poor hero, as to what has happened to him. He falls with all the perceptiveness of a stray animal being hit by a speeding bus. The tragic hero *must,* or so both tradition and taste would have it, assume the burden of his tragic fate with human dignity in order to achieve theatre of the truly classic dimension.

Hamlet restores justice to his native land and is willing to pay the price for it, whatever that price would have to be. Macbeth is willing to take the risk for the dangerous game he played, and stand up and fight, if for nothing else, at least for consistency's sake. Oedipus accepts his exile with the dignity of a redeemer which in fact he later becomes. Willie merely goes down blindly. He lives as a mole and so he dies. There is no human triumph here, only the morbidity of a purposeless life and the lingering stench of self-murder. This is not tragedy. The protagonist finds no measure of triumph and goes from weak and appealing to beaten and dead. This certainly cannot be the divine spark of the tragic muse. If it is, better then that it should be allowed to die out.

A View from the Bridge is another Miller attempt to create a modern tragedy. He creates for us in the dulling, spiritually deadening environment of the Brooklyn waterfront a character named Eddie Carbone, longshoreman. Eddie is generous, passionate, nominally Catholic, hard-working, a man who has, almost unknown to himself, become overly fond of his niece whom he has raised from early childhood.

Growing within the heart of Eddie Carbone is this incestuous attachment to the girl—an attachment so terrible in its implications that Eddie, an honest and decent fellow, can't even admit that it exists. He can't admit it to himself. It grows and grows, however, while the young girl responds quite healthily and glowingly to the love of a young man—an illegal immigrant who has taken shelter under the Carbone roof.

Gradually, with this most secret and shameful desire gnawing at his decent soul and wreaking havoc with his judgment, Eddie drags his own house down around his ears like a tortured Samson and dies miserably, the victim of a knife, in the dust of the street.

Obviously, Eddie has acted with something short of towering virtue. He has harbored passion in his heart—a passion that had no right to be. He has foully maligned the young man who loves his niece, he turns informer and betrays the boy and his impoverished brother to the immigration authorities, he treats his long-suffering wife wretchedly . . . he does all these things and they are wicked things. There's no denying his guilt. We cannot, however, say the play is bad because Eddie does these things or because the playwright takes note of these things.

The play does fail, however, in that it doesn't achieve the stature Miller himself seems so intent on its achieving. It again falls short of tragic stature as Eddie, with his last breath, cries, "Why?" Miller doesn't permit him to know—doesn't permit him a moment of final truth in which he sees the tangled skein of guilt running through his life. This is even more critical in the play's failure to reach tragic height than the matter of Eddie's stature. It, too, however, is a factor. Those who go to the theatre would not—and one need look at our audiences to see the truth of this—accept Eddie Carbone as an equal, much less a hero in whose fall they are involved. Despite the words of John Donne that "any man's death diminishes me," and despite the brotherhood theme in our literature and drama since Whitman, our audiences are reluctant to be any man's brother—particularly if he drinks beer, belches, unloads ships, crosses himself, and is named Eddie Carbone.

There is no question that Miller is a good playwright. He misses greatness, but he writes ever so well for a theatre which is distressingly short of great talent. (pp. 138-40)

Richard A. Duprey, "An Enema for the People," in his Just Off the Aisle: The Ramblings of a Catholic

Critic *(copyright © 1962 by The Newman Press),
Newman Press, 1962, pp. 135-45.**

HENRY POPKIN

Miller expresses regret, in the Introduction to his *Collected
Plays,* that he failed to make his villains sufficiently wicked;
he thinks now that he should have represented them as being
dedicated to evil for its own sake. I suspect that most students
of *The Crucible* will feel that he has made them quite wicked
enough. For one thing, he has established their depravity by
inserting a number of clear references to the investigators and
blacklisters of his own time. He has made Proctor ask, significantly: "Is the accuser always holy now?" To the automatic
trustworthiness of accusers he has added the advantage of
confession (always efficacious for former Communists), the
necessity of naming the names of fellow-conspirators, the accusation of "an invisible crime" (witchcraft—or a crime of
thought), the dangers threatening anyone who dares to defend
the accused, the prejudice of the investigators, the absence of
adequate legal defense for the accused, and the threat that those
who protest will be charged with contempt of court. Most of
these elements constitute what might be called a political case
against the accusers and especially against the magistrates,
Danforth and Hawthorne. Miller builds an economic case as
well, suggesting that the original adult instigators of the witchcraft trials were moved by greed, particularly by a desire for
the victims' lands. The whole case is stated only in Miller's
accompanying notes, but much of it is given dramatic form.

The viciousness of the children, except for Abigail, is less
abundantly explained. We are evidently to assume that when
they make their false charges they are breaking out of the
restrictive forms of proper, pious, Puritan behavior to demand
the attention that every child requires. The same rebelliousness has led them to dance in the moonlight and to join in Tituba's
incantations. The discovery of these harmless occupations has
led then to their more destructive activity. Curiously, Miller
chooses not to show us any good children—a category to which
the Proctors' offspring surely belong. (p. 145)

Over against the bad individual, the vengeful adults, and the
lying children, Miller sets the basically sound community, in
which the saintly Rebecca Nurse's benefactions are known even
to the stranger Hale. At best, Salem is a bad, quarrelsome
place; the good community is more warmly depicted in Miller's
earlier plays, but even in Salem it exists, and it furnishes twenty
honest souls who will not confess to witchcraft, even to save
their lives. The underlying presence of the good community,
however misruled it may be, reminds us that Miller, even in
face of his own evidence, professes to believe in the basic
strength and justice of the social organism, in the possibility
of good neighbors. If he criticizes society, he does so from
within, as a participant and a believer in it.

The deliberately antique language surely reflects Miller's self-
consciousness regarding his emphatically heroic hero and the
extreme situation in which he finds himself. Issues are never
made so clear, so black and white in any of Miller's other
plays. And so, naturally, the statement of these issues must be
colored, must be, to use Bertolt Brecht's term, "alienated"
by quaint, unfamiliar ways of speech. Certainly, the peculiar
speech of *The Crucible* is not a necessity, even in a play set
in the seventeenth century. . . . The purpose of the quirkish
English of *The Crucible* is not only to give the impression of
an antique time, although that is part of it; the purpose is to

alienate us, to make us unfamiliar in this setting, to permit
distance to lend its enchantment to this bare, simplistic confrontation of good and evil, and also to keep us from making
too immediate, too naive an identification between these events
and the parallel happenings of our own time. The issues are
too simple, much more simple than the modern parallels. Language imposes a necessary complexity from without.

Any final comment must dwell upon *The Crucible* as a play
of action and suspense. It falls short as a play of ideas, which
is what it was originally intended to be. It falls short because
the parallels do not fit and because Miller has had to adulterate—the pun is intentional—Proctor's all too obvious innocence to create a specious kind of guilt for him; he is easily
exonerated of both crimes, the real one and the unreal one, so
easily that no ideas issue from the crucible of this human
destiny. And yet, *The Crucible* keeps our attention by furnish-
ing exciting crises, each one proceeding logically from its predecessor, in the lives of people in whom we have been made
to take an interest. That is a worthy intention, if it is a modest
one, and it is suitably fulfilled. (p. 146)

*Henry Popkin, "Arthur Miller's 'The Crucible'"
(copyright © 1964 by the National Council of Teachers of English; reprinted by permission of the publisher and the author), in* College English, *Vol. 26,
No. 2, November, 1964, pp. 139-46.*

R. H. GARDNER

Some have interpreted [*Death of a Salesman*] as an attack upon
the "American dream"—which I take to mean the idea that
ours is a land of unlimited opportunity in which any ragamuffin
can attain riches and any mother's son become President. Others have chosen to regard it as a contemporary *King Lear*—
the tragedy of the common old man of today, as opposed to
that of the extraordinary old man of Shakespeare's time. The
symbolic significance of the hero's name (low man) and the
fact that Mr. Miller gave him an occupation associated in the
public's mind with the average white-collar worker have both
been cited as evidence to support this view. Still others have
sought to explain the play thematically, as the tragic consequence of false dreams. (p. 123)

The American dream, as I interpret the term, embodies the
concept of this country as a land of opportunity, where the
lowliest of men may become the greatest. The means for effecting this transition are (in accordance with the nineteenth-
century spirit of rugged individualism, of which the concept
is a product) hard work, shrewdness, and luck. I am no authority on the Horatio Alger school of fiction, but I doubt that
any of his characters became successful by being stupid or
lazy. The very vehemence with which nineteenth- and early
twentieth-century immigrants applied themselves to the task of
making a living indicates that, even for those most afflicted
with this dream, there was no substitute for effort.

Next door to Willy lives a man named Charley, whose son,
Bernard, is Biff's and Happy's schoolmate. A physically unattractive, spectacles-wearing lad, Bernard's chief claim to fame
rests upon the fact that he is the boy who furnishes Biff, the
school hero, with the right answers at exam time. In exchange
for this privilege, Biff lets Bernard carry his shoulder pads into
the locker room at game time and, in other small ways, bask
in his glory—which is all the glory Bernard can aspire to,
since, as Biff explains to his tickled father, Bernard is not
"well liked."

It is, therefore, interesting to note that, not well liked though he may be, Bernard, through persistent application of his native intelligence, grows up to be an eminent lawyer who, the day Biff and Willy are finally forced to face the unpleasant facts of their lives, embarks for Washington to plead a case before the Supreme Court. That Mr. Miller chose to contrast Willy's and Biff's failures with an obvious example of how one *can* succeed in this country makes it difficult to interpret the play as an attack upon the American system, either as constituted or as popularly imagined. Bernard is, in fact, living proof of the system's effectiveness, an affirmation of the proposition that persistent application of one's talents, small though they may be, pays off. And this, after all, is the substance of the American dream.

Death of a Salesman would have represented an attack upon the system—and a telling one at that—had Mr. Miller elected to reverse the situation and make Charley the central character and Bernard a failure. Had Bernard, following the axiom that hard work is the key to success, failed, while Biff, striving only for popularity, succeeded, the American dream would have exploded with a bang. Such a play might even have been closer to the truth.

Too often do we find examples of Americans who have succeeded not because of hard work, but rather because they possess personal charm or a gift of glibness that encourages those in power to help them. Movie stars, politicians, television personalities, apart from whatever merits they may possess as individuals, usually become famous through their capacity to make a favorable impression on the public. They are, in other words, "well liked."

The very machinery by which we place people in public office helps to substantiate Willy's point of view. We know of at least one man, Warren G. Harding, who became President of the United States because he happened to radiate the sort of personal charm the behind-the-scenes politicians considered necessary to swing the election in their favor. The two-time defeat of Adlai Stevenson by Dwight Eisenhower is attributed by some political analysts to the same phenomenon. Eisenhower's professional manner made him popular with the voters; Stevenson's didn't. In view of such matters, I find it impossible to interpret *Death of a Salesman* as an attack upon the system. If anything, the reverse is true.

We thus pass to the next possibility: that Willy was meant to represent a Lear of the modern middle classes. As to this assumption, I can only say that, if such indeed was Mr. Miller's intention, why did he feel compelled to go so far? His hero is not so much a "low man" as the *lowest* man (at least from the standpoint of ability) one could conceive. He is not a person of mediocre gifts; he's just plain dumb and one of the biggest bores in all literature.

Can you imagine the groans that must have broken from the lips of those New England buyers when informed by their secretaries that Willy Loman awaited without? His rantings about the potential greatness of his children and the wonders of America are more ludicrous than pathetic. He never exhibits any deep feeling for his doggedly loyal but equally stupid wife. His concluding remark that "the woman has suffered" is not enough to convince one that he has such feelings and is, in fact, overshadowed by indications that his real reason for suicide (apart from his inability to go on) is to become a hero again in the eyes of his son.

Willy's mulish pride prevents his accepting a job from his old friend and neighbor, Charley, though that same pride does not keep him from applying for "loans" which both he and Charley know will never be repaid. Since this job might well be the solution to all his problems, Willy's refusal, from the standpoint of dramatic significance, seems less a product of his insanity than of his lifelong feeling of competition with Charley. Acceptance would have been tantamount to admitting that Charley's philosophy had proved to be the right one, and Willy simply isn't big enough a man to make such an admission.

Add to these characteristics—stupidity, lack of feeling for others, pride, inflexibility, the need to play the big shot—the fact that Willy has destroyed any chances his children might have had to succeed by deliberately indoctrinating them with ideas that, carried to their logical extreme, could only result in their becoming criminals, and you have the picture of a man who defies respect.

But Lear, one might argue, was much the same sort. There is, however, an enormous difference. Though starting out like Willy, Lear, before the play ends, *does* win our respect—first, by overcoming his insanity; second, by realizing his mistakes; and, third, by facing the consequences of those mistakes with true humility. One has only to compare the attitudes represented by the two speeches, "I am a man / More sinned against than sinning" and "I am a very foolish fond old man," to understand how radically Lear changes before the end of the play.

Willy, however, never changes. At the end he is still the same old Willy, babbling maniacally about how magnificent Biff is going to be with the $20,000 insurance money. Nor does he display the slightest understanding of his own culpability and weakness. The farthest he ventures in this direction is a momentary bewilderment as to how he could have gone wrong. Even in the last scene we find him trying to shift the blame to Biff with the accusation that the son has thrown his life away to spite the father. As for Willy's insanity, not only does he never emerge from it, but there are strong indications that his inability to perceive reality may have been the result of a mental quirk existing in him from birth. (pp. 124-28)

In answering the question of whether or not *Death of a Salesman* may be regarded as a contemporary *King Lear,* we must, then, decide whether or not a congenital madman of less than average ability can properly perform the function of a tragic hero. The very nature of tragedy, as we have defined it, will not tolerate such an assumption. Willy's problem . . . is simply too narrow and specialized to hold any universal significance. The conflict, intense though it may be, never transcends the particular. It might hold significance for students of psychiatry or an audience of mental patients, but for the comparatively healthy, the specific problems of the insane are—at least from the standpoint of drama—of only academic interest, though they may momentarily move one to amusement, horror or disgust. Otherwise, one cannot identify with them enough to feel anything stronger than curiosity or the "dumb animal" kind of pity. Nor does Linda's impassioned plea—that, since Willy is a suffering human being, "attention must be paid" to him—help to raise that suffering to a more universal level.

Because of his insanity we experience no sense of waste at Willy's death. On the contrary, we welcome it as the only means of putting him out of his misery. Biff may represent waste, but Biff is not important enough in the play to fulfill the requirements of a tragic hero. Linda might, since in her love and courage exists the germ of tragic greatness; but for her to function as such, the play would have to be rewritten so that she became the central character.

We conclude, therefore, that the "tragedy" in *Death of a Salesman* arises not so much from "false dreams" as from pathological delusions. The hero's inability to distinguish fact from fantasy leads him to develop an erroneous image of the world. When the pressures brought about by his lifelong allegiance to this image threaten to shatter it, the hero, unable to face the consequences, destroys himself. Mr. Miller has thus provided us with an impressive demonstration of one of the basic principles of Freudian psychology; he has not, however, made it into a great play. Why then, you might ask, is it effective? For there can be no doubt about its power. It stirs our emotions and, at the climax, moves us close to tears. How, if Willy is just a madman, does it manage to do this?

The secret, I think, lies in the technique. The playwright may not have given us much in the way of characters, but he has done a beautiful job putting their story together. His manipulation of time and space is like the movement of a magician's wand. We watch, mesmerized, confusing our interest in the method with interest in the story. This interest reaches its peak shortly after Willy loses his job and is having what was originally planned as a victory dinner with his two sons in a downtown restaurant. It is then that Mr. Miller drops the final fact into place. With horrified eyes, we behold the earlier scene (in which Biff, then a boy, discovers his father and the woman in the Boston hotel) intruding itself upon the festivities, and its human and dramatic significance is too much to resist; for, though Willy, in his madness, may not constitute a universal, the situation does. Like that one heart-rending line where Linda, having referred to Happy as a philandering bum, says "That's all you are, my baby," it touches something deep within us. Providing the final link in the chain, this hotel incident—in which we share the torment of a parent whose adoring child has caught him in an unsavory act—trips the mechanism, and we react to it and all that has gone before as an overpowering communication of form. It is his ability to create such patterns of meaning in a frame of much broader scope than [Tennessee] Williams that encourages one to hope that Mr. Miller may yet turn out a great play. (pp. 133-34)

> *R. H. Gardner, "Tragedy of the Lowest Man," in his* The Splintered Stage: The Decline of the American Theater *(reprinted with permission of Macmillan Publishing Company; copyright © R. H. Gardner 1965), Macmillan, 1965, pp. 122-34.*

C.W.E. BIGSBY

[In a sense], Miller could be said to have paved the way for that revival of the American theatre which started in 1959, for like O'Neill before him he was a playwright prepared to confront seriously aspects of the human situation ignored by a theatre obsessed with psychology and sociology. . . . His achievement lies not in his sensitivity to contemporary issues but in his ability to penetrate to the metaphysical implications of those issues. Nevertheless Miller never entirely shakes himself free of the influence of the commercial theatre while even in theatrical form he has tended towards conservatism. In his introduction to *The Collected Plays* . . . he disapproves of certain new trends and emphasizes that a play 'must end, and end with a climax' and that he aimed at 'a true climax based upon revealed psychological truths'. . . . In truth Miller is more of an elucidator than a pioneer. Even the 'continuous present' of *Death of a Salesman* is less adventurous when placed beside Strindberg's *A Dream Play* or even [Thornton] Wilder's *Our Town*. . . . If *Death of a Salesman* marked something of a

watershed in the development of American drama, however, its achievement was a mark of the victory of sensibility and theatrical power over intellectual and dramatic confusion. (pp. 26-7)

Miller's dramatic career started, thematically speaking, where O'Neill's left off for his first Broadway production, *All My Sons,* has parallels in Ibsen's *The Wild Duck*. . . . While a diffusion of moral purpose together with an obsessional concern with the process of plot leaves the play finally unsatisfactory, Miller does show something of Ibsen's suspicion of the ideal and sentimental attraction for the validity of illusion. The significance of Miller's work, for the purpose of this study, lies in the process whereby he progresses from this tentative affirmation of illusion towards his final belief in confrontation—a process in which the social and psychological become subordinate to the metaphysical. *All My Sons* is a play which suggests immediately both the deficiencies of Miller and the potential which made him for many the chief hope for a vital American drama, for it raises certain issues which, if they are not confronted here, do nevertheless suggest an awareness of concerns beyond the idealistic egalitarianism of a postwar world. (p. 28)

Ostensibly the moral spine of the play is embodied in the title with its overtones of Emersonian transcendentalism or the more recent Marxism of [John] Steinbeck. Joe Keller is brought from his disavowal of ultimate responsibility to his final acceptance of the rest of society as being, 'all my sons'. In the words of Steinbeck's *The Grapes of Wrath* . . . , 'Use' ta be the fambly was fust. It ain't so now. It's anybody'. It is thus not Joe's legal culpability which is of importance but his ability to accept the necessary relationship between self and society which is implied in his acceptance of the ideal of universal brotherhood. Yet if this post-war egalitarianism is indeed the core of Miller's moral purpose he subverts it in part through a failure of craft and in part through an empirical distrust of the ideal. Over-concerned, as Miller has admitted that he was, with 'telling the story' he succumbs to the temptation to over-emphasize the element of intrigue. While Joe's legal guilt should be subordinated to his moral awakening the chief crises of the play are centred on his admission of this legal guilt and on the discovery (through an outmoded theatrical device) of a direct connection between his crime and his son's death. So that his final statement that they were 'all my sons' follows proof of physical causality rather than moral conversion. More fundamentally, however, this victory of the ideal is undercut by the proliferating examples of savage and self-justifying 'idealists' which Miller presents in the persons of Chris, George—his fiancée's brother, and Jim the next-door neighbour.

If Joe Keller represents the immorality of a society which considers people to be less indispensible than an industrial process then Chris surely represents the immorality of the idealist whose motives . . . cannot be finally dissociated from individual justification. . . . His attempts to destroy his mother's illusions stem from his wish to marry Ann while Joe becomes a scapegoat for his own guilt. When he brutally insists on reading a letter in which his dead brother indicates that his death had been a suicide inspired by knowledge of his father's crime, the ideal of truth becomes suspect while 'justice' is secured only at the expense of compassion. So too George, Ann's brother, arrives at the house determined to secure some semblance of justice for his father, Joe's former partner. In effect, however, he too sees Joe as a scapegoat for his own inhumanity, an inhumanity stemming at base from idealism. On returning from the war he had refused to visit his father who as Joe's assistant had been jailed in his stead. He admits the enormity of his action, 'Annie—we did a terrible thing. We can never be forgiven. Not even to send him a card at Christmas. I didn't see him once since I got home from the war!' . . . . Even Jim, a next-door-neighbour, who as a doctor acknowledges a responsibility to man, shows the same disregard for individual men which does little to recommend the validity of his principles.

The play thus becomes a battle between justice and humanity—a battle in which Miller largely abdicates both moral and artistic control. Far from expressing a sense of conflicting principles, the moral confusion serves not as an expression of paradox but as an indication that Miller here lacks Ibsen's clarity of thought and sureness of vision. If his intellectual assent is given to the Marxian ending his sympathies clearly lie with those whose world has collapsed under the impact of truth. In this play, as in *The Wild Duck,* the idealist is left stunned by the destruction which he has caused. (pp. 29-30)

All My Sons is in many ways a compromise. It is a compromise between the social dramatist, eager to endorse the message of brotherhood and integrity, and the empiricist, all too aware of the reality behind the ideal. If his message in this play amounts essentially to an acceptance of Emersonian transcendentalism then the unresolved issues which persist below the surface reveal his flirtation with the oversoul as an uneasy relationship. Even Stockman, depicted as the outstanding example of the individual finding values in his own conscience and shunning the corruption of society, had evidenced a callousness towards his family which is hard to reconcile with his ideals. It is clear that transcendentalism does not incorporate the sense of guilt— a guilt surpassing the mere legal culpability of Joe Keller— which many of his characters feel. Neither does it account for the cruelty which seems a natural corollary of those individuals who are released from the illusions of success society. . . . It is not until *After the Fall* however that he finally resolves these issues and begins fully to understand their significance.

All My Sons remains an unsatisfactory play because of its failure to come to terms with the issues which it raises and because, in his desire to master form, Miller has produced an example of [Eugène] Scribe's *pièce bien fait.* . . . If its theme owes something to Ibsen so does its style. The painfully symbolic tree which dominates the stage at the beginning of the play is little more than ill-digested Ibsen while the final shot which echoes round the stage had similarly concluded many of the Scandinavian's plays.

Nevertheless while he demonstrates a continued concern with the moral absolutes of the nineteen-thirties he does avoid the immediate simplicities of caricature. Joe Keller is no hard-skinned business-man intent on making a fast buck at the expense of his fellow man. For all its faults *All My Sons* already demonstrates Miller's perception of issues which transcend the immediate social situation. Already his concern with identity, guilt and the need to re-affirm innocence indicate that for him the social and the psychological could ultimately be traced to their source in the metaphysical. Already, too, it is clear that even at the beginning of his career he could not fully endorse O'Neill's and Ibsen's faith in the validity of illusion and that for all his social-consciousness revolt had begun to retreat before affirmation. (pp. 31-2)

C.W.E. Bigsby, "Arthur Miller," in his Confrontation and Commitment: A Study of Contemporary American Drama, 1959-66 *(reprinted by permission of the author; ©1967 and 1968 by C.W.E. Bigsby), University of Missouri Press, 1968, pp. 26-49.*

LOIS GORDON

Willy Loman, the salesman who sacrifices himself upon the altar of the American dream, has become as much of an American culture hero as Huck Finn. Like [Mark] Twain's boy, Willy has met with enormous public success and is capable of moving the middlebrow audience as well as the intellectual sophisticate. The latter, however, has belabored *Death of a Salesman* to no end with two questions: Is the play primarily a socio-political criticism of American culture, or, does Willy Loman fall far enough to be a tragic figure?

While these issues are continually provocative, they, as Miller points out in his famous Introduction to the *Collected Plays,* have been explored ad nauseum and to the point of meaninglessness. Perhaps Miller's stand arises from his awareness that either conclusion is too simple and too pat, each utterly destroying the other's possibility. Certainly a play cannot be both tragic and social, as Eric Bentley notes, for the two forms conflict in purpose. Social drama treats the little man as victim and arouses pity but no terror (for man is too little and passive to be the tragic figure), whereas tragedy destroys the possibility of social drama, since the tragic catharsis "reconciles us to, or persuades us to disregard precisely those material conditions which the social drama calls our attention to and protests against."

It seems to me that the brilliance of *Death of a Salesman* lies precisely in its reconciliation of these apparent contrarieties, that Arthur Miller has created a sort of narrative poem whose overall purpose can be understood only by a consideration of its poetic as well as narrative elements. *Death of a Salesman,* the major American drama of the 1940s, remains unequalled in its brilliant and original fusion of realistic and poetic techniques, its richness of visual and verbal texture, and its wide range of emotional impact. (pp. 273-74)

[Miller] presents a sort of total theater and, in a sense, is the transitional genius of the American stage, 1930-68. As [T. S.] Eliot might say, on the one hand he represents the turning point of the literary current, for he continues the human values and forms of the past in the terms of the present. He concentrates upon human endeavor and heroism with the contemporary, fragmented, anguished (in existential terms) world of the middle class citizen. But on the other hand, considering once again the drama preceding and following *Death of a Salesman,* he recreates a total theater by harmonizing subjective and objective realism, or in theatrical jargon, expressionism and realism. (p. 275)

Miller finds the appropriate concrete symbols for the social realities of his time and place. He achieves through a series of emotional confrontations among the members of a single family an emotionally valid psychological statement about the particular conflicts of the American family, as well as the universal psychological family struggle. And by placing all of these events within the context of one man's thoughts, rambling over his past and present life, he achieves an internal drama of a man's epic journey to self-knowledge through experience. The entire play is, in this last sense, a recognition scene. (p. 276)

Willy, as victim of [the] inexorable social system which drives its men to frantic, all-consuming dreams of success, is doomed not only by their grandiosity but also by their inherent contradictoriness. And as social victim, he is given his elegy in the last scene by his friend Charley, who, ironically, by a kind of indifference and lack of dream, has succeeded within the American system. Charley points out that a salesman must dream of great things if he is to travel the territory "way out there in the blue," but that he is also a man who really has no trade like the carpenter, lawyer, or doctor, and when the brilliant smile that has brought his success begins to pale, he must fall, though "there is no rock bottom."

Because this portrait rings true, the play seems to indict a system that promises and indeed demands total commitment to success without regard to human values, a system that, as Willy says to Howard, will "eat the orange and throw the peel away." (pp. 276-77)

It is a system symbolized ultimately in the play by the car, that strange, uniquely American obsession, which Willy and his sons (in Willy's glorious recollection scene in the first act) polish, love and cherish as a manifestation of their manly glory. But the car is something that wears out and breaks down, and soon enough, unless one can afford an ever-shinier, newer one, he is driving an old Studebaker, smashed up many times, with a broken carburetor. He is driving the symbol of an outlived usefulness. (p. 277)

Even more than this social theme, it is undeniably Miller's psychological drama—his story of a family with its multiple loves and antagonisms, its conflicting aims and yet total involvement—that drives his audience to tears shortly after the play's beginning. Miller's psychological setting is particularly American, for we are largely a second and third generation country.

The first generation (Willy's father) has been forced, in order to make a living, to break up the family. But, while Willy's father achieved and was creative, he left behind him a wife, a young son-become-fatherless, and an older son driven to find success at the expense of love.

Willy, the second generation, is his father's victim. While he wants to love and "do right" by his sons, (His poignant "Was I right?" echoes throughout his lifetime), he is driven to use them as heirs to the kingdom that he believes must be built. Thus, he must pass on to them not only love but the doomed dream. He cannot relent even now, in the present time of the play, with his son thirty-four years old, a boy obviously not destined to achieve the greatness Willy wanted for him. Willy must still, at the expense of endless quarrels and his son's hatred and contempt, give Biff minute instructions in big business morality. . . . (p. 278)

Yet because Willy did remain at home with his mother and receive more in the way of love and human affection, he has come to know their value. For this reason he stays in New York with his wife Linda, whom he loves, rather than go to the New Continent; he looks forward to being with his boys more than travelling; and, at the play's end, he finally knows an exultant peace in a momentary spiritual communion with his son.

In recalling his father, Willy says to Ben in pride: "Please tell about Dad. I want my boys to hear. I want them to know the kind of stock they spring from." But his comment is filled with an anguish that permeates and gives richness to Willy as a man: "Dad left when I was such a baby and I never had a chance to talk to him and I still feel—kind of temporary about myself." Willy has searched for a father's approval throughout his life, through living out his fantasy of what his father was

and would have wanted. So too, Willy's sons are trapped by their father's fantasy, even more hollow for them, and its fulfillment remains their means to gain his love. (pp. 278-79)

Biff is the third generation, a representative of the sons of the middle class for whom the middle class dream has failed but for whom the only alternatives are various, all-embracing idealisms totally free from social structure. He is the beatnik, the hippie, and the radical, in whom one cannot help but see that the potent part of idealism is rebellion against the father and the father's way of life but in whom a desperate longing for father-love remains.

Hap, the younger son, less favored by nature and his father, perhaps as Willy was in comparison with Ben, has escaped the closeness with his father that destroys Biff in social terms. Thus worshipping his father from afar, Hap has never fully come to realize that phony part of his father and his father's dreams. He does have longings to be outdoors and to get away from the crippling fifty-weeks-of-work-a-year routine, but because he has never seen his father's feet of clay, he has more fully than Biff accepted his father's dream. He is not a social rebel, and he will carry on with the life of a salesman, and, one suspects, go on to the death of a salesman. He will violate the boss' wife out of some lonely desperation, as Willy sought support and solace in his Boston woman. He will also prove his manliness with fast cars and fancy talk, but again like Willy, he will never really believe in his own manliness in any mature way. Just as Willy is called a kid throughout, and referred to as the diminutive Willy by everyone except Ben, . . . Happy has been trapped by the infantile American *Playboy* magazine vision of the male.

Linda, as the eternal wife and mother, the fixed point of affection both given and received, the woman who suffers and endures, is, in many ways, the earth mother who embodies the play's ultimate moral value—love. But in the beautiful, ironic complexity of her creation, she is also Willy's and their sons' destroyer. In her love Linda has accepted Willy's greatness and his dream, but while in her admiration for Willy her love is powerful and moving, in her admiration for his dreams, it is lethal. She encourages Willy's dream, yet she will not let him leave her for the New Continent, the only realm where the dream can be fulfilled. She wants to reconcile father and son, but she attempts this in the context of Willy's false values: She cannot allow her sons to achieve that selfhood that involves denial of these values.

While these are the basic social and psychological themes of the play, they subserve its central theme. (pp. 279-80)

Death of a Salesman is a drama of a man's journey into himself; it is a man's emotional recapitulation of the experiences that have shaped him and his values, a man's confession of the dreams to which he has been committed; and it is also a man's attempt to confront, in what is ultimately a metaphysical sense, the meaning of his life and the nature of his universe.

The play has been criticized because there is no recognition scene in the traditional sense. There is a notable absence, it has been said, of the classic, tragic, articulated awareness of self-delusion and final understanding. But, in emotional terms, the entire play is really a long recognition scene. Willy's heroism and stature derive not from an intellectual grandeur but from the fact that, in an emotional way, he confronts himself and his world. As Lear in madness comes to truth, so does Willy Loman. (pp. 280-81)

The road and Willy's car, for all their social and psychological significance, have metaphysical meaning. Willy's soul can no longer travel the road; it has broken down because the road has lost meaning. That multiplicity within himself, his creative yearnings, and that part of himself which sees creativity as a moral value, now intrudes on consciousness. The woods burn, and he is thrown into a hell of disorder and conflicting value within himself. The two bags which are his salesgoods, his emblems of material success, the two bags which his sons would carry into the capitals of New England and so carry on the tradition of his dream, are now too heavy. His sons will never bear them for him, and the values which they represent are now the overwhelming burden of his existence.

The refrigerator and the house, though paid for, will never house the totality of his yearnings. They will never be the monuments to his existence that he has sought to make them. His sons, who would also have been the immortality of his dreams, his mark on the world, have failed him. As the play progresses and Willy's sons finally leave him kneeling in a bathroom to take their chippies, in consonance with the manliness they have learned from him, they leave him alone to face the void within his soul.

In the play Willy has no traditional religion; his religion has been the American Dream; his gods have been Dave Singleman, Ben, and his father, but they are now all dead—to the world and as meaningful values for himself. When Willy goes to Howard to demand his just due and winds up confronting a babbling recording machine, which he cannot turn off, he is confronting the impersonal technologic society which metes out its own impersonal justice. But he is also confronting a world without justice, a world where final truth is a babble. Ironically, the capitals which elsewhere function as symbols of the pioneer spirit and Willy's pride in his own travels, are now controlled by a child, and Willy's own sword of battle is turned against him.

The play is about *the death* of a salesman. The wares which Willy has sold, as well as being symbolic of his role in a capitalistic society, are, as Miller has said, "himself." In the final analysis, it does not matter what he sold, or in objective terms, how well he succeeded. (pp. 281-82)

Willy's death is not just his driving a car to a suicide which will bring some much needed money to his family. It is Willy's soul in triumphant revenge upon the dream that has broken him. It is a final act of will in defiance of a chaos which he cannot end, and it is made possible by his realization of a human value, his son's love, which he cannot live by, because the world is too complex, but which he can die for. If it is ironic, it is because fate, social law, psychological law, and the illusions of life are necessary, inevitable and always, of course, victorious over the individual man in the end. (p. 283)

Lois Gordon, "'Death of a Salesman': An Appreciation," in The Forties: Fiction, Poetry, Drama, edited by Warren French (copyright © 1969 by Warren French), Everett/Edwards, Inc., 1969, pp. 273-83.

JOHN H. FERRES

For a play that was often dismissed as a political tract for the times, Arthur Miller's *The Crucible* has survived uncommonly well. In addition to wide use in English and drama courses, it has become a staple of courses in American Civilization both in high school and college. In the theater its popularity continues undiminished, both in this country and abroad. . . . Next to *Death of a Salesman, The Crucible* remains Miller's most popular play. (p. 8)

The contemporary appeal of *The Crucible* can hardly be attributed to any analogy it draws between the Salem witch hunts of 1692 and Joe McCarthy's Communist hunts, however, since the majority of those who see or read the play today are probably too young to remember the Wisconsin Senator. Foreign audiences must be even less conscious of the analogy. Why then has *The Crucible* held up so well? What makes it still worth reading and performing? One can perhaps begin to answer these questions by quoting something that Miller said in an interview about his later play, *After the Fall:* "I am trying to define what a human being should be, how he can survive in today's society without having to appear to be a different person from what he basically is." Despite his seventeenth-century setting, he might have been talking about a central theme of *The Crucible,* not only for audiences of the McCarthy years but today as well. Certainly the play more than bears out Miller's belief that drama is "the art of the present tense."

Put simply, Miller believes a man must be true to himself and to his fellows, even though being untrue may be the only way to stay alive. Out of the ordeal of his personal crucible, each of the principal characters comes to know the truth about himself. A man must strip away the disguises society requires him to wear in order to confront his essential self, to discover that self in the void between being and seeming. John Proctor, refusing at the moment of truth to sell his friends, tears up his confession. . . . Once the self has been revealed by this process, a man must be true to it. Much more than Proctor's or the Cold War period, ours is a time when traditional values are eroding. The individual feels compelled to look inward for new ones. A man must either stand or fall alone, once the fog of old standards has been burned away in the crucible of crisis. Stand or fall, though, he can achieve wholeness of being or "a sense of personal inviolability," in Miller's words, that justifies new faith in himself.

The possibility for genuine self-awareness is a remote one for most people today—not so much because few are tested as Miller's characters are, but because few, to paraphrase [Henry David] Thoreau, are able to live deliberately and confront the essential facts of life. The concern of writers with the loss of the self in modern society has given rise to a whole literature of existential search for identity. It is precisely his identity, his "name," that Proctor will not surrender. The size, complexity, and diversity of our urban technological civilization, in alliance with Madison Avenue techniques for manipulating the mind and stereotyping the personality to a collection of consumer wants, make it difficult to identify the essential self beneath the layers of pseudo-self. The real measure of Proctor's heroism as a standard for today lies in this ultimate discovery that life is not worth living when lies must be told to one's self and one's friends to preserve it.

Since self-understanding implies dissent, the spirit of dissent is strong in *The Crucible,* as strong perhaps as it was among the original Puritans. In the play the word "authority" always means authority without inner sanction and always implies skepticism. Whether it ought to or not, Proctor's "I like not the smell of this 'authority'" strikes a responsive chord at present. The struggle of Proctor and the others against the theocracy's repressive, irrational, and destructive use of authority is not without parallel in times more recent than the early 1950's. Proctor's gradual rejection of it is a paradigm of the intellectual misgivings of many today. He is shown first to be merely independent-minded about going to church. His excuse is that he needs the extra workday if his farm is to produce to capacity. We learn next that the real reason is his resentment of the Reverend Mr. Parris' grasping materialism, hypocritically concealed behind a facade of piety, and also his preoccupation with his congregation's possible future in hell instead of its actual spiritual needs in the present. Though Proctor has never "desired the destruction of religion," . . . he can "see no light of God" . . . in Parris and is "sick of Hell." . . . His disillusionment is not complete, however, until he is arrested for witchcraft. At that point he is convinced that "God is dead!" (pp. 8-10)

If not dead, then certainly He has withdrawn His blessing from a system engaged in persecutions worse than the Anglican Church's persecution of the Pilgrims, from which they had sought refuge in the New World. Like many revolutionaries and reactionaries today, Danforth and Hathorne are convinced that since their cause—the extirpation of Satan and all his works from the New Canaan—is right and just, any means is justifiable in serving that end. (p. 10)

Proctor rebels against the essentially totalitarian view of society that Danforth and Hathorne uphold. It is the view that the state knows best how a man should think and act. Carried to its extreme, as it was in the witchcraft trials, it bears out [Friedrich] Nietzsche's dictum that the basis of society is the rationalization of cruelty. Proctor represents the view of society held by the Enlightenment thinkers—that society should be founded on the common good, as agreed upon by all reasonable men. This may be seen in his attitude toward adultery with Abigail. He feels guilt not so much because the Church has decreed adultery a sin as because it goes against "his own vision of decent conduct." . . . Rather than an oppressively paternal state prescribing what he does, man needs a community whose essence is human with friends who share common goals and beliefs. The witch trials demonstrate that the theocracy in effect suppresses the growth of such a community by inducing and finally forcing people to betray one another.

The position of the theocracy in 1692 was that witchcraft was both a sin and a crime, albeit an invisible one. Its very invisibility, however, showed it to be a phenomenon of great mystery and, as such, best dealt with by those qualified to deal with mysteries, namely the civil and ecclesiastical officers of the theocracy. The Proctors, and finally Hale, want no part of mystery when a man is on trial for his life. Nevertheless, Americans are a people who religious roots bind them to a belief in mystery. They are also a people whose traditions, both secular and religious, bind them to a belief in rationalism. Miller believes the American audience will side with Proctor in his encounter with Hale in Act One. When Hale arrives in Salem with armfuls of books on witchcraft, Parris takes some and remarks on how heavy they are. To Hale's reply that they are "weighted with authority," . . . Proctor says that he has heard Hale is "a sensible man" . . . and hopes he will leave some sense in Salem. (p. 11)

The Salem episode can be seen as the inevitable explosion of a social schizophrenia suppressed for sixty years. To the extent that this condition was the product of real or imagined threats from without the Puritan enclave, war with the pagan Indians or the French Papists might have been the result. But in fact the Salemite found exorcism of his schizophrenia in the hysteria of the witch trials and the sacrifice of the twenty scapegoat victims. The Reverend Mr. Hale, comprehending at last the

enormity of the witch trials, denounces them at the same moment that Proctor concludes God is dead. A churchman in conflict with the Church, a convert to humanism opposed to all he once epitomized, Hale denounces the theocratic system. Faced with a Church that will hand a person on the strength of a controversial passage of Scripture, Hale concludes that "Life . . . is God's most precious gift; no principle, however glorious, may justify the taking of it." . . . One of these Scriptural principles was the charitable obligation of each Christian to be his brother's keeper, a principle which in 1692 had been perverted to sanction malicious gossip and informing. If the witch trials marked the end of the theocracy's power in Massachusetts, it was because the theocracy had ossified into a monument to dead ideas as far as the John Proctors were concerned. . . . In the play the failure of the parents to see through the children's pretense of witchcraft is consistently ludicrous until it becomes tragic. Expecting children to behave as adults, the Puritans nevertheless refused to respect them as adults. In this way they assured rebellion against their authority, whether in the form of a childish prank that gets tragically out of hand, or the plain refusal of a Mary Warren to stand for whippings and being ordered to bed. "I am eighteen and a woman," she says. (pp. 12-13)

It must be said, in extenuation perhaps, that the Puritans believed in witchcraft much more firmly than they understood the natural penchant for mischief of the young, which could also be assigned to a diabolical source. Even had they understood, doubtless they would have felt that to dismiss the phenomenon before their eyes as a childish prank was exactly what Satan wanted them to do. They had no knowledge of child psychology, much less the psychology of hysteria. Rebecca Nurse is the only one to state what seems so obvious to us, but no one listens. A mother of eleven children, Rebecca has "seen them all through their silly seasons, and when it comes on them they will run the Devil bowlegged keeping up with their mischief. . . . A child's spirit is like a child, you can never catch it by running after it; you must stand still, and, for love, it will soon itself come back." . . .

Part of the contemporaneity of *The Crucible* lies in its universality. The right of dissent versus the claims of authority makes up a conflict as old as organized society. Both Sophocles' *Antigone* and Shaw's *Joan of Arc* afford parallels with *The Crucible* in this connection. Names like Roger Williams, Anne Hutchinson, Henry Thoreau, Martin Luther King and indeed the whole tradition of minority dissent in America come to mind. The witch trials confront the mind with another age-old question too: how should we respond to evil? and its equally ancient corollary: what if the evil lie in us? (p. 13)

[If] *The Crucible* is a social play it applies to all societies rather than to any particular one. The setting of 1692 and the sociopolitical climate of 1953 take on the quality of timelessness found in Greek or Shakespearean tragedy. The persecution of both periods becomes the persecution of any period. But although Miller is careful to show how personal interest can infect society, the play seems less concerned now with a social condition than with a moral dilemma that continues to be part of the human condition for each one of us. In the same way perhaps *King Lear* is not, at least for modern readers, a tragedy about the social, much less the cosmic, effects of a king's misrule, but rather the personal consequences of an old man's perversity for himself and his immediate circle. (p. 14)

From a literary standpoint, the best reason for reading or performing *The Crucible* today is simply that it is a good play. It has always been recognized as absorbing theater, with Miller's skill in sustaining excitement and suspense never in question. But the tendency among earlier critics was to over-stress the defects that accompany these virtues. Certainly most of the cliches indispensable to courtroom melodrama are present in the trial and prison scenes. We learn virtually nothing of the background of even the major characters, and all of them fall too neatly into groups: those who grow morally like the Proctors and Hale; those who remain static like Danforth, Hathorne and Abigail; and those who flounder somewhere in between like Parris, Tibuba and the girls. It is a question, too, whether Proctor's guilt as an adulterer is not more of a box-office device than an adequate foundation for the larger implications of the play. Structurally, the action seems slow in getting under way because of the clutter of minor characters and the clumsiness of the exposition in Act One—a clumsiness the more surprising in view of Miller's awareness that exposition is "the biggest single dramatic problem." The fourth act, too, omits the scene of confrontation between John and Abigail which the play has been building toward. Once these concessions have been made, the play can hold its own.

To classify it as a morality play is to misread it badly. The Proctors, together with Giles and Rebecca Nurse, have human failings which make their goodness more convincing, and Danforth and Hathorne among the villains are also men of conscience and principle. Their principles are not wrong simply because they are inflexible. One of the most baleful ironies in the play is that both Proctor and Danforth believe they are fighting against the same evils of irrationality and ambiguity in the administration of justice and against their anarchic influence. Locked into the "contention of the state . . . that the voice of Heaven is speaking through the children," . . . Danforth must in conscience regard attacks upon the court as attacks upon God—which is to say the theocracy. Proctor is convinced the theocracy is an offense against God because it would deny the humanity of His creatures. (His equally stern conscience reflects a kind of secular Puritanism, as rigid and self-righteous in its way as Danforth's orthodox variety). Though he must seem obtuse to us, Danforth does not know the trials are a fraud, as Proctor alleges he does; and it is conscience as well as egotism that virtually closes his mind to this possibility. He is fully aware that he has already condemned seventy-two people to death for witchcraft. . . . It is noteworthy, too, that at least one critic of the court's methods plays fast and loose with the evidence himself. Giles Corey's "proof" that Putnam is conniving to gain a neighbor's property by having his daughter cry witch upon the neighbor is that Putnam admitted as much to an "honest man" who told Corey. Since Corey refuses, however, to name the man, he cannot be called to testify and the evidence remains purely hearsay. (pp. 15-16)

As for belief in witchcraft, the characters cannot be easily classified as enlightened skeptics on the one hand and superstitious dupes on the other. Knowing their neighbors and themselves, the Proctors believe that the origin of the troubles in Salem is all too human. Yet they do not deny that witches exist, simply that there are any in Salem. And as Miller says, "Danforth seems about to conceive of truth." The girls regard witchcraft as "sport," but Abigail does choke down some chicken blood, believing in its power to kill Elizabeth. It may be, too, that in Act One Betty Parris is not merely dissembling, but in a state of shock and fearful guilt after the escapade of the previous night. . . . Given the common belief in witchcraft, which the girls may have shared, it is possible that any inclination to nervous instability combined with suspected malice

in others could have produced the psychosomatic effects found in Betty and Ruth Putnam. Similarly, in the superstitious society of the Australian aborigine, a scapegoat may become paralyzed and eventually die as a result of psychological terror induced by the witch doctor's pointing a bone at him.

The language of the play should also be remarked. Miller has received consistently poor marks for the leaden realism of the dialogue in his other plays. In this, his first "history play," he has again chosen prosaic characters, but their historical remoteness allows him to use a semiarchaic language whose stark, rough eloquence nevertheless lends the drama much of the immediacy of the realistic mode. The language is a means of escaping the bonds of conventional dramatic realism at no sacrifice of strength. On the whole the attempt is successful, since the language not only avoids the extremes of melodrama inherent in the playwright's subject, but fuses feeling and awareness in a way that had previously eluded him. Biblical-sounding, seventeenth-century speech rhythms often serve to charge events with a momentous, awesome significance, and at the end lift the language to the agonized lyricism of the speeches of the Proctors and Hale. Like the mind of its hero, the play's language is informed by a "heightened consciousness" that can manifest a much greater degree of self-awareness on the part of the characters than the tortured rhetoric of Joe Keller, Willy Loman, or Eddie Carbone. (pp. 17-18)

John H. Ferres, "Still in the Present Tense: 'The Crucible' Today," in University College Quarterly (© 1972 by the Board of Trustees of Michigan State University), Vol. 17, No. 4, May, 1972, pp. 8-18.

MARVIN KITMAN

It is hard for me to say whether I liked [*Playing for Time*] itself. Ice cream is something you like, vanilla or chocolate. The movie was a morbid, frequently horrifying drama—as sickening and shocking a television experience as I've had since *Holocaust*. . . .

The situation was not helped by the German guards coming across as music lovers, making you think at times that Auschwitz was a perverted camp in the Berkshires. Especially disturbing was the incomplete portrait of Dr. Mengele, Herr Kommandant. What did this little man in the white lab coat do, I kept thinking, aside from listening to good classical music?

The basic shortcoming was Miller's script. He never really managed to tell us why the Nazis were torturing the poor people we saw. For three hours the movie showed us how cruel the human race can be. But what did it all mean? You had to read between the lines for any kind of historical context.

Television dramas usually are starkly simple. All conflict is presented in black and white, so that we can get the point quickly. Here, suddenly, we were given subtlety. How inappropriate for a presentation recapitulating such awful events almost four decades after they occurred. The assumption, I suppose, was that everyone watching already knew what went on during World War II. I'm not so sure. Certainly for most young TV viewers, World War II is *Hogan's Heroes*.

What should Miller's message have been? I usually leave such questions to the playwright, but as a starter how about "This is bad." There seems little point in a dramatist getting involved in a project like this one unless he can shout something to the sky: "Look at what they did" or "How are we going to prevent it from ever happening again?" Miller is one of the great moralists of our day, according to the New York *Times*, yet he apparently couldn't find a lesson in all the horrifying experiences he was portraying, couldn't make a simple statement for the masses. There is more morality in an episode of M*A*S*H than in all of *Playing for Time*.

Maybe it was a mistake to have a Jew like Miller do the script in the first place. Perhaps the assignment should have gone to William Styron, who covered similar ground in *Sophie's Choice*. A WASP dramatist might at least have been appalled by the material. I'll bet Miller would have drawn a powerful moral if he was dramatizing the My Lai story. Anything about Vietnam would have stirred his rage.

Miller had our horrified attention for three hours. What a moment for him as a playwright and as a moralist. Yet he blew it. (p. 22)

Marvin Kitman, "Playing for Bucks," in The New Leader *(© 1980 by the American Labor Conference on International Affairs, Inc.), Vol. LXIII, No. 20, November 3, 1980, pp. 21-2.**

NEIL CARSON

An individual's assessment of Miller as a playwright will depend, . . . on his own biases and presuppositions. If he is primarily interested in theatrical experimentation and novelty, he will find little to interest him in the plays. Miller's explorations of form have never taken him far from the highroad of realism. . . . From the rich storehouse of theatrical trickery accumulated in this century by the expressionists, symbolists, surrealists or absurdists, Miller has borrowed practically nothing.

This is not to suggest that Miller has been indifferent to dramatic form. Quite the contrary. Indeed each new play has been a fresh attempt to find a suitable vehicle for his dramatic vision. When he has experimented with modernist techniques, however, it has always been in an effort to make his characters more psychologically real, never to render them mechanical, faceless or depersonalised. It has been to render the causal connections between things more understandable, not to suggest a world without meaning. To Miller, whatever their limitations, reason and language remain man's most reliable tools for understanding himself and his world, and attempts to discredit them or to substitute a 'poetry of the theatre' for poetry in the theatre have seemed misguided.

Miller's experiments with symbols, stylised or free-form settings, or choral figures to suggest a 'generalized significance' have not, on the whole, been particularly successful. Where he has made a significant contribution is in his creation of an effective stage speech combining the power of formal rhetoric with an impression of colloquial conversation. His most extreme experiment with deliberately heightened speech is *The Crucible* where the historical setting gives a certain licence for highly figurative dialogue. Miller's evocation of seventeenth-century language in this play has been much admired, but it seems to me less successful than his metamorphosis of contemporary American speech in several of his other works. Willy Loman's indignant or despairing outcries ('a man is not a piece of fruit' or 'the woods are burning') or Gregory Solomon's expostulations ('five hundred dollars they'll pay a lawyer to fight over a bookcase it's worth fifty cents') are random examples of the way in which Miller transmutes the idiom of the New York streets into something powerfully moving. Such

approximations of the language really used by men seem to my mind greatly superior to the 'antique' locutions of *The Crucible* or the improbable rhetoric of Linda's 'Attention, attention must be finally paid.' Miller's best dialogue is that based on the slangy, wise-cracking speech of ill-educated or bilingual New York immigrants, mainly Jewish and Italian. Within this seemingly narrow compass of regional idiom the playwright expresses a remarkable range of feeling.

Miller's contribution to the development of a distinctively American stage rhetoric is important, but it is his attempts to extend the limits of conventional realism that will win him whatever reputation he achieves as an innovator. . . . It is [the] symbiotic relationship between man and his social and intellectual environment that has always fascinated Miller, and he has gone further than any dramatist of his time in his exploration of the subjective on the stage. Earlier playwrights had used devices such as masks and soliloquies to reveal the unspoken thoughts of stage characters, but no one had dramatised the inner life of a character as Miller did in *Death of a Salesman*. . . . What is most novel is not the 'flashback' technique of dramatising events from the past so much as Miller's skilful interweaving of memory and reality. In this play Miller found a way to explode the chronological framework of conventional realism, and substitute for it the subjective reality of a continual present. It is precisely this ability of the brain to relate an event to a whole universe of memories, ideas, dreams and hopes that Miller has always wanted to duplicate on stage.

As he found in *Death of a Salesman* (and still more in *After the Fall*), however, the 'stream of consciousness' drama has as many drawbacks as advantages. Among the former is the lack of accepted conventions that enable the playwright and the audience to set boundaries to the stage world. In the absence of some means of establishing 'objective' reality, there is a real danger that instead of suggesting a universal experience, a subjective play like *After the Fall* will seem no more than self-indulgent narcissism. (pp. 149-52)

It is not the 'formalists' who are attracted to the work of Arthur Miller so much as the critics who continue to see in the drama one of man's most powerful means of exploring his own destiny. To such critics, Miller's determination to deal with the eternal themes of life, death and human purpose is one of his greatest virtues. But even Miller's admirers have not always been able to agree about the relative importance of various elements in his work.

Some see him primarily as a 'social dramatist'. Considered in this perspective, Miller is part of a tradition which descends from Ibsen through Shaw and the playwrights of the 1930s. Such dramatists, so the theory goes, present man in conflict with a repressive social environment. The underlying implications of their plays are that society is flawed, that the majority of men are too blind, superstitious or venial to see it, and that what is needed is a radical re-examination of conventional ideas in preparation for a complete overhauling of the system. . . . But few of his plays are 'social' in the usual sense of that term. Their thrust does not seem to be outward toward the changing of political systems so much as inward towards the world of private relations and emotions. This has led some critics to describe Miller as essentially an observer of the family.

There is no question that one of Miller's greatest strengths is his penetrating insight into familial relationships. But to call him a dramatist of the family is also misleading if only because the range of his plays is surprisingly narrow. The typical Miller family consists of an ill-educated father, a mother with some cultural aspirations, and two sons. Sisters, grandparents and very young children hardly ever appear nor are their problems discussed. Furthermore, the families are almost invariably lower-middle-class. There are no 'movers and shakers' in the plays, and little concern with the problems of the 'rulers', whether these are considered to be politicians, scientists, engineers, financiers, or even writers and artists. The professional class is represented almost exclusively by lawyers, and the intellectual questions raised in the plays are discussed, for the most part, by non-intellectuals.

Even within this limited family unit it is only the men who are convincingly portrayed. It is one of the weaknesses of the plays as a whole that Miller fails to create believable women. The female characters in the plays are rarely shown except in their relationship to some man. They are not presented as individuals in their own right, but rather as mothers, wives or mistresses. The moral dilemma in a Miller play is almost invariably seen from a man's point of view, and to a large extent women exist outside the arena of real moral choice, because they are either too good (Linda, Beatrice, Catherine) or too bad (Abigail). They never experience the career or identity crises that affect men, nor are they shown having trouble relating to their parents or lovers. (pp. 152-53)

Miller's tendency to see society as a 'home' and the family in terms of politics has led some critics to suggest that he should make up his mind which he is really interested in—sociology or psychoanalysis, politics or sex, Marx or Freud. But Miller never makes such distinctions. For him man is inescapably social . . . , and it is impossible to understand an individual without understanding his society. What distinguishes Miller from some other 'social' dramatists is his recognition that the social environment is a support as well as a prison. Unlike Ibsen, for example, whom he otherwise resembles, Miller never shows self-realisation as a desirable end in itself. Selfishness in its various forms of materialism or self-indulgence is one of the cardinal sins in Miller's world. Man finds his highest good in association with others. On the other hand, that association must be voluntary, not coerced. Thus the other evil in the plays is an uncritical other-directedness (the handing over of conscience to others, or the pathetic desire to be thought well of by the neighbours). Miller focuses on the point of intersection between the inner and outer worlds, sometimes approaching it from one side, sometimes from the other.

It becomes apparent, I think, that in the final analysis Miller can best be described as a religious writer. He is not so much concerned with establishing utopias as with saving souls. This is why he is always more interested in the individual than the group. Systems—whether they be capitalism, socialism, McCarthyism or even Nazism—are not Miller's prime concern. They provide the fire in which the hero is tested. But it is not the nature of the precipitating crises that interests Miller; it is the way in which the protagonist responds in that crisis. It is in this context that one can speak of 'sins' and indeed Miller

sometimes seems almost medieval in his concern with such topics as conscience, presumption, despair and faith. Miller is quintessentially an explorer of the shadowy region between pride and guilt. His characters are a peculiar combination of insight and blindness, doubt and assertiveness, which makes them alternately confront and avoid their innermost selves. To the tangled pathways between self-criticism and self-justification there is probably no better guide.

Miller's heroes undoubtedly reflect many of the playwright's personal concerns. His entire career as a writer can be seen as an attempt to find justification for his own hope. In his youth he believed in the inevitability of socialism; later he sought salvation in personal relationships; in his most recent work he seems to have formulated for himself a kind of existential optimism. Miller's disillusion with an early faith and determined effort to find an acceptable substitute are in many ways the quintessential 'modern' experience. They can be duplicated repeatedly in the pages of literature from [William] Wordsworth at the beginning of the nineteenth century through [Alfred, Lord] Tennyson, [Thomas] Carlyle, John Stuart Mill up to the present. Where Miller differs from many of his contemporaries, however, is in his guarded optimism in the face of the great mass of evidence that has accumulated in the twentieth century to undermine it. This is partly a matter of temperament, and partly because his experiences have been different from those of the European intellectuals who have been most articulate in their expressions of despair and nihilism. The Depression (the most formative crisis in Miller's life) was in many ways a positive force in that it often brought people together and elicited the best from individuals. The experiences of war, occupation and the Nazi terror (which were the nursery of existentialism and absurdism) tended to alienate people and bring out the worst in human nature. Miller's refusal to believe that man is a helpless victim of circumstances, therefore, is not so much his 'naïveté' as his exposure to different facts.

Miller is the spokesman for those who yearn for the comfortable certainty of a belief, but whose critical intelligence will not allow them to accept the consolations of traditional religions. What seems certain to ensure his continued popularity in a world grown weary of the defeatism of so much modern literature is his hopefulness. Like the Puritan theologians of old, Miller has come to realise that the greatest enemy to life is not doubt, but despair. And against despair, the individual has only faith and hope. In *Playing for Time* Miller presents the artist as the individual who refuses to avert his eyes from the horrors of the concentration camp in order that he may bear witness before heaven and mankind. It is Miller's chief merit as an artist that the evidence he presents in his plays seems, on the whole, more balanced than that of some of his contemporaries. If he has not hesitated to look on the evil in himself and in mankind, neither has he been willing to shut his eyes to the good. (pp. 154-56)

Neil Carson, in his Arthur Miller *(reprinted by permission of Grove Press, Inc.; copyright © 1982 by Neil Carson), Grove Press, 1982, 167 p.*

Farley (McGill) Mowat

1921-

Canadian novelist, short story writer, nonfiction writer, scriptwriter, and editor.

Mowat is a popular and prolific writer for young people and adults. A naturalist, Mowat is an avid lover of the Canadian wilderness, of animals, and of nature and peoples unspoiled by the corruption of technological advances. Much of his writing is based upon his own experiences and adventures.

Mowat has been criticized for mixing fiction with fact, especially in his controversial book *People of the Deer*, in which he blames the Canadian government and traders for the ruin of a once-flourishing Eskimo tribe. He apparently feels that a writer's message is more important than accurate data, for in defense of his "subjective nonfiction" he has said, "Never let facts interfere with the truth."

Perhaps Mowat's best-known work for young adults is *Lost in the Barrens*, which won the Governor General's Award in 1957. This work effectively portrays his concern with the individual's struggle against natural forces. For Mowat, true human dignity lies in the ability to achieve an existence in harmony with nature. Mowat has a special affinity for young adults who, he feels, are not yet affected by the dehumanization of the modern world. He has written: "Writing for children, or rather for young people, is a particular pleasure since most of them have not yet been molded into the formal shapes of technological man; they remain really natural, and therefore really human in my eyes."

(See also *Contemporary Authors*, Vols. 1-4, rev. ed.; *Contemporary Authors New Revision Series*, Vol. 4; and *Something about the Author*, Vol. 3.)

Photograph by Paul Orenstein

ALBERT HUBBELL

["**People of the Deer**"] is a book about the inland Eskimos of the Barrens—the half-million square miles of plains, lakes, and low hills west of Hudson Bay. It is a record of two years the author spent among one tribe of these people—the Ihalmiut—in the late nineteen-forties, and in that sense is a travel book. But it is more, too, because Mr. Mowat is something of a fanatic about the tribe—or what is left of it after twenty years of slow starvation. His book is another contribution to the growing literature that employs a new approach in evaluating primitive men and cultures, one that quite properly avoids judging aboriginal societies by standards and ethical codes of higher—or at least different—civilizations. (p. 138)

"**People of the Deer**" is a complete amateur anthropology. It is probably a definitive one, too, for the Ihalmiut are at the end of their tether. In 1900, Mowat says, thousands of them roamed the Barrens and prospered off the deer; today, there are less than forty left, among them only two women able to bear children. Until the first white traders came to the fringes of their territory, the Ihalmiut lived as they had since the Stone Age. Four times a year, when the caribou migrated, the men of the tribe intercepted the hordes at selected passes and fords and slaughtered them with bows and spears. . . . When the

traders started edging into the Barrens, they wanted fox pelts. They gave the Ihalmiut rifles and ammunition and persuaded them to shoot the arctic fox, and in exchange for the pelts gave them more ammunition and food—not meat, which had been the tribe's sole diet from earliest times, but white flour, sugar, lard, and baking powder. . . . Around the end of the nineteen-twenties, the world market for arctic-fox fur collapsed and the traders decamped, leaving the Ihalmiut with rifles for which there was no ammunition. The supplies of white man's food, of course, stopped, too. The Eskimos, having relied for a generation on what was for them an unnatural diet, began to starve. . . . The Ihalmiut are puzzled by what has happened to them, but they bear no rancor. Rancor is apparently a development of more complicated civilizations. (pp. 138-39)

To study the Ihalmiut, Mowat not only lived with them but undertook to learn the Eskimo language—something few white explorers or travellers have ever bothered to do. Two men of the tribe instructed him. Mowat did not know it at the time, but they devised a "basic" Eskimo for his lessons, teaching him only one noun, and none of its variants, for a given object, and only one verb form for an action. The Ihalmiut spoke to him solely in this pidgin tongue and used it exclusively when talking among themselves in his presence. . . . He later became aware that the language is extraordinarily flexible and complex, that it can express many shades of meaning and many abstract thoughts, and that, grammatically, it is one of the toughest languages in the world, with verbs that can have up to five hundred endings and nouns that have nine cases. Mowat cites this experience as typical of the Eskimos' code of politeness and helpfulness; he believes that the Ihalmiut, who have respect for the white man but no very high opinion of his powers, felt that he would never be able to learn their language properly in the year or so he would be among them. (pp. 139-40)

Mowat heard stories of the famines that have depleted the Ihalmiut in recent years, and of winters when whole families sat huddled in their igloos, the useless rifle propped against the wall, and waited for death. As a consequence, he is not disposed to censure the people for infanticide or for their refusal to feed the old when the grinding pressure of starvation is on them—two of the Eskimos' classic crimes in the eyes of missionaries and other outsiders. (p. 140)

It is not often that a writer finds himself the sole chronicler of a whole human society, even of a microcosmic one like the Ihalmiut, and Mowat has done marvellously well at the job, despite a stylistic looseness and a tendency to formlessness. Also, his justifiable anger at the Canadian government's neglect of the Ihalmiut, who are its wards, intrudes in places where it doesn't belong, but then, as I said, Mowat is something of a fanatic on this subject. His book, just the same, is a fine one. (pp. 140-41)

Albert Hubbell, "Two from Up North," in The New Yorker *(© 1952 by The New Yorker Magazine, Inc.), Vol. XXVIII, No. 10, April 26, 1952, pp. 138-41.***

T. MORRIS LONGSTRETH

["**People of the Deer**"] issues from [Mowat's] fondness for these People of the Deer and from his concern over their plight. Between these covers he has packed exploration of a region seen by few, an unforgettably vivid cyclorama of the caribou, an ethnological study of the Ihalmiut, an unconscious full-length portrait of himself, and a peppery denunciation of governmental paralysis or worse.

It is a serious moral document which would have been strengthened by less passion. But this Canadian war veteran was too outraged by situations brought home to him by human anguish to present both sides of the picture. He is right to be outraged, and fortunately he goes beyond sweeping statements and accusations to outline practical steps looking to a more intelligent conduct toward the northern races. One hopes his single-handed crusade will have effect.

The general reader, however, will thank Mr. Mowat chiefly for his striking account of the caribou and his intimate revelation of the Ihalmiut. He came to love these gentle, generous, and friendly Eskimos, and his feeling for them carried him through vicissitudes of a life rigorous in the extreme. The author builds up this life for us by factual details which only a sharp-eyed sharer would summon. Nearly every phase of Ihalmiut life is conveyed, and some phases are revolting. Yet the squeamish had better persevere, for nothing is magnified for sensation's sake, and the good far outweighs the bad.

T. Morris Longstreth, "'Song-Cousin's' Tribute," in The Christian Science Monitor *(reprinted by permission from* The Christian Science Monitor; *© 1952 The Christian Science Publishing Society; all rights reserved), May 1, 1952, p. 15.*

CLIFFORD WILSON

A very long review would be needed to point out all the errors and misleading statements in [*People of the Deer,* a] well-written and plausible book, and to document them with references, so the present review will have to be confined to a discussion of the main points the author tries to make, in his charges against white men in the Canadian Arctic. (pp. 295-96)

[Perhaps] the weakest point in the whole book is that his tale of the starvation of the "Ihalmiut" is based on accounts given to him by a couple of Eskimos who spoke no English. Mr. Mowat tries to persuade us that he understood what they were saying to him. But since it takes years of contact with the Eskimos to understand their simplest phrases, and since he spent only 47 days in the Barrens, his long and involved tale of their misfortunes during the past half-century can hardly be accurate.

The author's "statistics" of their population, given on page 260, on which his claims of decimation are largely based, are vague, to say the least: "There *must have been* more than a thousand in 1880 and *probably* twice that many in *the later years*." (The italics are not his.) Indeed, one cannot escape the impression that he prefers readability to accuracy, and that, as he says on page 165, he believes "It matters little whether things happened as they are said to have happened." (p. 296)

Clifford Wilson, in his review of "People of the Deer," in The Canadian Historical Review *(© University of Toronto Press 1952), Vol. XXXIII, No. 3, September, 1952, pp. 295-96.*

THE TIMES LITERARY SUPPLEMENT

[*People of the Deer*] describes what has happened to the deer and the people since the white man began to trade in the Arctic. . . . It is at once a confession of regained faith in humanity by contact with a remnant of its most primitive and hard-pressed elements, a notable field study in human ecology and anthropology, and a sombre crusade against the decimation of Arctic natives by the fluctuations in the fur trade. . . .

[Mr. Mowat] traces with a beautiful clarity the material and spiritual bonds between land, deer and people, and the precarious ecological balance which had been struck between the forefathers of this handful of men and the antlered multitude. The fat of this forbidding land, he points out, is literally the fat of the deer. Without it the Ihalmiut die though their rivers teem with fish, their sky with birds and their land with other animals, just as the health of the coastal Eskimo depends absolutely on the blubber of sea mammals. Disaster, of which Mr. Mowat saw the concluding stages, came to the tribe when the trading companies presented them with guns and ammunition and persuaded them to hunt the white fox. . . .

However reluctant one may be to go the whole way with [Mr. Mowat] in his merciless analysis of the past of this people or in his passionate plea that in cherishing the future of the Arctic natives we defend our own economic interests and our strategic security, there is no doubt that this is the most powerful book to come out of the Arctic for some years. Much of its story is so tragic that any words recording it would wring the heart. But many of these pages do much more than that, they strongly uplift it. When Mr. Mowat transcribes the fantastic myth of the creation of the Ihalmiut world, he does so in the simplest prose, and makes a fine poem.

"A Barren Land," in The Times Literary Supplement *(© Times Newspapers Ltd. (London) 1952; reproduced from* The Times Literary Supplement *by permission), No. 2641, September 12, 1952, p. 599.*

SCOTT YOUNG

A literary battle without modern parallel in Canada has been banging and crashing just below the horizon for the last few months. The fight is over the book called **"People of the Deer"** by Farley Mowat. . . . The antagonists are the author and a magazine called *The Beaver*, which is published by the Hudson's Bay Company.

In its June issue *The Beaver*, among whose functions is that of professional debunker of all views of the North which do not conform to the Hudson's Bay Company's long and not entirely distinguished experience in that area, blasted Mowat's book in a review. . . . The review was written by A. E. Porsild, an Arctic expert employed by the Government, which Mowat criticizes more strongly even than northern traders in his book. . . .

Mowat did write a reply to *The Beaver's* review, admitting certain errors, all minor, but in all major aspects answering the charges levelled at him by the reviewer. *The Beaver* has refused to publish this reply in its editorial columns. (p. 16)

One factor which gives this controversy an importance (even above the moral one that an author called a liar has been refused the right to defend himself) is that the book has been such a success here and abroad. . . . [A] French anthropologist who is also an Eskimo linguist has called the book "certainly one of the best books ever written about the Eskimo," and he also verified in general material Mowat gained (in the Keewatin district of the Northwest Territories) by conversations with Eskimos of the dwindling tribe of caribou-eaters called the *Ihalmiut* with which the book is mainly concerned. This French anthropologist thus supported Mowat on a point which was the object of some of *The Beaver's* strongest ridicule—the very possibility that Mowat could learn the Eskimo tongue well enough to understand it, after only a few months of work at it. If one is to believe *The Beaver*, most career Arctic specialists find no time to learn the language.

"People of the Deer" is, to me and to many other readers, a magnificent book, an unforgettable portrayal of the present and past of a victimized people. Its enthusiastic public acceptance here and abroad attests its basic appeal, which is that of any vital, well told story. The attempts by these old Arctic hands of the Hudson's Bay Company and the government to discredit it seem to reflect the narrowness of their approach to the Eskimo problem. Any real humanist among them must admit that the major contentions of the book are true—that before we came the Eskimos were happy aborigines, able to combat their natural enemies, but that the weapons and diseases of white men have corrupted them to the extent that they no longer can cope with the forces that are destroying them.

I write this in the hope that the attempted discrediting of Farley Mowat and his book by *The Beaver* and its voice-of-government review can be halted. I have read the book, *The Beaver* review, Mowat's reply, and a letter stating the Hudson's Bay Company's refusal to print that reply. Most of Mowat's errors, which he admits in his reply, seem minor—such things as whether caribou do have antlers while carrying calves; one or two misleading travel details which were seized upon by the

reviewer; and so on. His major premise, that the Eskimos have been badly treated and that unless something is done quickly, they will soon become extinct, or a pitiful race of trading post bums, is so well known that it cannot be refuted. Indeed, *The Beaver*, review makes no serious effort to argue against that premise, merely attempting by concentration on niggling details to damn the entire book. If it were possible to discredit Einstein by ridiculing his haircuts, or to charge the entire Hudson's Bay Company with moral delinquency on the basis of the peccadillos of a few of its trading post factors, then it would be possible to to discredit Mowat by the few real inaccuracies to which *The Beaver* drew attention. Fortunately, we are all smarter than that. Or I hope we are anyway. (pp. 16,42)

Scott Young, "Storm Out of the Arctic" (copyright ©1952 by Saturday Night; *reprinted by permission of the author), in* Saturday Night, *Vol. 69, No. 2, October 18, 1952, pp. 16,42.*

JANET ADAM SMITH

In 1935 a boy of fifteen looked out of the train window on the line from Winnipeg to Fort Churchill in Hudson's Bay; there, across the track, flowed a great brown river a quarter of a mile wide—not of water, but of caribou: the annual migration which the first French explorers had called *la Foule*. From that moment he was infected with the Arctic fever; and it was this disease of the imagination that brought him back to the Barren Lands in 1947. He was dropped by aeroplane on a frozen lake near an abandoned trading-post. . . . That summer Mr. Mowat . . . made his first contacts with the Eskimos of the Barrens, the Ihalmiut, before canoeing back to Churchill. Next year, with a zoologist companion, he came back to learn the language of the Ihalmiut, study the deer, and follow their migration north to Angkuni Lake.

Such was the plain record of Mr. Mowat's travels; what raises [*People of the Deer*] well above the level of plain records, however freshly written, is his power of grasping the underlying pattern of life in the Barrens as well as enduring its physical rigours. He noticed how, as the deer swept over the isthmus by Angkuni, other life came too, with the ravens, gyrfalcons and gulls wheeling and swooping round the herd, the wolves and silver foxes barking on the outskirts. The new light in the face of the Eskimo Ohoto

> was not simply due to the prospect of gorging on meat. Rather it was as if the endless lines of the deer imparted to Ohoto something of their own immeasurable vitality. It was borne in on me again that the affinity between the Ihalmiut and the deer was more than a merely physical tie.

By living with this tribe, and learning their language, he came to piece together their side of the history which he had learnt in part from official statistics and reports. . . .

[There] is an undercurrent of anger throughout the narrative which swells in the last chapter to a considered denunciation of official policy towards the Ihalmiut. The Canadian Government has at moments been kind; but kindness alone, not backed by full understanding, may have disastrous results. There were only a few families of Ihalmiut in 1948; there are probably fewer to-day; but in his white-heat of feeling Mr. Mowat persuades us that it is not just a question of a tiny minority having a raw deal, but of men tragically misunderstanding their fellow-men and, through them, the forces of life itself—a lesson of far wider application than in the Barrens. Mr. Mowat is practical: he suggest measures, he can point to the Greenland Eskimos as an example of how a primitive race can be encouraged to develop along lines in harmony with their natures and the land they live in. But this can never be done by persons "whose interests in the land were measured in dollars and cents."

Mr. Mowat impresses us, in the last instance, because he has a poet's as well as an ecologist's grasp of the connection between a landscape and the life in it. The Mountie whom he once asked about the Barrens was prompt in his reaction: "That damn and bloody space—it just goes on and on until it makes you want to cry, or scream—or cut your own damn throat." Mr. Mowat makes us see it in different terms: the huddle of tents, the mounds of bleached bones and antlers, the brown river of deer, the line of the Inukok stretching into the distance—those stone men whom the Ihalmiut traveller built as he passed, not signposts, nor landmarks, but "the guardians who stolidly resisted the impalpable menace of space uncircumscribed, which can unhinge the finite minds of men."

Janet Adam Smith, "In the Barrens," in The New Statesman & Nation (© 1952 The Statesman & Nation Publishing Co. Ltd), Vol. XLIV, No. 1129, October 25, 1952, p. 486.

A. E. PORSILD

In his recent article: "Storm over the Arctic" [see excerpt above], Mr. Young imputes certain rather farfetched motives for my review of Farley Mowat's **"People of the Deer"** . . . . Actually my review was quite objective, and written solely from the point of view of a scientist whose work has brought him in close contact with the Arctic and with Arctic problems, but not necessarily with the actual responsibility of administration of the North. . . .

I speak the language of the Eskimo, I know a good deal about their customs and problems, and I am deeply concerned with their future welfare, for I have found among them some of the finest people I have ever known.

Unfortunately, the problem of what to do with and for the Eskimo is a very difficult one. And for it there is no entirely satisfactory solution because conditions vary so greatly from tribe to tribe over the many thousand miles of Arctic coastline along which our few thousand Eskimo live. (p. 17)

It is well known that for a number of years there has been a decline and a worsening of conditions among the more primitive Eskimo tribes in Canada. Owing to improved means of transportation, even the most remote tribes have at last come into contact with civilization. The impact upon them has almost invariably been disastrous because they were unprepared for it, and unable quickly to adapt themselves to the white man's food, his tools and his diseases. But the question whether the Government could or should have prevented this contact, is at best academic. It may safely be assumed that if it had, there would have been no lack of critics who would have found such a policy high-handed and unrealistic.

This lengthy preamble is to show that I am interested in the future of the Eskimo for their own sake and that, Mr. Young notwithstanding, my review of **"People of the Deer"** was not a "whitewash" of the policy of the Canadian Government in dealing with our native peoples any more than it was a defence of the past or present policy of our northern trading companies.

That of the Hudson's Bay Company, at least, can well speak for itself. My only concern was to show that Mowat's book, notwithstanding the favorable views expressed by numerous reviewers, is misleading and utterly worthless as a crusade against alleged maladministration, because the premises upon which its conclusions are built are wrong or even fictitious.

To prove this, it was necessary to cite some of the more glaring examples of errors and misleading statements. Scott Young pronounces these errors unimportant and trivial. They might be in a work of fiction, but not in a book which claims to be factual. If the author of such a book, whether through ignorance or by design, is consistently wrong about his "facts", how can his conclusions be other than worthless?

In posing as an authority on Eskimo and Arctic problems, Mowat leads his readers to believe that he has lived in the Arctic for considerable time, or to be exact, two years. Thus, on P. 89, when speaking about the Barrenlands, he says: ". . . after two years in the land. . ." and in a letter printed in *The Globe and Mail* on March 31, 1952, he categorically states: "I myself spent two years in the so-called barrenlands."

An examination of official reports and Government files actually shows that Mowat was in the Barrenlands no more than 47 days altogether and that, during 1947 and 1948, he spent no more than six months all told in the Northwest Territories. Such "inaccuracies" may seem trivial to Mr. Young but they make me wonder about the reliability of Mowat's memory. . . . (pp. 17-18)

My argument that Mowat could not possibly have attained even an elementary knowledge of the Eskimo language, does not impress Scott Young as much as Mowat's claim, that an unnamed French anthopologist and linguist verbally pronounced his book "one of the best ever written on Eskimo". One wonders if this is what Mr. Young means by "a balanced and unbiased view"? Or take the now famous case of the dried deer tongues. Mowat, on P. 78 of his book, reported that "one outpost of a world-famous trading concern actually encouraged the sale of tremendous quantities of ammunition to the Northern Indians by offering to buy all the deer tongues that were brought in! Many thousands of dried deer tongues passed through that post, while many thousands of carcasses, stripped only of their tongues, remained to rot in the spring thaws." Fortunately, as pointed out in the March, 1952, issue of *Beaver*, "deer tongue", in northern trade parlance means the leaf of a certain plant, used in the flavoring of tobacco!. . . [Also Mowat has not] explained that mysterious tribe—the Ihalmiut—that, as far as I can see, was created solely as a vehicle for his attack on Government administration and on the wicked traders. There never was such a tribe. Nor is there even a shred of evidence in support of his claim that there ever was a tribe of Eskimo, several thousand strong, living on the upper Kazan River. In fact, the very idea that there might ever have been enough game to support such numbers of people, is utterly ridiculous. (p. 18)

Most telling is Mowat's claim that he obtained his evidence and background information, including such matters as folklore, history and religion, direct from Eskimo who knew no English at all, and without the aid of an interpreter. To get around this difficulty he claims to have learned to speak the Eskimo language in just one month. (pp. 18-19)

To have learned French or German in a month's time would have been a considerable accomplishment. Since philologists agree Eskimoic is one of the most complicated languages known, this claim shows how utterly worthless his evidence is.

To judge from the Oct. 18 article by Scott Young, and from the numerous favorable reviews of **"People of the Deer"**, Mowat's style must somehow be convincing to writers who know little or nothing about the Arctic and who do not care to check statements. But it seems to me that such reviewers should be content to discuss only the literary merits or demerits. . . . (p. 19)

> *A. E. Porsild, "Arctic Storm in Reverse" (copyright © 1952 by Saturday Night; reprinted by permission of the Literary Estate of A. E. Porsild), in Saturday Night, Vol. 69, No. 3, October 25, 1952, pp. 17-19.*

HOWARD BOSTON

Across northern Canada stretch the Barrens, a region of swamps in summer and windswept, ice-encrusted plains in winter. Into this forbidding country, young Jamie Macnair and his Cree friend Awasin [the protagonists of **"Lost in the Barrens"**] accompany a hunting party of desperate Chipeweyans—the tribe of the Deer Eaters. The boys are separated from the rest of the group, and, with winter coming, are forced to hole up. How they face up to their predicament and learn—the hard way—to go along with nature rather than to fight it is the main theme. Illuminating it are the struggle for life's necessities; encounters with caribou, wolverine, grizzly bear and supposedly hostile Eskimos; and the discovery of Viking cairns.

Survival in the wilds has been a favorite theme since [Daniel Defoe's] "Robinson Crusoe." Here Farley Mowat develops it skillfully. . . . [He] seems to know all there is to know about the Barrens—as well as a good deal about human nature under stress. An engrossing, well-constructed tale, sharp with the tang of the north land.

> *Howard Boston, "Fight for Survival," in The New York Times Book Review (© 1956 by The New York Times Company; reprinted by permission), August 12, 1956, p. 24.*

ROSE FELD

To [**"The Dog Who Wouldn't Be"**], the portrait of Mutt, puppy and dog, Mr. Mowat brings a tender memory, a sharp eye for observation and a gift of expression that holds both poetry and humor. The development of Mutt as a hunting dog, from the day of his first hunt when he frightened the ducks by racing and screaming at them to the high point in his career when, on a bet, he retrieved a stuffed grouse for want of the real thing, is told with a nostalgic warmth rooted in a man's devotion to a beloved childhood friend.

Besides painting the portrait of an unusual dog, Mr. Mowat also paints the portrait of the author as a boy. The same adjective, "unusual," may be applied to him, for his interests and his pursuits were out of the ordinary. Encouraged by teachers and parents, the boy early showed the marks of an ardent naturalist.

Knowledgefully and amusingly, Mr. Mowat writes of his association with snakes, gophers, cormorants, owls and skunks. . . .

This book is one of reminiscence rather than fiction and is the work of an inspired nature writer.

> *Rose Feld, "Yes, Sir, This Dog Could Do Anything," in New York Herald Tribune Book Review (© I.H.T. Corporation; reprinted by permission), August 18, 1957, p. 8.*

HAL BORLAND

It would be much simpler to describe [**"The Dog Who Wouldn't Be"**] as a dog story, a good tale about an unusual dog, and let it go at that. But Mutt wasn't just a dog—indeed, as Farley Mowat says, Mutt was never content with being just a dog; he always wanted to be something more, and he pretty well succeeded. This is a good deal more than a dog story, for it is the story of a boy and his parents and dozens of neighbors and friends, tame and wild, human and almost-human. And it is a story about Canada, both the high, dry plains and the well watered area.

Mutt was a dog that Farley Mowat's mother bought from a small boy peddling baby ducks. The pup was an afterthought and cost Mrs. Mowat four cents. . . . This is his story, with the variations noted above; it is, in a sense, also the story of the Mowat family during a number of turbulent, fantastic years. Mutt was naturally in the midst of every predicament, every trial, every triumph.

Life in Canada, particularly in Saskatchewan, was much like life in the Midwest in the United States at the same time, some thirty years ago. And young Farley was a typical boy. . . . Farley and his father, and Mutt of course, had such duck hunts as never before occurred. They had vacations on a dry-land slough, with Mutt making new traditions, new folk lore. Mutt retrieved a stuffed partridge and won a fantastic bet. Mutt climbed ladders and trees, learned to walk fence-tops like a cat. . . .

If this seems to be the usual material of boy-dog tales, set that down to the deadening effect of summarization. Add to it the nature lore—Farley Mowat is a naturalist of note—and the human anecdote, salt it all with uninhibited humor, and you have a grand tale, one of the best stories of boyhood this reviewer has read in a long time.

> *Hal Borland, "The Story of Mutt," in The New York Times Book Review (© 1957 by The New York Times Company; reprinted by permission), August 18, 1957, p. 10.*

WALTER O'HEARN

Canada's angriest young man is Farley Mowat, who writes out of a desperate concern for the vanishing Eskimo. . . .

Mr. Mowat has told some of [the Ihalmiut's story] in his earlier book **"People of the Deer."** Last year, with military penetration and bureaucratic muddle added to their woes, the People of the Deer, the proto-Eskimo, were no longer a dying tribe. Only a handful were left. Soon they will have vanished.

Mr. Mowat's anger is honest; it is understandable. In rich words, whose poetry only rarely spills over to become rhetoric, he has built a solid emotional case. The Deer People, who breed leaders and rivalries worthy of a great empire, were fascinating and a writer's understanding made them lovable. Their lives and deaths were tragic, because they were heroic. They were never degraded into pathos.

When the author takes off to indict the whole Canadian approach to the Eskimo problem [in **"The Desperate People"**], he may be on more dubious ground. "We Canadians looked askance at the South African exponents of *apartheid*," he writes, "at the segregationists in the southern United States; and we gazed with holy horror upon the inhumanities which we were told were being perpetrated upon primitive people under the rule of communism. Indeed, we looked virtuously in all directions; except northward into our own land."

How can a reviewer who has never seen an Eskimo confront this indictment? By noting, perhaps, that Canadians recently have shown a desperate if muddled concern for the northern aborigine. By observing—as Mr. Mowat himself observes—that authorities on Northern affairs have taken issue with him. By conceding something he virtually admits, an anti-missionary, anti-government bias.

Nevertheless if we are at last fumbling toward a grasp of the Eskimo problem, the goading of Farley Mowat is one of the reasons. He has convictions and he can express them in prose that sears the conscience.

Walter O'Hearn, "People of the Deer," in The New York Times Book Review (© 1959 by The New York Times Company; reprinted by permission), November 1, 1959, p. 12.

IVAN SANDERSON

One of the most difficult tasks any author can perform is to write a book that cannot be put down once one has started reading it—particularly when its theme is a pitiable cry in a wilderness. Farley Mowat has succeeded in achieving this with **"The Desperate People,"** . . . a well-written, sensitive, and lucid account of one of the most horrible sidelights of modern history.

It is hard, if not impossible, even to attempt to review a book when its contents raise your most elemental passions to such a white heat that you find tears in your eyes over and over again—tears as much of frustration as of horror and fury. Yet this book was never by the wildest stretch of imagination intended as a tear-jerker. To the contrary, it is a straightforward report and documented by the author with tape-recordings of the accounts of those persons whose personal histories are chronicled therein. Withal, the book is a righteous howl of anguish on the part of a man with a soul, rendered the more dramatically ghastly by the fact that he predicted these events almost to the sentence eight years ago. It is a damning indictment of just about every aspect of our culture, ethics, and religion—but most of all of our blazing stupidity and its outcome.

In 1952 Mr. Mowat wrote a book entitled **"The People of the Deer,"** which was a startling document about his first-hand investigations of the then-current situation of the inland Eskimos of the Keewatin District of Canada's Northwest Territories. It was a pretty ghastly book, too, in the sense that it showed the actual decimation of these people by rapacious idiots unwilling or unable even to read the reports of their own scientists on the biological changes in that country. . . .

[**"The Desperate People"**] is the story of the ruthless extermination of these proud little people over the last decade by the four insensate forces of stupidity: the government; the two churches (Catholic and Protestant); the much-vaunted Royal Canadian Mounted Police, entrusted with the affairs of these

people, and the Hudson's Bay Company, which alone seems to have at least once or twice *tried* to do something. While in the opinion of this reviewer, Mr. Mowat leans over backwards to be fair to these groups, pointing out that their executives and executors were probably all basically men of good will, and, while this may be true, it is still no excuse for outright stupidity and obtuseness. One had always thought of Canada as a fine land with a heart and above-average intelligence in moral and political matters. I can only say, and I *can* say it as a Britisher, that I am both nauseated and appalled.

There are many damning quotes in this book. The pay-off is probably that of a government official, a Dr. Porsild, who stated, after the publication of Mr. Mowat's former book, "I am sure that Farley Mowat is pleased with [an] award and perhaps a little amused too—for he has a keen sense of humor—that his plea for 'the understanding help without which these people will vanish from the earth' has been heard. What worries me is that the Ihalmiut [the inland Eskimos concerned] people never did exist except in Mowat's imagination." So speaks authority, science, religion, and non-Eskimo "humanity." Not only the Ihalmiuts' existence but their plight has been fully documented for almost two decades in the files of the Canadian Government's departments concerned with their affairs.

The book itself is clear and unpretentious. . . . **"The Desperate People"** makes most engrossing reading, but I must warn you that, unless you are completely insensible to pure horror, you are in for a profound emotional experience. Accounts of millions deliberately killed in prison camps are bad enough, but the story of a gentle people just as deliberately starved into virtual extinction in the name of "kindness" and religious "soul-saving" is so utterly disgusting that it comes very close to destroying any respect one may have remaining for our own race.

Ivan Sanderson, in his review of "The Desperate People," in Saturday Review (© 1959 Saturday Review Magazine Co.; reprinted by permission), Vol. XLII, No. 48, November 28, 1959, p. 27.

JIM LOTZ

North of the Canadian mainland lies a vast archipelago of islands, surrounded by a drifting, ever-changing mass of pack ice. Wind and tide so change the extent and location of this shifting ice, that any ship venturing into these regions can be trapped, held and sometimes crushed and sunk in a matter of hours. And yet, through this archipelago lay the way to Asia—the Northwest Passage. . . .

How did the first explorers fare in this huge, dreary labyrinth of bare land and ever-moving ice as they sought the way west by sea? Farley Mowat, in [**"Ordeal by Ice"**], lets them speak for themselves. He has rescued from obscurity many fine accounts of early Arctic exploration, and, by careful selection and editing, draws a vivid picture of man's struggle against ice and weather in the Arctic. . . . A running commentary by Mr. Mowat links the excerpts. . . .

The prose in all of these selections matches the Arctic scene in its starkness and beauty. . . . The early accounts, even when describing death and disaster, have a singularly refreshing air about them.

Mr. Mowat shows that, until the intruders into the north began to learn from its inhabitants, they had little or no success. Early contacts with the Eskimos were marked by mutual suspicion. . . . Only slowly did the European explorers come to admire, and then to imitate, the Eskimo way of life. . . .

As early as 1830, John Ross, as the excerpt from the narrative of his second voyage shows, had an appreciation, if not an understanding, of the Eskimo diet. Leopold McClintock, whose expedition recovered the only written record of the Franklin party, refined sledding techniques and equipment, although he traveled by man-hauling his sled, and did not use dogs. It remained for Charles Hall, a Cincinnati blacksmith, to take the ultimate step and live like an Eskimo. In the excerpt from his book, however, he gives the impression of almost totally relying on his Eskimo companions. . . .

In his connecting narrative, Mr. Mowat is perhaps too credulous in accepting Eskimo reports of men of the Franklin expedition being alive as late as 1862, and he ascribes greater feats to the early Norse and pre-Columbian Arctic explorers than the scanty evidence suggests. Today, work and travel in the Arctic is a comparatively comfortable business. "Ordeal by Ice" eloquently illustrates the sufferings of those who first showed the way north.

> *Jim Lotz, "Summer Was Unseasonable," in* The New York Times Book Review *(© 1961 by The New York Times Company; reprinted by permission), June 4, 1961, p. 7.*

HAL BORLAND

In his delightful all-ages book, **"The Dog Who Wouldn't Be,"** Farley Mowat briefly told about the owls, Wol and Weeps. They deserved a book of their own, and here it is—[**"Owls in the Family,"**] a wonderful tale of boys, owls and warm family life in Saskatoon, Saskatchewan. Mutt, the incredible dog, is here too, but only as a minor character. Wol was rescued as a pathetic owlet from a storm-wrecked nest. Weeps came out of an old oil barrel in an alley. They grew up together in the Mowat family and, like Mutt, wanted to be people too. . . .

Mowat's charm and humor make his pictures of boyhood and family life memorable. His story is rich with unobtrusive natural history, and he achieves a rare combination of simplicity, grace and distinction in the writing.

> *Hal Borland, in his review of "Owls in the Family," in* The New York Times Book Review *(© 1962 by The New York Times Company; reprinted by permission), March 11, 1962, p. 30.*

E.B. GARSIDE

On Sept. 14, 1948, the Leicester, a former Liberty ship of the ill-starred "Sam" series (so named after Uncle Sam) found herself several hundred miles at sea due east of Cape Cod, bound empty and in ballast from London to New York. At this point she ran into a great cyclonic storm, known only as Hurricane VII on weathermen's maps of that year. . . . Within hours the ship was wallowing helplessly in enormous seas, canted at the almost unbelievable angle of 70 degrees. Yet against all odds the Leicester refused to go down. Two days later all aboard were taken off by an American and an Argentine freighter. The Liberty, lying on her side, was allowed to drift away, doomed, as it seemed, at any moment to take her final plunge.

Thus the stage was set for one of the most remarkable salvage operations of all time. . . . How this operation was carried out

by two deep-sea tugs of the Foundation Company of Canada is a saga that Farley Mowat, himself a Canadian, and already known for other fine stories of man against nature, is peculiarly fitted to tell. The prize was worth a million dollars; the men committed to seize it were Newfoundland seamen taught in a hard, hard school. Driving them on was a man of demonic will. Foundation's salvage master, Robert Featherstone. . . .

Mr. Mowat has caught the very mood and feeling of this unique episode in the annals of the sea. He tells his tale with the precision of a ship's log, and in the same hard and driving manner which must have informed the actual event. As a result, reading his book is almost a physical experience.

> *E. B. Garside, "Salvage Isn't Easy," in* The New York Times Book Review *(© 1962 by The New York Times Company; reprinted by permission), May 13, 1962, p. 10.*

HARRY C. KENNEY

Farley Mowat, official biologist for the Canadian government, plane hitch-hiked far to the Canadian north into the heart of the Keewatin Barren Lands to find out how wolves lived.

While his new book [**"Never Cry Wolf"**] seems to start slowly, it quickens considerably when a decrepit and creaky airplane, resuscitated by an ex-R.A.F. pilot, flew Mr. Mowat and a mountain of supplies out of Churchill onto a Barrens frozen lake the exact location of which neither the pilot, nor Mr. Mowat knew.

But the biologist, by a quirk of good fortune, had arrived safely at his "base." He was on his own. Now to find some wolves to see what they were up to. In the course of events, this took an Arctic summer. . . .

Eventually, Mr. Mowat found a den of wolves—four young ones and the parents and right where he could conveniently observe them with power glasses and telescope. . . .

From here on the narrative, touched with humor, takes Mr. Mowat through the lives of a wolf family. He started calling the male "George" and the female "Angeline." Later on a single male baby-sitter for the four mischievous cubs, "Uncle Albert" came into the family.

With a lively sense of story, Mr. Mowat unravels the complex tactics of the wolves slowly but factually. He learned to nap when they napped, ate the summertime wolf diet—mice—fished the way they fish.

He learned something of their language and how they conveyed "news" over great distances. He found out the meaning behind the Eskimo saying, "The wolf keeps the caribou strong," rather than the common belief that the wolf destroys herds of caribou. He observed the strong family ties among wolves and he ended up his long assignment by having great compassion toward them. And he concluded with the realization that the wolf in fact is very different from the wolf of legend.

"Never Cry Wolf" delightfully and instructively lifts one into a captivating animal kingdom.

> *Harry C. Kenney, "Amber Eyes in the Arctic," in* The Christian Science Monitor *(reprinted by permission from* The Christian Science Monitor; *© 1963 The Christian Science Publishing Society; all rights reserved), October 3, 1963, p. 11.*

GAVIN MAXWELL

Farley Mowat is a trained scientist with a skeptic's mind. There is need to recall this at the outset, because in ["**Never Cry Wolf**"] he strains his readers' credulity to a point at which it would certainly snap in less trustworthy hands. . . .

To some, no doubt, it will be a surprise that he found every wolf fable a fallacy, and over the months developed a profound affection and admiration for his study subjects, which he found to be kingly creatures possessed of every virtue and no vice, neighbors who accepted his presence with neither fear nor ferocity. He had names for each of them, and the book is dedicated to the wolf bitch: "For Angeline—the angel." He found the wolves capable of something akin to speech—the conveyance, that is, of more or less complex thought between wolf and wolf. Their staple food during the summer months he found to be mice, and he confirmed what he learned from Ootek—that wolves kill only old or sickly caribou, thus tending to keep the herds in health. The slaughterer of the caribou was man, a conservative 112,000 head being killed by trappers in this area every year to feed themselves and their huskies, to say nothing of airborne "safaris" landing on frozen lakes and murdering 30 or so beasts for the sake of a single pair of antlers. He realized that these were figures he could not use in his reports "unless I wished to be posted to the Galapagos Islands to conduct a ten-year study on tortoise ticks."

None of this is particularly hard to believe, but where I found my own credulity twanging dangerously was over Ootek's ability to understand wolf language as easily as human. Ootek, the author was told, could hear and understand so well that he could quite literally converse with wolves.

This is a fascinating and captivating book, and a tragic one, too, for it carries a bleak, dead-pan obituary of the wolf family that Mr. Mowat had learned to love and respect. It is an epilogue that will not endear the Canadian Wildlife Service to readers of "**Never Cry Wolf.**" We must presume Angeline—the angel—and her family to have been wantonly and agonizingly poisoned in the face of all the evidence which an impartial counsel adduced for them. Once more it is man who displays the qualities with which he has tried to damn the wolf.

> Gavin Maxwell, "The Villains Wore Sheep's Clothing," in Book Week—The Sunday Herald Tribune (© 1963, The Washington Post), November 24, 1963, p. 6.

LAURENCE ADKINS

[Farley Mowat] has already introduced the owls Wol and Weeps in a previous book, **The Dog Who Wouldn't Be.** [In **Owls in the Family**] their adventures are recorded for young readers, and their escapades are told with good humour and an accuracy which indicates an affection for the subject. It does not matter that the setting is Saskatchewan; children will respond to the genuine honesty and sensitive manner of the narrative. So rarely are animals allowed to remain their natural selves, that this is not an opportunity to be missed. Though Weeps is quite pathetic in his fondness for Wol, the relationship is never made the subject of slushy sentimentality.

> Laurence Adkins, in his review of "Owls in the Family," in The School Librarian and School Library Review, Vol. 12, No. 1, March, 1964, p. 99.

GAVIN WHITE

"**Never Cry Wolf**" is a humourous tale on the pattern of the "Eye-Opener," beginning with an hilarous take-off on that mine of comedy, the former Department of Mines and Resources. On their behalf the author is sent to study wolves in the Barrenlands, and specifically to determine the extent to which they eat caribou. He concludes that wolves do not eat caribou, they eat mice. If wolves occasionally do eat caribou, it is good for the caribou, who ought to like it.

As the study of wolves develops, not all of which is to be taken seriously, one basic conclusion emerges. Once you get under their skins, wolves are very human, but if you get under the skin of a human being you will find he's a bloodthirsty predator. Mr. Mowat depicts himself as a baffled innocent, fed on mediaeval European legends of wolves plus new legends invented by the Dominion Wildlife Service, gradually discovering that the wolf is a much maligned creature and a model citizen of this great country. (pp. 119-20)

There is a serious note at the end of the book; the author is much concerned about the depravations of humans who have upset the ecological balance of the North, using the wolf as a scapegoat. On this score he lambasts the government, not for the first time, nor for the second. But the book as a whole is no polemic, it is a pleasing tale in which humour and zoology are expertly blended. Typical is the footnote on page 228: "There is no authentic report of wolves ever having killed a human being in the Canadian North; although there must have been times when the temptation was well-nigh irresistible." (p. 120)

> Gavin White, "Baffled Innocent," in The Canadian Forum, Vol. XLIV, No. 523, August, 1964, pp. 119-20.

VIRGINIA KIRKUS' SERVICE

[**The Curse of the Viking Grave** is an] unnecessary sequel to **Lost in the Barrens** . . . and an anticlimax compared to that book, **The Black Hole** . . . , and the author's other excellent adventure stories set in the wilderness of northern Canada. In **Barrens,** the Scotch boy Jamie and his Cree Indian friend Awasin had been lost for a winter in the Barrenlands and finally rescued by Peetyuk and his Eskimo tribe. Here, Jamie, Awasin and Peetyuk make plans to go trapping and then in the summer to return to the region to investigate what they believe to be evidence of Vikings. . . . Awasin's sister is foisted off on the expedition, and despite the accounts of her athletic prowess as well as physical charm, readers are likely to agree with Jamie that she doesn't belong on this trip. The boys should be approaching the adult years, but sound younger when they talk, particularly when they are around the girl—Jamie is schoolboyishly clumsy and inexperienced about addressing her; Peetyuk, who wants to marry her, carries on an adolescent flirtation while the other two give him a dreary razzing. The mixture of dialects makes the book especially dismal.

> A review of "The Curse of the Viking Grave," in Virginia Kirkus' Service (copyright © 1966 Virginia Kirkus' Service, Inc.), Vol. XXXIV, No. 13, July 1, 1966, p. 635.

ROBERT COHEN

As is usual with Mr. Mowat's books, [in **The Curse of the Viking Grave**] we are presented with excellent descriptions of the terrain and inhabitants of the Northlands. He presents an Eskimo group that is quite different in their history and culture from their better-known cousins. We are instructed in the ways of the Barrens and the people who dwell there without the slightest hint of pedantry. Those readers unfamiliar with *Lost in the Barrens* will find this a well-written and interesting story of adventure in the Northlands. Those who loved the earlier book will be disappointed. In the earlier book the boys had to pit all their skill against the deadly power of winter in the Barrens and their survival was constantly in doubt. The drama was real and intense for the stakes were unlimited. In the present book there is, comparatively, a lack of urgency and danger. Throughout the present book there are choices of action. They face danger and hardship voluntarily and can usually turn back if the going gets too rough. In most instances, failure would result in a waste of effort, time, and great embarrassment, but not in utter disaster. In the earlier book a cold, impersonal, Arctic death was their adversary.

It would perhaps have been better if the present story had not been a sequel. Knowing what our young adventurers had been through the previous year, robs the present book of much of the excitement that it might otherwise engender.

> Robert Cohen, in his review of "The Curse of the Viking Grave," in Young Readers Review (copyright © 1966 Young Readers Review), Vol. III, No. 3, November, 1966, p. 10.

MARGUERITE BAGSHAW

Sequels are often disappointing and [*The Curse of the Viking Grave*] lacks the spontaneity, careful planning and craft of *Lost in the Barrens*. Frequently the story seems forced or contrived and the characters suffer too in a plot which to all appearances has been hastily thrown together. This is somewhat compensated for by the author's knowledge of the North and by his concern for the Eskimo.

> Marguerite Bagshaw, in her review of "The Curse of the Viking Grave," in In Review: Canadian Books for Children, Vol. 1, No. 1, Winter, 1967, p. 38.

CLINTON J. MAGUIRE

Farley Mowat's effort [in *The Boat Who Wouldn't Float*] is to show that a vessel may have a mind of its own such as to constitute a continuing frustration to its owner. Jocose the statement may be; many sailors will insist that a fabrication of wood, or even steel, into an "artificial contrivance used, or capable of being used as a means of transportation on water", can result in a being with understanding and will which must be cajoled, coaxed, entreated and persuaded before the human in control can get, or get to, what he wants—and sometimes cannot.

Mowat and a partner decided to spend $1000 on a vessel which they could use to make voyages to exotic places and it was agreed that Newfoundland was the one place where such a gem might be found. . . .

The boat, named "Happy Adventure", then took eight years to get off the south coast of Newfoundland, chiefly because of refusal of its engine to start, or to stop, or to reverse, and its tendency to sink wherever it might be. During the course of these years, the vessel, by reason of the ingenuity of the seafarers of the French island of Saint Pierre, became the only

ship in the world under the Basque flag, with its name in Basque on bow and stern.

Ultimately Happy Adventure made it to Montreal for Expo '67. Since the vessel has not sunk in over a year, Mowat now vows to return it to its saltwater habitat.

The first two-thirds of this history, covering the first two years up to the time Happy Adventure manages to get away from Saint Pierre et Miquelon, are sheer delight. Mowat's style is impeccable, his ear and eye for people and places are sharp and faithful instruments of recordation, and his humor is evident. . . . It is, perhaps, too much to expect that the tour-de-force could be extended to cover six years of relative inactivity. This does not, however, prevent a hearty endorsement for the general reader interested in a congenial evening with a perceptive and witty observer of unusual persons and places, whether one is especially a sea-buff or not.

> Clinton J. Maguire, in his review of "The Boat Who Wouldn't Float," in Best Sellers (copyright 1970, by the University of Scranton), Vol. 30, No. 1, April 1, 1970, p. 4.

ROBERT BERKVIST

The best boats float. Ask Farley Mowat, who bought one that wouldn't. Oh, his floated all right, after he'd had her hauled from the muck of a Newfoundland harbor and rebuilt her somewhat (from stem to stern, that is); but there was something about the Happy Adventure *(sic)* that made her more interesting than most pleasure craft *(sic)*. She loved to fill herself with water and head for the bottom. Perhaps she really wanted to be a submarine. God knows, she tried often enough, the miracle being that Mr. Mowat lived to tell the tale [in **"The Boat Who Wouldn't Float"**].

But she met her match in her doughty sea-crazed skipper, who raised her, patched her, polished her, caulked her endlessly, talked her into believing she was a trim, obedient little schooner, not a mud turtle, and sailed her—or, rather, sailed with her; he acknowledges the uneasy compromise—into most of the nooks and crannies of Canada's easternmost province. . . .

Despite her maddening queer ways, the Happy Adventure paid dividends . . . , introducing [Mowat] to a land and a people of remarkable character. He tells her story, and theirs, with great good humor and insight in this very funny and often touching tribute to a love affair that saner, duller souls would no doubt christen Farley's Folly.

> Robert Berkvist, in his review of "The Boat Who Wouldn't Float," in The New York Times Book Review (© 1970 by The New York Times Company; reprinted by permission), May 10, 1970, p. 18.

THE TIMES LITERARY SUPPLEMENT

Fabulous events are rare and even rarer is a fabulist worthy of them. *A Whale for the Killing* is a magnificent instance of this conjunction, perhaps because Farley Mowat was not merely the chronicler of this little tragedy which provides a microcosm of our planetary condition, but also the fabulously conscious participant.

The scene was Aldridge Pond, a salt-water enclosure on the southern side of Newfoundland, not far from Burgeo. Burgeo used to be one of many small "outposts" from which fishermen would catch cod in the time-honoured way, but when New-foundland was merged with Canada, Joe Smallwood, the New-foundland Prime Minister, pursued a policy of industrialization at any price.

Burgeo became a fish-factory town, with independent fishing families from other outports now working as cheap labour for outside bosses. . . .

In January 1967 a pod of fin whales appeard off Burgeo, as it had done for a few winters previously. The herring were in glut and the pod chased them into the cove near Aldridge Pond. Their method of hunting is far superior to, and more economical than, the most advanced human seiner with all its electronic sonar equipment. . . .

In this pod, all members had had their fill, except the mother whale, which was pregnant (with a baby whale which at birth would have measured some 20 feet). The need to support her-self and the baby led her to pursue the herring into Aldridge Pond. . . .

Once in Aldridge Pond, she was imprisoned, despite outlets from either end, until the next spring tide four weeks later. By a freak of chance, man had been given an opportunity to study and to help his marine peer, whose mastery of the oceans by virtue of size, intelligence and natural grace had been unchal-lenged until man had, without avowing it, conducted a gen-ocidal war.

The male fin whale could not join his mate in the pool. But for the next ten days he remained outside, "sounding" when she "sounded", driving herring into the pond by feigned at-tacks which panicked them towards his pregant wife. . . .

The baiting of the mother fin whale began in a small way with the firing of soft-nosed bullets which embedded themselves in her blubber without apparent harm. Then some 400 nickel bullets were fired at this huge pregnant female desperately circling her prison in search of food and a way to return to her mate. Though Mr. Mowat does not say so, the imprisoned whale became the symbol of a creature out of its element. Fishermen who had become factory workers, smart boys from St. John's who had put them to hire, wanted to kill the whale because she stood for the sort of servitude in which both classes stood. . . .

In this curious love story of a faithful male fin whale and his dying pregnant wife, who ended by being towed tail first out of the pond, floating easily because the gases of her dissolution made her so buoyant but might in ending the shame of Burgeo have sunk a dory or something bigger, Mr. Mowat has written a parable. This parable is an eloquent plea to stop industrial plunder not merely of whales, which may result soon in their extinction, but also of herring on which they feed and the whole submarine kingdom which we are devastating, while we wran-gle nationally about who can annihilate most first.

> *"Captive Whale of Aldridge Pond," in* The Times Literary Supplement *(© Times Newspapers Ltd. (London) 1973; reproduced from* The Times Literary Supplement *by permission), No. 3702, February 16, 1973, p. 182.*

PATRICK O'FLAHERTY

Farley Mowat is the latest in a rather long list of foreign and mainland authors of distinction who have come to Newfound-land, settled for a time, and written books about their expe-

riences here. I think it is fair to say that all of them have created distorted images of life in the province in their books, but some have nevertheless illuminated in a striking and original way the particular aspects of Newfoundland which interested them. . . . The outsiders who have given significant responses to Newfoundland have been those with no axes to grind, who came, suppressed their own egos and theories, and simply observed and shared experiences. . . .

There is no such sense conveyed in Farley Mowat's *Wake of the Great Sealers.* . . . Mowat's [book] is ultimately about Mo-wat himself. This statement can be made about all of Mowat's books on Newfoundland and perhaps about everything he has written. Every book by him, no matter what locale ostensibly provoked it, is in essence another parading of his own per-sonality and favourite hobbyhorses. Mowat cannot seem to get beyond his pleasure over his own uniqueness. He is instinc-tively drawn to subjects which appear to reinforce elements in his personality and corroborate his already formed opin-ions. . . . Mowat's *This Rock within the Sea* . . . [supports] his image of himself as a hairy primitive combatting mechanization and technology; and now the sealers, "a breed of men whose certainty and hardihood, whose courage and tenacity, linked them more closely to the ancestors of our species than to our-selves," are made to resemble his own strutting masculinity. And so it goes. Mowat does not record phenomena as inter-esting or worthwhile in themselves. He wanders around the world remaking it in his own image. In *Wake of the Great Sealers* this process is brought to a daring but logical extreme by his choosing to tell the story of the oldtime seal fishery in the first person, as if he were a sealer himself. This, I suppose, is likely to be termed an impertinence by some, since Mowat in fact never did go to the ice, never lived in a pre-confederation outport, and never to my knowledge lived for an extended period in that part of Newfoundland from which the sealers used to come. But he goes ahead anyway, adopting the tactic of the first person, he says, for "literary reasons." What those "literary reasons" are may elude critics, but since the book is just another self-display of an amiable *poseur,* I for one do not find his playing at being a sealer to be dishonest. Even sen-tences like "I supposes 'twas a hard life, accordin' to what they says nowadays, but it never seemed so to we" will not give offence when interpreted correctly. This is Mowat the romantic primitive (and amateur linguist) puffing and blowing in his usual way. Of course the sealer's life never seemed hard to *him.* He didn't live it, that's why.

Readers who think they will enjoy witnessing another unfolding of Mowat's psyche may find this book worth the money.

> *Patrick O'Flaherty, in his review of "Wake of the Great Sealers," in* The Canadian Forum, *Vol. 54, No. 642, July, 1974, p. 35.*

SHEILA EGOFF

No definition quite encompasses or fits animals like Mutt, the Prince Albert (?) retriever, the hero of Farley Mowat's *The Dog Who Wouldn't Be* . . . , written for adults and adopted by children, or Wol and Weeps, the equally surprising owls of Mowat's *Owls in the Family* . . . , written for children and adopted by adults. Both books brought joy and exuberance and a sense of fun and mischief for the first time into Canadian children's literature.

Mutt, the dog who wouldn't be, was a dog all right, but he was also sensitive to his appearance and to comments made

about him. He early learned to avoid trouble with more com-
bative dogs by balancing on the top of back fences; then he
graduated to tree and ladder climbing. He was a traveller,
sailing on the Saskatchewan River with Farley's father and on
land in the Mowat car, suitably dressed in dark glasses. He
became the most noted, but not always the most loved, dog in
Saskatoon, maybe because of, maybe in spite of, the competition offered him by Farley's madcap father. Though a super-
canine, Mutt was not immortal, and in old age he did not evade
the destructiveness of the hit-and-run driver. Death on a back
road in eastern Ontario ends his story—the ending does not
come as a surprise: it is inevitable. The fast and furious sense
of fun has been gradually disappearing and the reality of the
ending casts an aura of credibility, even over the bizarre incidents that have gone before.

All the Mowat animals are presented as eccentric individualists,
memorable for their refusal to accept the limitations of an
animal's life. The truth or untruth of any particular incident is
immaterial; disbelief is suspended and the reader does not doubt
either the genuineness or the exaggerations of the Mowat way
of life. If animals do take on the characteristics of the family
with whom they live, then Mutt is completely credible.

Owls in the Family is an extension of one of the episodes in
The Dog Who Wouldn't Be. No more readily classifiable than
its predecessor, it purports to be a factual account of a family
and its peculiar pets. The element of realism does exist—the
owls are owls and the boys are boys—and there is a sharp
sense of prairie sky and sun and cottonwoods. . . . Most of
all, it is an autobiography, recalling and conveying with humour, sometimes farcical and sometimes wry, a sympathetic
but unsentimental feeling for animals and the values the author
holds important: generosity, justice, and compassion. And it
always rings true, for the boy who recounts the tale is honest
and sensitive, and as colloquial as only a boy can be.

Mr Mowat is a natural writer for children. He writes from his
own experience, both childhood and adult. With his direct,
simple, and lively style he can reveal aspects of life that are
necessary in good children's literature if it is to have any enduring value. Qualities such as cruelty, irony, satire—gentled
of course—give life and depth to children's literature and they
are present in all Mowat's animal stories. They are implied in
the style and confronted squarely in the realistic details. (pp.
120-22)

Sheila Egoff, "The Realistic Animal Story," in her
The Republic of Childhood: A Critical Guide to Ca-
nadian Children's Literature in English *(© Oxford
University Press, Canadian Branch, 1975; reprinted
by permission), Oxford University Press, Canadian
Branch, 1975, pp. 105-26.**

SHEILA EGOFF

The combination of dramatic setting and narrative skill that
makes for a compelling tale is best exemplified in the books
of Roderick Haig-Brown and Farley Mowat. These writers
stand far above their Canadian contemporaries and rank high
internationally.

Both Haig-Brown and Mowat have come to the writing of
outdoor books almost inevitably. Confirmed naturalists who
have given years of their lives to exploring the Canadian wilderness, active and dogged campaigners for conservation, they
have a feeling for the Canadian land and a knowledge of it
that are genuine and deep. More important, they are thoroughly

professional writers who have learned how to shape their feelings rather than just express them; they know that even in
children's stories a character remains vivid long after the most
ingenious contrivances of plot have been forgotten. (pp. 164-
65)

Farley Mowat's stories are somewhat more conventionally adventurous and less thoroughly realistic than Haig-Brown's. *Lost
in the Barrens* . . . recounts the experiences of a white boy,
Jamie, and an Indian boy, Awasin, who become separated from
the Indian band. They encounter every test the North can impose upon them. They suffer near-starvation and snow blindness. They fight to the death with a Barren Lands grizzly and
with almost unbearable suspense they miss by a hair's breadth
the Indian band they were supposed to join for the return.
Somehow they survive it all and grow up in the process.

Mowat's strength lies in the sense of pace and breathless suspense he gives to his tale. The boys almost reel from crisis to
crisis. But Mowat is far too good a writer, and he knows the
North too well, to strain credibility in the interest of narrative.
Beneath the overlay of adventure there is always the solid
substance of the North itself and the kind of character development it imposes on those who live there. Awasin, the son
of a Cree chieftain, explains to Jamie, the city boy, that one
must conform to the North rather than fight it, and so the
interest of the story is fundamentally based on the way that
adaptation is made rather than on the events that precipitate it.

Mowat's steady hand on the world of reality can be seen even
more clearly in his modern pirate story, *The Black Joke.* . . .
Here are the hard economic facts of life in the Newfoundland
outports in the 1930s. The power of the traders, the father's
need to find a profitable cargo so as to retain his ship, form a
springboard for the incidents. *The Black Joke* is also a first-
class tale of the sea in the grand, a-little-larger-than-life tradition: seafaring boys navigating in stormy waters, brave seamen and scheming merchants, rum-runners and castaways, a
fine schooner shipwrecked and seized but brought home safely
to port. Mowat's beautifully outrageous imagination is shown
particularly in the gusto with which he delineates character.
His villains are properly evil. There is even a touch of grandeur
about Captain Smith: 'Back to the ship,' he bellowed, 'or I'll
drill the rotten lot of you'—an imprecation in the best tradition
of pirates' curses. Yet all this is set against a background of
precise detail, whether Mowat is describing a Newfoundland
outport or catching a salmon or sailing a ship through the fog.
The humour in the story is not particularly subtle, though perhaps it is well calculated for its audience. The two young
heroes, Peter and Kye, who are capable of doing a man's job
in sailing the *Black Joke,* indulge in pranks dear to their age—
squirting bilgewater at the unpleasant trader, Mr Barnes, and
frying salt pork when he is seasick. The style, as in *Lost in
the Barrens,* is simple, exact, and detailed, in the tradition of
the plain English of [Daniel] Defoe and [Jonathan] Swift. (pp.
167-69)

[Plain] words are often the prelude to momentous events. 'It
was a magnificent night,' says Mowat quietly, and then launches
into the crescendo of the story in which the boys cause an
explosion on the *Black Joke* and rout the villains. These pages
are probably the most exciting in Canadian children's literature.
The Black Joke is a latter-day *Treasure Island,* a story whose
gusto and toughness are generally lacking in Canadian books
for children.

Mowat and Haig-Brown owe most of their success to their
respect for their craft and for their readers. There is no sense

of writing down—they write on equal terms with their readers, like Stevenson, and, most important, they have a lot to say to them. (p. 169)

Sheila Egoff, "And All the Rest: Stories," in her The Republic of Childhood: A Critical Guide to Canadian Children's Literature in English *(© Oxford University Press, Canadian Branch, 1975; reprinted by permission), Oxford University Press, Canadian Branch, 1975, pp. 161-206.**

JIM HARRISON

Depending on one's immediate mood, a lot can be found wrong in the writing of Farley Mowat: all sorts of laughable excesses, from sloppy style, overweening sentimentality, a kind of con brio enthusiasm for windmill tilting, to the sort of verbal keening one associates with a traditional Boston Irish wake, with the whisky flowing so freely one forgets just who is dead and why.

This is not so much a disclaimer as an announcement of fact, and in Mowat's very particular case the fact doesn't matter. Of Farley Mowat's 19 or so books I've read 12, and after a few weeks' mulling over his latest it seems to me that **"The Snow Walker"** is the best. The precious sniping of the littérateur is simply not relevant here. **"The Snow Walker"** is a book of tales about the Eskimo, stories ranging from the ancient to the overwhelmingly modern. It is passionate, harsh, with a mythic density that puts a great strain on the reader. In fact, the reader will assuredly come up feeling more than vaguely unclean.

History is forgetful but ultimately unforgiving, and in **"The Snow Walker"** Mowat draws us into the beauty and anguish of an extirpated culture; perhaps more than a culture, a microcosmic civilization. The beauty of the tales purge, exhaust, draw us out of our skin, but the pain involved is so deep that we feel the free-floating remorse that characterizes modern man on those rare occasions he has the wit and humility to turn around and look at his spoor.

In the reading of this book we should first of all forget all the Brotherhood of Man nonsense. We have nothing in common with the Eskimo and he has nothing in common with us other than our accidental simultaneity on earth. It is not profitable to look for similarities, to make a unity of us all in the usual ritual of breast-beating. The simple fact is the Canadian Government has no better track record with the Eskimo than we with the American Indian in our mutual courses of empire. (p. 4)

The main character of **"The Snow Walker"** is the cold and the snow. The "snow walker" itself is death. We have an old man telling Mowat a tale going back so far that it recedes into the bottom layer of a glacier—how men with metal helmets with horns on them and wearing breastplates came in a long boat one year. They had blond beards, sang songs and taught the Eskimo how to build the crossbow. There are tales of starvation, cannibalism out of love, the giving of one body to another with the poignancy of the Eucharist. There are tales so simple and strong you read them again to make sure you haven't been tricked into feeling a story in your stomach for a change. There is a tale of a man and an arctic fox in a suicide pact, and a tale about a woman named Soosie that exceeds any story I've ever read, save in Kafka, for convincing bureaucratic horror. There is a tale that is a Romeo and Juliet for grownups—romanticism loses its perversity and becomes convincing. In

"The Snow Walker" Mowat is presenting the essence of his 30-year obsession with the Arctic and its people. (p. 5)

Jim Harrison, "The Main Character Is the Cold and the Snow," in The New York Times Book Review *(© 1976 by The New York Times Company; reprinted by permission), February 22, 1976, pp. 4-5.*

MICHAEL A. PETERMAN

[When] a book is as dull, repetitive and simplistic as *The Snow Walker* too often is, one can only hope that readers will quickly learn to mistrust McClelland and Stewart's unblushing declaration that this collection of short stories "is among Farley Mowat's finest contributions to Canadian literature."

This is not to say that *The Snow Walker* is without virtues. . . . The title story summarizes what might be called the thematic heart of the collection—the noble, dignified yet troublingly fatalistic manner in which the undiluted Innuit nature chooses to meet death, the spirit of the Snow Walker. These twice-told . . . tales reveal many interesting aspects of Innuit life and folklore. Native myths, legends, mysteries and attitudes to love, death and animals are interwoven into the stories, as are some curious, for the most part unexplored, ambivalences to the land itself.

The problem is that, as a collection, *The Snow Walker* is a tedious experience. . . . Mowat—if these stories be sufficient evidence—lacks the wit, audacity, inventiveness, curiosity and range necessary to enliven a group of stories so dependent on effect. If these tales reveal anything at all, they reveal the limits of Mowat's mind and imagination and the unabashed commercialism which seems to characterize his approach to writing. Upon reading them as a group, one is left with the sense of having witnessed a tremendous material and opportunity wasted, or at least left sadly unrealized.

Uniformly, the stories of *The Snow Walker* are solemn, high-minded and despairing; they share a unity of approach, tone and point of view, despite the fact that Mowat ostensibly introduces different narrators and narrative devices. Consistently a reverence for the struggling Innuit is juxtaposed to an overwhelming contempt for the white man, be he priest, trader or explorer. Mowat's sincerity in this regard becomes his enemy, not his ally, especially after the reader has read several selections. Because he insists so relentlessly on his point of view, Mowat sacrifices both realistic analysis and psychological penetration in presenting his material. Always the formulaic storyteller, he relies on the dramatic thump, the elegaic thrill or the staggering sense of loss and defeat in order to seduce the reader into the uncritical feeling that he is getting something authentic and important. His pursuit of effects is made to sugarcoat the unlifelike simplicity of the message. One is left in the end with an accumulation of stereotypes, a potpourri of sentimental cliches ("he was still in the full vigour of young manhood"), a sense of the heavy-handed treatment of the Innuit as a modern-day Noble Savage, of the clumsiness of the Hemingwayesque dialogue, and of the relentless focus of Mowat's biases.

Clearly, the real trouble lies with the biases. They are the basis for the morally simplistic conclusions one is forced to derive from the stories; they are also the basis for the insistent melodrama. [Edgar Allan] Poe, were he alive and spouting his characteristic critical venom, would doubtless and rightly accuse Mowat of "the heresy of the didactic". Story after story presents the pure and noble Innuit life (especially in the past) in simple juxtaposition to the cruel, self-serving and greedy habits of the white trader, a being apparently incapable of sensitivity either to the landscape or to the Eskimo. Mowat's natives can do little wrong in his eyes; the intruding bourgeois can do little right. Because Mowat so seldom moves beyond this fixed idea and seldom avoids his tendency to preach, the reader tires of the message after a time, even as an alert, young sensibility naturally tires of the repetitive moralizing of uni-maginative Sunday school teachers. The fault in both cases lies less with the message than with the mode of presentation.

In short, then, Mowat in *The Snow Walker* hurts his own case— the good case of the Innuit—by turning these sagas of the North into a medium for a grating and repetitive sort of jingoism of injustice. Mordecai Richler's Jake Hersh rather astutely di-agnosed this characteristic phenomenon of our modern "in-tellectual" life in *St. Urbain's Horseman*. To use Jake's phrase, Mowat comes in these stories to seem more an "injustice col-lector" than a man of cogent imagination. He quite overtly plays upon the feelings of guilt and unease shared by the readers who buy his book. Though Mowat claims to be interested in the "inner lives" of the Eskimoes and in what he romantically calls "the shadowy distances of Innuit history" he diminishes these important interests by insisting on the same, simplistic idea of truth story after story—the beauty, nobility, heroism and harmony of Innuit life has been abused and destroyed by the intruding, materialistic white man.

It is not surprising, then, that Mowat makes his best and most informative statements concerning the Innuit dilemma in those few among the stories based apparently on factual evidence rather than the author's formulaic imagination. . . . The actual facts provide more forcefulness and a greater ring of authen-ticity which in the other stories is blunted by the melodrama, moralizing and the accumulating tedium of repetition. It is too bad, really. But perhaps Farley Mowat deserves it. One can't help wondering, ironically, if Mowat, in amassing the profits from such a volume isn't as much the victimizer of the Eskimo as those rapacious company traders he stereotypes. (pp. 34-5)

Michael A. Peterman, "Injustice Collector," in The Canadian Forum, *Vol. LV, No. 659, March, 1976, pp. 34-5.*

ALEC LUCAS

Mowat's children's books (and all are boy's books) demon-strate his desire, on the one hand, to indoctrinate boys with his social concepts and values and, on the other, to retain the pleasant memories of his childhood.

For the most part Mowat skilfully disguises his didactic intent. He hides it under narrative motifs and themes that have to do with wish-fulfillment, with the search for affection and secu-rity, with animals as a way of satisfying a child's wish to love and be loved, and with success achieved through brave and noble deeds or through skill and resourcefulness. These motifs and themes are not only those of much adult fiction, but also (especially those relating to deeds) of much of Mowat's non-fiction, despite what would seem radical differences between his juvenile and his adult books. (p. 41)

Like his motifs and themes, Mowat's subjects are the old time-tested children's story standbys of pets and family life, Eski-mos, Indians, and pirates, but in his books they take on new life. Mutt and his "owlish" playmates, Wol and Weeps, defy

classification with animals and birds. Mowat's Eskimos may be friendly, but they are far from the fat-cheeked and jolly creatures of the general run of children's books about them, and his Indians live as Indians, not as noble savages, or as blood-thirsty warriors, or as sentimentalized vanishing Amer-icans. Vanishing they may be, but Mowat is indignant rather than sentimental about their plight. Mowat's "pirates" are boys, and their booty, far from the usual, is a treasure-trove of bootleg whiskey!

The settings of Mowat's stories have a freshness about them. His northland is far more realistic than [Robert Michael] Bal-lantyne's, E. R. Young's, and [James MacDonald] Oxley's, and there is also a convincing verisimilitude about the maritime world of *The Black Joke*. . . . As for the animal stories, Mowat relives his childhood in them and has simply to recreate, not invent, their settings. The fact that Mowat wrote from expe-rience may limit his scope somewhat, but it makes his books more vivid and more interesting. He is no arm-chair naturalist or yacht-club seaman. He lived in the Canadian North and sailed the eastern seaboard and the coasts of Newfoundland, and he succeeds in imparting his knowledge of, and feeling for, these regions in his stories.

If Mowat is impressive for his handling of his settings, subjects, and themes, he is no less so for his skill as a story-teller and for the liveliness of his humour. He creates suspense by hinting at future events or by withholding information and by dram-atizing or describing exciting episodes in which disaster is only a hair's breadth away. As is standard, also, in fiction of event, the characters are types with just enough individuality to set them apart from each other, but not so much as to preclude the reader's identification with them, or to hinder the flow of the narrative. Mowat is little concerned with analyzing per-sonality. His interest centres on the physical world and the life of action. This interest unquestionably attracts young readers, but it also seems to have contributed much to the popularity of his books for adults. (pp. 41-2)

Mowat's first juvenile book, *Lost in the Barrens* . . . , is ob-viously a by-product of [his earlier] *People of the Deer*. Both are set in the Keewatin District, the barren lands west of Hud-son Bay. Both aim not only at creating sympathy for the ab-origines of the north, but also at a greater understanding of the north itself and the way of life appropriate to it. It could be argued that *Lost in the Barrens* represents Mowat's response to the failure of officialdom to take prompt and appropriate action following his *exposé* in *People of the Deer* of their in-adequacies. An indignant book aimed at immediate remedies, it had received indignant replies in its turn. *Lost in the Barrens,* by the very nature of its genre, is a more moderate book than *People of the Deer,* and though it takes its stand on the same issues, it puts its trust in a future when its young readers, having become adults, will help bring about a changed attitude toward our native peoples. (p. 42)

Mowat embeds his rough-hewn anthropology and history with some nature lore . . . in a story of high adventure or misad-venture in which two boys in search of a viking tomb lose touch with their hunting companions and have to winter on the barrens. The boys move from crisis to crisis, after the tradi-tional fashion of boy's stories, and finally all ends happily, thanks to Peetyuk, a half-white Eskimo. The most distinguished section of the book by far, however, revolves around the boys' lives in Hidden Valley. Mowat, like [Daniel] Defoe, could make the most of a situation in which man and nature meet, not as rivals but as partners. Although storms blow violently in Hidden Valley, it is always cosy in the cabin, thanks to human ingenuity and to nature's bounty in supplying food and fuel and, as evidence of even greater largess, a caribou fawn so that the boys have an opportunity to satisfy their "wish to love and to be loved," the motif of so many pet animal stories. . . .

Mowat, again like Defoe, also made the most of a deep psychological realism by describing minutely all the boys' activities in building their wilderness home, getting in their supplies, making their clothes, building their fires, and cooking their meals. . . .

On the surface the central theme of the book may appear to be that of survival, but Mowat celebrates no such negative concept, not the merits of mere dogged persistency, for beneath the surface lies evidence that he has dedicated his story to positive values through which one asserts a joy in the vitality of living. (p. 43)

Ten years after *Lost in the Barrens,* Mowat turned to the north again in another book for boys, *The Curse of the Viking Grave.* . . . Like the former, it also stems from a preceding adult's book, in this case a history, *Westviking.* . . . (p. 44)

All the ingredients of *The Curse of The Viking Grave*—sizzling caribou chops over cheery campfires, dangerous rivers, ancient treasures, Indian and Eskimo hunters—ought to have produced another exciting tale. But the book proves the conjurer's old adage, "never twice," for Mowat seems to have lost his magic in it. Perhaps he was exhausted after the big book *Westviking,* or perhaps *Lost in the Barrens* had expended his imaginative capital as regards the north.

The Curse of the Viking Grave again uses quest and chase to create suspense and achieve unity. The heroics of Jamie, Awasin, Peetyuk, and this time Marie, Awasin's sister, derive from a trek to a mysterious viking tomb to secure treasures buried there and at the same time to avoid the RCMP officers who are out to get their man, Jamie—to send him back to school in the south. Not even the RCMP can stir up much excitement, however, for Mowat has too palpable a design upon the reader. Again there is a plea for understanding of the natives who, as the fellowship of the travellers proves, are worthy people by any standard worth holding by white civilization. In this book, however, Mowat has a new cause to take up. He is convinced that the vikings once settled in northern Canada. He accepts the Kensington Stone (and the Beardmore relics) as genuine and as almost certain proof of the viking presence there, as the long recitations of vikings legends in the book demonstrate. Even if justified as history, they clog the narrative, for Mowat drags them in as support of a theory and not as part of the plot. The story involving the police trails off completely early in the book, and the story of the treasure hunt loses itself in a thicket of anthropological and geographical details. Furthermore, no account could carry the weight of the description of an almost interminable journey through country that is endlessly the same, particularly since, from the very beginning, the treasure seems hardly worth the trouble, even if it is to be sold to help the native cause, and since the awful curse of the Eskimo medicine man seems little more than a joke to the younger people.

Mowat's attempt to write a thriller about the north fails because the story proper is mainly a travelogue and hence lacks any dramatic tension. "Where do the characters go next?" is a bare substitute for "what do they do next?" or "what happens next?" as a narrative device. Moreover the characters do not have the personalities to supply the interest that the plot lacks.

They are theme-ridden, Jamie obviously acting as spokesman for the author when, early in the book, he cries out against white man's indifference and injustice towards the Cree Indians: "Jamie clenched his hands, wadded the letter into a ball and flung it onto the ice. There was bitter defiance in his voice. '*My* people? They aren't mine! They'd let the whole lot of you die without lifting a hand to help. Don't call them *my* people, Alphonse!'" The romance between Peetyuk and Marie is out of place, cute, and heavily propagandistic. Fiction with four protagonists, no villains, and two adolescent lovers sets up obstacles that *The Curse of the Viking Grave* never overcomes.

Mowat's only other adventure story, *The Black Joke* . . . , is a tale of the sea, but, unlike the books set in the north, it centres on the struggles of man with man, not man in nature. If it lacks the psychological insight that the experience of the two boys in their winter camp reveals, it does not have to carry any of the kind of message that *The Curse of the Viking Grave* collapses under. Mowat again makes heroes of the unsophisticated—this time of the Newfoundland fishermen with their skills as seamen and their inherent loyalty and honesty. In *The Black Joke,* however, the qualities he admires are implicit in the story, so that it contains little upstage moralizing.

If the northern books gave the teen-ager a chance to "play" Indian, *The Black Joke,* the story of a boat, lets him identify with three modern boy "pirates" who rescue her from the rum-runners and restore her to her rightful owner, the father of one of these good "pirates." The story focuses on a plot leading to a typical "virtue triumphant" conclusion thanks to the shrewdness and derring-do of the three boys (this time a white, his white-Indian cousin, and a French boy) who prove too much for a whole crew of rum-runners.

The northern books, though stories of event, do not depend on the conflict between hero and villain for their interest. Mowat prefers a positive and general approach to the virtues of the northern people over one in which he would set out the weaknesses of the white man in his treatment of the aborigines by selecting some individual trader or trapper as a villain. Not that the white men were not worthy of the role, but Mowat avoided isolating one for such a part; he feared he would run the risk of defeating his purpose of revealing the general callousness or indifference of the white man outside the world of the natives, if he based his attack on the specific evils of an individual within it. He wishes most of all to disclose the attitudes, customs, and values of a good society, the members of which he thinks have long been treated as inferior citizens. Only once he toys with the idea of a villain—strangely, an Indian—who falls from grace apparently because he made improper proposals to Marie, destined by love (and theme) for Peetyuk, a white-Eskimo.

In *The Black Joke,* white villains take centre stage. Mowat has no need here to concentrate on enlightening the reader about a different way of life in a primitive society. Twice he alludes to the running sore of social injustice by which a government declares as contraband cheap food that could have been a godsend to the impoverished outports of Newfoundland during the Depression era, but otherwise he comes at the problem indirectly by devising a story and by creating characters who in themselves demonstrate the evils of modern materialism—Barnes, a business man (the standard whipping boy for such purposes in fiction), who secretly arranges to seize Jonathan Spence's *Black Joke,* a French judge who puts money above the law and Jonathan's rights, and Smith, a blow-hard American rum-runner, who indirectly controls all three. Mowat squares accounts somewhat with two good Frenchmen (Basques and poor fishermen), but the business man, the lawyers, and the American have no similar counterbalances, although Bill Smith's brave deeds (and his admiration of the three boys for their boldness) "redeem" the American in the end. There are no subtleties here. Mowat makes no attempt to analyze his views; he assumes their validity. The good guys and the bad, all type, static characters like those of most juvenile fiction, are clearly distinguishable, and the issues—unsophisticated integrity and honesty versus sophisticated chicanery and avarice—are no less obvious, despite the fact that the boys set fire to the *Black Joke*. They act for justice, for true law and order and, in doing so, enable the honest poor of Newfoundland to defeat the less morally pure privileged and wealthy who would subjugate them to economic serfdom. Even in his children's books Mowat did not hesitate to deride establishment values.

As Canadian children's books go, *The Black Joke* belongs in the "rough and tough" school. Yet the boys do have a chance to have some fun on the island of Miquelon. They fish and hunt and, moreover, learn that, as Awasin had also admonished, "It is not good to kill more than one needs." In such comments, however, Mowat leaves "need" undefined, perhaps because hunters belong with his red-blooded men of action, or because he still has a yen for hunting himself, associated as it is with his youthful years in Saskatchewan. For all that, his children's books disclose his intense interest in the natural world, not as romantic love of the pretty or as awe of grandeur, but as a sincere appreciation of the whole dynamic process it manifests. In the books about the north he tries to inculcate something of the feeling that vast land with its rivers, lakes, caribous, and Eskimos invoked in him. *The Black Joke* reveals a similar fascination with the sea and the fishermen who meet its challenge knowingly, yet unflinchingly, in their daily lives, and the story ends, after all its turbulence, with a tribute to their world:

> The wind was fresh from the southeast. Under the combined power of her sails and her diesel engine, *Black Joke* was soon logging a full twelve knots. It was still daylight when she began to close with the shores of Newfoundland. The massive sea-cliffs rose up close ahead, and the roar of bursting seas echoed back from the great rocks. Snoring through the water, the black-hulled ship bore down through the shadows of the evening.
>
> *Black Joke* was home at last.

This is the traditionally happy ending of children's stories. Simon Barnes's black joke has failed, turned back on him as it has been by the clever and brave boys. Yet it is more than a formula ending or a variant of the epic conclusion in which the long absent traveller finally returns home. It hints at Mowat's sympathy with the way of life of what he calls the "natural" man—the "simple life" as it is termed in the so-called agrarian myth. If the books about Indians and Eskimos speak for the pleasure of escape into the natural world, *The Black Joke*, the other side of the coin, implies the pleasure of escape from corrupted urban life.

Mowat has written four books about animals. Of these the publisher has classified "For Young Readers" only *Owls in the Family*. Yet since it is a sequel to *The Dog Who Wouldn't Be*, the latter also . . . belongs in the same category. *Never Cry Wolf* and *A Whale for the Killing*, despite being animal

stories, however, are books for adult readers, for their subject concerns the adult world and the cause of conservation of natural wildlife.

Within the genre of the animal story, *The Dog Who Wouldn't Be* belongs to the very popular class in which pets are the protagonists. (pp. 44-7)

Mowat's book stands apart from [Marshall Saunders's *Beautiful Joe*, R. M. Ballantyne's *The Dog Crusoe*, E. R. Young's *Hector, My Dog*, and Morley Callaghan's *Luke Baldwin's Vow*] and from Roberts's and Seton's stories with their attempts to examine animal psyche and character. It could be argued easily that Mowat satirizes all of these in his book, for it treats lightheartedly and even irreverently everything that they took so seriously, that Mutt, the animal hero or anti-hero (the very name suggests anti-elitism), embodies Mowat's own sense of fun in a world of make-believe, or that Mutt and Wol reflect something of the revolt against the *status quo* of the time as the dogs of the earlier books reflected the attitudes of their day and age.

Whatever the matrix of *The Dog Who Wouldn't Be*, on the surface it is an animal-cum-family children's story that has proved very popular. . . . Written in the first person about the author's childhood, it allows both the child and the adult reader to identify with the story teller's "I," as wish-fulfillment for the one in a world of mischievous but affectionate pets, and as a detour into the past for the other, for there is a common denominator in the autobiography of childhood lacking in that of maturity. Actually the book is broken-backed, for the protagonist, Mutt, fades from the middle of the story for some eighty pages. Because the book is episodic and anecdotal, the break does little harm, however, especially since the story never slackens pace from its remarkable *in medias res* beginning, whether Mutt, Father, or the owls are in the spotlight.

Lost in the Barrens, with its crises, issues, and serious purpose had no place for humour, nor had *The Curse of the Viking Grave* or *The Black Joke*, except for a practical joke or two, played against a shy lover in the former and, of course, against the villains in the latter. It is quite otherwise in *The Dog Who Wouldn't Be*, with its alleged recreation of events and people from the writer's happy, boisterous boyhood. Much of the humour is tongue-in-cheek, and, indeed, the whole story is a tall tale, for Mowat describes a dog who uses a diving board to go swimming, who climbs trees, fences, ladders, and mountains, and who challenges the very science of biology with his chattering teeth. This principle of exaggeration leads most frequently to slap-stick scenes, which Mowat occasionally garnishes with fine dialect dialogue. . . . (pp. 47-8)

The verbal, descriptive, and situational humour of *The Dog Who Wouldn't Be* is never subtle. Unfortunately the verbal humour is sometimes forced or obnoxiously prurient, and the descriptive and situational is hackneyed (at least in the tired old "dog and skunk confrontation") or coarse (as when Mutt falls foul of a cormorant in its nest). Humour of character often combines with humour of situation in *The Dog Who Wouldn't Be* in the battle of the sexes (as it does much less successfully in *The Black Joke*) during the mild skirmishes between Father and Mother Mowat, but especially in Father Mowat's misadventures afield and afloat. Although they are not the bland and sentimentalized parents of many children's stories, they are traditional, however, in that their ancestors have had long and distinguished careers in life-with-father comedies—a naive wife (who thinks Mutt chases cows because beef is a "dreadful price''), a blustering husband (who loves boats but moves to the dust-bowl prairies), and a precocious child (who acts as innocent commentator, observer, and prankster). All of these make for the fun Mowat has—hilarious is a favourite work word with the critics—but it is Mutt, not the father in the familiar roles of green-horn nimrod or sailor or foolish eccentric, nor the owls, who gives the story distinction. (p. 48)

Essentially, **The Dog Who Wouldn't Be** is a modern beast fable. Although neither typically allegorical nor heavily moralistic, it fits the genre, for it employs an animal to satirize man. Aside from the family comedy, there are inklings of a deeper satiric intent, also, in Mowat's grumbling about Ontario's lack of culture and Paul Sazalski's shrewd business practices: here Mowat, the social critic, surfaces too obviously. But it is Mutt who focuses the irony of the story. If, as Mowat says, Mutt is not human, he has, mingled with the canine, many of the characteristics of the human. Like a small boy he dislikes to wash (and so furtively swallows the soap), eats cherries and spits out their pits (against all rules of etiquette), and chews gum and swallows it (much to Mother's disapproval). As a naive actor he unconsciously makes a mockery of hunting, that holy of holies activity of the outdoors man. He dislikes rising in the cold dawn, he plays a practical joke on the hunters to the benefit of the hunted when he bounces from the duck blind before the firing starts (and it is he who saves the wounded ducks and geese from a slow death), and he even retrieves a mounted grouse from a hardware store, whereby his master saves face in a boastful and silly bet. Finally Mutt enables the son (and the reader) to learn of the father's pretentiousness and false pride and, along with Wol and Weeps, is the vehicle for an irony that pokes good-natured fun at the adult world. Although Mutt's innocence may be Tom Sawyerlike, Mutt does make a case for astute, individualistic behaviour as against mere eccentricity. For all his extraordinary ways as animal, Mutt makes more sense than the master of the house. Again, when, at the end of the book, a truck kills Mutt, it brings an animal story to a sad conclusion, but it also seems to imply much about this technological age.

Four years after **The Dog Who Wouldn't Be,** Mowat published his second animal story in which Mutt, Wol, and Weeps appear, but this time the owls are the stars of the piece. **Owls in the Family** is, however, more than sequel, for not only are the characters identical, but so also are many of the scenes, probably the result of the pleasures of memory rather than a flagging imagination. The owls are good copy, besides, and are never cute and cuddly, and play some very good scenes—Wol contributes a dead skunk to a dinner party, frightens a visiting minister, disrupts a French class, and plays squeeze-tail with poor Mutt. Many of the bizarre events have as common denominator not only the farcical but also the satiric overtones of **The Dog Who Wouldn't Be.** The trick of breaking up the Eaton's parade with a rattlesnake hidden in a box is more than trick. It is a joke played on a tinselly society, for until the box is opened, the "special pet in reserve" wins great praise from a successful business man as "smart merchandising." Actually Mowat speaks out directly once about his conviction that man is an inferior animal, Wol killing only out of need and man out of greed and his aggressiveness, he says, though he must have had war, not hunting, in mind in making the comment. But even iconoclast Mowat has not gone unscathed among modern socio-literary critics. Apparently he has been rocking only one side of the boat with his criticism of middle-class attitudes, for his **Owls in the Family** has recently been singled out for attack for its allegedly stereotyped, bourgeois attitude toward a black boy.

Despite Mutt's highly anthropomorphic traits, Mowat readily secures a willing suspension of disbelief because of the vigour of his narrative and humour, and because the whole story is a wonderful spoof that discloses some inner truths about man and his little ways. **Owls in the Family** maintains the same realistic-fanciful (if not fantastical) perspective as **The Dog Who Wouldn't Be,** but since owls, unlike dogs, are neither familiar pets nor common literary subjects, the remarkable antics and habits of Wol, the brashly confident, and Weeps, the timid (whose role it is to win sympathy for the animal world), add something to the book as realism, but they do not and cannot reveal (few readers having the knowledge needed as a standard of reference) the outlandish imagination that enabled Mowat to make Mutt so attractive and original.

If natural history goes awry in Wol's deliberately calling crows, acting as a mother prairie chicken, or failing to remember "whether he had finished his dinner or not," it certainly does not go astray in the western setting. Here, as in the descriptions of hunting in **The Dog Who Wouldn't Be,** Mowat's feeling for nature comes through clearly. The search for the owl's nest, to give one example, bears witness to the fact.

Some of Mowat's success depends on the choice of suitable themes, but much more depends on his talent in dramatizing them, on his lively descriptions of settings and situations, and on the verve of his narrative and humour. In short, on his prowess as a story teller. Beyond the wit, the farce, and the melodrama, the excitement and the fun, however, Mowat shows a seriousness of purpose: on the one hand he is in sympathy with the down-trodden and abused, and, on the other, he is out of sympathy with white society. Moreover, if his human characters sometimes support stereotyped concepts about certain aspects of human behaviour, his animals never do. They echo the anti-establishment attitude of some of his books for adults. One may disagree with Mowat's views, but it is they that contribute much of the intensity that makes his children's books far superior to the general run in our literature. (pp. 49-50)

    Alec Lucas, "Farley Mowat: Writer for Young People," in Canadian Children's Literature: A Journal of Criticism and Review (Box 335, Guelph, Ontario, Canada N1H6K5), Nos. 5 & 6, 1976, pp. 40-51.

PAT BARCLAY

In common with the majority of his previous works, **The Snow Walker** provides Mowat with a convenient platform from which to expound his passionately held convictions about the North and its people, but it also proves, to this reviewer's satisfaction at any rate, that Farley Mowat can be counted among the top story-tellers writing in Canada today.

There are nine short stories in **The Snow Walker,** each of which plays some variation on the general theme of character in conflict with environment, and two non-fictional pieces which are used to introduce and conclude them. (p. 129)

[The] concluding piece in **The Snow Walker, "Dark Odyssey of Soosie",** is vintage Mowat. . . . In it he documents the true and tragic story of a group of Eskimo families whom the Canadian government and the Hudson's Bay Company shunted from one bleak and hopeless location to another over a period of 30 years, refusing to return them to their original home.

Mowat's description of the Eskimos' ordeal, culminating in a murder trial; of the trial itself, and of its aftermath are as gripping as anything he has ever written.

Yet despite its power, **"Dark Odyssey of Soosie"** may seem out of place in a collection of short stories until we recollect that *The Snow Walker* is, after all, a book by Farley Mowat. Leaving well enough alone, or appreciating the Eskimo experience from a comfortable aesthetic distance, would be as foreign to Mowat's purpose as a baobab on Baffin Island. Though each of his fictional pieces is a self-contained story which can be enjoyed purely as a story, each is also in some measure a fierce and uncompromising sermon directed against white arrogance, ignorance and greed. Read as an epilogue, **"Dark Odyssey of Soosie"** goes a long way towards justifying Mowat's sermonizing. Truth, it demonstrates, is both stranger and more terrible than fiction.

All of which may seem to relegate the stories themselves to second place, which may well be precisely what their author had in mind. Yet looking back on the book as a whole it is Mowat's fictional characters, especially his animal characters, which spring to mind.

The life of the Eskimo in Farley Mowat's Arctic is stripped to its elements: love, death, hunger, work and tradition, and gives rise not to despair, but to moral purification. The plot of each story is generally a straightforward explanation of a mystery or an anomaly. All of the stories, sooner or later, deal with some aspect of the theme of brotherhood or self-sacrifice. Narration is divided equally between Eskimo characters and Mowat himself.

But it is Mowat's prose style, even more than the sometimes spectacularly dramatic stories he has to tell, which makes *The Snow Walker* exceptional. His vocabulary is large and knowledgeable; he is rich in the wiles of the born and practised storyteller; his ability to select the best of all possible words at the ideal moment is first rate. (pp. 129-30)

> *Pat Barclay, "Fiction Stranger than Fact" (reprinted by permission of the author), in* Canadian Literature, *No. 76, Spring, 1978, pp. 129-30.*

DAVID WEINBERGER

In *And No Birds Sang* Mowat tries to do what in the midst of war he knew he could not: make those far removed from battle understand what it was like. Even after almost 40 years, the material is too powerful to accommodate itself to a personal memoir. . . .

Through anecdote and story, the book does entertain.

But surely this is not what Mowat intends, for as he makes the war interesting its tedium remains hidden. Mowat is at pains not to glamorize his subject, yet there remains something glamorous about his tales of crashing shells, impossible treks and scaling cliffs. For war memoirs to succeed, they must subvert the romanticism which naturally accrues to the record of war without becoming as hard to get through as the war years themselves. The personal memoir may be the worst format for accomplishing this, for the author tells of his own growth (as if war were therapeutic), tells of the experiences burned deepest into him (as if war comprises only dramatic events). And because the narrator survives, it is harder for him to overcome the civilian's belief that death is something that happens only to others.

Everybody knows that war is hell; it is the author's task to transform that knowledge into understanding. At times Mowat succeeds, at times the writing bogs down in adjectives and ellipsis. We do learn about Farley Mowat: the book makes plausible the unlikely combination of pacific naturalist and gun-toting foot soldier, although since he is unsure that he ever killed anyone a certain expected dimension of moral reflection is absent. . . . The power of war is apparent in its refusal to be expressed in Mowat's book. It takes a writer of stature—both as an author and as a moral, sensitive person—to make the attempt as valiantly as Mowat has.

> *David Weinberger, "Delayed Dispatch from the Front," in* Maclean's Magazine (© 1979 by Maclean's Magazine; *reprinted by permission), Vol. 93, No. 41, October 8, 1979, p. 58.*

CHRISTOPHER LEHMANN-HAUPT

Veterans of bloody battle are not inclined to reminisce. Farley Mowat, the Canadian naturalist and author of some two dozen books, is no exception. According to the epilogue of his latest book, "So awful" was his experience of World War II "that through three decades I kept the deeper agonies of it wrapped in the cotton-wool of protective forgetfulness." . . . [Presumably] to demonstrate that it is not at all sweet and honorable to die for one's country, he decided to unwrap his deeper agonies and write **"And No Birds Sang."**

He paints the horrors of war gruesomely in this deceptively conventional account of his participation in the Mediterranean campaign of 1943-44 as a young lieutenant in a Canadian regiment attached to Montgomery's Eighth Army. At first he seems to be writing nothing more than the standard war memoir. . . .

There follow the familiar scenes: the rejection-by-the-Air-Force-because-of-too-little-weight scene; the settling-for-father's-old-infantry-regiment scene; the hazing-and-camaraderie-of-training scenes; the last-of-virginity scene; and the scene in which the neophyte longs fervently for real action and a chance to prove his manhood. True, the predictability of it all is broken up by a good yarn or two. . . . But for all that the narrative absorbs us, we keep wondering during the first third of the book why this story had to be retold nearly 40 years after it occurred.

Then bit by bit we begin to notice Mr. Mowat's growing preoccupation with what he will eventually name the Worm That Never Dies—gut-twisting fear. It doesn't bother him much at first, during a night landing on the southeast tip of Sicily, or during his platoon's initial victorious skirmishing with remnants of the German Army rapidly retreating to the north. But images of death accumulate in Mr. Mowat's mind—men cut in half, decapitated, blown to bits, or just driven mad—and the desire to fight steadily drains out of him. (p. 149)

But it isn't so much the violence that finally undoes him, as the constancy of the pressure—his having to go back and back and back into battle even after his nerves have failed him and the Worm has consumed his guts. In the middle of a night of "black, nauseous dread," "I began to weep." With that he ends his narrative.

It is all quite terrifying—one of the grimmer and more unromantic depictions of war I have read in as long as I can remember. And it is made all the more stark by Mr. Mowat's refusal to indulge in subjective wailing, and his determination to stick to the objective facts. But does it persuade us of the falseness of the statement, "Dulce et decorum est pro patria mori!"? It certainly convinces us that it isn't "sweet" to die for one's country, as if we needed much further convincing. But on the matter of the "honorableness" of doing so: Mr. Mowat never really engages the relevant issues.

He writes at the beginning of his book, "I believed that every healthy young man in the freedom-espousing countries was duty-bound to take up arms against the fascist plague and, in particular, the singularly bestial German brand." But he never returns to this theme at the end. He simply concludes: "Spurned in Hell long before Homer sanctified it," (though I believe it was Horace who wrote "Dulce et decorum est") "and goading men to madness and destruction ever since, that Old Lie *has to be put down!*"

Does he mean then that under no circumstances is it honorable to die for one's country? I suspect that Mr. Mowat would be pained if he were asked if that were all his book is intended to convey. I trust he would say, no, that is not all he meant; he only wished to tell us of the horror of war, so that nations might think twice before engaging in it again. Still, he would conclude, in the remote eventuality that absolutely no one on the face of the earth believed anymore that it is honorable to die for one's country, why then warfare would have to end forever. (pp. 149-50)

Christopher Lehmann-Haupt, in his review of "And No Birds Sang," in The New York Times, *Section III (© 1980 by The New York Times Company; reprinted by permission), February 19, 1980 (and reprinted in* Books of the Times, *Vol. III, No. 4, 1980, pp. 149-50.*

TED MORGAN

[In **"And No Birds Sang"** Mowat has written about his experiences as a soldier in World War II] in a departure from his usual subject matter, natural history, which he covered in such fine books as **"Never Cry Wolf"** and **"A Whale for the Killing."**

His purpose in doing so, he informs us, is to put down the lie that it is worthwhile to die for one's country. The discovery he made, in the shell-pitted hills and valleys of Italy nearly 40 years ago, is that there are no good wars. One resists the urge to tell him: You are not alone. It would take a writer of considerably more power than Mr. Mowat can summon to bring any freshness of feeling to this worn theme. Most of us know by now that in war men are killed unfairly. But some of us might still argue that there were worthwhile reasons for fighting World War II, and that the strategic reasons for the invasion of Italy were sound.

But Mr. Mowat is not concerned with the complexity of war. Beyond "getting Jerry" he has no interest in the purpose of the battles he fought in, or in the men outside his platoon. Indeed, he does not mention his divisional commander, the young and inexperienced Guy Simonds. Even the sketches of his fellow soldiers are perfunctory. The author's one theme—and who can blame him?—is "WHAT IS HAPPENING TO ME?" And yet the soldier's single aim, survival, as Randall Jarrell once wrote, "is nonsense to the practice of the centuries." The result is a book in which the action is oversimplified, as in a cartoon strip, with the dialogue seeming to come out of the soldiers' mouths in balloons.

Even so, Mr. Mowat is worth reading, if for no other reason than that there are too few war memoirs from the subaltern level, and I had a fine time comparing his account with those of his commanders. Generals, in their memoirs, with their lofty strategic outlook and their Monday-morning quarterbacking, tend to sanitize war. They provide the overview, while Mr. Mowat gives us what might be called the underview. (pp. 12-13)

Ted Morgan, "Subaltern in Sicily," in The New York Times Book Review *(© 1980 by The New York Times Company; reprinted by permission), February 24, 1980, pp. 12-13.*

TOM O'BRIEN

Mowat is probably best known for **"Never Cry Wolf"** and **"A Whale for the Killing,"** two accounts of his close personal involvement with these maligned and abused animals, written long before their causes became fashionable. His is a "world" of tundra and outcrop rock, a place where "only the disembodied whistling of an unseen plover gave any indication that life existed anywhere in this lunar land where no tree grew." Like the scenes before him, his writing is lean, evocative, haunting. And beneath his "achromatic landscapes," Mowat uncovers surprise, complexity, magnificence. . . .

In such a world, nature can seem sublimely inhuman, vast, terrible. Yet Mowat avoids either sentimental falsification of its harshness or the opposite fallacy of denying any feeling whatsoever for nature. His understanding encompasses both the beauty and necessities of the natural world, and his work seems more trustworthy for recording both.

Another aspect of Mowat's truthfulness is his humor. His prose sparkles with occasional comic gems. . . .

The stories [collected in **"The World of Farley Mowat"**] arranged by editor Peter Davison according to their sequence in Mowat's life, amount to quasi-autobiography. And yet the winnowing process has caused some problems; the isolated passages from **"A Whale for the Killing"** fail to capture the full power and pathos of that work. And the excerpts from **"Never Cry Wolf"** relate too little of the history of the delightful wolf family Mowat got to know.

The most satisfyingly replete piece is taken from an aptly titled study of Newfoundland, **"This Rock Within the Sea."** Its description of the land is loving and intimate, as if Mowat had pored over each acre of stone and sea spew. Recounting how the heritage of the region's old fishing villages was destroyed by industrialization, the story becomes a prose hymn to the lost tradition. What Mowat offers is not primitivism but genuine conservatism—a concern with, as Wordsworth phrased it at the beginning of the Industrial Revolution, "things gone silently out of the world, things violently destroyed."

Mowat explains that as a young man, on setting off to study wolves, his aim was to pursue *biology* in its literal sense, "the study of life." He complains that "too many of my contemporaries tended to shy away from living things as far as they could get, and chose to restrict themselves instead to the aseptic atmosphere of laboratories." Mowat was right about this imbalance in science, but efforts such as his have helped foster a newer scientific approach that regards life in its context—not as a specimen.

In **"The World of Farley Mowat,"** the wholeness of life is beautifully treated by a man whose heart and head, whose sharp eyes and wide grin are in strong union. His own wholeness permeates the book, and binds its parts with a shaman's magic.

Tom O'Brien, "Finding Surprise and Magnificence in Barren Northern Landscapes" (reprinted by permission of the author), in The Christian Science Monitor, *October 15, 1980, p. 17.*

WAYNE GRADY

Farley Mowat has written twenty-four books since *People of the Deer* (1952)—which Hugh MacLennan called "the finest thing of its sort to come out of Canada"—and it's a rare and lonely season when no new Mowat graces the stands. This season Peter Davison has saved us with *The World of Farley Mowat* [a collection of Mowat's work]. Mowat's immense popularity has remained as constant and as changing as his favourite elements, snow and sea. . . . Adored by the masses and ignored by the critics, Mowat wouldn't have it any other way. He described himself in 1977 as a "storyteller who is far more concerned with reaching his audience than with garnering kudos from the arbiters of literary greatness." When asked more recently where he would place his own work in the mansion of Canadian letters, he bellowed emphatically: "Nowhere! I'm in a room by myself. I'm considered pretentious and artistic by the commercial guys, and too commercial by the artistic guys. And I'm perfectly happy in that position."

Such an ambiguous reflection is difficult to catch in an anthology. (p. 67)

The selections in *The World of Farley Mowat* are arranged biographically. . . . The contrast between Mowat's Walt Disney childhood in Saskatoon . . . and his instant manhood overseas is stunning and instructive, exactly what an anthology of this sort ought to be. Each experience illuminates the past and informs the future.

The same is true of Section III, taken from four of Mowat's Arctic books. After the war Mowat spent almost two years in the Keewatin Barrens, studying first wolves and caribou . . . and, after graduating from the University of Toronto in 1949, the once-thriving Ihalmiut. . . . Returning south, Mowat spent his war gratuity on a log cabin near Palgrave, Ontario, and there wrote his first ten books, including most of the stories later collected in *The Snow Walker* . . . His first story was rejected by every magazine in Canada. . . . Mowat ignored [W. O. Mitchell's advice to write "boy-girl stories"] and promptly sold the story to the *Saturday Evening Post* for $750. *The Snow Walker* is represented here by **"Snow,"** which is really an essay, and by **"The White Canoe,"** which is really a tale.

The fifth section includes Mowat's first two Newfoundland books, *This Rock Within the Sea* and *The Boat Who Wouldn't Float* . . . , the former a quasi-historical account of the island's hardy seafarers, the latter an extended anecdote about his voyage with Jack McClelland on the *Happy Adventure,* in which those same hardy seafarers are satirized as oafish, illiterate clowns. This is the beginning of Mowat's "literary menopause". . . . What happened?

The answer comes partly out of this anthology, for if we survey Mowat's work for that period, only one book stands out as having been *written*—as distinct from being edited or revised—in Mowat's favourite first-person, furious style: *A Whale for the Killing*. . . . (pp. 67-8)

In 1967, a great Fin whale somehow got caught in Aldridges Pond near Burgeo, and Mowat watched in helpless fury as the local, deracinated population shot at it with rifles, took great gouging runs at it with their mail-order powerboats, and harassed the poor beast to death. In public retaliation Mowat wrote *A Whale for the Killing* to "blacken Burgeo's name from one end of Canada to the other"; privately he was dismayed that his hardy, natural seafarers could be "just as capable of being utterly loathesome as the bastards from the cities." It was a bitter realization; it changed Mowat's life, and—to judge from *And No Birds Sang*—it changed his philosophy and his writing.

What sort of writer emerges from this collection? Certainly on one level Mowat is the saga man, the wandering minstrel whose egotistical but essentially hollow task is to commit other people's deeds to memory or to history, to keep pale campfires of thought alight in the mindless badlands of civilization. Lear's fool, time's goat, Mowat is a fiercely devoted lover of anyone who has refused to let his survival instinct be lulled to sleep by the herd instinct, and in defence of that refusal he is sometimes willing to let his bleeding heart run away with his bloody head. But his books praise decency, courage, and endurance in the teeth of implacable fate and human stupidity, and there is nothing wrong with that.

The essence of Farley Mowat can be found in this book, but it's a slippery thing. It can be glimpsed, perhaps, in a comparison of these lines from one of Mowat's earliest stories, **"The White Canoe,"** with which Davison concludes *The World of Farley Mowat.* The lines describe the nightmare of the old Eskimo, Katalak: "I dreamt I was alone in a deserted place where no birds sang, no wolves howled, nothing moved except me, and the sky was growing darker and darker, and I knew that when the night came it would never be followed by another dawn." (p. 68)

Wayne Grady, "The Elemental Farley Mowat" (copyright ©1980 by Saturday Night; *reprinted by permission of the author), in* Saturday Night, *Vol. 95, No. 9, November, 1980, pp. 67-8.*

Kin Platt

1911-

American novelist and cartoonist.

Platt writes novels for young adults that range from rollicking adventure stories to introspective portrayals of troubled teenagers. In one of his earliest novels, *Sinbad and Me*, Platt follows the adventures of his protagonist, Steven Forrester, and Steve's bulldog, Sinbad. Full of rousing action, treasure hunts, and secret codes, *Sinbad and Me* won the 1967 Mystery Writers of America Edgar Award for juvenile mystery.

Platt has also written several novels about emotionally troubled young adults. *The Boy Who Could Make Himself Disappear* depicts the anxieties of a schizophrenic; *Hey, Dummy* is the story of Neil Comstock and Alan, the mentally retarded boy Neil calls "Dummy." *Hey, Dummy* follows the breakdown of Neil's ignorance and the friendship that evolves out of his eventual acceptance of Alan's handicap. Platt's series of "Chloris" books chronicle a young girl's attempt to deal with her parents' divorce, her mother's dating and remarriage, and her father's suicide.

Platt has been attacked for the unconventional subject matter of some of his novels. Perhaps his most controversial book is *Headman*, which Robert Berkvist has called a novel about "growing up dead in the . . . ghettos of Los Angeles." Critics have disputed Platt's use of violence and, especially, his casual use of foul language in this book. To Platt, this is reality. He has written: "The future I see for my own work is an ever widening and deepening spiral to get the most out of myself and my readers. . . . There is always resistance to new ideas, enlightening concepts, or attacks on societal structures, but at times some will be permitted to filter through and reach and hopefully influence our growing audience."

(See also *Contemporary Authors*, Vols. 17-20, rev. ed. and *Something about the Author*, Vol. 21.)

Photograph by Jerry Eisenberg

ROBERT BERKVIST

The moral of Kin Platt's slightly wacky thriller, "**The Blue Man**," seems to be that any red-blooded American teen-ager is bound to be more than a match for any blue-bodied whatsit that might choose to drop in from the Milky Way or from that house down the street (the one where the shades are always drawn). Another moral, this one for authors, is that when you trot out a villain with a lovely cerulean complexion, your explanation had better be good. Unfortunately, after Mr. Platt has introduced his blue bully-boy and allowed him to strike down the favorite uncle of our hero, Steve Forrester, there isn't much left except The Chase. Steve plunges off in pursuit of the fellow (or things) and pretty soon there isn't a lawman from Maine to New York who needs to be convinced that it's true what they say about the younger generation. Readers who take to Steve, a sort of whole-wheat Holden Caulfield, probably won't mind the trip or the dénouement.

Robert Berkvist, "Visiting Villain," in The New York Times Book Review *(© 1961 by The New York Times Company; reprinted by permission), September 24, 1961, p. 40.*

MIRIAM S. MATHES

Written in short, choppy, ungrammatical schoolboy vernacular by a boy who describes himself as "too old for camp and too young for anything good," [*The Blue Man*] is a wild yarn about a murderer, bright blue in appearance, and the boy's chase to apprehend him. The vernacular is so exaggerated and details of the plot so fantastic that even with the final more or less plausible explanation, the book cannot be recommended for purchase.

Miriam S. Mathes, in her review of "The Blue Man," in School Library Journal, *an appendix to* Library Journal *(reprinted from the November, 1961 issue of* School Library Journal, *published by R. R. Bowker Co./A Xerox Corporation; copyright © 1961), Vol. 8, No. 3, November, 1961, p. 54.*

VIRGINIA KIRKUS' SERVICE

[Platt] has been a syndicated cartoonist and a writer for some of the best known comedians, and the narration [in *Sinbad and Me*] is consistently lively and imaginative. Unfortunately, however, there's a little too much of too many good things here, and Steve's long-winded spouting on the subject of old houses (his major interest) drags the story out to unnecessary length.

The whole thing is wildly illogical—and readers will like it that way.

A review of "Sinbad and Me," in Virginia Kirkus' Service (copyright © 1966 Virginia Kirkus' Service, Inc.), Vol. XXXIV, No. 13, July 1, 1966, p. 630.

PHYLLIS COHEN

[Sinbad and Me] is a mystery story with character! It's breezy, funny, brash, clever, and frightening in turn. There are a number of puzzles all tied up in one good solution, and though it may sound as if the author has tried to work in every time-tested gimmick, the book doesn't sound tired and old-hat. It's fast moving!

There are all of these familiar elements—wonderful dog, pirate treasure, secret panels, caves, codes, ciphers, gamblers, family feuds, counterfeiting, old-world superstitions, haunted house, unsolved murder, missing map, invisible ink, and more.

But the young hero is not typical. For one thing, his hobby is old houses and antiques, and he is quite knowledgeable about these. For another, he has flunked his science course and is attending summer school to make it up. (He likes his teacher, he can pass the course, but he is completely disinterested in the subject—and remains unreconstructed.) He has tenacity and perseverance just like Sinbad, his wonderful bulldog. He doesn't set out to solve mysteries or play a lone hand. He reports odd happenings to the sheriff who is an intelligent, interesting, and observant man. (Hooray!)

Steve's friends are unusual, too. Herky is an authentic genius with total recall and a photographic memory. Mrs. Teska is old and crippled, speaks broken English, and is shrewd and kind. The science teacher skin dives and collects coins. Steve takes it for granted that there's more to people than appears on the surface and friends are where you find them. Though the story, as is the case with all children's mysteries, is wildly improbable, the characters and swift pace hold the attention completely. The puzzles will be fun for code lovers (solutions to the two ciphers are given at the end) and the author does not omit a single clue. It is a logically constructed, cleverly contrived, very involved plot. So involved is it, that about midway through the book, the hero is forced to list about thirty-five clues which he has collected. And that's only half-way through the book. This is a funny book. So few mysteries are genuinely funny, that this one stands out like a beacon! . . . The dialogue may be breezy, but the plot is solid—certainly one of the cleverest mysteries for youngsters I've ever read. (pp. 1-2)

Phyllis Cohen, in her review of "Sinbad and Me," in Young Readers Review (copyright © 1966 Young Readers Review), Vol. III, No. 2, October, 1966, pp. 1-2.

BEST SELLERS

[Sinbad and Me] will prove a delight for young readers. Young Steve Forrester is left behind to work out a science course during the summer when his parents leave for the Maine woods. In a short time Steve becomes involved, with his English bulldog, Sinbad, in a series of adventures. The adventures lead to the solution of the town's favorite mystery, the disappearance of Big Nick Murdock and his boat, "River Queen." The pleas-ant style, lively narrative and spirited action all contribute to make a delightful book for the mystery-loving young reader.

A review of "Sinbad and Me," in Best Sellers (copyright 1966, by the University of Scranton), Vol. 26, No. 13, October 1, 1966, p. 251.

SARAH LAW KENNERLY

A most unusual book is Kin Platt's Sinbad and Me . . . , a long and lively story told by its 12-year-old hero, Steve. While his parents are out of town, Steve and Sinbad, his English bulldog, disrupt the peace and harmony of Hampton, New Jersey, unravel an 18th-century mystery, find a hidden million-dollar treasure, outwit some pretty unsavory underworld characters, and find Big Nick Murdock, who disappeared years before when his floating gambling casino sank. Steve puzzles out riddles on tombstones and ciphers in a pirate's cave to solve much of the mystery, and his precocious knowledge of architecture and old houses does the rest. The whole story is outrageously illogical, long and rambling, and refreshingly funny.

Sarah Law Kennerly, in her review of "Sinbad and Me," in School Library Journal, an appendix to Library Journal (reprinted from the December, 1966 issue of School Library Journal, published by R. R. Bowker Co./A Xerox Corporation; copyright © 1966), Vol. 13, No. 4, December, 1966, p. 71.

KIRKUS SERVICE

Kin Platt's Sinbad and Me was a real spine-tingler but there's no mystery about [the protagonist of The Boy Who Could Make Himself Disappear]: he's a schizophrenic. In a combination of flashback, stream of consciousness and almost equally interior narrative, Roger reacts to his parents' abrupt divorce, to the tempo and impersonality of New York, and especially . . . constantly . . . to his inability to pronounce the letter r. As a small child he burned his tongue on a styptic pencil; thanks to a singularly monstrous set of parents, the impediment has mushroomed until the simplest conversation is agony. A few people reach him: the impetuous model in the penthouse and her boyfriend, who learned endurance in the Resistance; a girl who's crippled but not cramped; his current speech therapist, a solid, forthright, feeling woman. It is the latter who holds on when Roger withdraws into an infantile autistic state and the Frenchman who may lead him out. Obviously this is not child's play; neither is it good psychology—Roger's parents are too brutal, his benefactors too heroic. And as an approximation of adult fiction, it's not sufficiently well structured or written to be worth recommending.

A review of "The Boy Who Could Make Himself Disappear," in Kirkus Service (copyright © 1968 The Kirkus Service, Inc.), Vol. XXXVI, No. 10, May 15, 1968, p. 556.

BEST SELLERS

["The Boy Who Could Make Himself Disappear"] lacks the humor of the author's "Sinbad and Me", which was published in 1966. But the same understanding of youth is present as the story dips into the confused existence of young Roger Baxter. Roger is living in New York with his mother, following the divorce of his parents. His father has always been busy and his mother is only concerned with herself. The boy makes friends, but eventually breaks down from the emotional strain.

Young readers might have trouble with the story, but the insights into family life and its importance will not be lost on older students. (pp. 173-74)

> *A review of "The Boy Who Could Make Himself Disappear," in* Best Sellers *(copyright 1968, by the University of Scranton), Vol. 28, No. 8, July 15, 1968, pp. 173-74.*

ZENA SUTHERLAND

Although it is a little difficult to believe in the sustained cruelty of Roger's mother, [**The Boy Who Could Make Himself Disappear**] is a story so moving and so well written that one must accept her as a person whose aberrant behavior, deeply sadistic and selfish, has gone without notice because most of it is directed, in private, toward her only child. . . . [Roger's] sad musings on incidents of the past, his efforts to cope with his mother's hostility, and his valiant efforts to cooperate with the speech therapist are brilliantly told. (pp. 14-15)

> *Zena Sutherland, in her review of "The Boy Who Could Make Himself Disappear," in* Bulletin of the Center for Children's Books *(reprinted by permission of The University of Chicago Press; copyright 1968 by The University of Chicago), Vol. 22, No. 1, September, 1968, pp. 14-15.*

JOHN GILLESPIE

[**The Boy Who Could Make Himself Disappear** is an] unusual and disturbing novel which is apt to be controversial because of its theme and the way in which that theme is developed. The central character is seventh-grader Roger Baxter, handicapped by a severe speech impediment which resulted from a childhood accident and has been compounded by emotional problems with his parents, who have just been divorced and are both indifferent to the boy's welfare. . . . The novel ends on a faintly hopeful note when Roger, now in a mental hospital, makes tentative contact with someone who wants to help him. The reading is not easy; the author uses many flashbacks, and some passages verge on stream-of-consciousness. Nor is the book without flaws—Roger's mother, for example, seems at times unbelievably heartless. But in its painful honesty, this, like the YA favorite, [Hannah Green's] *I Never Promised You a Rose Garden*, is a book that will remain with thoughtful young people long after it is read.

> *John Gillespie, in his review of "The Boy Who Could Make Himself Disappear," in* School Library Journal, *an appendix to* Library Journal *(reprinted from the October, 1968 issue of* School Library Journal, *published by R. R. Bowker Co./A Xerox Corporation; copyright © 1968), Vol. 15, No. 2, October, 1968, p. 172.*

SARAH LAW KENNERLY

Mystery of the Witch Who Wouldn't . . . is the sequel to *Sinbad and Me*. . . . But readers who expect more of the same should be warned immediately: this one is all about witchcraft and only for aficionados. Hero Steve, his bulldog Sinbad, and his friend Minerva Landry, the sheriff's daughter, get involved with a little old lady witch, Aurelia Hepburn, who tells Minerva not to let her father open any package tied with string. When the sheriff does open one, it explodes, and he ends up in the hospital. Steve and Minerva investigate, aided, of course, by

Aurelia, who's subsequently captured by the criminals. They try to make her read the secret-formula-containing mind of a scientist they've captured, but Aurelia calls up her demons, weaves a spell that brings about a spectacularly successful hurricane, and performs other magic feats which unnerve the criminals. A kind of juvenile, watered down *Rosemary's Baby*, full of witchery and lacking a plot.

> *Sarah Law Kennerly, in her review of "Mystery of the Witch Who Wouldn't," in* School Library Journal, *an appendix to* Library Journal *(reprinted from the December, 1969 issue of* School Library Journal, *published by R. R. Bowker Co./A Xerox Corporation; copyright © 1969), Vol. 16, No. 4, December, 1969, p. 64.*

KIRKUS REVIEWS

The theme [of *Hey, Dummy*] is involvement: Neil's protective interest in and eventually, total identification (by means of an "altered personality due to an existing anxiety state from unknown psychogenic . . . causes") with a brain-dramaged boy. But the inept interior monologues (meant to convey the "Dummy's" state of mind), long-winded lectures on the facts of mental retardation, and heavy-handed reliance on the scapegoat motif impede any reader empathy. Just as we begin to plumb Neil's disintegrating psyche, the plot goes haywire—with a dead girl, a lynch mob and an improbable escape—and this well-intentioned, potentially enlightening, foray into abnormal psychology loses its own grip on reality. The result is stylistic confusion and, in the end, the exploitation of Neil's sensitively defined mental anguish for its shock value.

> *A review of "Hey, Dummy," in* Kirkus Reviews *(copyright © 1971 The Kirkus Service, Inc.), Vol. XXXIX, No. 22, November 15, 1971, p. 1213.*

BETSY BYARS

Bringing the tragedy of mental retardation to the printed page is difficult. Only the simplest truth is needed, and yet nothing that is said ever seems quite enough. Through the wry, sensitive Neil Comstock, Kin Platt says more than anybody so far, and he says it with gentleness and guts.

["**Hey, Dummy**"] begins with a three-man football game in which the Dummy becomes unwittingly involved when he picks up the stray ball. Boyish violence ensues, leaving Neil disturbed. "Thinking about that Dummy just lying there and saying 'Aaaah' after I hit him, ruined my game."

Neil's involvement with the Dummy increases. . . .

[Soon Neil] is attempting to look at the world as the Dummy does. He tries to put himself into Alan's skin. . . .

The build-up to the final tragedy is slow and sure. A young girl is attacked in the park, and the Dummy becomes the target of mob action. Neil, totally committed now, helps him escape. His evaluation of the situation is one of the most poignant moments of the novel. "I'm in big trouble . . . I'm sure I had to do what I did but it just didn't work out the way things are supposed to when you feel you're doing right." And then the agonized, "If only he wasn't such a Dummy!"

Despite an occasional jarring note (Would any bakery attendant stand by while the Dummy helped himself to nine cakes?) the book has a realistic feel to it. This is largely due to the dimension of the characters. The Dummy and Neil dominate, but Neil's kooky sister could be a book in herself. And Mr. Alvarado, a Mexican-American teacher, in three appearances comes off as a complex and wholly believable character.

There are flashes of humor in this compelling novel, but the nature of mental retardation does not lend itself to a happy ending. And the last word, uttered by Neil, is the same sound with which the Dummy tries to communicate throughout the book, the confused, helpless, "Aaaah."

One closes the book and hears the wry voice of Neil Comstock, "So what did you expect?"

> Betsy Byars, in her review of "Hey, Dummy," in The New York Times Book Review (© 1972 by The New York Times Company; reprinted by permission), March 12, 1972, p. 8.

ZENA SUTHERLAND

[In *Hey, Dummy*] Neil is at first both amused and repelled by the retarded boy who has moved into the neighborhood and is attending his school, but he soon begins to feel sympathy for Alan (the "Dummy" of the title) and to defend him when others tease him. And Alan responds, following Neil affectionately. Soon rejected by his other friends, worried by Alan's situation (autistic sister, withdrawn mother, father in an institution, home a shambles) and bitterly conscious of the harshness and hostility of his own parents, Neil is driven to run off with Alan. When they are caught, tension has pushed Neil to the breaking-point, and his sympathy for Alan results in his identifying with Alan. There has been, throughout the book, a train-of-consciousness reaction from the retarded Alan, and the startling ending has the same disjointed and monosyllabic speech (always italicized) only this time it is Neil. He has become a dummy, too. Not quite as effective as Platt's other study of a disturbed child (perhaps because the focus is broader here and therefore more diffuse) this is, nevertheless, a perceptive treatment of a child's sensitivity. Artistically it suffers somewhat because there is so little relief from the almost universal reactions of suspicion, intolerance, fear, and hostility on the parts of the adult characters.

> Zena Sutherland, in her review of "Hey, Dummy," in Bulletin of the Center for Children's Books (reprinted by permission of The University of Chicago Press; © 1972 by The University of Chicago), Vol. 25, No. 10, June, 1972, p. 162.

KIRKUS REVIEWS

In our opinion, Kin Platt's portraits of disturbed children have not always hit the mark. But Chloris [protagonist of *Chloris and the Creeps*]—in her violent hatred of the "creeps" her mother dates—and her rejection of her new stepfather in favor of an idealized memory of her dead (suicided) one—is totally believable. . . . Platt's strength lies in his ability to show Chloris both from her mother's point of view as a disturbing and disturbed child, and through the more intimate, non-judgmental eyes of her sympathetic sister. . . . Unlike the hero of *Hey, Dummy* . . . whose regression seemed both insufficiently motivated and dramatically unsubstantiated, Chloris is simply one of those people who has trouble letting go of her past; and as such she will be familiar to readers of all ages.

> A review of "Chloris and the Creeps," in Kirkus Reviews (copyright © 1973 The Kirkus Service, Inc.), Vol. XLI, No. 4, February 15, 1973, p. 188.

KRISTIN E. HAMMOND

[*Chloris and the Creeps* is another] novel about the problems caused by divorce, with the added complication of parental suicide. . . . Chloris' growing neurosis . . . is well handled, but her sudden reversal seems hard to believe. The divorce and suicide are never sufficiently explained, and children may not understand that these are the reasons for Chloris' unhappiness. Jenny is not consistently portrayed, and the mother and stepfather are stock characters. A Room Made of Windows by Eleanor Cameron . . . and Lillian by Gunilla Norris . . . treat similar problems more realistically.

> Kristin E. Hammond, in her review of "Chloris and the Creeps," in School Library Journal, an appendix to Library Journal (reprinted from the April, 1973 issue of School Library Journal, published by R. R. Bowker Co./A Xerox Corporation; copyright © 1973), Vol. 19, No. 8, April, 1973, p. 69.

ZENA SUTHERLAND

Any man who wants to marry her mother is a creep, Chloris thinks, her bitter resentment recorded by her [eight-year-old] sister Jenny [in *Chloris and the Creeps*]. . . . When their mother marries the gentle, patient Fidel Mancha, Chloris is venomous. With great skill, Kin Platt develops the slow, reluctant shedding of Chloris' fantasies about a hero-father and her acceptance of Fidel, whose intelligent sympathy does more to help Chloris than her mother's exasperated love or Jenny's careful allegiance to her sister. While the style is not convincing as that of a child of eight, the fidelity and insight of the author's conception and development far outweigh that one flaw in a moving and realistic story.

> Zena Sutherland, in her review of "Chloris and the Creeps," in Bulletin of the Center for Children's Books (reprinted by permission of The University of Chicago Press; © 1974 by The University of Chicago), Vol. 27, No. 5, January, 1974, p. 84.

KIRKUS REVIEWS

[*Headman* is] Durango Street updated, not only in language which is uncensored street talk throughout, but—more important—in the ending, where your suspicion that Owen doesn't have a chance is confirmed. . . . It's [a] kid with a corkscrew who gets him in the end, but Owen's decision to form his own gang of four in self defense sort of brings it on. And so we leave him—going down, dizzy, unable to speak, and in his head the perfect phrase to summarize it all: "What the fuck?" It's at least a generation too late for this kind of dead end realism to carry a real jolt, but Platt does give Owen enough good breaks to keep the options open, while at the same time making forcefully clear what he's up against.

> A review of "Headman," in Kirkus Reviews (copyright © 1975 The Kirkus Service, Inc.), Vol. XLIII, No. 14, July 15, 1975, p. 783.

ALIX NELSON

[In "Chloris and the Freaks"] Mom starts cheating on her second husband (Fidel, a sculptor, who lives only "to create," but can discourse on men, women and divorce at the drop of a mallet) while leaving her two semi-demented daughters to their own devices. What devices? Chloris, the elder, has a seance nightly with "dear Daddy's spirit" (he killed himself for reasons I will spare you, after marrying his second wife); Chloris plans to oust the pontificating Fidel and get rid of a new contender too. Jenny, the younger, eschews such signs of insanity and prefers instead to follow the signs of the zodiac, treating us to everyone's daily horoscope. You might say it's a mixture of psychology à la Dr. Franzblau and your local one-flight-up astrologist, and I, for one, find either medium a tedium. (p. 52)

Alix Nelson, "Fractured Families," in The New York Times Book Review *(© 1975 by The New York Times Company; reprinted by permission), November 16, 1975, pp. 50, 52.**

JACK FORMAN

Owen Kirby [protagonist of *Headman*], whose father was killed long ago in a fight and whose mother is an alcoholic, is sentenced to a rehabilitative "camp" after his knife work on three others, while defending himself in a street attack. At the camp which is liberally run, Owen makes friends and seems to be adapting to this life, but his term is cut short due to his mother's illness. . . . Again, he takes to the street and at the end of the story finds himself at the wrong end of a switchblade. This fast-paced novel is written for the same age group as *Durango Street* . . . yet the point of [Frank] Bonham's novel has been inverted here: social institutions are irrelevant to the Owen Kirbys of this country; the only law which is real is the law of the street. The language is street talk—sharp and quick and punctuated by a litany of fucks, shits, mothers, and the like. The language, however, is used to make the character of Owen believable and the setting credible. Provocative and engrossing, this is an especially good choice for the category of readers who need "high interest, low reading level" material.

Jack Forman, in his review of "Headman," in School Library Journal *(reprinted from the December, 1975 issue of* School Library Journal, *published by R. R. Bowker Co./A Xerox Corporation; copyright © 1975), Vol. 22, No. 4, December, 1975, p. 61.*

ROBERT BERKVIST

"You got to have gangs. You got to run. . . . The way the street is you got to have gangs. You by yourself, man, you got no chance. On the streets, it's the gangs what do the talking. . . . How else you going to go about your business without being cut or stomped out?" The speaker is Justin Dye; "headman" of the Nomads, a black street gang in Kin Platt's taut and very tough novel ["*Headman*"] about growing up dead in the white, black and Chicano ghettos of Los Angeles. Platt's book isn't about Justin; it's about Owen Kirby, a young white slum-dweller who knows that Justin's way is the only way. . . .

[Unreality never] creeps into "*Headman*," which is as direct as a hammer-blow. The language of "*Headman*," by the way, is the language of the streets, with hardly a four-letter word omitted. Obscenities abound in Owen Kirby's world, but none more obscene than that world itself, which most of us, given the chance, close our eyes to.

Robert Berkvist, in his review of "Headman," in The New York Times Book Review *(© 1975 by The New York Times Company; reprinted by permission), December 14, 1975, p. 8.*

KIRKUS REVIEWS

[*Chloris and the Freaks*] leans heavily on a few devices: Jennie's use of the daily paper's astrology column as a crutch; a frazzled teacher who functions as a stand-up comedian on the subject of marital discord; even Fidel's sometimes mushy philosophizing. And it takes a long time to recap Chloris' old problems. Nevertheless, Chloris continues to be a startlingly truthful portrait of a psychologically mixed-up girl, grimly determined to revenge the wounds of her mother's divorce and her father's suicide by breaking up this second marriage. And what we learn here about Daddy's death and Mom's continued immaturity adds a new, strengthening dimension. Jenny herself continues to be loyal to Chloris yet uncompromising in her struggle to disassociate herself from Chloris' delusions. The loss of Fidel's reassuring presence seems cruel but it's strictly logical. Platt's hard-edged California moderns may not be the most likable people, but one can't resist getting involved. And this unhappy episode is sure to create anxious demand for still more news of Chloris. (pp. 1379-80)

A review of "Chloris and the Freaks," in Kirkus Reviews *(copyright © 1975 The Kirkus Service, Inc.), Vol. XLIII, No. 24, December 15, 1975, pp. 1379-80.*

ZENA SUTHERLAND

In [*Chloris and the Freaks*] sequel to *Chloris and the Creeps*, in which Chloris' fanatical devotion to her dead father made her hostile to a stepfather, Fidel, the fourteen-year-old girl is even more bitter and antagonistic. . . . There's no sweetness and light here. Save for Fidel Mancha, a wise and kind man, all the adult characters are the "freaks" Chloris so contemptuously dubs them. The book has some flaws: an alcoholic teacher talks of his personal life to his class in unconvincing fashion, and the book is oversaturated with Jenny's preoccupation with astrology. Too bad, because the author writes with incisive candor and clarity, albeit a bitter clarity. (pp. 131-32)

Zena Sutherland, in her review of "Chloris and the Freaks," in Bulletin of the Center for Children's Books *(reprinted by permission of The University of Chicago Press; © 1976 by The University of Chicago), Vol. 29, No. 8, April, 1976, pp. 131-32.*

JACK FORMAN

[*The Doomsday Gang*] is a bleaker and less dramatic variation on Platt's *Headman*. . . . Led by tough 15-year-old Coby (he's been on the street since age 10), five Los Angeles teens who've been losers all their lives (they call themselves "fuck-ups") form the Doomsday Gang. . . . In trying to follow five characters, Platt is unable to develop any of them as much as he did Owen Kirby in *Headman*. Platt's message in both stories—there's nothing in gangs, but that's all there is—is driven home here with less impact and more cynicism.

Jack Forman, in his review of "The Doomsday Gang," in School Library Journal *(reprinted from the May, 1978 issue of* School Library Journal, *published by R. R. Bowker Co./A Xerox Corporation; copyright © 1978), Vol. 24, No. 9, May, 1978, p. 79.*

BETSY HEARNE

Another entertaining yet cutting picture of contemporary California family life, [*Chloris and the Weirdos*] finds sisters Chloris

(15) and Jennifer (13) coping with the aftermath of their mother's second divorce, along with their own adolescent exploration of dating. Ever the stable Libra of the family, Jen suddenly finds herself in love with a very sweet, non-sexist, red-haired skateboarder; she also discovers a capacity for unexpected explosions as her mother and sister constantly clash over freedom, responsibility, and male relationships. Platt really knows these characters and their situation, revealing a flair for funny dialogue in conjunction with serious issues that involve both children and adults, neither of which he idealizes or puts down. This has the same high appeal as, and a more natural flow than, *Chloris and the Freaks*. . . .

> *Betsy Hearne, in her review of "Chloris and the Weirdos," in* Booklist *(reprinted by permission of the American Library Association; copyright © 1978 by the American Library Association), Vol. 75, No. 26, November 15, 1978, p. 548.*

JAMES NORSWORTHY

[In *The Doomsday Gang*] white teenagers in Los Angeles form the Doomsday Gang in an attempt to survive a violent world. By publishing this book, Kin Platt and Greenwillow have surely created a new genre of children's literature—vulgarism. Realistic stories about the problems of modern youth living in far less than ideal conditions have been enjoyed by the many fans of S. E. Hinton and Frank Bonham, but neither of these authors and countless others had to writher in the slime of language to project their stories for children and young adults. Each page is literally loaded with obscenities, and will certainly offend everyone.

> *James Norsworthy, in his review of "The Doomsday Gang," in* Catholic Library World, *Vol. 50, No. 5, December, 1978, p. 236.*

PATTY CAMPBELL

Kin Platt, like J. D. Salinger a generation ago, has evidently been doing a lot of listening [to young adults], because *The Doomsday Gang* has the most accurate reproduction of the speech of urban male teenagers since *Catcher in the Rye*. Not only do four-letter words appear on every page, they appear in nearly every sentence, and in their variant forms they substitute for almost any noun, verb, or adjective. The effect, as in the original, is numbing and very effectively conveys the flatness and boredom of the limited lives of street kids. In this reviewer's opinion the language of *The Doomsday Gang* is completely justified by the subject; this is the way these hostile, abandoned kids would talk, and anyone who prefers that they say "Goodness gracious!" instead of "What the fuck!" is opting for dishonesty. (p. 340)

The real selection problem with *The Doomsday Gang* stems not from the language, but from Platt's unintentional cultural slur and from the undeniable fact that the book makes violence sound like fun. The climactic scene is a rumble in which the massed Chicano gangs close in on a bunch of naive and uppity kids from the suburbs. This is no innocent Hollywood slugfest, but a bloody massacre with broken bottles and tire chains, where skulls are fractured and guts are spilled. Nevertheless, we find ourselves drawn into the fierce joy of combat, and we cheer when the Doomsday Gang roars into the battle on stolen motorcycles.

Later, when the survivors lie talking it over in the hospital, we realize that none is going to survive much longer—their violent lives in the streets are going to be very short. Yet somehow the shortness of these lives seems a fair trade for the intensity and excitement of unleashed violence. (pp. 340-41)

It may not be moral to say that violence is fun, but it may be honest. The basic question seems to be this: Have we the right to demand that books for young adults make a moral statement? (p. 341)

> *Patty Campbell, in her review of "The Doomsday Gang," in* Wilson Library Bulletin *(copyright © 1978 by the H. W. Wilson Company), Vol. 53, No. 4, December, 1978, pp. 340-41.*

ZENA SUTHERLAND

Jenny writes about her problems and her sister Chloris in [*Chloris and the Weirdos*], a sequel to *Chloris and the Creeps* and *Chloris and the Freaks*. Jenny's thirteen, Chloris fifteen and difficult. Chloris had hated the stepfather Jenny loved, and she's bitterly resentful when their mother has a date; angry, and fearful that Mom may marry again. Jenny's more understanding, aware of her mother's loneliness, and she's happily establishing a relationship with her first boyfriend, Harold. Platt does a marvelously perceptive and amusing job with Jenny and Harold; they are nervous but candid with each other, neither wanting to be too committed and both finding joy in friendship as well as excitement at being in love. When an exasperated Chloris flounces off for a forbidden weekend at the same time Mom is making her gesture of independence (a weekend date) there's a showdown. The characters have vitality and conviction, the relationships are perceptively drawn, and there's an abundance of humor—especially in the dialogue between Jenny and her skateboard-addict Harold.

> *Zena Sutherland, in her review of "Chloris and the Weirdos," in* Bulletin of the Center for Children's Books *(reprinted by permission of The University of Chicago Press; © 1979 by The University of Chicago), Vol. 32, No. 7, March, 1979, p. 124.*

BOOKLIST

In [*Dracula, Go Home!*, a] seriocomic takeoff on the Dracula theme, Larry Carter, the affable, high school-age narrator, becomes curious enough about a ghoulish-looking hotel guest (who frequents the local cemetery and sports a black cape) to do some checking. Although he eventually discovers his imagination is a bit overactive and Count Dracula has not returned in the person of the creepy Mr. A. R. Claud, Larry does link the guest's unusual activities to some jewel thefts several summers before. An agreeable change of pace from the many problem-oriented books written for those with reading difficulties.

> *A review of "Dracula, Go Home!" in* Booklist *(reprinted by permission of the American Library Association; copyright © 1979 by the American Library Association), Vol. 75, No. 18, May 15, 1979, p. 1435.*

PATRICIA CAMPBELL

[In *Chloris and the Weirdos*, Mr. Platt] has done an excellent job with the character of Jennifer, portraying her problems and her solutions to those problems in a way that is easy for middle class preteens to identify with and learn from. His other characters do not come across as well. Harold is the perfect non-stereotyped adolescent, who is frequently just too good to be true. Jennifer's sister Chloris and her mother are portrayed as somewhat one dimensional, while her grandmother is portrayed in a negative manner that contributes nothing to the story.

The writing is smooth and easy as the book moves toward what seems to be its inevitable conclusion of Jennifer resolving her concerns about Harold and her mother's dating. Then Jennifer's mother goes away for a weekend with a man and Chloris runs away. The resulting family discussion on what family members owe each other and what they owe themselves is well done, although the reader is left hanging somewhat as to how the mother-daughter conflicts will be resolved. Perhaps that will be included in the next book in the series.

In general the book is a reasonably good one, although somewhat weakened by its negative portrayal of the grandmother. It can be of value to the preteen children of divorced parents trying to come to grips with both their own and their mothers' sexuality.

> *Patricia Campbell, in her review of "Chloris and the Weirdos," in* Interracial Books for Children Bulletin *(reprinted by permission of* Interracial Books for Children Bulletin, *1841 Broadway, New York, N.Y. 10023), Vol. 10, No. 7, 1979, p. 15.*

ZENA SUTHERLAND

Larry, who [narrates **Dracula, Go Home!**], is spending the summer helping his aunt run a hotel. He's convinced there's something eerie about the tall, secretive man who rents a room as A. R. Claud: Why does the man never use the hotel dining room? Why does he prowl about in the dark? And why does nobody ever see Claud coming down the stairs? Larry investigates old local papers and looks over the hotel register, discovering that the same handwriting as Claud's has been used for other names—always the same room. Is he really a vampire? No, but he is a criminal. There's some humor and plenty of action, some suspense, and certainly an element of mystery in a not-very-convincing story that will probably appeal to many readers because of the brisk pace and the suggestion of looming danger. Since the vocabulary difficulty is low, this should prove useful for slow older readers.

> *Zena Sutherland, in her review of "Dracula Go Home!" in* Bulletin of the Center for Children's Books *(reprinted by permission of The University of Chicago Press; © 1979 by The University of Chicago), Vol. 33, No. 1, September, 1979, p. 16.*

BOOKLIST

Fifteen-year-old Eddie Hall [protagonist of **The Ape Inside Me**] seems unable to control his temper. Plagued, in addition, by frustrations at home and a lack of self-confidence, he invents a macho alter ego (Kong) to which he assigns blame for the numerous fights he always getting into. Platt casts Eddie as surprisingly likable and uncomplicated, despite his volatility, and Eddie's struggles to gain control of his temper (which he eventually does) will strike a responsive chord among teenagers facing their own individual growing pains. Those in search of the "realistic" stuff of Platt's earlier books won't find it here. What teenagers will find, however, is a simply written, positive

story with an obvious, but not too overbearing, message—an appealing combination especially for reluctant readers.

> *A review of "The Ape Inside Me," in* Booklist *(reprinted by permission of the American Library Association; copyright © 1980 by the American Library Association), Vol. 76, No. 9, January 1, 1980, p. 662.*

CLAIRE M. DYSON

Fifteen year old Eddie [protagonist of **The Ape Inside Me**] is a "scrapper" often involved in violent clashes which, he insists, are encouraged by the "ape" inside him. Eddie calls the ape "Kong" and conveniently blames him when things get out of hand. Interestingly, most of the trouble encountered has not been initiated by Eddie (or Kong); it is simply a reaction to injustice, whether it be visited upon himself or upon others. . . .

The book covers a brief period in Eddie's life, yet we become fully aware of the circumstances of his home environment, his school, and the socio-economic climate of the community. The characters are well drawn; painfully poignant is that of Eddie's mother whose desperation in trying to retain her housemate suggests a pitiable lack of self-esteem.

A first person narrative is difficult but Kin Platt's character is wholly believable, and because he is an adolescent wrestling with the onset of maturity, the tiresome self-analysis which attends the I/Me tomes of the adult genre is absent here. The concluding chapter is unashamedly idealistic, so hold the moment close! . . . It's a singular joy to imagine just once "all things bright and beautiful" working together.

> *Claire M. Dyson, in her review of "The Ape Inside Me," in* Best Sellers *(copyright © 1980 Helen Dwight Reid Educational Foundation), Vol. 39, No. 11, February, 1980, p. 410.*

ZENA SUTHERLAND

There's some humor and plenty of action in [**The Ghost of Hellsfire Street**] in which the narrator, Steve, is the ever-suspicious, ever-tenacious detective despite his youthfulness. Steve's wildest suspicions are doubted by his friend Miranda and by her father, Sheriff Landry, but all of them prove to be true. One wonders if Platt has made an effort to see just how heavily he can lay it on: there's a kidnapped scientist, a medium who bilks a credulous old woman out of a million dollars, a pirate ghost, a dignified Shinnecock chieftain who lends Steve his sacred spirit bag, a venal politician, and so on. And a fire. Steve talks and talks to his dog. Everything comes out right, and it's all quite predictable and rather boring. Too bad, since Platt can do better.

> *Zena Sutherland, in her review of "The Ghost of Hellsfire Street," in* Bulletin of the Center for Children's Books *(reprinted by permission of The University of Chicago Press; © 1980 by The University of Chicago), Vol. 34, No. 3, November, 1980, p. 62.*

JACK FORMAN

[In **Flames Going Out**] Tammy, a disturbed 16 year old from an upper-middle-class family, plays a game that becomes a metaphor for her mental illness. Tammy lights a match, talks to it, and becomes one with it; as the match burns, she feels alive and creative, but when it dissipates into smoke, her reality disappears. Dr. Greengold, her psychiatrist (a biting but witty and understanding person), helps Tammy develop a self based in reality. Unfortunately, her association with her doctor leads to a romantic involvement with Greengold's hopelessly drug-addicted son, which ends in tragedy for both. The stark realism of Platt's gang stories (*Headman* . . . , etc.) doesn't work here, however. Tammy is more than a societal problem, and to make her believable requires more than fast plot action, direct language (punctuated by various uses of the word "fuck"), and some hackneyed attempts to explain Tammy's illness in flashback bits and pieces (an uncle who fondled her and a teen party where she was almost raped). The flame burns brighter and with more substance in Green's *I Never Promised You a Rose Garden* . . . , [Judith] Guest's *Ordinary People* . . . and, for younger readers, [John] Neufeld's *Lisa, Bright and Dark*. . . . (pp. 63-4)

> *Jack Forman, in his review of "Flames Going Out," in* School Library Journal *(reprinted from the December, 1980 issue of* School Library Journal, *published by R.R. Bowker Co./A Xerox Corporation; copyright © 1980), Vol. 27, No. 4, December, 1980, pp. 63-4.*

DREW STEVENSON

[*The Ghost of Hellsfire Street*] is a rip-roaring mystery. Steve Forrester and his pet bulldog Sinbad are faced with four mysteries: a scientist who may not have been kidnapped as thought, a weird psychic who may be trying to defraud an old woman, a new political party trying to oust Steve's friend Sheriff Landry and a pirate's ghost who keeps appearing in Steve's bedroom. The mysteries are all related to a plot to cheat the local Indians out of a hidden oil deposit on their reservation, but before the villains can be rounded up, Steve, Sinbad and friends have to face a trial by fire in a secret cave. Platt's dialogue is barbed, there's enough going on for several books and by story's end everything is wrapped up nice and tight. More please!

> *Drew Stevenson, in his review of "The Ghost of Hellsfire Street," in* School Library Journal *(reprinted from the December, 1980 issue of* School Library Journal, *published by R. R. Bowker Co./A Xerox Corporation; copyright © 1980), Vol. 27, No. 4, December, 1980, p. 74.*

PATTY CAMPBELL

Since a major function of adolescent literature is to provide reality checks for the reader's self-image, YA novels about teens who struggle through mental illnesses can be useful if they present an accurate picture of deviant behavior.

Recently there have been a number of books in which young adults who are overwhelmed by their problems commit suicide, starve themselves, or just plain act weird. Most of the authors of these books seem to have made at least some responsible efforts to research the symptoms and prognosis of the unhealthy behavior they are depicting.

This reviewer, however, has been intrigued (and a bit disturbed) to notice a difference between the plot structure of the books with a female protagonist and those with a male as the main character. The boys carry through with their willful self-destruction in a determined even heroic way, leaving their

girlfriends to agonize over their own ineffectiveness in preventing the tragedy. See, for example, *Tunnel Vision* by Fran Arrick or *About David* by Susan Beth Pfeffer. The disturbed girls, on the other hand, vacillate and waffle and are eventually salvaged by their boyfriends' steadfast love. (p. 454)

Kin Platt pulls a switch on this formula in *Flames Going Out*. Tammy has only a tentative hold on reality and must reassure herself of her continued existence by secretly lighting matches to see the flames that have come to symbolize life to her. When she falls in love with Jonathan, the emotion is her lifeline back to sanity. Even though he is even more disturbed than she and eventually succeeds in destroying himself, his death is the event that shocks her into taking charge of her life. (pp. 454-55)

[However, in Platt's novel and three other YA books about mental illness, Frank Bonham's *Gimme an H, Gimme an E, Gimme an L, Gimme a P*, Anne Snyder's *Goodbye, Paper Doll*, Mary Alexander Walker's *Maggot*], the female characters are unable to achieve healing without the guiding strength or example of the male characters. Their salvation comes through the transforming effect of admitting their love, a not-unfamiliar literary theme but an unfortunate example for young women just learning to stand on their own feet. The message is clear: nutty girls should look around for a stalwart boy to save them.

This search is simplified if the girl is beautiful. . . . [In *Flames Going Out*] Tammy is the target of leering eyes and grabbing hands whenever she sets foot outside her door. (Although Kin Platt has demonstrated in other books that he considers this the normal state of feminine interaction with the rest of humanity.) . . .

Of course, it would be unrealistic to project the cure of mental illness without a helping hand from the medical establishment. The warm, all-knowing psychiatrist has become a stock character in adolescent fiction, taking the place of the omnipotent deus ex machina parent of an earlier tradition. Counseling sessions have provided some of the liveliest scenes in recent YA fiction, especially when the therapist is witty as well as wise. . . .

[In *Flames Going Out*] Tammy's counselor is Jonathan's father, and he has survived the embarrassment of a disturbed son with his professional dignity intact—the implication is that Jonathan is crazy in spite of, rather than because of, his father. . . .

Because these books follow a predictable pattern, they should not be devalued as adolescent literature. All four are interesting stories with believable characters, and all work up a good head of page-turning steam. . . . In *Gimme an H* . . . and *Flames Going Out*, Bonham and Platt have both surpassed anything they have written for years. In spite of some sexist assumptions, these are four novels that represent YA fiction at its best. (p. 455)

> *Patty Campbell, in her review of "Flames Going Out," in* Wilson Library Bulletin *(copyright © 1981 by the H. W. Wilson Company), Vol. 55, No. 6, February, 1981, pp. 454-55.**

JOYCE MILTON

Kin Platt's reputation as the author of "controversial" books for teen-agers is based on the not unreasonable assumption that anyone who manages to shock so many adults must be telling it like it is. In the past, Mr. Platt's candor has served him well, but *Flames Going Out* . . . is, just as the title suggests, a fizzle.

When we first meet his heroine Tammy Darling (the name passes for irony) she is a mentally disturbed 16-year-old who has decided to resolve her sexual confusion through an affair with the drug-addict son of her Beverly Hills psychiatrist. Tammy's pursuit of this unlikely, and at times unwilling, love object is graphically portrayed, but this girl has so few resources for survival that one begins to feel like a voyeur for reading on to the inevitable conclusion. The setting of Tammy's odyssey, by the way, is decadent L.A., where her schoolmates are involved in fast sex, loud disco and hard drugs. A novel that challenged our preconceived notions of this scene could hardly have failed to be engaging, but it is hard to imagine how Los Angeles mores, even if accurately described, could be responsible for Tammy's problems. And the prospect of this being read, as the publisher's catalogue copy suggests, as "the story of young lovers . . . star-crossed by their times" is rather chilling.

Joyce Milton, in her review of "Flames Going Out," in The New York Times Book Review (© 1981 by The New York Times Company; reprinted by permission), February 1, 1981, p. 28.

ZENA SUTHERLAND

[*Flames Going Out*] is a depressing, unrelievedly negative novel: Platt handles the shifting of time adequately and the writing style is competent, and he conveys, as he did years (and many books) ago in *The Boy Who Could Make Himself Disappear,* with bitter brilliance the conflicts within a psychotic personality. As a novel, however, this seems too monochrome, too intricate, too directionless to reach readers. (pp. 159-60)

Zena Sutherland, in her review of "Flames Going Out," in Bulletin of the Center for Children's Books (reprinted by permission of The University of Chicago Press; © 1981 by The University of Chicago), Vol. 34, No. 8, April, 1981, pp. 159-60.

ZENA SUTHERLAND

Fifteen-year-old Monty [protagonist of *Brogg's Brain*] is on the track team, but he has little ambition and little expectation of winning races. It's his father who keeps pushing Monty, who talks things over with the coach, who pushes so hard he almost makes the boy lose interest. One night he and Cindy (a mild but growing love interest) see a movie called "Brogg's Brain," and—as in the movie—a disembodied voice seems to spur Monty on to win a race. This is not, however, the formula last-minute victory: Monty's win brings him no new status, no kudos, just some personal satisfaction. Although this has less surface sophistication, it is in some ways more mature than other (not all) Platt novels, knitting the theme of the reluctant sportsman, the basic father-son relationship, the growing self-confidence, and the increasing relaxation in the boy-girl relationship into a sturdy and effective whole. (pp. 35-6)

Zena Sutherland, in her review of "Brogg's Brain," in Bulletin of the Center for Children's Books (reprinted by permission of The University of Chicago Press; © 1981 by The University of Chicago), Vol. 35, No. 2, October, 1981, pp. 35-6.

KEVIN KENNY

[*Brogg's Brain*] is an extremely compelling story of one youngster's battle for identity and self-confidence. Monty's confusion about what constitutes a worthwhile goal, and his decision to leave an easily attained mediocrity for the more demanding world of winning form the heart of a light, but credible, plot. Like *The Ape Inside Me,* Platt has once again served up a winning story for YAs, one whose simple style and engaging characters make it a worthy read for all and a clear possibility for reluctant readers. Several female athletes play significant roles in shaping Monty's decision, and their presence should serve to broaden appeal across sex lines.

Kevin Kenny, in his review of "Brogg's Brain," in Voice of Youth Advocates (copyright 1981 by Voice of Youth Advocates), Vol. 4, No. 5, December, 1981, p. 34.

NANCY STEINBECK

Who should follow Dracula (*Dracula, Go Home*) but Frankenstein? Kin Platt's fantastic slapstick version [*Frank and Stein and Me*] of the classic merely changes the names and plot "to protect the innocent."

Thanks to his sister's mumps, Jack Hook, basketball player, is awarded Glop Oil's contest trip to Paris. Armed with his trusty basketball, Jack agrees to carry the mysterious stranger's birthday cake for his dear old mom in Paris. When the "cake" proves to be grass, Jack, on the run from customs agents and in search of comedic smugglers, Alphonse and Gaston, is rescued by black-bearded Dr. Stein who looks like Freud and acts like Frankenstein. Dr. Stein's horrifying "baby" Frank, created out of an ex-circus strongman and assorted concrete and iron, helps Jack capture the smugglers atop the Eiffel Tower and ends up with both a Glop Oil commercial contract and its beautiful representative.

I admire Kin Platt's talent for telling an interesting, even exciting tale with simple, not simple-minded vocabulary—and with wit. . . .

Frank and Stein is a silly spoof (second cousin to *Get Smart*) based on common, garden-variety Frankenstein lore. But the cardboard characters are so inept as to be engaging. The contrived ending is appropriate; Jack has won another free trip—this time to Slobovia. Though designed for high/lows, the novel will amuse anyone with an appreciation of the ridiculous.

Nancy Steinbeck, in her review of "Frank and Stein and Me," in The High/Low Report, Vol. 4, No. 1, September, 1982, p. 3.

Sidney Poitier
1924?-

Black American film director and actor.

Poitier's most successful films as a director are entertaining comedies geared toward a family audience. In his autobiography, *This Life*, Poitier vigorously expressed his concern over the content of Blaxploitation films popular during the early 1970s. Poitier contends that black youths exposed to a constant stream of black actors and actresses portraying drug pushers, pimps, and prostitutes might idolize these characters. Poitier's films are seen as refreshing alternatives to these violent works.

Poitier's first film, *Buck and the Preacher,* is a semihistorical account of the emigration of ex-slaves to the western frontier. Although the film contains predictable conflicts between the settlers and ex-Confederate soldiers, most critics believe that Poitier added fresh insight to the genre of "the Western." *Uptown Saturday Night* is the first of a series of comedies directed by Poitier. This film combines slapstick and farce in its story of two friends in search of a stolen lottery ticket. Many critics feel that Poitier's casting of top black performers such as Bill Cosby and Richard Pryor contributed to the critical success of both *Uptown Saturday Night* and its sequel, *Let's Do It Again. A Piece of the Action* is considered Poitier's weakest film. Some critics find condescending his intention to promote self-improvement ideals to black youths. In *Stir Crazy,* Poitier's most popular film, his role as director was overshadowed by the performances of Gene Wilder and Richard Pryor.

Poitier is well known as an actor and he received an Academy Award in 1964 for his performance in *Lilies of the Field.* In contrast to the seriousness of his dramatic roles, Poitier has directed films that emphasize social values less than the universal need to laugh.

Photograph by Ron Galella

Vincent Canby, in his review of "Buck and the Preacher," in The New York Times *(© 1972 by The New York Times Company; reprinted by permission), April 29, 1972 (and reprinted in* The New York Times Film Reviews: 1971-1972, *The New York Times Company & Arno Press, 1972, p. 254).*

VINCENT CANBY

"Buck and the Preacher," Sidney Poitier's first film as director as well as star, is a loose, amiable, post-Civil War Western with a firm though not especially severe Black Conscience. The film is aware of contemporary black issues but its soul is on the plains once ridden by Tom Mix, whom Poitier, astride his galloping horse, his jaw set, somehow resembles in the majestic traveling shots given him by the director. . . .

"Buck and the Preacher" is . . . a perfectly ordinary example of the kind of Western that seeks to prove that the West was not lily-white. The movie West, of course, has never been completely lily-white. There have always been a certain number of Indians horsing around, scalping, drinking, shooting, getting shot, and being poorly dealt with by just about everybody, including the movie makers.

For the most part, however, blacks showed up on the frontier only as servants or, occasionally, as outcasts and loners, most notably in [John] Ford's "Sergeant Rutledge" and "The Man Who Shot Liberty Valance." If they do nothing else, these new Soul Westerns may serve to desegregate our myths, which have always been out of the jurisdiction of the Supreme Court.

COLIN L. WESTERBECK, JR.

[Maya Angelou once claimed that] "Black men talk about change when what they really mean is exchange. They want to take over the positions of power white men have." Certainly Buck and the Preacher, the title characters in the new Sidney Poitier-Harry Belafonte film, would agree. The themes of exchange are obviously what appealed to Mr. Poitier when he chose the script for this black Western [*Buck and the Preacher*], which is his first assignment as a director. Poitier plays Buck as the latest word in self-reliant, soft-spoken, straight-shooting cowboys. At one point, while escaping a trap laid by his white nemeses, Buck even executes a running mount that would have made Yakima Canute proud. Yet I don't want to give the impression that Buck and his unscrupulous sidekick, the Preacher . . . are just Roy Rogers and Gabby Hayes in black face. There is also an undertone in the film whispering benignly, "Up against the wall, M----- F----: this is a stickup!" The best-

357

received scene in the film was the one where Buck and the Preacher robbed one of whitie's banks. (pp. 285-86)

[**Buck and the Preacher** is] more than just a Western. It has some fresh polemical intentions. It begins with a prologue informing us that black wagonmasters bravely tried to guide ex-slaves to homesteads in the West after the Civil War. The prologue briefs us on some of the extraordinary white discouragement and hardship faced by these wagonmasters. (Buck turns out to be a prototype of the breed.) At last the prologue dedicates the film to these men, "whose graves today lie as unmarked as their place in history." One purpose of this film, then, is to desegregate history. This strikes me as a feasible purpose for a work of popular art like a movie. (p. 286)

> *Colin L. Westerbeck, Jr., in his review "Buck and the Preacher," in* Commonweal *(copyright © 1972 Commonweal Publishing Co., Inc.; reprinted by permission of Commonweal Publishing Co., Inc.), Vol. XCVI, No. 12, May 26, 1972, pp. 285-86.*

GORDON GOW

A change from familiar Western customs is afforded by [**Buck and the Preacher,** a] mildly comic and moderately dramatic account of the troubles that befell some of the freed slaves after the Civil War, when they headed for pastures new, but were impeded by white nightriders who wanted to keep them in the South to go on picking cotton for peanuts. It might not sound like a subject for laughter; and when it begins in beautifully moody sepia it looks as if it will be a solemn tale. But shortly after the colour has crept subtly into the frames, the fun begins as well. . . .

Poitier has directed here for the first time, but with only a slight indication of freshness in Western style. He is much assisted, of course, by the unusual circumstances of the plot, as well as by the appropriately parched Mexican locations which give place at length to green and bounteous country. Some marvellously twangy music by Benny Carter lends a zip to numerous spates of action that might otherwise be routine. And it must be said that Poitier and Belafonte between them lift the comedy aspect into quite a tolerable caper, if perhaps a little obviously show-bizzy underneath the period realism. What I mean is best illustrated by a sequence where Belafonte surprises the nightriders in a brothel, and charms them as much as he shocks the 'madam' with his quasi-religious prattle about the sin of fornication: the preacher, in fact, is merely creating a diversion so that Buck can leap into action and make a surprise attack upon his enemies. In its way, this is breezy stuff and highly entertaining. And yet one feels that the racial connotations, so emphatic at times, ought not to be mixed with japes that are quite so calculated. Better than piling on the agony, of course; but I thought the balance uneasy.

> *Gordon Gow, in his review of "Buck and the Preacher" (© copyright Gordon Gow 1972; reprinted with permission), in* Films and Filming, *Vol. 18, No. 9, June, 1972, p. 54.*

JOSEPH McBRIDE

Buck and the Preacher, a likeably unpretentious Western which marks the directorial debut of Sidney Poitier, gains much of its charm from the sly manipulation of genre conventions. It's about a taciturn ex-cavalryman and a shifty preacher leading a wagon train westward under repeated attack by a gang of bandits. Nothing much new here, except perhaps the mating of the Ford tradition (many echoes of *Wagon Master*) with modern anti-heroism. The real twist, though, is that the pioneers are black, the bandits are white trash, and the wagon train is rescued not by the cavalry but by the Indians.

Buck and the Preacher is saved from being a mere stunt like the black *Hello, Dolly!* by its creative use of the conventions it turns inside out. It mocks them at the same time it allows black audiences (and, vicariously, whites) the pleasure of usurping the mythology which the Western has long used to keep minorities in their place. Poitier's entrance scene is a thrill, both for its intrinsic beauty and for the echoes it carries: several blacks gazing into the distance, a solitary horseman appearing in the extreme background, and a fast panning shot of the horseman swiftly galloping and wheeling his steed in a circle, silhouetted in a blaze of sunlight. As Gordon Parks did in *Shaft*, Poitier is compensating for the black's traditionally impotent cinema image by playing macho heroism to the hilt— when Buck . . . dispatches the bad guys, it's one of the most phallic bits of gunplay ever, a barrage from the hip with two sawed-off shotguns, the camera angling up from boot level. . . .

Ernest Kinoy's **Buck and the Preacher** script is sometimes faulty in its plotting—every time a catastrophe befalls the wagon train, Buck is conveniently off on a scouting trip, and there aren't enough scenes devoted to life in the train itself, which is mostly background filler. But it makes some sharp points about the peculiar role of blacks in the winning of the West. Begging for arms to defend his people against a sheriff's posse, Buck tells the Indian chief that they are brothers, but the chief refuses him because Buck fought against Indians in the cavalry. Still, when push comes to shove and Buck and the Preacher are cornered by murderous whites, the Indians appear on the mountain to save them. Poitier's deftest use of stock Western imagery comes when the Indians suddenly rise up over a ridge and form a cordon to let Buck and the Preacher escape. It's not guilt or masochism which makes the white audience cheer along with the black audience at this point. It's the shared realization that the turnabout is fair play.

> *Joseph McBride, in his review of "Buck and the Preacher," in* Rolling Stone *(by Straight Arrow Publishers, Inc. ©1972; all rights reserved; reprinted by permission), Issue 113, July 20, 1972, p. 58.*

JUDITH CRIST

A Warm December is a "black" film in that its protagonists . . . are black and that Poitier directed it. But it's essentially a non-racial and non-ethnic movie, with a bit of [William Wyler's] *Roman Holiday* and a dab of [Arthur Hiller's] *Love Story* to schmaltz up the highly literate Lawrence Roman script. It's the story of an American doctor on holiday in London, his encounter with a mystery girl, their romance and, with the solution of her mystery, their bittersweet parting.

It's a dashing, slick old-Hollywood romance—and the sort of movie that the popcorn-and-Kleenex crowd (count me in on rare occasions) can really wallow in. . . .

Militants may scoff at schmaltz (our heroine does not die at film's end, I hasten to note) or at the love-vs.-duty or I-want-to-live issues. But this is exactly what Poitier had in mind, to *my* mind, some years ago when he said he made *For Love of Ivy* so that his children could identify with characters in a middle-class movie. The maid and the gambler in that one weren't quite middle-class to anybody's mind. But the value of *A Warm December* is that its protagonists are black, products of a slick fiction though they may be, and romantic heroes and heroines to identify with who aren't pushing dope or pimping, who aren't out to kill whitey and who make us empathize and care. Isn't that what screen entertainment entails? (p. 73)

> *Judith Crist, ''The Old Fox and His New 'Jackal''' (reprinted by permission of the author), in* New York Magazine, *Vol. 6, No. 22, May 28, 1973, pp. 72-3.*

CLYDE JEAVONS

Although apparently intent on saying something meaningful about emergent Africa, Sidney Poitier's second feature as director [*A Warm December*] turns out to be an amorphous transposition of *Love Story*, employing familiar push-button techniques to spring one's emotions. The dark continent is sentimentalised in the worst traditions of [Zoltan Korda's] *Sanders of the River* by the interpolation halfway through of an achingly pretty Swahili folksong, while the fictitious and unconvincing state of Torunda has closer ties with those speculative, wind-of-change television dramas of the Sixties . . . than with the turbulent political arena of Amin, Kaunda and Co. Saddled with an aimless script, Poitier is marginally more effective in front of the camera than behind it, responding with understandable warmth to the pretty [Catherine] and participating in some incongruous motocross events whenever the plot runs out of steam.

> *Clyde Jeavons, in his review of ''A Warm December,'' in* Monthly Film Bulletin *(copyright © The British Film Institute, 1973), Vol. 40, No. 473, June, 1973, p. 135.*

COLIN L. WESTERBECK, JR.

Sidney Poitier's new film, *Uptown Saturday Night,* is some less-structured, coherent kind of TV fare—a variety show, perhaps, a black Ed Sullivan Show or Dean Martin Comedy Hour. The plot has to do with an honest but poor man named Steve . . . who has stolen from him a lottery ticket which, a few days later, wins the million-dollar prize. Needless to say the fellow tries to get his ticket back, persisting in his search even when the ticket turns out to be in the possession of a bunch of gangsters.

Though this might sound like an action film, a thriller of some sort, it isn't. On the contrary, it's a series of character studies, cameos really, which are never anything more than vaguely connected either to the plot or each other. Even in the big chase scenes at the end, where Steve clings to the luggage rack of a car from which hoodlum Geechie Dan . . . is shooting at him, the camera work minimizes the action and accentuates the character acting. A close-up isolates Steve from his hazardous circumstances, dissipating any tension that might inhere in the situation in order to give Poitier a chance to do a bit more mugging.

[The] black comedians and character actors who get to do their *shtick* in the movie are Bill Cosby, Flip Wilson, Richard Pryor, Paula Kelly, Calvin Lockhart and Roscoe Lee Browne. Including the principals, that's a total of eight stars in this movie, or, as a little simple math will tell us, a new character every thirteen minutes. Obviously a script that machine-guns new roles at us like this is going to end up riddled to pieces. Not

every role can score a hit either. Like all vignette comedy, the roles in this film are stereotypes. . . . When the stereotypes are upset or are played in unexpected ways, the results can be funny. . . .

A few years ago when black films first began to be produced, it looked as if they would quickly choke on their own bile and die off as a genre. But that hasn't happened. If *Uptown Saturday Night* [is] any indication, it now seems more likely that the black film will die from blandness instead.

> *Colin L. Westerbeck, Jr., in his review of ''Uptown Saturday Night,'' in* Commonweal *(copyright © 1973 Commonweal Publishing Co., Inc.; reprinted by permission of Commonweal Publishing Co., Inc.), Vol. CI, No. 3, October 18, 1973, p. 66.*

VINCENT CANBY

"Uptown Saturday Night" is essentially a put-on, but it's so full of good humor and, when the humor goes flat, of such high spirits that it reduces movie criticism to the status of a most nonessential craft.

The star as well as director of "Uptown Saturday Night" is Sidney Poitier, a man whose way with comedy is reminiscent of Stanley Kramer's in "It's a Mad, Mad, Mad, Mad World." It's less instinctive than acquisitive. He himself can't make anyone laugh but he knows people who can. Mr. Poitier has had the good sense to hire a lot of exceptionally talented and funny people, including Richard Wesley, who wrote the screenplay for "Uptown Saturday Night."

The film combines blunt, rollicking observations on life—the kind favored by black comedians—with the sort of fabulous narrative that has always been a staple of American comedy, from today's Woody Allen back through silent comedy to frontier literature.

Until recently true black comedy (not to be confused with black humor) has been something of an unknown frontier for most Americans who didn't have access to Harlem's Apollo Theater, Moms Mabley, Redd Foxx and the other headliners. Today, of course, Moms, Redd and the others are television headliners, and it's now apparent that a lot of the comedy of Freeman Gosden and Charles Correll (Amos and Andy) was a good deal more witty and accurate than it was fashionable to admit in the nineteen-fifties and sixties.

"Uptown Saturday Night" is an exuberant black joke that utilizes many of the stereotypical attitudes that only black writers, directors and actors can decently get away with. You've never seen so much eye-popping fear and unwarranted braggadocio used in the service of laughs. Yet the result is not a put-down comedy but a cheerful jape that has the effect of liberating all of us from our hangups.

"Uptown Saturday Night," once it gets started (and that takes a bit of time), is about a pair of stupendously ill-equipped innocents, Steve Jackson . . . , a factory worker, and Wardell Franklin . . . , a taxi driver, who set out to recover a winning lottery ticket contained in a wallet stolen during the pair's one and only visit to a fancy black after-hours club.

The course of their search takes them through a gallery of rogues, dead-beats and affable con-artists. . . .

Mr. Poitier's intelligence and taste are most noticeable in the film's casting, in the leeway he gives his actors, and in his ability at times to make himself seem physically small and downright intimidated. For a man of his stature, that cannot be easy.

The title of the film refers to neither a time nor a place (the setting seems to be Los Angeles where, as far as I know, there is no uptown). It defines, instead, a film fantasy in which fun needn't have boring consequences, in which gangsters shoot it out without anyone's getting bloodied up, and in which it's possible to have a high old time without fear of a hangover.

Vincent Canby, in his review of "Uptown Saturday Night," in The New York Times *(© 1974 by The New York Times Company; reprinted by permission), June 17, 1974 (and reprinted in* The New York Times Film Reviews: 1973-1974, *The New York Times Company & Arno Press, 1974, p. 222).*

MAURICE PETERSON

[*Uptown Saturday Night*] has no pretense of relevance whatsoever. It doesn't have a drop of blood, no obscenity, nudity or any of the other ingredients usually considered essential for a successful Black-oriented movie. What it does have is frivolity. The only real concern of the *Uptown* folks—aside from having a good time—is a winning $50,000 lottery ticket that has been stolen by a greedy gang. . . .

Uptown Saturday Night is Poitier's most ambitious directorial assignment to date. After a dazzling debut with *Buck and the Preacher* and the rather soggy *A Warm December,* he has undertaken a highly complex endeavor full of crowd scenes, intricate effects and delicately timed dialogs, and brought them all together. I would hesitate to say he has accomplished a masterwork, however. He does evoke shining performances from most of the stars. . . . But Director Poitier fails to fully develop Calvin Lockhart, who seems to be imitating Belafonte imitating [Marlon] Brando. And Richard Pryor is just a bit too intense in his sequence, which is somewhat awkwardly staged and timed. There are several other flaws in Poitier's conception and execution, but the overall glory of *Uptown Saturday Night* still should not be challenged. To point out errors here would be tantamount to looking for lint in a shag rug. Poitier has now moved to the front of the Black directors' pantheon.

Maurice Peterson, "They're Just in for Laughs" (reprinted by permission of the author), in Essence, *Vol. 5, No. 6, October, 1974, p. 16.*

PAULINE KAEL

Let's Do It Again is like a black child's version of [George Roy Hill's] *The Sting*—an innocent, cheerful farce about an Atlanta milkman . . . and a factory worker . . . who go to New Orleans and pull off a great scam. They outwit the black mobsters . . . and win enough money for their lodge back home, The Sons and Daughters of Shaka, to put up a new meeting hall. Nobody is hurt, and everybody who deserves a comeuppance gets it. Their con involves hypnotizing a spindly prizefighter. . . . (p. 66)

It's apparent why Sidney Poitier set this project in motion and directed it: he's making films for black audiences that aren't exploitation films. *Let's Do It Again* is a warm, throwaway slapstick, and the two leads are conceived as black versions of Bing Crosby and Bob Hope in the *Road* series. Poitier is trying to make it possible for ordinary, lower-middle-class black people to see themselves on the screen and have a good time. The only thing that makes the film remarkable is that

Poitier—who has been such a confident actor in the dozens of roles he has played under other people's direction since his first film, in 1949—gives an embarrassed, inhibited performance. As casual, lighthearted straight man to Bill Cosby, he is trying to be something alien to his nature. He has too much pride and too much reserve for low comedy.

Clearly Poitier is doing something that he profoundly believes in, and there can't be any doubt that he is giving the black audience entertainment that it wants and has never had before. Probably there was no one else who was in a position to accomplish this. One cannot simply say that he is wrong to do it. Many groups have been demanding fantasies in their own image, and if this often seems a demand for a debased pop culture, still it comes out of a sense of deprivation. But for an actor of Sidney Poitier's intensity and grace to provide this kind of entertainment is the sacrifice of a major screen artist. In a larger sense, he's doing what the milkman is doing in the movie: swindling like a Robin Hood, for the good of his lodge, his church. But it's himself Poitier is robbing. . . . As a director, Poitier is overly generous with the actors: he isn't skilled enough to shape sequences so that the actors can benefit from their closeups (nobody could benefit from all those tacky reaction shots). Jimmie Walker is used unimaginatively, but he's well cast—you can't help wanting him to win his fights, and he has a Muhammad Ali routine in his dressing room, shouting "I am the champ," that is very funny. (pp. 66-7)

It's not a disgraceful movie—I liked the people on the screen better than I liked the people in *The Sting*—but what I can't get out of my head is the image of Sidney Poitier doing primitive-fear double takes, like Willie Best in the old days, only more woodenly. For the fact is that black audiences roar in delight at the very same stereotypes that have been denounced in recent years. It's true that the context is different in these movies, but the frozen, saucer-eyed expressions when Poitier and Cosby are caught doing something naughty or something they can't explain go right back to little Farina in the *Our Gang* comedies. *Let's Do It Again* isn't the first of Poitier's two-black-buddies features: he also directed and appeared in *Buck and the Preacher* and *Uptown Saturday Night.* It amounts to a doggedly persistent skewering of his own talent. (p. 67)

Sidney Poitier, who was able to bring new, angry dignity to black screen acting because of the angry dignity inside him, is violating his very essence as a gift to his people. (p. 68)

Pauline Kael, "Horseplay" (originally published in The New Yorker, *Vol. LI, No. 37, November 3, 1975), in her* When the Lights Go Down *(copyright © 1975, 1976, 1977, 1978, 1979, 1980 by Pauline Kael; reprinted by permission of Holt, Rinehart and Winston, Publishers), Holt, Rinehart and Winston, 1980, pp. 62-8.**

JONATHAN ROSENBAUM

Despite a frankly nonsensical plot full of formula antics and an unnecessarily protracted running time, *Let's Do It Again* is a healthy reminder of the relative verve, energy and talent to be found nowadays in the so-called 'black exploitation' film— a somewhat loaded term considering the fact that no one ever speaks of 'white exploitation', and particularly inappropriate in relation to such a high-spirited yet unassuming entertainment as this. Modestly directing himself as a straight man for much of the time, Sidney Poitier gives most of the show over to the ebullient Bill Cosby, and the latter takes every advantage of the opportunity. . . . Working with such a patently ludicrous intrigue, Poitier for the most part keeps things moving lightly on the strengths of his enjoyable cast, with a nicely handled chase thrown in for good measure. But a few happy moments are occasionally offered by lines in Richard Wesley's script. Threatening the absurdly named Biggie Smalls over the phone while pretending to be a big-time Chicago operator, Billy Foster . . . offers the following challenge: "I understand you're six feet and good-lookin'—how'd you like to be four feet and ugly?"

> *Jonathan Rosenbaum, in his review of "Let's Do It Again," in* Monthly Film Bulletin *(copyright © The British Film Institute, 1976), Vol. 43, No. 511, August, 1976, p. 166.*

TOM ALLEN

Consider sit-com's ability to trivialize. After two decades of inexorable social enlightenment, the Brooklyn Sweathogs have substituted infantile pranks for the switchblade rock of [Richard Brooks's] *The Blackboard Jungle,* a classroom that has, incidentally, graduated at least three actor-directors in Paul Mazursky, Vic Morrow, and Sidney Poitier. The last, Poitier, seems particularly comfortable in the classroom. *The Blackboard Jungle* gave him a start; [James Clavell's] *To Sir, With Love* was a boost at mid-career; and now some of the strongest moments of his several directions appear in *A Piece of the Action,* in which he allows a younger generation, fresh faces in a ghetto class, their pause in the melodramatic limelight. Poitier's film, which inserts an ode to classroom reform within a caper story, is much too long and no model of neat construction. But in going for that old liberal uplift of *A Man Ten Feet Tall* and [Stanley Kramer's] *The Defiant Ones,* he has reached for the true schmaltz, not the treacly brand of some of his past films as director. I would judge from some of the more intense moments of *A Piece of the Action* that he is finally letting feelings get in the way.

> *Tom Allen, "'Oh, God!' and Other Third World Films" (reprinted by permission of* The Village Voice *and the author; copyright © The Village Voice, Inc., 1977), in* The Village Voice, *Vol. XXII, No. 42, October 17, 1977, p. 53.**

JOHN COLEMAN

Sidney Poitier probably shouldn't be accused so basely, but he does have a habit—since he turned actor-director—of making films that seem aimed at a black-white market and condescending to both shades. There is something for everyone in *A Piece of the Action* . . . : [the emphases rest] on jolly robbers, ghetto adolescents, even real problems. But the outcome of a largely black-staffed movie, with good intentions, does seem to turn on income: not what the film will make at the box-office but the way it chooses to deploy money in its inspissated plot. Poitier and the fine Bill Cosby are gentle villains who find themselves blackmailed into caring for a bunch of black dropouts at a community centre. While trying to suss out who has got them into this fix, they begin to bother about the prospective delinquents in their charge. Allow that there is some harsh language ('all you prissy-assed, middle-class niggers,' says an angry girl to a weeping teacher), but counter this with Poitier's cure: shelling out torn-in-half dollars against improved behaviour. Apart from a great deal of action, which lost me in its twists—there really appear to be three or four *kinds* of film

uneasily cohabiting here—the central theme is rehabilitation, making things better, doing it (up to a point) the tough route. Alas, then, that travesties like *Guess Who's Coming to Sinner?* or *A Piece at Any Price* suggest themselves as alternative titles.

> *John Coleman, "Show Trials," in* New Statesman *(© 1978 The Statesman & Nation Publishing Co. Ltd.), Vol. 95, No. 2461, May 19, 1978, p. 684.**

CARRIE RICKEY

Bruce Jay Friedman's gear-shifting script and Sidney Poitier's lackluster pacing sink *Stir Crazy.* Whenever Friedman needs a joke, he takes castration fear out of his pocket: a New York cabbie clamps pliers on the balls of a recalcitrant fare in order to get paid; an inmate confides to Pryor in the prison hospital, "I came in here for a hernia operation, but instead they cut off my nut"; the warden trying to beat Wilder makes him ride an *Urban Cowboy* motorized bull to no avail—"Him being from the East," rationalizes the warden, "I thought he was a little soft in the crotch." Friedman's getting a little soft in the head if he continually has to go below the belt for a yuk. An abler director than Poitier could have trimmed the fat, shortened scenes, but this is a film where if it takes someone a minute to make a prison break, it takes a minute-and-a-half on screen.

> *Carrie Rickey, "Polanski Makes Good" (reprinted by permission of* The Village Voice *and the author; copyright © News Group Publications, Inc., 1980), in* The Village Voice, *Vol. XXV, No. 50, December 10-16, 1980, p. 66.**

RICHARD COMBS

Against all the odds, Sidney Poitier's last directorial venture, *A Piece of the Action*—a loose bundle of heist movie, sit-com and moral uplift—pulled itself through on sheer naivety and patent sincerity. Something of the same mix might be said to work for *Stir Crazy,* which displays an untoward delight in recoining comedy stereotypes. And the populist nerve that Poitier seemed to be playing towards in *A Piece of the Action* has been resoundingly hit—in box-office terms anyway—in *Stir Crazy.* . . . It begins none too promisingly, with a lame reversal of the out-of-towner joke as two Manhattanites, playwright Gene Wilder and actor Richard Pryor, decide to quit the city (despite a credit montage, and title sign "Who Needs Hollywood?", which invokes the usual New York paranoia about out-there) for the inspirational spaces of the West. But the film thereafter remains convincingly split between optimistic naivety and paranoid trepidation—anchored respectively in Wilder and Pryor—about what this pioneer experience might involve. In turn, the genial, wide-open spaces of Poitier's direction seem to allow the duo more room than usual to expand on their accustomed personae, and the script offers less constrictive material than their *Silver Streak* pairing. . . . [The] film's mood remains consistent until the introductions are made in prison and then it switches, just as anonymously and personably at the same time, into its *Great Escape* finale. Of the self-improving sentiments espoused in *A Piece of the Action* there is not much sign here—except for the fact that, as they are being set up as bank robbers, not only are our heroes to be seen innocently eating their lunch, but tidily disposing of the wrappers. (p. 79)

> *Richard Combs, in his review of "Stir Crazy," in* Monthly Film Bulletin *(copyright © The British Film*

Institute, 1981), Vol. 48, No. 567, April, 1981, pp. 78-9.

DAVID ANSEN

If [Arthur Hiller's] ''Silver Streak'' was a brazen knockoff of [Alfred] Hitchcock, [**''Hanky Panky''**] is a knockoff of a knockoff, with [Gene] Wilder playing a ''wrong man'' who stumbles into a nasty struggle over a top-secret government tape. As [Richard] Widmark's thugs pursue him from one end and the frazzled Feds close in from the other, Wilder gets plenty of opportunity to exhibit the hapless hysteria that is his all-too-familiar trademark. Wilder needs a new shtik; [Gilda] Radner needs any shtik at all. As the sidekick/love interest, she is saddled with a mirthless role that requires of her the one thing not in her repertoire—sex appeal. Sidney Poitier directs this endless chase with a certain impersonal slickness that substitutes for high spirits. He has gotten little help from writers Henry Rosenbaum and David Taylor, who have raided the screenwriter's manual of tight squeezes but forgotten to embellish the handbook with anything resembling wit.

David Ansen, ''Dead End,'' in Newsweek *(copyright 1982, by Newsweek, Inc.; all rights reserved; reprinted by permission), Vol. XCIX, No. 25, June 21, 1982, p. 65.*

RICHARD COMBS

For a while, in *A Piece of the Action,* director Sidney Poitier seemed about to become Frank Capra reborn in the unlikely venue of bland, middle-of-the-road, caper-cum-comedy vehicles. But that film's agreeable mixture of improving sentiments and loose performance comedy now seems to have got lost in the stampede to repeat the box-office bonanza of *Stir Crazy*. . . . But *Hanky Panky* has not only forsaken the casualness that was so infectious about both those films, it doesn't even have a comedy pairing to carry its aggressive concoction of bad jokes, mistimed jokes and just plain non-jokes. . . .

Some American reviews have suggested that this is a belly-laugh variation on [Alfred Hitchcock's] *North by Northwest,* though given its mystic vision of the Grand Canyon leading to a secret government testing ground, one might as reasonably say that it is Hitchcock as strained through [Steven Spielberg's] *Close Encounters of the Third Kind*. Nothing like *hommage,* parody or pastiche, at any rate, ever infects the garbled anonymity of the film's telling, and it seems most likely that the makers simply grabbed at the first borrowings that came to mind. The plot . . . rushes hither and yon at the slightest excuse without ever adding up to very much. Even McGuffins are supposed to make more sense than this.

Richard Combs, in his review of ''Hanky Panky,'' in Monthly Film Bulletin *(copyright © The British Film Institute, 1982), Vol. 49, No. 584, September, 1982, p. 199.*

The Police

Stewart (Armstrong) Copeland (1952-) American-born English songwriter.

Sting (born Gordon Matthew Sumner) (1951-) English songwriter.

Andy Summers (born Andrew James Summers) (1942-) English songwriter.

The Police is one of the most critically and commercially successful groups to have emerged from the New Wave movement of the late 1970s. Their music contains elements of reggae, pop, rock, rhythm and blues, funk, and New Wave, resulting in a sound at once energetic and melodic, frenzied and lyrical.

The Police's first album, *Outlandos d'Amour*, contains what later became one of their most popular hit singles, "Roxanne." This song, which is about a man's love for a prostitute, typifies their early emphasis on love and the unique twists they bring to standard romance. Their subsequent albums, including *Ghost in the Machine*, show an increasing concern with political, social, and personal awareness. *Synchronicity*, their recent fifth album, continues in this direction, revealing an even darker, more bitter and pessimistic outlook toward contemporary society.

ED NAHA

One of the most exciting groups to slither out of the U.K. in the last five years, the Police are a harried hybrid of recent musical trends. They mesh hard rock with reggae rhythm, punk power, pop melody and Monty Python poetry to create a sound that is as distinctively exuberant as it is unnerving. At first listen, the Police sound like *just* a decent, melodic rock outfit. A few spins of [*Outlandos D'Amour*] later, one realizes the true dementia of the band. . . .

[The songs are catchy] and crazy. "Be My Girl-Sally" is a pop poem dedicated to an inflatable rubber mate . . . , "Peanuts" is a frenzied swipe at stardom . . . , and "Roxanne" is an anguished, driving reggae which pledges tortured but undying love to a hooker. . . .

All the siren songs on the Police's debut lp are similarly strange and never less than wonderful. Energetic, loud and melodic, *The Police* are as inventive as they are insane.

> Ed Naha, "Police Police Me," in Feature *(copyright © 1979 Feature Publishing Co., Inc.; all rights reserved; reprinted by permission), No. 95, April, 1979, p. 73.*

JON TIVEN

About 15 years ago albums by pop groups were just cheap exploitations of singles—you'd put one or two hits together with eight or 10 mediocre tracks and that was an album. Along came the Beatles and the Rolling Stones and it was a whole different ballgame; they'd put out an album with (in some cases) 15 songs of which 13 were of consistent good quality,

and suddenly most groups felt they had to do the same. The Police, despite their talent, have reverted the back to the old formula where you only need one or two good songs per album, and from initial indications audiences are lapping it up.

Can't Stand Losing You is a pretty good rock 'n' reggae tune, and *Roxanne* is exceptionally good and deserving of hit singledom, but I must add that the rest of ["*Outlandos d'Amour*"] is strictly third rate. . . . [The Police are] a rock group with a reggae twist, occasionally attempting New Wave (*Next To You*] and vaguely political (*Born in the Fifties* almost makes it but doesn't quite) tunes. I suppose for a first album by a new group, having two hot tracks isn't bad, but considering the pre-album hype I was expecting maybe the next big thing, and I'm sitting here instead wondering if *Roxanne* is just a fluke.

> Jon Tiven, in his review of "Outlandos d'Amour," in Audio *(© 1979, CBS Publications, The Consumer Publishing Division of CBS Inc.), Vol. 63, June, 1979, p. 115.*

TOM CARSON

[If the Police display a certain] stylish art-rock elegance, their music still sounds unpolished and sometimes mean enough to let them pass for part-time members of the New Wave—even

363

though it's a brand of New Wave sufficiently watered down to allow these guys to become today's AOR darlings. And yet their hybrid of influences has been fused into a streamlined, scrappy style, held together by the kind of knotty, economical hooks that make a song stick out on the radio. Musically, *Outlandos d'Amour* has a convincing unity and drive.

It's on the emotional level that it all seems somewhat hollow. Posing as a punk, Sting, as both singer and songwriter, can't resist turning everything into an art-rock game. He's so archly superior to the material that he fails to invest it with much feeling. Deft and rhythmically forceful though they are, the songs work only as posh collections of catch phrases ("Can't stand losing you" or "Truth hits everybody") thrown out at random to grab your attention: lyrical hooks to punch up musical hooks, with nothing behind them.

By trying to have it both ways—posturing as cool art-rockers and heavy, meaningful New Wavers at the same time—the Police merely adulterate the meanings of each. Their punk pose is no more than a manipulative come-on. For all its surface threat, there's no danger in this music, none of the spontaneity or passion that punk (and reggae) demands. Even when Sting says, "There's a hole in my life," he can't convince us it's keeping him up nights—we know it's just another conceit. And the larger the implied emotions, the tinnier he makes them sound. A gimmicky anthem manufactured out of whole cloth, **"Born in the 50's"** reaches for Who-style generational myth making . . . , but Sting can't make us see that there's anything special about this generation, because he knows there really isn't. . . .

As entertainment, *Outlandos d'Amour* isn't monotonous—it's far too jumpy and brittle for that—but its mechanically minded emptiness masquerading as feeling makes you feel cheated, and more than a little empty yourself. You're worn out by all the supercilious, calculated pretense. The Police leave your nervous system all hyped up with no place to go.

> *Tom Carson, in his review of "Outlandos d'Amour," in* Rolling Stone *(by Straight Arrow Publishers, Inc. © 1979; all rights reserved; reprinted by permission), Issue 293, June 14, 1979, p. 96.*

MARK KIDEL

[The Police], for all their success on both sides of the Atlantic, seem a little pallid. *Reggatta de Blanc* . . . has its good moments, but it is too clearly programmed for success, lacking in spontaneity, with its nods to New Wave Energy, reggae rhythm and Dub echo. Sting has a distinctive voice, the lyrics are fashionable 'concerned' and some of it is very danceable, but the album misses the bite that would make its chart success seem more than a very clever calculation. (pp. 867-68)

> *Mark Kidel, "Highstreet Madness," in* New Statesman *(© 1979 The Statesman & Nation Publishing Co. Ltd.), Vol. 98, No. 2541, November 30, 1979, pp. 867-68.*

JOHN MILWARD

Call the Police exploitative if you must, but *Reggatta de Blanc*'s title at least shows that they can be funny as well—chilly players who are nevertheless capable of a warm, pleasurable outburst like **"Roxanne."** It's the old story—black music played by white faces for maximum profit—but there's a twist. Lots

of Jamaicans live in Britain (another old story, colonialism), so the reggae these new-wavish enforcers have grafted onto their pop is nothing more than the exploitation of a natural resource. (p. 92)

The Police are more razor cut than dreadlocks, a cool mixture of influences—icily modern (and generally thin) lyrics, a winning sense of hard-rock dynamics . . . , and Sting's voice, which floats in the arrangements like bubbles in Perrier. Their detached approach to pop riffers like **"Can't Stand Losing You"** and **"So Lonely"** (from the generally rockier *Outlandos d'Amour*) and **"Message in a Bottle"** (from the overtly reggaeish new album) also mixes stylistic commitments: though driven by a new-wavish drums-guitar propulsion, the sound is rendered commercially clean by Sting's simple bass lines and arch, syncopated voice. The result is both too frenetic for mainstream rock and too clean for hard-core new wave. By being nothing to nobody, the Police can be everything to everybody.

The lyrics don't blow their cover. Instead of burnin' and lootin', their reggae complains that **"The Bed's Too Big Without You,"** but that's only proper. And while the one-dimensional sexual attitudes that inform the lyrics can be hard to swallow, a Rastafarian it's-a-man's-world rap would hardly be an improvement. **"Roxanne,"** which Peter Tosh reportedly adores, has the singer out to make a prostitute his girlfriend: "You don't have to put on the red light," Sting gulps and stutters, though his blase attitude toward her profession leads one to believe that, like a fickle john, he'd likely turn sour if it stopped burning incandescent for him. But that's beside the point— **"Roxanne"** is a song about the loose-lipped laugh that starts the tune, the choppy guitar that frames the verse, and the upbeat chorus that creates the climax. (p. 95)

> *John Milward, "The Police: Razor Cut Dreadlocks" (reprinted by permission of* The Village Voice *and the author; copyright © News Group Publications, Inc., 1979), in* The Village Voice, *Vol. XXIV, No. 50, December 10, 1979, pp. 92, 95.*

JON TIVEN

The Police's first album [**"Outlandos d'Amour"**] showed an exciting rock band with reggae inclinations that could kill with two songs but barely get off the ground with the remainder. On their second album [**"Reggatta de Blanc"**] they've forsaken most of their rock base and turned strictly into a reggae band with white faces, and unfortunately the move doesn't work to their advantage. The lack of consistency becomes even more apparent, and while Sting's vocal comparisons to Bob Marley made for entertainment when he sang a tune like *Can't Stand Losing You,* an entire LP of a white Marley singing reggae isn't nearly as exciting. The single, *Message in a Bottle,* is truly exceptional . . . but the rest of the album just doesn't hold water, if you pardon the pun.

> *Jon Tiven, in his review of "Regatta de Blanc," in* Audio *(© 1980, CBS Publications, The Consumer Publishing Division of CBS Inc.), Vol. 64, No. 3, March, 1980, p. 83.*

JERRY MILBAUER

When the Police first hit with **"Roxanne,"** they were welcomed and hated by opposite camps for the same reason: making new wave accessible to Top 40 audiences. Their use of reggae elements provoked a similarly split reaction; did they co-opt and dilute the form, or were they introducing it to new listeners who might then become interested in real Jamaican riddim? (p. 42)

What everyone missed in the ensuing turmoil—and what the third Police album, **Zenyatta Mondatta,** continues to illustrate—is that this is a band of three extremely inventive, smooth and technically gifted musicians whose individual abilities add up to a seamless, symbiotic whole. New wave or reggae they're not, nor do they claim to be, but the Police's unique brand of pop definitely raises the level of AM (and even FM) radio several notches.

Bassist Sting is still writing catchy, reggae-inflected tunes. **"Don't Stand So Close to Me"** is deceptively simple, but contains tricks like a contrapuntal vocal over the chanting chorus at the end. Occasionally, as in this song, cleverness isn't enough; here, what we really want to know is what happens to the older man and the Lolita he's lusting after—and we don't find out.

Social commentary or "relevance," however, is not what the Police is about, although on this album they do try. **"Driven to Tears"** deals with the band's tour to Bombay, Bangkok, etc. "Too many cameras and not enough food," Sting observes, hiding his face in his hands as he declares that "protest is futile." On the next (answer?) song he decides to a discoish beat, **"When the World Is Running Down, You Make the Best of What's Still Around"**—which for him consists of watching James Brown in the *TAMI Show* movie.

Not that we should care about the Police's world view; they're too much fun to listen to. At their best, on a bouncy number like **"De Do Do Do, De Da Da Da,"** they're catchy *and* creative, with a controlled way of putting sounds together. Even at their worst—the rambling throwaway **"Voices Inside My Head,"** for example—there's always Sting's slightly raspy, wailing voice. (pp. 42-3)

As a trio, the Police can be airtight for driving rhythm or a pop feel, or loose to show off their chops. They avoid, or at least rearrange, clichés (by putting them into a new context), and they just *sound* so damned good. And that's the whole idea, isn't it? (p. 43)

> *Jerry Milbauer, in his review of "Zenyatta Mondatta," in* Trouser Press *(copyright © 1981 by Trans-Oceanic Trouser Press, Inc.), Vol. 7, No. 12, January, 1981, pp. 42-3.*

STEVE SIMELS

Sooner or later it happens to every band, however talented or well intentioned: caught with an album due and little or nothing to say. This time it's happened to the Police. Apparently they've been so busy touring out-of-the-way markets (such as India) and coming to grips with the pressures of their sudden world-wide success that their songwriting has suffered. [**Zenyatta Mondatta**] is padded, thinly produced, and rushed sounding. . . .

Only the British and American singles from this album (**Don't Stand So Close** and **De Do Do Do,** respectively) have the sensuous instrumental interplay, melodic grace, and lyrical smarts we have come to expect from the Police. The rest is merely sound effects and aimless riffing. Granted, there are precious few groups, New Wave or otherwise, that can tread water this

skillfully, but from these guys one wants something a little more . . . er, arresting.

> *Steve Simels, in his review of "Zenyatta Mondatta," in* Stereo Review *(copyright © 1981 by Ziff-Davis Publishing Company), Vol. 46, No. 2, February, 1981, p. 96.*

DEBRA RAE COHEN

Ghost in the Machine feels unsettlingly crowded.

Which is as it should be, since that's what the album is about: overload, media explosion, the global village, the behavioral sink. The Police's platform, a spinoff from Marshall McLuhan, Alvin Toffler, et al., is hardly news . . . , yet it's strongly stated, consistent and compelling. The thrashing, denatured funk of **"Too Much Information,"** the whirlpool riff that punctuates **"Omegaman"** and the oppressive, hymnlike aspects of **"Invisible Sun"** all bespeak claustrophobia and frustration, and the lyrics bear them out. The Police skillfully manipulate musical details to underscore their points. Sting brays "infor*ma*tion" as if to demonstrate how words, when repeated often enough, can disassemble into meaninglessness. In **"Rehumanize Yourself,"** the singsong circus-calliope mood of the music works as a taunt to the raw seriousness of the lyrics: "Billy joined the National Front / He always was a little runt / Got his hand in the air with the other cunts. . . ."

They're still not the Clash—neither the National Front nor the situation in Belfast (broodingly addressed in **"Invisible Sun"**) is an especially risky target—but the Police display more commitment, more real anger, on *Ghost in the Machine* than ever before. It's as if their roles as self-anointed pop ambassadors have shown them the difficulty of healing gestures. For example, the heart-rending joyousness with which **"Every Little Thing She Does Is Magic"** bursts from the grooves proves its discontinuity with all of the other songs. It's a moment of liberation, of tossed-off shackles, whereas the rest of the record (even, to some extent, the obsessive **"Hungry for You"**) emphasizes constraints—if not those imposed by society, then those accepted as responsibility. . . .

Even **"One World—(Not Three),"** a sort of reggae march that's the closest the LP comes to an anthem, is a kind of trial: by attacking the concept of such categorizations as the Third World, the tune turns inward to interrogate the Police themselves, implicitly questioning the attitudes involved in their rock-around-the-world crusades. . . .

The Police's smarts have always been greatest when they didn't show—in making unorthodox career decisions or disguising the subtlety of their songwriting as simplicity. Now that the group has been rewarded with success, it's time to change, to challenge old assumptions. Having seen the world, these guys are starting to look more closely at themselves. (p. 83)

> *Debra Rae Cohen, "The Police Investigate Themselves," in* Rolling Stone *(by Straight Arrow Publishers, Inc. ©1981; all rights reserved; reprinted by permission), Issue 358, December 10, 1981, pp. 81, 83.*

RICHARD FRIEDMAN

The Police is a group, like Steely Dan, whose music makes you change speeds when one of their songs comes on your car radio. Clean, direct choruses that keep your ears blinking to attention, emotional hooks every 30 seconds, and lushly produced melodies make both groups irresistible. With the release of **Ghost In The Machine,** their fourth album, the Police prove they're able to merge diverse pop idioms into complex music that will carry a mass audience where the group wants to take them. . . .

Sting, Summers, and Copeland use any means at their disposal to create vital contemporary music. . . .

Rehumanize Yourself, [for example], throws everything in—sirens, synthesizer tremolos, racing guitars—to advise wayward youths and the authorities alike: "Policeman put on his uniform / He'd like to have a gun just to keep him warm / Cause violence here is a social norm / You got to humanize yourself." With songs like this and the mystic cymbal/tape magic reggae-like **One World,** the Police add an evangelical fervor to their exploitation of electronics, hoping to wrench the ghost out of the machine.

> *Richard Friedman, in his review of "Ghost in the Machine," in* down beat *(copyright 1982; reprinted with permission of* down beat*), Vol. 49, No. 3, March, 1982, p. 31 [the excerpt from the lyrics by The Police used here was taken from "Rehumanize Yourself" (used by permission of Reggatta Music/Illegal Songs, Inc.)].*

STEPHEN HOLDEN

Synchronicity is a work of dazzling surfaces and glacial shadows. Sunny pop melodies echo with ominous sound effects. Pithy verses deal with doomsday. A battery of rhythms—pop, reggae and African—lead a safari into a physical and spiritual desert, to **"Tea in the Sahara."** *Synchronicity,* the Police's fifth and finest album, is about things ending—the world in peril, the failure of personal relationships and marriage, the death of God. (p. 54)

Though the Police started out as straightforward pop-reggae enthusiasts, they have by now so thoroughly assimilated the latter that all that remains are different varieties of reggae-style syncopation. The Police and coproducer Hugh Padgham have transformed the ethereal sounds of Jamaican dub into shivering, self-contained atmospheres. Even more than on the hauntingly ambient **Ghost in the Machine,** each cut on *Synchronicity* is not simply a song but a miniature, discrete soundtrack.

Synchronicity's big surprise, however, is the explosive and bitter passion of Sting's newest songs. Before this LP, his global pessimism was countered by a streak of pop romanticism. Such songs as **"De Do Do Do, De Da Da Da"** and **"Every Little Thing She Does Is Magic"** stood out like glowing gems, safely sealed off from Sting's darker reflections. On *Synchronicity,* vestiges of that romanticism remain, but only in the melodies. In the lyrics, paranoia, cynicism and excruciating loneliness run rampant.

The cuts on *Synchronicity* are sequenced like Chinese boxes, the focus narrowing from the global to the local to the personal. But every box contains the ashes of betrayal. **"Walking in Your Footsteps,"** a children's tune sung in a third-world accent . . . , contemplates nothing less than humanity's nuclear suicide. "Hey Mr. Dinosaur, you really couldn't ask for more /

You were god's favorite creature but you didn't have a future," Sting calls out before adding, "[We're] walking in your footsteps."

In **"O My God,"** Sting drops his third-world mannerisms to voice a desperate, anguished plea to a distant deity: "Take the space between us, and fill it up, fill it up, fill it up!" This "space" is evoked in an eerie, sprinting dub-rock style, with Sting addressing not only God but also a woman and the people of the world, begging for what he clearly feels is an impossible reconciliation.

The mood of cosmic anxiety is interrupted by two songs written by other members of the band. Guitarist Andy Summers' corrosively funny **"Mother"** inverts John Lennon's romantic maternal attachment into a grim dadaist joke. Stewart Copeland's **"Miss Gradenko,"** a novelty about secretarial paranoia in the Kremlin, is memorable mainly for Summers' modal twanging between the verses.

The rest of the album belongs to Sting. **"Synchronicity II"** refracts the clanging chaos of **"Synchronicity I"** into a brutal slice of industrial-suburban life, intercut with images of the Loch Ness monster rising from the slime like an avenging demon. But as the focus narrows from the global to the personal on side two, the music becomes more delicate—even as the mood turns from suspicion to desperation to cynicism in **"Every Breath You Take," "King of Pain"** and **"Wrapped around Your Finger,"** a triptych of songs about the end of a marriage, presumably Sting's own. As the narrator of **"Every Breath You Take"** tracks his lover's tiniest movements like a detective, then breaks down and pleads for love, the light pop rhythm becomes an obsessive marking of time. Few contemporary pop songs have described the nuances of sexual jealousy so chillingly.

The rejected narrator in **"King of Pain"** sees his abandonment as a kind of eternal damnation in which the soul becomes "a fossil that's trapped in a high cliff wall/ . . . A dead salmon frozen in a waterfall." **"Wrapped around Your Finger"** takes a longer, colder view of the institution of marriage. Its Turkish-inflected reggae sound underscores a lyric that portrays marriage as an ancient, ritualistic hex conniving to seduce the innocent and the curious into a kind of slavery.

"Tea in the Sahara," *Synchronicity*'s moodiest, most tantalizing song, is an aural mirage that brings back the birdcalls and jungle sounds of earlier songs as whispering, ghostly instrumental voices. In this haunting parable of endless, unappeasable desire, Sting tells the story, inspired by the Paul Bowles novel *The Sheltering Sky,* of a brother and two sisters who develop an insatiable craving for tea in the desert. After sealing a bargain with a mysterious young man, they wait on a dune for his return, but he never appears. The song suggests many interpretations: England dreaming of its lost empire, mankind longing for God, and Sting himself pining for an oasis of romantic peace.

And that is where this bleak, brilliant safari into Sting's heart and soul finally deposits us—at the edge of a desert, searching skyward, our cups full of sand. (pp. 54-5)

> *Stephen Holden, "The Police: No More Silly Love Songs," in* Rolling Stone *(by Straight Arrow Publishers, Inc. © 1983; all rights reserved; reprinted by permission), Issue 398, June 23, 1983, pp. 54-5.*

Chaim Potok

1929-

American novelist, short story writer, and historian.

Potok's reputation as an American Jewish novelist was established with his first novel, *The Chosen*. In this, as in his succeeding four novels, his inspiration and focal concern is traditional Judaism. That tradition becomes the source of conflict for his central characters, as they seek their identities in contemporary, secular society. Potok, an ordained rabbi, combines scholarly knowledge with his thematic concerns to present informative fiction about American Jewish life.

This scholarly aspect of Potok's writing is not always an asset, for critics point out that his prose style is sometimes stilted and that his plots are contrived. However, he has sustained enough interest in his characters and their lives to make his books popular and, in general, critical successes.

(See also *CLC*, Vols. 2, 7, 14 and *Contemporary Authors*, Vols. 17-20, rev. ed.)

KARL SHAPIRO

[*The Chosen*] is a deeply considered exegesis of modern Judaism. Formally, it should be ticketed as an allegory. The plot is simple and slight, though strong and graceful: the plot carries the deadly weight of the argument through seas almost too stormy for the mind to bear. The style has a *solo* quality, in the sense that Charles A. Lindbergh flew alone across the Atlantic, every second in peril of death. The style is beautifully quiet and gentle. One is amazed that so frail a structure can make it into port with such a freight of grief. It does so, heroically.

The story is set in the Williamsburg district of Brooklyn in the 1940s, the moment before the full horror of Hitlerism bursts upon the 20th century. There are only four characters to reckon with, two fathers and two sons. One father is a Hasid whose son will inherit his rank and prestige. The other father is a mere Orthodox Jewish scholar, despised by the mystical sect of Hasidists. *His* son, however, will become a rabbi. The son of the Hasid will defect and become a psychologist. This exchange of roles defines the limits of the plot. . . .

The allegory is dramatized on the level of the two sons, who engage in a spiritual battle of love and hate. The argument of the book concerns the level of survival of Judaism, whether it shall remain clothed in superstition and mysticism, or whether it shall convey the message of humanitarianism, with the secular Jew as the prophet of gentleness and understanding.

The action revolves, simply and allegorically, around a baseball game between two Jewish parochial schools. Reuven Malter is pitcher for the Rationalists, as it were. Danny Saunders, son and heir of the Hasid rabbi, wants to murder the *apikorsim*, the rationalist infidels. Saunders slams a ball pitched by Malter directly at his head, almost blinding him. But while Malter is recovering in the hospital, the two boys become spiritual and intellectual brothers. The author paces the unfolding of this relationship with care and love. In the absence of "action"

the intellectual drama takes over and the depths of religious bigotry are revealed. (p. 4)

The split between the Jewish Enlightenment of the post-ghetto Jews and the Polish ex-mystics helps define the dilemma of modern Judaism. Any true reconciliation between the Hasid Reb Saunders and the enlightened orthodox Europeanized scholar, Reuven's father, is unthinkable. Each Jew respects the other; each turns his back on the other. The crisis occurs with the realization of Zionism. The Hasids denounce the founding of a Jewish state by non-Hasids. . . . But when the reality of Hitlerism dawns upon the consciousness of Reb Saunders, his spirit crumbles; he gives permission for his brilliant son to become a psychologist—"a tzaddik for the world," not merely for the Jews. It is the symbolic end of Hasidism for him, possibly the end of Hasidism itself. (pp. 4, 12)

The governments of the Western World, or the Allies, were completely aware of the German plan to exterminate the Jews during the Second World War. Anthony Eden spoke of it in Parliament; but neither England nor America offered its hospitality to the stricken Jews. The revelation of Reb Saunders occurs at this point: since the Enlightenment has failed to enlighten Christianity, even the Chosen (the Hasidim) must come to the aid of the Jewish "goyim." The mystique of suffering, which the Hasid purveys, collapses before the reality of anti-

Semitism, German, British, or American. That the world must replace its Jews is the message of this novel. It is a good, true, and beautiful message. (p. 12)

Karl Shapiro, "The Necessary People," in Book Week—World Journal Tribune (© 1967, The Washington Post), April 23, 1967, pp. 4, 12.

ELIOT FREMONT-SMITH

["**The Chosen**"] starts with a rousing softball game between two Jewish parochial schools that quickly explodes into a bloody holy war. This is, unfortunately, the dramatic highpoint of the novel, and it's over by page 37.

Thereafter, until an emotionally charged resolution near the very end, we have a long, earnest, somewhat affecting and sporadically fascinating tale of religious conflict and generational confrontation in which the characters never come fully alive because they are kept subservient to theme: They don't have ideas so much as they represent ideas. . . .

Mr. Potok offers a great deal of fascinating information about Jewish customs, the intricacies of Talmudic study, the origins of Hasidism, the constant strain in being both religiously Jewish and American, and, obliquely, the importance of women in the lives of [the] four males, which is apparently nil. Otherwise, the book is suffused with Wisdom and Empathy to the frequent point of disbelief.

In sum, "**The Chosen**" is an interesting but awkward novel, and both the interest and the awkwardness are because of its heavy emphasis on theme. One wants to like the book very much, and does somewhat.

Eliot Fremont-Smith, "Sons and Fathers," in The New York Times (© 1967 by The New York Times Company; reprinted by permission), April 24, 1967, p. 31.

HUGH NISSENSON

["**The Chosen**"] is Chaim Potok's first novel and—let's face it—there's something rough and unpolished about his style. Narrated in the first person by Reuven Malter, his speech rhythms are sometimes awkward, and the imagery blurred. And yet, while Reuven talks we listen because of the story he has to tell; and, long afterwards, it remains in the mind, and delights. It is like those myths that, as C. S. Lewis reminds us, do not essentially exist in words at all. Potok's style is transcended because he has given us a configuration of events which grip the imagination on their own.

The plot is simple enough. Two boys—Reuven and Danny Saunders—become friends, are estranged, and renew their relationship. (p. 4)

[Their] backgrounds are utterly different. Reuven is merely Orthodox; Danny is a Hasid, the son of a rabbi, and destined by his father to take his hereditary place as *tzaddik*—"a righteous one," who is a teacher, spiritual adviser, mediator between his community of followers and God, and living sacrifice who takes the suffering of his people—of all Israel—upon himself. But Danny is also a genius—and it is a tribute to Potok's talent that he makes this completely convincing—with a photographic memory, and a remarkably creative intelligence obsessed by the revelations of modern psychology. Thus, in one sense, the novel is about Danny's conflict between his

craving for secular knowledge and his spiritual obligations. In another, it is something much more. It is a mythic Sacred Rite, a ritual mystery which initiates a human soul.

In simplest terms, we are mystified by Rabbi Saunders's silence. He has taken a vow to raise his beloved son without communicating with him, except to discuss the Talmud. . . . But why? He loves the boy—adores him—and, as much as he suffers, Danny knows it. Even Reuven, who fears and hates the old man, realizes this. Then what is the reason for his behavior?

It is here that Potok's imaginative grasp of his material is most apparent. It is the very essence of the Hasidic—and Kabbalistic—conception of the nature of divine reality, and the origin of evil, which he dramatically objectifies and even transmutes into poetry in spite of the limitations of his language. It is the idea of the "spark" and the "shell."

"A man is born into this world with only a tiny spark of goodness in him. The spark is God," Rabbi Saunders explains to the boys at last. "It is the soul; the rest is ugliness and evil, a shell. . . . [A] *heart* I need for my son," he cries out. "Righteousness, mercy, strength to suffer and carry pain, that I want for my son, not a mind without a soul."

His silence has been explained. It has initiated his son into a comprehension of the meaning of suffering, and taught him compassion.

"Let Daniel become a psychologist," the Rabbi says. "I have no fear now. All his life he will be a *tzaddik*. He will be a *tzaddik* for the world."

Danny's conflict between the secular and spiritual life has been daringly, and brilliantly resolved.

Yet an even greater silence permeates the book: the silence of God. The history of the time, reverberating from the radio, and glimpsed in the newspapers, is the background against which the narrative is enacted: the war, the death camps, the struggle in Palestine, and the reestablishment of the Jewish state. Reuven's father is a Zionist. A frail, gentle Hebrew scholar, his work for the cause almost costs him his life. Like Rabbi Saunders, he has taken the suffering of his people upon himself. But actively. Unlike the *tzaddik*, he cannot passively accept the destruction of European Jewry as a manifestation of the mysterious will of God. (pp. 4-5, 34)

[He tells his son:] "We have a terrible responsibility. We must replace the treasures we have lost. . . . Now we need teachers and rabbis to lead our people."

Reuven eventually takes him at his word. A gifted mathematician, who at first wants to be a professor, he decides to become a rabbi. The structural pattern of the novel, the beautifully wrought contrapuntal relationship of the two boys, and their fathers, is complete. We rejoice, and even weep a little, as at those haunting Hasidic melodies which transfigure their words. (p. 34)

Hugh Nissenson, "The Spark and the Shell," in The New York Times Book Review (© 1967 by The New York Times Company; reprinted by permission), May 7, 1967, pp. 4-5, 34.

CAROLINE SALVATORE

Once a man named Chaim Potok wrote a story called *The Chosen*. It was a good story and he told it skillfully. It was deeply evocative and called forth from the marrow of the heart certain memories of its own which still haunted the city streets of childhood. It was a story about Jews and the Jewishness of the characters, their embodiment of encounter and conflict between two ancient factions, gave to the tale an exquisite flavor of vinegar and honey; but its life and meaning derived from their humanity, which was something much deeper. It was, above all, a story which cracked barriers so that we were made to look each other full in the face and see—not stereotypes and shadow but flesh and blood.

> *Caroline Salvatore, in her review of "The Chosen,"*
> *in* Book World—Chicago Tribune *(© 1968 Postrib*
> *Corp.; reprinted by permission of* Chicago Tribune
> *and* The Washington Post*), March 23, 1968, p. 3.*

CURT LEVIANT

Burdened with the same protagonists and the same unvital prose as *The Chosen, The Promise* suffers from the same faults, primarily Mr. Potok's utter pretentiousness, which makes his work pseudo-literary rather than literary. The artificiality is apparent in several aspects of the work.

First there is the monochromed, mono-rhythmed rhetoric, which gives a dubious unity to the novel. . . . The book is also burdened with a purposeless running literary allusion from Joyce's *Ulysses* ("Molly Bloom big with seed"), and festooned with fancy epigraphs from Pascal, Kafka, Joyce, the Midrash and the Rebbe of Kotzk. In addition, events are journalistically summarized rather than recreated. . . . Conversations generally have a stilted edge; people sound as if they were reading at each other rather than talking naturally. . . .

Crowning all this is the irritating pseudo-Hemingway style, which assumes that half a dozen phrases scotch-taped by "ands" magically become poetry. . . . What Mr. Potok does not realize is that beyond the deceptively artless Hemingway style lurks a firm sense of esthetics, literary discipline and, above all, a harmonious fusion of language to theme, the latter obviously nonexistent in *The Promise*.

The omnipresent air of "creative writing" prevents the alert reader from suspending his disbelief. By being continually conscious of the attempt, the reader is soured on the result. . . .

Another problem is characterization. Although a host of figures appear in the novel, most of them, with the exception of Reuven's father and, less so, Rav Kalman, are stiff and phoney. The book's biggest phonies are Michael's aunt and his professorial parents. . . . (p. 37)

As was its predecessor, *The Promise* is ridden with two levels of facts: The first is the cataloguing of objects, a Sears, Roebuck listing in words that do not bite and lines that do not sing. The second is the description of scenes to provide information for the wandering tourist. An interesting one is the ordination examination. . . . Another peek at Jewish exotica is the engagement ceremony at Reb Saunders's house. It is in these spheres that Potok's reportorial strengths lie. Familiar with this way of life, he can present it with credibility and without sounding pompous. The trouble, however, is that the narrative bears more resemblance to socio-anthropology—an attempt to record the folk-and mindways of an inaccessible group—than to fiction.

Reuven, the idealized first-person narrator, is too much a goody-goody to be true. Kind, pious, humble, he is the author's vision of the flawless future rabbi. . . .

In *The Promise* one looks in vain for a touch of poetry, the imaginative slant or extra-dimensional quality that makes reading a delight. (p. 38)

> *Curt Leviant, in his review of "The Promise," in*
> Saturday Review *(© 1969 Saturday Review Maga-*
> *zine Co.; reprinted by permission), Vol. LII, No. 38,*
> *September 20, 1969, pp. 37-8.*

MICHAEL J. BANDLER

"The Promise" is a longer work than its predecessor; in a sense, it is a more depressing book—one that concentrates less upon the beauty of the Hasidic world and more upon the tribulations and conflicts within traditional Jewry itself. Although the in-fighting represents merely one example of the many love-hate relationships that are woven together to form "The Promise," it serves as a catalyst for the other displays of passion.

"The Chosen" was a simpler book than its successor. In "The Promise," the author deals not only with the myriad worlds of Judaism, but also with the realm of psychology. It takes the conflicts unveiled in "The Chosen," and describes how they manifest themselves in a troubled and somewhat twisted mind. . . .

From the book's inception—a carnival scene that is as critical to "The Promise" as the furious baseball game is to the infrastructure of "The Chosen"—the author's personal attitudes, prejudices and outlooks are openly presented. . . . Potok is troubled by the growing influence of the right-wing Orthodoxy upon American Jewish life. However, on the other hand, he empathizes with them, recognizing that their ranks swelled after World War II with the remnants of the concentration camps. . . .

To a great extent, what is missing in Mr. Potok's second book is the joy and warmth that endeared the author to many readers. Only once—when he describes the ecstatically wild dancing and outpouring of gladness at an engagement ceremony—does the beauty and majesty leap forth, drawing the reader vicariously into the circle of merrymakers.

If the sequel is more pensive and less comforting than its predecessor, there is no doubt about its merits as a novel and its first-cousin relationship to "The Chosen."

> *Michael J. Bandler, "A Sequel to 'The Chosen',"*
> *in* The Christian Science Monitor *(reprinted by per-*
> *mission from* The Christian Science Monitor; *© 1969*
> *The Christian Science Publishing Society; all rights*
> *reserved), December 16, 1969, p. 13.*

STANLEY REYNOLDS

I have no qualms about praising Chaim Potok's *The Promise*, a novel as orthodox as a Hasidic earlock, a novel which follows a definite canon of clarity, and which enters a most difficult terrain of experience without stumbling upon the obscure. . . . [The] ability to grasp village life and breathe into it the troubles of the world is not new to Jewish writing. One thinks, after the Old Testament, of S. Y. Agnon, who died this month. But Chaim Potok is a step onward, writing not about the Diaspora but about New York in the 1950s. Reuven Malter (the hero of Potok's *The Chosen*) is a student at a tightly Orthodox yeshiva. He is caught in a series of situations which force him to make certain basic choices affecting his family, friends and teachers. To say simply that the novel's conflict is about Reuven trying to reconcile the old, Eastern European traditions with those of enlightened modern scholarship makes it sound dull and denies Chaim Potok's logic, humanity and art. *The Promise* has a clarity and intensity of style which makes the interplay of characters and ideas take on a wholly appropriate allegorical significance.

Stanley Reynolds, "Quipped the Raven," in New Statesman (© 1970 The Statesman & Nation Publishing Co. Ltd.), Vol. 79, No. 2033, February 27, 1970, p. 300.*

THE TIMES LITERARY SUPPLEMENT

[In *The Promise,* Mr. Chaim Potok handles his] material with a lucidity and compassion, and an intimate yet objective knowledge of detail which produces both a touching, convincing picture of family and synagogue and a wider comment on spiritual inflexibility and spiritual triumph.

Mr. Potok's Brooklyn is a severe, insulated community, sometimes even rather too remote and self-sufficent in its own values to be credible. The outside world impinges only in so far as Senator (Joe) McCarthy is frightening as a persecutor or reassuring because he has Jewish aides, Messrs. Cohn and Schine; and there is a moment of distasteful complacency about the fate of the Rosenbergs. These faults apart, *The Promise* is a moving, continually absorbing, account of how people come to terms with a puritanical background, discarding its (understandable) severities and deriving strength from its virtues. Mr. Potok's narrative is rigorously and beautifully straightforward: the crises of the story are resolved with the aid of the Jewish virtues, but entirely without the *schmaltz* that sometimes lurks just under the surface in some distinguished Jewish novelists; and there is none of the familiar self-torment and turgidity. Against all the odds, with incomparable skill and resource, the author makes the conflict between Orthodox and Reformed theologians not only comprehensible but enthralling, the kind of dilemma it presents vivid to all who have understood the anguish of divided loyalties.

"Back to the Fold," in The Times Literary Supplement (© Times Newspapers Ltd. (London) 1970; reproduced from The Times Literary Supplement by permission), No. 3549, March 5, 1970, p. 241.

SAM BLUEFARB

The conflict in Chaim Potok's novel *The Chosen* functions at several levels. These are: the generational conflict; the temperamental; the conflict between head and heart; the opposition between a petrified fanaticism and a humane tolerance; and, finally, the split between two visions of God and man's relationship to Him. Of all of these, however, it is the opposition between the head and the heart which predominates. . . .

Although much of the story's direction is determined by the conflict between Hassidic and Misnagdic traditions in Judaism (as respectively represented by the Saunders and Malter families), it is the conflict between two generations and the Hawthornesque split between the obsessions of the head and the impulses of the heart that carry the major thrust of *The Chosen.* (p. 402)

While it is true that the Misnagdim in *The Chosen* did not actively oppose the Hassidim, the baseball game between the Misnagdic and the Hassidic schools on which the novel opens,

not only triggers the conflict but determines the direction the novel will take. In a sense, *The Chosen* is a kind of exercise in the "Hegelian" dialectic which the Hassidim and the Misnagdim have engaged in for the last two and a half centuries; however, in doing so, they have articulated their respective visions toward life and God, and, in a sense, have managed to exert some beneficial influence on each other.

One of the central problems in *The Chosen* is communication —or lack of it. Part of this is deliberate and "chosen." Reb Saunders, in his oddly "Talmudic" way, believes that he can best teach his son the language and wisdom of the heart by forbidding, or discouraging, what he considers "frivolous" discourse—what most of us might think of as the minimal conversational civilities. Thus Reb Saunders denies Danny what Mr. Malter the yeshiva teacher freely gives to his son Reuven: warmth, communication, and understanding. (p. 403)

In the instance of Reb Saunders it is an admixture of pride and fanatic pietism that prevents any intimacy between himself and his son (rationalized by the elder Saunders' commitment to the Talmudic *A word is worth one coin; silence is worth two*). In Danny's case it is simply fear of his father that prevents any viable relationship between the two. (p. 404)

What we find in *The Chosen* is a kind of *doppelgänger* effect— minus the *doppelgänger* itself. For Reuven and Danny are symbolically two halves of a single (perhaps ideal? Jewish?) personality, each half searching for its complement, which we already know can never be found in an imperfect world. . . . In short, no perfection is to be attained, except in unity. But that is precisely the problem of the characters in *The Chosen:* theirs is a search for that elusive (or illusory) goal. For neither of these two boys growing into manhood can really be said to exist at their fullest potential unless they retain some sort of relationship with each other. . . . (pp. 404-05)

Reuven, whose father allows his son forays into symbolic logic, the mathematics of Bertrand Russell, ends up a rabbi! Danny, who throughout the novel is coerced into following Hassidic tradition, and is expected to succeed Reb to the leadership of the sect on his father's death, ultimately breaks away. Danny, for want of a better word—the word has been overly used and abused, though it applies here—has been alienated—from his father, from Hassidism, and finally from the Hassidic community itself. In a sense Danny is recapitulating (suffering through) the transitions and adjustments so traumatically demanded by the exodus from the Old World to the New, adjustments required of his father and his followers, "pilgrims" who came to America from the East European *shtetle* one step ahead of Hitler's kill-squads. (p. 405)

More significant than the conflict of belief in *The Chosen* is the conflict between the generations—each of which is so often collateral with the other. The novel itself could as easily, if not originally, have been called *Fathers and Sons.* For it is as much about the old split between the fathers and their offsprings as it is about the conflicts between religious views and personalities. The sons have been molded by the fathers, though in the case of Danny that influence is a negative one. For Reb Saunders is a fanatic, or at least has those propensities; he represents the archetypal, God-intoxicated Hassid. And it is he who has caused Danny to grow into a tense, coldly introverted personality. Reuven's father, on the other hand, is the tolerant (albeit religious) humanist, opposed both in mind and in heart to the cold scholasticism of the Saunderses.

In the growing estrangement between Danny and his father, the conflict of generations and of visions toward life surfaces.

And it is America that is catalyst: the old East European ambiance is gone (unless one accepts Williamsburg as a pale substitute milieu for the vanished *shtetle*); and in the second instance the old ghetto traditions have become influenced, perhaps eroded—the old acculturation-assimilation story—by the pressures of urbanism and secular intellectualism.

The relationship between Reuven Malter and his father is rooted organically, not in principle—self or externally imposed—but in tolerance and mutual respect. Mr. Malter is a yeshiva teacher, yet he can comfortably discuss the secular philosophers with Reuven as Danny's father, the Hassidic Reb Saunders, never can with him. . . . Reuven's father allows his son to seek truth in his own way (possibly because of his own exposure to the rationalist winds of Western philosophy). Where Danny is coerced into the study of a specific mode of religious thought, Reuven is allowed by his father to roam free through the country of ideas. This seemingly minor approach to pedagogical technique—both fathers are teachers in their own ways—will determine the direction each of the boys will later take as young men. (pp. 405-06)

[Fanaticism] and intolerance go to form the iron board that binds Danny to his father. What is important here, though, is that Danny becomes an object, manipulated by his father, rather than a person one relates to. This determines Danny's ultimate hostility toward Hassidism itself, so that when he rebels, he not only rebels against a religious movement but against his father, who is its representative. The worship of God gives way, in the first flush of enthusiasm, to his admiration, if not worship, of a substitute god, Sigmund Freud. (pp. 406-07)

Ultimately, though, *The Chosen* is a paradigm of two visions that have not only sundered Judaism but have affected other areas of life—the split between head and heart. The Saunderses seem to have an excess of head in their (paradoxical streak of zealousness and emotion) makeup; but the Malters have heart *and* head: they are in balance. For Reuven is not only an outstanding student of Talmud but he "has a head" for mathematics and symbolic logic. Like his father, he also has a spark of tolerance which illuminates his own knowledge of human essences as opposed to ritualistic forms.

Reuven's studies are "brain" disciplines—logic, mathematics, philosophy—yet it is he who finally turns out to have more "heart" than the brilliant son of a Hassid. Danny, on the other hand, having been raised in the tradition of the *Ba'al Shem*, should have been a "heart-and-joy specialist." Yet it is he who is all brain. And this produces a keen irony, since Hassidism, a movement that was originally a revolt against arid scholasticism became (as portrayed in *The Chosen*) transformed into its opposite. Piety, joy, even learning (a latecomer to Hassidism) becomes pietism, rote learning, memorization. (p. 407)

The major irony, then, is that Hassidism—the brand portrayed in Potok's novel—though presumably a religious movement of the heart, has become transformed into its opposite.

I should like to say a few words about the symbolic symmetry of *The Chosen.* Potok seems to have extended himself beyond plausibility here. For the conclusion of this otherwise fine and sensitive work is marred by contrivance. Perhaps this can be ascribed to a symmetry which, while possible in life, somehow doesn't ring true when placed in fictional context. In this symmetry Danny escapes the confines of the Hassidic sect while Reuven stays within the wider boundaries of a more tolerant form of Judaism. Further, in this kind of resolution, Potok

unintentionally (and unfortunately) reveals his intentions long before the novel ends. It takes no great effort to guess, even early in the novel, that Danny will rebel, while Reuven, the "nice Jewish boy," will become a rabbi.

Reb Saunders' "conversion"—his resignation to Danny's break with Hassidism—doesn't convince. The novel is too mechanical in this sense—with Danny, who was to have inherited his father's leadership going off to become a clinical or behavioral psychologist, while Reuven turns to the rabbinate.

The climax of the novel is illustrated by the following exchange the two young men engage in: Danny tells Reuven: "'I can't get over your becoming a rabbi.'" Whereupon Reuven answers: "'I can't get over your becoming a psychologist.'" . . . Even the dialogue is weak here, betraying the Procrustean ending; it is virtually the antithesis to the brilliant verbal fencing—stychomythia—that the great dramatists from Shakespeare to Shaw were such virtuosos at. In this instance, the dialogue verges on the cliché.

Thus, as Reuven moves closer to Misnagdic—non-Hassidic—Judaism, so Danny moves away from its Hassidic counterpart, giving the novel this mechanical symmetry. The saving feature in spite of the contrived ending is that the choices of the two young men are as much determined by motive and character (or lack of it) as by superimposed plot strictures.

The almost explicit theme of *The Chosen,* then, is that the more repression one is forced to knuckle under to (no matter the noble intentions), the greater will be the rebellion against the source of that repression. . . . (pp. 408-09)

Still—and this I mean to stress—the "contrivance of symmetry" with which the novel ends is a minor flaw in a larger pattern: that of tolerance against intolerance, empty ritual against the vital deed, rote learning against eager wonder. In any effective fiction it is the process rather than the outcome that is more important. This is especially true in *The Chosen.* For in this novel Chaim Potok gives us as keen an insight into the split between head and heart, tolerance and fanaticism, the strictures of tradition against the impulses of *rachmonis* (pity) as has appeared in the Jewish-American novel in a long time. (p. 409)

> Sam Bluefarb, "The Head, the Heart and the Conflict of Generations in Chaim Potok's 'The Chosen'," in CLA Journal (copyright, 1971 by The College Language Association; used by permission of The College Language Association), Vol. XIV, No. 4, June, 1971, pp. 402-09.

ANTHONY BARSON

Why is it no one seems able to write a convincing novel about the life work of a painter? . . .

Chaim Potok, I'm afraid, is one more name to add to the list of failures. His dull, ponderous, humorless account of the rise of Asher Lev, Jewish artist extraordinary [**"My Name Is Asher Lev"**], cannot convince anyone who has held a brush loaded with oil paint and tried to make some meaningful strokes on a canvas, that *this* is what it's like.

The childhood and youth of the burning genius are recounted in some detail but Asher never really comes to life, and when we read the descriptions of his pictures, his final success seems unlikely. The break with his parents comes with the exhibition of a painting of his mother crucified on the living-room window, her head in three: one segment regards the artist, her son, to her left; one, her husband (with briefcase) to her right; and one looks upward.

Asher's parents don't like this sort of stuff, and though Mr. Potok plainly intends us to accept it as Great Art, my sympathies lay with Mama and Papa.

Anthony Barson, "The Artist As a Novel," in The Christian Science Monitor (reprinted by permission from The Christian Science Monitor; © 1972 The Christian Science Publishing Society; all rights reserved), June 14, 1972, p. 11.

THE TIMES LITERARY SUPPLEMENT

The difficulties inherent in the creation of a fictional genius have undone this extremely interesting book [*My Name Is Asher Lev*], which is ironic since it brilliantly transcends the impediment of being yet another novel about a Jewish family in New York, by reason of its seriousness and doggedness for truth. . . .

The prayers, greetings, customs and attitudes of Hasidic Jews toll through the book; the writer is on intimate, respectful, but his own terms with them, and they are naturally and objectively conveyed. The opening of the boy's eyes to the riches, the compelling possibilities in every fall of light, in every demonstration of life in nature or in a human face, is marvellously done: one really believes in Asher's awakening powers.

But as the gift flowers in the book, the book topples. Jacob Kahn, the famous sculptor to whom the wise Rebbe apprentices the thirteen-year-old Asher, is entirely too full of dedication and wisdom, his conversation all lecture and sermon. The descriptions of Asher's first struggles ring so clear you feel you have seen the drawings of which they speak. His later work is smoothly announced as art of genius, but the triumphant struggle has left the painting and the writing about the painting, and we no longer believe in either.

"In the Goyish Mould," in The Times Literary Supplement (© Times Newspapers Ltd. (London) 1972; reproduced from The Times Literary Supplement by permission), No. 3683, October 6, 1972, p. 1184.

THE NEW YORKER

Chaim Potok's previous novel, **"My Name Is Asher Lev,"** was about a young painter torn between religion and art. His new novel [**"In the Beginning"**], about a gifted Bronx boy who becomes a Biblical scholar, suggests that the author has decided in favor of religion. The book has an ascetic, stoical, almost self-punishing tone, established with its first line, "All beginnings are hard," and sustained through the painful and sometimes repetitive actions of the story. From shortly after birth, in the nineteen-twenties, David Lurie is plagued by chronic sinus illnesses that prove to be emblematic of his growing up. . . . David's inner life, tortured with fears and bad dreams, is followed through the Depression, which nearly ruins his family; through the late thirties and forties, as the news from Europe grows more and more dreadful; and into his budding years as a scholar, when he learns that curiosity can be a dangerous enemy of faith. His story could be described as a Hebrew "Pilgrim's Progress" or as a spiritual Horatio Alger story, and so it can't be recommended to everyone. Its prose is simple and smooth, but a heavy earnestness pervades it all. (pp. 193-94)

A review of "In the Beginning," in The New Yorker ©1975 by The New Yorker Magazine, Inc.), Vol. LI, No. 39, November 17, 1975, pp. 193-94.

CHRISTOPHER LEHMANN-HAUPT

"In the Beginning" seems radically different from [Potok's earlier novels, **"The Chosen"** and **"The Promise"**]. True, the shift in its locale and time period is only slight. . . . But he does seem to have taken up new and profoundly more complex themes.

For one thing, he appears to be exploring the nature of evil in human affairs. **"In the Beginning"** unfolds against the background of the mounting persecution of European Jewry, first in Eastern Europe during and after World War I, then in Germany during the rise of Nazism. And Mr. Potok seems to be trying to mirror that evil by visiting a series of "accidents" on his young hero, David Lurie, a precocious reader and brilliant student of Jewish scriptures. . . . The accidental aspect of [certain] . . . incidents in the story is heavily underscored by Mr. Potok. It is as if he is setting us up for some comment on the meaning of accidents (do they have a secret cause? or are they random events in an indifferent universe?), which will prove by extension an explanation of the evil occurring in Europe.

For another thing, Mr. Potok seems to be questioning how Jews ought to respond to this evil, whatever its nature. . . . In the mirror world, David is being persecuted by an anti-Semitic Polish immigrant and his cousin, and the most dramatic question posed by the first third of the novel (to me, at least) is how David will react to his persecutors—with hatred or forgiveness.

Finally, Mr. Potok appears to be tying his story to scriptural themes with unaccustomed complexity. . . . [One] of the passages that David puzzles over at length in his study of the Torah is the one concerning Noah's nakedness and his curse of Canaan. So when David's Polish persecutors attack him and remove his clothes so that they may see his circumcision, I felt certain that Mr. Potok was developing a parallel to Noah's emasculation. And even the most literal-minded reader cannot fail to be struck by a sequence in which David first investigates the relationship of the Jews to Jesus Christ, then contemplates the fact that he himself owes his life to the death of his namesake uncle who died in a pogrom ("He died and I am David"), and then accidentally receives a wound in his foot "almost directly above the instep." I confess this is all rather vague, but surely Mr. Potok was up to *something*.

Alas, he is not; none of these complications add up to anything. The many accidents that happen to David are merely random events that serve to illustrate the unhappiness of his childhood. David's Polish persecutors simply move away when the Depression reduces their parents' financial circumstances. And the Biblical parallels turn out to be *ignes fatui* conjured up by your reviewer's feverish imagination.

What **"In the Beginning"** finally boils down to is a story in which its hero must eventually confront—yes—the conflict between orthodox and modern approaches to the scriptures. Beneath its surface complexities, it's the same story all over again. . . .

Of course, there's nothing fundamentally wrong about telling the same story over and over again. Most novelists do, when you come right down to it. And I may have done Mr. Potok a gross disservice by even imagining that he was up to something different. Still, I'd like to believe that he was trying, and that it all got so complicated that he had to fall back on the story he has told before. I'd like to think he'll follow all the way through the next time he writes a novel. Or maybe the time after that.

> *Christopher Lehmann-Haupt, "New Promises, Familiar Story," in* The New York Times *(© 1975 by The New York Times Company; reprinted by permission), December 3, 1975, p. 43.*

JULIAN BARNES

[Chaim Potok] follows growing up Jewish in Brooklyn in the Fifties (*The Promise*) with growing up Jewish (and Polish-Jewish at that) in the Bronx in the Thirties and Forties [*In the Beginning*]. A trifle Brucknerian in pace, and told completely straight except for a closing flicker of fantasy, this novel about a Jewish brainbox puzzling at the irrationality of history, turns out unexpectedly moving. Partly, one suspects, because the European holocaust, which shadows the lives of the whole community, is kept offstage and reflected in microcosm: the street-corner humiliations, the tough gangs of goyim forcing copies of *Social Justice* on Semitic-looking schoolboys, offer much more controllable leverage on our emotions than, say, being slugged with Belsen. It is this careful focus which ensures that the conclusion works. With five million dead in Europe and a race about to make a new beginning, a decision to abandon orthodox Jewish study and see what goyische learning has to offer might seem less than a climax. It is a measure of Mr. Potok's plausibility and characterisation that the act (viewed as treachery by the community) comes across as necessary, heroic, and loyal to a deeper Jewish tradition.

> *Julian Barnes, "Zion Tamers," in* New Statesman *(©1976 The Statesman & Nation Publishing Co. Ltd.), Vol. 91, No. 2351, April 9, 1976, p. 478.**

MICHAEL IRWIN

In the Beginning relates the changing fortunes and attitudes of the Luries, a Jewish family living in the Bronx. In particular it is the story of David, the narrator, and of the shaping of his character and vocation by the influences among which he grows up. . . .

Chaim Potok has remarkable gifts of recall. He catches beautifully the atmosphere of a family party or a school quarrel. Rarer than this is the skill with which he shows how what a child learns and what it experiences are fused and transformed by the imagination. As an evocation of a religious childhood *In the Beginning* is impressive. But the author is aiming at something much larger than this. What David Lurie learns of scripture or history, what he hears about his parents' past, what he endures himself in the way of accident or cruelty all become aspects of a single experience—the Jewish experience.

Despite the resulting fullness and complexity the author has miscalculated. His patterning is too careful, too insistent. When every small episode or description is made thematically relevant there is a loss of the spontaneity that Mr Potok's fluid, associative mode of reminiscence seems to require. He proceeds too cautiously, as though fearful of spilling a drop of his meaning. An incidental effect is to make Jewishness seem an exhaustingly full-time condition imposing a conversational style that moves only between the gnomic and the wry.

But the most important aspect of the miscalculation is that, within the larger context the author has created, his hero is insufficiently interesting.

> *Michael Irwin, "A Full-time Condition," in* The Times Literary Supplement *(© Times Newspapers Ltd. (London) 1976; reproduced from* The Times Literary Supplement *by permission), No. 3865, April 9, 1976, p. 413.*

JAY L. HALIO

In the Beginning, Chaim Potok's fourth novel, is again about urban life, about a young Jewish boy growing up in New York City and experiencing the strains that modern, assimilationist America can put upon a deeply religious, orthodox sensibility. . . . [Many] of the dramatic tensions in the novel develop through Max Lurie's active leadership in a society to help others emigrate to America. But the primary one derives from young David's situation in an environment that cherishes the old ways of life and Yeshiva study, while he becomes more and more conscious of a need to move out of that environment into the larger world of non-orthodox, even non-Jewish intellectual life—move out of it, moreover, without relinquishing it utterly. This is the theme of Potok's earlier novels, and while he treats it with great sensitivity and depth, he is dangerously close to repeating himself. He is unique among Jewish-American novelists in being able to write directly out of the context of lived orthodox experience . . . , and thus offers new perspectives on our visions of America. But other aspects of experience, particularly adult experience, should engage his interest more fully, as Max Lurie's does to a considerable though secondary extent in this fiction. (pp. 843-44)

> *Jay L. Halio, "American Dreams" (copyright, 1977, by Jay L. Halio), in* The Southern Review, *Vol. 13, No. 4, October, 1977, pp. 837-44.**

BOOK WORLD—THE WASHINGTON POST

Babylonian chroniclers wrote, in two columns, the histories of Assyria and Babylonia side by side; during their captivity in Babylonia, Jewish scribes adopted the practice as they synchronized the histories of Judah and Israel. In a way, Chaim Potok now has done the same thing [in *Wanderings*], matching the reigns of Abraham and Saul and David to the advancing civilizations of Mesopotamia, Egypt, Greece, Rome, and tracing the movements of the Hebrew peoples eventually through the development of Islam and Christianity. It is an intriguing concept, and one which lends a more solid basis to the ambiguous history related in the Bible. Unfortunately, Potok, who has formerly stuck to fiction for his explorations of Judaic culture, cannot prevent these massive civilizations from overshadowing the Hebrew tribes. As a matter of organization, he has left the Hebrews for last in each section, so that they seem tacked on. Potok has little control over his style, which staggers from prose to preachment to homily. And, he slips into pseudo-Biblical language ("Now these are the achievements of Solomon son of David, king of Judah and Israel"). With its clumsy and sometimes even ungrammatical style, and its excessive punctuation, reading this book is like traversing the Rocky Mountains one hill at a time.

> *"Diaspora," in* Book World—The Washington Post *(© 1978, The Washington Post), December 3, 1978, p. E5.*

DAVID WINSTON YORK

Potok has accomplished an amazing work [in *Wanderings*]: he has given us a long, well-researched history of the Jewish people, yet he does so with a narrative that is very personal and human. If he seems to scan centuries leaving gaps in the history, he does so because as a self-imposed editor, he must give space to the more important aspects of history which demand space. If he does not know how certain things happened, he offers the reader his own conjecture on the events, and how they came about. He includes the Bible as a record of fact, yet supports the stories within the Bible with a historical perspective. Potok's "wanderings" are passages through the history of his people, and not surprisingly, the peoples of other lands and other cultures.

> *David Winston York, in his review of "Wanderings," in* West Coast Review of Books *(copyright 1979 by Rapport Publishing Co., Inc.), Vol. 5, No. 1, January, 1979, p. 36.*

ERICH ISAAC

The novelist's hand is evident in the flow of the narrative and the often felicitous turns of phrase [in *Wanderings: Chaim Potok's History of the Jews*]. Despite the fact that it is not the work of a historian, it is sophisticated and judicious in its use of professional sources. Yet as the title makes clear, this is meant as a personal history, and its personal character is emphasized through the deliberate intrusion of the author into the narrative. (p. 84)

This sort of thing has a purpose: to help Potok formulate a perspective on Jewish history, and especially . . . on the Jewish confrontation with other cultures and civilizations. Yet considered as history, the volume never makes its thesis clear. And considered as personal history, it never makes clear how Potok's own faith has been reshaped, as he says it has been, by his encounter with non-Jewish, particularly Eastern, cultures.

The title, *Wanderings,* is suggestive of a perspective. Wanderings normally lack direction; they are not pilgrimages but random movements, perhaps searches for something whose exact location is elusive. . . . But despite the title and the frequent repetition of the idea in the book, I do not think that Potok's central thesis is that the Jews are a wandering people. Indeed, the book reveals the extent to which Jews in the last two thousand years have been at home in various civilizations. . . .

There is another problem with finding this book's perspective. It is possible to come away from Potok's narrative with a clear impression of the fabulous achievements of Sumer and Akkad, Egypt and Persia, Greece and Rome, Christendom and Islam, and also of what Potok calls "modern paganism"—all the civilizations through which the Jews have passed—but without any real understanding of what the Jewish role in these civilizations has been. Potok's volume leaves one with the sense that even Christianity and Islam, in all but their earliest stages, show little or no trace of Jewish influence.

Why should this be so? According to Potok: "The central idea of biblical civilization was the covenant . . . the central idea of rabbinic civilization was the Messiah." In his book, the covenantal idea is fully discussed. . . . No such treatment, however, is accorded to the messianic strain in Judaism—precisely that element in Jewish thought and life which perhaps

has made the greatest impact on others, and whose influence continues to be felt to this day. (p. 85)

For this reader there are also difficulties with Potok's division of Jewish history into two chronological civilizations, separated by the destruction of the Second Temple. Potok never defines what he means by a Jewish civilization. He says only that the central idea of the first is the covenant; of the second, messianism. But this is to say both too much and too little. It is too much because messianism predates rabbinic Judaism and because the covenant remained a central idea even after the maturation of the messianic concept. It is too little because a definition of Jewish civilization in terms of these two themes alone is oversimplified. The true distinctiveness of Jewish civilization both before and after the destruction of sovereignty lay in Jewish religious law and in the life that it shaped—biblical law in the first instance, rabbinic law in the second. Yet about this element of key importance Potok has relatively little to say. . . .

At the end we are told that a third civilization of the Jews may be at hand. . . . The reader may be forgiven a certain skepticism on this point. . . .

It would be possible to reverse the upbeat prophecies of Potok's final paragraph, in which he affirms his faith in the renewal of the Jewish people. The Jew is not solidly inside the affairs of the world. What surrounds him is a fresh wave of hate that has managed to encompass much of the so-called Third World, whole areas of the globe that never concerned themselves with Jews before. If, as Potok says, there will nevertheless be peace and renewal for Israel, the day seems as far distant now as it has ever been. (p. 86)

> *Erich Isaac, in his review of "Wanderings: Chaim Potok's History of the Jews," in* Commentary *(reprinted by permission; all rights reserved), Vol. 67, No. 4, April, 1979, pp. 84-6.*

JOHANNA KAPLAN

Beginning with his first novel, **"The Chosen,"** Chaim Potok has illuminated for a vast and rightly fascinated audience the little-known and frequently misunderstood milieu of those communities of very pious Jews who live their lives in contemporary America entirely within the structure and strictures of the Old World orthodoxy of their forebears. In this dense, highly ordered, exceptionally demanding world—especially in the range of its proscriptions—Mr. Potok's brooding, passionately knowledge-hungry young protagonists commonly come to grief. In the course of their growing up, they become desperate to reach outside the prescribed confines of their religious education. Most of Mr. Potok's novels end with the unusually gifted, conflicted young protagonists leaving—and, in a sense, watching themselves leave—the community that bred and nourished them, and their protracted leave-takings are freighted, as the reader imagines their lives will always be, with shadowy self-indictment. For though they remain religious Jews, they have chosen not to take on the obligations and burdens they were taught would be theirs from birth.

"The Book of Lights," Mr. Potok's fifth novel, is the story of the dark and baffling inner journey of Gershon Loran, a morose, isolated rabbinical student who appears, in the words of one of his professors, to "have no enthusiasm," to be "without the feeling of possession by the divine." (p. 14)

[At a non-Orthodox rabbinical seminary, Gershon] meets the two men whose lives and ideas accompany him spiritually for the duration of the novel. Professor Jakob Keter, a celebrated secularist German-Jewish Kabbalah scholar, perceives in Gershon an extraordinary talent and spiritual affinity for the reading of Jewish mystical texts, and he encourages him to pursue this study. . . . In singling Gershon out and offering him discipleship, Keter is in effect choosing a spiritual son, but Gershon wavers.

This father-son dilemma is embodied more directly in the character of Arthur Leiden, Gershon's roommate. The cultivated, sophisticated Arthur is the tormented son of a famous physicist, one of the scientists responsible for the development of the atom bomb. That his father has used knowledge to create devastation is Arthur's single obsession. . . . (pp. 14-15)

Gershon begins to experience the spiritual fire he has been wanting when, upon ordination, he is sent to Korea as a military chaplain. In this alien environment, he reads and immerses himself in Kabbalistic texts and is often visited by visions. On his brief trips to Japan, a country utterly untouched by Judaism, and hence for Gershon unshadowed by reminders of the Jewish past, he approaches a transcendent apprehension of beauty and holiness previously denied to him. "He was being taught the loveliness of God's world in a pagan land," and this troubles him.

When the guilt-haunted Arthur Leiden joins him as a fellow chaplain in Korea, the two friends, each for his own reasons, together embark on a feverish, partly phantasmagoric journey to Japan that is the emotional climax of the novel. But this episode is greatly clouded by Gershon and Leiden's near hysteria. So much so that when Gershon, in a dialogue with his visionary voices, indiscriminately indicts not only the rationalist Jewish scientists but also his own biological father and his various spiritual fathers, Keter included, it is hard to ascertain what his harsh charges really signify. At times he appears to be linking all exponents of Jewish rationalist thinking with the destructiveness wrought by the bomb. The rage is unfocused, and there is a strange confusion between the private and public realms.

In Mr. Potok's earlier novels, the sons refuse to take their fathers' places; in **"The Book of Lights,"** he appears to be suggesting that the undertakings of the fathers, "the giants of the century," have so devastated the world their sons have inherited that there are no places left to take. This is a dark and puzzling vision, and despite the author's attempts to provide a more optimistic conclusion, the novel does not ultimately transcend the gloom at its core. In **"The Book of Lights,"** Chaim Potok has written a powerful, controversial and enigmatic novel. As always, he raises difficult and interesting issues, and addresses them throughout with seriousness and passion. (p. 15)

> *Johanna Kaplan, "Two Ways of Life," in* The New York Times Book Review *(© 1981 by The New York Times Company; reprinted by permission), October 11, 1981, pp. 14-15, 28.**

DIANE CASSELBERRY MANUEL

The many lights in Chaim Potok's **"Book of Lights"** shine with allegorical splendor.

In his descriptions of tenement fires in a decaying Brooklyn neighborhood, the flash of the first atomic bombs at Alamogordo and Hiroshima, and the "light that is God" of mystical Jewish texts, Potok writes of luminous truths and darkly threatening evils. . . .

Like his previously acclaimed novels, **"The Book of Lights"** is the story of an American Jew's search for identity and faith in the 1950s. . . .

A story that draws much of its meaning from ancient Hebrew writings could be perplexing, if not boring, for the non-Jewish reader. But Potok cares too much for the ideas he's setting forth to lose them in abstract reasoning. We're caught up with Loran's questions because they're the questions we all have to answer. His quest isn't exclusively Jewish—it's a quest for the things of the spirit.

In a narrative style that's an intriguing blend of one-word sentences and flowing stream-of-consciousness paragraphs, Chaim Potok mixes intellectual probing and irreverent humor in equal parts, to keep his message from slipping into a soulful or guilt-driven apologia. He's writing about issues of the heart here and should attract readers who have hearts, not just card-carrying believers.

> *Diane Casselberry Manuel, "Potok's Journey toward Light" (reprinted by permission of the author), in* The Christian Science Monitor, *October 14, 1981, p. B4.*

RUTH R. WISSE

Chaim Potok in *The Book of Lights* has adapted his by now standard structure to the story of yet another mild Jewish insubordinate. In each of Potok's previous novels, a representative of Jewish tradition comes into conflict with some incursion of modernity—psychology, comparative philology, art—and makes the perilous move to the other side. His present hero moves from the accepted province of talmudic law to the Kabbalah, the source of a more mysterious, and currently more fashionable, light.

Gershon Loran, the central character in *The Book of Lights,* is a troubled rabbinical student at the Riverside Hebrew Institute—a thinly-veiled fictional version of the Jewish Theological Seminary—in the early 1950's. He is torn between the required study of Talmud and an attraction to Jewish mysticism. The book includes certain staples of Potok's fiction: a friendship between the hero and a young man from a different sociopolitical stratum, in this case the son of a prominent physicist who has been involved in the development of the atom bomb; and the guiding presence of a mentor. . . . The historicity of the novel is selective, with current attitudes and cultural trends superimposed on events of three decades ago.

The rabbinical students are required to serve in the chaplaincy overseas—the book takes place during and immediately after the Korean war—and though Loran's academic performance wins him the alternative of graduate work, he decides after all to serve. The greater part of the novel, no doubt based on the author's own experiences as a chaplain in Korea, is set in that country after the war's conclusion. There the sheltered Judaism of the young rabbi is put to the test of alien surroundings, physical hardship, and personal confrontations with unsympathetic superiors. A more serious problem is faced by Loran's friend, who bears the guilt of his father's "complicity" in the bombing of Hiroshima and comes to East Asia to do penance. Drawn compulsively back to Japan, he is killed in a plane crash which leaves his parents childless.

His experiences in Korea and the death of his friend force upon the hero a spiritual crisis, from which he emerges with professional resolve. Without explaining precisely how this is so, the book suggests that the light of the Kabbalah is more effective than the Talmud when it comes to coping with such natural and human mysteries as physics and war. (p. 47)

Potok's overly tried formula of a confrontation between tradition and some encroaching challenge has resulted in quite a bad book—despite some occasionally interesting descriptions of the life of a chaplain in Korea. The author does not appear to be nearly so comfortable with the mystical inclinations of Gershon Loran as he was with the down-to-earth adolescents of his first two works, *The Chosen* and *The Promise*. (pp. 47-8)

More interesting than the book itself is its place in the author's development. Potok once seemed to be the writer for whom the American Jewish community had been waiting—an educated Jew who knew Jewish life from the inside and could give it authentic representation. As against the second-generation sons and daughters who inhabited most American Jewish fiction, figures estranged from the culture of their parents, with attitudes ranging from indifference to contempt, he presented a generation still raised in traditional homes and only tentatively facing the challenges of the Enlightenment. At the start of each of his early books, Potok's characters feel as if they are emerging out of the pre-modern period, and are only beginning to make an adjustment.

By now, however, the author himself has made an adjustment, one that is apparent in this novel in various ways. During his stay in Korea, for example, the hero tries to prove himself a good chaplain and a good Jew. As a demonstration of his honesty he gives preference to a hard-working Mormon over a Jewish boy from Brooklyn who tries to invoke "tribal familiarity" as the key to a cushy job. The scene bears an unmistakable similarity to Philip Roth's early story, "Defender of the Faith," but at least in the Roth story both Jews are seen to be suspect, the one for trying to use the Jewish connection for personal gain, the other for his discomfort in acknowledging it. Potok is less complex: he differentiates between the good Jew, his hero, who serves the army selflessly, and the bad Jew, who puts his comfort above the common weal. He puffs up his hero at the cost of employing a classical anti-Semitic stereotype, with none of the mitigating irony or sympathy that marks Philip Roth's treatment of the same moral dilemma.

Potok's oddest innovation is his attempt to Judaize the development of the atom bomb, one of the few modern events with which the Jews, as Jews, have happily not heretofore been associated. In one episode in the first part of the book, the seminary grants an honorary degree to Albert Einstein, in the presence of many who have been responsible for the bomb's creation; in the denouement, the son of one of them is sacrificed by the author in a symbolic atonement. Not only the boy's father, but his mother too is shown to have been implicated;

as a noted art scholar, she had dissuaded the Secretary of War from bombing the beautiful city of Kyoto. "You helped save Kyoto and helped destroy Hiroshima," says her husband, trying to establish their common share in the deed. Of course their involvement was inadvertent, but "it was [their] part in all the inadvertence that [their son] had found unendurable."

We did not need Chaim Potok to tell us that Jews have an uncommon talent for cultivating guilt, but he is more than the bearer of the tale here. The book, in fact, takes a peculiar relish in this drama of Jewish self-accusation and expiation. The insensitivity this shows to the Jews may actually endear the novel to a kind of self-lacerating Jewish reader, but at least its trivialization of Hiroshima should not pass unnoticed.

The nature of the dilemma in this novel is the clearest indication of the author's present concerns. To have chosen the Kabbalah over the Halakhah might have been noteworthy within the rabbinate in 1950, but in a novel of the 1980's—after Harold Bloom and all America have approved Jewish mysticism—it is no more than what the publisher ordered. All the learned discussions and quotations from Jewish sources that run through the book, as they do through the author's work generally, do not add up to any perceptible interest in Judaism, the scholarship under discussion, or the Jews. A writer who began by validating traditional Judaism now takes his cues from the culture at large. (p. 48)

Ruth R. Wisse, "Jewish Dreams," in Commentary *(reprinted by permission; all rights reserved), Vol. 73, No. 3, March, 1982, pp. 45-8.**

MONTY HALTRECHT

The Book of Lights is set in the 1950s. . . . [Its] core is the hero's inner development. His questing nature is shown by his choice of a non-orthodox seminary, his first step away from safety and certainty, and his interest lies rather with the Kabbalah, the Jewish mystical writings, than with the safer Talmud. . . .

Isaac Bashevis Singer has given the occult element in life a poetic resonance, be it in the Polish shtetl before the holocaust or among the survivors in America. Potok is alive to the same Hassidic tradition. But he does not have a sense of dramatic effect, he doesn't vary the pace or highlight important moments—everything has equal emphasis, so it is difficult to see, except in retrospect, what is significant. . . .

Potok has chosen a difficult and exalted theme, but the development of the hero is not sufficiently related to the experiences he undergoes during his quest; nor are the changes themselves made vivid or interesting. For all the emphasis on light, this proves to be rather a glum Odyssey.

Monty Haltrecht, "In the Shadow of Giants," in The Times Literary Supplement *(© Times Newspapers Ltd. (London) 1982; reproduced from* The Times Literary Supplement *by permission), No. 4130, May 28, 1982, p. 594.*

Richard Pryor

1940-

Black American comedian and actor.

Pryor is recognized as one of the most original comedians of this era. His great achievement, in the opinion of many critics, is to point to the sometimes hilarious means by which mankind attempts merely to live. His is a comedy of the human condition, shaped by a broad and humane vision of the world.

Although Pryor's portrayals of tough-talking, hard-living blacks receive the most publicity, his characters are generally a mixed group and his satires are aimed at blacks and whites with equal intensity. Critics maintain that Pryor's characters have a stirring universality. Rich and poor, black and white, the young and the very old are portrayed deftly through a combination of visual and verbal techniques. Some observers attribute Pryor's evenhandedness to a sensibility which sees a mystical continuity and order beneath the surface of diverse lives.

Although his albums That Nigger's Crazy, Is It Something I Said?, *and* Bicentennial Nigger *all won Grammy awards, Pryor was not considered "acceptable entertainment" by many audiences until the late 1970s, when the language and subject matter of his routines became more commonplace in the work of other performers. Pryor's films continue to receive "restricted" ratings, but he is now extremely popular with both black and white audiences. Having nearly burned to death in an accident in June, 1980, Pryor returned in 1982 in the film* Richard Pryor Live on the Sunset Strip. *This work, like his film* Richard Pryor Live in Concert, *is often described as one of Pryor's most compelling and effective efforts.*

JAMES McPHERSON

Almost singlehandedly, [Richard Pryor] is creating a new style in American comedy, a style that some of his admirers have called "theater" because there is no other category available for what he does. His style relies on extremely subtle dimensions which must be observed and heard at the same time in order to be completely understood and appreciated. Indeed, there is no way his brand of comedy can be described in writing without the generous use of parentheses noting nuances in sound and facial expression. Mel Brooks, one of his admirers, has called him a comic of "*outré* imagination." Rolling Stone magazine has said that Pryor's comic style is "a new type of realistic theater," a theater which presents "the blemished, the pretentious, the lame—the common affairs and crutches of common people." Most black audiences love Richard Pryor. . . . But because of the particular nature of his art, because of the materials on which he draws, Pryor will probably have great difficulty reaching the wider white public. (pp. 20, 22)

The characters in his humor are winos, junkies, whores, street fighters, blue-collar drunks, pool hustlers—all the failures who are an embarrassment to the black middle class and stereotypes in the minds of most whites. The black middle class fears the glorification of those images and most whites fear them in general. Pryor talks like them; he imitates their styles. Almost always, he uses taboo words which are common in their vo-

cabularies. And he resists all suggestions that he modify his language, censor his commentary. As a result, Pryor's audiences have been limited to those who attend his night-club and concert engagements. These are mostly black people. When he does appear on television, it is only as a guest; and even then he is likely to say something considered offensive to a larger and more varied audience.

Although his routines seem totally spontaneous, his work has moved away from the stand-up comic tradition employed by comedians like Lenny Bruce. Pryor improvises, but his improvisations are structured, usually springing from within his characters. He seldom throws out one-liners just to haul in laughter, unless it is social commentary leading to the depiction of a character. Instead, he enters into his people and allows whatever is comic in them, whatever is human, to evolve out of what they say and how they look into a total scene. It is part of Richard Pryor's genius that, through the selective use of facial expressions, gestures, emphases in speech and movements, he can create a scene that is comic and at the same time recognizable as profoundly human. His problem is that he also considers certain aspects of their language essential to his characters.

"I couldn't do it just by doing the words of the person," he says. "I have to *be* that person. I *see* that man in my mind and go with him. I think there's a thin line between being a Tom on them people and seeing them as human beings. When I do the people, I have to do it true. If I can't do it, I'll stop right in the middle rather than pervert it and turn it into Tomism. There's a thin line between to laugh *with* and to laugh *at*. If I didn't do characters, it wouldn't be funny.'' Here Pryor pauses. "When I didn't do characters, white folks loved me."

There are many whites, however, who do admire Pryor. Like his black audiences, they seem to recognize he has completely abandoned the "cute" and usually paternalistic black comic images of the sixties, popularized mainly by Bill Cosby. Pryor's people are real and immediately recognizable by anyone who has had contact with them, whether in a black skin or a white one. He does not allow them to get away with anything, If it is true, as Henri Bergson has suggested, that laughter is a corrective, a social gesture that has as its purpose the punishment of rigid or inelastic conduct, Richard Pryor is giving a public airing to some of the more unadmirable styles of the urban black community and making his audiences recognize them for what they are. Any good comedian can do this, but it is Pryor's special genius to be able to make his audiences aware that the characters, though comic, are nonetheless complex human beings. (p. 22)

Most people, black or otherwise, would find it difficult not to respond to some of the characters of Richard Pryor's humor. Among them are a philosophical wino who hands out advice to passersby, including Dracula and a junkie; the denizens of an after-hours joint; a meek blue-collar drunk who picks his weekly fight in a barroom, is beaten, then goes home to his wife bragging that he will make love to her, only to fall asleep; a pool shark named The Stroker; a braggart named Oilwell who showers policemen with muscular rhetoric; a white policeman named Officer Timson; a whore named Big Black Bertha; black preachers, hillbillies and assorted minor characters—all of whom have individualized qualities. Not one is a stereotype. Their scenes are introduced from within them and conform strictly to the patterns of their individual experiences. Pryor presents them with such thoroughness and fidelity to their speech, gestures, flaws and styles in general that the same characters are recognizable to audiences in all parts of the country. Pryor's characters are human, and only that. (p. 32)

For all of its appeal, Richard Pryor's comic style is not for everyone, although, watching him portray a character in a comic scene, one realizes that Pryor's people have always existed. In Elizabethan England, a period with a lower class whose manners and styles resembled some of those found in urban black communities, Oilwell might have been called Pistol, Big Black Bertha might have been called Doll Tearsheet or Mistress Quickly, the boys on the block might have been named Bardolph, Peto, Gadshill and Poins. There might have been a sly old man, curiously resembling Redd Foxx, with the name Jack Falstaff. During that period, a genius who knew all levels of his society made a place for them in his historical plays. He produced great drama. Richard Pryor's is a different kind of genius. He knows intimately only one level of his society. But at least he is reminding us, in his special kind of theater, that such people still exist. (p. 42)

James McPherson, "The New Comic Style of Richard Pryor," in The New York Times Magazine *(© 1975 by The New York Times Company; reprinted by permission), April 27, 1975, pp. 20-43.*

ROBERT DUNCAN

[The] problem with reviewing comedy records is eventually the problem with comedy records themselves. Just how many times can you hear the same punchline and laugh? After the second or third time around, you're just remembering past pleasure, and beyond that these records tend to become a rather grim experience.

But the ephemerality of comedy is something the "new" comedians are trying to eliminate by rendering their material more—if you'll pardon the expression—relevant. The new comedians—this category usually includes Pryor, Carlin, Lily Tomlin, and in his worst moments Robert Klein—are working towards something along the line of spoken literature heavily dosed with—again, pardon my sixties—social commentary. Unfortunately the new comedians are not the new literati and their social commentary quickly becomes predictable. And since they took the *jokes* away the whole thing is turning into an out-and-out drag.

Richard Pryor is an extraordinarily funny guy. But his social viewpoint is just becoming all that much more familiar with [his album *Is It Something I Said?*], and so the twists and endings (punchlines?) to his bits are that much more predictable. But still it is Pryor. Right, so **"Eulogy"** was very funny the first two times around, and **"Just Us"** (Justice, get it?) holds up into the third or fourth spins. The major opus here, **"Mudbone,"** is a cut of about 15 minutes length wisely divided between sides one and two, is a captivating piece of hyperbolic black folklore (folk *literature*) and a great bit of acting that one would love to see but it's not really very funny. **"Our Text For Today"** is a surprising low point for Pryor. It's supposed to be funny that this preacher takes the lyrics from Stevie Wonder's "Livin' For The City" as his Sunday text. But has Richard really been subjected to one of those "new" preachers yet, those guys who try to make church "relevant"? Perhaps he's misjudged their impact. Because those cats is deadly dull.

Robert Duncan, in his review of "Is It Something I Said?" in Creem *(© copyright 1975 by Creem Magazine, Inc.), Vol. 7, No. 6, November, 1975, p. 84.*

FRED DeVAN

If you hear [Richard Pryor's album *Is It Something I Said?*] and find it offensive, outrageous, gross, unbelievable, and otherwise distasteful, you are perfectly normal. You probably will have to fight with your own tastes and the social conditioning that helped form them. The reason why you will listen is that your imagination will take over for your will. This record is the funniest thing I have heard in a long time. . . . [Pryor's] delivery is totally ethnic. His references are those of a portion of the Black community. His concepts are of a reality that only exists in his own head. But his messages are universal and universally funny. As long as you are familiar with American basic social elements and colloquial English, you will find Richard Pryor the funniest man alive! It must be something he said.

Fred DeVan, in his review of "Is It Something I Said?" in Audio *(© 1976, CBS Publications, The Consumer Publishing Division of CBS Inc.), Vol. 60, No. 3, March, 1976, p. 80.*

TOM CARSON

Bill Cosby may rent his smile to Ford while Dick Gregory retreats into sanctimonious oblivion, but Pryor is still a defiant, freakily incorrigible survivor—someone who's far too strung out on his own funky, rage-filled wavelength to even consider going respectable. His new, live double [album], *Wanted* (a reference to the legal and personal hassles that practically put him out of action last year), shows him to be top banana.

Though Pryor's raps are as unstructured as Steve Martin's, his high-flying, cheerfully scabrous style keeps the listener moving too fast to notice. Some introductory remarks to the audience segue into a routine on white obscenity versus black obscenity—Pryor's impersonations of white voices are deadly accurate, absolutely hilarious—that then turns into a skit about Andrew Young walking into the Oval Office with his cock in his hand ("'Scuse me, Mrs. Carter. . . ." "Oh, that's all right."). This comic speeds almost effortlessly from sports to sex to life in the ghetto, his fast-paced spiel the only link between topics. In Richard Pryor's world, animals, inanimate objects and even the various parts of his body all have their own voices, which are locked in constant argument—each of them both threatening and scared to death at the same time.

Pryor's bias toward his black fans (which comes through more clearly here than on his studio LPs) is hardly something one can complain about, but I do think it sometimes limits him: a bit on Muhammad Ali, for instance, evolves into another Us versus Them confrontation instead of assaulting the white-liberal infatuation with Ali that this white reviewer sees as its natural, more telling target. *Wanted*'s humor, however, is political for the same reason that the rock & roll of the Clash is political—not out of dogma, but as an inevitable reflection of the circumstances of the artist's life. Pryor's blunt, no-bullshit manner keeps his anger from ever turning into mere counterculture piety, and he's often so good he transcends the boundaries of his own satire. A routine about being beaten by his grandmother climaxes with a line that could have come from Ralph Ellison's *Invisible Man:* "Don't you run from me, don't you ever run from me—as long as you're black, don't you run from me."

As fine as it is, this record has a few problems. Some of the comedy (especially toward the end) is lost because it depends too heavily on visual impact. And even ideas as excellent as Pryor's, stretched over four sides, get somewhat repetitive. But these are minor flaws. *Wanted* is a first-rate document and one of the real finds of any year. At a time when everyone else is struggling to be accepted, it's heartening to note that Richard Pryor is still alive—and running too fast to ever be in or out of fashion. (p. 89)

Tom Carson, "Peeling the Top Bananas," in Rolling Stone *(by Straight Arrow Publishers, Inc. © 1979; all rights reserved; reprinted by permission), Issue 285, February 22, 1979, pp. 87-9.**

DAVID FELTON

Those familiar with Pryor's previous stage work [will be surprised by the film *Richard Pryor Live in Concert*]. His material—all seventy-eight minutes of it—is brand-new, conceived and assembled in the previous five months. And his performance is more unified and more personal, the best example yet of his ability to see and convey the humor in pain.

The difference is that, in the past, much of his material was inspired by the pain around him—the pimps, drunks, cons and junkies of the street, members of his family and his circle of friends. In *Richard Pryor Live in Concert*, the pain seems pretty

much his own, particularly the pain of this last year [in which he suffered a heart attack]. Maybe that's how he survived it. (p. 50)

The heart attack is a perfect metaphor for the show. It's as if in seventy-eight minutes his life passes before him. And us. He shows it to us with such accuracy and honesty that we laugh. It's weird, watching a whole audience laughing at a man dying onstage, and maybe it's a weird kind of laughter, something that comes from a little deeper inside; but the evidence is right there on film. They laugh.

Pryor shows us his childhood, getting whipped, going to a funeral, fighting with his father and grandmother, hunting deer in the forest, fighting in the ring. He doesn't just tell us about the stuff, like most comedians, telling jokes. He brings it to life and exposes its soul. (p. 52)

While there are characters Pryor's done before that I prefer to almost anything in [*Richard Pryor Live in Concert*]—his preachers, drunks and junkies, and a wonderful old man named Mudbone—this film has another dimension; it's as if Pryor, in examining his life during this chaotic year, has grown. . . . (p. 54)

David Felton, "Richard Pryor's Life in Concert," in Rolling Stone *(by Straight Arrow Publishers, Inc. © 1979; all rights reserved; reprinted by permission), Issue 290, May 3, 1979, pp. 50-5.*

STANLEY KAUFFMANN

[*Richard Pryor Live in Concert*] is simply a filmed record of a solo show that Pryor did in Long Beach, California, not long ago. Several cameras were set up, and the show went on, that's all. Aside from the steamy language, it's like watching a live TV broadcast. . . .

The life in the thing is Pryor's. I've seen him in a number of films—[Paul Schrader's] *Blue Collar*, [John Badham's] *Bingo Long* and others—in which he has been very funny and, sometimes, quite moving; his stand-up comic self was only a rumor. Not anymore. In the first 15 minutes or so, I thought this was a new Lenny Bruce, with a blistering tongue, a nastily knowing jab, an anger working itself out through savage but good jokes. For Bruce, the world was divided into people and gentiles: for Pryor, it's people and whites. And he scorches through those opening minutes with a blowtorch humor that compels laughs from those getting vindication and those harboring guilts.

After that opening, the monologue slips into merely (merely!) funny *shtick*, continuingly raunchy but designed only for yoks. Which it gets. In the course of the act Pryor does, possibly for the first time in history, a hilarious bit on having a heart attack (which, I gather, he has had); a pantomime on why blacks walking through woods don't get bitten by snakes but whites do; sharp mimicry of Wasps, John Wayne, and—believe it or not—a deer drinking, a Doberman pinscher and a salacious monkey. If the act doesn't sustain what it promises at the start—a real social blast—it's still a fast hour and 20 minutes. (p. 24)

Stanley Kauffmann, "Alive and Otherwise" (reprinted by permission of Brandt & Brandt Literary Agents, Inc.; copyright © 1979 by Stanley Kauffmann), in The New Republic, *Vol. 180, No. 18, May 5, 1979, pp. 24-5.**

VINCENT CANBY

Only the incomparable Richard Pryor could make a comedy as determinedly, aggressively sentimental as **"Bustin' Loose,"** which is about eight needy orphans and a $15,000 mortgage that's due, and still get an R-rating. Vulgar language is the reason, but because vulgar language is a basic part of the Pryor comedy method, one longs for his every assault on genteelism in **"Bustin' Loose,"** a film that would otherwise be painful. . . .

[The film] is Mr. Pryor's somewhat obsequious attempt to capture the family audience, though I suspect there are plenty of family audiences who prefer him at his more obscene. This movie is a cheerfully hackneyed, B-picture vehicle . . . , based on his own original story. It's about a footloose parolee (Mr. Pryor) who is assigned to drive the eight displaced children and their pretty social worker-guardian (Cicely Tyson) from Philadelphia to a farm in the state of Washington, where the kids can grow up clean and untroubled. . . .

"Bustin' Loose" is not unbearable, though a soft-hearted Richard Pryor is not a terribly funny Richard Pryor. There are occasional flashes of the real Pryor comedy, as in a confrontation with the Ku Klux Klan, whose members he tricks into pushing the bus out of the mud, and in another sequence in which Mr. Pryor attempts to con some professional con artists who are in the process of setting up a trapezoid club (as opposed to a pyramid club) in a small town.

Most of the time, Mr. Pryor gives the impression of holding himself in, of being on his best behavior but itching to do something in epic bad taste. . . .

One longs to see not what's happening on the screen but the story that precedes the opening of the film, hints of which are given in the prologue when we see Mr. Pryor in his role as ineffectual thief with a record that includes, among other things, the impersonation of a truant officer and the counterfeiting of Christmas Seals.

That, of course, would be another movie, and not the sort of movie that Mr. Pryor and his associates wanted to make. The aim of **"Bustin' Loose"** . . . is to convince us that Richard Pryor is just as sweet and jolly as Santa Claus. Believe it or not.

> Vincent Canby, " 'Bustin' Loose' Stars Richard Pryor Gone Softy," in The New York Times (© 1981 by The New York Times Company; reprinted by permission), May 22, 1981, p. C13.

DAVID DENBY

[*Bustin' Loose*] doesn't aim high. It's a family comedy with a formula plot and a horribly corny ending, and the movie almost succeeds in domesticating Richard Pryor—certainly enough to make some of his fans squirm and mutter under their breath. Yet the whole picture is friendly and good-hearted in ways that are hard to resist. Family comedy is a genre usually left to television and the Disney people, a genre despised and ignored by critics. I found myself enjoying almost all of *Bustin' Loose* and laughing helplessly more than once. . . .

Looking a little puffy and perhaps a little sadder around the eyes than before his accident, Richard Pryor is as funny as ever—at times incandescently funny. His role here as an unsuccessful burglar and con artist is less a character than a set of comic opportunities, but that's fine with me. Like millions

of others, I could be content watching Pryor simply *walk*. (p. 51)

Richard Pryor's physical comedy seems to spring directly from his unconscious (an illusion produced by hard work). Verbally, he's articulate beyond belief—a tempest of bluster relieved by vicious muttered asides. A querulous, put-upon man, somehow always a victim, he's capable of working up high-pitched accusations of racism against white people while he's in the very act of ripping them off. He falls into bluffs and scams instinctively, trying to swindle a hostile world through sheer speed. *Bustin' Loose* is so funny because the kiddies on the bus, who are really a bit crazy, turn their fantasies on him, and he can't outsmart or outtalk them. A blind boy who maniacally insists on driving the bus isn't faking; he's possessed, and so is a black girl who presents Pryor with a large teddy bear that has to pee every ten minutes or so. In fact, you would have to go back to the Depression-era *Our Gang* comedies . . . to find such an odd bunch of movie kids. They all try to push through dull reality with their fantasies, which is exactly what Pryor does with his frauds and put-ons, so he's on their wavelength in a way that stern, noble [co-star] Cicely Tyson can't be. No one could mistake *Bustin' Loose* for a good movie, especially since Pryor turns into a teddy bear himself at the end, but it has some of the same shambling pleasures as the W. C. Fields pictures, which were also largely a mess. (pp. 51-2)

> David Denby, "Richard Pryor on the Road," in New York Magazine (copyright © 1981 by News Group Publications, Inc.; reprinted with the permission of New York Magazine), Vol. 14, No. 23, June 8, 1981, pp. 51-2.

DAVID DENBY

Bending low, microphone in hand, Richard Pryor turns himself into two cheetahs calmly stalking a herd of gazelles in his new performance film, **Richard Pryor Live on Sunset Strip.** He's been recalling a trip to Africa in which he observed the animals—a mean mother African rabbit with a twitchy nose, so terrifying that Pryor wouldn't get out of his car; a hungry lion, rotating its haunches before the kill. Pryor assumes the body of each animal, and gives it a voice. His two cheetahs, companionably rubbing shoulders as they watch the doomed gazelles, could be a couple of debonair bloods in silks and Borsalinos sizing up the neighborhood on Saturday night. He's brilliantly anthropomorphic, but he doesn't merely imitate animals. He does everyone and everything: As you watch him, the whole world comes alive for you. In an episode that brings hilarity to the point of terror, he re-creates his "accident" of a few years ago, and tells us what his privates said to his chest as his whole body went up in flames. . . .

Richard Pryor Live on Sunset Strip is a perfect entertainment— 88 minutes of brilliant comedy without any repetitions or low spots. Richard Pryor is hilarious, but it's not enough to say that he's the funniest of the professional funny men. He keeps extending his material and his range. After all, the man doesn't make topical jokes about politics or TV (Johnny Carson); he's not a gag comedian (Henny Youngman); a pop culture satirist (Robin Williams); or a spooky, hostile, put-on artist (Steve Martin); and his mimicry goes a lot further than getting the voices and attitudes right (Rich Little). Richard Pryor works directly with the life around him, and he digs deeper into fear and lust and anger and pain than many of the novelists and playwrights now taken seriously. Like any great actor, he dramatizes emotion with his whole body, but his mind is so quick and his moods so volatile, he's light-years ahead of any actor delivering a text. Working from deep inside his own experience and understanding of what a human being is and is capable of, he can shake you to your roots. More than once during this nightclub act I found myself close to tears, and not just tears of laughter. . . .

After his initial complaints about the increase in chastity during the Reagan administration (as Vincent Canby said, his dirty jokes are obscene in language but not in feeling), he announces that he's not very angry anymore. As we listen, we realize it's true—there's a new evenhandedness in his comedy. In that Africa routine, he not only acts the cheetahs, he acts the gazelles. Richard Pryor identifies with both hunter and quarry, killer and victim; his mimicry captures the frightened surface blandness of so many Americans and also the raging anger underneath. (p. 63)

Like Lenny Bruce, Pryor is completely undeceived about most people's motives (including his own). But he's turned his back on Bruce's nihilism: He's not so eager to shock, nor so gleefully determined to pull the rug out from under the audience at all costs. Richard Pryor has a mean, dirty streak in him, of course, but there's also a part of him that wants to find some common ground that we can all stand on. At this point he's probably as fearlessly unsentimental on the issue of race as anyone in the country. . . . In Africa, he's excited and moved by the realization that "there are no niggers here." He's hardly the first American black to bring that experience home, but who else would have the courage the next minute to build a hilarious routine about the body odor of a tribesman picked up on the road? The simple solidarity of black brotherhood is not for him; life keeps getting in the way.

Richard Pryor may be loved as fervently as he is because he can tell stories of his own disgrace without masochism or self-pity; he's genuinely outraged that anyone could act so stupidly, and he expects us to share that outrage. He tells us that he was so stoned when he blew himself up that he didn't realize, at first, that the pretty blue light coming off his body was fire. Recreating his addiction for us, he turns it into an epic battle between himself and his cocaine pipe in which the pipe, speaking in a calm, soothing, rational voice, like a corporation lawyer, offers haven and rest and tells him to ignore his career and friends. As it goes on, the dialogue begins to sound like a modern Temptation. Man confronts Satan, and man loses, despite the intervention of an angel of light (in the person of Jim Brown). From his hospital bed, swathed in bandages, Pryor watched a TV newsman announce that he had died five minutes earlier. He's a modern Lazarus: He's raised himself from the dead and turned the whole bizarre experience into the best material any comic ever had. (pp. 63-4)

> *David Denby, "Lazarus Laughs," in* New York Magazine *(copyright © 1982 by News Group Publications, Inc.; reprinted with the permission of* New York *Magazine), Vol. 15, No. 13, March 29, 1982, pp. 63-5.**

PAULINE KAEL

When [Charlie] Chaplin began to talk on-screen, he used a cultivated voice and high-flown words, and became a deeply unfunny man; if he had found the street language to match his low-life, tramp movements, he might have been something like Richard Pryor, who's all of a piece—a master of lyrical obscenity. Pryor is the only great poet satirist among our com-

ics. His lyricism seems to come out of his thin-skinned nature; he's so empathic he's all wired up. His 1979 film **"Richard Pryor Live in Concert"** was a consummation of his years as an entertainer, and then some. He had a lifetime of material at his fingertips, and he seemed to go beyond himself. He personified objects, animals, people, the warring parts of his own body, even thoughts in the heads of men and women—black, white, Oriental—and he seemed to be possessed by the spirits he pulled out of himself. To those of us who thought it was one of the greatest performances we'd ever seen or ever would see, his new one-man show **"Richard Pryor Live on the Sunset Strip"** may be disappointing yet emotionally stirring. His new routines aren't as fully worked out. . . . Pryor doesn't seem as prickly now—he doesn't have the hunted look, or the old sneaky, guilty gleam in his eyes. He says he isn't angry anymore, and he seems to have been strengthened—he's more open. (pp. 184-85)

Pryor doesn't appear sweetened, exactly. Even in the films in which he has played Mr. Nice Guy to children or whites, the stickiness hasn't clung to him; he's shed it. And he's always come clean with the audience. Pryor's best jokes aren't jokes in the usual sense—they're observations that are funny because of how he acts them out and because of his inflections. He constantly surprises us and makes us laugh in recognition. He tells us what we *almost* knew but shoved down, so when we laugh at him we feel a special, giddy freedom. That hasn't changed—he isn't soft in **"Sunset Strip."** He tries on some benign racial attitudes and then drops them very fast—that's how you know he's still alive and kicking. He's different, though. You may sense that there has been a deepening of feeling, that there's something richer inside him, something more secure.

At the same time, he's adrift as a performer, because he isn't sure that he's got his act together. And he hasn't. The pressure of a one-man show before a huge crowd and on camera must be just about heart-stopping if you haven't been working in front of big live audiences. And that first film made him a legend; he has the pressure here of an audience expecting history to be made. This film doesn't build the performance rhythm that the 1979 film did; it's very smoothly put together, but in a meaningless way—you don't feel that you're experiencing *Pryor's* rhythms. . . . [Pryor] has trouble getting going. He has hunches—he touches on things and you wait to see what he'll do with them. And most of the time he doesn't do anything with them; they don't develop into routines—he just drops them. Midway, he starts getting into his swing, in a section about his experiences during the filming of parts of [Sidney Poitier's] "Stir Crazy" in the Arizona State Prison. He goes on to talk about a trip he took to Africa, and it's a scene—he can live it. He turns himself into a rabbit, a bear, a lion, a couple of cheetahs, and a fearful gazelle. You feel his relief when he does the animals; a lot of the time he has been looking for his place on this stage, and now he has something physical to do. But then there's a sudden break. Voices, ostensibly from the audience, can be heard. One of them calls, "Do the Mudbone routine," and, rather wearily, saying that it will be for the last time, Pryor sits on a stool and does the ancient storyteller Mudbone, who in the seventies was considered one of his great creations. And the movie goes thud. This section feels like an interpolation—it doesn't have the crackle of a performer interacting with an audience. It's almost as dead as what happens when Johnny Carson asks an aging celebrity to tell the joke he used to tell that always broke Johnny up. Pryor looks defeated, shot down. The sudden dullness is compounded by his sitting: we're used to seeing him prowling—accompanied, when the spots hit the curtain behind him, by wriggling shadows.

When he picks up his act again, he talks about freebasing, and the feelings he had about his pipe—it talks to him, and he becomes the pipe. We feel as if we were actually listening to his habit talking to him. And he builds up a routine about his wife and his friend Jim Brown telling him what cocaine was doing to him. But "the pipe say, 'Don't listen.'" And then he tells about the hospital and about Jim Brown's visiting him every day. He's a great actor and a great combination of mimic and mime; he's perhaps never more inspired than when he assumes the personality of a rebellious organ of his body or of an inanimate object, such as that pipe—or Jim Brown. This is the high point of the film. When he becomes something or someone, it isn't an imitation; he incarnates the object's soul and guts. But he doesn't have enough material to work up the rhythmic charge he reached before Mudbone. What he has in **"Sunset Strip"** is the material for a forty-minute classic.

The picture is full of wonderful bits, such as his demonstration of how he loses his voice when he's angry at his wife, and to those unfamiliar with Pryor's infectiousness and truthfulness and his unfettered use of obscenity, and to all those who missed his 1979 film, it may be a revelation. But the greatness of **"Richard Pryor Live in Concert"** was in the impetus of his performance rhythm—the way he kept going, with all those characters and voices bursting out of him. When he told us about his heart attack, he was, in almost the same instant, the helpless body being double-crossed by its heart, the heart itself, a telephone operator, and Pryor the aloof, dissociated observer. We registered what a mysteriously original physical comedian he is, and we saw the performance sweat soaking his collarless red silk shirt. (There's no visible sweat this time.)

If he fulfilled his comic genius in **"Live in Concert,"** here he's sampling the good will the public feels toward him. Audiences want him, they love him, even in bum movies, and he appears to be experiencing a personal fulfillment. But he hasn't yet renewed himself as an artist; it may seem cruel to say so, but even the routine on his self-immolation is a pale copy of his heart attack. In the first film, there was a sense of danger; when he used the word "nigger," it was alive and raw. When he uses it here, it just seems strange. He's up against something very powerful: the audience may have come expecting to see history made, but history now is also just seeing Richard Pryor. He knows that he doesn't have to do anything. All he has to do is stand there and be adored. And he knows there's something the matter with this new situation, but he doesn't know how to deal with it. (pp. 185-88)

Pauline Kael, "Comedians" (© 1982 by Pauline Kael), in The New Yorker, *Vol. LVIII, No. 7, April 5, 1982, pp. 180, 183-88.**

ROBERT HATCH

Like other professions, that of the comedian has its own hierarchy. Pryor is a jester, a high rank that can be defined as a clown who goes armed. . . . [His] charm is boundless, but of a sort that one would not want to presume upon. His grin is inviting but his eyes are watchful, and he responds to acclamation with a breathless, almost suppressed laugh that seems private, a little ambiguous. He can be charming, all right, but hardly playful, and at times he is not even pleasant.

He opens [his film *Richard Pryor Live on the Sunset Strip*] by announcing that he will speak first "about fucking." It is a bold, if somewhat obvious, way to seize the attention of an audience. What depressed me was that Pryor, having decided on this ploy, described the activity in a way to deny its joy or even its momentary pleasure. Was he hitting us, I wondered, with what he thought we thought was the level of his sensitivity? I was troubled, too, by his use of "shit," "fuck" and their derivatives as substitutes for almost every word in the language save "and" and "but." The effect is not shocking and has not been so for years; it is merely punishing. I was acutely aware of that quiet laugh.

It is clear that Pryor is far from insensitive and has a vocabulary ample for the points he wants to make. A memorable example is his discourse on "nigger." It is a term, he says, that doesn't so much make a black man angry as it knocks the wind out of him. You're having a hot argument with a white man (sometimes with another black), when suddenly he calls you "nigger." You think, Christ! I'm having a fight with this fellow and now he makes me stop and deal with that shit. (There, for once, the word is apposite.) "I wish," Pryor says plaintively, "they would stop doing it." At another point, he got to me with a skit on the illusion of bravery and the reality of danger, his brush with the Mafia providing the text. Later, he evokes the history of his narcotics addiction, staging a dialogue between himself and the drug that was a desperately comic and I thought chilling insight into the cloistral life of a junkie. To my bewilderment, the audience roared with laughter.

Perhaps those viewers were not to be blamed, for by then Pryor had worked them up to a pitch where they screamed when he so much as paused for a drink of water. Not that what he says is so irresistibly funny; at least, I can recall no cascades of incapacitating wit. It means little to commend Pryor for his sense of timing; every stand-up comic knows how to pace an act. Beyond that, he has grace the gift of allusion. His body speaks constantly and elliptically. His miming and mimicry do not studiously imitate their targets, a procedure that is at best mechanical and often tedious. Instead, he catches the essence of what he wants to expose (with Mafiosi, it is the way they hug you), and sketches it with a few strokes so accurate and economical that the wit is in the efficiency of the surgery. If, as I suspect, he is sometimes chastising his admirers for the vulgarity of their suppositions, he pays them the compliment of assuming that they can catch intelligence on the wing.

All in all, he is a somewhat frightening, very useful man. Kings employed jesters to school them in humility. We pay at the box office for Pryor to undermine our complacency. (pp. 536-37)

Robert Hatch, in his review of "Richard Pryor—Live on the Sunset Strip," in The Nation *(copyright 1982 The Nation magazine, The National Associates, Inc.), Vol. 24, No. 17, May 1, 1982, pp. 536-37.*

STANLEY KAUFFMANN

[*Richard Pryor Live on the Sunset Strip*] has a sprinkling of high spots—the animal imitations, a scene with the Mafia—but the direct confrontation of Pryor and audience encourages sentimentalities in him, both of heart-tug and profanity. Also, it puts a double load on him, of performing and being the whole show as well. I don't mean that he improvises everything in these shows; he uses some of his standard bits. But the selections, the relative lengths of bits, the pacing, all make demands on him that he has to keep in mind while he's also performing, with no help from anyone else.

Many cultures have developed genius clowns who do much more than make their audiences laugh, they remind and chide and reassure and rive—Karl Valentin in Brecht's Bavaria, for instance, Dario Fo in terrorized Italy today. In his own style, vastly empowered by film, Pryor is becoming our culture's prime clown and actor. . . . Partly because he is black and uses his blackness as he does, largely through his powerful talents, he is making his films into some of the best political art we now have, whatever the scripts may literally be. (pp. 22-3)

> *Stanley Kauffmann, "Pryor Engagement" (reprinted by permission of Brandt & Brandt Literary Agents, Inc.; copyright © 1982 by Stanley Kauffmann), in* The New Republic, *Vol. 186, No. 18, May 5, 1982, p. 22-3.**

COLIN L. WESTERBECK, JR.

I like Pryor. I think he's funny. But I've never thought he was off the charts, absolutely hilarious. A few years ago he did [a performance film], and I found it amusing, but not great. I feel much the same about the [*Richard Pryor Live on the Sunset Strip*]. Nonetheless, I have to admit that his brush with death does bring a certain patina, a new aura, to his work. It certainly brings a new level of rapture to his audience, which clearly loved this film beyond all reason. Magic is a word thrown around a lot in show biz, but Pryor's magic is now enhanced by a more potent kind, the sort you have to have not to die when you burn up. (p. 273)

Having burnt himself half to death with cocaine, Pryor could step on stage in *Richard Pryor Live* and say anything he wanted, and we would go along with him. He has the license of Lazarus. We are accustomed to comics who take all manner of liberties with life, who treat us to the most grotesque and far-out views of it imaginable, without having anything like Pryor's credentials for doing so. Yet Pryor himself does not do so, amazingly. The only wisdom Pryor has to offer is that, as he says at one point in his monologue, "People are the same everywhere. The ones that work in the airports in Africa f— over your luggage just like they do in New York." None of life's hassles ultimately seem worse to him than that battered luggage. That someone who has virtually come back from the dead should take such a normative, unremarkable view of life seems very encouraging. He has gone to the other side, and come back the same good-natured goof he always was. Pryor continues to do the whole repertoire of ethnic types—Mafiosi and blacks and WASPs and Mudbone. His comedy still aspires to the universal humanity they represent, and now he's had perhaps the only human experience that might validate such routines. This does give them a new dimension, a certain resonance and bounce they never had before. (p. 274)

> *Colin L. Westerbeck, Jr., "Pryor Restraint: Up from Burnout," in* Commonweal *(copyright © 1982 Commonweal Publishing Co., Inc.; reprinted by permission of Commonweal Publishing Co., Inc.), Vol. CIX, No. 9, May 7, 1982, pp. 273-74.**

MICHAEL H. SEITZ

[Richard Pryor] is at his best in the recently released "concert" film, *Richard Pryor Live on the Sunset Strip*. Although the witless pop comedies he's held together single-handedly through the past decade [(Arthur Hiller's *Silver Streak*, Michael Schultz's *Greased Lightning*, Herbert Ross's *California Suite*, Sidney Poitier's *Stir Crazy*)] draw upon his talents in a parsimonious way, he seems to me unquestionably the most gifted and inventive comic working today. . . .

Pryor's work in *Live on the Sunset Strip* represents a fusion of his unrestrained abilities as a writer . . . , stand-up comic, and actor of increasing range and versatility—and it is both unexpectedly moving and wildly funny. (p. 52)

The funny stuff, almost seamlessly stitched together in this performance, runs a thematic range from sex to money, success, lawyers, marriage, prisons, courage, racism, the search for roots, Africa, caged and uncaged animals, cultural relativism, and Pryor's recent, notorious self-immolating "accident." What the movie-goer sees and hears has doubtless been well rehearsed, but there is a commanding sense of improvisation, and one is held on edge by a feeling that this shameless, hyperimaginative wild man might say or do absolutely anything. Pryor goes in for smoker language in a big way, but while the dirty talk adds flavor to the act, his comedy is far from dependent on it. He grounds his work on human feelings, often the most intimate sort, and social and psychological perceptions, and I know of no one better at turning such material into comedy. (pp. 52-3)

> *Michael H. Seitz, "A Few Laughs," in* The Progressive *(reprinted by permission from* The Progressive, *409 East Main Street, Madison, Wisconsin 53703; copyright © 1982 by The Progressive, Inc.), Vol. 46, No. 6, June, 1982, pp. 52-3.**

JONATHAN ROSENBAUM

At the center of Richard Pryor's comedy is his grasp of poverty and weakness, pain and defeat—the very reverse of that strength and self-confidence which he can project so powerfully on a stage. Within the taut dynamics of his performance art, complex attitudes about success and failure, pride and shame, wealth and poverty, love and self-interest are constantly being formulated in relation to one another—guaranteeing the authenticity of his popular appeal, and the beauty and honesty of his self-scrutiny.

To get some measure of the imaginative empathy that Pryor can invest in his creations, his capacity to examine the reverse side of every coin, one need only compare his deer hunt in *Richard Pryor Live in Concert* (1979) with [the one in Michael Cimino's Oscar-winner *The Deer Hunter*]. For a big-time auteur like Cimino, intent on filling out a grand mythic design, the question of how a frightened deer drinks water never gets posed. Pryor does more than pose it; he *becomes* a frightened deer drinking water—along with himself as a kid and his father watching—in order to find out.

This has a lot to do with the art of a Chaplin as well. *Limelight*, for instance, set in London's East End around the turn of the century, was made the very same year that the father of the film's star, director, writer, producer, and composer—a music-hall performer and alcoholic, also named Charlie Chaplin—died in poverty. Thus Chaplain's speculative portrait of himself in 1952 as a has-been and failure is possibly based on what he might have become had he remained in English music halls, and reflects the fate of his own father, whom he barely knew.

The way that, even at his most egotistical and self-indulgent, Chaplin was able to construct an auto-critique founded on the antithesis of his fame and fortune, helps to define what makes him a great filmmaker, and Richard Pryor a great performer. Theirs is an art of rigorous dialectics shared with a mass audience, a game that few comics are capable of sustaining. Correspondingly, it is the absence of such dialectics in the work of Woody Allen—the literal absence of non-whites on the streets of his classy travel-poster *Manhattan,* or marginal working-class types in the Gothic recesses of his *Stardust Memories*—that prevents him from becoming major.

As it happens, Chaplin and Pryor also take in Woody Allen's key subject, the spectacle of middle-class consumption. . . . But Pryor and Chaplin never make the mistake that Allen does, of confusing the part with the whole, or middle-class Manhattan with the universe.

One might argue, in fact, that all three comics can be defined by their separate constituencies, and judged by their individual relationships to them, which amount to political mandates. Woody Allen betrayed his own middle-class mandate in *Stardust Memories* by insulting it; at the end of **Richard Pryor Live on the Sunset Strip,** Pryor thanks his audience for supporting him through his near-brush with death—"You gave me a lotta love when I wasn't feeling well"—and then gently chides them for telling nasty jokes, like the sight gag equating a moving lit match with Pryor as jogger.

According to Pauline Kael [see excerpt above], the new Pryor concert movies "goes thud" when Pryor, in response to requests from the audience, sits down on a stool and goes into his Mudbone routine, because this section "doesn't have the crackle of a performer interacting with an audience." Perhaps Kael would also fault Chaplin's speech at the end of *The Great Dictator*—that unnerving moment when the Jewish barber changes imperceptibly into Chaplin himself—on similar grounds, and it's easy to see why. But it must be acknowledged that these are the parts of both films that matter the most *politically,* as testaments and acts of witness: Chaplin's collapse of his own fiction; Pryor's presentation of his own gaudy success seen through the eyes of a poor rural black from Mississippi, uneducated yet skeptical. . . . In both cases, the comic finds he has to step outside his customary persona in order to speak the truth. For Pryor, this logically precedes his detailed account of his near-fatal accident from freebasing cocaine.

What are Chaplin and Pryor each doing here but reminding us who they are? In a way, the total "inadequacy" of Chaplin's speech as a response to Hitler in 1940 becomes the key truth that the film has to offer. Annihilating the Tramp before our eyes in order to speak as himself, Chaplin simultaneously resurrects the Tramp more profoundly, through exposure (however unwitting) of his own helplessness. He's revealing, in short, that even the famous Charlie Chaplin can't save the world, just as Pryor is revealing candidly that on one level, even a powerless nitwit like Mudbone from Tupelo has more smarts than *he* does when it comes to self-preservation.

Let's bring a final self-witness into the act. Leonard Maltin has pointed out that Jerry Lewis, while playing an unemployed circus clown in *Hardly Working,* still wears his Cartier wristwatch and other expensive jewelry to signal to his audience that he's a hotshot celebrity as well as an out-of-work fun-

nyman. This rather grotesque (or at least mannerist) application of dialectics remains operative on several levels throughout Lewis' last feature, which was largely a hit because of its working-class audience.

Richard Pryor is essentially caught in the same dilemma now; it is fascinating to see in his latest work how he deals, from moment to moment, with this problematical inpasse. Living (as Chaplin did) in a country where success constitutes no less deadly a trap than failure, and where a success such as his own is intimately tied up with his grasp of failure, he walks a very narrow tightrope that can snap at any moment, inviting us to watch his progress. Like any jazz musician, he depends vitally on this sexy form of suspense that keeps everyone off-balance. (pp. 17-18)

Unfortunately, unlike Chaplin, Allen, and Lewis, Pryor doesn't make movies; he gives performances. And apart from his two concert films, where the performance more closely equals the movies, his performances are taken by other people to make *their* movies out of them. (p. 18)

Live in Concert—an act of boundless courage, generosity, beauty, imagination, and wit—presented a lot of heavy-duty shit: Pryor's heart attack (expressed collectively by a chorus of different characters and voices, some of them white); Pryor shooting his wife's car with a Magnum (perishing tires and motor both lovingly recreated); his father's death; whites and blacks crying differently at funerals; women he has sex with who can't come; getting beaten with switches and fists by grandmother and father; finding roaches in his grandmother's cooking. By contrast, **Live on the Sunset Strip** is a piece of cake, and he knows it. He also knows what he can do now, and that's the major disappointment; in the earlier film, he was still discovering his capacities, finding his strength, and luxuriating in the power of that knowledge.

The latest concert movie, much less funny and Shakespearean (and structured with all the apparent "spontaneity" of a fireside chat), is largely concerned with Pryor's simple fears: A black mass-murderer encountered at Arizona State Penitentiary, whites who give rebel yells at night, and the chummy Mafia gangster he worked for at a nightclub in Youngstown, Ohio, when he was nineteen; also his simple day-to-day preoccupations with money, lawyers, marital fidelity, and memories of learning how to masturbate. His degree of candor remains admirable and touching; he even comments on his own tension about doing well, knowing how much is expected of him. Yet he mainly seems interested in keeping himself protected, under wraps—like most of Susan Sontag's writing since her own close brush with death. . . .

There are times when one can speak of Pryor as one spoke of Charles Mingus—or as film theorist Raymond Bellour once wrote of Fritz Lang's two Indian films, when he alluded to "an inability to lie carried to the point of tragedy." Pryor's aversion to slickness and predictability can sometimes keep him interesting and truthful in the most threadbare projects, even when it works against his material. (p. 18)

Jonathan Rosenbaum, "The Man in the Great Flammable Suit" (copyright © 1982 by Jonathan Rosenbaum; reprinted by permission of the author), in Film Comment, *Vol. 18, No. 4, July-August, 1982, pp. 17-20.*

Paul (Joseph) Schrader

1946-

American film director, screenwriter, editor, and critic.

Schrader is noted for his realistic studies of human anxiety and pain. The theme of individual redemption through violent behavior is prevalent throughout his films, and his climactic scenes often explode in brutal massacres. The film that best exemplifies this theme is *Taxi Driver*, a controversial story of an alienated man whose search for identity evolves into a psychotic trail of violence and death.

In his first directorial effort, *Blue Collar*, Schrader examines the systematic emasculation of three assembly line workers in an automobile factory. The script, coauthored by Schrader, has been commended for its realistic dialogue. *Hardcore* is the first of Schrader's works to probe the debasement of human sexuality. In this film, a deeply religious man travels through the subculture of pornography in search of his runaway daughter, who performs in pornographic films. *American Gigolo*, one of Schrader's most popular films, analyzes the world of male prostitution through the eyes of protagonist Julian Kay. Some critics believe that Schrader reached the height of his apparent obsession with sex and violence in *Cat People*. He altered the 1942 version of the film into an intense, sensual horror fantasy about a brother and sister who could make love only to one another lest they release an ancient family curse.

Schrader has been influenced greatly by French director Robert Bresson. In his scholarly book *Transcendental Style in Film*, Schrader analyzes the filmic techniques of Bresson, Carl Dreyer, and Yasujiro Ozu, and he has been criticized for blatantly copying the moralistic themes and stark settings of Bresson's work. Although many critics have tired of his "obsession with sleaze," Schrader's films maintain interest because he captures the sordidness hidden in modern American society.

(See also *Contemporary Authors*, Vols. 37-40, rev. ed.)

STANLEY KAUFFMANN

[*Taxi Driver*, written by Paul Schrader, centers on Travis Bickle, an ex-Marine] who becomes a New York taxi driver, who is willing to drive at night even in the riskiest parts of town, who lives a lonely, grubby life even though he makes an adequate living, who keeps a journal, who goes from ten hours' nightwork straight to porno films because he can't sleep, who develops a crush on a distant blonde beauty, fails with her, then assumes a knightly stance toward a twelve-year-old prostitute in the East Village. He shows increasing signs of psychosis, arms himself with a knife and several pistols, attempts the life of a political candidate for whom the blonde works, fails, then kills the pimps of the child-whore. There is a postlude after the presumed finish, intended to be ironic but which only blazons the defects of what has gone before and crystallizes the picture's ultimate insignificance.

Schrader is the author of a book called *Transcendental Style in Film*, a study of three directors including Robert Bresson, and it's apparent that, despite the torrent of violence and violent

© *Jerry Bauer*

language, he has based this script on Bressonian models. . . . But the more that this script reminds us of Bresson, the more Schrader reveals a recurrent fault in latter-day American filmmaking: the imitation of the form and movement of a good European model without rooting the work in sources like those from which the model grew. The hero of *Pickpocket* is, for Bresson, a tiny, lonely digit in the infinite calculus of God. The hero of *Taxi Driver* is a psychotic, nothing more, and his story is a case history, nothing more. It's as if one were to copy *Macbeth* including the murders for career-advancement but omitting the spiritual withering of the murderer.

The episode with the blonde shows further Schrader's bungling, strategically and tactically. After [Bickle] makes clear his adoration and near-reverence, the girl—seemingly impressed by his fervor and his awe—consents to go out with him. Where does he take her? To a hard-core porno flick. She soon leaves in disgust and refuses to speak to him again. His choice of films might be seen as a symptom of a kind of innocence: he himself goes to porno flicks, apparently not for arousal, and if we could believe his statement that he doesn't know there is any other kind of movie, we could see the disaster of this date as the vengeance of the world on the unworldly—a Bressonian strophe. But we can't believe him. [Bickle] spends a great deal of time fulminating against the sexual filth in New York that he sees as he drives, that takes place even in his cab.

He hates it and says often that all the garbage in New York should be flushed down the toilet. How could he possibly dissociate what he sees on the porno screen from the male and female whoring he loathes in the streets, even if he did somehow believe that this was the only kind of movie in existence? Far from naïveté, the scene comes out at best as further proof of the hero's insanity; and also of Schrader's imposition on his script of gestures of innocence, in imitation of his model, instead of drawing them from inner sources as Bresson does. (pp. 200-01)

The ending confirms the fakery of what has gone before. (I debated whether to reveal this ending, but if the work is really serious, then surprise should be irrelevant; and this film claims to be serious.) [Bickle] has a very long, very bloody shootout with the two men who protect the child-whore; he himself is shot at least twice. At the end of this protracted hideous violence [Bickle] sprawls, barely conscious, next to one of the corpses. [Martin] Scorsese then takes his camera high above the scene and, moving overhead, goes back over the bloodstains to the other body. It's like a deceptive cadence in music: we expect the closing chord. Instead we suddenly cut to the epilogue. [Bickle] has recovered, has been hailed as a hero for rescuing the child, is back driving a cab, and accidentally re-meets the blonde, who is now in awe of *him*. He snubs her and drives off.

What in heaven's name does this ending mean? A dream? Whose? Irony, obviously, but about what? Society's inability to detect a homicidal psychotic? The fact that, from this "hero," more killing will surely come? Is that what this heavy, grittily detailed film has been building up to? Or does it all merely lead up to the cute shift of awe from him to the blonde? Or are we supposed to swallow the psychically incredible proposition that [Bickle] has now had his emotional explosion and will henceforth live normally? No matter how you slice it, it's a Happy Ending. When F. W. Murnau and his writer, Carl Mayer, stuck an arbitrary happy ending on *The Last Laugh*, they at least had the Brechtian honesty to laugh at it, so that it obliquely ratified the grimness that had gone before. Schrader, with Scorsese, only ratifies the hollowness of what has gone before. (p. 202)

Stanley Kauffmann, in his review of "Taxi Driver" (originally published in The New Republic, *Vol. 174, No. 10, March 6, 1976), in his* Before My Eyes: Film Criticism and Comment *(copyright © 1976 by Stanley Kauffmann; abridged by permission of Harper & Row, Publishers, Inc.), Harper & Row, 1980, pp. 200-03.*

PATRICIA PATTERSON AND MANNY FARBER

Basing its tortured hackie hero vaguely on the pasty-faced Arthur Bremer, who, frustrated in his six attempts to kill Nixon, settled on maiming George Wallace for life, *Taxi Driver* not only waters down the unforgettable (to anyone who's read his diary) Bremer, but goes for traditional plot sentimentality. Bremer, as he comes across in his diaries, was mad every second, in every sentence, whereas the Bickle character goes in and out of normality as the Star System orders. The Number One theme in the Arthur Bremer diary is I Want to Be A Star. Having dropped this obsession as motivation, the movie falls into a lot of motivational problems, displacing the limelight urge into more Freudian areas (like sexual frustration) and into religious theories (like ritual self-purification). The star or celebrity obsession is a Seventies fact—the main thing that drives

people these days—compared to the dated springboards in Paul Schrader's script. Instead of Bremer's media dream, getting his name into the *New York Times* headlines, this script is set on pulp conventions: a guy turns killer because the girl of his dreams rejects him. The girl of his dreams, a squeaky-clean WASP princess, is yet another cliché assumption: that the outsiders of the world are yearning to connect to the symbols of well-washed middle-class gentility.

Busily trying to turn pulp into myth, the movie runs into all kinds of plot impossibles:

(1) A shy guy converts himself into a brutal killer after scenes in which he is a smart-ass with an FBI agent, a near matinee idol with his Miss Finishing School, and an unsophisticated, normal Lindbergh type with a teen prostitute. The latter girl similarly goes from street-hardened and cynical to open and cheerful, well-nourished and unscarred, in one twelve-hour time interval.

(2) The cabbie, after having readied himself with push-ups, chin-ups, burning dead flowers, and many hours of target practice, guns down a black thief in a Spanish deli. The brutality, which is extended by the store-owner golfing the victim's corpse with a crowbar, is never touched by the police.

(3) A taxi driver who's slaughtered three people, been spotted twice by the FBI, and has enough unlicensed artillery strapped to his body to kill a platoon, is hailed as a liberating hero by the New York press.

(4) A Secret Service platoon, grouped around a rather minor campaign speech on Columbus Circle, fails to spot and apprehend a fantastic apparition: a madly grinning young man who is wearing an oversized jacket on a summer day, sunglasses, and has his head shaved like a Mohawk brave, with a strip of carpeting for the remaining hair.

Although *Taxi Driver* is immeasurably more gritty, acrobatic, and zigzagging than the *Jeremiah Johnson* mythicizing of mountain men, the two films (one moves blandly forward on snow shoes, the other sets a grueling pace) are remarkably similar in their linear structure and ideology. Both are odes to Masculine Means in which a mysterious young man appears out of indistinct origins; learns the lore of survival warfare in a hostile land; after a heartbreak, lashes out in a murderous rampage; fades into a mythic haze. The lore Jeremiah-Travis learns has to do with manly self-reliance: the first learns to kill a bear, catch a fish barehanded; the "hackie in Hell" becomes a one-man commando unit. Both inhabit a world—an unpeopled wilderness and a callous jungle—where no one can be counted on for help. Women are the spurs to the climactic bloodbath: Jeremiah's Indian wife is murdered, while Travis's efficient blond tease rejects him, confirming him in his conviction that blood is the only solution.

The character of the Loner, which dominates American films from Philip Marlowe to Will Penny to Dirty Harry Callahan, has seldom been given such a double-sell treatment. The intense [Travis Bickle] is sold as a misfit psychotic and, at the same time, a charismatic star who centers every shot and is given a prismatic detailing by [Martin Scorsese], who moves like crazy multiplying the effects of mythic glamour and down-to-earth feistiness in his star. (pp. 27-8)

What's really disgusting about *Taxi Driver* is not the multi-faced loner but the endless propaganda about the magic of guns. The movie's pretty damn cunning *mise-en-scène* is a mystical genuflection to The Gun: what a .44 Magnum can do to woman's face and pussy, the continuous way in which male brotherhood is asserted by one man pointing his pistol finger at the other and saying "pow." If the male population isn't exchanging this payoff gesture, they're addressing each other with "Hyah, Killer. How's the killer, today." The film's funky, insinuatingly ripe surface comes from a steady litany of "I'll kill you" shrieks, a collaging of sinister inserts, anal allusions, so many references to the sewer, "wiping the come and sometimes the blood off the seat," a giant lotus of steam enveloping a cab like fumes from Hell. Each item of this mélange is used as a metaphor for the destructive blasting of a gun. Even the cab, moving forward with ominous slowness, is felt as either death machine or coffin. (p. 28)

Seldom since John Ford's epics of Joad and Lincoln in the 1939-40 period has there been such oily, over-definition of the lower classes. How colorful these workers are: a one man compendium of champion jazz drummers studied for three minutes ("now Gene Krupa's syncopated style"); or [the] incredibly garish pimp, decked out with tight-muscled mannerisms, the weirdest clothing, an appetizing voice that tries to score on every word. One standout example of an over-detailed shtick: a snarling, aggressive guy who hires cabbies and overreacts wildly to Travis's small attempt at a joke with a ferocious "Are you going to break my chops? . . . If you are, you can take it on the arches right now." Twenty seconds later, he melts with brotherhood and warmth, learning they're both ex-Marines. . . .

Taxi Driver is a half-half movie: half of it is a skimpy story line with muddled motivation about the way an undereducated misfit would act, and the other half is a clever, confusing, hypnotic sell. End to end, behind as well as in front of the camera, is the sense of propagandists talking about power, scoring, and territory. The movie's ad campaign . . . is revelatory of what the filmmakers feel it takes to move, score, and hold your territory in a competitive USA society.

Reconstituting pulp is central to both the movie's writing and filming, always juicing up or multiplying a cliché notion so that the familiar becomes exotically humorous. Pumping up clichés runs inevitably into moral problems. A scene that's been grooved a thousand times on TV crime shows, not to mention late *film noir* like [Robert Aldrich's] *Hustle* (a store heist recorded with the camera on an unexposed customer who then guns down the surprised marauder), is super-charged out of the cliché by showing the store-owner brutally beating up the black corpse. Are there any moviegoers left who aren't fed up with personal reform through Atlas physical exercises? The hero suddenly stops "mistreating his body," goes into a regimen of musclebuilding, target practice, and health food. This situation is juiced up with a comedy scene that throws audiences in the aisles. Bickle, strapped up with his special equipment and guns, faces himself in the mirror: "You talkin' to me, You Fuck! You must because I'm the only one here." The sneering monologue refurbishes two or three clichés, it sneers at anyone who isn't a gunsel or muscle boy, and puts a glamorous sanction, a good gunman seal of approval, on the movie's future holocausts.

A chief mechanism of the script is power: how people either fit or don't fit into the givens of their status, and the power they get from being socially snug. Travis's dream girl has power because she has a certain golden beauty and doesn't question or rebel against her face or her position as political campaigner. Various pimps are shown as editorialized icons of illegal power. The cabbies, more or less at peace with themselves, are glimpsed as a gang not fighting job or status. The movie shows the facts of being in or out. Everyone plays this power game but Travis—he can't figure what kind of game he wants to play. While this misfit moves toward his massacre in a Twelfth Street bordello, the movie's heart is an ensemble of chesty people jockeying to score points. The script sets up a world where people constantly score off each other, releasing petty hostilities. Little Iris's professional command: "You better get to it, Mister, because when that cigarette goes out, your time is up." Some sexual invitation. . . . (p. 29)

The importance of humor is one of the movie's trumps, as well as one of its bad cards. When people try to jokingly tease [Travis], he can't throw it back. He tries to joke with the cab employer and the guy explodes. Betsy doesn't get his "organazized" joke. This sealed-off guy's problems with humor—his crestfallen, embarrassed, or shamed responses—are always poetically right; and the movie is almost always good when it's dealing with his communicative impotence. (pp. 29-30)

Taxi Driver is actually a Tale of Two Cities: the old Hollywood and the new Paris of [Robert Bresson–Jacques Rivette–Jean-Luc Godard]. More importantly, its immoral posture on the subject of blacks, male supremacy, guns, women, subverts believability at every moment in favor of the crucial decal image that floats around the world—a lean, long-legged loner in cowboy boots who strides down the center of a city street, knowing he cuts a striking figure. . . . [Travis's] image, looming over his vague environment, is voiced everywhere in the script: "Around his eyes, in his gaunt cheeks, one can see the dark stains caused by a life of terror, emptiness, and loneliness." The next line is great: "He seems to have wandered in from a land where it is always cold." (p. 30)

Patricia Patterson and Manny Farber, "The Power and the Gory," in Film Comment *(copyright © 1976 by The Film Society of Lincoln Center; all rights reserved), Vol. 12, No. 3, May-June, 1976, pp. 26-30.*

MICHAEL DEMPSEY

In *Taxi Driver,* New York City is a steaming, polluted cesspool and Travis Bickle's cab a drifting bathysphere from which he can peer at the "garbage and trash" which obsess him: whores, pimps, junkies, wandering maniacs, maggotty streets, random violence. It's definitely a subjective vision—the film locks us into his consciousness—yet not solipsistic, inasmuch as the grisly avenues and their cargo of human flotsam could be observed by anyone walking or riding there at night. The screenwriter, Paul Schrader, also wrote a book entitled *Transcendental Style in Film,* and he has gone out of his way to make us take one of its subjects, Robert Bresson, for his main inspiration. Actually, it is Bresson's *Four Nights of a Dreamer* (released after the book was published) which *Taxi Driver* suggests most. (p. 37)

[Schrader must have had] the desire to have the movie conform to his formulation of "transcendental style." Any brief summary of its elements is bound to be oversimplified. But, as he analyzes it, its constituent parts are: a detailed, nondramatic presentation of *everyday* life, in which "nothing is expressive" of psychology, ideas, or any sort of readily paraphrasable meaning; the *disparity* which results when "human density" is added to this cold, flat mundaneness, causing us to be emotionally stirred and to accept on faith the *decisive action* taken by a character in order to break through it; and a concluding *stasis,* defined as "a form which can accept deep, contradictory emotion and transform it into an expression of something unified, permanent, transcendent." The style seeks to embody everything in life which cannot be explained psychologically, economically, dramatically, or through any other kind of rational means. It attempts to express "the inner unity of all things," to "maximize the mystery of existence." Schrader declares Bresson and Ozu its prime practitioners, adds elsewhere that he wrote his first script under its guidance, and has undoubtedly thought of it in connection with *Taxi Driver.*

But, leaving aside any debate over the validity of the style, the film has become a travesty of it. (pp. 39-40)

Taxi Driver cannot hope to attain either [disparity or decisive action] because of its slippery plotting, which deprives its movement toward violence of any fatalistic quality. Just before he buys a load of guns in preparation for his attempt on Palantine's life, Travis's diary states that, after days and days of life's uneventful drift, "suddenly there is change." Like the narration which precedes his first conversation with Betsy, this remark seems intended to make us view what follows—in this case, the violence—as fated. In his book, Schrader cites the religious paradox of becoming truly free by choosing one's predestined fate. But if one's fate is indeed predestined, then so is one's choice (or rejection) of it. Travis's narration would have us believe that he is taking "decisive action" by accepting a fate which he cannot alter. But bad plotting, rather than predestination, has brought him to this point. Like the fate in Godard's *My Life to Live,* this one is, as Pauline Kael put it, "cross-eyed." So is the coda, during which Travis, acclaimed by the media because the pimps he killed turned out to be gangsters, accepts Betsy as a passenger in his cab, drops her off, then drives away, rejecting her tentative interest but retaining her image in his rear-view mirror. Has his explosion purged him of his rage? Permanently or temporarily? The first seems unbelievable, and the second renders the whole movie a virtually pointless psychodrama. Instead of stasis, the scene expresses the desperation of the filmmakers to find a playable ending for the movie.

Schrader's allusions to Bresson tend to seem almost as forced. From *The Diary of a Country Priest,* he has borrowed its protagonist's Holy Agony—with both words operative, because his goal seems to be the canonization of Travis as a mythic icon or secular saint, a lowlife Christ come to cleanse the temple of moneylenders. When Palantine pontificates about the suffering of "we the people," the phrase seems calculated to include Travis, who even wears a "We the people" campaign button during his failed attempt on the candidate's life. When a fence lays out his inventory of guns for Travis, painstakingly cataloguing the caliber and power of each, the movie becomes laughably fetishistic. But the intention was apparently sacramental; Travis and the fence handle the weapons like chalices, set them down in their cases like hosts on a paten at High Mass. The miscalculation is almost sublime. With much of the audience simply gasping at the arsenal and turning on to the scene's sexual undertones, its tonier aspirations become a joke, like Travis's Bressonian lament that "I think I've got stomach cancer." Travis has neither the religion of Bresson's priest nor the Dostoyevskian rationale of his pickpocket. (pp. 40-1)

When it finally comes, the climax of *Taxi Driver* certainly does have a rush of emotion which could be palmed off as characteristic of the transcendental "decisive action." But it is only a revenge movie cliché; like the shark attacks in [Steven Spielberg's] *Jaws,* it provides a purely physical jolt and obtains nothing more than a reflex reaction. When necks are gushing, blown-off hands are flying, and brains are spattering the wall, we cannot help jumping with shock (pleasurable or otherwise), but that has nothing to do with anything as lofty as redemption. During this scene, *Taxi Driver* reduces itself almost to the squalid level of [Michael Winner's] *Death Wish,* the kind of adrenalin-pumping, unprincipled revenge melodrama which will do anything to arouse its audience.

Despite the current cry in Hollywood for "pure entertainment" and a return to old-fashioned storytelling, most of today's screenwriters are no better at either than Schrader is, which is why they so often head straight for this genre. It's the easiest type of script to plot; just establish a lantern-jawed hero, kill off his wife and kids and dog, throw in some picturesque torture such as breaking both his legs or grinding off his hand in a garbage disposal, then turn him loose. As simple-minded as this mechanism is, its raw power is irresistible to many audiences no matter how stupidly and cynically it is used. *Taxi Driver* never becomes this simplistic, but the revenge movie's relentless build-up to a bloody climax is hard to derail once it gets going and perhaps too brutally driving to be contained by even a flawless application of transcendental style. When Travis prepares for violence with calisthenics, target practice, dieting, fast-draw exercises before a mirror, and a Mohawk haircut, these ritual preparations, this Puritan shriving of the body, looks like a weird cross between a bull-fighter donning his suit of lights and a priest vesting for Mass. It does no good to remember that this is an ancient movie gimmick . . . or even that Lee Marvin parodies it hilariously in [Elliott Silverstein's] *Cat Ballou.* The inherent roller-coaster force of this sequence can neither be denied nor, in this movie at least, controlled. As a result, during the shootout, the audience doesn't get redeemed; it just gets off—or gets sick. . . .

If *Taxi Driver* had unleashed its firestorm, say, halfway through its running time and then had gone on to show Travis dealing with the changes in his life brought on by this catharsis and the resulting fame, it might have become an analysis of contemporary confusion rather than an example of it. In any sense of the term, [*Taxi Driver*] fails to transcend because its makers are caught in too many contradictions. Scorsese has an enviable feeling for film, Schrader a knack for evocative premises in addition to an often incisive critical mind. But, separately or together, both need a healthy dose of redemption from half-baked ideas. (p. 41)

Michael Dempsey, in his review of "Taxi Driver," in Film Quarterly *(© 1976 by The Regents of the University of California; reprinted by permission of The Regents), Vol. XXIX, No. 4, Summer, 1976, pp. 37-41.*

RICHARD COMBS

[Paul Schrader seems] to have succumbed to a paralysed narcissism. His cinephile enthusiasms, which have run to simply but powerfully motivated blood and thunder plots, graced with metaphysical ironies ranging from Bresson to [Alfred] Hitchcock, have locked in *Rolling Thunder* on the most primitive, exploitative level. Ex-Vietnam POW Charles Rane . . . returns home to San Antonio, Texas, and discovers that his wife wants to leave him for his best friend. However, a gang of thugs erupt into his home in search of one of his valuable coming home gifts, beat and torture him (prompting some flashback allusions to how he endured similar treatment in Vietnam) and leave with the loot after shooting his wife and child. Putting himself into training to streamline his newly acquired artificial hand into a lethal weapon, Rane sets off in pursuit with a Vietnam buddy . . . more obviously traumatised by the war.

The most revealing thing about this concoction is neither its emotionally over-driven construction, nor its rampaging gratuitous violence, but Schrader's clear grinding down of the ingredients of 'serious' movies like *Taxi Driver*. In this respect, *Rolling Thunder* is actually of a different species from [George Romero's] *Martin* and [John Carpenter's] *Assault on Precinct 13*. Its movie lore is channelled into the creation of one sustained, gut-wrenching effect, where the pleasures of the other films are more diffuse—their creativity served rather than exhausted by their multiple allusions and borrowings. The collaboration of Schrader and director John Flynn actually fits with Hollywood's standard, carbon-copying processes, along with such low-grade genre rip-offs as Robert Clouse's *The Pack* and any number of television series at a further, diluted end of the spectrum. (p. 59)

> *Richard Combs, in his review of "Rolling Thunder,"* in Sight and Sound *(copyright © 1978 by The British Film Institute), Vol. 47, No. 1, Winter, 1977-78, pp. 58-9.*

STANLEY KAUFFMANN

Paul Schrader, who wrote the dubious script of *Taxi Driver* and the undubiously awful script of *The Yakuza,* wrote [*Blue Collar* with his brother Leonard]. . . . The script has its waverings. . . . [*Blue Collar*] starts as a breezy comedy about three friends, two black men and a white man who work on the same assembly line, who bowl together with their wives and who ball with other women at cocaine parties. At the beginning the script handles their strapped financial situations farcically. A scene with an IRS man is an updated black remake of a similar scene in [Frank Capra's] *You Can't Take It with You;* then there's a comic robbery with ludicrous Halloween masks, a touch of [Mario Monicelli's] *Big Deal on Madonna Street;* then, because of something the three friends discover in the union local's safe that they rob, the script suddenly turns heavily dramatic; and then it tries to turn tragic. It's almost as if Schrader didn't know where he was heading when he started.

But along the way, inside each of the sections, inside the scenes within those sections, life is made. The homes, the bar, the parties, the plant squabbles, the union meetings, the snoopings by the FBI have the smell of authenticity: of dailiness dramatized as most documentaries cannot do it. And the dialogue, except for an occasional touch of the unduly prophetic, is raunchily real. (p. 228)

[*Blue Collar*] is Schrader's first directing job, and the best elements in the script fit his ability like a role tailored for an actor. His work is easy and quick, imaginative but not ostentatious. The long shots of the auto plant and a filling station tell us that he has seen [Michelangelo Antonioni's] *Red Desert* and [George Lucas's] *American Graffiti,* his traveling shots of the assembly line are reminders of Godard, but as long as he isn't merely imitating, why shouldn't a young director learn from older ones? In the grittiness of this workers' world, Schrader is much less strained and arty than Scorsese was in directing Schrader's *Taxi Driver* script, much more intent on revealing than displaying. (pp. 228-29)

Two principal themes connect under the clanky plot. The first is the changed status of the American worker: from the poverty of poverty to the higher-paid poverty of inflicted consumerism. Where he used to struggle for bread and shelter, now he struggles—not much less painfully—for back taxes and braces for his daughter's teeth. The second theme is the changed relation with the union, and the changed union. . . .

Blue Collar hits hard at this union, the UAW, in the instance of this local. The leaders are drawn as liars, crooks, users of race prejudice, brutes and murderers. We see the services that the union provides for its members, and we see the tyrannies leveled in exchange. I won't presume to pass judgment on the accuracy of this portrayal, though the newspapers are not exactly free of stories about union malfeasance. But I certainly can't believe that American unions, which have been blessings to millions, are free of American vices. There is a clear recurrence of anti-union feeling these days, in advertising campaigns and elsewhere, yet only the extremely nervous will see *Blue Collar* as anti-unionist. Truth, for those who care about it, can be uncomfortable, not really inimical; and in the view of general experience, these union actions ring true. (p. 229)

> *Stanley Kauffmann, in his review of "Saturday Night Fever" and "Blue Collar"* (originally published in The New Republic, *Vol. 178, No. 6, February 11, 1978), in his* Before My Eyes: Film Criticism and Comment *(copyright © 1978 by Stanley Kauffmann; abridged by permission of Harper & Row, Publishers, Inc.), Harper & Row, 1980, pp. 226-30.**

PAULINE KAEL

Blue Collar has to be one of the most dogged pictures ever produced. Making his début as a director, Paul Schrader, the phenomenally successful young screenwriter, has approached directing as a painful, necessary ritual—the ultimate overdue term paper. He goes at it methodically, and gets through it with honors but without flair, humor, believability. *Blue Collar* is an exercise, an idea film in which each scene makes its point and is over. (p. 406)

Blue Collar says that the system grinds all workers down, that it destroys their humanity and their hopes. At the start, under the titles, there's the ominous, heavy rock beat of "Hard Workin' Man"—like the hammer of oppression. The music is calculatedly relentless. It's to make us feel the throbbing noise of the assembly line, so that we'll grasp how closed-in the men's universe is. Noise isn't just noise in this movie, it's fate. The meaning of *Blue Collar* is in its dark, neon tones, its pounding inexorability, its nighttime fatalism. There's no feeling of fresh air, and even the sunlight has a suggestion of purgatory. The *film noir* style of nightmare realism, which in the thirties and forties was used in high-strung thrillers about loners in the city or outlaws on the lam or prisoners threatened by brutal guards or innocents who got on the wrong side of the law and were hounded, is here applied to American blue-collar workers. When Jerry, thinking to escape from the blackmail mess, says "Maybe I'll go to Canada," he gets the classic *film noir* answer—"Wherever you go, they'll find you." Smokey, in the deep voice of a man who knows, spells out the conditions in the automotive industry: "Everything they do, the way they pit the lifers against the new boys, the old against the young, the black against the white, is meant to keep us in our place." And when at the end Zeke and Jerry raise their arms against each other it's the proof that they were pre-ordained to be victims and that the system has won. In all probability, the automotive industry wants to keep the assembly lines running, and doesn't want any dissension among the men which might slow the lines down. But this film's jukebox Marxism carries the kind of cynical, tough-minded charge that encourages people in the audience to yell "Right on!"

The entertaining *noir* movies usually had some neurotic tension; they revelled in sleaziness and shadows, in cheaters and femmes fatales and twisty plots. And they were marvellously well suited to black-and-white cinematography; the oppression had a sleek theatricality—jagged patterns, shivery contrasts, highlighting. The oppression here is really oppressive—blue and drab. . . . *Blue Collar* has a consistent dark, threatening scheme, and some of the sequences in the auto plant (particularly the opening montage) are strong and feverish. But several of the most critical dramatic scenes are weakly staged, with no visual energy: the actual robbery doesn't have an ounce of tension, and seems to be lighted with a fifteen-watt bulb. The shortcoming of Schrader's direction is that, with all the ominousness and threat in the percussive music and the visual design, there's no suspense. When the fatalistic style was used in crime thrillers, even with doom hovering in the air luck might change; there was a chance, a hope, some poetic radiance. (If there wasn't, the picture flopped.) Schrader doesn't yet know how to create that tingling sense of possibilities, or that suggestion of delirium, which might make his doominess vibrant and funny. What he's got is a mulish driving force. The script . . . is plodding in a shrewd, manipulative way, and he lets the dull story play itself out. That could be his swindling genius; he's a propagandist without a cause. In puritan tones, he tells us that the world is an ugly place and you can't change a thing. If you stick up your head, they chop it off. So you might as well be a flunky to the bosses and make things easier on yourself.

The risky astuteness is in having [Zeke (rather than Jerry)] . . . the one who's bought out by the union officials. . . . Zeke is lean, a lightweight griper and joker, boyishly corruptible. He's a brooder, but with a short attention span, and in some fundamental way he's not connected up right. . . . In Schrader's thinking, to survive men either allow themselves to be used or become users; Smokey, who balks at the first and is constitutionally incapable of the second, has to die. He's the only man of substance in the entire film. . . . [But] Jerry is the character the writers did the least for (even his motivation for taking part in the robbery—that his daughter needs braces for her teeth—is tacky, since the U.A.W. has a dental plan). . . . As it is, there's no interplay [between the characters], nothing to suggest that there's a history to the friendship. All their responses to each other are so programmed they might have met the day before—they're pals because the movie needs them to be. In the same way, the three men have an accomplice in the robbery because an accomplice is needed to rat on them, and at the end Jerry goes back to his locker at the factory so there can be the confrontation between him and Zeke. (pp. 406-08)

Most of what happens in the movie has no intrinsic interest; it's for the sake of the plot. When there's an incident at the plant which doesn't serve the plot directly, such as . . . [the bit with] a man enraged by a food dispenser that doesn't work, it's a relief. There's not nearly enough detail of what the men say and do at home or at the union meeting or the bowling alley or the beer tavern. No one ever talks about quitting; there's no indication of the rapid turnover of auto workers, of the fact that perhaps thirty per cent a year get fed up with the gruelling,

noisy, hard work and leave (so that auto workers get younger all the time). If the film recognized that men can step sidewise in the society, can try to move on to something easier, or something that doesn't grind them down, its cosmic hopelessness would look overcooked.

In this movie, even the men's buying worthless things on the installment plan is part of the bosses' grand design. *Blue Collar* is about the malaise of the workingman, trapped in all his comfort. Schrader isn't interested in the men's lives; it's only the system—a symbol of evil—that quickens his blood. There's anger in this movie (there is in most of the films Schrader has had a hand in—that's what makes his scripts sell), and his hostile, melancholy tone unifies this amalgam of pilfered pieces of old pictures and ideologies. The big flaw in *Blue Collar* is that Schrader has imposed his personal depression on characters who, in dramatic terms, haven't earned it. He's given Zeke, Smokey, and Jerry no will but the will to destroy themselves. (pp. 408-09)

People can be impressed by a movie this low in entertainment value; they can assume that it's thinking of higher things. But chances are that when Paul Schrader gets his bearings as a director he'll put his manipulative cynicism to more sparkling uses. (p. 409)

> *Pauline Kael, "The Cotton Mather of the Movies"*
> *(originally published in* The New Yorker, *Vol. LIV,*
> *No. 2, February 27, 1978), in her* When the Lights
> Go Down *(copyright © 1975, 1976, 1977, 1978,*
> *1979, 1980 by Pauline Kael; reprinted by permission*
> *of Holt, Rinehart and Winston, Publishers), Holt,*
> *Rinehart and Winston, 1980, pp. 406-10.**

ANDREW SARRIS

[In *Blue Collar* Schrader] seems to have been influenced by both Godard and Antonioni—the former in the deadening ritual of the assembly line itself, and the latter in the chromatic utilization of industrial artifacts as art objects in their own right. The movie has an interesting look to it as Schrader tries to make a painterly comment on the pathetic bleakness of low-level industrial landscapes.

But the pacing is something else again, as much of *Blue Collar* turns out to be stylistically and thematically indecisive, inarticulate, and incoherent. At first the movie seems to be striving for a comically absurdist tone on the order of Rene Clair's *A Nous la Liberte* and Charles Chaplin's *Modern Times*. . . . [We] are slowly made to understand that something more serious is afoot. Zeke, Jerry, and Smokey are propelled with minimal preparation into a robbery of the union treasury. But the model for this caper is less [John Huston's] *The Asphalt Jungle* than *Big Deal on Madonna Street*. Unfortunately, Schrader seems very wary of any possibility of laughter in the audience, and he throws away some very promising gags arising from the cliches of synchronizing watches and wearing masks (with dangling eyeballs yet!).

Somehow the bunglers succeed in spiriting away the union safe, only to discover that they have made off with a few hundred bucks in petty cash. But the safe also yields up an accounting ledger with records of incriminating payoffs to racketeers. The burglars are thus transformed into blackmailers, with very mixed results for the three: One receives a major promotion; one dies in a car-painting room from a choking blizzard of blue paint, as if to express in Antoniesque terms the blue collar blues; and one turns informer for the FBI in the manner of Marlon Brando's Terry Malloy in [Elia Kazan's] *On the Waterfront.*

In a voice-over commenting on the final freeze frame of the two surviving buddies about to come to blows, we hear the dead Smokey's Brechtian words about "Them" in the Establishment pitting black against white, young against old, and whatever against whatever as a way of keeping the masses in line. Consequently the characters are taken off the hook for any of their actions because they have been merely puppets of the class struggle. . . . (pp. 32-3)

This Brechtian voice-over alone may account for the judgment of some highbrow observers that *Blue Collar* is the first American Marxist film in the classical tradition of cinema since Abraham Polonsky's *Force of Evil* back in the late '40s. A French intellectual of my acquaintance has argued to the contrary that *Blue Collar* is actually a Fascist film because of its inclination to resolve all its problems violently, and its mistrust of all collective effort. My own view is that Schrader is promoting a radical individualism in line with his own romantic impulses.

In *Blue Collar* he seems to be fantasizing about what he would feel and do if he himself were trapped on an assembly line. Unlike most workers, however, Schrader has a very short fuse, and thus he tends to mix his genres. The patience required to live ordinary, average life is not part of his aesthetic, and so all the tacky details of working-class life take on a furtive, fleeting quality on the way to a bloody confrontation with personal destiny.

It is not surprising, therefore, that Schrader hits all these tacky details so hard that they strike false notes. . . . [People] who are actually living out the delusions of the American Dream do not make self-mocking speeches about it, at least not in so many words. For that matter, the so-called Oreo cookie gang never convinces us that they have achieved genuine rapport between the races. And if they had, the Brechtian voice-over at the end would have been discredited from the beginning.

There is, of course, much truth to the notion that management encourages dissension among its workers to keep them docile, but bigotry and xenophobia have never needed too much help from capitalists. To argue otherwise is to succumb to the most sentimentally Stalinist aesthetics of yesteryear. Still, Schrader only confuses the issue further when he resolves the lives of his characters in the context of the supposed omnipotence of organized crime, and its omnipresence throughout all social institutions. (p. 33)

Andrew Sarris, "Off the Assembly Line: One Lemon, One Authentic Model" (reprinted by permission of The Village Voice *and the author; copyright © The* Village Voice, *Inc., 1978), in* The Village Voice, *Vol. XXIII, No. 9, February 27, 1978, pp. 32-3.**

ARTHUR SCHLESINGER, JR.

[In *Blue Collar,* one feels that Paul Schrader] has a distinctive imagination and eye without as yet a sure directorial instinct. The discordant elements in the film—comedy, melodrama, social message—are imperfectly fused. But *Blue Collar*'s vitality and drive generally prevail over technical flaws. It is continuously fresh, surprising, and absorbing. . . .

Blue Collar, for all its documentary verve, does have two grievous faults. There is a grave disjunction in its internal logic. The key message, uttered mid-film by the wise ex-con and

repeated behind a freeze finish, is straight out of the Thirties: The company's purpose, as the old black warns his comrades, is to preserve its power by setting the workers at one another's throats. The particular idea, Paul Schrader subsequently told an interviewer, was to show "how racism is used as a device by the corporate structure to keep the men divided and their statuses perpetuated."

But in fact the company is at best an ancillary villain. The central villain is the union; and the crooked union officials are stealing for themselves, not for the company. No doubt they have been corrupted in some larger sense by the ethos of an acquisitive society, but the film shows no specific collusion between the union and the "corporate structure." On the contrary, the film's implicit message is that the class war today is not between the workers and the corporations but between the workers and the unions. The alleged message, when repeated at the end, simply does not connect with the plot of the film.

The other grievous fault is that the film's target is the United Auto Workers—the union of all unions that has striven most carefully and energetically to prevent precisely the kind of labor racketeering the movie indicts. The union in the movie is called the AAW—presumably the Associated Auto Workers—but the photographs of Walter Reuther hanging on the walls in the office of the crooked union boss leave no doubt about the union [Paul and Leonard Schrader] had in mind.

For a movie with documentary pretensions, this is hard to forgive. *On the Waterfront,* for example, took on Joe Ryan's notoriously corrupt International Longshoremen's Association. If the Schraders had really wanted to make a courageous movie about union corruption, they would have made *Blue Collar* about the Teamsters—and, in so doing, might have given much-needed support to the group of valiant Teamsters who have organized to overthrow the unsavory dictatorship of Frank Fitzsimmons. . . .

One is sorry that when Paul Schrader decided to make a movie about union corruption, he also decided to play it so awfully safe.

Arthur Schlesinger, Jr., "Villainy among the Proletariat," in Saturday Review *(© 1978 Saturday Review Magazine Co.; reprinted by permission), Vol. 5, No. 14, April 15, 1978, p. 65.*

VINCENT CANBY

[The films of Paul Schrader] are difficult to get hold of. They are not only about contradictions, they deal in them. As often as not they employ shock effects that appear to pander to what the moralists among us would call our baser instincts. . . .

Once upon a time when we went to the movies, there was never any doubt about what we were supposed to think. We knew who were the good guys and who were the bad. Some of this had to do with typecasting but, basically, it was the result of the laws laid down by the old Production Code, which said that crime could not pay except, of course, for the producers who made films showing us the manifold ways in which crime could not pay again and again and again.

Moral outrage, though prefabricated, was built into our films. The Production Code made things simpler then. But so, too, did the times. . . .

The extent to which things have changed today is reflected in the sort of films Mr. Schrader is making, particularly in **"Hardcore,"** which will, I'm sure, upset a lot of people, principally because it gives every indication of exploiting the permissiveness about which it seems to have very mixed feelings. Even the title can be seen as a cheap come-on. Yet the movie isn't to be dismissed. It's a serious film, seriously conceived and executed. . . .

"Hardcore" is not much more than straightforward melodrama that takes its audience on a sightseeing tour of the porn world that a lot of people haven't before had the interest (or perhaps courage) to see for themselves. Sleaze is the style, and there are those for whom sleaze is essential to the art of pornography. Among the characters that Jake [the protagonist] meets are porn movie producers, actors, actresses, hookers, hustlers, drifters and, most important, a pretty, pathetic, half-baked would-be porn star named Niki. . . .

"Hardcore" has a lot of faults, not the least of which (some will say) is the entertaining way it allows us to look inside this particular underworld without fear of contamination or discovery. A more serious problem is the manner in which the movie asks us to take a lot of its psychological underpinnings on faith. . . .

Mr. Schrader asks us to make a lot of assumptions but I'm inclined to make them, understanding that what he set out to do was to make a conventional melodrama in a milieu that itself is the reason for the picture. I don't mean only the Southern California porn world, but the good, solid, prosperous, Protestant, middle-American world that has produced Jake and his family.

As in his **"Blue Collar,"** Mr. Schrader here demonstrates an extraordinary sensitivity to the realities of the American heritage that are seldom even thought about on screen, much less dramatized. His characters are complex. Unfortunately the melodrama seldom matches their complexity. It is blunt, clumsy—melodrama that seems not to reflect life but the way lives are led in movies.

At its best, **"Hardcore"** is an inventory of opposing forces in contemporary American life as revealed in the course of Jake's search. The movie is constructed of opposites, even visually. There is tension before the credits are over in the contrast between the film's lurid title and the background shots we see of children playing in the snow. We know that the security of the happy family we see sitting down to Christmas dinner is going to be shattered, but not quite how. Climate is emblematic. Snow and cold are the old way of life that one knew how to cope with. Southern California's sun and warmth suggest a world where faith is no longer required: you don't have to work to keep warm. No wonder people fall apart in California. Life is too easy. If one grew up in the fierce winters of the upper Middle West (as Mr. Schrader did), Southern California is the devil's paradise.

"Hardcore" raises more questions than it has any interest in answering, and Mr. Schrader is ambivalent in his feelings toward the society that created Jake, [his teenage daughter] Kristen and (another assumption on my part) the filmmaker himself. He has sympathy for these people who, in spite of their right-mindedness, cannot deal with the world as it really is. He also has affection for the lost and the muddled, like Niki, who at one point says to Jake, "We are alike, you know." Jake: "We are not!" Niki: "You think so little of sex you never do it. I think so little of it I don't care who I do it with."

Everyone, finally, is in the same boat.

"Hardcore" expresses no easily identifiable moral outrage. It means to be an entertaining chase film that gets all the mileage it can from its exotic backgrounds. This is the way things are, it says. This is where America is. The old values no longer hold, and there are no new ones for people like Kristen and Niki, who wanly describes herself as "a Venusian." I suspect that some part of Mr. Schrader agrees with Jake when he launches into a tirade about the part that television, movies and advertising are playing in the changing of the scene, but Mr. Schrader also knows such tirades are futile. The world that Jake would deny continues to exist. What can one do? Mr. Schrader has made a movie about it that can be seen either as a cynical rip-off or as a position paper prepared by someone who is concerned but not dropping out. Take your pick.

> *Vincent Canby, "'Hardcore': Bring Your Own Morality," in* The New York Times, *Section 2 (© 1979 by The New York Times Company; reprinted by permission), February 11, 1979, p. 15.*

DAVID DENBY

Hardcore must be the most perversely priggish movie in the history of the American cinema. It's impossible to think of another film that approaches its bizarrely knotted interweaving of prurience and dismay, lurid excitement and icy disgust. . . . [Paul Schrader has] combined his personal background and his violent obsessions into a single, uneasy package. Schrader's story is about the moral testing of a religious man—Jake VanDorn . . . , a businessman in Grand Rapids who adheres to the Calvinist absolutism of the Dutch Reformed Church.

The premise is simple: VanDorn's teenage daughter, Kristen, mysteriously runs away during a trip to Los Angeles and joins the porno-movie and sex-show underworld. After a dissolute private eye . . . fails to find the girl, VanDorn moves to L.A. himself and begins prowling the squalid night world of brothels and bookstores, bars and movie houses. What he sees fills him with revulsion, and as he averts his eyes and cringes and suffers, he begins to rage at our whole modern media culture in which "everything is based on sex, sold on sex." . . .

The movie's plot resembles Schrader's earlier script for *Taxi Driver,* which featured another angry, obsessed man . . . trying to save a young teenager . . . from prostitution. But *Taxi Driver* was an infinitely more expressive movie. . . .

Directing his own material (a schematic, overexplicit, emotionally dead screenplay) . . . , Schrader creates the least sensual images possible. In the early section shot in Michigan, the sequences break down into discontinuous fragments—bleak, snowy landscapes; dirty industrial buildings; gloomy, gray-brown interiors of an ugly house in which adults stand around stiffly at a dull Christmas party for children. For a while, I assumed the discontinuities and coldness were intentional—a way of conveying the dourness of a provincial, religion-centered existence. No one seems to connect here, and we see the daughter, Kristen, only briefly, registering little more than the image of a shy, slender girl who looks like Patty Hearst. However, when the movie shifts to Los Angeles the narrative and visual style stay the same. Los Angeles itself (and also other locations in California) is made to look as shoddy, sordid, and alienating as possible. Either the director sees everything this way or he can't get much rhythm going visually, not even in the neon-lit, city-of-night sequences. Furthermore, the performers seem cold and disconnected from one another. . . .

As Schrader presents it, then, the porno scene is vicious and pathetic and that's all there is to it. But why make a movie to tell us that? And why, in that case, would a young girl be attracted to the scene? Since Schrader has shown us nothing about Kristen, we're left with little to identify with but VanDorn's sense of personal degradation as he searches for her. When VanDorn first sees a film of her having sex with two young men, Schrader rightly concentrates on the man's anguish. But then, later in his search, VanDorn puts on a wig and mustache and poses as a porno-film producer in order to infiltrate the scene, and rather than playing this adventure for comedy and excitement, Schrader gives us more humiliation: A stud lowers his pants in an audition, and VanDorn covers his face in misery. That the young actor might also feel degraded isn't a possibility; he's simply scum, and VanDorn is shown as justified a few minutes later when he smashes in the face of another porno actor. And so it goes. Linking up with an unhappy young hooker . . . who might lead him to Kristen, he cuts her off every time she tries to explain herself.

In other words, *Hardcore* lacks moral curiosity; indeed, the film isn't moral at all, it's *moralistic*—superior and preachy. And it isn't truly religious or spiritual either, since VanDorn never feels even slightly tempted by anything he sees. His perfection is inviolate. What, then, is the point of this exercise in rectitude? I fear that Schrader . . . [has] given way to the kind of meaningless indignation that is usually the province of hysterical right-wing radio commentators: "Wake up, America! If your fourteen-year-old daughters appear in sex films with professional sadists, it won't be good for them!" But does anyone really need to be warned? This pointless movie is all knotted up. The director, teasing us with sensational material only to show us he's superior to it, is like a man standing on the edge of experience, afraid to take a look at what lies beyond.

> *David Denby, "What Fools These Moralists Be," in*
> New York *Magazine (copyright © 1979 by News*
> *Group Publications, Inc.; reprinted with the permission of* New York *Magazine), Vol. 12, No. 7,*
> *February 12, 1979, p. 84.*

ANDREW SARRIS

As a charter member and prime theoretician of the American *nouvelle vague*, Schrader has gone a long way in *Hardcore* toward defining his strengths and weaknesses. One can see in certain mysteriously lateral movements the author of a book on the transcendental art of Bresson, Dreyer, and Ozu. Schrader has written also, and with considerable expertise, on the parameters of the *film noir*. His formulas, consequently, are in opposition to those of the Philco Playhouse school of anti-genre humanist playwrights with their endless explanations and motivations. Schrader goes to the other extreme of dissolving character in action. Curiously, his projects seem more lurid and violent in their conception than in their execution, which is to say his latest movie is neither as opportunistic nor as sensational as its shrewd and succinctly commercial title would suggest.

At the outset he shows us two young girls, standing side by side, one a cute, curvaceous blonde, the other a skinny, angular, comparatively plain brunette. From what many of us have heard of the scenario, we know that one of these two girls is to be violated, and the dirty old man in some of us

hopes that it will be the blonde. Having set up this peculiar Judgment of Paris situation, Schrader turns away from erotic exploitation and toward sociological probability. Jake's soon-to-be-scandalous daughter is the brunette—a wise move in terms of the "realism" of runaways. But Schrader makes no effort to prepare us for what is to happen. The almost idyllic home-town scenes are always cluttered, communal, and convivial, with no hint of oppression and frustration. Schrader indulges in a bit of self-conscious architectural analysis of Grand Rapids, reminiscent of his very methodical inspection of the milieu in *Blue Collar,* but we remain completely outside of the people in the absence of any subjective insights from the editing. The young people on the bus to California cheer when the bus pulls out, but only Jake's daughter becomes a runaway, and we are never shown why. From Grand Rapids we descend into the wickedness of the West Coast, a neon jungle comparable in its catatonia and malignancy to the New York of *Taxi Driver*. . . .

Out on the coast, Schrader's tone shifts from unvarying blandness to a split-level perception of the porn scene, by turns satiric and melodramatic. Jake is assisted at one time or another by an embarrassingly horny, but otherwise okay private eye named Andy Mast . . . , and a good-natured hooker and self-styled "Venusian" named Niki. . . . Unfortunately, neither Andy Mast nor Niki is a strong enough character to provide Jake with a forum to communicate his innermost feelings. It is never even clearly established whether Jake is widowed, divorced, or separated. All we know for sure is that there is no Mrs. VanDorn on the premises. Both in Michigan and in California Jake displays a tendency to bully people, and, consequently, we may infer that his daughter was unloved. Inference, however, is not the stuff of dramatic spectacle. Gradually Jake's daughter becomes something of a Macguffin in absentia as her tawdry trail leads [Jake] and his growing entourage from Los Angeles to San Diego to San Francisco. There, Schrader's predilection for anarchic individualism produces a bizarre shoot-out and an unconvincing reunion. By this time one feels that Schrader and his cast are winging it on sheer momentum. We end up with neither the mythology of [John Ford's] *The Searchers* nor the psychology and sociology of the Philco Playhouse.

Still, *Hardcore* on the whole strikes me as an honorable film with a permissibly puritanical attitude toward its subject. Where it is notably deficient is in its lack of curiosity and confessional candor. Having established a horrifying premise, Schrader seems to shy away from its more profound implications. What is it that a father really feels for his daughter? How does he cope with all his guilt and ambivalence? And why are we titillated by the situation even as we nod in agreement with the self-righteous editorializing of Schrader and [Jake]. Perhaps Schrader has ultimately cheated on his subject by eschewing the eroticism. What price redemption without temptation? Or is it merely the sleaze rather than the sin from which *Hardcore* turns in revulsion? I can't help feeling that the whole subject, with its attendant backlash, is somewhat out of date. Children are still running away from their parents, and parents are still searching for their children. But there is a new chill in the air, and a subtler decadence. Schrader is right to remind us that there are still millions of people who don't really care what happens in the gossip columns, but this has always been true. The Grand Rapids side of America has been flourishing through the '60s and '70s. I am not sure that I welcome a Holy Crusade from the boondocks into the Times Squares and Market Streets of America. One never knows where such crusades will end. . . .

Anti-porn politics aside, the individual scenes in *Hardcore* never seem to come alive with emotion and conviction. Much of the time people seem to be walking on eggshells. I am sorely tempted to suggest that Schrader has never completely escaped from Grand Rapids, and that he is thereby unable to exorcise the demons of repression in his protagonist. But I shall resist the temptation, since it is with such speculative flights that auteurism has acquired its heady reputation.

Andrew Sarris, "A Puritan's Progress" (reprinted by permission of The Village Voice *and the author; copyright © The Village Voice, Inc., 1979), in* The Village Voice, *Vol. XXIV, No. 7, February 12, 1979, p. 51.**

PAULINE KAEL

Paul Schrader has powerful raw ideas for movies, but he attempts to function as a writer-director without ever developing his ideas or his characters. . . . [Jake's search through the porno-prostitution world for his daughter in *Hardcore*] might be a great fiery subject if we could feel what the girl was running away from and if the father were drawn into experiences that scared him, sickened him, shook him up. In old movies that warned viewers about the vices lying in wait for their daughters (white slavery, prostitution, drugs), there was something to attract the audience: the thrill of sin. Even when the cautionary aspect of the films was just a hypocritical ploy, there was something at stake; the temptations of the Devil were given their due. In *Taxi Driver* . . . , the protagonist, Travis Bickle, had a fear and hatred of sex so feverishly sensual that we experienced his tensions, his explosiveness. But in *Hardcore* Jake feels no lust, so there's no enticement—and no contest. The Dutch Reformation Church has won the battle for his soul before the film's first frame. (p. 543)

Schrader, who has said that Jake is modelled on his father, doesn't explore the possibility that it's what Jake, in his firm religious morality, denies and excludes from his life that drives his daughter to sexual degradation. In this film, there's nothing between fundamentalism and licentiousness—no forms of sexual expression or pleasure that aren't degraded, and no way to have any sexual freedom without going to porno hell. (pp. 543-44)

Schrader shot in actual porno bookshops and massage parlors and peep shows, yet he missed out on the atmosphere—there's none of the pulsation of sleazy dives, no details strike our imaginations. Schrader doesn't enter the world of porno; he stays on the outside, looking at it coldly, saying, "These people have nothing to do with me." The girls are displayed like pieces of meat in a butcher's counter, under fluorescent glare. And since the film doesn't regard these girls as human there's no horror in their dehumanization—only frigid sensationalism. It has never been difficult to feel out the psychological mechanism of how pimps draw and hold runaway teen-agers: the girls are brutalized in the porno world, yet they also get the attention they've always wanted, and any attention can seem better than none. *Hardcore* treats them as if they weren't worth attention. The only person who attempts to reveal something of her feelings is Niki . . . , a young girl who guides Jake in his search. Niki's poorly written dialogue makes her seem realistically self-aware—she has no illusions to sustain her, no psychological defenses against the truth of her situation. She's very straight, and Schrader leads us to expect that she will get through to Jake—warm him up, change him, make him human. At the end, when Niki is brushed aside and we're told that she belongs where she is, we feel completely baffled and cheated. Jake will go on being the same self-contained moralist whose

daughter ran away, but because . . . he single-mindedly pursued Kristen, found her, and took her home, we're supposed to see him as a man whose principles have triumphed. (p. 544)

The tone of the film is cautious and maddeningly opaque. There's no feeling of suspense, because the characters are all prejudged and they stay the same from scene to scene while Schrader holds the camera on them for an extra instant to make them look empty, or plays with photographing them from different angles. . . . There may never have been another American director as lacking in spontaneity as Paul Schrader. The Europeans, such as Bresson and Dreyer, whose methods have been deliberate and studied (and whom he emulates) have achieved their effects through rigorous design. But Schrader doesn't have that control and precision. There is no radiance to the color in *Hardcore,* and there's no indication of a visual plan. Every now and then, there's a shot with an exact kind of garish density—a travelling shot of the equipment in a sex shop, or a mirror image. But it just seems an effect applied to a scene—it isn't integral. The film can't resist such gaudy pulp flourishes as the white-suited Ratan . . . , who materializes in order to provide a last-minute shoot-'em-up ending. Ratan, we're told in awed tones, deals in pain and produces "snuff" movies; the implication is that Kristen might be the next victim. . . .

It's not merely that Schrader went to porno places and missed them—he went home to Grand Rapids and missed that, too. There are lovely shots of the downtown area and of Christmas snow scenes, but they're edited in a random way that dulls the effect, and we feel as alienated from the family life there as we do from the porno environment. It's hard to distinguish between the furniture in Jake's factory and the family members he sits down to dinner with. They don't inquire after Kristen once she has vanished, and don't show any anxiety about what might have happened to her. (p. 545)

Who *does* matter to this director? He presents everyone in the same detached, affectionless way; even the sound is hollow. His scenes are so inexpressive that it could be he simply doesn't have enough interest in other people's emotions to loosen up the performers and bring something out of them, and doesn't have an instinctive sense of film rhythm. There's the same determined ploddingness in this movie as in his 1978 *Blue Collar,* but it's much worse here. The possibility also comes to mind that the porno world is Schrader's metaphor for show business, and that, in some corner of his mind, he is the runaway who became a prostitute. He has sometimes said that he regards working in the movie business as prostitution, and *Hardcore* looks like a film made by somebody who finds no joy in moviemaking. . . . Several veteran directors are fond of calling themselves whores, but, of course, what they mean is that they gave the bosses what was wanted. They're boasting of their cynical proficiency. For Schrader to call himself a whore would be vanity: he doesn't know how to turn a trick. (pp. 545-46)

Pauline Kael, "No Contest" (originally published in The New Yorker, *Vol. LV, No. 1, February 19, 1979), in her* When the Lights Go Down *(copyright © 1975, 1976, 1977, 1978, 1979, 1980 by Pauline Kael; reprinted by permission of Holt, Rinehart and Winston, Publishers), Holt, Rinehart and Winston, 1980, pp. 543-47.**

VINCENT CANBY

Having now seen **"American Gigolo," "Hardcore"** and **"Taxi Driver,"** . . . I can't tell whether Mr. Schrader seizes on these sensational subjects because he is a canny picture-maker or because he is fascinated by moral sleaziness. I don't mean that he's just idly curious but that he is obsessed in the manner of a person who was brought up in a strict religious faith, as Mr. Schrader (Dutch Reformed Church) was, and somewhat late in life discovered what he takes to be the real nature of the world.

"American Gigolo" is a laughable movie but it's not without interest, if only because Mr. Schrader seems to be genuinely convinced of the worth of his hero, Julian Kay . . . , an almost physically perfect young man who makes a very good living as an expensive Los Angeles prostitute. (pp. D15, D42)

However, Mr. Schrader's interest in Julian quickly comes to look less like concern for the hustler's soul than like uncontrolled adoration. This is especially true in the way the camera focuses on [Julian's] mostly expressionless face, on his body and on those objects that the director has placed in Julian's apartment in a failed attempt to give the guy some class. Because the character met early in the movie would seem to have difficulty reading People magazine from cover to cover, it's a sight-laugh when Mr. Schrader's camera, in panning across Julian's belongings, just happens to spy works by Vladimir Nabokov and Colin Wilson.

Does he have a bookish cleaning lady?

The major difficulty with **"American Gigolo"** is that Mr. Schrader has too effectively established Julian as high-priced sex-machine to make the character work as the consciousness-raised hero he's supposed to be in the murder-mystery that takes over the second half of the movie.

Not terribly significant, perhaps, but much more believable are Julian's narcissism that takes pride in having been able to lead to sexual climax an older (very rich) woman who'd been abandoned by her husband and thought herself frigid. The scene in which Julian tells us about this triumph is hilarious, not because it is exploitative but because the movie maker is being so dumbfoundingly sincere. I don't doubt at all that a prostitute like Julian would talk this way, but Mr. Schrader, incurable naif that he seems to be, takes everything Julian says at face value when a little irony might have been in order.

Julian is a trivial character. Mr. Schrader might have transformed him into something other had he (Mr. Schrader) maintained a tiny bit of skepticism or seen Julian as another aspect of our junk-food generation. That, I suspect, is beyond Mr. Schrader. He gives every indication of being as dazzled by Julian as everyone else is. He's also dazzled by the life Julian leads, by all of the terrible, disgusting, kinky, sleazy, *immoral* things one has to do to put a little money in the bank. . . .

When, at the end of **"American Gigolo,"** Julian's soul is salvaged, it's salvaged not by God or by some breakthrough in understanding but by a plot device learned from all of those Hollywood movies that Mr. Schrader, as a little boy in Michigan, was not allowed to see. . . .

I believe there are characters like Julian Kay living the fast life in Hollywood at this moment. Mr. Schrader knows how real people of all kinds talk and behave, and he has deep sympathy for them, as was beautifully manifest in the small-town sequences in **"Hardcore."** Sometimes, though, his real people, like Julian Kay, resolutely refuse to be canonized by melodramatic violence. They remain stubbornly trivial. (p. D42)

> *Vincent Canby, "Fine Manners Can't Disguise Petty People," in* The New York Times *(© 1980 by The*

New York Times Company; reprinted by permission), February 3, 1980, pp. D15, D42.*

ROGER ANGELL

In **"American Gigolo,"** Julian Kay (Richard Gere) skims around the Southern California freeways in a shiny black Mercedes 450-SL convertible, often with the top down, so that we can study his narrow eyes behind his tortoiseshell shades, his expensively cut hair, and his extraordinary but uninteresting good looks. When he alights, we see him buying expensive clothes at Juschi's boutique, on Rodeo Drive in Beverly Hills (or, rather, being bought clothes: a woman is paying the bill); or having a drink at the Polo Lounge (he keeps an odd jacket or two with the hat-check girl there, in case of social emergencies); or dining at Perino's or Chasen's; or discussing business with a beautiful female pimp (Nina Van Pallandt) at her Malibu beach house, where the sundeck is crowded with half-naked women catching some rays; or visiting other women in Westwood and Bel Air and Palm Springs. A great many older but well-kept-up women pay him hundreds of dollars to make love to them, for Julian is a top-level, 450-SL-model male prostitute, and Michelle (Lauren Hutton), the terrific-looking but unhappy wife of a California state senator, is in love with him. Inescapably, irresponsibly (we feel terrible about it, really), we find ourselves beginning to have the wrong thoughts about him: This cat has really got it *made!* What we are probably meant to think about Julian is to wonder where he comes from—in both the Webster's and the Cyra McFadden senses of the phrase—but the script of **"American Gigolo"** (by Paul Schrader, who also directed the picture) is generally unhelpful. Julian lies to one woman when he tells her that he used to be a pool boy at the Beverly Hills Hotel, and to another when he says he was "born in Torino but studied in Nantes" (he is said to speak five or six languages); finally, alone with the senator's wife, he exclaims, "I'm not *from* anywhere—I'm from this bed." He has scruples ("I don't do fags or couples"), and he prides himself on his ability to bring sexual pleasure to sad old women. This is ugly but promising. What else are we going to discover about Julian? Unfortunately, that's about it. Now and then, in his pad, he picks up a vase or a painting and studies it enigmatically, but he spends more of his time opening the drawers of his bureau and the doors of his closet, so that he and we can gaze at length on his rich, muted shirtings, his narrow fifty-dollar ties, and his sleek Giorgio Armani jackets and suits. Late in the picture, Julian murmurs to Michelle, "All my life I've been looking for something—I don't know what it is. Maybe it's you," and at last we understand. Julian has, like, lost touch with his *feelings*. He is not in a good space. Poor Julian.

Paul Schrader is an earnest filmmaker (he directed **"Blue Collar"** and wrote the screenplay for Martin Scorsese's **"Taxi Driver"**), but **"American Gigolo"** gives the impression that he was distracted by the looks of things in the picture and allowed himself and his audience to become tourists of these expensive places and people. Perhaps sensing the absence of anything serious or moving at the end of the road, he more or less gave up on the search for Julian's soul, and instead involved his hero in a sadomasochistic murder, a silly frameup, and a brutal accidental killing: television-series stuff. . . .

"American Gigolo" will inevitably be measured against Hal Ashby's **"Shampoo,"** because of the films' similar themes and settings, but the comparison is deadly. Warren Beatty's George—scooting around town on that motorcycle, with his hair dryer tucked in his belt—was so whipped and confused and rewarded and harassed by his own violently libidinous attractiveness that the scattered scenes and beds in the picture could hardly contain its energy and surprises. "Shampoo" was so sexy that it was funny, but "**American Gigolo**" presents a humorless, *Penthouse* kind of sex, all dolled up with expensive "real" settings, foreign cars, hi-fi sets, and designer clothes, but barely alive at its glum, soft core. (pp. 107-08)

Roger Angell, "Up from Possum Gully," in The New Yorker (© 1980 by The New Yorker Magazine, Inc.), Vol. LV, No. 51, February 4, 1980, pp. 105-09.*

ANDREW SARRIS

[*American Gigolo* is] the most elegant of Schrader's directorial exercises, and there are never any lapses of tone. What's lacking, as always, are narrative flow, dramatic development, and psychological coherence. . . . [Up to now Schrader's] style has seemed either too obviously derivative, or too disruptive in terms of the very lurid material with which he has chosen to work. It is as if Bresson were trying to direct a [Luis] Bunuel script.

Curiously, *American Gigolo* is less lurid than it might have been because Julian Kay is never smug or jaded, and Schrader does not hold any of his characters in contempt. [Michelle] is strangely, if awkwardly, sincere as the great love of Julian's life. Schrader clearly lacks the flair for articulating this love with appropriate dialogue, but the iconic eye contact works just the same. Significantly, [Julian and Michelle] seem closest at precisely those moments when they are separated physically, but connected optically. As soon as the bedcovers are turned down Schrader seems to revert to an academic collage of flesh-signs suggested by Godard's two-dimensional skin shots in *Une Femme Mariee*.

When the plot takes a sudden twist into a frame-up for murder Schrader finds himself in much the same bind that [Francis Ford] Coppola did at the end of *The Conversation,* with realism giving way to stylization, observation to intuition, and experience to ritual. . . . Somehow the picture keeps moving along until that very startling moment when Schrader boldly lifts Bresson's leap-of-faith ending from *Pickpocket* virtually intact, along with the deadpan declaration of a completely irrational, and, in dramatic terms, completely unearned love. . . .

[For] the first time ever I find myself on Schrader's side as he strains to transfer dangerously internalized feelings onto the dynamic surfaces of the cinema. . . . [Under] the best circumstances Schrader would never entirely overwhelm me with his formal and cerebral tendencies. But *American Gigolo* remains nonetheless an honorable and fascinating work by an American artist, who just happens to be spiritually abstracted from the world at large.

Andrew Sarris, "Different Strokes . . ." (reprinted by permission of The Village Voice and the author; copyright © News Group Publications, Inc., 1980), in The Village Voice, Vol. XXV, No. 5, February 4, 1980, p. 43.*

RICHARD COMBS

With **American Gigolo,** Paul Schrader seems to have found his footing as a director—and achieved a measure of distance from (might one say transcended?) his obsessions as a writer. Not

that he has really relaxed his Calvinist grip on the plot mechanism: characters are stuffed willy-nilly down a determinist tunnel, and one feels a tortured Providence-as-dramatist—rather than any inner necessity or logic—behind their every move and utterance. The hero of *American Gigolo* is more fortunate than most in that he doesn't have to say very much, though there is one grotesque moment of 'naked' truth in which he stands undressed by a window—the barred lighting that falls across him will be repeated to more ominous effect in a later scene—and professes his pride in having done "something very worthwhile" by taking three hours to bring a neglected woman to orgasm. He is spared the spiritual ordeal of the outraged father in *Hardcore,* who plunges through a meretricious purgatory to a hypocritical redemption. Though Julian Kay is presented from the beginning as being in a kind of hell: the camera prowls after him into the pinkly glowing inferno of a night-club, or snakes along much closer to the floor towards the bed in which Julian is doing something particularly loathsome (talking 'dirty' over the phone to one of his clients). That movement is repeated later in the film when Julian reaches the pit of this particular Hades, a disco which seems to epitomise everything ('fag tricks', 'kink') which Julian has ruled out of his repertoire. The real hell, of course, is inside Julian (in Schrader's words, "He is only able to give. He is unable to receive, and so he has perfected himself into giving"), and on one level the novelty of *American Gigolo* is that the hero's inevitable release is somewhat less violent than the Schrader norm (". . . what he is building toward is not an explosion but an implosion"). The concluding passage comes, however, as a rather forced epiphany. The characters seem to emerge too late from the determinist tunnel into the sunlight of spiritual tranquillity: Julian, in prison awaiting trial for the murder for which he has been framed, is detached, not to say lackadaisical, about his own defence. The rhythm of the film slows—and its spiritual space, presumably, opens—to accommodate long fades to black in between scenes, and Michelle's self-sacrificing action on his behalf brings Julian to an acceptance of love, and Schrader to his most determinedly Bressonian moment. In the last shot, Julian lays his head on the partitioning glass next to Michelle's hand and murmurs, "It's taken me so long to come to you". . . . What is notable about *American Gigolo,* however, is that Schrader's 'European' pretensions for the first time seem to have been integrated with the style of the film: the camera, here almost deliriously liberated from its prosaic functions in **Blue Collar** and **Hardcore,** drifts through the neighbourhoods of Los Angeles and some rather splendid scenery on Julian's drive to Palm Springs in a way that almost out-Antonionis *Zabriskie Point.* The detachment for which the plot has to work so hard is quite gracefully achieved at this level. In the process, Schrader's 'transcendental cinema' even incorporates other models: the sequence in which Julian, now suspecting the plot against him, rips his room apart looking for a plant, observed by a camera stealthily tracking at a very high angle, conjures [Bernardo] Bertolucci in its lighting and staging . . . , and love-making between Julian and Michelle becomes a montage of body geometry, à la the Godard of *Une Femme Mariée.* (p. 88)

Richard Combs, in his review of "American Gigolo," in Monthly Film Bulletin (copyright © The British Film Institute, 1980), Vol. 47, No. 556, May, 1980, pp. 87-8.

DAVID DENBY

Raging Bull is about a man with an iron skull and no brains inside, an enduring but mysteriously wretched man who can't trust anyone or enjoy himself and who finally destroys all his relationships through jealousy, paranoia, and fear. [Jake La Motta's] smile says that he's crazy and that his inhuman strength comes out of the craziness. Just as in the sentimental and melodramatic fight movies of the forties, to which this movie is a sour rejoinder, Jake is a Bronx slum boy, and the mob wants a piece of him. Only this time there's no upbeat ending: Jake may break free of the mob, but he can't break free of himself.

Directed by Martin Scorsese . . . and written by Mardik Martin and Paul Schrader, *Raging Bull* is a kind of morose American passion play, a chronicle of the successive stages of a fighter's disintegration. Starting in 1941, when Jake was a fierce young contender, punching in rapid volleys out of a closed-in crouch, the movie passes, in brief, violent scenes, through the great six-match rivalry with Sugar Ray Robinson, the 1948 title fight against Marcel Cerdan, and the loss of the title to Robinson. It ends with a long, pathetic coda devoted to Jake's miserable time as a nightclub owner in Miami and as a lewd comedian— a fourth-rate Joe E. Lewis—introducing strippers in cruddy bars. Along with the fights, we see the volatile neighborhood life and urban hellishness . . . and also Jake's hapless efforts as husband and brother. Even when he holds the title, Jake never feels like a champ—there he is in his tacky Pelham Parkway apartment, with its broken TV and its figurine lamps, hassling his wife over nothing. It's a pitiless, unrelenting, terribly sad movie. The aging Jake, corpulent and heavy-jowled in a way that suggests a corresponding coarsening of the spirit . . . , is a piteous and terrifying figure: Isn't this what we all fear—that we might simply get older and thicker, learning nothing at all?

We never do discover why Jake is such a surly crumb-bum— though explanation enough can be found in La Motta's 1970 autobiography (same title), in which the ex-fighter amply describes the violence and criminality of his youth, the guilt and rage arising from feelings of unworthiness, the bouts of impotence that made him so hostile to women. Of his first serious fight (in a reformatory) La Motta writes, "I felt that if I didn't destroy [my opponent], he would destroy me, and that for some reason he had a right to destroy me. And that enraged me more—the fact that I felt he had that right. And that's what I went out to fight, to kill." This is terrific stuff, but none of it is in the movie. The mean, obsessive Jake isn't given a past or any particular motives, drives, ideas. Nor is there any hint of the rascally humor found in the book. The throbbing soundtrack music (out of Mascagni's operas), all Italianate lamentation, tells us that this dumb beast is ruled by powerful emotions that he can't understand or control. But surely it's an artist's task to illuminate. I admire *Raging Bull* immensely for its beautiful period detail and its brutal humor, but I find it a monomaniacal, crabbed, limited work. Everyone knows that Jake La Motta was a bad guy, but the filmmakers diminish him too much, reducing him to mere instinct, almost as if they thought that putting an opaque and dislikable man at the center of a movie were itself a mark of honor. (p. 61)

David Denby, "Brute Force," in New York *Magazine (copyright © 1980 by News Group Publications, Inc.; reprinted with the permission of* New York *Magazine), Vol. 13, No. 47, December 1, 1980, pp. 61-3.**

COLIN L. WESTERBECK, JR.

[The end of] *Raging Bull* is a continuation of the scene with which the film begins, one where the aging Jake La Motta . . .

rehearses a nightclub act he does after retiring from the ring. The scene is like a variation on that old cliché of having the fighter's life pass before his eyes in flashback between the counts of nine and ten, and this isn't the only instance in which the film seems to rely on fight-film conventions. Scorsese and at least one of his scriptwriters, Paul Schrader, . . . always work very much in the shadow of movie history. They're aware of the many ways that La Motta's story follows the standard plot line of boxing classics like *Body and Soul*. Like John Garfield in Robert Rossen's film, La Motta got mixed up with a dame and a gangster who both brought him grief. [This] film even suggests that La Motta himself is aware of such parallels between his life and the fighters in movies. The material Jake rehearses in that opening and closing scene includes a monologue based on Brando's speech to his brother—"I coulda' been a contenda, Chahley"—in *On the Waterfront*. The dive that La Motta once had to take was also set up by his own brother.

What sets *Raging Bull* apart, however, is the way that Scorsese and Schrader play against the grain of these fight-film conventions which their own film invokes. . . . In the movies, the hero of a fight film always has a character that develops slower than his body. But in the end, his character does develop. He changes dramatically. He grows up. He gets rid of the floozies and tells off the gangster. "Everybody dies," as John Garfield says to the fuming gangster for whom he has just refused to throw the title fight at the end of *Body and Soul*. The stoicism of this remark is a new-found wisdom for him, a radical transformation of his character.

Jake doesn't change. . . . [The] key to his character is his obduracy. This is what made him both a great fighter and a rather tragic person. . . . In effect, Jake's stance as a fighter is his stance toward life. He moves in relentlessly in a low crouch, taking his beating, waiting for his chance to lash out at his opponent with his trip-hammer barrage of lefts and rights. But as the film goes on, the opening that he's looking for, the chance to strike back and score the knockout he wants, occurs less and less. (p. 20)

Before even the opening scene where Jake is rehearsing his night-club act, we catch a glimpse of him in the ring, all alone, as he warms up before a fight by doing a little shadowboxing. At the end of the movie, when it's time for him to go on stage at the night club, he concludes the warm-up he's been doing this time with a little more shadowboxing in front of the dressing-room mirror. In between these two rounds of self-sparring, everything that usually happens to the hero in a fight film happens to Jake. He marries a hot tomato named Vickie . . . , who drives him crazy and finally leaves him. . . . Jake has to take [a] dive because no matter how many other contenders he beats, he can't get a title shot without doing the local don a favor. ("It's an embarrassment to me," the mobster explains to Joey. "I can't even deliver a boy from my own neighborhood.") Jake wins the title, and then loses it. He gets his own club in Miami and loses that too. He even loses the love and loyalty of his brother, and ends up a deadbeat comic in other people's sleazy clubs.

Yet while everything has changed for him, nothing has changed. That's the point of the opening and closing shots where he is shadowboxing with himself. It wasn't Vickie who ruined his life. She turned out to be a good wife and only left him after putting up with years of his suspicions that everybody from hoodlums to his own brother was sleeping with her. It wasn't Joey or the Mob that ruined Jake, either. After Jake threw that fight, he and Joey wept bitterly in the dressing room. He'd done such a lousy job of taking the dive that the boxing commission investigated him. But he still got his title shot as the gangsters promised, and he won and lost the championship with no fix in. No, the only fate Jake ever really has to struggle against is being Jake. It is his own intractability, his inability to change, to learn from life the way the clean-cut kid played by John Garfield does. That's what finally defeats Jake in the end. The truth is that he's spent his whole career boxing with shadows, faking himself out, throwing punches at his own paranoid delusions.

Because La Motta is seen this way by Scorsese, Schrader, and maybe even La Motta himself, whose memoir was the basis of the movie, *Raging Bull* ultimately becomes not an old-fashioned fight film, but a peculiarly modern story. It is the sort of flat, anti-dramatic, almost documentary narrative so typical of contemporary films and fiction. La Motta's story is appealing as a modern Everyman play because he did a kind of work which allowed him to act out, physically, the character he possessed. (pp. 20-1)

Colin L. Westerbeck, Jr., "Shadowboxing: A Fighter's Stance Toward Life," in Commonweal *(copyright © 1981 Commonweal Publishing Co., Inc.; reprinted by permission of Commonweal Publishing Co., Inc.), Vol. CVIII, No. 1, January 16, 1981, pp. 20-1.*

LAWRENCE O'TOOLE

Paul Schrader's remake of the 1942 [Val Lewton/Jacques Tourneur] classic, *Cat People*, is no pussycat. Where the original wove a subtle spell, the new version goes for the throat. The difference between the two may well be an indication of how esthetic responses by film-makers to suspense and horror have become knee jerk and jejune. That is certainly not to say *Cat People* isn't effective—it's astonishingly and crudely so—but some may resent being pounced upon by such schlock. (p. 62)

Obviously, Schrader wanted to eroticize the original story, which he does on the most superficial level. There is probably no better example of the anthropomorphically erotic than the panther—the lean, taut, muscular body and the soft, padded feet and tail—but Schrader doesn't pursue the possibilities, opting for a fade-out just when our interest is pricked. Instead, he goes for the gore: a trainer's arm being ripped from its socket; a gruesome autopsy on a big cat; and a hotel-room seduction ending in a blood bath. Such shocks are random and furious; they don't seem earned, merely exploited.

The violence of the original *Cat People* lay in its powers of suggestion, mostly through the interplay of light and shadow caught by the tracking camera. Schrader's *Cat People* is a Fiesta-ware movie—a lot of lime green and rich, peachy tones—and the New Orleans locations (which are curiously underpopulated) aren't used for their exotic, ripe and suggestive powers. . . . *Cat People* is a terrific movie subject, having the potential to arrest visually and psychologically. But Schrader never once lets his movie stalk—or purr. (pp. 62-3)

Lawrence O'Toole, "Going for the Throat," in Maclean's Magazine *(© 1982 by Maclean's Magazine; reprinted by permission), Vol. 95, No. 15, April 12, 1982, pp. 62-3.*

DAVID DENBY

[In *Cat People*] Schrader and screenwriter Alan Ormsby are trying for an obsessive "dark" myth of monstrous couplings, births, transformations. The movie is full of blood-stained floors and sheets, steaming, gelatinous gunk, alligators moaning in the night. [The original storyline] has been crassly refashioned so as to produce juicy Freudian horrors—sex as annihilation, as ultimate taboo—and after a while we seem to be watching not the possibilities that were always inherent in the material but the mucky personal fantasies that have been loaded onto it.

Paul Schrader's last two films, *Hardcore* and *American Gigolo*, were also weighted with a heavy load of sexual obsession; by this time I think it's obvious that this man is trying to tell us something. Schrader and Ormsby have invented a brother for Irena, given him the director's first name, and cast an actor who looks like him. . . . Glowering Paul keeps trying to seduce or rape Irena. Why? Because they're both cat people, and so they can safely sleep only with each other—if anyone else arouses them, they turn into leopards and must kill someone before returning to human form. Our heroine refuses, of course, so Paul goes on a rampage. A sequence in which a hooker chats away happily, thinking that her client is in the bathroom, while a black tail thumps expectantly under the bed has a charge of perverse wit in it that makes the bloody scene that follows easier to bear. But I can't say I enjoyed looking at the hacked-up body of another woman, a friendly blonde who does her best to excite Paul. Since Schrader is generally solemn about his far-out conceits, the movie seems slightly mad. In the original *Cat People* the notion that sex could turn the heroine into a beast was a witty metaphor for men's fears of being overwhelmed by sexually ravenous women. Now that the whole notion is worked out *literally*, and applied to men too, it looks like a pretentiously macho way of making sex dangerous. (p. 60)

This farrago of lust and fear might have been exciting, even grimly impressive, if the movie had developed some visual poetry and urgency, but it's a rhythmless, inexpressive mess. . . . The original, black-and-white *Cat People* made wonderful use of shadow, but much of this version is merely dark, and Schrader adds to the portentousness by sending the camera gliding here or there, or drifting up to some high angle, where it takes in, say, a statue of a leopard below. There are gaps in the narration, inexplicable lapses of intelligence in supposedly bright characters, and too many climaxes—instead of working out a visual and dramatic strategy that accumulates power, Schrader settles for making us jump.

Paul Schrader's intellectualized, humorless concepts about what he's doing lead him into absurdities that an ordinary horror-film director would avoid. The flashbacks to the primal leopard past, designed by "visual consultant" Ferdinando Scarfiotti and filled with black animals gathered at a gnarled tree against a background of pink-orange clouds, cannot be deemed an improvement over such dim forties camp as the Maria Montez classic *Cobra Woman*. And Schrader has contributed one absolute howler to film history. Led to the tree by [Paul, Irena] looks up at one of the black beasts and fervently intones, "Mother!" (p. 61)

David Denby, "Puss in Boots," in New York Magazine *(copyright © 1982 by News Group Publications, Inc.; reprinted with the permission of* New York Magazine*), Vol. 15, No. 15, April 12, 1982, pp. 60-1.**

PAULINE KAEL

There's no American director who gives his movies a tonier buildup than Paul Schrader does. His interviews about his new **"Cat People"** . . . might make the picture seem mouth-watering to those who hadn't seen his **"Blue Collar,"** **"Hardcore,"** and **"American Gigolo."** But if you did see that last one you know his trouble: his movies are becoming almost as tony as the interviews. . . . Schrader is perfecting an apocalyptic swank. When his self-puffery about magic and myth and eroticism and about effecting a marriage between the feeling of [Jean] Cocteau's "Orpheus" and the style of Bertolucci's "The Conformist" is actually transferred to the screen in **"Cat People,"** each shot looks like an album cover for records you don't ever want to play.

While trying to prove himself a heavyweight moralist, Schrader has somehow never mastered the rudiments of directing. He doesn't shape his sequences. In **"American Gigolo,"** the design was stunning and the camera was always moving, but the characters were enervated and the film felt stagnant, logy; it's only energy was in Deborah Harry's singing "Call Me" during the opening credits. And in **"Cat People,"** . . . , Schrader repeatedly kills your pleasure. Just when a scene begins to hold some interest, he cuts away from it; the crucial things seem to be happening between the scenes. He's trying for a poetic, "legendary" style—which turns out to be humorless, comatose, and obscure. You can fake out interviewers if you're as smart as Schrader is, but he may be falling for his own line of gaudy patter. **"Cat People"** has all the furnishings for a religious narrative about Eros and Thanatos, but what's going on is that [Irena and Paul]—the sister and brother with black leopards inside them—are jumping out of their skins and leaving little puddles of guck behind. According to the film's newly minted legend, the two of them can have sex only with each other; sex with anyone else releases the beast inside, who devours the lover. The picture is often ludicrous (especially in the orange-colored primal-dream sequences), yet you don't get to pass the time by laughing, because it's so queasy and so confusingly put together that you feel shut out. You're brought into it only by the camera tricks or the special-effects horrors, or, perhaps, the nude scenes, or a strange image—such as the façade of an Art Deco church covered in lights. (pp. 130-31)

The dialogue that the actors are given to speak is dead. Eventually, [Irena], who's in love with the zookeeper, pleads with him—"Kill me. You must free me." He says, "I can't," and you want to yell, "Oh, go ahead and kill her." (p. 131)

> *Pauline Kael, in her review of "Cat People" (© 1982 by Pauline Kael), in* The New Yorker, *Vol. LVIII, No. 11, May 3, 1982, pp. 124, 126, 128, 130-31.**

RICHARD COMBS

Without the compulsive plot mechanism that usually draws [Schrader's] characters ineluctably towards their destiny . . . , *Cat People* tends to disintegrate into a series of notations. That these in themselves remain watchable enough, and at times quite fascinating, is a testament—yet another paradox—to the extent that Schrader's transcendentalist cinema has transcended his own limitations as a writer. *American Gigolo* marked the point where the force-feeding of characters through the plot mechanism (which became an actual meat-grinder in *Rolling Thunder*) could be suspended in favour of more meditatively visual comment. Ferdinando Scarfiotti, Bertolucci's collaborator and Schrader's "visual consultant" on *American Gigolo,* is also at work here: one notices the colour co-ordination between a high shot of the multi-coloured décor of a church and a gaggle of children seen entering the zoo, and the rust-tinted prologue—a brief family history and anthropology of the cat folk—persuades one to accept its tongue-in-cheek hokum as psychological groundwork (an effect [Roger] Corman used to achieve simply by doing things on the cheap).

But such visual elaboration, which lent *American Gigolo* both a seductive and a quizzical European gloss, is too easily subsumed by the exoticism of *Cat People.* This is not so much inevitable as the result of another perversity on Schrader's part, who not only keeps harping on the feline transformations as a Tennessee Williams-ish skeleton in the family closet—with [Paul], to revise the metaphor, as the unrepentant black sheep—but rather breaks the back of his plot by returning, two-thirds of the way through, to the mythological landscape of the beginning. Just at the point, in effect, where Irena's reluctance to accept Oliver [the zookeeper], out of fear of what sex might release in her, has begun to intersect interestingly with Oliver's reluctance to take her, out of preference for the ideal she represents. But as Irena trudges back through the red dust, accompanied by her now supposedly dead brother, to be reacquainted with her cat family before being sent back to the world of men (for no very explicable reason), she is more or less consigned to another literal-minded special-effects horror movie. . . .

It is immediately after this—almost as if signalling a loss of direction—that Schrader returns most explicitly to the Lewton/Tourneur original, recreating the fearful walk through the park (here become a jog) and the episode in the swimming-pool. Given the way the film up to this point has confidently detached itself from its source—though the swapping of a city jungle for the lusher environment of New Orleans is not that rewarding—these *hommages* tend to look more like temporary crutches. They also invoke a theme, the jealousy between Irena and Alice over Oliver, which was central to the original *Cat People* but which this film is not capable of making much of. Its psychic energy is too tied up in the love postponed between Oliver and Irena—Calvinists both—to take in love actively pursued by a third party. In a comparable fashion, the hobgoblins of an actual horror movie—as opposed to its displaced equivalent in, say, *Taxi Driver*—aren't easily translatable into the demons that haunt a Schrader hero on his way to a religious transcendence that is also a renunciation. (p. 157)

> *Richard Combs, in his review of "Cat People," in* Monthly Film Bulletin *(copyright © The British Film Institute, 1982), Vol. 49, No. 583, August, 1982, pp. 156-57.*

Sandra Scoppettone

1936-

American novelist, playwright, and scriptwriter.

Scoppettone is known to most young adults as the author of realistic and unsentimental novels on serious social problems. In *Trying Hard to Hear You*, she addresses the subject of homosexuality; teenage alcoholism is the focus of *The Late Great Me*.

Her next two novels, *Happy Endings Are All Alike* and *Such Nice People*, are generally considered controversial for their graphic violence. *Happy Endings* confronts the subjects of rape and lesbianism; *Such Nice People* tells the story of a middle-class teenage boy who plans and carries out the slaughter of his family. The pervasive message of Scoppettone's recent book, *Long Time between Kisses*, is that difficult and painful introspection is necessary for self-discovery.

While some critics contend that Scoppettone's novels are unnecessarily violent and erotic, her defenders feel that she has provided young readers with subjects which reflect their concerns.

(See also *Contemporary Authors*, Vols. 5-8, rev. ed. and *Something about the Author*, Vol. 9)

© Nancy Crampton

KIRKUS REVIEWS

No doubt Camilla Crawford's "terrifically" trendy, affectedly blase monologue [in *Trying Hard to Hear You*] is intentionally slanted to reveal a certain cliquish pseudo-sophistication. Still, these Long Island teen-agers, whose lives revolve around a little theater production of *Anything Goes*, may turn readers off long before Cam's problems with her buddy Jeff and new boyfriend Phil coalesce around the discovery that the two boys are homosexual lovers. Despite the group's much-flaunted worldliness, the revelation proves shattering and leads to the boys' persecution by cruel teasing, an attempted tar and feathering, and eventually the death in an auto accident of Phil and the girl who had offered to help him "prove" himself. Though the tragic outcome may seem overblown, it is logical in the context of the group's well-established pattern of self-dramatization and acting out. The message about homosexuality is well handled both factually . . . and in terms of kids' emotional reactions, which in Camilla's case don't keep pace with her growing intellectual acceptance of the situation. One can't help suspecting that other areas of Cam's snobbish immaturity . . . are being exploited. But for all the soap-operations, the approach to homosexuality is honest and substantial enough to justify the discussion it will no doubt generate.

A review of "Trying Hard to Hear You," in Kirkus Reviews (copyright © 1974 The Kirkus Service, Inc.), Vol. XLII, No. 20, October 15, 1974, p. 1110.

THE BOOKLIST

[*Trying Hard to Hear You* focuses on the summer of '73, which for] narrator Camilla Crawford, a 16-year-old aspiring actress, revolves around the Youth On Stage production in which her whole crowd participates. . . . During the course of rehearsals Cam falls for Phil Chrystie, who seems to reciprocate her feelings but puzzles her by his inordinate interest in her best friend Jeff Grathwohl. When Phil and Jeff are caught kissing during a Fourth of July party everyone turns on them making them a continuing butt of cruel jokes. . . . Jeff is able to cope, but the pressure overwhelms Phil, who is baited into dating a girl, drinks too much, and is killed with her in an automobile crash. In trying to comfort Jeff, Cam comes to realize what has been done to the boys, while she and most of her friends gain an understanding and greater acceptance of homosexuality. Plot threads are credibly interwoven, adult as well as teenage characters are well developed and interrelated, dialog is natural, and the author's thesis is skillfully though obviously projected in a teenage story of unusual depth for mature readers.

A review of "Trying Hard to Hear You," in The Booklist (reprinted by permission of the American Library Association; copyright © 1974 by the American Library Association), Vol. 71, No. 6, November 15, 1974, p. 340.

ALICE BACH

[*Trying Hard to Hear You*] is one of this year's most affecting novels. . . . Without a trace of moralizing and never skirting the issue, Sandra Scoppettone has examined the underlying bitterness and prejudice even supposedly "hip" teenagers have toward homosexual activity. (pp. 51-2)

Alice Bach, in her review of "Trying Hard to Hear You" (reprinted by permission of The Village Voice *and the author; copyright © The Village Voice, Inc., 1974), in* The Village Voice, *Vol. XIX, No. 50, December 16, 1974, pp. 51-2.*

ANNIE GOTTLIEB

[In **"Trying Hard to Hear You"**], Scoppettone has taken an inherently condescending form and pumped it full of "nature" content; the result is a little like reading "Double Date" in post-hippie costume and language (words like "masturbate" and "vomit" are bravely in place), with the obligatory moral punchline adjusted to 70's liberal pieties: not "save your virginity for marriage," but "as long as you don't hurt anyone else, you have a right to be whatever you want to be." . . .

The story tells what Camilla and her crowd go through when they discover that Camilla's best friend Jeff and her crush, Phil, love each other and are lovers. They react, predictably, with bewilderment, fear, disgust and, in some cases, violence; the confrontation between the gentle sincerity of the lovers and the tittering shock of the "straights" is, while a bit of a set piece, the most emotionally genuine and moving thing in the book. . . .

[The] whole hygienic list is here: homosexuality, death, alcohol, women's liberation—all set rakishly askew in the old strawberry-soda format, and in the bright relentless voice of a grownup pretending to be a precocious kid. I am probably being too harsh, because this book *could* be educational, provided its young readers are naive enough about writing not to hear the screaming clash between the medium and the message.

Annie Gottlieb, in her review of "Trying Hard to Hear You," in The New York Times Book Review *(© 1975 by The New York Times Company; reprinted by permission), January 12, 1975, p. 8.*

ALLEEN PACE NILSEN

Trying Hard to Hear You is a fourth book to put on the shelves next to [Lynn Hall's *Sticks and Stones*, Isabelle Holland's *Man Without a Face*, and John Donovan's *I'll Get There It Better Be Worth the Trip*]. These are all books touching on the subject of homosexuality. In some ways *Trying Hard* is similar. For example, the people involved in the homosexual relationship are both males, and again there is a tragedy (death) at the end of the book. But it's also different in that both boys had both parents, so there's no implication that being a homosexual relates to coming from an incomplete family as in the other three books. Another difference is that the boys, who are the same age, are actually homosexual. Although it's done with taste, the author doesn't stop short to leave readers wondering; there is an open discussion of the homosexuality. The story is told through the eyes of Camilla Crawford, a high school junior. . . . Her mother is a psychologist, so, luckily, at Camilla's invitations, she can occasionally interject little comments and observations which have the ring of authority. (pp. 81-2)

Just as in *Sticks and Stones*, the tragedy [in *Trying Hard to Hear You*] was not so much the homosexuality as it was people's reaction to it. And it was refreshing that the author made it clear that the other boy is "alive and well," and off to college:

. . . he wrote to me that he's met someone he likes a lot. He says that the boy, Richard, will never take Phil's place . . . but then, no one should ever take anyone's place. He thinks they'll have a nice relationship and he's planning to bring him home for Thanksgiving. . . .

(p. 82)

Alleen Pace Nilsen, "Grandly Revolutionary? or Simply Revolting?" (copyright © 1975 by the National Council of Teachers of English; reprinted by permission of the publisher and the author), in English Journal, *Vol. 64, No. 6, September, 1975, pp. 80-3.**

PUBLISHERS WEEKLY

[**The Late Great Me**] is centered on a problem rather than on empathetic characters. Geri Peters counts herself among the "freaks" in high school. Her mother keeps urging the girl to make friends with the popular crowd and is overjoyed when Geri announces she has a date. So is Geri, for her squire is handsome Dave Townsend, a new boy who passes up the girls in the "in" crowd. The girl's triumph, however, leads to disaster. For Dave introduces Geri to the world of booze. Before you can say AA, she's nipping from a stashed bottle in her closet at home and another in her school locker. Not scandal, blackouts, hangovers nor even the death of Dave's alcoholic mother slow Geri's compulsive drinking. That takes the author's too pat resolution and a sympathetic teacher.

A review of "The Late Great Me," in Publishers Weekly *(reprinted from the November 10, 1975 issue of* Publishers Weekly, *published by R. R. Bowker Company, a Xerox company; copyright © 1975 by Xerox Corporation), Vol. 208, No. 19, November 10, 1975, p. 47.*

KIRKUS REVIEWS

The Late Great Me could easily have been published as a "young adult problem novel" . . . since that's the audience which will primarily listen to the Late Great Me whose name is Geri. She's one of the post-pot teenagers who switched to juice, inadvertently really, after her first date, attractive Dave, introduced her to wine. Before that, alone with her only two friends . . . she'd been most unpopular with nothing to do except feed her resentment of [her] mother. . . . In time, she and Dave switch to Scotch and some nondescript sex. Only her teacher Kate Laine, an AA, spots her at once, offers her the help she keeps refusing although she does attend one boring meeting of the ten rules and twelve steps, while she goes on drinking, gaining weight, hoping to lick the problem alone, and witnessing one awful happening after another (her brother's dog is run over—by them; Dave's mother, also a lush, chokes on her own vomit). This, then, is one of those eye-opened candids with a kind of confessional volubility you'll not find hard to keep up with—the flip side of a record you're hearing more and more.

A review of "The Late Great Me," in Kirkus Reviews *(copyright © 1975 The Kirkus Service, Inc.), Vol. XLIII, No. 22, November 15, 1975, p. 1304.*

KAREN McGINLEY

The Late Great Me is the depressingly impressive story of Geri Peters, one of the half-million teenage alcoholics in this country. Although [Geri] is a fictional character, Ms. Scoppettone acknowledges that much of herself is to be found in her.

This is the story of Geri's descent to the hell of alcoholism after she first tasted wine in her junior year of high school. At fifteen Geri considered herself a freak at Walt Whitman High because she was not a part of any group, "the Straights," "the Jocks," "the Greasers," or the "Juicers," i.e., the drinkers. Then a new student, handsome David Townsend, befriends her and together they join the Juicers. As Geri and Dave sink more deeply into the world of alcohol, their lives become blurred trying to hide their alcohol and believing they will be able to stop drinking at any time.

While presenting a vivid picture of a teenager's problems, Ms. Scoppettone also studies hangups of the parents and their co-horts, such as those of Geri's mother, who was continuously playing songs of the Fifties and fantasizing about her past while refusing to recognize her daughter's expanding problems.

The Late Great Me is a book which will make us all more aware of a problem that is growing around us. It will help us to grow in our own awareness and understanding.

> Karen McGinley, in her review of "The Late Great Me," in Best Sellers (copyright © 1976 Helen Dwight Reid Educational Foundation), Vol. 36, No. 2, May, 1976, p. 40.

PUBLISHERS WEEKLY

Scoppettone's **"Trying Hard to Hear You"** . . . was a sensitive, well-written novel about young male homosexuals. [**"Happy Endings Are All Alike"**], though, seems based on ventriloquist's dummies, mouthing the author's unoriginal opinions about sexism, intolerance and what-not. It's a pity that Scoppettone doesn't do justice to a vital subject.

> A review of "Happy Endings Are All Alike," in Publishers Weekly (reprinted from the July 24, 1978 issue of Publishers Weekly, published by R. R. Bowker Company, a Xerox company; copyright © 1978 by Xerox Corporation), Vol. 214, No. 4, July 24, 1978, p. 100.

KIRKUS REVIEWS

Those who consider YA novels according to the handling and breakthrough value of their messages will give [*Happy Endings Are All Alike*] a high rating for depicting an unambiguous, freely accepted lesbian relationship, with a brutal rape to muster outrage, a moral battle bravely undertaken, and—except perhaps for the police chief—false stereotypes carefully avoided. (Both girls are pretty, had swell mothers, don't "hate men," etc.) What's more, none of it creaks; Scoppettone is a master of smooth, soapy readability. With all that, it's probably too much to ask that the "mature" subject matter be matched with any depth of observation or genuine literary imagination.

> A review of "Happy Endings Are All Alike," in Kirkus Reviews (copyright © 1978 The Kirkus Service, Inc.), Vol. XLVI, No. 18, September 15, 1978, p. 1022.

CATHOLIC LIBRARY WORLD

[*Happy Endings Are All Alike* is] a candid novel about a very controversial subject, lesbianism. The author handles the topic

delicately, yet, frankly. She does not back down on moral values but faces the issue in such a manner that it could lead to an intelligent, unbiased discussion.

> A review of "Happy Endings Are All Alike," in Catholic Library World, Vol. 50, No. 3, October, 1978, p. 117.

PATTY CAMPBELL

Happy Endings Are All Alike deals . . . with lesbian teen love and is a much stronger political and sexual statement [than *Trying Hard to Hear You*].

The story is told by one of the participants, not an observer, making explicit scenes of at least foreplay inevitable. The author has also worked in a steamy heterosexual rape scene, so that she can get in the fashionable clichés on that subject, too. It is to Scoppettone's credit as a writer that, in spite of all this propaganda overload, she has created a touching love story with interesting characters and some suspense. And at last, as the title slyly suggests, young adult literature has a novel about homosexuality that does not end with the obligatory grisly sudden death of one of the lovers.

> Patty Campbell, in her review of "Happy Endings Are All Alike," in Wilson Library Bulletin (copyright © 1978 by the H. W. Wilson Company), Vol. 53, No. 4, December, 1978, p. 341.

LINDA R. SILVER

Dimensionless characters, a formless, melodramatic plot, and dialogue that substitutes repetitive jargon for human speech merge [in *Happy Endings Are All Alike*] to present an encapsulated version of the spectrum of society's attitudes and prejudices toward lesbianism and rape. Jaret's and Peggy's love affair flowers during the summer between high school graduation and college and flounders after Jaret's rape by a deranged boy—a most brutal scene—who has seen the girls making love. While Peggy and Jaret gush, coo, and spat in a manner that embarrasses more than it enlightens, the girls' families and friends serve as convenient exemplars of various attitudes toward lesbianism. The range of prejudices that emerge after Jaret's rape are from the text according to Brownmiller, voiced and refuted in slogans. The title is irrelevant to the story and the story is irrelevant to any understanding of lesbianism or rape, displaying a lack of integrity and a willingness to address the concerns and interests of young people simplistically, sensationally, and spuriously.

> Linda R. Silver, in her review of "Happy Endings Are All Alike," in School Library Journal (reprinted from the February, 1979 issue of School Library Journal, published by R. R. Bowker Co./A Xerox Corporation; copyright © 1979), Vol. 25, No. 6, February, 1979, p. 65.

LENORE GORDON

There is virtually no validation for the lesbian teenager, and not only is her right to self-respect opposed by adult institutions, but she is also subject to emotional and/or physical abuse from homophobic peers. Scoppettone deals with such problems, including the rape of one of the protagonists, with depth and sensitivity in *Happy Endings*. . . . Her book concerns the lesbian relationship (already in progress) between Jaret and

Peggy, upper-middle-class high school seniors in a small eastern town.

The central drama involves the rape of Jaret by her brother's friend Mid, who has secretly happened upon the young women's love-making in the woods. He is apparently psychotic, but he also epitomizes the essential misogyny and fear of lesbians within this society. . . .

The rape is jarring, but treated responsibly. The author's intent is not to shock, but to leave the reader with no illusions about the violence inherent in the act. The rape's consequences, the response of the police when they learn of Jaret's lesbianism, and Jaret's own decision to prosecute all serve to be alternately rage-provoking and intensely moving. Scoppettone depicts, with great accuracy, a police investigator who embodies society's typical treatment of rape and lesbianism. Rape is not a subject most young-adult authors dare to tackle, and this one does so admirably.

Scoppettone also deals in a thoughtful manner with the issue of family, allowing each member's point of view into the drama. In both families, siblings have a particular difficulty in adjusting to their sisters' relationship, as do Jaret's parents and Peggy's recently widowed father. Unfortunately, all of the parents are treated somewhat superficially. . . .

The presentation of the small community's prejudice is more realistic, and by the end of the book it is clear that both the young women and their families are enduring the hostility of a community that views Jaret as either "whore" or "queer." The problems that ensue between Peggy and Jaret are not uncommon in the lesbian community. When Jaret chooses to prosecute the rapist, thus publicly asserting her identity as a lesbian, Peggy temporarily pulls out, fearing the consequences. Rather than judge one choice or the other, Scoppettone compassionately deals with the complexity of each young woman's feelings, emphasizing how societal pressures make their decision more painful. The way in which Peggy and Jaret ultimately deal with their individual needs within the relationship serves as a valuable model to readers of any sexual orientation. (p. 16)

> *Lenore Gordon, in her review of "Happy Endings Are All Alike," in* Interracial Books for Children Bulletin *(reprinted by permission of* Interracial Books for Children Bulletin, *1841 Broadway, New York, N.Y. 10023), Vol. 10, No. 6, 1979, p. 16.*

GERALDINE DeLUCA

[*Happy Endings Are All Alike*] is Scoppettone's second work to deal with homosexuality, and it is a far more positive and assertive treatment of the subject than her first. The earlier work, *Trying Hard to Hear You,* dealt with a furtive, guilt-ridden, male relationship that ended in tragedy. But this work, perhaps buoyed by the women's movement and a more vocal stance on the part of homosexuals in the culture, recognizes that young adult literature must, from time to time, acknowledge homosexuality as more than a passing phase in some adolescents' development. The book depicts the struggles of two young women discovering and affirming their love for each other even when one of them is raped and the rapist uses his knowledge of their lesbian relationship as blackmail. The plot may sound sensational, but the treatment is not. And though the book has its exaggerated, oversimplified moments, as a whole it presents a balanced exploration of two highly sensitive issues.

What initially disappointed me about the work was the familiar poverty of the prose. Though she doesn't use the first person, Scoppettone nevertheless binds herself to the voice of youth. Her style is a combination of the speech patterns of adolescence and the jargon-ridden, albeit often valid insights of psychotherapy. . . . The prose never does more than tell the story. Once one accepts this limitation, however, one can begin to notice the book's strengths. It is well paced, it provides some insight into almost every character, and its subject matter is never exploited. As a whole the work has a sense of proportion and dignity, and Scoppettone's encouragement of tolerance is a valuable message for teenagers. (pp. 126-27)

[*Happy Endings Are All Alike*] is wiser and says more than any of its stiff summaries or individual lines of dialogue would suggest. For it is a book that challenges many of our conventional assumptions about life, particularly the belief that certain patterns lead to happiness and that they are the same for all of us. And it encourages the individual to stand for what he or she needs and believes.

In giving us a story of a lesbian relationship that moves us and allows us to identify, Scoppettone conversely exposes the prejudices of those who feel threatened by homosexuality or who achieve a vapid sense of superiority, regardless of the emptiness of their own lives, by virtue of feeling "normal." She also asserts firmly that rape is not an act of desire but of violence, and that the circumstances of a woman's life have nothing to do with determining the guilt of the rapist. The work urges women to speak out, implying that fearful silence may be more damaging than the risk of scandal. It also urges families to support each other, to recognize that their children's or their siblings' lives should not be evaluated as a measure of acceptance or rejection of their own. The book also acknowledges that in some cases people will fail to give support. (pp. 129-30)

One must fight for one's choices, Scoppettone insists. . . . For as the title suggests, Scoppettone recognizes that the formulas that are supposed to bring life-long happiness are often inadequate, and that sensing where one's happiness actually lies, and being willing to struggle for it, is by far the braver and wiser choice. (p. 130)

> *Geraldine DeLuca, "Taking True Risks: Controversial Issues in New Young Adult Novels," in* The Lion and the Unicorn *(copyright © 1980 The Lion and the Unicorn), Vol. 3, No. 2, Winter, 1979-80, pp. 125-48.**

KIRKUS REVIEWS

[In *Such Nice People*], Scoppettone wants you to meet the Nash family of Logan, Pa.—a clean-cut, well-fed, all-American clan with seething craziness just beneath the surface. Cole, the father: over-protective of the kids, inhibited, zombie-like, pops Valium, is bitter about giving up a hot affair, dreams of escape. Mother Anne: daughter of an alcoholic, miserable, longing to consummate an affair with nice Jim. Older daughter Kit: normal, a little over-hungry for sex maybe. Younger daughter Sara: fat, compulsive eater, feels deprived of love because of older siblings growing up and away. Likewise younger sons Steven and Max: Steve's a marijuana freak, Max has the occasional violent fit. And then there's 17-year-old Tom—handsome, charming, athletic—who's totally bonkers behind his boy-next-door facade: he has visions, hears voices, believes he's being directed by a deity called SOLA, and plans to kill his entire family (except Kit) at Christmastime. And even after Tom waves a gun at neighbor Esther, tells everyone about SOLA, and is seen by the other kids masturbating and raping himself with a toilet plunger . . . , the family's so uptight that they just wait around to be killed: Tom butchers two neighbors, both parents, grandma, and three siblings. The basic point— that those photogenic WASPy families sometimes are just as crazy as ethnic ones—has been made before. . . . [Scoppettone] merely lays it on indiscriminately, in a shallow jazzy style full of flashbacks that's effective only in the few well-observed glimpses of kids acting normally. So: enough family pathology to keep a Psych. 101 class busy all semester—but the clinical potpourri doesn't add up, leaving this an unconvincing and unimaginative sick-a-thon that's ultimately just exploitational and more than a little loathsome.

A review of "Such Nice People," in Kirkus Reviews *(copyright © 1980 The Kirkus Service, Inc.), Vol. XLVIII, No. 5, March 1, 1980, p. 319.*

MICHELE M. LEBER

[*Such Nice People*] could have come from page one of the sensational press, and it may be based in fact. But translating it to fiction (with a lurid masturbation-sodomy scene and graphic details of seven murders) seems indefensible unless cause and motivation are explored; and despite smatterings of psychological jargon, a mysterious "chemical break" is the only explanation. Scoppettone's readable enough style and canny handling of adolescent characters are not reasons enough to buy this.

Michele M. Leber, in her review of "Such Nice People," in Library Journal *(reprinted from* Library Journal, *April 15, 1980; published by R. R. Bowker Co. (a Xerox company); copyright © 1980 by Xerox Corporation), Vol. 105, No. 8, April 15, 1980, p. 1005.*

KATE WATERS

Such Nice People covers a five-day period during which 17-year-old Tom, second child and first son of a family who collectively have every problem in vogue in YA literature, carries out instructions from SOLA, a phosphorescent ruler, to kill his family with the exception of older sister Kit who is to be Duchess in the new order. . . . Kit, a doctoral candidate in psychology, lives away from home but is due to arrive for the holidays. She is in therapy to work through the residue of various love affairs. Sara, a younger sister, is fat. Steven and Max, Tom's young brothers, follow him one evening to a shed and see his solitary sexual writhings that involve his penis and a plunger. They hear him speak to the air in a voice that is not his. On the appointed day, Tom takes a gun from close family friends and calmly butchers one and shoots the other. He cleans up and gaily returns home where he stabs his father repeatedly. His mother [Anne] and Steven are next. Max has slipped out a window . . . and gone to the neighbors for help. Anne's lover senses that something is wrong because the phone is out of order, picks up his gun and drives to the house where, finding everyone dead, he shoots and kills Tom. Kit, delayed by a flat tire, finds little Max on the side of the road. A week later, Anne's lover is in the hospital in deep shock. Max has gone to live with cousins. Kit thinks, "I'll never be the same, but God Almighty, I'm alive. For a moment she felt guilty. And then she didn't." Assuming that Scoppettone's purpose is to

describe the child victim of parental emotional abuse, . . . she has failed. Her latest has no place in YA collections.

Kate Waters, in her review of "Such Nice People," in School Library Journal *(reprinted from the May, 1980 issue of* School Library Journal, *published by R. R. Bowker Co./A Xerox Corporation; copyright © 1980), Vol. 26, No. 9, May, 1980, p. 92.*

LIZ WILLIAMS

Long Time Between Kisses is a refreshing and well-written novel that explores the discovery and change inherent in adolescence. Billie James, the story's narrator and protagonist, lives in a loft in New York City's SoHo with her mother . . . and three cats. In the summer of her sixteenth year, she chops off her boring brown hair and dyes the remainder purple, hoping that this radical physical alteration will substitute for what she considers to be an unremarkable personality. In the course of the novel, however, she and the reader come to recognize her uniqueness. . . . [Billie] is gifted with the capacity to care for other people. She rescues an old man from starvation and loneliness, cares about her best friend Elissa's problems and feelings, and is concerned with the well-being of her parents, both of whom have a great many of their own anxieties. Most significantly, she helps the boy with whom she falls in love to recognize his fears and feelings, though she must give up her relationship with him to do so.

Scoppettone weaves her story skillfully. Billie and her friends are realistically portrayed, and the adult characters are also believable—malapropistic Aunt Ruthie from the Bronx deserves special mention. The dialogue is convincing and often funny. *Long Time Between Kisses* addresses many significant issues—feminism, handicaps, moral dilemmas—but never pedantically. It is well worth reading, and young adults will enjoy it. (pp. 57-8)

Liz Williams, in her review of "Long Time between Kisses," in Young Adult Cooperative Book Review Group of Massachusetts, *Vol. 18, No. 4, April, 1982, pp. 57-8.*

ANNIE GOTTLIEB

Sixteen-year-old Billie James, heroine of Sandra Scoppettone's *Long Time Between Kisses* . . . has grown up in SoHo and Greenwich Village, and she dodges drug dealers and street crazies with aplomb. Harder to take lightly are her divorced parents: her mother, a failed artist turned carpenter . . . , and her father, a failed musician who freaks out on angel dust and has to be dragged away in a straitjacket. What can Billie do under the circumstances but cut her hair very short and dye it purple? This precipitates a breakup with her boyfriend, and soon Billie believes she's in love with a mysterious "older man" of 21 about to be confined to a wheelchair with multiple sclerosis.

Weird, huh? Yet this relentlessly up-to-date scenario camouflages a conventional Y.A. plot: basically good kid learns basic moral lessons—like doing the right thing hurts but it's better than selfish fantasy, and you don't have to dye your hair purple to be noticed. The emotional dimension of the book rings true; Sandra Scoppettone handles the tension between Billie's surface jive and her deeper loneliness very nicely. But the moralizing has that whiff of condescension; under the hip surface is a sugar pill.

Annie Gottlieb, "Young but Not Innocent," in The New York Times Book Review (© 1982 by The New York Times Company; reprinted by permission), April 25, 1982, p. 44.*

JOSEPH A. SZUHAY

[In *A Long Time Between Kisses,* the] author presents experiences facing many teen-agers in center city and creates situations that are both funny and sad, illustrating the problems of growing up and maturing during a short time span in the game of life. Attitude modification about the disabled is presented—personal and public attitudes about persons with multiple sclerosis. Sandra Scoppettone did her homework to be able to describe the various feelings and defense mechanisms of disabled individuals as well as many of the misconceptions and myths about them among the general public. . . .

The repeated use of The Mother, The Father, The Organic Woman, etc., was disturbing but should not be a problem for the *more mature adolescent* who is "with it" or "where it's at." This story is a serious yet humorous presentation of life not too infrequently faced by our youth.

Joseph A. Szuhay, in his review of "A Long Time between Kisses," in Best Sellers *(copyright © 1982 Helen Dwight Reid Educational Foundation), Vol. 42, No. 3, June, 1982, p. 123.*

JORJA DAVIS

[In *Long Time Between Kisses*] Billie James must make some major changes in her life—or go [crazy]. . . . So—Billie cuts off her hair in a sort of butchered crew-cut, and dyes it purple to "express her self." It's been a long time between kisses for Billie, until Captain Natoli—old, senile, living on dog food, and ignored by family and friends, and Mitch, young, handsome, and suffering from MS, and running away from family and friends come into her life. To both she gives a helping hand and to Mitch she gives her heart. Wit and humor, and finely drawn characters . . . work together to flesh out this bittersweet identity crisis and first love. Inconsistencies in tense are disturbing, but otherwise a good read. . . .

Jorja Davis, in her review of "Long Time between Kisses," in Voice of Youth Advocates *(copyrighted 1982 by* Voice of Youth Advocates), *Vol. 5, No. 3, August, 1982, p. 36.*

BARBARA J. CRAIG

As in Scoppettone's other books, excellent writing and lively characterizations grace a heartwarming "it could happen to me" story. [*Long Time Between Kisses*] tells the story of a sixteen-year-old girl who misinterprets the confused feelings, self-negation, and rebelliousness common to adolescence as love for a man with multiple sclerosis (who is himself confused and rebellious).

And, as in the author's earlier writings, my only reservation about *Long Time Between Kisses* lies with the portrayal of Billie, the main character. Her artsy east coast language and habits (such as sipping a daily cappuccino) may diminish the story's realism for some readers.

Billie's emotional states are too subtle for most pre-teens to grasp. But *Long Time Between Kisses* is an excellent reading selection for girls thirteen and up. (Boys might find it enjoyable and thought-provoking, too, if we could get them to read a "girl's" book.)

Barbara J. Craig, in her review of "Long Time between Kisses," in The ALAN Review, *Vol. 10, No. 1, Fall, 1982, p. 17.*

Carly Simon

1945-

American songwriter.

Simon is best known for writing lyrics that honestly and realistically evaluate life's predicaments. In her first popular success, "That's the Way I've Always Heard It Should Be," Simon views marriage as a complex social institution which inhibits individuality yet protects people from loneliness. Simon deals with the bitter aspects of personal relationships in many of her songs, including "You're So Vain." However, the emotions and situations in her best lyrics, and her treatment of the problems of the upper-middle-class woman, are understood by all types of listeners.

Carly Simon, her debut album, was both a critical and commercial success. Her later records, however, have received mixed reviews. Some critics believe that Simon has lost interest in writing about social hypocrisy and putting forth a universal message since her marriage to songwriter James Taylor. Although she collaborates on some of her lyrics, most often with Jacob Brackman, critics attribute Simon's popularity to her ability to sensitively and confidently analyze complicated human situations.

Lynn Goldsmith/LGI © 1982

TIMOTHY CROUSE

Carly Simon [is] a very beautiful, if very different, album. . . .

[Carly's] style is difficult to pin down. She is a Sarah Lawrence graduate and she unabashedly writes like one. Much more than Randy Newman, who was once carelessly labelled "the king of the suburban blues," Carly writes songs dedicated to the proposition that the rich, the well-born and the college-educated often find themselves in the highest dues-paying brackets. Some of the songs on this album sound like [John] Updike or [J. D.] Salinger short stories set to music.

These are personal songs written by a woman caught in a classic post-graduation bind: she has a fierce desire for independence; at the same time, frightened of loneliness, she longs for the security of marriage. In song after song, she gives in and opts for marriage, sometimes to find that her man has lost patience and split. . . .

The loneliness of the sophisticated city girl in Carly's songs is mitigated by a career, travel, college friends (all these things are alluded to in the lyrics)—and no doubt, by a psychotherapist or two. But what this persona lacks in intensity, she makes up for in complexity. The woman in these songs is at once passionately romantic and cynically realistic. . . .

[What] makes this record exceptional is its subject matter. Like very few recent records, it strikes close to a lot of middle class homes.

> Timothy Crouse, in his review of "Carly Simon," in Rolling Stone (by Straight Arrow Publishers, Inc. © 1971; all rights reserved; reprinted by permission), Issue 79, April 1, 1971, p. 50.

BRUCE HARRIS

If [*Carly Simon*] was Carly Simon's tenth album it would have been an amazing feat. But it is only her first album, and that makes it something in the order of a miracle.

It is a rarity indeed to have an artist on her first album emerge as a totally developed talent. But Carly Simon is that rarity. . . .

Her lyrics are pointed, searing, and honest. She writes of experiences between people, and so her songs, though deeply personal, have a painful universality to them. When she sings in *Reunions* of people who used to be friends trying desperately to perpetuate dead friendships, she is singing for all of us. . . .

Carly's thinking, like her artistry, is mature. She has a lot of fire, but she also has the ability to channel that fire and make it work for her. Rather than screaming about tearing down the walls and about the blood in the streets, she sings powerfully and realistically of personal revolutions in which each individual confronts the challenges of his life on his own terms and conquers the demons of the world by first conquering the demons at home. In her hit single, *That's The Way I've Always Heard It Should Be,* for instance, Carly deals with the social traps that lead so many of us into lives of quiet desperation. . . . (p. 49)

Carly Simon is more than just another great find. She is it. Past all the hypes and the hits, Carly is the most exciting new artist we've got going these days. With a first album like this, the future looks very bright indeed. (pp. 49-50)

Bruce Harris, in his review of "Carly Simon" (© 1971 by Jazz & Pop Inc.; reprinted by permission of the author), in Jazz & Pop, *Vol. 10, No. 5, May, 1971, pp. 49-50.*

RICHARD WILLIAMS

It's terribly easy to put ["Carly Simon"] on once, decide that it's very pleasant, and then forget it. Unlike [Laura] Nyro, Simon doesn't have any immediately identifiable trademark which gets the ear hooked straight away. What's so good about her, then? . . . [She] writes songs of an unassuming excellence. Take the opening cut, **"That's The Way I've Always Heard It Should Be."** . . . [It's] so honest and unfashionable that it has to be autobiographical, and it's one of the most piquant love songs I've heard in ages. . . . [There's] enough in the other songs to suggest that Carly Simon will become a major force. She's possessed by that valuable ability to articulate the personal and, in the process, convert it into the universal.

Richard Williams, in his review of "Carly Simon," in Melody Maker *(© IPC Business Press Ltd.), May 15, 1971, p. 27.*

STEPHEN DAVIS

If there are traces of an emerging, strong female consciousness on [*Anticipation*], they appear as much in [Carly Simon's] attitude to her role as a musician and singer as in the music itself. The music of *Anticipation* consists of starkly frank and carefully manicured songs about the vagaries of the male/female saga. They are a strange set of love songs, more like a cycle of the wide range of the emotional pulls and tugs that love connotes. She sings sometimes as an acute observer of the life conditions of a fellow human, sometimes as an equal partner in a shattered affair, sometimes as a bemused annotater of losing battles and the highly-charged moment flying away.

The title song is the first cut. **"Anticipation"** is a spirited examination of the tensions involved in a burgeoning romantic situation in which nobody has any idea of what's going on or what's going to happen. . . .

"Legend in Your Own Time" is about anyone who has achieved a measure of fame and has been working at it since their youth. That the most famous folks are often the loneliest is one of the tiredest truisms in show-biz, but Carly convinces the listener that her story is a personal one rather than a generalization. **"Our First Day Together"** is a re-creation of just that. It's a quiet song, lovely and quite enigmatic. . . .

"The Garden" and **"Three Days"** are a pair of disparate love songs, the first an image-filled idealization, the second a lovely, wistful realization of a pair of musicians in love, people who have to travel away from each other after three shared days of intensity. . . .

I don't think Carly Simon wants anything to do with her image as the Woman of the Future. All she is really is a maturing musician who is a woman and who is making excellent music, and that should be enough for anyone. Forget the labels, listen to the music.

Stephen Davis, "Carly Simon's Second," in Rolling Stone *(by Straight Arrow Publishers, Inc. © 1971; all rights reserved; reprinted by permission), Issue 98, December 23, 1971, p. 66.*

NOEL COPPAGE

Carly Simon's work on melodies *and* words bears the same tool marks as Kris Kristofferson's. . . . [As] lyricists, both tend to be self-centered even for this generation. Whatever ambiguities are thrown in for a wide audience to identify with are almost branded as such—tag-lines or aphorisms interjected or pinned on. Carly's *Anticipation* goes through a specific description of how unpredictable the author finds a new love affair. . . . Both are romantics, and no doubt think of themselves as *tough-minded* romantics. . . . Both are concerned with writing intelligent lyrics that are nonetheless simple enough to reach the listener on an emotional level. That remains one of the toughest jobs in the business, and Carly is almost as good at it as Kris is. (p. 59)

Noel Coppage, "Troubadettes, Troubadoras, and Troubadines . . . or . . . What's a Nice Girl Like You Doing in a Business Like This?" in Stereo Review *(copyright © 1972 by Ziff-Davis Publishing Company), Vol. 29, No. 3, September, 1972, pp. 58-61.**

ROBERT CHRISTGAU

Except for **"One More Time,"** Simon's compositions [on *Carly Simon*] sound stiff and overperformed, typical rock-as-art jive. At the time I closed my ears and hoped she would go away. (p. 292)

"That's the Way I Always Heard It Should Be" is in the noble tradition of "Leader of the Pack" and "Society's Child." In all three a young woman's challenge to the social limitations of romance is milked for melodrama, and in all three, realistically enough, she capitulates. Of course, Simon's song comes on more sophisticated, although it's worth noting that "Society's Child" seemed equally sophisticated five or six years ago. In any case, sophistication ruins Simon's song. Only in such a painstakingly precise song would the hazy outline of its persona—who talks like a recent college graduate yet claims that her college friends have already alienated their children, a process that normally takes ten years or so—be so noticeable. And only in such a wordy song would the basic principles of schlock pop-melodrama production be flouted so arrogantly. Its shock absorbed, the song was simply no fun to hear. (pp. 292-93)

As her career progressed, I liked her less. It seemed to me that she epitomized women's lib as an upper-middle-class movement. Girls and young women empathized with her problems and her projected independence without understanding that her independence was primarily a function of economic privilege. . . .

And then there was **"You're So Vain,"** a record so wondrously good-bad that it eventually overcame every one of my prejudices. Verbally, it is so overblown that I can only assume Simon is parodying her own hubris. Why else would she rhyme "yacht" (in a simile that shilly-shallies instead of specifying), "apricot" (in one of the song's numerous syntactical awkwardnesses), and "gavotte" (a dance that has been dead for two hundred years) or stick in impossibly clumsy qualifiers like "strategically'' and ''naturally''? What does ''clouds in my coffee'' mean? Why does she transgress against colloquial speech rhythms at every opportunity? And who cares?

Not me, because the song is recorded the way I always thought **"That's the Way I Always Heard It Should Be"** should be. . . . [The] song is a schlock masterpiece. It puts Ms. Simon exactly in her place.

In the name of honesty, in the name of what is fair, I have to admit that Simon's third album, *No Secrets,* is much superior to the first two. This time it is the Brackman lyrics that sound forced, while most of Simon's own songs are likable enough. Significantly, **"Embrace Me You Child,"** a song about how good her own family was for her, works best. Simon's independent pose is crumbling fast, and that's just as well—the task of redefining the female image can be left to stronger, braver women. It is appropriate that the song that establishes Simon's stardom more or less permanently, **"You're So Vain,"** is about the aristocracy of pop decadence in which she moves so easily, albeit with all the usual easy misgivings. (pp. 293-94)

> *Robert Christgau, "Carly Simon As Mistress of Schlock," in* Newsday *(copyright © Newsday, Inc., 1973; reprinted by permission), January, 1973 (and reprinted as "Weird Scenes After the Gold Rush: Carly Simon As Mistress of Schlock," in his* Any Old Way You Choose It: Rock and Other Pop Music, 1967-1973, *Penguin Books, 1973, pp. 291-94).*

STEPHEN HOLDEN

In the degree of its intelligence and forthrightness [*No Secrets*] is the equal of its predecessors. . . .

The obvious highlight of *No Secrets* is the hit single, **"You're So Vain,"** an affectionately high-spirited putdown of a male chauvinist glamour boy. . . .

[Of the album's] other cuts, five take up the subject of time— lovers' time versus childhood time—playing variations on Carly's favorite theme. The implicit assumption behind these songs is the difficulty of being happy, especially when in love, without over-analyzing one's happiness so as to dissipate its intensity. The realization that emotion and rationalization are often irreconcilable is most painfully expressed in Carly's ballad, **"We Have No Secrets."** . . . With the exception of **"You're So Vain,"** Carly's lyrics are stronger than her tunes.

> *Stephen Holden, in his review of "No Secrets," in* Rolling Stone *(by Straight Arrow Publishers, Inc. © 1973; all rights reserved; reprinted by permission), Issue 125, January 4, 1973, p. 64.*

ED KELLEHER

[*No Secrets* is Carly Simon's] third try at making a good lp and it offers neither the curious changeability of the first nor the refined mediocrity of the second. But it is undeniably one of the most commercial records of the past year. . . .

As a songwriter, Carly has a few shortcomings. Sometimes she reminds me of an overzealous Thom McAn's clerk as she shoehorns lyrics into musical position. But far more distressing is her apparent lack of anything to say. Anything very original, that is. Conventional generalities and staid value judgments abound. Her formative years must have been fraught with a whole carload of doubts and perils. The spectres of God, Daddy,

the Next Door Neighbors, Girlfriends and Disapproving Relatives always seem to be lurking around the next phrase. . . . Now there's certainly nothing wrong with writing about the commonplace but, for God's sake, you don't have to endorse it! . . .

Nineteen-seventy-three will probably go down as the year of Carly Simon, which goes to prove that you don't have to go into the mousetrap business to have people beating a path to your door. Just find a producer who understands commercialism.

> *Ed Kelleher, in his review of "No Secrets," in* Crawdaddy *(copyright © 1973 by Crawdaddy Publishing Co., Inc.; all rights reserved; reprinted by permission), April, 1973, p. 77.*

LORAINE ALTERMAN

[**"Hotcakes"**], Carly Simon's fourth album, demonstrates her continuing concern with basic human relationships. . . . **"Hotcakes"** reflects Simon's perceptions about sharing her life with someone she loves. The album's first song, **"Safe And Sound,"** states the premise that the whole world may be topsy-turvy crazy, but it's somehow safer to go through it all with another human being. . . .

It seems to set the scene for the rest of the album. . . .

"Misfit" and **"Haven't Got Time For The Pain"** delve more deeply into the love relationship. Each song says in its own way how being involved with another person can help one overcome his or her own problems. **"Misfit"** is tough and even sarcastic whereas **"Haven't Got Time For The Pain"** is directly emotional. . . .

Simon also probes family relationships in **"Older Sister"** which I think is the best cut on the LP. The song explains with a great deal of wit and understanding exactly how a kid sister feels. . . .

Though nothing on this album is as instantly catchy as **"You're So Vain,"** there is more than enough proof that Simon is a remarkable talent.

> *Loraine Alterman, "Sing a Song of Rock Romance," in* The New York Times, *Section 2 (© 1974 by The New York Times Company; reprinted by permission), January 27, 1974, p. 8.**

MICHAEL OLDFIELD

Love is a many splendoured thing and all that—but sometimes it's not necessarily all you need. **"Hotcakes"** is a case in point. One of the strengths of Carly Simon's previous albums has been her lyrics; they carry a sting in the tail that few other singer-songwriters can match. She's also capable of communicating invective—**"You're So Vain"**—that shows up the railing against the world in general adopted by so many singers for the embarrassments they are. It's quite a skill to be nasty in a song—and Carly's got it. She also has a knack for writing about specific events rather than abstractly painting a word picture of a mood or a feeling. Loneliness at the top, for example, is a subject that's always been popular with songwriters; few have tackled it as eloquently as her in **"Legend In Your Own Time."** Like her best numbers it's sad; **"Hotcakes"** on the other hand is a happy album. It's mainly a collection of love songs—not surprising, perhaps, considering she's only recently married. **"Mind On My Man"** (beautifully executed), **"Forever My Love"** (co-written with her husband James Taylor) and **"Haven't Got Time For The Pain"** (co-written with Jacob Brackman) are all plain and simple romantic cuts. **"Just Not True"** and **"Misfit"** on the other hand are almost the "hard" Carly Simon; but just when she's about to deliver the coup de grace she adds a happy ending. One of her obsessions has lasted though: childhood. **"Older Sister"** is the best cut on the album. . . . The other childhood cut, **"Grownup"** isn't quite up to this standard, but still very attractive. . . . Taking the album as a whole, on the credit side is Carly's lovely voice, slick playing, and fine arrangements. But without the bite in the lyrics, it only adds up to very hip Muzak.

> *Michael Oldfield, "Plain and Simple Simon: 'Hotcakes',"* in Melody Maker *(© IPC Business Press Ltd.), March 16, 1974, p. 32.*

SUSIN SHAPIRO

Hotcakes wants to sizzle but when you take that first serious chew, the flake falls away and the words are runny, underdone.

Gone is the soft loneliness and sad cynicism of Carly's *Anticipation* album. . . . [Carly] seems to have lost that adrenal-inspiration only touring can ignite. It's been replaced by maritally exuberant content and a stay-at-home pace, doubtless totally fulfilling to live but less fun to eavesdrop on. **"Forever My Love"** . . . extols this bliss best.

Carly's songs have never been "heavy" or involving, but there was always enough successfully sublimated social comment and repetitive rhythms to make you whistle along in the shower or hum in the subway buzz. (p. 73)

If I dare compare, Carly's got the pyrotechnics but [Joni Mitchell's] got control. Carly fails to enlarge her stylistic idiom; Joni dares not miss that chance. Carly once wrote: "Whoever you want is exactly what I'm willing to be." Where are the assertive seeds of independence that women are supposed to be nurturing these days? Carly can't and doesn't speak for the common woman . . . and that's why *Hotcakes* is ho-hum. "Come home with me, we'll turn on the TV." Yawn. "She rides in the front seat, she's my older sister . . . She goes to bed an hour later than I do . . . I'd like to be my older sister." Snork. Not terribly scintillating. . . .

What I miss most is the growth. Richard Perry [the album's producer] has widened Carly's music, but being well-fed is not growing taller. If an artist is content to rest on his childhood flannel blanket then we must let her/him know in some manner that we're too big to crawl alongside them. Buy quality, not predictability. Accept no substitutes, sweet or otherwise. (p. 74)

> *Susin Shapiro, in her review of "Hotcakes,"* in Crawdaddy *(copyright © 1974 by Crawdaddy Publishing Co., Inc.; all rights reserved; reprinted by permission), April, 1974, pp. 73-4.*

MICHAEL WATTS

Having listened to [**"Playing Possum"**] more than half a dozen times now, what clear and precise thoughts does it provoke? The answer is, to the best of my ability, that there's little provocation at all, beyond, that is, the picture on the cover. . . .

The songs within comprise music of controlled sensuality, but the mood is too languorous to generate much real heat. Carly Simon's a tease and a society broad. You knew it with **"You're So Vain,"** but on **"Playing Possum"** she extends that role, even to the point of including a song called **"Are You Ticklish."** . . . It's tempting to think of her as Joni Mitchell without depth; even her sensuality seems mere artfulness, the refined and coolly calculated product of the debs' finishing school. Although the title cut is really a reference to the present attitude of sixties activists, it can be interpreted as expressing the emotional low-profile of the whole album. . . .

[It] must be worrying for Ms. Simon's commercial aspirations that there aren't any really memorable tunes or hook-lines here, although the single that's been released, **"Attitude Dancing,"** enjoys a pleasant rhythmic propulsion in the chorus. Certainly there's nothing as obviously infectious as **"You're So Vain."** . . .

It should be said . . . that she does have moments as a writer. Anyone who can write, in **"After the Storm"**—"the wind's pulling the moon down, underneath the eiderdown," has some talent going for them; lyrically, in fact, it's a finely-felt song about screwing, probably the best on the album. Her problem, here at any rate, is an inability to translate that vital impulse into music with the same emotional impact.

> *Michael Watts, "Carly: Sensual Promise, but No Hot Cakes: 'Playing Possum',"* in Melody Maker *(© IPC Business Press Ltd.), June 14, 1975, p. 36.*

STEPHEN HOLDEN

The cover of Carly Simon's enjoyable new album is an indication of its best songs, which celebrate the body at play. *Playing Possum* represents a breakthrough of sorts for Simon. Earlier albums, through *Hotcakes,* depicted adolescent and postadolescent growing pains, family relationships and especially an aching romantic ardor. Simon's new, bolder stance was probably inevitable—it's certainly welcome—since her previous four albums have defined a slow but steady movement away from the "sensitive singer/songwriter" role toward that of "rock" songstress. . . .

With *Playing Possum,* Simon has largely abandoned plaintive balladeering for a blunt style that means to be aggressively sexy. Aggressive it is—and characteristically ingratiating—but not particularly sexy except on one song, **"Attitude Dancing."** (p. 63)

While **"Attitude Dancing"** stands as the album's showstopper, six other original songs comprise the core of *Playing Possum*'s thematic material. In **"After the Storm,"** . . . Simon promotes the domestic squabble as a tool for sexual stimulation: "And doesn't anger turn you on." **"Love out in the Street"** explores voyeuristic fantasy, suggesting, if not a mass orgy, at least greater sexual relaxation. In a softer style, **"Look Me in the Eyes"** extols the ecstasy of eye contact during sex. **"Waterfall"** likens lust to drowning in a waterfall. And **"Are You Ticklish,"** an old-fashioned waltz, describes a childlike playfulness that can precede sex. The album's "heaviest" erotic song, **"Slave,"** cowritten with Jacob Brackman, describes very straightforwardly what it's like to be madly in love. That **"Slave"** may be taken by some as an antifeminist statement seems to me beside the point. . . .

Playing Possum's title cut ends the album on a sociological rather than erotic note. The song traces the history of the generation just turned 30, suggesting that its political, spiritual and utopian ideals have dissipated into a desire for the bourgeois "easy life." Simon questions whether or not "there might be something more." Like many of Simon's songs, "**Playing Possum**" sounds more like a well-crafted writing exercise than a fully imagined reminiscence. A somewhat similar aesthetic distance characterizes Simon's "body" songs as well as her performances of them. . . .

Cuts like "**You're So Vain**" and "**Attitude Dancing**" represent paragons of commercial craft that command attention like wonderful new toys. It's a shame that each Carly Simon album contains only one such cut and even more of a shame that below their surfaces there is no soul, nothing to evoke the subliterate, primal responses that the greatest rock music can make happen. I suggest that Carly Simon knows "there might be something more"—it's just beginning to creep into some of her lyrics and around the edges of her voice—and is aware of the terrible risks involved in trying to find it. *Playing Possum* is at least good enough for a start. (p. 65)

> *Stephen Holden, in his review of "Playing Possum," in* Rolling Stone *(by Straight Arrow Publishers, Inc. © 1975; all rights reserved; reprinted by permission), Issue 189, June 19, 1975, pp. 63, 65.*

PETER REILLY

Carly Simon's new album "**Playing Possum**" . . . is an intelligent, mind-warming romp and an almost continuous musical joy. . . . [She] has gotten her head together, in 1975 terms, better than any other young female composer-performer around.

The sexual revolution? Put such pedestrian back-numbers out of your mind. Carly has clearly moved beyond all that. Listen to her in *Look Me in the Eyes*. . . . Quite frank, as we used to say, but also as clear-eyed, healthily straightforward, and up-to-the-minute as can be for an honest woman dealing with these matters today.

Slightly more ambivalent is her approach to the Lib game in *Slave*. . . . [The] song is a statement of fact, how things are, and not a cry of impotent rage. The point is that it's *all* role playing; we cannot choose *no* role, but we can choose among the number available, even the one called the path of least resistance. And choice is not without its dangers too, according to Carly (and Jacob Brackman) in *Attitude Dancing*— . . . for even choosing can become a habit, a role, condemning the player to a life of confused, directionless (even though self-manipulated) jostling. The best song here, however, is the title song, *Playing Possum*. It's about whatever happened to The Revolution, it echoes with little whispers of frustrated cultural possibilities, perhaps sinister, perhaps pathetic, and it will make you think. (pp. 73-4)

[The album] at least temporarily sums up a number of current social conundrums better than might any learned dissertation by one of the paper pundits of the media. (p. 74)

> *Peter Reilly, "A Thoughtful Report from the Home Front by Investigator Carly Simon," in* Stereo Review *(copyright © 1975 by Ziff-Davis Publishing Company), Vol. 35, No. 2, August, 1975, pp. 73-4.*

ALLAN JONES

["**The Best of Carly Simon**"] is really quite unremarkable in that it reveals her to be, despite (or even because of) her undeniable popularity, a relatively minor talent. And, although we are presented here with a selection of work which covers

the last five years of her career, there is an absence of any thematic or musical development. Despite the early promise of "**Carly Simon,**" . . . represented by "**That's The Way I've Always Heard It Should Be,**" and "**Anticipation**"—the title track and "**Legend In Your Own Time**" are featured here— she has not matured like her contemporary, Joni Mitchell. She lacks, too, the vivid perception which characterises the work of the sadly-neglected Laura Nyro. One has, however, to acknowledge Simon's facility for composing (most often in collaboration with Jacob Brackman) songs of a certain intelligence and discrimination. Her better songs, for instance, are thankfully free of any contrived emotional pyrotechnics (although "**No Secrets**" is a little mawkish). It's her consistency which is most admirable, though this has to be balanced against the fact that she has—with the exception of "**You're So Vain,**" perhaps—written little that is either particularly memorable or demanding. . . . If her career is to be saved from the decline indicated by her most recent album, "**Playing Possum,**" a drastic re-think is necessary.

> *Allan Jones, in his review of "The Best of Carly Simon," in* Melody Maker *(© IPC Business Press Ltd.), December 20, 1975, p. 31.*

COLIN IRWIN

For someone who's produced albums of the substantial bite of "**No Secrets**" and "**Anticipation,**" Simon's capable of the most crass banalities. On half of ["**Another Passenger**"] she appears to be striving to recapture the sardonic wit of "**You're So Vain**" but falling miserably short, while the rest show all the symptoms of half-hearted fillers. . . . When she tries to rock she ends up in a trot, and her attempts at tenderness finish flat. On the few occasions that she captures the right mood in her performance, the songs are either frivolous or lacking in credibility. The good track is "**In Times When My Head,**" a ballad which deals with the guilt complex of an unfaithful woman, but even that has suspicions of cliché, though it's the only time the song and performance are consistent. "**Be With Me**" is a moderately pretty love song. . . . But otherwise she tackles subjects which may be terribly meaningful to their author, but sound a little ridiculous when exposed to the world in such splendour. Like the tale of Texas millionaire Donald Swan who married a French lady called Simone and that's about the sum of the story; or "**Fairweather Father,**" about the guy who has no interest in the baby until mother walks out and he's instantly remorseful. Heavy stuff eh? . . . The track that might have saved it, or at least covered it with a bit more credit, is "**Darkness 'Til Dawn.**" . . . But Carly comes up with the same moody hardness she uses on all the tracks, from . . . the passably poppy "**Libby**" and "**Dishonest Modesty,**" which is "**You're So Vain**" with the sex changed and the impact squandered.

> *Colin Irwin, in his review of "Another Passenger," in* Melody Maker *(© IPC Business Press Ltd.), August 7, 1976, p. 18.*

KEN TUCKER

"**Cowtown,**" a song Carly Simon has written for *Another Passenger,* tells the story of a cagey French woman named Simone Swann who marries a Texas millionaire for his money, and because she's lonely. In the second verse, Swann prepares to accompany the Texan to his native land. . . . [Simon's song] is the sort of lucid, humorous and concise observation for which

Randy Newman, say, would be praised to the skies. I'll venture a guess that Carly Simon won't be huzzahed for her verbal dexterity and wit, however. If past reviews are any indication, a goodly number of her notices will consist of arch compliments of the gams displayed on the back cover.

Another Passenger is Carly Simon's best record. (p. 60)

True, Carly Simon has produced a lot of average music, but what is more important is that she has never abandoned her original themes, something she might easily have done at any time. Simon is not a very original songwriter. Her melodies are similar; often her lyrics seem as if she had not worked very hard at them, taking the first clever rhyme that came to mind. But at her best she conveys the monied angst of the leisured with moving conviction, something no one else has ever done. Additionally, she is always further explicating and enhancing an exploration of her ego and her sexuality. It is extraordinary for a woman to say without a speck of self-consciousness or irony, as she does here on **"In Times When My Head,"** that she "Know[s] none could compare with me/In my airy skirts and cool retreats."

This may not seem like much to radical prose writers, but it is still jolting stuff for pop music. (pp. 60, 62)

> *Ken Tucker, "Fire, Rain & Ennui, The Discreet Charm of James & Carly: 'Another Passenger',' in* Rolling Stone *(by Straight Arrow Publishers, Inc. © 1976; all rights reserved; reprinted by permission), Issue 219, August 12, 1976, pp. 60, 62.*

PETER REILLY

Carly Simon's back, smarter, more ironically perceptive, and more engaging than ever. . . . ["**Another Passenger"**] is another totally classy job from a foxy lady who not only knows where it's all at, but doesn't mind letting you know, in an offhand way, that her pearls of wisdom have cost her a pretty penny or two in the purchase. . . . *In Times When My Head* [is not] precisely about staying cool at all costs: . . . [it] is as good a description of self-destructive jealousy as one would really care to hear about. This ability to deal honestly and directly with emotional life has always been one of Carly's major strengths, and it permeates all her songs here. (pp. 88-9)

Carly Simon, *chansons à clef* and all, is a grown-up joy to have around. Over the past couple of years she's been recording observed scenes from her life, and this latest collection is as filled with insight, humor, truthfulness, and, yes, modesty as was the early literary work of Mary McCarthy. The nicest thing about her is that her laser-beam eye and rifle-mike ear are both softened by a civilized disinclination to judge. But oh my, what a witness! (p. 89)

> *Peter Reilly, "The Laser-Beam Eye and Rifle-Mike Ear of the Engaging Carly Simon," in* Stereo Review *(copyright © 1976 by Ziff-Davis Publishing Company), Vol. 37, No. 5, November, 1976, pp. 88-9.*

M. MARK

[On *Boys in the Trees* Carly Simon is] obscure and artsy in her ruminations about sexual insecurity. *Boys in the Trees* includes a couple of songs that say without-my-man-I'm-worthless-and-he'll-leave-me-'cause-I'm-worthless. The new single, **"You Belong to Me,"** presents her response—mostly desperate, with

a neat hint of egocentrism—to her man's announcement that he's in love with someone else. There's still a high school feel to her songs—it's *boys* in the trees—but Carly seems less anguished over whether she'll get asked to the prom.

Which is smart. She's too sleek and well-adjusted to be a credible victim; if Carly went up to Saratoga, guess whose horse would win. *Boys in the Trees* is relatively light on wallflowerism and turgid ballads. Exceptions are **"Haunting,"** [which is] arcane and ostentatious . . . , and **"In a Small Moment,"** the pompous, moralistic recounting of a fall from grace. But **"Back Down to Earth"** acknowledges that a grown-up woman can survive the breakup of a love affair, and **"You're the One"** acknowledges that she can stop being passive. It's a likable album.

And it has what may be Carly's best song since **"You're So Vain"**—a calypso **"De Bat (He Fly in Me Face)."** . . . A song that's witty, funny, sly—how *do* you get de wings on the cat? But there's a little problem: rich white girl puts on brownface, plays minstrel, has good time. . . .

Although she's begun to consider the injustices of the prom world, she apparently hasn't thought much about walking away from that old demeaning dance of courtly love. It's way past time for Carly Simon to define herself: She'll always get asked to the prom, and she doesn't have to say yes.

> *M. Mark, "Carly Simon: Belle of the Ball" (reprinted by permission of* The Village Voice *and the author; copyright © The Village Voice, Inc., 1978), in* The Village Voice, *Vol. XXIII, No. 20, May 15, 1978, p. 65.*

JANET MASLIN

[*Boys in the Trees* suggests a] feeling of grateful, hopeful and also slightly cautious contentment. . . .

Boys in the Trees is Carly Simon's most serene accomplishment to date, but its moods vary dramatically enough to indicate that peace of mind comes at a high price. . . .

The scrubbed-down Simon is a mightily seductive creature and also a somewhat mocking one, but for once these elements are firmly controlled. . . .

Boys in the Trees has a few holes, but there are no major craters—and for an artist as erratic as Simon once was, achieving this kind of consistency amounts to a major breakthrough. . . . [**"Haunting"**] is a throwback to Carly Simon's more pretentious days. But for the most part, she's become quite a reliable songwriter, even at the cost of being repetitive (**"Back Down to Earth"** is a direct recycling of **"Haven't Got Time for the Pain"**). And the confidence and clarity of her delivery mesh beautifully with the mature intelligence that's at work in so much of her material. (p. 91)

> *Janet Maslin "Paul & Carly: Family Affairs," in* Rolling Stone *(by Straight Arrow Publishers, Inc. © 1978; all rights reserved; reprinted by permission), Issue 267, June 15, 1978, pp. 89, 91-2.**

JON YOUNG

Carly Simon used to be dangerous. Remember? She had to her credit a lethal attack on marriage (**"That's the Way I've Always Heard It Should Be"**) and one of the most quotable put-down songs ever (**"You're So Vain"**). Those were the days.

But she threw it all away. After having scored a direct hit on the institution of holy matrimony, she had the gall to go and get hitched! Shocking. For whatever reason, her music consequently lost much of that restless and abrasive (some said obnoxious) quality so crucial to its personality. Indeed, so important had that edge been that, without it, her albums' statements were made by the silly covers rather than the contents. . . .

Simon's failure to keep up her credibility can be tied directly to the fact that she lacked the massive egotism and exhibitionistic tendencies that make Joni Mitchell, Neil Young and even hubby James Taylor such genuinely fascinating public displays. Unlike them, she always seemed concerned with more superficial things than the state of her eternal soul, as if she didn't consider herself sufficient subject matter. And lacking unusual circumstances, she generally offered self-effacing radio fare, hardly as exciting as inner torment.

Boys in the Trees is full of little psychological clues from the reticent Ms. Simon that mean great fun for the amateur shrink but trying listening for anyone else. A trio of bland songs with domestic references casts a pall over the rest of the album. . . .

At the other extreme, three undeniable winners are tucked away on side two. Here Simon temporarily loses her self-conscious reserve and risks abandoning her safe stance. As a result, both **"You're the One"** . . . and **"For Old Times' Sake"** . . . have an emotional honesty she elsewhere declines to attempt. It's frustrating she doesn't do this sort of thing more often, yet nice to know she's still got the knack. But her greatest triumph is the gemlike **"In a Small Moment."** Freed from the spotlight by a third-person perspective, Carly examines the germ of corruption. . . . It's a "small" song, but its perceptive resonance is wide and deep. Perfect.

Occupying the middle ground are three bittersweet, pressed-flower tunes with wistful lyrics that allude to experience without getting too close. Curiously, the intended throwaways are much more memorable, being irritating and unappealing. . . .

Why Carly Simon won't make a greater commitment to her own records is beyond the domain of a humble review, but an understanding of that insecurity would no doubt explain why this album is so hollow. . . . *Boys in the Trees* is plenty of pleasantries with a tantalizing dash of substance.

Jon Young, "Branchin' Out: 'Boys in the Trees'," in Crawdaddy *(copyright © 1978 by Crawdaddy Publishing Co., Inc.; all rights reserved; reprinted by permission), July, 1978, p. 68.*

STEPHEN HOLDEN

As the social queen of East Coast pop-rock, Carly Simon can be counted on to put out well-tailored product that defines "class" (lots of money tastefully spent) to the industryites and consumers who regard the pop world as a toney horse race. With their tense fake-natural glamor, Simon's albums amount to aural fashion shows. Each year, an expensive name producer is engaged to design a collection that cautiously incorporates the latest trends and squeezes one or two hits out of the star's new material, thus validating her writing talents and recertifying her first-lady status commercially. (p. 50)

I've long thought that if Simon would scrap all but the best of her own songs and concentrate on singing other people's ma-

terial, she might actually come up with a great album, instead of the tasteful teases we've grown used to.

Spy, Simon's latest, is no breakthrough. . . . [It's] typical Carly Simon—trendy-sexy with a soupçon of intellectual vigor. There are no killer cuts like **"You're So Vain"** or **"You Belong to Me"** and no personal narratives as interesting as the best songs on *Another Passenger,* the album that falsely signaled a breakthrough in Simon's writing. The conflict between Simon's arty aspirations and her rock & roll drive is, if anything, more glaring than ever.

Spy takes its title from an Anais Nin quote, and most of its material touches on the war between the sexes. But when Simon tries to be serious, she becomes impenetrable. The album's big shot at "art" is a klunking eight-and-a-half-minute pop-jazz-classical fusion called **"Memorial Day"** that brushes more grooves than the rest of the album put together without actually settling into any of them. It's as rambling and nondescript as Joni Mitchell's "Paprika Plains," which might have been a model. The content of the text—a girl in a limo finds herself in a desert wilderness witnessing a primal sexual battle—is as dull as its versification. Dream sequences in art are usually cheap substitutes for direct self-expression, and this one is typical.

Spy's better moments are its lighter ones. In **"Vengeance,"** Simon titillatingly banters with a hot cop. . . . The most arresting lyric, **"We're So Close,"** describes the frustration of loving someone who forestalls communication by saying things like "in speaking one can be so false." There are hints of real rage in this song, but not enough to cut beneath it's glossy easy-listening surface; as in most of Simon's other semi-autobiographical outpourings, the confessional impulse is muted by an evasive decorousness. So *Spy* remains a pleasant album; the listening is painless at best, the hooks catchy, and the star still teasingly unavailable. (p. 56)

Stephen Holden, "Carly Simon: This Year's Model" (reprinted by permission of The Village Voice *and the author; copyright © News Group Publications, Inc., 1979), in* The Village Voice, *Vol. XXIV, No. 29, July 16, 1979, pp. 50, 56.*

PETER REILLY

Carly's songs on ["**Spy**"] show her at her tough-minded best, asking no quarter and offering none. Like her literary counterparts Mary McCarthy and Joan Didion, Carly Simon sees and allows herself to feel a great deal more than the average privileged, upper-middle-class young woman—probably much more than she'd like to. In *We're So Close* she offers a clear-eyed description of one of those strangely bloodless relationships so many people cling to these days. . . . [No] matter how much it may chill the marrow of sentimentalists or romantics, Carly Simon has the courage to tell it like it is.

She also has the courage to touch on something that's rarely discussed: violent female rage. *Vengeance* tells of a woman stopped by a policeman for a traffic violation; he uses his position of authority to molest her verbally with gross sexual innuendo, and finally she strikes back. . . . It's a strong song. . . .

Memorial Day shows courage of another kind, for instead of taking the role of a car hop, a bar girl, or some other of the not-so-beautiful losers who are the typical protagonists of most pop songs, Carly portrays herself as the relatively secure and immune person she really is, insulated by her wealth and celebrity from most of the rough and tumble of ordinary life. . . .

But it's not all social realism. **"Spy"** includes plenty of simple entertainment, such as *Pure Sin,* about a girl posing chastely for her portrait while planning something a good bit livelier for later, the unsticky but romantic *Love You by Heart,* and the very funny and touching *Coming to Get You,* about a country mother talking on the phone with her runaway child. . . .

[**"Spy"**] is one of the best albums of the year and . . . Carly Simon is carving out a unique place for herself in American pop as a sort of Sister Courage.

Peter Reilly, "Carly Simon: 'Spy'," in Stereo Review *(copyright © 1979 by Ziff-Davis Publishing Company), Vol. 43, No. 4, October, 1979, p. 120.*

DEBRA RAE COHEN

All too often on *Spy,* the small, significant personal questions that the songwriter is capable of asking are obscured by a lascivious "Does she or doesn't she?" Even the Rolling Stones-style backup vocals on the catchy **"Pure Sin"** can't rescue its central oxymoron from tedium, because the extremes simply aren't that interesting. Though Simon's not the artistic wallflower she presents in **"Memorial Day"** . . . , she's no rakish hot mama either. Indeed, the dreary mock twang of **"Coming to Get You"** reminds me of academicians who write in dialect.

All of this cartoons-for-adults posturing doesn't disguise the fact Simon gives away very little of herself on *Spy.* She's always been of two minds about exposure: a confessional singer with patrician reticence. Her best songs, from **"No Secrets"** to **"In Times When My Head"** (and the new record's gem, **"We're So Close"**), have transmuted and exploited this conflict, simultaneously serving as rueful commentary on her own reserve while homing in on the role of honesty in love. . . .

Simon's quite aware of her potential as gossip fodder—remember **"You're So Vain"**?—but she's forfeiting emotional intensity now by offering hints, rather than insights, about her marriage. Perhaps that's why [some lines] . . . have an air of calculated self-exposure that makes Carly Simon, in her trench coat, seem more like a flasher than a spy.

Debra Rae Cohen, "Carly Simon's Trench-Coat Flasher: 'Spy'," in Rolling Stone *(by Straight Arrow Publishers, Inc. © 1979; all rights reserved; reprinted by permission), Issue 301, October 4, 1979, p. 58.*

KEN TUCKER

On *Come Upstairs,* Carly Simon's instincts are bold, but her music betrays her. Confronting a self-imposed semiretirement, declining disc sales and the pervasive peppiness of the New Wave, Simon has responded with a comely perversity by writing a batch of new songs that are either loose and trashy or tight and morose. . . .

[The] current album is so confused and boring that it almost sounds resigned to its own aesthetic failure. *Come Upstairs* commences with some promisingly slick, bitchy pop (the title track, **"Stardust"**), then quickly sheds its allure with witless paranoia (**"Them"**) and ballads oozing with cliched imagery

(**"Jesse," "James"**). The peak of discomfort is **"In Pain,"** in which Carly Simon (who's spent a career proving that she can be aggressive and vulnerable with equal ferocity) falls apart in the service of primal Muzak, yowling: "Pain, in pain/I'm in pain."

The awful thing is that you can't believe her for a second.

Ken Tucker, in his review of "Come Upstairs," in Rolling Stone *(by Straight Arrow Publishers, Inc. © 1980; all rights reserved; reprinted by permission), Issue 325, September 4, 1980, p. 51.*

PETER REILLY

[**"Come Upstairs"**] is not only filled with risks, some daring and impromptu, others cannily calculated, but also with a wry, grown-up self-awareness that is light years away from the squishy self-absorption of so many of [Carly Simon's] contemporaries. And it is an album that continues the upward arc of a career that's been a success almost from its very beginnings. . . . She has at least three songs in this new collection that are as good as anything she's done before; they offer further proof that she is the possessor of a dynamic sensibility unerringly in tune with the kind of world we're living in at the moment.

Come Upstairs and *The Three of Us in the Dark* are both brilliant examples of her ability to explore contemporary sexual tensions in a uniquely ambivalent style. She's moved away from her earlier intellectualized, girlish, even rather angry stance (*You're So Vain, Vengeance, We're So Close*) to a softer, more catlike subtlety, engaged but not committed. Her work somehow seems a lot more womanly for it and therefore a lot more appropriate to the Eighties. . . . *Come Upstairs* is either about passion suddenly lit between two people who've known each other for years or about passion rekindled. It's a Carly Simon song, so of course you're never quite sure. But the precise meaning isn't nearly as important as the rich variety of moods that suffuses the lyric from initial impulse to final lines. . . . *The Three of Us in the Dark* is perhaps about the memory of a past lover intruding upon a current relationship, maybe about another, more critical self doing the same. But, then again, it *is* the Eighties, and one never knows about these new designs for living, do one? Anyway, it's a lovely song. . . . (p. 79)

There are other good things here too, such as *Stardust,* a rock number about that by-now fairly tattered and quite justly abused figure the Macho Rock Star, and *Them,* yet another exercise in ambiguity; it might be about any minority group (Short People?), but it has a special poignancy in that it is seen through the eyes of a girl who, though she vowed to resist Them, has instead become one of their conquests.

"Come Upstairs" is one of those albums that it's a pleasure to report on because it not only dignifies but enlarges the pop scene. . . . [It] can't be denied that she's been making records for quite a while now that have consistently been more than a shade better than those of any of her contemporaries. What distinguishes her work here is what has distinguished it in the past: enormous musical vitality combined with a fierce intelligence that keeps on risking, winning, and maturing. (pp. 79-80)

Peter Reilly, "Carly Simon: Enormous Vitality, Fierce Intelligence," in Stereo Review *(copyright © 1980 by Ziff-Davis Publishing Company), Vol. 46, No. 4, October, 1980, pp. 79-80.*

Aleksandr I(sayevich) Solzhenitsyn

1918-

Russian novelist, short story writer, poet, dramatist, and critic.

Solzhenitsyn attained world prominence with *One Day in the Life of Ivan Denisovich*, an authentic portrayal of life in Joseph Stalin's labor camps, where Solzhenitsyn himself had spent eight years. The novel was among the first works critical of the Stalin era to be published in the Soviet Union. It is widely read by young adults for its powerful treatment of the loss of freedom and for its emotional and philosophical impact. Solzhenitsyn's persistent activities as a dissident and outspoken critic of literary censorship led to his expulsion from the Soviet Union in 1969 and the censorship of his subsequent publications in Russia.

Now living in the United States, Solzhenitsyn continues to write in exile of the oppression in his own land, as well as to speak of his concern for the political and moral problems of the West. Rejecting the precepts of socialist realism, he writes from a Christian point of view, depicting the suffering of the innocent in a world where good and evil vie for the human soul. In this he is thematically linked to the great Russian writers of the nineteenth century. His writing, distinguished by its austere, simple style, shows his compassion and moral concern. Solzhenitsyn was awarded the Nobel Prize for Literature in 1970.

(See also *CLC*, Vols. 1, 2, 4, 7, 9, 10, 18 and *Contemporary Authors*, Vols. 25-28, rev. ed., 69-72.)

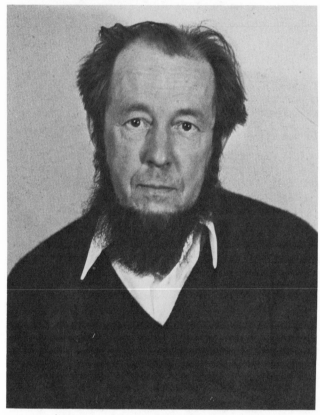

Hedrick Smith/NYT PICTURES

MARVIN L. KALB

On November 20, 1962, *Novy Mir*, a monthly Soviet literary magazine, published a short novel by an unknown Russian writer, Alexander Isayevich Solzhenitsyn, entitled *One Day in the Life of Ivan Denisovich*. It was an immediate literary and political sensation. . . . [The] title character, Ivan Denisovich Shukhov, was quickly recognized throughout the country as a touching symbol of the suffering which the Russian people had endured under the Stalinist system.

Was there anything special about Ivan that sparked this lightning response? Not really. Ivan was an ordinary Russian caught up in the swirl and chaos of World War II. Like millions of other Russians, he served uncomplainingly in the Red Army for four years, surviving the bitter cold and hunger of the Western front. In 1945, he and a friend were captured by the Germans. After a few days they managed to escape and returned to Russian lines. Ironically, instead of being decorated for heroism and loyalty, Ivan was arrested by Stalin's supersensitive secret police, who accused him of high treason and charged that he had returned only to spy for the Germans. Confused and helpless, afraid that he would be shot if he tried to explain, Ivan "confessed." He was sentenced to ten years in a Siberian concentration camp. Solzhenitsyn's book describes one day in that camp, one day no better and no worse than any of the other three thousand six hundred and fifty-two days of Ivan's sentence. Ivan's experience was no isolated miscarriage of justice; it was typical of the Stalinist system, under which the labor camps of Siberia were crowded with Russians whose "crime" may have been nothing greater than

a careless remark about Stalin to a tattletale neighbor. There is hardly a Russian family today that managed to escape this tragic fate. Almost every one of them had a father or a husband or a son or a cousin who "sat"—the Russian euphemism for serving a term, generally unwarranted, in the camps. That is why *One Day,* the first book about this black page of the Stalin era ever to appear in the Soviet Union, has had such a profound impact on the Russian people. By its brevity and simple power, it forces a Russian reader to remember the days of Stalin.

Many Russians do not want to remember: the victims of Stalinist injustice find it too painful; and the accomplices find it too shattering—especially now, after several years of relative normalcy. But there are others—[Nikita] Khrushchev among them—who want Russia to remember. Although Solzhenitsyn is undoubtedly a writer with bold views, it is important to note that his novel was published at this time because it suited Khrushchev's domestic policy. Its unstated but obvious message—the devastating impact of Stalinism on ordinary Russians—fits neatly into the pattern of Khrushchev's continuing attack against Stalin's abuses. (pp. 5-6)

Even without this official encouragement, the book would have been a sensation in Russia—not only because of its sensitive subject but also because of its literary merit. *One Day* represents no literary innovation. Its form and style are conventional, following the nineteenth-century Russian tradition of the "social protest" novel. But it tells a story about little people trapped in a merciless political machine in a way that lifts it high above the level of the average Soviet "man-loves-tractor" school of literature.

Solzhenitsyn's language is direct and powerful, reminding some Russian critics of the young [Fedor] Dostoevsky, who, in his *Notes from Underground*, managed to convey a unique impression of nineteenth-century Russia through the eyes and thoughts of a man holed up in a basement. Using this same effective literary device—seeing and understanding the world through the eyes and mind of the leading character—Solzhenitsyn presents an unadorned and starkly disturbing picture of life in a Russian concentration camp. He traces one day in Ivan's life, from reveille to lights-out. He never intrudes in Ivan's story, and the reader quickly identifies with Ivan the man and Ivan the prisoner. (pp. 7-8)

Solzhenitsyn conveys the power and drama of prison life in a style marked by understatement. (p. 9)

It is difficult to imagine Khrushchev endorsing a different kind of literary sensation—for example, one in which the main character openly denounces the Communist Party itself, rather than Stalin, for the evils of the labor camps. It is certainly a step toward internal liberalization when a cutting attack such as Solzhenitsyn's can be published in Moscow; but Russia still has a long way to go before *Doctor Zhivago*s can be published and freely discussed. (p. 11)

> Marvin L. Kalb, "Introduction" (1962), in One Day in the Life of Ivan Denisovich *by Alexander Solzhenitsyn, translated by Ralph Parker (translation copyright © 1963 by E. P. Dutton & Co., Inc., New York, and Victor Gollancz, Ltd., London; reprinted by permission of the publisher, E. P. Dutton, Inc.), Dutton, 1963, pp. 5-11.*

ALEXANDER TVARDOVSKY

The raw material of life which serves as a basis for A. Solzhenitsyn's [*One Day in the Life of Ivan Denisovich*] is unusual in Soviet literature. It carries within itself an echo of the painful features in our development related to the cult of personality that has been debunked and repudiated by the Party. . . . (p. 13)

One Day in the Life of Ivan Denisovich is not a document in the sense of being a memoir, nor is it notes or reminiscences of the author's personal experiences, although only such personal experiences could lend this story its sense of genuine authenticity. This is a work of art and it is by virtue of the artistic interpretation of this material from life that it is a witness of special value, a document of an art which up to now had seemed to have few possibilities.

The reader will not find in A. Solzhenitsyn's story an all-encompassing portrayal of that historic period which is particularly marked by the bitter memory of the year 1937. The content of *One Day* is naturally limited in time and place of action and the horizons of the main hero of the story. But in the writing of A. Solzhenitsyn, who here enters the literary scene for the first time, one day in the life of the camp prisoner, Ivan Denisovich Shukhov, develops into a picture which gives extraordinary vitality and fidelity to the truthfulness of its human characters. Herein above all lies the uncommon power of the work to impress. The reader can visualize for himself many of the people depicted here in the tragic role of camp inmates

in other situations—at the front or at postwar construction sites. They are the same people who by the will of circumstance have been put to severe physical and moral tests under special and extreme conditions.

In this story there is no deliberate concentration of terrible facts of the cruelty and arbitrariness that were the result of the violation of Soviet legality. The author chose instead to portray only one of the most ordinary of days in the life at camp from reveille to retreat. Nevertheless this "ordinary" day cannot but arouse in the heart of the reader a bitter feeling of pain for the fate of the people who, from the pages of this story, rise up before us so alive and so near. Yet the unquestionable victory of the artist lies in the fact that the bitterness and the pain have nothing in common with a feeling of hopeless depression. On the contrary, the impression left by this work is so extraordinary in its unvarnished and difficult truth that it somehow frees the soul of the burden of things unsaid that needed to be said and at the same time it strengthens one's manly and lofty feelings. (pp. 13-15)

One Day is alive and distinctive in its very everyday ordinariness and outward unassumingness; it is least of all concerned with itself and is therefore full of an inner dignity and force. (p. 15)

> *Alexander Tvardovsky, in his foreword to* One Day in the Life of Ivan Denisovich *by Alexander Solzhenitsyn, translated by Ralph Parker (translation copyright © 1963 by E. P. Dutton & Co., Inc., New York, and Victor Gollancz, Ltd., London; reprinted by permission of the publisher, E. P. Dutton, Inc.), Dutton, 1963, pp. 13-15.*

SIDNEY MONAS

One Day in the Life of Ivan Denisovich happens to be a masterpiece, but not exactly festive. . . .

On one level it is an account of a prison; on another, a parable of life anywhere in Stalin's Russia. (p. 118)

[Solzhenitsyn] spent eight years in concentration camps. . . .

This is not, however, a book carried off by force of personal involvement alone, an amateur's book. I have read many accounts of concentration camps, Nazi and Soviet, all of them horrifying, some of them acute in their understanding of the role of the camps in totalitarian society and in their observations on the behavior of guards and inmates. Yet none of these accounts has the immediacy, the direct quality of an experience lived, that distinguishes Solzhenitsyn's book. Dostoevsky's *Notes from the House of the Dead* immediately suggests itself as an apt comparison. But even that great parable of life as a prison, beside *One Day*, seems a little intellectualized, a little contrived.

Prison, for those who are innocently there, assaults the will to survive and that minimal, basic sense of worth on which the will to survive depends. If the prisoner is to live through conditions of the utmost physical hardship (and *to* what? sentences in the concentration camps were indeterminate), conditions which force him into a constant and terrifying awareness of his own fragility, he must keep his identity when for everyone else he is a mere number. The concentration camp is ironically named, for its inmate is forced to concentrate, not merely on his soul, but on that frightening dependence of the soul on the bowels. The most meager events become fraught with significance.

Solzhenitsyn conveys all this in a style heavy with camp jargon, but clear, controlled, terse, understated and completely transparent, as though there were no obstacle between the reader and the life represented. The terrifying logic of the body's rebellion against hardship is contrasted with the terrifying absurdity of the camp's routine.

There is no expression of horror or amazement, no attempt at analysis or explanation. Ivan Denisovich Shukhov has been in the camp ten years. Conditions are what they are. He scrounges for food and protects himself against the cold. . . . He does not try to understand his presence in the camp. (p. 119)

There are no atrocities, no acts of heroism. Ivan Denisovich himself could not be more ordinary. Yet everything he does, thinks or sees is invested with an enormous pathos. . . . (p. 120)

Sidney Monas, "Ehrenburg's Life, Solzhenitsyn's Day," in The Hudson Review *(copyright © 1963 by The Hudson Review, Inc.; reprinted by permission), Vol. XVI, No. 1, Spring, 1963, pp. 112-21.**

GEORG LUKÁCS

The central problem of socialist realism today is to come to terms critically with the Stalin era. Naturally this is the major task of all socialist ideology. Here I will confine myself to the field of literature. If socialist realism—which in consequence of the Stalinist period became at times a disdainful term of abuse, even in the socialist countries—desires to regain the level it had reached in the nineteen-twenties, then it must rediscover the way to depict contemporary man as he actually is. However, this way necessarily leads through a faithful portrayal of the Stalinist decades with all their inhumanities. Against this, the sectarian bureaucrats raise the objection that one should not rake up the past, but only describe the present. The past is said to be done, already completely outmoded, vanished from the present. Such a claim is not only untrue—the way in which it is presented demonstrates the still extremely influential presence of the Stalinist cultural bureaucracy—but it is also completely meaningless. (pp. 10-11)

Without uncovering the past . . . there is no discovery of the present. Solzhenitsyn's *One Day in the Life of Ivan Denisovich* is a significant overture to this process of literary rediscovery of the self in the socialist present.

The point here is not—at least not primarily—the horrors of the Stalin era, of the concentration camps, etc. This theme has existed for some time in Western literature. Moreover, since the XXth Congress placed a critique of the Stalinist period on its agenda, these horrors have lost their initial shock effect, above all in the socialist countries. Solzhenitsyn's achievement consists in the literary transformation of an uneventful day in a typical camp into a symbol of a past which has not yet been overcome, nor has it been portrayed artistically. Although the camps epitomize one extreme of the Stalin era, the author has made his skilful grey monochrome of camp life into a symbol of everyday life under Stalin. He was successful in this precisely because he posed the artistic question: what demands has this era made on man? Who has proved himself as a human being? Who has salvaged his human dignity and integrity? Who has held his own—and how? Who has retained his essential humanity? Where was this humanity twisted, broken, destroyed? His rigorous limitation to the immediate camp life permits Solzhenitsyn to pose the question simultaneously in quite general and quite concrete terms. The constantly changing

political and social alternatives which life places before free human beings are in the nature of the case eliminated, but resistance or collapse are treated so directly in terms of concrete being or non-being of living people that every solitary decision is raised to the level of a true-to-life generalization and typification.

The entire composition, the details of which we will discuss later, serves this purpose. The slice of everyday camp life already described, as the central figure stresses at the end, presents a "good" day in camp life. And in fact nothing unusual, no special atrocity occurs on that day. We see the normal order of the camp and its inmates' typical reactions based on that order. In this way the typical problems can be sketched firmly, and it is left to the reader's imagination to visualize the effects on the characters of even greater tribulations. This almost ascetic concentration on essentials is matched exactly by the extreme economy of presentation. Of the outer world only the elements indispensable for their effect on the inner working of man are shown; of the emotional world of man only those reactions which are directly connected with their human substance in immediately comprehensible ways—and he is most sparing even with these. Thus this work—which is not even symbolically conceived—can exert a strong symbolic effect; thus the problems of everyday life in the Stalinist world—even though they have nothing immediately in common with camp life—are commented on implicitly in this description.

Even this extremely abstract synopsis of Solzhenitsyn's work shows that stylistically it is a story, a novella, and not a novel (however short), despite his efforts to achieve the greatest possible completeness and a mutual complementing of types and fates through concrete description. Solzhenitsyn consciously avoids any perspective. Camp life is represented as a permanent condition; the very few allusions to the expiration of individual terms are kept extremely vague—and the dissolution of the camp does not even appear in daydreams. In the case of the central figure, it is merely stressed that his home has changed very much in the meanwhile, and that he can by no means return to the familiar old world; this too increases the seclusion of the camp. Thus the future is heavily veiled in all directions. What is foreseeable are similar days, better or worse, but not radically different. The past is likewise represented with economy. (pp. 14-15)

The world of socialism today stands on the eve of a renaissance of Marxism, a renaissance whose task it will be not only to eliminate Stalinist distortions and point to the way forward, but above all adequately to encompass the new facts of reality with the old-new methods of genuine Marxism. In literature, socialist realism faces a similar task. . . . In this process of transformation and renewal, which signifies an abrupt departure from the socialist realism of the Stalin era, the role of landmark on the road to the future falls to Solzhenitsyn's story. (pp. 15-16)

Readers have felt this one day of Ivan Denisovich to be a symbol of the Stalin era. Yet there is not a trace of symbolism in Solzhenitsyn's descriptive method. He presents a genuine, realistic slice of life in which no single aspect obtrudes itself simply for effect or exaggerated effect or for any symbolic motive. To be sure, the typical fate, the typical behaviour of millions is concentrated into this slice. This straightforward fidelity to nature in Solzhenitsyn's work has nothing whatever in common with naturalism—either with direct naturalism or the kind brought about with technical refinement. (p. 17)

Solzhenitsyn's tale stands in marked contrast to all the trends within naturalism. We have already discussed the extreme economy of his descriptive method. The consequence of this in his work is that his details are always highly significant. (p. 19)

The detail in Solzhenitsyn's work has a peculiar function which grows out of the nature of his material: it renders conspicuous the suffocating constriction of everyday camp life, its monotony shot through with peril, the never-resting capillary movements, barely sufficient for the preservation of life. Every detail presents an alternative between survival and succumbing, every object is a trigger of a salutary or destructive fate. In this way the adventitious existence of individual objects is inseparably and visibly bound up with the curves of individual fates. Thus the concentrated totality of camp life is evoked with the very greatest economy, the sum and system of this mean, threadbare reality results in a humanly significant symbolic totality which illuminates an important aspect of human life.

On this experimental basis Solzhenitsyn builds a particular form of the novella whose parallels and contrasts with the . . . great modern novellas of the bourgeois world cast light on the historical situation of both. In both groups man struggles against an all-powerful and hostile environment whose cruelty and inhumanity reveal its nature-like essence. In [Joseph] Conrad or [Ernest] Hemingway, this hostile environment is actually nature. (Storm or calm in Conrad; but even where strictly human destinies are at work, as in *The End of the Tether*, growing blind—the cruelty of his own biological nature—is what the old captain has to contend with.) The social nature of human relationships is thrust into the background and often pales to the point of disappearing altogether. Man is set against nature itself; either he must stand up to it relying on his own strength or he must perish. (pp. 20-1)

In Solzhenitsyn's works too, the totality portrayed has nature-like features. (p. 21)

[But survival] or the failure to survive are also seen in directly social terms; even if this is never openly stated, they refer to a future real life, to a life in freedom among other free men. Of course contained in this is also a "nature-like" element of immediate physical survival or immediate physical destruction, but the dominant factor is objectively the social one. (pp. 21-2)

This leads back to the symbolic effect of Solzhenitsyn's story: it results, implicitly, in a concentrated prelude to the approaching artistic debate with the Stalinist period in which such slices of life did in fact symbolize everyday reality. This was a prelude to the portrayal of the present, of the world of the people who—directly or indirectly, actively or passively, strengthened or broken—have passed through this "school" [of human education], and whose present-day lives and activities were formed in it. Herein lies the paradoxical character of Solzhenitsyn's literary position. His laconic expression, his refraining from any allusion that would point beyond the immediacy of camp life nevertheless sketches in the central human and moral problems without which contemporary man would be objectively impossible and subjectively incomprehensible. Precisely in its concentrated, economical reserve, this immediate, extremely limited slice of life is an overture to the great literature of the future. (pp. 22-3)

Georg Lukács, "Solzhenitsyn: 'One Day in the Life of Ivan Denisovich'" (1964), in his Solzhenitsyn, *translated by William David Graf (translation copy-right* The Merlin Press, 1970; *originally published under a different title in his* Solschenizyn, *Luchterhand, 1970),* Merlin Press, 1970 *(and reprinted by* The MIT Press, 1971), *7-33.*

LEONID RZHEVSKY

The writer's craft begins with his language.

Solzhenitsyn is undoubtedly an innovator in the field of language. His efforts to enliven the modern Russian language with the freshness and richness of popular speech, to soften the congealed bookishness, lifelessness, and platitudes in the literary language with living conversational elements, which are themselves based on the honesty and directness characteristic of common speech—these are his innovations. (p. 19)

Sincerity—merciless, courageous, and honest—is the essence of Solzhenitsyn's literary creations, a sincerity in which poetic and ethical elements merge into one definitive feature of his style and craft.

But sincerity demands the categorical rejection of clichés and hypocrisy, which had become rooted in the language of the literature contemporary to Solzhenitsyn. He had to find an equivalent mode of expression for sincerity. (pp. 23-4)

There was a need to find if not a "sting" (even though Solzhenitsyn uses satire), then a language which, as [Nikolai] Gogol wrote "tore itself from the very heart, . . . seethed and surged," a language with a peculiar inner brilliance, clarity, and warmth—spontaneous and more sincere.

Solzhenitsyn discovered this language by turning to the colloquial conversational language, in an original oral *počvennost'*—just as some time ago Dostoevsky after four years in prison found a redefinition of his views in *počvennost'*. (p. 24)

Solzhenitsyn's turning to popular speech is not of course confined to its vocabulary. It includes the entire syntactic-stylistic system, rhythm, sound—the entire structure of oral expression. From popular speech Solzhenitsyn borrows its spontaneity, its emotional overtones, its figurative expression. [Alexander] Pushkin once said that [Nikolai] Karamzin restored freedom to the Russian language, "turning it towards the living sources of popular speech." No comparison intended, one can say something close to this about Solzhenitsyn: his verbal innovation makes him the creator of a new style of modern prose. (p. 25)

[Speaking of] the innovation in Solzhenitsyn's stylistic manner as a whole, one unusually important literary device must be mentioned. This very device significantly creates that spontaneous, sincere, and intelligible tonality of oral communication that is perceived as the chief distinction of Solzhenitsyn's prose.

When introducing a character's speech, Solzhenitsyn almost plunges his story into the speech pattern of that character. This device slightly resembles the form of "indirect speech," but in Solzhenitsyn's case the device is structurally quite different. It is not simply two or three of the character's words or expressions that sprinkle the author's words, but a kind of organic fusion between the language of the author and that of the dialogue. This is based on the fact that both of these languages (the author's and the character's) are inspired by the folk elements of speech. (pp. 29-30)

In Solzhenitsyn's books there are quite a few characters who from time to time become the author's focal point. Thus a very interesting and original polyphony of narrative speech emerges. (p. 30)

> *Leonid Rzhevsky, in his* Solzhenitsyn: Creator & Heroic Deed, *translated by Sonja Miller (translation copyright ©1978 by Leonid Rzhevsky; reprinted by permission of the author; originally published as his* Tvorets i Podvig, *Possev-Verlag, Frankfurt am Main, Federal Republic of Germany, 1972), The University of Alabama Press, 1978, 124 p.*

CHRISTOPHER MOODY

Alexander Solzhenitsyn has been described by different critics as both an old-fashioned writer and a genuine innovator. Paradoxically, both of these views are correct. In the early 1930s, when his fame in the Soviet Union was at its height, the official aesthetic of socialist realism, with its emphasis on optimism and education, was beginning to give way to a more candid and exploratory approach to Soviet life. Writers were being admitted to those dark areas of social and political evil which they had hitherto been obliged to by-pass. They were acquiring the freedom to question the assumptions which they had been expected to affirm. They were gaining the right to express private thoughts and exercise their consciences on moral and ethical problems, independently of official ideology. In other words, Soviet literature was quietly repossessing the traditions of critical realism bequeathed to it by its nineteenth-century forebears. (p. 28)

Solzhenitsyn's stories were, by common consent of those who liked them and those who did not, the most important contributions to this new literature of 'exposure'.

The difference between most of the new writers and the Stalin Prize novelists of the 1940s and 1950s was not as great as some Western critics imagined it to be. For one thing, they were still 'social command' writers, responding to, and ultimately controlled by, current Party dictates. They differed mainly in the degree of truthfulness with which they approached their subjects. And it was not only the critical stance and moral seriousness of the nineteenth-century novelists which inspired them. They also followed their manner of writing. They were still realists. The basic principles which governed the new wave of Soviet writing were still those of socialist realism, demanding a direct and rational treatment of surface reality. Cut off for nearly forty years from their own modernist movement and virtually unaffected by Western experimental developments, few Soviet writers knew anything different. They had been brought up on their own national classics and remained heavily in debt to them. (p. 29)

Solzhenitsyn's artistic range is not as restricted as that of most of his contemporaries. Indeed, it is an indication of the breadth of his literary education that critics have been able to detect in his work the influence of nearly all the major nineteenth-century prose styles and writers. But he, too, has responded only to the realist traditions. Solzhenitsyn owes nothing [to] the Symbolists or later modernist trends. . . . There is little *arrière-plan* of meanings in his work, no distorted chronology, and sparing use of such figurative devices as metaphor and simile. Although he is said to be well read in foreign literatures, no critic has found this reflected in his own writing. On the contrary, Solzhenitsyn is intensely, even aggressively Russian in his outlook. . . . He frequently exhibits an almost mystical

reverence for old Russian customs; his ideas reveal the inspiration of such nineteenth-century Russian thinkers as [Vladimir] Solovyov and Dostoevsky; and in the language of his books as well as in his own speech, he deliberately eschews the numerous foreign borrowings which have, he considers, disfigured the Russian language during the last two and a half centuries. (pp. 29-30)

Solzhenitsyn may be regarded as an old-fashioned writer in the sense that nearly all contemporary Soviet writers are old-fashioned. He has made no contribution to the advancement of the novel or the short story as a genre. Nor does he display the influence of those who have been advancing it in the West. That he is a significant figure in world literature, worthy of a Nobel Prize, is due to the fact that, besides being acutely sensitive to the issues confronting his native land, his themes and his treatment of them transcend local conditions and have a universal relevance in the latter half of the twentieth century. Perhaps most important of all, he is a remarkable artist with words and, at his best, an impeccable stylist. (p. 30)

One Day was published exactly one hundred years after Dostoevsky's *Notes from the House of the Dead,* in which he described his own experience during a four-year term in a Siberian penal colony. The coincidence is fortuitous, but a comparison is instructive on both literary and historical grounds. The similarities between the two works are in fact superficial, but both writers had the avowed aim of exposing, as never before, the camps to the Russian public. Dostoevsky chose to present a broad view of the camps, through the eyes of an aristocrat, an intellectual who could rationalise his experience and philosophise about crime. Solzhenitsyn's hero Shukhov, however, is a simple peasant, innocent of any crime and able to comprehend little beyond the day-to-day problems of survival. Although, unlike Dostoevsky's story, ***One Day*** is not a first person narration, the point of view and even the language are consistently Shukhov's. Solzhenitsyn himself does not interpose extended comment, and thus the deeper thoughts of the more sophisticated prisoners are left unexpressed. Such questions as how communists and other thinking people explain to themselves the injustice which has condemned them to the camps, or how they have become reconciled to a twenty-five-year sentence, are left unanswered. There is no explicit generalisation in ***One Day***. There are no politically motivated characters and Solzhenitsyn refrains from any overt political statement on the burning issues raised by the very existence of the camps. (p. 31)

Solzhenitsyn does not build up his characters or the episodes in their lives from an accumulation of minute detail. The reader gains only a vague idea of Shukhov's appearance. Solzhenitsyn's technique of evoking a whole impression by means of a few carefully selected, emotionally neutral, facts, is Chekhovian. And the artistry with which he accomplishes his effects is comparable with [Anton] Chekhov's. He needs no more than two laconic sentences to convey fully the sensation of the cold and the early morning at the beginning of the story: 'The intermittent sounds barely penetrated the window panes on which the frost lay two fingers thick, and they ended almost as soon as they had begun. It was cold outside, and the campguard was reluctant to go on beating out the reveille for long.' . . . And the simple remark 'the snow creaked under their boots' conjures up the entire image of the freezing snow-covered camp.

As Solzhenitsyn takes his little hero through every stage of an ordinary camp day, he builds up a comprehensive account of all the essential activities in a *zek*'s life and a picture of the camp itself and of its inmates, both prisoners and guards. Without distorting the simple central thread of the action he employs, though sparingly, the common devices of realistic narrative to give breadth and perspective to his picture. (p. 32)

Comment is generally confined to Shukhov's own frequently interposed remarks, which although reflecting a limited point of view, nevertheless impart a personal eye-witness quality to the story. Solzhenitsyn, in fact, rarely intrudes at all in the capacity of omniscient author. (p. 33)

There is not a trace of romanticism in Solzhenitsyn's description of Ivan Denisovich's day. (p. 34)

It is unlikely that had Solzhenitsyn tried to emulate Dostoevsky, and elaborated his own opinions, *One Day* would have been published. But it was an artistic choice which led him to describe the undramatic experience of such an ordinary hero (he has even been called an anti-hero) as Shukhov. Shukhov is a simple, even naive, man whose perception of the world is purely physical. He does not search for meanings or draw conclusions. He doesn't possess the mental equipment to do so. He happily accepts the folklore explanation of the behaviour of the moon and stars. His one cry of protest is very muted by comparison with Dostoevsky's: 'You see, Alesha,' Shukhov explained to him, 'somehow it works out all right for you: Jesus Christ wanted you to sit in prison and so you are—sitting there for His sake. But for whose sake am I here? Because we weren't ready for war in forty-one? For that? But was it *my* fault?' (pp. 34-5)

The choice of detail in Solzhenitsyn's picture of the labor camp is effectively Shukhov's. Things are presented as they appear to him. The language is colourful and rhythmical because it reflects the cadences of Shukhov's peasant speech, with frequent use of aphorism. But there is no sentimentality in the descriptions, no lyricism such as [Ivan] Turgenev might have brought even to this harsh scene. The narrative is confined to the unembellished facts, conveyed dispassionately in spare prose with an elliptical economy of words. [Georg] Lukács has called this method 'non interpretative description'. It is a measure of Solzhenitsyn's self-discipline and control over his medium that he is able to maintain a consistent tone and pace from the first page of his story until the last.

Soviet critics complained at the apparent absence of indignation and civic protest in *One Day*. They were unable to appreciate that Solzhenitsyn's restraint, his unpretentious and even artless simplicity, were a more eloquent protest than emotionally charged rhetoric, that his artistic detachment disguised a passionate engagement. (pp. 34-5)

A Soviet reader of *One Day* might identify many practices familiar in Soviet life—the callous attitude of authority and the need to outwit it (the worksheets), the self-seeking, scrounging and working on the side. A comparison between human behaviour in the camps and in *Matryona's Home*, which depicts life beyond the wire, is revealing. Solzhenitsyn shows how many of the negative features of camp life have their exact counterparts among the inhabitants of an ordinary Russian village. There one finds a heartless collective-farm management, the authorities confiscating the peasants' fuel, falsified school records, unsympathetic medical services and a general lust for private gain. This comparison of a place of confinement with the outside world is a favourite source of irony with Solzhenitsyn. Shukhov wonders whether life will be any better if he

is released and several times in *One Day*, Solzhenitsyn underlines the paradox that in general, it will not be. (pp. 37-8)

By choosing peasants as the central protagonists of his first two stories, Solzhenitsyn was upholding one of the enduring traditions of Russian literature. For the aristocrats of the nineteenth century, the peasant held an almost mystical fascination. He was idealised by [Leo] Tolstoy, Turgenev and [Nikolai] Nekrasov in their search for truth, as the repository of natural wisdom and simplicity. It was this wishful image which Chekhov and [I. A.] Bunin attempted to correct with their ruthlessly objective glimpses of peasant life at the end of the century. Soviet critics were quick to see both these views reflected in Solzhenitsyn's stories. (p. 39)

There is a superficial resemblance between Shukhov and Tolstoy's Platon Karataev, skilfully sewing a shirt for the French corporal. Karataev 'knew how to do everything, he was always busy', while Shukhov 'knew how to manage everything.' But the parallel between the two is confined to their external characteristics. In Shukhov there is nothing of 'the unfathomable, rounded, eternal personification of the spirit of simplicity and truth' which Pierre thought he had found in Karataev. Nor is Shukhov in any meaningful sense a religious believer. Solzhenitsyn does not idealise Shukhov or hold him up as the embodiment of some abstract principle. It happens to be Shukhov's nature that he is simple and submissive. Such qualities were cultivated as the essential prerequisites for survival even by more assertive characters like Tiurin. It is the lesson of the camps which Buinovsky must learn. And Shukhov's practical wisdom and adroitness are no more than refinements in a man accustomed to earn his living by the use of his hands. (p. 40)

The portrait which emerges of Ivan Shukhov, is of an unexceptional little man, wielding the practical guile native to the Russian peasant, simple but not innocent, sly but not dishonest, insulted but not a weakling, and submissive but not degraded. A man with sufficient force of character not only to preserve his primitive moral sense and feelings of common decency but even to benefit in some small way from his ordeal. Shukhov commands pity but also respect. Those who complained that his behaviour in camp was unworthy of a Soviet man were doing him less than justice. But if they meant that none of the qualities exhibited by Shukhov and the other prisoners were particularly attributable to their Soviet or socialist upbringing they were right. . . . In *One Day*, there is no suggestion that the virtues which enabled the prisoners to endure came from anywhere but their own inner being. As in *The First Circle* and *Cancer Ward* each prisoner is ultimately thrown back on his own personal resources. . . . In *One Day*, the only character to invoke the name of communism is the Captain, a camp novice. And he must learn to sublimate his ideals, not parade them. If there is a doctrine which fortifies the prisoners in the camp, it is the camp itself. It is the camp which has toughened Shukhov just as it made Kostoglotov in *Cancer Ward* 'sharp as an axe.' The hardy Tiurin is also 'a true son of Gulag'. It was this lack of clear ideological orientation which finally disqualified *One Day* from official favour when a more orthodox interpretation of socialist realism began to be applied after Khrushchev's departure. (pp. 42-3)

Solzhenitsyn depicts his characters *in extremis*, but the situations in which they find themselves are all such as Solzhenitsyn has himself experienced or witnessed. The dilemmas they face are the fundamental problems of human existence, in *One Day* how to live, and in *Cancer Ward* how to die. But Solzhenitsyn's characters are also social beings and he identifies and examines the values which govern human relationships. Political values are ultimately irrelevant. . . . Nor is it possible to discover a metaphysical dimension to Solzhenitsyn's thinking, beyond the occasional glimpses of mystical intuition. Christianity, although it attacts Solzhenitsyn's sympathy, is practically irrelevant too. (p. 48)

The destinies of all Solzhenitsyn's characters are in their different ways subject to the interplay of good and evil, which are in turn the product of the presence or the absence of conscience and justice; conscience at a personal level and justice as the expression of the communal conscience. The all-pervading theme of Solzhenitsyn's work at every level is the quest for justice. (p. 49)

Christopher Moody, in his Solzhenitsyn *(copyright © Christopher Moody 1973; reprinted by permission of the author), Oliver & Boyd, 1973, 184 p.*

GARY KERN

The structural framework of **One Day** is obvious: Ivan Denisovich is described from the time of waking to the time of falling asleep. We follow him step by step through his daily routine, witnessing all of his tasks, experiences, and thoughts. We see the sun rise and set, the sky change colors, the moon rise, the stars come out. We notice also that the day falls into three periods (before work, work, after work), and that this imparts a certain "natural" symmetry to the piece: Alyoshka says a prayer in the beginning and at the end, Ivan hides his bread in his mattress in the morning and recovers it at night, Buinovsky is sentenced in the morning and taken to the cooler at night, the men march to work and back from work. The list could be extended, because the parallels are not simply natural but composed. The author places them on each side of the work period, making the period the epicenter of the novella with parallels radiating out from it. Such is the overall scheme of the piece.

Within this scheme, the descriptions are scattered. With very few exceptions, no person or procedure is described to completion in any one passage. Of course, this may happen in any novel, but here the technique is extreme: essential features of a character's appearance, history, and personality are cut up and strewn throughout the work in no easily comprehended manner. We have to keep a record of the characters, and even then we cannot visualize them well on a first reading. Such scattering produces an unusual esthetic effect: pleasure is postponed, and confusion and discomfort are stimulated. The parcelling of information has another effect: the units of this prison society cannot be comprehended until they are totalled up. And only when they are totalled up can the moral argument become known. It seems likely, in the Soviet context, that this would serve the purpose of baffling potential censors, but it also corresponds to the impressions of an initiate (the reader) into the labor camp.

The devices of chronology, parallelism, and scattering may be observed in the description of the prison camp's conditions. Again, the chronology is most prominent, since it is simply added to bit by bit. A schedule emerges: 5 AM—reveille, 6:30 AM—roll call, 8 AM to 6 PM—work (shortened winter hours), 9 PM—roll call, 10 PM—lights out. Parallels fall into place: Ivan's personal tasks—before the morning and evening mess; mess—before the roll calls; friskings and countings—before and after work, etc. But the scattering of information, in this case, acquires something like a reverse movement, a subtrac-

tion. The units usually do not add up in a cumulative way, but rather negate what has been given. It works out something like this: the author first states a condition (e.g., the food ration) along with its rule (e.g., the time to eat) or its limitation (e.g., weight). The reader assumes that this is poor, but at least it's something. Then the author discloses a further limitation (e.g., cuts in the ration) and then still another limitation, so that the reader is left with impoverished poverty. It's like a bitter joke with not just one punchline but a whole series of "toppers." (pp. 5-6)

[For example, the] zeks do not have to work in blizzards, but the days lost are made up on Sundays. Sundays are considered days off, but when there are five in one month the zeks must work on two of them. And on the Sundays off they are made to do odd jobs—clean-ups, inspections, check-ups. In other words, there are no days off. (p. 7)

The effect of these ironic reductions, naturally, is to increase the feeling of deprivation. In a sense, the entire day of Ivan Denisovich is a bitter joke: it is an excellent day for him, with a number of little successes and unexpected rewards. But if this is an excellent day, the reader can surmise what is a terrible one. And, as the author jokes in conclusion, there are 3653 days in the 10-year term—with the three extra days for the leap years. (p. 8)

Thus the details of the prison camp's conditions are not thrust upon the reader in a way that will shock him, but rather in a way that will cause him to think—to add, subtract, and compare. He will not receive much immediate esthetic pleasure (there are other deterrents, such as the camp lingo), but if he goes on thinking and if he calculates, the impression will deepen. The effect of **One Day** is much greater after the first reading. (pp. 8-9)

The curse words are the novella's most shocking element, unprecedented in the entire history of Russian literature: "you fu-u-ck off! Stu-u-pid prick! Cheater! Dirty squealer! Filthy slime! Rotten hunk of meat! . . . Bastard! Puke! Rotten turd!" . . . The sheer abundance of these vulgarisms may blind us to the fact that everyone uses them and uses them against everyone else. However, if we follow the word *gad* (snake, vermin, pest, skunk, stinker, stoolie, disgusting person) through the novella, we shall see that such is the case. . . . [Everyone] curses and is cursed: the curses create an environment of brutalization.

This brutalization is underscored by the metaphorical scheme of the work, based almost entirely on animal images. The zeks in a convoy are driven like a flock (*stado*) of sheep . . . ; they are "a black flock of zeks" . . . , a flock of calves. . . . They are driven by guards with dogs . . . and are themselves often compared to dogs. . . . There are other derogatory animal images: the hateful Der is a bloodsucker and a pig's snout . . . , the rapacious storeroom guard is a rat . . . , and the frightened Moldavian is a little mouse. . . . (pp. 10-11)

All of these examples emphasize their subhuman condition. . . .

The last motif we will consider is that of the law (*zakon*). The zeks, almost to a man imprisoned on false charges, must master new concepts of the law. Ivan recalls the words of an old camp wolf: "The law here, boys, is the taiga. But people can still live here. In a camp the guy who croaks is the guy who licks bowls, the guy who depends on the infirmary, and the guy who raps at the door of the godfather (i.e., squeals to the security officer . . .)''. This law serves Ivan well; he knows what to avoid. And so long as he follows the rules of the camp, he will earn his rightful (*zakonnaya*) gruel. . . . However, the law of this camp is not always the same as the Soviet law. . . . And neither law is reliable: when your sentence is up, you may get another. ''The law can be twisted any way you like,'' thinks Ivan. . . . But the Soviet law is omnipotent. (p. 12)

The motifs examined here, by their consistency and their wealth of detail, establish the social and economic conditions of the camp. Within these conditions, the zeks must struggle for physical and spiritual survival. They must satisfy the laws of the camp to survive; they have a degree of choice in their method of survival. The more they oppress or deprive others to survive, the more they degrade themselves. The more they achieve self-sufficiency and even helpfulness to others, the more they gain dignity and self-respect. (pp. 12-13)

Ivan does not work for immediate rewards. To demonstrate this point, Solzhenitsyn constructs a situation free from any utilitarian benefit, one which epitomizes Ivan's spiritual contradiction to the pressures of his environment. This occurs at the end of the work period. Ivan is finishing his fifth row of bricks, the activity of the entire gang has converged on this work, but they must immediately run back for the counting. Tyurin tells them to dump the remaining mortar (''Ekh, who cares about that shit!'' . . .), but Ivan does not want to waste it. He tells the others to turn in their tools and leave him to finish the row with his extra trowel—Klevshin can hand him the bricks. Everyone leaves but the two. Ivan finishes up, and Klevshin runs down the ladder with the hod. Ivan is alone. There is not a moment to spare, no work to be done, and yet he remains:

> But Shukhov, even if the convoy guards should set the dogs after him now, ran back over the floor, took a look. Not bad. Now he ran right up—and along the wall, from the left, from the right. Heh, an eye like a water-level! Even! The hand hasn't gotten too old. . . .

This scene may be called an epiphany—the moment in which Ivan's nature and the argument of the book are most fully revealed. For this single, dangerous moment of self-congratulation, Ivan has had to oppose all obstacles, work superbly, and again endanger his life. No one gives him this moment; no one would even permit him to take it. He must seize it for himself as the most precious moment of his day—the moment which preserves his spirit and consequently his self. (pp. 22-3)

This does not make Ivan a so-called ''individualist,'' an alienated being with a hateful and superior attitude toward others. Although he has a singular role in the novella, the features of his portrayal mark him as an ''ordinary'' man, a simple honest worker. . . . In effect, by this portrayal of an ordinary man, Solzhenitsyn has turned the Marxist formula upside-down: it is not Ivan or anyone like him who is alienated from this society, but the society which is alienated from him. His is the positive force, enacted regardless of circumstances. It is the society, not Ivan, who has failed its human potential. It is this society which experiences ''false consciousness.''

Therefore it is quite natural that Ivan escapes subjective alienation entirely. One writer has listed five states of subjective, or psychological alienation: powerlessness, meaninglessness, normlessness, isolation, and self-estrangement. Ivan does not experience any one of these states. He feels powerful when working on the wall; he finds meaning in a good job; he makes his own norms despite chaotic conditions; he overcomes isolation by directing the gang, and he realizes himself in his self-congratulation. And yet, let us remember, he is in a concentration camp, working under extreme duress. How does he achieve this miracle of non-alienation? Is this only a fictional dream?

I think the answer lies in the insufficiency of Marx's theory—which, after all, is no less a fictional construct than Solzhenitsyn's novella. Marx assumes that man makes himself in his work and that this work is essentially practical, utilitarian. In this view of man's ''praxis,'' Marx eliminated man's spiritual needs: he did not conceive of artful performance as a human need apart from any material benefit; he neglected the realm of man's thought and activity which requires no utilitarian motive; he forgot about the sense of wonder and joy which comes from no calculation. Surely man is alienated by systems of exploitation, but he alienates himself when he accedes to pure practicality. A man makes himself by the totality of his physical and spiritual life, and anything that prevents its expression may alienate him. Complete alienation would be total external control. Solzhenitsyn, in his portrait of Ivan Denisovich, and especially in his description of Ivan's *celebration of labor*, reminds us of man's power to realize himself, whatever his circumstance.

Let us consider another aspect of alienation—religious alienation. From a Marxist viewpoint, it would be natural for Ivan to seek escape from his oppressive circumstance by the projection of his own thwarted potential onto an imaginary omnipotent being and the expectation of a reward in a fictional afterlife. But Ivan refuses this escape: he cannot believe in heaven and hell—no doubt, because the prison camp is hell enough. . . . Yet he does believe in God. . . . From [certain] episodes we may conclude that Ivan has a basic faith in God and calls on him when in danger, but does not rely on religion to help him through the normal course of the day. It is his work and his services which perform this function, as well as his camp cunning. In this sense, Ivan is not alienated—estranged from his environment or himself—by his belief in God. For him, God helps those who help themselves.

We must remember, however, that **One Day** was originally a Soviet text. It would have been completely impossible to draw a hero as a Christian believer and expect to publish the work. Ivan's superstitions, criticisms of the priest, and irony about prayers fall well within acceptable Soviet practice and serve to undercut his religious beliefs. They also seem to refute the utterances of his bunk-mate, Alyoshka. It is only from other works of Solzhenitsyn that we can understand that Alyoshka's message is very close to the heart of the author: ''If you will keep your faith and say to the mountain—move!—it will move.'' . . . Needless to say, the author rejects outright the whole notion of religious alienation. He is closer to the traditional, pre-Marxist understanding of alienation as separation from God.

But a problem still lingers. Even if we accept the argument that Ivan does not alienate himself in his labor and does not seek escape in religion, can we overlook the fact that he benefits the system? He is treated as a slave and yet returns quality work. Whatever the value to his self-esteem as a skilled worker, he produces for a state which robs and degrades him. In a sense, he perpetuates the system by overcoming its injustices. This would seem to be self-alienating, in the sense that it helps those who mean to crush Ivan. On the other hand, a renunciation of his work-ethic would diminish his own self-esteem and alienate him from his labor. Ivan appears to be caught in a paradoxical situation, where the only choice is self-alienation.

This is by no means a semantic problem, but a real and vital issue to anyone attempting to survive in conditions of coercive labor. (pp. 25-8)

[Ivan] cannot opt for the alienation of sloppy work or sabotage, and his benefit to the present system is absolved by his benefit to future generations. As a result, Ivan does not entirely alienate himself by benefiting the system. When good work is stolen from you, in some instances you can regard it as a gift. On his return to the camp, Ivan is frisked in the future public square, where someday, as he imagines, there will be parades.

Therefore, Ivan benefits the system and in this sense alienates himself, but he also benefits future generations and so absolves himself. Does his tactic not help to undermine the system and turn it from bad to good? Does he not subvert the system by refusing to crack, by proving himself each day? These are questions which admit no final answers. We know only that Ivan does the best he can do; he creates the most freedom he can within a coercive system. (p. 29)

> *Gary Kern, "Ivan the Worker," in* Modern Fiction Studies *(© 1977 by Purdue Research Foundation, West Lafayette, Indiana 47907, U.S.A.), Vol. 23, No. 1, Spring, 1977, pp. 5-30.*

PHILIP RAHV

A completely authentic account of life in the forced-labor camps under Stalin, [*One Day in the Life of Ivan Denisovich*] is cast in a fictional form superbly adapted to its subject. Its narrative tone and method, relying on the selective accumulation of minute factual particulars, finely controls the powerful emotional content, never getting out of hand, never descending to rhetorical presentation or to any sort of preaching and moralizing. (p. 232)

The experience recorded in *One Day* no doubt parallels [Solzhenitsyn's] own, but he is not the novel's protagonist. That role, from first page to last, is reserved for the simple village workman, Ivan Denisovich Shukhov, who has no head for politics or any kind of "learned conversation." He is a wonderful creation, exhibiting certain traits that are new as well as traits deeply rooted in the Russian literary tradition. The figure in that tradition he most reminds me of is Tolstoy's Platon Karatayev. But there is also a significant difference between them. For Karatayev, standing somewhat apart from the other characters in *War and Peace,* who were portrayed with surpassing realism, is in the main a mythic figure, an abstraction of Christian goodness, while Shukhov, in no way dependent on religious doctrine or precept, is invested with a goodness that is altogether credible, altogether imbedded in the actual. He fills in every crevice of his own nature, without appeal to higher powers, or utopian and ambiguous dreams of saintliness.

As all ideologies are alien to Shukhov, so none can ruin him. Neither hero nor saint, existing in an environment where the only time the prisoners are not marched out to work in the early mornings is when the thermometer goes down to forty-two degrees below zero, he yields neither to hope nor despair but depends for survival on his own largely unconscious and invulnerable humanity. Though in no way exceptional, he is the unbeatable human being whom the regime can at any time destroy but never convert nor make over in its own image, thus giving the lie to [George] Orwell's nightmare of total demoralization in 1984. Humble yet extremely resourceful in small ways, a man whose self-respect demands that he do his work properly and even joyfully, Shukhov has been "walking this earth for forty years. He'd lost half his teeth and was getting bald. He'd never given or taken a bribe from anybody, and he hadn't learned that trick in the camp either." . . . And why was Shukhov put in a concentration camp? He had escaped from a German prisoners-of-war cage and upon returning to his own lines found himself accused of treason. Though guiltless, he was forced to give evidence against himself: "The way he figured, it was very simple. If he didn't sign, he was as good as buried. But if he did, he'd still go on living for a while. So he signed." Shukhov's fate is the essence of the Stalinist terror-system.

However, the way in which the author chiefly succeeds in his characterization of Shukhov is not by harping on his innocence or putting any kind of political gloss on his ordeal but by depicting him throughout as a person in his own right—not merely a victim and least of all a symptom but always a person, even when ill, starving, and freezing. The secondary characters, such as Alyoshka the Baptist and Tyurin the boss of the work squad, are portrayed with equal responsiveness to their personal qualities. Now it is precisely this newly won and truly existential personalization of vision, so long outlawed in the Communist theory and practice of literature, which surprises and impresses us most in *One Day.* As a novel it is not, in my view, the "great work of art" that some people say it is; its scale is too small for that. But it is a very fine book in which not a false note is struck. (pp. 232-33)

> *Philip Rahv, in an extract from "Two Subversive Russians" (originally published in a slightly different form as "House of the Dead?" in* The New York Review of Books, *Vol. I, No. 1, 1963), in his* Essays on Literature and Politics: 1932-1972, *edited by Arabel J. Porter and Andrew J. Dvosin (Copyright © 1978 by Arabel J. Porter and Andrew J. Dvosin. Reprinted by permission of the Estate of Philip Rahv), Houghton Mifflin, 1978, pp. 232-34.*

EDWARD E. ERICSON, JR.

Early reviews [of *One Day in the Life of Ivan Denisovich*], even in the most orthodox of Soviet sources, were overwhelmingly favorable. *Pravda* remarked on Solzhenitsyn's "profound humanity, because people remained people even in an atmosphere of mockery." Zhores Medvedev, who was later to write *Ten Years after Ivan Denisovich,* emphasized the artistry of the novel. But most responses, in keeping with Khrushchev's motivation for allowing publication, centered on the book's political significance. Importantly, most Western reviews also emphasized the political dimension; the book's publication was viewed as an event illustrating the increasing thaw within the Soviet Union, thus auguring well for future East-West relations. So from the beginning Solzhenitsyn's work was viewed through the wrong lens.

A political approach does not penetrate to the heart of *One Day.* The novel is not, in its essence, about Stalin's inhumanity to man; it is about man's inhumanity to man. Stalin is not some aberration in an otherwise smooth progression of humaneness in history. The evil of the human heart is a universal theme: this is Solzhenitsyn's approach.

Perhaps never has the political appropriation of a work of art by state authorities backfired so dramatically and totally as in the case of *One Day*. Once having been catapulted into the limelight of world attention, Solzhenitsyn would not be silent. Now he had a platform, and his sense of duty urged him on. Khrushchev had let out of the bottle a genie which his successors could not put back in. (pp. 35-6)

Despite the fact that some critics consider *One Day in the Life of Ivan Denisovich* the best piece Solzhenitsyn ever has written, he seems to have felt that he was still at a kind of apprenticeship stage. (p. 36)

If *One Day* was part of a period of apprenticeship, it stands near the end of that period. The author was about to embark on those long novels of his maturity. And this novel is a piece of such consummate artistry that to call it the work of an apprentice seems ultimately inadequate. Had Solzhenitsyn written nothing after *One Day,* his reputation as an author of note would have been secure. With this short novel he had arrived, whatever his further ambitions. His literary situation at this stage is interestingly parallel to that of [John] Milton: had Milton written nothing after "Lycidas," he would still be an anthologized poet; but he went on to *Paradise Lost, Paradise Regained,* and *Samson Agonistes.*

The novel depicts a single day in the life of a simple peasant, Ivan Denisovich Shukhov, who has been unjustly thrown into a prison camp. While we see many of his fellow zeks, the focus remains rather tightly fixed on Shukhov. (pp. 36-7)

Solzhenitsyn shows great respect for his title character. . . . The clearest sign of respect is in the mere naming of the hero. The combination of given name (Ivan—significantly, the most common of Russian names) and patronymic (Denisovich—son of Denis) is a polite form most readily used for persons of high station or intrinsic importance. Solzhenitsyn applies it to a simple peasant. The author deems his character worthy of the respect usually reserved for "important" people.

The most memorable technical trait of *One Day* is its understatement. The novel depicts horrors which might well elicit white-hot anger—or, if not that, a kind of sentimentality over the suffering of innocents. The novel makes no such explicit claim on our emotions. Rather, it describes the day of Shukhov and his fellows as not too bad, as almost a good day. (p. 37)

As is typical of Solzhenitsyn's works, *One Day* shows us suffering humanity *in extremis*. But because of Shukhov's limited perspective, suffering here is depicted as primarily physical. . . . [Still], the suffering of the body takes on a metaphysical dimension—through the mediation of the author, who can go beyond the ken of the main character. The inhospitably cold climate becomes a symbol of the inhumane setting for human life in general, and the reader comes away feeling moral outrage rather than mere vicarious physical pain. When a medical assistant finds the feverish Ivan not ill enough to exempt from the day's work, the author queries, "How can you expect a man who's warm to understand a man who's cold?" It is one of those microcosmic remarks from which ray out large symbolic meanings. The warm man is the one open to perpetrating injustice. Solzhenitsyn devotes his life to making warm men feel the cold. (pp. 38-9)

The arbitrariness of the life of the zeks is all-governing. The guards are not allowed to recognize the diversity and unpredictability of life; only two zeks may be sick per day; only two letters per zek may be mailed out per year. "Soviet power,"

Solzhenitsyn satirizes, has decreed that the sun stands highest in the sky not at noon but an hour later. Being dehumanized entails being denatured.

Given the collectivist ideology of the Soviets, an ironic effect of their prison regimen is that it breaks down the sense of human solidarity. Solzhenitsyn, who speaks consistently on behalf of individual dignity, always speaks with equal consistency on behalf of human solidarity. So he laments that in a zek's mind it is another zek who is one's worst enemy. Occasional displays of solidarity, which should be a natural outflowing of the zeks' common humanity and their shared plight, usually succumb to the camp attitude, "You croak today but *I* mean to live till tomorrow."

Nevertheless, however much the grim environment and the need to adapt somehow to it may reduce the basic humanity of the zeks, such pressures can never eradicate the human essence. To be sure, Shukhov is constantly and instinctively concerned with self-preservation. When he was accused, absurdly, of high treason for surrendering to the Germans with the intention of betraying his country, he coolly calculated: "If he didn't sign, he was as good as buried. But if he did, he'd still go on living a while. So he signed." . . . But there is more. A man will assert his wants as well as his needs. For instance, he wants to smoke; it is an unnecessary small pleasure, but he will find a way. Then, there is satisfaction in work. Ivan works poorly only when given meaningless tasks. Laying bricks well pleases him, even if in prison. Constructive work brings out in him the ennobling quality of self-validation through creative effort. . . . The camp system would grant him the status only of an animal, a workhorse. It is up to him to insist, however inarticulately, that he is more than that, that he is spiritual, too, and not only material.

The greatest of all human capacities demonstrated by Ivan Denisovich is his capacity to absorb pain and yet to endure with at least some vestiges of humanity intact. This enduring humanity is one of Solzhenitsyn's most important themes, and it is his great consolation as he weeps for mankind. The best efforts to reduce humanity to the level of the animal are never entirely successful; and, by definition, a process of dehumanization which is not totally successful is a failure: some humanity remains. (pp. 39-40)

Ivan Denisovich's attitude toward religion is much like Matryona's in **"Matryona's House."** Both show little interest in formal religion, either ecclesiastical or credal. Yet both breathe a kind of natural piety, and religious references pepper their everyday talk. Ivan's ready response to his tribulations in prison is, "As long as you're in the barracks—praise the Lord and sit tight." (pp. 40-1)

Ivan's faith is naive and unreasoned, and includes a sizeable dose of superstition. He believes in God: "When He thunders up there in the sky, how can you help believe in Him?" . . . Atheistic rulers may curtail the growth of religion "The Russians didn't even remember which hand you cross yourself with," . . . but it is beyond their power to shake the faith of the Matryonas and Ivans.

While Solzhenitsyn clearly admires Ivan's faith, Ivan does not represent his religious ideal. A character who comes closer to doing so is Alyosha (or Alyoshka) the Baptist. It is intriguing that Solzhenitsyn, who has returned to his ancestral Russian Orthodox Church, gives the deepest religious sentiments in this novel to a character who is hostile to Orthodoxy. . . . The fact is that the author is simply being faithful to the quality of the persons whom he knew in the camps. In addition, Solzhenitsyn's handling of Alyosha shows that his primary religious concerns are not with the particularities of Orthodoxy but with those central aspects of the Christian faith held in common by all Christians.

The climactic conversation of the novel is between Ivan and Alyosha. Alyosha's prominence here has been prepared for by frequent earlier depictions of him as a good worker and kind person. Alyosha's faith does not incapacitate him for survival. On the contrary, it is a source of the inner strength that so often characterizes Solzhenitsyn's little heroes, the small people who somehow are able to withstand everything that a soulless bureaucracy inflicts on them. (pp. 41-2)

The climactic conversation begins when Alyosha, reading his Bible, overhears Ivan's routine, day's end prayer and says, "Look here, Ivan Denisovich, your soul wants to pray to God, so why don't you let it have its way?" . . . But Ivan, for whom camp experience is a microcosm of all of life, doubts the efficacy of praying. . . . (p. 42)

Ivan does not want to be misunderstood. Although disillusioned by a bad priest, he insists that he believes in God. "But what I don't believe in is Heaven and Hell." . . . The afterlife, after all, is not open to empirical verification, as are monthly new moons and falling stars. When he prays, he says, it will be for something real, like release from prison. This attitude scandalizes Alyosha, who consciously suffers for Christ. He counters, "What do you want your freedom for? What faith you have left will be choked in thorns. Rejoice that you are in prison. Here you can think of your soul." . . . This spiritual focus, which Solzhenitsyn elsewhere asserts in his own person, affects Ivan: "Alyosha was talking the truth. You could tell by his voice and his eyes he was glad to be in prison." . . .

Solzhenitsyn admires the Baptist's ability to give a positive meaning to his prison experience; Alyosha is the only character in the novel who can do so. Ivan admires that, too. But it just will not do for him. (p. 43)

Ivan and Alyosha are brothers under the skin. Both are models of humanity in the midst of inhumanity; both care for others as much as for themselves. Ivan represents the best possible from a man without an articulated faith; a man can act very well without faith in a transcendent reality. Such a one is in no position, however, to explain the mystery of suffering. This crucial matter, which Ivan deeply needs, is what Alyosha can add. Without Alyosha, the novel would be much diminished. Ivan, as good as he is, needs Alyosha's insight to complete the picture. (pp. 43-4)

Edward E. Ericson, Jr., in his Solzhenitsyn: The Moral Vision *(copyright © 1980 by Wm. B. Eerdmans Publishing Co.; used by permission), Eerdmans, 1980, 239 p.*

Rosemary Sutcliff

1920-

English novelist.

Sutcliff is one of England's foremost writers of historical fiction for young adults. She is especially noted for her ability to bring history alive for her readers. Whether she is retelling a traditional legend or chronicling actual historical events, her expertise at realistically conveying a particular sense of time and place enables young adults to see history as a "continuous process of which they themselves are a part." By focusing as much on the dramatic external action as on the inner life of the protagonist struggling to pass into maturity, Sutcliff succeeds in creating historical fiction relevant to contemporary youth.

Perhaps the best known of her works is her trilogy about the rise and fall of Roman Britain consisting of *The Eagle of the Ninth, The Silver Branch,* and *The Lantern Bearers.* Sutcliff won the Carnegie Medal award in 1960 for *The Lantern Bearers.* Her other trilogy, depicting Arthurian legends, was recently completed with the publication of *The Road to Camlann.*

(See also *Contemporary Authors,* Vols. 5-8, rev. ed. and *Something about the Author,* Vol. 6.)

LOUISE S. BECHTEL

"Simon" is the longest and best written of Miss Sutcliff's books, appealing more to readers over twelve. It pictures England of the Civil War in 1640, focusing on the campaign in Devon and the west country, showing how a teen-age boy came to take his share in the fighting, and what happened to his friendship for his neighbor and friend who fought with the Royalists. The battles, the journeys, the narrow escapes, are done with vigorous realism. The setting, always vivid with this writer, is most memorable here, for this is country she knows well. There is romance, for the older girls who like "costume" stories, but chiefly it is for those boys who love old battles with youth as hero whether or not the war is one they have met already in history.

Louise S. Bechtel, in her review of "Simon," in New York Herald Tribune Book Review (© I.H.T. Corporation), May 16, 1954, p. 21.

NAOMI LEWIS

One of the most interesting writers of children's historical novels today is Rosemary Sutcliff; her new book, *The Eagle of the Ninth,* seems to me a work of real distinction. It concerns a young Roman's first few years in Britain, and his journey into the Caledonian north, after a wound has put him out of Army service, to see if any trace can be found of the mysteriously vanished Ninth Legion. Second-century Britain may not seem an enticing period; yet Miss Sutcliff writes so evocatively and well, and with so skilful an avoidance of pitfalls, that I would recommend her book not only to older boys and girls but to any adult who likes, in reading, the serious historical story, the enigma and the quest.

Courtesy of Murray Pollinger Literary Agency

Naomi Lewis, "The Young Supernaturalist," in The New Statesman & Nation (© 1954 The Statesman & Nation Publishing Co. Ltd.), Vol. XLVIII, No. 1230, October 2, 1954, p. 404.*

LAVINIA R. DAVIS

When the young centurion Marcus Aquila took over his first command in a frontier garrison in ancient Britain his heart was set on a long and glorious military career. He was also determined to find out about his father who had been lost ten years earlier when the Ninth Legion had mysteriously vanished on its way to quell a rebellion in North Britain. A crippling wound in his first battle put an early end to Marcus' military career. How he achieved his second ambition, even to restoring the Eagle, the bronze standard of the lost Ninth, and clearing his father's name, makes an exceptionally fine historical novel ["The Eagle of the Ninth"].

The two main characters, Marcus and his former slave, a Briton named Esca, are well drawn. Their adventures, whether in battle, on the lonely hills, or in the forbidden temple where the Eagle was finally found, are invariably exciting and credible.

Lavinia R. Davis, "In Ancient Britain," in The New York Times Book Review (© 1955 by The New York

Times Company; reprinted by permission), January 9, 1955, p. 24.

LOUISE S. BECHTEL

With each of her historical stories for older boys and girls, [Rosemary Sutcliff] writes better. Her "**Eagle of the Ninth**" was a stirring recreation of life in Roman Britain. Keeping to the same period, she now tells [in "**Outcast**"] an almost equally thrilling tale of a Roman boy brought up as a Briton, then rejected by his tribe, made a slave when he goes back to Rome, and . . . sent to the galleys. The plot finally takes him back to Britain, the land he truly loves, to find his father, his freedom, and his own true love.

The background has startling reality. Those "good readers" over twelve, who appreciate as fine and as long a story as this, will be absorbed, not only in the exciting action, the battles and escapes, but in the remarkably interesting details of life in Rome, of the sufferings of the galley slaves, of the Roman engineering that drained the Romney Marshes.

Louise S. Bechtel, in her review of "Outcast," in New York Herald Tribune Book Review (© I.H.T. Corporation; reprinted by permission), February 26, 1956, p. 9.

ELIZABETH HODGES

[In "**The Shield Ring**"] Rosemary Sutcliff tells the story of young Bjorn, unsure of his own courage but determined to prove himself worthy of the noble traditions of his people [the Vikings]. How he does this, and how his friendship for the Saxon girl, Frytha, gradually changes into love, makes an absorbing tale, peopled with three-dimensional characters and filled with stirring events. Admittedly, the author's precise care in recreating a period and place, her use of archaic words such as garth and schoon, her concern with character motivations make for slow and sometimes difficult reading. Nevertheless, this is a well-written, richly colored historical novel which can be warmly recommended. . . .

Elizabeth Hodges, "The Defenders," in The New York Times Book Review (© 1957 by The New York Times Company; reprinted by permission), March 17, 1957, p. 40.

MARGARET SHERWOOD LIBBY

A deeply stirring historical tale, one like "**The Shield Ring**," is rare. The characters are forceful, sympathetic and interesting. There is a startlingly vivid picture of life in hut and Great Hall in a Viking settlement or *steading* among the northern hills and lakes of England in the eleventh century while the Normans harass its borders. . . .

Splendid as was the "**Eagle of the Ninth**," this is finer. The intelligent reader over twelve will be caught by the sweep and power of it and by its wild, poetic atmosphere. It cannot be pigeonholed as just for the "young". . . .

Margaret Sherwood Libby, in her review of "The Shield Ring," in New York Herald Tribune Book Review (© I.H.T. Corporation; reprinted by permission), May 12, 1957, p. 8.

J. O. PRESTWICH

Rosemary Sutcliff has won a reputation as a writer of historical novels for children which always show care and sensitivity and sometimes distinction. Her recent work has been rather sombre in tone and over ornate in style. **The Silver Branch**, a story of Roman Britain, is a sequel to **The Eagle of the Ninth**, and shows Miss Sutcliff at her best. The time is the close of the third century: the theme the recovery of Britain by Rome after the reign of Carausius and the coup of Allectus. . . . It is a carefully constructed book with a firm dramatic theme, many admirable descriptive passages and vivid characters. (pp. 658-59)

J. O. Prestwich, in a review of "The Silver Branch," in New Statesman (© 1957 The Statesman & Nation Publishing Co. Ltd.), Vol. LIV, No. 1392, November 16, 1957, pp. 658-59.

LAVINIA R. DAVIS

As in an earlier book, "**The Eagle of the Ninth**," Rosemary Sutcliff paints here a colorful and convincing picture of Roman Britain ["**The Silver Branch**"], this time in the latter part of the third century. The story begins during the rule of Carausius, and centers on Justin, newly come to Albion to take up his post of junior surgeon. Uneasily aware of intrigue and unrest about him, Justin and his kinsman Flavius, a young centurion, think at first the turmoil is centered in the conflict between Carausius and his corrupt, self-seeking Finance Minister. But when the Emperor is murdered and the two are forced into hiding, they realize that the whole hope of a civilized and united Britain is at stake. It is only after two years of exile and of adventures with an outcast native tribesman, an ex-gladiator and other members of the loyal underground that Justin and Flavius see Roman justice and order emerge triumphant.

All the characters—the shy young surgeon, his dashing companion—even the Emperor's jester, whose branch of silver bells gives the book its title—are entirely credible. The detailed but never redundant descriptions create a brilliant background for a vigorous and unusually moving narrative.

Lavinia R. Davis, "Turmoil in Britain," in The New York Times Book Review (© 1958 by The New York Times Company; reprinted by permission), June 29, 1958, p. 18.

ERIC HOOD

A bronze-age boy had to kill a wolf single-handed before he could wear the warrior's scarlet, the mantle of manhood. For Drem, the test was doubly difficult because of a crippled right arm. . . .

This tale of the testing of Drem [**Warrior Scarlet**] is a splendid excursion into the past, a fine reconstruction of prehistoric rituals. Set in southern England, the novel is evocative in mood and revealing in detail. The courage and determination of the handicapped hero are implied through actions that speak louder than words. Young people will read the author's message and be grateful for the absence of patronizing explanations and sentimentality. Style and taste lift this novel well above the average tale of adventure. It is smooth stuff, showing a steady hand on the narrative and an eye for color.

Eric Hood, "Mantle of Manhood," in The New York Times Book Review (© 1959 by The New York Times

Company; reprinted by permission), January 4, 1959, p. 26.

THE TIMES LITERARY SUPPLEMENT

Miss Sutcliff's *The Lantern Bearers* ends, it is true, with a victory, but a victory in a war which, the reader is aware throughout the story, is inevitably lost. For this is a story of the decline of Roman Britain. Miss Sutcliff has written most sensitively in two previous books about other aspects of this theme. In each the ultimate disaster has lain like a shadow across the action. In the Place of Life, deep in the mists of Caledonia, Marcus the Centurion had felt it (in *The Eagle of the Ninth*), and his descendant Flavius had read it in the flames of Calleva (in *The Silver Branch*). Now Aquila tastes the last bitterness of humiliation when he deserts the Eagles to stay in Britain when the last Legions pull out. The three novels belong together. Together they make perhaps the most interesting achievement of this remarkable writer.

It is well known that Miss Sutcliff owes her initial inspiration to [Rudyard] Kipling. There is much of Kipling in *The Lantern Bearers,* in the idea, in the sweep of the story, in—it must be confessed—certain stylistic mannerisms which from time to time stick out their uncomfortable spikes. Miss Sutcliff has so many talents and so much promise that one must wish that she would eschew Fine Writing. She handles her narrative with superb skill, particularly in scenes of violent action, but holds up the movement too often with passages of mannered prose. It is a hint of immaturity in a writer who has matured almost beyond recognition in the nine years since *The Queen Elizabeth Story.* There is increasing evidence in her recent books, and most of all in *The Lantern Bearers,* that she is ceasing to be a writer for children. The complex characters, the difficult motives, if not the toughness of the action, belong more obviously to writing for adults.

Miss Sutcliff is at her best in the invention of vividly seen, memorable episodes, in the management of colour and of sharp contrasts of light and dark. Aquila's "defiance against the dark" when, as the last Legions sail from Rutupiae, he lights the beacon in the Pharos, is a fine example of her love for the bold larger-than-life gesture. The first sight of the little boy who is to be Artos the Bear, the historic Arthur, is more subtle, and not less memorable. It is in such touches, as much as in those more spectacular set pieces, the battle scenes, that she shows her growing mastery.

"Old Unhappy Far-Off Things," in The Times Literary Supplement *(© Times Newspapers Ltd. (London) 1959; reproduced from* The Times Literary Supplement *by permission), No. 3014, December 4, 1959, p. vii.**

MARGARET SHERWOOD LIBBY

"We are the Lantern Bearers, my friend; for us to keep something burning, to carry what light we can forward into the darkness and the wind."—so, at the end of the latest and one of the finest of Rosemary Sutcliff's historical novels ["**The Lantern Bearers**"], does Ambrosius, who had held off the Saxon hordes for a time, speak to his young aid Aquila, adding that "morning always grows again out of the darkness, though maybe not for the people who saw the sun go down." Aquila, the hero of the story, had let his troop sail without him when the Romans abandoned Briton forever, and great had been his

subsequent sufferings. . . . His story, exciting, thoughtful, mature, the story of a man's steadfast adherence to a difficult choice that brought both bitterness and satisfaction, is for young people ready for adult books. The characterizations are vivid, varied and convincing, the setting a superb recreation of an unfamiliar period in English history, and the plot, both interesting and plausible, has its significance heightened by the recurring symbolism of light in dark days, first introduced in an early chapter when Aquila, having let his fellows sail for Gaul, impulsively lights once more the great beacon light of Rutupiae which would be quenched forever after the departure of the legions.

Margaret Sherwood Libby, in her review of "The Lantern Bearers," in New York Herald Tribune Book Review *(© I.H.T. Corporation; reprinted by permission), February 14, 1960, p. 11.*

C. S. BENNETT

[*Knight's Fee* is] a splendid rendering of upper-middle-class values. It is set in that Kiplingesque region of English history where Saxon and Norman are being made one. The hero is a lowly Celtic hound boy, in touch with the surviving magic of earth and folk. . . . [His] loyal steadfastness (and the accidents of fate) finally win him victory over the class barrier and inheritance of the knight's fee. The feudal background is vivid; the political intrigue murky. Miss Sutcliff's strength is her almost poetic feeling for people and places and things; but this can sometimes betray her into fine writing. (p. 742)

C. S. Bennett, "Varlets, Nabobs, Governesses," in New Statesman *(© 1960 The Statesman & Nation Publishing Co. Ltd.), Vol. LX, No. 1548, November 12, 1960, pp. 742, 744.**

THE TIMES LITERARY SUPPLEMENT

Rosemary Sutcliff is a master of the concrete detail which brings home to us that our ancestors, though men like ourselves, lived in very different conditions. . . . [*Knight's Fee*] which tells how a poor dog-boy rose by faithful service to knighthood under King Henry I. . . .

The reader is told what people ate and at what times, as well as what they wore. The characters are not deeply explored, but the sketches of chivalrous knights and turbulent barons are adequate for the purpose of an exciting story.

In fact this would be a perfect introduction to the Middle Ages, from which older children might learn all they need of its daily life, if one great medieval preoccupation had not been completely omitted. We are told almost nothing about religion or the Church. . . .

Miss Sutcliff does not suggest that her Saxons and Normans were agnostics; she supposes that most of them practised a pagan fertility cult. On the last page she writes flatly: "William Rufus belonged to the Old Faith", as though it were a fact universally admitted by historians. But the clerks who knew William Rufus personally wrote him down a wicked Christian or perhaps an atheist. Thus to state as a fact the fancies of modern anthropologists is to incur the danger of misleading untutored minds, even in a work of fiction.

"The Blanket of the Dark," in The Times Literary Supplement *(© Times Newspapers Ltd. (London) 1960; reproduced from* The Times Literary Supple-

ment *by permission), No. 3065, November 25, 1960, p. xv.**

CAROLYN HOROVITZ

Rosemary Sutcliff's *The Eagle of the Ninth* combines the presentation of the historic era of the Roman occupation of Britain with an acute sense of place. A feeling of belonging to a certain landscape becomes a vital part of the plot structure. She portrays remarkably the conflict between the Celtic tribal customs and the Roman way of imposing its own civilization wherever it went. The two elements are finally welded into an inseparable unity by one force of nature—the country itself. . . . Place works its will, not only on the buildings of the Romans but on the characters of the Romans as well. The hero of the story, Marcus, is at the end of the novel free to go where he wishes, back to the loved land of his childhood. But he elects to stay; Britain has become his home. This conclusion is no mere noble decision but the inevitable result of the strong sense of place inherent in this novel from the beginning. By the time the novel is finished, the reader even feels homesick, homesick not only for a certain essence of country and climate but for another time.

While the action in the plot is dignified and utterly credible, it moves to a climactic chase which crests onward to the conclusion. There is never any question about the appropriateness of this time and place as background; the characters are drawn out of the past; they behave in a way consistent with their times and still are utterly comprehensible. Much about the past is illuminated by this novel, particularly the relationship between Celt and Roman, the dynamics of two civilizations clashing. Used in a masterly, symbolic way to emphasize the underlying theme is the incident of the wolf cub and his allegiance, as a free animal, to his master. The author points out, through the wolf cub and also the Celtic freedman, that loyalty, allegiance, and friendship have value only when freely rendered. This idea is presented not as a moral but as dramatic development within the plot. If the plot is to have meaning it must be in the deepening of our understanding of man's relationship to man. That this presentation of the past does so with sharpness and acuity is not only a tribute to the writer's scholarship, her careful proportioning of a good story with believable characters, but is also a measure of her philosophical depth. She brings a degree of greatness to the feeling of love that a man from another place, a man of a conquering people, can have for a country not his birthplace, a people not his own. (pp. 142-43)

> *Carolyn Horovitz, "Dimensions in Time, a Critical View of Historical Fiction for Children" (copyright, 1962, by The Horn Book, Inc., Boston; reprinted by permission of the author), in* The Horn Book Magazine, *Vol. XXXVIII, No. 3, June, 1962 (and reprinted in* Horn Book Reflections: On Children's Books and Reading, Selected from Eighteen Years of The Horn Book Magazine—1949-1966, *edited by Elinor Whitney Field, Horn Book, 1969, pp. 137-52).**

MARGARET MEEK

[Rosemary Sutcliff's] first four books are for younger children: *The Chronicles of Robin Hood* (1950), *The Queen Elizabeth Story* (1950), *The Armourer's House* (1951), and *Brother Dusty-Feet* (1952). They are stories of imaginative fancy set in an historical period which provides the framework, but the fairies

and the magic are more important than the kings and queens. Into each story the author reweaves some of the legends which are links with her own childhood delight. (p. 16)

Rosemary Sutcliff's historical novels show her strong attachment to Kipling. The writing of both authors is shot through with the spirit of the English countryside and the sense of its continuity which links the present with the past. To Kipling, the fact that the Sussex he loved was the same land the Bronze Age villagers knew, the Saxons ploughed and the Normans conquered was to be wondered at. This wonder gives saga, legend and myth modern significance. Miss Sutcliff shares this feeling, and her readers respond to her enthusiasm. Without some communication of feeling for the past the historical novel is lost. When Randal in *Knight's Fee* sits on the hill with the shepherd (the timeless occupation) and handles the flint axe-head which the initiated reader knows was, perhaps, that of Drem in *Warrior Scarlet,* we are made to feel that continuity is important. (p. 27)

This sense of place and continuity can be seen in Alison Uttley's *A Traveller in Time* (1939). It is a historical novel with a double time illusion in which the heroine seems to live both in the present and in the past. Although Rosemary Sutcliff has never used this device in a book, one feels that part of her success comes from her ability to do what Miss Uttley demonstrates, to talk 'with people who lived alongside but out of time, moving through a life parallel to my own existence'. (pp. 27-8)

These elements of continuity in place and time, together with a much greater involvement in a series of historical events, came out strongly in *Simon* (1953), Rosemary Sutcliff's first important historical novel. (p. 28)

Although *Simon* does not deal with the central issues of the [Civil War], . . . idealism is the dominant theme. It is a significant book in Miss Sutcliff's development as a writer, for it showed her where her strength lay. It does what she demands history should do, brings to vivid life the actuality of the last campaign of the Civil War which was fought in the combes and across the farmlands of Somerset and North Devon. Miss Sutcliff immersed herself totally in the details and emerged with, for her, a new kind of novel, where pageant is replaced by theme, and all the story-teller's skill is challenged by battles, sieges, troop movements, documentation of personages and events, and the need to account for action in terms of motive as well as circumstance.

Simon is the Roundhead, Amias the Cavalier. Their childhood friendship is wrecked by the war and their conflicting loyalties. No one who had read the early novels would have foreseen that Miss Sutcliff could describe the beating of a deserter, the battle of Torrington and the harsh discomfort of the sick and wounded so evocatively that the waste, pain, misery, glory and excitement of war are held together in a plot compellingly detailed and yet fast-moving. (pp. 28-9)

Many an author has described a battle with exactness, but Miss Sutcliff's method of settling on the felt details that remain in the mind, driven along the nerves of the hero, is even more convincing than the historian's account. The intensity of the inner life of the author, at which the earlier books hinted, has been projected into the teeming outside world of the Civil War. Her sympathies are shared, but her bias is towards the Roundheads. To grasp the quality and personal involvement, one can compare *Simon* with [Geoffrey] Trease's *The Grey Adventurer* which is equally skilful but much more detached. Sometimes

Miss Sutcliff is carried away by the pressure of detail, but the line of action is held taut throughout the book. (pp. 30-1)

In *Simon* Miss Sutcliff leaves the sheltered world of childhood and enters the realm where public excellence is tested and recognized. Her heroes are separated by differing sympathies in the war, but they are true to what they believe, so that their friendship is sealed at the very moment they fight each other. The theme is for a reader older than any Miss Sutcliff had in mind before this. Loyalty and devotion, the conflicts and complexities of war, are beyond the immediate grasp of the undertens but within the compass of the twelve-year-old who is beginning to recognize these very conflicts in his own terms. Both author and reader are identified with the hero's development, and both have grown in stature as a result.

As this happens, the conscious narrative tone of the earlier books falls away. A greater breadth of vocabulary and longer sentences are possible. With *Simon*, Rosemary Sutcliff becomes a writer for the child who is a discriminating reader, one who asks that his books should extend his experience and stretch his ability to the full.

Not only is *Simon* longer, more complex, and more strongly felt than the earlier books, it also shows a new depth of characterization and a totally unexpected skill in dialogue based on the rhythms of local Devonshire speech. . . . With new vigour and conviction Rosemary Sutcliff moved away from the tempting delight of historical tales for the younger reader and the threat of escapism. Now real history, the kind that demands not only passion and zeal in the telling but also painstaking checking of detail and careful assimilation of the spirit of an age, had superseded the lure of legend. Looking back, one can see *Simon* as a turning point in Rosemary Sutcliff's career. It has all the seeds of promise that flowered later. Interestingly, the hero is robust and finely-balanced within himself from the start. He has depths of sense and sensibility unusual in adventure story heroes; he suffers anguish from his divided loyalties, but keeps faith above all, and comes through by virtue of a sound constitution and an even temper. None of the heroes who follow begin with these advantages. (pp. 31-2)

Rosemary Sutcliff has written four books which deal with [the twilight period when the Romans were evacuating Britain]: *The Eagle of the Ninth* (1954), *The Silver Branch* (1957), *The Lantern Bearers* (1959) and *Outcast* (1955). The first three form a sequence in that they deal with the fortunes of the family of Marcus Flavius Aquila, the centurion who came to Britain in the hope of finding what happened to his father's legion, the legendary Ninth, when it marched beyond the Wall and was never heard of again. *Outcast* is about the life of a slave in the galleys which brought the legions to Britain. *Dawn Wind* (1961) is the chronological sequel to *The Lantern Bearers*. It links the books of the first Roman period with the coming of the Christian missionaries to Kent. (pp. 34-5)

These books enjoy widespread popularity both here and abroad and have contributed most to Miss Sutcliff's reputation. (pp. 34-5)

[The] vital spark of Rosemary Sutcliff's books, from *The Eagle of the Ninth* onwards, is the total imaginative penetration of the historical material. The books seem to be written from the inside, so that the reader's identification with the chief character carries him further into the *felt* life of the time than many other books which are made up of the skilful but detached articulation of the fruits of research. One feels that Rosemary Sutcliff is less concerned to write historical narrative than to reconstruct, in the child's response to her creative imagination, a strong feeling for and involvement with the people of this mist-bound, huddling, winter-dark island at the periods when the invaders came, Romans, Saxons, Norsemen.

This magic has certain recognizable elements; the names of the characters are chosen with a poet's care, the dogs have a central place and are characterized with the loving attention children recognize and approve. The villains, such as Placidus in *The Eagle of the Ninth* and Allectus in *The Silver Branch* are acidly etched, although there is more reliance on traditional enmity and feud than on personal evil to provide the dark side. Episodic characters, singly or in groups, have a miniaturist's clarity of outline. . . . [Her characters] all carry a dignity and heroism that link this series of tales with the legends Miss Sutcliff loves to tell. Indeed, part of the difficulty in evaluating the achievement of these books comes from the thickly woven texture which is as closely wrought as in many adult novels of quality. (pp. 36-7)

Each plot is full of incident and suspense, the construction is taut but supple. Each book has a unified theme, yet they are linked together. (p. 38)

In narrative, *The Eagle of the Ninth* is the most workmanlike; each incident has a bold outline, fire-clear details, and is told with passion and skill. The others cover larger stretches of time and the canvas is more crowded. As the subtlety of plot and theme grows more complex, so the author looks to older readers. (p. 39)

The theme of each book is the light and the dark. The light is what is valued, what is to be saved beyond one's own lifetime. The dark is the threatening destruction that works against it. The heroes are serious young men schooled in the Roman virtues of *pietas* and *gravitas* which demand loyalty to family, country, friend and cause, exactly those things which call out the idealism of adolescents whose inner world is full of this kind of thinking. Marcus goes to look for his father's eagle as an act of piety and also that he may compensate for the loss of his own command. In so doing, he learns other loyalties, to the land of Britain as well as to Rome, to his slave who becomes his friend, and about the nature of loyalty itself, how it grew hollow in the lost legion, how men mistake the true for the false, that honour must be paid for many times, that freedom is not simply manumission. To become adult is to learn these things in different ways. As in *Simon*, public excellence is seen as the extension of private virtues. It is recognized by men of all tribes, by those who move in the darkness beyond the Wall as well as by those to whom duty is the clear call of a military trumpet. This is what the young want to know about in an age when they are faced by equivocal adult standards and general cynicism.

This theme is extended in *The Silver Branch* with increased subtlety, for the creativeness of the Roman peace is now threatened by the wanton destructiveness of the Saxons and the darkness at the heart of those who threaten the order that Rome brought to the barbarians. (pp. 40-1)

The chances of saving the light are no stronger than the little silver branch carried by the Emperor's fool, 'shining drops distilled out of the emptiness'. This may be a partial view of the Pax Romana, but it speaks to the young who are constantly reminded of past glories when these are now so obviously lacking, and who have no firm assurance that their world will emerge from the darkness that threatens it.

The Lantern Bearers is the most closely-woven novel of the trilogy. . . . In it the hero bears within himself the conflict of dark and light, the burden of his time and of himself. When he fires the beacon of Rutupiae light for the last time 'as a defiance against the dark' and goes wilful-missing to stay in Britain, to which he feels he belongs, Aquila is carrying the Roman *virtus* into the next age. At the end of the book he says, 'I wonder if they will remember us at all, these people on the other side of the darkness'. To this theme there is a rich counterpoint of personality and event, motive and action, more intricately interwoven than in any novel so far.

After his thralldom with the Jutes, Aquila's darkness is at his heart, for loyalties betrayed and vengeance sought. All gentleness is shut out. At moments of the greatest turbulence when the darkness is closing round, Aquila realizes that the light men carry within them, which is the only safeguard against the greater darkness of despair, is their concern for each other and what is dear to them. . . . A man may serve a cause so that his public excellence can be recognized, and yet one who remains untouched by family love and warmth for others is still in darkness, for all his *virtus*. The glory that was Rome is no longer; all that remains is an ideal in the hearts of men who have risen above common vengeance, and the races must learn to be at peace together.

This theme is continued in *Dawn Wind*. Owain has more than served his time as a thrall, yet he does not leave the family he has lived with because he made a promise to his master that was more binding than his thrall ring. (pp. 41-3)

This intricacy of theme is kept jewel-clear in all the books by an adept handling of symbolic material, a ritualism which young readers appreciate. It is full of surcharged emotion which need not be uttered: Marcus setting up his little altar to Mithras and sacrificing the bird of carved olive wood, symbolizing his childhood and former life, the Dolphin ring which links the family through the ages, the fish symbol drawn in the ashes of the hearth by the legionary, the tattooed dolphin on Aquila's shoulder, the recurrent symbolism of flowers, herbs, colours, and the ritual return of seasons, blossom and fruit, sowing and sacrifice.

Remembering the gentle cosiness of Miss Sutcliff's early books, one might be surprised to find the uncompromising cruelty of the battles portrayed with equally uncompromising clarity. The white heat of Aquila's controlled emotion in *The Lantern Bearers*, its total rejection of comfort and gentleness, has no precedent in her work. Treachery, hardship, the ferocity of friend and foe are set down with an intensity of imaginative passion, as if the author were concerned to prove the lasting qualities of the virtues that are tried in the fire of conflict. (pp. 43-4)

When we examine [the] particular instances of Miss Sutcliff's craft we see that the effectiveness of the whole, which moves with the speed and sweep of the narrative to the climax of each episode, is nevertheless composed of minute attention to detail: the colour of the sky, the shape of the hills, the mane of a horse, a bowl of apples or words carved on a rock, all are invested with meaning.

In these Roman stories the problem of dialogue has been solved by the invention of timeless cadences in a slightly shifted word order, the surest safeguard against stilted archaism or colloquialism, even though the fall of the phrase is sometimes unreal, or occasionally the modern speaker peeps out. Also the girls, who were not so well-drawn as the boys, have gradually assumed more weight. Ness, Aquila's wife, is a character of quality, whereas Cottia, Marcus's friend, is altogether too babyish. As her characters mature, so does the author's handling of dialogue.

In between the books of the trilogy are three others: *Outcast* (1955), *The Shield Ring* (1956) and *Warrior Scarlet* (1958) and a short story of life on the Roman Wall, *The Bridge Builders*, which although published in 1959 seems from the author's note to have been written before *The Shield Ring* was completed. Although Miss Sutcliff has developed into a story-teller who is at her best in a long narrative, this short sketch has her unmistakable individuality.

Outcast, the story of Beric, can be mentioned here as it has a link with the others discussed in this chapter, and it throws light on an important aspect of the novels. Beric is washed up on the shores of Britain and adopted by a tribe which later casts him out. He is carried off to Rome as a slave. In making a bid for freedom he is recaptured and sent to the galleys where, after unspeakable treatment, he attacks an overseer, is lashed and dropped into the sea for dead. The sea casts him up again, this time on Romney Marsh where he falls into the hands of Justinius, the 'Builder of Roads and Drainer of Marshes', who adopts him as his son. Together they fight the great gale that threatens the dyke and the work to which Justinius's life is dedicated.

This is another fast-moving story, yet the plot depends to a greater extent than usual on coincidence, legitimate as this is, and is more loosely episodic. The two outstanding features are the descriptive reality of the life of a galley slave and the dark misery of the outcast, which anticipates Aquila's torments in *The Lantern Bearers*. Beric belongs nowhere; he has no tribe, his Roman master give him another name, a galley slave has no identity. Finally Justinius seems to have mistaken him for someone else, the son he had never seen.

To the adolescent the theme of 'Who am I?' is a compelling one. In his desire to be accepted for the person he is, to establish his identity in the adult world, to find a role he can play, he identifies himself with the outcast, a part which, for all its misery, he fully understands. The characterization of Beric might well have fallen into sentimentality, but this is avoided. It is debatable, however, whether it avoids altogether an excess of self-laceration that is more than the realistic cruelty conventional in the Roman tales of other writers, notably those of Henry Treece. Adult reviewers have objected to the scenes of lashings, while young people have told Miss Sutcliff that they enjoyed them. They are neither excessive nor distasteful, but they hint at something deeper in the plight of the hero, which the other three Roman books also illustrate.

After his first battle Marcus, in *The Eagle of the Ninth,* endures rough-and-ready doctoring and later penetrating surgery to search his wounds which leave him with a limp and exclude him from regular military service. He undertakes his special mission with a handicap. Justin, in *The Silver Branch* is a disappointment to his father as he is a surgeon, not a fighting man. He stutters and lacks self-assurance in his dealings with people. Aquila, in *The Lantern Bearers,* has withdrawn from close human relationships and is something of a maimed personality. The scar on his brow is the merest outward sign of his inward scars. Beric distrusts all kindness as the result of the treatment he has undergone. . . . (pp. 45-8)

Only in their relationship with others, the ideal companion, the blood brother, the wise man, do these wounds heal. (p. 48)

One feels in reading these books that the inner life of the hero is as important as any outward action. The heroic man is of a certain cast of temper, a mould, a balance, which is no more and no less than we learn in [Homer's] *Iliad* and the tales of Arthur. The conflict of the light and the dark is the stuff of legend in all ages. Miss Sutcliff's artistry is a blend of this realization in her own terms and an instructive personal identification with problems which beset the young, problems of identity, of self-realization. Children see in stories of maimed and hurt children struggles with conscience rather than with the outside world. Extended into adolescence these struggles increase in intensity. . . . As the heroes come to see that one must learn to carry one's scars lightly by acceptance and concern for others, so do the readers.

Being an outcast may mean that one feels rejected, different, but it is also an attitude of mind by which one takes revenge on others. One is less of a person if one is preoccupied with one's own hurts. Only by being involved in something creative, the search for the Eagle, the maintenance of law in a disordered world, the building of a wall against the sea, the farming of the land, does one find oneself.

In *Dawn Wind* one sees that internal battles in England solve fewer and fewer problems. The different tribes and races must learn to live with each other. The last conquest is still to come, but the lesson holds good. (pp. 49-50)

We have seen that Rosemary Sutcliff can not only revivify the twilight period between the age of Imperial Rome and the coming of Christianity, but also create heroes whose standards of values reflect her readers' awareness of the conflict between private conduct and public excellence in a way that extends beyond the limits of formula fiction. In another three books, *The Shield Ring, Warrior Scarlet* and *Knight's Fee,* written in between the Roman stories, Miss Sutcliff tackles the most pressing problem of all: how does one win one's place in the world of men? What are the conditions of acceptance? To a writer like Miss Sutcliff, whose circumstances as a child cut her off from much that other children could take for granted, this question had a special significance. Miss Sutcliff is fully identified with everything she writes, and we have traced her development as a writer in the growing complexity of the themes she has chosen. The books of this chapter highlight three specific 'traces' of importance to an understanding of her work and her personality. They concern the permanence of landscape, which is the Kipling tradition; the settling in England of races or peoples who learn to live together so that their original identity is blended in a new nationality, and the *rite de passage* from youth to manhood, which is, I feel, the central theme.

All three traces are present in *The Shield Ring,* the story about Norsemen who withstood the entry of King William's Norman troops into the Lake District at the making of the Domesday Book. The tribal valour and clan loyalty of the Norsemen formed a 'shield ring' and the Normans were lured up a specially made road that led to nowhere and slaughtered in ambush. From a study of place names and local legend, the author has recreated Lakeland as it was in Jarl Buthar's day, not only as a scholar, but as an artist whose eye can select the details, which, combined with intensity of narration, bring alive the fells, lakes and rock ledges as the tale unfolds. . . . (pp. 51-2)

The landscape in *Warrior Scarlet* is the Sussex Downs, those same hills that Kipling found so full of historical significance.

Warrior Scarlet is set in the Bronze Age, the age of the heroic Golden People. But long before their time an unknown ancient warrior slept under the Hill of Gathering, the Bramble Hill of *Knight's Fee,* which deals with the Sussex Downs when Senlac fight was a living memory. The Little Dark People who lived there before the Golden People came are still there in the Conqueror's day in the shepherd and the wise woman. So the earth remains. This spell of continuity, Miss Sutcliff's best legacy from Kipling, is woven long and wide in a way that Kipling no more than hinted at. The plots of Miss Sutcliff's three stories are bound fast to the soil. The Norsemen know that they will gradually blend with the people round about; the Normans learn that they must settle disputes in accordance with customs now long established. This feeling for the continuing survival of the land is the true historical sense of Miss Sutcliff's novels. Where other novelists for children have portrayed this sense of continuity they have been involved in the chronicle aspects of their material, the unwinding of a tale of successive generations, as in a novel like *The Land the Ravens Found,* by Naomi Mitchison, so that although we could retrace the steps of the families which moved from Caithness to Iceland, so vivid and exact are the details, we miss the mounting tension of *The Shield Ring* which concentrates on a single climax. In it there is the deep brooding fear of being hunted that haunts each episode, a feeling that only by supreme efforts, by surpassing themselves, will the Norsemen survive. The countryside takes on the significance of a human character, especially at night or in time of battle. It is never simply a setting. (pp. 53-4)

It is well for a critic to confess a preference. *Warrior Scarlet* has been kept until last because I am persuaded that it shows Rosemary Sutcliff's art at its best and combines the qualities of the other tales with a controlled intensity of writing which produces a work of great power and authenticity. Also, I feel that in this book author and reader are most truly identified. For the reader the theme is the one which most concerns the adolescent, that of becoming adult. For the writer the problem is to vivify a period beyond written record, to write a book about the heroic age as compelling as legend itself.

Because we no longer have any recognizable ceremony of initiation, adolescents begin to demand recognition as adults as soon as they can adopt adult roles. Society complicates matters by allowing them to drive a car, enlist in the army, marry, vote, all at different ages, and the certainty of having gained adult status seems elusive. They are also expected to act responsibly before they are given responsibility. In *Warrior Scarlet* the reader sees the problem in clear outline against the background of a heroic age where the demands of the tribe are unequivocal: after a wolf is slain in single combat, the boy hunts with the Men's Side. What if he fails? He is no longer of the Golden People. He is an outcast and keeps sheep with the Little Dark People whom the golden warriors once dispossessed of their lands and to whom tribal privileges no longer extend.

In *Warrior Scarlet* Rosemary Sutcliff has widened her range to cover the hinterland of history and realized, with the clarity we have come to expect, every aspect of the people of the Bronze Age, from hunting spears and cooking pots to king-making and burial customs, from childhood to old age. The book is coloured throughout with sunset bronze. (pp. 57-8)

No summary of the plot can do justice to the power and sweep of this tale and the depth of the relationships portrayed. (p. 60)

Drem's coming to manhood is more than his growing skill to conquer his disability. He sees the power and beauty of the swan he killed. . . .

He learns to see sheep as a shepherd sees them and to put his own concerns aside while looking after them. He comes to realize that although his world had been 'a harsh one in which the pack turned on the weakest hound, in which little mercy was asked or given', the real achievement is to face the fear, to carry the disability, to save one's life by risking it entirely.

Miss Sutcliff shows again her great artistry in dealing with the menace of dark rituals. The making of New Spears, a ritual scene which first appeared in *The Eagle of the Ninth,* is built into a thrilling climax of darkness and light. (p. 61)

The essential Englishness in both theme and location suggests that Rosemary Sutcliff would find her public restricted, but this is by no means the case. Her publishers report that she is well-known in North America, where *The Shield Ring, Warrior Scarlet, The Lantern Bearers* and *Knight's Fee* were named Notable Children's Books by the American Library Association. Several books have been translated into German and the Scandinavian languages. There is also a version of *Warrior Scarlet* in Serbo-Croat.

During the last few years the historical novel has increased in popularity, scope and effectiveness. In this form of writing for children one can confidently say that the highest standards of artistry and craftsmanship prevail. Rosemary Sutcliff's work is characterized by a degree of intensity akin to poetic fervour. Her imaginative reconstruction of the past and the themes of heroic legend find an echo in the idealism of the modern adolescent. She combines great talent and industry with the incomparable gifts of the true story-teller. Praise for her work, simply because it is amongst the best of its kind, is bound to seem excessive, but the more exacting the criticism, the more favourable the final judgment must be. (p. 69)

Margaret Meek, in her Rosemary Sutcliff *(© The Bodley Head Ltd 1962; reprinted by permission of The Bodley Head), Bodley Head, 1962, 72 p.*

MARCUS CROUCH

Rosemary Sutcliff is an intuitive historian. This is not to say that she is not most careful and exact in research, but that her ability to think herself back into the past transcends scholarship. Her acknowledged master is Kipling who had the same gift for feeling history through his nerves and seeking it through the soil. Rosemary Sutcliff began her career with *The Queen Elizabeth Story* [1950], a gentle, charmingly written story with an element of fantasy and a pervading sweetness which bordered on sentimentality. This was the vein of several succeeding stories until suddenly, in *Simon* [1953] the author found her strength in a brilliant realistic picture of life in the civil wars. In later books she developed her gift for strong vigorous narrative and replaced the sentimentality with an increasing harshness. *The Eagle of the Ninth* [1954], a story of Roman rule in Britain, and *The Shield Ring* [1956], which described the last stand of the Viking settlers in Buttermere against the Normans, represent the finest flower of her early maturity. In later stories, like *Warrior Scarlet* [1958] a story of the Bronze Age, and *The Lantern Bearers,* a pendant to *The Eagle of the Ninth,* describing the break-up of Roman Britain after the departure of the Legions . . . , she has introduced difficult social and emotional motives which seem to threaten that she is ceas-

ing to be a writer for children; but in the splendidly Kipling-esque *Knight's Fee* [1960], a story of England under William Rufus, she has returned to the powerful striding narrative of her finest manner.

Rosemary Sutcliff is one of the very few major writers to appear in England since the war. She is a master of the declining art of storytelling with an exact sense of timing, pace and invention. She has at times shown a weakness for 'fine' writing which is her only sign of immaturity. Her most remarkable quality is an ability to create atmosphere, to let the reader see and hear and smell the past. (pp. 127-28)

Marcus Crouch, ''Widening Horizons,'' in his Treasure Seekers and Borrowers: Children's Books in Britain 1900-1960 *(© Marcus Crouch, 1962), The Library Association, 1962, pp. 112-38.**

ROBERT PAYNE

In the best historical novels, history goes out of the window and love remains.

So it is in Rosemary Sutcliff's new novel **"Sword at Sunset"**—which is only theoretically concerned with King Arthur. As history, it is unconvincing. Miss Sutcliff's king has almost nothing to do with the familiar Arthur of folklore. She has reinvented him, given him a character of her own choosing and placed him outside the accepted legends altogether—in a closed world where nothing happens except at the dictates of her imagination. In this way—though the first-person narrator she presents is more mysterious than ever—he is somehow more credible than his legends.

This is not the Arthur of the history-books—the figure that scholars have puzzled over in the sparse chronicles of his time. At another level, he is not the central figure of [Sir Thomas] Malory's ''Morte d'Arthur,'' or the more conventional hero of [Alfred, Lord] Tennyson's ''Idylls of the King.'' This time, he is a living presence who moves in a brilliantly lit and fantastic landscape only remotely connected with ancient England. And why not? The author, we feel sure, has studied all the sources—and then, it would seem, discarded them. What remains is an expression of the purest affection for the Arthur of her heart.

The tale she tells is an odd one indeed: as rich and sumptuous as the world described in the ''Mabinogion,'' as gay and menacing as ''The Tale of Genji.'' . . . [Arthur] is always in character. He wanders across France to buy horses in Narbonne. He is seduced by his sister. He fights battle after battle against the marauding Picts and the even more murderous Saxons (who destroy entire villages for the pleasure of destruction). Though he is depicted as a man of culture, he is most at home among the Dark People, the aboriginal inhabitants of England, who practice cannibalism and weave spells and provide a shadowy background to the brightness of Arthur, Artos the Bear.

Guinevere goes into her nunnery; Arthur is crowned in a circle of seven swords; the Saxons go down to defeat at Badon Hill, and the smoke rises over the burned-out villages—it is the smoke one remembers most vividly as it clouds the landscape and suddenly vanishes to reveal Arthur in his anguish or Guinevere at her love-making, and then there is smoke again, and the passing of armies.

Rosemary Sutcliff is a spellbinder. While we read, we believe everything she says. She has hammered out a style that rises and falls like the waves of the sea—colorful and admirably suited for the set pieces like the battles and the astonishingly successful coronation scene.

> Robert Payne, "Britain's Warrior-King," in The New York Times Book Review (© 1963 by The New York Times Company; reprinted by permission), May 26, 1963, p. 26.

PADRAIC COLUM

Ever since Standish O'Grady published his bardic history of Ireland in the nineties, storytellers and poets have been exalting Cuchulain. . . .

Cuchulain's story is the grand episode of the epic tale of pagan Ireland, and, like a good deal of Irish romance, has much of supernatural and irrational in it. Here is the hero who is to die young, the one who defends his uncle's kingdom against the forces of the whole of Ireland, who has to meet a well-loved friend in single combat, who unwittingly slays his son and whose love story is charming in a way that is rare in ancient romance.

Rosemary Sutcliff, who has finely presented the Anglo-Saxon Beowulf, makes a stirring narrative out of Cuchulain's career ["**The Hound of Ulster**"]. Here and there she misses a trick. The ancient storytellers had to make Cuchulain undefeatable. His victorious returns become monotonous as Miss Sutcliff relates them. There is one episode that would have provided relief: his courtship of Emer, a sophisticated damsel, who could be occult as well as charmingly coquettish. It would have been a relief from the raids and the slaughters. At the end, however, not the sternness but the pathos that was in the life of Cuchulain is brought out. She has sensitively presented the superman who is also gentle, loving and chivalrous.

> Padraic Colum, "Legend of the Past, Parable of the Present: 'The Hound of Ulster'," in The New York Times Book Review (© 1964 by The New York Times Company; reprinted by permission), May 3, 1964, p. 26.

SHEILA EGOFF, G. T. STUBBS, AND L. F. ASHLEY

For those who submit willingly to magic, Rosemary Sutcliff's new novel, *The Mark of the Horse Lord,* will cast its spell no less powerfully than any of her books since *The Eagle of the Ninth.* This is her fifteenth book for children, the flowering since 1950 of a remarkable talent which enchants readers old and young, exercises critics, and makes irrelevant the notion that the historical novel is barely concealed didacticism or an escape from the difficulty of writing for adolescents about contemporary problems. Miss Sutcliff's books have an organic unity which sets them apart from the extrovert 'good yarn' or historical fiction, and they make no concessions to ideas of what is a suitable book for children. (p. 249)

Timid as they now seem, her early books are not without significance, especially as historical stories for the under-tens are thin on the ground. *The Chronicles of Robin Hood, The Queen Elizabeth Story, The Armourer's House,* and *Brother Dusty-Feet* enjoy a continuing popularity with the young who identify history with legend. The heroes and heroines are the idealized playmates of the only child. *Simon* is the first novel to show the power that the later books developed. Miss Sutcliff sketches a vigorous hero and shows unexpected skill in describing battles.

In discussing the novels after *Simon* one moves back and forth between the relevance of the thematic material to the growing points of adolescence and the varied response of the readers. . . . [The] Roman books, notably the trilogy of *The Eagle of the Ninth, The Silver Branch,* and *The Lantern Bearers,* are the most generally appreciated. The grave virtues of the maimed heroes chime in with the serious idealism of adolescence. Miss Sutcliff's theme is the struggle of the Roman ideal, the light, against the dark ignorance of the barbarians. Aquila in *The Lantern Bearers* learns that an ideal persists even when empires totter, and the reader knows that history is the continuity of the past and present; the soil and the people remain. Owain in *Dawn Wind* discovers that a nation grows when warring tribes join in a common cause. These books provide the definition of authentic Sutcliff material: symbolic action, the heroic figure who surmounts his disability, the father figure, the links with the past in the timeless characters of seers and 'little dark people'. There are hosts of other good books for children on the Roman period; these are among the best because the universality of Miss Sutcliff's themes is balanced by detailed description.

The secret of their success is the close identification of the author, reader, and hero. The books seem to be written from the inside so that the author's imagination is fused with the reader's response. . . . Adolescents recognize the adult complexity of Miss Sutcliff's themes and respond to it while continuing to read the stories with the total involvement which is the best feature of the reading done by children.

This becomes even clearer in *Warrior Scarlet,* which is central in Miss Sutcliff's development. In this book many strands come together—awareness of historical continuity, the significance of the countryside, tribal rituals—to explore the theme of initiation into manhood. . . . *Warrior Scarlet,* with its flashing bronze and gold colouring, its archetypal issues and conflicts, is the strongest emotional experience Miss Sutcliff provides and is outstanding among children's books of any kind.

Where the historical record is scant the author's penetrative imagination has the greater scope. Miss Sutcliff illuminates the blank pages with an intensity which comes from her reading of heroic legends which *are* the history of these times in that they portray what greatness, fealty, and sacrifice meant to the followers and descendants of the warrior kings. She is fortunate in that she has no self-consciousness when writing about sublimity. Her style rises to a bardic strain and, while some passages are over-written, there is, on the whole, more restraint than excess. (pp. 250-52)

In her modern versions of Beowulf and the stories of Cuchulain in *The Hound of Ulster,* Miss Sutcliff returns to the sources of her inspiration. Her Arthurian novel, *Sword at Sunset,* which was written for adults, is a working-out at length of her preoccupation with the 'leader whose divine right is to die for his people'. *The Mark of the Horse Lord* has traces of all three. In action and tone it is the most truly epic of the novels and, so far as readers are concerned, the most adult. It shows how far Miss Sutcliff has come from the wounded Marcus in *The Eagle of the Ninth.* (p. 252)

[An] awareness that public excellence is the extension of private integrity links [*The Mark of the Horse Lord*] with *The Lantern Bearers, Warrior Scarlet,* and *Knight's Fee.* The familiar elements recur: the dark patch of history, the tribal feud, the hunts, the battles. The plot is slight, apart from the central action, so that each scene is described in detail to carry the intensity of the feud. The reader needs more experience than can generally be assumed of eleven-year-olds. For the first time in her novels for the young Miss Sutcliff may have outstripped her readers. (p. 253)

The Horse Lord becomes larger than life until he becomes Arthur, Cuchulain, and Beowulf in one. There is enough artistry and complexity to extend an adolescent's experience. Undoubtedly the book is another success for Miss Sutcliff. The battle scenes are as grand as ever, but even in the descriptive passages there is a sharper edge on the prose which makes the style more taut. . . .

The Mark of the Horse Lord shows the coming-of-age of Miss Sutcliff's hero and the total assurance of the writing indicates an author fully in command of her power. (p. 254)

> Sheila Egoff, G. T. Stubbs, and L. F. Ashley, "The Search for Selfhood: The Historical Novels of Rosemary Sutcliff," in The Times Literary Supplement (© Times Newspapers Ltd. (London) 1965; reproduced from The Times Literary Supplement by permission), No. 3303, June 17, 1965 (and reprinted in Only Connect: Readings on Children's Literature, Sheila Egoff, G. T. Stubbs, and L. F. Ashley, eds., Oxford University Press, Canadian Branch, 1969, pp. 249-55).

JOAN V MARDER

Miss Sutcliff's first book, a retelling of the Robin Hood legends, and the three which followed, are written for younger children and, while they give pleasure, they do not suggest the range and power of the later books. Signs of this developing potential came with the publication of *Simon* in 1953, a story with a Civil War setting, whose hero fights for the Parliamentary cause. Teachers welcome this book as a counterweight to the over-romantic view of the war seen from the Royalist camp which is commonly propounded in historical novels; but to the child reading the book, it is very much more than a *roman à thèse*, it is a story about timeless and enduring problems. Simon, the name character, has to resolve the rival claims of friendship and loyalty to a cause, to grow up and to move from the protection of his family to an adult life with public responsibilities. This blending of historical setting and timeless problems is the mark of all Rosemary Sutcliff's later work, and one of the main reasons for its popularity with children. (p. 138)

In the year after *Simon* appeared, *Eagle of the Ninth* was published, and marked the beginning of a sequence of novels which explore many aspects of Roman Britain from the full flush of Roman power until long after the legions had departed, and Rome was only a memory and a hope in the hearts of a few men—a civilisation, a way of life, 'the last brave glimmer of a lantern very far behind'. In each of the novels, the hero has his personal conflict, his particular quest. Aquila, in *The Lantern Bearers*, has to overcome the bitterness left by the destruction of all he held dear in his youth and to learn the importance of personal relationships and the value of family love. Owain, in *Dawn Wind*, keeps his ideal of Roman civilisation before him through all his years as a Saxon thrall, and he too discovers the importance of his obligations to his fellow-men. Phaedrus, in *The Mark of the Horse Lord*, wins his freedom in the arena and, with Roman fortitude, gives his life for the safety of the tribe which had made them their lord. These and other heroes express the adolescent's need to work out a

code of behaviour, to discover his public loyalties, and to establish his personal integrity.

Beside the Romano-British sequence, there are three novels which explore similar personal problems in different historical settings. These are: *The Shield Ring,* a story of the Norse community in Lakeland which maintained its freedom and way of life for a generation after the Norman Conquest; *Knight's Fee,* set in Norman Sussex; and *Warrior Scarlet,* set in Bronze Age Sussex. Perhaps even more strongly than in the Romano-British novels, the reader is aware of the theme of quest, of overcoming handicap, of the adolescent's urgent need to play his part in the life around him. Drem, in *Warrior Scarlet,* has the handicap of a crippled right arm. Society's demands are uncomplicated and uncompromising. To take his part in the life of the tribe, he must kill his wolf in ritual battle and be able to take his place in the warrior band; if he cannot fulfil these demands, then he must be banished to live with the conquered Neolithic people, the shepherds and servants of the tribe. Randal, in *Knight's Fee,* is physically whole but spiritually crippled—abandoned as a baby, he has learned to keep alive by lying and stealing—and he has to learn a more ordered way of life. For both Drem and Randal, the major problem is to conquer their handicap, to learn not to allow resentment to colour their relations with their fellows, and to give and accept friendship.

To the history teacher, Rosemary Sutcliff's novels are a valuable teaching aid. The novelist's imagination illuminates and brings to life periods and ways of life that are remote and difficult to understand. Norman land-tenure is a complex study, but the rights and duties of knight-service are the very stuff of the plot of *Knight's Fee,* as is the Romanisation of Britain in such books as *The Silver Branch, The Lantern Bearers,* and *Dawn Wind.* We are today cushioned from the elements, but Rosemary Sutcliff can make us feel the famine that lurked at winter's end, the threat of wolves making each winter night dangerous. We can feel the narrow boundaries, the constriction of the tribal world, or the stretching of the known world under the Roman Empire. The impression of space, of the difficulties of journeying from one settlement to another, and the time consumed in doing so, come with a shock of surprise to the child of today's world of easy transport; to one growing up in this overcrowded island. (pp. 139-40)

> Joan V Marder, "The Historical Novels of Rosemary Sutcliff" (1968), in Good Writers for Young Readers, edited by Dennis Butts (copyright 1977 Hart-Davis Educational), Hart-Davis Educational, 1977, pp. 138-41.

ELEANOR CAMERON

[The] power of imagination Rosemary Sutcliff needed in order to cast herself back into the minds and feelings of the Bronze Age peoples in *Warrior Scarlet* is fully as vital and astounding as that required by any of the great fantasists. Sutcliff's quality of imagination is different from theirs, no doubt, for there are many different kinds, but it is just as truly a wizard power to exist so completely in the past that the reader never stops once to question any action, any name, any practice or statement or habit of these ancient people. There is never once a false or hollow ring; on the other hand, every scene is packed with evocation and reality. We feel deeply what her boy Drem felt in that far-off time, not only because of his own nature, but because of the nature and history of his culture. A sense of profound conviction is conjured out of this fusion of research and empathy and imagination. (pp. 263-64)

> Eleanor Cameron, "'The Dearest Freshness Deep Down Things'" (originally published in a different form in The Horn Book Magazine, Vol. XL, No. 5, October, 1964), in her The Green and Burning Tree: On the Writing and Enjoyment of Children's Books (copyright © 1962, 1964, 1966, 1969 by Eleanor Cameron; reprinted by permission of Little, Brown and Company in association with The Atlantic Monthly Press), Atlantic-Little, Brown, 1969, pp. 258-76.*

THE TIMES LITERARY SUPPLEMENT

[So] great is the output of legends retold nowadays, amounting almost to a minor industry, that one is entitled to ask not only if the story is well told, but also if it was really worth the telling.

Rosemary Sutcliff's *Tristan and Iseult* deserves the highest praise on both counts. The Arthurian cycle is a defining element in our culture, as the Trojan war was in the ancient Greek, and the Tristan story is one of its loveliest strands. Miss Sutcliff tells it with her admirable mastery of that difficult thing, an epic style—never incongruously modern, never fusty or obscure, believable even in dialogue. The pace and shape of the narrative are superbly managed.

> "The Stuff of Dreams," in The Times Literary Supplement (© Times Newspapers Ltd. (London) 1971; reproduced from The Times Literary Supplement by permission), No. 3618, July 2, 1971, p. 764.*

JOHN ROWE TOWNSEND

Day to day, minute to minute, second to second the surface of our lives is in a perpetual ripple of change. Below the immediate surface are slower, deeper currents, and below these again are profound mysterious movements beyond the scale of the individual life-span. And far down on the sea-bed are the oldest, most lasting things, whose changes our imagination can hardly grasp at all. The strength of Rosemary Sutcliff's main work—and it is a body of work rather than a shelf of novels—is its sense of movement on all these scales. Bright the surface may be, and vigorous the action of the moment, but it is never detached from the forces underneath that give it meaning. She puts more into the reader's consciousness than he is immediately aware of.

She is not—in terms of the novel in general rather than of the children's list—a fashionable writer, or even very well known. . . . It may be that Miss Sutcliff's virtues are not fundamentally a novelist's virtues. The novel is much more concerned with individual character and day-to-day living than were the ancient forms that came before it. Rosemary Sutcliff's work is rooted more in myth, legend and saga than in the English novel.

She was a slow starter. The promise of her early books was not outstanding. *The Queen Elizabeth Story* (1950), *The Armourer's House* (1951) and *Brother Dusty-Feet* (1952) were innocuous, episodic historical stories for quite young children of perhaps eight to eleven. The backgrounds were already solid, and the storytelling, as distinct from story-construction, was already effective. In each case the story covers a period of many months, and the chapters are strung like beads on a thread; they do not often rise out of each other. . . . [There]

is no real life in any of them. The atmosphere is almost cosy; as it is, too, in the retold *Chronicles of Robin Hood,* published in 1950. . . . The tone of voice is sometimes condescending, and simplicity can sink into naïvety or be misleading, as, for instance, in the presentation of the life of a company of strolling players as one of innocent good-fellowship.

Simon (1953) has an English Civil War setting and is a transitional book. Miss Sutcliff is writing for an older age-group and with more complexity. The action, as in so many later books, is spread over several years. *Simon* is not to my mind a success. It gives the impression that a good deal of military history has been imperfectly transposed into fiction; the conflict of loyalties in a friendship that cuts across the civil-war lines is rather obvious, and the hero a dull fellow. (pp. 193-94)

Miss Sutcliff's big C-major theme comes in with *The Eagle of the Ninth* (1954). This book is perhaps more of a complete novel, more satisfying in itself, than any other of her books so far; yet at the same time it is the first stage in a complex construction of which a great deal of her later work can be said to form part.

There are three 'Roman novels', the second and third being *The Silver Branch* (1957) and *The Lantern Bearers* (1959); but the break between the Roman books and their successors really comes early in *The Lantern Bearers,* when the galleys leave Britain and the hero, Aquila, though a Roman citizen and officer, decides to stay in the small benighted island where he was born. The theme, as Margaret Meek pointed out in her Bodley Head monograph on Rosemary Sutcliff [see excerpt above], is 'the light and the dark'. In *The Lantern Bearers* the light is carried, weak and guttering, into the darkness. The events of this book are followed by those of the adult novel *Sword at Sunset* (1963) where Arthur is presented as a British war leader fighting a doomed rearguard action against the invading hordes. In *Dawn Wind* (1961) the theme and the metaphor are extended; there is not only 'the last gleam of a lantern far behind', but there is also 'the hope of other light as far ahead' in the prospect of a union of Briton and Saxon in the Christian faith.

But 'the light and the dark' is not the only theme; nor does it cover all that the author thinks and feels about civilization and barbarism. An overriding subject, extended over many books, is the making of Britain. This goes back to the Bronze Age in *Warrior Scarlet* (1958); and forward to *The Shield Ring* (1956), in which Norseman meets Norman, and *Knight's Fee* (1960) where the Norman Conquest is over and Normans too are beginning to lose themselves in a common identity. And Miss Sutcliff moves sideways, as it were, from Roman Britain in *The Mark of the Horse Lord* (1965), in which Phaedrus the Gladiator first impersonates, then becomes identified with, the leader of the Gaelic 'horse people'. Peoples mix, conquerors are absorbed, and all along, timeless and patient, from *Warrior Scarlet* right through to *Knight's Fee* two thousand years later, are the Little Dark People, who endure and survive.

Miss Sutcliff's link with Kipling—especially of *Puck of Pook's Hill*—is well known and acknowledged, and in this theme of continuity it is seen at its strongest. Continuity is emphasized by the recurrence of symbolic objects: the flawed emerald ring in the Roman novels, and in *Sword at Sunset* and *Dawn Wind;* the silver branch in the book to which it gives its name and also in *Sword at Sunset* and *The Mark of the Horse Lord;* the weathered flint axe-head, found on the Downs, that links Randal in *Knight's Fee* with Drem, right back in *Warrior Scarlet.*

And 'the light and the dark' is not a division between good and bad. Just as Kipling, a man of the West, could respect and appreciate the different values of the East (see especially *Kim*), so Miss Sutcliff, who strikes me as a rather Roman writer herself, can understand qualities which from a Roman point of view might be called barbarian. (pp. 194-96)

The last great Sutcliff theme, again running through all the major books, is at the most basic level of all. This is death and rebirth as a condition of the continuance of life. Appropriately, this is most explicit in *Warrior Scarlet,* the earliest book in its subject-matter. (p. 196)

A further preoccupation of Miss Sutcliff, which gives her books their special relevance for young people but nevertheless goes far beyond any such sectional appeal, is that of the proving of the hero. This theme recurs so often that I need not link it with a succession of titles. It seems to me that this is part of the major theme just mentioned. It is necessary to come through a testing ordeal in order to die as a boy—or unproved man— and be reborn as man and warrior. Nearly all Miss Sutcliff's heroes are warriors. They are also leaders, and two of them are, for practical purposes, kings. Leadership has its price, and the greater the leadership the greater the price. It is the duty and privilege and ultimate glory of a king to die that his people may flourish. So die Arthur in *Sword at Sunset* and Phaedrus in *The Mark of the Horse Lord.* We are in the shadow of the Golden Bough. (p. 197)

Although it is not too difficult to find differences among Rosemary Sutcliff's heroes, they nevertheless seem to me to be from the same mould. They are brave but not reckless, thoughtful but limited, conscientious, reliable, true to their friends, stiff-upper-lipped. They face and overcome their difficulties, though not with ease. They are not gay or dashing; they suggest the Service officer rather than the independent adventurer, or— however humble their origins may be—the common man. They are not artists, and one feels that although they would try dutifully to appreciate the worth of the artist they would never enter his world. There is a revealing sentence at the end of *Knight's Fee* when the minstrel Herluin, though indebted to the hero Randal for his freedom, thinks it 'more than likely' that he would find life dull with Randal on his Downland manor. The reader may well agree. Some of the Sutcliff heroes are unexciting, though worthy. . . .

The fiery girls who make up Miss Sutcliff's little band of feminine characters are thinly sketched, and only just exist as people. Her villains, major and minor, come straight from stock; her most notable successes in characterization may well be her tetchy old men. She rarely practises the novelist's art of building up tension towards a single climax, and she is not above making excessive use of coincidence.

Yet there can be few writers who cope anything like so well as she does with the passage of time, who can speed or slow up the narrative so effortlessly as it leaves or arrives at its significant points. Miss Sutcliff's writing is highly pictorial. At the same time she has a splendid gift for the stirring account of swift action, and she can combine these qualities most effectively. (p. 198)

There is a great deal of violent action in her books, but it is never meaningless violence, violence for violence's sake, violence that in the end defeats itself and deadens the reader's response. Always one has a sense of what it is all about. At the same time there is little that is abstract, and there are no painstaking and lifeless reconstructions. For Rosemary Sutcliff the past is not something to be taken down from the shelf and dusted. It comes out of her pages alive and breathing and now. (p. 199)

John Rowe Townsend, "Rosemary Sutcliff," in his A Sense of Story: Essays on Contemporary Writers for Children *(copyright © 1971 by John Rowe Townsend; reprinted by permission of Harper & Row, Publishers, Inc.), Lippincott, 1971, pp. 193-99.*

MAY HILL ARBUTHNOT AND ZENA SUTHERLAND

Most critics would say that at the present time the greatest writer of historical fiction for children and youth is unquestionably Rosemary Sutcliff. Her books are superior not only because they are authentic records of England's earliest history with its bloody raids and its continuous wars for occupation by Norsemen, Romans, Normans, and Saxons, but also because every one of her memorable books is built around a great theme. Her characters live and die for principles they value and that men today still value.

The theme of all her stories, as Margaret Meek points out [see excerpt above], is "the light and the dark. The light is what is valued, what is to be saved beyond one's own lifetime. The dark is the threatening destruction that works against it." In *The Lantern Bearers* . . . the blackness of despair is concentrated in the heart of Aquila, a Roman officer. . . .

No briefing of these stories can give any conception of their scope and power, and when young people read them they live with nobility. The sooner our children can begin to read these Sutcliff books the better, as they will help to build intellectual maturity. Nevertheless, these are difficult books, not because of vocabulary problems, but because of the complexities of the plots in which many peoples are fighting for dominance. (p. 508)

Fortunately, *Dawn Wind* . . . , one of the finest of the books, is also the least complex. Chronologically it follows *The Lantern Bearers,* but it is complete in itself and will undoubtedly send some readers to the trilogy. For the fourteen-year-old hero Owain, the light of the world seems to have been extinguished. He finds himself the sole survivor of a bloody battle between the Saxons and the Britains in which his people, the Britains, were completely destroyed. In the gutted remains of the city from which he had come, the only life the boy finds is a pitiable waif of a girl, lost and half-starved. At first Owain and Regina are bound together in mutual misery, but eventually they are united in respect and affection. So when Regina is sick and dying, Owain carries her to a Saxon settlement, even though he knows what will happen to him. The Saxons care for the girl but sell Owain into slavery. . . . After eleven years, he is freed and sets out at once to find his people and Regina, who has never doubted he would come for her.

So life is not snuffed out by the night. A dawn wind blows and two people start all over again with those basic qualities that have always made for survival. . . . Rosemary Sutcliff gives children and youth historical fiction that builds courage and faith that life will go on and is well worth the struggle. (pp. 508-09)

May Hill Arbuthnot and Zena Sutherland, "Historical Fiction: 'The Lantern Bearers' and 'Dawn Wind'," in their Children and Books *(copyright © 1972, 1964, 1957, 1947 by Scott, Foresman and Company; reprinted by permission), fourth edition, Scott, Foresman, 1972, pp. 508-09.*

FEENIE ZINER

[In "**The Capricorn Bracelet**" Rosemary Sutcliff] returns to subject matter she treated 20 years ago in her first big novel, "**The Eagle of the Ninth.**"

"**The Capricorn Bracelet**" is a collection of short stories spanning the Roman occupation of Britain from the first to the fifth century. The bracelet, awarded for distinguished military service, affirms the tradition of the Roman Legions. . . .

No one writes more convincing battle scenes than Miss Sutcliff. Her landscapes are alive with movement and color. Yet her heroes are curiously stereotyped, unchanged, whether the power they serve is on the rise or falling apart at the seams. They are all brave, decent young men concerned with the esteem of their peers, never entertaining a doubt about their obligations.

"**The Capricorn Bracelet**" is not Miss Sutcliff at her best. Still it is very good.

> Feenie Ziner, "King King Kangalo, Hadrian's Wall and One Cool Buzzard," in The New York Times Book Review (© 1973 by The New York Times Company; reprinted by permission), September 30, 1973, p. 8.

JILL PATON WALSH

[It] is now a long time since there was a new major piece of writing from Rosemary Sutcliff. *Blood Feud* will be eagerly welcomed by admirers of her long and distinguished body of work.

Is *Blood Feud* then more of the same? In some ways, yes. We find ourselves once more with a hero suspended between worlds in transition—half Celtic, half English, Viking slave and Byzantine soldier, he is swept up on that epic movement of the Viking expansion eastwards, so fascinatingly unfamiliar to most of us. We find ourselves also in a moral world where courage and loyalty count overwhelmingly, and men are ruled by a ferocious code—blood binds them as brothers or as enemies. Once again we are brought through darkness to a faint dawn; the hero is suspended between duty to kill and duty to heal, and finds himself defined by the choice he makes.

Rosemary Sutcliff's mastery of her chosen vein of writing is complete, beyond praise. The evocation with a few vivid, always concrete strokes of remote scenes, of battles, journeys, camps, is superb. She can catch the manly tones of voices uttering tough or grand or commonplace sentiments in a language which never seems outré, and never sounds the false contemporaneity which is the bane of so much historical writing. The tale moves swiftly across a crowded and believable world. And this book is as finely crafted as anything Rosemary Sutcliff has done.

And yet this is not quite more of the same. Rosemary Sutcliff's central subject in the past has been "The Matter of Britain" the welding of those manifold strands which made our country; Jestyn of this book is not part of that—he is almost literally a spin-off, thrown violently on a long path that leads him for ever away from home. And though Jestyn never really feels at one with the duty to kill that the old code lays upon him, the inner drama is faintly drawn compared with the sweeping grandeur of the outward one.

And if a little of the zest has gone, and if this is not the Sutcliff novel one would recommend above all the rest, it is still an admirable book, and a splendid read, and we can never have enough work of this quality.

> Jill Paton Walsh, "Go East, Young Man," in The Times Literary Supplement (© Times Newspapers Ltd. (London) 1976; reproduced from The Times Literary Supplement by permission), No. 3900, December 10, 1976, p. 1545.

MARGERY FISHER

Rosemary Sutcliff is never obvious in her interpretation of old causes lost and won. . . . *Blood Feud* is in fact what the book is about, the obligation for vengeance not for gain but so that the shades of the dead may rest in peace. (p. 3064)

Relatively short, concentrated, enriched with pictorial detail, the book has an emotional force which relates it, for me, to Rosemary Sutcliff's best work and especially with *Eagle of the Ninth*. Everything in the book—battle scenes, the discovery of love in various forms, weather and landscape, religious polemic—is reflected through Jestyn, the waif whose life is ruled by accident. . . . The first-person reminiscence distances old tragedies and conflicts, as Jestyn, now a physician, sends his thoughts back over the years. It is a narrative method well suited to this richly personal chronicle. (p. 3065)

> Margery Fisher, "Causes and Conflicts," in her Growing Point, Vol. 15, No. 8, March, 1977, pp. 3064-67.*

SARAH HAYES

Rosemary Sutcliff has always enjoyed the idea of the outsider, of the odd one who is isolated by fate to perform some special act. Though it has become almost a formula now, the magic lingers on—even in her new novel [*Sun Horse, Sun Moon*] which verges on self-parody. . . .

All the Sutcliff hallmarks are here: the sonorous descriptions, the perfect evocation of an alien culture, the stilted quasi-primitive dialogue (with its unique use of the soothing phrase "na-na"). And, at about a third of the length of the earlier novels, this spare tale could easily be taken for a faint copy. But it is not. Though it lacks detail and human warmth, it conveys instead the mystery of ancient civilizations: the bleak unadorned style and story suit an age that remains dark and impenetrable to this day. The plot is a simple one, but the use of contrasting images of horses, shadows, birds, and cold winds give it a complex patterning that is the verbal equivalent of early Celtic jewelry.

> Sarah Hayes, "The Breath of Life," in The Times Literary Supplement (© Times Newspapers Ltd. (London) 1977; reproduced from The Times Literary Supplement by permission), No. 3949, December 2, 1977, p. 1415.

PAULINE CLARKE

Rosemary Sutcliff has given us [in *Song for a Dark Queen*] a rounded, convincing and (very properly) rather frightening portrait of Boudicca, queen of the Iceni, who led the tribes to the sack of Roman Colchester, St. Alban's and London. In the lyrical, loving, and doomladen tale of Cadwan the harper, she grows from a brave defiant infant to a proud unwilling bride, a happy mother and a vengeful widow, her private self always contrasted with her public, queenly role. . . .

The Roman point of view, and the Legions' movements in meeting the rebellion, are recounted by young Agricola on his first service. . . .

All Rosemary Sutcliff's well-known skills are here: the lovely descriptions of the seasons in a subtly prehistoric East Anglian scene . . . : the brilliant evocation of atmosphere, whether happy, foreboding, or sinister (as in the sacred grove, where the atrocious sacrifices detailed by the historian Dio Cassius are more subtly dealt with by this author): the assured narrative power in handling crowded and dramatic scenes, which pile up as this superbly exciting, albeit bloodthirsty story rises to its tragic climax in the battle: the sense of contrast between the "civilized" and the "barbarian", in their own and each other's estimation: the masterly telescoping of the passing years, the skilful indications of the underlying reasons for the uprising. With her usual confidence she describes Celtic ritual and the worship of the mother goddess: the choosing of the royal bridegroom, the marriage, the funerals, the corn dancing. Her sympathies are totally engaged, so that, despite her refusal to minimize any of the savageries of the British, the reader's are too.

In basing her treatment on the theory that the Iceni were a matriarchy she has surely added great force to Boudicca's thirst to avenge her dishonoured queenship and royal daughters: and there may be a Pictish parallel. But all that Tacitus says is: "In Britain there is no rule of distinction to exclude the female line from the throne or the command of armies".

> *Pauline Clarke, "The Power Behind the Throne," in* The Times Literary Supplement *(© Times Newspapers Ltd. (London) 1978; reproduced from* The Times Literary Supplement *by permission), No. 3979, July 7, 1978, p. 766.*

ELAINE MOSS

[What] is impressive about *Frontier Wolf* is not the story itself, nor the gradual winning through of Alexios from disgrace to honour. It is Rosemary Sutcliff's extraordinary capacity for recreating a visual and emotional picture, many-textured, of the life of a Roman garrison on the Antonine Wall as the Empire crumbled. She has the writer's equivalent of a musician's "absolute pitch"; her certainty enables her to use language that fore-echoes the future (the Votadini speak with a recognizable Celtic lilt), and to engender situations and characters that carry with them an authenticity and complexity that defy the conventional textbook image of Roman times.

> *Elaine Moss, "Outposts of the Empire," in* The Times Literary Supplement *(© Times Newspapers Ltd. (London) 1980; reproduced from* The Times Literary Supplement *by permission), No. 4051, November 21, 1980, p. 1323.*

ANN EVANS

Very occasionally, the opening sentence of a book works a small miracle on the reader. It is as if a shutter sprang open momentarily, to reveal the essence and truth of the entire book within a single visionary second. There is nothing obviously spectacular about the first sentence of *The Sword and the Circle* but the magic is there and with it the certainty that riches lie ahead.

Many followers of Rosemary Sutcliff must have waited and hoped for her to bring her own particular distinction to a re-

telling of the legends of King Arthur and the Knights of the Round Table. There are other available versions, of course, some of them admirable . . . , but *The Sword and the Circle* stands far above any collection known to me, and should be seized on by anybody providing books for children upwards of ten years old.

With her usual scrupulous regard for authenticity, Rosemary Sutcliff has rooted the stories deep in history. . . .

For some, Rosemary Sutcliff's writing may perhaps be over-rich (though much less so than twenty years ago). It has the stately measure of seventeenth-century English prose, the sharp pathos of an old ballad and an echo of Homer in its beautifully tuned imagery, and yet it can be as homely and unpretentious as an old kitchen table. This way of writing has evolved over the years into a style unmistakably her own—so much so that it could be said to be too pervasive, like an over-heavy perfume, masking the individuality of each separate book. For most readers, I suspect, it provides the perfect vehicle for each of the stories she has to tell, and if in this collection the romantic influence of Malory is strong, Rosemary Sutcliff rises above it, a minstrel in her own right.

Of her many gifts as a writer for all ages, perhaps two are especially to be valued: the first, that of involving the reader with a character at a human and emotional level while still preserving the historical perspective; the second, that of gauging the pace of a book to such perfection. The tension is never allowed to slacken and yet there is time to laugh at a pompous ass of a knight being unhorsed backwards, time to ponder the sad truth that even in the Dark Ages a man could be torn apart because he loved his best friend's wife. It is for qualities like these that Rosemary Sutcliff's name will be remembered and revered long after others have been forgotten.

> *Ann Evans, "The Real Thing," in* The Times Literary Supplement *(© Times Newspapers Ltd. (London) 1981; reproduced from* The Times Literary Supplement *by permission), No. 4069, March 27, 1981, p. 341.*

MARCUS CROUCH

Rosemary Sutcliff has dwelt so long, imaginatively, in the Dark Ages that she seems not quite at ease in bringing Arthur into the age of chivalry. Future literary historians, assessing her contribution to the literature of our age, will find profitable exercise in comparing her approach to the figure of Arthur in *The Lantern Bearers,* in the adult novel *Sword at Sunset,* and in this rather more conventional exploration of Malory and other medieval sources [*The Sword and the Circle*].

Perhaps it is some evidence of her incomplete ease that Miss Sutcliff returns here to some of the stylistic devices of her earlier books. There is much elegant and atmospheric writing, a little less of the terse, hard lines which have distinguished the later novels for children.

This having been said, let me hasten to add that this is as good a retelling of the ancient stories as we have had in this half-century.

> *Marcus Crouch, in his review of "The Sword and the Circle," in* The Junior Bookshelf, *Vol. 45, No. 3, June, 1981, p. 127.*

HILARY WRIGHT

It can hardly have been by chance that in 1960 it was Rosemary Sutcliff who wrote the Bodley Head monograph on the children's books of Rudyard Kipling, nor is it surprising that in it she remarked ". . . of all the writers of my childhood, he made the strongest impact on me, an impact which I have never forgotten," . . . for no reader of her own books—except one totally ignorant of Kipling—can fail to be aware of her debt to him. Quite apart from certain identities of subject, there is an underlying identity of theme: what one might call the Conflict of Duty and Inclination. In the monograph she wrote that the Mowgli stories are ". . . a following-out of divided life and divided loyalties, the unbearable choice that has to be made and has to be borne" . . . ; this might equally well be said of her own works, since she has scarcely a hero who does not have to make that "unbearable choice," with the making of and abiding by that choice very often the mainspring of the book. Just how deeply she has been influenced by Kipling I suspect that even she is not fully aware; that it goes beyond a casual borrowing of subject material may be shown in a review of her major works. . . . (p. 90)

Simon is the first Sutcliff work to have a recognizably Sutcliffian—one might almost say epic—flavour. It has many of the typical Sutcliff ingredients: young adult rather than child hero, a David-and-Jonathan friendship, above all a central conflict of Duty and Inclination. Simon has to choose between his duty to Parliament—his own and his father's political creed—and his friendship with Royalist Amias, just as Mowgli must choose between the Jungle and his humanity. . . . Simon, too, could easily be the typical Kipling subaltern as he learns his job in the New Model Army with the covert help of his troop. If the book has still a certain amount of Elizabeth Goudge (the dominant influence of the earlier works) it has yet come a long way from the mere prettiness of *The Queen Elizabeth Story* or *The Armourer's House.*

With *The Eagle of the Ninth* . . . Rosemary Sutcliff achieved full maturity and did it with a significant dash of Kipling. Her Marcus is a blood-brother of Parnesius and Pertinax, those Roman subalterns of *Puck of Pook's Hill*, and her picture of the Roman army is rather more akin to Kipling's than to a historian's. (pp. 90-1)

Yet despite the Roman setting of *The Eagle of the Ninth* and its sequels it is not they but *Outcast* . . . which is the clearest example of Kipling's effect on Rosemary Sutcliff. It too has a Roman background, but it does not derive from the Parnesius stories. Consider, rather, where one would find the classic story of a boy reared from infancy among a people not his own, cast out by them on the verge of manhood through fear of his difference, meeting with incomprehension and ill-treatment among his "own" people and, after various adventures, ending as the trusted servant of a conquering and imperial power. The answer, of course, is Mowgli, but remove the Jungle and the answer is equally Beric in *Outcast.* (p. 91)

Characters apart, *Outcast,* like most of Rosemary Sutcliff's work, is full of verbal echoes of Kipling. It can hardly be a coincidence that the Druid speaks of the Dumnonii as "the Free People" just as so often in *The Jungle Book* the Wolves are "the Free People," or that Cathlan in his leavetaking of Beric gives him the Jungle farewell "Good hunting!" From Kipling must come the almost invariable reference to any baby or child as "cub" or "cubling" . . . , but not, I think, that other typically Sutcliffian formula "wolf kind," "Saxon kind," "shepherd kind," and so on.

Outcast was followed by *The Shield Ring* . . . , the least Kiplingesque of Rosemary Sutcliff's major works. It owes nothing to Kipling in either geographical or historical setting . . . or, indeed, in theme. It seems significant that it is the only major Sutcliff work to focus on a heroine rather than a hero, though of course for much of the book we share Frytha's preoccupation with Bjorn. Nevertheless there are certain reminders of Kipling. The poor, broken-witted mazelin, whose wits return only at the end, seems to derive from "half-caulked" Penn in *Captains Courageous*—interestingly, the only echo from a book which Rosemary Sutcliff says in *Rudyard Kipling* that she did not meet until "well after I was grown up." . . . But the true derivative of Kipling's Norman stories was yet to come. (pp. 93-4)

The Lantern Bearers has very little surface Kipling; *Knight's Fee* . . . not only has a great deal, but is very nearly a sequel to Kipling's Norman stories centring on Sir Richard Dalyngridge. There is the same post-Conquest period, the same small Sussex manor, the same old Norman knight close to his stern but kindly overlord, each with his "glimmering gown" of chain mail, "nut-shaped" helmet, and notable sword. Both stories have an element of pre-Tenchebrai treason which may involve the loss of the beloved manor. . . .

There are other, smaller likenesses. Both tales include a horse called Swallow [both greys], make play with "the Custom of the Manor" and involve voyaging with a Viking seaman. . . .

But the main essence of *Knight's Fee* is the friendship of Randal and Bevis, with Bevis's death the fee Randal must pay for knighthood and manor, and though Kipling writes often enough of comradeship he never touches on that typically Sutcliffian subject, the parting—whether temporary or permanent—of twin-souled friends. Nor does Rosemary Sutcliff ever use Kipling's real-life experience of marriage to the sister of a dead companion. Even for a parallel with Sir Richard's marrying of Hugh's sister (though Hugh is not dead) we have to go right back to *Simon.* (p. 96)

Knight's Fee is, however, the Sutcliff story which bears most obviously those marks of Kipling which show in her books "like shadows on the Downs." It is also the last of her major works to do so at all. Neither *Dawn Wind* . . . nor *The Mark of the Horse Lord* . . . have more than a touch or two of Kipling. (p. 97)

[We] can now see that the prevailing sources of [Kipling's] influence appear to be the Mowgli stories and the Norman and Roman sequences in *Puck of Pook's Hill* and *Rewards and Fairies*. Other books and stories have their echoes, but it is these which dominate. (p. 98)

But if it does seem that very often Rosemary Sutcliff has taken the kernel of a story or a point of detail from something in Kipling she has always developed it in her own way. It is not at all that she is imitating Kipling but rather that she has sometimes used the same stones to build something quite different. *Outcast,* for example, is not merely the Mowgli story in Roman dress, but a deeply realised description of rejection and reintegration. With Kipling we are nearly always given external views from a detached and objective angle; feelings and motives are very often understated or left to our own deduction. With Rosemary Sutcliff we are always at the heart of the action and experiencing it through a hero of whose feelings and motives we are piercingly aware. Kipling, in short, is on the outside looking in; Rosemary Sutcliff is on the inside looking out. (pp. 98-9)

The influence of Rudyard Kipling on Rosemary Sutcliff may well be said ''to show and fade / Like shadows on the Downs,'' but it no more shapes her individuality than the marks alter the basic shapes of the Downs. (p. 101)

Hilary Wright, "Shadows on the Downs: Some In-fluences of Rudyard Kipling on Rosemary Sutcliff," in Children's literature in education *(© 1981, Aga-thon Press, Inc.; reprinted by permission of the pub-lisher), Vol. 12, No. 2 (Summer), 1981, pp. 90-102.*

NEIL PHILIP

If there is one story with which every child growing up in Britain should be familiar, it is the story of King Arthur. There is no shortage of retelling, but most of them are hack rewritings which debase their source material. Even the best attempts . . . seem to lack the vital spark which animates the early sources, and which received its classic expression in the prose writings of Sir Thomas Malory.

Rosemary Sutcliff's version, told in three books, **The Sword and the Circle, The Light Beyond the Forest** and **The Road to Camlann,** is now complete, and stands . . . as a valiant attempt to bring the often tragic, violent and sensual tales within the compass of children's understanding without cutting the heart from them. While story and language stay close to Malory, the shaping spirit is recognisably that of the author of **The Eagle of the Ninth, The Mark of the Horse Lord** and that splen-did novel of an historicised Arthur, **Sword at Sunset.**

The Road to Camlann is the best of the three volumes, perhaps because its interwoven stories all tend to the same end. The theme of the book is the destruction of the fellowship of the Round Table through the machinations of Arthur's incestuous bastard Mordred. The stories centre on Lancelot: his threefold rescue of Guenevere and his bitter wars with Arthur and Ga-wain. To children his betrayal of his best friend out of passion can seem mere treachery, and his slaying of Gareth and Gaheris ''unarmed and unwares'' unforgivable. Rosemary Sutcliff, by conveying so skilfully ''the grete curtesy that was in Sir Laun-celot more than in only other man'', blocks such a damaging response. Lancelot is a rounded, convincing character. . . .

Neil Philip, "Completing the Circle," in The Times Educational Supplement *(© Times Newspapers Ltd. (London) 1981; reproduced from* The Times Edu-cational Supplement *by permission), No. 3408, Oc-tober 23, 1981, p. 30.*

MARCUS CROUCH

[**The Road to Camlann**] takes up the story [of King Arthur] with Mordred at Camelot, insidiously undermining the fellow-ship and the spiritual values on which the Round Table was based. There follows the love of Guenever and Lancelot, the wars and the final battle. The story ends with the death of Lancelot at Glastonbury.

In this, the most familiar of all the Arthurian stories, there is not much room for individual interpretation, and Miss Sutcliff stays close to Malory, even to the use of actual speeches and phrases at climactic moments where modern words, even those as resounding as this writer's, might have struck the wrong note. Miss Sutcliff captures the profound sadness of the story and the hopelessness of its preordained doom. She writes with conscious nobility of style, as befits the material, using the techniques of the chronicler rather than the novelist, although

she shows her characteristic understanding in dealing with the motives of Lancelot and Arthur. Here, young readers and their parents may be assured, is the best of a great and lasting story matched with the best of one of this age's great writers. Those who, later in life, move on to Malory will discover that the spirit of the Arthurian legends has been conveyed without fal-sification, and that the transition to the fifteenth-century orig-inal can be made with no effort.

Marcus Crouch, in his review of "The Road to Cam-lann," in The Junior Bookshelf, *Vol. 45, No. 6, December, 1981, p. 251.*

SHEILA A. EGOFF

A virtually perfect mesh of history and fiction can be found in the writing of Rosemary Sutcliff. She seems to work from no recipe for mixing fact and imagination and thus, like fantasy, which it also resembles in its magic qualities, her writing defies neat categorization. Still, what cannot be defined can be ob-served. Thus what one perceives is that Sutcliff begins with a very well stored mind and an affinity for a given period in the distant past that she sets forth as if it were something she herself had once experienced, richly remembers, and recounts—much as some ordinary person talks about the memories of childhood or a trip. Sutcliff easily, unobtrusively, and naturally seems able to supply just the right detail at just the right time to make both setting and plot utterly convincing. Her persuasion is so compelling that readers are imperceptibly led back into the past with such subtlety they feel they are living side by side with her characters. (pp. 163-64)

With her first major novel, **The Eagle of the Ninth** . . . , Sut-cliff brought a new dimension into historical fiction for chil-dren, indeed into children's literature. . . . [She] gives all her characters universal, human problems while making them vital and recognizable in their own time. And with all this she also tells a great story. (p. 164)

Sutcliff is a ''hot'' novelist in strong contrast to the cooler, more cerebral, and lucid approach of a Hester Burton or a Barbara Willard. Like all modern writers she does not open her books with long descriptive passages to set the period but thrusts the reader immediately into the stir and terror of great, grim events. . . .

Sutcliff's perennial theme is that of personal responsibility, particularly if the protagonist is in a position of leadership. Her characters frequently resemble Beowulf, the King of the Geats, facing the dragon alone in his last battle. Most of her major novels have this epic quality. (p. 176)

Like the myths, Sutcliff's works are by no means monochro-matic. Her works are filled with images of light as well as dark. Amidst the clang and clash of war, the horrors of a slave ship or arena, or in the picture of the dark people who live beyond the Roman Wall in Britain, she also imparts a sense of the necessity for and the profundity of a culture. Above all, even in depicting the most harrowing tragedies, she suggests that these may be the steps we've been taking on our slow, hard climb to real humanity. (p. 177)

Sheila A. Egoff, "Historical Fiction," in her Thurs-day's Child: Trends and Patterns in Contemporary Children's Literature *(copyright © 1981 by the Amer-ican Library Association),* American Library Asso-ciation, *1981, pp. 159-92.*

NEIL PHILIP

[Rosemary Sutcliff] cherishes cultural diversity even while she stresses continuity. And while she upholds such unfashionable virtues as duty, courage, integrity, she has in her treatment of the theme of male comradeship provided the most sensitive and sustained representation of male homosexual feeling in children's literature.

The main body of her work, the sequence of major novels ranging from the Bronze Age *Warrior Scarlet,* through the great Roman trilogy (published in one volume as *Three Legions*) to the eleventh century *Knight's Fee,* is a magnificent achievement. To call the books historical novels is to limit them disgracefully; the very phrase implies a deadness . . . and a distancing which is the opposite of her intention. She does not bring "history" to the reader, but involves the reader in the past—not just for the duration of a book, but for ever. She can animate the past, bring it to life inside the reader in a most personal and lasting way.

This ability is a magical one, and there perhaps lies the key to her success. She is not essentially a novelist but a storyteller. She has the oral storyteller's instinctive grasp of pace, slowing her action till the reader is aware of every breath her characters take, then triumphantly whirling into battle, enmeshing the reader in confusion which seems to pass too quickly for the eye to take it in, yet never losing her grip on her material. And she has a bardic attitude to language. She re-uses phrases which appeal to her, sometimes several times in a book; in her descriptions of downland and heath she can become intoxicated with detail, as if the very thought of the open air exults her. Her "one plot; a boy growing up and finding himself" has done her and her readers proud.

> Neil Philip, *"Romance, Sentiment, Adventure,"* in The Times Educational Supplement (© *Times Newspapers Ltd. (London) 1982; reproduced from* The Times Educational Supplement *by permission), No. 3425, February 19, 1982, p. 23.*

MARGERY FISHER

[In *The Road to Camlann*] Rosemary Sutcliff has assumed a bardic style, rhythmic and full of poetic archaism and reflecting in some ways the manner of medieval poetry. From this source, perhaps, come the delicate natural touches that refresh a tale of intrigue and cruelty—the flowers that herald spring, the dark forest reaches: but the author uses nature for something more than decoration. [For example, the] last battle at Dover in which Mordred and Arthur strike their last blows is full of the harshness of winter, used almost as a symbol. . . .

Battles and single combat are described strongly but in formal tones, and in formal terms, too, Rosemary Sutcliff outlines the love between Lancelot and the Queen in its latter years, bringing tension to her tale with a felt contrast between their passion and the courtly restraints in which it has to be expressed. The destructive element in this love is recognised as one cause of the final dispersal of Arthur's knights and, with equal importance, the incestuous parentage of Mordred, a parentage which caused his jealousy and led him to undermine Arthur's power and peace of mind. This romantic interpretation of historical chronicle and fifteenth century narrative is finely done in its grave, pictorial style.

> Margery Fisher, *"Imagined Past,"* in her Growing Point, *Vol. 20, No. 6, March, 1982, pp. 4030-33.*

ANNE DUCHÊNE

Autobiography, however much one may try to modify the fact, is essentially the raising of a monument to oneself: an impulse which society may long have acknowledged as legitimate and healthy, but which still runs counter to inherited traditions of modesty and reticence. Rosemary Sutcliff, an honourable retailer and reteller of romance and epic, is the daughter of a naval officer, and a mother who taught her never to cry, always to conceal the fox beneath her cloak. Moreover, she was their only child, and physically handicapped. Deciding to record her early life—from infancy to the acceptance of her first book, in her early twenties—risks flouting the disciplines ingrained in her. It also means that we, the public, are invited to intrude on private griefs, and joys, without being fully admitted to more than one or two of them.

At most points where the story might be deemed remarkable, Miss Sutcliff's training usually denies its singularity. . . . Like all handicapped children, Miss Sutcliff says, she accepted [her physical] limitations: life wells up to fill whatever circumference it is allowed. Comparisons and complications only set in later.

Later, indeed, since she was, as she just allows herself to stress, as much prone to falling in love as those with limbs of more average efficiency—a blissful but doomed marriage of true minds, just after the war, could find no consequence then (could it more easily now?) because of the discrepancies of the flesh, or, in her case, more strictly, of the flesh and the bone. . . . This is the only point where feelings are strong enough to threaten the book's smooth surface; but it is not her intention to be contentious, and they are put down again—welcomed, even, as teaching her about feelings she could use later in her books.

Other limitations are accepted just as stoically. . . . [The] texture of her disparate parents' relationship is never discussed.

Nor—a greater gap—is her mother, who seems likely, from the illustrations, to have been as vividly lovely and changeable as her daughter says, but who remains a vast, imponderable, unassuaged presence in the background. . . . [The] subject is virtually dismissed as early as page 14. . . .

Given this, much of the book has to be taken up with accounts of aunts and uncles who are mostly acknowledged as rather dull; of childhood friendships, by circumstance fleeting; of family dogs, always marvellously tenderly recalled; and of early ecstasies over wild flowers. Education ended at fourteen. . . . Early reading was dominated by Kipling, and Arthur Rackham's drawings, and such; first attempts at writing by such sophisticates as Jeffrey Farnol and Warwick Deeping. The mixture, here still, of scrupulous exactness and ingenuous opacity makes it enjoyable to trace these influences, for those old enough to recognize the signs.

> Anne Duchêne, *"The Burden of Reticence,"* in The Times Literary Supplement (© *Times Newspapers Ltd. (London) 1983; reproduced from* The Times Literary Supplement *by permission), No. 4177, April 22, 1983, p. 396.*

Paul Weller

1958-

British songwriter.

Until his recent departure from the group, Weller wrote for the Jam, who were tentatively linked with Punk and New Wave rock and roll. In common with the bands in these movements, the Jam were young and enthusiastic and played simple, energetic music. Weller's lyrics, however, were more serious and socially oriented than those of most other songwriters. In contrast to the outrageous dress of many rock stars in the 1970s, the Jam had the unadorned appearance of 1960s mods—short haircuts, black mohair suits, white shirts, and black ties. Weller's songs and the group's music were influenced by the early Who, but the Jam updated their sound to make it fresh and exciting.

Weller directs his songs toward the under-twenty audience; he believes that bands like the Rolling Stones, Led Zeppelin, and Genesis no longer have anything to say to this age group. His songs often deal with such issues as corruption, alienation, waste, and class conflicts. Besides being socially relevant, Weller's lyrics describe the problems, aspirations, and hopes of young adults. The Jam were a huge success in England, but had only a cult following in America; nevertheless, most critics consider Weller to be one of the finest songwriters of the New Wave movement.

BRIAN HARRIGAN

The Jam are a young three-piece band who have the potential of becoming the most commercially successful of the new wave outfits. I say new wave advisedly, since the Jam bear no relation to the mass conception of punk—whether it be quasi-anarchist politics or out and out mindless aggression.

The Jam are simply new, young and part of today's extensive musical reaction against the dinosaur bands who have dominated rock for the last eight years. Thus, they are new wave. . . .

The Jam, comprehensive school educated, have played extensively in social clubs and dingy pubs for a considerable part of their two-year existence and the music they are making now represents the release of the frustration to which such a restricted environment must give birth.

On the evidence of ["**In the City**"], however, they've also controlled this outburst with a rare skill in musicians of their age and have produced tightly composed and performed songs. They've elected to include on this album just two of the half-dozen or more non-original songs they use in their normal repertoire—Larry Williams' "Slow Down" and Neal Hefti's "Batman Theme." The former is worthy of inclusion, the latter not. . . .

[The Weller-composed songs] are anything but an embarrassment. In fact, he has a deft touch that, for me, places his material on a much higher plateau than almost anything his new wave contemporaries have attempted. . . .

Apart from the title track, "**In The City**," which, to these ears, is the very best of the new wave anthems, the stand-out title

Michael Putland/Retna Ltd.

is "**Non-Stop Dancing**," which is a medium-paced chunk of R&B boogie and features an aggressive choked-off vocal and even a reference in the lyrics to James Brown, which in itself underlines the band's commitment to the spirit of the early Sixties. . . .

Understandably, many potential buyers will be put off this album because of the band's tenuous links with punk, but not giving it at least one listen would be a mistake. Lay down your prejudices and give them a try—they're guaranteed not to disappoint.

Brian Harrigan, "Who? It's the Jam," in Melody Maker *(© IPC Business Press Ltd.), May 28, 1977, p. 23.*

DAN OPPENHEIMER

On their debut album, *In the City,* the Jam . . . present 12 tracks without a ballad among them, tracks that come from the center of a very live, alive, lively performing band. . . . The band's power and flair as a working-class trio is attractive; even more important, Weller's lyrics are as intriguing on paper and in your head as they are between chord changes. . . .

They are dealing with the problem of *authority* and what the hell to do about it, but so subtly they're veritably Zen Buddhist compared to those who would batter down walls by knocking their heads against them. You see, anyone serious about trashing fat cats does so by simply ignoring those fucks and going their own way. It's the antithesis of the graffiti truism: "If it's illegal, it's fun." If you believe the scrawl, it follows that you won't do what you're allowed to do and that you must do what you ain't. The Jam realize that angry young men are no less boring than they ever were. But to build great music because things ain't right—yes, indeed. . . .

They have a way with words . . . , as in Weller's lyric for ["**I Got By in Time**"], which show him to be conscious of self but not preoccupied with it: "Saw a girl that I used to know / I was deep in thought at the time / Didn't recognize her face at first / Because I was prob'ly looking at mine . . . we were young, we were full of ideas . . . " . . .

[In] "**Time for Truth**," Weller takes on a certain Uncle Jimmy, who may be a straw man or a real character in his life. Weller hints that this character is just another poor fuck, but says with finality, "You lost, Uncle Jimmy, you lost." And then he growls, "What ever happened to the *great empire*?"

My God, that's what I always wanted to know. I could care less about glue and safety pins.

> *Dan Oppenheimer, "Jam Shakes Like This" (reprinted by permission of* The Village Voice *and the author; copyright © The Village Voice, Inc., 1977), in* The Village Voice, *Vol. XXII, No. 35, August 29, 1977, p. 73.*

DAVE MARSH

The Jam is totally unheralded, but it is one of the most interesting groups to come out of Britain's punk scene. The group's obsession—probably guitarist/vocalist/writer Paul Weller's—with the Who is only slightly veiled: the band even goes so far as to cover Neal Hefti's "Batman Theme," which is definitely Keith Moon out of Jan and Dean if you ask me. And the title song [of *In the City*], of course, is modeled after Pete Townshend's song of the same name from the first Who LP.

Jam has a penchant for vulgarity unrivaled by anyone save Patti Smith, though this group's point is less poetical. The promotional copies of the LP carry a warning, advising DJs that "**Art School**" and "**Time for Truth**" contain "language that segments of your audience might find offensive." . . . Such a word to the wise ought to be sufficient.

> *Dave Marsh, in his review of "In the City," in* Rolling Stone *(by Straight Arrow Publishers, Inc. © 1977; all rights reserved; reprinted by permission), Issue 249, October 6, 1977, p. 89.*

CHRIS BRAZIER

As the title ["**This Is the Modern World**"] makes clear, the album's ostensible theme is the modern world, and contains . . . obviously contemporary lyrics. . . .

Yet, as everyone knows, the Jam hark back to the mod mid-Sixties and Swingin' London. . . .

[Even] some of the song-themes smack of the Sixties—complaints about "**London Traffic**" were rife then; "**London Girl**" is [David] Bowie's "London Boys" revisited (though no less relevant for that); and they've admitted that "**Here Comes The**

Weekend" was a reworking of [The Easybeats's] "Friday On My Mind."

None of this matters as long as the material is fresh and exciting and transcends the limitations of a museum tribute. . . . Much of the record suffers, though, precisely because it's typical Jam—"**Standards**," "**Here Comes The Weekend**," "**In The Street Today**" and "**The Modern World**" are all adequate, but thoroughly ordinary, and don't represent any development on their first album, "**In The City**."

Some of the songs are lyrically weak as well. Take these well-meaning but ridiculous lines from a description of a frantic weekend's pleasure-seeking, much less effective than the Clash's "48 Hours." "If we tell you that you got two days to live / Then don't complains 'co that's one more than you got in Zaire / So don't hang around and be foolish / Do something constructive with your weekend." The expression is redolent of the earnest excess of sixth-form writing, but I prefer that to the aggressive self-satisfaction which leads Weller to write glib words like "All my life has been the same / I've learned to live by hate and pain," and foolishly complacent ones like "I've learned more than you'll ever know" (both from the colourless new single "**The Modern World**"). "**Standards**" seems to ridicule the kind of Tory attitude Weller once espoused, which is fine, but again the attack is too glib and exaggerated. Hate and war aren't the only things we've got today—the over-riding evils are the numbing influences, as to the lilting finale to "**The Combine**" recognises, with its collage of features of an ordinary life.

All the same, existence does have its highs and it's when Paul Weller is glorying in it that he seems to write best. "**I Need You (For Someone)**" tends towards the banal, but it's refreshing to find an unashamedly simple love-song in this context. . . .

Conclusive proof that introspective optimism suits the Jam lies in "**Life From A Window**" and "**Tonight At Noon**," two really fine songs in the same class as the debut album's stand-out track, "**Away From The Numbers**." . . .

Paul Weller should mature into one of our best songwriters, provided he keeps his mind open and floats free of a rigid Sixties base. . . .

> *Chris Brazier, "Jam: Mod and Modern," in* Melody Maker *(© IPC Business Press Ltd.), November 12, 1977, p. 25 [the first excerpt of Paul Weller's lyrics used here was taken from "Here Comes the Weekend" (copyright © 1977 And Son Music; reprinted by permission of And Son Music Ltd.), the second excerpt was taken from "The Modern World" (copyright © 1977 And Son Music; reprinted by permission of And Son Music Ltd.)].*

KEN EMERSON

This Is the Modern World is at once more intriguing and less exciting [than *In the City*] because, this time around, Weller's music lags behind his thought.

In less than a year, Weller's sensibility seems to have made a giant leap from *The Who Sings My Generation* to *Tommy* and especially *Quadrophenia*. On the most interesting of his new songs, punk desperation and truculence have given way to a wistful, reflective resignation that brings to mind not only later Pete Townshend but also Ray Davies: "**Life from a Window**" is a New Wave "Waterloo Sunset" and nearly as poignant, while . . . [some sentiments hark] back to *The Kinks Are the Village Green Preservation Society*.

> *Ken Emerson, in his review of "This Is the Modern World," in* Rolling Stone *(by Straight Arrow Publishers, Inc. © 1978; all rights reserved; reprinted by permission), Issue 259, February 23, 1978, p. 52.*

ED WARD

With the release of their third album, *All Mod Cons,* the Jam find themselves in a jam. Careful never to identify too closely with either punk or the more artsy new wave, they share with both camps so many points of reference—right down to the time they emerged—that I, for one, can't help continuing to lump them among bands I know they shouldn't share quarters with. Yeah, I know they aren't jumping onto bandwagons; yeah, I know they don't offer a wholesale repudiation of the past. But they sound enough like the bands that do that I mix Jam records in with the punks and would-bes and they sound just fine. Maybe not this time though. *All Mod Cons* is a much less self-assured album than the first two this brazen bunch put out, and contains some of the best and worst work they've yet done. They seem confused, stopped at a multiple crossroad, getting passed at high speed on the left and right.

If the Jam have decided not to pursue the political/aesthetic points the punks were making a lot more loudly and visibly, well and good, but what makes *All Mod Cons* feel so tentative is that they don't seem to know the boundaries of the new territory they want to stake out. And they've done all the things you'd expect in such an insecure situation. They've rewritten **"Away from the Numbers"** from their first album as **"In the Crowd,"** and even give it away by singing **"Numbers"** in the fadeout. . . .

Paul Weller, the Jam's guitarist and main writer, has outdone himself lyrically on **"Down in a Tube Station at Midnight."** Yet another song about racially inspired mugging, except that this one is different—unlike the Clash's "Safe European Home" or 10cc's "Dreadlock Holiday," it deals with right-wing white toughs mugging a Pakistani, and is told from the Pakistani's viewpoint. It's hard to tell whether he's badly hurt, killed, or what, and the song builds (and doesn't release) the tension well. On the other hand, along with an undue quantity of simply mediocre material, we have **"English Rose,"** an acoustic-guitar-accompanied love song which features the line "No bonds can ever keep me from she" not only ending the verses, but serving as the musical/lyrical hook. Ouch. . . .

All Mod Cons is a transitional album by a very talented band, nothing more or less. You could do a lot worse, and they could do a lot better.

> *Ed Ward, "The Jam Ain't Punks—Ain't Kinks Either" (reprinted by permission of* The Village Voice *and the author; copyright © News Group Publications, Inc., 1979), in* The Village Voice, *Vol. XXIV, No. 14, April 2, 1979, p. 60.*

DAVE MARSH

For two albums, the Jam made leader Paul Weller's obsession with Pete Townshend and the early Who stand up as an acceptable substitute for personal vision. With *All Mod Cons,* Weller makes his move. The trouble is he can't decide between branching out into Ray Davies and the Kinks' bogus nostalgia

for things never known or becoming an illiterate version of Bryan Ferry. The result is a record that's nearly catastrophic, weak at the surface and almost rotten underneath. (p. 74)

[Weller has] gone in for some of the most pretentious writing I've heard on a rock & roll record in years. **"English Rose"** is a half-witted schoolboy's rewrite of Sir Walter Scott, while **"Fly"** has all the disenchantment and none of the erudition of Bryan Ferry.

Paul Weller is at his best when he's indulging in fantasies. **"Mr. Clean"** is the Kinks' "A Well Respected Man" turned mad-dog vicious. It fails because straight suburbanites are safe targets. (The forebodings Weller has about his peers in **"In the Crowd"** are a lot more interesting.) Similarly, **"Down in a Tube Station at Midnight"** would work better if its hero had been stomped by his own kind rather than by right-wing creeps. The quintessential paranoia, though, is **" 'A' Bomb in Wardour Street,"** which is as much a miniature rewrite of Pete Townshend's "Won't Get Fooled Again" as it is anything. (pp. 74-5)

[Somewhere] the Jam has lost its punch. In **"Billy Hunt,"** a song about a discontented laborer, Weller says: "No one pushes Billy Hunt around, / Well they do but not for long." This notion about the inconsequential—that every gesture's *only* a gesture—probably speaks very directly to the gamesmanship of current rock. But what's rock & roll worth without a sense of triumph, and the feeling that every gesture is also a blow for identity? (p. 75)

> *Dave Marsh, in his review of "All Mod Cons," in* Rolling Stone *(by Straight Arrow Publishers, Inc. © 1979; all rights reserved; reprinted by permission), Issue 291, May 17, 1979, pp. 74-5 [the excerpt of Paul Weller's lyrics used here was taken from "Billy Hunt" (© 1978 And Son Music Ltd.; reprinted by permission of And Son Music Ltd.)].*

PAULO HEWITT

Within the framework of songs that form the entire bulk of the Jam's work to date lie two recurring themes. Theme One concerns itself with the documentation of the Great British Animal and its times. It's a line that can be followed through the lifestyles of such characters as the **"London Girl"** and **"Mr. Clean"**, as well as taking in the pastimes (**"Here Comes the Weekend"**), violence (**"A-Bomb In Wardour Street"**) and aspirations of (male) British working-class youth.

Theme Two is a bit more complex, and has surfaced in such songs as **"Away From The Numbers"**, **"Life From A Window"** and **"In The Crowd"**. It's the punk problem of balancing both the enforced isolation that craft and success demand, while remaining as near as possible to the all-important source material—in this case the Great British Animal. The trick is to avoid the dead-end imprisonment that bands such as Sham have run head on into without compromising the qualities that brought success in the first place. Progression is the key word here, and this album is the evidence.

Based around a thinly-veiled concept, [**"Setting Sons"**] reveals the Jam, and more pertinently Paul Weller, breaking away from the confinements of mod, punk, call it what you will. Weller has resolved this problem by shifting his viewpoint substantially to the (and I use the term kindly) middle of the road. Whereas before he railed at the absurdities and injustices of the Modern World, now he's coolly taking stock of all the evidence, and supplying us with his bleakest picture yet.

The album itself divides into two halves, but still remains a satisfying whole. The first of these parts is the concept angle, which can be detected only through a process of elimination. It's no more a story than a reflection of the ideals and values that society foists upon us at an early age, and which ultimately tear us apart as we grow up.

Though it's part of a concept, which I'd better point out is based around three friends torn apart by a civil war some time in the future, this forms one of the album's major concerns, namely that of the effect of our present political system on people and their relationships.

By using a concept device, Weller is able to put forward two opposing points of view, one from a guy who is able to state boldly "These days I find that I can't be bothered / To argue with them / Well what's the point?" while his friend proudly boasts "We ruled the world / We killed and robbed / The fucking lot / But we don't feel bad / It was done beneath the flag of democracy."

Outside of this concept, the picture is just as nasty. **"Private Hell"**, for one, examines the lot of a housewife, cut off from friends and relations, trying to come to terms with the fact that her sanity lies in her own hell. . . . It's a mark of Weller's increasingly confident handling of his material that the portrait is so convincing. . . .

The Jam have never sounded better. Yet this album is going to cause them problems, because sooner or later people are going to want answers instead of battle-reports, action in preference to bugle-calls. But, as Weller so unnervingly points out in **"Saturday Kids"**, "It's the system, hate the system / What's the system?????" Paul Weller is 21.

> *Paulo Hewitt, "Taking Stock," in* Melody Maker *(© IPC Business Press Ltd.), November 17, 1979, p. 27 [the first excerpt of Paul Weller's lyrics used here was taken from "Saturday's Kids" (© 1979 And Son Music Ltd.; reprinted by permission of And Son Music Ltd.), the second excerpt was taken from "Little Boy Soldiers" (© 1979 And Son Music Ltd.; reprinted by permission of And Son Music Ltd.)].*

RICHARD HOGAN

On *Setting Sons*, Weller's structures are getting more ambitious. *Setting Sons*, with its twin-stranded story lines, interlocking images and frequent tempo changes, the LP is in its way as unlikely a bidder for the Top 20 as the first Kinks singles were. Weller's lyrics allude to Eliot and Orwell; though his voice is raw, he seems to be talking down to the rock audience by paying far more attention to language than to conventional melody. . . . The biggest problem with Weller's nine new songs is that you have to pay close attention to what they say.

Setting Sons plunges further into the Jam's pet themes—conformity, aging, corruption, propaganda, and alienation, and imperialism. Frequently, Weller and [Bruce] Foxton deal in situations rather than characters, the better to decry modern England. . . .

It's odd that writers and musicians with as much depth as Weller and the Jam haven't broken in America. . . . Maybe the current emphasis on melody in rock is bound to force a

band whose greatest strengths are its lyrics and arrangements into second-class status. But for their verbal scope, as well as their pulsing, scurrying rhythms and '60s-inspired sound, the Jam should command more respect than they get.

> *Richard Hogan, "The Jam: Orwell Rocks" (reprinted by permission of* The Village Voice *and the author; copyright © News Group Publications, Inc., 1980), in* The Village Voice, *Vol. XXV, No. 11, March 17, 1980, p. 63.*

SIMON FRITH

The Jam's first two LPs, *In the City* and *This Is The Modern World,* were full of powerful street images, fire and skill, but the group were celebrating the images, not the streets. They are a reactionary group in that their musical dreams lie in a golden rock past—schoolboy dreams. . . .

The peculiarities of the Jam are Paul Weller's. He's a prickly auto-didact. . . . [He] still hears the great era of rock lyric writing as the 60's, Pete Townshend and Ray Davies, social relevance wth Mod nonchalance. (p. 43)

I ask Paul Weller if he will run out of things to say, exhaust the experience—dreary youth—that still informs his songs, but he takes himself seriously, doesn't value spontaneity anyway. *All Mod Cons,* the Jam's third LP, is a wonderfully clever record, particularly when you hear through its Mod artifacts and references, scattered about like debris from a party that went on too long. It's a record about disillusion, Weller's success songs, weariness/wariness at the top and all that. And, more powerfully, it's a record about the vacant heart of crowd culture, the teenage apathy that is the other side of the coin of rock's community. The Jam's best street song is here: **"Down At The Tube Station At Midnight,"** a sour slab of London violence, tight and vengeful, skins and fascists, Dr. Marten's apocalypse. The truth is that the other punks, the Pistols and the Clash, were naive, cheerful, romantic. The Jam, last of the big three, have never been romantic. Love, as Weller says, is about hard work.

Setting Sons, the Jam's new album, is Paul Weller's most ambitious work. It is more diffuse than *All Mod Cons,* less immediately sharp, but its sophistication, depth, control, could open American ears at last to a classic British group. Weller is using increased artiface—puns and imagery, the Jam orchestra—to explore his sense of waste. The record is packaged, like *All Mod Cons,* in debris, but literal war relics now, uniforms and spent shells, the sense of victory promise: 1918, 1945, Britain and the land fit for heroes. And it is 1980, every promise long forgotten. People have grown old in work that only made sense if something better came. It didn't.

"Hate the system! What is the system?" the Jam chant, like yobbos and then, on **"Eton Rifles"** tell us, as Weller takes on punk populism and marvels, mockingly, at a class consciousness that struts through the streets in safety pins. The punks, at long last, take on the nobs (on the playing fields of Eton). They find out what the Jam knew all along: in this sort of cultural clash, ruling class wit will always win. The kids troop back to Slough, and the Jam's new music has got the mood just right. Britain is swinging into the 80's with a government which is calling on folk memories of patriotism and promise and adjusting us to the sharpest decline in the standard of ordinary living we have ever known. Waste indeed, the move is from punk refusal to the Mod sense of fate. (pp. 43, 61)

Simon Frith, "Winkle-Pickers into the Void: The Jam is Packed Off to America," in Creem (© copyright 1980 by Creem Magazine, Inc.), Vol. 11, No. 11, April, 1980, pp. 41-3, 61.

TOM CARSON

[With] *Setting Sons*, Weller seems to have come into his own.

Because it ultimately refers to class conflict, all English rock & roll is in a sense political—you almost can't avoid it, maybe because the island is just too goddamn small to let you ignore anything. Indeed, throughout *Setting Sons*, the world and history are closing in. The compositions here mesh and collide to create a dark, tightly packed, peculiarly British landscape of desolation. Memories of Empire clash with Welfare State shoddiness, while the vagaries of the caste system lock in dubious battle with a frustrated proletarian violence that's no longer revolutionary but simply a way of staving off boredom. In the street-fighting **"Saturdays Kids,"** Weller interrupts his "Hate the system" chant to ask in bewilderment, "What's the system?," before jumping headlong back into the fray. **"Burning Sky,"** the LP's urgent, tensely beautiful opener, uses rattling drums and martial guitars to turn a sellout's declaration that accepting repression is a kind of freedom into a cryptic, strangely stirring call to arms.

Such social paradoxes are reminiscent of the questing Clash of *Give 'Em Enough Rope* and the impassioned pop dialectics of Elvis Costello's *Armed Forces*—and even more so of middle-period Kinks. But Paul Weller isn't as complacent in his alienation as is Ray Davies. Instead he's torn, his voice hunting from anger to irony to helpless vulnerability and back again as he looks for his place—and wonders if it's worth having one—in this crumbling society. If, in **"Strange Town,"** he's an outsider, "betrayed by [his] accent and manners," he can still remember the punk solidarity that's betrayed in **"Thick as Thieves"** or degenerates into the mindless, endless gang wars of the grim **"Eton Rifles,"** a brutalization that, Weller knows, is merely a uniform away from the futile deaths of **"Little Boy Soldiers."** . . .

Wellers' writing has grown both more direct and more complex—and almost desperately literate, as if his intelligence were the only thing left he could count on. . . . **"Private Hell"**— with its . . . blend of compassion, bitterness and sharp detail— is Weller's rewrite of the Rolling Stones' "Mother's Little Helper," this time from the viewpoint of the mother. Its effect is riveting and doom laden.

Trading punk polemics for an alert, passionate and bloody-but-unbowed maturity, *Setting Sons* is the Jam's best album. Nothing captures their new outlook better than the closing cut, **"Wasteland,"** probably the most intensely felt composition they've ever recorded. The title suggests no-future sloganeering. Instead, a tootling recorder, at once sprightly and wistful, leads you gently into the song. Then Weller enters to deliver a lover's plea that's both simple and touchingly brave. "Meet me on the wastelands," he says.

Tom Carson, in his review of "Setting Sons," in Rolling Stone *(by Straight Arrow Publishers, Inc. © 1980; all rights reserved; reprinted by permission), Issue 316, May 1, 1980, p. 53.*

PAULO HEWITT (Interview with PAUL WELLER)

Let's talk about your lyrics . . .

I find it hard talking about lyrics. It's what it is and it's hard for me to explain lyrics sometimes, unless I can gauge someone's reactions on what they feel the lyrics are about. Sometimes people come up with their own explanations, on what the lyric is about, which is better than I started out to do. . . .

[You] said that you're a lot happier these days. Any reason for that?

No. None that I can give you. I just think you've got to remain a little optimistic. On "Setting Sons" for instance, I think a lot of the lyrics are trying to face up to things and I didn't see any kind of solutions at all. But this year I'm thinking you've got to be a bit optimistic, otherwise you go under and join the numbers.

That was one of the first things that struck me about that album, the bleak scenarios you were dealing with.

It is pretty bleak really . . . but I think it's all true.

Was that how you were leading your life at that time?

It's hard to say because I change so quickly. I get in different frames of minds, but I still think a lot of the things written, especially on that LP, are in a real general sense and pretty realistic. But what I'm saying is that now, I feel different. I still feel pretty hopeful, pretty optimistic. But next year I don't know. I just think about now.

In what sense do you feel optimistic?

I'm trying not to get too cynical. I'm trying not to give up and accept it, because what's the point? If you're all agreed that you've got nothing anyway, you might as well be hopeful about it, because something might turn up. But I mean it's impossible in these days to think of anything in any long term way. It's so unstable that you just don't know.

Do you think any of your songs go beyond that though. Like **"Tube Station"** *will probably stand for ever, the sentiments behind it, I mean.*

I'm not sure. It might be true of songs that I haven't written for the album yet. I've got one new song (**"Scrapeaway"**) and that's looking at that real, bitter, twisted social consciousness that everyone seems to have these days. I'm trying to look beyond that, because you've got to. It's either that or you give up. . . .

A lot of people would say music is escapist anyway.

It is to a certain extent, but I also think music can transcend that as well.

Is that what your songs try and do?

I'm not sure what I try and do when I write a song. Mainly I write because I think a lot about things quite deeply, so therefore it's a means for me to express it, without trying to sound too cliched, that's what it is. But at the same time I try and write in a general sense so that other people . . . maybe it'll make them think as well, and to me it's as simple as that really. If I wasn't writing songs then I'd try and write something else, like books or poetry or anything. (p. 58)

Paulo Hewitt, in an interview with Paul Weller, in Melody Maker *(© IPC Business Press Ltd.), October 11, 1980, pp. 33, 58.*

ADAM SWEETING

Weller is virtually alone in this wonderful world of pop in conspicuously giving a damn. The effort nearly cripples him at times too, but when it works it's blinding. **"A Town Called Malice"** [from **"The Gift"**] for example, once over that razor-slash rhythm guitar and the restlessly pumping bass and drums, Weller suddenly unleashes lines like "It's enough to make you stop believing when tears come fast and furious / In a town called Malice".

It's when he backs off and lets the details fill themselves in that Weller's writing really cuts to the bone. When he tries for living-room drama, it's a bit like looking at a badly-lit TV studio on video tape. . . .

There's a strong streak of the romantic in Paul Weller. It inevitably tends to colour his perceptions, and make his vision of class struggle and the indignity of labour seem over-simplified and at times almost Dickensian. . . .

[Despite] the potency of some of the images, it's only when Weller uses his imagination and not just his eyes that the song [**"The Planner's Dream Goes Wrong"**], achieves anything more than impotent rage. . . .

[There] has to be a special mention for **"Ghosts"**, probably the most haunting and haunted song Weller has written. . . . Weller exorcises a few demons of his own: "That ain't no ghost—it's a reflection of you." . . .

It's probably pretentious to start picking up key images from these songs, but the mirror as instrument of revelation appears again in a sombre Kinks-like number on side two called **"Carnation"**: "Look no further than the mirror—because I am the Greed and Fear / And every ounce of Hate in you". Melodrama? Maybe. It works, though.

In a couple of weeks I should know for sure whether **"The Gift"** is a classic or merely a very good record. At the moment I can't get it off the turntable.

> *Adam Sweeting, "Get Weller Soon," in* Melody Maker *(© IPC Business Press Ltd.), March 6, 1982, p. 17 [the first excerpt of Paul Weller's lyrics used here was taken from "A Town Called Malice" (copyright © 1982 by Chappell & Co., Ltd.; published in the U.S.A. by Chappell & Co., Inc.; all rights reserved; used by permission); the second excerpt was taken from "Carnation" (© 1982 by Morrison Leahy Music Ltd.; reprinted by permission of Morrison Leahy Music Ltd.)].*

STEVE POND

The Gift is the kind of solid but unspectacular effort that will mean a lot to fans but little to the unconverted.

Paul Weller is still absorbed in the plight of the British workers, and the closing tracks on each side offer solutions: on side one, **"Trans-Global Express,"** posits an international workers strike, while the little track makes the simpler, funkier suggestion. "Groove groove—to the beat of this drum." But the former song's ambitious lyrics are buried beneath the most pointlessly murky sound on the record, while the Jam's funk workouts are their least assured and most overextended outings. What's left, though, is a varied and enjoyable Jam record, highlighted by **"Running on the Spot"** and **"Town Called Malice."** On these tunes, Weller's complaints find the big, full sound that matches their fervor. It'll probably put them at the top of a few more

English polls, but *The Gift* is not the record that will take them beyond this point.

> *Steve Pond, in his review of "The Gift," in* Rolling Stone *(by Straight Arrow Publishers, Inc. © 1982; all rights reserved; reprinted by permission), Issue 369, May 13, 1982, p. 67.*

DAVID FRICKE

Paul Weller is always one to take his responsibilities seriously. The Jam have become Mother Britain's top post-'77 band because—more so than ambulance-chasing leftists the Clash—the articulate high-octane anger and no-lead passion at the heart of this flash trio's mod-ified thrash speak directly to the people who feel it most, the disenfranchised youth quickly growing up into that country's broken, dispirited adults. With Bruce Foxton and Rick Buckler's Union Jacked-up bass and drums thunder and Weller's Rickenbacker slam, they still can't help sounding like the Who. But it is that sound that has always given Weller's lyrical barrage of apocalyptic prophecy and working class cheerleading . . . its explosive force.

Weller is aware that the comfy rock life can reduce the strongest anger and heartiest passion to pretentious fizz, and *The Gift* . . . is his confrontation not only with the usual foes—racism, economic fascism, apathy—but the possibility of his own failing. Contrast **"Happy Together,"** classic Jam crash'n' burn . . . , with the headbanging frustration of **"Running On The Spot,"** a scathing indictment of liberal knee-jerking and a confession of his own ineffectualness. (p. 102)

He has a tendency to tilt at too many windmills and then wonder if he's spread himself too thin. But there's no question Paul Weller's causes have effect. . . . The revolution could receive no greater gift. (pp. 102, 104)

> *David Fricke, in his review of "The Gift," in* Musician *(© 1982 by* Musician*), No. 46, August, 1982, pp. 102, 104.*

PAOLO HEWITT

Faced with [**"Dig The New Breed"**], the final Jam LP, the temptation to wax lyrical, (not to mention boringly), about the group, their music and What It All Meant to thousands of people, is obvious; especially when you consider their importance and influence throughout the late Seventies/early Eighties.

That seductive allure of nostalgia and sentimentality is one, though, which defeats the object of The Jam in the first place. They may have been "about" a lot of things—some great music, youth excitement and trust—but as *I* remember it, The Jam always tried to look forward rather than backward and that's the way it should be. Unlike The Who, say, The Jam never bothered with tradition as such, and Paul Weller's decision to break up the band, coupled with the silver line of integrity he always sought in his songs and attitudes, was a prime example of this.

It was this stance that triggered an almost frightening degree of loyalty from his audience, and saw him tagged as a miserable, dour personality simply because he took his music SERIOUSLY. That doesn't matter now. But what his critics failed so patently to realise was that it was this dogged belief, garnered from punk days, that was one of the Jam's main attractions. Words like honesty and integrity are words that have no real relevance to the music business, but The Jam tried to

447

breathe life into them and it's one of the over-riding factors on **"Dig The New Breed"**.

Of course, such theorising is nonsense if there aren't the songs to go with it and **"DTNB"** has quite a few of these as well. Never that well produced, The Jam always made more sense live simple because their belief and passion could be given proper breathing space on stage. As **"DTNB"** fits over their career willy-nilly, so the conviction the band displayed onstage holds the package together.

From the brash hardness of **"In the City"** . . . to the haunting tenderness of **"Ghosts"** . . . , there's a belief and urgency here—a *need* to communicate—that is rarely displayed else-where.

It is fitting that The Jam should bow out with a live LP, and one that takes a few chances, refuses to fit into the established mould of greatest hits regurgitated ad infinitum. It would also be nice to think that a few other groups, established or oth-erwise, will follow the example The Jam have set, but I'm too cynical to imagine that happening.

Quite simple we shan't see their like again for a long time.

Paolo Hewitt, "The Long Goodbye," in Melody Maker *(© IPC Business Press Ltd.), December 4, 1982, p. 20.*

Maia (Teresa) Wojciechowska

1927-

Polish-born novelist, biographer, poet, and translator.

Wojciechowska won the Newbery Medal in 1965 for *Shadow of a Bull*, which, according to the awards committee, "epitomizes all humanity's struggle for conquest of fear and knowledge of self." The novel, set in Spain, relates a boy's agonizing decision not to follow his famous father as a bullfighter, but to establish his own identity. The need to become one's true self and to refuse to accept an identity based on others' expectations is a recurring theme in Wojciechowska's fiction. Her protagonists strive to find courage within themselves to confront and resolve problems that are usually the result of family or societal pressures.

While some critics complain of a didactic prose style that leads to contrived resolutions, most praise Wojciechowska's presentation of the struggle to assert oneself. Both *Shadow of a Bull* and *Till the Break of Day*, an account of Wojciechowska's adolescent flight during the Nazi invasion of Poland and her later anti-Nazi efforts, are viewed as important works and are strongly recommended for young adults. Although Wojciechowska turned away from young adult fiction in the mid-1970s, she remains an influential figure in young adult literature.

(See also *Children's Literature Review*, Vol. 1; *Contemporary Authors*, Vols. 9-12, rev. ed.; *Contemporary Authors New Revision Series*, Vol. 4; and *Something about the Author*, Vols. 1, 28.)

Photograph by Milton Ackoff

JOHN R. TUNIS

["**Shadow of a Bull**"] deals with fear in the heart of Manolo Olivar, a 12-year-old Spanish boy, son of a great bullfighter who had been killed in the ring.

The book is tight, . . . done by a writer whose native language is not English. Miss Wojciechowska knows bullfighting and, more important, she is a magnificent writer. In spare, economical prose she makes one feel, see, smell the heat, endure the hot Andalusian sun and shows one the sand and glare of the bullring. Above all, she lifts the veil and gives glimpses of the terrible loneliness in the soul of a boy.

Perhaps the ending was ever so slightly contrived. But the whole is so good it does not detract from an eloquent, moving book. . . . This book is a must; buy it, read it. If you do, I promise two things: anyone who starts "**Shadow of a Bull**" will finish it in a single sitting. Second, he won't be quite the same person he was before reading the book.

> *John R. Tunis, in his review of "Shadow of a Bull,"* in The New York Times Book Review (© *1964 by The New York Times Company; reprinted by permission), March 22, 1964, p. 22.*

EMILY MAXWELL

["**Shadow of a Bull**"] is about a little Spanish town whose heart is the market place and whose soul is the bull ring. The hero—or anti-hero—is the ten-year-old son of a famous bullfighter. In the main square is a huge statue of his father, and in the cemetery, marking his father's grave, is another. The boy was three when his father was killed in the ring, and doesn't even remember him. Because of his father, he is treated with more respect than other boys, he is taken to the bullfights, he is allowed to see the bullfighters dressing and eating and waiting their turn in the ring, and to listen to their conversation. The men of the town talk to him incessantly of his father, and though he is unable to summon the courage to jump from a hay wagon with the other boys, he is expected to enter the bull ring alone when he is twelve and kill his first bull. . . . He wishes that he had not been born the son of his father, that he had not been born at all. It is a theme worthy of [Joseph] Conrad. The book's only weakness is its ending. So often, good fiction for children has a contrived ending—as if a book were a nursery that had to be tidied up, and the characters put back on their proper shelves, and the door firmly closed. But then the same thing is true of fiction for adults. Miss Wojciechowska knows everything there is to know about bullfighting and a lot about fear and courage.

> *Emily Maxwell, in her review of "Shadow of a Bull,"* in The New Yorker (© *1964 by The New Yorker Magazine, Inc.), Vol. XL, No. 42, December 5, 1964, pp. 224-25.*

NEWSWEEK

["**Shadow of a Bull**"] is disarmingly simple; yet nuances of feeling continually break through, and their subtlety astonishes the adult reader who supposes that a book for children is necessarily . . . childish.

"**Shadow of a Bull**" is the story of Manolo Olivar, age 9 when the tale opens, and 11 when it concludes. He is the son of the man who had been the greatest bullfighter in Spain. (p. 103)

But Manolo lacks the fire of *afición*, the true love of the archaic contest—the ritual confrontation of a brave man with a brave bull, "the victory of man over death" which the Spanish call *la fiesta brava*. A sensitive, brooding, introspective boy, he knows this; but he is the son of his father, and that is a great burden as well as an exalted privilege. . . .

A new illumination comes when he assists an old doctor in treating the wounds of a gored torero—and knows that healing is his true vocation.

Nevertheless, he engages in a novice fight. He is brilliant with the cape—but he is not born to the art and fails finally, cannot go through with the *faena*, the finale leading to the kill. But he has vindicated his honor, and now he can become a healer of wounds, and in that sense, a killer of death.

As accomplished and colorful as this prize-winning book is, it still poses interesting questions concerning the nature of children's literature. It can be argued that the ending is false and bathetic, Pollyanna plus American middle-class values. "My son, the doctor" does not translate easily into Andalusian Spanish. Manolo would far more likely become a peasant, or a hanger-on at bars where aficionados gather to while away the nights with epic tales of stupendous deeds of valor.

But if scrupulous emotional truth is asking too much of a book for children, this will have to do—a touching story told with finesse and delicacy, arresting in its cape-work, even dazzling, but in the end—at the faena, where it matters most—questionable. (p. 104)

> *A review of "Shadow of a Bull," in* Newsweek *(copyright 1965, by Newsweek, Inc.; all rights reserved; reprinted by permission), Vol. LXV, No. 11, March 15, 1965, pp. 102, 104.*

BEST SELLERS

The author may well be proud of [*Odyssey of Courage: The Story of Alvar Nunez Cabeza de Vaca,* a] history that reads like fiction, with a style that is flawless. Maia Wojciechowska has chosen to write about a man who is relatively unknown, but one who deserves much more recognition. Cabeza de Vaca's overland journey from Florida to Mexico, seeking for those cities of pure gold, is one of amazing endurance and courage, as exciting as any tale that [Walt] Disney could imagine. . . . [Cabeza de Vaca] tried to bring peace and freedom where only brutality and avarice existed. His enemies saw to it that he was imprisoned, misunderstood and misrepresented, that he would die a broken man with only his dreams and ideas and fervent love of God intact. But his principles live on to this day and young readers of the present will feel privileged to read this wonderful account.

> *A review of "Odyssey of Courage: The Story of Alvar Nunez Cabeza de Vaca," in* Best Sellers *(copyright 1965, by the University of Scranton), Vol. 25, No. 4, May 15, 1965, p. 102.*

SAUL MALOFF

Knowing perfectly well that only the certifiably insane believe it, I am all for instilling in legal infants the tragic sense of life, ideas of radical evil, existential decision, the intolerable certainty of death—though I would not, of course, deny them healthy play and sufficient sunlight. I have the lunatic, indefensible conviction that it is good for them—morally and aesthetically. I realize, by some monstrous irony of history and human perversity, that the great "children's books" are among the most unbearable of all books. Take the Brothers Grimm, and [Lemuel] Gulliver, and Huck [Finn], and [Robinson] Crusoe. Like any other great work of art, they tell the truth, they tell it pitilessly; and the truths they tell are often ugly, sometimes very nearly insupportable—which is simply to say that they tell the truth. (pp. 321-22)

We have so many ways of lying, so few of telling the truth. And lying is of the very essence of bad art. Lies are always prettier than the truth. They come in soft pastels and they smell nice. They seem more suitable—certainly for children. We tell ourselves they're not ready for the truths we know. After enough feedings, lies become the only truths they know. . . .

The 1964 winner [of the Newbery Award] is Maia Wojciechowska's **Shadow of a Bull,** a book which seems to me to be a case in point. Although it contains some drawings, it is no picture book for tots. It is a short novel intended for kids who can read a sustained narrative of a certain complexity all by themselves, with no one breathing down their necks.

Shadow is a harmless little book, sweet in its way, and instructive. Among other things, it is a guide to bullfighting, its technique and mystique, both, tricked out with a glossary of terms in Spanish and English, a how-to manual, and rather vivid descriptions of the balletic moves. The small protagonist, Manolo Olivar, . . . is the only son of the great Juan Olivar . . .—the superlative *numero uno,* killed in the ring. All Arcangel—his Andalusian town—lives for the time when Manolo will redeem all Spain by becoming his father's even greater successor. Like a primitive people awaiting the advent of a rain-king, all Spain awaits the "birth of a bullfighter." That will be the meaning of his life, and theirs.

But Manolo, a gentle, sensitive, introspective boy, lacks the true passion, the fires of *aficion*—the overriding intensity of feeling for the "victory of man over death" which the Spanish call *la fiesta brava*, the ritual confrontation of a brave man with a brave bull. At the heart of his torment is the sacred code of *pundonor*—the special gravity, dignity, and solemnity which the Spanish attach to the quasi-religious idea of personal honor. (p. 322)

Manolo is a boy "who could hardly watch a fly being killed without feeling its pain, its loss." Reluctantly, doubting himself, he apprentices himself to *aficionados,* spectral figures whose only desire is to recreate in the boy his great father. He undergoes the arduous training—in torment; a boy preparing himself for the rigors of a kind of priesthood for which he has no true vocation.

The possibilities for fiction are interesting; but at this point the game is rigged. Starkness begins to give way to sentimentality. An old doctor—an Andalusian Lionel Barrymore—enters out of nowhere to practice his healing arts on the gored body of a matador, with Manolo's assistance. And there is no possible mistaking the form the cop-out will take. The pressure thus removed—by the author, for the sake of the gentle reader—Manolo can be allowed to vindicate himself in safety. The reader knows the boy is in good hands. No harm can come to him now. He goes ahead with his novice fight. He is superb with the cape—a young master; but he cannot go through with the *faena,* the approach to the kill. Such high drama as the book contains lies there—in the portrayal of the beauty and nobility, the ceremonial grace and irrational meaning of the tragic encounter in the ring. Our moral misgivings—humane, bourgeois, queasy—are made to seem irrelevant, trivial—as, indeed, they should. Not in life (that is not the point); but in *this* fiction.

But life need not necessitate tragic choice. Pathos can always be got round, if you are sly enough. You can have it all ways. Manolo, aged 12, can be a dazzling virtuoso in the ring. And who should appear in the stands at the fight? Who but the old doctor, looking every inch the *deus ex machina*? looking every inch the Way Out?

This Andalusian boy, like any other good American boy, will go off, led by that kindly light, to become a doctor, opting for the supreme middle-class choice: a long and happy life at good pay. Once again, just as we stood on the brink of some painful discovery, we have been spared. It could have been a nightmare, but mother called it a bad dream, and she knows best. Hemingway knew, sometimes anyway, that we are in fact defeated—that defeat is one of the terms of employment.

If *Shadow of a Bull* were not a skillful performance, my argument would be even more fatuous than it is. I return to my absurd supposition—that sensibilities are shaped by what we feed them while they are still malleable; and arguing from that suggest a spirit trained up on the aesthetic of the compromise and the cop-out cannot later be expected to stand too much reality. (pp. 322-23)

> *Saul Maloff, "Teaching Johnny to Cop Out," in* Commonweal *(copyright © 1965 Commonweal Publishing Co., Inc.; reprinted by permission of Commonweal Publishing Co., Inc.), Vol. LXXXII, No. 10, May 28, 1965, pp. 321-23.**

ALDEN T. VAUGHAN

The exploits of the Spanish conquistadors are not always considered proper fare for children's books: the truth about them is too harsh, too cruel, too immoral. Maia Wojciechowska, . . . faces the facts squarely in [**"Odyssey of Courage: The Story of Alvar Nuñez Cabeza de Vaca"**] her brief, vigorous biography of the man who first explored much of the area that became the southern United States and who later served as Spanish Governor of Paraguay.

The story is not a pretty one. The Spanish explorers and settlers display the full range of human crimes and vices: avarice and treachery, murder and slavery—even cannibalism. Yet overshadowing all the brutality and terror are the courage, fortitude and humanity of Cabeza de Vaca. Almost alone Cabeza practiced Christian ethics in a part of the 16th-century world that paid lip service to God, but worshiped gold. . . .

Miss Wojciechowska has based most of her book on Cabeza de Vaca's own "Relation," from which she quotes often and effectively. She employs imaginary dialogue skillfully if sometimes fancifully. **"Odyssey of Courage,"** part fact, part plausible fiction, makes a fascinating, often shocking story of one man's courage in the face of appalling physical hardships and human opposition.

> *Alden T. Vaughan, in his review of "Odyssey of Courage: The Story of Alvar Nuñez Cabeza de Vaca," in* The New York Times Book Review *(© 1965 by The New York Times Company; reprinted by permission), June 13, 1965, p. 24.*

HOUSTON L. MAPLES

[In *A Kingdom in a Horse*] a young teenager, David Earl, . . . feels betrayed and thwarted by his father, a daredevil rodeo clown. A rodeo catastrophe has convinced the father that his son must not follow his career. Retirement to a Vermont village brings an end to David's dreams and a period of bewilderment and pain. The horse is a tentative gift from the father. While David's love goes out to it immediately, he refuses to accept the horse and it is sold to a lonely widow, Sarah Tierney. With mounting enthusiasm the author describes the growing significance the horse comes to have for this elderly woman. It is the rebirth of loving, caring, giving—an Indian summer of fulfillment after helpless bereavement. Sarah's autumnal romance seems to reflect a greater degree of personal involvement for the author. One is carried along and persuaded, because Miss Wojciechowska . . . is a skillful writer: a suspicion lingers, however, that her interest in David declines as the story proceeds. Horse-story fans will relish the vivid portrait of a beautiful animal, probably without worrying about the significance of the horse. More thoughtful readers may be disappointed in the baldly convenient happy ending, which undermines the integrity of the whole. (p. 41)

> *Houston L. Maples, "Growing Pains," in* Book Week—The Sunday Herald Tribune *(© 1965, The Washington Post), October 31, 1965, pp. 20, 41.**

ELLEN LEWIS BUELL

It's well known that horse lovers are dedicated—some to the point of nuttiness—yet it is distressing to read [in **"A Kingdom in a Horse"**] of a 64-year-old woman as enamored of her first horse as any teen-age heroine. It is also hard to believe that Sarah, a Vermont farm woman, though newly widowed and lonely, would spend most of her waking and some of her sleeping hours with her mare.

One can believe in 13-year-old David Earl, though, whose life is briefly but momentously entwined with Sarah's and that of her mare, Gypsy. . . . [Maia Wojciechowska] poignantly evokes David's desperation when his father, a rodeo clown, retires after a nearly fatal goring. David, who has dreamed of being his father's partner, feels betrayed and retreats into sullen loneliness until he succumbs to Gypsy's charms and, eventually, to Sarah's generosity. David, in his hurt and natural self-centeredness, is the real thing but Sarah is an awkward invention. It follows that their story is fantasy, rather than the moving study of friendship between youth and age it might have been.

> *Ellen Lewis Buell, in her review of "A Kingdom in a Horse," in* The New York Times Book Review, Part II *(©1965 by The New York Times Company; reprinted by permission), November 7, 1965, p. 20.*

MAIA WOJCIECHOWSKA

I saw her, for the first and only time, on a rainy November afternoon in 1962. We both boarded the Fifth Avenue bus, going downtown, at Forty-second Street. We both found seats at the back of the bus, and she sat across the aisle from me.

She wore glasses, had straight, long, mousey brown hair, an armful of books, an alpaca-lined raincoat, and a sad, small face. She was ugly and she knew it.

I imagined that she was the only child of an intellectual couple no longer married to each other. Her mother had a full-time job and would not be home until six. At least two evenings a week the mother took courses toward her master's, maybe once a week she went out with a man. Her father was a writer addicted to collecting, and adding to, obscure reference books. When she was little, before her parents were divorced, she was the center of their world. Now she was very much alone. Her intelligence made her a displaced person. It isolated her from other children and, even more, from adults. . . . Among her schoolbooks were two library books with their spines away from me, but with the stamp of the New York Public Library system on the accordion of pages. They were too thick to be children's books. (p. 142)

I stared at the girl until she looked at me, wrinkled her nose, and turned her head away. With that visual dismissal I suddenly knew that what I really wanted to do with my life was to write the kind of books she would like. Not adult books, which she read even now, but books for her—for her age, for her needs, for her intelligence.

This special girl, unlike the others, would not grow older. For me she would always be twelve, her mind fifteen. She would never be part of my world, and I would never be part of hers. The only thing that I could hope for was to build a bridge for her, a bridge of books. Not from her world into mine, but from her childhood into her adulthood. If I could only do that, she need never jump, for the jump from one world to the other is a long and dangerous one—and I did not want this child to fall.

That evening I began to rewrite *Shadow of a Bull*. I had recently finished it as a short story, and already it had been rejected by a magazine. I decided to use the story I wrote for adults as an outline of a children's book. Not any children's book. It was to be *her* book. As I converted thirteen pages into fourteen chapters, I was worried about the unlucky publisher who might publish this book intended for an audience of one.

When the book did come out, I began to wait for a letter from the kid on the bus. (pp. 142-43)

I still have not heard from my girl. Maybe one day she will write; maybe she won't. Whether she does or doesn't, I have already written an answer to her: (p. 143)

Shadow was mostly about pride and being locked in. I say pride rather than self-respect, because in Spain the word *pride* encompasses so much—honor and dignity and self-esteem. You'll find that sort of pride in others, more often in the poor than in the rich, and you'll find it in yourself. Because you are you, you'll respect it wherever you find it in spite of what others may say about it. That sort of pride, sometimes—most of the time—makes life harder than it needs to be. But without pride, life is less.

About being locked in. Sometimes one lives in a prison without a key, without hope of a pardon. Sometimes one never gets out. And sometimes, when one gets out, it is at a cost in pride, and sometimes at a cost in success. It all depends on who built the prison. If you've built the prison yourself, you should never

pay in pride. If others have built it, I hope you'll pay them in success. So, you see, *Shadow of a Bull* is not a book about bullfighting after all.

I have written another book for you, *Odyssey of Courage,* and that one is all about failure. The kind that deprives one of less than it gives. Not a personal failure. For there is so much that others have confused for you. They have put labels on things, and then they got the labels all mixed up. You'll see many doors labeled SUCCESS, but often, on going through those doors, you will have passed into FAILURE. So I wrote *Odyssey* not about a man called Cabeza de Vaca, but about how he discovered that one door had the wrong label on it.

I hope to live a long time, because I want to keep writing for you. You see, while waiting for your letter, and even before, I decided that you'll never grow old; but of course you will. No matter. I will still write for you as if you could not get past your thirteenth birthday. And that's an important time. It is a time of finding out about what life will be like. I want to give you a glimpse of the choices you have before you, of the price that will be asked of you. And don't fool yourself; you will be asked to pay.

When you know what life has to sell, for how much, and what it can give away free, you will not live in darkness. I hope that in books you'll find your light, and that by this light you may cross from one shore of love to another, from your childhood into your adulthood. I hope that some of the light will come from my books and that, because of this light, life will lose its power to frighten you. (pp. 145-46)

> *Maia Wojciechowska, "Shadow of a Kid" (origi-nally a paper delivered in acceptance of the Newbery and Caldecott Awards in 1965), in* Newbery and Caldecott Medal Books: 1956-1965, *edited by Lee Kingman (copyright © 1965, by The Horn Book, Inc., Boston), Horn Book, 1965, pp. 140-52.*

GERALD GOTTLIEB

Maia Wojciechowska is an extremely gifted writer. But in [*The Hollywood Kid*] it is painful to say, the excellence of her writing cannot mask the fact that what she is dishing out is specious. *The Hollywood Kid* is a stark little tale that begins at the bottom of despair and swiftly descends. Bryan Wilson, the 15-year-old only child of Hollywood's greatest movie queen, sits morosely beside his mother's huge swimming pool and asks: "Does life need to be so crummy?"

Bryan and his one friend, a 12-year-old girl named Martha, are lonely, sophisticated, cynical, bright, world-weary kids, drenched in luxury but thirsty for emotional life, deprived not only of love but also of anything resembling a normal home. They are frightened, hypersensitive, withdrawn and thoroughly bewildered. Both kids are casualties of destroyed marriages and disordered family lives, and both suffer from indifferent, egotistical and usually absent parents. And when Bryan tries to go outside himself and cope with the world the results are either dismal or disastrous. Each time, he builds brave illusions that then are promptly smashed, leaving him bruised and reeling and hopeless. But Bryan suddenly realizes what life is all about and what he can do to reverse his downward spiral.

Yes, you did read it correctly: he Suddenly Realizes. It's meant to be uplifting, but in fact it's enough to make strong psychiatrists shudder. The idea that a kid as seriously troubled and alienated as this one can be redeemed in a miraculous flash of self-knowledge is (a) incredible and (b) simplistic and dangerous, for it holds out to questing adolescents a totally false and cruel hope. There is some similarity between the situation of Bryan Wilson and that of young Manolo, the bullfighter's timorous son, in Miss Wojciechowska's very well received earlier book, *Shadow of a Bull*. Both boys, their real selves obscured by the shadows of famous parents, are desperately pining for identities they can live with. But when the melancholy Spanish lad frees himself of guilt and fear and manages to take a step on his own, the author has laid some groundwork that makes the step reasonably believable for the reader. This is, alas, not at all the case with the Hollywood kid, who seems just about as doomed a boy at the end of his gloomy little story as he was at the beginning.

> Gerald Gottlieb, "Growing Pains and Pleasures," in Book Week—The Washington Post *(© 1966, The Washington Post), October 30, 1966, p. 28.*

SCHOOL LIBRARY JOURNAL

In [*The Hollywood Kid*] Miss Wojciechowska does succeed in conveying some idea of what life in the Hollywood milieu must be like for a sensitive adolescent boy. Despite this, the book is a blatant failure mainly because it is a pseudo-adult rather than a juvenile novel. Hollywood families obviously have problems which are quite different from those of average families. And, the 15-year-old hero's problems arise from his life: it is certainly difficult to be the son of a famous movie star, to live amidst the glamour and phoniness of Hollywood, to lose two fathers—the real one by divorce, the stepfather by death. Bryan's search for help somehow strikes the wrong note and the solution to his problems does not ring true. In many scenes, Bryan seems to be an adult masquerading as a teen-ager, in other scenes he is realistic and appealing. The conversations between Bryan and Martha, his 12-year-old friend, and Paula Wing, an ex-movie star, are stilted and embarrassingly false. The style of writing is contrived and there is a basic flaw in the use of point of view. The first five chapters of the book are written from the boy's point of view, but in chapter six (and throughout the rest of the book) the author begins a violent switching back and forth between Bryan's thoughts and those of various other characters which destroys the reader's identification with the hero. The author had a good idea which hasn't come off, because she seemingly can't reconcile herself here to writing for young people.

> A review of "The Hollywood Kid," in School Library Journal, *an appendix to* Library Journal *(reprinted from the November, 1966 issue of* School Library Journal, *published by R. R. Bowker Co./A Xerox Corporation; copyright © 1966), Vol. 13, No. 3, November, 1966, p. 105.*

A. H. WEILER

[Maia Wojciechowska] again illustrates, through **"The Hollywood Kid,"** her sensitive insight into the enigma of a genuinely troubled juvenile born to the purple of picture royalty. . . .

Miss Wojciechowska's taut, precise prose makes it plain that she knows the heart and mind of an unusual lad struggling to free himself from a tinseled world he never made or wanted.

The author's expertise extends to the man-made planet bounded by Hollywood Studio sets with their frustrations and tensions, the exclusive menages of Bel Air, the manufactured merriment of Disneyland. She writes as though she had had first-hand contact with Bryan as he lives through the turbulent death of the stepfather-director he admired; the brief contacts with the poet-teacher father he scarcely knows; and the neuroses of the glamorous mother, whose compulsive need for his presence threatens his dream of freedom in an Eastern prep school.

> A. H. Weiler, in a review of "The Hollywood Kid," in The New York Times Book Review, *Part II (© 1966 by The New York Times Company; reprinted by permission), November 6, 1966, p. 8.*

JANET MALCOLM

The distinguishing characteristic of [**"The Hollywood Kid"**] . . . is its author's profound contempt for the mental capacity of her readers. . . .

[The protagonist, Bryan,] is the only son of a beautiful movie actress who puts stardom before motherhood and devotes just half an hour every day to her son—an arrangement, considering the quality of his conversation, one can hardly blame her for. When the book begins, the boy's stepfather has just died. He had been a movie director and the one person, besides a Polish cleaning woman, "who ever said anything to Bryan that he remembered." The dull-witted boy, however, is considerably less affected by his stepfather's death than he is exercised about the décor of the mortuary chapel where the body lies. "Why did everything in California have to be phony or a lie?" he wonders. The mother takes the director's death at its face value—as the plot device it is—and dutifully assumes the tired part of the mother trying to extract from her son the love she never gave him and has no right to expect from him. The book records at great length how the boy comes to terms with her and learns to feel sorry for the awful people in California instead of hating them. In the climactic scene, which takes place in Disneyland, the mother is mobbed by her fans, and the boy goes to the rest room and throws up. A man appears and explains that the fans are "just a bunch of poor slobs" who "do all that because they need love. . . . That's what they lack, all those slobs, love and beauty." The boy "sees," and stops hating people. "Life, he was sure, was a sort of struggle," and he decides to take up writing "as an exercise" to "help him understand about people."

"The Hollywood Kid" is just one of many children's books as confused and derivative, and I have singled it out as a typical rather than a unique instance. Its author was honored in 1965 with the Newbery Medal, the highest award for children's fiction in the industry, and she takes her calling very seriously, hoping, she says on the book jacket, "to infect them [children], through my books, with love of life and a sense of what's important." Miss Wojciechowska writes her books for readers between eleven and fourteen—an age at which she believes children "tend to be intellectually snobbish." They may be that (whatever it means), but I'm afraid they are not as stupid as most authors of children's books would like them to be, and that they are just as quick to spot pretension and shoddy thinking as the members of book-award juries seem to be slow to. (pp. 217-18)

> Janet Malcolm, in her review of "The Hollywood Kid," in The New Yorker *(© 1966 by The New Yorker Magazine, Inc.), Vol. XLII, No. 43, December 17, 1966, pp. 217-19.*

KIRKUS SERVICE

[In *A Single Light,* a] deaf-and-dumb girl whom the world has rejected, a pedant and a priest who have, each in his own way, rejected the world, are brought together by a marble statue of the Christ Child concealed in a remote Spanish church. . . . Roughly the first half is the girl's story, and it has the undeniable heart-tug of a Jane Wyman movie at a more measured pace. With the advent of Larry Katchen, the American, the somber absorption is blasted into facetious fragments; although he has a chance to recover his humanity, the book never recovers even a sympathetic conviction. It becomes a crypto-parable that masticates love and morality into pulp. (pp. 344-45)

A review of "A Single Light," in Kirkus Service *(copyright © 1968 Virginia Kirkus' Service, Inc.), Vol. XXXVI, No. 6, March 15, 1968, pp. 344-45.*

EDWARD FENTON

Maia Wojciechowska is obviously on the side of the angels. Her new book [*A Single Light*] is a legend imbued with the desperation of the human need for love. Its vivid setting is the harsh, gnarled landscape of Spanish Andalucia. In it lies a poverty-ridden town named, symbolically, Almas—Spanish for "souls." Its heroine is a deaf-and-dumb girl, so unloved by her widower father that he has even neglected to name her. She is a creature of seraphic simplicity, unsentimentally portrayed. . . .

It is after her "miracle," her discovery of [a lost statue of the infant Christ], that a middle-aged American art expert appears on the scene. A failure, as rejected and as thirsty for human love as the Andalusian deaf mute, his adult life has been a single-minded quest for this very statue—a missing work by a Renaissance sculptor.

As the villagers learn of their unsuspected treasure's value, the story turns into an ironic study of human greed. It concludes with a miracle of understanding and regeneration which some readers may find a little too pat.

Maia Wojciechowska's message of love and understanding is somewhat impaired by didacticism and over-simplification. And yet, although her new book is not entirely successful, it is a far better one than most, which are less ambitious and do succeed.

Edward Fenton, in his review of "A Single Light," in Book World—Chicago Tribune *(© 1968 Postrib Corp.; reprinted by permission of* Chicago Tribune *and* The Washington Post*), May 5, 1968, p. 22.*

JOHN R. TUNIS

["*A Single Light*"] is a short book, not more than 30,000 words. (How often good books are short!) I read it twice, to see whether it was as fine as it seemed. It was even better.

Basically a parable, "A Single Light" is a message of love and need, hung round a deaf-and-dumb girl. . . .

The unnamed girl's story is told in the simplest terms. As it moves to its climax, we see how her presence changes the lives of those around her: the priest, his housekeeper, the townspeople—even the visiting art-expert from America, who discovers a priceless Renaissance sculpture of the Christ Child hidden in the local church.

The girl, who has long since accepted the statue as the counterpart of a real child she once nursed, flees with it to the woods. The people of Almas, deciding she is a witch, are prepared to kill her, until the local hunchback gives his life to turn the human stampede aside. Later, the priest and the art-expert find the girl beside a forest stream, with the statue cradled in her arms. The American wants to take her away for "rehabilitation." The priest, who has gone through a moral catharsis of his own, insists that she stay on in Almas. Together, he says, they will teach their neighbors to love instead of hate.

But the overtones in Maia Wojciechowska's book defy synopsis. The finale, in the hands of a less skillful craftsman, could have seemed overdone, even spurious. Here, it is both austere and moving. The whole tale moves and flows, like life. Hope for the future of man is its essence. . . .

Will it be read by young Americans today? Who knows? Those who do read it will carry it with them all their lives.

John R. Tunis, "That Day in Almas," in The New York Times Book Review, *Part II (© 1968 by The New York Times Company; reprinted by permission), May 5, 1968, p. 3.*

BERNICE LEVINE

Told with controlled pathos, the plight of a young deaf and dumb girl, who grew up unwanted in an Andalusian village, and the impact of her presence on the villagers, the local priest, and an American art expert traveling in search of a priceless lost sculpture makes a strong story [in *A Single Light*]. The themes are the overwhelming human need for love and the possibility for even the meanest persons to change. Because of the appeal which these universal themes have for young people and the smooth and unobtrusive quality of the writing, the book should have a wide readership.

Bernice Levine, in her review of "A Single Light," in Library Journal *(reprinted from* Library Journal, *July, 1968; published by R. R. Bowker Co. (a Xerox company); copyright © 1968 by Xerox Corporation), Vol. 93, No. 13, July, 1968, p. 2738.*

LAURA POLLA SCANLON

The horror and despair of the drug scene is conveyed in this excellent book [*Tuned Out*] without romance or sensation. The book's substance is the journal of a 16-year-old boy, his record of the summer that Kevin, his older brother and idol, returned from the University of Chicago.

For Jim the summer is a nightmare. Kevin learned to "turn on and tune out" at school. LSD is his bag now. The family is respectable, middle class. The parents are kind but incredibly dense and unaware of any change in Kevin. Jim bears the burden of caring for him through his last freak-out. The journal tells more than Kevin's story. It reveals much about the family and about the complex relationship between the two boys. The author is so skillful that the narrator's own ambivalence and anger is effectively expressed, sometimes through subtle changes in the journal's style. The book offers no pat resolution. The author knows too much about human nature to indulge in that.

Laura Polla Scanlon, in her review of "Tuned Out," in Commonweal *(copyright © 1968 Commonweal Publishing Co., Inc.; reprinted by permission of*

Commonweal Publishing Co., Inc.), Vol. LXXXIX, No. 8, November 22, 1968, p. 289.

ANITA MacRAE FEAGLES

Nothing is fudged up [in "**Tuned Out**"]; the sadder parts of the drug scene are left out (the sexual indiscrimination common among female users, for example), but the essential story is told.

We are shown in convincing detail the effects of pot and acid; the whole drug scene is handled with authority, from the hippie pad to the mental hospital. The differences among the drugs are clearly spelled out; finally, someone has said how important it is to lump marijuana with the more dangerous hallucinogens. The story is vivid enough to need no moralizing. Motivation is clear and readers know what happened. Not everyone else has been so lucky.

If one is slightly uneasy at remaining dry-eyed in the face of Jim's sensitivity and misery, perhaps it's because it's hard for a female author to carry off a boy's story—in first person. Or perhaps it's because one becomes impatient with Jim's consuming adoration of his brother.

The father and mother, as Jim sees them, don't come off too well, but then older people seldom do these days. Although they are constantly advised to trust their children, they must also, according to some of the fatuous remarks made by young people on the back jacket, be perpetually alert to horrid possibilities. This is a tough assignment, and I would not agree that "**Tuned Out**" should be a ready-reference work for parents. It is certainly worthwhile reading for young people for whom fictionalized material is likely to be more meaningful.

Anita MacRae Feagles, in her review of "Tuned Out," in The New York Times Book Review *(© 1968 by The New York Times Company; reprinted by permission), November 24, 1968, p. 42.*

JANE MANTHORNE

Anguish and fear cry out in [*Tuned Out,* a] rare, moving novel about two brothers sucked into deepest despondency by the world of drugs. So intense is the conflict, so satanic the power of "grass" and "acid," that the drama seems to proceed on two levels: the desperate struggle of Jim to save Kevin's soul and sanity, and the universal war between good and evil. . . . [When] Kevin takes his trip with LSD, Jim stays behind as a terrified onlooker, battling against Kevin's nightmare visions and the strangling circles which reduce the boy to a quaking, terrified animal. No recent novel or factual treatment succeeds as well in showing the self-deception, the sense of alienation, the bitterness against the established order of today, which drives the Kevins toward the touted pleasures and release of drugs. (pp. 714-15)

Jane Manthorne, in her review of "Tuned Out," in The Horn Book Magazine *(copyright © 1968 by The Horn Book, Inc., Boston), Vol. XLIV, No. 6, December, 1968, pp. 714-15.*

JOHN NEUFELD

Maia Wojciechowska is often a fine writer. ["**Don't Play Dead Before You Have To**"] is nearly one of those times.

There are good things. Here is an attempt to write about the kid in-between—neither college nor slum-bound, neither bright nor deadeningly dumb, not ambitious but aware—the middle achiever who is too frequently ignored. There is an honest, moving, yet oddly oblique look at the depression and attempted suicide of a very bright child whose parents are separating. And there is a lovely *coup de théâtre* as an old man, a once-famous philosopher, allows a television interview knowing he will die on camera.

There are some not-so-good things, too. The contrivance on which the entire novel rests. An inconsistency of focus. A confusion about how perceptive, how alone our hero is really to be.

Can a book's basic flaws be overcome by enough shining albeit scattered moments? Miss Wojciechowska's other books have been alternately very good and very much less so. But there is an additional, happy feeling in "**'Don't Play Dead Before You Have To'**"—that of an author "getting it all together" for a new, and real, event. Perhaps, soon, a book as honest and moving as "**Shadow of a Bull**"?

John Neufeld, in his review of "Don't Play Dead Before You Have To," in The New York Times Book Review *(© 1970 by The New York Times Company; reprinted by permission), August 16, 1970, p. 22.*

JOHN W. CONNER

Record the voice of an adolescent as he speaks and writes to a child for a three-year-period and you will have an interesting account of that adolescent's growth. This is the device employed by Maia Wojciechowska in her new novel, "***Don't Play Dead Before You Have To.***" The device is as pretentious as the quotation marks about the title of this brief novel.

It doesn't work. Byron, the adolescent, is an unbelievable, average guy who is sincerely concerned about the problems and welfare of a five-year-old boy for whom he babysits. . . . A reader learns a great deal about Byron through these oral and written conversations with Charlie. But what a reader learns does not contribute to the character the author tries to develop.

The language in which Byron couches his ideas lacks credibility. Byron's sentences contain an occasional four-letter epithet but they are never incomplete. His expressions are not those of a mid-adolescent. Near the end of this brief novel, Byron defends his swearing, because, he says, it is similar to long hair. Both, he says, don't mean a thing. I'm afraid "***Don't Play Dead Before You Have To***" doesn't mean a thing either. (pp. 277-78)

John W. Conner, in his review of "Don't Play Dead Before You Have To" (copyright © 1971 by the National Council of Teachers of English; reprinted by permission of the publisher and the author), in English Journal, *Vol. 60, No. 2, February, 1971, pp. 277-78.*

PAMELA D. POLLACK

Despite her obvious attempt to speak for contemporary young people in her newest novel [*The Rotten Years*] Maia Wojciechowska succeeds only in tediously preaching at them. The barest essentials of characterization and plot are summarily disposed of in the first two chapters which introduce the protagonists: 14-year-old Denise Brown, whose "rotten years" (here arbitrarily defined as ages 12 through 15) are further complicated by her paranoid, Agnew-spouting, fanatically religious mother; and Elsie Jones, the "resident subversive" high school history teacher at Mark Twain Junior High School. . . . The bulk of the book is devoted to the activities of Mrs. Jones' experimental class set up to mobilize her students for a children's crusade against American "moral depression." . . . Denise Brown is scarcely mentioned after the opening pages but the italicized paragraphs which precede chapters are apparently passages from her diary. From these we learn of her growing rebellion against her mother; in the final entry which concludes the book she discusses the arson/death of Mrs. Jones at the hands of her now totally insane mother. Elsie Jones is clearly the vehicle for the author's beliefs and very obtrusive biases, and the rest—a militant mother who wants only black studies taught; foster parents whose charges "[mean] no more than a monthly check"; etc.—are clay pigeons set up to be shot down.

> *Pamela D. Pollack, in her review of "The Rotten Years," in* School Library Journal, *an appendix to* Library Journal *(reprinted from the November, 1971 issue of* School Library Journal, *published by R. R. Bowker Co./A Xerox Corporation; copyright © 1971), Vol. 18, No. 3, November, 1971, p. 127.*

BENJAMIN DeMOTT

[The] defects that mar most problem political [books for juveniles] are of two kinds—excessive detachment (inability to feel the exciting, promising newness of politics to youth) and excessive righteousness (lack of responsiveness to the humanity, however ignorant, of the benighted opposition). And neither of this season's interesting political juveniles—Nat Hentoff's "In the Country of Ourselves" and Maia Wojciechowska's **"The Rotten Years"**—is free of one or the other of those defects. (p. 3)

[The] impression left by ["In the Country of Ourselves"] as a whole—namely that politics is boring—is under-nourishing and false.

A nearly opposite failing scars Maia Wojciechowska's **"The Rotten Years."** The book's heroine, Elsie Jones, is a high school history teacher, a worshiper of Bobby Kennedy and Lecomte du Noüy, a thoroughly passionate activist. Mrs. Jones secures her principal's permission to conduct a 30-day experiment in intensive moral education with one class. ("During that month," she tells her students, "you can become potential saviors of mankind . . . addicted for life to the search for truth.") The experiment enrages the community, the teacher herself is burned to death in a fire set by the demented mother of one of her students, and the event is perceived as martyrdom. The strength of the book—it's less negligible than the story in summary can suggest—is the author's fine enthusiasm for great moral and political undertakings. **"The Rotten Years"** doesn't stand back from "causes" and commitment: it embraces them with a quickness and force that's the best kind of answer to the question, Does injustice matter?

But, as counsel against self-righteousness, the book is ineffective, and its refusal of its imaginative obligations to the community it means to "save" is a serious shortcoming. Miss Wojciechowska continually sets youth and community in confrontation: "From 3:30 to 5:30 PM today I'd like you to be downtown smiling at people. You may stand on street corners, go inside supermarkets and other stores, hang around bus stops,

walk the streets smiling at people. . . . [Later] we shall write a news paper story about your experiences downtown."

Now and then she invites her students to work their way through to knowledge of why elders think and feel as they do. But the martyrdom of Mrs. Jones, together with the paucity of concrete attempts to reach for understanding of other men's fears and anxieties, becomes at the end a powerful incitement to youthful self-pity. (Can the suspicion and hatred felt for Elsie Jones by the demented parent be decently judged without a comment on the suffering of those who have nothing between themselves and total loneliness, no defense except rage against the seductive exotic ways of snobbish college-bred teachers seemingly bent on stealing their kids?) Miss Wojciechowska is remarkable for her willingness to chide the young for pettiness—as when she complains about a boy who would "speak about a chore demanded by his father with as much resentment as when he talked about the injustice of poverty." And her summons to earnestness of mind and social awareness is bracing. But if it's superficial to reduce political positions and commitments to personal traits, it's equally so to reduce political conflict to wars of saints and knaves. **"The Rotten Years,"** like "In the Country of Ourselves," is a less than perfect problem book. (pp. 3, 22)

> *Benjamin DeMott, in his review of "The Rotten Years," in* The New York Times Book Review, *Part II (© 1971 by The New York Times Company; reprinted by permission), November 7, 1971, pp. 3, 22.*

JOHN W. CONNER

Maia Wojciechowska says that [*The Rotten Years*] is her only important book. It is certainly her best book since *Shadow of a Bull*. The editorial gimmicks the author has been intrigued by in recent books are skillfully handled in *The Rotten Years* contributing valuable effects: headlines scream actual news events; the succession of letters written by parents to Mrs. Elsie Jones come as a natural result of the activities in the story; varieties in type size call legitimate attention to important distinctions in speakers.

The Rotten Years recounts one month in the lives of Mrs. Elsie Jones and her seventh-grade class in American history. . . . During this month Mrs. Jones vows (with her principal's blessing) to put aside traditional texts and homework and try to instill some of her own great respect for human life in her students. Her students become their own texts, studying themselves and their relationships with their parents and other human beings. In a carefully prepared series of lesson plans, Mrs. Jones tries to make her students aware of the conventional ways in which children are molded into adults like their parents before them, and the compromises adults make to achieve adulthood. Mrs. Jones believes that the evils in this system could be rectified by one generation of children. She asks this group of children to spearhead that movement.

Much of the author's passion for moral and spiritual truth springs from the text of *The Rotten Years* in a torrent of love. A reader easily senses the author's real concerns in those of Mrs. Elsie Jones.

Is this a book for adolescents? Possibly. Adolescents are rarely enthusiastic about adult philosophy thinly disguised as adolescent fiction.

Is this a book for teachers of adolescents? Definitely. I doubt that a teacher could have ambivalent feelings about this book: A teacher will love it or hate it. Elsie Jones commits herself wholly to her profession. She serves as a teacher, mentor, and guide for her students as long as they desire. A teacher who is afraid of such involvement will not like *The Rotten Years*.

Is this book for parents of adolescents? Yes. Maia Wojciechowska reveals the subtle influences which penetrate a thirteen-to-fifteen-year-old's defenses. A parent who is easily turned off by his child's divergence from an accepted norm (and aren't we all?) may reconsider his obligations to his child after reading *The Rotten Years*. (pp. 604-05)

> *John W. Conner, in his review of "The Rotten Years"*
> *(copyright © 1972 by the National Council of Teachers of English; reprinted by permission of the publisher and the author), in* English Journal, *Vol. 61, No. 4, April, 1972, pp. 604-05.*

JEAN FRITZ

The theme [of **"Through the Broken Mirror with Alice"**] is Man Against Man; nature has . . . been eliminated and, as far as one can see, all good men, including fathers and grandfathers, have been killed off. The scene is Harlem; the heroine is Alice who has been kicked out of her 12th foster home with only an imaginary bee to keep her company and a copy of [Lewis Carroll's] "Through the Looking Glass." Bee and book are both important: the bee to buzz inside Alice's head whenever life becomes too much, the book to convert the unhappy world of Harlem into the chessboard world of Lewis Carroll.

Alice, of course, becomes a pawn; the local librarian is the White Queen, the school history teacher is the Black Queen ("All the black ways around here belong to me," the Black Queen says. "And all the white ways belong to me," the White Queen adds); the school principal and the school psychiatrist become Tweedledum and Tweedledee ("Trust us, child," they tell Alice, "we know better than you who you are"); the welfare worker is Humpty Dumpty who believes in people staying "where they're at."

The most dangerous character, however, who pursues Alice throughout the book (and is finally rejected by her) takes on no Lewis Carroll disguise. In the old days when he felt loved, he was known as Uncle Sam, but now he is simply Sam, the Pusher Man who promises everyone safety inside his castle of dreams. A bitter and clever book with the air of a "West Side Story."

> *Jean Fritz, "Mostly Losers by Newbery Winners,"*
> *in* The New York Times Book Review *(© 1972 by The New York Times Company; reprinted by permission), April, 1972, p. 8.**

MARILYN GARDNER

Two volumes of World War II memoirs may appeal as much to parents—for whom the war was reality—as to their teenagers, for whom it is merely history. . . . [Johanna Reiss's *The Upstairs Room* and Maia Wojciechowska's *Till the Break of Day*] both offer straightforward, not-to-be-missed accounts of what it was to leave childhood abruptly behind as Europe entered and endured world war.

Their victory-over-adversity themes are nothing new. But they present them with such disarming freshness and candor that it is difficult sometimes to remember the authors are drawing on 30-year-old memories. . . .

Maia Wojciechowska was 12 when Germany invaded her native Poland in 1939. From then until the family went to America in 1942, her life became a series of personal vendettas against the Nazis that belied both her age and sex. She reveled in fear and danger, flirted with the idea of her own early death, and seemed to thrive on the close calls that resulted from her reckless courage.

But she was also vulnerable: her father's absence was a source of constant pain. By admitting her weaknesses as well as her precocious strength and independence, Miss Wojciechowska has put together an amazing, admirable story. In revealing herself here she also adds dimension to her other books for teens, and the reasons for her success (and theirs) become obvious.

> *Marilyn Gardner, "In the Last Days of Childhood,"*
> *in* The Christian Science Monitor *(reprinted by permission from* The Christian Science Monitor; *© 1972 The Christian Science Publishing Society; all rights reserved), November 8, 1972, p. B7.**

MARY M. BURNS

Confession may be good for the soul, but confessional writing may not be good reading unless the penitent is blessed, as is the author of [*Till the Break of Day, Memories: 1939-1942*] remarkable document, with an understanding of life's absurdities, a sense of the dramatic, and a felicitous talent for precise, vivid description. Because [Maia Wojciechowska has] these qualities, her reminiscences of a turbulent adolescence during the Second World War are both intensely personal and yet recognizable as a universal statement on the tragicomic conditions which are a necessary part of maturation. The Foreword, comparing the writing of autobiography to the making of a movie, makes use of a particularly apt analogy, for the narrative techniques—employing flashbacks and montages of impressionistic detail—suggest contemporary cinematography. And only a wide screen with stereophonic sound would be appropriate for a heroine who, in three short years, conducted a personal war against the Nazis, become involved with a strangely romantic and mysterious ballerina, and at fifteen, finding life unbearable, decided to die magnificently—like all the great women of fiction. Frank in its delineation of the adolescent's romantic fantasizing, painful in its exploration of the daughter's yearning for her hero-father's approval, provocative in its appraisal of war's effects on family and social relationships, the book is a dazzling blend of emotional pyrotechnics and disciplined structure.

> *Mary M. Burns, in her review of "Till the Break of Day, Memories: 1939-1942," in* The Horn Book Magazine *(copyright © 1972 by The Horn Book, Inc., Boston), Vol. XLVIII, No. 6, December, 1972, p. 609.*

KIRKUS REVIEWS

There is no overall tone or mood to unify the ten brief folk tales included [in *Winter Tales from Poland*. And] it's hard to know what to make of the unfolksy opener, with its pointed putdown of people who are greedy or who distrust what is different, about a Polish poet-angel with clipped wings. In the same moral vein is **"The Freak,"** about a "baby" who is born as an old man into an unheeding village that is soon destroyed by war—but there are also conventional fairy tales featuring riddles and tests of love, a stepmother who appears as a mare and a prince in disguise who marries the princess. The flimsiest tale concerns an incompetent witch who falls in love; the one about a tailor so skinny he can only eat spaghetti is both funnier and more fully treated in [Virginia] Haviland's *Favorite Fairy Tales Told In Poland*. . . .

> *A review of "Winter Tales from Poland," in* Kirkus Reviews *(copyright © 1972 The Kirkus Service, Inc.), Vol. XL, No. 23, December 1, 1972, p. 1358.*

PUBLISHERS WEEKLY

[Wojciechowska] presents legendary folktales of her native country [in *Winter Tales from Poland*]. One is about a baby born an old man, with the power of speech. He asks the villagers why they engage in battles every 10 years, and if they can remember what was the last just cause they had fought for. But he's killed by a bullet before they can answer. Some of the stories are light and entertaining but most have a heavy moral; all are tightly structured and engrossing.

> *A review of "Winter Tales from Poland," in* Publishers Weekly *(reprinted from the February 12, 1973 issue of* Publishers Weekly, *published by R. R. Bowker Company, a Xerox company; copyright © 1973 by Xerox Corporation), Vol. 203, No. 7, February 12, 1973, p. 68.*

SHIRLEY WEINSTEIN

With great candor, humor, and vividness, Maia Wojciechowska gives an autobiographical account of how she lived through the years 1939-1942 [in *Till the Break of Day*]. . . . Her family managed to escape from Poland and went from town to town in France and then to Madrid, Lisbon, London, and finally the United States. At each stopover Maia waged her personal war against the Germans. For example, in France she and her brother were willing to risk death in order to shoot at the Germans. Frustrated in this attempt, they harassed the enemy by stealing hundreds of their bicycles, slashing tires, wrecking truck motors. Many of Maia's escapades and lucky breaks will make the reader gasp. In describing herself Maia gives a true picture of the adolescent. Her obsession with ideals, death, love, self-hatred will strike a responsive chord. This is a book for everyone.

> *Shirley Weinstein, in her review of "Till the Break of Day," in* Best Sellers *(copyright 1973, by the University of Scranton), Vol. 33, No. 2, April 15, 1973, p. 47.*

GERTRUDE B. HERMAN

[*Winter Tales from Poland* is a collection of] freely adapted and embellished Polish folk tales [which] contain all of the elements familiar to that folklore: the mixture of mysticism and common sense; the presence of angels and death in human guise; and, the testing of wits or virtue by riddles and dilemmas. Readers will recognize Joseph Nitechka (here Josef Niteczka), the jolly tailor who is so thin he can only eat noodles and who saves a village from flood by mending a hole in the sky. The vigor and humor of [Lucia Merecka] Borski and [Kate B.] Miller's *The Jolly Tailor and Other Fairy Tales* . . . are less evident here, where the balance falls to more somber themes.

However, Wojciechowska effectively carries the cadence of folk telling, and this book is pleasant in style and content.

> *Gertrude B. Herman, in her review of "Winter Tales from Poland," in* Library Journal *(reprinted from* Library Journal, *July, 1973; published by R. R. Bowker Co. (a Xerox company); copyright © 1973 by Xerox Corporation), Vol. 98, No. 13, July, 1973, p. 2198.*

I. V. HANSEN

Reviews of a number of the novels of Maia Wojciechowska contain phrases like 'a blatant failure', 'too blurred to be effective', 'succeeds only in tediously preaching', and 'the pretentiously allegorical parades of stereotypes'. These are hardly the sentiments to encourage readership and there is a sense in which Wojciechowska is her own worst enemy. It is not too fanciful to suggest that her personal life has been so exotic that she finds it very difficult to communicate with ordinary mortals. . . .

It is a pity, . . . that two of [Wojciechowska's] novels from the 1960s are in danger of being lost. They are *Shadow of a Bull* (1964) and *A Single Light* (1968). Both are set in Spain. It is the Spain of the tourists and the guidebooks, of stark and barren hillsides, of *paella* and the muezzin cry of flamenco songs, of olive groves and hot sun. (p. 186)

There is much [of Ernest] Hemingway in the atmosphere of [*Shadow of a Bull*]. There are references to the killer of death in the bullring, for instance. Bracketed together in Manolo's education are Belmonte and Joselito, photographs of whom appear in fact on the same page in Hemingway's study of the *Fiesta Brava* (in *Death in the Afternoon*). There is a starkness and simplicity in the telling of *Shadow of a Bull* very reminiscent of *Death in the Afternoon*.

The wrench Manolo feels between loyalty and the need to be himself is finally realised, despite the rather contrived ending. It is an eminently teachable novel for boys and draws with a sure hand the terrible loneliness in a boy's heart; it is finally convincing for the young reader. The theme of the sense of solitariness is pure existentialism.

Less well known is *A Single Light.* In this novel, too, is the theme of loneliness and lack of understanding. (p. 187)

The conclusion of the novel is very open, too open perhaps for young readers. Wojciechowska is not strong on endings: *Shadow of a Bull* has three different endings, the most satisfactory, in my view, dealing with Manolo's killing of the bull. *A Single Light* is, in its last pages, too miraculous in promise and too pat. The hope of regeneration for an embittered people is perhaps pious to the point of incredibility. However, the contrast of violence and innocence is sustained throughout and the novel from time to time takes on a [strength akin to William Blake's proverbs]. (p. 188)

A Single Light has the qualities of a legend. The writing, as in *Shadow of a Bull,* is austere and often haunting: the way the girl fills her emptiness is movingly expressed. . . . The novel is suited to a patient rehearsal with twelve- or thirteen-year-old girls. The theme of the great human need for love is stated firmly but without pretentiousness.

In both the novels, the resolution is forced by outsiders, in the case of Manolo, by the old doctor, and in the case of the girl, by the art historian. This invites a charge of contrivance, but Wojciechowska is in difficulties here; there is a tension between the existentialism in the novels and her own inherited Catholic orthodoxy. The priest, in *A Single Light,*

> had thought the world perpetually in a state of war, divided into two camps—the white army of virtue and the black army of sin. And he had delighted in staging battles between these two forces. . . .

(pp. 188-89)

Wojciechowska really wants to operate from this premise and as a result her novels tend to over-simplification and preaching. Nevertheless, she demonstrates in our present case two clear capacities. Firstly, she is able with skill to fill in for the young reader a convincing if exotic background. Her descriptions of the Spanish setting, all too brief and underplayed, are vivid and often momentarily powerful; she can tell us a great deal about bullfighting and about the life of an Andalusian village. And secondly, she underscores the pressures from the adult world upon young people without the tediousness we find in her other novels. (p. 189)

There is much in these two novels that the adult reader could cavil at. Wojciechowska sees herself as 'a midwife to society'; she is unashamedly didactic, a kind of religious social worker. Like Manolo himself and the Count de la Casa, a bullfight impresario who lives in France most of the year, she is a tourist, using the setting for her own purposes and less for the purposes of the narratives; there is a Manolo in both books, there are Garcias in both. The writer's arguments are simplistic and her endings a sell-out. She tackles issues without really resolving them; the failure of the priest, who claims in *A Single Light* that he has never done anything for his people, is a complex issue not examined with anything like thoroughness. Wojciechowska moralises to a point where we as older readers become impatient.

Classroom experience suggests to me that this impatience is an adult phenomenon. . . . In the affairs of people, animals and even things, the young teenager is still attracted by the bald contrast between good and evil, beauty and ugliness, calm and convulsion, courage and fear, all part of these Spanish novels. For these novels breathe a myth-quality that makes some sense of a violent world of pain, uncertainty and rejection. Young readers want to feel that, after all, people are just. All too soon they will learn bitterly that this is not so, learn it perhaps in the world of Leon Garfield, where things are not as they seem (e.g. *The Pleasure Garden*). (p. 190)

I. V. Hansen, "The Spanish Setting: A Re-appraisal of Maia Wojciechowska," in Children's literature in education *(© 1981, Agathon Press, Inc.; reprinted by permission of the publisher), Vol. 12, No. 4 (Winter), 1981, pp. 186-91.*

Yevgeny (Alexandrovich) Yevtushenko

1933-

(Also transliterated as Evgeni or Evgeny Evtushenko) Russian poet.

Yevtushenko is perhaps the most publicized living Russian poet, known throughout the world for dramatic readings of his own work. A large part of his popularity is attributed to the youthful vitality and dynamic personality which flavor his writing as well as his public performances.

Yevtushenko's poems are loosely categorized into two types: declamatory poems, which express his political and social concerns, and personal poems, which focus on self-doubt and self-reflection. Although the latter sometimes border on narcissistic self-absorption, most critics believe that the energy and authenticity of these personal poems endow them with greater literary value than is usually found in his political poems.

Yevtushenko's political poems show affection for the United States and criticize contemporary Soviet society, but at the same time demonstrate Yevtushenko's essential loyalty to Russia. *Babyi Yar* and *The Heirs of Stalin* are perhaps his best-known political poems. *Babyi Yar* breaks a traditional silence in Russia by directly commenting on Soviet involvement in the horrors of anti-Semitism. *The Heirs of Stalin* unsparingly attacks the former Russian ruler and his followers. Although Yevtushenko generally remains within the limitations set by Soviet censors, he has occasionally provoked criticism from the authorities (as with the publication of *Babyi Yar*). In several instances he has been denied leave to travel and perform due to his political "indiscretions."

Recent years have shown an increase in speculation about Yevtushenko's literary talents. When D. M. Thomas looked beyond the poet's personality, he found the poems themselves to be constructed with a "stylistic crudity and spiritual hollowness." However, Yevtushenko remains widely read at home and abroad. Yevtushenko's recent collection, *Invisible Threads*, reveals his talents as a photographer and poet. In this work he focuses on the need for international unity. Alternately optimistic and pessimistic, this cry for world peace can be heard throughout most of his work.

(See also *CLC*, Vols. 1, 3, 13 and *Contemporary Authors*, Vols. 81-84.)

MARC SLONIM

There was a stir, a feeling of discontent among [Russian youth in the 1960's], a critical attitude toward society, a growing interest in fresh ideas, an impatient rejection of boring formulas. . . . This explains the terrific response the poets of the "new wave" (mostly in their twenties) drew from their audiences. (p. 324)

This extraordinary popularity of the poets gave special significance to their work: from a literary phenomenon it grew into a social-political event. A case in hand was Evtushenko whose tempestuous career reflected the contradictions and aspirations of his generation. . . . He was 23 when he made a brilliant debut in 1956 with his long poem **"Station Zima"** (*zima* in

Ken Regan/Camera 5

Russian means winter). It was a "soul searching" lyrical confession with strong patriotic overtones—"glorious deeds, not weaknesses Russia expects from us"—but also possessing a spirit of daring, a drive for independence, and a consciousness that "the writer is not a ruler but a guardian of thoughts."

Within a few years he had become famous not only in Moscow, but also in Paris, London, and New York. He was permitted to travel extensively and was received everywhere as an unofficial delegate of post-Stalinist Russia. Foreign audiences in Europe, America, Asia, and Cuba were entranced by this tall, handsome, outgoing Siberian, an athletic, devil-may-care fellow, who personified youth and poetry. There was rebellion and hope, something exotic and yet something still highly familiar in this messenger from the Communist world. . . . Slightly intoxicated by his international success and his ever increasing influence at home, Evtushenko made the mistake of overestimating his possibilities as a free agent. In 1962, while in Paris, he published a French version . . . of his *Precocious Autobiography* in which he wrote daringly about himself and conditions in Russia. Summoned back to Moscow at a moment when Party controls were being tightened again after the Cuba crisis, Evtushenko was officially blamed and indicted . . . and he underwent a temporary eclipse. All his impending appearances abroad were canceled, and he retired to his Siberian village. He did not make a comeback until the end of [1963] and in early 1964.

His vertiginous rise and fall were the result of a conjunction of political pressures and personal characteristics. Evtushenko was endowed with an almost animal vitality, a zest for life, a passion for new experiences, for love, for travel, for action. (pp. 324-25)

His general outlook and his poetics were basically Communist, but his rebellious nature prevented him from becoming a slave of the Establishment. . . . Sincerely interested in other countries and cultures, he was strongly attracted by the diversity and innovations of modern European art. His own verse is abrupt, expressive, filled with jokes, jingles, and ironical hints. The scanning of the lines, the loud orchestration of broken rhythms, the vernacular used for the de-poetization of the language, come from [Vladimir] Mayakovsky; like other poets of his age, he learned from [Boris] Pasternak how to believe in the "truth of the word" and how to look for unusual metaphors; yet, he could never forget [Aleksandr] Blok's "harps and violins" and [Sergei] Essenin's melancholic complaints: they recur in his pieces on love, parting, and solitude. But above all, he is a declamatory poet, possessed of the same "oratorical passion" which engendered Mayakovsky's "civic odes." Evtushenko also wanted to have a dialogue with his epoch, to take part in political struggle, to employ poetry as a weapon, to put lyrical sensitivity at the service of a cause. Whether he depicted France or praised Cuba, his brisk forays or revolutionary hymns contained a purpose and a message. This was his main weakness and also the reason for his popularity. Some of his poems were like explosions; this was especially true of "Babyi Yar." . . . He depicted the ravine in Kiev, "unmarked by any monument" where thirty-four thousand Jews were exterminated by the Nazis. In a highly emotional way, he evoked the horrors of the massacre and launched a fierce attack against the anti-Semites in the Soviet Union. . . .

"Babyi Yar" was very embarrassing to the Party leaders who kept denying the existence of anti-Semitism in their own ranks and in the Soviet Union, and they blamed the poet for his "exaggerations." (p. 326)

No sooner had the polemics about "Babyi Yar" subsided than Evtushenko came out with "Stalin's Heirs." . . . This time he certainly received preliminary blessings from Khrushchev because the poem suited the Party line of the moment. Evtushenko demanded that the guards around Stalin's grave be doubled and tripled lest the dictator rise from the dead and bring back the past with him. . . .

These declamatory poems had dubious poetic value but their political impact was shattering. (p. 327)

> Marc Slonim, "The Newcomers," in his Soviet Russian Literature: Writers and Problems (copyright © 1964 by Oxford University Press, Inc.; used by permission), Oxford University Press, New York, 1964, pp. 324-37.*

VERA S. DUNHAM

The sensational rise of Yevgeny Yevtushenko's fame in the West some five years ago and its decline, especially in the United States, in the last two years or so have been unrelated to the literary merit of his poetry. Yevtushenko's stance—that of a rebel and envoy, performing artist and civil libertarian—has perplexed readers on both sides of the border. . . .

Two kinds of themes can be distinguished in Yevtushenko's poetry: the civic and the intensely personal. These two strands were refreshingly interlaced in the early poetry of the mid-fifties ("Weddings," for instance).

At about the time of his first flamboyant trips abroad, his poetry bifurcated. Some civic pieces became bombastic and his personal lyrics took on a somewhat whining tone. It is hard to deny that Yevtushenko lacks self-discipline. He writes too much and reveals himself too frantically.

Despite his hurried and at times heavy manner, there is ample evidence of the existence of substantial poetic resources. . . .

["The Poetry of Yevgeny Yevtushenko 1953 to 1965"] includes the sensational "Babii Yar" and "The Heirs of Stalin," though a number of important poems are absent. . . .

In Yevtushenko's lyrics, the theme of a dogged search of the self is couched in so much ambiguity that ambiguity itself emerges as a major theme, as in "Envy" and "Prologue." . . .

Yevtushenko is neither a modernist nor a strict adherent to tradition. When a somewhat hectic and not unattractive narcissistic self-examination is expressed through his favorite devices, he comes into his own. He is a narrative poet whether his pieces are long or short, and as a narrator and reciter he plays skillfully with language. Within conventional limits, he exploits frequent repetition, near rhymes, sustained and sonorous echoes.

Punning is an important device for him, as it is for most good young poets, and he revels in the game of verbal association which, until not so long ago, was almost illicit in Soviet poetry. Yevtushenko's dactylic rhymes do more than mark the ends of his lines. They bind and mirror associations.

> Vera S. Dunham, "Public Poet," in The New York Times Book Review (© 1965 by The New York Times Company; reprinted by permission), December 26, 1965, p. 17.

MARGARET DALTON

"The new young Mayakovsky of today," says Herbert Marshall of Yevgeny Yevtushenko. And there is indeed some parallel between the personalities and works of these two poets. If Mayakovsky was the poet of the Revolution, Yevtushenko occupies a similar position in the post-Stalin thaw. Something of Mayakovsky's personal dynamism and public appeal is present, though to a weaker degree, in Yevtushenko. In tone, language and form, Yevtushenko is at times very close to Mayakovsky. This is especially the case in his rhetorical poetry, declaimed "at the top of the voice" and addressed to the masses rather than to the "chosen few." . . .

Like Mayakovsky, Yevtushenko is primarily a "civic" poet (though not to the exclusion of personal, lyric poetry), involved in contemporary issues and committed to the ideology of the Communist regime. Yet the dissimilarities which become apparent at closer scrutiny—caused by different political and intellectual climates and by differing poetical personalities—may possibly be more fundamental and decisive than are the points of contact. The revolutionary and post-revolutionary periods in which Mayakovsky was active were characterized by material deprivation and cruelty, but also by creative freedom and enthusiasm. Mayakovsky and his "co-Futurists" fervently believed that they were creating new art for a new and better society. . . . None of this ebullient optimism was present in the fifties, the starting point for Yevtushenko's poetry. Despite the thaw, the memories of the terror of the thirties and the privations of one of the most devastating wars in Russian history were still vivid. Yevtushenko is representative of those young poets who were slowly groping their way toward more individual and less prescribed art; but they were hardly daring innovators: they looked back to poets like Mayakovsky, just as they looked back to the Revolution as a distant ideal which had been darkened and corrupted.

Compared to Mayakovsky, Yevtushenko is more restrained, more narrow in his emotional scale and, possibly, more lyrical. Although he will avoid the "lapses" and vulgarity of Mayakovsky, his tendency at overt moralizing strikes at times an unpleasantly pedantic note as compared to Mayakovsky's expansiveness. Despite the fact that Yevtushenko is still developing, it seems fairly certain that he will never approach the linguistic genius and emotional *élan* of Mayakovsky. . . . (p. 271)

> *Margaret Dalton, "At the Top of the Voice," in* The Nation *(copyright 1966 The Nation magazine, The Nation Associates, Inc.), Vol. 202, No. 10, March 7, 1966, pp. 271-72.*

ROSEMARY NEISWENDER

Bratsk Station, which is as heroically ambitious as its subject, is a 5,000-line, 35-poem cycle commemorating the construction of a vast hydroelectric power complex in Siberia. The light-giving Bratsk station is seen as a symbol of faith and human progress, and is contrasted with an Egyptian pyramid, seen as the epitome of slave labor and lack of faith. Within this context, Yevtushenko employs a variety of verse forms, from classic poetic diction to a conversational, colloquial style. . . . [It is] a significant contribution by the most publicized living Soviet poet (and possibly the most talented). . . . (pp. 86-7)

> *Rosemary Neiswender, in her review of "Bratsk Station and Other New Poems," in* School Library Journal, *an appendix to* Library Journal *(reprinted from the January, 1967 issue of* School Library Journal, *published by R. R. Bowker Co./A Xerox Corporation; copyright © 1967), Vol. 13, No. 5, January, 1967, pp. 86-7.*

JULIAN SYMONS

It is very easy for any book reader to see that parts of Yevtushenko's loose series of poems that make up a hymn of praise to *The Bratsk Station* (a new Siberian hydro-electric development) would sound magnificent at a public reading, particularly those with a strong repetitious thrust like *The Execution of Stenka Razin* and *Envoys are Going to Lenin.* Yet one feels with these poems . . . that there are verbally intoxicated writers who don't worry much about putting down the right words in the right order.

There are several important exceptions to this intoxication—a delicate poem of Yevtushenko's called *The Far Cry* [is an example] . . .—but it is impossible not to feel that [he has] sacrificed too much for the sake of immediate intelligibility. . . . I suppose if you are a public poet like Yevtushenko, consciously a Russian patriot, you are bound to produce extravagantly phrased poems on large themes, and one would like to feel that a comparison is possible with our own early

anonymous ballads, or [Thomas] Percy's *Reliques.* The trouble is that Yevtushenko's poems often look much more like [Thomas] Macaulay.

> *Julian Symons, "Cooked and Raw," in* New Statesman *(© 1967 The Statesman & Nation Publishing Co. Ltd.), Vol. 74, No. 1897, July 21, 1967, p. 87.*

THE TIMES LITERARY SUPPLEMENT

Is [Yevgeny Yevtushenko], as Anthony Burgess remarked recently . . . , "easy to do, but hardly worth doing" . . . ? Reading George Reavey's fairly substantial collection of Yevtushenko translations [*The Poetry of Yevgeny Yevtushenko*] . . . together with the poet's own fat volume *Idut belye snegi* (a full retrospective of the best poems from earlier books, plus some recent work), one would be forced to a rather different view. He is only "easy to do" in the sense that the obvious interest of his subject-matter can be made to sponsor loose, publicistic translations which make no attempt to reproduce his often very pointed rhymes and sound-effects. And that he is "hardly worth doing" is surely a hasty judgment, hinging again on a negative reaction to his "civic" concerns, but forgetting the not inconsiderable bulk of deeply felt lyrical and meditative poems. . . . Yevtushenko seems entitled to some defence, if only because in his best personal poems of troubled, questioning feeling he shows that the matter of poetry, even in a western sense, is in him. Washing the soiled linen of the age is perhaps nothing more unusual than what [Ezra] Pound and [T. S.] Eliot—and Dante—might have claimed to be doing before him. But a lot depends on the detergent, as well as on the state of the linen. What one objects to in Yevtushenko is his proprietorial adoption of the role of international vigilante, skimming from Copenhagen to Helsinki, from Fairbanks to Beirut, from Taormina to New York, and never failing to hold up a few dirty garments to public view as each place, each encounter suffers instant versification. A bullfight in Spain, a right-wing provocation at a conference in Finland, homosexuals meeting in the shadows of the Coliseum in Rome—all are conventionally rapped as this Siberian archangel passes over.

With America, however, he has a deeper involvement, and his poems on that country, whether soiled linen poems or not, have a great interest. In the present Russian volume he has a section devoted to his more recent American poetry. This includes a highly improbable **"Monologue of Dr. Spock"** ("I'm a troublemaker. I'll trouble you to love your children!"), and a rather unoriginal **"Monologue of a Broadway Actress"** on the theme of the absence of proper roles in modern society, but also some genuinely shocked, probing, concerned poems on the violence of American events. In the **"Monologue of an American Poet"**, dedicated to Robert Lowell, he seems to put on Lowell's darkly brooding mantle to speak of the loss of love, friends, hope, confidence of everything except the possibilities of the next generation. **"The Whales' Graveyard"** draws a strange imaginative parallel between the much-persecuted whale ("You're ugly if you're big") and the doomed family of Kennedys; at least, he says, there are no hypocritical flowers in the Eskimos' graveyard, the bones themselves are the flowers. And in **"The Mark of Cain"**, which is in memory of Robert Kennedy, the chain-reactions of a nation bent on fratricide are chosen as the central image, the poem ending strikingly: "Wind whipped and slapped, wet with invisible blood, as if the pages of the Bible were beating me on the face." (p. 1389)

> *"From Blok to Yevtushenko," in* The Times Literary Supplement *(© Times Newspapers Ltd. (London)*

1970; reproduced from The Times Literary Supplement by permission), No. 3587, November 27, 1970, pp. 1389-90.*

ALAYNE P. REILLY

Yevtushenko has come close to being an ideal socialist-realist poet, lending his talents to the exposition of social and political themes as well as to the intimate lyrical expression of personal feelings. He is a gifted poet, but his dual dedication to Marx and Apollo has resulted in a somewhat uneven performance: his poems range from propagandist doggerel to truly expressive lyrics. . . . (p. 173)

Yevtushenko made his first trip to the United States . . . during the spring of 1961. The trip seems to have had a profound effect on him, for soon after it a subtle but very significant change began to manifest itself in his political poems. The first evidence of this change is found in the *absence* of a barrage of anti-American poems after the trip. This is important for two reasons: first, because negative reports are expected of Soviet writers who visit America, and second, because Yevtushenko had previously excelled in the writing of anti-American poems. (p. 174)

Yevtushenko launched his career as a poet with propaganda verses among which was a somewhat naïve but powerful anti-American poem, "A Boxer's Fate." It relates the history of Jim, the World Boxing Champion, who is deprived of his title and livelihood in retaliation for having signed a petition against the North Atlantic Treaty, and whose sole comfort these cold, hungry days on the streets in New York is a portrait of Stalin given him by a Russian soldier during the war. (pp. 174-75)

The poem is typical propaganda verse: a hero of the masses suffers at the hands of the capitalist bosses for his pro-Communist gesture, but is calmed by visions of freedom inspired by thoughts of Comrade Stalin. Yevtushenko's poetics here is rather primitive. There is not one genuine poetic image in the entire poem, which is composed of prose statements syntactically rearranged to provide occasional rhyme. There is no poetic meter. (p. 176)

Propagandist clichés abound in the poem: "capital of profit," "boss," "breathe freedom," "Stalin's inspired ideas," "property of the people," and so forth. Nevertheless, the poem is quite an ambitious undertaking for a sixteen-year-old, and clearly shows the potential talent that Yevtushenko was later to develop, as polemicist as well as poet.

It is this polemical spirit, however, that seems unusually silent as Yevtushenko confronts America herself. He seems a bit overwhelmed and unsure of what to say. The first poem from his American trip [is] "An American Nightingale." . . . The poem is an impression from the poet's visit to Cambridge. It is a weak poem, replete with oversimplification ("In the land of perlon and dacron, / and of science that has become a fetish"); awkward metaphor (a nightingale in the city of Cambridge); journalistic cliché ("half-truths and lies," "black deeds," "millions of questionnaires," "shark-like bodies of rockets"); saccharine sentimentality ("And somewhere in the heart of Russia / . . . his little Russian brother sang"); and banal observation (nightingales speak the same language; men don't understand one another).

Technically, the poem is rather loosely constructed and the poet's thoughts seem unmotivated and disconnected. For instance, the line "A bird is no load for a branch" is awkward

and contributes little to the poem. The poet jumps from "the land of perlon" to "a bird on a branch," to "students on a spree," to "rockets ready for action" without much motivation or cohesion of content or of mood. Such a lack of inner consistency suggests a lack of conviction on the part of the poet as to what to say about America. The poem also seems rather drawn out and inflated in comparison with its simple presentation of the theme of nonunderstanding. Moreover, the confrontation with this nonunderstanding seems to engender strangely little regret. Hence the poet's thought appears insincere and superficial. His use of contrastive epithets such as "mournfully he sang, and happily" and unusual simile such as "the music, like a blizzard lashed" conveys an impression more of ostentatious display than of poetic depth or firm conviction, and underscores the superficiality of the poem's impressionism. At the same time, one cannot fail to mark the absence of the usual criticisms of the American scene. The students are described as happy, the weather is pleasant, and something in the surroundings apparently reaches out to the poet, calling to mind one of the tenderest images of Russian poetry, the nightingale. However untypical of the American scene this association may be, it is a sharp contrast to the "vultures of capitalism" often found in propaganda. (pp. 177-78)

Yevtushenko recovers his balance a bit in his next American poem, "Girl Beatnik." The scene is New York, the world is a "moralist who's been howled down." The beatnik is pictured as running away even from herself, finding truth only in the "twist." . . . The lines are clever and striking. . . . The imagery stresses the emptiness and confusion of the beatnik's world, where enmity exists, but no love. Yevtushenko delights in composing such maxims, and his poetry is full of them.

"Girl Beatnik" describes the despairing world of a beatnik, supposedly an American, but the reference to "spiked heels" is a curious one for American beatniks who usually go barefoot or, at best, wear sandals. Soviet girls, on the other hand, are quite style-conscious and almost always wear high heels. The relative anonymity of this beatnik, together with the absence of a comparison to "happy" Soviet youth, distinguishes it from the didactic mood of propagandist writings such as "A Boxer's Fate." "Girl Beatnik" is a much better constructed poem than "An American Nightingale," and some of its imagery is captivating. There is a striking comparison of the moon moving along its heavenly route with a drunken beatnik staggering along a well-lighted avenue. . . . The poem is a cry of despair. However, while it was supposedly written about America, the words "New York" in the first line could easily be changed to "Paris" or "Moscow" without disrupting the rest of the poem. Thus, as a concern with morality instead of ideology, it transcends political or geographical boundaries, and becomes a statement of the spiritual condition of man.

The third poem about Yevtushenko's visit to America, "Monologue of the Beatniks," is quite ambiguous. Although it was written in New York, there is nothing in the text to identify it as a description of America. It, too, is a personal poem, a statement of youth—perhaps of New York, perhaps of Moscow, perhaps of the world. The poem bears signs of Yevtushenko's growing mastery: thoughts are expressed with imagination and poignance. The imagery shows a poet, not a propagandist, at work. . . . [The poet] uses assonance and alliteration with great effectiveness. . . . The image of ideas being scattered like dandelions is vivid and expressive, showing Yevtushenko at his creative best. The self-negating essence of irony is astutely captured in a later stanza: "Irony, you have

---

turned from our savior into our executioner.'' And literary imagery is even more successfully employed in this poem than in **"Girl Beatnik":** ''Irony, to you we've sold our soul. / receiving no Margaret in return.''

The simple and direct exposition, as well as the absence of cliché and *non-sequitur*, attest to the poem's sincerity and depth, and suggest an intimate acquaintance of the poet with his theme. As such the poem may be interpreted as Yevtushenko's commentary on what he knows best: Soviet life. The ambiguity of this poem is an early example of the trend of Soviet writers in the 1960s to use their trips to America in part as camouflage for observations that do not necessarily concern America.

These three poems give some idea of the range of Yevtushenko's poetics and the long way he has come from his teenage verses of puppet-propaganda to thoughtful reflection on the capitalist world. Upon personal acquaintance, he seems to find it not so alien nor so one-dimensional. The two beatnik poems especially show the beginnings of a change in Yevtushenko's attitude towards America, notably: the absence of political cliché, didacticism, or a denunciatory tone, the concern with moral rather than political values, and the ambiguity of his references. **"An American Nightingale"** and **"Girl Beatnik"** present us with at least a hint of admiration as well—of Cambridge and New York as beautiful cities.

Thus, though Yevtushenko's exposition of his impressions of America is rather limited on this first trip, his hesitation may be interpreted as a not unfavorable reaction to the country of capitalism. For once the young poet-polemicist seems speechless, as if his confrontation with the real America comes into conflict with the preconceived notions of propaganda. America begins to emerge as an attractive image in his poetry. (pp. 179-82)

This change in the poet's attitude toward America is accompanied by the beginning of some vacillation in Yevtushenko's political ideology. The teen-ager's utopia begins to show signs of fallibility. It may be significant that two outspoken poems against abuses within the Soviet Union, the famous poems **"Babii Yar,"** decrying the persistence of antisemitism in the Soviet Union, and **"The Heirs of Stalin,"** about the continuation of Stalinist policies by his ideological heirs, were written after his visit to America. (p. 183)

The poem, **"A Letter to John Steinbeck,"** marks Yevtushenko's return to political poetry in the war against capitalism. The poet reproaches Steinbeck for not protesting the war in Vietnam. . . . The poet's description of July days as ''the winter of our discontent'' (a reference to Steinbeck's novel by that name) borders on bathetic cliché. The ''poem'' is versified prose rather than poetry, and is full of the political cliché, bathos, and didacticism that are typical of propaganda.

The first poems to appear after Yevtushenko's second trip to America are strongly anti-American. **"Slippery Ice in New York"** extends the image of slippery ice in the streets to slippery politics in a rather crude caricature. . . . (pp. 183-84)

America is portrayed as a Natasha Rostov (the heroine of Tolstoy's *War and Peace* and one of the most beloved feminine images in Russian literature), running through the streets, wanting only peace and a happy world ''free from baseness and bombs.'' But someone keeps pouring icy lies beneath her feet.

The poem ends with the moralistic condescension of the skilled propagandist:

> Be more careful crossing the icy streets.
> Give me your hand,
>   I'll take you across.

The poem is an apparent denunciation of the Vietnam War, and possibly the poet's ''payment'' for his trip to America. . . . [The] strength of feeling conveyed through the consistency of the imagery does suggest some inner conviction on the part of the poet. The angry young polemicist has caught his second wind. This is Yevtushenko's most powerful anti-American poem. The crude imagery, political cliché, and contemptuous tone mark it as propaganda.

On the other hand the ending of the poem may be interpreted as the emergence of a new American image in Yevtushenko's work—an America divorced from capitalism, an innocent girl, a Natasha Rostov, to be saved by the poet. Some later poems will show that the chivalry aroused in the poet by his first visit to America (his desire to salvage the reputation of her ''gringo'' sons) has grown in measure with reacquaintance.

A second poem, **"A Ballad of Nuggets,"** tells the story of a drunken prospector in Alaska whose search for gold bankrupts him. The poet meets him in a bar complete with a ''stripeskimo'' and hears his sad tale. . . . [Amusing] images break up the moralizing of the poem which exposes the ravages of gold fever. It is a poorly written poem, indicating perhaps that the poet's interest in it was not great.

His debt to the Party paid, as it were, with these two unfavorable poems about America, Yevtushenko returns to work on a cycle of verse that continues his exploration of himself and develops into allegorical commentary about the Soviet Union as well. The first of these poems, **"Cemetery of Whales,"** published two months later, is again about Alaska. The sight of whale bones on the frozen wastes calls various associations to the poet's mind. He compares the fate of the whales to the vulnerability of other giants . . . whose greatness is impossible to hide. . . . The Russian is very concise here and the images well chosen. (pp. 185-86)

[The] conciseness of the Russian is very forceful, due to the crisp iambic trimeter and the dramatic assonance of the rhyme. The poet concludes that life is better among the Eskimos, who have some ''tact'' and sense of decency before the dead.

"Cemetery of Whales" is a powerfully written poem that points toward the beginning of an allegorical tendency in Yevtushenko's poems about America. There is little ambiguity here—the poet himself defines his symbols quite clearly. Later poems become more cryptographical as the poet finds his candor ill rewarded. . . . (p. 187)

Significantly enough [in the later cryptographical poems, such as **"Monologue of a Fox on an Alaskan Fur Farm,"**] America seems to have become a personified female figure whom the poet treats with great tenderness and affection and to whom he reaches out in times of despair. This has formerly been a role reserved for Russia. That Yevtushenko, like [Andrei] Voznesensky, is strongly attracted to the capitalist beauty cannot be doubted. There is something in America with which both poets strongly identify. For Yevtushenko capitalist America becomes ''my America,'' right beside ''my Russia.'' America has not supplanted Russia in the poet's soul—he remains deeply attached to his motherland. But if Russia is his mother, his stern parent, America is perhaps his sister, his understanding friend. She is no longer the cause of all the miseries of the world, as Communist propaganda suggests, but a covictim of the suffocating times. The poet would like to save her as well as himself, but he does not know how. (pp. 189-90)

Artistically, [the later poems] about America are among the best of Yevtushenko's creative work. The imagery is concise and powerful. The precise employment of assonances, internal rhymes, and unusual associations marks a profound maturation of his poetics. The inner consistency and simplicity of theme attest to the poet's sincerity and depth of conviction. . . . The confusion of his first poems about America has given way to despair over his own purposelessness, and disenchantment with the morality of the world on both sides of the globe. A strong desire to save the world alternates with cynicism over its seemingly hopeless state. (p. 196)

As the soul of America offers him solace and companionship, so the form of America offers him allegorical camouflage for the outpourings of his own soul. (pp. 199-200)

> *Alayne P. Reilly, "Allegory: Yevgeny Yevtushenko, Poems," in her* America in Contemporary Soviet Literature *(reprinted by permission of New York University Press; copyright © 1971 by New York University), New York University Press, 1971, pp. 173-204.*

ANDREI SINYAVSKY

[In 1965] Yevgeny Yevtushenko published a long poem [**"Bratsk Hydroelectric Station"**]—at once summary and programmatic for his own art, and intended to communicate the experience of the modern age and to connect this with the experience of the past, with the history of Russia. The poem unfolds a panorama of varied human destinies and ordeals, of work and struggle. As the author states in his Foreword, the unifying principle is the dispute between two themes: "the theme of unbelief," comprised in the monologues of an Egyptian pyramid, and the "theme of faith," expressed in the monologues of a hydroelectric station and by figures, episodes, and lyrical meditations connected with its construction. Before us arise the outlines of a vast monumental scheme, and indeed in respect to its size Yevtushenko's poem clearly exceeds the customary scale of most modern poems, just as it outwardly wishes to match the structure that gave it its life and name—the Bratsk Hydroelectric Station.

To be sure Yevtushenko also explains in his Preface: "Perhaps this is not a poem, but simply my thoughts united by the dispute of the two themes." . . . Digressions and monologues, thoughts and discussions—even if they fill up the whole poem—can be interesting and poetically justified. We shall take advantage of the appearance of such a responsible work, presented to us by Yevtushenko in the unconstrained conversation he carries on with the reader, and we shall involve ourselves in this and try—even if digressions are needed—not to restrict ourselves to an evaluation of this poem, but to touch on some general problems that his work poses for modern poetry.

The first problem is Yevtushenko himself, a man who enjoys extraordinary success with a wide, mainly youthful audience. Even persons who are reserved or skeptical about his verse (among them, let us speak frankly, the author of this article) are forced to confess that the poet's fame both at home and abroad, perhaps the most loudly trumpeted of recent times, has a real foundation. (pp. 167-68)

Yevtushenko owes his popularity first of all to himself—to the very vivid and fundamental qualities of his character and poetic talent, which permit him, for better or worse, to rule over the minds of his time within a certain circle, and to a limited degree to fill the gap left in poetry by the departure of Mayakovsky. After a long interval he has given back to us the sense of a lyrical *biography*, which unfolds before our eyes in a series of poems sustained by a single subject, namely the personality and life of the poet. (p. 168)

[However], Yevtushenko, for all his proneness to self-display, lacks the stamp of an exclusive personality, the idea of a vocation or of a great and terrible fate which would impart to the poet's destiny something providential and not to be resisted, and at the same time would allow him to develop his own biography like a legend, in which personal life is raised to the level of a unique saga, half real, half invented, and created day by day before an astonished public. . . . Yevtushenko's hero seems like an ordinary man. His attractive features and high ideals do not prevent him from being "like everyone else," and from most often appearing in the role of "a fine fellow" or "a good guy," who is interesting, good, bold, but by no means one of the elect. He is far from that myth-making about one's own personality that so attracted Yesenin and Mayakovsky, to say nothing of Blok and [Marina] Tsvetayeva, and he is far from their spiritual storms and messianic pretensions. Nevertheless Yevtushenko, like them, introduces into his poetry credible details of his own life and surroundings. . . . He tells about his appearance and character, and thereby sustains in his verse the illusion of *acquaintance* with a living man. . . . (p. 169)

It is quite a different matter with the tradition of Mayakovsky's civic poetry, which Yevtushenko inherits and continues, since he is one of the most keenly topical poets of the new generation and eagerly assumes the role of tribune. Civic feelings largely dictated **"Bratsk Hydroelectric Station"** too, which has a special chapter in honor of Mayakovsky, who serves the author as an example of steadfastness, nobility, and revolutionary purity.

But the affective verse of Mayakovsky, if not supported from within by a personality of the same charge and caliber, sounds often on his lips rather bare and rarefied and declamatory, and it easily passes into a mere publicist's work. . . . On the other hand Yevtushenko, even in the role of fighter, tribune, or agitator represents something different, a weaker variant of citizenship. Yevtushenko does not have the forcefulness of Mayakovsky, who always went straight and headlong to his goal, allowing no circumlocutions or false ideas; therefore Yevtushenko is forced to resort to maneuvers, ambushes, detours, and camouflage. ("We managed to get orders and do it all the other way around.") He has even worked out his own special "battle strategy." For him the poet "retreats in order to attack," maneuvers, lures, dodges. (pp. 172-73)

Much, it is obvious, has changed and grown more complex since the time when the poet made no secret of the flank on which he concentrated ("Who steps to the right there? To the left, left, left!"), when he strode to the attack straight and to the front, "deploying on parade" his troops. It is hard to reproach Yevtushenko for the changes which have occurred, and still one cannot fail to notice with chagrin that his warlike temperament, boldness, and implacability toward "the scum" coexist in a startling way with compliance and adroitness, and all his complicated distribution of troops and their regrouping now on the right, now on the left flank, in short all his "battle strategy" turns out to be a very simple adjustment to the situation. He maneuvers so skillfully that you may admire his unexpected fencing sallies, but you can't feel much confidence in following him: he is capable of leading you anywhere at all, and for the sake of the next maneuver may leave you in the lurch.

Yevtushenko himself is fully aware of the compliance and halfway policy of his civic muse, and therefore the highest "strategic" considerations with which he justifies himself now and then are exchanged for other avowals: "Sometimes I am not exactly afraid, but still not very bold"; "I was as if a middle thing between wax and metal." Since he feels himself to be the poet of a time of transition, a poet still incomplete and not fully consistent, he welcomes the artist of the future who will realize his good intentions and fulfill what he has not dared to begin. . . . (pp. 173-74)

At the same time these reproaches against him have a better basis than his self-praise. By not making himself into a willing paragon of virtue, but by very often confessing his weaknesses and deficiencies, the poet strengthens our feeling of contact with a living person who for all his simplicity is not so simple and by no means naive. Most of all, these confessions tell us that he is capable of doubt and self-analysis which allow him to take a sober look at reality in all its complexity and contradictions, to reflect on his own unsure position in the world and thus to step aside from his self of yesterday, and to rise above himself and reveal some other potentialities. This is the psychological basis for a number of Yevtushenko's best poems, for example his earlier **"Boots,"** and more recently some verses under the general title of **"A Trip to the North."** . . . (pp. 174-75)

Yevtushenko is a poet of undefined possibilities and of frequent reappraisals of his career in life and poetry. He snatches at everything and is ready to refuse everything in order to take a new chance, try himself in a new arena and finally take the road to his "real self" which is still only just getting ready to live. More than ten years ago he expressed the fear: "Shall I not really turn out to be anything, not really result?" And he still continues to worry about this theme, as though all his books were only a test of his pen, preparation, a running start, and a tuning-up. This gives his work the stamp of haste, instability, and diffuseness. He writes a lot, eagerly and often carelessly, without depth, as if he were chasing somebody he wished to overtake—most likely himself, who still has not "resulted."

But those same qualities in him which made one feel the living development of a human personality full of conflicts appealed strongly to the young. Youth too stands half-way on the road to itself, is also in a hurry to live and does not know what will result; it is full of doubt, makes choices, reappraises, seeks, finds, and does not find itself. With Yevtushenko this process has been rather extended and has assumed sharper forms, which is perhaps due to certain specific moments in his life as a writer, a life accompanied alternately by applause and reprimands and combining rare "good luck" and success with official half-recognition—and this has formed the habit in the poet of striving for something and of justifying himself in some respect or other. . . . Perhaps that is why his sincere "anxiety about himself" ("Character is knit together from one's first anxiety about oneself") at times suddenly smacks of vanity and the desire to "seem" overpowers the urge to "be"; the concern for "What am I like?" is interrupted by anxiety about "How do I look?"; the problems of the poet's fate is reduced to the trivial success of winning. (pp. 175-76)

Something else is wrong too: the attitude toward oneself as a lottery ticket which may win if the occasion is right and the number turns up, but on which in reality nothing depends—a *disrespectful* attitude toward one's own personality can by this one gesture erase all the lofty monologues about faith in a humanity which has become the master of its own fate.

Fortunately there are opposed to these moods . . . other motifs which recently have become stronger: dissatisfaction with himself, the desire to break out of the magic circle, to rest, catch his breath, and reflect . . . These are the motifs which mark the cycle **"A Trip to the North"** mentioned above, the most mature and significant work, in our view, that he has written up to now. The experiences narrated here are perhaps grievous and sad and contradictory, but they can serve as a condition for a more profound view of the world; they testify to a growing exactingness in the poet and leave the impression that the constant hurry and fuss have for a while left him, yielding their place to serious thoughts about life, about himself. (pp. 176-77)

The notes of dissatisfaction with himself and his environment and the endeavor to review the familiar, boring round of occupations and habits are to be heard clearly in **"Bratsk Hydroelectric Station,"** which was written for the most part somewhat earlier. The appearance of the poem was motivated to a significant degree by these new needs: the poet wishes to waste no more time on trivialities, does not wish to glide over the surface, and renounces certain widespread sins of his past and that of others. (p. 177)

Yevtushenko is easy for the reader and hard for the critic. He knows how to please, win favor, and evoke sympathy. He is the first to criticize himself in such a way that he gives any critic a hundred points bonus. . . . And although his poems are not complex or difficult to understand, it is difficult to catch their inward essence which is inclined to change, so to speak, as the play continues. Perhaps the conditions that formed him have taught him flexibility, perhaps as a person he has not achieved final form and therefore easily loses the course he has taken, distracted by fresh ideas and impressions; or perhaps finally the historical vocation of Yevtushenko consists in removing from actuality, for the present, only the "top layer." However that may be, as you follow the logic of his art, you are often astonished at his skill in touching the acute and painful questions of our time without stating them profoundly; you are also astonished by his ability to meditate on everything in the world but not to speak to the essence of anything; and by his knack for sincerely proclaiming one thing and then just as sincerely doing something completely different. This is not always the case with him, but it can happen, and it does in **"Bratsk Hydroelectric Station."** (pp. 178-79)

Andrei Sinyavsky, "In Defense of the Pyramid (On Yevtushenko's Poetry)" (originally published in a different form as "On Evtushenko," translated by Henry Gifford, in Encounter, *Vol. XXVIII, No. 4, April, 1967), in his* For Freedom of Imagination, *translated by Laszlo Tikos and Murray Peppard (copyright © 1971 by Holt, Rinehart and Winston; reprinted by permission of Holt, Rinehart and Winston, Publishers), Holt, Rinehart and Winston, 1971, pp. 167-96.*

MICHAEL SCHMIDT

Translations of contemporary poetry are a kind of dust-sheet. Beneath it, the reader tries to distinguish the solid furniture. [Arthur Boyars and Simon Franklin, the] translators of Yevtushenko's new collection of more than 60 poems [*The Face behind the Face*], have chosen an idiomatic dust-sheet: plain English, the rhythms prosaic rather than spoken or sung. They have not attempted any approximation to Yevtushenko's forms or metres. It is his matter, his images, his ideas that we experience, without the prosodic tact that harmonises them and elevates the commonplace, the opinion, into memorable and occasionally self-transcending language. Before we look for the face behind the face, we have to locate the poem behind the translation.

I think I recognise several fine poems concealed here. The best may be **'Love of Solitude'**, about an old woman in Budapest who is devoted to Russian poetry and lives alone with it. 'I love being alone!' she insists. . . . There are other poems here which suggest the writer is still alive to his own and others' experience: **'But Before'**, **'A Tear'**, **'Iron Staircase'**, **'Potato Flower'** and **'A Father's Son'** are in various ways remarkable. Most of the work takes anecdotal form. **'Snow in Tokyo'**, the longest poem in the book, is a tedious narrative allegory. Beside it, two other oblique narratives about women artists—**'Poet at the Market'** and **'Lampshades'**—look especially strong.

As Yevtushenko has travelled abroad more, it seems to me he has become more narrowly Russian. As a young man, writing of lived experience, of the land which had given him his nature and his voice, he achieved those statements which even in English could shake a reader. As a tourist, Yevtushenko registers impressions, indignations, as a journalist might. Something has happened since he burst on the West in the early Sixties. I think what has happened is *audience*. . . .

Some readers prefer the fully public Yevtushenko. I prefer the poet who could surprise us by the tensions he achieved between private and public worlds, who without making *himself* representative could make his experience so. I sense in this book the absence of the private world. The limelight may have faded the poet, for in a sense he has lost all chance of the privacy out of which his large early statements grew.

Of course, like his masters, Esenin and Mayakovsky, he is a declamatory poet. But where in the earlier work he said 'I', he now says 'we', forcing complicity. He exploits vague personifications. We meet Fear, Despair, Hope, Wisdom, Folly, Friendship, History, Love and other terms, generally bald and unsubstantiated by the experience contained in the poetry.

Yevtushenko appears to have moved on from being a witness, with all that this implies, to being a directly didactic poet. His most public poems enunciate an orthodox message. His are the aggressively normative aims native to his ideology. The old lady in **'Love of Solitude'** is portrayed as humanly inadequate *because* she likes to be alone. No other explanation occurs to the poet. In his homilies, there is a curious loss of proportion, a dependence on the verbal gesture for effect. His comprehensive soul is pained by the petal of a flower as by the deaths of men. The question of rigorous truth, of particular witness, is no longer the burning question.

Some of the homilies are vivid. Others tend towards allegory. . . . Yevtushenko declares a sensible preference for 'verse that comes out of the air' over 'verse that is worked out in advance'. But it is a common error among poets in a vital rhetorical tradition to imagine words are gifts of the air when, in fact, they are dictated by a chosen form. Such work is not discovered but derived, and the fluency with which it comes may have more to do with a poet's technical proficiency than with the informing power of his muse.

Yevtushenko's preface to this book is a confused romantic rhapsody, and the book is an extension of that confusion: the excellent lies cheek by jowl with the merely silly and the factitious. What is wrong, some may ask, with a poet address-

ing an audience in the terms it wants to hear? For a poet with Yevtushenko's proven powers, it seems to me a waste. He is no philosopher. He is not even an unacknowledged legislator. He is at his best a man of intuitions grounded in specific experience. The best poems in this collection prove that fact. The worst are those which try to think, categorise and communicate in terms that do not extend poetry, language or perception. Let poets with lesser gifts preach to the converted. Yevtushenko seemed to be a writer on a larger scale.

Michael Schmidt, "'I' and 'We'" (© British Broadcasting Corp. 1979; reprinted by permission of Michael Schmidt), in The Listener, *Vol. 101, No. 2604, March 29, 1979, p. 466.*

ANDREW MOTION

Like most of his modernist contemporaries, Eliot believed that 'The progress of an artist is a continual self-sacrifice, a continual extinction of personality'. In recent years, few poets have disagreed more conspicuously than Yevgeny Yevtushenko. His reputation depends to a large extent on the inflation of personality—apparent radicalism, a charismatic background, and good looks have ensured him an enthusiastic public reception. Private reception is a different matter: what commands the stage at readings is vulnerable to charges of solipsism on the page. Yevtushenko obviously realises this, and defends himself at length in the introduction to *The Face Behind The Face*. He disapproves of masks because they are associated with 'the idea of forced collectivism', and frankly admits that, 'despite the kaleidoscope of geographical and psychological situations' in his book, it has a single hero: himself. The face behind—and in front of—the face is always his own, and its expression is unashamedly self-absorbed.

One might expect this to herald a collection of rewarding intimacy. But for all his emphasis on individuality, Yevtushenko reveals remarkably little. Rather than soul-searching, he gives advice—often of spectacular banality. . . . In his attempts to describe an obscure personal crisis, the same tendency to bluster about abstracts and absolutes persists. He is so inhibitingly aware of his role as a poet that words like 'pity', 'love' and 'forgiveness' become blank cards. They are dealt out with all the paraphernalia of concern, but find little human application. And when he turns his attention to poetic theory, they appear even more smugly didactic. . . . (p. 562)

Andrew Motion, "Self's the Man," in New Statesman *(© 1979 The Statesman & Nation Publishing Co. Ltd.), Vol. 97, No. 2509, April 20, 1979, pp. 562-63.**

ALAN BROWNJOHN

[Might] not a volume with the title *The Face Behind the Face* contain some clues about the "real" man behind the public image?

On the surface, it doesn't. All the poems in this [collection of Yevgeny Yevtushenko's works] . . . are immensely readable. Most of them are engaging, and vital in their own way. Yet neither the Whitmanesque avocations of [Yevtushenko's] Introduction ("You have to look into the mirror and be able to see . . . a multiplicity of other faces, without which there is no you.") nor the argument of the title poem carry a lot of conviction. . . . The real interest here lies in the corners illuminated by shafts of self-doubt; and in the poet's zeal to prove that poets and poetry still retain some status, in his world and ours. . . . And it is possible to see many of the poems in this new book as the extrovert side of a coin which is stamped on the obverse with a deal of self-questioning. Fear is telling him, "Write, write, Before your very soul has vanished"; despair has to be pushed out with the aid of an elusive hope, "like a drop of heaven in a sieve"; he is worried about growing older; and concerned with the problem of cutting the right figure. . . . This vulnerable, more complicated Yevtushenko provides a small quota of fully achieved, intriguingly subtle poems among the routine protests and exhortations. **"Chance Encounters"** see-saws between attraction and alarm. . . . And **"Kompromise Kompromisovich"** adroitly chastises the little victories of comfortable self-deception. . . . *The Face Behind the Face* also has its unhappy quota of feeble and embarrassing work; and yet the familiar, lyrical Yevtushenko is at his sharpest and best in new poems like **"Somewhere Above the Victim"**, **"A Father's Ear"** and **"Alder Catkin."** (pp. 69-70)

> *Alan Brownjohn, "Untidy Moments," in* Encounter *(© 1979 by Encounter Ltd.), Vol. LII, No. 6, June, 1979, pp. 68-72.*

EMMA FISHER

[In his long poem *Ivan the Terrible and Ivan the Fool*], Yevtushenko puts his money on the workers, on the blue-eyed, illused, unstoppable Ivan the Fool, against Ivan the Terrible, the disastrous but not entirely guilty autocrat. The second Ivan takes many forms, and a panorama of Russian history sweeps by, growing from the central incident of the founding in 1905 of one of the earliest soviets at a calico factory in Ivanovo-Voznesensk. . . . [We] are denied the musical resources that contained the thoughts, and have to follow only the thoughts themselves, uncomfortable in an English unused to conscious rhetoric. Like a black and white photo of a coloured picture, the translation shows the shapes and subjects, not the living tones. The tone is hard to pin down: is he serious? Or is he laughing at himself for saying 'Remain unsullied, proletarian firmament'? Or wringing his hands at the unlikeliness of his objurgation's being obeyed? Or getting carried away by the impetus of his own argument, without necessarily wanting to act on it, like a character in [an Ivan] Turgenev novel? The cleverness of the translation [by Daniel Weissbort], with its natural-sounding clanging rhymes, makes the decision more difficult; but I think he is probably deadly serious, which makes the poem for me, less interesting. (p. 22)

> *Emma Fisher, in her review of "Ivan the Terrible and Ivan the Fool," in* The Spectator *(© 1979 by The Spectator; reprinted by permission of* The Spectator*), Vol. 242, No. 7875, June 16, 1979, pp. 21-2.*

FRANCIS B. RANDALL

Some twenty years ago, a young Russian poet named Yevgeny Yevtushenko went to one of the terrible places of the world, a ravine near Kiev called Babi Yar, where the Nazis, in September 1941, had massacred at least 34,000 Ukrainian Jews in two days, and according to some over 100,000. He was shocked to find that in a land brimming with memorials to the millions of victims of Nazi terror, the Communists, his fellow Russians, had done nothing to mark this major site of Nazi terror against Jews. He wrote a memorable poem with a memorable line: *There is no monument at Babi Yar.*

He excoriated the complicitous indifference to the mass murder of Jews and the continuing antisemitism of the Communists and most of the Russian people, so contrary to all of their highest ideals. He touched the heart even of the then dictator Khrushchev, who allowed the publication of the poem and authorized the construction of a monument, of sorts, at Babi Yar. The poem and the poet became world famous. . . .

Since then, Yevtushenko has reached no such heights. Inside and outside the USSR he has been increasingly regarded as a flamboyant personality, like his model from the early Communist period, Vladimir Mayakovsky, but, unlike Mayakovsky, as only a second-rate poet. (p. 1212)

Now we are presented with his *Ivan the Terrible and Ivan the Fool*. . . . It is a small book containing in eight cantos and an epilogue, the kind of middle-length poem (this one is 872 lines) which Russians call a *poema* (as distinct from shorter "verses" or a much longer epic). It is indeed modeled on Mayakovsky's works in the genre, with somewhat irregular and often broken lines, dramatic images (but not so startling as Mayakovsky's), rapid changes of subject-matter and mood, and, to a Russian Communist, noble patriotic, popular, and revolutionary sentiments, not very Partyish, disturbingly personal, unorthodox, and two-edged.

There is no "story." Things go back and forth in time as well as in mood. The earliest characters dealt with are Czar Ivan the Terrible—ambivalently, a great builder of the Russian land but also the bloody tyrant who unleashed Russia's first great police terror—and Ivan Fyodorov the First Printer, a real hero of Yevtushenko's, who under the Terrible's patronage printed the first book in 1564. But later the Czar drove his printer from Russia as a subversive; hilariously, bandits try to rob him in his flight of his font of leaden print, but give it up as useless. (pp. 1212-13)

The real, Russian title of this poem is *Ivanovo Calicoes*, fabrics which were noted for their blood-red color and small-flowered patterns (still our image of what the Russian *babushka* wears). A sustained image in this poem is precisely the flowers and blood color of the calicoes, which become in various ways the flowering and simultaneously bloody aspects of Russian history. . . .

It is probably not a great poem and Yevtushenko is not a great soul. But whatever his compromises, this sort of exhortation to earlier idealism and broader tolerance tries to make Communists better, not worse. (p. 1213)

> *Francis B. Randall, "A Melancholy Tale," in* National Review *(© National Review, Inc., 1980; 150 East 35th St., New York, NY 10016), Vol. XXXII, No. 20, October 3, 1980, pp. 1212-13.*

EDWIN MORGAN

It is very clear from the prefatory poems, from the introduction and from the dedication to Edward Steichen, that [Yevgeny Yevtushenko's *Invisible Threads*] is a book with a purpose. In the introduction, Yevtushenko says what a revelation he found Steichen's *The Family of Man* photographs at the American Exhibition in Moscow in 1957. They were "like a gigantic poem by [Walt] Whitman, written not in words but with a camera. Through Steichen's photography, the invisible threads binding one nation to another had been made visible." The impact of Steichen's images of real people from different countries seemed to shatter the abstract clichés of the Cold War.

When he saw that his own poetry was aiming at a wide audience, and especially at people who were not normally poetry-readers, it was a natural step for Yevtushenko to take up photography with its "potential as an international language". . . .

A few of the photographs have a straightforward beauty that scarcely needs any added comment: a horse with startling blond mane cropping grass; a girl's head seen through the interlaced lozenges of a wall in Samarkand. Sometimes there is a documentary interest which again seems to be mostly self-contained, as in a shot of Japanese pearl-divers with white masks, white diving suits and orange wooden tubs; a Moscow cheerleader holding up a ghastly card of Pollyanna verses for mass singing; a view of Zima Station in Siberia. Some images are strange, even bizarre: a man on a bench about to have his bare belly patted by a friend, a fur-hatted man leaning against a picture of Christ painted on a lane in Baku. Some are lucky shots that both make and call for comment: a crippled veteran under a wall of fluttering want ads, a boy like a young Napoleon caught as he pauses behind the Director-General's microphone at Unesco in Paris. And some, it must be said, are banal or too obviously message-bearing: most of the shots of London, many of the shots of children, two lovers embracing against a background of national flags.

The caption-poems, which are brief—even at times epigrammatic—vary in persuasiveness. At times they preach or merely spell out in verbal terms what the eye has already taken from the photograph; but many of them are able to use the pictures as springboards into something which is imaginative or moving and only to be expressed in words. . . .

Yevtushenko's theme of the yearning for peace and harmony, for a globe without frontiers, for a strengthening of the "invisible threads" his title-poem speaks of, in a world where a tear in Paraguay "will fall as a snowflake onto the cheek of an Eskimo", is a dream everyone can sympathize with. Both photography and poetry, however, (and one might add science) provide evidence that diversification may be a greater evolutionary key than coming together. . . . I hope it is not a back-handed compliment to Yevtushenko to say that his book forcefully stimulates these wider thoughts and counter-thoughts.

> *Edwin Morgan, "The Poet and His Camera," in* The Times Literary Supplement *(© Times Newspapers Ltd. (London) 1981; reproduced from* The Times Literary Supplement *by permission), No. 4101, November 6, 1981, p. 1288.*

MARTIN BOOTH

Not since **"Zima Junction"** has Yevtushenko written such an astounding poem [as **"A Dove in Santiago"**]. His skill at the long, narrative form comes from a vast tradition in Russian verse, going back to [Alexander] Pushkin, but Yevtushenko has given it new vitality and range and a contemporary relevance.

Sub-titled "a novella in verse", the book is a 52-page poem in blank and free verse about an art student, Enrique, living in Chile during the Presidency of Allende. . . . The reality is a poignant story, but reconstructed by the poet it is a major literary document of life and death. . . .

Yevtushenko is uncompromisingly blunt in his poem, writing with pathos and understanding yet in a documentary style, or perhaps that of a parable. The sense of reportage only highlights the tragedy of a man striving to remain civilised in a world of barbarism.

> *Martin Booth, "Document of Life and Death" (reprinted by permission of the author), in* Tribune, *Vol. 46, No. 45, November 5, 1982, p. 9.**

PUBLISHERS WEEKLY

Set in the Chile of the Pinochet coup, [Yevgeny Yevtushenko's **"A Dove in Santiago"**] is the tragic story of 21-year-old Enrique. As an artist, Enrique is torn between the opposing views of his two teachers. As a lover, he divides his affections between an older woman and a younger, his secrecy towards each a deep betrayal. The young man's soul is divided, too, between politics and art, and even between his parents—an ailing mother and father who abandoned him. Enrique's situation and those around him drive him to despair and eventual suicide. Although he never intended harm to anyone, his death brings much suffering. And in a cruel twist of fate, his body plummeting to earth crushes a dove, marking another death that should never have occurred. . . . [Yevtushenko's] strong, descriptive, and very accessible verse . . . tells a graceful and memorable tale.

> *A review of "A Dove in Santiago," in* Publishers Weekly *(reprinted from the December 3, 1982 issue of* Publishers Weekly, *published by R. R. Bowker Company, a Xerox company; copyright © 1982 by Xerox Corporation), Vol. 222, No. 23, December 3, 1982, p. 55.*

Paul Zindel

1936-

American novelist, dramatist, and screenwriter.

Zindel's informal narrative style and his candid approach to subjects of interest to young people have made him one of the most popular writers of contemporary young adult literature. His teenage characters often feel betrayed by the adult world and cynical towards life in general; but, though they lose their innocence, these protagonists learn to be more self-reliant while maintaining hope for a better future.

Zindel is especially adept at depicting amoral, free-spirited teenagers who learn that carefree living has risks and that people must account for their actions. According to critics, this message comes through most effectively in *The Pigman*, Zindel's first young adult novel. In this story the young protagonists, John and Lorraine, take advantage of the one sympathetic adult in their lives; only upon his death (which they have caused inadvertently) do they realize the responsibilities they owe to themselves and others. Zindel's subsequent novels, including *My Darling, My Hamburger* and *Pardon Me, You're Stepping on My Eyeball!*, offer various perspectives on male-female relationships among adolescents.

Zindel's play *The Effect of Gamma Rays on Man-in-the-Moon Marigolds,* which centers on a domineering mother and her two daughters, appeals to both teenagers and adults. The play earned for Zindel the 1971 Pulitzer Prize in drama.

(See also *CLC,* Vol. 6; *Children's Literature Review,* Vol. 3; *Contemporary Authors,* Vols. 73-76; *Something about the Author,* Vol. 16; and *Dictionary of Literary Biography,* Vol. 7.)

© 1983 Martha Swope

DIANE FARRELL

[*The Pigman* is] a "now" book, a thoroughly contemporary, sensitive—and shocking—first novel. Lorraine and John are high-school sophomores: Are they villains or victims? Wild, wise kids whose selfish, irresponsible actions cause an old man's death? Or frightened children, clinging to the never-never land of their Staten Island childhood, prolonging innocence with foolish clowning and silly games? At the edge of adulthood, escaping from the example set by neurosis-ridden, anxiety-laden parents, they stumble into a relationship, tender and complex, humorous and heartbreaking, with an ugly, lonely old man. Few books that have been written for young people are as cruelly truthful about the human condition. Fewer still accord the elderly such serious consideration or perceive that what we term senility may be a symbolic return to youthful honesty and idealism.

> *Diane Farrell, in her review of "The Pigman," in* The Horn Book Magazine *(copyright © 1969 by The Horn Book, Inc., Boston), Vol. XLV, No. 1, February, 1969, p. 61.*

ZENA SUTHERLAND

[The protagonists of *The Pigman*, John and Lorraine,] have two great bonds: they are both in conflict with their parents

and they both have capricious and inventive minds. Out of this comes their friendship with an elderly man they call the Pigman (his name is Pignati and he collects china pigs) whom they met when pretending to be collecting for a charity. They are not criminal, but John and Lorraine have the pliant amorality of the young. Mr. Pignati comes home from the hospital to find a wild party going on; shocked by his young friends' behavior, the trusting and loving Pigman succumbs to a stroke. For John and Lorraine, "there was no one to blame anymore . . . And there was no place to hide . . . Our life would be what we made of it—nothing more, nothing less." Although the writing (by John and Lorraine, alternately) has the casual flavor of adolescence, the plot has an elemental quality. Sophisticated in treatment, the story is effective because of its candor, its humor, and its skilful construction.

> *Zena Sutherland, in her review of "The Pigman,"* in Bulletin of the Center for Children's Books *(reprinted by permission of The University of Chicago Press; © 1969 by The University of Chicago), Vol. 22, No. 8, April, 1969, p. 136.*

THE TIMES LITERARY SUPPLEMENT

John and Lorraine in *The Pigman* are not immediately attractive figures with whom to identify. They are out of sympathy with home and school, disturbed even, so that when they encounter old Mr. Pignati, who is senile, they are delighted to have him for a fairy godfather but unwilling to be responsible in their attitude to him. In their total absorption in their own needs they neglect his. This is an abrasive, tragic encounter: an unpleasant book in some ways, but the issues are starkly real.

> *"Themes for the Salad Days," in* The Times Literary Supplement *(© Times Newspapers Ltd. (London) 1969; reproduced from* The Times Literary Supplement *by permission), No. 3501, April 3, 1969, p. 355.**

MARILYN R. SINGER

[*My Darling, My Hamburger* is a] skillfully written story of four high school seniors . . . that has tremendous appeal on the entertainment level, but that totally cops out on the issues raised: sex, contraception, abortion. The action in the story happens to Liz and Sean; Maggie and Dennis, there to register and transmit what's happening emotionally, are sensitive, insecure alter egos for those glamorous, hip loners. The teenagers here are the most realistic of any in high-school novels to date: they have appropriate feelings and relationships; smoke, drink, swear; have refreshingly normal sexual thoughts and conflicts. The dialogue and description are so natural and entertaining (and often very funny) that the author disarms his audience (anyone who writes so convincingly must be a friend) while planting mines of moralism: *pot and sex are destructive.* Sean pressures Liz into having sex which she finally does, not out of passion, but anger at her parents; and her fears of pregnancy are soon realized. Sean, too immature, backs out of marriage but pays for her abortion. Liz immediately turns recluse out of shame, and she, Sean, and the issues are never really faced again. Only Maggie is left to carry a totally irrelevant ending—thoughts and clichés on graduation and growing up. Yesterday's ideas seductively disguised for today's teens. (pp. 137-38)

> *Marilyn R. Singer, in her review of "My Darling, My Hamburger," in* School Library Journal, *an appendix to* Library Journal *(reprinted from the November, 1969 issue of* School Library Journal, *published by R. R. Bowker Co./A Xerox Corporation; copyright © 1969), Vol. 16, No. 3, November, 1969, pp. 137-38.*

JOHN ROWE TOWNSEND

["**My Darling, My Hamburger**"] seems to me to be a better novel than "**The Pigman.**" . . . It's the story of two couples in their senior year at high school. One pair, Maggie and Dennis, are squareish, not too attractive, unsure of themselves and each other. The other pair, Liz and Sean, are desperately in love, and the boy is importunate. And he gets his way. (The girl's resistance is ended, convincingly, not by persuasion or passion but because her stepfather is nasty to her.) And Liz becomes pregnant. Sean says he'll marry her but is dissuaded by his worldly-wise father. She has an abortion. Maggie is with her, thinks it has gone wrong and gives the game away to Liz's parents.

And that's it. The book ends with the graduation-day scene, from Maggie's viewpoint. Liz is conspicuously absent. Nothing much has happened to Maggie, and her friendship with Dennis has fizzled out, but here she is, a year older, a year wiser, ready for what comes next.

It's a simple enough story. It proves for the millionth time that you can get along quite well without a brilliant plot. The book is concerned single-mindedly with sex and growing up; more precisely, it's about the predicament—funny, bitter and nerve-racking—of men and women who are also children. . . .

True, the story is value-laden; but then, the subject is value-laden. It's made plain, without being pointed out in so many words, that the girl still pays and that abortion is what it is, not just a fashionable talking-point. The writing is professional in the extreme. Some of the important action takes place off-stage—for instance, Liz's telling the boy of her pregnancy and her parents' discovery of what's happened. We don't need these scenes; they're standard; we can picture them well enough. But it's not so obviously sound to skip (between parts one and two) from Liz's capitulation to the news, months later, that she's pregnant. . . . This is too near the heart of the story to be skipped; this is where the author's quick leap is an evasion, and he misses the chance to supersede at last the row of asterisks or the strictly-clinical account or the romantic euphemisms. We could have done to see these two as lovers. (Happy lovers? Perhaps.)

The facsimiles of letters and announcements and whatnot that decorate the text strike me as gimmickry, and here and there, especially at the end of the book, there's a patch of sogginess where we want it to be crisp. As a work of literary art this is more a promise than an achievement, but it's quite a big promise and it's not a negligible achievement. (p. 2)

> *John Rowe Townsend, "It Takes More than Pot and the Pill," in* The New York Times Book Review, *Part II (© 1969 by The New York Times Company; reprinted by permission), November 9, 1969, pp. 2, 48.**

DIANE GERSONI-EDELMAN

[In his *My Darling, My Hamburger*], Zindel copped out on his likable, interest-sustaining characters by resolving their problems in a pat, moralizing manner. The moralizing in *I Never Loved Your Mind* is just as obtrusive—and the characters are more superficial (particularly the female protagonist, who's a caricature embodying the worst traits of the clichéd hippy). In a relentlessly flip, trying-to-be-funny, first-person narrative punctuated by unclever footnoted comments, Dewey, a superior 17-year-old dropout and the son of parents he amiably refers to as "the librarian" and "the engineer," tells of his love for Yvette Goethals, whom he meets while working as a respiration therapist. Yvette is a tough petty thief, ardent vegetarian, and part-time nudist, who shares a pad with her brother and the other two members of the rocking Electric Lovin' Stallions. One day at her home she initiates a massage session with Dewey that slips over into lovemaking, but Yvette later dumps him, informing him she's never loved his mind. Throughout the book, Dewey's sincerity and openness to people are contrasted with Yvette's pseudo-idealism and cynicism, but the irritating self-consciousness of his narrative strains reader empathy for both characters. And while Zindel zonks readers with a glittering verbal battery of pungent dialogues, apt descriptions, bon mots, and some four-letter words, it's a virtuosity that masks rather than reveals characters; an unsuccessful attempt to illuminate serious teen conflicts—dropping out versus working within the Establishment, resolving attitudes about sex, etc.—via sophisticated humor. Still, flawed as this book is, it makes better reading than most simply because Zindel is a more technically proficient writer than most producing novels for post-child, pre-adult readers.

Diane Gersoni-Edelman, in her review of "I Never Loved Your Mind," in Library Journal *(reprinted from* Library Journal, *June 15, 1970; published by R. R. Bowker Co. (a Xerox company); copyright © 1970 by Xerox Corporation), Vol. 95, No. 12, June 15, 1970, p. 2317.*

THE TIMES LITERARY SUPPLEMENT

[Paul Zindel's] problem as a writer is what to do when you are writing about [the non-conforming young in America] as an outsider to their current revolutionary values and life-style. He solves it [in *I Never Loved Your Mind*] in an immensely clever way which leaves a mild trace of anxiety. Dewey Daniels . . . has career problems. For want of anything else, he gets a job as a hospital assistant on leaving high school. Telling a first person narrative, Mr. Zindel wins our identification with the humorous, heartless, uninvolved Dewey, who tells himself "What the hell!" and finds the hospital one pretty funny sick joke; but is, deep down somewhere, a straight, very nice guy. Dewey also finds Yvette, a glamorous, heavy-breasted girl colleague . . . who eats broccoli sandwiches and steals hospital equipment for the counter-culture commune she lives in with a group called the "Electric Lovin' Stallions". Gradually, through a bizarre tale told with great pace and fantastic humour (Mr. Zindel's readers would seem about to get to Kurt Vonnegut), Yvette demonstrates the vacuity of her life and beliefs: the message is, firmly and unobtrusively, that the world is an awful, corrupt place but Yvette's free-loving, macrobiotic values are no answer. Better be Dewey, chastened and solidified by his experience of both hospital and of Yvette's bed, who decides at the end to turn purposeful, and train to be a doctor. Mr. Zindel understands his young people, but also knows what he would like them to be. He might be right, but his book is a slightly too clever plea for conformity which will leave his most alert readers more than a little suspicious.

"Looking for a Life-Style," in The Times Literary Supplement *(© Times Newspapers Ltd. (London) 1971; reproduced from* The Times Literary Supplement *by permission), No. 3605, April 2, 1971, p. 385.**

MARY SILVA COSGRAVE

The effect of a tragic home environment on three tormented souls—a widow and her two teen-age daughters—is tautly dramatized in . . . [*The Effect of Gamma Rays On Man-In-The-Moon Marigolds*. Paul Zindel] has drawn upon his fond recollections of his mother's preposterous schemes for getting rich quick to tell a sad and sometimes funny story. The characters in the play, like the marigolds in the scientific experiment, undergo mutations, some good, some bad. The mother is embittered by a life of disappointments and shattered dreams; a woman scorned and scornful, she is cruel, though capable of compassion. One daughter is beyond hope, jealous and vindictive, full of fears, and subject to convulsive seizures. The other, having been inspired by a science teacher, wins a prize for her experiment on marigolds and discovers there are galaxies out beyond her harsh world which offer her the kind of chance her mother lost and her sister never had.

Mary Silva Cosgrave, in her review of "The Effect of Gamma Rays on Man-in-the-Moon Marigolds: A

Drama in Two Acts," in The Horn Book Magazine *(copyright © 1971 by The Horn Book, Inc., Boston), Vol. XLVII, No. 3, June, 1971, p. 308.*

ZENA SUTHERLAND

[*Let Me Hear You Whisper* is a touching and trenchant two-act play. It] reads beautifully, with good dialogue and characterization, an original plot, and a theme that should appeal to young people. [Helen, a] cleaning woman who has just begun working for an experimental biology laboratory, learns that the dolphin in a laboratory tank has failed to learn to talk and is therefore to be killed. Helen is a gentle, ingenuous person who has chattered with pity and affection to the dolphin. And it talks to her when they are alone, although it will not speak to the staff. She learns that the dolphin knows it was meant to be used for warfare and would not cooperate; the dolphin tells her of a plan: she must get him into a large hamper and take him to the sea. Helen is caught talking to the dolphin, which she's been told not to do, and dismissed. The dolphin says one word, "love," and everybody hears it. If Helen can be brought back and the dolphin speaks to her again, it will not be killed . . . but it is too late, an angry Helen will not return.

Zena Sutherland, in her review of "Let Me Hear You Whisper," in Bulletin of the Center for Children's Books *(reprinted by permission of The University of Chicago Press; © 1974 by The University of Chicago), Vol. 27, No. 11, July-August, 1974, p. 188.*

BEVERLY A. HALEY AND KENNETH L. DONELSON

[Paul Zindel] speaks to young people about man's cruelty and "matters of consequence" in three novels, [*The Pigman, My Darling, My Hamburger,* and *I Never Loved Your Mind*] . . . , and one drama, *The Effect of Gamma Rays on Man-in-the-Moon Marigolds*. . . . In these amusing, provocative, and very-much-of-our-time works, Zindel presents questions to his readers, and if they care (and they do), they will search for answers. Their *own* answers. (p. 941)

He looks at the world through the eyes of adolescents, many kinds of adolescents, all trying to find some meaning in a world apparently gone mad, all concerned with man's cruelty and "matters of consequence." By selecting an adolescent point of view, Zindel forces the reader to look at the world as if he were awakening to it for the first time, a kind of rebirth.

The titles of Zindel's works suggest a first need for today's society, fun and humor. . . . Zindel's adolescents try to find some fun in life for themselves, even though the adults that surround them are humorless.

In *The Pigman,* the home lives of both major characters, John Conlan and Lorraine Jensen, are devoid of anything bordering on humor. John's father is interested only in the world of stocks and bonds. His mother is so meticulous a housekeeper that no one dares touch anything, and this perfection consumes her entire mind and time and life. Lorraine's father is dead, and her mother sees life as one long struggle to keep the "wolf" (metaphorically representing both poverty and men, mostly men) from the door. Both John's and Lorraine's parents are so involved in themselves that they are indifferent to their children except as the children reflect on their parents' public images. For both adolescents, there is no fun in their lives at home.

But they find fun when they meet and rapidly become friends with the "Pigman," Angelo Pignati, a lonely widower in his late fifties. Mr. Pignati brings fun and joy and meaning and life into the lives of two adolescents in some ways far lonelier than he is. Simple things—roller skating in a department store, visiting Bobo the baboon, buying delicacies and savoring every morsel with friends, moaning at the zoo keeper who simply doles out food to sea lions when he could make a game out of it. Changing routine into fun, that's what the Pigman does for John and Lorraine's lives and what they do for him.

Then, inadvertently, John and Lorraine cause the Pigman's death. Reality and cruelty enter into an almost family-like relationship. What seemed to be something good turns into evil. . . . [But] out of evil and the loss of John and Lorraine's innocence comes self-awareness and a promise of something good, a comment on "matters of consequence" and the question, why are we so cruel to each other? . . . If John had evaded any sense of responsibility for his actions earlier in the book, he begins [in the end] to accept responsibility for his actions. (pp. 941-42)

Several themes run through all four works. The search for identity and meaning. The theme of youthful questioning of traditional values. The theme of the loneliness of the individual in the crowd. The theme of man's inability to communicate in a world of instantaneous communication. All these themes are universal and most of them classic. Zindel makes these primordial themes believable and relevant and significant to young people. . . .

In each story, the protagonists are basically lonely because they are unable to establish communication with their parents. Ironically, the adolescents themselves seem to understand *why* the parents behave as they do and to forgive them while the parents are too self-centered to make any real effort to establish any communication link with their teenagers. The instinctive wisdom of youth seems superior to the learned wisdom of adults. (p. 943)

In *The Pigman*, John and Lorraine first try to escape through beer drinking and mischievous games. Then they find a "substitute parent" in Mr. Pignati, a childless widower, who becomes the parent neither has ever known, as they become the children he has never had. Their situation reminds the reader of a lamentable but obvious fact of our society, that it is denying young people the uniquely vital child-parent and child-grandparent relationship typical of previous generations.

In *My Darling, My Hamburger*, Liz turns from her mother and her new stepfather to try to find meaning through relating to her boyfriend and her best girlfriend. . . . All four adolescents in this novel are insecure and lonely, but at the end of the story Maggie and her boyfriend Dennis show some promise of maturing into positive young people.

In *I Never Loved Your Mind*, Yvette and Dewey have dropped out of school and left their homes in their loneliness and inability to communicate with their parents. Yvette seeks her answer in communal life, but her moving from one place to the next, never really finding what she is searching for, makes clear Zindel's point that merely moving from one unhappy situation does not necessarily imply any happiness. Dewey is torn between what Yvette believes in and what the "establishment" represents. He comes close to communicating with and caring about two people, Yvette and the "senior citizen" invalid Irene, but even with them he fails. In an atmosphere of old age, death, and illness in the hospital where Dewey

works and plays, Dewey stands near the brink of discovering what life means to him.

In *The Effect of Gamma Rays on Man-in-the-Moon Marigolds*, the sisters Tillie and Ruth try vainly to please their mother Beatrice, a woman already regarded by the community as more than slightly looney. . . . Both sisters suffer loneliness because of the mother's self-indulgent pity, a mother who will not permit her children to relate to a world because she herself cannot relate to it. Despite all the odds, Tillie emerges a potential winner, for her thirst for knowledge and her scientific experiment with the marigolds have given her confidence in her own self-worth.

The duality and paradox of the theme of loneliness is that in a crowded, urban society with instant and inescapable communication, loneliness has become a major source of other problems. (pp. 943-44)

Some of the values most highly regarded by tradition are questioned in these four works. Is the "establishment" always right? Is motherhood a "holy" institution? Can mothers do no wrong? Is school educating young people in any worthwhile sense? Are adults necessarily wiser than young people? Are sex and drinking moral wrongs? Is the family unit the best way for people in our society to learn communication? Is the well-adjusted life *the* worthwhile goal of young people?

The family suffers mightily in all four works, the role of the mother coming under particular fire. Mothers are portrayed as self-centered beings who have established wrong or invalid or dubious priorities. Materialism seems to be the prime goal of adults. In none of the homes is there warmth and understanding and communication, much less love or a "haven from the cruel, outside world."

School is devalued not only by the young people themselves in these books, but often by the parents themselves. For example, both Mrs. Jensen in *The Pigman* and Beatrice in *The Effect of Gamma Rays on Man-in-the-Moon Marigolds* keep their daughters out of school to help the mothers do housekeeping. Beatrice is unwilling or unable to see how important Ruth's science project is to Ruth's life. Mrs. Jensen thinks it a simple matter for Lorraine to make up the Latin test she misses. Other parents care only that their offspring's grades be "respectable" so the parents will not be disgraced. School comes off as a "place to go because there's nothing better to do," and the leading characters in *I Never Loved Your Mind* have found something better to do, at least temporarily, in working in the hospital.

Sex in any puritanical sense hardly exists for Zindel's adolescents, but a free-sex philosophy is equally non-existent. . . . Sex is constantly on the mind of Dewey in *I Never Loved Your Mind*, but except for a sexual episode near the close of the novel, it stays in Dewey's mind only as his number one ambition and frustration. But sex is the central problem in *My Darling, My Hamburger* from the first lines, when Maggie and Liz discuss a sex education class, to the horrors of Liz's abortion. Liz worries that Sean will not respect her if she does what he wants, but she is even more afraid that she will lose his love if she does not give in. The duality theme is strong in this work, for when Liz gives her total love to Sean, it results in his deserting her, leaving her alone instead of receiving love in return. In *I Never Loved Your Mind*, Yvette leaves Dewey puzzled, alone, and insecure just at the moment when he had discovered the meaning of real love. Liz and Dewey have been cast aside by both parents and their lovers. But again, the reader senses that each has learned and grown from these bitter experiences.

Paul Zindel examines our society, realizes the pathos and sometimes the bathos of its condition, and finally presents an affirmation of his faith in people, particularly young people, of the basic worth of the individual human being and the collective human spirit. (pp. 944-45)

> *Beverly A. Haley and Kenneth L. Donelson, "Pigs and Hamburgers, Cadavers and Gamma Rays: Paul Zindel's Adolescents" (copyright © 1974 by the National Council of Teachers of English; reprinted by permission of the publisher and the author), in Elementary English, Vol. 51, No. 7, October, 1974, pp. 940-45.*

ISABEL QUIGLY

Paul Zindel's people seem to take over his book entirely and live so vividly you forget there's a narrator at all. [J. D.] Salinger managed the same effect in *The Catcher in the Rye* with an adolescent narrator who seemed to pickle a generation forever in his chat (which some found insufferably coy). Nobody thought his book suitable for Holden Caulfield's contemporaries in those days, or put it on the children's shelf.

Pardon Me, You're Stepping On My Eyeball! is a lot more outspoken and explicit and is now considered suitable for readers the age of its characters, which shows, I suppose, how life has caught up with fiction (rather than the other way round). It recalls Salinger in its zest and funniness and, like so much good teenage fiction, is an adult novel that happens to have a young viewpoint, but is not so much (or so necessarily) about a pair of fifteen-year-olds as about the pressures of American life upon them. Pressures to succeed, to belong, to be popular, to come out on top in every competition, particularly the sexual.

Edna's parents are so distraught that she hasn't a boyfriend that they rush to the school psychiatrist. Marsh's mother is so obsessed with his randiness that he invents a randy life to match her fantasies. Meantime, from California, letters pour in from a mysteriously absent father, prodding, advising, keeping up Marsh's spirits and telling him to be sure no one treads on his eyeball. It doesn't take Edna long to find that Marsh's father is in fact in an urn under Marsh's bed, what's left of him, that is . . . And so to Washington, with urn and rocket, symbolically launched into river and sky. . . .

The quality of this [novel] lies in its understanding of the incoherence as well as the precocious intelligence of its young, and its wry reaction to those damaging comics, their elders; to the stand it takes on every point that matters and its attractive understanding of what doesn't matter. Above all, it catches what Kingsley Amis has called "the adolescent's coldly wondering stare".

> *Isabel Quigly, "Son of Salinger," in The Times Literary Supplement (© Times Newspapers Ltd. (London) 1976; reproduced from The Times Literary Supplement by permission), No. 3900, December 10, 1976, p. 1549.**

ZENA SUTHERLAND

[In *Pardon Me, You're Stepping on My Eyeball!* two] members of a high school therapy group run by the school psychologist grope toward real friendship and understanding, in a story that is ebulliently zany, at times seeming exaggerated, at times very funny. Edna is withdrawn, resisting her mother's constant nagging about getting a date; "Marsh" Mellow is a borderline psychotic who tries to convince Edna to help him rescue his father, whose letters he produces. . . . Marsh and Edna have several wild experiences (a house party at which most of the adolescent guests have stripped, and at which the house burns down) before the final escapade, in which Marsh coaxes Edna to run off with him to help save his father. Their car is wrecked, and the two land in a cemetery where Marsh admits, for the first time, that his father is dead; he wrote the letters himself. The story is sophisticated, candid, not quite believable in what happens—but it is more than convincing in its perceptiveness and its sensitivity to the anguish of the unhappy adolescent. In their own way, Edna and Marsh, for all the abrasion they feel at times, help each other move toward self-acceptance and stability.

> *Zena Sutherland, in her review of "Pardon Me, You're Stepping on My Eyeball!" in Bulletin of the Center for Children's Books (reprinted by permission of The University of Chicago Press; © 1977 by The University of Chicago), Vol. 30, No. 8, April, 1977, p. 136.*

ISABEL QUIGLY

Like the other heroes of Paul Zindel's books [Chris Boyd, hero of *Confessions of a Teenage Baboon*], can explain, in language that comes convincingly from a sixteen-year-old, what the bizarre circumstances of his life have brought him to. His mother is a kleptomaniac nurse who takes him round to her patients' houses when she's hired. In between jobs they live out of two suitcases and three shopping bags in a rundown rooming house called the Ritz Hotel. So, no home, no stability, and—since he ran off when Chris was five and then died—no father. Chris's baboonery strikes no one till he and his mother land up looking after an apparently sweet old lady with an apparently alcoholic, violent son of thirty called Lloyd. The sweet old lady turns out to have some odd habits (such as biting people) and her son some socially suspect attitudes and ways of behaving. But he does seem to care that Chris is being crushed by his mother and is lonely, dissatisfied, hopeless, and a loser; a degree of psychic disorder that calls for tough treatment, which, in his way, Lloyd seems to try and give him. The result: the police, blackmail, violence, death.

Is Lloyd a corrupter of local youth, as seems clear to most outsiders, certainly to anyone who accepts today's sexual and psychological clichés? Or a Socratic figure who gives youngsters self-knowledge and self-respect, and, out of his own failures, tries to teach them to overcome theirs?

Paul Zindel makes his points about compassion and the unlikely forms of human goodness with tender eccentricity of expression. His action is fast, noisy, explosive; people's behaviour in it makes one uneasily aware of one's own snap judgments and cowardice in the face of the ambiguous or the half-understood: the Lloyds around us, so easily labelled and then comfortably dismissed.

Needless to say, it is not the stuff that teenage novels used to deal with; but then the stuff of teenage life is not what it used to be, either, and what counts is the way Paul Zindel handles it, with a delicacy at once funny and heartfelt, outspoken and sensitive. He comments on the mess that adults have made of the world their children inherit by showing, with candour but a certain gentleness as well, a young-eyed view of it. His children are never type-cast, nor are the situations he puts them in. They show the variety as well as the weirdness of behaviour and of life itself; thus stretching teenage experience and, more importantly, imagination.

Isabel Quigly, "Banking on Lloyd," in The Times Literary Supplement *(© Times Newspapers Ltd. (London) 1978; reproduced from* The Times Literary Supplement *by permission), No. 3966, April 7, 1978, p. 383.*

STANLEY HOFFMAN

Approaching a new Paul Zindel novel is something of an adventure. . . . The reason is that, unless he changes radically as a writer of "young adult novels" (a phrase with which I've never been entirely comfortable), one is bound to be either wildly wild about Zindel's books or wildly disappointed. It is a simple matter, although somewhat coarse and irritatingly unsophisticated too: ask, say, a twelve-year-old what he thinks of a particular movie he's just seen and he will look you squarely in the eye and without hesitation answer, "Terrific!" or "It stinks!"

Simple.

Thus it was when the galley copy of Mr. Zindel's latest effort, *The Undertaker's Gone Bananas* . . . , fell into my excited clutches. And like the twelve-year-old moviegoer . . . , I cast all other "matters of consequence" aside, snuggled up in my bed and, with a full bag of Doritos for company, dove in. I wanted to like it—no, craved to *love* it, wanted to jump up and shout "Terrific!"

Damn it. I think it stunk.

And because of that, this will not be as pleasant as I would have wanted. (p. 78)

My first contact with Paul Zindel was *The Pigman*. John, Lorraine, lonely old Mr. Pignati.

I cried.

I actually cried.

I loved it.

Next came *My Darling, My Hamburger*. I didn't love it nearly as much but certain parts moved me deeply. Maggie growing up, Liz disillusioned, Sean and Dennis going where? Not much plot, really, but plenty of feeling. Kind of nice.

I Never Loved Your Mind followed. Something was changing which I think a lot of readers didn't like. Unlike *Pigman* and *Hamburger*, novels which, like nearly all of Zindel's works, revolved around the actions of couples—boy meets girl and they team up to move the plot along—the "couple" in *I Never Loved Your Mind* rarely team up and one of them doesn't even live with her family. This last fact is a major departure for Zindel and the atmosphere of the novel, in part because of this, weaves a spell of potential hopelessness. Dewey, the male of the couple, may move forward at novel's end but the commune-living, free-loving Yvette might not turn out as fortunate. As with all of Zindel's couples, along the way of the story a certain innocence is lost, but the innocence is often heavy baggage without which the real world can be seen more clearly—and the clearer one can see, the better one might be able to cope. Indeed, if there is any one "message" that runs through Zindel's works, it has to be this: if reality is ugly, in facing it we can prepare ourselves to see beyond the ugliness to something hopeful. Thus, Dewey, after all his tribulations at Yvette's hands, closes out the novel on an up note. (pp. 79-80)

The detractors of Zindel—a growing number, I suspect, though it's a safe bet his admirers are also on the increase—point to his seeming inevitable pessimism and its potential infectiousness on the young reader. Representative of this view is Myles McDowell, who writes, . . .

> There is such an overall cynical depressive quality about Zindel's books, which seems to me to be destructive of values before values have properly had time to form. It is the depression I would want to protect emergent minds from.

McDowell is, I think, both right and wrong. Cynical depression is assuredly a large part of Zindel's teenage universe, yet to "protect emergent minds" from it recalls John Milton's warning in *Areopagitica* to the effect that "A cloistered virtue is no virtue at all." The question is whether Zindel's world is a real one and, if it is, should it be kept hidden from impressionable young minds. (p. 80)

[If] Zindel is dangerous then we are all in trouble. More to the point seems to be not whether Zindel is dangerous as a philosopher, but rather whether his approach to the realities of life is vastly oversimplified. By that I mean are his novels constructed along formulated, predictable lines which ultimately render them shallow—the worst sin of a novelist, short of being boring, being that of emptiness. And, if so, why is he so popular? Is it because he does have something vital to offer or simply that he has fooled so many? I think the answer lies somewhere in between and is best discovered in his two latest books, *Confessions of A Teenage Baboon* and *The Undertaker's Gone Bananas*.

Next to *Pigman*, I think that *Baboon* is Zindel's most haunting novel in the best sense of that word. It stays with you long after it's been read and presents the most curious—and believable—adult character in any of his works. Indeed, the pathetic, lonely booze-hound, Lloyd, whose mother is days away from death in the room next to his, is even more poignant than Mr. Pignati in Zindel's first book. Similarly, the fifteen-year-old narrator of the novel, Chris, is Zindel's most moving—and believable—teenager. (pp. 80-1)

Baboon may be, in fact, Zindel's best novel precisely because it breaks with the formulas of his past books. In a like manner, *Undertaker* may well be his worst because in it he reverts back to the formulas of old. Where *Baboon* is fresh, direct, a tiny sparkling gem of a story, *Undertaker* is stale, contrived, at times—God, I hate to say this—an embarrassment to read. Amazing that these two books are only a year apart; what that might say about the development of one writer's craft is, at the least, puzzling. Zindel may be the Jekyll and Hyde of modern young adult fiction; his books get better, worse, better, worse, and one never knows what will come next. Yes, it is an adventure, each separate path as unpredictable as the one before it and to follow.

In *Baboon*, Chris treks along with his insensitive domineering mother. . . . Theirs is a semi-vagabond existence, their lives, to put it mildly, in a state of constant uncertainty and chaos. The mother is a high-strung neurotic who thrives on hysteria and yelling; Chris is a mellower neurotic whose major fetish centers around his dead father's gigantic Chesterfield coat which he takes with him from household to household. The present household, bizarre in the extreme, finds Chris's mother tending one Carmelita Diparti, an old woman stricken with terminal cancer coming home to die, a fact which permeates the novel's atmosphere. Her family consists of Lloyd Diparti, a strange, bitter, brooding man in his late 30's who throws nightly parties in the house. His constant companion is Harold, a fifteen-year-old who is Lloyd's cook and maid, and the house is always filled with boisterous teenagers. Apparently, Lloyd has no adult friends whatsoever.

The relationship formed between Lloyd and Chris—formed like a slow, masterful ballet, inching forward, quickly retreating, going back and forth in disarrayed but growing harmony—is the path to the latter's enlightenment, an enlightenment both profound and very possibly permanent. Lloyd is that pathetic, though all-too-real adult who has true wisdom to impart to everyone save himself. He knows the Truth that can potentially set everyone but him free. (pp. 81-2)

[Later, Lloyd shoots] himself, the scene fully witnessed by Chris. Hours later, [Chris] is walking with his new friend, Rosemary, beneath the moonlit sky when all that Lloyd has tried to impart to him finally rings true. . . .

> Even for a full moon there is always its dark side which can never be seen, which can never be fully known, and which will always be the mystery that is called Life. And I was ready to accept that, and yet for some reason I was most interested in the things in my life I *could* change. The things I could see if I tried hard enough. The things I *deserved*, as Lloyd had told me.

This from a boy who at book's beginning had to ask not to be despised for telling us "that the days of being Huckleberry Finn are gone forever." It is Zindel's most moving tribute to the possibilities of boys growing into men. Certainly *not* the product of cynicism and despair.

One would expect—would naturally *want* to expect—that the follow-up novel to this would be, if not superior, then at least brimming with a somewhat similar profundity—writers, like others, hopefully growing as they get older and a little wiser. Unfortunately, neither is the case here. *The Undertaker's Gone Bananas* is a shamelessly contrived story, disappointing in the extreme. It circles—as in *The Pigman*—around the adventures of two lonely teenagers, Bobby and Lauri, who live in a new luxury high-rise in New Jersey, so new and so luxurious that—conveniently for the story about to unfold—most of the apartments are unoccupied. To add to the artificial eeriness of this, neighbors soon move in next door to Bobby, one Mr. and Mrs. Hulka, a boozing, arguing couple approaching the ennui of middle-age and stable affluence. Mr. Hulka is an undertaker, his wife—well, she is apparently just his wife. (pp. 83-4)

The Hulka family presence in the book seems pointless until one day Bobby hears screaming coming from their apartment and, looking into their terrace window (conveniently adjoining his own), the boy sees what he thinks is Mr. Hulka pummelling his wife to death. The police are called, but what Bobby thought is obviously not the case (Mrs. Hulka enters alive and well) and the cops leave with angry warnings on their tongues.

It is here where the plot strains our credulity to the breaking point. Strange noises come from the Hulka apartment—chains rattle, machines roar, finally the trash compactor is employed. Bobby is convinced that Hulka has indeed now killed his wife

for sure, cut her up as only a veteran undertaker can and is about to take her out as literal garbage. He tells Lauri—whose skepticism at Bobby's imaginings is only surpassed by the reader's—who indulges him just for the sake of playing the game. Things follow swiftly now as Bobby closes in on the Hulkas' mystery. Without elaborating further—not for fear of spoiling the story but simply because there's little point—the truth is finally revealed when, snooping in the Hulka apartment, Lauri comes across Mrs. Hulka's dismembered head in the interior of the TV set, warm dripping blood and all. Wild chases ensue, including, even before the discovered head, Bobby swiping Mr. Hulka's hearse and driving it into the neighborhood McDonald's where not even his "peers" (though, except for Lauri, Bobby rather understandably has no peers) believe him. At the end, Hulka is nabbed, Bobby believed and—who knows, one guesses that's a "happy" ending of sorts.

What makes these outrageous contrivances even more embarrassing is Zindel's attempts to include them in a story where the two main characters are potentially so memorable and even charming. What happens, though, is that this potentiality gets buried under the spotty movements of the plot. . . . All one can sense is the idea of brilliant characterization which has somehow failed in the execution, sacrificed to a plot that shouldn't be. Never has the possibility for brilliance been so hinted at without being realized. It is a shame.

Perhaps Zindel, at least in this genre, has few places left to go. If so, one would hope he comes to realize this and goes on to expand his evident talent elsewhere. At best, the erratic quality of his novels is disappointing; at worst, upsetting in the extreme. (pp. 84-5)

[But] even when Zindel is downright bad, it is so evident that we can learn from it. He is hardly ever mediocre and that, I think, is a virtue. And if he isn't always successful with his "young adults" he almost always hits the mark with older people, especially parents. Lloyd, though not a parent, is the next closest thing and his character may be Zindel's best. Chris's mother is also memorable and unique—a singularly unlikeable woman—and Zindel spares us nothing when dealing with these supposed adults. (pp. 85-6)

[Zindel] is absurdly uneven, but so what? Better to have him risk terrible books—trial and error is often the writer's lot; if we sometimes become subject to it, that is the risk of the reader—because somewhere he's bound to come up with another winner. To repeat, anything is better than the smooth, content consistency of mediocrity. And Paul Zindel can certainly never be accused of that. (p. 87)

Stanley Hoffman, "Winning, Losing, but Above All Taking Risks: A Look at the Novels of Paul Zindel," in The Lion and the Unicorn *(copyright © 1978 The Lion and the Unicorn), Vol. 2, No. 2, Fall, 1978, pp. 78-88.*

JOYCE MILTON

Paul Zindel has been a trendsetter in young-adult fiction since 1968. Significantly, his latest book ["**The Undertaker's Gone Bananas**"] features a teen-age girl who's obsessed with death, a boy who's obsessed with practical jokes and an undertaker who's a homicidal maniac. Significantly, too, Mr. Zindel turns these elements into a zany farce. . . . The most striking feature of Mr. Zindel's story is the setting—a white elephant luxury-apartment complex on the Palisades Cliffs. The tenants, mostly refugees from other urban nightmares, are surrounded by unrented and perhaps unrentable apartments, and Mr. Zindel's hero [Bobby Perkins], who can't get anyone to believe that he has witnessed a murder on his neighbor's terrace, is the most isolated of all. This book is like a screenplay waiting to happen. The imagery is terrific, but, I confess, I'm not sure what the images mean. Do today's young people really feel so bereft and abandoned? Or are we witnessing the death wish of a genre? I don't think we could, or should want to, go back to the days when the author of a young-adult novel could seriously be charged with "nihilism" for writing a story with a depressing ending. On the other hand, we do seem to have run out of taboos to shatter. (p. 88)

Joyce Milton, "Sweet 16 No More," in The New York Times Book Review (© 1978 by The New York Times Company; reprinted by permission), December 10, 1978, pp. 87-8.*

MAXINE FISHER

[Paul] Zindel is the recipient of a Pulitzer Prize as well as the New York Drama Critics Circle Award; The New York Times has included four of his books in recent lists of outstanding children's books. It is especially distressing, in light of his enormous prestige, to discover that [The Undertaker's Gone Bananas] could not have been more outrageously sexist if that had been Zindel's explicit goal.

Bobby is a brash fifteen-year-old who has virtually no friends. He views himself as a kind of superboy and attributes his rejection by his peers as stemming from the fact that, "I happen to hold poetry, goodness, and beauty above all qualities." When faced with examples of injustice in the world, he responds automatically with physical violence. His only and recently found friend is Lauri. He describes his initial impression of her as "a timid delicate angora cat." . . . Two entire pages are devoted to listing all of the unlikely things which she fears will blot out her life at any moment. Bobby feels, "here is one girl who needed someone to look after her" and that "God or Nature had appointed him to assure her that life was really worth living." Bobby's strategy is to "psychologize" her out of her fears (rooted in a neighbor's death by fire) by planning adventures that will divert her mind. It is not in any way a relationship between equals.

Other relationships are equally sexist. In a typical domestic scene, Lauri's father reads the newspaper while his wife and daughter prepare dinner. (Lauri also frequently serves Bobby; he, in turn, "orders" her to make tea, etc.) The father "checks up" on things in the kitchen (" 'Test the sausage,' Mrs. Geddes said seductively," to him). Watching this exchange, Lauri is inspired to daydream about herself and Bobby in sex roles modeled after those set by her parents. She dreams that he is a famous writer, and that she is a student of his ("and you're teaching me everything I know"). In an imaginary love letter to him she says: "every night I say my prayers and hope I turn into a very lovely girl, and that I'm smart and modern enough for you. . . ." In another she says: "I have dreams about you saving me . . . you're always my savior . . . if you think my hair is too straight, I'll get it cut and curl it for you."

Significantly, Bobby and Lauri think of each other as characters in conventionally sexist fairy tales. Lauri thinks of Bobby as a reincarnated Jack of the Beanstalk, while he thinks of her as Sleeping Beauty. Later in the story she muses that she is probably a mixture of Snow White and Sleeping Beauty and hopes that Bobby will be the prince who rescues her from death (or

in her case, her chronic fear of death) by taking a romantic interest in her. He, however, remains committed to less sexual adventuring. In their adventures they are partners until it appears that their position is genuinely dangerous. Then, Bobby dismisses Lauri, telling her to go home to safety while he forges ahead. She agrees, but halfway home, torn between her own fear and her concern for his welfare, she feels "like a mouse standing in front of a maze." She returns. (pp. 15-16)

Aside from a group of women gathered at the apartment building pool, whom Bobby assumes to be "a lot of desperate secretaries" who are "throwing whammies to attract whatever unmarried men there were," only two other female characters appear momentarily in these pages. One is Bobby's mother, an artist who has failed "at practically every known material and technique of artistic expression known to man." The other is Mrs. Hulka, the source of Bobby and Lauri's concern. [Mrs. Hulka is described as "a very plastic woman" and as "a high-class Barbie doll."] . . . In sum, there isn't a single female character here worthy of emulation; all of the women—even those only briefly noted—are limned by an extremely chauvinistic male with a highly jaundiced eye. . . .

Bobby is forever proclaiming that he wants to save the world from the greedy and unjust, but his attitude toward the various working-class people in the book is so consistently hostile and lacking in empathy that we must wonder who he thinks is victimized by whom. He seems to have an elitist view of service employees as parasites on the members of his class. . . .

A moving van crew looks to Bobby like "a trio of pre-humanoid creatures . . . little hairy apes." A doorman looks like "a nasty little dwarf" and "drools like a dragon"; a garage attendant has "such a twisted little sneaky face" that Bobby suspects him of robbing the apartments. Throughout, in fact, characters make assumptions about people's moral character on the basis of their physical appearance. Nowhere do the protagonists—or reader—learn that there is anything questionable about such judgments. (p. 16)

Maxine Fisher, in her review of "The Undertaker's Gone Bananas," in Interracial Books for Children Bulletin (reprinted by permission of Interracial Books for Children Bulletin, 1841 Broadway, New York, N.Y. 10023), Vol. 10, No. 5, 1979, pp. 15-16.

JACK FORMAN

Whatever one expects of a novel by Paul Zindel, [A Star for the Latecomer] is not it. (It is co-authored by his wife.) There are no drunk mothers, wayward fathers, and "off the wall" kids trying to find one another. There is not even the ambiguous mixture of cynicism and hope which has become the Zindel trademark. What there is is a sugar-coated though surprisingly moving family story and teen romance about a 16-year-old, Long Island girl named Brooke Hillary, who attends a Manhattan high school for potential stars in the performing arts. (Brooke's mother has convinced her that she will be a great dancer someday.) With an appealing, sometimes hard-to-believe naivete, Brooke narrates the past year of her life—a time when she learns of her mother's terminal illness, experiences "first love" and "disappointment" (in the tradition of soda shops and good night kisses), and discovers that her real aspirations have nothing to do with her mother's dream for her. What makes this story so unusual is the warm, close relationship Brooke has with her mother—and the involving, heart-rending scenes of Brooke seeing her mother waste away physically while fighting valiantly against pain to maintain her dignity and strong support for Brooke. The rest of the characters are one-dimensional and almost incidental to the story. . . . (pp. 129-30)

Jack Forman, in his review of "A Star for the Late-comer," in School Library Journal *(reprinted from the April, 1980 issue of* School Library Journal, *published by R. R. Bowker Co./A Xerox Corporation; copyright © 1980), Vol. 26, No. 8, April, 1980, pp. 129-30.*

CYRISSE JAFFEE

Death is not an easy subject to deal with in children's books. Attempts to reassure young people too often create saccharine prose; attempts to confront the issue can result in a grim and unappealing tone. Alas, **"A Star for the Latecomer"**—the story of a young girl trying to come to terms with her mother's approaching death from cancer—tries to find a middle ground but fails. Like Roni Schotter's "A Matter of Time," concerning a similar situation, the story is overwhelmed by its messages. The authors, intent on their topic, have produced prose that is repetitive and tends toward preachiness. And from the opening paragraph, when the narrator says, "I feel somehow you'll understand because you're probably around my age *or once upon a time you were my age*" (italics mine), they don't really seem to know whom they are speaking to.

Brooke Hillary, 16, has always been close to her mother and has tried, valiantly, to live up to parental expectations that she become a show-biz success. Brooke attends a special school, goes to auditions, but her fantasies are considerably less glamorous: "I had dreams of falling in love with a fabulous boy and having three kids I would take to the park." The knowledge that her mother is dying sharpens the conflict. In spite of lengthy passages where Brooke reflects naively and somewhat tediously on her problems . . . , the reader becomes involved enough so that the final scenes between mother and daughter are heartfelt. Brooke's grief is assuaged by relief, and she resolves to become a star only "in my own dreams."

Brooke's rapid adjustment to the loss, given her attachment to her mother, seems unrealistic. Her sense of loneliness and betrayal is consistent with the trauma she is experiencing, but where are other family members (father and brother are barely developed) or friends? Brooke is simply not a credible adolescent. Although she speaks frequently of feeling pressured and at odds with her mother's demands, she is not rebellious. "I never minded that she arranged everything for me," Brooke says, "because I knew no one would hurt me as long as she was around." Must a young person suffer the death of a parent to become an individual?

Paul Zindel is a popular young adult author and has written many fine novels, but this husband and wife collaboration lacks the vigor his fans expect.

Cyrisse Jaffee, in her review of "A Star for the Late-comer," in The New York Times Book Review *(© 1980 by The New York Times Company; reprinted by permission), July 20, 1980, p. 17.*

SALLY HOLMES HOLTZE

Four months after the end of **The Pigman** . . . , John and Lorraine discover Gus, a sick, lonely old man, living inside Mr. Pignati's house and force themselves on him in friendship.

They tell the story [in **The Pigman's Legacy**] in the same alternating first-person chapters; similarities from the plot (Gus dies at the novel's climax) to small incidents (Gus initiates a psychoanalyzing parlor game as Mr. Pignati did), to vocabulary and jokes . . . parrot **The Pigman,** but the strong characterization, credibility, and skilled story development is missing. Gus is stereotypically "feisty"; John and Lorraine seem pallid versions of their former selves, and their narratives are almost interchangeable. The boy who once set off bombs in the school bathrooms suddenly gets along with his parents, defends a janitorial worker from the harassment of fellow schoolmates, and sets out boy scout-like to save a stranger from loneliness. The plot loosely chronicles the wild adventures of John and Lorraine: they gamble in Atlantic City (never mind that they are minors); they provide a priest who performs a marriage ceremony for Gus in an intensive care ward (forget that blood tests or marriage licenses are required); they even manage to bring Gus' dog into the ward. A romance between John and Lorraine, too timid for 16 year olds, is chronicled in clumsily injected sections; and out of nowhere, John professes a lifelong commitment, stretching credibility even further.

Sally Holmes Holtze, in her review of "The Pigman's Legacy," in School Library Journal *(reprinted from the October, 1980 issue of* School Library Journal, *published by R. R. Bowker Co./A Xerox Corporation; copyright © 1980), Vol. 27, No. 2, October, 1980, p. 160.*

PETER FANNING

It seems that a good story will not lie down; and there are not that many around. After **The Pigman, The Pigman's Legacy** (followed, I suppose by *The Pigman's Return*), several titles and 11 years later, Paul Zindel picks up John and Lorraine. He finds them almost as fresh and eccentric as they were just before the Pigman died. . . .

[**The Pigman's Legacy** has] a much simpler plot. All the old man does is die; and all the children do is make his final days a little easier. The cycle of birth, infatuation and death is heavily scored in the final chapters. But if the moral tone is just a little more sententious, the hijinks more hollow and the Overwhelming Question a lot more overwhelming, **The Pigman's Legacy** emerges as a serious sequel rather than a souped up rerun of a book that launched a thousand imitations.

Peter Fanning, "Nasties in the Woodshed," in The Times Educational Supplement *(© Times Newspapers Ltd. (London) 1980; reproduced from* The Times Educational Supplement *by permission), No. 3361, November 21, 1980, p. 32.*

DAVID REES

There is something peculiarly subversive about Zindel's books that appeals to the adolescent. Adults, particularly authoritarian figures like policemen or teachers, are usually portrayed in a bad light, and the reader can feel himself happily encapsulated in an immature world in which the young are wronged, misunderstood, and generally knocked about; where the battle-lines between the generations are very clearly drawn; and the teenager who thinks he's got problems can be at ease, identify with the central characters, or find he's not the only misfit, unsuccessful at home or at school, with his friends, with the opposite sex. Whether life is really like this is another matter.

For the adult, reading the collected works of Paul Zindel is a slightly tedious process, which is not the experience one has with some writers of teenage fiction. The world, in fact, is not as distorted as it appears to be in these books: it isn't so narrow, so neurotic as this. The point of view is as out of focus as if someone had quite literally stepped on the narrator's eyeball. There is also the problem of narrowness of range in the material; though there are differences in theme and emphasis, Zindel seems essentially to be covering the same ground again and again, and never appears to do it quite so well as he did it in his first novel, *The Pigman*. And there is the famous "style."

Zindel's style is often praised for being the authentic voice of the modern teenager. . . . Zindel's voice, in fact, is specifically that of the New Yorker, and a special kind of New Yorker, too: intellectually very bright and probably of East European origin. It is doubtful whether anybody in real life actually talks like a Zindel character; the hyperboles, the verbal fireworks, the enormous width of vocabulary and cross-reference, though often exceedingly clever and funny, are just too much to accept as everyday speech. His voice is a very useful vehicle for looking at life in the peculiarly lop-sided poses Zindel's characters adopt, but it probably has its origins as much in literature as in reality. As I've said before, it's not so far removed from the voice of Holden Caulfield [the protagonist of J. D. Salinger's *The Catcher in the Rye*, published in 1951]. . . . In 1951 the American young were dancing fox-trots and worrying about being drafted for Korea. Holden Caulfield would have known nothing of the drug scene, the beat generation, flower power, sexual permissiveness, Vietnam, pollution, the energy crisis, and a thousand other things that have interested the young since Holden was sixteen. It seems strange, then, to a British adult reader of the same age as Holden would be that today's kids still talk as he does in so many American books.

One only has to open *The Catcher in the Rye* and read the opening sentences to see the similarity to the first paragraph of Zindel's *I Never Loved Your Mind*. . . . Even the titles have something in common. [Salinger's] "A Perfect Day for Bananafish" or "Just Before the War with the Eskimos" are as joky and esoteric as *My Darling, My Hamburger*, or *Pardon Me, You're Stepping on My Eyeball!*

This kind of writing, if taken in small doses, is witty enough, but read *in extenso* it becomes tiresome. It relies far too much on hyperbole. No car, for instance, ever goes fast in a Zindel novel; it is always burning rubber, or going like a bat out of hell, or traveling at the speed of a Batmobile. People's eyes always widen to the size of balloons or grapefruit. The imagery searches too self-consciously and too often for the exotic, the grotesque, and the ridiculous, so that the reader longs for just one ordinary homely metaphor to leaven the unpalatable richness of the fare. Is Staten Island, for example, really a "sort of geographical version of a detached retina"? Or would a boy in fact look like "a constipated weasel"? Or someone's hair stick out so much that it "seemed to give him a type of energy like his fingers were jammed into some 220 electric socket"? . . . It makes the reader doubt the offered realism, the supposed reflection of actualities. Where most of us go, there isn't the unusual.

Most irritating of all is the repetitiveness. John's mother in *The Pigman* "runs around like a chicken with its head cut off," but so do Jacqueline *and* Miss Conlin in *Pardon Me, You're Stepping on My Eyeball!* In the latter book there are "wall-to-wall crooks," and in *The Undertaker's Gone Bananas* "wall-to-wall teenagers," though Mae West did that one first with

"wall-to-wall men," long before the Second World War. When somebody is disliked, he's always "retarded" or has "a low IQ" (even a peacock in *The Pigman* has a low IQ) or he's "Neanderthal" or "Cro-magnon man" or has a memory "like that of a titmouse with curvature of the brain." Amusing once, yes; half a dozen times, no. (pp. 25-8)

One suspects that the mouthpiece in all Zindel's books is not really the character—John Conlan or Dewey Daniels—but Paul Zindel: and that may well be the reason why reading him is, in some ways, a disappointing experience for the adult. People who write novels for children and teenagers may well be using the creative process as a way of rearranging the patterns of their childhood or adolescence, as an exorcism of their hang-ups—indeed we are, all of us, probably doing that—but the art of it is to disguise it so well that it doesn't show through. There is something so frenetic and hysterical about some of Zindel's work that one suspects personal experiences which may underlie some of the material in the books are still uncomfortable and too emotionally close for him to become sufficiently detached to give them a separate life of their own in a novel.

The Pigman, his first book, is probably his best. It is a somber and chastening story that gets better and better as it goes on, and despite the linguistic irritations, it deserves its high reputation and wide readership. More than any other of his novels it has coherent shape and direction, and its climax is particularly good: a chilling, sobering, morality-tale conclusion. It also has several finely-wrought verbal felicities. . . . Lorraine and John are credible realistic characters, telling us more, strangely, about each other in their first-person narrations than about themselves. Effective, too, is the emphasis laid by the author on the fact that it is a combination of their own selfishness and Mr. Pignati's that leads to the old man's death—not some vague malevolent adult world outside that is responsible, which is the point made in some of the other books. Mr. Pignati's premature senility and the dangerously unstable state of his mind are quite unrecognized by the children and provide the necessary recipe for disaster; one watches the collision of these two utterly different life-styles—the Pigman's and the children's—knowing all along that, whatever the pleasures each may give to the other, tragedy is bound to be the outcome, because none of the protagonists can ever see beyond what is happening at the present moment. It is a fine book, but one can't help feeling that a completely different change of direction might have been best for Zindel in his second novel.

The characters in *My Darling, My Hamburger* are less sharply individualized; in fact they seem little more than four standard teenage types—blond attractive girl with lots of poise, mousy introverted girl with no poise, rich and handsome boy, plain and not so well-to-do boy. The main theme of the book—Liz's abortion—is dealt with fairly well; the whole business comes over, as it should, as an ugly, emotionally messy, squalid experience. But the dice are far too heavily loaded against Liz. Quirks of fate play a large role in what happens, and her encounters with the unbelievably nasty Rod Gittens seem a little too much when added to the chain of circumstantial events that leads to her and Sean Collins making love without any contraceptive precautions. Also the book seems, ten years later, rather unmodern. The horror of the back-street abortion, even if still with us, is not now necessarily the outcome of an unwanted pregnancy, and the whole atmosphere of the teenage romance as portrayed here has a passé feeling to it with its formal dates and dances. It's as if the author felt as unrelaxed as his characters. Maybe the trouble is that the book is too didactic, and that not enough space is devoted to developing what goes on inside the characters: one feels curiously uninvolved with them, unlike, say, in *The Pigman.*

Or in *I Never Loved Your Mind.* The verbal pyrotechnics of this novel are more mannered and excessive than in most of the others, and some of the situations—the nude vacuum-cleaning scene, for instance—are somewhat unreal, yet Dewey Daniels is a complex, sympathetic character who holds our attention throughout. . . . It is impressive that Zindel is honest enough to admit that Dewey's chase of Yvette is not because he loves her, but simply because he wants to go to bed with her (a common enough teenage situation, surely, but one not frequently acknowledged as being normal and healthy in teenage fiction). Indeed, who could love such a monster of selfish egotism as Yvette? One is less convinced when, having slept with her, he does fall in love with the creature, neatly ironic though that may be. Yvette's world of unrecognized double standards, hypocrisy and parasitism—Zindel's comment on the worst excesses of flower power and the whole late-sixties dropout scene—is done with a great deal of panache and excellent satirical humor, and though the details of that particular era are a phenomenon of the recent past rather than the present, they don't have the dated feeling of his treatment of the Senior Prom stuff of *My Darling, My Hamburger.* They are brought to life much more persuasively. The ending is good, too; Dewey's decision to abandon "that Love Land crap" in order to do something "phantasmagorically different" yet not "to give civilization a kick in the behind" is not a suggestion that he's going to join the nine-to-five rat-race, but rather that he will follow a path of self-fulfilment, whatever that may turn out to be. (pp. 30-3)

Pardon Me, You're Stepping on My Eyeball! and *Confessions of a Teenage Baboon* are Zindel's least impressive books. It's difficult, in fact, to say anything good about either of them. The plots are improbable, the tone unrelievedly hysterical, and most of the characters so grotesque that it's almost impossible to suspend disbelief at any point. The few ordinary kids—Edna in *Pardon Me, You're Stepping on My Eyeball!* and Chris and Rosemary in *Confessions of a Teenage Baboon*—seem so out of place in this world of nightmare that one wonders what they're doing there at all, let alone being allowed to grow up and come to terms with their problems. It's more likely that they'd collapse and be carted off to a lunatic asylum. It's not easy to believe that someone as normal, as nice and sensible as Edna is, would be in the care of a school psychiatrist, labeled as one of the most maladjusted of children, unless the whole world has gone completely mad. It's equally difficult to accept the idea that Chris would be so attracted, so spell-bound by the neurotic, dangerous, suicidal Lloyd, no matter what flashes of common sense and insight a thirty-year-old who's never grown up may have. This is a pity, because the man who has failed to mature, who still wants as an adult to be King of the Teenagers, is an interesting idea. But Zindel fails to breathe real life into Lloyd. He's too bizarre, far too strange to have the attraction to the young that Zindel says he has. Such a figure *is* dangerous, just as the senile Mr. Pignati is dangerous, but the disaster that occurs would be much more effective if the reader could be allowed to feel sympathy for Lloyd similar to that which he feels for the Pigman. It's as if Zindel had approached his material too emotively and had not properly sized up all the delicate nuances of a complex situation. The characters in these books indulge in too much self-pity; there

is too much straining after big emotional effects: the reader is left unconvinced and, again, uninvolved.

The Undertaker's Gone Bananas shows some signs of the new direction which Zindel should perhaps have pursued after *The Pigman,* or at the very latest after *I Never Loved Your Mind.* The world of this novel is a younger world, though the central characters, we are told, are fifteen. But despite Bobby's ability to drive a car, and other small details which suggest that particular age, he and Lauri give the feeling, emotionally and psychologically, of being younger—thirteen-year-olds perhaps. The mechanics of the plot, too, belong to a species of children's fiction—kids outwit police in catching crooks—that is the property of readers younger than those who would enjoy *I Never Loved Your Mind.* In fact the story is very well handled: Bobby seeing the next door neighbor, Mr. Hulka, murdering his wife, and the police refusing to believe him, may sound a bit old hat as a plot but it's told with skill, humor, and real excitement, proving in fact to be an excellent addition to what one might think was an overworked genre. Bobby's precociousness and daring is nicely balanced by Lauri's caution and good sense, and for once the adults—the Hulkas excepted—are not seen as totally unsympathetic monsters, but normal credible people. Even the grumbles and threats of the police are the reactions of uncorrupt ordinary men trying to do a difficult job. It's as if Zindel has at last worked something out of his system, and is now able to look at his creations in a more objective light, and, as a result, do something that is much more satisfactory than the two previous books.

The Undertaker's Gone Bananas is a welcome development. Zindel had clearly more than exhausted, with *Confessions of a Teenage Baboon,* a very narrow and limited kind of material. *The Undertaker's Gone Bananas* certainly shows greater control than *Confessions of a Teenage Baboon*—the language is more restrained, the climaxes are not spoiled by being too frenetic, the view of things is no longer that of a squashed eyeball. The world is here a richer, more varied place than it seemed previously. (pp. 33-5)

> David Rees, "Viewed from a Squashed Eyeball," in his The Marble in the Water: Essays on Contemporary Writers of Fiction for Children and Young Adults *(copyright © 1979, 1980 by David Rees), The Horn Book, Inc., 1980, pp. 25-35.*

PAXTON DAVIS

["The Pigman's Legacy" is] a mystery of sorts and also a tale of second chances for both John and Lorraine, not to mention the puzzled beneficiary of their ministrations and an elderly cleaning woman whom they bring into their derring-do. But . . . it's a rousing adventure yarn too. Mr. Zindel is an old hand at plunging from one episode to the next in such whirlwind fashion that a few implausibilities are concealed along the way. Here he deepens his narrative by alternating narrators chapter-by-chapter between John and Lorraine, which gives us not only John's headlong zest for action and Lorraine's perspective on what's happening but a fine change-of-pace that keeps the tale turning.

Sequels are risky, of course, as they too often merely try to imitate a previously successful formula. But Mr. Zindel is on to something bolder here: Instead of merely tacking it on, he's wrapped his sequel around its precursor, returning to old themes but enlarging and deepening them. The result is a story in which we become involved with recognizable youths who grow and mature. And as they mature, their tale takes on broader implications; it is a surprising, beautiful and even profound story.

Paxton Davis, in his review of "The Pigman's Legacy," in The New York Times Book Review (© 1981 by The New York Times Company; reprinted by permission), January 25, 1981, p. 27.

JUDITH N. MITCHELL

[In *The Girl Who Wanted a Boy*] Sibella Cametta, 15 year old clod and scientific whiz, learns that it is better to have loved and lost than not to have loved at all. Zindel's adolescent novels are not everyone's cup of tea, but I love them. This one, too, is a fun house ride where one careens from heartache to hilarity without time to adjust to the author's antic zaniness. Sibella's mother and sister are faintly likeable horrors, the object of her affections is a poor girl's [Marlon] Brando, and Sibella herself has a juggernaut methodology that invests her quest for a boy-friend with genuine black comedy. Perhaps it's this term black comedy, hastily borrowed from stage parlance, that is the key to Zindel's adolescent novels: he is to the teen novel what [Edward] Albee is to drama. It's a mistake to chide him for fantastic plot shifts, or a gallery of grotesqueries masquerading as normal people. His exaggerations pin point the absurdities of normalcy, and his novels carry the theme of loving and being loved like contraband with a homing device.

That is not to say that there are no flaws in *The Girl Who Wanted a Boy;* Sibella's father is a bloodless oracle, and her mother's insightfulness comes a little too late in the story. . . . What is new and compelling is the force with which Sibella's pain is delineated—she knows what she wants, and she is utterly without the proper resources to procure it. Her misery and her refusal to be done in by that misery will communicate to kids and haunt adults.

Judith N. Mitchell, in her review of "The Girl Who Wanted a Boy," in Voice of Youth Advocates (copyrighted 1981 by Voice of Youth Advocates), Vol. 4, No. 4, October, 1981, p. 40.

MARGERY FISHER

There is, I am sure, much good sense and sound advice for adolescents in *The Girl who wanted a Boy*. The trouble is that to find these desirable qualities you have to hack your way through a jungle of slang, hyperbole and clotted verbiage so dense that I do not believe even American readers will find the exercise an easy one. This is not so much a story as a situation, the outline of an encounter between a schoolgirl of fifteen and a lad of nineteen who conveniently blames his casual nature on nagging parents. For that matter, one of Sibella's parents nags too, and the somewhat different tone has much the same effect. To her assertion that 'boys don't want to caress an electro magnet' her capable fixer of a daughter replies 'Look, Mom, I think there's a big difference between being an electro magnet and lassoing every used-car salesman who comes along'. But in the end, however strong the girl's reaction against her mother's boy-friends, Sibella has to recognise that they offer her mother a companionship that goes beyond the physical, and her pursuit of handsome Dan Douglas, with her tool-bag and accumulated savings, inept and painful as it is, brings the first lesson she has to learn about the definition of love. . . . I only wish the author had been a little less explosive and obscure in putting over his message. (p. 3971)

Margery Fisher, "Close Encounters," in her Growing Point, Vol. 20, No. 4, November, 1981, pp. 3967-71.*

A. THATCHER

[*The Girl Who Wanted a Boy*, written] by an author who certainly understands American teenagers, is a brilliantly and sensitively written story of Sibella's search for her ideal of love. She rejects offers of help and advice from her mother and sister, and turns instead to a book called "How to Pick Up Boys."

She "falls in love" with a newspaper photograph of a nineteen year old boy called Dan, and hunts him down. He is as unsure and unstable as she is, but Sibella is unable to accept this. She loves him, so he must be something special, and her love and belief in him must be able to work miracles. The story moves inexorably towards the inevitable rejection and heartache. At least, she does learn a great deal about herself and her emotions from this traumatic experience.

I found the book very disturbing and I cannot believe that this kind of probing and analysis can do any good for those emotionally so immature. I found very distasteful the emphasis placed on sex experience for those too young to appreciate it as anything more than an appetite to be satisfied. The casual acceptance as "normal" for parents to write-off their teenage children when they get difficult I found very hard to swallow.

A. Thatcher, in a review of "The Girl Who Wanted a Boy," in The Junior Bookshelf, Vol. 6, No. 1, February, 1982, p. 40.

Appendix

THE EXCERPTS IN *CLC*, VOLUME 26, WERE REPRINTED FROM THE FOLLOWING PERIODICALS:

The ALAN Review
America
The American Scholar
Analog Science Fiction/Science Fact
The Antioch Review
Appraisal
Arizona Quarterly
The Atlantic Monthly
Audio
Best Sellers
Book Week—New York Herald Tribune
Book Week—The Sunday Herald Tribune
Book Week—The Washington Post
Book Week—World Journal Tribune
Book Window
Book World—Chicago Tribune
Book World—The Washington Post
Booklist
Books in Canada
Books Today
Bulletin of the Center for Children's Books
Canadian Children's Literature: A Journal of
   Criticism and Review
The Canadian Composer
The Canadian Forum
The Canadian Historical Review
Canadian Literature
Catholic Library World
Catholic World
Chicago Tribune
Children's Book Review
Children's Book Review Service
Children's Literature
Children's literature in education
Choice
The Christian Science Monitor
Christianity Today
CLA Journal

College English
Commentary
Commonweal
Crawdaddy
Creem
Cue
down beat
Elementary English
Encounter
English Journal
English Studies in Africa
Esquire
Essence
Fantasy Newsletter
Feature
Film Comment
Film Heritage
Film Quarterly
Films and Filming
Growing Point
Harper's
High Fidelity
The High/Low Report
The Horn Book Magazine
Hudson Review
In Review: Canadian Books for Children
Interracial Books for Children Bulletin
Jazz & Pop
Journal of Popular Culture
Journal of Reading
The Junior Bookshelf
Junior Libraries
The Kenyon Review
Kirkus Reviews
Kirkus Service
Kliatt Young Adult Paperback Book Guide
Language Arts
Library Journal

The Lion and the Unicorn
The Listener
Literature/Film Quarterly
Lively Arts and Book Review
Los Angeles Times Book Review
Maclean's Magazine
The Magazine of Fantasy and Science
   Fiction
Melody Maker
MELUS
Modern Fiction Studies
Monthly Film Bulletin
Musician
The Nation
National Review
The Negro History Bulletin
The New Leader
New Letters
The New Republic
New Scientist
New Statesman
The New Statesman & Nation
New York Herald Tribune Book Review
New York Magazine
The New York Review of Books
The New York Times
The New York Times Book Review
The New York Times Magazine
The New Yorker
Newsday
Newsweek
The Progressive
Publishers Weekly
The Quarterly Journal of Speech
Quill and Quire
Records and Recording
Rolling Stone
Saturday Night

Saturday Review
Saturday Review of the Arts
The School Librarian
The School Librarian and School Library
   Review
School Library Journal
Science Books
Science Fiction Review
Scientific American
Sight and Sound
The Social Studies
South Atlantic Quarterly
The Southern Humanities Review

The Southern Review
The Spectator
Sports Illustrated
Stereo Review
Studies in Black Literature
Studies in Short Fiction
Theatre Arts
Time
The Times Educational Supplement
The Times Literary Supplement
Tribune
Trouser Press
University College Quarterly

University Review
The Village Voice
Virginia Kirkus' Service
Virginia Quarterly Review
Voice of Youth Advocates
West Coast Review of Books
Wilson Library Bulletin
The World of Children's Books
The Yale Review
Young Adult Cooperative Book Review
   Group of Massachusetts
Young Readers Review

THE EXCERPTS IN *CLC*, VOLUME 26, WERE REPRINTED FROM THE FOLLOWING BOOKS:

Aldiss, Brian W. Billion Year Spree: The True History of Science Fiction. *Doubleday, 1973, Schocken Books, 1974.*

Arbuthnot, May Hill, and Sutherland, Zena. Children and Books. *4th ed. Scott, Foresman, 1972.*

Barry, Elaine. Robert Frost. *Ungar, 1973.*

Baskin, Barbara H., and Harris, Karen H. Books for the Gifted Child. *Bowker, 1980.*

Bigsby, C.W.E. Confrontation and Commitment: A Study of Contemporary American Drama, 1959-66. *University of Missouri Press, 1968.*

Butler, Francelia, ed. Children's Literature: Annual of the Modern Language Association Seminar on Children's Literature and The Children's Literature Association, Vol. 4. *Temple University Press, 1975.*

Butts, Dennis, ed. Good Writers for Young Readers. *Hart-Davis Educational, 1977.*

Cameron, Eleanor. The Green and Burning Tree: On the Writing and Enjoyment of Children's Books. *Atlantic-Little, Brown, 1969.*

Carson, Neil. Arthur Miller. *Grove Press, 1982.*

Christgau, Robert. Any Old Way You Choose It: Rock and Other Pop Music, 1967-1973. *Penguin Books, 1973.*

Church, Richard. Eight for Immortality. *J. M. Dent & Sons Ltd., 1941, Books for Libraries Press, 1969.*

Clareson, Thomas D., ed. Voices for the Future: Essays on Major Science Fiction Writers, Vol. 1. *Bowling Green University Popular Press, 1976.*

Crouch, Marcus. Treasure Seekers and Borrowers: Children's Books in Britain 1900-1960. *The Library Association, 1962.*

Dixon, Bob. Catching Them Young 1: Sex, Race and Class in Children's Fiction. *Pluto Press, 1977.*

Donelson, Kenneth L., and Nilsen, Alleen Pace. Literature for Today's Young Adults. *Scott, Foresman, 1980.*

Duprey, Richard A. Just Off the Aisle: The Ramblings of a Catholic Critic. *Newman Press, 1962.*

Egoff, Sheila. The Republic of Childhood: A Critical Guide to Canadian Children's Literature in English. *Oxford University Press, 1975.*

Egoff, Sheila. Thursday's Child: Trends and Patterns in Contemporary Children's Literature. *American Library Association, 1981.*

Egoff, Sheila; Stubbs, G.T.; and Ashley, L. F., eds. Only Connect: Readings on Children's Literature. *Oxford University Press, 1969.*

Ericson, Edward E., Jr. Solzhenitsyn: The Moral Vision. *Eerdmans, 1980.*

Field, Elinor Whitney, ed. Horn Book Reflections: On Children's Books and Reading, Selected from Eighteen Years of The Horn Book Magazine—1949-1966. *Horn Book, 1969.*

Franklin, H. Bruce. Robert A. Heinlein: America As Science Fiction. *Oxford University Press, 1980.*

French, Warren, ed. The Forties: Fiction, Poetry, Drama. *Everett/Edwards, Inc., 1969.*

Gambaccini, Peter. Billy Joel: A Personal File. *Quick Fox, 1979.*

Gardner, R. H. The Splintered Stage: The Decline of the American Theater. *Macmillan, 1965.*

Graves, Robert. Introduction *to* Selected Poems of Robert Frost, *by Robert Frost. Holt, Rinehart and Winston, 1963.*

Gunn, James. The Foundations of Science Fiction. *Oxford University Press, 1982.*

Harris, Kathryn Gibbs, ed. Robert Frost: Studies of the Poetry. *G. K. Hall & Co., 1979.*

Heins, Paul, ed. Crosscurrents of Criticism: Horn Book Essays, 1968-1977. *The Horn Book, Incorporated, 1977.*

Hurrell, John D., ed. Two Modern American Tragedies: Reviews and Criticism of ''Death of a Salesman'' and ''A Streetcar Named Desire.'' *Charles Scribner's Sons, 1961.*

Kael, Pauline. When the Lights Go Down. *Holt, Rinehart and Winston, 1980.*

Kalb, Marvin L. Introduction to One Day in the Life of Ivan Denisovich, *by Alexander Solzhenitsyn. Translated by Ralph Parker. Dutton, 1963.*

Kauffmann, Stanley. Living Images: Film Comment and Criticism. *Harper & Row, Publishers, 1975.*

Kauffmann, Stanley. Before My Eyes: Film Criticism and Comment. *Harper & Row, 1980.*

Keith, W. J. The Poetry of Nature: Rural Perspectives in Poetry from **Wordsworth** to the Present. *University of Toronto Press, 1980.*

Killam, G. D. The Writings of Chinua Achebe. *Rev. ed. Heinemann, 1977.*

King, Bruce. The New English Literatures: Cultural Nationalism in a Changing World. *Macmillan, 1980.*

King, Bruce, ed. Introduction to Nigerian Literature. *Africana, 1972.*

Kingman, Lee, ed. Newbery and Caldecott Medal Books: 1956-1965. *Horn Book, 1965.*

Lukács, Georg. Solzhenitsyn. *Translated by William David Graf. Merlin Press, 1970, The MIT Press, 1971.*

Meek, Margaret. Rosemary Sutcliff. *Bodley Head, 1962.*

Monroe, Harriet. Poets and Their Art. *Rev. ed. Macmillan, 1932.*

Moody, Christopher. Solzhenitsyn. *Oliver & Boyd, 1973.*

Olander, Joseph D., and Greenberg, Martin Harry, eds. Isaac Asimov. *Taplinger, 1977.*

Olander, Joseph D., and Greenberg, Martin Harry, eds. Robert A. Heinlein. *Taplinger, 1978.*

Pearce, Roy Harvey. The Continuity of American Poetry. *Princeton University Press, 1961.*

Peters, Jonathan. A Dance of Masks: Senghor, Achebe, Soyinka. *Three Continents Press, 1978.*

Rahv, Philip. Essays on Literature and Politics: 1932-1972. *Edited by Arabel J. Porter and Andrew J. Dvosin. Houghton Mifflin, 1978.*

Rees, David. The Marble in the Water: Essays on Contemporary Writers of Fiction for Children and Young Adults. *The Horn Book, Inc., 1980.*

Reilly, Alayne P. America in Contemporary Soviet Literature. *New York University Press, 1971.*

Riley, Dick, ed. Critical Encounters: Writers and Themes in Science Fiction. *Ungar, 1978.*

Roscoe, Adrian A. Mother Is Gold: A Study in West African Literature. *Cambridge University Press, 1971.*

Rzhevsky, Leonid. Solzhenitsyn: Creator & Heroic Deed. *Translated by Sonja Miller. The University of Alabama Press, 1978.*

Scholes, Robert, and Rabkin, Eric S. Science Fiction: History, Science, Vision. *Oxford University Press, 1977.*

Shores, Edward. George Roy Hill. *Twayne, 1983.*

Simon, John. Reverse Angle: A Decade of American Film. *Clarkson N. Potter, Inc./Publishers, 1982.*

Sinyavsky, Andrei. For Freedom of Imagination. *Translated by Laszlo Tikos and Murray Peppard. Holt, Rinehart and Winston, 1971.*

Slonim, Marc. Soviet Russian Literature: Writers and Problems. *Oxford University Press, 1964.*

Townsend, *John Rowe.* A Sense of Story: Essays on Contemporary Writers for Children, *Lippincott. 1971.*

Townsend, *John Rowe.* A Sounding of Storytellers: New and Revised Essays on Contemporary Writers for Children. *J. B. Lippincott, 1979.*

Tvardovsky, *Alexander. Foreword to* One Day in the Life of Ivan Denisovich, *by Alexander Solzhenitsyn. Translated by Ralph Parker. Dutton, 1963.*

Warren, *Robert Penn.* Selected Essays. *Random House, 1958.*

Warrick, *Patricia S.* The Cybernetic Imagination in Science Fiction. *The MIT Press, 1980.*

Warshow, *Robert.* The Immediate Experience: Movies, Comics, Theatre & Other Aspects of Popular Culture. *Doubleday, 1962.*

Whipple, *T. K.* Spokesmen: Modern Writers and American Life. *Appleton, 1928.*

Cumulative Index to Authors

Author Index

Author Index

Cumulative Index to Critics

Aaron, Daniel
Thornton Wilder 15:575

Aaron, Jonathan
Tadeusz Różewicz 23:363

Aaron, Jules
Jack Heifner 11:264

Abbey, Edward
Robert M. Pirsig 6:421

Abbott, John Lawrence
Isaac Bashevis Singer 9:487
Sylvia Townsend Warner 7:512

Abeel, Erica
Pamela Hansford Johnson 7:185

Abel, Elizabeth
Jean Rhys 14:448

Abel, Lionel
Samuel Beckett 2:45
Jack Gelber 6:196
Jean Genet 2:157
Yoram Kaniuk 19:238

Abernethy, Peter L.
Thomas Pynchon 3:410

Abicht, Ludo
Jan de Hartog 19:133

Ableman, Paul
Brian Aldiss 14:14
Beryl Bainbridge 22:45
Jurek Becker 19:36
William S. Burroughs 22:85
J. M. Coetzee 23:125
Len Deighton 22:116
William Golding 17:179
Mary Gordon 13:250
Mervyn Jones 10:295

Piers Paul Read 25:377
Mary Renault 17:402
Anatoli Rybakov 23:373
Andrew Sinclair 14:489
Scott Sommer 25:424
D. M. Thomas 22:419
Gore Vidal 22:438

Abley, Mark
Margaret Atwood 25:65
Harry Crews 23:136
William Mitchell 25:327
Agnès Varda 16:560

Abraham, Willie E.
William Melvin Kelley 22:249

Abrahams, Cecil A.
Bessie Head 25:236

Abrahams, William
Elizabeth Bowen 6:95
Hortense Calisher 2:97
Herbert Gold 4:193
Joyce Carol Oates 2:315
Harold Pinter 9:418
V. S. Pritchett 5:352

Abrahamson, Dick
Sue Ellen Bridgers 26:92
John Knowles 26:265
Norma Fox Mazer 26:294

Abrams, M. H.
M. H. Abrams 24:18
Northrop Frye 24:209

Abramson, Doris E.
Alice Childress 12:105

Abramson, Jane
Peter Dickinson 12:172
Christie Harris 12:268
Rosemary Wells 12:638

Acheson, James
William Golding 17:177

Acken, Edgar L.
Ernest K. Gann 23:163

Ackerman, Diane
John Berryman 25:97

Ackroyd, Peter
Brian Aldiss 5:16
Martin Amis 4:19
Miguel Ángel Asturias 8:27
Louis Auchincloss 6:15
W. H. Auden 9:56
Beryl Bainbridge 8:36
James Baldwin 5:43
John Barth 5:51
Donald Barthelme 3:44
Samuel Beckett 4:52
John Berryman 3:72
Richard Brautigan 5:72
Charles Bukowski 5:80
Anthony Burgess 5:87
William S. Burroughs 5:92
Italo Calvino 5:100; 8:132
Richard Condon 6:115
Roald Dahl 6:122
Ed Dorn 10:155
Margaret Drabble 8:183
Douglas Dunn 6:148
Bruce Jay Friedman 5:127
John Gardner 7:116
Günter Grass 4:207
MacDonald Harris 9:261
Joseph Heller 5:179
Mark Helprin 10:261
Russell C. Hoban 7:160
Elizabeth Jane Howard 7:164
B. S. Johnson 6:264
Pamela Hansford Johnson 7:184

G. Josipovici 6:270
Thomas Keneally 10:298
Jack Kerouac 5:215
Francis King 8:321
Jerzy Kosinski 10:308
Doris Lessing 6:300
Alison Lurie 4:305
Thomas McGuane 7:212
Stanley Middleton 7:220
Michael Moorcock 5:294
Penelope Mortimer 5:298
Iris Murdoch 4:368
Vladimir Nabokov 6:358
V. S. Naipaul 7:252
Joyce Carol Oates 6:368
Tillie Olsen 13:432
Grace Paley 6:393
Frederik Pohl 18:411
Davi Pownall 10:418, 419
J. B. Priestley 9:441
V. S. Pritchett 5:352
Thomas Pynchon 3:419
Frederic Raphael 14:437
Simon Raven 14:442
Peter Redgrove 6:446
Keith Roberts 14:463
Judith Rossner 9:458
May Sarton 4:472
David Slavitt 5:392
Wole Soyinka 5:398
David Storey 4:529
Paul Theroux 5:428
Thomas Tryon 11:548
John Updike 7:488; 9:540
Gore Vidal 8:525
Harriet Waugh 6:559
Jerome Weidman 7:518
Arnold Wesker 5:483
Patrick White 4:587

Critic Index

Roger Zelazny **21**:469

Adam, G. F.
Rhys Davies **23**:143

Adamowski, T. H.
Simone de Beauvoir **4**:47

Adams, Agatha Boyd
Paul Green **25**:197

Adams, Alice
Lisa Alther **7**:14

Adams, George R.
Lorraine Hansberry **17**:190
Ann Petry **18**:403

Adams, J. Donald
Erich Maria Remarque **21**:327

Adams, Jacqueline
Al Young **19**:479

Adams, James Truslow
Esther Forbes **12**:206

Adams, John
Roy A. Gallant **17**:131

Adams, Laura
Norman Mailer **11**:340

Adams, Leonie
John Crowe Ransom **4**:428

Adams, M. Ian
Juan Carlos Onetti **10**:376

Adams, Percy
James Dickey **7**:81

Adams, Phoebe-Lou
Chinua Achebe **26**:11, 13
Richard Adams **18**:2
Joy Adamson **17**:3
Beryl Bainbridge **5**:40
Ann Beattie **18**:38
David Bradley, Jr. **23**:81
André Brink **18**:68
Robert Cormier **12**:133
Margaret Craven **17**:80
Roald Dahl **18**:109
G. B. Edwards **25**:151
John Fowles **15**:234
Dick Francis **22**:150
Günter Grass **22**:196
Dashiell Hammett **5**:161
James Herriot **12**:282
George V. Higgins **18**:234
Jamake Highwater **12**:285
Bohumil Hrabal **13**:290
P. D. James **18**:275
David Jones **7**:189
Garson Kanin **22**:232
Jerzy Kosinski **6**:285
William Kotzwinkle **14**:311
Halldór Laxness **25**:292, 300
Harper Lee **12**:341
Yukio Mishima **9**:385
N. Scott Momaday **19**:317
Berry Morgan **6**:340
Joyce Carol Oates **6**:374
Tillie Olsen **13**:433
Sylvia Plath **17**:352
Reynolds Price **6**:426
Jean Rhys **19**:394
João Ubaldo Ribeiro **10**:436
Philip Roth **15**:452

Françoise Sagan **17**:419
Khushwant Singh **11**:504
Jean Stafford **19**:431
Christina Stead **8**:500
R. G. Vliet **22**:441
Joseph Wambaugh **18**:532

Adams, Richard
Robert Newton Peck **17**:338

Adams, Robert M.
Adolfo Bioy Casares **13**:87
R. V. Cassill **23**:105
John Cheever **25**:121
Eleanor Clark **19**:105
Edward Dahlberg **7**:63
Peter Matthiessen **11**:361
Mary McCarthy **14**:362
Alberto Moravia **18**:348
Robert M. Pirsig **4**:404
Severo Sarduy **6**:485
Mary Lee Settle **19**:409
Edmund Wilson **24**:469

Adams, Robert Martin
John Barth **10**:24
Samuel Beckett **14**:74
Jorge Luis Borges **10**:66
Richard Brautigan **12**:61
Anthony Burgess **10**:90
Lawrence Durrell **13**:185
T. S. Eliot **10**:171
William Faulkner **11**:201
Carlo Emilio Gadda **11**:215
William H. Gass **2**:154
José Lezama Lima **10**:321
Vladimir Nabokov **11**:393
Flann O'Brien **10**:363
Thomas Pynchon **11**:453
Alain Robbe-Grillet **10**:437
J.R.R. Tolkien **12**:586
Angus Wilson **2**:472

Adams, Robin
Frank Herbert **12**:279
Roger Zelazny **21**:470

Adams, S. J.
Ezra Pound **13**:453

Adams, Timothy Dow
Leon Rooke **25**:394

Adcock, Fleur
John Berryman **13**:83
Robert Lowell **11**:331
Peter Porter **13**:453

Adelman, Clifford
John Berryman **3**:71

Adelman, George
Frank B. Gilbreth, Jr. and
Ernestine Gilbreth Carey
17:156

Adereth, M.
Louis Aragon **22**:36

Adkins, Laurence
Eilís Dillon **17**:96
Farley Mowat **26**:336

Adler, Bill
Marvin Gaye **26**:132

Adler, Dick
Ross Macdonald **1**:185

Adler, Joyce
Wilson Harris **25**:207

Adler, Renata
Mel Brooks **12**:75
Francis Ford Coppola **16**:232
Joan Micklin Silver **20**:346

Adler, Thomas P.
Edward Albee **11**:13
Harold Pinter **15**:424
Sam Shepard **17**:446

Aers, Lesley
Philippa Pearce **21**:284

Agar, John
Jonathan Baumbach **6**:32
Laurie Colwin **5**:107

Agee, James
Frank Capra **16**:156
Charles Chaplin **16**:193
Maya Deren **16**:251
Carl Theodor Dreyer **16**:256
Alfred Hitchcock **16**:339, 342
John Huston **20**:158, 160
Buster Keaton **20**:188
Laurence Olivier **20**:234
Billy Wilder **20**:456

Agee, Joel
Aharon Appelfeld **23**:38

Agena, Kathleen
Charles Wright **13**:613

Aggeler, Geoffrey
Anthony Burgess **2**:86; **5**:85;
13:123; **22**:69

Aghazarian, Nancy
Milton Meltzer **26**:304

Agius, Ambrose, O.S.B.
Edward Dahlberg **7**:64

Ahearn, Kerry
Wallace Stegner **9**:509

Ahokas, Jaakko A.
Paavo Haavikko **18**:206
Frans Eemil Sillanpää **19**:418

Ahrold, Robbin
Kurt Vonnegut, Jr. **3**:501

Aiken, Conrad
William Faulkner **8**:206
St.-John Perse **11**:433
I. A. Richards **24**:370
Karl Shapiro **15**:475

Aiken, David
Flannery O'Connor **10**:365

Aiken, William
David Kherdian **6**:281

Aithal, Rashmi
Raja Rao **25**:373

Aithal, S. Krishnamoorthy
Raja Rao **25**:373

Aitken, Will
Carlos Saura **20**:319

Alazraki, Jaime
Jorge Luis Borges **19**:45
Pablo Neruda **2**:309; **7**:261

Albers, Randall
Ai **14**:8

Albert, Walter
Blaise Cendrars **18**:90

Albertson, Chris
Laura Nyro **17**:313
Stevie Wonder **12**:662

Aldan, Daisy
Phyllis Gotlieb **18**:193

Alderson, Brian W.
Leon Garfied **12**:226
William Mayne **12**:395, 401

Alderson, S. William
Andre Norton **12**:464, 466, 470

Alderson, Sue Ann
Muriel Rukeyser **10**:442

Alderson, Valerie
E. M. Almedingen **12**:6
Noel Streatfeild **21**:412

Aldiss, Brian
J. G. Ballard **3**:33
Frank Herbert **12**:272

Aldiss, Brian W.
Isaac Asimov **26**:38
Robert A. Heinlein **26**:162

Aldrich, Nelson
Piri Thomas **17**:497

Aldridge, John W.
James Baldwin **4**:42
Donald Barthelme **2**:39
Saul Bellow **2**:49, 50
Louis-Ferdinand Céline **7**:47
John Cheever **3**:105
John Dos Passos **4**:131
James T. Farrell **4**:157
William Faulkner **3**:150
William Gaddis **3**:177; **6**:193
Joseph Heller **5**:177
Ernest Hemingway **3**:231, 233
James Jones **3**:261
Jerzy Kosinski **2**:231
Alison Lurie **5**:260
Norman Mailer **1**:193; **2**:258
Mary McCarthy **3**:327, 328
Wright Morris **3**:342; **18**:352
John O'Hara **2**:323
Katherine Anne Porter **3**:392
Philip Roth **4**:459
Alan Sillitoe **3**:447
William Styron **3**:472
John Updike **2**:439
Gore Vidal **22**:431
Robert Penn Warren **1**:356
Eudora Welty **2**:461
Colin Wilson **3**:536
Edmund Wilson **2**:474
P. G. Wodehouse **2**:478

Aldridge, Judith
Ruth M. Arthur **12**:27
Honor Arundel **17**:14, 15, 18

Alegria, Fernando
Jorge Luis Borges **2**:71

Critic Index

Critic Index

Critic Index

Critic Index

Critic Index

Critic Index

Critic Index

Critic Index

Critic Index

Critic Index

Critic Index

Critic Index

CUMULATIVE INDEX TO CRITICS   *CONTEMPORARY LITERARY CRITICISM, Vol. 26*

Critic Index

Critic Index

Critic Index

Critic Index

Critic Index

Critic Index

Critic Index

Critic Index

Critic Index

Critic Index

Critic Index

Critic Index

Critic Index

Critic Index

Critic Index